Sortuc (+1)

Constitutional
Law SECOND EDITION

MALCOLM M. FEELEY
University of California, Berkeley

SAMUEL KRISLOV
University of Minnesota

SCOTT, FORESMAN/LITTLE, BROWN HIGHER EDUCATION
A Division of Scott, Foresman and Company
Glenview, Illinois   London, England

Acknowledgment

Pages 44–49 excerpted from Thomas C. Grey, "Do We Have an
Unwritten Constitution?" *Stanford Law Review,* Volume 27 (February 1975),
pp. 703–718. Copyright 1975 by the Board of Trustees of the Leland
Stanford Junior University. Reprinted by permission.

Library of Congress Cataloging-in-Publication Data

Feeley, Malcolm.
   Constitutional law / Malcolm M. Feeley, Samuel Krislov. — 2nd ed.
     p.   cm.
   ISBN 0-673-39690-8
   1. United States — Constitutional law — Cases. I. Krislov, Samuel.
II. Title.
KF4549.F37   1990
342.73'00264 — dc20
[347.3020264]
                                  89-38593
                                      CIP

Artwork, Illustrations, and other materials supplied by the publisher.

1 2 3 4 5 6 — RRD — 94 93 92 91 90 89

to the memory of Hal Chase

Preface

These are pivotal times for the Supreme Court. The Court is assuming a sensitive role in shaping the powers of Congress and the President, while its own inner structure is precarious. As of this writing there is an unprecedented number of octogenarian justices; consequently, the Court's balance of power and its ideological direction could change at any moment. This coincidence of impressive power and lack of direction is unprecedented in the Court's history, and is especially significant in light of the Court's major role in defining public policy.

In the 1950s, under Chief Justice Earl Warren, the Supreme Court set in motion an ambitious agenda of social reform that continues today. Under Warren Burger the Court slowed down, and occasionally reversed, Warren Court initiatives in some areas. But in other areas, the Burger Court moved with the tide of social change. In response to women's rights it was much more creative and activist than its predecessor. While its motives were usually more conservative, the Burger Court was no less concerned with social policy, and no less inclined than its immediate predecessor to second-guess and reverse other agents of government. Vincent Blasi observed that the "rootless activism of the Burger Court" was an activism maintained by no particular vision of the future, but one that produced constant changes in small and not necessarily consistent ways.

Now, with the elevation of William Rehnquist to Chief Justice, and the appointment of more conservative justices, and with still more changes expected in the near future, the future of the Court is problematic and critical. During the next few years a radically reconstituted Court will continue to rethink such key issues as abortion, affirmative action, criminal justice, governmental roles in regulating the environment, separation of church and state, federalism, and executive-legislative division of power. These issues go to the core of major national political controversies.

Therefore, the study of constitutional law is much more than merely a preview of law school. The study of constitutional law is the study of legal discourse, and legal discourse is the language of American public policy and the grammar of its politics. To be an informed observer of public policy requires a general familiarity with legal methods and approaches; to participate demands more than just familiarity. Either role requires a basic understanding of the American constitutional framework and an appreciation of the evolution and history of specific constitutional doctrines. Without understanding the allocation of national power, the mechanics of federalism, and the history of such specific topics as incorporation of the Bill of Rights, the fundamental features of American public policy are almost incomprehensible.

This casebook, then, is designed to meet the needs of informed observers of government affairs rather than the needs of professional preparation. For that reason, it combines philosophical, historical, and evolutionary approaches on each major topic. Another of its purposes is to temper an awareness of political factors with a healthy respect for legal craftsmanship, the power of precedent, and the relative autonomy of the Court. This casebook is not restricted to a hard-line development of any approach or perspective, because it is oriented toward a liberal arts core course that is quite distinct from separate courses on the judicial process or criminal justice.

In preparing the first edition of this volume we incurred many debts. The late Hal Chase advised us about which cases to include, as did Susan Olson, David Fellman, Joel Grossman, and Jerry Skolnick. Reference librarians at Minnesota, Wisconsin, and Berkeley Universities, and at the Institute of Advanced Legal Studies at the University of London, were patient with our requests to photocopy mountains of materials and to track down dozens of references. We also wish to acknowledge the office staffs in the Political Science Departments at Minnesota and Wisconsin and in the Jurisprudence and Social Policy Program at Boalt Hall, Berkeley, who were patient with our requests to type and retype materials.

While research assistants and students too numerous to list helped us at various stages of our long project, we must single out several for special acknowledgment: Rosann Greenspan for various forms of help, including preparation of the list of justices (Appendix II); Alison Dundees for some last-minute reference checking and proofreading; and Silvio Pucci for proofreading the final draft.

In preparing the second edition of the volume we were aided by Maria Cuzzo, David Sousa, Daniel Krislov, Mary Ellen Otis, and Celia Ronis, who typed and coordinated the many revisions. We are especially grateful to Jonathan Simon, who, just after completion of the Court's 1983 term, provided us with a penetrating reading of the chapter on criminal procedure, and to Jeremy Elkins, who reviewed the material on affirmative action and abortion.

Throughout the development of this book we have benefited from the advice of many people. When preparing the first edition John Brigham, Stanley Brubaker, Lief Carter, Herbert Jacob, Michael McCann, Mark Silverstein, and Elliot Slotnick commented on successive drafts of our essays and on the selection and editing of the cases, and saved us from numerous errors, made us rethink and tighten many of our arguments, and offered useful advice on format and style. We were especially appreciative of the sustained commentary provided by Michael McCann. The diligence of this group significantly improved our work.

When preparing this second edition we were aided by the comments of many of our colleagues who offered us help based on their experiences teaching from the first edition. Among them are Woody Howard, Robert Kagan, Henry Balfe, Charles Miller, Susan Olson, Chris Perry, and Kenneth Street. We are especially appreciative of the detailed comments provided by Jerry Goldman.

Our original editor at Little, Brown was Don Palm, who merits more than the small line of acknowledgment we offer here. He was the proper mixture of cheerful friend and stern taskmaster needed to see us through a project much larger than either of us had imagined at the outset. John Covell, who took over those functions and helped us with many rough spots, saw us through this revision. Ron Newcomer ably handled production for this second edition, and Elliot Simon did an outstanding job of copyediting.

No doubt there are some errors in this volume, but there are many fewer than there would have been had we not been fortunate enough to draw on the help of the many people we have just acknowledged. We would be grateful if our readers — students and instructors alike — would call attention to the remaining errors, and for that matter, to comment on what are seen as the strengths of this volume.

M. M. F.
S. K.

A Note on Citations and Justices' Votes

Before 1875, Supreme Court decisions were published by authorized reporters whose names were incorporated into the citations: Dallas (Dall.) 1789-1900; Cranch (Cr.) 1801-1815; Wheaton (Wheat.) 1816-1827; Peters (Pet.) 1828-1842; Howard (How.) 1843-1860; Black (Bl.) 1861-1862; and Wallace (Wall.) 1863-1874. Thus *Marbury* v. *Madison,* for example, is cited as 1 Cr. 137 (1803), meaning that the case was decided in 1803 and is reported in Volume 1 of Cranch's reports at page 137. Since 1874 the Supreme Court has had its own official Supreme Court Reports (U.S. Government Printing Office), which are cited as United States (U.S.). For instance, *Brown* v. *Board of Education,* 347 U.S. 483 (1954), was handed down in 1954; the decision is found in Volume 347 of the Supreme Court Reports at page 483.

There are also two private reporting systems, the Supreme Court Reporter (West Publishing Company, abbreviated S.Ct.) and the United States Supreme Court Reports, Lawyers Edition (Lawyer's Cooperative Publishing Company, abbreviated L.Ed.). *Brown* v. *Board of Education,* 347 U.S. 483 (1954) is also found in 74 S.Ct. 686 (1954) and 98 L.Ed. 873 (1954). As is obvious, volume and page numbers in these two private re-

porters differ from the official reporter. Both private reports, however, contain information so that their citations can be translated quickly into official citations, and vice versa. Thus, with only an official citation the student can easily locate a case in either of the two private reporters. There is still one more reporting system which merits comment. The Bureau of National Affairs publishes *Law Week,* a biweekly pamphlet throughout the year which contains Supreme Court decisions handed down within the prior two weeks. It is generally cited as LW. Thus the Court's 1989 abortion decision, *Webster* v. *Reproductive Health Services,* is cited as 57 LW 5023.

Cases referred to or included in this text are generally cited in the official citation system (the authorized private reporters to 1874, and the U.S. Reports after that). However, to save space we give a full citation only where a case is first mentioned. An index of all cases referred to or included in this volume, with full official citations, is found at the end of the book.

At any point in the book the student may wish to read other decisions mentioned in our essays or case introductions. For this purpose we have distinguished typographically between references to cases that are in our book (set in capitals) from references to cases that must be looked up elsewhere (set in italics). For example, BROWN V. BOARD OF EDUCATION may be found among the cases in Chapter 10, but *Sweatt* v. *Painter* may not. Note, however, that in reprinting the Court's decisions we have thought it best not to alter the style of the original publication.

For each case reprinted in this volume, we have reported the voting total of the majority and minority. For the most part this is a simple process; in recent years the Court has become more fragmented than ever before. One consequence is an increasing number of separate opinions. On many occasions as many as six or seven justices have penned their own opinions. Even more confusing is the fact that justices who write their own opinions may also concur in those of other justices. Such combinations of alternatives allow justices to concur in part with one or more opinions, write a separate partial dissent, and concur in part with still another dissent. All this means that, in a number of recent cases, it is impossible to report voting in terms of a simple majority/minority division. In those cases where we have not been able to characterize mixed positions in terms of either majority or minority positions, we have created a third, middle position. Thus some votes are reported as, for example, 5–1–3 or even 3–1–2–3.

Because there is no standard convention on reporting the names of participating justices when opinions are reprinted in casebooks, we have developed our own rules of thumb. We see no value in reporting all the names and voting positions of all the justices in all the cases reprinted in this volume. However, we always identify the authors of the opinions we have reprinted. In those cases that represent a continuing ideological division on the Court, we make an effort to indicate the positions of each of the justices. In a handful of cases, this seemingly simple effort is taxing, for the reasons identified in the preceding paragraph.

Contents

(Those cases in brackets appear in previous chapters.)

Part I

Chapter 3

The Problems of Yesteryear:
National Authority over
Commerce and Taxation   170

Chapter 4

The Other Side of Federalism:
State Powers over
Commerce and Taxation   266

Part II

Chapter 9

Chapter 10

Chapter 11

Social Change and the
Fourteenth Amendment: The
"New Equal Protection" and the
Right of Privacy and Autonomy   797

The "New Equal Protection" 797

The Right of Privacy and Autonomy 870

Appendix I

Appendix II

Part I

CHAPTER 1

Judicial Review and Court Power

Judicial Review: Theoretical Justification

The Supreme Court is the most powerful judicial body in the world. Its multiple functions and many powers far surpass those of any other court. Those few judicial bodies with similar power were all created in conscious imitation of the American example.

In part, the special power of the Supreme Court comes from its place at the apex of an unusually active legal system. "Scarcely any political question arises in the United States that is not resolved sooner or later into a judicial question," De Tocqueville wrote in 1835. And American courts have become far more important in recent years. The simple fact of federalism — and two largely independent sets of laws and lawgivers — forces people to turn to the courts for clarification and choice of law more than in most nations. This may have established the pattern of high judicial involvement in public matters, in striking contrast to the low profile of courts in most countries.

But the U.S. Supreme Court's prestige and power also flow from its right of judicial review — the power to declare unconstitutional (1) laws of Congress and (2) laws of state governments, as well as (3) actions and regulations of the executive. This power gives to the Supreme Court glamour and a decisive weapon that allows it to compete on a plane of equality with the other and more active branches of government. When the Burger Court invalidated the legislative veto in a 1983 decision, I.N.S. v. CHADHA (see Chapter 2), it was declaring some two hundred laws unconstitutional in a single decision. These were laws enacted over a fifty-year period, many after lengthy political bargaining within Congress or with the President. Most decisions of unconstitutionality are less dramatic, but the Court enhances its position even where it sustains the actions of another branch, or where it exercises less far-reaching and more routine judicial authority. The power of judicial review is the wedge by which courts have assumed progressively expanding authority over public issues, policies, and institutions.

This power has troubled thinkers both on and off the bench. Why should nine lifetime appointees make such momentous decisions for a majoritarian society? Why should five justices be able to set aside the actions of a Congress and Presidency, who are responsible to the electorate? The justification of judicial power is neither easy nor obvious.

Oddly, the Constitution does not explicitly call for judicial review. The Supreme Court, however, decided in MARBURY V. MADISON (1803) that it had the power, and in spite of the obvious peculiarity of its authority resting upon its own decision, the Court has been able to make that decision stick.

Judicial review would undoubtedly be more firmly rooted if the Constitution did provide explicitly for such a role. Chief Justice Marshall, in MARBURY, argues that the Constitution really does just that. But at best, he shows there is wording compatible with judicial review, even suggestive of this power, but not compelling such an interpretation.

The justification of judicial review, then, must be a more complex and subtle one. There are many arguments to that justification, summarized below under six headings: (1) the argument from intent: A weaker form of arguing direct authorization, it suggests the Framers must have wanted judicial review, deduced from a total pattern of behavior, even though there is no explicit delegation; (2) historical acceptance, deriving legitimacy from the general support given the Supreme Court and judicial review through most of our history; (3) the counter-majoritarian argument, which finds restraints on the "tyranny of the majority" as a strengthening rather than a dilution of democracy; (4) the educative and moral role that the Court can play when it issues reasoned decisions, as it did in striking down segregation in BROWN V. BOARD OF EDUCATION (1954); (5) the Court's role in dealing with issues that politically might be incurably divisive but can be resolved through the symbolism of the law and the myth of the Constitution; and (6) judicial review as a balancing device of federalism, which seems explicit in Article Six and suggests the legitimacy of even broader Court power.

The Argument from Intent

Marshall's opinion in MARBURY drew heavily on Hamilton's argument in *Federalist 78* and is an impressive bit of argumentation, al-

though in the end the opinion is neither conclusive nor unanswerable.

Essentially, Marshall advanced three major justifications of Court power: (1) the nature of written constitutions implies limits on legislative power enforceable in the courts; (2) the nature of the judicial function is to declare what law is, with judicial review being a special form of this task; and (3) the constitutional text indirectly orders review.

That written constitutions must be obeyed and that limits set by them must be judicially enforced is argued strongly in *Federalist 78*:

It is not otherwise to be supposed, that the Constitution could intend to enable the representatives of the people to substitute their *will* to that of their constituents. It is far more rational to suppose, that the courts were designed to be an intermediate body between the people and the legislature, in order, among other things, to keep the latter within the limits assigned to their authority. The interpretation of the laws is the proper and peculiar province of the courts. A constitution is, in fact, and must be regarded by the judges, as a fundamental law. It therefore belongs to them to ascertain its meaning, as well as the meaning of any particular act proceeding from the legislative body. If there should happen to be an irreconcilable variance between the two, that which has the superior obligation and validity ought, of course, to be preferred; or, in other words, the Constitution ought to be preferred to the statute, the intention of the people to the intention of their agents.

But as many have pointed out, including Judge Gibson in EAKIN AND OTHERS V. RAUB AND OTHERS (1825), the argument for limited government does not require judicial enforcement. Constitutions are also addressed to Congress, the President, and the public. Other countries have adopted constitutions, both before and after 1804, and have trusted political forces to respect constitutional limits.

Much the same reply can be made to the second argument of MARBURY and the *Federalist;* namely, that judicial review is required by the very existence of the judiciary. That argument suggests the power to declare laws unconstitutional is a burden, part of the dilemma of deciding a case. In settling a controversy, judges must choose between laws and inevitably must choose the higher law, the Constitution.

The obvious answer to this argument is that throughout history judges in other countries have not found the power of judicial review to be necessary. It is also obvious that it simplifies the judicial process, and makes the task of a judge clearer, if the judiciary assumes that the "law" is what the legislature enacts and that the legislatures, being aware of the Constitution, have obeyed it. The "burden" of judicial review is one that Marshall wanted to take on, not one that forces itself upon the judge.

Marshall is only a bit more convincing when he goes to the Constitution itself. His weakest argument of all is that judges are required to swear allegiance to the Constitution, ignoring the fact that so are other government officials. Indeed, the President's oath is the only one the Constitution prescribes word for word (art. II, §1, cl. 8).

Arguing from the Supremacy Clause (art. VI, §2) is much more effective. This provision specifies that treaties, the Constitution, and laws "in pursuance thereof" are the supreme law of the land and binding upon state judges. Marshall reads "in pursuance thereof" to mean "consistent with," and he concludes that state judges can refuse to enforce acts in conflict with the Constitution, i.e., not "in pursuance thereof." The actions of state judges dealing with federal matters are reviewable by the Supreme Court, so the justices also must have the power to sustain or invalidate acts.

This is a plausible, but not absolutely compelling, interpretation of the Supremacy Clause. "In pursuance thereof" might be a stylistic flourish or might mean "passed after adoption of the Constitution."

Marshall's interpretation of the Supremacy Clause received powerful support from actions of members of the Constitutional Convention in subsequent official capacities. The Federal Judiciary Act of 1789, another portion of which was at issue in MARBURY, provided for Supreme Court review of state court cases in which the constitutionality of a federal law "is drawn into question." This Act is an unambiguous restatement of the Supremacy Clause's "in pursuance thereof," as Marshall interpreted it. The Act was passed by the very first Congress, which was dominated by Founding Fathers, who must have known what the Constitution intended. Further, justices who sat in judgment before Marshall reached the Court, in several cases (e.g., CALDER V. BULL and *Hylton* v. *U.S.*, 1796) carefully considered invalidating the statutes in question and painfully sustained them. Obviously, the act of reviewing constitutionality indicates that these judges felt they could declare laws unconstitutional. While the evidence to support Marshall's view is strong, it remains perplexing that the Founders left so vital an issue to be decided by inference when plain language would have been easy. It seems clear that they did not envision the full-blown power of judicial review as we now know it and did not consider judicial review an important tool of governance.

The Argument from Acceptance

Court power has been controversial from time to time in American history. But the controversy has been surprisingly muted. Few serious frontal attacks have been mounted against judicial power, and nothing approaching a successful constitutional amendment to curtail the basic power of judicial review has ever been advanced.

Furthermore, both controversy over the basic grant of power and efforts to curtail it have actually diminished over time. It is fair to say that two centuries of acceptance constitute a significant claim to legitimacy.

The Jeffersonians were the most determined nay-sayers to judicial power. They brought impeachment proceedings against Justice Chase, who was acquitted by the Senate, and by Act of Congress forbade the sitting of the Supreme Court for a full year. Jefferson wrote darkly of the need to take away the Court's monopoly over review. But little came of all this except the

Eleventh Amendment, which still is the only amendment directly aimed at curtailing court power. (The Eleventh Amendment, adopted in 1798, provides that citizens of one state may not sue another state in federal court.)

Populist-progressive forces (1890–1925) were highly critical of Supreme Court actions and backed a proposal for the recall of state judges. This non sequitur underlined the standing of the Supreme Court in the eyes of the public and how much opponents shied away from direct confrontation. President Roosevelt's Court-packing proposal (1937), talk of impeaching Warren Court justices, and the Nixon administration's efforts to remove Justice Fortas (successful) and Justice Douglas (unsuccessful) were other indirect attacks on the Court through its membership.

Much more common have been efforts to change specific decisions. These have included amendments to effectively reverse specific decisions; for example, the Sixteenth Amendment nullifying the Court's anti-income tax decision in POLLACK V. FARMERS' LOAN AND TRUST CO. (1895). Congress, in recent times, has also threatened to use its power over Supreme Court jurisdiction and its power of defining liberties under the Fourteenth and Fifteenth Amendments to affect doctrinal changes.

But this brief accounting underscores the fact that criticism of the Court has generally been either vague and unfocused, or else dealing with particular policies or decisions. Challenges to the basic grant of power are few and far between, and only one relatively technical challenge to Court power has been constitutionally successful. Judicial review itself has not faced tough political challenges, and this is a negative form of validation.

The Counter-Majoritarian Argument

Probably the strongest justification of judicial review is that it helps control runaway temporary majorities. The Founders believed in a republic, one that limited democracy. The system they created has many checks on simple majorities, such as the equal vote in the Senate of states with widely differing populations, and the need for special majorities in both Congress and the states to amend the Constitution.

Compared to such serious and permanent departures from simple majority rule, judicial power is seen as less capricious and less harsh. While granting special power to minorities in the political process may be permanently vesting a veto power in representatives of a particular interest or sectional group, the judiciary is reasonably independent from such considerations. And while political figures such as senators are responsive almost exclusively to their own constituencies, judges are aware of the power that Congress and the President have over major bases of Court authority. The "political branches" can change Supreme Court jurisdiction and alter the number and composition of judges (though impeachment of sitting judges is limited and very difficult). Congress may also alter laws, thus requiring judgments in future cases to be different. When Congress and the President agree on criticism of Court decisions, history has shown that legal compromise or outright capitulation by the courts is the result. So, it is argued, judicial review is a check on temporary majorities but not a bar to strong, enduring majorities.

The life tenure of judges allows them the luxury of standing against momentary fads. Their legal training and the force of precedent can give them a more philosophical view derived from history. In fact, the Supreme Court has emerged in the last half century as the defender of freedom of expression. And judicial responsibility for taking the long view has been given new emphasis.

Courts are also defended as valued supplements to simple head counting, since they add reasoned judgment and technical competence to the process of decision making. Judges present justifications of their decisions in opinions that are analyzed, criticized, and defended. The justices sign their opinions, and Justice Brandeis once suggested that the real prestige of the Supreme Court derived from their being the last people in Washington doing their own work, instead of relying upon staff aides. Some concern is expressed over the growing work load of the justices, the resulting increase in the number of their law clerks, and the growing reliance on such help. Still, many opinions are recognizably the work of the individual justices, distinctive in style, and open to evaluation by professors and lawyers in law reviews and other judges in legal opinions.

Justice Stone's famous footnote in the CAROLENE PRODUCTS (1938) case pointed to other justifications for judicial review. Majorities could vote to curtail democracy itself. Courts, he argued, have a special responsibility to eliminate majoritarian measures that deprive people of equal political power. Censorship laws prevent critics of censorship laws from organizing to eliminate such abuses. A temporary majority could take away all voting rights from a minority that otherwise could work to become a majority.

And Stone also argued that some groups — religious and racial minorities — might be so seriously cut off from political power that they needed special protection against the majority. These imperfections in a democratic order, and judicial protection of the system, are then defended as only superficial violations of democracy since, in reality, they are designed to ensure the democratic process itself.

The Supreme Court as Educator: The Argument from Principle and Decision Making

The reality of reasoned decision making is also invoked to suggest another defense of judicial review. Courts educate the public in democratic values and principles of fairness and of group justice. They do this, it is argued, by example — in the very process of hearing and deciding cases, and in their enunciation of rules and principles which guide them. In turn, these principles infect public discussion and direct other aspects of democratic life. The Supreme Court is thus seen as an educator and advocate for our constitutional order.

The strongest advocate of this position was Herbert Wechsler, who found the essence of law and the authority of the Court to lie in its ability to formulate "neutral general principles." Such principles, he argued, must apply to all who come within its compass. They must not be formulated for particular parties or because claimants have an unusually sad story to tell.

Examples of Wechsler's "neutral principles" abound. When Ku Klux Klan supporters wished to meet in a border state, and American Nazis wanted to march through a largely Jewish suburb outside Chicago, their lawyers successfully invoked precedents established in the course of black civil rights demonstrations in the 1960s led by the martyred Martin Luther King. In this sense, the Supreme Court helps teach that the law is not a narrow partisan but a respector of rights for all persons.

Critics of the "neutral principles" notion suggest its truth is highly limited. They cite novelist Anatole France's biting comment on "the majestic equality of the law" that forbids rich and poor alike "to sleep under bridges and beg in the streets." On some matters, particularly those relating to procedure and method in law and in politics, we take turns in different roles, so that laws are neutral. In others, such as the regulation of the rights of the blind, the appearance of generality may be a sham.

The case that principled opinion making generates public support of democratic behavior is a weak one. Clearly, the Court has been in the forefront of opinion on desegregation, school prayer, and such emotional matters as exemption from saluting the flag. The public has come to strongly support these positions. Yet, while the Supreme Court has affected public opinion, there is little evidence that the specific general principles enunciated have been an important part of the public debate, even on these issues.

The very process of Supreme Court decision aggregation works against clean, decisive general principles emerging. Since Marshall's time, Supreme Court opinions have been assigned to a member of the majority in the Court's conference, who generally tries to keep together or even add to the majority. Within limits of conscience, opinion writers try to write a decision that does not alienate other justices. The nonwriting justices, in turn, seek changes to bring the opinion closer to their own view. The product is a negotiated text, a joint product, and all too often reads that way. Justice Blackmun, the author of the much-criticized abortion decision—even scholars who support the outcome are unhappy with the text and its reasoning—has openly indicated that its sometimes contradictory approaches were necessary to gain a majority opinion. This is not unusual.

Perhaps the most important educative role is, in fact, played by dissenting opinions. These are often solo efforts, so dissenting justices feel free to express themselves pungently. As they usually need to please only themselves, dissenters often write more decisive and coherent opinions, based on simple direct principles. Many famous dissents, particularly those of the first Justice Harlan and Justices Holmes and Brandeis, were not only more famous in their times than the majority views, but have since been vindicated by new majorities overruling those precedents. Of course, the mere fact that we not only permit public dissent by our officials but print and disseminate such disagreements is itself a profound symbolic act.

The Mystic Function of Judicial Review

Some see the contribution of judicial review as lending legitimacy and "sacredness" to the laws. In this view, the Court and the Constitution play some of the role that royal families played in nineteenth-century constitutional monarchies or priests play in some societies even today—not actually governing, but lending an aura

of continuity and mystery to the process. The argument is somewhat at variance with the notion that the Supreme Court educates through neutral principles, but perhaps the thought is that different segments of our society respond to different aspects of the judicial function.

Of course, legitimation occurs only if the population is convinced the Court has made a genuine inquiry into the constitutionality of a statute or policy. Thus, oddly, the function of legitimation entails invalidation of some laws in order that the Supreme Court has the authority to validate other laws.

Judicial Review and Federalism: The Court as Umpire

The English judge and legal philosopher Lord Devlin has spoken of the legal vacuums created by federalism. It is striking that most of the legal systems that have judicial review are federal systems. There is an affinity, a symbiotic relationship, between judicial review and divided government.

Federalism in the U.S. embraces the national legal order and those of the fifty states. Courts must mediate and choose between conflicting laws of these multiple systems. For the Supreme Court, it is advantageous to be seen as objective and posed above the battle, rather than as the agent of national power.

The Supreme Court has historically been "the Court of the Union," preserving a balance between nation and state. It has found national measures unconstitutional, as encroaching on state power, though such decisions are rare today. It has more often found that state measures intrude upon national commerce power or prevent the free flow of persons or goods among the states.

The notion of the Supreme Court as system umpire was historically more attractive because of the assumption that courts were not merely dispassionate, but also rather weak and fragile. The *Federalist* authors note many times that the judiciary is inherently "the least dangerous branch" of government. Paradoxically, this perceived weakness has been a source of strength allowing the Court to generally enjoy public support and confidence. Periodically, however, the power of the court system has become a public issue.

The notion of the Court as umpire is somewhat tainted by its role as a creature of the national government. Its power and privilege can be directly affected by the President and Congress in ways that state governments cannot. Its functional role is also different with respect to the federal division of authority. Both in theory and in practice it has less ability to constrain national power than to constrain state power. And both John Marshall and Oliver Wendell Holmes Jr. thought the need for judicial control over congressional authority to be less vital than control over the states. As Marshall emphasized, an individual state could gain selfish advantage over others or over the national government. The national government (with states strongly represented, especially in the Senate) was politically unlikely to move against the states, unless majorities within most states wished such a move.

The clue to the Court's continued vitality as umpire is in Marshall's analysis. The Court has seldom been out of pace with public opinion in its balancing act between nation and state.

Marshall himself, largely by force of personality, kept the Court nationalistic as states'-rights notions became predominant in American politics. This was rather significant in establishing a firm constitutional order. Still, his court moved toward accommodating new patterns, permitting states to regulate even when purists might have seen in-fringement of national power, particularly in the area of interstate commerce. The Taney Court hastened the spread of local authority but more as a modification than a reversal of Marshall.

After the Civil War, the Court was again mainly a nationalizing instrumentality, encouraging and abetting the growth of a national economy. Its reluctance to permit social regulation and redistribution measures put it out of step with growing sentiment for such measures, but it bobbed and weaved its way effectively until the Great Depression.

What the Court did from roughly 1896 to 1937 was to create two lines of precedent, one emphasizing national authority, the other the Tenth Amendment prerogatives of the states. Which line was used to test the constitutionality of a measure depended mainly on the social nature of the legislation. National power was upheld with respect to regulating meat plants and stockyards — most justices are not vegetarians — but not as to wages or work hours for children. The power of umpiring federalism became a power to regulate social policy.

With the changes in constitutional doctrine after 1937, the Court's role in federalism relations became less pronounced and less controversial. Where controversy has grown is in a new and different line of development — a set of decisions applying the provisions of the Bill of Rights to the states. Here the Court acts as quite a different kind of umpire, not between nation and state, but between individual citizen and state. This transformation of the Court's leading role is dramatic and significant. The Commerce Clause remains a major base of Court explication and adjudication. But the Fourteenth Amendment has surpassed it, transforming the Court's place in our system.

Judicial Review in Action

In practice, the Supreme Court has used judicial review sparingly. There are few periods in our history in which invalidation of congressional actions were frequent. Most of these periods were quite recent.

As the table nearby indicates, the peak periods of invalidation of federal legislation were the Taft-Hughes Courts of the 1920s and 1930s and the Warren and early Burger years. While invalidation of Acts of Congress is usually emphasized in dis-

Legislative Action Nullified by the
Supreme Court, 1789–1978

	Acts of Congress	State legislation	Local ordinances
1789–1800	0	0	0
1801–1820	1	8	0
1821–1840	0	10	1
1841–1860	1	17	0
1861–1880	12	61	2
1881–1900	9	71	10
1901–1920	17	138	29
1921–1940	25	207	18
1941–1960	6	104	23
1961–1978	33	282	41
	104	898	124

Source: Library of Congress, *Constitution of the United States of America: Analysis and Interpretation.* Washington: Government Printing Office, 1973, and Supplement, 1979. Since standards for such listings are subjective, no attempt to update was made to preserve comparability.

cussion of judicial review, invalidation of state laws is more frequent. Significantly, the pattern of high activity and low activity is remarkably similar for both types of judicial invalidation — of federal or state laws.

While the historical pattern is revealing, the decision in IMMIGRATION AND NATURALIZATION SERVICE V. CHADHA (1983) has upset all the charts. That decision alone put into jeopardy provisions of over two hundred congressional statutes, perhaps tripling the exercise of judicial review.

The Pre-Marshall Period,
1789–1801

Certainly the institution of judicial review began slowly and burgeoned only over time. The period before Marshall saw little evidence of Court influence. No less than three Chief Justices were confirmed by Congress in little over a decade. A few major cases were decided, e.g., CALDER V. BULL (1798) and *Ware* v. *Hylton* 3 Dall.

199 (1796). In the latter, at least implicitly, the power of the Court to declare acts unconstitutional was involved. It is also likely that an act of Congress was invalidated by a non-Supreme Court decision in *U.S.* v. *Yale Todd* (1794), but the opinion is turgid and the issue — whether judges could function as a board to set veterans' pensions — so trivial that no notice was taken.

The John Marshall Epoch,
1801–1835

Marshall brought to the Court dignity, power, and continuity. He ended the practice of individual opinions by the justices and hammered out a unanimous opinion of the Court. He believed this enhanced the authority of the justices. Marshall tried to prevent any dissents, and we know from Justice Story that he authored at least three major opinions whose outcome he personally disagreed with. Not until a Jeffersonian majority was long established did Marshall's grip slip enough to allow individual concurrences and dissents, but the practice of an "opinion of the Court" survives.

Marshall's great decisions sustained national power and congressional authority. The skill and persuasiveness of those opinions have earned him high marks as an architect of the American nation.

Marshall, of course, was the author of MARBURY V. MADISON (1803), which established the power of judicial review and constituted its first exercise by the Supreme Court. Still, what is amazing about Marshall's performance in MARBURY is the dazzling way he advances the power of the Court while avoiding any act that directly challenged the power of potential enemies. In MARBURY, to be sure, the Court declared the President at fault and invalidated an act of Congress, but its bottom-line action was to do nothing for the plaintiffs, which was precisely what the Jeffersonians wanted. And Marshall was just as cautious in later years, avoiding any finding of unconstitutionality at the federal level throughout his term of office.

The Taney Period, 1836–1864

With the advent of a Jacksonian Chief Justice, many expected the undoing of Marshall's major doctrines. Instead, Taney's leadership was cautious and consolidating, modifying and perfecting Marshallian decisions rather than overturning them. So the great decision in COOLEY V. BOARD OF WARDENS (1852) reconciles opposing views of the Commerce Clause in a masterful way, while the CHARLES RIVER BRIDGE (1837) decision mitigates the DARTMOUTH COLLEGE (1819) case without completely undermining Marshall's assumption that a governmental grant to private persons is protected by the Contract Clause of the Constitution. The direction of the modifications were generally to strengthen states' rights. The Taney court shared the localism of the President and Congress and had little desire or need to challenge them.

This characteristic care and caution was thrown to the winds in the most famous and most disastrous decision of the Taney court, the DRED SCOTT (1857) case, which was also its one use of judicial review at the national level. The invocation of a power previously only used in rather trivial ways to solve the most difficult social issue the nation has ever faced proved foolhardy. Charles Evans Hughes listed the DRED SCOTT case and two others as "self-inflicted wounds" of the Supreme Court. But in fact, it also wounded the nation and helped precipitate the Civil War. The prestige of the Court was drastically undermined by the decision, which was explicitly overruled by the Fourteenth Amendment. (That Amendment firmly proclaims all persons born in the U.S. to be citizens and establishes national citizenship as primary over state citizenship.) The Court was all but ignored by the Lincoln administration, and observers feared a move to abolish it.

The Court Comes Back! The Chase (1864–73) and Waite (1874–88) Years

From this nadir the Court made a remarkable comeback. The outbreak of conflict between the President and Congress, which per-sisted throughout the Reconstruction period, probably created the opportunity for this comeback by an institution capable of resolving and minimizing acrimony. The problems of reintegrating the southern states and of new forms of financing and taxation arising from the Civil War also presented legal problems of immense importance.

The great Civil War Amendments also required legal exposition. Under the influence of states' rights Democrats, the Court tried to minimize the import of the Amendments, especially the Fourteenth Amendment. But as industrial-minded, nationalistic capitalists like Justice Field began to assert themselves, the Amendments were gradually given broader interpretation. Intended to protect newly freed slaves, the Amendments were first used to aid the growth of big business; only later were they applied to individuals.

The High Point of Power: The Fuller (1888–1910), White (1910–1920), and Taft (1924–1930) Eras

By the turn of the century, the Court had developed great power over state legislation through the Due Process Clause of the Fourteenth Amendment and the "negative implications" of the commerce power. National legislation could be sustained by invoking granted powers, especially the power to regulate commerce, or invalidated as an invasion of states' rights under the Tenth Amendment. Constitutional doctrine emphasized "dual federalism"—the notion that each level of government must be confined to protect the other. The Court was seen as the guardian of this balance.

As a national economy emerged, the Court grudgingly permitted national regulatory power to grow. It did so by developing dual lines of precedents that could be invoked to permit national power to deal with some problems but used to strike down other types of legislation. Liberals like Holmes, Brandeis, and, later, Stone, who wished to sustain broad congressional power, condemned this as hypocritical. So did rock-rib conservatives like Sutherland and Van Devanter, who would rather have sharply curtailed all national regulatory power. The balance of power was held by conservative pragmatists like Hughes and McKenna and even Taft, and the Court exercised something close to a policy veto over economic legislation during this time.

Crisis and Doubt: The Hughes (1930–41), Stone (1941–45), and Vinson (1946–53) Years

As the New Deal of Franklin Roosevelt unfolded with its sometimes desperate efforts to cope with the Great Depression, the justices became increasingly alarmed. The pragmatists, Hughes and Roberts, increasingly sided with the conservatives; even Brandeis was shocked by what he saw as collectivist and anti-Federalist moves. The Court struck down a whole series of New Deal programs almost on the eve of the 1936 election, which witnessed Roosevelt's sweeping vindication.

The President sought revenge with his court-packing bill. Alarmed, the justices obliged him by overturning states' rights doctrines and retiring from the Court. Roosevelt was to appoint more justices than any other President since Washington, and to see new constitutional doctrines triumph.

The new judges followed the Holmes-Brandeis-Stone approach and scuttled dual federalism, bringing back Marshallian national supremacy to the interpretation of commerce and other granted powers. The national government was one of limited specified powers, but once again those powers could be exercised to the hilt. The Court was no longer to be the arbiter of economic policy. Judicial invalidation of congressional enactments fell to a level not seen since the Civil War. The Court was unsure of its very reason for being, strife-ridden and poorly led. The tide of McCarthyism and spy chasing engulfed the Court, which deferred to the congressional findings of a communist threat.

Chief Justice Warren and the Activist Era (1953–1969)

President Eisenhower's choice of Earl Warren as Chief Justice proved momentous. The most important item before the Court was the issue of segregation in schools, and the new Chief Justice was able to lead his colleagues to a unanimous decision ultimately undermining the "separate but equal" decision of PLESSY V. FERGUSON (1896). The cautiously courageous decision in BROWN V. BOARD OF EDUCATION (1954) was to restore to the Court its lost honor and to propel it to new heights of power. Warren, less than a great legal craftsman, was to retire to the plaudits of some as the greatest Chief Justice since Marshall.

The Warren Court plunged enthusiastically into a new role that Stone and Black had advanced only slightly — the development of an expansive and aggressive protection of individual rights. This had been advocated even earlier by the first Justice Harlan and by Brandeis, but now gained momentum as a major function of the Court with respect to both national and state governments. Judicial control over criminal law, emphasis upon the rights of underprivileged groups under the Equal Protection Clause, and unprecedented expansion of rights of expression and privacy were all part of the legacy of the Warren years.

These substantive changes also drastically altered the political and social role played by the Court. Traditionally, it had used constitutional provisions to protect property interests (vested rights, just compensation, due process in regulation) or to define federal-state powers. By converting the provisions of the Bill of Rights, which had formerly applied only to the national government, into limits on state power, the Court moved to control more and more of state government regulations. In turn, it was to utilize these new doctrines to limit the national power as well. The Court became a libertarian citadel. The old business interests could turn to the Court for only a limited share of the older agenda. New groups— libertarian and egalitarian—became the new supporters of the Court, even as the old support groups grew colder to it.

The Court was activist in yet other ways. It was more receptive to new types of law suits, relaxed technical requirements for parties bringing suits, and embraced creative approaches to enforcement of decisions.

Critics argued that the Court was abandoning old law for their own predilections. The justices were accused of coddling criminals and being preoccupied with technicalities rather than issues of guilt and innocence. By turning over precedents at an unprecedented pace, they were, it was suggested, contributing to the social turbulence of the 1960s. And by their willingness to ignore legal forms, it was suggested, they were destroying the boundaries between the judiciary and the legislature.

Retreat: From Warren to Warren Burger (1969–1986)

President Nixon appointed Warren Burger on the premise that he would end judicial activism, making decisions in accordance with the Constitution, not politics. The hope, presumably, was that the Court would sharply reverse its line of decisions in three areas of controversy: criminal law regulation, pornography, and religion in education.

In fact, the Burger Court, like the Taney Court, sometimes modified but largely consolidated Warren Court decisions in most areas. In the area of women's rights, it was aggressively innovative. Its decision on abortion rivals in public controversy any Warren Court case. Even the criminal law and pornography regulation changes of the Burger Court were modest. And the Court did not con-vince critics that its decisions were dictated by the Constitution.

Still, the Burger Court proved its objectivity and continuity with the past in a series of major decisions involving the Nixon administration. Almost all were decided contrary to the interests of Nixon. This included such landmarks as the decision permitting the *New York Times* to print the famous Pentagon Papers, though classified as top secret. Even more dramatic was the decision by the Court, including Nixon appointees, requiring the President to turn over to the special prosecutor the tapes of White House conversations that established Nixon's early involvement in the Watergate coverup and led to his resignation only days later.

While the Burger Court did restate the tests of obscenity and pornography to permit regulation of a broader run of materials and also to judge materials by local rather than national standards, it basically stood by its abortion decisions and expanded the scope of affirmative action. As a result it was epitomized by one writer as representing "the counterrevolution that wasn't." This epithet proved a bit premature, however, for in the last months of the Burger Court a significant abridgment of the MIRANDA doctrine finally occurred. The majority found that where police had acted in "good faith," the fact that material was seized illegally did not require exclusion from evidence. Another decision sustained governmental rights to hold high-risk criminals in jail awaiting trial as a form of preventive detention. Burger's avowed program of tougher treatment of accused criminals was at a high-water mark.

The Rehnquist Years (1980–   ): Which Way for the Court?

When Burger stepped down at the end of the 1985–86 term, President Reagan quickly elevated William Rehnquist, the most conservative member of the Court, to Chief Justice and nominated Antonin Scalia, a Court of Appeals judge and University of Chicago Law School professor, for the vacancy. There was only mild opposition to either nomination. Though Scalia was known as a libertarian conservative, he was replacing a conservative and was the first Italian-American Supreme Court Justice.

When Justice Powell retired the following year, however, the nomination of Robert Bork was hotly contested. Liberal groups were opposed to Bork, who had for decades been a scathing critic of most major Supreme Court decisions — many of which at the confirmation hearings he now professed to accept. Bork's hearings were extensive, and senators probed his attitudes toward constitutional matters to an unprecedented degree. In the end he failed to convince senators that his view was not one of drastically revising and rolling back important judicial protections of freedom. Although Bork was considered a distinguished legal thinker and a successful soliciter general and judge, his rejection was based on asserted extremes of ideology, a claim the Senate had not really put forward much in this century, though it had in earlier years. Crucial was the feeling that the Court was evenly balanced and that an extreme figure would radically tilt that balance away from center. Finally, Judge Anthony Kennedy, a California conservative acceptable to almost everyone, was confirmed.

Chief Justice Rehnquist, personally popular with the justices, has been a brisk administrator under whose direction Court business has been completed significantly earlier than under Burger and, superficially at least, with less acrimony. In his first years the Court has continued to follow both moderate liberal and moderate conservative doctrine.

But the 1988–89 term seems to point definitively to a new conservatism, with Justice Kennedy emerging both as a strong conservative and an articulate spokesman. Key issues such as the abortion decision, the interpretation of race discrimination, and police discretion have been modified in significant ways, and overruling of some decisions seems likely as the Rehnquist court finally emerges with the conservative majority so long sought by Presidents Nixon and Reagan.

Judicial Activism and Judicial Restraint

Judicial Restraint

Traditionally, judges embrace notions of limited authority and constrained activity, for such a position is at the same time a shield and a claim. If judging is limited to a tiny segment of political claims made in a society, then the judiciary can truly advertise itself as the least dangerous branch of government. If it functions within a sphere of legally defined and rather precise circumstances, the judiciary can claim it is acting in obedience to that mandate and not volitionally.

The notion that the power of declaring legislative acts unconstitutional should be exercised with circumspection arises from Marshall's seminal opinion in MARBURY. The Supreme Court, he suggests, should use the power only when there is a collision of law and the Constitution, and only in clear cases of conflict. Some critics have suggested that limiting the power to "clear cases" is a confession of doubt as to whether it is appropriate at all. At any rate, Marshall acknowledged that congressional action represents the voice of the people-in-day-to-day-politics. It is the superior voice of the people-as-Constitution-makers that the judges implement.

The argument for limited use of judicial review helped keep the Court in check for the better part of a century. Only as regular invalidation became the pattern did a sustained critique of judicial review emerge.

The clearest exposition of a highly limited judicial role was developed by J. B. Thayer, a great

Harvard law professor, who deeply impressed many students, including Justice-to-be Felix Frankfurter. In a classic essay on "The Origin and Scope of the American Doctrine of Constitutional Law," Thayer made the case for delimiting judicial review as a highly exceptional incursion on majority review. Whether one looked at the rhetoric of judges about the power, or the actual behavior of courts in using judicial review, most of the first century of our experience clearly showed it was not conceived of as a routine matter. Thayer, writing in 1893, suggested the Courts were beginning to depart from this pattern of deference to legislatures and violating the Marshallian injunction to invalidate only in clear cases. Statutes, Thayer argued, should be invalidated only when clearly irrational or when in clear repudiation of the Constitution. His critics suggested Thayer wanted the Court to function as a "lunacy commission" sustaining "rational" legislation and invalidating it only when the legislature had gone mad. Supporters suggested such a line of demarcation was necessary if we were to avoid substituting government by "nine old men" for majority rule.

On the Court, a parallel argument was being advanced by Justice Oliver Wendell Holmes, later joined by Justice Louis Brandeis. The former was a philosopher and legal historian of the highest order, the latter a legal technician and social architect; together they constituted a formidable duo. Justice Harlan Stone experienced a complete transformation under their influence. Justice Frankfurter, their friend and disciple, was to continue the argument until his own retirement in 1962.

The Holmes-Brandeis argument substantially emphasized the primacy of the will of the majority and the duty of the judges to defer to that will. "Courts are not the only agency of government that are presumed to have the capacity to govern," Justice Stone sarcastically suggested in one dissent. The right of review was also circumscribed. Whether the enacting agency had the power to deal with a subject was a legitimate inquiry. But the wisdom of the legislation was not a subject that ought to concern judges.

Brandeis also perfected a series of techniques to limit the judiciary. Taking seriously Marshall's suggestion that the Court act on constitutionality only when confronted by the dilemma of contradiction between Constitution and statute, he suggested ways by which the Court should minimize such contradictions — for example, by reinterpreting statutes wherever possible to avoid unconstitutionality. Brandeis meticulously scanned past opinions to produce his masterful ASHWANDER (1935) rules. This gem of legal craftsmanship purports to be merely summary (which in part it was, of course) of rules by which the Court avoids exercise of judicial review. By force of its compilation, the ASHWANDER summary influenced future cases and made it less seemly for justices to plunge into constitutional rulings when they could be avoided.

This two-pronged effort pushed the Court in one direction: Except under extreme conditions, courts should avoid making social policy, avoid standing in the way of making social policy, and avoid standing in the way of popular majorities. To help ensure this, judges should construe strictly their own jurisdiction, ruling on questions only when stringent requirements for court action were met.

The Brandeis-Holmes-Stone classic articulation of this philosophy of restraint was developed in response to a Court trying to constrain both national and state governments to economic formulae regarded by most as obsolete. By the mid-1940s, the classic Holmes-Brandeis-Stone dissents had prevailed, but Justice Frankfurter felt their truths still applied to efforts to use the judiciary to promote civil liberties. Recognizing a special judicial obligation to the Bill of Rights, Frankfurter insisted the judicial role in such matters was not substantially different from the judge's function in, say, preventing taking of property or protecting free movement of goods in interstate commerce. Most of the key protections of the individual against governmental intrusion on "economic" or "civil" liberty are commingled throughout the Constitution; often they are cheek-by-jowl, as in the Fifth Amendment, which protects both against taking of property and against compulsory self-incrimination. The judiciary, Frankfurter insisted, had no more right to bifurcate the Bill of Rights and create hierarchies of rights than the Taft Court had to hallow the liberty of contract above all other privileges. Ultimately, he argued, if judges were seen as the real defenders of liberty of expression and the equalizer of all, the public would never learn the fundamental truth that freedom required majority support to survive. Both because he respected majority rule and because he felt majority lapses from full freedom should become object lessons in the cost of such lapses, Frankfurter argued against heavy-handed judicial creativity, even in the interest of liberty and equality.

The Warren Court found Frankfurter's approach less and less attractive, and his influence waned over the last years. Still, John Marshall Harlan, like Frankfurter a highly respected craftsman, and Lewis Powell made the argument of judicial restraint uniquely their own.

Off the Court, too, there have been significant contributions to the argument for judicial restraint. Herbert Wechsler, a great criminal law innovator as well as constitutional expert, suggested that activism and "result-oriented" decision making undercut the basic contribution of law, which is the development of "neutral general principles." (A dramatic example of such general principles in action occurred when American Nazis were allowed to march in Chicago under legal doctrine developed in response to the civil rights marches of Dr. Martin Luther King in the 1960s.)

Alexander Bickel, an admirer of Frankfurter, also contributed to concepts of restraint. Noting that the eye of the journalist catches the dramatic assertion of power, Bickel exalted the "passive virtues" of courts that knew when not to intervene, either for reasons of lack of authority or, even, for tactical reasons. Certainly, the Taney Court might have profited from a moral lecture suggesting that there are times when Courts should not decide, in a case before them, every fundamental issue they can think of.

Result-Oriented Law: Judicial Activism

Doubts about the legal power of the Court were historically those of the democratic, majoritarian left, who saw the Court as a facade by which their cause was continuously thwarted. The departure from democracy was seen as usurpation. As the Court now has served their purposes for four decades, liberals generally have made their peace with Court action. Although the political right is more inclined to see the Court as a legal rather than a political institution, the Republican platform of 1980, with an explicit call for pledges from prospective appointees on key issues, is the clearest example of accepting the Court as a pure instrument of policy.

In terms of actions of the justices, the result-oriented approach has been called "activism." The recourse to legal techniques for limiting court intervention is labeled "judicial restraint." By and large, the terms have been fighting labels of the "restraint" people — Frankfurter, Harlan, and Lewis Powell. Those justices most accused of "activism" — like Black, Douglas, Murphy, and Warren — never accepted the label or acknowledged its applicability. It is indeed difficult to see how a judge could officially accept such a description without losing effectiveness both on and off the Court.

One of the most impassioned pleas for activism is the dissenting opinion of Sutherland, for himself and the other members of the ultraconservative bloc of the 1930s. Stung by Stone's widely praised dissent in U.S. v. BUTLER (1936), which sternly warned against judicial abuse of power and called for exercise of restraint, Sutherland replied effectively, if a year late, in WEST COAST HOTEL CO. V. PARRISH (1937):

... [R]ational doubts must be resolved in favor of the constitutionality of the statute. But whose doubts, and by whom resolved? Undoubtedly it is the duty of a member of the court, in the process of reaching a right conclusion, to give due weight to the opposing views of his associates; but in the end, the question which he must answer is not whether such views seem sound to those who entertain them, but whether they convince him that the statute is constitutional or engender in his mind a rational doubt upon that issue. The oath which he takes as a judge is not a composite oath, but an individual one. And in passing upon the validity of a statute, he discharges a duty imposed upon *him,* which cannot be consummated justly by an automatic acceptance of the views of others which have neither convinced, nor created a reasonable doubt in his mind. If upon a question so important he thus surrender his deliberate judgment, he stands forsworn. He cannot subordinate his convictions to that extent and keep faith with his oath or retain his judicial and moral independence.

The suggestion that the only check upon the exercise of the judicial power, when properly invoked, to declare a constitutional right superior to an unconstitutional statute is the judge's own faculty of self-restraint, is both ill considered and mischievous. Self-restraint belongs in the domain of will and not of judgment. The check upon the judge is that imposed by his oath of office, by the Constitution and by his own conscientious and informed convictions; and since he has the duty to make up his own mind and adjudge accordingly, it is hard to see how there could be any other restraint.

Today's activists essentially are still the intellectual heirs of the Holmes-Brandeis-Stone tradition and have usually found it necessary to distance themselves from this suggestion that the Constitution is simply the product of its impact on the minds of five justices.

Paradoxically, modern activists find their justifications in one of the most distinctive contributions of Mr. Justice Stone's, his famous footnote in the CAROLENE PRODUCTS case. Like scripture, Stone can be quoted with great power, on both sides of this debate.

Stone's basic notion is attractive and simple. Economic and other social policies should be decided, in the main, by majoritarian agencies in a democratic society. If bad policies are adopted, the hue and cry will cause reappraisal. Good causes will be convincing causes. They do not require judicial protection.

Restrictions on freedom of expression, however, are not only bad policies. They also prevent appeal to the corrective mechanism, the thinking process of the community. The special class of laws that simultaneously change the right of political effectiveness and prevent redress includes not only political expression (press, speech, political organization), but also apportionment, voting, and representation. In this domain, judges with technical knowledge and a broad view of constitutional history can bring something special to bear. Because they do not act as representatives of an economic class and are not involved in immediate social conflicts, the judges are more able to take the long view than persons in other branches of government.

The Court's detachment, Stone suggested, also allows it to protect those politically isolated groups that find it hard to protect themselves in the majoritarian arena. The protection of the unpopular group or the weak or politically isolated is, in this approach, a special responsibility of a nonpolitical, principled process. The Warren Court, in particular, saw its mission as the "elimination of nonpersons" in American law, which entailed expanding the groups specially protected. Among those were small religious groups, social radicals, criminals, the indigent, the illegitimate, and the mentally disturbed. While critics saw this mission as quixotic and arbitrary, its social appeal was manifest in its continuation and expansion, though at a slower pace, under the Burger Court.

Activism has rallied around this attractive role and gone well beyond it. Stone, Frankfurter, and Jackson, who were initially eager to see the Court protect liberty more, came to feel that new doctrines were undermining majority rule.

Still, the implications of liberal activism were barely spelled out in their lifetimes. It was, as we have noted, the Warren Court, garlanded with its triumph in ending legal segregation, that went on to tackle other social issues, including de facto segregation, with less clearcut results.

Racial discrimination was not merely attacked by the courts under their constitutional authority. Congress passed broad statutes instructing courts to protect all kinds of minorities, in treatment by government, with respect to housing, schooling, right of employment, pay, and conditions of employment. The effect was to blur the boundaries of courts acting under Fourteenth Amendment standards and under specific statutes. It also cast federal courts in unfamiliar, and even administrative, tasks.

Nor is this bursting of legal patterns limited to minority rights. It includes expanding legal protections for women (who are numerically the majority). Similarly, the administration of programs nominally for the benefit of "weaker" groups such as welfare recipients, the handicapped, prisoners, and the mentally ill has been closely scrutinized by courts in recent years. This is in sharp contrast to norms prevailing before the 1960s, when such matters involving "grants" rather than "entitlements" would have been seen as free-will gifts governments could offer with whatever conditions and brusqueness they wished. The domains of consumer protection, production safety for employees, and environmental protection, though statutory in origin, have also involved the courts in unprecedented ways with the issues involved and the very mode of court interaction with society.

The leading interpreter of these developments is Abram Chayes, a Harvard law professor, who sees federal courts as constructively moving slowly away from preoccupation with relatively trivial disputes between two private parties and moving toward a "public law" concern. Elaborating Chayes' notions, Owen Fiss suggests that judges now have taken broad responsibility to affect structural reform; that is, the courts have undertaken institutional supervision and reconstruction. As government bureaucracies become both larger and less visibly accountable, society (including Congress) expects the courts to be troubleshooters and supervisors of those structures.

The new activism is currently even more characteristic of lower courts than of the more conservative Supreme Court, but the Burger Court did not move in any decisive way to stem the tide. Rather, its moves were small-scale, generally resulting in multifaceted rules that maximized its own decision-making power, and therefore aggravated the problem of judicial policy making.

Donald Horowitz has sharply criticized the courts for intruding into areas that transcend their capacities, into social engineering, where the judges try to predict what effect policies will have on public behavior — a role best left, he asserts, to the legislative branches. Another leading critic, Nathan Glazer, a neoconservative sociologist, suggests the Court has destroyed the old limits imposed by technical rules of standing of litigants, ripeness of review, and doctrines of restraint like the political questions doctrine. At the same time they have, he suggests, become convinced political reprisals are ineffectual. Remedies for court overreaching are available in the President, in Congress' control over jurisdiction, in congressional power over the number of justices on the Court, and even in the right of impeachment. But efforts to "curb the court" have failed miserably over nearly four decades. Thus we have created, in Glazer's view, an "imperial judiciary."

But judicial activism need not be seen as completely subjective and arbitrary. As Thomas Grey argues, principled doctrine can be formulated around constitutional words. These principles, in turn, if carefully chosen and articulated, create a legal imperative that leads to still other decisions. It is at least arguable that the main reason the Burger Court was not able to reverse Warren Court doctrine is precisely because the Warren Court's somewhat sloppy decisions concealed reliance on persuasive principles. Critics of the Warren Court may have underestimated the force of long-standing doctrine, as did those who admired it precisely because they thought the liberal justices had abandoned the boundaries of legal rules.

In general, result-oriented law is a dangerous game for the Court. If it is indeed a question of will and not law, why should lawyers have a monopoly? And why so small a group as the Supreme Court? And why not a court whose membership is replenished more regularly?

At present there is little challenge to the general legitimacy of judicial review and Supreme Court power — even federal court power — over policy on principles. There are strong pockets of criticism of specific lines of decision — abortion, busing, police control, school prayer — that have persisted for some time and have won some on-Court or off-Court victories. There also is a broad intellectual challenge to the continued expansion of judicial power. Yet pragmatically we turn in that direction on more and more matters. There is tension and trouble inherent in that contradiction. It is not clear that the Rehnquist court will content itself with less activism. It seems likely, in fact, that it will merely alter the values aggressively defended.

Federal and State Court Systems

The peculiarities of federalism are emphatically reflected in our complex legal system. Basically the federal judicial order serves to deal with litigation based upon congressional legislation, federal crimes, and violations of treaties. By and large, state systems are independent and handle the bulk of their cases without federal appeal. In terms of numbers, federal cases constitute only a few thousand a year. State cases have never been thoroughly enumerated but may be estimated at some seven or eight million a year. The regular federal courts, then, are an elite corps of only some 650 judges with a highly select load.

The structure of the federal courts is basic. The lowest federal court is the district court, with at least one such court in each state. As of the mid-1980s, the districts were organized into eleven circuits (plus the District of Columbia), with a court of appeals (of from four to twenty-three judges) in each. Generally, appeals are heard by a panel of three appellate judges, although in cases of exceptional significance a full court may hear the case in what is called an en banc proceeding. Another special procedure, in cases deemed urgent, is a mixed three-person court composed of both district and appellate judges, with appeal direct to the Supreme Court. In addition, there is a new Court of Appeals for the Federal Circuit, with power over specified special courts.

Most federal appeals follow the ordinary route and end with the court of appeals. Cases may also originate within administrative units, especially the independent regulatory commissions, and are heard either at the district court or court of appeals, as Congress has prescribed.

The Supreme Court has been given virtually complete authority over its docket, mainly in two important steps — in 1925 and in 1988. The Judges' Act of 1925 allowed most cases to come up under a writ of certiorari. Under this form of review the Justices have complete discretion whether to take jurisdiction or not. In keeping with a commitment made by Chief Justice Taft to Congress on passage of the Judges' Act, certiorari is granted even with one less than a majority. (This is known as the Rule of Four, though when a full Court is not sitting it can require only three positive votes.)

For over sixty years after that the Court operated under congressional requirement that it automatically review certain decisions, e.g., when a federal court invalidated a state statute or when a state court declared federal legislation. Over the years these cases constituted up to 20 percent of the Supreme Court's load. As pressure on Court capacity developed, the Court began to treat "mandatory" appeals much as it treated requests for certiorari. Cases under mandatory appeal were decided without oral argument. Instead of rejection by the curt formula "certiorari denied," the case was "dismissed for want of a substantial federal question" — hardly more helpful. Yet cases denied certiorari technically created no precedent and mandatory appeals did — without real guidance to lower courts.

Congress essentially ended this state of affairs in 1988. With very minor remaining exceptions the Supreme Court's mandatory jurisdiction ended in September of that year, except for "grandfathered" cases already docketed or appealable to the Supreme Court at the date of the law's effectiveness. It will take a year or two of experience to see if this provides the Court much relief or changes its mix of cases.

Another basis for Supreme Court action is a lower court request for clarification of a matter of law. This is called "certification" and is quite infrequently invoked.

The net effect of all this is that the Supreme Court is now in a position to make its choices of the 150 or so cases fully argued before it with more freedom. Virtually all cases will uniformly come to it as petitions for certiorari.

Cases appealed from state courts to the federal system go directly to the Supreme Court. Often the plaintiffs will have an option to file in the federal courts at the beginning of their dispute, or the defendants may convince a judge that the appropriate forum is the federal court. But generally, proceedings undertaken at the state level must be pursued to the highest state court having authority over such cases. The party must "exhaust local remedies" if machinery for redress exists. The case cannot be appealed to the Supreme Court on simple error of fact or even on most questions of law. Rather, a federal question—a violation of a federal statute, a treaty, or a violation of constitutional provision—must be involved. In recent decades a violation of the Fourteenth Amendment has become the most common basis of appeal. However, if the Supreme Court finds for the plaintiff, it seldom decides such a case in its basic form or "on the merits." Only the federal question is resolved, and the case is then remanded to the state court, often with the litany "for proceedings not inconsistent with this decision."

Even among federal cases, constitutional law issues come up only in a tiny fraction. Bankruptcy and immigration cases bulk large in terms of numbers, but only a few are of importance to those not involved in the proceedings. Antitrust or tax cases may involve millions (or even billions) of dollars, take years to decide, and affect the lives of millions. But constitutional law issues—by which we mean issues affecting the legal relations between major governmental units or between individuals and such units—can arise in trivial cases

as well as expensive or complex ones. Constitutional law cases of note have arisen, for example, in *U.S.* v. *Twelve 200 Foot Reels of Super 8 mm film* or *U.S.* v. *43 Gallons of Whiskey*. The setting may be a conflict between a President and a Congress that has reason to believe he is a lawbreaker (U.S. v. NIXON), or arise out of a property dispute (SHELLEY V. KRAEMER), or involve a man who shoots a few birds (MISSOURI V. HOLLAND). The great decisions that sometimes flow from trivial fact situations give the courts a human touch absent in big bureaucratic settings or in the bustle of legislative traffic.

Federal judicial jurisdiction is grounded in Article III of the Constitution, but Congress has wide, almost untrammeled, latitude in allocating it. Only a Supreme Court is specified, and Congress may create any number of inferior courts. Though the Constitution seems to confer automatic jurisdiction on the Supreme Court, subject to exceptions by Congress, the Court has operated under the assumption that Congress has ultimate authority here and that nonconferral is as decisive as express denial. (See EX PARTE MCCARDLE, 1869.) This may be a response to the comprehensiveness of admirably drawn statutes. At any rate, Hart and Wechsler note that Congress has not acted as drastically in some of the reallocations in past history as is assumed. They speculate that under no conditions could the Supreme Court be deprived of so much review authority that it would become inferior to one of the inferior courts mentioned in Article III.

Jurisdiction is based upon either the nature of the parties or the source of law. Suits between states, or involving official foreign representation, or involving citizens of different states (diversity jurisdiction), or against the United States are examples of the first. Admirality law, constitutional treaty law, and claims under U.S. legislation or administrative provisions are examples of federal matters by nature of the law involved.

Suits against consuls and ambassadors and between states are specified as part of the original jurisdiction of the Supreme Court. The Court would act as the trial court, hearing witnesses, and reaching conclusions. However, Congress has also delegated such proceedings to lower courts. It would appear, then, that Congress may subtract from, but not add to, original jurisdiction (see MARBURY). In suits between states, usually boundary or water rights cases, the Court generally appoints a Master acquainted with the technical problems and rubber-stamps the results. Any authorization for citizen suits against states was theoretically nullified by the Eleventh Amendment. Such cases now come up, whether on appeal or through certiorari, as proceedings against state officials, so technically they do not violate the Amendment.

Diversity jurisdiction (suits between citizens of different states) was once regarded as highly necessary, for fear that the courts of a state would heavily favor its own citizens. Today's mobility and the national scope of business affairs seem to make this an anachronism. With federal courts busy implementing broad social policy and a reluctance to expand the federal courts, there is considerable support for eliminating diversity jurisdiction, thereby forcing such cases back into the state courts. (Diversity cases, which constitute a high percentage of federal bench time, would be a tiny proportion of state time and might be absorbed, in large part, without personnel increases, it is argued.)

Congress' power to allocate jurisdiction to various courts can be (and has been) exercised on the basis of subject matter, the dates cases are filed, the nature of the parties, the amounts involved — virtually every reasonable classification. The power is subject to constitutional limits, particularly of the Due Process Clause of the Fifth Amendment. For example, when the Nixon administration backed a provision prohibiting courts from ordering busing in desegregation for a period of years, most constitutional authorities expressed concern and the measure never passed. (The question mooted was, if a court found that busing was the sole remaining measure to vindicate rights, how could Congress proscribe it?)

If Congress provided that no busing cases could be appealed to the Supreme Court, it almost certainly would be within its powers. In view of the special requirements for courts and Congress as to race under the Fourteenth and Fifteenth Amendments, it probably could not delegate all authority over desegregation to state courts, though it might have a chance of being sustained by delegating all educational questions to them. It is doubtful, though, that any action short of a constitutional amendment could preclude totally some federal court ruling on properly raised constitutional questions. (See YAKUS V. UNITED STATES, 1944.)

When Congress is unhappy with a Court decision it can easily move to reverse the doctrine but not the result as to the immediate parties, if what is involved is interpretation of an Act of Congress. Constitutional decisions normally can be altered only by amendments. But reversal through alteration of jurisdiction — cutting the courts out of the picture — is, practically speaking, extremely difficult. To eliminate review by the Supreme Court is to permit different decisions to prevail in different parts of the country, to bring the country back to a preconstitutional stage. Furthermore, legislation about jurisdiction is always technical and subject to judicial interpretation. While pro-segregation interpositionists tried to use this power of Congress as a weapon to punish the Court in the 1960s, the efforts failed, though sometimes by hairline margins.

Under President Nixon, a commission recommended creation of a National Court to hear routine cases, subject to Supreme Court authority to review decisions of this body. Supreme Court liberals remain suspicious that such a court would be used to curtail judicial power through manipulation of jurisdiction.

During the Reagan administration there were ingenious proposals of various kinds to alter the drift of Supreme Court decisions. The most ingenious was the attempt to overrule ROE V. WADE (1973), the abortion decision, by a legislative finding that the term *person* in the Fourteenth Amendment encompasses the fetus. In effect, Congress would amend the Fourteenth Amend-

Simplified Organizational Chart of the Federal Court System

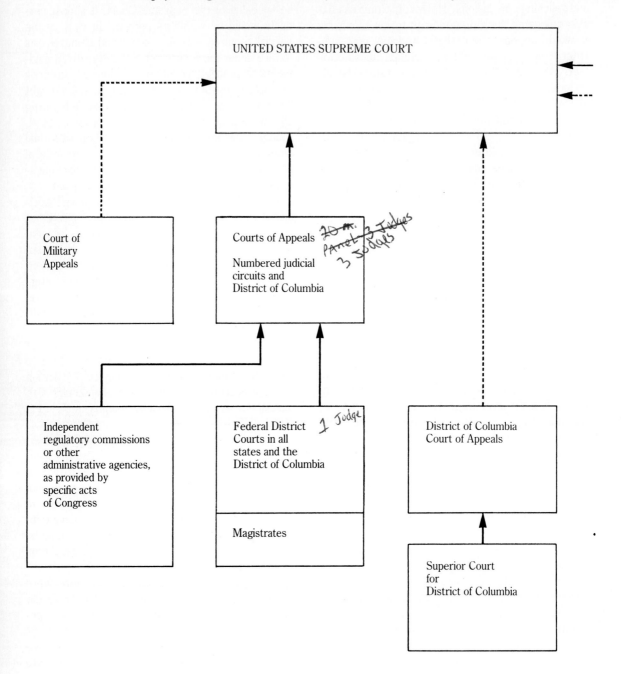

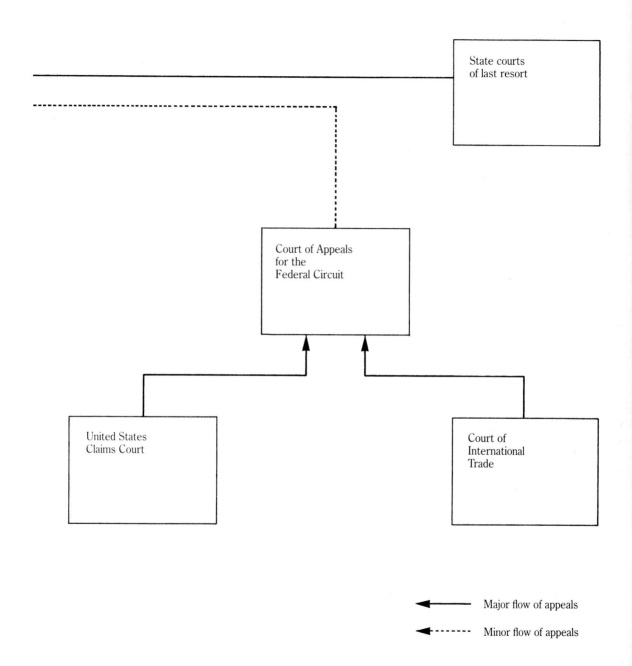

State courts
of last resort

Court of Appeals
for the
Federal Circuit

United States
Claims Court

Court of
International
Trade

◄──────── Major flow of appeals

◄------- Minor flow of appeals

ment to encompass the fetus, and it would do so through legislation. This is superficially sanctioned by some careless judicial language in civil rights cases by liberal opinion writers, but is basically an ultraconservative effort to deal with the sense of powerlessness created by Court decisions. Conservative figures like Robert Bork have warned against the action while approving the objective, since it could undercut judicial review itself.

The Supreme Court in Operation

The Supreme Court is a humanized institution, with a life and charm of its own. When the present stately building was inaugurated, one justice described himself and his colleagues as "nine black-robed beetles in the Temple of Karnak," but in fact the Court operates with great style, some intimacy, and usually with courtliness. Conferences start with mutual handshakes — forty-five in all. A year before the appointment of Justice O'Connor, the Court dropped the traditional

"Mr. Justice" in its proceedings, not simply to avoid embarassment to the newcomer but to signal the appropriateness of a woman's being appointed to the Court.

The publication of Woodward and Armstrong's *The Brethren,* a book about personal conflict, rivalry, and other human emotions on the Court, came as a source of titillation to some, but hardly a surprise to students of psychology, institutions, or the law. The Court has had its share of all types, including McReynolds, a crabbed, narrow man who refused to speak to colleagues out of prejudice, and Douglas, a brilliant, restless, and difficult man whose real interests were off the Court. In writing about the Court, commentators have usually emphasized the admirable, the heroic, and the detached. Other commentators have written with perspicacity about human interrelations and human frailty within the constraints of legal institutions. Beveridge's *Marshall,* Mason's *Stone,* and Walter Murphy's *Elements of Judicial Strategy* all present a more penetrating view of the Supreme Court justice as a real-life decision maker.

Limits on the Courts

Hamilton, in *Federalist* 78, referred to the courts as "the least dangerous" branch. Marshall, as we have noted, repeated the argument in many cases. Courts are not in a position to go out to do business; they only react to dilemmas in the course of trying ordinary cases. Then they must answer questions, including constitutional ones. They also are dealing with legislation subject to change by other agencies of government; indeed a court's right to hear cases is subject to control by the other, aggressive, "more dangerous branches," which can create policies and programs whenever they wish and can act on their own timetables in initiating, modifying, and enforcing policies. Courts must wait for parties to ask before they answer, must respect limits in the law, and must depend on the executive branch to

enforce their pronouncements. They control, as Hamilton said, neither purse nor sword.

No matter how different its powers are, the United States Supreme Court, in its manner of accepting cases, functions as an ordinary court. In many ways its rules are stricter than most. Care in taking on cases is even a protection to the Court, a mark of its own respect for legal precision.

Historically, the Court has elaborated rules of abstention regarding where it is improper for it to intervene. For a case to be heard, there must be a clear collision of interests in a concrete way. The parties must be in a position to demonstrate the conflict, to make a request for concrete remedies, and to prove they are appropriate representatives of each claim. This has been consistently held to be the meaning of the Court's right to hear "cases" and "controversies" (art. III, §2), which is changeable only by constitutional amendment. Many courts, including American courts, have the right to issue advisory opinions (e.g., as to the constitutionality of a statute or the meaning of an agreement), if proper governmental authorities seek guidance. This has consistently been rejected for federal courts. (The precedent, oddly, was established in an exchange of letters between President Washington and Chief Justice Jay.)

Another limit is jurisdiction (or the authority to decide a case) as conferred or denied by the Constitution or Congress. The Court has generally accepted the highly deferential tone toward legislative power over jurisdiction, represented here by MCCARDLE. This deference is far less complete than appears on the surface. Courts usually have the last word as specific and complex cases arise, and congressional composition and attitudes are usually more fluid and fickle than judicial ones. Courts can, therefore, reinterpret statutes in many instances, even those intended originally to limit them. By and large, however, the constitutional language leaves little room — though, as noted, some leeway — for thwarting congressional supremacy over jurisdiction.

There are derivative principles that the Court has felt followed from this basic reality. Justice Brandeis pulled together a list of these principles in a case, ASHWANDER V. T.V.A., and that list is often cited as an authoritative compilation of "rules of the game" in Supreme Court proceedings. Brandeis was that unusual combination — a fervent, activist public servant, whom Holmes called "Isaiah" for his intensity, yet one of the greatest legal sticklers ever to serve as a Supreme Court justice. His listing of when Court action or interference is improper has special significance in the light of its compiler, and it has highly influenced subsequent Supreme Court discussions.

In recent years critics like Nathan Glazer, who speaks of an "imperial judiciary," have charged that the courts have run roughshod over the notion of technical restraints and have adopted the idea that they are free-floating censors of public policy, fairy godfathers who have the right to wave wands and correct any evil they see. Supporters of the Court say there has been a relaxation of formalism but that legal action is still channelled and restricted. Glazer also suggests the courts are now too insulated from political pressure and that the sense that courts are not primary policy makers has unfortunately been eliminated. Presumably, he would welcome the legislative attacks of the 1980s on constitutional decisions (though perhaps hoping for their failure), to remind the courts of the restraint which Hamilton and Marshall believed was the essence of their role.

Cases, Controversies, and Standing

As noted, the federal courts have strict rules about hearing cases. Since a "case or controversy" is required, the question of who may bring an action becomes vital. This issue is called "standing," and the law has moved in differing ways on this. In one sense, our sensitivity has grown to the appearance of collusion or false controversy. In an early case, *Hylton* v. *U.S.* (1796), it was alleged by Hylton that he had "125 chariots for hire." This was an absurd claim, made only to allow the case to meet the required dollar amount for standing. Still, there was a real controversy over the tax, the fiction being only about the amount involved. More recently, in CARTER V. CARTER COAL CO. (1936), Mr. Carter sued his own, completely owned, company to challenge a federal tax. In fact, the U.S. government as "intervenor" defended that tax, not the nominal party, the company. But under today's standards neither case would be allowed.

A broader view of what is a genuine controversy now prevails. Using devices developed in equity law, the federal courts permit third parties clearly involved in a controversy and affected by a decision to become "intervenors," or regular participators in a three-or-more-handed suit. Those who individually have small or minor interests may amalgamate into a "class action" suit. So, for example, where drug companies were found guilty of price-fixing on a specific remedy, many millions of dollars could be returned to a very large group of people (each with claims of only a few dollars) on the basis of one proceeding.

The courts also have shown greater sensitivity to "legal interests" that are nonmonetary but have a general benefit. There are limits, as indicated by *Sierra Club* v. *Morton* (1972). It is almost certain, though, that had members of the Sierra Club alleged they were campers who would use the facilities and so lose a benefit, standing would have been granted. The Club wished to expand further the tendency of the Warren Court to treat standing generously. They claimed the right to intervene solely because they were interested in conservation as a policy, and if granted, this would have drastically changed the concept of standing. One of the Burger Court tendencies was to slow down and even roll back concepts of standing, particularly of class actions (see WARTH V. SELDIN, 1975). Burger Court decisions as to notifying members of the alleged class and allowing them to object had this effect, for it raised the question of when and whether a half-dozen people can claim to really represent millions. (At the same time, Congress may define a class with a clear right to litigate, e.g., blacks or women, and the courts do operate quite differently when a legislatively defined class is involved in the litigation.)

One form of standing the federal courts had not allowed for half a century was taxpayer suits, unless an identifiable tax was being challenged, or if clear differences accrue to the litigant if the specific expenditure was prohibited. Otherwise, a taxpayer would have needed only a rather general right to sue wherever expenditure is involved. Still, most states allow such suits. In FROTHING-HAM V. MELLON (1923), a federal rejection of such suits was decided. It was not totally clear whether the Supreme Court was refusing because there was no "case or controversy" (a constitutional and unchangeable basis), or if this was a rule of convenience, created by the justices, so that federal courts would not have to deal with such a trivial and remote interest. A clue that it was the latter was that taxpayer suits, where the taxpayer lost at the state level, were permitted On Appeal at the Supreme Court level as early as 1947.

The definitive answer did not come until FLAST V. COHEN (1968), although Congress had seriously considered ordering the courts to move in that direction a decade earlier. The issue in FLAST had been discussed at elaborate length in congressional hearings.

Some provisions of the Constitution appear litigation-proof even if they are violated, if normal concepts of standing are used. One obvious example is the provision prohibiting an establishment of religion under conditions when all religions receive payments. (The provisions listed by the late Justice Jackson as "disaster potentials," seemingly beyond the reach of the courts, are the war powers and the taxing and spending provisions. Interestingly, in both instances Congress has now given the courts a handle to deal with such problems.)

The Court's decision in FLAST is a very curious one, indeed. The taxpayer rule clearly is labeled a rule of convenience, an extension of the *de minimus* principle: "The law does not concern itself with trifles." Exceptions will be made, it seems, for religious expenditure cases and for other basic constitutional rights, left undefined, when normal rules of standing to sue will not permit reasonable Court review. FLAST is a very ad hoc, maybe even ad lib, decision, serving notice that hit-and-miss exceptions can be expected. No other application of the FLAST special dispensation rule has occurred.

The central meaning is striking. Formal rules of standing (which were developed largely in this century) will be relaxed under proper circumstances to follow the basic constitutional mandate. To admirers this is following the banner of justice. To others the judges have abandoned regularity. Oddly, this wild-card rule, hardly applied, still arouses controversy.

Expansion of Court Activity Illustrated: The Decline of the Political Questions Doctrine

A very special form of Court abnegation has historically been the "political questions" doctrine, a vague but intriguing concept. Beginning with Marshall's decision in *Martin* v. *Mott* (1827), the Court has suggested it should not intrude when another branch of government exercises discretion that is properly within its domain. The concept adds a family relationship to the concept of judicial restraint.

John P. Frank has suggested four elements enter into the Court's evaluation of a matter as a political question: (1) where there is a need for a quick and single policy; (2) areas of obvious judicial incompetence; (3) clear prerogative of another branch of government; and (4) avoidance of unmanageable situations. The political questions doctrine has little to do with whether politics or controversy is involved, but is closer to a notion of separation of powers that emphasizes each branch in its own place, where it can deal with a matter effectively.

Critics of the concept have suggested it was a beautifully crafted cop-out, an escape hatch by which the justices avoided making decisions that were awkward or embarrassing or politically dangerous. As judicial activism became more conspicuous, the doctrine has been challenged and confined. The Warren Court sharply limited its sway.

The areas where the political questions doctrine has been most prominent are foreign affairs and national defense. There the tests coalesce. It is difficult to see the Court coming forth with a good invasion plan for Normandy Beach or an opinion of what the precedents suggest we do about Russian intervention in Afghanistan. A policy (say, a deployment of troops) subject to later overruling by a 5-to-4 judicial decision is not going to be one enthusiastically supported by our European allies.

And daily events are not easily processed by courts. For all of these reasons, the doctrine has held here, even in an era in which it has had little support in other areas.

But the political questions doctrine has been scuttled or diminished almost everywhere else. The first retreat occurred in the area of reapportionment. The leading precedent was of short vintage and doubtful authority but was defended ferociously by Justice Frankfurter and his coterie. The decision in *Colegrove* v. *Green* (1946) was made by a short-handed Court, and the leading opinion actually had the support of only three justices, who thought apportionment was a political question. Three dissenters wished to do something about the gross inequities developed. The swing justice—Justice Rutledge—felt that the shortness of time until election prevented equitable action by the Court.

This very curious and fragile lineup was somehow projected into the solid line of precedent Frankfurter saw as undermined by BAKER V. CARR (1962). In that case the majority of the Court decided that courts could deal with the apportionment of legislatures. The decision, Frankfurter warned, would lead to an ungovernable situation. How could a Court force an entire legislative body to enact legislation it had refused to pass previously?

In point of fact, action against legislatures has proven remarkably easy. In cases where membership is at stake, an order to the clerk not to pay (or to pay) a salary is completely effective. In parallel matters—for example, where judges have found that prisons with four prisoners crowded into one-person cells violate the "cruel and unusual punishment" provision of the Constitution—dealing with the problem also has not been especially difficult. Efforts to order expenditures directly have not been effective, but such remedies as ordering no new prisoners admitted until standards are met gives judges the leverage they need.

Far from not being able to direct events, federal courts have been more and more involved in such controls, and on less and less clear constitutional pretexts. There have been political protests of some intensity and critiques arguing that courts are not equipped to choose among the policy complexities involved. (Donald Horowitz's *The Courts and Social Policy* points to several cases where more and more intricate court orders covering minute details were issued without solving the basic problem.) All of this is a long way from the disaster predicted by Frankfurter. On the contrary, even when not remarkably successful, it is heady stuff for the judges and growing in scope.

It has proved remarkably easy for the courts to move against authorities at the state level. Indeed, it seems likely that the political questions doctrine no longer exists in state-federal relations but is now confined to relations between the branches at the national level. This does not mean the federal courts have abolished the idea of state prerogatives or repudiated the claims of federalism. It does mean that those prerogatives are weighed as one of many factors, and that deference to governors or legislatures is not in itself a complete or dispositive argument, as would be the case if the test were the political questions standard.

Encouraged by the sweep of their success at the state level, the justices have also curtailed the political questions doctrine at the federal level. This has emerged most clearly in dealing with Congress. POWELL V. MCCORMACK (1969), a technically impressive performance (a rarity for the Warren Court, and perhaps even rarer for the Burger Court), distinguished between the right of expulsion by a two-thirds vote and the power to seat an elected member, which requires a majority vote only. By mentioning both and indicating the basis for the exercise of the latter, the Constitution clearly required such matters as Powell's financial behavior to come under the expulsion process.

All of this is a good object lesson in the decline of the doctrine. Under the old interpretations, such matters as refusing to seat Victor Berger during World War I for opposition to the war was solely for the House to decide. Today, litigation would be expected and the Supreme Court would have the last word.

While the Court has rejected claims and supported congressional positions, it does the weighing and deciding. This means it is more vulnerable and more conspicuous when politically dangerous cases arise. It is now harder for the Court to decide not to decide, which was a safer posture in the past. To be sure, such considerations as lie at the basis for the political questions doctrine are still part of the decision. The factors that make judicial proceedings inefficient ways to deal with foreign policy and the historical prerogatives of the executive will be weighed against the asserted claim. Similarly, Congress' inherent control over the taxing and spending power is approached with deference by the judges. But when the decision is reached, it is on the level of constitutionally channelled policy making, rather than because judicial action is precluded by the logic of the system itself. The Court must put itself on the line and make a choice, leaving itself open to criticism. The decline of the "political questions" doctrine adds to the power of, but also the risk for, the Court of the future.

Cases

Marbury v. Madison

1 Cranch 137 (1803)
Vote: Unanimous

Marbury is the great precedent for judicial review, the first Supreme Court exercise of the power. The argument is anticipated in *Federalist* 78, and there are lower court precursors. Nevertheless, Marshall's opinion is much admired and studied.

The case arose out of the first changeover of party control, a tense and unprecedented scene. The Federalists created a number of new positions and rushed through the Senate a number of "midnight judges." Adams and his lame duck Secretary of State, John Marshall, the new Chief Justice, left behind them a number of commissions of appointment, and President Jefferson and his new Secretary of State, Madison, refused to deliver them to the Senate confirmees, denying them their positions. Marbury and others then sued for a writ of mandamus.

OPINION OF THE COURT. At the last term, on the affidavits then read and filed with the clerk, a rule was granted in this case, requiring the secretary of state to show cause why a *mandamus* should not issue, directing him to deliver to William Marbury his commission as a justice of the peace for the county of Washington, in the district of Columbia. . . .

. . . .

1. The first object of inquiry is — Has the applicant a right to the commission he demands?

. . . .

Mr. Marbury, then, since his commission was signed by the president, and sealed by the secretary of state, was appointed; and as the law creating the office, gave the officer a right to hold for five years, independent of the executive, the appointment was not revocable, but vested in the officer legal rights, which are protected by the laws of his country. To withhold his commission, therefore, is an act deemed by the court not warranted by law, but violative of a vested legal right.

2. This brings us to the secondary inquiry; which is: If he has a right, and that right has been violated, do the laws of his country afford him a remedy?

The very essence of civil liberty certainly consists in the right of every individual to claim the protection of the laws, whenever he receives an injury. One of the first duties of government is to afford that protection. . . .

The government of the United States has been emphatically termed a government of laws, and not of men. It will certainly cease to deserve this high appellation, if the laws furnish no remedy for the violation of a vested legal right. . . .

It is, then, the opinion of the Court: 1st. That by signing the commission of Mr. Marbury, the President of the United States appointed him a justice of peace for the county of Washington, in the district of Columbia; and that the seal of the United States, affixed thereto by the secretary of state, is conclusive testimony of the verity of the signature, and of the completion of the appointment; and that the appointment conferred on him a legal right to the office for the space of five years. 2d. That, having this legal title to the office, he has a consequent right to the commission; a refusal to deliver which is a plain violation of that right, for which the laws of his country afford him a remedy.

3. It remains to be inquired whether he is entitled to the remedy for which he applies? This depends on — 1st. The nature of the writ applied for; and 2d. The power of this court.

1st. The nature of the writ. Blackstone, in the 3d volume of his Commentaries, page 110, defines a *mandamus* to be "a command issuing in the king's name, from the court of king's bench, and directed to any person, corporation or inferior court of judicature, within the king's dominions, requiring them to do some particular thing therein specified. . . ."

. . . .

This, then, is a plain case for a *mandamus*, either to deliver the commission, or a copy of it from the record; and it only remains to be inquired, whether it can issue from this court?

The act to establish the judicial courts of the United States authorizes the supreme court, "to issue writs of *mandamus,* in cases warranted by the principles and usages of law, to any courts appointed or persons holding office, under the authority of the United States." The secretary of state, being a person holding an office under the authority of the United States, is precisely within the letter of this description; and if this court is not authorized to issue a writ of *mandamus* to such an officer, it must be because the law is unconstitutional, and therefore, absolutely incapable of conferring the authority, and assigning the duties which its words purport to confer and assign.

The constitution vests the whole judicial power of the United States in one supreme court, and such inferior courts as congress shall, from time to time, ordain and establish. This power is expressly extended to all cases arising under the laws of the United States; and consequently, in some form, may be exercised over the present case; because the right claimed is given by a law of the United States.

In the distribution of this power, it is declared, that "the supreme court shall have original jurisdiction, in all cases affecting ambassadors, other public ministers and consuls, and those in which a state shall be a party. In all other cases, the supreme court shall have appellate jurisdiction." It has been insisted, at the bar, that as the original grant of jurisdiction to the supreme and inferior courts, is general, and the clause, assigning original jurisdiction to the supreme court, contains no negative or restrictive words, the power remains to the legislature, to assign original jurisdiction to that court, in other cases than those specified in the article which has been recited; provided those cases belong to the judicial power of the United States.

If it had been intended to leave it in the discretion of the legislature, to apportion the judicial power between the supreme and inferior courts, according to the will of that body, it would certainly have been useless to have proceeded further than to have defined the judicial power, and the tribunals in which it should be vested. . . .

The question, whether an act, repugnant to the constitution, can become the law of the land, is a question deeply interesting to the United States; but, happily, not of an intricacy proportioned to its interest. It seems only necessary to recognise certain principles, supposed to have been long and well established, to decide it. That the people have an original right to establish, for their future government, such principles as, in their opinion, shall most conduce to their own happiness, is the basis on which the whole American fabric has been erected.

The exercise of this original right is a very great exertion; nor can it, nor ought it, to be frequently repeated. The principles, therefore, so established, are deemed fundamental: and as the authority from which they proceed is supreme, and can seldom act, they are designed to be permanent.

This original and supreme will organizes the government, and assigns to different departments their respective powers. It may either stop here, or establish certain limits not to be transcended by those departments. The government of the United States is of the latter description. The powers of the legislature are defined and limited; and that those limits may not be mistaken or forgotten, the constitution is written. To what purpose are powers limited, and to what purpose is that limitation committed to writing, if these limits may, at any time, be passed by those intended to be restrained? The distinction between a government with limited and unlimited powers is abolished, if those limits do not confine the persons on whom they are imposed, and if acts prohibited and acts allowed, are of equal obligation. It is a proposition too plain to be contested, that the constitution controls any legislative act repugnant to it; or that the legislature may alter the constitution by an ordinary act.

. . . .

Between these alternatives, there is no middle ground. The constitution is either a superior paramount law, unchangeable by ordinary means, or it is on a level with ordinary legislative acts, and, like other acts, is alterable when the legislature shall please to alter it. If the former part of the alternative be true, then a legislative act, contrary to the constitution, is not law; if the latter part be true, then written constitutions are absurd attempts, on the part of the people, to limit a power, in its own nature, illimitable.

Certainly, all those who have framed written constitutions contemplate them as forming the fundamental and paramount law of the nation, and consequently, the theory of every such government must be, that an act of the legislature, repugnant to the constitution, is void. This theory is essentially attached to a written constitution, and is, consequently, to be considered, by this court, as one of the fundamental principles of our society. It is not, therefore, to be lost sight of, in the further consideration of this subject.

If an act of the legislature, repugnant to the constitution, is void, does it, notwithstanding its invalidity, bind the courts, and oblige them to give it effect? Or, in other words, though it be not law, does it constitute a rule as operative as if it was a law? This would be to overthrow, in fact, what was established in theory; and would seem, at first view, an absurdity too gross to be insisted on. It shall, however, receive a more attentive consideration.

It is, emphatically, the province and duty of the judicial department, to say what the law is. Those who apply the rule to particular cases, must of necessity expound and interpret that rule. If two laws conflict with each other, the courts must decide on the operation of each. So, if a law be in opposition to the constitution; if both the law and the constitution apply to a particular case, so that the court must either decide that case, conformable to the law, disregarding the constitution; or conformable to the constitution, disregarding the law; the court must determine which of these conflicting rules governs the case; this is of the very essence of judicial duty. If then, the courts are to regard the constitution, and the constitution is superior to any ordinary act of the legislature, the constitution, and not such ordinary act, must govern the case to which they both apply.

Those, then, who controvert the principle, that the constitution is to be considered, in court, as a paramount law, are reduced to the necessity of maintaining that courts must close their eyes on the constitution, and see only the law. This doctrine would subvert the very foundation of all written constitutions. It would declare that an act which, according to the principles and theory of our government, is entirely void, is yet, in practice, completely obligatory. It would declare, that if the legislature shall do what is expressly forbidden, such act, notwithstanding the express prohibition, is in reality effectual. It would be giving to the legislature a practical and real omnipotence, with the same breath which professes to restrict their powers within narrow limits. It is prescribing limits, and declaring that those limits may be passed at pleasure. That it thus reduces to nothing, what we have deemed the greatest improvement on political institutions, a written constitution, would, of itself, be sufficient, in America, where written constitutions have been viewed with so much reverence, for rejecting the construction. But the peculiar expressions of the constitution of the United States furnish additional arguments in favor of its rejection. The judicial power of the United States is extended to all cases arising under the constitution. Could it be the intention of those who gave this power, to say, that in using it, the constitution should not be looked into? That a case arising under the constitution should be decided, without examining the instrument under which it arises? This is too extravagant to be maintained. In some cases, then, the constitution must be looked into by the judges. And if they can open it at all, what part of it are they forbidden to read or to obey?

There are many other parts of the constitution which serve to illustrate this subject. . . .

The constitution declares 'that no bill of attainder or *ex post facto* law shall be passed.' If, however, such a bill should be passed, and a person should be prosecuted under it; must the court condemn to death those victims whom the constitution endeavors to preserve?

'No person,' says the constitution, 'shall be convicted of treason, unless on the testimony of two witnesses to the same *overt* act, or on confession in open court.' Here, the language of the constitution is addressed especially to the courts. It prescribes, directly for them, a rule of evidence not to be departed from. If the legislature should change that rule, and declare one witness, or a confession out of court, sufficient for conviction, must the constitutional principle yield to the legislative act?

From these, and many other selections which might be made, it is apparent, that the framers of the constitution contemplated that instrument as a rule for the government of courts, as well as of the legislature. Why otherwise does it direct the judges to take an oath to support it? This oath certainly applies in an especial manner, to their conduct in their official character. How immoral to impose it on them, if they were to be used as the instruments, and the knowing instruments, for violating what they swear to support!

The oath of office, too, imposed by the legislature, is completely demonstrative of the legislative opinion on this subject. It is in these words: 'I do solemnly swear, that I will administer justice, without respect to persons, and do equal right to the poor and to the rich; and that I will faithfully and impartially discharge all the duties incumbent on me as ———, according to the best of my abilities and understanding, agreeably to the constitution and laws of the United States.' Why does a judge swear to discharge his duties agreeably to the constitution of the United States, if that constitution forms no rule for his government? if it is closed upon him, and cannot be inspected by him? If such be the real state of things, this is worse than solemn mockery. To prescribe, or to take this oath, becomes equally a crime.

It is also not entirely unworthy of observation, that in declaring what shall be the supreme law of the land, the constitution itself is first mentioned;

and not the laws of the United States, generally, but those only which shall be made in pursuance of the constitution, have that rank.

Thus, the particular phraseology of the constitution of the United States confirms and strengthens the principle, supposed to be essential to all written constitutions, that a law repugnant to the constitution is void; and that courts, as well as other departments, are bound by that instrument.

The rule must be discharged.

Eakin and Others v. Raub and Others

12 Sergeant and Rawle
330 (Pa. 1825)
Vote: Gibson dissenting

Marshall's logic in MARBURY has been criticized by many, but Gibson's dissent in this Pennsylvania case has been considered the most cogent. Gibson was dealing with the Pennsylvania Constitution and was obviously unable to convince his colleagues. Later, he was to change his views, first because the legislature had acquiesced, through silence, in judicial review, and second, "from experience of the necessity of the case."

GIBSON J., dissenting.

The constitution of *Pennsylvania* contains no express grant of political powers to the judiciary. But to establish a grant by implication, the constitution is said to be a law of superior obligation; and consequently, that if it were to come into collision with an act of the legislature, the latter would have to give way; that is conceded. But it is a fallacy, to suppose, that they can come into collision *before the judiciary*. What is a constitution? It is an act of extraordinary legislation, by which the people establish the structure and mechanism of their government; and in which they prescribe fundamental rules to regulate the motion of the several parts. What is a statute? It is an act of ordinary legislation, by the appropriate organ of the government; the provisions of which are to be executed by the executive or judiciary, or by officers subordinate to them. The constitution, then, contains no practical rules for the administration of *distributive justice,* with which alone the judiciary has to do; these being furnished in acts of

ordinary legislation, by that organ of the government, which, in this respect, is exclusively the representative of the people; and it is generally true, that the provisions of a constitution are to be carried into effect immediately by the legislature, and only mediately, if at all, by the judiciary. In what respect is the constitution of *Pennsylvania* inconsistent with this principle? Only, perhaps, in one particular provision, to regulate the style of process, and establish an appropriate form of conclusion in criminal prosecutions: in this alone, the constitution furnishes a rule for the judiciary, and this the legislature cannot alter, because it cannot alter the constitution. In all other cases, if the act of assembly supposed to be unconstitutional, were laid out of the question, there would remain no rule to determine the point in controversy in the cause, but the statute or common law, as it existed before the act of assembly was passed; and the constitution and act of assembly, therefore, do not furnish conflicting rules *applicable to the point before the court;* nor is it at all necessary, that the one or the other of them should give way.

The constitution and the *right* of the legislature to pass the act, may be in collision; but is that a legitimate subject for judicial determination? If it be, the judiciary must be a peculiar organ, to revise the proceedings of the legislature, and to correct its mistakes; and in what part of the constitution are we to look for this proud preeminence? Viewing the matter in the opposite direction, what would be thought of an act of assembly in which it should be declared that the supreme court had, in a particular case, put a wrong construction on the constitution of the *United States,* and that the judgment should therefore be reversed? It would, doubtless, be thought a usurpation of judicial power. . . .

But it has been said to be emphatically the business of the judiciary, to ascertain and pronounce what the law is; and that this necessarily involves a consideration of the constitution. It does so: but how far? If the judiciary will inquire into anything beside the form of enactment, where shall it stop? There must be some point of limitation to such an inquiry; for no one will pretend, that a judge would be justifiable in calling for the election returns, or scrutinizing the qualifications of those who composed the legislature.

. . . For instance, let it be supposed that the power to declare a law unconstitutional has been exercised. What is to be done? The legislature must acquiesce, although it may think the construction of the judiciary wrong. But why must it acquiesce? Only because it is bound to pay that respect to every other organ of the government, which it has a right to exact from each of them in turn. This is the argument. But it will not be pretended, that the legislature has not, at least, an equal right with the judiciary to put a construction on the constitution; nor that either of them is infallible; nor that either ought to be required to surrender its judgment to the other. Suppose, then, they differ in opinion as to the constitutionality of a particular law; if the organ whose business it first is to decide on the subject, is not to have its judgment treated with respect, what shall prevent it from securing the preponderance of its opinion by the strong arm of power? . . .

It may be alleged, that no such power is claimed, and that the judiciary does no positive act, but merely refuses to be instrumental in giving effect to an unconstitutional law. This is nothing more than a repetition, in a different form, of the argument — that an unconstitutional law is *ipso facto* void; for a refusal to act under the law, must be founded on a right in each branch to judge of the acts of all the others, before it is bound to exercise its functions to give those acts effect. No such right is recognised in the different branches of the national government, except the judiciary (and that, too, on account of the peculiar provisions of the constitution), for it is now universally held, whatever doubts may have once existed, that congress is bound to provide for carrying a treaty into effect, although it may disapprove of the exercise of the treaty-making power in the particular instance. A government constructed on any other principle, would be in perpetual danger of standing still; for the right to decide on the constitutionality of the laws, would not be peculiar to the judiciary, but would equally reside in the person of every officer whose agency might be necessary to carry them into execution.

. . . .

The power is said to be restricted to cases that are free from doubt or difficulty. But the abstract existence of a power cannot depend on the clearness or obscurity of the case in which it is to be exercised; for that is a consideration that cannot present itself, before the question of the existence of the power shall have been determined; and if its existence be conceded, no considerations of policy, arising from the obscurity of the particular case, ought to influence the exercise of it. . . .

But the judges are sworn to support the constitution, and are they not bound by it as the law of the land? . . . The oath to support the constitution is not peculiar to the judges, but is taken indiscriminately by every officer of the government, and is designed rather as a test of the political principles of the man,

than to bind the officer in the discharge of his duty. . . . [T]he foundation of every argument in favor of the right of the judiciary, is found, at last, to be an assumption of the whole ground in dispute. . . .

But do not the judges do a *positive* act in violation of the constitution, when they give effect to an unconstitutional law? Not if the law has been passed according to the forms established in the constitution. The fallacy of the question is, in supposing that the judiciary adopts the acts of the legislature as its own; whereas, the enactment of a law and the interpretation of it are not concurrent acts, and as the judiciary is not required to concur in the enactment, neither is it in the breach of the constitution which may be the consequence of the enactment; the fault is imputable to the legislature, and on it the responsibility exclusively rests. In this respect, the judges are in the predicament of jurors, who are bound to serve in capital cases, although unable, under any circumstances, to reconcile it to their duty to deprive a human being a life. . . .

But it has been said, that this construction would deprive the citizen of the advantages which are peculiar to a written constitution, by at once declaring the power of the legislature, in practice, to be illimitable. I ask, what are those advantages? The principles of a written constitution are more fixed and certain, and more apparent to the apprehension of the people, than principles which depend on tradition and the vague comprehension of the individuals who compose the nation, and who cannot all be expected to receive the same impressions or entertain the same notions on any given subject. But there is no magic or inherent power in parchment and ink, to command respect, and protect principles from violation. . . .

For these reasons, I am of opinion, that it rests with the people, in whom full and absolute sovereign power resides, to correct abuses in legislation, by instructing their representatives to repeal the obnoxious act. . . . the judiciary is not infallible; and an error by it would admit of no remedy but a more distinct expression of the public will, through the extraordinary medium of a convention; whereas, an error by the legislature admits of a remedy by an exertion of the same will, in the ordinary exercise of the right of suffrage — a mode better calculated to attain the end, without popular excitement. It may be said, the people would probably not notice an error of their representatives. But they would as probably do so, as notice an error of the judiciary; and beside, it is a *postulate* in the theory of our government, and the very basis of the superstructure, that the people are wise, virtuous, and competent to manage their own affairs. . . .

The Dred Scott Case

19 Howard 393 (1857)
Vote: 7–2

The *Dred Scott* case represents judicial review at its worst. The Supreme Court attempted to resolve the most divisive issue facing the nation by a final and definitive judicial decision. As much as any other single action, this helped lead to the Civil War. The Fourteenth Amendment (1868) effectively overruled *Dred Scott*. The antisegregation decision, BROWN V. BOARD OF EDUCATION (1954), was only a small reparation.

Dred Scott, a slave, was taken by his master to Fort Snelling in the Louisiana Territory and then to Missouri, a slave state. His suit argued that once he was taken into free territory he ceased to be a slave.

The complex opinion deals with two interrelated questions. (1) Was Dred Scott a "citizen" who could sue in federal courts? (2) Was he in fact set free by moving into free territory and therefore losing the status of property? In a sweeping decision, the Court ruled Congress could neither free Dred Scott nor give him citizenship. Congress could not, Taney argued, deprive the slaveholder of property, there being no provision in the Constitution allowing Congress such powers in the territories. (This invalidated the Missouri Compromise, though it left open the possibility mentioned by Douglas in the Lincoln-Douglas debates that the residents of a territory could, like people of a state, do what the Congress could not — forbid slavery.)

As extreme as its position on the freeing of slaves was, the Taney Court went further. Distinguishing sharply between state citizenship and federal citizenship, it suggested federal citizenship was fixed at the definitions prevailing in 1789, and that no state could ever confer U.S. citizenship on

blacks. Only Congress might possibly do so as a national measure, not in its rule over territories. So states could grant freedom, state citizenship, even voting rights to blacks, but blacks and their descendants could never be entitled to the rights of U.S. citizens.

Justice Curtis objected on grounds of the basic notion itself, pointing out that blacks were citizens in at least five of the original thirteen states. He pointed to the incredible problems this odd theory of citizenship would create.

As we now know, the Fourteenth Amendment did away with this racism, and the confusion it would have created, by providing "All persons born or naturalized in the United States . . . are citizens of the United States and the State wherein they reside."

MR. CHIEF JUSTICE TANEY delivered the opinion of the court:

The question is simply this: can a negro, whose ancestors were imported into this country and sold as slaves, become a member of the political community formed and brought into existence by the Constitution of the United States, and as such become entitled to all the rights, and privileges, and immunities, guarantied by that instrument to the citizen. One of these rights is the privilege of suing in a court of the United States in the cases specified in the Constitution.

It will be observed, that the plea applies to that class of persons only whose ancestors were negroes of the African race, and imported into this country, and sold and held as slaves. The only matter in issue before the court, therefore, is, whether the descendants of such slaves, when they shall be emancipated, or who are born of parents who had become free before their birth, are citizens of a state, in the sense in which the word "citizen" is used in the Constitution of the United States. And this being the only matter in dispute on the pleadings, the court must be understood as speaking in this opinion of that class only; that is, of those persons who are the descendants of Africans who were imported into this country and sold as slaves.

. . . .

The words "people of the United States" and "citizens" are synonymous terms, and mean the same thing. They both describe the political body, who, according to our republican institutions, form the sovereignty, and who hold the power and conduct the government through their representatives. They are what we familiarly call the "sovereign people," and every citizen is one of this people, and a constituent member of this sovereignty. The question before us is, whether the class of persons described in the plea in abatement compose a portion of this people, and are constituent members of this sovereignty. We think they are not, and that they are not included, and were not intended to be included, under the word "citizens" in the Constitution, and can, therefore, claim none of the rights and privileges which that instrument provides for and secures to citizens of the United States. On the contrary, they were at that time considered as a subordinate and inferior class of beings, who had been subjugated by the dominant race, and whether emancipated or not yet remained subject to their authority, and had no rights or privileges but such as those who held the power and the government might choose to grant them.

It is not the province of the court to decide upon the justice or injustice, the policy or impolicy of these laws. The decision of that question belonged to the political or lawmaking power, to those who formed the sovereignty and framed the Constitution. The duty of the court is to interpret the instrument they have framed, with the best lights we can obtain on the subject, and to administer it as we find it, according to its true intent and meaning when it was adopted.

In discussing this question, we must not confound the rights of citizenship which a state may confer within its own limits, and the rights of citizenship as a member of the Union. It does not by any means follow, because he has all the rights and privileges of a citizen of a State, that he must be a citizen of the United States. He may have all the rights and privileges of the citizen of a State, and yet not be entitled to the rights and privileges of a citizen in any other State. For, previous to the adoption of the Constitution of the United States, every State had the undoubted right to confer on whomsoever it pleased the character of a citizen, and to endow him with all its rights. But this character, of course, was confined to the boundaries of the State, and gave him no rights or privileges in other States beyond those secured to him by the laws of nations and the county of States. Nor have the several States surrendered the power of conferring these rights and privileges by adopting the Constitution of the United States. Each State may still confer them upon an alien, or any one it thinks proper, or upon any class or de-

scription of persons: yet he would not be a citizen in the sense in which that word is used in the Constitution of the United States, nor entitled to sue as such in one of its courts, nor to the privileges and immunities of a citizen in the other States. The rights which he would acquire would be restricted to the State which gave them. The Constitution has conferred on Congress the right to establish a uniform rule of naturalization, and this right is evidently exclusive, and has always been held by this court to be so. Consequently, no State, since the adoption of the Constitution, can, by naturalizing an alien, invest him with the rights and privileges secured to a citizen of a State under the federal government, although, so far as the State alone was concerned, he would undoubtedly be entitled to the rights of a citizen, and clothed with all the rights and immunities which the Constitution and laws of the State attached to that character.

It is very clear, therefore, that no State can, by any Act or law of its own, passed, since the adoption of the Constitution, introduce a new member into the political community created by the Constitution of the United States. It cannot make him a member of this community by making him a member of its own. And for the same reason it cannot introduce any person, or description of persons, who were not intended to be embraced in this new political family, which the Constitution brought into existence, but were intended to be excluded from it.

The question then arises, whether the provisions of the Constitution, in relation to the personal rights and privileges to which the citizen of a state should be entitled, embraced the negro African race, at that time in this country, or who might afterwards be imported, who had then or should afterwards be made free in any State; and to put it in the power of a single State to make him a citizen of the United States, and endue him with the full rights of citizenship in every other State without their consent. Does the Constitution of the United States act upon him whenever he shall be made free under the laws of a State, and raised there to the rank of a citizen, and immediately clothe him with all the privileges of a citizen in every other State, and in its own courts?

The court think the affirmative of these propositions cannot be maintained. And if it cannot, the plaintiff in error could not be a citizen of the State of Missouri, within the meaning of the Constitution of the United States, and, consequently, was not entitled to sue in its courts.

It is true, every person, and every class and description of persons, who were at the time of the adoption of the Constitution recognized as citizens in the several States, became also citizens of this new political body; but none other; it was formed by them, and for them and their posterity, but for no one else. And the personal rights and privileges guarantied to citizens of this new sovereignty were intended to embrace those only who were then members of the several state communities, or who should afterwards, by birthright or otherwise, become members, according to the provisions of the Constitution and the principles on which it was founded. It was the union of those who were at that time members of distinct and separate political communities into one political family, whose power, for certain specified purposes, was to extend over the whole territory of the United States. And it gave to each citizen rights and privileges outside of his State which he did not before possess, and placed him in every other State upon a perfect equality with its own citizens as to rights of person and rights of property; it made him a citizen of the United States.

It becomes necessary, therefore, to determine who were citizens of the several States when the Constitution was adopted. And in order to do this, we must recur to the governments and institutions of the thirteen Colonies, when they separated from Great Britain and formed new sovereignties, and took their places in the family of independent nations. We must inquire who, at that time, were recognized as the people or citizens of a State, whose rights and liberties had been outraged by the English Government; and who declared their independence, and assumed the powers of government to defend their rights by force of arms.

In the opinion of the court, the legislation and histories of the times, and the language used in the Declaration of Independence, show, that neither the class of persons who had been imported as slaves, nor their descendants, whether they had become free or not, were then acknowledged as a part of the people, nor intended to be included in the general words used in that memorable instrument.

It is difficult at this day to realize the state of public opinion in relation to that unfortunate race, which prevailed in the civilized and enlightened portions of the world at the time of the Declaration of Independence, and when the Constitution of the United States was framed and adopted. But the public history of every European nation displays it, in a manner too plain to be mistaken.

They had for more than a century before been regarded as beings of an inferior order; and altogether unfit to associate with the white race, either in social or political relations; and so far inferior, that they had no rights which the white man was bound to respect; and that the negro might justly and lawfully be reduced to slavery for his benefit. . . .

But it is said that a person may be a citizen, and entitled to that character, although he does not possess all the rights which may belong to other citizens; as, for example, the right to vote, or to hold particular offices; and that yet, when he goes into another State, he is entitled to be recognized there as a citizen, although the State may measure his rights by the rights which it allows to persons of a like character or class, resident in the State, and refuse to him the full rights of citizenship.

This argument overlooks the language of the provision in the Constitution of which we are speaking.

Undoubtedly, a person may be a citizen, that is, a member of the community who form the sovereignty, although he exercises no share of the political power, and is incapacitated from holding particular offices. Women and minors, who form a part of the political family, cannot vote; and when a property qualification is required to vote or hold a particular office, those who have not the necessary qualification cannot vote or hold the office, yet they are citizens.

So, too, a person may be entitled to vote by the law of the State, who is not a citizen even of the State itself. And in some of the States of the Union foreigners not naturalized are allowed to vote. And the State may give the right to free negroes and mulattoes, but that does not make them citizens of the State, and still less of the United States. And the provision in the Constitution giving privileges and immunities in other States, does not apply to them.

Neither does it apply to a person who, being the citizen of a State, migrates to another State. For then he becomes subject to the laws of the State in which he lives, and he is no longer a citizen of the State from which he removed. And the State in which he resides may then, unquestionably, determine his status or condition, and place him among the class of persons who are not recognized as citizens, but belong to an inferior and subject race; and may deny him the privileges and immunities enjoyed by its citizens.

But so far as mere rights of person are concerned, the provision in question is confined to citizens of a State who are temporarily in another State without taking up their residence there. It gives them no political rights in the state as to voting or holding office, or in any other respect. For a citizen of one State has no right to participate in the government of another. But if he ranks as a citizen of the State to which he belongs, within the meaning of the Constitution of the United States, then, whenever he goes into another State, the Constitution clothes him, as to the rights of person, with all the privileges and immunities which belong to citizens of the State. And if persons of the African race are citizens of a state, and of the United States, they would be entitled to all of these privileges and immunities in every State, and the State could not restrict them; for they would hold these privileges and immunities, under the paramount authority of the Federal Government. . . .

. . . . [I]t may be safely assumed that citizens of the United States who migrate to a territory belonging to the people of the United States, cannot be ruled as mere colonists, dependent upon the will of the general government, and to be governed by any laws it may think proper to impose. The principle upon which our governments rest, and upon which alone they continue to exist, is the union of States, sovereign and independent within their own limits in their internal and domestic concerns, and bound together as one people by a general government, possessing certain enumerated and restricted powers, delegated to it by the people of the several States, and exercising supreme authority within the scope of the powers granted to it throughout the dominion of the United States. A power, therefore, in the general government to obtain and hold Colonies and dependent Territories, over which they might legislate without restriction, would be inconsistent with its own existence in its present form. Whatever it acquires, it acquires for the benefit of the people of the several States who created it. It is their trustee acting for them, and charged with the duty of promoting the interests of the whole people of the Union in the exercise of the powers specifically granted.

But the power of Congress over the person or property of a citizen can never be a mere discretionary power under our Constitution and form of government. The powers of the government and the rights and privileges of the citizen are regulated and plainly defined by the Constitution itself. And when the territory becomes a part of the United States, the Federal Government enters into possession in the character impressed upon it by those who created it. It enters upon it with its powers over the citizen strictly defined, and limited by the Constitution, from which it derives its own existence, and by virtue of which alone it continues to exist and act as a government and sovereignty. It has no power of any kind beyond it; and it cannot, when it enters a territory of the United States, put off its character,

and assume discretionary or despotic powers which the Constitution has denied to it. It cannot create for itself a new character separated from the citizens of the United States, and the duties it owes them under the provisions of the Constitution. The territory being a part of the United States, the government and the citizen both enter it under the authority of the Constitution, with their respective rights defined and marked out; and the Federal Government can exercise no power over his person or property, beyond what that instrument confers, nor lawfully deny any right which it has reserved.

A reference to a few of the provisions of the Constitution will illustrate this proposition.

For example, no one, we presume, will contend that Congress can make any law in a territory respecting the establishment of religion or the free exercise thereof, or abridging the freedom of speech or of the press, or the right of the people of the territory peaceably to assemble and to petition the government for the redress of grievances. . . .

. . . .

These powers, and others in relation to rights of person, which it is not necessary here to enumerate, are, in express and positive terms, denied to the general government; and the rights of private property have been guarded with equal care. Thus the rights of property are united with the rights of person, and placed on the same ground by the fifth amendment to the Constitution, which provides that no person shall be deprived of life, liberty and property, without due process of law. And an Act of Congress which deprives a citizen of the United States of his liberty or property, merely because he came himself or brought his property into a particular Territory of the United States, and who had committed no offense against the laws, could hardly be dignified with the name of due process of law.

. . . .

Now, as we have already said in an earlier part of this opinion, upon a different point, the right of property in a slave is distinctly and expressly affirmed in the Constitution. The right to traffic in it, like an ordinary article of merchandise and property, was guaranteed to the citizens of the United States, in every State that might desire it, for twenty years. And the government in express terms is pledged to protect it in all future time, if the slave escapes from his owner. This is done in plain words — too plain to be misunderstood. And no word can be found in the Constitution which gives Congress a greater power over slave property, or which entitles property of that kind to less protection than property of any other description. The only power conferred is the power coupled with the duty of guarding and protecting the owner in his rights.

Upon these considerations, it is the opinion of the court that the Act of Congress which prohibited a citizen from holding and owning property of this kind in the territory of the United States north of the line therein mentioned, is not warranted by the Constitution, and is therefore void: and that neither Dred Scott himself, nor any of his family, were made free by being carried into this territory; even if they had been carried there by the owner, with the intention of becoming a permanent resident.

MR. JUSTICE CURTIS, dissenting.

. . . .

It has been often asserted that the Constitution was made exclusively by and for the white race. It has already been shown that in five of the thirteen original States, colored persons then possessed the elective franchise, and were among those by whom the Constitution was ordained and established. If so, it is not true, in point of fact, that the Constitution was made exclusively for the white race. And that it was made exclusively for the white race is, in my opinion, not only an assumption not warranted by anything in the Constitution, but contradicted by its opening declaration, that it was ordained and established by the people of the United States, for themselves and their posterity. And as free colored persons were then citizens of at least five States, and so in every sense part of the people of the United States, they were among those for whom and whose posterity the Constitution was ordained and established.

. . . .

Slavery being contrary to natural right, is created only by municipal law. . . .

Is it conceivable that the Constitution has conferred the right on every citizen to become a resident on the Territory of the United States with his slaves, and there to hold them as such, but has neither made nor provided for any municipal regulations which are essential to the existence of slavery?

Is it conceivable that the Constitution has conferred the right on every citizen to become a resident on the Territory of the United States with his State are property only to the extent and under the conditions fixed by those laws: that they must cease to be available as property, when their owners voluntarily place them permanently within another jurisdiction, where no municipal laws on the subject of slavery exist: and that, being aware of these principles, and having said nothing to interfere with or displace them, or compel Congress to legislate in any

particular manner on the subject, and having empowered Congress to make all needful rules and regulations respecting the Territory of the United States, it was their intention to leave to the discretion of Congress what regulations, if any, should be made concerning slavery therein?

Roe v. Wade

410 U.S. 113 (1973)
Vote: 7–2

Roe v. *Wade* addresses the right of a state to deal with and forbid abortion. It finds a need to balance the rights of the mother against the state's interests, which include protection of the fetus. The mother's claims are protected by a "right to privacy," a right not mentioned in the Constitution but held by the justices in GRISWOLD V. CONNECTICUT (1965) to be protected. This case remains a center of controversy well after the decision. It raises the question of what legal tools or specialties would entitle judges, predominantly older males, to decide a question of special importance to women.

Roe was dramatically distinguished and its future put in jeopardy by the 1989 decision of *Webster* v. *Reproductive Health Services* 57 LW 5023, (see Chapter 11). The controversy was hardly abated as *Webster* keeps the judicial pot boiling while turning many issues back to the state legislatures and political confrontation.

MR. JUSTICE BLACKMUN delivered the opinion of the Court.

. . . .

We forthwith acknowledge our awareness of the sensitive and emotional nature of the abortion controversy, of the vigorous opposing views, even among physicians, and of the deep and seemingly absolute convictions that the subject inspires. One's philosophy, one's experiences, one's exposure to the raw edges of human existence, one's religious training, one's attitudes toward life and family and their values, and the moral standards one establishes and seeks to observe, are all likely to influence and to color one's thinking and conclusions about abortion.

In addition, population growth, pollution, poverty, and racial overtones tend to complicate and not to simplify the problem.

Our task, of course, is to resolve the issue by constitutional measurement free of emotion and of predilection.... We ... place ... some emphasis upon medical and medical-legal history and what that history reveals about man's attitudes toward the abortive procedure over the centuries. We bear in mind, too, Mr. Justice Holmes' admonition in his now vindicated dissent in *Lochner* v. *New York* (1905):

> It [the Constitution] is made for people of fundamentally differing views, and the accident of our finding certain opinions natural and familiar or novel and even shocking ought not to conclude our judgment upon the question whether statutes embodying them conflict with the Constitution of the United States.

. . . .

Jane Roe, a single woman who was residing in Dallas County, Texas, instituted this federal action in March 1970 against the District Attorney of the county. She sought a declaratory judgment that the Texas criminal abortion statutes were unconstitutional on their face, and an injunction restraining the defendant from enforcing the statutes.

Roe alleged that she was unmarried and pregnant; that she wished to terminate her pregnancy by an abortion "performed by a competent, licensed physician, under safe, clinical conditions"; that she was unable to get a "legal" abortion in Texas because her life did not appear to be threatened by the continuation of her pregnancy; and that she could not afford to travel to another jurisdiction in order to secure a legal abortion under safe conditions. She claimed that the Texas statutes were unconstitutionally vague and that they abridged her right of personal privacy, protected by the First, Fourth, Fifth, Ninth, and Fourteenth Amendments. By an amendment to her complaint Roe purported to sue "on behalf of herself and all other women" similarly situated.

James Hubert Hallford, a licensed physician, sought and was granted leave to intervene in Roe's action. In his complaint he alleged that he had been arrested previously for violations of the Texas abortion statutes and that two such prosecutions were pending against him....

John and Mary Doe, a married couple, filed a companion complaint to that of Roe. They also named the District Attorney as defendant, claimed like constitutional deprivations, and sought declaratory and injunctive relief. The Does alleged that they were a childless couple; that Mrs. Doe was suffering from a "neuralchemical" disorder; that her physician had "advised her to avoid pregnancy until such time as her condition has materially improved" (although a

pregnancy at the present time would not present "serious risk" to her life)....

... The court held that Roe and Dr. Hallford, and members of their respective classes, had standing to sue, and presented justiciable controversies, but that the Does had failed to allege facts sufficient to state a present controversy and did not have standing. It concluded that, with respect to the requests for a declaratory judgment, abstention was not warranted. On the merits, the District Court held that the "fundamental right of single women and married persons to choose whether to have children is protected by the Ninth Amendment, through the Fourteenth Amendment," and that the Texas criminal abortion statutes were void on their face because they were both unconstitutionally vague and constituted an overbroad infringement on the plaintiffs' Ninth Amendment rights....

We are next confronted with issues of justiciability, standing, and abstention. Have Roe and the Does established that "personal stake in the outcome of the controversy," *Baker* v. *Carr* (1962), that insures that "the dispute sought to be adjudicated will be presented in an adversary context and in a form historically viewed as capable of judicial resolution," *Flast* v. *Cohen* (1968), and *Sierra Club* v. *Morton* (1972)? And what effect did the pendency of criminal abortion charges against Dr. Hallford in state court have upon the propriety of the federal court's granting relief to him a plantiff-intervenor?

. . . .

Viewing Roe's case as of the time of its filing and thereafter until as late as May, there can be little dispute that it then presented a case or controversy and that, wholly apart from the class aspects, she, as a pregnant single women thwarted by the Texas criminal abortion laws, had standing to challenge those statutes.

. . . .

The appellee notes, however, that the record does not disclose that Roe was pregnant at the time of the District Court hearing on May 22, 1970, or on the following June 17 when the court's opinion and judgment were filed. And he suggests that Roe's case must now be moot because she and all other members of her class are no longer subject to any 1970 pregnancy.

The usual rule in federal cases is that an actual controversy must exist at stages of appellate or certiorari review, and not simply at the date the action is initiated.

But when, as here, pregnancy is a significant fact in the litigation, the normal 266-day human gestation period is so short that the pregnancy will come to term before the usual appellate process is complete.

If that termination makes a case moot, pregnancy litigation seldom will survive much beyond the trial stage, and appellate review will be effectively denied. Our law should not be that rigid. Pregnancy often comes more then once to the same woman, and in the general population, if man is to survive, it will always be with us. Pregnancy provides a classic justification for a conclusion of nonmootness. It truly could be "capable of repetition, yet evading review. . . ."

. . . .

It perhaps is not generally appreciated that the restrictive criminal abortion laws in effect in a majority of States today are of relatively recent vintage. Those laws, generally proscribing abortion or its attempt at any time during pregnancy except when necessary to preserve the pregnant woman's life, are not of ancient or even of common law origin. Instead, they derive from statutory changes effected, for the most part, in the latter half of the 19th century.

. . . .

Three reasons have been advanced to explain historically the enactment of criminal abortion laws in the 19th century and to justify their continued existence.

It has been argued occasionally that these laws were the product of a Victorian social concern to discourage illicit sexual conduct. Texas, however, does not advance this justification in the present case, and it appears that no court or commentator has taken the argument seriously. The appellants and *amici* contend, moreover, that this is not a proper state purpose at all and suggest that, if it were, the Texas statutes are overbroad in protecting it since the law fails to distinguish between married and unwed mothers.

A second reason is concerned with abortion as a medical procedure. When most criminal abortion laws were first enacted, the procedure was a hazardous one for the women. This was particularly true prior to the development of antisepsis. Antiseptic techniques, of course, were based on discoveries by Lister, Pasteur, and others first announced in 1867, but were not generally accepted and employed until about the turn of the century. Abortion mortality was high. Even after 1900, and perhaps until as late as the development of antibiotics in the 1940's, standard modern techniques such as dilation and curettage were not nearly so safe as they are today. Thus it has been argued that a State's real concern in enacting a criminal abortion law was to protect the pregnant woman, that is, to restrain her from submitting to a procedure that placed her life in serious jeopardy. . . . Mortality rates for women undergoing early abortions, where the procedure is legal, appear to be as low as or lower than the rates for normal childbirth. Consequently, any interest of the State in protecting the woman from an inherently hazardous procedure, except when it would be equally dangerous for her to forgo it, has largely disappeared. Of course, important state interests in the area of health and medical standards do remain. The State has a legitimate interest in seeing to it that abortion, like any other medical procedure, is performed under circumstances that insure maximum safety for the patient. This interest obviously extends at least to the performing physician and his staff, to the facilities involved, to the availability of after-care, and to adequate provision for any complication or emergency that might arise. The prevalence of high mortality rates at illegal "abortion mills" strengthens, rather than weakens, the State's interest in regulating the conditions under which abortions are performed. Moreover, the risk to the woman increases as her pregnancy continues. Thus the State retains a definite interest in protecting the woman's own health and safety when an abortion is proposed at a late stage in pregnancy.

The third reason is the State's interest — some phrase it in terms of duty — in protecting prenatal life. Some of the argument for this justification rests on the theory that a new human is present from the moment of conception. The State's interest and general obligation to protect life then extends, it is argued, to prenatal life. Only when the life of the pregnant mother herself is at stake, balanced against the life she carries within her, should the interest of the embryo or fetus not prevail. Logically, of course, a legitimate state interest in this area need not stand or fall on acceptance of the belief that life begins at conception or at some other point prior to live birth. In assessing the State's interest, recognition may be given to the less rigid claim that as long as at least *potential* life is involved, the State may assert interests beyond the protection of the pregnant woman alone.

. . . .

The Constitution does not explicitly mention any right of privacy. In a line of decisions, however, going back perhaps as far as *Union Pacific R. Co.* v. *Botsford* . . . (1891), the Court has recognized that a right of personal privacy, or a guarantee of certain areas or zones of privacy, does exist under the Constitution. In varying contexts the Court or individual Justices have indeed found at least the roots of that right in the First Amendment, *Stanley* v. *Georgia* . . . (1969); in the Fourth and Fifth Amendments, *Terry* v. *Ohio* . . . (1968), *Katz* v. *United States* . . . (1967), *Boyd* v. *United States* . . . (1886), see *Olmstead* v. *United States* . . . (1928) (Brandeis, J., dissenting); in the penumbras of the Bill of Rights, *Griswold* v. *Connecticut* . . . (1965); in the Ninth Amendment, . . . (Goldberg, J., concurring); or the concept of liberty guaranteed by the first section of the Fourteenth Amendment, see *Mayer* v. *Nebraska* . . . (1923). These decisions make it clear that only personal rights that can be deemed "fundamental" or "implicit in the concept of ordered liberty," *Palko* v. *Connecticut* . . . (1937), are included in this guarantee of personal privacy. They also make it clear that the right has some extension to activities relating to marriage, *Loving* v. *Virginia* . . . (1967), procreation, *Skinner* v. *Oklahoma* . . . (1942), contraception, *Eisenstadt* v. *Baird* . . . (1972), . . . (WHITE, J., concurring), family relationships, *Prince* v. *Massachusetts* . . . (1944), and child rearing and education, *Pierce* v. *Society of Sisters* . . . (1925), *Meyer* v. *Nebraska, supra.*

This right of privacy, whether it be founded in the Fourteenth Amendment's concept of personal liberty and restrictions upon state action, as we feel it is, or, as the District Court determined, in the Ninth Amendment's reservation of rights to the people, is broad enough to encompass a woman's decision whether or not to terminate her pregnancy. The detriment that the State would impose upon the pregnant woman by denying this choice altogether is apparent. . . .

On the basis of elements such as these, appellants and some *amici* argue that the woman's right is absolute and that she is entitled to terminate her pregnancy at whatever time, in whatever way, and for whatever reason she alone chooses. With this we do not agree. Appellant's arguments that Texas either has no valid interest at all in regulating the abortion decision, or no interest strong enough to support any limitation upon the woman's sole determination, is unpersuasive. The Court's decisions recognizing a right of privacy also acknowledge that some state regulation in areas protected by that right is appropriate. As noted above, a state may properly assert important interests in safeguarding health, in maintaining medical standards, and in protecting potential life. At some point in pregnancy, these respective interests become sufficiently compelling to sustain regulation of the factors that govern the abortion decision. The privacy right involved, therefore, cannot be said to be absolute. In fact, it is not clear to us that the claim asserted by some *amici* that one has an unlimited right to do with one's body as one

pleases bears a close relationship to the right of privacy previously articulated in the Court's decisions. The Court has refused to recognize an unlimited right of this kind in the past. *Jacobson* v. *Massachusetts* . . . (1905) (vaccination); *Buck* v. *Bell* . . . (1927) (sterilization).

We therefore conclude that the right of personal privacy includes the abortion decision, but that this right is not unqualified and must be considered against important state interests in regulation.

. . . .

Where certain "fundamental rights" are involved, the Court has held that regulation limiting these rights may be justified only by a "compelling state interest," *Kramer* v. *Union Free School District* . . . (1969); *Shapiro* v. *Thompson* . . . (1969), *Sherbert* v. *Verner* . . . (1963), and that legislative enactments must be narrowly drawn to express only the legitimate state interests at stake. *Griswold* v. *Connecticut* . . . (1965); *Aptheker* v. *Secretary of State* . . . (1964); *Cantwell* v. *Connecticut* . . . (1940); see *Eisenstadt* v. *Baird* . . . (1972) (WHITE, J., concurring).

In the recent abortion cases, cited above, courts have recognized these principles. Those striking down state laws have generally scrutinized the State's interest in protecting health and potential life and have concluded that neither interest justified broad limitations on the reasons for which a physician and his pregnant patient might decide that she should have an abortion in the early stages of pregnancy. Courts sustaining state laws have held that the State's determinations to protect health or prenatal life are dominant and constitutionally justifiable.

The District Court held that the appellee failed to meet his burden of demonstrating that the Texas statute's infringement upon Roe's rights was necessary to support a compelling state interest, and that, although the defendant presented "several compelling justifications for state presence in the area of abortions," the statutes outstripped these justifications and swept "far beyond any areas of compelling state interest." . . .

A. The appellee and certain *amici* argue that the fetus is a "person" within the language and meaning of the Fourteenth Amendment. In support of this they outline at length and in detail the well-known facts of fetal development. If this suggestion of personhood is established, the appellant's case, of course, collapses, for the fetus' right to life is then guaranteed specifically by the Amendment. The appellant conceded as much on reargument. On the other hand, the appellee conceded on reargument that no case could be cited that holds that a fetus is a person within the meaning of the Fourteenth Amendment.

The Constitution does not define "person" in so many words. Section 1 of the Fourteenth Amendment contains three references to "person." The first, in defining "citizens," speaks of "persons born or naturalized in the United States." The word also appears both in the Due Process Clause and in the Equal Protection Clause. "Person" is used in other places in the Constitution: in the listing of qualifications for representatives and senators. . . . But in nearly all these instances, the use of the word is such that it has application only postnatally. None indicates, with any assurance, that it has any possible pre-natal application.

All this, together with our observation, *supra,* that throughout the major portion of the 19th century prevailing legal abortion practices were far freer than they are today, persuades us that the word "person," as used in the Fourteenth Amendment, does not include the unborn. . . .

B. The pregnant woman cannot be isolated in her privacy. She carries an embryo and, later, a fetus, if one accepts the medical definitions of the developing young in the human uterus. See Dorland's Illustrated Medical Dictionary, 478–479, 547 (24th ed. 1965). The situation therefore is inherently different from marital intimacy, or bedroom possession of obscene material, or marriage, or procreation, or education, with which *Eisenstadt, Griswold, Stanley, Loving, Skinner, Pierce,* and *Meyer* were respectively concerned. As we have intimated above, it is reasonable and appropriate for a State to decide that at some point in time another interest, that of health of the mother or that of potential human life, becomes significantly involved. The woman's privacy is no longer sole and any right of privacy she possesses must be measured accordingly.

Texas urges that, apart from the Fourteenth Amendment, life begins at conception and is present throughout pregnancy, and that, therefore, the State has a compelling interest in protecting that life from and after conception. We need not resolve the difficult question of when life begins. When those trained in the respective disciplines of medicine, philosophy, and theology are unable to arrive at any consensus, the judiciary, at this point in the development of man's knowledge, is not in a position to speculate as to the answer.

. . . .

In view of all this, we do not agree that, by adopting one theory of life, Texas may override the rights of the pregnant woman that are at stake. We repeat,

however, that the State does have an important and legitimate interest in preserving and protecting the health of the pregnant woman, whether she be a resident of the State or a nonresident who seeks medical consultation and treatment there, and that it has still *another* important and legitimate interest in protecting the potentiality of human life. These interests are separate and distinct. Each grows in substantiality as the woman approaches term and, at a point during pregnancy, each becomes "compelling."

With respect to the State's important and legitimate interest in the health of the mother, the "compelling" point, in the light of present medical knowledge, is at approximately the end of the first trimester. This is so because of the now established medical fact . . . that until the end of the first trimester mortality in abortion is less than mortality in normal childbirth. It follows that, from and after this point, a State may regulate the abortion procedure to the extent that the regulation reasonably relates to the preservation and protection of maternal health. Examples of permissible state regulation in this area are requirements as to the qualifications of the person who is to perform the abortion; as to the licensure of that person; as to the facility in which the procedure is to be performed, that is, whether it must be a hospital or may be a clinic or some other place of less-than-hospital status; as to the licensing of the facility; and the like.

This means, on the other hand, that, for the period of pregnancy prior to this "compelling" point, the attending physician, in consultation with his patient, is free to determine, without regulation by the State, that in his medical judgment the patient's pregnancy should be terminated. If that decision is reached, the judgment may be effectuated by an abortion, free of interference by the State.

With respect to the State's important and legitimate interest in potential life, the "compelling" point is at viability. This is so because the fetus then presumably has the capability of meaningful life outside the mother's womb. State regulation protective of fetal life after viability thus has both logical and biological justifications. If the State is interested in protecting fetal life after viability, it may go so far as to proscribe abortion during that period except when it is necessary to preserve the life or health of the mother.

Measured against these standards, Art. 1196 of the Texas Penal Code, in restricting legal abortions to those "procured or attempted by medical advice for the purpose of saving the life of the mother," sweeps too broadly. The statute makes no distinction between abortions performed early in pregnancy and those performed later, and it limits to a single reason, "saving" the mother's life, the legal justification for the procedure. The statute, therefore, cannot survive the constitutional attack made upon it here.

. . . .

To summarize and to repeat:

1. A state criminal abortion statute of the current Texas type, that excepts from criminality only a *life saving* procedure on behalf of the mother, without regard to pregnancy stage and without recognition of the other interests involved, is violative of the Due Process Clause of the Fourteenth Amendment.

(a) For the stage prior to approximately the end of the first trimester, the abortion decision and its effectuation must be left to the medical judgment of the pregnant woman's attending physician.

(b) For the stage subsequent to approximately the end of the first trimester, the State, in promoting its interest in the health of the mother, may, if it chooses, regulate the abortion procedure in ways that are reasonably related to maternal health.

(c) For the stage subsequent to viability the State, in promoting its interest in the potentiality of human life, may, if it chooses, regulate, and even proscribe, abortion except where it is necessary, in appropriate medical judgment, for the preservation of the life or health of the mother.

. . . .

This holding, we feel, is consistent with the relative weights of the respective interests involved, with the lessons and example of medical and legal history, with the lenity of the common law, and with the demands of the profound problems of the present day. The decision leaves the State free to place increasing restrictions on abortion as the period of pregnancy lengthens, so long as those restrictions are tailored to the recognized state interests. The decision vindicates the right of the physician to administer medical treatment according to his professional judgment up to the points where important state interests provide compelling justifications for intervention. Up to those points the abortion decision in all its aspects is inherently, and primarily, a medical decision, and basic responsibility for it must rest with the physician. If an individual practitioner abuses the privilege of exercising proper medical judgment, the usual remedies, judicial and intra-professional, are available.

MR. JUSTICE STEWART, concurring.

In 1963, this Court, in *Ferguson* v. *Skrupa*, 372 U.S. 726, purported to sound the death knell for the doctrine of substantive due process, a doctrine under which many state laws had in the past been held to violate the Fourteenth Amendment. As Mr. Justice Black's opinion for the Court in *Skrupa* put it: "We have returned to the original constitutional proposition that courts do not substitute their social and economic beliefs for the judgment of legislative bodies, who are elected to pass laws." *Id.,* at 730.

Barely two years later in *Griswold* v. *Connecticut,* 381 U.S. 479, the Court held a Connecticut birth-control law unconstitutional. In view of what had been so recently said in *Skrupa,* the Court's opinion in *Griswold* understandably did its best to avoid reliance on the Due Process Clause of the Fourteenth Amendment as the ground for decision. Yet, the Connecticut law did not violate any provision of the Bill of Rights, nor any other specific provision of the Constitution. So it was clear to me then, and it is equally clear to me now, that the *Griswold* decision can be rationally understood only as a holding that the Connecticut statute substantively invaded the "liberty" that is protected by the Due Process Clause of the Fourteenth Amendment. As so understood, *Griswold* stands as one in a long line of pre-*Skrupa* cases decided under the doctrine of substantive due process and I now accept it as such. . . . The Constitution nowhere mentions a specific right of personal choice in matters of marriage and family life, but the "liberty" protected by the Due Process Clause of the Fourteenth Amendment covers more than those freedoms explicitly named in the Bill of Rights.

. . . .

Clearly, therefore, the Court today is correct in holding that the right asserted by Jane Roe is embraced within the personal liberty protected by the Due Process Clause of the Fourteenth Amendment.

It is evident that the Texas abortion statute infringes that right directly. Indeed, it is difficult to imagine a more complete abridgment of a constitutional freedom than that worked by the inflexible criminal statute now in force in Texas. The question then becomes whether the state interests advanced to justify this abridgment can survive the "particularly careful scrutiny" that the Fourteenth Amendment here requires.

The asserted state interests are protection of the health and safety of the pregnant woman, and protection of the potential future human life within her. These are legitimate objectives, amply sufficient to permit a State to regulate abortions as it does other surgical procedures, and perhaps sufficient to permit a State to regulate abortions more stringently or even to prohibit them in the late stages of pregnancy. But such legislation is not before us, and I think the Court today has thoroughly demonstrated that these state interests cannot constitutionally support the broad abridgment of personal liberty worked by the existing Texas law. Accordingly, I join the Court's opinion holding that that law is invalid under the Due Process Clause of the Fourteenth Amendment.

MR. JUSTICE REHNQUIST, dissenting.

. . . I have difficulty in concluding, as the Court does, that the right of "privacy" is involved in this case. Texas by the statute here challenged bars the performance of a medical abortion by a licensed physician on a plaintiff such as Roe. A transaction resulting in an operation such as this is not "private" in the ordinary usage of that word. . . .

The Court eschews the history of the Fourteenth Amendment in its reliance on the "compelling state interest" test. See *Weber* v. *Aetna Casualty & Surety Co.* . . . (1972) (dissenting opinion). But the Court adds a new wrinkle to this test by transposing it from the legal considerations associated with the Equal Protection Clause of the Fourteenth Amendment to this case arising under the Due Process Clause of the Fourteenth Amendment. Unless I misapprehend the consequences of this transplanting of the "compelling state interest test," the Court's opinion will accomplish the seemingly impossible feat of leaving this area of the law more confused than it found it.

MR. CHIEF JUSTICE BURGER, concurring.

I agree that, under the Fourteenth Amendment to the Constitution, the abortion statutes of Georgia and Texas impermissibly limit the performance of abortions necessary to protect the health of pregnant women, using the term health in its broadest medical context.

MR. JUSTICE WHITE, with whom MR. JUSTICE REHNQUIST joins, dissenting.

. . . The Court simply fashions and announces a new constitutional right for pregnant mothers and, with scarcely any reason or authority for its action, invests that right with sufficient substance to override most existing state abortion statutes. The upshot is that the people and the legislatures of the 50 States are constitutionally disentitled to weigh the relative importance of the continued existence and development of the fetus on the one hand against a spectrum of possible impacts on the mother on the other hand. As an exercise of raw judicial power, the Court perhaps has authority to do what it does today; but in my view its judgment is an improvident

and extravagant exercise of the power of judicial review which the Constitution extends to this Court.

The Court apparently values the convenience of the pregnant mother more than the continued existence and development of the life or potential life which she carries. Whether or not I might agree with the marshalling of values, I can in no event join the Court's judgment because I find no constitutional warrant for imposing such an order of priorities on the people and legislatures of the States. In a sensitive area such as this, involving as it does issues over which reasonable men may easily and heatedly differ, I cannot accept the Court's exercise of its clear power of choice by interposing a constitutional barrier to state efforts to protect human life and by investing mothers and doctors with the constitutionally protected right to exterminate it. This issue, for the most part, should be left with the people and to the political processes the people have devised to govern their affairs.

Do We Have an Unwritten Constitution?*

Thomas C. Grey

Cases like the abortion decision prompt discussion of how far the Court is limited in its creative use of language of the Constitution. Professor Grey summarizes the criticism, but defends activism firmly.

In reviewing laws for constitutionality, should our judges confine themselves to determining whether those laws conflict with norms derived from the written Constitution? Or may they also enforce principles of liberty and justice when the normative content of those principles is not to be found within the four corners of our founding document? Excluding the question of the legitimacy of judicial review itself, that is perhaps the most fundamental question we can ask about our fundamental law.

THE PURE INTERPRETIVE MODEL

For many years this most basic question has not much engaged the explicit attention of constitutional scholars or of the courts or judges themselves, with

*From *Stanford Law Review,* 27 703 FF (1975). Reprinted by permission.

at least one important exception. That exception was Mr. Justice Black. Throughout his long and remarkable career on the bench, the most consistently reiterated theme of his constitutional jurisprudence was the need for fidelity to the constitutional text in judicial review, and the illegitimacy of constitutional doctrines based on sources other than the explicit commands of the written Constitution.

It now appears that as a final mark of Mr. Justice Black's achievement, his jurisprudential view of constitutional adjudication may be returning to favor. In the last few years, distinguished commentators on constitutional law have begun to echo Mr. Justice Black's central theme, criticizing constitutional developments in terms that have scarcely been heard in the scholarly community for a generation.

The criticism has centered around the new "fundamental interest" branch of equal protection doctrine, and the emerging libertarian right of privacy in familial and sexual matters. The strand of criticism that I wish to focus on here has not alleged the impolicy of the new doctrines, or their lack of internal coherence or principled articulation—those are the familiar themes of contemporary constitutional commentary. Rather it has urged that because the new developments rest on principles not derived by normal processes of textual interpretation from the written Constitution, they represent a wholly illegitimate mode of judicial review.

This is the strand of criticism that sounds in the jurisprudence of Mr. Justice Black. It has been put most forcefully by Solicitor General (then Professor) Bork:

> [T]he choice of "fundamental values" by the Court cannot be justified. Where constitutional materials do not clearly specify the value to be preferred, there is no principled way to prefer any claimed human value to any other. The judge must stick close to the text and the history, and their fair implications, and not construct new rights.

Mr. Bork calls this the requirement of "neutral derivation" of constitutional principle, and makes clear that he regards it as additional to the requirement of "neutral application" of principle so much debated in the 1950's and 1960's.

In a thoughtful and stimulating review and extension of that familiar "neutral principles" debate, Professor Hans Linde has likewise urged a return to the commands of the constitutional text as the sole legitimating source for judicial review:

> The judicial responsibility begins and ends with determining the present scope and meaning of a decision that the nation, at an earlier time, articulated and enacted into constitutional text. . . .

The last example of this recent trend that I will cite—though not the last I could cite—is Professor John Ely's powerful assault on the Supreme Court's recent decision in the Abortion Cases. Professor Ely charges that in those decisions, based on a right of "privacy" drawn by no imaginable arts of construction or interpretation from the constitutional text, the Court has violated its "obligation to trace its premises to the charter from which it derives its authority." He goes on:

> A neutral and durable principle may be a thing of beauty and a joy forever. But if it lacks connection with any value the Constitution marks as special, it is not a constitutional principle and the Court has no business imposing it.

I do not think that the view of constitutional adjudication outlined by these commentators is sufficiently broad to capture the full scope of legitimate judicial review. It seems to me that the courts do appropriately apply values not articulated in the constitutional text, and appropriately apply them in determining the constitutionality of legislation.

This view, it seems to me, tacitly underlies much of the affirmative constitutional doctrine developed by the courts over the last generation. The trouble is that the view has been too tacit. It has not been clearly stated and articulately defended, as basic constitutional doctrine should be. Nor, for that matter, has the opposing general view received adequate theoretical statement and defense—except by Mr. Justice Black. Unfortunately, the professional world concerned with constitutional law has not taken Mr. Justice Black's theoretical position sufficiently seriously. Perhaps there was too much of a tendency to accept at face value the great Justice's pose as a rather old-fashioned and simple-minded country lawyer, with sound intuition and a good nose for the concrete issues, but lacking any claim to jurisprudential sophistication.

If the articles by Messrs. Bork, Linde, and Ely mark the emergence of an important trend—as I suspect they do—this basic theoretical issue will no longer be swept under the rug. These critics simply cannot be dismissed as unsophisticates or out-of-date legal primitives.

The truth is that the view of constitutional adjudication that they share with Mr. Justice Black is one of great power and compelling simplicity. That view is deeply rooted in our history and in our shared principles of political legitimacy. It has equally deep roots in our formal constitutional law; it is, after all, the theory upon which judicial review was found in *Marbury* v. *Madison*.

The chief virtue of this view is that it supports judicial review while answering the charge that the practice is undemocratic. Under the pure interpretive model (as I shall henceforth call the view in question), when a court strikes down a popular statute or practice as unconstitutional, it may always reply to the resulting public outcry: "We didn't do it — you did." The people have chosen the principle that the statute or practice violated, have designated it as fundamental, and have written it down in the text of the Constitution for the judges to interpret and apply. The task of interpretation of the people's commands may not always be simple or mechanical; there is no warrant to condemn Mr. Justice Black or his allies with the epithet "mechanical jurisprudence." But the task remains basically one of interpretation, the application of fixed and binding norms to new facts.

BEYOND INTERPRETATION

The contrary view of judicial review, the one that I espouse and that seems to me implicit in much of the constitutional law developed by the courts, does not deny that the Constitution is a written document, expressing some clear and positive restraints upon governmental power. Nor does it deny that part of the business of judicial review consists of giving effect to these explicit commands.

Where the broader view of judicial review diverges from the pure interpretive model is in its acceptance of the courts' additional role as the expounder of basic national ideas of individual liberty and fair treatment, even when the content of these ideals is not expressed as a matter of positive law in the written Constitution. It must at once be conceded that such a role for our courts is more difficult to justify than is the role assigned by the pure interpretive model. Why, one asks, are the courts better able to discern and articulate basic national ideals than are the people's politically responsible representatives? And one recalls Learned Hand's remark that he would find it "most irksome to be ruled by a bevy of Platonic Guardians, even if I knew how to choose them, which I assuredly do not."

These grave difficulties no doubt explain, although they do not excuse, the tendency of our courts — today as throughout our history — to resort to bad legislative history and strained reading of constitutional language to support results that would be better justified by explication of contemporary moral and political ideals not drawn from the constitutional text. Of course, this tendency of the courts in noway helps to establish the legitimacy of noninterpretive judicial review. Indeed, standing alone it tends to establish the opposite; for if judges resort to bad interpretation in preference to honest exposition of deeply held but unwritten ideals, it must be because they perceive the latter mode of decisionmaking to be of suspect legitimacy.

. . . .

In the academic teaching of constitutional law, the general question of the legitimacy of judicial review is addressed largely through the vehicle of *Marbury* v. *Madison*. Students examine the arguments made for judicial review by Chief Justice Marshall, and perhaps contrast them with some of the counter-arguments of later judges or commentators. The discussion concludes with the point that, whatever the validity of those arguments as an original matter, history has firmly decided in favor of judicial review. Thereafter, debates about judicial review focus on the question of how "activist" and how "deferential" *it* should be. *It* is always assumed to be the single unitary practice established and justified in *Marbury*.

This seems to me a seriously misleading way of proceeding. *Marbury* defends (and its detractors attack) what I have here called the pure interpretive model of judicial review. The case itself involves the close interpretation of a technical and explicit constitutional provision, which is found, upon conventional linguistic analysis, to conflict with a statute. The argument for judicial review as a general matter is made in terms appropriate to that sort of case. Chief Justice Marshall's stress is on the *writtenness* of the Constitution, and on its supremacy in cases of clear conflict with ordinary law. His heuristic examples all involve obvious conflicts between hypothetical (and unlikely) statutes on the one hand, and particularly explicit constitutional commands on the other.

All this makes *Marbury* a most atypical constitutional case, and an inappropriate paradigm for the sort of judicial review that has been important and controversial throughout our history, from *Dred Scott* to the *Legal Tender Cases* to *Lochner* to *Carter Coal* and so on to *Brown* v. *Board of Education*, *Baker* v. *Carr*, and the Dealth Penalty and Abortion cases in our own day. In the important cases, reference to and analysis of the constitutional text plays a minor role. The dominant norms of decision are those large conceptions of governmental structure and individual rights that are at best referred to, and whose content is scarcely at all specified, in the written Constitution — dual federalism, vested rights, fair procedure, equality before the law.

. . . .

Much of our substantive constitutional doctrine is of this kind. Where it arises "under" some piece of constitutional text, the text is not invoked as the source of the values or principles that rule the cases. Rather the broad textual provisions are seen as sources of legitimacy for judicial development and explication of basic shared national values. These values may be seen as permanent and universal features of human social arrangements — natural law principles — as they typically were in the 18th and 19th centuries. Or they may be seen as relative to our particular civilization, and subject to growth and change, as they typically are today. Our characteristic contemporary metaphor is "the living Constitution" — a constitution with provisions suggesting restraints on government in the name of basic rights, yet sufficiently unspecific to permit the judiciary to elucidate the development and change in the content of those rights over time.

This view of constitutional adjudication is at war with the pure interpretive model. As Mr. Justice Black said often and forcefully enough, he had no truck with the notion of changing, flexible, "living" constitutional guarantees. The amendment process was the framers' chosen and exclusive method of adopting constitutional values to changing times; the judiciary was to enforce the Constitution's substantive commands as the framers meant them.

This is not to say that the interpretive model is incompatible with one limited sense of the concept of a "living" constitution. The model can contemplate the application of the framers' value judgments and institutional arrangements to new or changed *factual* circumstances. In that sense, its proponents can endorse Chief Justice Marshall's view of the Constitution as "intended to endure for ages to come, and consequently, to be adapted to the various crises of human affairs."

But the interpretive model cannot be reconciled with constitutional doctrines protecting unspecified "essential" or "fundamental" liberties, or "fair procedures," or "decency" — leaving it to the judiciary to give moral content to those conceptions either once and for all or from age to age. That sort of "interpretation" would drain from the interpretive model its animating strength. Once it was adopted, the courts could no longer honestly defend an unpopular deci-

sion to a protesting public with the transfer of responsibility: "We didn't do it — you did." No longer would the Court's constitutional role be the technical and professional one of applying *given* norms to changing facts; instead the Court would assume the large and problematic role of discerning a society's most basic contemporary values.

THE IMPLICATIONS OF THE PURE INTERPRETIVE MODEL

. . . .

A striking point overlooked by contemporary interpretivists is that the demise of substantive due process must constitutionally free the federal government to engage in explicit racial discrimination. There is no textual warrant for reading into the due process clause of the fifth amendment any of the prohibitions directed against the states by the equal protection clause.

Equally strikingly, the application of the provisions of the Bill of Rights to states cannot be justified under an interpretive model — unless one strains to accept, as the Court clearly has declined to do, the flimsy historical evidence that the framers of the 14th amendment intended this result. Freedom of speech, freedom of religion, and the requirement of just compensation in the taking of property, as well as the procedural provisions of the fourth, fifth, sixth, and eighth amendments must then no longer be seen as federal constitutional restraints on state power.

All of the "fundamental interests" that trigger "strict scrutiny" under the equal protection clause would have to be discarded, if the interpretive model were to control constitutional adjudication. Most obviously, the large body of doctrine that has grown up around the interests in the franchise and in participation in the electoral process could not stand. If the values implicit in the equal protection clause are limited only to those that its framers intended at the time of enactment, the clause clearly does not speak to questions of eligibility for the franchise or of legislative apportionment.

Thus far, it seems to me there is little room for disagreement that the premises of the pure interpretive model would require the conclusions I have drawn from it. For those who have not yet had enough, and coming to slightly more doubtful matters, there is serious question how much of the law prohibiting state racial discrimination can survive honest application of the interpretive model. It is clear that the equal protection clause was meant to prohibit *some* forms of state racial discrimination, most obviously those enacted in the Black Codes. It is equally clear from the legislative history that the clause was *not* intended to guarantee equal political rights, such as the right to vote or to run for office, and perhaps including the right to serve on juries.

It is at least doubtful whether the clause can fairly be read as intending to bar any form of state-imposed racial segregation, so long as equal facilities are made available. Professor Bickel's careful study of the legislative history revealed little evidence of intent to prohibit segregation, which at the time was widespread in the North. Professor Bickel did conclude that the original understanding of the amendment was consistent with the decision in the School Segregation Cases, but only in the sense that the general language of the clause *licensed* the courts (and Congress) to enforce evolving ideals of racial justice. Yet this is a classic invocation of the notion of the "living constitution," and as such is not permitted by the interpretive model.

Finally, under the interpretive model, modern applications of the provisions of the Bill of Rights based on their capacity to grow or develop with changing social values would have to be discarded. Prominent among the discarded doctrines would be the prevailing view that the eighth amendment's prohibition of cruel and unusual punishments must be "interpreted" in light of society's "evolving standards of decency." It is doubtful that much of modern first amendment doctrine could be defended on the basis of value choices attributable to the framers, and similar doubts must cast a shadow on some of the law of the fourth amendment. The doctrine that the sixth amendment guarantees appointed counsel for indigent defendants is likewise in serious jeopardy, if historically intended meaning must be the only legitimate guide in constitutional adjudication.

While one might disagree with this rough catalogue on points of detail, it should be clear that an extraordinarily radical purge of established constitutional doctrine would be required if we candidly and consistently applied the pure interpretive model. Surely that makes out at least a prima facie practical case against the model. Conservatives ought to be cautious about adopting any abstract premise which requires so drastic a change in accepted practice, and liberals presumably will be dismayed by the prospect of any major diminution in the courts' authority to protect basic human rights.

. . . .

For the generation that framed the Constitution, the concept of a "higher law," protecting "natural rights," and taking precedence over ordinary positive law as a matter of political obligation, was widely shared and deeply felt. An essential element of American constitutionalism was the reduction to written form — and hence to positive law — of some of the principles of natural rights. But at the same time, it was generally recognized that written constitutions could not completely codify the higher law. Thus, in the framing of the original American constitutions it was widely accepted that there remained unwritten but still binding principles of higher law. The ninth amendment is the textual expression of this idea in the federal Constitution.

As it came to be accepted that the judiciary had the power to enforce the commands of the written Constitution when these conflicted with ordinary law, it was also widely assumed that judges would enforce as constitutional restraints the unwritten natural rights as well. The practice of the Marshall Court and of many of its contemporary state courts, and the writings of the leading constitutional commentators through the first generation of our national life, confirm this understanding.

A parallel development during the first half of the 19th century was the frequent attachment of unwritten constitutional principles to the vaguer and more general clauses of the state and federal constitutions. Natural-rights reasoning in constitutional adjudication persisted up to the Civil War, particularly with respect to property and contract rights, and increasingly involving "due process" and "law of the land" clauses in constitutional texts. At the same time, an important wing of the antislavery movement developed a natural-rights constitutional theory, built around the concepts of due process, of national citizenship and its rights, and of the human equality proclaimed in the Declaration of Independence.

. . . .

The late 19th century saw the most controversial phase in our history of unwritten constitutional law, with the aggressive development by state and federal judges of constitutional principles protecting "liberty of contract" against labor regulation, and restraining taxation and the regulation of prices charged by private business. The reaction to this tendency marked the beginning of sustained intellectual and political attack on the whole concept of unwritten constitutional principles.

Politically, emergent and eventually dominant social forces continued to press for the legislation that was being invalidated under these constitutional principles. Intellectually, the 18th-century philosophical framework supporting the concept of immutable natural rights was eroded with the growth of legal positivism, ethical relativism, pragmatism, and historicism.

Under the combined assault of these social and intellectual forces, the courts retreated from the doctrines of "economic due process," abandoning them in the 1930's. However, although the more sweeping attack on the whole tradition of unwritten constitutional principles gained some important adherents within the judiciary and still more among academic critics, it did not ultimately prevail.

For at almost the same time as the doctrines protecting the laissez-faire economy were passing out of constitutional law, the judiciary began the active development of new civil libertarian constitutional rights whose protection was deemed "essential to the concept of ordered liberty" — for example, rights against state governments of freedom of speech and religion, rights to "fundamentally fair" proceedings, and rights to familial autonomy in childrearing and education.

The last generation has seen further development of constitutional rights clearly — and sometimes avowedly — not derived by textual interpretation, notably the right of privacy, the right to vote, the right to travel, and generally the rights resulting from application of "equal protection of the laws" to the federal government. The intellectual framework against which these rights have developed is different from the natural-rights tradition of the founding fathers — its rhetorical reference points are the Anglo-American tradition and basic American ideals, rather than human nature, the social contract, or the rights of man. But it is the modern offspring, in a direct and traceable line of legitimate descent, of the natural-rights tradition that is so deeply embedded in our constitutional origins.

CONCLUSION

I recognize that there are a host of controversial assertions in this little historico-legal sketch. Had the natural-rights arguments that played so large a role in the American Revolution passed out of fashion and favor when the Constitution was framed? Was not the ninth amendment meant merely to express a principle of federalism? How clear are the natural-rights, antislavery origins of the 14th amendment?

Perhaps the most significant question raised is not one of historical fact so much as legal principle and political theory. Conceding the natural-rights origins of our Constitution, does not the erosion and abandonment of the 18th-century ethics and epistemology on which the natural-rights theory was founded require the abandonment of the mode of judicial review flowing from that theory? Is a "fundamental law" judicially enforced in a climate of historical and cultural relativism the legitimate offspring of a fundamental law which its exponents felt expressed rationally demonstrable, universal, and immutable human rights?

These questions remain to be debated and further investigated before the legitimate pedigree of noninterpretive judicial review can be established. I certainly make no claim that they have been answered here. I have only argued in this Essay that very little of our constitutional law of individual rights has any firm foundation in the model of judicial review which traces from *Marbury* v. *Madison* to the jurisprudence of Mr. Justice Black. And I have suggested that the reflexive resort to variants of this model, so common a rhetorical response of constitutional scholars in the *Lochner* era, seems to be reviving today, and therefore requires more direct critical scrutiny than it has had in the recent past.

U.S. v. Carolene Products

304 U.S. 144 (1938)
Vote: 8–1

Perhaps the most influential exposition of the potential of the U.S. Supreme Court is found in a mere footnote in an otherwise only modestly significant case. The ideas behind the footnote have been employed by justices on many sides — sometimes even in the same case.

U.S. v. *Carolene Products* involved a question of regulation of commerce and permission to ship and sell "filled milk," a sort of liquid oleo. Justice Stone suggested in this case that judges were *not* the appropriate officials to make economic judgments. Legislatures are chosen by the people to make those choices.

The footnote appears as almost an afterthought, dealing with what *is* the province of courts. At bottom there is a notion that politics and democracy work well, but there are occasions when majority rule is distorted or weakened. Then courts must step in.

There may be narrower scope for operation of the presumption of constitutionality when legislation appears on its face to be within a specific prohibition of the Constitution, such as those of the first ten amendments, which are deemed equally specific when held to be embraced within the Fourteenth. . . .

It is unnecessary to consider now whether legislation which restricts those political processes which can ordinarily be expected to bring about repeal of undesirable legislation, is to be subjected to more exacting judicial scrutiny under the general prohibitions of the Fourteenth Amendment than are most other types of legislation. . . .

Nor need we enquire whether similar considerations enter into the review of statutes directed at particular religious, . . . or national, . . . or racial minorities . . . whether prejudice against discrete and insular minorities may be a special condition, which tends seriously to curtail the operation of those political processes ordinarily to be relied upon to protect minorities, and which may call for a correspondingly more searching judicial inquiry. Compare *McCulloch* v. *Maryland,* 4 Wheat. 316, 428; *South Carolina* v. *Barnwell Bros.,* 303 U.S. 177, 184, n. 2, and cases cited.

Yakus v. U.S.

321 U.S. 414 (1944)
Vote: 6–3

During World War II, the United States had price controls to minimize the inflation generated by a war-production economy going at full blast and a shortage of goods for domestic consumption. Violations were crimes that could be tried in federal district courts and appealed to a special court. These proceedings could not rule on the constitutionality of the statute or the regulations. Essentially, through clever draftmanship, the price administration legislation deferred judicial review of constitutionality until after the war. The Supreme Court majority upheld these arrangements, under reasoning similar to that in MCCARDLE. Judicial review was separated from appeal but was theoretically possible by other means. Justice Rutledge dissented, arguing Congress might exclude courts from an administrative process, but if the courts are to be involved, they must have full freedom to act as courts. While there is no definitive word on what would be decided today, Rutledge's dissent is probably more respected and influential than the majority view.

MR. JUSTICE RUTLEDGE, dissenting.
. . . .

The crux of this case comes, as I see it, in the question whether Congress can confer jurisdiction upon federal and state courts in the enforcement proceedings, more particularly the criminal suit, and at the same time deny them "jurisdiction or power to consider the validity" of the regulations for which enforcement is thus sought. This question which the Court now says "presents no novel constitutional issue" was expressly and carefully reserved in *Lockerty* v. *Phillips, supra.* The prohibition is the statute's most novel feature. . . .

It is one thing for Congress to withhold jurisdiction. It is entirely another to confer it and direct that it be exercised in a manner inconsistent with constitutional requirements or, what in some instances may be the same thing, without regard to them. Once it is held that Congress can require the courts criminally to enforce unconstitutional laws or statutes, including regulations, or to do so without regard for their validity, the way will have been found to circumvent the supreme law and, what is more, to make the courts parties to doing so. This Congress cannot do. There are limits to the judicial power. Congress may impose others. And in some matters Congress or the President has final say under the Constitution. But whenever the judicial power is called into play, it is responsible directly to the fundamental law and no other authority can intervene to force or authorize the judicial body to disregard it. The problem therefore is not solely one of individual right or due process of law. It is equally one of the separation and independence of the powers of government and of the constitutional integrity of the judicial process, more especially in criminal trials.
. . . .

Clearly Congress could not require judicial enforcement of an unconstitutional statute. The same is true of an unconstitutional regulation. And it is conceded that Congress could not have compelled judicial enforcement of all price regulations, without regard to their validity, if it had not given opportunity for attack upon them through the Emergency Court or if that opportunity is inadequate. But because the opportunity is afforded and is deemed adequate in the unusual circumstances, at any rate for some of its purposes, and because it was not followed, the Court holds that criminal enforcement must be given and the enforcing court cannot consider the question of validity.
. . . .

A procedure so piecemeal, so chopped up, so disruptive of constitutional guaranties in relation to trials for crime, should not and, in my judgment, cannot be validated, as to such proceedings, under the Constitution. Even war does not suspend the protections which are inherently part and parcel of our criminal process. . . .

War requires much of the citizen. He surrenders rights for the time being to secure their more permanent establishment. Most men do so freely. According to our plan others must do so also, as far as the nation's safety requires. But the surrender is neither permanent nor total. The great liberties of speech and the press are curtailed but not denied. Religious freedom remains a living thing. With these, in our system, rank the elemental protections thrown about the citizen charged with crime, more especially those forged on history's anvil in great crises. They secure fair play to the guilty and vindication for the innocent.... Not yet has the war brought extremity that demands or permits them to be put aside. Nor does maintaining price control require this....

Different considerations, in part at any rate, apply in civil proceedings. But for the trial of crimes no procedure should be approved which dispenses with trial of any material issue or splits the trial into disjointed segments, one of which is summary and civil, the other but a remnant of the ancient criminal proceeding.

The judgment should be reversed.

I am authorized to say that MR. JUSTICE MURPHY joins in this opinion.

Ashwander v. T.V.A.

297 U.S. 288 (1936)

Although Brandeis was a passionate activist, he was also a stickler for legal rules. He believed that the courts could best serve society by faithfully observing prescribed limits. In *Ashwander*, Brandeis assembled an impressive set of limits on court power from previous decisions of the Supreme Court. These rules have assumed a semiconstitutional status and are cited by the Court, in reverential tones, in cases which faithfully follow the limits, as well as in the arguably larger number of cases in which the Court sidesteps them.

MR. JUSTICE BRANDEIS, concurring.
. . . .

The court developed, for its own governance in the cases confessedly within its jurisdiction, a series of rules under which it has avoided passing upon a large part of all the constitutional questions pressed upon it for decision. They are:

1. The Court will not pass upon the constitutionality of legislation in a friendly, non-adversary, proceeding....

2. The Court will not "anticipate a question of constitutional law in advance of the necessity of deciding it."...

3. The Court will not "formulate a rule of constitutional law broader than is required by the precise facts to which it is to be applied...."

4. The Court will not pass upon a constitutional question although properly presented by the record, if there is also present some other ground upon which the case may be disposed of. This rule has found most varied application. Thus, if a case can be decided on either of two grounds, one involving a constitutional question, the other a question of statutory construction or general law, the Court will decide only the latter. *Siler* v. *Louisville & Nashville R. Co.*, 213 U.S. 175, 191; *Light* v. *United States*, 220 U.S. 523, 538. Appeals from the highest court of a state challenging its decision of a question under the Federal Constitution are frequently dismissed because the judgment can be sustained on an independent state ground. *Berea College* v. *Kentucky*, 211 U.S. 45, 53.

5. The Court will not pass upon the validity of a statute upon complaint of one who fails to show that he is injured by its operation. *Tyler* v. *The Judges*, 179 U.S. 405; *Hendrick* v. *Maryland*, 235 U.S. 610, 621....

6. The Court will not pass upon the constitutionality of a statute at the instance of one who has availed himself of its benefits. *Great Falls Mfg. Co.* v. *Attorney General*, 124 U.S. 581; *Wall* v. *Parrot Silver & Copper Co.*, 244 U.S. 407, 411–412; *St. Louis Malleable Casting Co.* v. *Prendergast Construction Co.*, 260 U.S. 469.

7. "When the validity of an act of the Congress is drawn in question, and even if a serious doubt of constitutionality is raised, it is a cardinal principle that this Court will first ascertain whether a construction of the statute is fairly possible by which the question may be avoided." *Crowell* v. *Benson*, 285 U.S. 22, 62....

Ex parte McCardle

7 Wallace 506 (1869)
Vote: Unanimous

After the Civil War, the South was administered under the authority of the military, acting under the Reconstruction Acts. When McCardle, a southerner, was arrested, he sought a writ of habeas corpus, arguing that, as the hostilities had ceased, only civil courts could try him. Faced with this serious legal challenge to their entire Reconstruction policy, the Radical Republicans who dominated Congress hastily repealed the 1867 statute under which McCardle's lawyers had filed. The Supreme Court had already begun proceedings, but they backed away from the proceedings completely, the most dramatic show of congressional control in history.

Was it also the most far-reaching legally? That depends on how one reads the last paragraph of the opinion. It is certainly factually correct. It also might mean "this can be done, since it still leaves judicial review in place by another route." If so, *McCardle* would be a much less significant precedent.

THE CHIEF JUSTICE delivered the opinion of the court.

The first question necessarily is that of jurisdiction; for, if the act of March, 1868, takes away the jurisdiction defined by the act of February, 1867, it is useless, if not improper, to enter into any discussion of other questions.

It is quite true, as was argued by the counsel for the petitioner, that the appellate jurisdiction of this court is not derived from acts of Congress. It is, strictly speaking, conferred by the Constitution. But it is conferred, "with such exceptions and under such regulations as Congress shall make."

It is unnecessary to consider whether, if Congress had made no exceptions and no regulations, this court might not have exercised general appellate jurisdiction under rules prescribed by itself. For among the earliest acts of the first Congress, at its first session, was the act of September 24th, 1789, to establish the judicial courts of the United States. That act provided for the organization of this court, and prescribed regulations for the exercise of its jurisdiction. . . . In the case of *Durousseau* v. *The United States,* particularly, the whole matter was carefully examined, and the court held, that while "the appellate powers of this court are not given by the judicial act, but are given by the Constitution," they are, nevertheless, "limited and regulated by the act, and by such other acts as have been passed on the subject." The court said, further, that the judicial act was an exercise of the power given by the Constitution to Congress "of making exceptions to the appellate jurisdiction of the Supreme Court." "They have

described affirmatively," said the court, "its jurisdiction, and this affirmative description has been understood to imply a negation of the exercise of such appellate power as is not comprehended within it."

The exception to appellate jurisdiction in the case before us, however, is not an inference from the affirmation of other appellate jurisdiction. It is made in terms. The provision of the act of 1867, affirming the appellate jurisdiction of this court in cases of *habeas corpus* is expressly repealed. It is hardly possible to imagine a plainer instance of positive exception.

We are not at liberty to inquire into the motives of the legislature. We can only examine into its power under the Constitution; and the power to make exceptions to the appellate jurisdiction of this court is given by express words.

What, then, is the effect of the repealing act upon the case before us? We cannot doubt as to this. Without jurisdiction the court cannot proceed at all in any cause. Jurisdiction is power to declare the law, and when it ceases to exist, the only function remaining to the court is that of announcing the fact and dismissing the cause. . . .

It is quite clear, therefore, that this court cannot proceed to pronounce judgment in this case, for it has no longer jurisdiction of the appeal; and judicial duty is not less fitly performed by declining ungranted jurisdiction than in exercising firmly that which the Constitution and the laws confer.

Counsel seem to have supposed, if effect be given to the repealing act in question, that the whole appellate power of the court, in cases of *habeas corpus,* is denied. But this is an error. The act of 1868 does not except from that jurisdiction any cases but appeals from Circuit Courts under the act of 1867. It does not affect the jurisdiction which was previously exercised.

The appeal of the petitioner in this case must be
Dismissed for want of jurisdiction.

Frothingham v. Mellon

262 U.S. 447 (1923)
Vote: 9–0

A childless woman, objecting to the use of federal funds for maternity facilities in hospitals, wished to argue that the federal government had no right to spend taxes for such purposes. The State of Massachusetts wished to make the same claim. The federal government argued neither was a proper party. Frothingham's taxes were not hinged to the particular program in question, and she would probably pay the same tax with or without the existence of the program. Massachusetts could not really claim to represent the interests of its citizens in court on this matter; many residents would benefit from the program and probably approve. (A state can represent its citizens politically, of course. And on such matters as, for example, garbage coming downstream from another locality, the interests of the citizens of the state seem sufficiently similar that a state government might well be a proper spokesperson in court.)

It is appropriate to note how often cases hinge not upon the merits but upon who has the right to appear where. Compare MARBURY (right complainant, wrong court) and DRED SCOTT (wrong court system entirely) with COLEMAN V. MILLER (courts don't decide such matters). Compare *Frothingham* and WARTH V. SELDIN (you can't be heard) with POWELL V. MCCORMICK (you can be heard).

MR. JUSTICE SUTHERLAND delivered the opinion of the Court.

. . . .

It is asserted that these appropriations are for purposes not national, but local to the States, and together with numerous similar appropriations constitute an effective means of inducing the States to yield a portion of their sovereign rights. . . . In the *Massachusetts* case [*Commonwealth of Massachusetts v. Mellon,* companion case to Frothingham] it is alleged that the plaintiff's rights and powers as a sovereign State and the rights of its citizens have been invaded and usurped by these expenditures and acts; and that, although the State has not accepted the act, its constitutional rights are infringed by the passage thereof and the imposition upon the State of an illegal and unconstitutional option either to yield to the Federal Government a part of its reserved rights or lose the share which it would otherwise be entitled to receive of the moneys appropriated. In the *Frothingham* case plaintiff alleges that the effect of the statute will be to take her property, under the guise of taxation, without due process of law.

We have reached the conclusion that the cases must be disposed of for want of jurisdiction without considering the merits of the constitutional questions.

In the first case, the State of Massachusetts presents no justiciable controversy either in its own behalf or as the representative of its citizens. The appellant in the second suit has no such interest in the subject-matter, nor is any such injury inflicted or threatened, as will enable her to sue.

. . . .

Probably, it would be sufficient to point out that the powers of the State are not invaded, since the statute imposes no obligation but simply extends an option which the State is free to accept or reject. But we do not rest here. Under Article III, §2, of the Constitution, the judicial power of this Court extends "to controversies . . . between a State and citizens of another State" and the Court has original jurisdiction "in all cases . . . in which a State shall be party." The effect of this is not to confer jurisdiction upon the Court merely because a State is a party, but only where it is a party to a proceeding of judicial cognizance. Proceedings not of a justiciable character are outside the contemplation of the constitutional grant.

. . . .

We come next to consider whether the suit may be maintained by the State as the representative of its citizens. To this the answer is not doubtful. We need not go so far as to say that a State may never intervene by suit to protect its citizens against any form of enforcement of unconstitutional acts of Congress; but we are clear that the right to do so does not arise here. . . . [T]he citizens of Massachusetts are also citizens of the United States. It cannot be conceded that a State, as *parens patriae,* may institute judicial proceedings to protect citizens of the United States from the operation of the statutes thereof. While the State, under some circumstances, may sue in that capacity for the protection of its citizens (*Missouri* v. *Illinois*, 180 U.S. 208, 241), it is no part of its duty or power to enforce their rights in respect of their relations with the Federal Government. In that field it is the United States, and not the State, which represents them as *parens patriae,* when such representation becomes appropriate; and to the former, and not to the latter, they must look for such protective measures as flow from that status.

Second. The attack upon the statute in the *Frothingham* case is, generally, the same, but this plaintiff alleges in addition that she is a taxpayer of the United States; and her contention, though not clear, seems to be that the effect of the appropriations complained of will be to increase the burden of future taxation and thereby take her property without due process of law. The right of a taxpayer to enjoin the execution of a federal appropriation act, on the ground that it is invalid and will result in taxation for illegal purposes, has never been passed upon by this Court. In cases where it was presented, the question has either been allowed to pass *sub silentio* or the determination of it expressly withheld. . . . The interest of a taxpayer of a municipality in the application of its moneys is direct and immediate and the remedy by injunction to prevent their misuse is not inappropriate. It is upheld by a large number of state cases and is the rule of this court. . . .

But the relation of a taxpayer of the United States to the Federal Government is very different. His interest in the moneys of the Treasury — partly realized from taxation and partly from other sources — is shared with millions of others; is comparatively minute and indeterminable; and the effect upon future taxation, of any payment out of the funds, so remote, fluctuating and uncertain, that no basis is afforded for an appeal to the preventive powers of a court of equity.

The administration of any statute, likely to produce additional taxation to be imposed upon a vast number of taxpayers, the extent of whose several liability is indefinite and constantly changing, is essentially a matter of public and not of individual concern. If one taxpayer may champion and litigate such a cause, then every other taxpayer may do the same, not only in respect of the statute here under review but also in respect of every other appropriation act and statute whose administration requires the outlay of public money, and whose validity may be questioned. The bare suggestion of such a result, with its attendant inconveniences, goes far to sustain the conclusion which we have reached, that a suit of this character cannot be maintained. . . .

The functions of government under our system are apportioned. To the legislative department has been committed the duty of making laws; to the executive the duty of executing them; and to the judiciary the duty of interpreting and applying them in cases properly brought before the courts. The general rule is that neither department may invade the province of the other and neither may control, direct or restrain the action of the other. . . . We have no power *per se* to review and annul acts of Congress on the ground that they are unconstitutional. That question may be considered only when the justification for some direct injury suffered or threatened, presenting a justiciable issue, is made to rest upon such an act. Then the power exercised is that of ascertaining and declaring the law applicable to the controversy. It amounts to little more than the negative power to disregard an unconstitutional enactment, which otherwise would stand in the way of the enforcement of a legal right. The party who invokes the power must be able to show not only that the statute is invalid but that he has sustained or is immediately in danger of sustaining some direct injury as the result of its enforcement, and not merely that he suffers in some indefinite way in common with people generally. If a case for preventive relief be presented the court enjoins, in effect, not the execution of the statute, but the acts of the official, the statute notwithstanding. Here the parties plaintiff have no such case. Looking through forms of words to the substance of their complaint, it is merely that officials of the executive department of the government are executing and will execute an act of Congress asserted to be unconstitutional; and this we are asked to prevent. To do so would be not to decide a judicial controversy, but to assume a position of authority over the governmental acts of another and co-equal department, an authority which plainly we do not possess.

Flast v. Cohen

392 U.S. 83 (1968)
Vote: 8–1; two concurrences.

As is discussed in Chapter 7, the Constitution provides for freedom of religion in two ways. It prohibits denial of free exercise of worship and also prohibits the establishment of religion — making a faith (or faiths) the official religion and providing funds for it. A complaint of a denial of worship can be heard by the courts without problems of standing, since the interest of a complainant is direct and clear. But if a program of government aid helps all faiths, it might be difficult to challenge the program under the Frothingham rule. Since 1947, the federal government has tried to find constitutional ways to aid the educational systems of religious movements by distinguishing secular and religious objectives. The line drawn has often been a thin and complex one. Yet in many instances citizens who were passionately concerned, and who believed the nature of the government was at stake, had no way of raising issues, since they were mere "taxpayers." But their claim was not really monetary.

Flast and others claimed a right to sue as federal taxpayers to prevent the Secretary of Health, Education and Welfare from providing funds to parochial schools for textbooks and other purposes. A three-judge federal court ruled that, under FROTHINGHAM, the plaintiffs had no standing.

MR. CHIEF JUSTICE WARREN delivered the opinion of the Court.

In *Frothingham* v. *Mellon* ... this Court ruled that a federal taxpayer is without standing to challenge the constitutionality of a federal statute. That ruling has stood for 45 years as an impenetrable barrier to suits against Acts of Congress brought by individuals who can assert only the interest of federal taxpayers. In this case, we must decide whether the *Frothingham* barrier should be lowered when a taxpayer attacks a federal statute on the ground that it violates the Establishment and Free Exercise Clauses of the First Amendment.

. . . .

The gravamen of the appellants' complaint was that federal funds appropriated under the Act were being used to finance instruction in reading, arithmetic, and other subjects in religious schools, and to purchase textbooks and other instructional materials for use in such schools. Such expenditures were alleged to be in contravention of the Establishment and Free Exercise Clauses of the First Amendment. . . .

II

This Court first faced squarely the question whether a litigant asserting only his status as a taxpayer has standing to maintain a suit in a federal court in *Frothingham* v. *Mellon* ... and that decision must be the starting point for analysis in this case. The taxpayer in *Frothingham* attacked as unconstitutional the Maternity Act of 1921, 42 Stat. 224, which established a federal program of grants to those States which would undertake programs to reduce maternal and infant mortality. The taxpayer alleged that Congress, in enacting the challenged statute, had exceeded the powers delegated to it under Article I of the Constitution and had invaded the legislative province reserved to the several States by the Tenth Amendment. The taxpayer complained that the result of the allegedly unconstitutional enactment would be to increase her future federal tax liability and "thereby take her property without due

process of law." 262 U.S., at 486. The Court noted that a federal taxpayer's "interest in the moneys of the Treasury ... is comparatively minute and indeterminable" and that "the effect upon future taxation, of any payment out of the [Treasury's] funds, ... [is] remote, fluctuating and uncertain." *Id.*, at 487. As a result, the Court ruled that the taxpayer had failed to allege the type of "direct injury" necessary to confer standing. *Id.*, at 488.

Although the barrier *Frothingham* erected against federal taxpayer suits has never been breached, the decision has been the source of some confusion and the object of considerable criticism. The confusion has developed as commentators have tried to determine whether *Frothingham* establishes a constitutional bar to taxpayer suits or whether the Court was simply imposing a rule of self-restraint which was not constitutionally compelled. The conflicting viewpoints are reflected in the arguments made to this Court by the parties in this case. The Government has pressed upon us the view that *Frothingham* announced a constitutional rule, compelled by the Article III limitations on federal court jurisdiction and grounded in considerations of the doctrine of separation of powers. Appellants, however, insist that *Frothingham* expressed no more than a policy of judicial self-restraint which can be disregarded when compelling reasons for assuming jurisdiction over a taxpayer's suit exist. The opinion delivered in *Frothingham* can be read to support either position. The concluding sentence of the opinion states that, to take jurisdiction of the taxpayer's suit, "would be not to decide a judicial controversy, but to assume a position of authority over the governmental acts of another and co-equal department, an authority which plainly we do not possess." ... Yet the concrete reasons given for denying standing to a federal taxpayer suggest that the Court's holding rests on something less than a constitutional foundation. For example, the Court conceded that standing had previously been conferred on municipal taxpayers to sue in that capacity. However, the Court viewed the interest of a federal taxpayer in total federal tax revenues as "comparatively minute and indeterminable" when measured against a municipal taxpayer's interest in a smaller city treasury. *Id.*, at 486–487. This suggests that the petitioner in *Frothingham* was denied standing not because she was a taxpayer but because her tax bill was not large enough. In addition, the Court spoke of the "attendant inconveniences" of entertaining that taxpayer's suit because it might open the door of federal courts to countless such suits "in respect of every other appropriation act and statute whose administration requires the outlay of public money, and whose validity may be questioned." Such a statement suggests pure policy considerations.

. . . .

III

The jurisdiction of federal courts is defined and limited by Article III of the Constitution. In terms relevant to the question for decision in this case, the judicial power of federal courts is constitutionally restricted to "cases" and "controversies." As is so often the situation in constitutional adjudication, those two words have an iceberg quality, containing beneath their surface simplicity submerged complexities which go to the very heart of our constitutional form of government. Embodied in the words "cases" and "controversies" are two complementary but somewhat different limitations. In part those words limit the business of federal courts to questions presented in an adversary context and in a form historically viewed as capable of resolution through the judicial process. And in part those words define the role assigned to the judiciary in the tripartite allocation of power to assure that the federal courts will not intrude into areas committed to the other branches of government. Justiciability is the term of art employed to give expression to this dual limitation placed upon federal courts by the case-and-controversy doctrine.

Justiciability is itself a concept of uncertain meaning and scope. Its reach is illustrated by the various grounds upon which questions sought to be adjudicated in federal courts have been held not to be justiciable. Thus, no justiciable controversy is presented when the parties seek adjudication of only a political question, when the parties are asking for an advisory opinion, when the question sought to be adjudicated has been mooted by subsequent developments, and when there is no standing to maintain the action. Yet it remains true that "[j]usticiability is . . . not a legal concept with a fixed content or susceptible of scientific verification. Its utilization is the resultant of many subtle pressures. . . ." *Poe* v. *Ullman* . . . (1961).

Part of the difficulty in giving precise meaning and form to the concept of justiciability stems from the uncertain historical antecedents of the case-and-controversy doctrine. For example, Mr. Justice Frankfurter twice suggested that historical meaning could be imparted to the concepts of justiciability and case and controversy by reference to the practices of the courts of Westminster when the Constitution was adopted. *Joint Anti-Fascist Committee* v.

McGrath . . . (1951) (concurring opinion); *Coleman* v. *Miller* . . . (1939) (separate opinion). However, the power of English judges to deliver advisory opinions was well-established at the time the Constitution was drafted. 3 K. Davis, Administrative Law Treatise 127–128, (1958). And it is quite clear that "the oldest and most consistent thread in the federal law of justiciability is that the federal courts will not give advisory opinions." C. Wright. Federal Courts 34 (1963). Thus, the implicit policies embodied in Article III, and not history alone, impose the rule against advisory opinions on federal courts. When the federal judicial power is invoked to pass upon the validity of actions by the Legislative and Executive Branches of the Government, the rule against advisory opinions implements the separation of powers prescribed by the Constitution and confines federal courts to the role assigned them by Article III. See *Muskrat* v. *United States* . . . (1911); 3 H. Johnston, Correspondence and Public Papers of John Jay 486–489 (1891) (correspondence between Secretary of State Jefferson and Chief Justice Jay). However, the rule against advisory opinions also recognizes that such suits often "are not pressed before the Court with that clear concreteness provided when a question emerges precisely framed and necessary for decision from a clash of adversary argument exploring every aspect of the multifaced situation embracing conflicting and demanding interests." *United States* v. *Fruehauf* . . . (1961). Consequently, the Article III prohibition against advisory opinions reflects the complementary constitutional considerations expressed by the justiciability doctrine: Federal judicial power is limited to those disputes which confine federal courts to a role consistent with a system of separated powers and which are traditionally thought to be capable of resolution through the judicial process.

Additional uncertainty exists in the doctrine of justiciability because that doctrine has become a blend of constitutional requirements and policy considerations. And a policy limitation is "not always clearly distinguished from the constitutional limitation." *Barrows* v. *Jackson* . . . (1953). For example, in his concurring opinion in *Ashwander* v. *Tennessee Valley Authority* . . . (1936), Mr. Justice Brandeis listed seven rules developed by this Court "for its own governance" to avoid passing prematurely on constitutional questions. Because the rules operate in "cases confessedly within [the Court's] jurisdiction," *id.,* at 346, they find their source in policy, rather than purely constitutional, considerations. However, several of the cases cited by Mr. Justice Brandeis in illustrating the rules of self-governance articulated purely constitutional grounds for decision. See, *e.g.,* *Massachusetts* v. *Mellon* . . . (1923). . . . The "many subtle pressures" which cause policy considerations to blend into the constitutional limitations of Article III make the justiciability doctrine one of uncertain and shifting contours.

It is in this context that the standing question presented by this case must be viewed and that the Government's argument on that question must be evaluated. As we understand it, the Government's position is that the constitutional scheme of separation of powers, and the deference owed by the federal judiciary to the other two branches of government within that scheme, presents an absolute bar to taxpayer suits challenging the validity of federal spending programs. The Government views such suits as involving no more than the mere disagreement by the taxpayer "with the uses to which tax money is put." According to the Government, the resolution of such disagreements is committed to other branches of the Federal Government and not to the judiciary. Consequently, the Government contends that, under no circumstances, should standing be conferred on federal taxpayers to challenge a federal taxing or spending program. An analysis of the function served by standing limitations compels a rejection of the Government's position.

Standing is an aspect of justiciability and, as such, the problem of standing is surrounded by the same complexities and vagaries that inhere in justiciability. Standing has been called one of "the most amorphous [concepts] in the entire domain of public law." Some of the complexities peculiar to standing problems result because standing "serves, on occasion, as a shorthand expression for all the various elements of justiciability." In addition, there are at work in the standing doctrine the many subtle pressures which tend to cause policy considerations to blend into constitutional limitations.

Despite the complexities and uncertainties, some meaningful form can be given to the jurisdictional limitations placed on federal court power by the concept of standing. . . . A proper party is demanded so that federal courts will not be asked to decide "ill-defined controversies over constitutional issues," *United Public Workers* v. *Mitchell* . . . (1947), or a case which is of "a hypothetical or abstract character," *Aetna Life Insurance Co.* v. *Haworth* . . . (1937). So stated, the standing requirement is closely related to, although more general than, the rule that federal courts will not entertain friendly suits, *Chicago & Grand Trunk R. Co.* v. *Wellman,* or those which are feigned or collusive in na-

ture, *United States* v. *Johnson* . . . (1943); *Lord* v. *Veazie* . . . (1850).

When the emphasis in the standing problem is placed on whether the person invoking a federal court's jurisdiction is a proper party to maintain the action, the weakness of the Government's argument in this case becomes apparent. The question whether a particular person is a proper party to maintain the action does not, by its own force, raise separation of powers problems related to improper judicial interference in areas committed to other branches of the Federal Government. Such problems arise, if at all, only from the substantive issues the individual seeks to have adjudicated. Thus, in terms of Article III limitations on federal court jurisdiction, the question of standing is related only to whether the dispute sought to be adjudicated will be presented in an adversary context and in a form historically viewed as capable of judicial resolution. It is for that reason that the emphasis in standing problems is on whether the party invoking federal court jurisdiction has "a personal stake in the outcome of the controversy," *Baker* v. *Carr* . . . (1952), and whether the dispute touches upon "the legal relations of parties having adverse legal interests." *Aetna Life Insurance Co.* v. *Haworth.* . . . A taxpayer may or may not have the requisite personal stake in the outcome, depending upon the circumstances of the particular case. Therefore, we find no absolute bar in Article III to suits by federal taxpayers challenging allegedly unconstitutional federal taxing and spending programs. There remains, however, the problem of determining the circumstances under which a federal taxpayer will be deemed to have the personal stake and interest that imparts the necessary concrete adverseness. . . . [O]ur decisions establish that, in ruling on standing, it is both appropriate and necessary to look to the substantive issues for another purpose, namely, to determine whether there is a logical nexus between the status asserted and the claim sought to be adjudicated.

The nexus demanded of federal taxpayers has two aspects to it. First, the taxpayer must establish a logical link between that status and the type of legislative enactment attacked. Thus, a taxpayer will be a proper party to allege the unconstitutionality only of exercises of congressional power under the taxing and spending clause of Art. I, §8, of the Constitution. It will not be sufficient to allege an incidental expenditure of tax funds in the administration of an essentially regulatory statute. This requirement is consistent with the limitation imposed upon state taxpayer standing in federal courts in *Doremus* v.

Board of Education . . . (1952). Secondly the taxpayer must establish a nexus between that status and the precise nature of the constitutional infringement alleged. Under this requirement, the taxpayer must show that the challenged enactment exceeds specific constitutional limitations imposed upon the exercise of the congressional taxing and spending power and not simply that the enactment is generally beyond the powers delegated to Congress by Art. I, §8. When both nexuses are established, the litigant will have shown a taxpayer's stake in the outcome of the controversy and will be a proper and appropriate party to invoke a federal court's jurisdiction.

. . . Our history vividly illustrates that one of the specific evils feared by those who drafted the Establishment Clause and fought for its adoption was that the taxing and spending power would be used to favor one religion over another or to support religion in general. . . .

. . . The taxpayer in *Frothingham* attacked a federal spending program and she, therefore, established the first nexus required. However, she lacked standing because her constitutional attack was not based on an allegation that Congress, in enacting the Maternity Act of 1921, had breached a specific limitation upon its taxing and spending power. The taxpayer in *Frothingham* alleged essentially that Congress, by enacting the challenged statute, had exceeded the general powers delegated to it by Art. I, §8, and that Congress had thereby invaded the legislative province reserved to the States by the Tenth Amendment. . . .

We have noted that the Establishment Clause of the First Amendment does specifically limit the taxing and spending power conferred by Art. I, §8. Whether the Constitution contains other specific limitations can be determined only in the context of future cases. . . .

While we express no view at all on the merits of appellants' claims in this case, their complaint contains sufficient allegations under the criteria we have outlined to give them standing to invoke a federal court's jurisdiction for an adjudication on the merits.

Reversed.

MR. JUSTICE DOUGLAS, concurring.

While I have joined the opinion of the Court, I do not think that the test it lays down is a durable one for the reasons stated by my Brother HARLAN. I think, therefore, that it will suffer erosion and in time result in the demise of *Frothingham* v. *Mellon*, 262 U.S. 447. It would therefore be the part of wisdom, as I see the problem, to be rid of *Frothingham* here and now.

. . . .

We have a Constitution designed to keep government out of private domains. But the fences have often been broken down; and *Frothingham* denied effective machinery to restore them. The Constitution even with the judicial gloss it has acquired plainly is not adequate to protect the individual against the growing bureaucracy in the Legislative and Executive Branches. He faces a formidable opponent in government, even when he is endowed with funds and with courage. The individual is almost certain to be plowed under, unless he has a well-organized active political group to speak for him. The church is one. The press is another. The union is a third. But if a powerful sponsor is lacking, individual liberty withers — in spite of glowing opinions and resounding constitutional phrases.

I would not be niggardly therefore in giving private attorneys general standing to sue. I would certainly not wait for Congress to give its blessing to our deciding cases clearly within our Article III jurisdiction. To wait for a sign from Congress is to allow important constitutional questions to go undecided and personal liberty unprotected.

. . . .

I would be as liberal in allowing taxpayers standing to object to these violations of the First Amendment as I would in granting standing of people to complain of any invasion of their rights under the Fourth Amendment or the Fourteenth or under any other guarantee in the Constitution itself or in the Bill of Rights.

MR. JUSTICE STEWART, concurring.

MR. JUSTICE FORTAS, concurring.

I would confine the ruling in this case to the proposition that a taxpayer may maintain a suit to challenge the validity of a federal expenditure on the ground that the expenditure violates the Establishment Clause. As the Court's opinion recites, there is enough in the constitutional history of the Establishment Clause to support the thesis that this Clause includes a *specific* prohibition upon the use of the power to tax to support an establishment of religion. There is no reason to suggest and no basis in the logic of this decision for implying, that there may be other types of congressional expenditures which may be attacked by a litigant solely on the basis of his status as a taxpayer.

... I believe, we must recognize that our principle of judicial scrutiny of legislative acts which raise important constitutional questions requires that the issue here presented — the separation of state and church — which the Founding Fathers regarded as fundamental to our constitutional system — should be subjected to judicial testing. This is not a question which we, if we are to be faithful to our trust, should consign to limbo, unacknowledged, unresolved, and undecided.

On the other hand, the urgent necessities of this case and the precarious opening through which we find our way to confront it, do not demand that we open the door to a general assault upon exercises of the spending power. The status of taxpayer should not be accepted as a launching pad for an attack upon any target other than legislation affecting the Establishment Clause. ...

MR. JUSTICE HARLAN, dissenting.
....

Presumably the Court does not believe that regulatory programs are necessarily less destructive of First Amendment rights, or that regulatory programs are necessarily less prodigal of public funds than are grants-in-aid, for both these general propositions are demonstrably false. The Court's disregard of regulatory expenditures is not even a logical consequence of its apparent assumption that taxpayer-plaintiffs assert essentially monetary interests for it surely cannot matter to a taxpayer *qua* taxpayer whether an unconstitutional expenditure is used to hire the services of regulatory personnel or is distributed among private and local governmental agencies as grants-in-aid. His interest as taxpayer arises, if at all, from the fact of an unlawful expenditure, and not as a consequence of the expenditure's form. Apparently the Court has repudiated the emphasis in *Frothingham* upon the amount of the plaintiff's tax bill, only to substitute an equally irrelevant emphasis upon the form of the challenged expenditure.

The Court's second criterion is similarly unrelated to its standard for the determination of standing. The intensity of a plaintiff's interest in a suit is not measured, even obliquely, by the fact that the constitutional provision under which he claims is, or is not, a "specific limitation" upon Congress' spending powers. ...

Although the Court does not altogether explain its position, the essence of its reasoning is evidently that a taxpayer's claim under the Establishment Clause is "not merely one of ultra vires," but instead asserts "an abridgment of individual religious liberty" and a "governmental infringement of individual rights protected by the Constitution." Choper, The Establishment Clause and Aid to Parochial Schools, 56 Calif. L. Rev. 260, 276. It must first be emphasized that this is apparently not founded upon any "preferred" position for the First Amendment, or upon any asserted unavailability of other plaintiffs. The Court's position is instead that, because of the Establishment Clause's historical purposes, taxpayers retain rights under it quite different from those held by them under other constitutional provisions.

The difficulties with this position are several. ...

Although I believe such actions to be within the jurisdiction conferred upon the federal courts by Article III of the Constitution, there surely can be little doubt that they strain the judicial function and press to the limit judicial authority. ...

Presumably the Court recognizes at least certain of these hazards, else it would not have troubled to impose limitations upon the situations in which, and purposes for which, such suits may be brought. Nonetheless, the limitations adopted by the Court are, as I have endeavored to indicate, wholly untenable. This is the more unfortunate because there is available a resolution of this problem that entirely satisfies the demands of the principle of separation of powers. This Court has previously held that individual litigants have standing to represent the public interest, despite their lack of economic or other personal interests, if Congress has appropriately authorized such suits. See especially *Oklahoma* v. *Civil Service Comm'n*, 330 U.S. 127, 137–139. Compare *Perkins* v. *Lukens Steel Co.*, 310 U.S. 113, 125–127. I would adhere to that principle. ...

Warth v. Seldin

422 U.S. 490 (1975)
Vote: 5–4

The question of standing, the right to adjudicate, is often linked to views of how much courts should set policy, as this case demonstrates.

A diverse group of ethnic minorities and home builders tried to challenge a prosperous suburb's allegedly discriminatory zoning policies. This had the earmarks of a "test case" challenging the pattern of American housing policy, which often involves class-stratified communities.

The lower courts held that the claims were too vague, impersonal, and generalized to give these plaintiffs standing. The Burger Court majority, with Justice Powell writing, agreed. Essentially, the Court served notice that they were moving back to stricter standards of justiciability and standing. Brennan's thoughtful dissent, in which Marshall and White joined, suggested that Powell confused proving a case with setting out a justification for standing. Douglas's dissent suggested, in true Warren Court tones, that technicalities should always give way to social justice.

MR. JUSTICE POWELL delivered the opinion of the Court.

Petitioners, various organizations and individuals resident in the Rochester, N.Y., metropolitan area, brought this action in the District Court for the Western District of New York against the town of Penfield, an incorporated municipality adjacent to Rochester, and against members of Penfield's Zoning, Planning and Town Boards. Petitioners claimed that the town's zoning ordinance, by its terms and as enforced by the defendant board members, respondents here, effectively excluded persons of low and moderate income from living in the town, in contravention of petitioners' First, Ninth, and Fourteenth Amendment rights and in violation of 42 U.S.C. §§1981, 1982, and 1983. The District Court dismissed the complaint. . . .

. . . .

Petitioners' complaint alleged that Penfield's zoning ordinance, adopted in 1962, has the purpose and effect of excluding persons of low and moderate income from residing in the town. In particular, the ordinance allocates 98% of the town's vacant land to single-family detached housing, and allegedly by imposing unreasonable requirements relating to lot size, setback, floor area, and habitable space, the ordinance increases the cost of single-family detached housing beyond the means of persons of low and moderate income. . . . Petitioners also alleged that "in furtherance of a policy of exclusionary zoning,". . . the defendant members of Penfield's Town, Zoning, and Planning Boards had acted in an arbitrary and discriminatory manner: they had delayed action on proposals for low- and moderate-cost housing for inordinate periods of time; denied such proposals for arbitrary and insubstantial reasons; refused to grant necessary variances and permits, or to al-

low tax abatements; failed to provide necessary support services for low- and moderate-cost housing projects; and had amended the ordinance to make approval of such projects virtually impossible.

. . .

Petitioners further alleged certain harm to themselves. The Rochester property owners and taxpayers — Vinkey, Reichert, Warth, Harris, and Ortiz — claimed that because of Penfield's exclusionary practices, the city of Rochester had been forced to impose higher tax rates on them and other similarly situated than would otherwise have been necessary. The low- and moderate-income, minority plaintiffs — Ortiz, Broadnax, Reyes, and Sinkler — claimed that Penfield's zoning practices had prevented them from acquiring, by lease or purchase, residential property in the town, and thus had forced them and their families to reside in less attractive environments. To relieve these various harms, petitioners asked the District Court to declare the Penfield ordinance unconstitutional, to enjoin the defendants from enforcing the ordinance, to order the defendants to enact and administer a new ordinance designed to alleviate the effects of their past actions, and to award $750,000 in actual and exemplary damages.

On May 2, 1972, petitioner Rochester Home Builders Association, an association of firms engaged in residential construction in the Rochester metropolitan area, moved the District Court for leave to intervene as a party-plaintiff. . . . An affidavit accompanying the motion stated that 17 of Housing Council's member groups were or hoped to be involved in the development of low- and moderate-cost housing, and that one of its members — the Penfield Better Homes Corp. — "is and has been actively attempting to develop moderate income housing" in Penfield, "but has been stymied by its inability to secure the necessary approvals. . . ."

Upon consideration of the complaints and of extensive supportive materials submitted by petitioners, the District Court held that the original plaintiffs, Home Builders, and Housing Council lacked standing to prosecute the action, that the original complaint failed to state a claim upon which relief could be granted, that the suit should not proceed as a class action, and that, in the exercise of discretion, Home Builders should not be permitted to intervene. . . . The Court of Appeals affirmed, reaching only the standing questions.

. . . .

In its constitutional dimension, standing imports justiciability: whether the plaintiff has made out a "case or controversy" between himself and the defendant within the meaning of Art. III. This is the threshold question in every federal case, determining the power of the court to entertain the suit. As an aspect of justiciability, the standing question is whether the plaintiff has "alleged such a personal stake in the outcome of the controversy" as to warrant *his* invocation of federal-court jurisdiction and to justify exercise of the court's remedial powers on his behalf. . . .

Apart from this minimum constitutional mandate, this Court has recognized other limits on the class of persons who may invoke the courts' decisional and remedial powers. First, the Court has held that when the asserted harm is a "generalized grievance" shared in substantially equal measure by all or a large class of citizens, that harm alone normally does not warrant exercise of jurisdiction. . . . Second, even when the plaintiff has alleged injury sufficient to meet the "case or controversy" requirement, this Court has held that the plaintiff generally must assert his own legal rights and interests, and cannot rest his claim to relief on the legal rights or interests of third parties. . . . Without such limitations — closely related to Art. III concerns but essentially matters of judicial self-governance — the courts would be called upon to decide abstract questions of wide public significance though other governmental institutions may be more competent to address the questions, and even though judicial intervention may be unnecessary to protect individual rights. . . .

. . . We turn first to the claims of petitioners Ortiz, Reyes, Sinkler, and Broadnax, each of whom asserts standing as a person of low or moderate income and, coincidentally, as a member of a minority racial or ethnic group. . . .

But the fact that these petitioners share attributes common to persons who may have been excluded from residence in the town is an insufficient predicate for the conclusion that petitioners themselves have been excluded, or that the respondents' assertedly illegal actions have violated their rights. Petitioners must allege and show that they personally have been injured, not that injury has been suffered by other, unidentified members of the class to which they belong and which they purport to represent. . . .

In their complaint, petitioners Ortiz, Reyes, Sinkler, and Broadnax alleged in conclusory terms that they are among the persons excluded by respondents' actions. None of them has ever resided in Penfield; each claims at least implicitly that he desires, or has desired to do so. Each asserts, moreover, that he made some effort, at some time, to locate housing in Penfield that was at once within his means and adequate for his family's needs. Each claims that his efforts proved fruitless. We may assume, as petitioners allege, that respondents' actions have con-

tributed, perhaps substantially, to the cost of housing in Penfield. But there remains the question whether petitioners' inability to locate suitable housing in Penfield reasonably can be said to have resulted, in any concretely demonstrable way, from respondents' alleged constitutional and statutory infractions. Petitioners must allege facts from which it reasonably could be inferred that, absent the respondents' restrictive zoning practices, there is a substantial probability that they would have been able to purchase or lease in Penfield and that, if the court affords the relief requested, the asserted inability of petitioners will be removed. . . .

We find the record devoid of the necessary allegations. . . . The fact that the harm to petitioners may have resulted indirectly does not in itself preclude standing. . . . But it may make it substantially more difficult to meet the minimum requirement of Art. III: to establish that, in fact, the asserted injury was the consequence of the defendants' actions, or that prospective relief will remove the harm.

Here, by their own admission, realization of petitioners' desire to live in Penfield always has depended on the efforts and willingness of third parties to build low- and moderate-cost housing. The record specifically refers to only two such efforts: that of Penfield Better Homes Corp., in late 1969, to obtain the rezoning of certain land in Penfield to allow the construction of subsidized cooperative townhouses that could be purchased by persons of moderate income; and a similar effort by O'Brien Homes, Inc., in late 1971. But the record is devoid of any indication that these projects, or other like projects, would have satisfied petitioner's needs at prices they could afford, or that, were the court to remove the obstructions attributable to respondents, such relief would benefit petitioners. Indeed, petitioners' descriptions of their individual financial situations and housing needs suggest precisely the contrary — that their inability to reside in Penfield is the consequence of the economics of the area housing market, rather than of respondents' assertedly illegal acts. . . .

. . . .

The petitioners who assert standing on the basis of their status as taxpayers of the city of Rochester present a different set of problems. These "taxpayer-petitioners" claim that they are suffering economic injury consequent to Penfield's allegedly discriminatory and exclusionary zoning practices. Their argument, in brief, is that Penfield's persistent refusal to allow or to facilitate construction of low- and moderate-cost housing forces the city of Rochester to provide more such housing than it otherwise would do; that to provide such housing, Rochester must allow certain tax abatements; and that as the amount of tax-abated property increases, Rochester taxpayers are forced to assume an increased tax burden in order to finance essential public services.

"Of course, pleadings must be something more than an ingenious academic exercise in the conceivable." United States v. SCRAP.... We think the complaint of the taxpayer-petitioners is little more than such an exercise. Apart from the conjectural nature of the asserted injury, the line of causation between Penfield's actions and such injury is not apparent from the complaint. Whatever may occur in Penfield, the injury complained of — increases in taxation — results only from decisions made by the appropriate Rochester authorities, who are not parties to this case.

But even if we assume that the taxpayer-petitioners could establish that Penfield's zoning practices harm them, their complaint nonetheless was properly dismissed. Petitioners do not, even if they could, assert any personal right under the Constitution or any statute to be free of action by a neighboring municipality that may have some incidental adverse effect on Rochester. On the contrary, the only basis of the taxpayer-petitioners' claim is that Penfield's zoning ordinance and practices violate the constitutional and statutory rights of third parties, namely, persons of low and moderate income who are said to be excluded from Penfield. In short the claim of these petitioners falls squarely within the prudential standing rule that normally bars litigants from asserting the rights or legal interests of others in order to obtain relief from injury to themselves....

. . . .

We turn next to the standing problems presented by the petitioner associations — Metro-Act of Rochester, Inc., one of the original plaintiffs; Housing Council in the Monroe County Area, Inc., which the original plaintiffs sought to join as a party-plaintiff; and Rochester Home Builders Association, Inc., which moved in the District Court for leave to intervene as plaintiff. There is no question that an association may have standing in its own right to seek judicial relief from injury to itself and to vindicate whatever rights and immunities the association itself may enjoy. Moreover, in attempting to secure relief from injury to itself the association may assert the rights of its members, at least so long as the challenged infractions adversely affect its members' associational ties....

. . . .

Petitioner Metro-Act's claims to standing on its own behalf as a Rochester taxpayer, and on behalf of its members who are Rochester taxpayers or per-

sons of low or moderate income, are precluded by our holdings in Parts III and IV. Metro-Act also alleges, however, that 9% of its membership is composed of present residents of Penfield... deprived of the benefits of living in a racially and ethnically integrated community....

. . . .

... We do not understand Metro-Act to argue that Penfield residents themselves have been denied any constitutional rights, affording them a cause of action under 42 U.S.C. §1983. Instead, their complaint is that they have been harmed indirectly by the exclusion of others. This is an attempt to raise putative rights of third parties, and none of the exceptions that allow such claims is present here....

. . . .

Home Builders' prayer for prospective relief fails for a different reason. It can have standing as the representative of its members only if it has alleged facts sufficient to make out a case or controversy had the members themselves brought suit. No such allegations were made. The complaint refers to no specific project of any of its members that is currently precluded either by the ordinance or by respondents' action in enforcing it. There is no averment that any member has applied to respondents for a building permit or a variance with respect to any current project. Indeed, there is no indication that respondents have delayed or thwarted any project currently proposed by Home Builders' members, or that any of its members has taken advantage of the remedial processes available under the ordinance. In short, insofar as the complaint seeks prospective relief, Home Builders has failed to show the existence of any injury to its members of sufficient immediacy and ripeness to warrant judicial intervention.

A like problem is presented with respect to petitioner Housing Council. The affidavit accompanying the motion to join it as plaintiff states that the Council includes in its membership "at least seventeen" groups that have been, are, or will be involved in the development of low- and moderate-cost housing. But, with one exception, the complaint does not suggest that any of these groups has focused its efforts on Penfield or has any specific plan to do so. Again with the same exception, neither the complaint nor any materials of record indicate that any member of Housing Council has taken any step toward building housing in Penfield, or has had dealings of any nature with respondents. The exception is the Penfield Better Homes Corp. As we have observed above, it applied to respondents in late 1969 for a zoning variance to allow construction of a housing project designed for persons of moderate income. The affidavit in support of the motion to join Housing Council refers specifically to this effort, the supporting materials detail at some length the circumstances surrounding the rejection of Better Homes' application. It is therefore possible that in 1969, or within a reasonable time thereafter, Better Homes itself and possibly Housing Council as its representative would have had standing to seek review to respondents' action. The complaint, however, does not allege that the Penfield Better Homes project remained viable in 1972 when this complaint was filed, or that respondents' actions continued to block a then-current construction project....

The rules of standing, whether as aspects of the Art. III case-or-controversy requirement or as reflections or prudential considerations defining and limiting the role of the courts, are threshold determinants of the propriety of judicial intervention.... We agree with the District Court and the Court of Appeals that none of the petitioners here has met this threshold requirement. Accordingly, the judgment of the Court of Appeals is

Affirmed.

MR. JUSTICE DOUGLAS, dissenting.

....

[C]ases such as this one reflect festering sores in our society; and the American dream teaches that if one reaches high enough and persists there is a forum where justice is dispensed. I would lower the technical barriers and let the courts serve that ancient need. They can in time be curbed by legislative or constitutional restraints if an emergency arises.

MR. JUSTICE BRENNAN, with whom MR. JUSTICE WHITE and MR. JUSTICE MARSHALL join, dissenting.

....

... [T]he portrait which emerges from the allegations and affidavits is one of total, purposeful, intransigent exclusion of certain classes of people from the town, pursuant to a conscious scheme never deviated from. Because of this scheme, those interested in building homes for the excluded groups were faced with insurmountable difficulties, and those of the excluded groups seeking homes in the locality quickly learned that their attempts were futile. Yet, the Court turns the very success of the allegedly unconstitutional scheme into a barrier to a lawsuit seeking its invalidation. In effect, the Court tells the low-income minority and building company plaintiffs they will not be permitted to prove what they have alleged — that they could and would build and live in the town if changes were made in the zoning ordinance and its application — because they have not succeeded in breaching, before the suit was filed, the very barriers which are the subject of the suit.

... The Court does not, as it could not, suggest that the injuries, if proved, would be insufficient to give petitioners the requisite "personal state in the outcome of the controversy as to assure the concrete adverseness which sharpens the presentation of issues...." Rather, it is abundantly clear that the harm *alleged* satisfies the "injury in fact, economic or otherwise,"... requirement which is prerequisite to standing in federal court. The harms claimed — consisting of out-of-pocket losses as well as denial of specifically enumerated services available in Penfield but not in these petitioners' present communities, see nn. 3 and 4, *supra* — are obviously *more* palpable and concrete than those held sufficient to sustain standing in other cases....

Instead, the Court insists that these petitioners' allegations are insufficient to show that the harms suffered were *caused* by respondents' allegedly unconstitutional practices, because "their inability to reside in Penfield [may be] the consequence of the economics of the area housing market, rather than of respondents' assertedly illegal acts."

....

Thus, the Court's real holding is not that these petitioners have not *alleged* an injury resulting from respondents' action, but that they are not to be allowed to prove one, because "realization of petitioners' desire to live in Penfield always has depended on the efforts and willingness of third parties to build low- and moderate-cost housing...."

... Obviously, they cannot be expected, prior to discovery and trial, to know the future plans of building companies, the precise details of the housing market in Penfield, or everything which has transpired in 15 years of application of the Penfield zoning ordinance, including every housing plan suggested and refused. To require them to allege such facts is to require them to prove their case on paper in order to get into court at all....

Luther v. Borden

7 Howard 1 (1849)
Vote: 5–1

In 1841–42, Rhode Island was wracked by a civil war known as Dorr's Rebellion, after the man chosen as "governor" by the rebel government. Luther, a supporter of Dorr, was arrested by Borden, a member of the state militia. Luther sued Borden for trespass, and, when a jury found for Borden, appealed on writ of error. In effect, he was asking that the established government be declared unlawful, which would mean that Borden was not a government agent when he came to Luther's house. (In the course of events, President Tyler, responding to an appeal from the governor of the established government, promised to provide military help if needed.)

MR. CHIEF JUSTICE TANEY delivered the opinion of the court.

This case has arisen out of the unfortunate political differences which agitated the people of Rhode Island in 1841 and 1842.

It is an action of trespass brought by Martin Luther, the plaintiff in error, against Luther M. Borden and others, the defendants, in the Circuit Court of the United States for the District of Rhode Island, for breaking and entering the plaintiff's house. The defendants justify upon the ground that large numbers of men were assembled in different parts of the State for the purpose of overthrowing the government by military force, and were actually levying war upon the State; that, in order to defend itself from this insurrection, the State was declared by competent authority to be under martial law; that the plaintiff was engaged in the insurrection; and that the defendants, being in the military service of the State, by command of their superior officer broke and entered the house and searched the rooms for the plaintiff, who was supposed to be there concealed, in order to arrest him, doing as little damage as possible. The plaintiff replied, that the trespass was committed by the defendants of their own proper wrong. .

The existence and authority of the government under which the defendants acted was called in question; and the plaintiff insists, that, before the acts complained of were committed, that government had been displaced and annulled by the people of Rhode Island, and that the plaintiff was engaged in supporting the lawful authority of the State, and the defendants themselves were in arms against it.

This is a new question in this court, and certainly a very grave one; and at the time when the trespass is alleged to have been committed it had produced a general and painful excitement in the State, and threatened to end in bloodshed and civil war.

The evidence shows that the defendants, in breaking into the plaintiff's house and endeavouring to arrest him, as stated in the pleadings, acted under the authority of the government which was established in Rhode Island at the time of the Declaration of Independence, and which is usually called the charter government. For when the separation from England took place, Rhode Island did not, like the other States, adopt a new constitution, but continued the form of government established by the charter of Charles the Second in 1663; making only such alterations, by acts of the legislature, as were necessary to adapt it to their condition and rights as an independent State. It was under this form of government that Rhode Island united with the other States. . . .

Thomas W. Dorr, who had been elected governor under the new constitution, prepared to assert the authority of that government by force, and many citizens assembled in arms to support him. The charter government thereupon passed an act declaring the State under marital law, and at the same time proceeded to call out the militia, to repel the threatened attack and to subdue those who were engaged in it. In this state of the contest, the house of the plaintiff, who was engaged in supporting the authority of the new government, was broken and entered in order to arrest him. The defendants were, at the time, in the military service of the old government, and in arms to support its authority.

It appears, also, that the charter government at its session of January, 1842, took measures to call a convention to revise the existing form of government; and after various proceedings, which it is not material to state, a new constitution was formed by a convention elected under the authority of the charter government, and afterwards adopted and ratified by the people; the times and places at which the votes were to be given, the persons who were to receive and return them, and the qualification of the voters, having all been previously authorized and provided for by law passed by the charter government. This new government went into operation in May, 1843, at which time the old government formally surrendered all its powers; and this constitution has continued ever since to be the admitted and established government of Rhode Island.

We do not understand from the argument that the constitution under which the plaintiff acted is supposed to have been in force after the constitution of May, 1843, went into operation. The content is confined to the year preceding. The plaintiff contends that the charter government was displaced, and ceased to have any lawful power, after the organization, in May, 1842, of the government which he supported, and although that government never was able to exercise any authority in the State, nor to command obedience to its laws or to its officers, yet he insists that it was the lawful and established government, upon the ground that it was ratified by a large majority of the male people of the State of the age of twenty-one and upwards, and also by a majority of those who were entitled to vote for general officers under the then existing laws of the State. The fact that it was so ratified was not admitted; and at the trial in the Circuit Court he offered to prove it by the production of the original ballots, and the original registers of the persons voting, verified by the oaths of the several moderators and clerks of the meetings, and by the testimony of all the persons so voting, and by the said constitution; and also offered in evidence, for the same purpose, that part of the census of the United States for the year 1840 which applies to Rhode Island; and a certificate of the secretary of state of the charter government, showing the number of votes polled by the freemen of the State for the ten years then last past.

The Circuit Court rejected this evidence, and instructed the jury that the charter government and laws under which the defendants acted were, at the time the trespass is alleged to have been committed, in full force and effect as the form of government and paramount law of the State, and constituted a justification of the acts of the defendants as set forth in their pleas. For, if this court is authorized to enter upon this inquiry as proposed by the plaintiff, and it should be decided that the charter government had no legal existence during the period of time above mentioned, — if it had been annulled by the adoption of the opposing government — then the laws passed by its legislature during that time were nullities; its taxes wrongfully collected; its salaries and compensation to its officers illegally paid; its public accounts improperly settled; and the judgments and sentences of its courts in civil and criminal cases null and void, and the officers who carried their decisions into operation answerable as trespassers, if not in some cases as criminals. . . .

. . . [t]he courts uniformly held that the inquiry proposed to be made belonged to the political power and not to the judicial; that it rested with the political power to decide whether the charter government had been displaced or not; and when that decision was made, the judicial department would be bound to take notice of it as the paramount law of the State, without the aid of oral evidence or the examination of witnesses. . . .

Judicial power presupposes an established government capable of enacting laws and enforcing their execution, and of appointing judges to expound and administer them. The acceptance of the judicial office is a recognition of the authority of the government from which it is derived. And if the authority of that government is annulled and overthrown, the power of its courts and other officers is annulled with it. . . .

Upon what ground could the Circuit Court of the United States which tried this case have departed from this rule, and disregarded and overruled the decisions of the courts of Rhode Island? Undoubtedly the courts of the United States have certain powers under the Constitution and laws of the United States which do not belong to the State courts. But the power of determining that a State government has been lawfully established, which the courts of the State disown and repudiate, is not one of them. Upon such a question the courts of the United States are bound to follow the decisions of the State tribunals, and must therefore regard the charter government as the lawful and established government during the time of this contest.

Besides, if the Circuit Court had entered upon this inquiry, by what rule could it have determined the qualification of voters upon the adoption or rejection of the proposed constitution, unless there was some previous law of the State to guide it? It is the province of a court to expound the law, not to make it.

The court had not the power to order a census of the freeholders to be taken; nor would the census of the United States of 1840 be any evidence of the number of freeholders in the State in 1842. Nor could the court appoint persons to examine and determine whether every person who had voted possessed the freehold qualification which the law then required. In the nature of things, the Circuit Court could not know the name and residence of every citizen, and bring him before the court to be examined. And if this were attempted, where would such an inquiry have terminated? And how long must the people of Rhode Island have waited to learn from this court under what form of government they were living during the year in controversy?

The fourth section of the fourth article of the Constitution of the United States provides that the United States shall guarantee to every State in the Union a republican form of government, and shall protect each of them against invasion; and on the application of the legislature or of the executive (when the legislature cannot be convened) against domestic violence.

The power given to the President in each case is the same, — with this difference only, that it cannot be exercised by him in the latter case, except upon the application of the legislature or executive of the State. The case above mentioned arose out of a call made by the President, by virtue of the power conferred by the first clause; and the court said, that, "whenever a statute gives a discretionary power to any person to be exercised by him upon his own opinion of certain facts, it is a sound rule of construction that the statute constitutes him the sole and exclusive judge of the existence of those facts." The grounds upon which that opinion is maintained are set forth in the report, and we think are conclusive. The same principle applies to the case now before the court. Undoubtedly, if the President in exercising this power shall fall into error, or invade the rights of the people of the State, it would be in the power of Congress to apply the proper remedy. But the courts must administer the law as they find it.

Much of the argument on the part of the plaintiff turned upon political rights and political questions, upon which the court has been urged to express an opinion. We decline doing so. . . . This tribunal, therefore, should be the last to overstep the boundaries which limit its own jurisdiction. And while it should always be ready to meet any question confided to it by the Constitution, it is equally its duty not to pass beyond its appropriate sphere of action, and to take care not to involve itself in discussions which properly belong to other forums. No one, we believe, has ever doubted the proposition, that, according to the institutions of this country, the sovereignty in every State resides in the people of the State, and that they may alter and change their form of government at their own pleasure. But whether they have changed it or not by abolishing an old government, and establishing a new one in its place, is a question to be settled by the political power. And when that power has decided, the courts are bound to take notice of its decision, and to follow it.

The judgment of the Circuit Court must therefore be affirmed.

Coleman v. Miller

307 U.S. 433 (1939)
Vote: 8–1

Coleman v. *Miller* is a classic "political questions" decision that, unlike many others, may be good law today. It involves the process of constitutional amendment, which, after all, is particularly inappropriate for judicial review. The very purpose of an amendment is to change the Constitution, and the court has come close to suggesting there is no such thing as an unconstitutional amendment. (Some theorists have suggested that the provision that a state must agree to lose equal voting power in the Senate cannot be changed by simple amendment, but most argue that repealing the equal vote provision and then changing the Senate, a two-step process, would meet even that objection.) The Constitution explicitly involves the Congress in the amendment process and gives it considerable discretion in methods of handling amendments. The lack of standards also would result in judicial exercise of unfettered judgment most appropriate to the "political" arms of the government.

Coleman contrasts with *Hawke* v. *Smith* (1920), where the Court invalidated an Ohio constitutional requirement that ratification of U.S. amendments would have to be by popular referendum. The Court noted that ratification is a national function. Using language similar to *Coleman*'s assertion of congressional authority, it observed that Congress had specified legislative, not popular, approval. But it also called attention to the fact that the Constitution provides for only two methods of ratification — by the state legislatures or by state conventions. Strickly speaking, a political questions approach would mean no scrutiny of congressional action at all, but the specificity of that provision might be a basis for partial review by the courts.

The issues raised and left unsettled by *Coleman* have surfaced in the struggle over the Equal Rights Amendment. The extension of the period for ratification was acted upon by Congress on the theory of sweeping powers and made more acceptable by the accident that the expiration date was included in a covering resolution instead of being in the text of the amendment, as had been the fashion. The issue of rescinding approval or agreeing after rejection has also been raised and suits threatened. If *Coleman* is still good law, what would be the decision?

Opinion of the Court by MR. CHIEF JUSTICE HUGHES, announced by MR. JUSTICE STONE.

In June, 1924, the Congress proposed an amendment to the Constitution, known as the Child Labor Amendment. In January, 1925, the Legislature of Kansas adopted a resolution rejecting the proposed amendment and a certified copy of the resolution was sent to the Secretary of State of the United States. In January, 1937, a resolution known as "Senate Concurrent Resolution No. 3" was introduced in the Senate of Kansas ratifying the proposed amendment. There were forty senators. When the resolution came up for consideration, twenty senators voted in favor of its adoption and twenty voted against it. The Lieutenant Governor, the presiding officer of the Senate, then cast his vote in favor of the resolution. The resolution was later adopted by the House of Representatives on the vote of a majority of its members.

This original proceeding in mandamus was then brought in the Supreme Court of Kansas by twenty-one members of the Senate, including the twenty senators who had voted against the resolution, and three members of the House of Representatives, to compel the Secretary of State to erase an endorsement on the resolution to the effect that it had been adopted by the Senate and to endorse thereon the words "was not passed," and to restrain the officers of the Senate and House of Representatives from signing the resolution and the Secretary of State of Kansas from authenticating it and delivering it to the Governor. The petition challenged the right of the Lieutenant Governor to cast the deciding vote in the Senate. The petition also set forth the prior rejection of the proposed amendment and alleged that in the period from June, 1924, to March, 1927, the amendment had been rejected by both houses of the legislatures of twenty-six States, and had been ratified in only five States, and that by reason of that rejection and the failure of ratification within a reasonable time the proposed amendment had lost its vitality.

. . . .

The [state] Supreme Court found no dispute as to the facts. The court entertained the action and held that the Lieutenant Governor was authorized to cast the deciding vote, that the proposed amendment retained its original vitality, and that the resolution "having duly passed the house of representatives and the senate, the act of ratification of the proposed amendment by the legislature of Kansas was final and complete. . . ."

. . . [T]he questions raised in the instant case arose under the Federal Constitution and these questions were entertained and decided by the state court. They arose under Article V of the Constitution which alone conferred the power to amend and determined the manner in which that power could be exercised. *Hawke* v. *Smith (No. 1)*, 253 U.S. 221, 227; *Leser* v. *Garnett*, 258 U.S. 130, 137. Whether any or all of the questions thus raised and decided are deemed to be justiciable or political, they are exclusively federal questions and not state questions.

. . . We think that these senators have a plain, direct and adequate interest in maintaining the effectiveness of their votes. Petitioners come directly within the provisions of the statute governing our appellate jurisdiction. They have set up and claimed a right and privilege under the Constitution of the United States to have their votes given effect and the state court has denied that right and privilege. . . .

Second. The participation of the Lieutenant Governor. — Petitioners contend that, in the light of the powers and duties of the Lieutenant Governor and his relation to the Senate under the state constitution, as construed by the supreme court of the state, the Lieutenant Governor was not a part of the "legislature" so that under Article V of the Federal Constitution, he could be permitted to have a deciding vote on the ratification of the proposed amendment, when the senate was equally divided.

Whether this contention presents a justiciable controversy, or a question which is political in its nature and hence not justiciable, is a question upon which the Court is equally divided and therefore the Court expresses no opinion upon that point.

Third. The effect of the previous rejection of the amendment and of the lapse of time since its submission.

1. The state court adopted the view expressed by text-writers that a state legislature which has rejected an amendment proposed by the Congress may later ratify. The argument in support of that view is that Article V says nothing of rejection but speaks only of ratification and provides that a proposed amendment shall be valid as part of the Constitution when ratified by three-fourths of the States; that the power to ratify is thus conferred upon the State by the Constitution and, as a ratifying power, persists despite a previous rejection. The opposing view proceeds on an assumption that if ratification by "Conventions" were prescribed by the Congress, a convention could not reject and, having adjourned

sine die, be reassembled and ratify. It is also premised, in accordance with views expressed by textwriters, that ratification if once given cannot afterwards be rescinded and the amendment rejected, and it is urged that the same effect in the exhaustion of the State's power to act should be ascribed to rejection; that a State can act "but once, either by convention or through its legislature."

... The question did arise in connection with the adoption of the Fourteenth Amendment. . . .

Thus the political departments of the Government dealt with the effect both of previous rejection and of attempted withdrawal and determined that both were ineffectual in the presence of an actual ratification. . . .

We think that in accordance with this historic precedent the question of the efficacy of ratifications by state legislatures, in the light of previous rejection or attempted withdrawal, should be regarded as a political question pertaining to the political departments, with the ultimate authority in the Congress in the exercise of its control over the promulgation of the adoption of the amendment.

The precise question as now raised is whether, when the legislature of the State, as we have found, has actually ratified the proposed amendment, the Court should restrain the state officers from certifying the ratification to the Secretary of State, because of an earlier rejection, and thus prevent the question from coming before the political departments. We find no basis in either Constitution or statute for such judicial action. Article V, speaking solely of ratification, contains no provision as to rejection. . . .

2. The more serious question is whether the proposal by the Congress of the amendment had lost its vitality through lapse of time and hence it could not be ratified by the Kansas legislature in 1937. . . .

We have held that the Congress in proposing an amendment may fix a reasonable time for ratification. . . . But petitioners contend that, in the absence of a limitation by the Congress, the Court can and should decide what is a reasonable period within which ratification may be had. We are unable to agree with that contention.

Where are to be found the criteria for such a judicial determination? None are to be found in Constitution or statute. . . . [T]he question of a reasonable time in many cases would involve, as in this case it does involve, an appraisal of a great variety of relevant conditions, political, social and economic, which can hardly be said to be within the appropriate range of evidence receivable in a court of justice and as to which it would be extravagant extension of judicial authority to assert judicial notice as the basis of de-

ciding a controversy with respect to the validity of an amendment actually ratified. On the other hand, these conditions are appropriate for the consideration of the political departments of the Government. The questions they involve are essentially political and not justiciable. They can be decided by the Congress with the full knowledge and appreciation ascribed to the national legislature of the political, social and economic conditions which have prevailed during the period since the submission of the amendment.

... If it be deemed that such a question is an open one when the limit has not been fixed in advance, we think that it should also be regarded as an open one for the consideration of the Congress when, in the presence of certified ratifications by three-fourths of the States, the time arrives for the promulgation of the adoption of the amendment. The decision by the Congress, in its control of the action of the Secretary of State, of the question whether the amendment had been adopted within a reasonable time would not be subject to review by the courts.

It would unduly lengthen this opinion to attempt to review our decisions as to the class of questions deemed to be political and not justiciable. In determining whether a question falls within that category, the appropriateness under our system of government of attributing finality to the action of the political departments and also the lack of satisfactory criteria for a judicial determination are dominant considerations. . . .

... [W]e think that the Congress in controlling the promulgation of the adoption of a constitutional amendment has the final determination of the question whether by lapse of time its proposal of the amendment had lost its vitality prior to the required ratifications. . . .

As we find no reason for disturbing the decision of the Supreme Court of Kansas in denying the mandamus sought by petitioners, its judgment is affirmed but upon the grounds stated in this opinion.

Affirmed.

Concurring opinion by MR. JUSTICE BLACK, in which MR. JUSTICE ROBERTS, MR. JUSTICE FRANKFURTER and MR. JUSTICE DOUGLAS join.

... To the extent that the Court's opinion in the present case even impliedly assumes a power to make judicial interpretation of the exclusive consitutional authority of Congress over submission and ratification of amendments, we are unable to agree.

... There is no disapproval of the conclusion arrived at in *Dillon* v. *Gloss,* that the Constitution impliedly requires that a properly submitted amendment must die unless ratified within a "reasonable time." Nor does the Court now disapprove its prior assumption of power to make such a pronouncement.... On the other hand, the Court's opinion declares that Congress has the exclusive power to decide the "political questions" of whether a State whose legislature has once acted upon a proposed amendment may subsequently reverse its position, and whether, in the circumstances of such a case as this, an amendment is dead because an "unreasonable" time has elapsed. No such division between the political and judicial branches of the government is made by Article V which grants power over the amending of the Constitution to Congress alone. Undivided control of that process has been given by the Article exclusively and completely to Congress. The process itself is "political" in its entirety, from submission until an amendment becomes part of the Constitution, and is not subject to judicial guidance, control or interference at any point....

Opinion of MR. JUSTICE FRANKFURTER.

It is the view of MR. JUSTICE ROBERTS, MR. JUSTICE BLACK, MR. JUSTICE DOUGLAS and myself that the petitioners have no standing in this Court.

In endowing this Court with "judicial Power" the Constitution presupposed an historic content for that phrase and relied on assumption by the judiciary of authority only over issues which are appropriate for disposition by judges. The Constitution further explicitly indicated the limited area within which judicial action was to move—however far-reaching the consequences of action within that area—by extending "judicial Power" only to "Cases" and "Controversies."...

In the familiar language of jurisdiction, these Kansas legislators must have standing in this Court. What is their distinctive claim to be here, not possessed by every Kansan?...

...[T]he claim that the Amendment was dead or that it was no longer open to Kansas to ratify, is not only not an interest which belongs uniquely to these Kansas legislators; it is not even an interest special to Kansas....

We can only adjudicate an issue as to which there is a claimant before us who has a special, individualized stake in it. One who is merely the self-constituted spokesman of a constitutional point of view can not ask us to pass on it....

...In seeking redress here these Kansas senators have wholly misconceived the functions of the Court....

MR. JUSTICE BUTLER, dissenting.

Baker v. Carr

369 U.S. 186 (1962)
Vote: 7–2

From 1901 to 1962, Tennessee did not change its allocation of seats in the legislature. Grave distortions occurred, and the situation was repeated in most states. Representatives of areas that had lost population were not eager to give up political power.

As Justice Brennan's opinion indicates, the courts had refused to intervene in such matters, but on vague and shaky grounds, Justice Frankfurter's dissent notwithstanding. Now a majority ruled unequivocally that there was no political questions doctrine barrier. Does the case imply that political questions are only at issue when cognate branches—Congress or the President— are involved?

The opinion holds that there was a dilution of the voting rights of citizens under the Equal Protection Clause of the Fourteenth Amendment. Later decisions made the basic rule "one man— one vote." Is that rule implied by the Fourteenth Amendment or by this decision? Could another plausible doctrine have been developed—for example, Justice Clark's "crazy quilt" argument? The courts allow reasonable latitude in the population arrangement. Is that a dilution? Is the U.S. Senate rendered unconstitutional?

MR. JUSTICE BRENNAN delivered the opinion of the Court.

...The complaint, alleging that by means of a 1901 statute of Tennessee apportioning the members of the General Assembly among the State's 95 counties, "these plaintiffs and others similarly situated, are denied the equal protection of the laws accorded them by the Fourteenth Amendment to the Constitution of the United States by virtue of the debasement of their votes...."

...In the more than 60 years since that action, all proposals in both Houses and the General Assembly for reapportionment have failed to pass.

Between 1901 and 1961, Tennessee has experienced substantial growth and redistribution of her population. In 1901 the population was 2,020,616, of whom 487,380 were eligible to vote. The 1960 Federal Census reports the State's population at 3,567,089, of whom 2,092,891 are eligible to vote. The relative standings of the counties in terms of qualified voters have changed significantly. It is primarily the continued application of the 1901 Apportionment Act to this shifted and enlarged voting population which gives rise to the present controversy.

. . . .

The District Court was uncertain whether our cases withholding federal judicial relief rested upon a lack of federal jurisdiction or upon the inappropriateness of the subject matter for judicial consideration — what we have designated "nonjusticiability." This distinction between the two grounds is significant. In the instance of nonjusticiability, consideration of the cause is not wholly and immediately foreclosed; rather, the Court's inquiry necessarily proceeds to the point of deciding whether the duty asserted can be judicially identified and its breach judicially determined, and whether protection for the right asserted can be judicially molded. In the instance of lack of jurisdiction the cause either does not "arise under" the Federal Constitution, laws or treaties (or fall within one of the other enumerated categories of Art. III, §2), or is not a "case or controversy" within the meaning of that section; or the cause is not one described by any jurisdictional statute. Our conclusion, see pp. 208–237, *infra*, that this cause presents no nonjusticiable "political question" settles the only possible doubt that it is a case or controversy. Under the present heading of "Jurisdiction of the Subject Matter" we hold only that the matter set forth in the complaint does arise under the Constitution and is within 28 U.S.C. §1343.

. . . . It is clear that the cause of action is one which "arises under" the Federal Constitution. The complaint alleges that the 1901 statute effects an apportionment that deprives the appellants of the equal protection of the laws in violation of the Fourteenth Amendment. Dismissal of the complaint upon the ground of lack of jurisdiction of the subject matter would, therefore, be justified only if that claim were "so attenuated and unsubstantial as to be absolutely devoid of merit," *Newburyport Water Co.* v. *Newburyport*, 193 U.S. 561, 579, or "frivolous," *Bell* v. *Hood*, 327 U.S. 678, 683. That the claim is unsubstantial must be "very plain." *Hart* v. *Keith Vaudeville Exchange*, 262 U.S. 271, 274. Since the District Court obviously and correctly did not deem the asserted federal constitutional claim unsubstantial and frivolous, it should not have dismissed the complaint for want of jurisdiction of the subject matter. And of course no further consideration of the merits of the claim is relevant to a determination of the court's jurisdiction of the subject matter. . . .

An unbroken line of our precedents sustains the federal court's jurisdiction of the subject matter of federal constitutional claims of this nature. . . .

The appellees refer to *Colegrove* v. *Green*, 328 U.S. 549, as authority that the District Court lacked jurisdiction of the subject matter. Appellees misconceive the holding of that case. The holding was precisely contrary to their reading of it. Seven members of the Court participated in the decision. Unlike many other cases in this field which have assumed without discussion that there was jurisdiction, all three opinions filed in *Colegrove* discussed the question. Two of the opinions expressing the views of four of the Justices, a majority, flatly held that there was jurisdiction of the subject matter. MR. JUSTICE BLACK joined by MR. JUSTICE DOUGLAS and Mr. Justice Murphy stated: "It is my judgment that the District Court had jurisdiction . . . ," citing the predecessor of 28 U.S.C. §1343(3), and *Bell* v. *Hood, supra.* 328 U.S., at 568. Mr. Justice Rutledge, writing separately, expressed agreement with this conclusion. 328 U.S., at 564, 565, n. 2. Indeed, it is even questionable that the opinion of MR. JUSTICE FRANKFURTER, joined by Justices Reed and Burton, doubted jurisdiction of the subject matter. Such doubt would have been inconsistent with the professed willingness to turn the decision on either the majority or concurring views in *Wood* v. *Broom, supra.* 328 U.S., at 551.

. . . .

A federal court cannot "pronounce any statute, either of a State or of the United States, void, because irreconcilable with the Constitution, except as it is called upon to adjudge the legal rights of litigants in actual controversies." *Liverpool Steamship Co.* v. *Commissioners of Emigration*, 113 U.S. 33, 39. Have the appellants alleged such a personal stake in the outcome of the controversy as to assure that concrete adverseness which sharpens the presentation of issues upon which the court so largely depends for illumination of difficult constitutional questions? This is the gist of the question of standing. It is, of course, a question of federal law.

The complaint was filed by residents of Davidson, Hamilton, Knox, Montgomery, and Shelby Counties. Each is a person allegedly qualified to vote for members of the General Assembly representing his county. These appellants sued "on their own behalf and on behalf of all qualified voters of their respective counties, and further, on behalf of all voters of the State of Tennessee who are similarly situated. . . ."

We hold that the appellants do have standing to maintain this suit. Our decisions plainly support this conclusion. Many of the cases have assumed rather than articulated the premise in deciding the merits of similar claims. And *Colegrove v. Green, supra,* squarely held that voters who allege facts showing disadvantage to themselves as individuals have standing to sue. A number of cases decided after *Colegrove* recognized the standing of the voters there involved to bring those actions.

These appellants seek relief in order to protect or vindicate an interest of their own, and of those similarly situated. Their constitutional claim is, in substance, that the 1901 statute constitutes arbitrary and capricious state action, offensive to the Fourteenth Amendment in its irrational disregard of the standard of apportionment prescribed by the State's Constitution or of any standard, effecting a gross disproportion of representation to voting population. The injury which appellants assert is that this classification disfavors the voters in the counties in which they reside, placing them in a position of constitutionally unjustifiable inequality *vis-à-vis* voters in irrationally favored counties. A citizen's right to a vote free of arbitrary impairment by state action has been judicially recognized as a right secured by the Constitution, when such impairment resulted from dilution by a false tally, cf. *United States v. Classic,* 313 U.S. 299; or by a refusal to count votes from arbitrarily selected precincts, cf. *United States v. Mosley,* 238 U.S. 383, or by a stuffing of the ballot box, cf. *Ex parte Siebold,* 100 U.S. 371; *United States v. Saylor,* 322 U.S. 385.

It would not be necessary to decide whether appellants' allegations of impairment of their votes by the 1901 apportionment will, ultimately, entitle them to any relief, in order to hold that they have standing to seek it. If such impairment does produce a legally cognizable injury they are among those who have sustained it. They are asserting "a plain, direct and adequate interest in maintaining the effectiveness of their votes," *Coleman v. Miller,* 307 U.S., at 438, not merely a claim of "the right, possessed by every citizen, to require that the Government be administered according to law. . . ." *Fairchild v. Hughes,* 258 U.S. 126, 129; compare *Leser v. Garnett,* 258 U.S. 130. They are entitled to a hearing and to the District Court's decision on their claims. "The very essence of civil liberty certainly consists in the right of every individual to claim the protection of the laws, whenever he receives an injury." *Marbury v. Madison,* 5 U.S. (1 Cranch) 137, 163.

We hold that this challenge to an apportionment presents no nonjusticiable "political question." The cited cases do not hold the contrary.

Of course the mere fact that the suit seeks protection of a political right does not mean it presents a political question. Such an objection "is little more than a play upon words." *Nixon v. Herndon,* 273 U.S. 536, 540. Rather, it is argued that apportionment cases, whatever the actual wording of the complaint, can involve no federal constitutional right except one resting on the guaranty of a republican form of government, and that complaints based on that clause have been held to present political questions which are nonjusticiable.

We hold that the claim pleaded here neither rests upon nor implicates the Guaranty Clause and that its justiciability is therefore not foreclosed by our decisions of cases involving that clause. The District Court misinterpreted *Colegrove v. Green* and other decisions of this Court on which it relied. Appellants' claim that they are being denied equal protection is justiciable, and if "discrimination is sufficiently shown, the right to relief under the equal protection clause is not diminished by the fact that the discrimination relates to political rights." *Snowden v. Hughes,* 321 U.S. 1, 11. To show why we reject the argument based on the Guaranty Clause, we must examine the authorities under it. But because there appears to be some uncertainty as to why those cases did present political questions, and specifically as to whether this apportionment case is like those cases, we deem it necessary first to consider the contours of the "political question" doctrine.

Our discussion, even at the price of extending this opinion, requires review of a number of political question cases, in order to expose the attributes of the doctrine — attributes which, in various settings, diverge, combine, appear, and disappear in seeming disorderliness. Since that review is undertaken solely to demonstrate that neither singly nor collectively do these cases support a conclusion that this apportionment case is nonjusticiable, we of course do not explore their implications in other contexts. The review reveals that in the Guaranty Clause cases and in the other "political question" cases, it is the relationship between the judiciary and the coordinate branches of the Federal Government, and not the federal judiciary's relationship to the States, which gives rise to the "political question."

We have said that "In determining whether a question falls within [the political question] category, the appropriateness under our system of government of attributing finality to the action of the political departments and also the lack of satisfactory criteria for a judicial determination are dominant considerations." *Coleman* v. *Miller,* 307 U.S. 433, 454–455. The nonjusticiability of a political question is primarily a function of the separation of powers. Much confusion results from the capacity of the "political question" label to obscure the need for case-by-case inquiry. Deciding whether a matter has in any measure been committed by the Constitution to another branch of government, or whether the action of that branch exceeds whatever authority has been committed, is itself a delicate exercise in constitutional interpretation, and is a responsibility of this Court as ultimate interpreter of the Constitution. To demonstrate this requires no less than to analyze representative cases and to infer from the analytical threads that make up the political question doctrine. We shall then show that none of those threads catches this case.

Foreign relations: There are sweeping statements to the effect that all questions touching foreign relations are political questions. Not only does resolution of such issues frequently turn on standards that defy judicial application, or involve the exercise of a discretion demonstrably committed to the executive or legislature; but many such questions uniquely demand single-voiced statement of the Government's views. Yet it is error to suppose that every case or controversy which touches foreign relations lies beyond judicial cognizance. Our cases in this field seem invariably to show a discriminating analysis of the particular question posed, in terms of the history of its management by the political branches, of its susceptibility to judicial handling in the light of its nature and posture in the specific case, and of the possible consequences of judicial action. . . .

While recognition of foreign governments so strongly defies judicial treatment that without executive recognition a foreign state has been called "a republic of whose existence we know nothing," and the judiciary ordinarily follows the executive as to which nation has sovereignty over disputed territory, once sovereignty over an area is politically determined and declared, courts may examine the resulting status and decide independently whether a statute applies to that area.

Dates of duration of hostilities: Though it has been stated broadly that "the power which declared the necessity is the power to declare its cessation, and what the cessation requires," *Commercial Trust Co.* v. *Miller,* 262 U.S. 51, 57, here too analysis reveals isolable reasons for the presence of political questions, underlying this Court's refusal to review the political departments' determination of when or whether a war has ended. Dominant is the need for finality in the political determination, for emergency's nature demands "A prompt and unhesitating obedience," *Martin* v. *Mott,* 25 U.S. (12 Wheat.) 19, 30 (calling up of militia). Moreover, "the cessation of hostilities does not necessarily end the war power. . . ."

Validity of enactments: In *Coleman* v. *Miller, supra,* this Court held that the questions of how long a proposed amendment to the Federal Constitution remained open to ratification, and what effect a prior rejection had on a subsequent ratification, were committed to congressional resolution and involved criteria of decision that necessarily escaped the judicial grasp. Similar considerations apply to the enacting process: "The respect due to coequal and independent departments," and the need for finality and certainty about the status of a statute contribute to judicial reluctance to inquire whether, as passed, it complied with all requisite formalities. *Field* v. *Clark,* 143 U.S. 649, 672, 676–677; see *Leser* v. *Garnett,* 258 U.S. 130, 137. But it is not true that courts will never delve into a legislature's records upon such a quest: If the enrolled statute lacks an effective date, a court will not hesitate to seek it in the legislative journals in order to preserve the enactment. *Gardner* v. *The Collector,* 73 U.S. (6 Wall.) 499. The political question doctrine, a tool for maintenance of governmental order, will not be so applied as to promote only disorder.

It is apparent that several formulations which vary slightly according to the settings in which the questions arise may describe a political question, although each has one or more elements which identify it as essentially a function of the separation of powers. Prominent on the surface of any case held to involve a political question is found a textually demonstrable constitutional commitment of the issue to a coordinate political department; or a lack of judicially discoverable and manageable standards for resolving it; or the impossibility of deciding without an initial policy determination of a kind clearly for nonjudicial discretion; or the impossibility of a court's undertaking independent resolution without expressing lack of the respect due coordinate branches of government; or an unusual need for unquestioning adherence to a political decision already made; or the potentiality of embarassment from multifarious pronouncements by various departments on one question.

Unless one of these formulations is inextricable from the case at bar, there should be no dismissal for nonjusticiability on the ground of a political question's presence. The doctrine of which we treat is one of "political questions," not one of "political cases." The courts cannot reject as "no law suit" a bona fide controversy as to whether some action denominated "political" exceeds constitutional authority. . . .

. . . A conclusion as to whether the case at bar does present a political question cannot be confidently reached until we have considered those cases with special care. We shall discover that Guaranty Clause claims involve those elements which define a "political question," and for that reason and no other, they are nonjusticiable. In particular, we shall discover that the nonjusticiability of such claims has nothing to do with their touching upon matters of state governmental organization.

Republican form of government: Luther v. *Borden,* 48 U.S. (7 How.) 1, though in form simply an action for damages for trespass was, as Daniel Webster said in opening the argument for the defense, "an unusual case."

Chief Justice Taney's opinion for the Court reasoned as follows: (1) If a court were to hold the defendants' acts unjustified because the charter government had no legal existence during the period in question, it would follow that all of that government's actions — laws enacted, taxes collected, salaries paid, accounts settled, sentences passed — were of no effect; and that "the officers who carried their decisions into operation [were] answerable as trespassers, if not in some cases as criminals." There was, of course, no room for application of any doctrine of *de facto* status to uphold prior acts of an officer not authorized *de jure,* for such would have defeated the plaintiff's very action. A decision for the plaintiff would inevitably have produced some significant measure of chaos, a consequence to be avoided if it could be done without abnegation of the judicial duty to uphold the Constitution.

(2) No state court has recognized as a judicial responsibility settlement of the issue of the locus of state governmental authority. Indeed, the courts of Rhode Island had in several cases held that "it rested with the political power to decide whether the charter government had been displaced or not," and that that department had acknowledged no charge.

(3) Since "[t]he question relates, altogether, to the constitution and laws of [the] . . . State," the courts of the United States had to follow the state courts' decisions unless there was a federal constitutional ground for overturning them.

(4) No provision of the Constitution could be or

had been invoked for this purpose except Art. IV, §4, the Guaranty Clause. Having already noted the absence of standards whereby the choice between governments could be made by a court acting independently, Chief Justice Taney now found further textual and practical reasons for concluding that, if any department of the United States was empowered by Guaranty Clause to resolve the issue, it was not the judiciary. . . .

Clearly, several factors were thought by the Court in *Luther* to make the question there "political": the commitment to the other branches of the decision as to which is the lawful state government; the unambiguous action by the President, in recognizing the charter government as the lawful authority; the need for finality in the executive's decision: and the lack of criteria by which a court could determine which form of government was republican. . . .

We come, finally, to the ultimate inquiry whether our precedents as to what constitutes a nonjusticiable "political question" bring the case before us under the umbrella of that doctrine. A natural beginning is to note whether any of the common characteristics which we have been able to identify and label descriptively are present. We find none: The question here is the consistency of state action with the Federal Constitution. We have no question decided, or to be decided, by a political branch of government coequal with this Court. Nor do we risk embarrassment of our government abroad, or grave disturbance at home if we take issue with Tennessee as to the constitutionality of her action here challenged. Nor need the appellants, in order to succeed in this action ask the Court to enter upon policy determinations for which judicially manageable standards are lacking. Judicial standards under the Equal Protection Clause are well developed and familiar, and it has been open to courts since the enactment of the Fourteenth Amendment to determine, if on the particular facts they must, that a discrimination reflects *no* policy, but simply arbitrary and capricious action.

This case does, in one sense, involve the allocation of political power within a State, and the appellants might conceivably have added a claim under the Guaranty Clause. Of course, as we have seen, any reliance on that clause would be futile. But because any reliance on the Guaranty Clause could not have succeeded it does not follow that appellants may not be heard on the equal protection claim which in fact they tender. True, it must be clear that the Fourteenth Amendment claim is not so enmeshed with those political question elements which render Guaranty Clause claims nonjusticiable as actually to present a political question itself. But we have found that not to be the case here.

In this connection special attention is due *Pacific States Tel. Co.* v. *Oregon,* 223 U.S. 118. In that case a corporation tax statute enacted by the initiative was attacked ostensibly on three grounds: (1) due process; (2) equal protection; and (3) the Guaranty Clause. But it was clear that the first two grounds were invoked solely in aid of the contention that the tax was invalid by reason of its passage. . . .

The due process and equal protection claims were held nonjusticiable in *Pacific States* not because they happened to be joined with a Guaranty Clause claim, or because they sought to place before the Court a subject matter which might conceivably have been dealt with through the Guaranty Clause, but because the Court believed that they were invoked merely in verbal aid of the resolution of issues which, in its view, entailed political questions. *Pacific States* may be compared with cases such as *Mountain Timber Co.* v. *Washington,* 243 U.S. 219, wherein the Court refused to consider whether a workmen's compensation act violated the Guaranty Clause but considered at length, and rejected, due process and equal protection arguments advanced against it. . . .

. . . And only last Term, in *Gomillion* v. *Lightfoot,* 364 U.S. 339, we applied the Fifteenth Amendment to strike down a redrafting of municipal boundaries which effected a discriminatory impairment of voting rights, in the face of what a majority of the Court of Appeals thought to be a sweeping commitment to state legislatures of the power to draw and redraw such boundaries.

Gomillion was brought by a Negro who had been a resident of the City of Tuskegee, Alabama, until the municipal boundaries were so recast by the State Legislature as to exclude practically all Negroes. The plaintiff claimed deprivation of the right to vote in municipal elections. The District Court's dismissal for want of jurisdiction and failure to state a claim upon which relief could be granted was affirmed by the Court of Appeals. This Court unanimously reversed. This Court's answer to the argument that States enjoyed unrestricted control over municipal boundaries was:

> Legislative control of municipalities, no less than other state power, lies within the scope of relevant limitations imposed by the United States Constitution. . . . The opposite conclusion, urged upon us by respondents, would sanction the achievement by a State of any impairment of voting rights whatever so

long as it was cloaked in the garb of the realignment of political subdivisions. 'It is inconceivable that guaranties embedded in the Constitution of the United States may thus be manipulated out of existence.' 364 U.S., at 344–345.

To a second argument, that *Colegrove* v. *Green, supra,* was a barrier to hearing the merits of the case, the Court responded that *Gomillion* was lifted "out of the so-called 'political' arena and into the conventional sphere of constitutional litigation" because here was discriminatory treatment of a racial minority violating the Fifteenth Amendment.

. . . .

We conclude that the complaint's allegations of a denial of equal protection present a justiciable constitutional cause of action upon which appellants are entitled to a trial and a decision. The right asserted is within the reach of judicial protection under the Fourteenth Amendment.

The judgment of the District Court is reversed and the cause is remanded for further proceedings consistent with this opinion.

Reversed and remanded.

MR. JUSTICE DOUGLAS, concurring.

. . . .

I agree with by Brother Clark that if the allegations in the complaint can be sustained a case for relief is established. We are told that a single vote in Moore County, Tennessee, is worth 19 votes in Hamilton County, that one vote in Stewart or in Chester County is worth nearly eight times a single vote in Shelby or Knox County. The opportunity to prove that an "invidious discrimination" exists should therefore be given the appellants.

It is said that any decision in cases of this kind is beyond the competence of courts. Some make the same point as regards the problem of equal protection in cases involving racial segregation. Yet the legality of claims and conduct is a traditional subject for judicial determination. Adjudication is often perplexing and complicated. An example of the extreme complexity of the task can be seen in a decree apportioning water among the several States. *Nebraska* v. *Wyoming,* 325 U.S. 589, 665. The constitutional guide is often vague, as the decisions under the Due Process and Commerce Clauses show. The problem under the Equal Protection Clause is no more intricate. See Lewis, Legislative Apportionment and the Federal Courts, 71 Harv. L. Rev. 1057, 1083–1084.

. . . .

With the exceptions of *Colegrove* v. *Green,* 328 U.S. 549; *MacDougall* v. *Green,* 335 U.S. 281; *South* v. *Peters,* 339 U.S. 276, and the decisions they spawned, the Court has never thought that protection of voting rights was beyond judicial cognizance. Today's treatment of those cases removes the only impediment to judicial cognizance of the claims stated in the present complaint.

MR. JUSTICE CLARK, concurring.

. . . I believe it can be shown that this case is distinguishable from earlier cases dealing with the distribution of political power by a State, that a patent violation of the Equal Protection Clause of the United States Constitution has been shown, and that an appropriate remedy may be formulated.

I

I take the law of the case from *MacDougall* v. *Green,* 335 U.S. 281 (1948), which involved an attack under the Equal Protection Clause upon an Illinois election statute. The Court decided that case on its merits without hindrance from the "political question" doctrine. . . .

The other cases upon which my Brethren dwell are all distinguishable or inapposite. The widely heralded case of *Colegrove* v. *Green,* 328 U.S. 549 (1946), was one not only in which the Court was bobtailed but in which there was no majority opinion. Indeed, even the "political question" point in MR. JUSTICE FRANKFURTER'S opinion was no more than an alternative ground. Moreover, the appellants did not present an equal protection argument. While it has served as a Mother Hubbard to most of the subsequent cases, I feel it was in that respect illcast and for all of these reasons put it to one side. . . .

II

The controlling facts cannot be disputed. It appears from the record that 37% of the voters of Tennessee elect 20 of the 33 Senators while 40% of the voters elect 63 of the 99 members of the House. But this might not on its face be an "invidious discrimination," *Williamson* v. *Lee Optical of Oklahoma,* 348 U.S. 483, 489 (1955). . . .

It is true that the apportionment policy incorporated in Tennessee's constitution, *i.e.,* state-wide numerical equality of representation with certain minor qualifications, is a rational one. . . . However, the root of the trouble is not in Tennessee's Constitution, for admittedly its policy has not been followed.

The discrimination lies in the action of Tennessee's Assembly in allocating legislative seats to counties or districts created by it. Try as one may, Tennessee's apportionment just cannot be made to fit the pattern cut by its Constitution. This was the finding of the District Court. The policy of the Constitution referred to by the dissenters, therefore, is of no relevance here. We must examine what the Assembly has done. The frequency and magnitude of the inequalities in the present districting admit of no policy whatever. . . . This is not to say that some of the disparity cannot be explained, but when the entire table is examined — comparing the voting strength of counties of like population as well as contrasting that of the smaller with the larger counties — it leaves but one conclusion, namely that Tennessee's apportionment is a crazy quilt without rational basis. . . .

Although I find the Tennessee apportionment statute offends the Equal Protection Clause, I would not consider intervention by this Court into so delicate a field if there were any other relief available to the people of Tennessee. But the majority of people of Tennessee have no "practical opportunities for exerting their political weight at the polls" to correct the existing "invidious discrimination." Tennessee has no initiative and referendum. I have searched diligently for other "practical opportunities" present under the law. I find none other than through the federal courts. The majority of the voters have been caught up in a legislative strait jacket. Tennessee has an "informed, civically militant electorate" and "an aroused popular conscience," but it does not sear "the conscience of the people's representatives." This is because the legislative policy has riveted the present seats in the Assembly to their respective constituencies, and by the votes of their incumbents a reapportionment of any kind is prevented. The people have been rebuffed at the hands of the Assembly; they have tried the constitutional convention route, but since the call must originate in the Assembly it, too, has been fruitless. They have tried Tennessee courts with the same result, and Governors have fought the tide only to flounder. It is said that there is recourse in Congress and perhaps that may be, but from a practical standpoint this is without substance. To date Congress has never undertaken such a task in any State. We therefore must conclude that the people of Tennessee are stymied and without judicial intervention will be saddled with the present discrimination in the affairs of their state government.

. . . .

In view of the detailed study that the Court has given this problem, it is unfortunate that a decision is not reached on the merits. The majority appears to hold, at least *sub silentio,* that an invidious discrimination is present, but it remands to the three-judge court for it to make what is certain to be that formal determination. . . . Nevertheless, not being able to muster a court to dispose of the case on the merits, I concur in the opinion of the majority and acquiesce in the decision to remand. However, in fairness I do think that Tennessee is entitled to have my idea of what it faces on the record before us and the trial court some light as to how it might proceed. . . .

MR. JUSTICE STEWART, concurring.

The separate writings of my dissenting and concurring Brothers stray so far from the subject of today's decision as to convey, I think, a distressingly inaccurate impression of what the Court decides. For that reason, I think it appropriate, in joining the opinion of the Court, to emphasize in a few words what the opinion does and does not say.

The Court today decides three things and no more: "(a) that the court possessed jurisdiction of the subject matter; (b) that a justiciable cause of action is stated upon which appellants would be entitled to appropriate relief; and (c) . . . that the appellants have standing to challenge the Tennessee apportionment statutes."

. . . My Brother Clark has made a convincing prima facie showing that Tennessee's system of apportionment is in fact utterly arbitrary — without any possible justification in rationality. My Brother Harlan has, with imagination and ingenuity, hypothesized possibly rational bases for Tennessee's system. But the merits of this case are not before us now. The defendants have not yet had an opportunity to be heard in defense of the State's system of apportionment; indeed, they have not yet even filed an answer to the complaint. As in other cases, the proper place for the trial is in the trial court, not here.

MR. JUSTICE FRANKFURTER, whom MR. JUSTICE HARLAN joins, dissenting.

The Court today reverses a uniform course of decision established by a dozen cases, including one by which the very claim now sustained was unanimously rejected only five years ago. The impressive body of rulings thus cast aside reflected the equally uniform course of our political history regarding the relationship between population and legislative representation — a wholly different matter from denial of the franchise to individuals because of race, color, religion or sex. Such a massive repudiation of the experience of our whole past in asserting destructively novel judicial power demands a detailed analysis of the role of this Court in our constitutional scheme. Disregard of inherent limits in the effective exercise of the Court's "judicial Power" not only presages the futility of judicial intervention in the essentially political conflict of forces by which the relation between population and representation has time out of mind been and now is determined. It may well impair the Court's position as the ultimate organ of "the supreme Law of the Land" in that vast range of legal problems, often strongly entangled in popular feeling, on which this Court must pronounce. The Court's authority — possessed neither of the purse nor the sword — ultimately rests on sustained public confidence in its moral sanction. Such feeling must be nourished by the Court's complete detachment, in face and in appearance, from political entanglements and by abstention from injecting itself into the clash of political forces in political settlements.

. . . .

. . . In effect, today's decision empowers the courts of the country to devise what should constitute the proper composition of the legislatures of the fifty States. If state courts should for one reason or another find themselves unable to discharge this task, the duty of doing so is put on the federal courts or on this Court, if State views do not satisfy this Court's notion of what is proper districting.

We were soothingly told at the bar of this Court that we need not worry about the kind of remedy a court could effectively fashion once the abstract constitutional right to have courts pass on a state-wide system of electoral districting is recognized as a matter of judicial rhetoric, because legislatures would heed the Court's admonition. This is not only an euphoric hope. It implies a sorry confession of judicial impotence in place of a frank acknowledgment that there is not under our Constitution a judicial remedy for every political mischief, for every undesirable exercise of legislative power. The Framers carefully and with deliberate forethought refused so to enthrone the judiciary. In this situation, as in others of like nature, appeal for relief does not belong here. Appeal must be to an informed, civically militant electorate. In a democratic society like ours, relief must come through an aroused popular conscience that sears the conscience of the people's representatives. . . .

. . . The influence of these converging considerations — the caution not to undertake decision where standards meet for judicial judgment are lacking, the reluctance to interfere with matters of state government in the absence of an unquestionable and effectively enforceable mandate, the unwillingness to make courts arbiters of the broad issues of political organization historically committed to other institutions and for whose adjustment the judicial process is ill-adapted — has been decisive of the settled line of cases, reaching back more than a century. . . . Appellants appear as representatives of a class that is prejudiced as a class, in contradistinction to the polity in its entirety. However, the discrimination relied on is the deprivation of what appellants conceive to be their proportionate share of political influence. This, of course, is the practical effect of any allocation of power within the institutions of government. Hardly any distribution of political authority that could be assailed as rendering government non-republican would fail similarly to operate to the prejudice of some groups, and to the advantage of others, within the body politic. . . .

What, then, is this question of legislative apportionment? Appellants invoke the right to vote and to have their votes counted. But they are permitted to vote and their votes are counted. They go to the polls, they cast their ballots, they send their representatives to the state councils. Their complaint is simply that the representatives are not sufficiently numerous or powerful — in short, that Tennessee has adopted a basis of representation with which they are dissatisfied. Talk of "debasement" or "dilution" is circular talk. One cannot speak of "debasement" or "dilution" of the value of a vote until there is first defined a standard of reference as to what a vote should be worth. What is actually asked of the Court in this case is to choose among competing bases of representation — ultimately, really, among competing theories of political philosophy — in order to establish an appropriate frame of government for the State of Tennessee and thereby all the States of the Union. . . .

Dissenting opinion of MR. JUSTICE HARLAN, whom MR. JUSTICE FRANKFURTER joins.

. . . .

I can find nothing in the Equal Protection Clause or elsewhere in the Federal Constitution which expressly or impliedly supports the view that state legislatures must be so structured as to reflect with approximate equality the voice of every voter. Not only is that proposition refuted by history, as shown by my Brother Frankfurter, but it strikes deep into the heart of our federal system. Its acceptance would require us to turn our backs on the regard which this Court has always shown for the judgment of state legislatures and courts on matters of basically local concern.

In the last analysis, what lies at the core of this controversy is a difference of opinion as to the function of representative government. It is surely beyond argument that those who have the responsibility for devising a system of representation may permissibly consider that factors other than bare numbers should be taken into account. The existence of the United States Senate is proof enough of that. To consider that we may ignore the Tennessee Legislature's judgment in this instance because that body was the product of an asymmetrical electoral apportionment would in effect be to assume the very conclusion here disputed. Hence we must accept the present form of the Tennessee Legislature as the embodiment of the State's choice, or, more realistically, its compromise, between competing political philosophies. The federal courts have not been empowered by the Equal Protection Clause to judge whether this resolution of the State's internal political conflict is desirable or undesirable, wise or unwise.

. . . .

In short, there is nothing in the Federal Constitution to prevent a State, acting not irrationally, from choosing any electoral legislative structure it thinks best suited to the interests, temper, and customs of its people. . . .

. . . I would hardly think it unconstitutional if a state legislature's expressed reason for establishing or maintaining an electoral imbalance between its rural and urban population were to protect the State's agricultural interests from the sheer weight of numbers of those residing in its cities. . . .

From a reading of the majority and concurring opinions one will not find it difficult to catch the premises that underlie this decision. The fact that the appellants have been unable to obtain political redress of their asserted grievances appears to be regarded as a matter which should lead the Court to stretch to find some basis for judicial intervention. . . . Thus, what the Court is doing reflects more an adventure in judicial experimentation than a solid piece of constitutional adjudication. Whether dismissal of this case should have been for want of jurisdiction or, as is suggested in *Bell* v. *Hood,* 327 U.S. 678, 682–683, for failure of the complaint to state a claim upon which relief could be granted, the judgment of the District Court was correct. . . .

Powell v. McCormack

395 U.S. 486 (1969)
Vote: 8–1

Congressman Powell was a talented and aggressive black Congressman and leader. His life-style was also rather flamboyant, especially as he was the minister of a major Baptist church in Harlem. As he began to have various run-ins with the law over financial matters, irregularities were demonstrated in his handling of accounts of the committee he chaired in the House of Representatives. Powell was refused his seat when a new Congress met in January 1967.

The previous year the Supreme Court had ruled that the Georgia legislature could not exclude Julian Bond, a black antiwar leader, solely because of anti-Vietnam speeches, which were legal and protected by the First Amendment. But that involved a legislative body's inappropriate intrusion of political outlook. And even more significantly, that involved the actions of a state agency no longer securely autonomous under the political questions doctrine. *Bond* v. *Floyd* (1966) made clear what BAKER V. CARR (1962) implied: the states could not rely very much, if at all, on the political questions doctrine.

Powell further dents the political questions approach at the federal level. But impressive legal reasoning allowed the Court to be ambiguous on the extent. It noted that initial seating is based on the House's power to judge qualifications. Misconduct is punishable through expulsion. The House had erred in its use of remedies.

(Powell got his seat, paid back the funds, but was subsequently defeated for reelection by his Harlem constituents.)

MR. CHIEF JUSTICE WARREN delivered the opinion of the Court.

. . . .

During the 89th Congress, a Special Subcommittee on Contracts of the Committee on House Administration conducted an investigation into the expenditures of the Committee on Education and Labor, of which Petitioner Adam Clayton Powell, Jr., was chairman. The Special Subcommittee issued a report concluding that Powell and certain staff employees had deceived the House authorities as to travel expenses. The report also indicated there was strong evidence that certain illegal salary payments had been made to Powell's wife at his direction. . . .

When the 90th Congress met to organize in January 1967, Powell was asked to step aside while the oath was administered to the other members-elect. . . .

. . . .

The resolution excluding Petitioner Powell was adopted by a vote in excess of two-thirds of the 434 Members of Congress — 307 to 116. 113 Cong. Rec. 1956–1957 (daily ed. March 1, 1967). Article I, §5, grants the House authority to expel a member "with the Concurrence of two thirds." Respondents assert that the House may expel a member for any reason whatsoever and that, since a two-thirds vote was obtained, the procedure by which Powell was denied his seat in the 90th Congress should be regarded as an expulsion not an exclusion. . . .

Although respondents repeatedly urge this Court not to speculate as to the reasons for Powell's exclusion, their attempt to equate exclusion with expulsion would require a similar speculation that the House would have voted to expel Powell had it been faced with that question. Powell had not been seated at the time House Resolution 278 was debated and passed. After a motion to bring the Select Committee's proposed resolution to an immediate vote had been defeated, an amendment was offered which mandated Powell's exclusion. Mr. Celler, chairman of the Select Committee, than posed a parliamentary inquiry to determine whether a two-thirds vote was necessary to pass the resolution if so amended "in the sense that it might amount to an expulsion." 113 Cong. Rec. 1942 (daily ed., March 1, 1967). The speaker replied that "action by a majority vote would be in accordance with the rules." *Ibid*. Had the amendment been regarded as an attempt to expel Powell, a two-thirds vote would have been constitutionally required. The Speaker ruled that the House was voting to exclude Powell, and we will not speculate what the result might have been if Powell had been seated and expulsion proceedings subsequently instituted.

Nor is the distinction between exclusion and expulsion merely one of form. The misconduct for which Powell was charged occurred prior to the convening of the 90th Congress. On several occasions the House had debated whether a member can be expelled for actions taken during a prior Congress and the House's own manual of procedure applicable in the 90th Congress states that "both Houses have distrusted their power to punish in such cases." Members of the House having expressed a belief that such strictures apply to its own power to expel, we will not assume that two-thirds of its members would have expelled Powell for his prior conduct had the Speaker announced that House Resolution 278 was for expulsion rather than exclusion. . . .

In *Baker v. Carr* we noted that a federal district court lacks jurisdiction over the subject matter (1) if the cause does not "arise under" the Federal Constitution, laws or treaties (or fall within one of the other enumerated categories of Article III); or (2) if it is not a "case or controversy" within the meaning of that phrase in Article III; or (3) if the cause is not one described by any jurisdictional statute. And, as in *Baker v. Carr,* our determination . . . that this cause presents no nonjusticiable "political question" disposes of respondents' contentions that this cause is not a "case or controversy."

Respondents first contend that this is not a case "arising under" the Constitution within the meaning of Article III. They emphasize that Art. I, §5, assigns to each house of Congress the power to judge the elections and qualifications of its own members and to punish its members for disorderly behavior. Respondents also note that under Art. I, §3, the Senate has the "sole power" to try all impeachments. Respondents argue that these delegations (to "judge," to "punish," and to "try") to the Legislative Branch are explicit grants of "judicial power" to the Congress and constitute specific exceptions to the general mandate of Article III that the "judicial power" shall be vested in the federal courts. Thus, respondents maintain, the "power conferred on the courts by Article III does not authorize this Court to do anything more than declare its lack of jurisdiction to proceed."

We reject this contention, Article III, §1, provides the "judicial Power . . . shall be vested in one supreme Court, and in such inferior Courts as the Congress may . . . establish." Further, §2 mandates that the "judicial Power shall extend to all Cases . . . arising under this Constitution. . . ." It has long been held that a suit "arises under" the Constitution if petitioners' claims "will be sustained if the Constitution . . . [is] given one construction and will be defeated if it [is] given another. . . ." Any bar to federal courts reviewing the judgments made by the House or Senate in excluding a member arises from the allocation of powers between the two branches of the Federal Government (a question of justiciability), and not from the petitioners' failure to state a claim based on federal law.

. . . .

In deciding generally whether a claim is justiciable, a court must determine whether "the duty asserted can be judicially identified and its breach judicially determined, and whether protection for the right asserted can be judicially molded." *Baker v. Carr, supra,* at 198. Respondents do not seriously contend that the duty asserted and its alleged breach cannot be judicially determined. If petitioners are correct, the House had a duty to seat Powell once it determined he met the standing requirements set forth in the Constitution. It is undisputed that he met those requirements and that he was nevertheless excluded.

Respondents do maintain, however, that this case is not justiciable because, they assert, it is impossible for a federal court to "mold effective relief for resolving this case." Respondents emphasize that petitioners asked for coercive relief against the officers of the House, and, they contend, federal courts cannot issue mandamus or injunctions compelling officers or employees of the House to perform specific official acts. Respondents rely primarily on the Speech or Debate Clause to support this contention.

We need express no opinion about the appropriateness of coercive relief in this case, for petitioners sought a declaratory judgment, a form of relief the District Court could have issued. The Declaratory Judgment Act, 28 U.S.C. §2201 (1964 ed.), provides that district court may "declare the rights . . . of any interested party . . . whether or not further relief is or could be sought."

1. Textually Demonstrable Constitutional Commitment.

Respondents maintain that even if this case is otherwise justiciable, it presents only a political question. It is well-established that the federal courts will not adjudicate political questions. See *e.g., Coleman v. Miller,* 307 U.S. 433 (1939); *Oetjen v. Central Leather Co.,* 246 U.S. 297 (1918). In *Baker v. Carr, supra,* we noted that political questions are not justiciable primarily because of the separation of powers within the Federal Government. After reviewing our decisions in this area, we concluded that on the surface of any case held to involve a political question was at least one of the following formulations:

> a textually demonstrable constitutional commitment of the issue to a co-ordinate political department; or a lack of judicially discoverable and manageable standards for resolving it; or the impossibility of deciding without an initial policy determination of a kind clearly for nonjudicial discretion; or the impossibility of a court's undertaking independent resolution without expressing lack of the respect due coordinate branches of government; or an unusual need for unquestioning adherence to a political decision already made; or the potentiality of embarrassment from multifarious pronouncements by various departments on one question. *Id.,* at 217.

Respondents' first contention is that this case presents a political question because under Art. I, §5, there has been a "textually demonstrable constitutional commitment" to the House of the "adjudicatory power" to determine Powell's qualifications. Thus it is argued that the House, and the House alone, has power to determine who is qualified to be a member.

In order to determine the scope of any "textual commitment" under Art. I, §5, we necessarily must determine the meaning of the phrase to "judge the qualifications of its members." Petitioners argue that the records of the debates during the Constitutional Convention, available commentary from the post-Convention, pre-ratification period, and early congressional applications of Art. I, §5, support their construction of the section. Respondents insist, however, that a careful examination of the pre-Convention practices of the English Parliament and American colonial assemblies demonstrates that by 1787, a legislature's power to judge the qualifications of its members was generally understood to encompass exclusion or expulsion on the ground that an individual's character or past conduct rendered him unfit to serve. When the Constitution and the debates over its adoption are thus viewed in historical perspective, argue respondents, it becomes clear that the "qualifications" expressly set forth in the Constitution were not meant to limit the long recognized legislative power to exclude or expel at will, but merely to establish "standing incapacities," which could be altered only by a constitutional amendment. Our examination of the relevant historical materials leads us to the conclusion that petitioners are correct and that the Constitution leaves the House without authority to *exclude* any person, duly elected by his constituents, who meets all the requirements for membership expressly prescribed in the Constitution.

. . . .

Had the intent of the Framers emerged from these materials with less clarity, we would nevertheless have been compelled to resolve any ambiguity in favor of a narrow construction of the scope of Congress' power to exclude members-elect. A fundamental principle of our representative democracy is, in Hamilton's words, "that the people should choose whom they please to govern them." 2 Elliot's Debates 257. As Madison pointed out at the Convention, this principle is undermined as much by limiting whom the people can select as by limiting the franchise itself. In apparent agreement with this basic philosophy the Convention adopted his suggestion limiting the power to expel. To allow essentially that

same power to be exercised under the guise of judging qualifications, would be to ignore Madison's warning. . . . In short, both the intention of the Framers, to the extent it can be determined, and an examination of the basic principles of our democratic system persuade us that the Constitution does not vest in the Congress a discretionary power to deny membership by a majority vote.

. . . .

Respondents' alternate contention is that the case presents a political question because judicial resolution of petitioners' claim would produce a "potentially embarrassing confrontation between coordinate branches" of the Federal Government. But, as our interpretation of Art. I, §5, discloses, a determination of Petitioner Powell's right to sit would require no more than an interpretation of the Constitution. Such a determination falls within the traditional role accorded courts to interpret the law, and does not involve a "lack of respect due [a] coordinate branch of government," nor does it involve an "initial policy determination of a kind clearly for nonjudicial discretion." *Baker* v. *Carr, supra,* at 217. Our system of government requires that federal courts on occasion interpret the Constitution in a manner at variance with the construction given the document by another branch. The alleged conflict that such an adjudication may cause cannot justify the courts' avoiding their constitutional responsibility. . . .

Nor are any of the other formulations of a political question "inextricable from the case at bar." *Baker* v. *Carr, supra,* at 217. Petitioners seek a determination that the House was without power to exclude Powell from the 90th Congress, which, we have seen, requires an interpretation of the Constitution — a determination for which clearly there are "judicially manageable standards." Finally, a judicial resolution of petitioners' claim will not result in "multifarious pronouncements by various departments on one question." For, as we noted in *Baker* v. *Carr, supra,* at 211, it is the responsibility of this Court to act as the ultimate interpreter of the Constitution. *Marbury* v. *Madison,* 1 Cranch 137 (1803). Thus, we conclude that petitioners' claim is not barred by the political question doctrine, and having determined that the claim is otherwise generally justiciable, we hold that the case is justiciable.

Mr. JUSTICE STEWART, dissenting.

I believe that events which have taken place since certiorari was granted in this case on November 18, 1968, have rendered it moot, and that the Court should therefore refrain from deciding the novel, difficult, and delicate constitutional questions which the case presented at its inception.

I

The essential purpose of this lawsuit by Congressman Powell and members of his constituency was to regain the seat from which he was barred by the 90th Congress. That purpose, however, became impossible at attainment on January 3, 1969, when the 90th Congress passed into history and the 91st Congress came into being. . . .

In short, dismissal of Powell's action against the legislative branch would not in the slightest prejudice his money claim, and it would avoid the necessity of deciding constitutional issues which, in the petitioners' words, "touch the bedrock of our political system [and] strike at the very heart of representative government." If the fundamental principles restraining courts from unnecessarily or prematurely reaching out to decide grave and perhaps unsettling constitutional questions retain any vitality, see *Ashwander* v. *TVA,* 297 U.S. 288, 346–348 (Brandeis, J., concurring), surely there have been few cases more demanding of their application than this one. . . .

CHAPTER 2

President and Congress: Separation of Power and the Balance of Authority

The Basic Pattern

Constitutions, it has been wisely observed, are written to control and contain the previous regime. Perhaps the genius of the American system inheres in its being the fruit of two such reactions—the perceived abuse of power by the British prior to the Revolution and the absence of power during the Articles of Confederation era. Definitions and limits of the principal divisions of government are set out in flexible terms permitting shifts in the balance of power.

The Founding Fathers thought they were constructing a variation of the parliamentary system they imagined Great Britain had. They were wrong on both scores. The British model for their handiwork was already well under way to becoming a system of cabinet-controlled government. The system the Founders established was to become a presidential system. The Founders saw the legislature as "the great vortex" into which all the other powers threaten to be drawn. But the Presidency was to emerge as the focal point of the Union, though unlike the British Parliament, Congress was not brought under cabinet or executive control.

Congress did not always wrestle with the President, but, unique among world legislatures, it has retained the major powers clearly allocated to it, and has therefore also retained the potential to claim those powers left ambiguous.

The distribution of power between national government and states — federalism—is dealt with extensively in Chapters 3 and 4. Here we are concerned with the division of powers within the national government. Most of the powers clearly granted to the national government are powers delegated to Congress and are found in Article I of the Consitition. Many of these may be delegated by legislation to executive agents, and the Presidency has laid claim to some of them on its own. Other powers are allocated to Congress in other parts of the Consitition; especially important are the powers to inforce the subject matter of the Thirteenth, Fourteenth, and Fifteenth Amendments, which involve rights of equality and voting rights.

Presidential authority is prescribed more in terms of roles and responsibilities than in terms of specific powers. Thus the President shall "take care that the laws are enforced," and he is "the Commander-in-Chief of the army and navy." The President's monopolistic authority over foreign affairs is inferred from the right to appoint and receive ministers and ambassadors. These broad and inferred presidential provisions contrast with the narrow and specific congressional grants and create overlap, ambiguity, and conflict, some of which was no doubt intended.

Constitutionally speaking, the problem of allocating power within the national government is one of drawing a line between President and Congress. The entire administration of the laws, the vast bureaucracy, is seen as controlled by the Chief Executive. Only in its giving Congress the power to delegate to someone other than the President the right to appoint "inferior officers" does the Constitution recognize the complexity of such an administrative structure. The Supreme Court has reached the convenient conclusion that the independent regulatory commissions are "quasi-legislative" and "quasi-judicial" and that therefore Congress may insulate them from presidential control.

The allocation of functions between the three branches of government is usually referred to as the *separation of powers*. This clear oversimplification of political reality is counterposed by the rival notion of checks and balances that the Framers also embraced. Presidents obviously share in the legislative process by vetoing legislation; they share in the judicial process by granting pardons. Congress may impeach officials and direct agencies in executive fashion. Courts, as we have noted, may rewrite or negate statutes and directly control aspects of prisons or welfare institutions, albeit on a temporary basis. As Justice Brandeis has suggested, the system of checks and balances promotes liberty through each agency's acting as a watchdog guarding the others. The intent is not to create efficiency but to maximize freedom by minimizing unchecked power.

Still, the separation of powers notion comes into play when one arm of government moves into what has been held to be the core of another branch's function — a sort of extension of the Court's own continued unwillingness to extend itself into the executive's foreign policy and defense roles or the legislature's monopoly over new taxation. (See THE PRIZE CASES for a prime example of Court avoidance of authority over war and money.) When Congress has attempted to punish specific government employees by withholding their salaries, the courts have found such actions to be bills of attainder and usurpations of judicial functions (*U.S.* v. *Lovett, U.S.* v. *Brown*). In a recent and far-reaching decision, the Court also decided that Congress may not give the President the right to legislate or reserve for either House the right to veto. This role reversal, it was held, violates the separation of powers and the clear wording of the Constitution [see IMMIGRATION AND NATURALIZATION SERVICE V. CHADHA (1983)]. The President may not abrogate legislation or act in defiance of the laws — rights asserted by President Nixon and his staff — though emergencies may permit executive actions not clearly authorized. (On both these points, see YOUNGSTOWN SHEET AND TUBE V. SAWYER (1952). The CHADHA and YOUNGSTOWN decisions, resting on "old-fashioned" separation of powers notions, are landmark cases of great import even though many writers consider their analysis oversimplified and archaic. Indeed, the more momentous and difficult the case, the more likely the Court is to turn to simple and basic "truths.")

In analyzing the distribution of power between the President and Congress under the Constitution, scholars have placed great stress upon the opening sentences of each article. These so-called "vesting clauses" were added by the Committee on Style, so perhaps their substantive significance is exaggerated, but the striking differences could not escape notice. Article I allocates "All legislative Powers herein granted" to a Congress. It is exclusive, but clearly limited. Article II vests "the executive Power" in the President, apparently despairing of forging precise definitions. By Article III, the judicial power is "vested in a Supreme Court and such inferior courts as the Congress . . . may establish." Section 2 of Article III further defines and constricts the judicial power.

Inevitably, these ambiguities and the legal overlapping of categories have produced conflicting claims and litigation. Let us now explore that evolution, the claims of Congress and the President, and the Supreme Court's resolution of these conflicts.

The Powers of Congress

The enumerated powers of Congress range from major policy areas — taxing and spending, the commerce power, and the war power — to such minor issues as the regulation of patents and bankruptcy. Some congressional powers, such as the power to grant letters of marque and reprisal, are obsolete. In sum, the powers of Congress are a great source of national power, and their definition largely defines the limits of federal authority over the states, as well as a good deal of the boundary between the federal government and the individual. Congress must legislate on the basis of powers assigned to it by the Constitution. Those powers are usually generously construed in accordance with the decision in McCULLOCH V. MARYLAND (1819). Each granted, enumerated, or express power (all terms used to describe those powers actually listed in the Constitution) implies other authority as well. For example, the power to operate post offices implies the power to hire postal carriers and issue stamps.

While congressional legislative power must constitutionally be traced to a specific provision, the liberal rules of construction set forth in McCULLOCH V. MARYLAND make each specific power a source of multiple potential powers. Marshall's decision in that case interpreted the provision that Congress could "make laws necessary and proper for carrying into Execution the foregoing Powers" as permitting expansion of federal authority. This "elastic clause" suggests that Congress is not limited to actions clearly permitted or even implied but may act where legislation is "conducive" or "useful" to the carrying out of a granted constitutional purpose. Congress' power is nonetheless circumscribed by the need to base action on some appropriate constitutional purpose.

Delegation

The exercise of national power is conditioned by implications of the separation doctrine, especially the notion of delegation of power. The Court has held that Congress alone may exercise legislative power, echoing an old Latin maxim that holds that a "delegated power may not be delegated." Having said this, the Court proceeded to decide that Congress may authorize the President or other officials to exercise wide discretion, assuming Congress provides guidelines and channels the discretion. The legal "explanation" is that under controlled and limited circumstances, this is an exercise of "administration" rather than an improper delegation of the power to legislate. The classic decision in J. W. HAMPTON, JR., AND CO. V. U.S. (1928) was not the first decision sustaining such delegation, but it comprehensively and clearly set out the approach. The President was authorized to change tariffs on foreign goods, but that power was conditioned on findings by an expert commission that comparable U.S. products were being undersold. The existence of standards meant the President was operating within congressional authority, not on his own.

Having established the notion that strict rules were needed to justify delegation, the Court proceeded to sustain all such legislation ever passed — until the New Deal period. Then in PANAMA REFINING CO. V. RYAN (1935), in SCHECTER POULTRY CORP. V. U.S. (1935), and in CARTER V. CARTER COAL CO. (1936), New Deal programs were held to exceed permissible limits. The legislation was said to permit "delegation run riot" without adequate congressionally prescribed standards. These decisions constitute a unique series of events. Congress continues to delegate authority to agencies, enjoining them to "eliminate unfair competition," "further the public interest," or "insofar as possible determine dangerous levels" of pollutants in the air. And the courts continue to sustain such authorizations as delegations within constitutional limits.

Realistically, the courts have been so generous because they recognize the dilemma faced by the Congress. The burgeoning of complex governmental programs presents obstacles to congressional control. Giving agencies discretion is not only a reasonable solution to Congress' problems, it has also been one of its more conservative ones.

A more adventurous form of delegation, the legislative veto, has been used by Congress with increasing frequency since 1937. By this device, Congress delegates authority to an agency to promulgate policies. The authorized agency must keep Congress informed of any new policy, and the policy only goes into effect if Congress does not nullify the action within a specified time. The result is to reverse normal roles of governance: the executive legislates, Congress vetoes.

In 1983, in the CHADHA decision, the Supreme Court invalidated those delegations that allowed veto by a single house or without presidential participation. Whether other forms of legislative veto are constitutional remains open. However, such acts as the War Powers Act, which require positive approval by Congress to permit continued executive initiative, still seem permitted by the reasoning in the CHADHA case.

Even more important than the effect of the CHADHA decision — which invalidated in one step more Acts of Congress than all previous decisions in history — is the development of a rigid, formal concept of separation of powers. BOWSHER V. SYNAR's (1986) invalidation of that part of the Gramm-Rudman budget bill that gave the Comptroller General a key role in the budgetary process was based on the technicality that that official, being removable only by Congress, was therefore in the legislative branch. That decision suggested that legislative employees were not permitted to perform executive functions.

Based on this theory, Oliver North and others challenged the constitutionality of the special prosecutor, who is chosen by judges. This device, authorized by an Act of Congress, was a solution to the Watergate scandal quandry as to how the Justice Department, under presidential political control, could investigate wrongdoing in and around the White House. The argument for its constitutionality is based on the textual right of Congress to vest appointment of "inferior officers" in heads of departments or the judiciary. Opponents claim that prosecutors are not "inferior officers" and are inherently exercising executive *functions*.

In 1988 the Supreme Court held, in *Morrison* v. *Olson,* that the office of special prosecutor was constitutional, and that the power vested in that office did not substantially detract from presidential authority, but rather was sensitively designed to preserve the separation of powers. (Only Justice Scalia held to a hard line on requiring functions deemed executive to be exercised only by presidential appointees.) The Chief Justice's opinion neatly places the Court in a position to even more closely adjust the boundary line between President and Congress. At the same time it represents a more practical and less strictly conceptual view of that boundary.

In a series of decisions, the Court has made it clear that it is no longer enthralled by Scalia's highly elaborate conceptions of separation of powers. In the most important of these *Mistretta* v.

U.S. 57 LW 4102 (1989) the Court upheld the creation of a U.S. sentencing commission. Designated, by law, as "an independent commission in the Judicial branch," and composed of seven appointees (at least three of whom must be judges) and the Attorney General or a representative, the commission sets guidelines for sentencing by federal judges. Neither the function nor the membership of judges troubled by the eight-justice majority, though they had some difficulty with presidential power to remove judges from the commission for cause. However, they upheld that power as well since the judges retained their judicial post and salary in any event.

Interestingly, during the New Deal years it was the liberals who advocated presidential power, and the conservatives who found the will of the people in Congress. Since the Presidency has recently been more often in conservative hands and Congress has remained more liberal, ideology has shifted radically. For example, Reagan's attorney general, Edwin Meese, argued that any executive official in the government is under direct control of the White House, a position Roosevelt or Truman never dared take. On the other hand, liberals deplore the growth of an "imperial" Presidency, particularly with respect to foreign affairs.

Investigation, Publicity, and Immunity

The same problem — declining legislative capacity to fully supervise the bureaucracy — has driven legislators to multiply congressional investigations. These range from serious, technical inquiries into governmental problems, to seminarlike discussions of widespread social problems, down to publicity-hungry abuse of witnesses' privacy or rights.

From the beginning of the Republic, President and Congress have been in disagreement over the question of the legislature's authority to obtain information from presidential subordinates on the conduct of the executive. As against the legislature's general responsibility for the conduct of programs, presidents have insisted on their right to confidential discussions with their principal subordinates. The rights of "executive privilege" have usually been tested in decisions on congressional investigations; for example, MCGRAIN V. DAUGHERTY (1927) and U.S. V. NIXON (1974). In such cases, presidents have refused to submit documents or to permit subordinates to testify, claiming that a need for confidential communication with a subordinate is vital. Recognizing not only that claim, but also Congress' need for information, the courts determine such claims case by case. The level of the subordinate is particularly significant to such a determination.

As Congress has become more active in these inquiries, the Court has been called upon to protect individual rights as well. The plethora of investigations has resulted in a series of decisions, many of them inconsistent. In general, the courts have recognized for over a century that congressional investigations may have some of the character of a criminal trial, and that Congress therefore must limit inquiries and provide basic elements of fair play to witnesses called before it. The era in which a committee chair would bark, "You have only the rights we grant you," has given way to a more circumscribed type of inquiry.

Investigations are only one area in which Congress' own procedures have been held reviewable. The prevailing attitude was that, in general, how a legislature comports itself is basically a political question. COLEMAN V. MILLER (1939) held that decisions on ratification of constitutional amendments were essentially nonjusticiable; each House of Congress was seen as sole master of its rules and proceedings. The paring down of the political questions doctrine culminated in POWELL V. MCCORMACK (1969), limiting sharply Congress' power to refuse to seat an elected member. Similarly, the privilege of members of the House of Representatives not to be accountable in courts for their actions in the House has been construed to cover reasonably confined circumstances — not including press conferences, even if given on congressional premises — though also interpreted liberally as to using votes in the Congress as evidence of bribery. Compare GRAVEL V. U.S. (1972) with *U.S.* v. *Helstocki* (1979). "Legislative acts" may not include in public releases wide-sweeping characterizations of private citizens, even if they are recipients of public funds. Similarly, congressional staff action under orders from a member of Congress are immune, although the Superintendent of Documents does not have legislative immunity in publishing material claimed to be defamatory [*Hutchinson* v. *Proxmire* (1979)].

Presidential Power: A Record of Aggrandizement?

The Presidency has been in a strong position politically, constitutionally, and situationally to aggrandize itself and to claim greater need for authority, especially in the twentieth century. Since Andrew Jackson, presidents have called attention to the fact that they (and their vice presidents) are the only officials in the system elected by all the people. While this is scarcely a legal argument, this "steward" or "tribune of the people" claim does enhance the Presidency politically. It also colors and supplements stricter arguments.

In general, the President's specific powers, except the power over legislation, are relatively less important than the vaguely granted ones. With respect to legislation, the President may "from time to time" inform Congress of situations and propose remedies. By custom there is an annual State-of-the-Union Address, but presidential initiatives are not restricted to such moments. By law, the President proposes a detailed annual budget, which is the basic governmental game plan but which Congress may alter or even ignore. Finally, the President has a potent weapon in the power to veto. A two-thirds vote in both Houses is required to override a veto, and few presidents find it difficult to mobilize 34 percent of at least one House. If Congress is adjourned, the President may kill a bill simply by refusing to sign, the so-called pocket veto. But if Congress is in session and the President neither signs nor vetos, after ten days the bill becomes law. The President may call special sessions of Congress. If the two chambers of Congress disagree over the time of adjournment, the President also may adjourn it.

The President may pardon offenses against the national government, and the recipient party has no right to refuse a pardon. The President may not pardon for an offense not yet committed, for this would be license to violate the law. A pardon also does not prevent impeachment and removal from public office. The most significant use of the pardoning power was President Ford's pardon of ex-President Nixon, in connection with the growing evidence that Nixon had directed a White House campaign to thwart the investigation of the Watergate break-in of Democratic party headquarters during the campaign of 1972. Whether Nixon (or any other President) could issue a pardon for himself on criminal charges remains an undecided question.

The President appoints a wide variety of civil and military officers with the consent of the Senate. Congress may, and has, provided for appointment of most officials by other means, especially civil service "merit" principles. Oddly, the Constitution does not provide for removal of officials, except for impeachment. This oversight has caused conflict, with the President arguing for an unlimited power of removal, and Congress claiming a role.

The Court has carved out a middle course on this issue. It rejected Congress' effort to require Senate consent to removal of "executive" officers originally confirmed by them [MYERS V. U.S. (1926)]. Subsequently, the Court has held that Congress may limit presidential removal power for "quasi-legislative" or "quasi-judicial" officials such as members of the Independent Regulatory Commissions [HUMPHREY'S EXECUTOR V. U.S. (1935)]. If no grounds are specified in the authorizing statute, the President may not remove such a "quasi-judicial" official at all. Removal may not occur at any level because of partisan affiliation, though a stratum of office-holders may be replaced to assure policy compatibility, a semantic but legally significant difference [*Elrod* v. *Burns* (1976)].

The Expansiveness of Roles

As important as these specific powers are on specific occasions, most tend to be secondary to the President's other more broadly or vaguely defined constitutional powers and roles. These include (1) power over the military by virtue of the role as Commander-in-Chief; (2) power over foreign affairs, which derives more by implication than from the plain words of the Constitution; (3) the role of Chief Executive, which involves direction and at least nominal control over much of the bureaucracy; and (4) the claim and expectation that the President can act in emergencies.

The Commander-in-Chief in War and Peace

The power of Commander-in-Chief of the armed forces was interpreted by George Washington as requiring him to don a uniform and actively direct troops, but later tradition sees it more as a civilian power of immense influence. The assertion of presidential authority to conduct "police-actions" in Korea and Vietnam brought to the fore Congress' own claims to peace making and authority over the armed forces. By and large, the courts did not intervene. The War Powers Act has yet to be fully tested by events, but the executive power does not appear much hemmed in by it.

Even more significant are presidential claims to domestic civilian authority as a result of war powers and the observable fact that the conduct of war increasingly encompasses more and more of everyday life. Decisions to intern civilian Japanese on the West Coast and to maintain martial law in Hawaii indefinitely were reviewed by the courts and mostly sustained during World War II. President Roosevelt's startling veto message to Congress on a tax bill during the war, asserting that if Congress did not provide an adequate excess profits tax he would put one into effect on his own authority, was never put to the test. Congress went along, but Roosevelt's claimed power over taxation is perhaps the most extreme ever asserted by a President.

At least two similar presidential efforts have been repudiated by the courts. President Truman sought to seize the steel industry to maintain production and avert a strike. Because Congress had prescribed methods of dealing with the matter, the Court ruled Truman could not claim exigent emergency. It is, perhaps, even more significant that the majority of justices conceded that, in the absence of legislation, the President did have emergency powers, however derived.

President Nixon's odd legal advisors continued to insist on his domestic authority to ignore explicit prohibitions and even to violate "search and seizure" provisions of the Constitution. This "doctrine" was never seriously presented by his lawyers to courts. It has no real basis in law and is a caricature of a pragmatic and constitutional argument of great subtlety and difficulty, one to which we shall return.

The President and Foreign Affairs

The President's authority over foreign relations is only indirectly referred to in the Constitution. The Commander-in-Chief, of course, influences foreign policy in a basic way, since military commitments play so prominent a role in international relations. The Constitution also gives to the President the authority to receive ambassadors and ministers and to appoint our representatives abroad. The courts continue to interpret this to give to the President unreviewable discretion to recognize foreign governments. The constitutional text, separation of powers, functional disability of courts, executive special competence, and the need for one decisive answer combined to make this authority the quintessential "political question."

The President is also authorized to negotiate treaties with foreign governments "with the advice and consent of the Senate." George Washington tried to confer with the Senate on a treaty, but that body feared they would be manipulated by a President actually sitting with them and deliberately left the President cooling his heels in an antechamber. Finally, Washington stalked off, muttering that he "would be damned if he would be found in that place again," according to the dairy of Senator McClay. At any rate, that ended any notion of using the Senate as a treaty-formulating, as opposed to a treaty-ratifying, body.

Other presidents have found the requirement of two-thirds approval by the Senate too exacting. The Senate may also offer reservations or amendments, which then must be renegotiated with the foreign governments. Between 1945 and 1971, over 25 percent of all treaties submitted to the Senate were either amended or bogged down entirely. As a result, Presidents enter into agreements with foreign countries that are not sent to the Senate for confirmation. The vast majority of such executive agreements — over 90 percent — are authorized by Congress and are not controversial. Still, Presidents may resort to executive agreements to avoid a tough Senate fight. Theodore Roosevelt once simply changed a treaty rejected by the Senate into an agreement. An embarrassed Senate finally approved the treaty after the identical agreement had been in operation for about a year.

Since 1972, the President must by law file with Congress the text of any agreements. Occasionally, as it did in 1973 over an agreement with

Czechoslovakia, Congress may indicate displeasure with some provision or other. In these few instances, the President has renegotiated. The legal situation is murky, but in practice these actions have disarmed critics of such diplomacy. After an extensive hearing in 1975, the Senate chose not to attempt to further limit the President's power.

Treaties are, like the Constitution and Acts of Congress, supreme law of the land; they are "self-executing" and immediately enforceable in the courts (except where expenditures or other Acts of Congress are needed to implement them). As far as domestic law is concerned, treaties are on a par with legislation. In case a law and a treaty conflict, whichever is later in time prevails. In *U.S.* v. *Belmont* (1937), the principle was established that executive agreements are constitutionally equivalent to treaties.

As will be seen in Chapter 3, both treaties and executive agreements may alter the domestic law of the United States and shift the domain of authority from state to nation. For example, the U.S. may enter into an extradition treaty and thereby get the right to arrest and deport a person who had committed no domestic offense. In fact, the President did agree that American companies and the hostages imprisoned in the American embassy in 1980 would not pursue legal claims against the Iranian government.

The public cry against such changes in law and rights by agreement with a foreign power has at various times been strong, particularly with respect to presidential agreements. However, the Court has made clear that such treaties or agreements cannot deprive citizens of constitutional rights. A treaty may not abolish trial by jury (REID v. COVERT). The Iranian Agreement ceded rights to proceed with claims against Iran, but since individuals and companies could pursue claims against the U.S. in our courts, there was no taking of property without just compensation, a Fifth Amendment right. (See *Dames and Moore* v. *Regan*, 1981.)

In a series of lower court cases, the principle seems to have emerged that a provision of a treaty or executive agreement can be set aside if the purpose of the provision is demonstrably not related to foreign affairs. The Supreme Court has not yet dealt with such a case in those terms.

Taking Care that the Laws Are Faithfully Executed

The President's domestic authority is no more clearly defined than in his authority over foreign relations. The only comprehensive provision is the requirement that he "shall take care that the laws be faithfully executed." The President's authority over subordinates is implied from the right to appoint them and from the right to obtain the opinion in writing of "the principal officer in each of the executive departments."

The executing of the statutes of the United States constitutes a broad mandate. There are myriad statutes. And the courts have been generous in their interpretation of how much leeway a President has in exercising this function.

Two examples will suffice. In IN RE NEAGLE (1890), the Supreme Court held a President could assign a U.S. marshall to defend a federal judge and that a killing caused by that marshall in line of duty was authorized. No statute specifically permitted such an assignment. Again, in *In re Debs* (1895), President Grover Cleveland's use of federal military to break the Pullman strike was sustained on the theory that the continued operation of railroads was needed to deliver the U.S. mail.

Still, as we have seen, the President's use of statutes to justify action is not unlimited, particularly when the action is not in accord with some statutory provisions [YOUNGSTOWN SHEET AND TUBE V. SAWYER (1952)]. Theodore Roosevelt argued that he could do anything not forbidden by the Constitution or laws. His successor, William Howard Taft, argued that the President could do only what was authorized by the Constitution or laws. It is clear that the Presidency has outgrown the Taft approach, if indeed it was ever appropriate. To date, the Court has neither accepted nor repudiated the Roosevelt claim.

War, Police Actions, and Constitutional Theory

John Locke, the British theorist whose work so profoundly influenced the American Revolution and Constitution, wrote of the "separation of powers" as four branches of government. Besides normal executive functions, he suggested, there was a "federative power," referring to the executive coping with dire emergencies and issues of life and death for the society as a whole. The shadow of that notion haunts the Presidency even today.

Emergencies aggrandize executive power because executives are continuously there, organized for decision, ready to move into action. Legislatures usually shrink from quick decisions, partly because they are so poorly structured to deal with them. Perhaps because the U.S. in this century has careened from emergency to emergency, presidential power has grown steadily,

although in between emergencies, the Court and Congress struggle to regain their hold on the executive.

The vague contours of presidential power invite and permit broad, bold assertions to bolster the few defined islands of authority. As we have seen, the actual allocation of presidential power by the Constitution is meager and lacks coherence. As Justice Jackson characterized it, presidential power surprises by the "poverty of really useful and unambiguous authority, applicable to concrete problems of executive problems of executive power as they actually present themselves." This paucity of "unambiguous power" has impelled theorists of the Presidency to resort to grandiose theories—hence the emphasis on popular support and claims that the President represents mass thought more faithfully than legislators, who are tuned to local—not national—interests. Lincoln argued, however, that once any immediate emergency was over, a President who acted beyond his authority had an obligation to justify the actions before normal political processes. So he sought authorization from Congress, after the fact, for raising armies and other actions in the early days of the Civil War and faced a free election even while hostilities raged.

Such assertions of a non-Constitutional nature are paralleled by those who believe that courts should permit any and all violations by the President during emergencies, and punish or judge possible violations only when it is clear the war or other emergency is successfully dealt with. This modern-day translation of the Roman maxim that "the laws are silent while arms clash" was hinted at by Justice Jackson in the Japanese exclusion cases and embraced by the leading constitutional student of emergency power, Clinton Rossiter, in his book with the intentionally oxymoronic title *Constitutional Dictatorship*.

There is a somewhat fanciful theory of federal authority in foreign affairs, which would almost completely remove it from the realm of review by courts, known as the Sutherland theory. The Presidency, of course, would be the chief beneficiary of such an approach. Sutherland, while a Senator and not yet a justice of the Supreme Court, argued that at the time of the American Revolution the individual colonies exercised domestic authority individually and could transfer or delegate it piecemeal. However, foreign and military authority was the prerogative first of the British Crown, then of the Continental Congress, and then, through a direct line of transfer, of the new constitutional government. The states never had foreign or military authority, so it was national and basically unbounded. In this view, neither the federal government nor its chief agent is much hampered by the Constitution; the President has essentially the foreign policy authority of an eighteenth-century king. Sutherland largely sold this argument to the Court in U.S. v. CURTISS-WRIGHT (1936). The Court upheld executive power when the President embargoed shipment of munitions to a South American country in a revolutionary situation. Some of the sweeping language of Holmes' decision in MISSOURI V. HOLLAND (1920) is also related to this theory. (See below, Chapter 3.)

The Supreme Court has avoided extreme emergency theories. The nebulousness of presidential power, particularly the war power, generally has allowed pragmatic sustaining of unusual actions without a clear basis for the approval. Congress, generally, also has passed legislation enabling the President to cope with unanticipated events in its name. And, as the Court has observed, when presidential discretion is linked with congressional authority to deal with urgent matters, national power is at maximum.

The Court has been wise to avoid strong assertions of extraordinary power. The justices have needlessly caused difficulties by using patriotic rhetoric to broadly defend minor constitutional decisions when adequate and limited constitutional grounds were present.

Marshall recognized differences in the sweep of Congress' power over commerce with foreign countries, as against commerce among the several states, even as he argued that the latter authority, where it existed, was "complete in itself." In short, there are functional differences and practical limits that must be recognized in dealing with these matters. The Constitution recognizes this explicitly in its repeated prohibition against states' engaging in foreign relations. The Court could have consistently based limited differences between domestic and foreign authority on the document itself.

The limited and backhanded recognition of emergency power that can be teased from the multiple opinions in YOUNGSTOWN SHEET AND TUBE V. SAWYER is, in contrast, a Court success. At the time, the justices' inability to join in a coherent statement was, quite simply, embarrassing. But in a case that denied a specific presidential claim to emergencies, the justices spelled out the need for a limited class of special broad authority. For vague and unpredictable contingencies, Justice Jackson's concurring opinion has emerged, as the majority opinion suggests in *Dames and Moore* v. *Regan,* as the source that "brings together as much combination of analysis and common sense as there is in this area."

The rejection of a "plenary and exclusive" emergency power of the Presidency in YOUNGS-TOWN, and its weak endorsement of a highly lim-ited and contingent emergency power based in part on congressional ability to constrain itself, has been amply vindicated. As the administrations of Lyndon Johnson and Richard Nixon demonstrated, presidents can concoct extreme theories of their own power without much encouragement from the Courts we rely on to contain just that kind of grandiosity.

President and Congress and Emergency Power: Constitutional Law

The context of presidential expansive-ness is emergency. War and depression result in expansion of congressional authority, but even more of the Presidency. To be sure, as Richard Pious emphasizes, the tide recedes after the emergency, but the high-water mark is easily reached and surpassed.

From the beginning of the Republic, presidential action was prominent. In domestic interventions [the Whiskey Rebellion, or the disturbances in-volved in *Martin* v. *Mott* (1827) and LUTHER V. BORDEN (1849)], executive use of troops was justified on both constitutional and legislative grounds. Presidents claimed the right to use their military and foreign policy powers in such matters as Jefferson's embargo of supplies to Britain dur-ing the Napoleonic Wars and Madison's decision to attack the Barbary Pirates, which at least claimed to be self-governing nations. But there were also claims of legislative authorization, as well as con-stitutional authority.

Lincoln's claims were more extensive; he even argued at times for the right to violate the Consti-tution in order to save it. As THE PRIZE CASES indi-cate, Lincoln declared an embargo on goods to the rebellious states and then requested Congress to authorize it. He suspended the writ of habeas cor-pus, though the power to do so appears — without specific indication of how — among the powers of Congress. The blurring of military control over civilian populations forms the background for the EX PARTE MILLIGAN case, and indicates how far the Civil War confused constitutional boundaries. Paradoxically, Lincoln insisted on holding a free election under fire, though he also established presidential claims justifying constitutional presi-dential dictatorship during war. (See Clinton Rossiter's justification of such a policy, *Constitu-tional Dictatorship,* which does not contain the re-markable aphorism that appeared in the original Ph.D. dissertation: "No price is too great to pay for democracy, even democracy itself.")

Smaller situations solidified some of the Lincoln view of the Presidency as responsible chiefly to the people. IN RE NEAGLE, where the President, without Congressional authorization, assigned a bodyguard to a justice who received threats to his life, illustrates the many small-scale, fast-breaking events where presidential discretion seems imperative — even if, as in this case, the interven-tion had unpredictably tragic consequences.

Foreign relations of less-than-earth-shaking dimensions still may require adjustments. Su-preme Court cases involving less dramatic fact situations have produced greater cohesion of views than some of the more extreme crises, such as the Steel Seizure Act, and therefore have sometimes had more impact. Two such cases were MISSOURI V. HOLLAND (1920) and U.S. v. CURTISS-WRIGHT (1936), where the strong nationalist expressions of their authors — respectively, Justices Holmes and Sutherland — have made these leading cases in the understanding of national and executive power in foreign policy matters.

In MISSOURI V. HOLLAND, at stake was an agreement between the U.S. and Canada to control and protect migratory birds. While Holmes' suggestion that this involved a national interest of "very nearly the first magnitude" seemed hyperbole even in those quiet years, a national agreement was clearly an appropriate mode for dealing with the problem. Holmes' language strayed beyond the needs of the case, however, in suggesting treaties might not need to conform to the Constitution.

The problem of when state control could be superseded by international agreement was rendered even more controversial when President Franklin Roosevelt reached an agreement to, at long last, recognize the Soviet Union and, in what was known as the Litvinov Assignment, agreed to transfer frozen Czarist bank assets to the USSR. The Superintendent of Banks in New York challenged the agreement, which was upheld in *U.S. v. Pink* (1942) and *U.S. v. Belmont* (1937), under reasoning similar to that in MISSOURI V. HOLLAND.

More recently, the President's power to settle claims involving foreign governments was tested via negotiations with the Khomeni regime to release American hostages held in the Iranian embassy by irregular means. The very complex financial agreements, which involved international transfers and a special tribunal to hear claims, also had the effect of limiting or preventing legal claims by U.S. citizens against Iran. With only Justice Powell dissenting in part, the Court overwhelmingly upheld the agreement, noting that congressional legislation through the years has recognized that such settlements are, as Louis Henkin writes, "established international practice reflecting traditional international relations theory." However, all three opinions noted the government's admission that claimants could now sue the

U.S. government for losses incurred in the Court of Claims [*Dames and Moore v. Regan* (1981)].

U.S. V. CURTISS-WRIGHT involved a presidential embargo to combatants in a South American dispute. Since a specific congressional authorization was enacted prior to the embargo, Sutherland's strong endorsement of a broad scope for foreign policy, far beyond domestic policy, is generous, but his arguably stronger endorsement of executive prerogative and inherent powers emerges as even gratuitous. But the case is basic.

During World War II, military necessity was invoked for extraordinary measures, especially with respect to citizens of Japanese descent. These measures were sustained during the early phases of the war, in KOREMATSU V. U.S. (1944) and *Hirabayashi v. U.S.* (1943), but were whittled down as the war progressed favorably or when heard subsequently. In *Duncan v. Kahanamoku* (1946), the invocation of martial law in Hawaii was found to have violated the MILLIGAN "open courts" rule.

In domestic affairs, Congress authorized rationing and price controls as war measures. These were upheld in such cases as *Bowles v. Willingham* (1944) and YAKUS V. U.S. (1944).

The YOUNGSTOWN STEEL case is a landmark, for both expansion and limitation of the executive. In declaring President Truman's seizure of the steel mills unconstitutional, in spite of the exigent fact of the Korean "police action," the Court clearly reaffirmed the reviewability of executive actions, even while the guns were shooting. Still, the three dissenters were not the only claimants that the executive had emergency power. Reading the many opinions individually shows a first judicial acknowledgment of this power. Especially influential was Justice Jackson's clarifying divisions of executive power, indicating it is at its maximum when yoked to congressional power, and at its minimum in opposition.

President Johnson employed this notion to his advantage. On the occasion of a now-disputed attack upon a U.S. ship by Vietnamese, he secured the famous Gulf of Tonkin Resolution from

Congress. He then treated the Resolution as something approximating a declaration of war, citing congressional approval as augmenting the President's, as he escalated our commitment in Vietnam.

However, it was during the Nixon administration that these claims of foreign and domestic presidential emergency power were largely litigated. The Supreme Court refused to rule upon external and military prerogatives of the President, suggesting Congress should act to limit alleged excesses. In domestic affairs, in U.S. v. U.S. DISTRICT COURT (1972), efforts to justify surveillance in a manner contrary to legislation was invalidated, and in NEW YORK TIMES V. U.S. (1971) an asserted power of the executive to prevent newspapers from printing leaked "secret" documents was found to be baseless.

Perhaps more important was the congressional reaction to this pattern of executive overreaching. The War Powers Act was analogous to the congressional effort on impoundment or the requirement that the President file executive agreements with Congress, thus permitting their repudiation. Like those measures, it allows Presidential initiative, but it also distinctly requires congressional approval if the "emergency" intervention persists longer than sixty days.

The war power is a shared power. Only Congress has the power to declare war, and it seems logical that Congress also has the power to declare peace. The War Powers Act builds on this by requiring the President to report the use of forces in conflict situations and Congress to act in approval or disapproval within sixty days. The Act has been interpreted restrictively by the White House, which decided, for example, that the commitment of Marines in Lebanon was not covered by its provisions. Congressional courage has so far not been much in evidence. But the pace of international affairs continually pushes the Congress into new potential confrontations with the President and demands that it employ its constitutional and legislative weapons.

The Nicaraguan situation stimulated the battle between executive and legislative power, for a Democratic Congress long was skeptical of the Reagan commitment to the Contras. Not only did Congress regularly refuse most appropriations for military aid, it also passed the Boland Amendment forbidding use of executive discretionary funds and personnel to aid the Contras. To circumvent this congressional cutting off of support, efforts were made to raise funds through private solicitation and from foreign governments, as well as via Colonel Oliver North's Iran arms deal. The conviction of Oliver North and indictment of his associates will in part test the ability of Congress to constrain executive discretion in foreign affairs.

On the whole, the Presidency continues to dominate the process. No President has fully complied with the process specified in the War Powers Act, arguing that even its limits on sole discretion of the executive to ninety days constitutes a serious handicap to foreign policy. Congress, in turn, snipes at specific details, finding it difficult to challenge a policy effectively and, especially, to agree on an alternative program.

Summary

The national governmental structure originally thought of as a legislatively based system is much more complex. In times of crisis the executive power is allowed to grow, becoming continually expansive in an era of crisis.

The Supreme Court has tried to evolve notions of legal control and constitutional order in such matters. It has made many decisions hemming in the executive, particularly on the basis of congressional action. By invoking such a partnership, the judicial and legislative branches can check the Presidency, much as the same sort of check develops from other combinations of the separate branches of government.

Congress does not have an easy time of it either. To maintain general power it has tried to evolve flexible methods of delegating day-to-day management to the executive while maximizing capability to assert its responsibility. Some of these methods appear of doubtful constitutional legality. To date, however, it has coped reasonably well with the problems of continuing budgetary power, sharing responsibility on appointment and removal, and informing the public about social problems.

Cases

McCulloch v. Maryland

4 Wheat. 316 (1819)
Vote: Unanimous

The National Bank established by Congress was a major political issue of early American politics. Maryland attempted to tax the Bank at prohibitive rates. In Court, the position of Maryland was that the National Bank was improper and, in any event, states could tax federal instrumentalities — an issue of recurring note, as we shall explore in Chapter 3. In this regard, Marshall's formulation of the legislative power in the Constitution is classic. Congress, he said, is not free to legislate on any subject, but it is not rigidly bound by the Constitution, which is flexible on its face.

This case was recognized as basic from its promulgation. It was attacked by leading Jeffersonian legalists, including Judge Spencer Roane of the Virginia Supreme Court, writing under the pseudonym "Hamden." Marshall replied as "A friend of the Constitution." (Today, this would be regarded as improper, but it was standard practice at the time.) The material is assembled by Gerald Gunther as *John Marshall's Defense of McCulloch v. Maryland* (Stanford, Calif.: Stanford University Press, 1969). The critique also involves an attack on the device of a Court opinion, as opposed to individual expression by the judges, and Marshall's defense of the device.

MARSHALL, CH. J., delivered the opinion of the court:

In the case now to be determined, the defendant, a sovereign state, denies the obligation of a law enacted by the legislature of the Union, and the plaintiff, on his part, contests the validity of an act which has been passed by the legislature of that state. . . .

The first question made in the cause is, has Congress power to incorporate a bank?

In discussing this question, the counsel for the state of Maryland have deemed it of some importance, in the construction of the constitution, to consider that instrument not as emanating from the people, but as the act of sovereign and independent states. The powers of the general government, it has beem said, are delegated by the states, who alone are <u>truly sovereign;</u> and must be exercised in subordination to the states, who alone possess supreme domination.

It would be difficult to sustain this proposition. The convention which framed the constitution was indeed elected by the state legislatures. But the instrument, when it came from their hands, was a mere proposal, without obligation, or pretensions to it. It was reported to the then existing Congress of the United States, with a request that it might "be submitted to a convention of delegates, chosen in each state by the people thereof, under the recommendation of its legislature, for their assent and ratification." This mode of proceeding was adopted; and by the convention, by Congress, and by the state legislatures, the instrument was submitted to the people. They acted upon it in the only manner in which they can act safely, effectively, and wisely, on such a subject, by assembling in a convention. It is true, they assembled in their several states — and where else should they have assembled? No political dreamer was ever wild enough to think of breaking down the lines which separate the states, and of compounding the American people into one common mass. Of consequence, when they act, they act in their states. But the measures they adopt do not, on that account, cease to be the measure of the people themselves, or become the measures of the state governments.

The government of the Union, then (whatever may be the influence of this fact in the case), is emphatically, and truly, a government of the people. In form and in substance it emanates from them. Its powers are granted by them, and are to be exercised directly on them, and for their benefit.

This government is acknowledged by all to be one of enumerated powers. The principle, that it can exercise only the powers granted to it, would seem too apparent to have required to be enforced by all those arguments which its enlightened friends, while it was depending before the people, found it necessary to urge. That principle is now universally admitted. But the question respecting the extent of the powers actually granted, is perpetually arising, and will probably continue to arise, as long as our system shall exist.

In discussing these questions, the conflicting powers of the general and state governments must be brought into view, and the supremacy of their respective laws, when they are in opposition, must be settled.

If any one proposition could command the universal assent of mankind, we might expect it would be this — that the government of the Union, though limited in its powers, is supreme within its sphere of action. This would seem to result necessarily from its nature. It is the government of all; its powers are delegated by all; it represents all, and acts for all. Though any one state may be willing to control its operations, no state is willing to allow others to control them. The nation, on those subjects on which it can act, must necessarily bind its component parts. But this question is not left to mere reason; the people have, in express terms, decided it by saying, "this constitution, and the laws of the United States, which shall be made in pursuance thereof," "shall be the supreme law of the land," and by requiring that the members of the state legislatures, and the offi-

cers of the executive and judicial departments of the states shall take the oath of fidelity to it.

The government of the United States, then, though limited in its powers, is supreme; and its laws, when made in pursuance of the constitution, form the supreme law of the land, "anything in the constitution or laws of any state to the contrary notwithstanding."

Among the enumerated powers, we do not find that of establishing a bank or creating a corporation. But there is no phrase in the instrument which, like the articles of confederation, excludes incidental or implied powers; and which requires that everything granted shall be expressly and minutely described. Even the 10th amendment, which was framed for the purpose of quieting the excessive jealousies which had been excited, omits the word "expressly," and declares only that the powers "not delegated to the United States, nor prohibited to the states, are reserved to the states or to the people;" thus leaving the question, whether the particular power which may become the subject of contest has been delegated to the one government, or prohibited to the other, to depend on a fair construction of the whole instrument.

. . . In considering this question, then, we must never forget that it is a constitution we are expounding.

Although, among the enumerated powers of government, we do not find the word "bank" or "incorporation," we find the great powers to lay and collect taxes; to borrow money; to regulate commerce; to declare and conduct a war; and to raise and support armies and navies. The sword and purse, all the external relations, and no inconsiderable portion of the industry of the nation, are entrusted to its government. . . .

But the constitution of the United States has not left the right of Congress to employ the necessary means for the execution of the powers conferred on the government to general reasoning. To its enumeration of powers is added that of making "all laws which shall be necessary and proper, for carrying into execution the foregoing powers, and all other powers vested by this constitution, in the government of the United States, or in any department thereof."

The counsel for the State of Maryland have urged various arguments, to prove that this clause, though in terms a grant of power, is not so in effect; but is really restrictive of the general right, which might otherwise be implied, of selecting means for executing the enumerated powers.

But the argument on which most reliance is placed, is drawn from the peculiar language of this clause. Congress is not empowered by it to make all laws, which may have relation to the powers conferred on the government, but such only as may be "necessary and proper" for carrying them into execution. The word "necessary" is considered as controlling the whole sentence, and as limiting the right to pass laws for the execution of the granted powers, to such as are indispensable, and without which the power would be nugatory. That it excludes the choice of means, and leaves to Congress, in each case, that only which is most direct and simple.

Is it true that this is the sense in which the word "necessary" is always used? Does it always import an absolute physical necessity, so strong that one thing, to which another may be termed necessary, cannot exist without that other? We think it does not. If reference be had to its use, in the common affairs of the world, or in approved authors, we find that it frequently imports no more than that one thing is convenient, or useful, or essential to another. To employ the means necessary to an end, is generally understood as employing any means calculated to produce the end, and not as being confined to those single means, without which the end would be entirely unattainable. Such is the character of human language, that no word conveys to the mind, in all situations, one single definite idea; and nothing is more common than to use words in a figurative sense. Almost all compositions contain words, which, taken in their rigorous sense, would convey a meaning different from that which is obviously intended. It is essential to just construction, that many words which import something excessive should be understood in a more mitigated sense — in that sense which common usage justifies. The word "necessary" is of this description. It has not a fixed character peculiar to itself. It admits of all degrees of comparison; and is often connected with other words, which increase or diminish the impression the mind receives of the urgency it imports. A thing may be necessary, very necessary, absolutely or indispensably necessary. This provision is made in a constitution intended to endure for ages to come, and, consequently, to be adapted to the various crises of human affairs. To have prescribed the means by which government should, in all future time, execute its powers, would have been to change, entirely, the character of the instrument, and give it the properties of a legal code. It would have been an unwise attempt to provide, by immutable rules, for exigencies which, if foreseen at all, must have been seen dimly, and which can be best provided for as they occur. To have declared that the best means shall not be used, but those alone without which the power given would be nugatory, would have been to deprive the legislature of the capacity to avail itself of experience, to exercise its reason, and to accommodate its legislation to circumstances. If we apply this principle of construction to any of the powers of the government, we shall find it so pernicious in its operation that we shall be compelled to discard it.

Take, for example, the power "to establish post-offices and post-roads." This power is executed by the single act of making the establishment. But, from this has been inferred the power and duty of carrying the mail along the post-road, from one post-office to another. And, from this implied power, has again been inferred the right to punish those who steal letters from the post-office, or rob the mail. It may be said, with some plausibility, that the right to carry the mail, and to punish those who rob it, is not indispensably necessary to the establishment of a post-office and post-road. This right is indeed essential to the beneficial exercise of the power, but not indispensably necessary to its existence.

In ascertaining the sense in which the word "necessary" is used in this clause of the constitution, we may derive some aid from that with which it is associated. Congress shall have the power "to make all laws which shall be necessary and proper to carry into execution" the powers of the government. If the word "necessary" was used in that strict and rigorous sense for which the counsel of the state of Maryland contend, it would be an extraordinary departure from the usual course of the human mind, as exhibited in compositon, to add a word, the only possible effect of which is to qualify that strict and rigorous meaning. . . . This clause, as contrued by the state of Maryland, would abridge, and almost annihilate this useful and necessary right of the legislature to select its means. That this could not be intended, is, we should think, had it not been already controverted, too apparent for controversy. We think so for the following reasons:

1st. The clause is placed among the powers of Congress, not among the limitations on those powers.

2d. Its terms purport to enlarge, not to diminish the powers vested in the government. It purports to be an additional power, not a restriction on those already granted. No reason has been, or can be assigned for thus concealing an intention to narrow the discretion of the national legislature under words which purport to enlarge it. . . . Let the end be legitimate, let it be within the scope of the constitution, and all means which are appropriate, which are plainly adopted to that end, which are not prohibited, but consist with the letter and spirit of the constitution, are constitutional.

It being the opinion of the court that the act incorporating the bank is constitutional, and that the power of establishing a branch in the state of Maryland might be properly exercised by the bank itself, we proceed to inquire:

2. Whether the state of Maryland may, without violating the constitution, tax that branch?

That the power of taxation is one of vital importance; that it is retained by the states; that it is not abridged by the grant of a similar power to the government of the Union; that it is to be concurrently exercised by the two governments; are truths which have never been denied. But, such is the paramount character of the constitution that its capacity to withdraw any subject from the action of even this power, is admitted. . . .

On this ground the counsel for the bank place its claim to be exempted from the power of a state to tax its operations. There is no express provision for the case, but the claim has been sustained on a principle which so entirely pervades the constitution, is so intermixed with the materials which compose it, so interwoven with its web, so blended with its texture, as to be incapable of being separated from it without rendering it into shreds.

This great principle is, that the constitution and the laws made in pursuance thereof are supreme; that they control the constitution and laws of the respective states, and cannot be controlled by them. From this, which may be almost termed an axiom, other propositions are deduced as corollaries, on the truth or error of which, and on their application to this case the cause has been supposed to depend. These are, 1st. that a power to create implies a power to preserve. 2d. That a power to destroy, if wielded by a different hand, is hostile to, and incompatible with these powers to create and to preserve. 3d. That where this repugnancy exists, that authority which is supreme must control, not yield to that over which it is supreme.

The sovereignty of a state extends to everything which exists by its own authority, or is introduced by its permission; but does it extend to those means which are employed by Congress to carry into execution—powers conferred on that body by the people of the United States? We think it demonstrable that it does not. Those powers are not given by the people of a single state. They are given by the people of the United States, to a government whose laws, made in pursuance of the constitution, are declared to be supreme. Consequently, the people of a single state cannot confer a sovereignty which will extend over them.

That the power to tax involves the power to destroy; that the power to destroy may defeat and render useless the power to create; that there is a plain repugnance, in conferring on one government a power to control the constitutional measures of another, which other, with respect to those very measures, is declared to be supreme over that which exerts the control, are propositions not to be denied. But all inconsistencies are to be reconciled by the magic of the word confidence. Taxation, it is said, does not necessarily and unavoidably destroy. To carry it to the excess of destruction would be an abuse, to presume which, would banish that confidence which is essential to all government.

But is this a case of confidence? Would the people of any one state trust those of another with a power to control the most insignificant operations of their state government? We know they would not. Why, then, should we suppose that the people of any one state should be willing to trust those of another with a power to control the operations of a government to which they have confided the most important and most valuable interests? In the legislature of the Union alone, are all represented. The legislature of the Union alone, therefore, can be trusted by the people with the power of controlling measures which concern all, in the confidence that it will not be abused. This, then, is not a case of confidence, and we must consider it as it really is.

If the states may tax one instrument, employed by the government in the execution of its powers, they may tax any and every other instrument. They may tax the mail; they may tax the mint; they may tax patent-rights; they may tax the papers of the customhouse; they may tax judicial process; they may tax all the means employed by the government, to an excess which would defeat all the ends of government. This was not intended by the American people. This did not design to make their government dependent on the states.

Gentlemen say they do not claim the right to extend state taxation to these objects. They limit their pretensions to property. But on what principle is this distinction made? Those who make it have furnished no reason for it, and the principle for which they contend denies it. They contend that the power of taxation has no other limit than is found in the

10th section of the 1st article of the constitution; that, with respect to everything else, the power of the states is supreme, and admits of no control. If this be true, the distinction between property and other subjects to which the power of taxation is applicable, is merely arbitrary, and can never be sustained. This is not all. If the controlling power of the states be established; if their supremacy as to taxation be acknowledged; what is to restrain their exercising this control in any shape they may please to give it? Their sovereignty is not confined to taxation. That is not the only mode in which it might be displayed. The question is, in truth, a question of supremacy; and if the right of the states to tax the means employed by the general government be coceded, the declaration that the constitution, and the laws made in pursuance thereof, shall be the supreme law of the land, is empty and unmeaning declamation.

It has also been insisted, that, as the power of taxation in the general and state governments is acknowledged to be concurrent, every argument which would sustain the right of the general government to tax banks chartered by the states, will equally sustain the right of the states to tax banks chartered by the general government.

But the two cases are not on the same reason. The people of all the states have created the general government, and have conferred upon it the general power of taxation. The people of all the states, and the states themselves, are represented in Congress, and, by their representatives, exercise this power. When they tax the chartered institutions of the states, they tax their constituents; and these taxes must be uniform. But, when a state taxes the operations of the government of the United States, it acts upon institutions created, not by their own constituents, but by the people over whom they claim no control. It acts upon the measures of a government created by others as well as themselves, for the benefit of others in common with themselves. The difference is that which always exists, and always must exist, between the action of the whole on a part, and the action of a part on the whole — between the laws of a government declared to be supreme, and those of a government which, when in opposition to those laws, is not supreme.

But if the full application of this argument could be admitted, it might bring into question the right of Congress to tax the state banks, and could not prove the right of the states to tax the Bank of the United States.

The court has bestowed on this subject its most deliberate consideration. The result is a conviction that the states have no power, by taxation or otherwise, to retard, impede, burden, or in any manner control the operations of the constitutional laws enacted by Congress to carry into execution the powers vested in the general government. This is, we think, the unavoidable consequence of that supremacy which the constitution has declared.

We are unanimously of opinion that the law passed by the legislature of Maryland, imposing a tax on the Bank of the United States, is unconstitutional and void.

This opinion does not deprive the states of any resources which they originally possessed. It does not extend to a tax paid by the real property of the bank, in common with the other real property within the state, nor to a tax imposed on the interest which the citizens of Maryland may hold in this institution, in common with other property of the same description throughout the state. But this is a tax on the operations of the bank, and is, consequently, a tax on the operation of an instrument of the Union to carry its powers into execution. Such a tax must be unconstitutional.

The Prize Cases

2 Black 635 (1863)
Vote: 5–4

During the early days of the Civil War, Lincoln proceeded unilaterally, declaring the states in rebellion, ordering various military actions, and prescribing punishments and pains for various actions. Among other actions, he announced a blockade of southern ports and authorized seizing of ships doing business with the South. The latter step is at question here. The government argued several somewhat contradictory rationales, namely: (1) the President has an inherent power and duty as Commander-in-Chief to resist military incursions, including Civil War; (2) the Acts of 1795 and 1807 delegated war power from Congress to the President; and (3) the special session of Congress in 1861 cured any problem by *retroactively* authorizing Lincoln's actions. Which theory does the Grier opinion adopt? What precedent, if any, does it create as to the relative authority of the President and Congress in emergencies?

MR. JUSTICE GRIER.

By the Constitution, Congress alone has the power to declare a national or foreign war. It cannot declare war against a State, or any number of States, by virtue of any clause in the Constitution.

If a war be made by invasion of a foreign nation, the President is not only authorized but bound to resist force by force. He does not initiate the war, but is bound to accept the challenge without waiting for any special legislative authority. . . . This greatest of civil wars was not gradually developed by popular commotion, tumultuous assemblies, or local unorganized insurrections. However long may have been its previous conception, it nevertheless sprung forth suddenly from the parent brain, a Minerva in the full panoply of *war.* The President was bound to meet it in the shape it presented itself, without waiting for Congress to baptize it with a name; and no name given to it by him or them could change the fact.

It is not the less a civil war, with belligerent parties in hostile array, because it may be called an "insurrection" by one side, and the insurgents be considered as rebels or traitors. It it not necessary that the independence of the revolted province or State be acknowledged in order to constitute it a party belligerent in a war according to the law of nations. Foreign nations acknowledge it as war by a declaration of neutrality. The condition of neutrality cannot exist unless there be two belligerent parties.

As soon as the news of the attack on Fort Sumter, and the organization of a government by the seceding States, assuming to act as belligerents, could become known in Europe, to wit, on the 13th of May, 1861, the Queen of England issued her proclamation of neutrality, "recognizing hostilities as existing between the Government of the United States of America and *certain States* styling themselves the Confederate States of America." This was immediately followed by similar declarations or silent acquiescence by other nations.

After such an official recognition by the sovereign, a citizen of a foreign State is estopped to deny the existence of a war with all its consequences as regards neutrals. They cannot ask a Court to affect a technical ignorance of the existence of a war, which all the world acknowledges to be the greatest civil war known in the history of the human race, and thus cripple the arm of the Government and paralyze its power by subtle definitions and ingenious sophisms.

Whether the President in fulfilling his duties, as Commander-in-chief, in suppressing an insurrection, has met with such armed hostile resistance, and a civil war of such alarming proportions as will compel him to accord to them the character of belligerents, is a question to be decided *by him,* and this Court must be governed by the decisions and acts of the political department of the Government to which this power was entrusted. "He must determine what degree of force the crisis demands." The proclamation of blockade is itself official and exclusive evidence to the Court that a state of war existed which demanded and authorized a recourse to such a measure, under the circumstances peculiar to the case.

If it were necessary to the technical existence of a war, that it should have a legislative sanction, we find it in almost every act passed at the extraordinary session of the Legislature of 1861, which was wholly employed in enacting laws to enable the Government to prosecute the war with vigor and efficiency. And finally, in 1861, we find Congress "*ex majore cautela*" and in anticipation of such astute objections, passing an act "approving, legalizing, and making valid all the acts, proclamations, and orders of the President, &c., as if they had been *issued and done under the precious express authority* and direction of the Congress of the United States."

Without admitting that such an act was necessary under the circumstances, it is plain that if the President had in any manner assumed powers which it was necessary should have the authority or sanction of Congress, that on the well known principle of law, "*omnis ratihabito retrotrahitur et mandato equiparatur,*" this ratification has operated to perfectly cure the defect.

The objection made to this act of ratification, that it is *expost facto,* and therefore unconstitutional and void, might possibly have some weight on the trial of an indictment in a criminal Court. But precedents from that source cannot be received as authoritative in a tribunal administering public and international law.

On this first question therefore we are of the opinion that the President had a right, *jure belli,* to institute a blockade of ports in possession of the States in rebellion, which neutrals are bound to regard.

We come now to the consideration of the second question. What is included in the term "*enemies' property*"?

The appellants contend that the term "enemy" is properly applicable to those only who are subjects or citizens of a foreign State at war with our own.

They contend, also, that insurrection is the act of individuals and not of a government or sovereignty; that the individuals engaged are subjects of law. That confiscation of their property can be effected only under a municipal law. That by the law of the land such confiscation cannot take place without any conviction of the owner of some offence, and finally that the secession ordinances are nullities and ineffectual to release any citizen from his allegiance to the national Government, and consequently that the Constitution and Laws of the United States are still operative over persons in all the States for punishment as well as protection.

This argument rests on the assumption of two propositions, each of which is without foundation on the established law of nations. It assumes that where a civil war exists, the party belligerent claiming to be sovereign, cannot, for some unknown reasons, exercise the rights of belligerents, although the revolutionary party may. Being sovereign, he can exercise only sovereign rights over the other party. The insurgent may be killed on the battle-field or by the executioner; his property on land may be confiscated under the municipal law; but the commerce on the ocean, which supplies the rebels with means to support the war, cannot be made the subject of capture under the laws of war, because it is *"unconstitutional!!!"* Now, it is a proposition never doubted, that the belligerent party who claims to be sovereign, may exercise both belligerent and sovereign rights (see 4 Cr., 272). Treating the other party as a belligerent and using only the milder modes of coercion which the law of nations has introduced to mitigate the rigors of war, cannot be a subject of complaint by the party to whom it is accorded as a grace or granted as a necessity. We have shown that a civil war such as that now waged between the Northern and Southern States is properly conducted according to the humane regulations of public law as regards capture on the ocean.

Under the very peculiar Constitution of this Government, although the citizens owe supreme allegiance to the Federal Government, they owe also a qualified allegiance to the State in which they are domiciled. Their persons and property are subject to its laws.

Hence, in organizing this rebellion, they have *acted as States* claiming to be sovereign over all persons and property within their respective limits, and asserting a right to absolve their citizens from their allegiance to the Federal Government. Several of these States have combined to form a new confederacy, claiming to be acknowledged by the world as a sovereign State. Their right to do so is now being decided by wager of battle.

MR. JUSTICE NELSON, dissenting.

The truth is, this idea of the existence of any necessity for clothing the President with the war power, under the Act of 1795, is simply a monstrous exaggeration; for, besides having the command of the whole of the army and navy, Congress can be assembled within any thirty days, if the safety of the country requires that the war power shall be brought into operation.

The Acts of 1795 and 1807 did not, and could not under the Constitution, confer on the President the power of declaring war against a State of this Union, or of deciding that war existed, and upon that ground authorize the capture and confiscation of the property of every citizen of the State whenever it was found on the waters. The laws of war, whether the war be civil or *inter gentes,* as we have seen, convert every citizen of the hostile State into a public enemy, and treat him accordingly, whatever may have been his previous conduct. This great power over the business and property of the citizen is reserved to the legislative department by the express words of the Constitution. It cannot be delegated or surrendered to the Executive. Congress alone can determine whether war exists or should be declared; and until they have acted, no citizen of the State can be punished in his person or property, unless he has committed some offence against a law of Congress passed before the act was committed, which made it a crime, and defined the punishment. The penalty of confiscation for the acts of others with which he had no concern cannot lawfully be inflicted.

MR. CHIEF JUSTICE TANEY, MR. JUSTICE CATRON and JUSTICE CLIFFORD, concurred in the dissenting opinion of JUSTICE NELSON.

Youngstown Sheet and Tube v. Sawyer

343 U.S. 579 (1952)
Vote: 6–3; however, every member of the majority filed a concurrence.

During the Korean "police action" (an undeclared war, which was conducted without congressional approval), a labor dispute developed in the steel industry, a crucial basis for armaments and other war-related production. While statutes provided ways in which a strike could be averted, Truman chose to seize the plants and conduct them as government enterprises. He preferred not to invoke the statutes because, as a Democratic President who had received strong labor backing, Truman thought his solution looked less antilabor. It would also assure continued steel production.

The Court was badly split. What answer emerges as to whether the President has emergency power? Are the lines of division on that question the same as the division on the decision of the Court?

MR. JUSTICE BLACK delivered the opinion of the Court.

We are asked to decide whether the President was acting within his constitutional power when he issued an order directing the Secretary of Commerce to take possession of and operate most of the Nation's steel mills.

Obeying the Secretary's orders under protest, the companies brought proceedings against him in the District Court. Their complaints charged that the seizure was not authorized by an act of Congress or by any constitutional provisions. The District Court was asked to declare the orders of the President and the Secretary invalid and to issue preliminary and permanent injunctions restraining their enforcement. Opposing the motion for preliminary injunction, the United States asserted that a strike disrupting steel production for even a brief period would so endanger the well-being and safety of the Nation that the President had "inherent power" to do what he had done — power "supported by the Constitution, by historical precedent, and by court decisions."

II

The President's power, if any, to issue the order must stem either from an act of Congress or from the Constitution itself. There is no statute that expressly authorizes the President to take possession of property as he did here. Nor is there any act of Congress to which our attention has been directed from which such a power can fairly be implied. Indeed, we do not understand the Government to rely on statutory authorization for this seizure. There are two statutes which do authorize the President to take both personal and real property under certain conditions. However, the Government admits that these conditions were not met and that the President's order was not rooted in either of the statutes. The Government refers to the seizure provisions of one of these statutes (§201(b) of the Defense Production Act) as "much too cumbersome, involved, and time-consuming for the crisis which was at hand."

Moreover, the use of the seizure technique to solve labor disputes in order to prevent work stoppages was not only unauthorized by any congressional enactment; prior to this controversy, Congress had refused to adopt that method of settling labor disputes. When the Taft-Hartley Act was under consideration in 1947, Congress rejected an amendment which would have authorized such governmental seizures in cases of emergency. Apparently it was thought that the technique of seizure, like that of compulsory arbitration, would interfere with the process of collective bargaining.

It is clear that if the President had authority to issue the order he did, it must be found in some provision of the Constitution. And it is not claimed that express constitutional language grants this power to the President. The contention is that presidential power should be implied from the aggregate of his powers under the Constitution. Particular reliance is placed on provisions in Article II which say that "The executive Power shall be vested in a President...": that "he shall take Care that the Laws be faithfully executed"; and that he "shall be Commander in Chief of the Army and Navy of the United States."

The order cannot properly be sustained as an exercise of the President's military power as Commander in Chief of the Armed Forces. The Government attempts to do so by citing a number of cases upholding broad powers in military commanders engaged in day-to-day fighting in a theater of war. Such cases need not concern us here. Even though "theater of war" be an expanding concept, we cannot with faithfulness to our constitutional system hold that the Commander in Chief of the Armed Forces has the ultimate power as such to take possession of private property in order to keep labor disputes from stopping production. This is a job for the Nation's lawmakers, not for its military authorities.

Nor can the seizure order be sustained because of the several constitutional provisions that grant executive power to the President. In the framework of our Constitution, the President's power to see that the laws are faithfully executed refutes the idea that he is to be a lawmaker. The Constitution limits his functions in the lawmaking process to the recommending of laws he thinks wise and the vetoing of laws he thinks bad. And the Constitution is neither silent nor equivocal about who shall make laws which the President is to execute. . . .

The President's order does not direct that a congressional policy be executed in a manner prescribed by Congress — it directs that a presidential policy be executed in a manner prescribed by the President. The preamble of the order itself, like that of many statutes, sets out reasons why the President believes certain policies should be adopted, proclaims these policies as rules of conduct to be followed, and again, like a statute, authorizes a government official to promulgate additional rules and regulations consistent with the policy proclaimed and needed to carry that policy into execution. The power of Congress to adopt such public policies as those proclaimed by the order is beyond question. The Constitution does not subject this lawmaking power of Congress to presidential or military supervision or control.

It is said that other Presidents without congressional authority have taken possession of private business enterprises in order to settle labor disputes. But even if this be true, Congress has not thereby lost its exclusive constitutional authority to make laws necessary and proper to carry out the powers vested by the Constitution "in the Government of the United States, or any Department or Officer thereof."

The Founders of this Nation entrusted the lawmaking power to the Congress alone in both good and bad times. It would do no good to recall the historical events, the fears of power and the hopes for freedom that lay behind their choice. Such a review would but confirm our holding that this seizure order cannot stand.

The judgment of the District Court is

Affirmed.

. . . .

MR. JUSTICE FRANKFURTER, concurring.

So-called constitutional questions seem to exercise a mesmeric influence over the popular mind. This eagerness to settle — preferably forever — a specific problem on the basis of the broadest possible constitutional pronouncements may not unfairly be called one of our minor national traits.

The issue before us can be met, and therefore should be, without attempting to define the President's powers comprehensively. I shall not attempt to delineate what belongs to him by virtue of his of-

fice beyond the power even of Congress to contract; what authority belongs to him until Congress acts; what kind of problems may be dealt with either by the Congress or by the President or both, cf. *La Abra Silver Mng. Co.* v. *United States,* 175 U.S. 423; what power must be exercised by the Congress and cannot be delegated to the President. It is as unprofitable to lump together in an undiscriminating hotch-potch past presidential actions claimed to be derived from occupancy of the office, as it is to conjure up hypothetical future cases.

It is one thing to draw an intention of Congress from general language and to say that Congress would have explicitly written what is inferred, where Congress has not addressed itself to a specific situation. It is quite impossible, however, when Congress did specifically address itself to a problem, as Congress did to that of seizure, to find secreted in the interstices of legislation the very grant of power which Congress consciously withheld. To find authority so explicitly withheld is not merely to disregard in a particular instance the clear will of Congress. It is to disrespect the whole legislative process and the constitutional division of authority between President and Congress.

MR. JUSTICE JACKSON, concurring in the judgment and opinion of the Court.

We may well begin by a somewhat over-simplified grouping of practical situations in which a President may doubt, or others may challenge, his powers, and by distinguishing roughly the legal consequences of this factor of relativity.

1. When the President acts pursuant to an express or implied authorization of Congress, his authority is at its maximum, for it includes all that he possesses in his own right plus all that Congress can delegate. In these circumstances, and in these only, may he be said (for what it may be worth) to personify the federal sovereignty. If his act is held unconstitutional under these circumstances, it usually means that the Federal Government as an undivided whole lacks power.

2. When the President acts in absence of either a congressional grant or denial of authority, he can only rely upon his own independent powers, but there is a zone of twilight in which he and Congress may have concurrent authority, or in which its distribution is uncertain. Therefore, congressional inertia, indifference or quiescence may sometimes, at least as a practical matter, enable, if not invite, measures on independent presidential responsibility.

3. When the President takes measures incompatible with the expressed or implied will of Congress, his

power is at its lowest ebb, for then he can rely only upon his own constitutional powers minus any constitutional powers of Congress over the matter. Courts can sustain exclusive presidential control in such a case only by disabling the Congress from acting upon the subject. Presidential claim to a power at once so conclusive and preclusive must be scrutinized with caution, for what is at stake is the equilibrium established by our constitutional system.

. . . .

I do not suppose, and I am not persuaded, that history leaves it open to question, at least in the courts, that the executive branch, like the Federal Government, as a whole, possesses only delegated powers. . . . However, because the President does not enjoy unmentioned powers does not mean that the mentioned ones should be narrowed by a niggardly construction.

MR. JUSTICE CLARK, concurring in the judgment of the Court.

. . . .

I conclude that where Congress has laid down specific procedures to deal with the type of crisis confronting the President, he must follow those procedures in meeting the crisis; but that in the absence of such action by Congress, the President's independent power to act depends upon the gravity of the situation confronting the nation. I cannot sustain the seizure in question because here, as in *Little* v. *Barreme*, Congress had prescribed methods to be followed by the President in meeting the emergency at hand.

. . . .

MR. JUSTICE BURTON, concurring. . . .

MR. JUSTICE DOUGLAS, concurring. . . .

MR. CHIEF JUSTICE VINSON, with whom MR. JUSTICE REED and MR. JUSTICE MINTON join, dissenting.

. . . Cases do arise presenting questions which could not have been foreseen by the Framers. In such cases, the Constitution has been treated as a living document adaptable to new situations. But we are not called upon today to expand the Constitution to meet a new situation. For, in this case, we need only look to history and time-honored principles of constitutional law — principles that have been applied consistently by all branches of the Government throughout our history. It is those who assert the invalidity of the Executive Order who seek to amend the Constitution in this case.

. . . .

A review of executive action demonstrates that our Presidents have on many occasions exhibited the leadership contemplated by the Framers when they made the President Commander in Chief, and imposed upon him the trust to "take Care that the Laws be faithfully executed." With or without explicit statutory authorization, Presidents have at such times dealt with national emergencies by acting promptly and resolutely to enforce legislative programs, at least to save those programs until Congress should act. Congress and the courts have responded to such executive initiative with consistent approval.

McGrain v. Daugherty

273 U.S. 135 (1927)
Vote: 8–0; Stone, Coolidge's Attorney General, did not participate.

Teapot Dome was a major scandal. Its corruption reached into President Harding's Cabinet; the former Attorney General, Harry Daugherty, was among those ultimately convicted. In *Field* v. *Clark* (1892), the Supreme Court had noted that a congressional investigation could not be a substitute for criminal proceedings. In dealing with the Attorney General's brother, Mally Daugherty, the government argued, Congress was ascertaining whether problems of governmental structure — the regulation of the Department of Justice — were involved. Mally Daugherty refused to participate, claiming his conduct was not a matter of public concern.

MR. JUSTICE VAN DEVANTER delivered the opinion of the court.

Harry M. Daugherty became the Attorney General March 5, 1921, and held that office until March 28, 1924, when he resigned. Late in that period various charges of misfeasance and nonfeasance in the Department of Justice after he became its supervising head were brought to the attention of the Senate by individual senators and made the basis of an insistent demand that the department be investigated.

. . . .

In the course of the investigation the committee issued and caused to be duly served on Mally S. Daugherty — who was a brother of Harry M. Daugherty and president of the Midland National Bank of

Washington Court House, Ohio. . . . A little later in the course of the investigation the committee issued and caused to be duly served on the same witness another subpoena commanding him to appear before it for the purpose of giving testimony relating to the subject under consideration. . . . The witness again failed to appear; and no excuse was offered by him for either failure. . . .

. . . After a reading of the report, the Senate adopted a resolution reciting these facts and proceedings as follows:

Resolved, That the President of the Senate pro tempore issue his warrant commanding the Sergeant at Arms or his deputy to take into custody the body of the said M. S. Daugherty wherever found. . . .

. . . [T]he principal questions involved are of unusual importance and delicacy. They are (a) whether the Senate — or the House of Representatives, both being on the same plane in this regard — has power, through its own process, to compel a private individual to appear before it, or one of its committees and give testimony needed to enable it efficiently to exercise a legislative function belonging to it under the Constitution, and (b) whether it sufficiently appears that the process was being employed in this instance to obtain this testimony for that purpose.

The committee was acting for the Senate and under its authorization; and therefore the subpoenas which the committee issued and the witness refused to obey are to be treated as if issued by the Senate. The warrant was issued as an auxiliary process to compel him to give the testimony sought by the subpoenas; and its nature in this respect is not affected by the direction that his testimony be given at the bar of the Senate instead of before his committee. If the Senate deemed it proper, in view of his contumacy, to give that direction it was at liberty to do so. . . .

. . . [T]here is no provision expressly investing either house with power to make investigations and exact testimony to the end that it may exercise its legislative function advisedly and effectively. So the question arises whether this power is so far incidental to the legislative function as to be implied.

In actual legislative practice power to secure needed information by such means has long been treated as an attribute of the power to legislate. It was so regarded in the British Parliament and in the Colonial legislatures before the American Revolution; and a like view has prevailed and been carried into effect in both houses of Congress and in most of the state legislatures.

This power was both asserted and exerted by the House of Representatives in 1792, when it appointed a select committee to inquire into the St. Clair expedition and authorized the committee to send for necessary persons, papers and records.

. . . .

Four decisions of this Court are cited and more or less relied on, and we now turn to them.

The first decision was in *Anderson* v. *Dunn*, 6 Wheat. 204. The question there was whether, under the Constitution, the House of Representatives has power to attach and punish a person other than a member for contempt of its authority — in fact, an attempt to bribe one of its members. The Court regarded the power as essential to the effective exertion of other powers expressly granted, and therefore as implied. . . .

The next decision was in *Kilbourn* v. *Thompson*, 103 U.S. 168. The question there was whether the House of Representatives had exceeded its power in directing one of its committees to make a particular investigation. The decision was that it had. The principles announced and applied in the case are — that neither house of Congress possesses a "general power of making inquiry into the private affairs of the citizen"; that the power actually possessed is limited to inquiries relating to matters of which the particular house "has jurisdiction" and in respect of which it rightfully may take other action; that if the inquiry relates to "a matter wherein relief or redress could be had only by a judicial proceeding" it is not within the range of this power, but must be left to the courts, conformably to the constitutional separation of governmental powers. . . . The Court pointed out that the resolution contained no suggestion of contemplated legislation; that the matter was one in respect to which no valid legislation could be had; that the bankrupts' estate and the trustee's settlement were still pending in the bankruptcy court; and that the United States and other creditors were free to press their claims in that proceeding.

. . . .

Next in order is *In re Chapman*, 166 U.S. 661. The inquiry there in question was conducted under a resolution of the Senate and related to charges, published in the press, that senators were yielding to corrupt influences in considering a tariff bill then before the Senate and were speculating in stocks the value of which would be affected by pending amendments to the bill. Chapman appeared before the committee in response to a subpoena, but refused to answer questions pertinent to the inquiry, and was indicted and convicted under the act of 1857 for his refusal. The Court sustained the constitutional validity of the act of 1857, and, after referring to the constitutional provision empowering either house to punish its members for disorderly behavior and by a vote of two-thirds to expel a member, held that the inquiry related to the integrity and fidelity of senators in the discharge of their duties, and therefore to a matter "within the range of the constitutional powers of the Senate" and in respect of which it could compel witnesses to appear and testify.

The latest case is *Marshall* v. *Gordon,* 243 U.S. 521. The question there was whether the House of Representatives exceeded its power in punishing, as for a contempt of its authority, a person — not a member — who had written, published and sent to the chairman of one of its committees an ill-tempered and irritating letter respecting the action and purposes of the committee. Power to make inquiries and obtain evidence by compulsory process was not involved. The Court recognized distinctly that the House of Representatives has implied power to punish a person not a member for contempt, as was ruled in *Anderson* v. *Dunn, supra,* but held that its action in this instance was without constitutional justification. The decision was put on the ground that the letter, while offensive and vexatious, was not calculated or likely to affect the House in any of its proceedings or in the exercise of any of its functions — in short, that the act which was punished as a contempt was not of such a character as to bring it within the rule that an express power draws after it others which are necessary and appropriate to give effect to it.

While these cases are not decisive of the question we are considering, they definitely settle two propositions which we recognize as entirely sound and having a bearing on its solution: One, that the two houses of Congress, in their separate relations, possess not only such powers as are expressly granted to them by the Constitution, but such auxiliary powers as are necessary and appropriate to make the express powers effective; and, the other, that neither house is invested with "general" power to inquire into private affairs and compel disclosures, but only with such limited power of inquiry as is shown to exist when the rule of constitutional interpretation just stated is rightly applied. . . .

. . . A legislative body cannot legislate wisely or effectively in the absence of information respecting the conditions which the legislation is intended to affect or change; and where the legislative body does not itself possess the requisite information — which not infrequently is true — recourse must be had to others who do possess it. Experience has taught that mere requests for such information often are unavailing, and also that information which is volunteered is not always accurate or complete; so some

means of compulsion are essential to obtain what is needed. All this was true before and when the Constitution was framed and adopted. In that period the power of inquiry — with enforcing process — was regarded and employed as a necessary and appropriate attribute of the power to legislate — indeed, was treated as inhering in it. . . .

The contention is earnestly made on behalf of the witness that this power of inquiry, if sustained, may be abusively and oppressively exerted. If this be so, it affords no ground for denying the power. The same contention might be directed against the power to legislate, and of course would be unavailing.

We come now to the question whether it sufficiently appears that the purpose for which the witness's testimony was sought was to obtain information in aid of the legislative function. The court below answered the question in the negative and put its decision largely on this ground, as is shown by the following excerpts from its opinion:

What the Senate is engaged in doing is not investigating the Attorney General's office; it is investigating the former Attorney General. What it has done is put him on trial before it. In so doing it is exercising the judicial function. This it has no power to do.

We are of opinion that the court's ruling on this question was wrong. . . .

It is quite true that the resolution directing the investigation does not in terms avow that it is intended to be in aid of legislation; but it does show that the subject to be investigated was the administration of the Department of Justice — whether its functions were being properly discharged or were being neglected or misdirected, and particularly whether the Attorney General and his assistants were performing or neglecting their duties in respect of the institution and prosecution of proceedings to punish crimes and enforce appropriate remedies against the wrongdoers — specific instances of alleged neglect being recited. Plainly the subject was one on which legislation could be had and would be materially aided by the information which the investigation was calculated to elicit.

We think the resolution and proceedings give no warrant for thinking the Senate was attempting or intending to try the Attorney General at its bar or before its committee for any crime of wrongdoing. Nor do we think it a valid objection to the investigation that it might possibly disclose crime or wrongdoing on his part.

We conclude that the investigation was ordered for a legitimate object; that the witness wrongfully refused to appear and testify before the committee and was lawfully attached; that the Senate is entitled to have him give testimony pertinent to the inquiry, either at its bar or before the committee; and that the district court erred in discharging him from custody under the attachment.

Final order reversed.

MR. JUSTICE STONE did not participate in the consideration or decision of the case.

Watkins v. U.S.

354 U.S. 178 (1957)
Vote: 6–1; Frankfurter concurring;
Burton and Whittaker not
participating.

Congressional investigations into sensitive areas such as labor unions, universities, and political affiliations have dealt with Communist and other "un-American" views, on a theory of danger to the Republic, which investigations might lead to legislation. In fact no, or insignificant, legislation has resulted. In earlier years the tradition had been that a witness had only the rights granted by the congressional committee, even with respect to such matters as having an attorney for advice in difficult situations. *Watkins* asserts a first broad right of a witness: to be informed of the purpose of the probe and the relevance of the question being asked.

MR. CHIEF JUSTICE WARREN delivered the opinion of the Court.

This is a review by certiorari of a conviction under 2 U.S.C. §192 for "contempt of Congress." The misdemeanor is alleged to have been committed during a hearing before a congressional investigating committee. It is not the case of a truculent or contumacious witness who refuses to answer all questions or who, by boisterous or discourteous conduct, disturbs the decorum of the committee room. Petitioner was prosecuted for refusing to make certain disclosures which he asserted to be beyond the authority of the committee to demand. The controversy thus rests upon fundamental principles of the power of the Congress and the limitations upon that power. We approach the questions presented with conscious awareness of the far-reaching ramifications that can follow from a decision of this nature.

We start with several basic premises on which there is general agreement. The power of the Congress to conduct investigations is inherent in the legislative process. That power is broad. It encompasses inquiries concerning the administration of existing laws as well as proposed or possibly needed statutes. It includes surveys of defects in our social, economic or political system for the purpose of enabling the Congress to remedy them. It comprehends probes into departments of the Federal Government to expose corruption, inefficiency or waste. But, broad as is this power of inquiry, it is not unlimited. There is no general authority to expose the private affairs of individuals without justification in terms of the functions of the Congress. This was freely conceded by the Solicitor General in his argument of this case. Nor is the Congress a law enforcement or trial agency. These are functions of the executive and judicial departments of government. No inquiry is an end in itself; it must be related to, and in furtherance of, a legitimate task of the Congress. Investigations conducted solely for the personal aggrandizement of the investigators or to "punish" those investigated are indefensible.

It is unquestionably the duty of all citizens to cooperate with the Congress in its efforts to obtain the facts needed for intelligent legislative action. It is their unremitting obligation to respond to subpoenas, to respect the dignity of the Congress and its committees and to testify fully with respect to matters within the province of proper investigation. This, of course, assumes that the constitutional rights of witnesses will be respected by the Congress as they are in a court of justice. The Bill of Rights is applicable to investigations as to all forms of governmental action. Witnesses cannot be compelled to give evidence against themselves. They cannot be subjected to unreasonable search and seizure. Nor can the First Amendment freedoms of speech, press, religion or political belief and association be abridged.

There was very little use of the power of compulsory process in early years to enable the Congress to obtain facts pertinent to the enactment of new statutes or the administration of existing laws. The first occasion for such an investigation arose in 1827 when the House of Representatives was considering a revision of the tariff laws. In the Senate, there was no use of a fact-finding investigation in aid of legislation until 1859. In the Legislative Reorganization Act, the Committee on Un-American Activities was the only standing committee of the House of Representatives that was given the power to compel disclosures.

It is not surprising, from the fact that the Houses of Congress so sparingly employed the power to conduct investigations, that there have been few cases requiring judicial review of the power. The Nation was almost one hundred years old before the first case reached this Court to challenge the use of compulsory process as a legislative device, rather than in inquiries concerning the elections or privileges of Congressmen. In *Kilbourn* v. *Thompson,* 103 U.S. 168, decided in 1881, an investigation had been authorized by the House of Representatives to learn the circumstances surrounding the bankruptcy of Jay Cooke & Company, in which the United States had deposited funds. The committee became particularly interested in a private real estate pool that was a part of the financial structure. The Court found that the subject matter of the inquiry was "in its nature clearly judicial and therefore one in respect to which no valid legislation could be enacted." The House has thereby exceeded the limits of its own authority.

Subsequent to the decision in *Kilbourn,* until recent times, there were very few cases dealing with the investigative power. The matter came to the fore again when the Senate undertook to study the corruption in the handling of oil leases in the 1920's. In *McGrain* v. *Daugherty,* 273 U.S. 135, and *Sinclair* v. *United States,* 279 U.S. 263, the Court applied the precepts of *Kilbourn* to uphold the authority of the Congress to conduct the challenged investigations. The Court recognized the danger to effective and honest conduct of the Government if the legislature's power to probe corruption in the executive branch were unduly hampered.

Following these important decisions, there was another lull in judicial review of investigations. The absence of challenge, however, was not indicative of the absence of inquiries. To the contrary, there was vigorous use of the investigative process by a Congress bent upon harnessing and directing the vast economic and social forces of the times. Only one case came before this Court, and the authority of the Congress was affirmed.

In the decade following World War II, there appeared a new kind of congressional inquiry unknown in prior periods of American history. Principally this was the result of the various investigations into the threat of subversion of the United States Government, but other subjects of congressional interest also contributed to the changed scene.

It was during this period that the Fifth Amendment privilege against self-incrimination was frequently invoked and recognized as a legal limit upon the authority of a committee to require that a wit-

ness answer its questions. Some early doubts as to the applicability of that privilege before a legislative committee never matured. When the matter reached this Court, the Government did not challenge in any way that the Fifth Amendment protection was available to the witness, and such a challenge could not have prevailed. It confined its argument to the character of the answers sought and to the adequacy of the claim of privilege.

A far more difficult task evolved from the claim by witnesses that the committees' interrogations were infringements upon the freedoms of the First Amendment. Clearly, an investigation is subject to the command that the Congress shall make no law abridging freedom of speech or press or assembly. . . . The First Amendment may be invoked against infringement of the protected freedoms by law or by lawmaking.

Abuses of the investigative process may imperceptibly lead to abridgement of protected freedoms. The mere summoning of a witness and compelling him to testify, against his will, about his beliefs, expressions or associations is a measure of governmental interference. And when those forced revelations concern matters that are unorthodox, unpopular, or even hateful to the general public, the reaction in the life of the witness may be disastrous. This effect is even more harsh when it is past beliefs, expressions or associations that are disclosed and judged by current standards rather than those contemporary with the matters exposed. Nor does the witness alone suffer the consequences. Those who are identified by witnesses and thereby placed in the same glare of publicity are equally subject to public stigma, scorn and obloquy. Beyond that, there is the more subtle and immeasurable effect upon those who tend to adhere to the most orthodox and uncontroversial views and associations in order to avoid a similar fate at some future time. That this impact is partly the result of non-governmental activity by private persons cannot relieve the investigators of their responsibility for initiating the reaction.

The Court recognized the restraints of the Bill of Rights upon congressional investigations in *United States* v. *Rumely,* 345 U.S. 41. The magnitude and complexity of the problem of applying the First Amendment to that case led the Court to construe narrowly the resolution describing the committee's authority. It was concluded that, when First Amendment rights are threatened, the delegation of power to the committee must be clearly revealed in its charter.

Petitioner has earnestly suggested that the difficult questions of protecting these rights from infringement by legislative inquiries can be surmounted in this case because there was no public purpose served in his interrogation. His conclusion is based upon the thesis that the Subcommittee was engaged in a program of exposure for the sake of exposure. The sole purpose of the inquiry, he contends, was to bring down upon himself and others the violence of public reaction because of their past beliefs, expressions and associations. In support of this argument, petitioner has marshalled an impressive array of evidence that some Congressmen have believed that such was their duty, or part of it.

But a solution to our problem is not to be found in testing the motives of committee members for this purpose. Such is not our function. Their motives alone would not vitiate an investigation which had been instituted by a House of Congress if that assembly's legislative purpose is being served.

Petitioner's contentions do point to a situation of particular significance from the standpoint of the constitutional limitations upon congressional investigations.

An essential premise in this situation is that the House or Senate shall have instructed the committee members on what they are to do with the power delegated to them. It is the responsibility of the Congress, in the first instance, to insure that compulsory process is used only in furtherance of a legislative purpose. That requires that the instructions to an investigating committee spell out that group's jurisdiction and purpose with sufficient particularity. . . .

The authorizing resolution of the Un-American Activities Committee was adopted in 1938. It defines the Committee's authority as follows:

> The Committee on Un-American Activities, as a whole or by subcommittee, is authorized to make from time to time investigations of (1) the extent, character, and objects of un-American propaganda activities in the United States. . . .

It would be difficult to imagine a less explicit authorizing resolution. Who can define a meaning of "un-American"? What is that single, solitary "principle of the form of government as guaranteed by our Constitution"? There is no need to dwell upon the language, however. At one time, perhaps, the resolution might have been read narrowly to confine the Committee to the subject of propaganda. The events that have transpired in the fifteen years before the interrogation of petitioner make such a construction impossible at this date.

. . . .

An excessively broad charter, like that of the House Un-American Activities Committee, places the courts in an untenable position if they are to strike a balance between the public need for a particular interrogation and the right of citizens to carry out their affairs free from unnecessary governmental interference. It is impossible in such a situation to ascertain whether any legislative purpose justifies the disclosures sought and, if so, the importance of that information to the Congress in furtherance of its legislative function. The reason no court can make this critical judgment is that the House of Representatives itself has never made it.

The problem attains proportion when viewed from the standpoint of the witness who appears before a congressional committee. He must decide at the time the questions are propounded whether or not to answer. As the Court said in *Sinclair* v. *United States*, 279 U.S. 263, the witness acts at his peril. He is ". . . bound rightly to construe the statute." *Id.*, at 299. An erroneous determination on his part, even if made in the utmost good faith, does not exculpate him if the court should later rule that the questions were pertinent to the question under inquiry.

It is obvious that a person compelled to make this choice is entitled to have knowledge of the subject to which the interrogation is deemed pertinent. That knowledge must be available with the same degree of explicitness and clarity that the Due Process Clause requires in the expression of any element of a criminal offense. The "vice of vagueness" must be avoided here as in all other crimes. . . . Fundamental fairness demands that no witness be compelled to make such a determination with so little guidance. Unless the subject matter has been made to appear with undisputable clarity, it is the duty of the investigative body, upon objection of the witness on grounds of pertinency, to state for the record the subject under inquiry at the time and the manner in which the propounded questions are pertinent thereto. To be meaningful, the explanation must describe what the topic under inquiry is and the connective reasoning whereby the precise questions asked relate to it.

The statement of the Committee Chairman in this case, in response to petitioner's protest, was woefully inadequate to convey sufficient information as to the pertinency of the questions to the subject under inquiry. Petitioner was thus not accorded a fair opportunity to determine whether he was within his rights in refusing to answer, and his conviction is necessarily invalid under the Due Process Clause of the Fifth Amendment.

We are mindful of the complexities of modern government and the ample scope that must be left to the Congress as the sole constitutional depository of legislative power. Equally mindful are we of the indispensable function, in the exercise of that power, of congressional investigations. The conclusions we have reached in this case will not prevent the Congress, through its committees, from obtaining any information it needs for the proper fulfillment of its role in our scheme of government. The legislature is free to determine the kinds of data that should be collected. It is only those investigations that are conducted by use of compulsory process that give rise to a need to protect the rights of individuals against illegal encroachment. That protection can be readily achieved through procedures which prevent the separation of power from responsibility and which provide the constitutional requisites of fairness for witnesses. A measure of added care on the part of the House and the Senate in authorizing the use of compulsory process and by their committees in exercising that power would suffice. That is a small price to pay if it serves to uphold the principles of limited, constitutional government without constricting the power of the Congress to inform itself.

The judgment of the Court of Appeals is reversed, and the case is remanded to the District Court with instructions to dismiss the indictment.

It is so ordered.

MR. JUSTICE FRANKFURTER, concurring.

... Until 1857, Congress was content to punish for contempt through its own process. By the Act of January 24, 1857, 11 Stat. 155, as amended by the Act of January 24, 1862, 12 Stat 333, Congress provided that, "in addition to the pains and penalties now existing" (referring of course to the power of Congress itself to punish for contempt), "contumacy in a witness called to testify in a matter properly under consideration by either House, and deliberately refusing to answer questions pertinent thereto, shall be a misdemeanor against the United States." *In re Chapman,* 166 U.S. 661, 672. This legislation is now 2 U.S.C. §192. By thus making the federal judiciary the affirmative agency for enforcing the authority that underlies the congressional power to punish for contempt, Congress necessarily brings into play the specific provisions of the Constitution relating to the prosecution of offenses and those implied restrictions under which courts function.

MR. JUSTICE CLARK, dissenting.

It may be that at times the House Committee on Un-American Activities has, as the Court says,

"conceived of its task as the grand view of its name." And, perhaps, as the Court indicates, the rules of conduct placed upon the Committee by the House admit of individual abuse and unfairness. But that is none of our affair. So long as the object of a legislative inquiry is legitimate and the questions propounded are pertinent thereto, it is not for the courts to interfere with the committee system of inquiry. To hold otherwise would be an infringement on the power given the Congress to inform itself, and thus a trespass upon the fundamental American principle of separation of powers. The majority has substituted the judiciary as the grand inquisitor and supervisor of congressional investigations. It has never been so.

. . . .

I am sure that the committees would welcome voluntary disclosure. It would simplify and relieve their burden considerably if the parties involved in investigations would come forward with a frank willingness to cooperate. But everyday experience shows this just does not happen. One needs only to read the newspapers to know that the Congress could gather little "data" unless its committees had, unfettered, the power of subpoena. In fact, Watkins himself could not be found for appearance at the first hearing and it was only by subpoena that he attended the second. The Court generalizes on this crucial problem saying "added care on the part of the House and the Senate in authorizing the use of compulsory process and by their committees in exercising that power would suffice." It does not say how this "added care" could be applied in practice; however, there are many implications since the opinion warns that "procedures which prevent the separation of power from responsibility" would be necessary along with "constitutional requisites of fairness for witnesses."

As to "fairness for witnesses" there is nothing in the record showing any abuse of Watkins. If anything, the Committee was abused by his recalcitrance.

Barenblatt v. U.S.

360 U.S. 109 (1959)
Vote: 5–4

The vagaries, political niceties, and legal technicalities involved in congressional hearings is illustrated by the turnabout in results in *Barenblatt,* only two years later. The facts were only a hair's-breadth different, the legislative authorization only a bit more focused, but the Court found the contempt conviction in order.

Barenblatt, though heavily criticized and somewhat modified by decisions such as *U.S.* v. *Russell* (1962), makes clear that the WATKINS principle of pertinency is mostly a technical protection of the witness and not a broad basis for judicial control of the subject matter of congressional investigations. But the fact of technical review of fairness in notice and procedure has forced Congress to clean up its act in regard to the treatment of witnesses, who previously had to make split-second judgments as to when and what to answer, without counsel, while often being badgered by multiple questioners, and sometimes in the dark as to the nature of the ultimate purpose of the inquiry. (Of course, sometimes this naiveté was a protective game, but in any event the witness was still invariably at a disadvantage.) The entering wedge of judicial review of pertinency has also kept hearings more or less focused, through authorizing legislation when controversial subjects are involved, rather than letting committees rove at will. To what degree this is because the political climate demands greater procedural correctness, and to what degree the Court has created such a climate, it is impossible to tell.

MR. JUSTICE HARLAN delivered the opinion of the Court.

Once more the Court is required to resolve the conflicting constitutional claims of congressional power and of an individual's right to resist its exercise. The congressional power in question concerns the internal process of Congress in moving within its legislative domain; it involves the utilization of its committees to secure "testimony needed to enable it efficiently to exercise a legislative function belonging to it under the Constitution." *McGrain* v. *Daugherty,* 273 U.S. 135, 160.

Broad as it is, the power is not, however, without limitations. Since Congress may only investigate into those areas in which it may potentially legislate or appropriate, it cannot inquire into matters which are within the exclusive province of one of the other branches of the Government. Lacking the judicial power given to the Judiciary, it cannot inquire into matters that are exclusively the concern of the Judiciary. Neither can it supplant the Executive in what exclusively belongs to the Executive. And the Congress, in common with all branches of the Government, must exercise its powers subject to the limitations placed by the Constitution on governmental action, more particularly in the context of this case the relevant limitations of the Bill of Rights.

. . . .

In the present case congressional efforts to learn the extent of a nation-wide, indeed world-wide, problem have brought one of its investigating committees into the field of education. Of course, broadly viewed, inquiries cannot be made into the teaching that is pursued in any of our educational institutions. When academic teaching-freedom and its corollary learning-freedom, so essential to the well-being of the Nation, are claimed, this Court will always be on the alert against intrusion by Congress into this constitutionally protected domain. But this does not mean that the Congress is precluded from interrogating a witness merely because he is a teacher. An educational institution is not a constitutional sanctuary from inquiry into matters that may otherwise be within the constitutional legislative domain merely for the reason that inquiry is made of someone within its walls.

Pursuant to a subpoena, and accompanied by counsel, petitioner on June 28, 1954, appeared as a witness before this congressional Subcommittee. After answering a few preliminary questions and testifying that he had been a graduate student and teaching fellow at the University of Michigan from 1947 to 1950 and an instructor in psychology at Vassar College from 1950 to shortly before his appearance before the Subcommittee, petitioner objected generally to the right of the Subcommittee to inquire into his "political" and "religious" beliefs or any "other personal and private affairs" or "associational activities," upon grounds set forth in a previously prepared memorandum which he was allowed to file with the Subcommittee. Thereafter petitioner specifically declined to answer each of the following five questions:

"Are you now a member of the Communist Party? [Count One].

"Have you ever been a member of the Communist Party? [Count Two.]

"Now, you have stated that you knew Francis Crowley. Did you know Francis Crowley as a member of the Communist Party? [Count Three.]

"Were you ever a member of the Haldane Club of the Communist Party while at the University of Michigan? [Count Four.]

"Were you a member while a student of the University of Michigan Council of Arts, Sciences, and Professions?" [Count Five.]

In each instance the grounds of refusal were those set forth in the prepared statement. Petitioner expressly disclaimed reliance upon "the Fifth Amendment."

SUBCOMMITTEE'S AUTHORITY TO COMPEL TESTIMONY

At the outset it should be noted that Rule XI authorized this Subcommittee to compel testimony within the framework of the investigative authority conferred on the Un-American Activities Committee. Petitioner contends that *Watkins* v. *United States, supra,* nevertheless held the grant of this power in all circumstances ineffective because of the vagueness of Rule XI in delineating the Committee jurisdiction to which its exercise was to be appurtenant. This view of *Watkins* was accepted by two of the dissenting judges below.

The *Watkins* case cannot properly be read as standing for such a proposition.... This Court reversed the conviction solely on that ground, holding that Watkins had not been adequately apprised of the subject matter of the Subcommittee's investigation or the pertinency thereto of the questions he refused to answer.

That the vagueness of Rule IX was not alone determinative is also shown by the Court's further statement that aside from the Rule "the remarks of the chairman or members of the committee, or even the nature of the proceedings themselves, might sometimes make the topic [under inquiry] clear." *Ibid.* In short, while *Watkins* was critical of Rule XI, it did not involve the broad and inflexible holding petitioner now attributes to it.

Petitioner also contends, independently of *Watkins,* that the vagueness of Rule XI deprived the Subcommittee of the right to compel testimony in this investigation into Communist activity. We cannot agree with this contention, which in its furthest reach would mean that the House Un-American Activities Committee under its existing authority has no right to compel testimony in any circumstances. Granting the vagueness of the Rule, we may not read it in isolation from its long history in the House of Representatives. The Rule comes to use with a "persuasive gloss of legislative hsitory," which shows beyond doubt that in pursuance of its legislative concerns in the domain of "national security" the House has clothed the Un-American Activities Committee with pervasive authority to investigate Communist activities in this country.

We are urged, however, to construe Rule XI so as at least to exclude the field of education from the Committee's compulsory authority. Two of the four dissenting judges below relied entirely, the other two alternatively, on this ground. Not only is there no indication that the House ever viewed the field of education as being outside the Committee's authority under Rule XI, but the legislative history affirmatively evinces House approval of this phase of the Committee's work.

PERTINENCY CLAIM

Undeniably a conviction for contempt under 2 U.S.C. §192 cannot stand unless the questions asked are pertinent to the subject matter of the investigation. But the factors which led us to rest decision on this ground in *Watkins* were very different from those involved here.

In *Watkins* the petitioner has made specific objection to the Subcommittee's questions on the ground of pertinency; the question under inquiry had not been disclosed in any illuminating manner; and the questions asked about the petitioner were not only amorphous on their face, but in some instances clearly foreign to the alleged subject matter of the investigation — "Communism in labor."

In contrast, petitioner in the case before us raised no objections on the ground of pertinency at the time any of the questions were put to him.

We need not, however, rest decision on petitioner's failure to object on this score, for here "pertinency" was made to appear "with undisputable clarity." First of all, it goes without saying that the scope of the Committee's authority was for the House, not a witness, to determine, subject to the ultimate reviewing responsibility of this Court. What we deal with here is whether petitioner was sufficiently apprised of "the topic under inquiry" thus authorized "and the connective reasoning whereby the precise questions asked relate[d] to it." *Id.,* at 215. In light of his prepared memorandum of constitutional objections there can be no doubt that this petitioner was well aware of the Subcommittee's authority and purpose to question him as it did. And, lastly, unlike Watkins, *id.,* at 182–185, petitioner refused to answer questions as to his own Communist

Party affiliations, whose pertinency of course was clear beyond doubt.

CONSTITUTIONAL CONTENTIONS

The precise constitutional issue confronting us is whether the Subcommittee's inquiry into petitioner's past or present membership in the Communist Party transgressed the provisions of the First Amendment, which of course reach and limit congressional investigations.

. . . Undeniably, the First Amendment in some circumstances protects an individual from being compelled to disclose his associational relationships. However, the protections of the First Amendment, unlike a proper claim of the privilege against self-incrimination under the Fifth Amendment, do not afford a witness the right to resist inquiry in all circumstances. Where First Amendment rights are asserted to bar governmental interrogation resolution of the issue always involves a balancing by the courts of the competing private and public interests at stake in the particular circumstances shown. These principles were recognized in the *Watkins* case, where, in speaking of the First Amendment in relation to congressional inquiries, we said (at p. 198): "It is manifest that despite the adverse effects which follow upon compelled disclosure of private matters, not all such inquiries are barred. . . . The critical element is the existence of, and the weight to be ascribed to, the interest of the Congress in demanding disclosures from an unwilling witness."

That Congress has wide power to legislate in the field of Communist activity in this Country, and to conduct appropriate investigations in aid thereof, is hardly debatable. The existence of such power has never been questioned by this Court, and it is sufficient to say, without particularization, that Congress has enacted or considered in this field a wide range of legislative measures, not a few of which have stemmed from recommendations of the very Committee whose actions have been drawn in question here. . . .

We think that investigatory power in this domain is not to be denied Congress solely because the field of education is involved. Indeed we do not understand petitioner here to suggest that Congress in no circumstances may inquire into Communist activity in the field of education. Rather, his position is in effect that this particular investigation was aimed not at the revolutionary aspects but at the theoretical classroom discussion of communism.

In our opinion this position rests on a too constricted view of the nature of the investigatory process, and is not supported by a fair assessment of the record before us. An investigation of advocacy of or preparation for overthrow certainly embraces the right to identify a witness as a member of the Communist Party.

Nor can we accept the further contention that this investigation should not be deemed to have been in furtherance of a legislative purpose because the true objective of the Committee and of the Congress was purely "exposure." So long as Congress acts in pursuance of its constitutional power, the Judiciary lacks authority to intervene on the basis of the motives which spurred the exercise of that power. . . .

Finally, the record is barren of other factors which in themselves might sometimes lead to the conclusion that the individual interests at stake were not subordinate to those of the state. There is no indication in this record that the Subcommittee was attempting to pillory witnesses. Nor did petitioner's appearance as a witness follow from indiscriminate dragnet procedures, lacking in probable cause for belief that he possessed information which might be helpful to the Subcommittee. And the relevancy of the questions put to him by the Subcommittee is not open to doubt.

We conclude that the balance between the individual and the governmental interest here at stake must be struck in favor of the latter, and that therefore the provisions of the First Amendment have not been offended. . . .

MR. JUSTICE BLACK, with whom THE CHIEF JUSTICE and MR. JUSTICE DOUGLAS concur, dissenting.

. . . On the Court's own test, the issue is whether Barenblatt can know with sufficient certainty, at the time of his interrogation, that there is so compelling a need for his replies that infringement of his rights of free association is justified. The record does not disclose where Barenblatt can find what that need is. There is certainly no clear congressional statement of it in Rule XI. Perhaps if Barenblatt had had time to read all the reports of the Committee to the House, and in addition had examined the appropriations made to the Committee he, like the Court, could have discerned an intent by Congress to allow an investigation of communism in education. Even so he would be hard put to decide what the need for this investigation is since Congress expressed it neither when it enacted Rule XI nor when it acquiesced in the Committee's assertions of power. Yet it is knowledge of this need — what is wanted from him and why it is wanted—that a witness must have if he is to be in a position to comply with the Court's rule that he balance individual rights against the requirements of the State. I cannot see how that knowledge can exist under Rule XI.

But even if Barenblatt could evaluate the importance to the Government of the information sought, Rule XI would still be too broad to support his conviction. For we are dealing here with governmental procedures which the Court itself admits reach to the very fringes of congressional power. In such cases more is required of legislatures than a vague delegation to be filled in later by mute acquiescence. If Congress wants ideas investigated, if it even wants them investigated in the field of education, it must be prepared to say so expressly and unequivocally. And it is not enough that a court through exhaustive research can establish, even conclusively, that Congress wished to allow the investigation.

The First Amendment says in no equivocal language that Congress shall pass no law abridging freedom of speech, press, assembly or petition. The activities of this Committee, authorized by Congress, do precisely that, through exposure, obloquy and public scorn. The Court does not really deny this fact but relies on a combination of three reasons for permitting the infringement: (A) The notion that despite the First Amendment's command Congress can abridge speech and association if this Court decides that the governmental interest in abridging speech is greater than an individual's interest in exercising that freedom, (B) the Government's right to "preserve itself," (C) the fact that the Committee is only after Communists or suspected Communists in this investigation.

(A) I do not agree that laws directly abridging First Amendment freedoms can be justified by a congressional or judicial balancing process. There are, of course, cases suggesting that a law which primarily regulates conduct but which might also indirectly affect speech can be upheld if the effect on speech is minor in relation to the need for control of the conduct. . . .

But we did not in *Schneider,* any more than in *Cantwell,* even remotely suggest that a law directly aimed at curtailing speech and political persuasion could be saved through a balancing process. . . .

But even assuming what I cannot assume, that some balancing is proper in this case, I feel that the Court after stating the test ignores it completely. At most it balances the right of the Government to preserve itself, against Barenblatt's right to refrain from revealing Communist affiliations. Such a balance, however, mistakes the factors to be weighed. In the

first place, it completely leaves out the real interest in Barenblatt's silence, the interest of the people as a whole in being able to join organizations, advocate causes and make political "mistakes" without later being subjected to governmental penalties for having dared to think for themselves. It is this right, the right to err politically, which keeps us strong as a Nation.

Finally, I think Barenblatt's conviction violates the Constitution because the chief aim, purpose and practice of the House Un-American Activities Committee, as disclosed by its many reports, is to try witnesses and punish them because they are or have been Communists or because they refuse to admit or deny Communist affiliations. The punishment imposed is generally punishment by humiliation and public shame. There is nothing strange or novel about this kind of punishment. It is in fact one of the oldest forms of governmental punishment known to mankind; branding, the pillory, ostracism and subjection to public hatred being but a few examples of it. Nor is there anything strange about a court's reviewing the power of a congressional committee to inflict punishment.

Ultimately all the questions in this case really boil down to one—whether we as a people will try fearfully and futilely to preserve democracy by adopting totalitarian methods, or whether in accordance with our traditions and our Constitution we will have the confidence and courage to be free.

I would reverse this conviction.

Gravel v. U.S.

408 U.S. 606 (1972)
Vote: 5–4; Stewart dissenting in part.

The case involved the Pentagon Papers, the politically sensitive material, classified by the Defense Department, and leaked to various sources, including Senator Gravel, the *New York Times,* and the *Washington Post.* Gravel read material from the Papers into his subcommittee record, and was rumored to be arranging for publication. The issue is the extent of personal immunity provided Gravel and his staff by the Constitution.

The growing activism of Congress members and their use of the media have presented the courts with various dilemmas. They have been forced to decide who has legislative immunity and under what circumstances. It is clear that an aide may be exercising a legislator's functions; also, that a member of Congress, when outside that body, sometimes has, and sometimes exceeds, legislative immunity.

Hutchinson v. *Proxmire* (1979) involved Senator Proxmire's award of his "Golden Fleece of the Month Award" to a research professor doing work funded by government grants. Proxmire incorrectly suggested, among other charges, that Hutchinson received funds from two sources for the same work. The Supreme Court held that Proxmire's speech in Congress was immune but that his newsletter to constituents and television interview statements were not. Subsequently, a settlement was reached by which the Senator apologized in a letter sent to academic departments throughout the country.

Opinion of the Court by MR. JUSTICE WHITE, announced by MR. JUSTICE BLACKMUN.

These cases arise out of the investigation by a federal grand jury into possible criminal conduct with respect to the release and publication of a classified Defense Department study entitled History of the United States Decision-Making Process on Viet Nam Policy. This document, popularly known as the Pentagon Papers, bore a Defense security classification of Top Secret-Sensitive.

It appeared that on the night of June 29, 1971, Senator Gravel, as Chairman of the Subcommittee on Buildings and Grounds of the Senate Public Works Committee, convened a meeting of the subcommittee and there read extensively from a copy of the Pentagon Papers. He then placed the entire 47 volumes of the study in the public record. Rodberg had been added to the Senator's staff earlier in the day and assisted Gravel in preparing for and conducting the hearing. Some weeks later there were press reports that Gravel had arranged for the papers to be published by Beacon Press and that members of Gravel's staff had talked with Webber as editor of M.I.T. Press.

The District Court overruled the motions to quash and to specify questions but entered an order proscribing certain categories of questions. *United Staes* v. *Doe,* 332 F. Supp. 930 (Mass. 1971). The Government's contention that for purposes of applying the Speech or Debate Clause the courts were free to inquire into the regularity of the subcommittee meeting was rejected. Because the Clause protected all legislative acts, it was held to shield from inquiry anything the Senator did at the subcommittee meeting and "certain acts done in preparation therefore." The Senator's privilege also prohibited "inquiry into things done by Dr. Rodberg as the Senator's agent or assistant which would have been legislative acts, and therefore privileged, if performed by the Senator personally." The trial court, however, held that private publication of the documents was not privileged by the Speech or Debate Clause. . . .

The Court of Appeals affirmed the denial of the motions to quash but modified the protective order to reflect its own views of the scope of the congressional privilege. *United States* v. *Doe,* 455 F. 2d 753 (CA1 1972). Agreeing that Senator and aide were one for the purposes of the Speech or Debate Clause and that the Clause foreclosed inquiry of both Senator and aide with respect to legislative acts, the Court of Appeals also viewed the privilege as barring direct inquiry of the Senator or his aide, but not of third parties, as to the sources of the Senator's information used in performing legislative duties. Although it did not consider private publication by the Senator or Beacon Press to be protected by the Constitution, the Court of Appeals apparently held that neither Senator nor aide could be questioned about it because of a common-law privilege akin to the judicially created immunity of executive officers from liability for libel contained in a news release issued in the course of their normal duties.

The United States petitioned for certiorari challenging the ruling that aides and other persons may not be questioned with respect to legislative acts and that an aide to a Member of Congress has a common-law privilege not to testify before a grand jury with respect to private publication of materials introduced into a subcommittee record. Senator Gravel also petitioned for certiorari seeking reversal of the Court of Appeals insofar as it held private publication unprotected by the Speech or Debate Clause and asserting that the protective order of the Court of Appeals too narrowly protected against inquiries that a grand jury could direct to third parties. We granted both petitions. 405 U.S. 916 (1972).

I

Because the claim is that a Member's aide shares the Member's constitutional privilege, we consider first whether and to what extent Senator Gravel himself is exempt from process or inquiry by a grand jury investigating the commission of a crime. Our frame of reference is Art. I, §6, cl. 1, of the Constitution:

> They shall in all Cases, except Treason, Felony and Breach of the Peace, be privileged from Arrest during their Attendance at the Session of their respective Houses, and in going to and returning from the same; and for any Speech or Debate in either House, they shall not be questioned in any other Place.

The last sentence of the Clause provides Members of Congress with two distinct privileges. Except in cases of "Treason, Felony and Breach of the Peace," the Clause shields Members from arrest while attending or traveling to and from a session of their House. History reveals, and prior cases so hold, that this part of the Clause exempts Members from arrest in civil cases only.... Nor does freedom from arrest confer immunity on a Member from service or process as defendant in civil matters, or as a witness in a criminal case.... It is, therefore, sufficiently plain that the constitutional freedom from arrest does not exempt Members of Congress from the operation of the ordinary criminal laws, even though imprisonment may prevent or interfere with the performance of their duties as Members.... Indeed, implicit in the narrow scope of the privilege of freedom from arrest is, as Jefferson noted, the judgment that legislators ought not to stand above the law they create but ought generally to be bound by it as are ordinary persons. T. Jefferson, Manual of Parliamentary Practice, S. Doc. No. 92–1, p. 437 (1971).

In recognition, no doubt, of the force of this part of §6, Senator Gravel disavows any assertion of general immunity from the criminal law. But he points out that the last portion of §6 affords Members of Congress another vital privilege—they may not be questioned in any other place for any speech or debate in either House.... His insistence is that the Speech or Debate Clause at the very least protects him from criminal or civil liability and from questioning elsewhere than in the Senate, with respect to the events occuring at the subcommittee hearing at which the Pentagon Papers were introduced into the public record. To us this claim is incontrovertible. The Speech or Debate Clause was designed to assure a co-equal branch of the government wide freedom of speech, debate, and deliberation without intimidation or threats from the Executive Branch. It thus protects Members against prosecutions that directly impinge upon or threaten the legislative process.

... [T]he United States strongly urges that because the Speech or Debate Clause confers a privilege only upon "Senators and Representatives," Rodberg himself has no valid claim to constitutional immunity from grand jury inquiry. In our view, both courts below correctly rejected this position. We agree with the Court of Appeals that for the purpose of construing the privilege of a Member and his aide are to be "treated as one...."

... Both courts recognize what the Senate of the United States urgently presses here: that it is literally impossible, in view of the complexities of the modern legislative process, with Congress almost constantly in session and matters of legislative concern constantly proliferating, for Members of Congress to perform their legislative tasks without the help of aides and assistants; ...

It is true that the Clause itself mentions only "Senators and Representatives," but prior cases have plainly not taken a literalistic approach in applying the privilege. The Clause also speaks only of "Speech or Debate," but the Court's consistent approach has been that to confine the protection of the Speech or Debate Clause to words spoken in debate would be an unacceptably narrow view. Committee reports, resolutions, and the act of voting are equally covered; ...

Rather than giving the Clause a cramped construction, the Court has sought to implement its fundamental purpose of freeing the legislator from executive and judicial oversight that realistically threatens to control his conduct as a legislator.

Dombrowski v. *Eastland, supra,* is little different in principle. The Speech or Debate Clause there protected a Senator, who was also a subcommittee chairman, but not the subcommittee counsel. The record contained no evidence of the Senator's involvement in any activity that could result in liability, whereas the committee counsel was charged with conspiring with state officials to carry out an illegal seizure of records that the committee sought for its own proceedings. The committee counsel was deemed protected to some extent by legislative privilege, but it did not shield him from answering as yet unproved charges of conspiring to violate the constitutional rights of private parties. Unlawful conduct of this kind the Speech or Debate Clause simply did not immunize.

Powell v. *McCormack* reasserted judicial power to determine the validity of legislative actions impinging on individual rights—there the illegal exclusion of a representative-elect—and to afford relief against House aides seeking to implement the invalid resolutions.

None of these cases adopted the simple proposition that immunity was unavailable to congressional or committee employees because they were not

Representatives or Senators; rather, immunity was unavailable because they engaged in illegal conduct that was not entitled to Speech or Debate Clause protection.

In each case, protecting the rights of others may have to some extent frustrated a planned or completed legislative act; but relief could be afforded without proof of a legislative act or the motives or purposes underlying such an act. No threat to legislative independence was posed, and Speech or Debate Clause protection did not attach. . . . On the other hand, no prior case has held that Members of Congress would be immune if they executed an invalid resolution by themselves carrying out an illegal arrest, or if, in order to secure information for a hearing, themselves seized the property or invaded the privacy of a citizen. Neither they nor their aides should be immune from liability or questioning in such circumstances.

II

We are convinced also that the Court of Appeals corectly determined that Senator Gravel's alleged arrangement with Beacon Press to publish the Pentagon Papers was not protected speech or debate within the meaning of Art. 1, §6, cl. 1, of the Constitution.

Historically, the English legislative privilege was not viewed as protecting republication of an otherwise immune libel on the floor of the House. . . .

That Senators generally perform certain acts in their official capacity as Senators does not necessarily make all such acts legislative in nature. Members of Congress are constantly in touch with the Executive Branch of the Government and with administrative agencies — they may cajole, and exhort with respect to the administration of a federal statute — but such conduct, though generally done, is not protected legislative activity.

. . . The heart of the Clause is speech or debate in either House. Insofar as the Clause is construed to reach other matters, they must be an integral part of the deliberative and communicative processes by which Members participate in committee and House proceedings with respect to the consideration and passage or rejection of proposed legislation or with respect to other matters which the Constitution places within the jurisdiction of either House. . . .

Here, private publication by Senator Gravel through the cooperation of Beacon Press was in no way essential to the deliberations of the Senate; nor does questioning as to private publication threaten the integrity or independence of the Senate by impermissibly exposing its deliberations to executive influence. The Senator had conducted his hearings; the record and any report that was forthcoming were available both to his committee and the Senate. Insofar as we are advised, neither Congress nor the full committee ordered or authorized the publication. We cannot but conclude that the Senator's arrangements with Beacon Press were not part and parcel of the legislative process. . . . The Speech or Debate Clause does not in our view extend immunity to Rodberg, as a Senator's aide, from testifying before the grand jury about the arrangement between Senator Gravel and Beacon Press or about his own participation, if any, in the alleged transaction, so long as legislative acts of the Senator are not impugned.

III

Similar considerations lead us to disagree with the Court of Appeals insofar as it fashioned, tentatively at least, a nonconstitutional testimonial privilege protecting Rodberg from any questioning by the grand jury concerning the matter of republication of the Pentagon Papers.

IV

Rodberg's immunity, testimonial or otherwise, extends only to legislative acts as to which the Senator himself would be immune. The grand jury, therefore, if relevant to its investigation into the possible violations of criminal law, and absent Fifth Amendment objections, may require from Rodberg answers to questions relating to his or the Senator's arrangements, if any, with respect to republication or with respect to third-party conduct under valid investigation by the grand jury, as long as the questions do not implicate legislative action of the Senator. Neither do we perceive any constitutional or other privilege that shields Rodberg, any more than any other witness, from grand jury questions relevant to tracing the source of obviously highly classified documents that came into the Senator's possession and are the basic subject matter of inquiry in this case, as long as no legislative act is implicated by the questions.

Because the Speech or Debate Clause privilege applies both to Senator and aide, it appears to us that paragraph one of the order, alone, would afford ample protection for the privilege if it forbade questioning any witness, including Rodberg: (1) concerning the Senator's conduct, or the conduct of his aides, at the June 29, 1971, meeting of the subcommittee; (2) concerning the motives and purposes behind the Senator's conduct, or that of his aides, at that meeting; (3) concerning communications between the Senator and his aides during the term of their employment and related to said meeting or any other legislative act of the Senator; (4) except as it proves relevant to investigating possible third-party crime, concerning any act, in itself not criminal, performed by the Senator, or by his aides in the course of their employment, in preparation for the subcommittee hearing. We leave the final form of such an order to the Court of Appeals in the first instance, or, if that court prefers, to the District Court.

MR. JUSTICE STEWART, dissenting in part.

The Court today holds that the Speech or Debate Clause does not protect a Congressman from being forced to testify before a grand jury about sources of information used in preparation for legislative acts. This critical question was not embraced in the petitions for certiorari. It was not dealt with in the written briefs. It was addressed only tangentially during the oral arguments. Yet it is a question with profound implications for the effective functioning of the legislative process. I cannot join in the Court's summary resolution of so vitally important a constitutional issue. . . . But even if the Executive had reason to believe that a Member of Congress had knowledge of a specific probable violation of law, it is by no means clear to me that the Executive's interest in the administration of justice must *always* override the public interest in having an informed Congress. Why should we not, given the tension between two competing interests, *each* of constitutional dimensions, balance the claims of the Speech or Debate Clause against the claims of the grand jury in the particularized contexts of specific cases? And why are not the Houses of Congress the proper institutions in most situations to impose sanctions upon a Representative or Senator who withholds information about crime acquired in the course of his legislative duties?

MR. JUSTICE DOUGLAS, dissenting.

I would construe the Speech or Debate Clause to insulate Senator Gravel and his aides from inquiry concerning the Pentagon Papers, and Beacon Press from inquiry concerning publication of them, for that publication was but another way of informing the public as to what had gone on in the privacy of the Executive Branch concerning the conception and pursuit of the so-called "war" in Vietnam. Alternatively, I would hold that Beacon Press is protected by the First Amendment from prosecution or investigations for publishing or undertaking to publish the Pentagon Papers.

One of the things normally done by a Member "in relation to the business before it" is the introduction of documents or other exhibits in the record the committee or subcommittee is making. The introduction of a document into a record of the Committee or subcommittee by its Chairman certainly puts it in the public domain. . . . The aides and agents such as Beacon Press must be taken as surrogates for the Senator and the confidences of the job that they enjoy are his confidences that the Speech or Debate Clause embraces.

Classification of documents is a concern of the Congress. It is, however, no concern of the courts, as I see it, how a document is stamped in an Executive Department or whether a committee of Congress can obtain the use of it. The federal courts do not sit as an ombudsman refereeing the disputes between the other two branches.

Forcing the press to become the Government's co-conspirator in maintaining state secrets is at war with the objectives of the First Amendment. That guarantee was designed in part to ensure a meaningful version of self-government by immersing the people in a "steady, robust, unimpeded, and uncensored flow of opinion and reporting which are continuously subjected to critique, rebuttal, and re-examination." . . .

Aside from the question of the extent to which publishers can be penalized for printing classified documents, surely the First Amendment protects against all inquiry into the dissemination of information which, although once classified, has become part of the public domain.

To summon Beacon Press through its officials before the grand jury and to inquire into why it did what it did and its publication plans is "abridging" the freedom of the press contrary to the command of the First Amendment.

MR. JUSTICE BRENNAN, with whom MR. JUSTICE DOUGLAS, and MR. JUSTICE MARSHALL, join, dissenting.

I fully agree with the Court that a Congressman's immunity under the Clause must also be extended to his aides if it is to be at all effective. The complexities and press of congressional business make it impossible for a Member to function without the close cooperation of his legislative assistants. Their role as his agents in the performance of official duties requires that they share his immunity for those acts. The scope of that immunity, however, is as important as the persons to whom it extends. In my view, today's decision so restricts the privilege of speech or debate as to endanger the continued performance of legislative tasks that are vital to the workings of our democratic system.

The Court seems to assume that words spoken in debate or written in congressional reports are protected by the Clause, so that if Senator Gravel had recited part of the Pentagon Papers on the Senate floor or copied them into a Senate report, those acts could not be questioned "in any other Place." Yet because he sought a wider audience, to publicize information deemed relevant to matters pending before his own committee, the Senator suddenly loses his immunity and is exposed to grand jury investigation and possible prosecution for the republication. The explanation for this anomalous result is the Court's belief that "Speech or Debate" encompasses only acts necessary to the internal deliberations of Congress concerning proposed legislation. "Here," according to the Court, "private publication by Senator Gravel through the cooperation of Beacon Press was in no way essential to the deliberations of the Senate."... Therefore, "the Senator's arrangements with Beacon Press were not part and parcel of the legislative process."...

Thus, the Court excludes from the sphere of protected legislative activity a function that I had supposed lay at the heart of our democratic system. I speak, of course, of the legislator's duty to inform the public about matters affecting the administration of government. That this "informing function" falls into the class of things "generally done in a session of the House by one of its members in relation to the business before it," *Kilbourn* v. *Thompson*, . . . (1881), was explicitly acknowledged by the Court in *Watkins* v. *United States*, . . . (1957). . . .

There is substantial evidence that the Framers intended the Speech or Debate Clause to cover all communications from a Congressman to his constituents. Thomas Jefferson clearly expressed that view of legislative privilege in a case involving Samuel Cabell, Congressman from Virginia. . . . Jefferson's protest is perhaps the most significant and certainly the most cogent analysis of the privileged nature of communication between Congressman and public.

J. W. Hampton, Jr., and Co. v. U.S.

276 U.S. 394 (1928)

Vote: Unanimous

The dividing line between the legislature and the executive is a thin one. Policy making blends with policy execution. A decision that is not implemented is simply a collection of empty words. But action without policy is arbitrary and unpredictable.

The U.S. courts follow the Latin maxim "*delegata potestas non potest delegari*" — a delegated power may not be delegated. The intent is to control executive law making, and therefore to try to limit administrators to carrying out the intent of Congress.

Logic and "the necessity of the case" lead to more flexible results. Delegation is permitted when the legislature lays down standards for action and thus places limits on executive discretion. In practice, only during the New Deal period (the PANAMA REFINING CO. case, SCHECHTER POULTRY CORP. V. U.S., and CARTER V. CARTER COAL CO.) was the lack of standards in delegated power considered so extreme that legislation was invalidated. And even then, there were hints that the problem lay not in delegating power to the executive, but in delegating it to nongovernmental groups of private interests.

The Hampton case remains an unusually clear and basic illustration of how delegation normally works. Does the President perform any legislative functions in these matters? Does the Congress effectively limit the administrative power? Could Congress attach conditions that were infringements on the executive?

MR. CHIEF JUSTICE TAFT delivered the opinion of the Court.

J. W. Hampton, Jr., & Company made an importation into New York of barium dioxide, which the collector of customs assessed at the dutiable rate of six cents per pound. This was two cents per pound more than that fixed by statute, par. 12, ch. 356, 42 Stat. 858, 860. The rate was raised by the collector by virtue of the proclamation of the President, 45 Treas. Dec. 669, T. D. 40216, issued under, and by authority of, §315 to Title III of the Tariff Act of September 21, 1922, ch. 356, 42 Stat. 858, 941, which is the so-called flexible tariff provision.

The President issued his proclamation May 19, 1924. . . .

"Whereas, under and by virtue of said section of said act, the United States Tariff Commission has made an investigation to assist the President in ascertaining the differences in costs of production of and of all other facts and conditions enumerated in said section with respect to... barium dioxide, ...

"Whereas in the course of said investigation a hearing was held, of which reasonable public notice was given and at which parties interested were given a reasonable opportunity to be present, to produce evidence, and to be heard;

"And whereas the President upon said investigation... has thereby found that the principal competing country is Germany, and that the duty fixed in said title and act does not equalize the differences in costs of production in the United States and in... Germany, and has ascertained and determined the increased rate of duty necessary to equalize the same.

"Now, therefore, I, Calvin Coolidge, President of the United States of America, do hereby determine and proclaim that the increase in the rate of duty provided in said act shown by said ascertained differences in said costs of production necessary to equalize the same is as follows:

"An increase in said duty on barium dioxide (within the limit of total increase provided for in said act) from 4 cents per pound to 6 cents per pound."

The issue here is as to the constitutionality of §315, upon which depends the authority for the proclamation of the President and for two of the six cents per pound duty collected from the petitioner. The contention of the taxpayers is two-fold—first, they argue that the section is invalid in that it is a delegation to the President of the legislative power, which by Article I, §1 of the Constitution, is vested in Congress, the power being that declared in §8 of Article I, that the Congress shall have power to lay and collect taxes, duties, imposts and excises. The second objection is that, as §315 was enacted with the avowed intent and for the purpose of protecting the industries of the United States, it is invalid because the Constitution gives power to lay such taxes only for revenue.

First. It seems clear what Congress intended by §315. Its plan was to secure by law the imposition of customs duties on articles of imported merchandise which should equal the difference between the cost of producing in a foreign country the articles in question and laying them down for sale in the United States, and the cost of producing and selling like or similar articles in the United States, so that the duties not only secure revenue but at the same time enable domestic producers to compete on terms of equality with foreign producers in the markets of the United States. It may be that it is difficult to fix with exactness this difference, but the difference which is sought

in the statute is perfectly clear and perfectly intelligible. Because of the difficulty in practically determining what that difference is, Congress seems to have doubted that the information in its possession was such as to enable it to make the adjustment accurately, and also to have apprehended that with changing conditions the difference might vary in such a way that some readjustments would be necessary to give effect to the principle on which the statute proceeds. To avoid such difficulties, Congress adopted in §315 the method of describing with clearness what its policy and plan was and then authorizing a member of the executive branch to carry out this policy and plan, and to find the changing difference from time to time, and to make the adjustments necessary to conform the duties to the standard underlying that policy and plan. As it was a matter of great importance, it concluded to give by statute to the President, the chief of the executive branch, the function of determining the difference as it might vary. He was provided with a body of investigators who were to assist him in obtaining needed data and ascertaining the facts justifying readjustments. There was no specific provision by which action by the President might be invoked under this Act, but it was presumed that the President would through this body of advisers keep himself advised of the necessity for investigation or change, and then would proceed to pursue his duties under the Act and reach such conclusion as he might find justified by the investigation, and proclaim the same if necessary.

The Tariff Commission does not itself fix duties, but before the President reaches a conclusion on the subject of investigation, the Tariff Commission must make an investigation and in so doing must give notice to all parties interested and an opportunity to adduce evidence and to be heard.

The well-known maxim *"Delegata potestas non potest delegari,"* applicable to the law of agency in the general and common law, is well understood and has had wider application in the construction of our Federal and State Constitutions than it has in private law. The Federal Constitution and State Constitutions of this country divide the governmental power into three branches. The first is the legislative, the second is the executive, and the third is the judicial, and the rule is that in the actual administration of the government Congress or the Legislature should exercise the legislative power, the President or the State executive, the Governor, the executive power, and the Courts or the judiciary the judicial power, and in carrying out that constitutional division into three branches it is a breach of the National fundamental law if Congress gives up its legislative power and transfers it to the President, or to the Judicial branch, or if by law it attempts to invest itself or its members with either executive power or judicial power. This is not to say that the three branches are not co-ordinate parts of one government and that each in the field of its duties may not invoke the action of the two other branches in so far as the action invoked shall not be an assumption of the constitutional field of action of another branch. In determining what it may do in seeking assistance from another branch, the extent and character of that assistance must be fixed according to common sense and the inherent necessities of the governmental co-ordination.

The field of Congress involves all and many varieties of legislative action, and Congress has found it frequently necessary to use officers of the Executive Branch, within defined limits, to secure the exact effect intended by its acts of legislation, by vesting discretion in such officers to make public regulations interpreting a statute and directing the details of its execution, even to the extent of providing for penalizing a breach of such regulations.

It is conceded by counsel that Congress may use executive officers in the application and enforcement of a policy declared in law by Congress, and authorize such officers in the application of the Congressional declaration to enforce it by regulation equivalent to law. But it is said that this never has been permitted to be done where Congress has exercised the power to levy taxes and fix customs duties. The authorities make no such distinction.

. . . In *Field* v. *Clark,* 143 U.S. 649, 680, . . . the Court said that while Congress could not delegate legislative power to the President, this Act did not in any real sense invest the President with the power of legislation, because nothing involving the expediency or just operation of such legislation was left to the determination of the President; that the legislative power was exercised when Congress declared that the suspension should take effect upon a named contingency. What the President was required to do was merely in execution of the act of Congress. It was not the making of the law. He was the mere agent of the law-making department to ascertain and declare the event upon which its expressed will was to take effect.

Second . . . It is contended that the only power of Congress in the levying of customs duties is to create revenue, and that it is unconstitutional to frame the customs duties with any other view than that of revenue raising. It undoubtedly is true that during the political life of this country there has been much discussion between parties as to the wisdom of the policy of protection, and we may go further and say as

to its constitutionality, but no historian, whatever his view of the wisdom of the policy of protection, would contend that Congress, since the first revenue Act, in 1789, has not assumed that it was within its power in making provision for the collection of revenue, to put taxes upon importations and to vary the subjects of such taxes or rates in an effort to encourage the growth of the industries of the Nation by protecting home production against foreign competition. It is enough to point out that the second act adopted by the Congress of the United States, July 4, 1789, ch. 2, 1 Stat. 24, contained the following recital.

"Sec. 1. Whereas it is necessary for the support of government, for the discharge of the debts of the United States, and the encouragement and protection of manufactures, that duties be laid on goods, wares and merchandises imported: Be it enacted, etc."

In this first Congress sat many members of the Constitutional Convention of 1787. This Court has repeatedly laid down the principle that a contemporaneous legislative exposition of the Constitution when the founders of our Government and framers of our Constitution were actively participating in public affairs, long acquiesced in, fixes the construction to be given its provisions. . . . Section 315 and its provisions are within the power of Congress. The judgment of the Court of Customs Appeals is affirmed.

Affirmed.

Immigration and Naturalization Service v. Chadha

103 S.Ct. 2764 (1983)
Vote: (6–1)–(1–1)

To deal with the realities of modern bureaucratic regulation, Congress turned increasingly to the *legislative veto.* Policy was delegated to an executive agency, which was required to report its decisions to Congress, while Congress retained the right to overturn the administrative action within a period of time specified by the delegating statute.

The legislative veto took many forms. Nullification was authorized by action of both Houses in some statutes, or by action of a single House in others. (Justice White explains in his opinion that it is as if new legislation were involved; the executive veto is represented via the administrative agency initiative, and defeat by either House of Congress would defeat a bill.) Vetoes by committees also have been provided for, though presidents have consistently opposed such delegations. They have generally accepted "one-House" vetoes in order to gain the additional authority while complaining about the string attached to it.

The Supreme Court here was dealing with a "one-House veto" measure, but it also chose to invalidate two-House vetoes. Committee vetoes, while mentioned only in passing in White's dissent, hopelessly fail to meet the standards suggested in *Chadha* and are clearly also invalid.

Presumably, similar provisions, such as those of the War Powers Act, which require that actions cease unless authorized by Congress within a certain time, are still constitutional.

There have been a number of suggestions as to how Congress can retain its power without contradicting this decision. One is that delegating statutes can provide that the administrative action go into effect only if approved by Congress, but the approval shall be deemed granted if no negative action has taken place within a certain period after the regulation is reported to Congress. The establishment of such a regulatory "unanimous consent" calendar is presumably within the absolute power of each House of Congress to control its own rules.

This approach, interestingly, would accept, to a large extent, the analysis of Justice White's dissent while technically comporting with the "plain words of the Constitution" approach of the majority.

CHIEF JUSTICE BURGER delivered the opinion of the Court.

Chadha is an East Indian who was born in Kenya and holds a British passport. He was lawfully admitted to the United States in 1966 on a nonimmigrant student visa. His visa expired on June 30, 1972.

After Chadha submitted his application for suspension of deportation, the deportation hearing was resumed on February 7, 1974. On the basis of evidence adduced at the hearing, affidavits submitted with the application, and the results of a character investigation conducted by the INS, the immigration judge, on June 25, 1974, ordered that Chadha's deportation be suspended. The immigration judge found that Chadha met the requirements of §244(a)(1): he

had resided continuously in the United States for over seven years, was of good moral character, and would suffer "extreme hardship" if deported. . . .

Once the Attorney General's recommendation for suspension of Chadha's deportation was conveyed to Congress, Congress had the power under §244(c)(2) of the Act, 8 U.S.C. §1254(c)(2), to veto* the Attorney General's determination that Chadha should not be deported.

On December 12, 1975, Representative Eilberg, Chairman of the Judiciary Subcommittee on Immigration, Citizenship, and International Law, introduced a resolution opposing "the granting of permanent residence in the United States to [six] aliens," including Chadha. . . . The resolution had not been printed and was not made available to other Members of the House prior to or at the time it was voted on. *Ibid.* So far as the record before us shows, the House consideration of the resolution was based on Representative Eilberg's statement from the floor that

> [i]t was the feeling of the committee, after reviewing 340 cases, that the aliens contained in the resolution [Chadha and five others] did not meet these statutory requirements, particularly as it relates to hardship; and it is the opinion of the committee that their deportation should not be suspended.

. . . Chadha filed a petition for review of the deportation order in the United States Court of Appeals for the Ninth Circuit. The Immigration and Naturalization Service agreed with Chadha's position before the Court of Appeals and joined him in arguing that §244(c)(2) is unconstitutional. In light of the importance of the question, the Court of Appeals invited both the Senate and the House of Representatives to file briefs *amici curiae.*

After full briefing and oral argument, the Court of Appeals held that the House was without constitutional authority to order Chadha's deportation. . . . The essence of its holding was that §244(c)(2) violates the constitutional doctrine of separation of powers. . . . Both Houses contend that the INS has already received what it sought from the Court of Appeals, is not an aggrieved party, and therefore cannot appeal from the decision of the Court of Appeals. We cannot agree.

*In constitutional terms, "veto" is used to describe the President's power under Art. I, §7 of the Constitution. See Black's Law Dictionary 1403 (5th ed. 1979). It appears, however, that Congressional devices of the type authorized by §244(c)(2) have come to be commonly referred to as a "veto. . . ."

The INS was ordered by one House of Congress to deport Chadha. As we have set out more fully, *ante* at 7, the INS concluded that it had no power to rule on the constitutionality of that order and accordingly proceeded to implement it. Chadha's appeal challenged that decision and the INS presented the Executive's views on the constitutionality of the House action to the Court of Appeals. But the INS brief to the Court of Appeals did not alter the agency's decision to comply with the House action ordering deportation of Chadha. The Court of Appeals set aside the deportation proceedings and ordered the Attorney General to cease and desist from taking any steps to deport Chadha, steps that the Attorney General would have taken were it not for that decision.

At least for purposes of deciding whether the INS is "any party" within the grant of appellate jurisdiction in §1252, we hold that the INS was sufficiently aggrieved by the Court of Appeals decision prohibiting it from taking action it would otherwise take....

Congress also contends that the provision for the one-House veto in §244(c)(2) cannot be severed from §244. Congress argues that if the provision for the one-House veto is held unconstitutional, all of §244 must fall. If §244 in its entirety is violative of the Constitution, it follows that the Attorney General has no authority to suspend Chadha's deportation under §244(a)(1) and Chadha would be deported. From this, Congress argues that Chadha lacks standing to challenge the constitutionality of the one-House veto provision because he could receive no relief even if his constitutional challenge proves successful.... Here, however, we need not embark on that elusive inquiry since Congress itself has provided the answer to the question of severability....

> If *any* particular provision of this Act, or the application thereof to *any* person or circumstance, is held invalid, *the remainder of the Act and the application of such provision to other persons or circumstances shall not be affected thereby.* (Emphasis added.)

Case or Controversy

It is also contended that this is not a genuine controversy but "a friendly, non-adversary, proceeding," *Ashwander* v. *Tennessee Valley Authority, supra,* 297 U.S., at 346 (Brandeis, J., concurring), upon which the Court should not pass. This argument rests on the fact that Chadha and the INS take the same position on the constitutionality of the one-House veto. But it would be a curious result if, in the administration of justice, a person could be denied access to the courts because the Attorney General of the United States agreed with the legal arguments asserted by the individual.

A case or controversy is presented by this case. First, from the time of Congress' formal intervention, see note 5, *supra,* the concrete adverseness is beyond doubt. Congress is both a proper party to defend the constitutionality of §244(c)(2) and a proper petitioner under §1254(1).... "*Every* Order, Resolution, or Vote to which the Concurrence of the Senate and House of Representatives may be necessary (except on a question of Adjournment) *shall be* presented to the President of the United States; and before the Same shall take Effect, *shall be* approved by him, or being disapproved by him, *shall be* repassed by two thirds of the Senate and House of Representatives, according to the Rules and Limitations prescribed in the Case of a Bill." Art. I, §7, cl. 3. (Emphasis added).

B

The Presentment Clauses

The records of the Constitutional Convention reveal that the requirement that all legislation be presented to the President before becoming law was uniformly accepted by the Framers. Presentment to the President and the Presidential veto were considered so imperative that the draftsmen took special pains to assure that these requirements could not be circumvented....

C

Bicameralism

The bicameral requirement of Art. I, §§1, 7 was of scarcely less concern to the Framers than was the Presidential veto and indeed the two concepts are interdependent. By providing that no law could take effect without the concurrence of the prescribed majority of the Members of both Houses, the Framers reemphasized their belief, already remarked upon in connection with the Presentment Clauses, that legislation should not be enacted unless it has been carefully and fully considered by the Nation's elected officials....

....

We see therefore that the Framers were acutely conscious that the bicameral requirement and the Presentment Clauses would serve essential constitutional functions. The President's participation in the legislative process was to protect the Executive Branch from Congress and to protect the whole people from improvident laws. The division of the Congress into two distinctive bodies assures that the legislative power would be exercised only after opportunity for full study and debate in separate settings. The President's unilateral veto power, in turn, was limited by the power of two thirds of both Houses of Congress to overrule a veto thereby precluding final arbitrary action of one person. See 1 M. Farrand, *supra,* at 99–104. It emerges clearly that the prescription for legislative action in Art. I, §§1, 7 represents the Framers' decision that the legislative power of the Federal . . .

Checks & Balances

IV

. . . .

Examination of the action taken here by one House pursuant to §244(c)(2) reveals that it was essentially legislative in purpose and effect. In purporting to exercise power defined in Art. I, §8, cl. 4 to "establish an uniform Rule of Naturalization," the House took action that had the purpose and effect of altering the legal rights, duties and relations of persons, including the Attorney General, Executive Branch officials and Chadha, all outside the legislative branch. Section 244(c)(2) purports to authorize one House of Congress to require the Attorney General to deport an individual alien whose deportation otherwise would be cancelled under §244. The one-House veto operated in this case to overrule the Attorney General and mandate Chadha's deportation; absent the House action, Chadha would remain in the United States. Congress has *acted* and its action has altered Chadha's status.

. . . .

The nature of the decision implemented by the one-House veto in this case further manifests its legislative character. After long experience with the clumsy, time consuming private bill procedure, Congress made a deliberate choice to delegate to the Executive Branch, and specifically to the Attorney General, the authority to allow deportable aliens to remain in this country in certain specified circumstances. It is not disputed that this choice to delegate authority is precisely the kind of decision that can be implemented only in accordance with the procedures set out in Art. I. Disagreement with the Attorney General's decision on Chadha's deportation — that is, Congress' decision to deport Chadha — no less than Congress' original choice to delegate to the Attorney General the authority to make that decision, involves determinations of policy that Congress can implement in only one way: bicameral passage followed by presentment to the President. Congress must abide by its delegation of authority until that delegation is legislatively altered or revoked.

Finally, we see that when the Framers intended to authorize either House of Congress to act alone and outside of its prescribed bicameral legislative role, they narrowly and precisely defined the procedure for such action. There are but four provisions in the Constitution, explicit and unambiguous, by which one House may act alone with the unreviewable force of law, not subject to the President's veto:

(a) The House of Representatives alone was given the power to initiate impeachments. Art. I, §2, cl. 6;

(b) The Senate alone was given the power to conduct trials following impeachment on charges initiated by the House and to convict following trial. Art. I, §3, cl. 5;

(c) The Senate alone was given final unreviewable power to approve or to disapprove presidential appointments. Art. II, §2, cl. 2;

(d) The Senate alone was given unreviewable power to ratify treaties negotiated by the President. Art. II, §2, cl. 2.

Clearly, when the Draftsmen sought to confer special powers on one House, independent of the other House, or of the President, they did so in explicit, unambiguous terms. These carefully defined exceptions from presentment and bicameralism underscore the difference between the legislative functions of Congress and other unilateral but important and binding one-House acts provided for in the Constitution. These exceptions are narrow, explicit, and separately justified; none of them authorize the action challenged here . . . .

. . . The bicameral requirement, the Presentment Clauses, the President's veto, and Congress' power to override a veto were intended to erect enduring checks on each Branch and to protect the people from the improvident exercise of power by mandating certain prescribed steps. To preserve those checks, and maintain the separation of powers, the carefully defined limits on the power of each Branch must not be eroded. . . .

. . . With all the obvious flaws of delay, untidiness, and potential for abuse, we have not yet found a better way to preserve freedom than by making the exercise of power subject to the carefully crafted restraints spelled out in the Constitution.

Affirmed.

JUSTICE POWELL, concurring in the judgment.
. . . In my view, the case may be decided on a narrower ground. When Congress finds that a particular person does not satisfy the statutory criteria for permanent residence in this country it has assumed a judicial function in violation of the principle of separation of powers. Accordingly, I concur in the judgment.

JUSTICE WHITE, dissenting.

Today the Court not only invalidates §244(c)(2) of the Immigration and Nationality Act, but also sounds the death knell for nearly 200 other statutory provisions in which Congress has reserved a "legislative veto." For this reason, the Court's decision is of surpassing importance. And it is for this reason that the Court would have been well-advised to decide the case, if possible, on the narrower grounds of separation of powers, leaving for full consideration the constitutionality of other congressional review statutes operating on such varied matters as war powers and agency rulemaking, some of which concern the independent regulatory agencies.

I

. . . .

The legislative veto developed initially in response to the problems of reorganizing the sprawling government structure created in response to the Depression. The Reorganization Acts established the chief model for the legislative veto. When President Hoover requested authority to reorganize the government in 1929, he coupled his request that the "Congress be willing to delegate its authority over the problem (subject to defined principles) to the Executive" with a proposal for legislative review. . . . Congress followed President Hoover's suggestion and authorized reorganization subject to legislative review. . . . Over the years, the provision was used extensively. Presidents submitted 115 reorganization plans to Congress of which 23 were disapproved by Congress pursuant to legislative veto provisions. . . .

. . . Congress and the President applied the legislative veto procedure to resolve the delegation problem for national security and foreign affairs. World War II occasioned the need to transfer greater authority to the President in these areas. The legislative veto offered the means by which Congress could confer additional authority while preserving its own constitutional role. During World War II, Congress enacted over thirty statutes conferring powers on the Executive with legislative veto provisions. President Roosevelt accepted the veto as the necessary price for obtaining exceptional authority.

Over the quarter century following World War II, Presidents continued to accept legislative vetoes by one or both Houses as constitutional, while regularly denouncing provisions by which Congressional committees reviewed Executive activity. . . .

During the 1970's the legislative veto was important in resolving a series of major constitutional disputes between the President and Congress over claims of the President to broad impoundment, war, and national emergency powers. The key provision of the War Powers Resolution, 50 U.S.C. §1544(c), authorizes the termination by concurrent resolution of the use of armed forces in hostilities. A similar measure resolved the problem posed by Presidential claims of inherent power to impound appropriations. Congressional Budget and Impoundment Control Act of 1974, 31 U.S.C. §1403. In conference, a compromise was achieved under which permanent impoundments, termed "rescissions," would require approval through enactment of legislation. In contrast, temporary impoundments, or "deferrals," would become effective unless disapproved by one House. This compromise provided the President with flexibility, while preserving ultimate Congressional control over the budget. . . .

Even this brief review suffices to demonstrate that the legislative veto is more than "efficient, convenient, and useful." *Ante,* at 23. It is an important if not indispensable political invention that allows the President and Congress to resolve major constitutional and policy differences, assures the accountability of independent regulatory agencies, and preserves Congress' control over lawmaking. Perhaps there are other means of accommodation and accountability, but the increasing reliance of Congress upon the legislative veto suggests that the alternatives to which Congress must now turn are not entirely satisfactory.

II

. . . Courts should always be wary of striking statutes as unconstitutional; to strike an entire class of statutes based on consideration of a somewhat atypical and more-readily indictable exemplar of the class is irresponsible. It was for cases such as this one that Justice Brandeis wrote:

> The Court has frequently called attention to the 'great gravity and delicacy' of its function in passing upon the validity of an act of Congress. . . . The Court will not 'formulate' a rule of constitutional law broader than is required by the precise facts to which it is to be applied.' . . .

If the legislative veto were as plainly unconstitutional as the Court strives to suggest, its broad ruling today would be more comprehensible. But, the constitutionality of the legislative veto is anything but clearcut. The issue divides scholars, courts, attorneys general, and the two other branches of the National Government. . . .

... We should not find the lack of a specific constitutional authorization for the legislative veto surprising, and I would not infer disapproval of the mechanism from its absence. From the summer of 1787 to the present the government of the United States has become an endeavor far beyond the contemplation of the Framers. Only within the last half century has the complexity and size of the Federal Government's responsibilities grown so greatly that the Congress must rely on the legislative veto as the most effective if not the only means to insure their role as the nation's lawmakers. But the wisdom of the Framers was to anticipate that the nation would grow and new problems of governance would require different solutions. ...

III

The Court holds that the disapproval of a suspension of deportation by the resolution of one House of Congress is an exercise of legislative power without compliance with the preclauses. There is no question that a bill does not become a law until it is approved by both the House and the Senate, and presented to the President. Similarly, I would not hesitate to strike an action of Congress in the form of a concurrent resolution which constituted an exercise of original lawmaking authority. ... All of this, the Third Part of the Court's opinion, is entirely unexceptionable.

It does not, however, answer the constitutional question before us. The power to exercise a legislative veto is not the power to write new law without bicameral approval or presidential consideration. The veto must be authorized by statute and may only negative what an Executive department or independent agency has proposed. On its face, the legislative veto no more allows one House of Congress to make law than does the presidential veto confer such power upon the President. Accordingly, the Court properly recognizes that it "must establish that the challenged action under §244(c)(2) is of the kind to which the procedural requirements of Art. I, §7 apply" and admits that "not every action taken by either House is subject to the bicameralism and presentation requirements of Art. I."

The wisdom and the constitutionality of these broad delegations are matters that still have not been put to rest. But for present purposes, these cases establish that by virtue of congressional delegation, legislative power can be exercised by independent agencies and Executive departments without the passage of new legislation. For some time, the sheer amount of law—the substantive rules that regulate private conduct and direct the operation of government—made by the agencies has far outnumbered the lawmaking engaged in by Congress through the traditional process. ... [T]he Court concedes that certain administrative agency action, such as rulemaking, "may resemble lawmaking" and recognizes that "[t]his Court has referred to agency activity as being 'quasi-legislative' in character. *Humphrey's Executor* v. *United States*, ... (1935)." Such rules and adjudications by the agencies meet the Court's own definition of legislative action for they "alter the legal rights, duties and relations of persons ... outside the legislative branch," *ante,* at 32, and involve "determinations of policy," *ante,* at 34. Under the Court's analysis, the Executive Branch and the independent agencies may make rules with the effect of law while Congress, in whom the Framers confided the legislative power, Art. I, §1, may not exercise a veto which precludes such rules from having operative force. If the effective functioning of a complex modern government requires the delegation of vast authority which, by virtue of its breadth, is legislative or "quasi-legislative" in character, I cannot accept that Article I—which is, after all, the source of the nondelegation doctrine—should forbid Congress from qualifying that grant with a legislative veto.

2

The central concern of the presentation and bicameralism requirements of Article I is that when a departure from the legal status quo is undertaken, it is done with the approval of the President and both Houses of Congress—or, in the event of a presidential veto, a two-thirds majority in both Houses. This interest is fully satisfied by the operation of §244(c)(2). The President's approval is found in the Attorney General's action in recommending to Congress that the deportation order for a given alien be suspended. The House and the Senate indicate their approval of the Executive's action by not passing a resolution of disapproval within the statutory period. Thus, a change in the legal status quo—the deportability of the alien—is consummated only with the approval of each of the three relevant actors. The disagreement of any one of the three maintains the alien's pre-existing status: the Executive may choose not to recommend suspension; the House and Senate may each veto the recommendation. The effect on the rights and obligations of the affected individuals and upon the legislative system is precisely the same as if a private bill were introduced but failed to receive the necessary approval. ...

....

... [I]t may be said that this approach leads to the incongruity that the two-House veto is more suspect than its one-House brother. Although the idea may be initially counter-intuitive, on close analysis, it is not at all unusual that the one-House veto is of more certain constitutionality than the two-House version. If the Attorney General's action is a proposal for legislation, then the disapproval of but a single House is all that is required to prevent its passage. Because approval is indicated by the failure to veto, the one-House veto satisfies the requirement of bicameral approval. The two-House version may present a different question. . . .

IV

The Court of Appeals struck §244(c)(2) as violative of the constitutional principle of separation of powers. It is true that the purpose of separating the authority of government is to prevent unnecessary and dangerous concentration of power in one branch. . . .

But the history of the separation of powers doctrine is also a history of accommodation and practicality. Apprehensions of an overly powerful branch have not led to undue prophylactic measures that handicap the effective working of the national government as a whole. The Constitution does not contemplate total separation of the three branches of Government. *Buckley* v. *Valeo,* . . . (1976). "[A] hermetic sealing off of the three branches of Government from one another would preclude the establishment of a Nation capable of governing itself effectively."

. . . .

Section 244(c)(2) survives this test. The legislative veto provision does not "prevent the Executive Branch from accomplishing its constitutionally assigned functions." First, it is clear that the Executive Branch has no "constitutionally assigned" function of suspending the deportation of aliens. "'Over no conceivable subject is the legislative power of Congress more complete than it is over' the admission of aliens. . . ." Nor can it be said that the inherent function of the Executive Branch in executing the law is involved. *The Steel Seizure Case* resolved that the Article II mandate for the President to execute the law is a directive to enforce the law which Congress has written. . . .

. . . .

Nor does §244 infringe on the judicial power, as JUSTICE POWELL would hold. Section 244 makes clear that Congress has reserved its own judgment as part of the statutory process. Congressional action does not substitute for judicial review of the Attorney General's decisions. . . .

V

I regret that I am in disagreement with my colleagues on the fundamental questions that this case presents. But even more I regret the destructive scope of the Court's holding. It reflects a profoundly different conception of the Constitution than that held by the Courts which sanctioned the modern administrative state. Today's decision strikes down in one fell swoop provisions in more laws enacted by Congress than the Court has cumulatively invalidated in its history. I fear it will now be more difficult "to insure that the fundamental policy decisions in our society will be made not by an appointed official but by the body immediately responsible to the people. . . ." I must dissent.

Bowsher, Comptroller General of the U.S. v. Synar, Member of Congress, et al.

478 U.S. 914 (1986)
Vote: 7–2

Responding to presidential criticism that it was responsible for the mounting budget deficits and to urgings that it should bite the bullet and cut expenditures, in 1985 the Congress enacted the Balanced Budget and Emergency Deficit Control Act, widely known as the Gramm-Rudman Act. Because in the past Congress had found it difficult to make deep cuts in the budget when it reviewed individual programs separately, it sought to devise across-the-board cuts and thereby to remove itself from the budget-cutting process. The reductions were to be accomplished under complicated provisions spelled out in Sections 251 and 252 of the Act. They required the directors of the Office of Management and Budget and the Congressional Budget Office to submit their deficit estimates and budget-reduction calculations to the Comptroller General, a public official appointed by the President from a list of nominees but removable by the Congress for reasons specified in legislation enacted in 1921. After reviewing the estimates and budget-reduction calculations, the Comptroller General was required by Section 251 to submit a report to the President, who was then required to issue a "sequestration" order mandating spending reductions specified by the Comptroller General. This order was to go into effect unless Congress legislated its own reductions in the interim. The Act also provided for a "fallback deficit-reduction process" in the event that Section 251 was invalidated by the Court.

CHIEF JUSTICE BURGER delivered the opinion of the Court.

. . . .

The Constitution does not contemplate an active role for Congress in the supervision of officers charged with the execution of the laws it enacts. The President appoints "Officers of the United States" with the advice and consent of the Senate. . . ." . . . Once the appointment has been made and confirmed, however, the Constitution explicitly provides for removal of Officers of the United States by Congress only upon impeachment by the House of Representatives and conviction by the Senate. An impeachment by the House and trial by the Senate can rest only on "Treason, Bribery or other high Crimes and Misdemeanors." . . . A direct congressional role in the removal of officers charged with the execution of the laws beyond this limited one is inconsistent with separation of powers.

This Court first directly addressed this issue in *Myers* v. *U.S.* . . . [A]t issue was a statute providing that certain postmasters could be removed only "by and with the advice and consent of the Senate." The President removed one such postmaster without Senate approval, and a lawsuit ensued. CHIEF JUSTICE TAFT, writing for the Court, declared the statute unconstitutional on the ground that for Congress to "draw to itself, or to either branch of it, the power to remove or the right to participate in the exercise of that power . . . would . . . infringe the constitutional principle of the separation of governmental powers." . . .

A decade later, in *Humphrey's Executor* v. *U.S.* . . . (1935), relied upon heavily by appellants, a Federal Trade Commissioner who had been removed by the President sought back pay. . . . The Court distinguished *Myers*, reaffirming its holding that congressional participation in the removal of executive officers is unconstitutional. JUSTICE SUTHER-

LAND's opinion for the Court also underscored the crucial role of separated powers in our system.

The Court reached a similar result in *Weiner* v. *U.S.* . . . (1958), concluding that, under *Humphrey's Executor*, the President did not have unrestrained removal authority over a member of the War Crimes Commission.

To permit an officer controlled by Congress to execute the laws would be, in essence, to permit a congressional veto. Congress could simply remove, or threaten to remove, an officer for executing the laws in any fashion found to be unsatisfactory to Congress. This kind of congressional control over the execution of the laws . . . is constitutionally impermissible.

The dangers of congressional usurpation of Executive Branch functions have long been recognized. "[T]he debates of the Constitutional Convention, and the Federalist Papers, are replete with expressions of fear that the Legislative Branch of the National Government will aggrandize itself at the expense of the other two branches." *Buckley* v. *Valeo* . . . (1976). Indeed, we also have observed only recently that "[t]he hydraulic pressure inherent within each of the separate Branches to exceed the outer limits of its power, even to accomplish desirable objectives, must be resisted." *Chadha*. . . . With these principles in mind, we turn to consideration of whether the Comptroller General is controlled by Congress.

. . . .

It is clear that Congress has consistently viewed the Comptroller General as an officer of the Legislative Branch. The Reorganization Acts of 1945 and 1949, for example, both stated that the Comptroller General and the GAO are "a part of the legislative branch of the Government." Similarly, in the Accounting and Auditing Act of 1950, Congress required the Comptroller General to conduct audits "as an agent of the Congress."

Over the years, the Comptrollers General have also viewed themselves as part of the Legislative Branch. In one of the early Annual Reports of Comptroller General, the official seal of his office was described as reflecting: "the independence of judgment to be exercised by the General Accounting Office, subject to the control of the legislative branch. . . .

. . . .

Congress of course initially determined the content of the Balanced Budget and Emergency Deficit Control Act; and undoubtedly the content of the Act determines the nature of the executive duty. However, as *Chadha* makes clear, once Congress makes its choice in enacting legislation, its participation ends. Congress can thereafter control the execution of its enactment only indirectly — by passing new legislation. By placing the responsibility for execution of the Balanced Budget and Emergency Deficit Control Act in the hands of an officer who is subject to removal only by itself, Congress in effect has retained control over the execution of the Act and has intruded into the executive function. The Constitution does not permit such intrusion.

We now turn to the final issue of remedy. Appellants urge that rather than striking down Section 251 and invalidating the significant power Congress vested in the Comptroller General to meet a national fiscal emergency, we should take the lesser course of nullifying the statutory provisions of the 1921 Act that authorizes Congress to remove the Comptroller General. At oral argument, counsel for the Comptroller General suggested that this might make the Comptroller General removable by the President. All appellants urge that Congress would prefer invalidation of the removal provisions rather than invalidation of Section 251 of the Balanced Budget and Emergency Deficit Control Act.

Severance at this late date of the removal provisions enacted 65 years ago would significantly alter the Comptroller General's office, possibly by making him subservient to the Executive Branch. [Because of this the Court rejects this alternative.]...

No one can doubt that Congress and the President are confronted with fiscal and economic problems of unprecedented magnitude, but "the fact that a given law or procedure is efficient, convenient, and useful in facilitating functions of government, standing alone, will not save it if it is contrary to the Constitution. Convenience and efficiency are not the primary objectives — or the hallmarks — of democratic government...."...

We conclude the District Court correctly held that the powers vested in the Comptroller General under Section 251 violate the command of the Constitution that the Congress play no direct role in the execution of the laws. Accordingly, the judgment and order of the District Court are affirmed.

Our judgment is stayed for a period not to exceed 60 days to permit Congress to implement the fallback provisions.

JUSTICE STEVENS, with whom JUSTICE MARSHALL joins, concurring in the judgment.

...I agree with the Court that the "Gramm-Rudman-Hollings" Act contains a constitutional infirmity so severe that the flawed provision may not stand. I disagree with the Court, however, on the reasons why the Constitution prohibits the Comptroller General from exercising the powers assigned to him by...the Act. It is not the dormant, carefully circumscribed congressional removal power that represents the primary constitutional evil. Nor do I agree with the conclusion of both the majority and the dissent that the analysis depends on a labeling of the functions assigned to the Comptroller General as "executive powers." Rather, I am convinced that the Comptroller General must be characterized as an agent of Congress because of his long-standing statutory responsibilities; that the powers assigned to him under the Gramm-Rudman-Hollings act require him to make policy that will bind the Nation; and that, when Congress, or a component or an agent of Congress, seeks to make policy that will bind the nation, it must follow the procedures mandated by Article I of the Constitution — through passage by both Houses and presentment to the President. In short, Congress may not exercise its fundamental power to formulate national policy by delegating that power to one of its two Houses, to a legislative committee, or to an individual agent of the Congress such as the Speaker of the House of Representatives, the Sergeant at Arms of the Senate, or the Director of the Congressional Budget Office.... That principle, I believe, is applicable to the Comptroller General.

....

In the statutory section that identifies the Comptroller General's responsibilities for investigating the use of public money, four of the five enumerated duties specifically describe an obligation owed to Congress....

....

Numerous other provisions strongly support the conclusion that one of the Comptroller General's primary responsibilities is to work specifically on behalf of Congress....

....

Everyone agrees that the powers assigned to the Comptroller General by...[the] Act are extremely important. They require him to exercise sophisticated economic judgment concerning anticipated trends in the Nation's economy, projected levels of unemployment, interest rates, and the special problems that may be confronted by the many components of a vast federal bureaucracy. His duties are anything but ministerial — he is not merely a clerk wearing a "green eye shade" as he undertakes these tasks. Rather, he is vested with the kind of responsibilities that Congress has elected to discharge itself under the fallback provision that will become effective if and when Section 251(b) and Section 251(c)(2) are held invalid. Unless we make the naive assumption that the economic destiny of the Nation could be safely entrusted to a mindless bank of computers, the powers that this Act vests in the Comptroller General must be recognized as having transcendent importance.

. . . .

In my opinion, Congress itself could not exercise the Gramm-Rudman-Hollings functions through a concurrent resolution. The fact that the fallback provision in Section 274 requires a joint resolution rather than a concurrent resolution indicates that Congress endorsed this view. I think it equally clear that Congress may not simply delegate those functions to an agent such as the Congressional Budget Office. Since I am persuaded that the Comptroller General is also fairly deemed to be an agent of Congress, he too cannot exercise such functions.

JUSTICE WHITE, dissenting.

The Court, acting in the name of separation of powers, takes upon itself to strike down the Gramm-Rudman-Hollings Act, one of the most novel and far-reaching legislative responses to a national crisis since the New Deal. . . . I cannot concur in the Court's action. Like the Court, I will not purport to speak to the wisdom of the policies incorporated in the legislation the Court invalidates; that is a matter for the Congress and the Executive, both of which expressed their assent to the statute barely half a year ago. I will, however, address the wisdom of the Court's willingness to interpose its distressingly formalistic view of separation of powers as a bar to the attainment of governmental objectives through the means chosen by the Congress and the President in the legislative process established by the Constitution. . . . [T]he Court's decision rests on a feature of the legislative scheme that is of minimal practical significance and that presents no substantial threat to the basic scheme of separation of powers. . . .

Realistic consideration of the nature of the Comptroller General's relation to Congress . . . reveals that the threat to separation of powers conjured up by the majority is wholly chimerical. The power over removal retained by the Congress is not a power that is exercised outside the legislative process as established by the Constitution, nor does it appear likely that it is a power that adds significantly to the influence Congress may exert over executive officers through other, undoubtedly constitutional exercise of legislative power and through the constitutionally guaranteed impeachment power. Indeed, the removal power is so constrained by its own substantive limits and by the requirement of presidential approval "that, as a practical matter, Congress has

not exercised, and probably will never exercise, such control over the Comptroller General that his nonlegislative powers will threaten the goal of dispersion of power, and hence the goal of individual liberty, that separation of powers serves." . . .

. . . The wisdom of vesting "executive powers" in an officer removable by joint resolution may indeed be debatable — as may be the wisdom of the entire scheme of permitting an unelected official to revise the budget enacted by Congress — but such matters are for the most part to be worked out between the Congress and the President through the legislative process, which affords each branch ample opportunity to defend its interests. The Act vesting budget-cutting authority in the Comptroller General represents Congress's judgment that the delegation of such authority to counteract ever-mounting deficits is "necessary and proper" to the exercise of the powers granted the Federal Government by the Constitution; and the President's approval of the statute signifies his unwillingness to reject the choice made by Congress. . . . Under such circumstances, the role of this Court should be limited to determining whether the Act so alters the balance of authority among the branches of government as to pose a genuine threat to the basic division between the lawmaking power and the power to execute the law. Because I see no such threat, I cannot join the Court in striking down the Act.

I dissent.

[JUSTICE BLACKMUN also dissented (and would have invalidated the 1921 Act providing for Congressional removal of the Comptroller General).]

In re Neagle

135 U.S. 1 (1890)
Vote: 6–2; Field not participating.

One theory of the Presidency — sometimes identified as the Buchanan or Taft or Whig Theory — is that there must be a specific authorization for any action. *In re Neagle* tested this view in a dramatic but simple way. President Cleveland assigned a guard to protect a justice whose life was threatened. The guard ultimately shot the threatener. The question tested was whether a federal or a state court would decide if the homicide was justifiable. Only if the President's action was proper, even without legislation or a constitutional provision, was Neagle acting in a federal capacity.

The case is called *In re Neagle* ("in the matter of Neagle") because it is a "one-sided" suit by Neagle to remove the case to the federal courts, with the State of California legally insisting it need not argue when the matter was before its courts. (This is a fictitious matter; a lawyer did actually argue the case, and it is referred to, e.g., in the *Supreme Court Reporter,* as *Cunningham* v. *Neagle.*)

Llewellyn has argued that every case is "Janus-faced." As a precedent, every case can be read for a minimum impact or maximum effect. *Neagle* is a perfect example. It seems a very limited expansion of presidential power. Can you see how it may be used to justify the most extreme assertions of presidential power?

Neagle as United States deputy marshal, acting under the orders of Marshal Franks, and in pursuance of instructions from the Attorney General of the United States, had, in consequence of an anticipated attempt at violence on the part of Terry against the Honorable Stephen J. Field, a justice of the Supreme Court of the United States, been in attendance upon said justice, and was sitting by his side at a breakfast table when a murderous assault was made by Terry on Judge Field, and in defence of the life of the judge the homicide was committed for which Neagle was held by Cunningham. The allegation was very distinct that Justice Field was engaged in the discharge of his duties as circuit justice of the United States.

MR. JUSTICE MILLER . . . delivered the opinion of the court.

 . . . .

. . . Without a more minute discussion of this testimony, it produces upon us the conviction of a settled purpose on the part of Terry and his wife, amounting to a conspiracy, to murder Justice Field. And we are sure that if Neagle had been merely a brother or a friend of Judge Field, travelling with him, and aware of all the previous relations of Terry to the Judge, — as he was, — of his bitter animosity, his declared purpose to have revenge even to the point of killing him, he would have been justified in what he did in defence of Mr. Justice Field's life, and possibly his own.

But such a justification would be a proper subject for consideration on a trial of the case for murder in the courts of the State of California, and there exists no authority in the courts of the United States to discharge the prisoner while held in custody by the State authorities for his offence, unless there be found in aid of the defence of the prisoner some element of power and authority asserted under the government of the United States.

This element is said to be found in the facts that Mr. Justice Field, when attacked, was in the immediate discharge of his duty as judge of the Circuit Courts of the United States within California; that the assault upon him grew out of the animosity of Terry and wife, arising out of the previous discharge of his duty as circuit justice in the case for which they were committed for contempt of court; and that the deputy marshal of the United States, who killed Terry in defence of Field's life, was charged with a duty under the law of the United States to protect Field from the violence which Terry was inflicting, and which was intended to lead to Field's death.

To the inquiry whether this proposition is sustained by law and the facts which we have recited, we now address ourselves.

Mr. Justice Field was a member of the Supreme Court of the United States, and had been a member of that court for over a quarter of a century, during which he had become venerable for his age and for his long and valuable service in that court. The business of the Supreme Court has become so exacting that for many years past the justices of it have been compelled to remain for the larger part of the year in Washington City, from whatever part of the country they may have been appointed. The term for each year, including the necessary travel and preparations to attend at its beginning, has generally lasted from eight to nine months.

But the justices of this court have imposed upon them other duties, the most important of which arise out of the fact that they are also judges of the Circuit Courts of the United States.

We have no doubt that Mr. Justice Field when attacked by Terry was engaged in the discharge of his duties as Circuit Justice of the Ninth Circuit, and was entitled to all the protection under those circumstances which the law could give him.

It is urged, however, that there exists no statute authorizing any such protection as that which Neagle was instructed to give Judge Field in the present case, and indeed no protection whatever against a vindictive or malicious assault growing out of the faithful discharge of his official duties; . . .

If a person in the situation of Judge Field could

have no other guarantee of his personal safety, while engaged in the conscientious discharge of a disagreeable duty, than the fact that if he was murdered his murderer would be subject to the laws of a State and by those laws could be punished, the security would be very insufficient. . . .

Where, then, are we to look for the protection which we have shown Judge Field was entitled to when engaged in the discharge of his official duties? Not to the courts of the United States; because, as has been more than once said in this court, in the division of the powers of government between the three great departments, executive, legislative and judicial, the judicial is the weakest for the purposes of self-protection and for the enforcement of the powers which it exercises. The ministerial officers through whom its commands must be executed are marshals of the United States, and belong emphatically to the executive department of the government. They are appointed by the President, with the advice and consent of the Senate. They are removable from office at his pleasure. They are subjected by act of Congress to the supervision and control of the Department of Justice, in the hands of one of the cabinet officers of the President, and their compensation is provided by acts of Congress. The same may be said of the district attorneys of the United States, who prosecute and defend the claims of the government in the courts.

The legislative branch of the government can only protect the judicial officers by the enactment of laws for that purpose, and the argument we are now combating assumes that no such law has been passed by Congress.

If we turn to the executive department of the government, we find a very different condition of affairs. The Constitution, section 3, Article 2, declares that the President "shall take care that the laws be faithfully executed," and he is provided with the means of fulfilling this obligation by his authority to commission all the officers of the United States, and, by and with the advice and consent of the Senate, to appoint the most important of them and to fill vacancies. He is declared to be commander-in-chief of the army and navy of the United States. The duties which are thus imposed upon him he is further enabled to perform by the recognition in the Constitution, and the creation by acts of Congress, of executive departments, which have varied in number from four or five to seven or eight, the heads of which are familiarly called cabinet ministers. These aid him in the performance of the great duties of his office, and represent him in a thousand acts to which it can hardly be supposed his personal attention is called,

and thus he is enabled to fulfil the duty of his great department, expressed in the phrase that "he shall take care that the laws be faithfully executed."

Is this duty limited to the enforcement of acts of Congress or of treaties of the United States according to their *express terms,* or does it include the rights, duties and obligations growing out of the Constitution itself, our international relations, and all the protection implied by the nature of the government under the Constitution?

We cannot doubt the power of the President to take measures for the protection of a judge of one of the courts of the United States, who, while in the discharge of the duties of his office, is threatened with a personal attack which may probably result in his death, and we think it clear that where this protection is to be afforded through the civil power, the Department of Justice is the proper one to set in motion the necessary means of protection. . . .

The result at which we have arrived upon this examination is, that in the protection of the person and the life of Mr. Justice Field while in the discharge of his official duties, Neagle was authorized to resist the attack of Terry upon him; that Neagle was correct in the belief that without prompt action on his part the assault of Terry upon the judge would have ended in the death of the latter; that such being his well-founded belief, he was justified in taking the life of Terry, as the only means of preventing the death of the man who was intended to be his victim; that in taking the life of Terry, under the circumstances, he was acting under the authority of the law of the United States, and was justified in so doing; and that he is not liable to answer in the courts of California on account of his part in that transaction.

MR. JUSTICE LAMAR (with whom concurred MR. CHIEF JUSTICE FULLER) dissenting.

The Chief Justice and myself are unable to assent to the conclusion reached by the majority of the court.

. . . [I]t is not pretended that there is any *single* specific statute making it, in so many words, Neagle's duty to protect the justice. The position assumed is, and is wholly, that the authority and duty to protect the justice did arise directly and necessarily out of the Constitution and positive congressional enactments. . . . Waving the question of the essentiality of any such protection to the existence of the government, the manifest answer is, that the protection needed and to be given must proceed not from the President, but primarily from Congress. Again, while it is the President's duty to take care that the laws be faithfully executed, it is not his duty to *make* laws or a law of the United States. . . .

... [i]f the killing of Terry was done "in pursuance of a law of the United States," that the law had somewhere an origin. There are under the general government only two possible sources of the law.

Now, what is it that constitutes the supreme laws, of which so much is said in this case? How distinctly, how plainly and how fully the Constitution answers! The Constitution itself, the treaties, and the laws made in pursuance of the Constitution. Made by whom? By Congress, manifestly. The two clauses already quoted give the power of legislation in the most sweeping terms. It alone has power to make any law. Anything purporting to be a law not enacted by Congress would not be "in pursuance of" any provision of the Constitution.

Thus we are driven to look for the source of this asserted law to some legislation of Congress — legislation made under either its express constitutional authority, or under its properly implied authority, it is immaterial which; and there is none of either class.

The authority is sought to be traced here through the self-preservative power of the federal judiciary implied from the Constitution; and then through the obligation of the executive to protect the judges, implied from the Constitution, whereas there is no such implication in either case, for the simple but all-sufficient reason that by the Constitution itself the whole of those functions is committed to Congress.

MR. JUSTICE FIELD did not sit at the hearing of this case, and took no part in its decision.

Myers v. U.S.

272 U.S. 52 (1926)
Vote: 6–3

The Constitution is strangely silent about the relationships of public officials in the executive branch to Congress and the President. In a parliamentary system, at least in theory, there is no dilemma; all officials are responsible through the Cabinet to Parliament. In our system the executive and legislature are separate and even antagonistic. The issue of who can remove a subordinate is one manifestation of the built-in ambiguity and conflict.

In 1876, the Radical Republicans in control of Congress passed the Tenure of Office Act, which provided that permission of the Senate was required to remove an appointee whose original appointment involved Senatorial approval. The course of litigation has its own imperatives, and it took a half-century for the measure to come before the Supreme Court. The Chief Justice, a former President, wrote the opinion stressing the context of the Constitutional Convention, but also the needs of the President in performing the great tasks incumbent on the office.

MR. CHIEF JUSTICE TAFT delivered the opinion of the Court.

This case presents the question whether under the Constitution the President has the exclusive power of removing executive officers of the United States whom he has appointed by and with the advice and consent of the Senate.

Myers, appellant's intestate, was on July 21, 1917, appointed by the President, by and with the advice and consent of the Senate, to be a postmaster of the first class at Portland, Oregon, for a term of four years. On January 20, 1920, Myers' resignation was demanded. He refused the demand. On February 2, 1920, he was removed from office by order of the Postmaster General, acting by direction of the President. . . .

On April 21, 1921, he brought this suit in the Court of Claims for his salary from the date of his removal, which, as claimed by supplemental petition filed after July 21, 1921, the end of his term, amounted to $8,838.71. . . .

The Court of Claims gave judgment against Myers, and this is an appeal from that judgment.

By the 6th section of the Act of Congress of July 12, 1876, 19 Stat. 80, 81, c. 179, under which Myers was appointed with the advice and consent of the Senate as a first-class postmaster, it is provided that

"Postmasters of the first, second and third classes shall be appointed and may be removed by the President by and with the advice and consent of the Senate and shall hold their offices for four years unless sooner removed or suspended according to law."

The Senate did not consent to the President's removal of Myers during his term. If this statute, in its requirement that his term should be four years unless sooner removed by the President by and with the consent of the Senate, is valid, the appellant, Myers' administratrix, is entitled to recover his unpaid salary for his full term, and the judgment of the Court of Claims must be reversed. The Government maintains that the requirement is invalid, for the reason that under Article II of the Constitution the President's power of removal of executive officers appointed by him with the advice and consent of the Senate is full and complete without consent of the Senate.

... A veto by the Senate — a part of the legislative branch of the Government — upon removals is a much greater limitation upon the executive branch and a much more serious blending of the legislative with the executive than a rejection of a proposed appointment. It is not to be implied. The rejection of a nominee of the President for a particular office does not greatly embarrass him in the conscientious discharge of his high duties in the selection of those who are to aid him, because the President usually has an ample field from which to select for office, according to his preference, competent and capable men. The Senate has full power to reject newly proposed appointees whenever the President shall remove the incumbents. Such a check enables the Senate to prevent the filling of offices with bad or incompetent men or with those against whom there is tenable objection.

The power to prevent the removal of an officer who has served under the President is different from the authority to consent to or reject his appointment. When a nomination is made, it may be presumed that the Senate is, or may become, as well advised as to the fitness of the nominee as the President, but in the nature of things the defects in ability or intelligence or loyalty in the administration of the laws of one who has served as an officer under the President, are facts as to which the President, or his trusted subordinates, must be better informed than the Senate, and the power to remove him may, therefore, be regarded as confined, for very sound and practical reasons, to the governmental authority which has administrative control. The power of removal is incident to the power of appointment, not to the power of advising and consenting to appointment, and when the grant of the executive power is enforced by the express mandate to take care that the laws be faithfully executed, it emphasizes the necessity for including within the executive power as conferred the exclusive power of removal.

A reference of the whole power of removal to general legislation by Congress is quite out of keeping with the plan of government devised by the framers of the Constitution. It could never have been intended to leave to Congress unlimited discretion to vary fundamentally the operation of the great independent executive branch of government and thus most seriously to weaken it. It would be a delegation by the Convention to Congress of the function of defining the primary boundaries of another of the three great divisions of government. The inclusion of removals of executive officers in the executive power vested in the President by Article II, according to its usual definition, and the implication of his power of removal of such officers from the provision of section 2 expressly recognizing in him the power of their appointment, are a much more natural and appropriate source of the removing power.

It is reasonable to suppose also that had it been intended to give to Congress power to regulate or control removals in the manner suggested, it would have been included among the specifically enumerated legislative powers in Article I, or in the specified limitations on the executive power in Article II. The difference between the grant of legislative power under Article I to Congress, which is limited to powers therein enumerated, and the more general grant of the executive power to the President under Article II, is significant. The fact that the executive power is given in general terms strengthened by specific terms where emphasis is appropriate, and limited by direct expressions where limitation is needed and that no express limit is placed on the power of removal by the executive, is a convincing indication that none was intended.

Made responsible under the Constitution for the effective enforcement of the law, the President needs as an indispensable aid to meet it the disciplinary influence upon those who act under him of a reserve power of removal. But it is contended that executive officers appointed by the President with the consent of the Senate are bound by the statutory law and are not his servants to do his will, and that his obligation to care for the faithful execution of the laws does not authorize him to treat them as such. The degree of guidance in the discharge of their duties that the President may exercise over executive officers varies with the character of their service as prescribed in the law under which they act. The highest and most important duties which his subordinates perform are those in which they act for him. In such cases they are exercising not their own but his discretion. This field is a very large one. It is sometimes described as political. ... Each head of a department is and must be the President's *alter ego* in the matters of that department where the President is required by law to exercise authority.

The duties of the heads of departments and bureaus in which the discretion of the President is exercised and which we have described, are the most important in the whole field of executive action of the Government. There is nothing in the Constitution which permits a distinction between the removal of the head of a department or a bureau, when he discharges a political duty of the President or exercises his discretion, and the removal of executive officers engaged in the discharge of their other normal duties. The imperative reasons requiring an unrestricted power to remove the most important of his subordinates in their most important duties must, therefore, control the interpretation of the Constitution as to all appointed by him.

But this is not to say that there are not strong reasons why the President should have a like power to remove his appointees charged with other duties than those above described. The ordinary duties of officers prescribed by statute come under the general administrative control of the President by virtue of the general grant to him of the executive power, and he may properly supervise and guide their construction of the statutes under which they act in order to secure that unitary and uniform execution of the laws which Article II of the Constitution evidently contemplated in vesting general executive power in the President alone. Laws are often passed with specific provision for the adoption of regulations by a department or bureau head to make the law workable and effective. The ability and judgment manifested by the official thus empowered, as well as his energy and stimulation of his subordinates, are subjects which the President must consider and supervise in his administrative control. Finding such officers to be negligent and inefficient, the President should have the power to remove them. Of course there may be duties so peculiarly and specifically committed to the discretion of a particular officer as to raise a question whether the President may overrule or revise the officer's interpretation of his statutory duty in a particular instance. Then there may be duties of a quasi-judicial character imposed on executive officers and members of executive tribunals whose decisions after hearing affect interests of individuals, the discharge of which the President can not in a particular case properly influence or control. But even in such a case he may consider the decision after its rendition as a reason for removing the officer, on the ground that the discretion regularly entrusted to that officer by statute has not been on the whole intelligently or wisely exercised. Otherwise he does not discharge his own constitutional duty of seeing that the laws be faithfully executed.

We come now to consider an argument advanced and strongly pressed on behalf of the complainant, that this case concerns only the removal of a postmaster; that a postmaster is an inferior officer; that such an office was not included within the legislative decision of 1789 which related only to superior officers to be appointed by the President by and with the advice and consent of the Senate. . . .

The power to remove inferior executive officers, like that to remove superior executive officers, is an incident of the power to appoint them, and is in its nature an executive power. The authority of Congress given by the excepting clause to vest the appointment of such inferior officers in the heads of departments carries with it authority incidentally to invest the heads of departments with power to remove. It has been the practice of Congress to do so and this Court has recognized that power. The Court also has recognized in the *Perkins* case that Congress, in committing the appointment of such inferior officers to the heads of departments, may prescribe incidental regulations controlling and restricting the latter in the exercise of power of removal. But the Court never has held, nor reasonably could hold, although it is argued to the contrary on behalf of the appellant, that the excepting clause enables Congress to draw to itself, or to either branch of it, the power to remove or the right to participate in the exercise of that power.

. . . We are now asked to adopt an adverse view, because the Congress of the United States did so during a heated political difference of opinion between the then President and the majority leaders of Congress over the reconstruction measures adopted as a means of restoring to their proper status the States which attempted to withdraw from the Union at the time of the Civil War. The extremes to which the majority in both Houses carried legislative measures in that matter are now recognized by all who calmly review the history of that episode in our Government, leading to articles of impeachment against President Johnson, and his acquittal. Without animadverting on the character of the measures taken, we are certainly justified in saying that they should not be given the weight affecting proper constitutional construction to be accorded to that reached by the First Congress of the United States during a political calm and acquiesced in by the whole Government for three-quarters of a century. . . .

. . . [T]he Tenure of Office Act of 1867, in so far as it attempted to prevent the President from removing executive officers who had been appointed by him by and with the advice and consent of the Senate, was invalid, and that subsequent legislation of the same effect was equally so.

For the reasons given, we must therefore hold that the provision of the law of 1876, by which the unrestricted power of removal of first class postmasters is denied to the President, is in violation of the Constitution, and invalid. This leads to an affirmance of the judgment of the Court of Claims.

Judgment affirmed.

MR. JUSTICE HOLMES, dissenting.

The arguments drawn from the executive power of the President, and from his duty to appoint officers of the United States (when Congress does not vest the appointment elsewhere), to take care that the laws be faithfully executed, and to commission all officers of the United States, seem to me spider's webs inadequate to control the dominant facts.

We have to deal with an office that owes its existence to Congress and that Congress may abolish tomorrow. Its duration and the pay attached to it while it lasts depend on Congress alone. Congress alone confers on the President the power to appoint to it and at any time may transfer the power to other hands. With such power over its own creation, I have no more trouble in believing that Congress has power to prescribe a term of life for it free from any interference than I have in accepting the undoubted power of Congress to decree its end. . . .

The separate opinion of MR. JUSTICE MCREYNOLDS.

A certain repugnance must attend the suggestion that the President may ignore any provision of an Act of Congress under which he has proceeded. He should promote and not subvert orderly government. The serious evils which follow the practice of dismissing civil officers as caprice or interest dictated, long permitted under congressional enactments, are known to all. It brought the public service to a low estate and caused insistent demand for reform. . . .

Constitutional provisions should be interpreted with the expectation that Congress will discharge its duties no less faithfully than the Executive will attend to his. The legislature is charged with the duty of making laws for orderly administration obligatory upon all. It possesses supreme power over national affairs and may wreck as well as speed them. It holds the purse; every branch of the government functions under statutes which embody its will; it may impeach and expel all civil officers. The duty is upon it "to make all laws which shall be necessary and proper for carrying into execution" all powers of the federal government.

MR. JUSTICE BRANDEIS, dissenting.

The contention that Congress is powerless to make consent of the Senate a condition of removal by the President from an executive office rests mainly upon the clause in §1 of Article II which declares that "The executive Power shall be vested in a President." The argument is that appointment and removal of officials are executive prerogatives; that the grant to the President of "the executive Power" confers upon him, as inherent in the office, the power to exercise these two functions without restriction by Congress, except in so far as the power to restrict his exercise of them is expressly conferred upon by Congress by the Constitution; that in respect to appointment certain restrictions of the executive power are so provided for; but that in respect to removal, there is no express grant to Congress of any power to limit the President's prerogative. The simple answer to the argument is this: The ability to remove a subordinate executive officer, being an essential of effective government, will, in the absence of express constitutional provision to the contrary, be deemed to have been vested in some person or body. . . . But it is not a power inherent in a chief executive. The President's power of removal from statutory civil inferior offices, like the power of appointment to them, comes immediately from Congress. It is true that the exercise of the power of removal is said to be an executive act; and that when the Senate grants or withholds consent to a removal by the President, it participates in an executive act. But the Constitution has confessedly granted to Congress the legislative power to create offices, and to prescribe the tenure thereof; and it has not in terms denied to Congress the power to control removals. To prescribe the tenure involves prescribing the conditions under which incumbency shall cease. . . .

It is also argued that the clauses in Article II, §3, of the Constitution, which declare that the President "shall take Care that the Laws be faithfully executed, and shall Commission all the Officers of the United States" imply a grant to the President of the alleged uncontrollable power of removal. I do not find in either clause anything which supports this claim. . . .

The practice of Congress to control the exercise of the executive power of removal from inferior offices is evidenced by many statutes which restrict it in many ways besides the removal clause here in question. Each of these restrictive statutes became law with the approval of the President. Every President who has held office since 1861, except President Garfield, approved one or more of such statutes.

The separation of the powers of government did not make each branch completely autonomous. It left each, in some measure, dependent upon the others, as it left to each power to exercise, in some respects, functions in their nature executive, legislative and judicial.

Checks and balances were established in order that this should be "a government of laws and not of men." As White said in the House, in 1789, an uncontrollable power of removal in the Chief Executive "is a doctrine not to be learned in American governments." Such power had been denied in Colonial Charters, and even under Proprietary Grants and Royal Commissions. It had been denied in the thirteen States before the framing of the Federal Constitution. The doctrine of the separation of powers was adopted by the Convention of 1787, not to promote efficiency but to preclude the exercise of arbitrary power. The purpose was, not to avoid friction, but, by means of the inevitable friction incident to the distribution of the governmental powers among three departments, to save the people from autocracy. . . .

Humphrey's Executor (Rathbun) v. U.S.

295 U.S. 602 (1935)
Vote: 9–0

Humphrey was a conservative member of the Federal Trade Commission. In 1933, at the height of the Depression, President Roosevelt decided to remove Humphrey for policy reasons, as the FTC had authority over many economic policies key to New Deal programs. Humphrey had been ill—he was to die in the course of litigation—but Roosevelt dismissed him on policy, as opposed to performance, grounds.

With Sutherland's opinion in this case, rather considerable changes in the position of the Independent Regulatory Commissions took place. Roosevelt's reliance on MYERS proved misplaced, and removal authority of the President was limited. While *Rathbun* seemed to be an affirmation of possible congressional authority, *Wiener* v. *U.S.* (1958)

later decided the President could remove such officials *only* with congressional authorization.

Examine Llewellyn's "Janus-faced" notion of precedents in the light of MYERS and *Rathbun*, then *Rathbun* and *Wiener*.

MR. JUSTICE SUTHERLAND delivered the opinion of the Court.

Plaintiff brought suit in the Court of Claims against the United States to recover a sum of money alleged to be due the deceased for salary as a Federal Trade Commissioner from October 8, 1933, when the President undertook to remove him from office, to the time of his death on February 14, 1934.

. . . .

William E. Humphrey, the decedent, on December 10, 1931, was nominated by President Hoover to succeed himself as a member of the Federal Trade Commission, and was confirmed by the United States Senate. He was duly commissioned for a term of seven years expiring September 25, 1938; and, after taking the required oath of office, entered upon his duties. On July 25, 1933, President Roosevelt addressed a letter to the commissioner asking for his resignation, on the ground "that the aims and purposes of the Administration with respect to the work of the Commission can be carried out most effectively with personnel of my own selection," but disclaiming any reflection upon the commissioner personally or upon his services. The commissioner replied, asking time to consult his friends. After some further correspondence upon the subject, the President on August 31, 1933, wrote the commissioner expressing the hope that the resignation would be forthcoming and saying:

"You will, I know, realize that I do not feel that your mind and my mind go along together on either the policies or the administering of the Federal Trade Commission, and, frankly, I think it is best for the people of this country that I should have a full confidence."

The commissioner declined to resign; and on October 7, 1933, the President wrote him:

"Effective as of this date you are hereby removed from the office of Commissioner of the Federal Trade Commission."

. . . .

"1. Do the provisions of section 1 of the Federal Trade Commission Act, stating that 'any commissioner may be removed by the President for inefficiency, neglect of duty, or malfeasance in office,' restrict or limit the power of the President to remove a commissioner except upon one or more of the causes named?

First. The question first to be considered is whether, by the provisions of §1 of the Federal Trade Commission Act already quoted, the President's power is limited to removal for the specific causes enumerated therein.

The statute fixes a term of office ... of seven years — any commissioner being subject to removal by the President for inefficiency, neglect of duty, or malfeasance in office. The words of the act are definite and unambiguous.

... [I]f the intention of Congress that no removal should be made during the specified term except for one or more of the enumerated uses were not clear upon the face of the statute, as we think it is, it would be made clear by a consideration of the character of the commission and the legislative history which accompanied and preceded the passage of the act.

The commission is to be non-partisan; and it must, from the very nature of its duties, act with entire impartiality. It is charged with the enforcement of no policy except the policy of the law. Its duties are neither political nor executive, but predominantly quasi-judicial and quasi-legislative. Like the Interstate Commerce Commission, its members are called upon to exercise the trained judgment of a body of experts "appointed by law and informed by experience."

The legislative reports in both houses of Congress clearly reflect the view that a fixed term was necessary to the effective and fair administration of the law.

The debates in both houses demonstrate that the prevailing view was that the commission was not to be "subject to anybody in the government but ... only to the people of the United States"; free from "political domination or control" or the "probability or possibility of such a thing"; to be "separate and apart from any existing department of the government — not subject to the orders of the President."

More to the same effect appears in the debates, which were long and thorough and contain nothing to the contrary. While the general rule precludes the use of these debates to explain the meaning of the words of the statute, they may be considered as reflecting light upon its general purposes and the evils which it sought to remedy. *Federal Trade Comm'n* v. *Raladam Co.,* 283 U.S. 643, 650.

Thus, the language of the act, the legislative reports, and the general purposes of the legislation as reflected by the debates, all combine to demonstrate the Congressional intent to create a body of experts who shall gain experience by length of service — a body which shall be independent of executive authority, *except in its selection,* and free to exercise its judgment without the leave or hindrance of any other official or any department of the government. To the accomplishment of these purposes, it is clear that Congress was of opinion that length and certainty of tenure would vitally contribute. And to hold that, nevertheless, the members of the commission continue in office at the mere will of the President, might be to thwart, in large measure, the very ends which Congress sought to realize by definitely fixing the term of the office.

We conclude that the intent of the act is to limit the executive power of removal to the causes enumerated, the existence of none of which is claimed here; and we pass to the second question.

Second. To support its contention that the removal provision of §1, as we have just construed it, is an unconstitutional interference with the executive power of the President, the government's chief reliance is *Myers* v. *United States,* 272 U.S. 52. That case has been so recently decided, and the prevailing and dissenting opinions so fully review the general subject of the power of executive removal, that further discussion would add little of value to the wealth of material there collected. ... The narrow point actually decided was only that the President had power to remove a postmaster of the first class, without the advice and consent of the Senate as required by act of Congress. In the course of the opinion of the court, expressions occur which tend to sustain the government's contention, but these are beyond the point involved and therefore do not come within the rule of *stare decisis.*

The office of a postmaster is so essentially unlike the office now involved that the decision in the *Myers* case cannot be accepted as controlling our decision here. A postmaster is an executive officer restricted to the performance of executive functions. He is charged with no duty at all related to either the legislative or judicial power. The actual decision in the *Myers* case finds support in the theory that such an officer is merely one of the units in the executive department and, hence, inherently subject to the exclusive and illimitable power of removal by the Chief Executive, whose subordinate and aid he is.

The Federal Trade Commission is an administrative body created by Congress to carry into effect legislative policies embodied in the statute in accordance with the legislative standard therein prescribed, and to perform other specified duties as a legislative or as a judicial aid. Such a body cannot in any proper sense be characterized as an arm or an eye of the executive. Its duties are performed without executive leave and, in the contemplation of the statute, must be free from executive control.

To the extent that it exercises any executive function—as distinguished from executive power in the constitutional sense—it does so in the discharge and effectuation of its quasi-legislative or quasi-judicial powers, or as an agency of the legislative or judicial departments of the government.

We think it plain under the Constitution that illimitable power of removal is not possessed by the President in respect of officers of the character of those just named.

Alexia Morrison, Independent Counsel v. Theodore B. Olson, et al.

56 LW 4835 (1988)
Vote: 7–1; Kennedy not participating

There is an obvious problem when high government officials are accused of crime in office. The Department of Justice, headed by the Attorney General, decides on prosecution. But the suspect may be the Attorney General, the President, or some high co-worker in the administration.

To deal with this dilemma Congress passed the 1978 Ethics in Government statute. It provides for a Special Division of the Court of Appeals that will select an independent counsel to investigate charges when made about a specified set of high officials. The Special Division can act only after an application by the Attorney General, who has sole power to decide if the charges are serious enough to warrant further inquiry.

Once chosen, the special counsel, which is supervised in minor ways by the Special Division and in other ways by the Department of Justice, essentially has autonomy on the conduct of the authorized investigation.

This case involved an independent counsel prosecuting alleged perjury by high Environmental Protection Agency officials in testifying before Congress. Defendants argued that the creation of the prosecutor's office was an unconstitutional limit on the powers of the President. Although the Attorney General had found, of course, that there was sufficient evidence to warrant investigation, the Department of Justice backed the defendants' view of the separation of powers. (Critics suggested that the fact that Attorney General Meese was the subject of two separate inquiries by independent counsel might have had some bearing on the department's stance.)

Notice Justice Scalia's argument that when the two branches of the national government collide, the normal presumption of constitutionality of laws does not hold. Did Brandeis agree? (See the *Ashwander* rules and the *Myers* case.) Where did Scalia get this rule?

The Court has also upheld the constitutionality of a sentencing commission commingling judges, the Attorney General, and appointed experts in *Mistretta* v. *U.S.* 1989, as well as referral to an American Bar Association committee of the names of judicial nominees for their evaluation, and the appointment by judges of temporary U.S. prosecutors, ending the specter of a new era of rigid separation of power decision.

CHIEF JUSTICE REHNQUIST delivered the opinion of the Court.

. . . The parties do not dispute that "[t]he Constitution for purposes of appointment . . . divides all its officers into two classes." *United States* v. *Germaine* . . . (1879). As we stated in *Buckley* v. *Valeo* . . . (1976), "[p]rincipal officers are selected by the President with the advice and consent of the Senate. Inferior officers Congress may allow to be appointed by the President alone, by the heads of departments, or by the Judiciary." The initial question is, accordingly, whether appellant is an "inferior" or a "principal" officer. If she is the latter, as the Court of Appeals concluded, then the Act is in violation of the Appointments Clause.

The line between "inferior" and "principal" officers is one that is far from clear, and the Framers provided little guidance into where it should be drawn. See, *e.g.,* 2 J. Story, Commentaries on the Constitution . . . (1858) ("In the practical course of the government there does not seem to have been any exact line drawn, who are and who are not to be deemed *inferior* officers, in the sense of the constitution, whose appointment does not necessarily require the concurrence of the senate"). We need not attempt here to decide exactly where the line falls between the two types of officers, because in our view appellant clearly falls on the "inferior officer" side of that line. Several factors lead to this conclusion.

First, appellant is subject to removal by a higher Executive Branch official. Although appellant may not be "subordinate" to the Attorney General (and the President) insofar as she possesses a degree of independent discretion to exercise the powers delegated to her under the Act, the fact that she can be removed by the Attorney General indicates that she is to some degree "inferior" in rank and authority. Second, appellant is empowered by the Act to perform only certain, limited duties. An independent counsel's role is restricted primarily to investigation and, if appropriate, prosecution for certain federal crimes. . . .

. . . .

Third, appellant's office is limited in jurisdiction. Not only is the Act itself restricted in applicability to certain federal officials suspected of certain serious federal crimes, but an independent counsel can only act within the scope of the jurisdiction that has been granted by the Special Division pursuant to a request by the Attorney General. Finally, appellant's office is limited in tenure. There is concededly no time limit on the appointment of a particular counsel. Nonetheless, the office of independent counsel is "temporary" in the sense that an independent counsel is appointed essentially to accomplish a single task, and when that task is over the office is terminated, either by the counsel herself or by action of the Special Division. Unlike other prosecutors, appellant has no ongoing responsibilities that extend beyond the accomplishment of the mission that she was appointed for and authorized by the Special Division to undertake. . . .

. . . .

This does not, however, end our inquiry under the Appointments Clause. Appellees argue that even if appellant is an "inferior" officer, the Clause does, not empower Congress to place the power to appoint such an officer outside the Executive Branch. They contend that the Clause does not contemplate congressional authorization of "interbranch appointments," in which an officer of one branch is appointed by officers of another branch. The relevant language of the Appointments Clause is worth repeating. It reads: ". . . but the Congress may by Law vest the Appointment of such inferior Officers, as they think proper, in the President alone, in the courts of Law, or in the Heads of Departments." On its face, the language of this "excepting clause" admits of no limitation on interbranch appointments. Indeed, the inclusion of "as they think proper" seems clearly to give Congress significant discretion to determine whether it is "proper" to vest the appointment of, for example, executive officials in the "courts of Law." . . .

We also note that the history of the clause provides no support for appellees' position. . . . [T]here was little or no debate on the question of whether the Clause empowers Congress to provide for interbranch appointments, and there is nothing to suggest that the Framers intended to prevent Congress from having that power.

. . . .

. . . We thus disagree with the Court of Appeals' conclusion that there is an inherent incongruity about a court having the power to appoint prosecutorial officers. We have recognized that courts may appoint private attorneys to act as prosecutor for judicial contempt judgments. . . . In *Go-Bart Importing Co.* v. *United States* . . . (1931), we approved court appointment of United States commissioners, who exercised certain limited prosecutorial powers. . . . In *Siebold,* as well, we indicated that judicial appointment of federal marshals, who are "executive officer[s]," would not be inappropriate. Lower courts have also upheld interim judicial appointments of United States Attorneys, . . . and Congress itself has vested the power to make these interim appointments in the district courts. . . . Congress of course was concerned when it created the office of independent counsel with the conflicts of interest that could arise in situations when the Executive Branch is called upon to investigate its own high-ranking officers. It if were to remove the appointing authority from the Executive Branch, the most logical place to put it was in the Judicial Branch. In the light of the Act's provision making the judges of the Special Division ineligible to participate in any matters relating to an independent counsel they have appointed, . . . we do not think that appointment of the independent counsels by the court runs afoul of the constitutional limitation on "incongruous" interbranch appointments.

. . . .

Appellees next contend that the powers vested in the Special Division by the Act conflict with Article III of the Constitution. We have long recognized that by the express provision of Article III, the judicial power of the United States is limited to "Cases" and "Controversies." . . .

. . . Clearly, once it is accepted that the Appointments Clause gives Congress the power to vest the appointment of officials such as the independent counsel in the "Courts of Law," there can be no Article III objection to the Special Division's exercise of that power, as the power itself derives from the Appointments Clause, a source of authority for judicial action that is independent of Article III. . . .

. . . This said, we do not think that Congress may give the Division *unlimited* discretion to determine the independent counsel's jurisdiction. In order for the Division's definition of the counsel's jurisdiction to be truly "incidental" to its power to appoint, the jurisdiction that the court decides upon must be demonstrably related to the factual circumstances that gave rise to the Attorney General's investigation and request for the appointment of the independent counsel in the particular case.

. . . .

. . . In this case, the miscellaneous powers described above do not impermissibly trespass upon the authority of the Executive Branch. Some of these allegedly "supervisory" powers conferred on the court are passive: the Division merely "receives" reports from the counsel or the Attorney General, it is not entitled to act on them or to specifically approve or disapprove of their contents. Other provisions of the Act do require the court to exercise some judgment and discretion, but the powers granted by these provisions are themselves essentially ministerial. The Act simply does not give the Division the power to "supervise" the independent counsel in the exercise of her investigative or prosecutorial authority. . . .

We are more doubtful about the Special Division's power to terminate the office of the independent counsel pursuant to §596(b)(2). As appellees suggest, the power to terminate, especially when exercised by the Division on its own motion, is "administrative" to the extent that it requires the Special Division to monitor the progress of proceedings of the independent counsel and come to a decision as to whether the counsel's job is "completed." §596(b)(2). It also is not a power that could be considered typically "judicial," as it has few analogues among the court's more traditional powers. Nonetheless, we do not, as did the Court of Appeals, view this provision as a significant judicial encroachment upon executive power or upon the prosecutorial discretion of the independent counsel.

We think that the Court of Appeals overstated the matter when it described the power to terminate as a "broadsword and . . . rapier" that enables the court to "control the pace and depth of the independent counsel's activities." . . . The provision has not been tested in practice, and we do not mean to say that an adventurous special court could not reasonably construe the provision as did the Court of Appeals; but it is the duty of federal courts to construe a statute in order to save it from constitutional infirmities. . . .

. . . The termination provisions of the Act do not give the Special Division anything approaching the power to *remove* the counsel while an investigation or court proceeding is still underway — this power is vested solely in the Attorney General. As we see it, "termination" may occur only when the duties of the counsel are truly "completed" or "so substantially completed" that there remains no need for any continuing action by the independent counsel. It is basically a device for removing from the public payroll an independent counsel who has served her purpose, but is unwilling to acknowledge the fact. So construed, the Special Division's power to terminate does not pose a sufficient threat of judicial intrusion into matters that are more properly within the Executive's authority to require that the Act be invalidated as inconsistent with Article III.

. . . .

We emphasize, nevertheless, that the Special Division has *no* authority to take any action or undertake any duties that are not specifically authorized by the Act. . . .

. . . Two examples of this were cited by the Court of Appeals, which noted that the Special Division issued "orders" that ostensibly exempted the independent counsel from conflict of interest laws. . . . In another case, the Division reportedly ordered that a counsel postpone an investigation into certain allegations until the completion of related state criminal proceedings. . . . The propriety of the Special Division's actions in these instances is not before us as such, but we nonetheless think it appropriate to point out not only that there is no authorization for such actions in the Act itself, but that the division's exercise of unauthorized powers risks the transgression of the constitutional limitations of Article III that we have just discussed.

We now turn to consider whether the Act is invalid under the constitutional principle of separation of powers. Two related issues must be addressed: The first is whether the provision of the Act restricting the Attorney General's power to remove the independent counsel to only those instances in which he can show "good cause," taken by itself, impermissibly interferes with the President's exercise of his constitutionally appointed functions. The second is whether, taken as a whole, the Act violates the separation of powers by reducing the President's ability to control the prosecutorial powers wielded by the independent counsel.

A

Two Terms ago we had occasion to consider whether it was consistent with the separation of powers for Congress to pass a statute that authorized a government official who is removable only by Congress to participate in what we found to be "executive powers."... We held in *Bowsher* that "Congress cannot reserve for itself the power of removal of an officer charged with the execution of the laws except by impeachment."... A primary antecedent for this ruling was our 1925 decision in *Myers* v. *United States*.... *Myers* had considered the propriety of a federal statute by which certain postmasters of the United States could be removed by the President only "by and with the advice and consent of the Senate." There, too, Congress' attempt to involve itself in the removal of an executive official was found to be sufficient grounds to render the statute invalid. As we observed in *Bowsher*, the essence of the decision in *Myers* was the judgment that the Constitution prevents Congress from "draw[ing] to itself... the power to remove or the right to participate in the exercise of that power. To do this would be to go beyond the words and implications of the [Appointments Clause] and to infringe the constitutional principle of the separation of governmental powers."...

Unlike both *Bowsher* and *Myers*, this case does not involve an attempt by Congress itself to gain a role in the removal of executive officials other than its established powers of impeachment and conviction. The Act instead puts the removal power squarely in the hands of the Executive Branch; an independent counsel may be removed from office, "only by the personal action of the Attorney General, and only for good cause."... There is no requirement of congressional approval of the Attorney General's removal decision, though the decision is subject to judicial review.... In our view, the removal provisions of the Act make this case more analogous to *Humphrey's Executor* v. *United States*... (1935), and *Wiener* v. *United States*,... (1958), than to *Myers* or *Bowsher*.

....

Appellees contend that *Humphrey's Executor* and *Wiener* are distinguishable from this case because they did not involve officials who performed a "core executive function." They argue that our decision in *Humphrey's Executor* rests on a distinction between "purely executive" officials and officials who exercise "quasi-legislative" and "quasi-judicial" powers. In

their view, when a "purely executive" official is involved, the governing precedent is *Myers*, not *Humphrey's Executor*.... And, under *Myers*, the President must have absolute discretion to discharge "purely" executive officers at will....

We undoubtedly did rely on the terms "quasi-legislative" and "quasi-judicial" to distinguish the officials involved in *Humphrey's Executor* and *Wiener* from those in *Myers*, but our present considered view is that the determination of whether the Constitution allows Congress to impose a "good cause"-type restriction on the President's power to remove an official cannot be made to turn on whether or not that official is classified as "purely executive." The analysis contained in our removal cases is designed not to define rigid categories of those officials who may or may not be removed at will by the President, but to ensure that Congress does not interfere with the President's exercise of the "executive power" and his constitutionally appointed duty to "take care that the laws be faithfully executed" under Article II. *Myers* was undoubtedly correct in its holding, and in its broader suggestion that there are some "purely executive" officials who must be removable by the President at will if he is to be able to accomplish his constitutional role.... But as the Court noted in *Wiener*,

> "The assumption was short-lived that the *Myers* case recognized the President's inherent constitutional power to remove officers no matter what the relation of the executive to the discharge of their duties and no matter what restrictions Congress may have imposed regarding the nature of their tenure."...

At the other end of the spectrum from *Myers*, the characterization of the agencies in *Humphrey's Executor* and *Wiener* as "quasi-legislative" or "quasi-judicial" in large part reflected our judgment that it was not essential to the President's proper execution of his Article II powers that these agencies be headed up by individuals who were removable at will. We do not mean to suggest that an analysis of the functions served by the officials at issue is irrelevant. But the real question is whether the removal restrictions are of such a nature that they impede the President's ability to perform his constitutional duty, and the functions of the officials in question must be analyzed in that light.

....

... This is not a case in which the power to remove an executive official has been completely stripped from the President, thus providing no means for the President to ensure the "faithful execution" of the laws. Rather, because the independent counsel may be terminated for "good cause," the Executive, through the Attorney General, retains ample authority to assure that the counsel is competently performing her statutory responsibilities in a manner that comports with the provisions of the Act. Although we need not decide in this case exactly what is encompassed within the term "good cause" under the Act, the legislative history of the removal provision also makes clear that the Attorney General may remove an independent counsel for "misconduct."... Here, as with the provision of the Act conferring the appointment authority of the independent counsel on the special court, the congressional determination to limit the removal power of the Attorney General was essential, in the view of Congress, to establish the necessary independence of the office. We do not think that this limitation as it presently stands sufficiently deprives the President of control over the independent counsel to interfere impermissibly with his constitutional obligation to ensure the faithful execution of the laws.

B

The final question to be addressed is whether the Act, taken as a whole, violates the principle of separation of powers by unduly interfering with the role of the Executive Branch....

We observe first that this case does not involve an attempt by Congress to increase its own powers at the expense of the Executive Branch....

The Act does empower certain members of Congress to request the Attorney General to apply for the appointment of an independent counsel, but the Attorney General has no duty to comply with the request, although he must respond within a certain time limit.... Other than that, Congress' role under the Act is limited to receiving reports or other information and oversight of the independent counsel's activities,... functions that we have recognized generally as being incidental to the legislative function of Congress. See *McGrain* v. *Daugherty*... (1927).

Similarly, we do not think that the Act works any *judicial* usurpation of properly executive functions. As should be apparent from our discussion of the Appointments Clause above, the power to appoint inferior officers such as independent counsels is not in itself an "executive" function in the constitutional sense, at least when Congress has exercised its power to vest the appointment of an inferior office in the "courts of Law." We note nonetheless that under the Act the Special Division has no power to appoint an independent counsel *sua sponte;* it may only do so upon the specific request of the Attorney General, and the courts are specifically prevented from re-

viewing the Attorney General's decision not to seek appointment, §592(f). In addition, once the court has appointed a counsel and defined her jurisdiction, it has no power to supervise or control the activities of the counsel....

Finally, we do not think that the Act "impermissibly undermine[s]" the powers of the Executive Branch... or "disrupts the proper balance between the coordinate branches [by] prevent[ing] the Executive Branch from accomplishing its constitutionally assigned functions."... It is undeniable that the Act reduces the amount of control or supervision that the Attorney General and, through him, the President exercises over the investigation and prosecution of a certain class of alleged criminal activity. The Attorney General is not allowed to appoint the individual of his choice; he does not determine the counsel's jurisdiction; and his power to remove a counsel is limited. Nonetheless, the Act does give the Attorney General several means of supervising or controlling the prosecutorial powers that may be wielded by an independent counsel. Most importantly, the Attorney General retains the power to remove the counsel for "good cause," a power that we have already concluded provides the Executive with substantial ability to ensure that the laws are "faithfully executed" by an independent counsel. No independent counsel may be appointed without a specific request by the Attorney General, and the Attorney General's decision not to request appointment if he finds "no reasonable grounds to believe that further investigation is warranted" is committed to his unreviewable discretion. The Act thus gives the Executive a degree of control over the power to initiate an investigation by the independent counsel. In addition, the jurisdiction of the independent counsel is defined with reference to the facts submitted by the Attorney General, and once a counsel is appointed, the Act requires that the counsel abide by Justice Department policy unless it is not "possible" to do so. Notwithstanding the fact that the counsel is to some degree "independent" and free from Executive supervision to a greater extent than other federal prosecutors, in our view these features of the Act give the Executive Branch sufficient control over the independent counsel to ensure that the President is able to perform his constitutionally assigned duties.

Reversed

JUSTICE SCALIA, dissenting.

... [I]t is ultimately irrelevant *how much* the statute reduces presidential control. The case is over when the Court acknowledges, as it must, that "[i]t is undeniable that the Act reduces the amount of control or supervision that the Attorney General and, through him, the President exercises over the investigation and prosecution of a certain class of alleged criminal activity."... It effects a revolution in our constitutional jurisprudence for the Court, once it has determined that (1) purely executive functions are at issue here, and (2) those functions have been given to a person whose actions are not fully within the supervision and control of the President, nonetheless to proceed further to sit in judgment of whether "the President's need to control the exercise of [the independent counsel's] discretion is *so central* to the functioning of the Executive Branch" as to require complete control....

Is it conceivable that if Congress passed a statute depriving itself of less than full and entire control over some insignificant area of legislation, we would inquire whether the matter was "*so central* to the functioning of the Legislative Branch" as really to require complete control, or whether the statute gives Congress "*sufficient* control over the surrogate legislator to ensure that Congress is able to perform its constitutionally assigned duties"?...

... Or to bring the point closer to home, consider a statute giving to non-Article III judges just a tiny bit of purely judicial power in a relatively insignificant field, with substantial control, though not total control, in the courts—perhaps "clear error" review, which would be a fair judicial equivalent of the Attorney General's "for cause" removal power here. Is there any doubt that we would not pause to inquire whether the matter was "*so central* to the functioning of the Judicial Branch" as really to require complete control, or whether we retained "*sufficient* control over the matters to be decided that we are able to perform our constitutionally assigned duties"?...

First, however, I think it well to call to mind an important and unusual premise that underlies our deliberations, a premise not expressly contradicted by the Court's opinion, but in my view not faithfully observed. It is rare in a case dealing, as this one does, with the constitutionality of a statute passed by the Congress of the United States, not to find anywhere in the Court's opinion the usual, almost formulary caution that we owe great deference to Congress' view that what it has done is constitutional... and that we will decline to apply the statute only if the presumption of constitutionality can be overcome.... That caution is not recited by the Court in the present case *because it does not apply.* Where a private citizen challenges action of the Government on grounds unrelated to separation of powers, harmonious functioning of the system demands that we ordinarily give some deference, or a presumption of validity, to the actions of the political branches in what is agreed, between themselves at least, to be

within their respective spheres. But where the issue pertains to separation of powers, and the political branches are (as here) in disagreement, neither can be presumed correct....

To repeat, Art. II, §1, cl. 1 of the Constitution provides:

> "The executive Power shall be vested in a President of the United States."

As I described at the outset of this opinion, this does not mean *some of* the executive power, but *all of* the executive power. It seems to me, therefore, that the decision of the Court of Appeals invalidating the present statute must be upheld on fundamental separation-of-powers principles if the following two questions are answered affirmatively: (1) Is the conduct of a criminal prosecution (and of an investigation to decide whether to prosecute) the exercise of purely executive power? (2) Does the statute deprive the President of the United States of exclusive control over the exercise of that power? Surprising to say, the Court appears to concede an affirmative answer to both questions, but seeks to avoid the inevitable conclusion that since the statute vests some purely executive power in a person who is not the President of the United States it is void.

. . . .

The independent counsel is not even subordinate to the President. The Court essentially admits as much, noting that "appellant may not be 'subordinate' to the Attorney General (and the President) insofar as she possesses a degree of independent discretion to exercise the powers delegated to her under the Act."... In fact, there is no doubt about it. As noted earlier, the Act specifically grants her the "*full* power and *independent* authority to exercise *all* investigative and prosecutorial functions of the Department of Justice,"... and makes her removable only for "good cause," a limitation specifically intended to ensure that she be *independent* of, not *subordinate* to, the President and the Attorney General....

Because appellant is not subordinate to another officer, she is not an "inferior" officer and her appointment other than by the President with the advice and consent of the Senate is unconstitutional.

. . . .

One can hardly grieve for the shoddy treatment given today to *Humphrey's Executor,* which, after all, accorded the same indignity (with much less justification) to Chief Justice Taft's opinion 10 years earlier in *Myers* v. *United States, supra*—gutting, in six quick pages devoid of textual or historical precedent for the novel principle it set forth, a carefully researched and reasoned 70-page opinion. It is in fact comforting to witness the reality that he who lives by the *ipse dixit* dies by the *ipse dixit*. But one must grieve for the Constitution. *Humphrey's Executor* at least had the decency formally to observe the constitutional principle that the President had to be the repository of *all* executive power, ... which, as *Myers* carefully explained, necessarily means that he must be able to discharge those who do not perform executive functions according to his liking. As we noted in *Bowsher,* once an officer is appointed " 'it is only the authority that can remove him, and not the authority that appointed him, that he must fear and, in the performance of his functions, obey.' " ... By contrast, "our present considered view" is simply that *any* Executive officer's removal can be restricted, so long as the President remains "able to accomplish his constitutional role." ... There are now no lines. ...

The notion that every violation of law should be prosecuted, including — indeed, *especially* — every violation by those in high places, is an attractive one, and it would be risky to argue in an election campaign that that is not an absolutely overriding value. *Fiat justitia, ruat coelum.* Let justice be done, though the heavens may fall. The reality is, however, that it is not an absolutely overriding value, and it was with the hope that we would be able to acknowledge and apply such realities that the Constitution spared us, by life tenure, the necessity of election campaigns. I cannot imagine that there are not many thoughtful men and women in Congress who realize that the benefits of this legislation are far outweighed by its harmful effect upon our system of government, and even upon the nature of justice received by those men and women who agree to serve in the Executive Branch. But it is difficult to vote not to enact, and even more difficult to vote to repeal, a statute called, appropriately enough, the Ethics in Government Act. If Congress is controlled by the party other than the one to which the President belongs, it has little incentive to repeal it; if it is controlled by the same party, it dare not. By its short-sighted action today, I fear the Court has permanently encumbered the Republic with an institution that will do it great harm. ...

U.S. v. Nixon

418 U.S. 683 (1974)
Vote: 8–0; Rehnquist did not
participate.

Only one President of the United States has been forced to resign with the im-

peachment process nipping at his heels. Richard Nixon gained this distinction through his role in the Watergate scandal.

Watergate involved two bungled break-ins at the National Democratic Party Headquarters during the 1972 presidential campaign. The burglars caught by the police were found to have both CIA and White House connections. To this day it is not clear what the purpose of the break-in was or whether Nixon knew about it in advance.

What gradually became clear, however, was that the White House was the center of an effort to prevent investigation of the incident. This involved use of presidential power to misdirect the Department of Justice and complex efforts to induce the defendants not to cooperate with the investigators. As evidence piled up that a whole series of the President's public statements on the case were not true, suspicions arose about the degree of his complicity. Two of his Attorneys General ultimately went to jail, and the growing evidence on their roles cast further doubts on the objectivity of their investigations.

To head off congressional legislation taking authority on the matter out of the hands of the Presidency, Nixon chose the highly respected Elliot Richardson as Attorney General. He in turn selected Archibald Cox, one of the most successful Solicitors General in U.S. history, to be a Special Prosecutor, with a written pledge of his independence.

In the course of congressional testimony, a White House aide revealed that Nixon had audiotapes of most conversations he had held. Cox subpoenaed the tapes as crucial evidence. When he persisted in this course, Cox was fired, and Attorney General Richardson resigned in protest.

The outcry against the "Saturday Night Massacre" strengthened the hands of Nixon's critics. He was forced to agree to a new Special Prosecutor, Leon Jaworski, with even greater autonomy. Jaworski proceeded with the suit to obtain the tapes, which ultimately convinced even the bulk of the congressional Republicans of Nixon's complicity.

Before the Supreme Court, Nixon argued that "executive privilege," the need for confidential advice from subordinates, protected his conversations or papers or dealings with John Dean, and that a coordinate branch (the courts) could not obtain his records.

Leon Jaworski, the Special Prosecutor, argued that executive privilege was conditional, not absolute. Normally the President's papers and effects were untouchable. But here the President was directly implicated in possible wrongdoing, sitting on relevant evidence in the name of executive privilege! Jaworski further proposed judicial private weighing of the needs of confidentiality for the President as against the evidence the tapes contained before making them available. This, he argued, was a careful and cautious course, while the President's argument would put the Presidency above the law.

MR. CHIEF JUSTICE BURGER delivered the opinion of the Court.

On March 1, 1974, a grand jury of the United States District Court for the District of Columbia returned an indictment charging seven named individuals with various offenses, including conspiracy to defraud the United States and to obstruct justice. Although he was not designated as such in the indictment, the grand jury named the President, among others, as an unindicted co-conspirator.... This subpoena required the production, in advance of the September 9 trial date, of certain tapes, memoranda, papers, transcripts, or other writings relating to certain precisely identified meetings between the President and others....

In the District Court, the President's counsel argued that the court lacked jurisdiction to issue the subpoena because the matter was an intra-branch dispute between a subordinate and superior officer of the Executive Branch and hence not subject to judicial resolution. That argument has been renewed in this Court with emphasis on the contention that the dispute does not present a "case" or "controversy" which can be adjudicated in the federal courts. The President's counsel argues that the federal courts should not intrude into areas committed to the other branches of Government. He views the present dispute as essentially a "jurisdictional" dispute within the Executive Branch which he analogizes to a dispute between two congressional committees. Since the Executive Branch has exclusive authority and absolute discretion to decide whether to prosecute a case, *Confiscation*

Cases, ... (1869), *United States* v. *Cox*, ... (CA5), cert. denied, ... (1965), it is contended that a President's decision is final in determining what evidence is to be used in a given criminal case. Although his counsel concedes the President has delegated certain specific powers to the Special Prosecutor, he has not "waived nor delegated to the Special Prosecutor the President's duty to claim privilege as to all materials ... which fall within the President's inherent authority to refuse to disclose to any executive officer." Brief for the President 47. The Special Prosecutor's demand for the items therefore presents, in the view of the President's counsel, a political question under *Baker* v. *Carr*, ... (1962), since it involves a "textually demonstrable" grant of power under Art. II.

The mere assertion of a claim of an "intra-branch dispute," without more, has never operated to defeat federal jurisdiction; justiciability does not depend on such a surface inquiry.

Our starting point is the nature of the proceeding for which the evidence is sought—here a pending criminal prosecution. It is a judicial proceeding in a federal court alleging violation of federal laws and is brought in the name of the United States as sovereign.... Under the authority of Art. II, §2, Congress has vested in the Attorney General the power to conduct the criminal litigation of the United States Government. 28 U.S.C. §516. It has also vested in him the power to appoint subordinate officers to assist him in the discharge of his duties. 28 U.S.C. §§509, 510, 515, 533. Acting pursuant to those statutes, the Attorney General has delegated the authority to represent the United States in these particular matters to a Special Prosecutor with unique authority and tenure. The regulation gives the Special Prosecutor explicit power to contest the invocation of executive privilege in the process of seeking evidence deemed relevant to the performance of these specially delegated duties....

So long as this regulation is extant it has the force of law.... [I]t is theoretically possible for the Attorney General to amend or revoke the regulation defining the Special Prosecutor's authority. But he has not done so. So long as this regulation remains in force the Executive Branch is bound by it, and indeed the United States as the sovereign composed of the three branches is bound to respect and to enforce it. Moreover, the delegation of authority to the Special Prosecutor in this case is not an ordinary delegation by the Attorney General to a subordinate officer: with the authorization of the President, the Acting Attorney General provided in the regulation that the Special Prosecutor was not to be removed without the "consensus" of eight designated leaders of Congress. . . .

The demands of and the resistance to the subpoena present an obvious controversy in the ordinary sense, but that alone is not sufficient to meet constitutional standards. In the constitutional sense, controversy means more than disagreement and conflict; rather it means the kind of controversy courts traditionally resolve. Here at issue is the production or nonproduction of specified evidence deemed by the Special Prosecutor to be relevant and admissible in a pending criminal case. It is sought by one official of the Government within the scope of his express authority; it is resisted by the Chief Executive on the ground of his duty to preserve the confidentiality of the communications of the President. Whatever the correct answer on the merits, these issues are "of a type which are traditionally justiciable." . . . The independent Special Prosecutor with his asserted need for the subpoenaed material in the underlying criminal prosecution is opposed by the President with his steadfast assertion of privilege against disclosure of the material. This setting assures there is "that concrete adverseness which sharpens the presentation of issues upon which the court so largely depends for illumination of difficult constitutional questions." . . . Moreover, since the matter is one arising in the regular course of a federal criminal prosecution, it is within the traditional scope of Art. III power. . . .

In light of the uniqueness of the setting in which the conflict arises, the fact that both parties are officers of the Executive Branch cannot be viewed as a barrier to justiciability. It would be inconsistent with the applicable law and regulation, and the unique facts of this case, to conclude other than that the Special Prosecutor has standing to bring this action and that a justiciable controversy is presented for decision.

A

. . . [W]e turn to the claim that the subpoena should be quashed because it demands "confidential conversations between a President and his close advisors that it would be inconsistent with the public interest to produce." App. 48a. The first contention is a broad claim that the separation of powers doctrine precludes judicial review of a President's claim of privilege. The second contention is that if he does not prevail on the claim of absolute privilege, the court should hold as a matter of constitutional law that the privilege prevails over the subpoena *duces tecum*.

In the performance of assigned constitutional duties each branch of the Government must initially interpret the Constitution, and the interpretation of its powers by any branch is due great respect from the others. The President's counsel, as we have noted, reads the Constitution as providing an absolute privilege of confidentiality for all presidential communications. Many decisions of this Court, however, have unequivocally reaffirmed the holding of *Marbury* v. *Madison* . . . (1803), that "it is emphatically the province and duty of the judicial department to say what the law is." . . .

No holding of the Court has defined the scope of judicial power specifically relating to the enforcement of a subpoena for confidential presidential communications for use in a criminal prosecution, but other exercises of powers by the Executive Branch and the Legislative Branch have been found invalid as in conflict with the Constitution. *Powell* v. *McCormack, supra; Youngstown, supra.* In a series of cases, the Court interpreted the explicit immunity conferred by express provisions of the Constitution on Members of the House and Senate by the Speech or Debate Clause, U.S. Const. Art. I, §6. *Doe* v. *McMillan* . . . (1973); *Gravel* v. *United States,* . . . (1973); *United States* v. *Brewster,* . . . (1972); *United States* v. *Johnson,* . . . (1966). Since this Court has consistently exercised the power to construe and delineate claims arising under express powers, it must follow that the Court has authority to interpret claims with respect to powers alleged to derive from enumerated powers.

Our system of government "requires that federal courts on occasion interpret the Constitution in a manner at variance with the construction given the document by another branch." *Powell* v. *McCormack, supra,* 549. And in *Baker* v. *Carr,* 369 U.S., at 211, the Court stated:

> [D]eciding whether a matter has in any measure been committed by the Constitution to another branch of government, or whether the action of that branch exceeds whatever authority has been committed, is itself a delicate exercise in constitutional interpretation, and is a responsibility of the Court as ultimate interpreter of the Constitution.

Notwithstanding the deference each branch must accord the others, the "judicial power of the United States" vested in the federal courts by Art. III, §1 of the Constitution can no more be shared with the Executive Branch than the Chief Executive, for example, can share with the Judiciary the veto power, or the Congress share with the judiciary the power to override a presidential veto.

We therefore reaffirm that it is "emphatically the province and the duty" of this Court "to say what the law is" with respect to the claim of privilege presented in this case. . . .

B

In support of his claim of absolute privilege, the President's counsel urges two grounds one of which is common to all governments and one of which is peculiar to our system of separation of powers. The first ground is the valid need for protection of communications between high government officials and those who advise and assist them in the performance of their manifold duties; the importance of this confidentiality is too plain to require further discussion. Human experience teaches that those who expect public dissemination of their remarks may well temper candor with a concern for appearances and for their own interests to the detriment of the decision-making process. Whatever the nature of the privilege of confidentiality of presidential communications in the exercise of Art. II powers the privilege can be said to derive from the supremacy of each branch within its own assigned area of constitutional duties. Certain powers and privileges flow from the nature of enumerated powers; the protection of the confidentiality of presidential communications has similar constitutional underpinnings.

The second ground asserted by the President's counsel in support of the claim of absolute privilege rests on the doctrine of separation of powers. Here it is argued that the independence of the Executive Branch within its own sphere, *Humphrey's Executor* v. *United States, . . . Kilbourn* v. *Thompson, . . .* (1880), insulates a president from a judicial subpoena in an ongoing criminal prosecution, and thereby protects confidential presidential communications.

However, neither the doctrine of separation of powers, nor the need for confidentiality of high level communications, without more, can sustain an absolute, unqualified presidential privilege of immunity from judicial process under all circumstances. The President's need for complete candor and objectivity from advisers calls for great deference from the courts. However, when the privilege depends solely on the broad, undifferentiated claim of public interest in the confidentiality of such conversations, a confrontation with other values arises. Absent a claim of need to protect military, diplomatic, or sensitive national security secrets, we find it difficult to accept

↑ IN Judges Chambers

the argument that even the very important interest in confidentiality of presidential communications is significantly diminished by production of such material for *in camera* inspection with all the protection that a district court will be obliged to provide.

The impediment that an absolute, unqualified privilege would place in the way of the primary constitutional duty of the Judicial Branch to do justice in criminal prosecutions would plainly conflict with the function of the courts under Art. III. . . . To read the Art. II powers of the President as providing an absolute privilege as against a subpoena essential to enforcement of criminal statutes on no more than a generalized claim of the public interest in confidentiality of nonmilitary and nondiplomatic discussions would upset the constitutional balance of "a workable government" and gravely impair the role of the courts under Art. III.

C

Since we conclude that the legitimate needs of the judicial process may outweigh presidential privilege, it is necessary to resolve those competing interests in a manner that preserves the essential functions of each branch. The right and indeed the duty to resolve that question does not free the judiciary from according high respect to the representations made on behalf of the President. *United States* v. *Burr,* . . . (1807).

The expectation of a President to the confidentiality of his conversations and correspondence, like the claim of confidentiality of judicial deliberations, for example, has all the values to which we accord deference for the privacy of all citizens and added to those values the necessity for protection of the public interest in candid, objective, and even blunt or harsh opinions in presidential decisionmaking. A President and those who assist him must be free to explore alternatives in the process of shaping policies and making decisions and to do so in a way many would be unwilling to express except privately. These are the considerations justifying a presumptive privilege for presidential communications. The privilege is fundamental to the operation of government and inextricably rooted in the separation of powers under the Constitution. In *Nixon* v. *Sirica, . . .* U.S. App. D.C. . . . 487 F. 2d 700 (1973), the Court of Appeals held that such presidential communications are "presumptively privileged," and this position is accepted by both parties in the present litigation. We agree with Mr. Chief Justice Marshall's observation, therefore, that "in no case of this kind would a court be required to proceed against the President as against an ordinary individual." *United States* v. *Burr....*

But this presumptive privilege must be considered in light of our historic commitment to the rule of law. This is nowhere more profoundly manifest than in our view that "the twofold aim [of criminal justice] is that guilt shall not escape or innocence suffer." *Berger* v. *United States,* ... (1935). We have elected to employ an adversary system of criminal justice in which the parties contest all issues before a court of law. The need to develop all relevant facts in the adversary system is both fundamental and comprehensive. The ends of criminal justice would be defeated if judgments were to be founded on a partial or speculative presentation of the facts. The very integrity of the judicial system and public confidence in the system depend on full disclosure of all the facts, within the framework of the rules of evidence. To ensure that justice is done, it is imperative to the function of the courts that compulsory process be available for the production of evidence needed either by the prosecution or by the defense.

... [T]he Fifth Amendment to the Constitution provides that no man "shall be compelled in any criminal case to be a witness against himself." And, generally, an attorney or a priest may not be required to disclose what has been revealed in professional confidence. These and other interests are recognized in law by privileges against forced disclosure, established in the Constitution, by statute, or at common law. Whatever their origins, these exceptions to the demand for every man's evidence are not lightly created nor expansively construed, for they are in derogation of the search for truth.

In this case the President challenges a subpoena served on him as a third party requiring the production of materials for use in a criminal prosecution on the claim that he has a privilege against disclosure of confidential communications. He does not place his claim of privilege on the ground they are military or diplomatic secrets. As to these areas of Art. II duties the courts have traditionally shown the utmost deference to presidential responsibilities....

In *United States* v. *Reynolds,* ... (1952), dealing with a claimant's demand for evidence in a damage case against the Government, the court said:

It may be possible to satisfy the court, from all the circumstances of the case, that there is a reasonable danger that compulsion of the evidence will expose military matters which, in the interest of national security, should not be divulged. When this is the case, the occasion for the privilege is appropriate, and the court should not jeopardize the security which the privilege is meant to protect by insisting upon an examination of the evidence, even by the judge alone, in chambers.

No case of the Court, however, has extended this high degree of deference to a President's generalized interest in confidentiality. Nowhere in the Constitution, as we have noted earlier, is there any explicit reference to a privilege of confidentiality, yet to the extent this interest relates to the effective discharge of a President's powers, it is constitutionally based.

The right to the production of all evidence at a criminal trial similarly has constitutional dimensions. The Sixth Amendment explicitly confers upon every defendant in a criminal trial the right "to be confronted with the witnesses against him" and "to have compulsory process for obtaining witnesses in his favor." Moreover, the Fifth Amendment also guarantees that no person shall be deprived of liberty without due process of law. It is the manifest duty of the courts to vindicate those guarantees and to accomplish that it is essential that all relevant and admissable evidence be produced.

In this case we must weigh the importance of the general privilege of confidentiality of presidential communications in performance of his responsibilities against the inroads of such privilege on the fair administration of criminal justice. The interest in preserving confidentiality is weighty indeed and entitled to great respect. However, we cannot conclude that advisers will be moved to temper the candor of their remarks by the infrequent occasions of disclosure because of the possibility that such conversations will be called for in the context of a criminal prosecution.

On the other hand, the allowance of the privilege to withhold evidence that is demonstrably relevant in a criminal trial would cut deeply into the guarantee of due process of law and gravely impair the basic function of the courts. A President's acknowledged need for confidentiality in the communications of his office is general in nature, whereas the constitutional need for production of relevant evidence in a criminal proceeding is specific and central to the fair adjudication of a particular criminal case in the administration of justice.

... [T]he District Court treated the material as presumptively privileged, proceeded to find that the Special Prosecutor had made a sufficient showing to rebut the presumption and ordered an *in camera* examination of the subpoenaed material. On the basis of our examination of the record we are unable to conclude that the District Court erred in ordering the inspection. . . .

[I]t is obvious that the District Court has a very heavy responsibility to see to it that presidential conversations, which are either not relevant or not admissible, are accorded that high degree of respect due the President of the United States. Mr. Chief Justice Marshall sitting as a trial judge in the *Burr* case, *supra,* was extraordinarily careful to point out that:

> [I]n no case of this kind would a Court be required to proceed against the President as against an ordinary individual. *United States* v. *Burr,* 25 Fed. Cases 187, 191 (No. 14.694).

Marshall's statement cannot be read to mean in any sense that a President is above the law, but relates to the singularly unique role under Art. II of a President's communications and activities, related to the performance of duties under that Article. Moreover, a President's communications and activities encompass a vastly wider range of sensitive material than would be true of any "ordinary individual." It is therefore necessary in the public interest to afford presidential confidentiality the greatest protection consistent with the fair administration of justice. . . . We have no doubt that the District Judge will at all times accord to presidential records that high degree of deference suggested in *United States* v. *Burr, supra,* and will discharge his responsibility to see to it that until released to the Special Prosecutor no *in camera* material is revealed to anyone. . . .

Affirmed.

MR. JUSTICE REHNQUIST took no part in the consideration or decision of these cases.

Ex parte Milligan

4 Wallace 2 (1866)
Vote: 5–4

A basic question of civilian rights under the Constitution was settled during the Civil War. Milligan was arrested on orders by the Indiana military command, tried by court martial, and sentenced to be hanged. On writ of habeas corpus, he argued that, as a civilian in a nonwar zone, he was not subject to military control. This case establishes the so-called "open court" rule.

Combatants, however, cannot invoke the rule, even in peaceful areas. In *Ex parte Quirin* (1946), eight Nazi saboteurs who attempted surreptitious entry into the U.S. during World War II were held to be properly tried by military procedures. (The saboteurs included one American citizen.)

An act of Congress—the Judiciary Act of 1789, section 14—enacts that the Circuit Courts of the United States "Shall have power to issue writs of *habeas corpus.*"

Another act—that of March 3d, 1863, "relating to *habeas corpus,* and regulating judicial proceedings in certain cases"—an act passed in the midst of the Rebellion—makes various provisions in regard to the subject of it. . . .

By proclamation, dated the 15th September following, the President reciting this statute suspended the privilege of the writ. . . .

With both these statutes and this proclamation in force, Lamdin P. Milligan a citizen of the United States, and a resident and citizen of the State of Indiana, was arrested on the 5th day of October, 1864, at his home in the said State. . . .

MR. JUSTICE DAVIS delivered the opinion of the court.

On the 10th day of May, 1865, Lamdin P. Milligan presented a petition to the Circuit Court of the United States for the District of Indiana, to be discharged from an alleged unlawful imprisonment. The case made by the petition is this: Milligan is a citizen of the United States; has lived for twenty years in Indiana; and, at the time of the grievances complained of, was not, and never had been in the military or naval service of the United States. On the 5th day of October, 1864, while at home, he was arrested by order of General Alvin P. Hovey.

On the 21st day of October, 1864, he was brought before a military commission convened at Indianapolis, by order of General Hovey, tried on certain charges and specifications, found guilty, and sentenced to be hanged.

On the 2d day of January, 1865, after the proceedings of the military commission were at an end, the Circuit Court of the United States for Indiana met at Indianapolis and empanelled a grand jury, who were charged to inquire whether the laws of the United States had been violated; and, if so, to make presentments. The court adjourned on the 27th day of

January, having, prior thereto, discharged from further service the grand jury, who did not find any bill of indictment or make any presentment against Milligan for any offence whatever; and, in fact, since his imprisonment, no bill of indictment has been found or presentment made against him by any grand jury of the United States.

The controlling question in the case is this: Upon the *facts* stated in Milligan's petition, and the exhibits filed, had the military commission mentioned in it *jurisdiction,* legally, to try and sentence him? Milligan, not a resident of one of the rebellious states, or a prisoner of war, but a citizen of Indiana for twenty years past, and never in the military or naval service, is, while at his home, arrested by the military power of the United States, imprisoned, and, on certain criminal charges preferred against him, tried, convicted, and sentenced to be hanged by a military commission, organized under the direction of the military commander of the military district of Indiana. Had this tribunal the *legal* power and authority to try and punish this man?

No graver question was ever considered by this court, nor one which more nearly concerns the rights of the whole people; for it is the birthright of every American citizen when charged with crime, to be tried and punished according to law. The power of punishment is, alone through the means which the laws have provided for that purpose, and if they are ineffectual, there is an immunity from punishment, no matter how great an offender the individual may be, or how much his crimes may have shocked the sense of justice of the country, or endangered its safety. By the protection of the law human rights are secured; withdraw that protection, and they are at the mercy of wicked rulers, or the clamor of an excited people. If there was a law to justify this military trial, it is not our province to interfere; if there was not, it is our duty to declare the nullity of the whole proceedings. The decision of this question does not depend on argument or judicial precedents, numerous and highly illustrative as they are. These precedents inform us of the extent of the struggle to preserve liberty and to relieve those in civil life from military trials. The founders of our government were familiar with the history of that struggle; and secured in a written constitution every right which the people had wrested from power during a contest of ages. By that Constitution and the laws authorized by it this question must be determined. . . .

The Constitution of the United States is a law for rulers and people, equally in war and in peace, and covers with the shield of its protection all classes of men, at all times, and under all circumstances. No doctrine, involving more pernicious consequences, was ever invented by the wit of man than that any of its provisions can be suspended during any of the great exigencies of government. Such a doctrine leads directly to anarchy or despotism, but the theory of necessity on which it is based is false; for the government, within the Constitution, has all the powers granted to it, which are necessary to preserve its existence; as has been happily proved by the result of the great effort to throw off its just authority.

Have any of the rights guaranteed by the Constitution been violated in the case of Milligan? and if so, what are they?

Every trial involves the exercise of judicial power; and from what source did the military commission that tried him derive their authority? Certainly no part of the judicial power of the country was conferred on them. . . .

But it is said that the jurisdiction is complete under the "laws and usages of war."

It can serve no useful purpose to inquire what those laws and usages are, whence they originated, where found, and on whom they operate; they can never be applied to citizens in states which have upheld the authority of the government, and where the courts are open and their process unobstructed. This court has judicial knowledge that in Indiana the Federal authority was always unopposed, and its courts always open to hear criminal accusations and redress grievances; and no usage of war could sanction a military trial there for any offence whatever of a citizen in civil life, in nowise connected with the military service. Congress could grant no such power; and to the honor of our national legislature be it said, it has never been provoked by the state of the country even to attempt its exercise. One of the plainest constitutional provisions was, therefore, infringed when Milligan was tried by a court not ordained and established by Congress, and not composed of judges appointed during good behavior. . . .

If it was dangerous, in the distracted condition of affairs, to leave Milligan unrestrained of his liberty, because he "conspired against the government, afforded aid and comfort to rebels, and incited the people to insurrection," the *law* said arrest him, confine him closely, render him powerless to do further mischief; and then present his case to the grand jury of the district, with proofs of his guilt, and, if indicted, try him according to the course of the common law. If this had been done, the Constitution would have been vindicated, the law of 1863 enforced, and the securities for personal liberty preserved and defended.

Another guarantee of freedom was broken when Milligan was denied a trial by jury....

The discipline necessary to the efficiency of the army and navy, required other and swifter modes of trial than are furnished by the common law courts; and, in pursuance of the power conferred by the Constitution, Congress has declared the kinds of trial, and the manner in which they shall be conducted, for offences committed while the party is in the military or naval service. Every one connected with these branches of the public service is amenable to the jurisdiction which Congress has created for their government, and, while thus serving, surrenders his right to be tried by the civil courts. *All other persons,* citizens of states where the courts are open, if charged with crime, are guaranteed the inestimable privilege of trial by jury. This privilege is a vital principle, underlying the whole administration of criminal justice; it is not held by sufferance, and cannot be frittered away on any plea of state or political necessity....

It is claimed that martial law covers with its broad mantle the proceedings of this military commission. The proposition is this: that in a time of war the commander of an armed force (if in his opinion the exigencies of the country demand it, and of which he is to judge) has the power, within the lines of his military district, to suspend all civil rights and their remedies, and subject citizens as well as soldiers to the rule of *his will;* and in the exercise of his lawful authority cannot be restrained, except by his superior officer or the President of the United States.

The statement of this proposition shows its importance; for, if true, republican government is a failure, and there is an end of liberty regulated by law. Martial law, established on such a basis, destroys every guarantee of the Constitution, and effectually renders the "military independent of and superior to the civil power"—the attempt to do which by the King of Great Britain was deemed by our fathers such an offence, that they assigned it to the world as one of the cases which impelled them to declare their independence. Civil liberty and this kind of martial law cannot endure together; the antagonism is irreconcilable; and, in the conflict, one or the other must perish.

This nation, as experience has proved, cannot always remain at peace, and has no right to expect that it will always have wise and humane rulers, sincerely attached to the principles of the Constitution. Wicked men, ambitious of power, with hatred of liberty and contempt of law, may fill the place once occupied by Washington and Lincoln; and if this right is conceded, and the calamities of war again befall us, the dangers to human liberty are frightful to contemplate. If our fathers had failed to provide for just such a contingency, they would have been false to the trust reposed in them. They knew—the history of the world told them—the nation they were founding, be its existence short or long, would be involved in war; how often or how long continued, human foresight could not tell; and that unlimited power, wherever lodged at such a time, was especially hazardous to freemen. For this, and other equally weighty reasons, they secured the inheritance they had fought to maintain, by incorporating in a written constitution the safeguards which *time* had proved were essential to its preservation. Not one of these safeguards can the President, or Congress, or the Judiciary disturb, except the one concerning the writ of *habeas corpus*....

It will be borne in mind that this is not a question of the power to proclaim martial law, when war exists in a community and the courts and civil authorities are overthrown. Nor is it a question what rule a military commander, at the head of his army, can impose on states in rebellion to cripple their resources and quell the insurrection. The jurisdiction claimed is much more extensive....

Martial law cannot arise from a *threatened* invasion. The necessity must be actual and present; the invasion real, such as effectually closes the courts and deposes the civil administration.

It is difficult to see how the *safety* of the country required martial law in Indiana. If any of her citizens were plotting treason, the power of arrest could secure them, until the government was prepared for their trial, when the courts were open and ready to try them....

It follows, from what has been said on this subject, that there are occasions when martial rule can be properly applied. If, in foreign invasion or civil war, the courts are actually closed, and it is impossible to administer criminal justice according to law, *then,* on the theatre of active military operations, where war really prevails, there is a necessity to furnish a substitute for the civil authority, thus overthrown, to preserve the safety of the army and society; and as no power is left but the military, it is allowed to govern by martial rule until the laws can have their free course.

THE CHIEF JUSTICE delivered the following opinion.

Four members of the court, concurring with their brethren in the order heretofore made in this cause, but unable to concur in some important particulars with the opinion which has just been read, think it their duty to make a separate statement of their views of the whole case.

The holding of the Circuit and District Courts of the United States in Indiana had been uninterrupted. The administration of the laws in the Federal courts had remained unimpaired. Milligan was imprisoned under the authority of the President, and was not a prisoner of war. No list of prisoners had been furnished to the judges, either of the District or Circuit Courts, as required by the law. A grand jury had attended the Circuit Courts of the Indiana district, while Milligan was there imprisoned, and had closed its session without finding any indictment or presentment or otherwise proceeding against the prisoner.

We think that Congress had power, though not exercised, to authorize the military commission which was held in Indiana.

We by no means assert that Congress can establish and apply the laws of war where no war has been declared or exists. Where peace exists the laws of peace must prevail. What we do maintain is, that when the nation is involved in war, and some portions of the country are invaded, and all are exposed to invasion, it is within the power of Congress to determine in what states or districts such great and imminent public danger exists as justifies the authorization of military tribunals for the trial of crimes and offences against the discipline or security of the army or against the public safety.

We cannot doubt that, in such a time of public danger, Congress had power, under the Constitution, to provide for the organization of a military commission, and for trial by that commission of persons engaged in this conspiracy. The fact that the Federal courts were open was regarded by Congress as a sufficient reason for not exercising the power; but that fact could not deprive Congress of the right to exercise it. Those courts might be open and undisturbed in the execution of their functions, and yet wholly incompetent to avert threatened danger, or to punish, with adequate promptitude and certainty, the guilty conspirators.

In Indiana, the judges and officers of the courts were loyal to the government. But it might have been otherwise. In times of rebellion and civil war it may often happen, indeed, that judges and marshals will be in active sympathy with the rebels, and courts their most efficient allies.

We have confined ourselves to the question of power. It was for Congress to determine the question of expediency. And Congress did determine it. That body did not see fit to authorize trials by military commission in Indiana, but by the strongest implication prohibited them. With that prohibition we are satisfied, and should have remained silent if the answers to the questions certified had been put on that ground, without denial of the existence of a power which we believe to be constitutional and important to the public safety.

Mr. Justice Wayne, Mr. Justice Swayne, and Mr. Justice Miller concur with me in these views.

Missouri v. Holland

252 U.S. 416 (1920)
Vote: 7–2

The question of national security is an awesome one and makes it difficult to assess constitutional relations. *Missouri* v. *Holland* is a thorny test of basic relations in a foreign policy situation. Involved was a treaty with Canada by which the countries undertook protection of certain migratory birds. Whether Congress had authority in the absence of a treaty was arguable. What is the limit imposed upon the treaty power, not by explicit limitations of the Constitution, as in the First Amendment, but by the generalized rule of construction that is the Tenth Amendment? Justice Holmes had been severely injured during the Civil War, and his opinion reflects a basic nationalism that goes beyond the needs of the case. Early decisions had made clear that Fifth Amendment rights and compensation for property could not be easily overridden by treaties, but left other rights in doubt.

The looseness of Holmes' language excited fears that a President could, by executive agreement, contract away our liberties (say, by agreeing that newspapers would not criticize the other country in the agreement), and that this would be enforceable in the Court. Such fears grew during the 1940s and 1950s, culminating in the proposed Bricker Amendment to the Constitution, which would have drastically limited treaties and agreements. The Supreme Court defanged the issue by making clear in such cases as Reid v. Covert (discussed shortly) that constitutional rights were not overridden by foreign agreements.

MR. JUSTICE HOLMES delivered the opinion of the court.

This is a bill in equity brought by the State of Missouri to prevent a game warden of the United States from attempting to enforce the Migratory Bird Treaty Act of July 3, 1918, c. 128, 40 Stat. 755, and the regulations made by the Secretary of Agriculture in pursuance of the same. The ground of the bill is that the statute is an unconstitutional interference with the rights reserved to the States by the Tenth Amendment, and that the acts of the defendant done and threatened under that authority invade the sovereign right of the State and contravene its will manifested in statutes.

On December 8, 1916, a treaty between the United States and Great Britain was proclaimed by the President. It recited that many species of birds in their annual migrations traversed certain parts of the United States and of Canada, that they were of great value as a source of food and in destroying insects injurious to vegetation, but were in danger of extermination through lack of adequate protection. It therefore provided for specified closed seasons and protection in other forms, and agreed that the two powers would take or propose to their law-making bodies the necessary measures for carrying the treaty out. . . . It is unnecessary to go into any details, because, as we have said, the question raised is the general one whether the treaty and statute are void as an interference with the rights reserved to the States.

To answer this question it is not enough to refer to the Tenth Amendment, reserving the powers not delegated to the United States, because by Article II, §2, the power to make treaties is delegated expressly. . . . If the treaty is valid there can be no dispute about the validity of the statute under Article I, §8, as a necessary and proper means to execute the power of the Government. The language of the Constitution as to the supremacy of treaties being general, the question before us is narrowed to an inquiry into the ground upon which the present supposed exception is placed.

It is said that a treaty cannot be valid if it infringes the Constitution, that there are limits, therefore, to the treaty-making power, and that one such limit is that what an act of Congress could not do unaided, in derogation of the powers reserved to the States, a treaty cannot do. An earlier act of Congress that attempted by itself and not in pursuance of a treaty to regulate the killing of migratory birds within the

States had been held bad in the District Court. . . . Those decisions were supported by arguments that migratory birds were owned by the States in their sovereign capacity for the benefit of their people, and that under cases like *Geer v. Connecticut,* 161 U.S. 519, this control was one that Congress had no power to displace. The same argument is supposed to apply now with equal force.

Whether the two cases cited were decided rightly or not they cannot be accepted as a test of the treaty power. Acts of Congress are the supreme law of the land only when made in pursuance of the Constitution, while treaties are declared to be so when made under the authority of the United States. It is open to question whether the authority of the United States means more than the formal acts prescribed to make the convention. We do not mean to imply that there are no qualifications to the treaty-making power; but they must be ascertained in a different way. It is obvious that there may be matters of the sharpest exigency for the national well-being that an act of Congress could not deal with but that a treaty followed by such an act could, and it is not lightly to be assumed that, in matters requiring national action, "a power which must belong to and somewhere reside in every civilized government" is not to be found. . . . What was said in that case with regard to the powers of the States applies with equal force to the powers of the nation in cases where the States individually are incompetent to act. We are not yet discussing the particular case before us but only are considering the validity of the test proposed. With regard to that we may add that when we are dealing with words that also are a constituent act, like the Constitution of the United States, we must realize that they have called into life a being the development of which could not have been foreseen completely by the most gifted of its begetters. It was enough for them to realize or to hope that they had created an organism; it has taken a century and has cost their successors much sweat and blood to prove that they created a nation. The case before us must be considered in the light of our whole experience and not merely in that of what was said a hundred years ago. The treaty in question does not contravene any prohibitory words to be found in the Constitution. The only question is whether it is forbidden by some invisible radiation from the general terms of the Tenth Amendment. We must consider what this country has become in deciding what that Amendment has reserved. . . . To put the claim of the State upon title is to lean upon a slender reed. Wild birds are not in the possession of anyone; and possession is the beginning of ownership. The whole foundation of the State's rights is the presence within their jurisdiction of birds that yesterday had not arrived, tomorrow may be in another State.

Here a national interest of very nearly the first magnitude is involved. It can be protected only by national action in concert with that of another power. The subject matter is only transitorily within the State and has no permanent habitat therein. But for the treaty and the statute there soon might be no birds for any powers to deal with. . . .

We are of opinion that the treaty and statute must be upheld. . . .

Decree affirmed.

Mr. Justice Van Devanter and Mr. Justice Pitney dissent.

U.S. v. Curtiss-Wright

299 U.S. 304 (1936)
Vote: 7–1

Acting under congressional authorization given that very day, the President embargoed arms shipments to participants in the Chaco conflict. Appellees were charged with violating the proclamation by providing Bolivia with arms. The case provides a number of basic answers to the question of the sweep of national power over foreign affairs. Among questions addressed were: Are the dimensions of foreign power and domestic power identical? Does the President have enhanced legal capability in foreign affairs? Is the President's power capable of augmentation by legislation? Together with the Youngstown Steel case, *Curtiss-Wright* emerges as a basic and illuminating discussion of fundamental issues.

Mr. Justice Sutherland delivered the opinion of the Court.

On January 27, 1936, an indictment was returned in the court below, the first count of which charges that appellees, beginning with the 29th day of May, 1934, conspired to sell in the United States certain arms of war, namely fifteen machine guns, to Bolivia, a country then engaged in armed conflict in the Chaco, in violation of the Joint Resolution of Congress approved May 28, 1934, and the provisions of a proclamation issued on the same day by the President of the United States pursuant to authority conferred by §1 of the resolution. . . .

Whether, if the Joint Resolution had related solely to internal affairs it would be open to the challenge that it constituted an unlawful delegation of legislative power to the Executive, we find it unnecessary to determine. The whole aim of the resolution is to affect a situation entirely external to the United States, and falling within the category of foreign affairs. The determination which we are called to make, therefore, is whether the Joint Resolution, as applied to that situation, is vulnerable to attack under the rule that forbids a delegation of the law-making power. In other words, assuming (but not deciding) that the challenged delegation, if it were confined to internal affairs, would be invalid, may it nevertheless be sustained on the ground that its exclusive aim is to afford a remedy for a hurtful condition within foreign territory?

It will contribute to the elucidation of the question if we first consider the differences between the powers of the federal government in respect of foreign or external affairs and those in respect of domestic or internal affairs. That there are differences between them, and that these differences are fundamental, may not be doubted.

The two classes of powers are different, both in respect of their origin and their nature. The broad statement that the federal government can exercise no powers except those specifically enumerated in the Constitution, and such implied powers as are necessary and proper to carry into effect the enumerated powers, is categorically true only in respect of our internal affairs. In that field, the primary purpose of the Constitution was to carve from the general mass of legislative powers *then possessed by the states* such portions as it was thought desirable to vest in the federal government, leaving those not included in the enumeration still in the states. *Carter v. Carter Coal Co.,* 298 U.S. 238, 294. That this doctrine applies only to powers which the states had, is self-evident. And since the states severally never possessed international powers, such powers could not have been carved from the mass of state powers but obviously were transmitted to the United States from some other source. During the colonial period, those powers were possessed exclusively by and were entirely under the control of the Crown. By the Declaration of Independence, "the Representatives of the United States of America" declared the United [not the several] Colonies to be free and independent states and as such to have "full Power to levy War, conclude Peace, contract Alliances, establish Commerce and to do all other Acts and Things which Independent States may of right do."

As a result of the separation from Great Britain by the colonies acting as a unit, the powers of external sovereignty passed from the Crown not to the colonies severally, but to the colonies in their collective and corporate capacity as the United States of America. Even before the Declaration, the colonies were a unit in foreign affairs, acting through a common agency — namely the Continental Congress, composed of delegates from the thirteen colonies. That agency exercised the powers of war and peace, raised an army, created a navy, and finally adopted the Declaration of Independence. Rulers come and go; governments end and forms of government change; but sovereignty survives. A political society cannot endure without a supreme will somewhere. Sovereignty is never held in suspense. When, therefore, the external sovereignty of Great Britain in respect of the colonies ceased, it immediately passed to the Union. . . .

The Union existed before the Constitution, which was ordained and established among other things to form "a more perfect Union." Prior to that event, it is clear that the Union, declared by the Articles of Confederation to be "perpetual," was the sole possessor of external sovereignty and in the Union it remained without change save in so far as the Constitution in express terms qualified its exercise. . . .

It results that the investment of the federal government with the powers of external sovereignty did not depend upon the affirmative grants of the Constitution. The powers to declare and wage war, to conclude peace, to make treaties, to maintain diplomatic relations with other sovereignties, if they had never been mentioned in the Constitution, would have vested in the federal government as necessary concomitants of nationality. . . .

Not only, as we have shown, is the federal power over external affairs in origin and essential character different from that over internal affairs, but participation in the exercise of the power is significantly limited. In this vast external realm, with its important, complicated, delicate and manifold problems, the President alone has the power to speak or listen as a representative of the nation. He *makes* treaties with the advice and consent of the Senate; but he alone negotiates. Into the field of negotiation the Senate cannot intrude; and Congress itself is powerless to invade it. As Marshall said in his great argument of March 7, 1800, in the House of Representatives, "The President is the sole organ of the nation in its external relations, and its sole representative with foreign nations. . . ."

It is important to bear in mind that we are here dealing not alone with an authority vested in the President by an exertion of legislative power, but with such an authority plus a very delicate, plenary and exclusive power of the President as the sole organ of the federal government in the field of international relations — a power which does not require as a basis for its exercise an act of Congress, but which, of course, like every other governmental power, must be exercised in subordination to the applicable provisions of the Constitution. It is quite apparent that if, in the maintenance of our international relations, embarrassment — perhaps serious embarrassment — is to be avoided and success for our aims achieved, congressional legislation which is to be made effective through negotiation and inquiry within the international field must often accord to the President a degree of discretion and freedom from statutory restriction which would not be admissible were domestic affairs alone involved. Moreover, he, not Congress, has the better opportunity of knowing the conditions which prevail in foreign countries, and especially is this true in time of war. He has his confidential sources of information. He has his agents in the form of diplomatic, consular and other officials. Secrecy in respect of information gathered by them may be highly necessary, and the premature disclosure of it productive of harmful results. Indeed, so clearly is this true that the first President refused to accede to a request to lay before the House of Representatives the instructions, correspondence and documents relating to the negotiation of the Jay Treaty — a refusal the wisdom of which was recognized by the House itself and has never since been doubted. . . .

The judgment of the court below must be reversed and the cause remanded for further proceedings in accordance with the foregoing opinion.

Reversed.

MR. JUSTICE McREYNOLDS does not agree. He is of opinion that the court below reached the right conclusion and its judgment ought to be affirmed.

MR. JUSTICE STONE took no part in the consideration or decision of this case.

Korematsu v. U.S.

323 U.S. 214 (1944)

Vote: 6–3

This case represents a high-water mark of American intolerance and of military discretion. Soon after Pearl Harbor, individuals of

Japanese ancestry were excluded from residency on the West Coast and ordered, in effect, to report to camps for continuing residence or relocation to another part of the country. (Since no argument was made about criminal behavior, it was assumed that the MILLIGAN test was irrelevant.) It is interesting to note that no inhabitant of Japanese descent was convicted, either on the continent or in Hawaii, of aiding the enemy.

The case is cited today, however, almost exclusively for Black's throwaway remark suggesting that racial categories are suspect in constitutional law, which remark has emerged as a cornerstone of modern equal protection law.

MR. JUSTICE BLACK delivered the opinion of the Court.

The petitioner, an American citizen of Japanese descent, was convicted in a federal district court for remaining in San Leandro, California, a "Military Area," contrary to Civilian Exclusion Order No. 34 of the Commanding General of the Western Command, U.S. Army, which directed that after May 9, 1942, all persons of Japanese ancestry should be excluded from that area. No question was raised as to the petitioner's loyalty to the United States.

It should be noted, to begin with, that all legal restrictions which curtail the civil rights of a single racial group are immediately suspect. That is not to say that all such restrictions are unconstitutional. It is to say that courts must subject them to the most rigid scrutiny. Pressing public necessity may sometimes justify the existence of such restrictions; racial antagonism never can....

Here, as in the *Hirabayashi* case, "... we cannot reject as unfounded the judgment of the military authorities and of Congress that there were disloyal members of that population, whose number and strength could not be precisely and quickly ascertained. We cannot say that the war-making branches of the Government did not have ground for believing that in a critical hour such persons could not readily be isolated and separately dealt with, and constituted a menace to the national defense and safety, which demanded that prompt and adequate measures be taken to guard against it."

Like curfew, exclusion of those of Japanese origin was deemed necessary because of the presence of an unascertained number of disloyal members of the group, most of whom we have no doubt were loyal to this country. It was because we could not reject the finding of the military authorities that it was impossible to bring about an immediate segregation of the disloyal from the loyal that we sustained the validity of the curfew order as applying to the whole group. In the instant case, temporary exclusion of the entire group was rested by the military on the same ground. The judgment that exclusion of the whole group was for the same reason a military imperative answers the contention that the exclusion was in the nature of group punishment based on antagonism to those of Japanese origin. That there were members of the group who retained loyalties to Japan has been confirmed by investigations made subsequent to the exclusion. Approximately five thousand American citizens of Japanese ancestry refused to swear unqualified allegiance to the United States and to renounce allegiance to the Japanese Emperor, and several thousand evacuees requested repatriation to Japan.

... [H]ardships are part of war, and war is an aggregation of hardships. All citizens alike, both in and out of uniform, feel the impact of war in greater or lesser measure. Citizenship has its responsibilities as well as its privileges, and in time of war the burden is always heavier. Compulsory exclusion of large groups of citizens from their homes, except under circumstances of direst emergency and peril, is inconsistent with our basic governmental institutions. But when under conditions of modern warfare our shores are threatened by hostile forces, the power to protect must be commensurate with the threatened danger.

It is argued that on May 30, 1942, the date the petitioner was charged with remaining in the prohibited area, there were conflicting orders outstanding, forbidding him both to leave the area and to remain there. Of course, a person cannot be convicted for doing the very thing which it is a crime to fail to do. But the outstanding orders here contained no such contradictory commands.

There was an order issued March 27, 1942, which prohibited petitioner and others of Japanese ancestry from leaving the area, but its effect was specifically limited in time "until and to the extent that a future proclamation or order should so permit or direct." 7 Fed. Reg. 2601. That "future order," the one for violation of which petitioner was convicted, was issued May 3, 1942, and it did "direct" exclusion from the area of all persons of Japanese ancestry, before 12 o'clock noon, May 9; furthermore it contained a warning that all such persons found in the prohibited area would be liable to punishment under the March 21, 1942 Act of Congress. Consequently, the only order in effect touching the petitioner's being in the area on May 30, 1942, the date specified in the information against him, was the May 3 order which prohibited his remaining there, and it was that same order, which he stipulated in his trial that he had violated, knowing of its existence. There is therefore no basis for the argument that on May 30, 1942, he was subject to punishment, under the March 27 and May 3 orders, whether he remained in or left the area.

It does appear, however, that on May 9, the effective date of the exclusion order, the military authorities had already determined that the evacuation should be effected by assembling together and placing under guard all those of Japanese ancestry," at central points, designated as "assembly centers," in order "to insure the orderly evacuation and resettlement of Japanese voluntarily migrating from Military Area No. 1...."

We are thus being asked to pass at this time upon the whole subsequent detention program in both assembly and relocation centers, although the only issues framed at the trial related to petitioner's remaining in the prohibited area in violation of the exclusion order. Had petitioner here left the prohibited area and gone to an assembly center we cannot say either as a matter of fact or law that his presence in that center would have resulted in his detention in a relocation center. Some who did report to the assembly center were not sent to relocation centers, but were released upon condition that they remain outside the prohibited zone until the military orders were modified or lifted. This illustrates that they pose different problems and may be governed by different principles....

Since the petitioner has not been convicted of failing to report or to remain in an assembly or relocation center, we cannot in this case determine the validity of those separate provisions of the order.

It is said that we are dealing here with the case of imprisonment of a citizen in a concentration camp solely because of his ancestry, without evidence or inquiry concerning his loyalty and good disposition towards the United States. Our task would be simple, our duty clear, were this a case involving the imprisonment of a loyal citizen in a concentration camp because of racial prejudice. Regardless of the true nature of the assembly and relocation centers — and we deem it unjustifiable to call them concentration camps with all the ugly connotations that term implies — we are dealing specifically with nothing but an exclusion order. To cast this case into outlines of racial prejudice, without reference to the real military dangers which were presented, merely con-

fuses the issue. Korematsu was not excluded from the Military Area because of hostility to him or his race. He *was* excluded because we are at war with the Japanese Empire, because the properly constituted military authorities feared an invasion of our West Coast and felt constrained to take proper security measures, because they decided that the military urgency of the situation demanded that all citizens of Japanese ancestry be segregated from the West Coast temporarily, and finally, because Congress, reposing its confidence in this time of war in our military leaders — as inevitably it must — determined that they should have the power to do just this. There was evidence of disloyalty on the part of some, the military authorities considered that the need for action was great, and time was short. We cannot — by availing ourselves of the calm perspective of hindsight — now say that at that time these actions were unjustified.

Affirmed.

MR. JUSTICE FRANKFURTER, concurring.

.... [T]he validity of action under the war power must be judged wholly in the context of war. That action is not to be stigmatized as lawless because like action in times of peace would be lawless....

The respective spheres of action of military authorities and of judges are of course very different. But within their sphere, military authorities are no more outside the bonds of obedience to the Constitution than are judges within theirs....

If a military order such as that under review does not transcend the means appropriate for conducting war, such action by the military is as constitutional as would be any authorized action by the Interstate Commerce Commission within the limits of the constitutional power to regulate commerce. And being an exercise of the war power explicitly granted by the Constitution for safeguarding the national life by prosecuting war effectively, I find nothing in the Constitution which denies to Congress the power to enforce such a valid military order by making its violation an offense triable in the civil courts.

MR. JUSTICE ROBERTS, dissenting.

I dissent because I think the indisputable facts exhibit a clear violation of Constitutional rights.

This is not a case of keeping people off the streets at night as was *Hirabayashi* v. *United States,* 320 U.S. 81, nor a case of temporary exclusion of a citizen from an area for his own safety or that of the community, nor a case of offering him an opportunity to go temporarily out of an area where his presence might cause danger to himself or to his fellows. On the contrary, it is the case of convicting a citizen as a punishment for not submitting to imprisonment in a concentration camp, based on his ancestry, solely because of his ancestry, without evidence or inquiry concerning his loyalty and good disposition towards the United States. . . .

We cannot shut our eyes to the fact that had the petitioner attempted to violate Proclamation No. 4 and leave the military area in which he lived he would have been arrested and tried and convicted for violation of Proclamation No. 4. The two conflicting orders, one which commanded him to stay and the other which commanded him to go, were nothing but a cleverly devised trap to accomplish the real purpose of the military authority, which was to lock him up in a concentration camp. The only course by which the petitioner could avoid arrest and prosecution was to go to that camp according to instructions to be given him when he reported at a Civil Control Center.

Again it is a new doctrine of constitutional law that one indicted for disobedience to an unconstitutional statute may not defend on the ground of the invalidity of the statute but must obey it though he knows it is no law and, after he has suffered the disgrace of conviction and lost his liberty by sentence, then, and not before, seek, from within prison walls, to test the validity of the law.

Mr. Justice Murphy, dissenting.

Being an obvious racial discrimination, the order deprives all those within its scope of the equal protection of the laws as guaranteed by the Fifth Amendment. It further deprives these individuals of their constitutional rights to live and work where they will, to establish a home where they choose and to move about freely. In excommunicating them without benefit of hearings, this order also deprives them of all their constitutional rights to procedural due process. Yet no reasonable relation to an "immediate, imminent, and impending" public danger is evident to support this restriction which is one of the most sweeping and complete deprivations of constitutional rights in the history of this nation in the absence of martial law.

It must be conceded that the military and naval situation in the spring of 1942 was such as to generate a very real fear of invasion of the Pacific Coast, accompanied by fears of sabotage and espionage in that area. The military command was therefore justified in adopting all reasonable means necessary to combat these dangers. In adjudging the military action taken in light of the then apparent dangers, we must not erect too high or too meticulous standards;

it is necessary only that the action have some reasonable relation to the removal of the dangers of invasion, sabotage and espionage. But the exclusion, either temporarily or permanently, of all persons with Japanese blood in their veins has no such reasonable relation. And that relation is lacking because the exclusion order necessarily must rely for its reasonableness upon the assumption that *all* persons of Japanese ancestry may have a dangerous tendency to commit sabotage and espionage and to aid our Japanese enemy in other ways. It is difficult to believe that reason, logic or experience could be marshalled in support of such an assumption.

That this forced exclusion was the result in good measure of this erroneous assumption of racial guilt rather than bona fide military necessity is evidenced by the Commanding General's Final Report on the evacuation from the Pacific Coast area. In it he refers to all individuals of Japanese descent as "subversive," as belonging to "an enemy race" whose "racial strains are undiluted," and as constituting "over 112,000 potential enemies . . . at large today" along the Pacific Coast. In support of this blanket condemnation of all persons of Japanese descent, however, no reliable evidence is cited to show that such individuals were generally disloyal, or had generally so conducted themselves in this area as to constitute a special menace to defense installations or war industries, or had otherwise by their behavior furnished reasonable ground for their exclusion as a group.

. . . A military judgment based upon such racial and sociological considerations is not entitled to the great weight ordinarily given the judgments based upon strictly military considerations.

I dissent, therefore, from this legalization of racism. . . .

Mr. Justice Jackson, dissenting.

Korematsu was born on our soil, of parents born in Japan. . . .

Korematsu, however, has been convicted of an act not commonly a crime. It consists merely of being present in the state whereof he is a citizen, near the place where he was born, and where all his life he has lived.

Had Korematsu been one of four—the others being, say, a German alien enemy, an Italian alien enemy, and a citizen of American-born ancestors, convicted of treason but out on parole—only Korematsu's presence would have violated the order. . . .

Now, if any fundamental assumption underlies our system, it is that guilt is personal and not inheritable. Even if all of one's antecedents had been convicted of treason, the Constitution forbids its penalties to be visited upon him, for it provides that "no attainder of treason shall work corruption of blood, or forfeiture except during the life of the person attainted." But here is an attempt to make an otherwise innocent act a crime merely because this prisoner is the son of parents as to whom he had no choice, and belongs to a race from which there is no way to resign. . . .

The armed services must protect a society, not merely its Constitution. The very essence of the military job is to marshal physical force, to remove every obstacle to its effectiveness, to give it every strategic advantage. Defense measures will not, and often should not be held within the limits that bind civil authority in peace. . . .

But if we cannot confine military expedients by the Constitution, neither would I distort the Constitution to approve all that the military may deem expedient. . . . [E]ven if they were permissible military procedures, I deny that it follows that they are constitutional. If, as the Court holds, it does follow, then we may as well say that any military order will be constitutional and have done with it. . . .

In the very nature of things, military decisions are not susceptible of intelligent judicial appraisal. They do not pretend to rest on evidence, but are made on information that often would not be admissible and on assumptions that could not be proved. Information in support of an order could not be disclosed to courts without danger that it would reach the enemy. Neither can courts act on communications made in confidence. Hence courts can never have any real alternative to accepting the mere declaration of the authority that issued the order that it was reasonably necessary from a military viewpoint.

Much is said of the danger to liberty from the Army program for deporting and detaining these citizens of Japanese extraction. But a judicial construction of the due process clause that will sustain this order is a far more subtle blow to liberty than the promulgation of the order itself. A military order, however unconstitutional, is not apt to last longer than the military emergency. Even during that period a succeeding commander may revoke it all. But once a judicial opinion rationalizes such an order to show that it conforms to the Constitution, or rather rationalizes the Constitution to show that the Constitution sanctions such an order, the Court for all time has validated the principle of racial discrimination in criminal procedure and of transplanting American citizens. The principle then lies about like a loaded weapon ready for the hand of any authority that can bring forward a plausible claim of an urgent need.

I should hold that a civil court cannot be made to enforce an order which violates constitutional limitations even if it is a reasonable exercise of military authority. The courts can exercise only the judicial power, can apply only law, and must abide by the Constitution, or they cease to be civil courts and become instruments of military policy.

Of course the existence of a military power resting on force, so vagrant, so centralized, so necessarily heedless of the individual, is an inherent threat to liberty. But I would not lead people to rely on this Court for a review that seems to me wholly delusive. The military reasonableness of orders can only be determined by military superiors. If the people ever let command of the war power fall into irresponsible and unscrupulous hands, the courts wield no power equal to its restraint. The chief restraint upon those who command the physical forces of the country, in the future as in the past, must be their responsibility to the political judgments of their contemporaries and to the moral judgments of history.

My duties as a justice as I see them do not require me to make a military judgment as to whether General DeWitt's evacuation and detention program was a reasonable military necessity. I do not suggest that the courts should have attempted to interfere with the Army in carrying out its task. But I do not think they may be asked to execute a military expedient that has no place in law under the Constitution. I would reverse the judgment and discharge the prisoner.

Reid v. Covert

354 U.S. 1 (1957)

Vote: 6–2; Whittaker not participating.

The special issue of treaties and constitutional law was, as we noted, a political as well as a legal issue. The Court dissipated this fear with a series of carefully considered decisions. *Reid* v. *Covert* involved an agreement with the Japanese to have American military courts try civilian dependents. The issue, therefore, was more nearly like the subsequent TIMES case than the earlier MISSOURI V. HOLLAND (1920), as specific constitutional protections were being compromised. This decision helped solidify a growing tendency to distinguish sharply between civilian crimes and military ones. (See the discussion of *Toth* v. *Quarles* in *Reid* and the decision in *O'Callahan* v. *Parker* (1969), where Justice Douglas summarized that development.) *Reid* also laid to rest fears generated by such cases as MISSOURI V. HOLLAND that the foreign affairs authority could drastically alter the domestic constitutional order.

MR. JUSTICE BLACK announced the judgment of the Court and delivered an opinion, in which THE CHIEF JUSTICE, MR. JUSTICE DOUGLAS, and MR. JUSTICE BRENNAN join.

These cases raise basic constitutional issues of the utmost concern. They call into question the role of the military under our system of government. They involve the power of Congress to expose civilians to trial by military tribunals, under military regulations and procedures, for offenses against the United States thereby depriving them of trial in civilian courts, under civilian laws and procedures and with all the safeguards of the Bill of Rights. These cases are particularly significant because for the first time since the adoption of the Constitution wives of soldiers have been denied trial by jury in a court of law and forced to trial before courts-martial.

In No. 701 Mrs. Clarice Covert killed her husband, a sergeant in the United States Air Force, at an air base in England. Mrs. Covert, who was not a member of the armed services, was residing on the base with her husband at the time. She was tried by a court-martial for murder under Article 118 of the Uniform Code of Military Justice. . . .

Counsel for Mrs. Covert contended that she was insane at the time she killed her husband, but the military tribunal found her guilty of murder and sentenced her to life imprisonment. . . .

[H]er counsel petitioned the District Court for a writ of habeas corpus to set her free on the ground that the Constitution forbade her trial by military authorities. Construing this Court's decision in *United States ex rel. Toth* v. *Quarles,* 350 U.S. 11, as holding that "a civilian is entitled to a civilian trial" the District Court held that Mrs. Covert could not be tried by court-martial and ordered her released from custody. The Government appealed directly to this Court under 28 U.S.C. §1252.

In No. 713 Mrs. Dorothy Smith killed her husband, an Army officer, at a post in Japan where she was living with him. She was tried for murder by a court-martial and despite considerable evidence that she was insane was found guilty and sentenced to life imprisonment.

The two cases were consolidated and argued last Term and a majority of the Court, with three Justices dissenting and one reserving opinion, held that military trial of Mrs. Smith and Mrs. Covert for their alleged offenses was constitutional.

Subsequently, the Court granted a petition for rehearing 352 U.S. 901. Now, after further argument and consideration, we conclude that the previous decisions cannot be permitted to stand. We hold that Mrs. Smith and Mrs. Covert could not constitutionally be tried by military authorities.

I

At the beginning we reject the idea that when the United States acts against citizens abroad it can do so free of the Bill of Rights. The United States is entirely a creature of the Constitution. Its power and authority have no other source. It can only act in accordance with all the limitations imposed by the Constitution. When the Government reaches out to punish a citizen who is abroad, the shield which the Bill of Rights and other parts of the Constitution provide to protect his life and liberty should not be stripped away just because he happens to be in another land. . . . While it has been suggested that only those constitutional rights which are "fundamental" protect Americans abroad, we can find no warrant, in logic or otherwise, for picking and choosing among the remarkable collection of "Thou shalt nots" which were explicitly fastened on all departments and agencies of the Federal Government by the Constitution and its Amendments. Moreover, in view of our heritage and the history of the adoption of the Constitution and the Bill of Rights, it seems peculiarly anomalous to say that trial before a civilian judge and by an independent jury picked from the common citizenry is not a fundamental right. . . .

The keystone of supporting authorities mustered by the Court's opinion last June to justify its holding that Art. III, §2, and the Fifth and Sixth Amendments did not apply abroad was *In re Ross,* 140 U.S. 453. The *Ross* case is one of those cases that cannot be understood except in its peculiar setting; even then, it seems highly unlikely that a similar result would be reached today. Ross was serving as a seaman on an American ship in Japanese waters. He killed a ship's officer, was seized and tried before a consular "court" in Japan. At that time, statutes authorized American consuls to try American citizens charged with committing crimes in Japan and certain other "non-Christian" countries. . . .

The consular power approved in the *Ross* case was about as extreme and absolute as that of the potentates of the "non-Christian" countries to which the statutes applied. Under these statutes consuls could and did make the criminal laws, initiate charges, arrest alleged offenders, try them, and after conviction take away their liberty or their life — sometimes at the American consulate. Such a blending of executive, legislative, and judicial powers in one person or even in one branch of the Government is ordinarily regarded as the very acme of absolutism. Nevertheless, the Court sustained Ross' conviction by the consul.

The Court's opinion last Term also relied on the "Insular Cases" to support its conclusion that Article III and the Fifth and Sixth Amendments were not applicable to the trial of Mrs. Smith and Mrs. Covert. We believe that reliance was misplaced. The "Insular Cases," which arose at the turn of the century, involved territories which had only recently been conquered or acquired by the United States. . . .

The "Insular Cases" can be distinguished from the present cases in that they involved the power of Congress to provide rules and regulations to govern temporarily territories with wholly dissimilar traditions and institutions whereas here the basis for governmental power is American citizenship. None of these cases had anything to do with military trials and they cannot properly be used as vehicles to support an extention of military jurisdiction to civilians. Moreover, it is our judgment that neither the cases nor their reasoning should be given any further expansion.

Article VI, the Supremacy Clause of the Constitution, declares:

> This Constitution, and the Laws of the
> United States which shall be made in
> Pursuance thereof; and all Treaties made, or
> which shall be made, under the Authority of
> the United States, shall be the supreme Law
> of the Land; . . .

There is nothing in this language which intimates that treaties and laws enacted pursuant to them do not have to comply with the provisions of the Constitution. Nor is there anything in the debates which accompanied the drafting and ratification of the Constitution which even suggests such a result. . . .

It would be manifestly contrary to the objectives of those who created the Constitution, as well as those who were responsible for the Bill of Rights — let alone alien to our entire constitutional history and tradition — to construe Article VI as permitting the United States to exercise power under an international agreement without observing constitutional prohibitions. In effect, such construction would permit amendment of that document in a manner not sanctioned by Article V. The prohibitions of the Constitution were designed to apply to all branches of the National Government and they cannot be nullified by the Executive or by the Executive and the Senate combined.

This Court has also repeatedly taken the position that an Act of Congress, which must comply with the Constitution, is on a full parity with a treaty, and that when a statute which is subsequent in time is inconsistent with a treaty, the statute to the extent of conflict renders the treaty null. It would be completely anomalous to say that a treaty need not comply with the Constitution when such an agreement can be overridden by a statute that must conform to that instrument.

There is nothing in *Missouri* v. *Holland,* 252 U.S. 416, which is contrary to the position taken here. There the Court carefully noted that the treaty involved was not inconsistent with any specific provision of the Constitution. The Court was concerned with the Tenth Amendment, which reserves to the States or the people all power not delegated to the National Government. To the extent that the United States can validly make treaties, the people and the States have delegated their power to the National Government and the Tenth Amendment is no barrier. . . .

The Government argues that the Necessary and Proper Clause when taken in conjunction with Clause 14 allows Congress to authorize the trial of Mrs. Smith and Mrs. Covert by military tribunals and under military law. The Government claims that the two clauses together constitute a broad grant of power "without limitation" authorizing Congress to subject all persons, civilians and soldiers alike, to military trial if "necessary and proper" to govern and regulate the land and naval forces. It was on a similar theory that Congress once went to the extreme of subjecting persons who made contracts with the military to court-martial jurisdiction with respect to frauds related to such contracts. In the only judicial test a Circuit Court held that the legislation was patently unconstitutional. . . .

It is true that the Constitution expressly grants Congress power to make all rules necessary and proper to govern and regulate those persons who are serving in the "land and naval Forces." But the Necessary and Proper Clause cannot operate to extend military jurisdiction to any group of persons beyond that class described in Clause 14 — "the land and naval Forces." Under the grand design of the Constitution civilian courts are the normal repositories of power to try persons charged with crimes against the United States.

. . . In *McCulloch* this Court was confronted with the problem of determining the scope of the Necessary and Proper Clause in a situation where no specific restraints on governmental power stood in the way. Here the problem is different. Not only does Clause 14, by its terms, limit military jurisdiction to members of the "land and naval Forces," but Art. III, §2 and the Fifth and Sixth Amendments require that certain express safeguards, which were designed to protect persons from oppressive governmental practices, shall be given in criminal prosecutions — safeguards which cannot be given in a military trial. In the light of these as well as other constitutional provisions, and the historical background in which they were formed, military trial of civilians is inconsistent with both the "letter and spirit of the constitution. . . ."

Just last Term, this Court held in *United States ex rel. Toth* v. *Quarles*, 350 U.S. 11, that military courts could not constitutionally try a discharged serviceman for an offense which he had allegedly committed while in the armed forces. It was decided (1) that since Toth was a civilian he could not be tried by military court-martial, and (2) that since he was charged with murder, a "crime" in the constitutional sense, he was entitled to indictment by a grand jury, jury trial, and the other protections contained in Art. III, §2 and the Fifth, Sixth, and Eighth Amendments. The Court pointed out that trial by civilian courts was the rule for persons who were not members of the armed forces. . . .

There have been a number of decisions in the lower federal courts which have upheld military trial of civilians performing services for the armed forces "in the field" during *time of war*. To the extent that these cases can be justified, insofar as they involved trial of persons who were not "members" of the armed forces, they must rest on the Government's "war powers." In the face of an actively hostile enemy, military commanders necessarily have broad power over persons on the battlefront. From a time prior to the adoption of the Constitution the extraordinary circumstances present in an area of actual fighting have been considered sufficient to permit punishment of some civilians in that area by military courts under military rules. But neither Japan nor Great Britain could properly be said to be an area where active hostilities were under way at the time Mrs. Smith and Mrs. Covert committed their offenses or at the time they were tried.

As this Court stated in *United States ex rel. Toth* v. *Quarles*, 350 U.S. 11, the business of soldiers is to fight and prepare to fight wars, not to try civilians for their alleged crimes. Traditionally, military justice has been a rough form of justice emphasizing summary procedures, speedy convictions and stern penalties with a view to maintaining obedience and fighting fitness in the ranks. Because of its very nature and purpose the military must place great emphasis on discipline and efficiency. Correspondingly, there has always been less emphasis in the military on protecting the rights of the individual than in civilian society and in civilian courts.

We recognize that a number of improvements have been made in military justice recently by engrafting more and more of the methods of civilian courts on courts-martial. In large part these ameliorations stem from the reaction of civilians, who were inducted during the two World Wars, to their experience with military justice. Notwithstanding the recent reforms, military trial does not give an accused the same protection which exists in the civil courts.

It is urged that the expansion of military jurisdiction over civilians claimed here is only slight, and that the practical necessity for it is very great. The attitude appears to be that a slight encroachment on the Bill of Rights and other safeguards in the Constitution need cause little concern. But to hold that these wives could be tried by the military would be tempting precedent. Slight encroachments create new boundaries from which legions of power can seek new territory to capture.

Mr. Justice Whittaker took no part in the consideration or decision of these cases.

Mr. Justice Frankfurter, concurring in the result.

The Government suggests that, if trial in an Article III court subject to the restrictions of the Fifth and Sixth Amendments is the only alternative, such a trial could not be held abroad practicably, and it would often be equally impracticable to transport all the witnesses back to the United States for trial. But, although there is no need to pass on that issue in this case, trial in the United States is obviously not the only practical alternative and other alternatives may raise different constitutional questions. The Government's own figures for the Army show that the total number of civilians (all civilians "serving with, employed by, or accompanying the armed forces" overseas and not merely civilian dependents) for whom general courts-martial for alleged murder were deemed advisable was only 13 in the 7 fiscal years, 1950–1956. It is impossible to ascertain from the figures supplied to us exactly how many persons were tried for other capital offenses, but the figures indicate that there could not have been many. There is nothing to indicate that the figures for the other services are more substantial. It thus appears to be a manageable problem within the procedural restrictions found necessary by this opinion.

I therefore conclude that, in capital cases, the exercise of court-martial jurisdiction over civilian dependents in time of peace cannot be justified by Article I, considered in connection with the specific protections of Article III and the Fifth and Sixth Amendments.

MR. JUSTICE HARLAN, concurring in the result.

I concur in the result, on the narrow ground that where the offense is capital, Article 2 (11) cannot constitutionally be applied to the trial of civilian dependents of members of the armed forces overseas in times of peace.

Since I am the only one among today's majority who joined in the Court's opinions of June 11, 1956, which sustained the court-martial jurisdiction in these cases, I think it appropriate to state the reasons which lead to my voting, first, to rehear these cases, and, now, to strike down that jurisdiction.

. . . I am satisfied that our prior holding swept too lightly over the historical context in which this Court upheld the jurisdiction of the old consular and territorial courts in those cases. I shall not repeat what my brother FRANKFURTER has written on this subject, with which I agree. But I do not go as far as my brother BLACK seems to go on this score. His opinion, if I understand it correctly, in effect discards *Ross* and the *Insular Cases* as historical anomalies. I believe that those cases, properly understood, still have vitality, and that, for reasons suggested later, which differ from those given in our prior opinions, they have an important bearing on the question now before us. . . .

[V]iewing Art. I, §8, cl. 14 in isolation, subjection of civilian dependents overseas to court-martial jurisdiction can in no wise be deemed unrelated to the power of Congress to make all necessary and proper laws to insure the effective governance of our overseas land and naval forces.

I turn now to the other side of the coin. For no matter how practical and how reasonable this jurisdiction might be, it still cannot be sustained if the Constitution guarantees to these army wives a trial in an Article III court, with indictment by grand jury and jury trial as provided by the Fifth and Sixth Amendments.

On this basis, I cannot agree with the sweeping proposition that a full Article III trial, with indictment and trial by jury, is required in every case for the trial of a civilian dependent of a serviceman over-

seas. The Government, it seems to me, has made an impressive showing that at least for the run-of-the-mill offenses committed by dependents overseas, such a requirement would be as impractical and as anomalous as it would have been to require jury trial for Balzac in Porto Rico. Again, I need not go into details, beyond stating that except for capital offenses, such as we have here, to which, in my opinion, special considerations apply, I am by no means ready to say that Congress' power to provide for trial by court-martial of civilian dependents overseas is limited by Article III and the Fifth and Sixth Amendments. Where, if at all, the dividing line should be drawn among cases not capital, need not now be decided. We are confronted here with capital offenses alone; and it seems to me particularly unwise now to decide more than we have to. Our far-flung foreign military establishments are a new phenomenon in our national life, and I think it would be unfortunate were we necessarily to foreclose, as my four brothers would do, our future consideration of the broad questions involved in maintaining the effectiveness of these national outposts, in the light of continuing experience with these problems.

MR. JUSTICE CLARK, with whom MR. JUSTICE BURTON joins, dissenting.

The Court today releases two women from prosecution though the evidence shows that they brutally killed their husbands, both American soldiers, while stationed with them in quarters furnished by our armed forces on its military installations in foreign lands. In turning these women free, it declares unconstitutional an important section of an Act of Congress governing our armed forces.

. . . It is unable to muster a majority. Instead, there are handed down three opinions. But, worst of all, it gives no authoritative guidance as to what, if anything, the Executive or the Congress may do to remedy the distressing situation in which they now find themselves.

MR. JUSTICE BURTON and I remain convinced that the former opinions of the Court are correct and that they set forth valid constitutional doctrine under the long-recognized cases of this Court.

My brothers who are concurring in the result seem to find some comfort in that for the present they void an Act of Congress only as to capital cases. I find no distinction in the Constitution between capital and other cases. In fact, at argument all parties admitted there could be no valid difference. My brothers are careful not to say that they would uphold the Act as to offenses less than capital. They unfortunately leave that decision for another day. This is disastrous to proper judicial administration as well as to law enforcement. . . .

New York Times v. U.S.

403 U.S. 713 (1971)
Vote: 6–3; every justice wrote an
   opinion.

A more specific testing of the boundary between emergency powers and individual rights occurred in connection with the *New York Times'* and *Washington Post's* printing of the same Pentagon Papers that figured in the GRAVEL case. The government asked that the classification of the material, signifying its vital connection with national defense, be regarded as closing the dispute and deciding that that alone precluded publication. Alternatively, they were prepared to argue the significance of the material.

The principal argument for the *New York Times* was made by Alexander Bickel, the late constitutional authority. He insisted that the argument *not* be an absolute rejection of any and all prior censorship. Rather, he argued: (1) that what was legally — in peacetime, at least — censorship must be most heavily justified and have minimal consequences; (2) that Congress must be the primary source of a policy for censorship of nongovernmental agencies; and (3) that the executive effort to withhold information must be internally enforced.

How much of the *Times'* position was adopted by the Court? Constitutionally, how could failure to contain the information permit the newspapers to proceed to publish?

It has been suggested that a major requirement for courts is that they decide what is before them and not anticipate problems. Does this conflict with the notion that the purpose of the Supreme Court is to provide broad legal guidance? Comparing the YOUNGSTOWN SHEET AND TUBE case and the *New York Times* case, do you think individual opinions (as opposed to a compromise majority opinion) are more helpful in providing future guidance? Do they enhance or diminish respect for

law? Do they provide the Court with more or less flexibility under new fact situations?

PER CURIAM.

We granted certiorari in these cases in which the United States seeks to enjoin the New York Times and the Washington Post from publishing the contents of a classified study entitled "History of U.S. Decision-Making Process on Viet Nam Policy."

"Any system of prior restraints of expression comes to this Court bearing a heavy presumption against its constitutional validity." *Bantam Books, Inc.* v. *Sullivan,* . . . (1963); see also *Near* v. *Minnesota,* . . . (1931). The Government "thus carries a heavy burden of showing justification for the enforcement of such a restraint." *Organization for a Better Austin* v. *Keefe,* . . . (1971). The District Court for the Southern District of New York in the *New York Times* case and the District Court for the District of Columbia and the Court of Appeals for the District of Columbia Circuit in the *Washington Post* case held that the Government had not met that burden. We agree.

The judgment of the Court of Appeals for the District of Columbia Circuit is therefore affirmed. The order of the Court of Appeals for the Second Circuit is reversed and the case is remanded with directions to enter a judgment affirming the judgment of the District Court for the Southern District of New York. The stays entered June 25, 1971, by the Court are vacated. The mandates shall issue forthwith.

So ordered.

MR. JUSTICE BRENNAN, concurring.

. . . So far as I can determine, never before has the United States sought to enjoin a newspaper from publishing information in its possession. The relative novelty of the questions presented, the necessary haste with which decisions were reached, the magnitude of the interests asserted, and the fact that all the parties have concentrated their arguments upon the question whether permanent restraints were proper may have justified at least some of the restraints heretofore imposed in these cases. Certainly it is difficult to fault the several courts below for seeking to assure that the issues here involved were preserved for ultimate review by this Court. But even if it be assumed that some of the interim restraints were proper in the two cases before us, that assumption has no bearing upon the propriety of similar judicial action in the future. To begin with, there has now been ample time for reflection and judgment; whatever values there may be in the preservation of novel questions for appellate review may not support any restraints in the future.

. . . Our cases, it is true, have indicated that there is a single, extremely narrow class of cases in which the First Amendment's ban on prior judicial restraint may be overriden. Our cases have thus far indicated that such cases may arise only when the Nation "is at war," *Schenck* v. *United States*, . . . (1919), during which times "no one would question but that a Government might prevent actual obstruction to its recruiting service or the publication of the sailing dates of transports or the number and location of troops." *Near* v. *Minnesota*, . . . (1931). Even if the present world situation were assumed to be tantamount to a time of war, or if the power of presently available armaments would justify even in peacetime the suppression of information that would set in motion a nuclear holocaust, in neither of these actions has the Government presented or even alleged that publication of items from or based upon the material at issue would cause the happening of an event of that nature.

. . . Thus, only governmental allegation and proof that publication must inevitably, directly and immediately cause the occurrence of an event kindred to imperiling the safety of a transport already at sea can support even the issuance of an interim restraining order. In no event may mere conclusions be sufficient: for if the Executive Branch seeks judicial aid in preventing publication, it must inevitably submit the basis upon which that aid is sought to scrutiny by the judiciary.

MR. JUSTICE STEWART, with whom MR. JUSTICE WHITE joins, concurring.

In the governmental structure created by our Constitution, the Executive is endowed with enormous power in the two related areas of national defense and international relations. This power, largely unchecked by the Legislative and Judicial branches, has been pressed to the very hilt since the advent of the nuclear missile age. For better or for worse, the simple fact is that a President of the United States possesses vastly greater constitutional independence in these two vital areas of power than does, say, a prime minister of a country with a parliamentary form of government.

In the absence of the governmental checks and balances present in other areas of our national life, the only effective restraint upon executive policy and power in the areas of national defense and international affairs may lie in an enlightened citizenry — in an informed and critical public opinion which alone can here protect the values of democratic govern-

ment. For this reason, it is perhaps here that a press that is alert, aware, and free most vitally serves the basic purpose of the First Amendment. For without an informed and free press there cannot be an enlightened people.

Yet it is elementary that the successful conduct of international diplomacy and the maintenance of an effective national defense require both confidentiality and secrecy. Other nations can hardly deal with this Nation in an atmosphere of mutual trust unless they can be assured that their confidences will be kept. And within our own executive departments, the development of considered and intelligent international policies would be impossible if those charged with their formulation could not communicate with each other freely, frankly, and in confidence. In the area of basic national defense the frequent need for absolute secrecy is, of course, self-evident.

I think there can be but one answer to this dilemma, if dilemma it be. The responsibility must be where the power is. If the Constitution gives the Executive a large degree of unshared power in the conduct of foreign affairs and the maintenance of our national defense, then under the Constitution the Executive must have the largely unshared duty to determine and preserve the degree of internal security necessary to exercise that power successfully. It is an awesome responsibility, requiring judgment and wisdom of a high order. I should suppose that moral, political and practical considerations would dictate that a very first principle of that wisdom would be an insistence upon avoiding secrecy for its own sake. For when everything is classified, then nothing is classified, and the system becomes one to be disregarded by the cynical or the careless, and to be manipulated by those intent on self-protection or self-promotion. . . .

. . . [I]t is clear to me that it is the constitutional duty of the Executive — as a matter of sovereign prerogative and not as a matter of law as the courts know law — through the promulgation and enforcement of executive relations, to protect the confidentiality necessary to carry out its responsibilities in the fields of international relations and national defense.

This is not to say that Congress and the courts have no role to play. Undoubtedly Congress has the power to enact specific and appropriate criminal laws to protect government property and preserve government secrets. Congress has passed such laws, and several of them are of very colorable relevance to the apparent circumstances of these cases. And if a criminal prosecution is instituted, it will be the responsibility of the courts to decide the applicability of the criminal law under which the charge is brought. Moreover, if Congress should pass a specific law authorizing civil proceedings in this field, the courts would likewise have the duty to decide the constitutionality of such a law as well as its applicability to the facts proved.

But in the cases before us we are asked neither to construe specific regulations nor to apply specific laws. We are asked, instead, to perform a function that the Constitution gave to the Executive, not the Judiciary. We are asked, quite simply, to prevent the publication by two newspapers of material that the Executive Branch insists should not, in the national interest, be published. I am convinced that the Executive is correct with respect to some of the documents involved. But I cannot say that disclosure of any of them will surely result in direct, immediate, and irreparable damage to our Nation or its people. That being so, there can under the First Amendment be but one judicial resolution of the issues before us. I join the judgments of the Court.

MR. JUSTICE WHITE, with whom MR. JUSTICE STEWART joins, concurring.

The Government's position is simply stated: The responsibility of the Executive for the conduct of the foreign affairs and for the security of the Nation is so basic that the President is entitled to an injunction against publication of a newspaper story whenever he can convince a court that the information to be revealed threatens "grave and irreparable" injury to the public interest; and the injunction should issue whether or not the material to be published is classified, whether or not publication would be lawful under relevant criminal statutes enacted by Congress and regardless of the circumstances by which the newspaper came into possession of the information.

At least in the absence of legislation by Congress, based on its own investigations and findings, I am quite unable to agree that the inherent powers of the Executive and the courts reach so far as to authorize remedies having such sweeping potential for inhibiting publications by the press. . . . To sustain the Government in these cases would start the courts down a long and hazardous road that I am not willing to travel at least without congressional guidance and direction.

It is thus clear that Congress has addressed itself to the problems of protecting the security of the country and the national defense from unauthorized disclosure of potentially damaging information. Cf. *Youngstown Sheet & Tube Co. v. Sawyer*, . . . (1952). . . . It has not, however, authorized the injunctive remedy against threatened publication. It

has apparently been satisfied to rely on criminal sanctions and their deterrent effect on the responsible as well as the irresponsible press.

MR. JUSTICE MARSHALL, concurring.

In this case there is no problem concerning the President's power to classify information as "secret" or "top secret." Congress has specifically recognized Presidential authority, which has been formally exercised in Executive Order 10501, to classify documents and information. . . . Nor is there any issue here regarding the President's power as Chief Executive and Commander-in-Chief to protect national security by disciplining employees who disclose information and by taking precautions to prevent leaks.

The problem here is whether in this particular case the Executive Branch has authority to invoke the equity jurisdiction of the courts to protect what it believes to be the national interest. . . . The Government argues that in addition to the inherent power of any government to protect itself, the President's power to conduct foreign affairs and his position as Commander-in-Chief give him authority to impose censorship on the press to protect his ability to deal effectively with foreign nations and to conduct the military affairs of the country. . . .

It would, however, be utterly inconsistent with the concept of separation of power for this Court to use its power of contempt to prevent behavior that Congress has specifically declined to prohibit. There would be a similar damage to the basic concept of these coequal branches of Government if when the Executive has adequate authority granted by Congress to protect "national security" it can choose instead to invoke the contempt power of a court to enjoin the threatened conduct. The Constitution provides that Congress shall make laws, the President execute laws, and courts interpret law. *Youngstown Sheet & Tube Co. v. Sawyer*, . . . (1952). It did not provide for government by injunction in which the courts and the Executive can "make law" without regard to the action of Congress. It may be more convenient for the Executive if it need only convince a judge to prohibit conduct rather than to ask the Congress to pass a law and it may be more convenient to enforce a contempt order than seek a criminal conviction in a jury trial. Moreover, it may be considered politically wise to get a court to share the responsibility for arresting those who the Executive has probable cause to believe are violating the law. But convenience and political considerations of the moment do not justify a basic departure from the principles of our system of government. . . .

MR. CHIEF JUSTICE BURGER, dissenting.

. . . In this case, the imperative of a free and unfettered press comes into collision with another imperative, the effective functioning of a complex modern government and specifically the effective exercise of certain constitutional powers of the Executive.

This case is not simple for another and more immediate reason. We do not know the facts of the case. No District Judge knew all the facts. No Court of Appeals judge knew all the facts. No member of this Court knows all the facts. . . .

I suggest we are in this posture because these cases have been conducted in unseemly haste. . . .

Here, moreover, the frenetic haste is due in large part to the manner in which the *Times* proceeded from the date it obtained the purloined documents. It seems reasonably clear now that the haste precluded reasonable and deliberate judicial treatment of these cases and was not warranted. The precipitous action of this Court aborting a trial not yet completed is not the kind of judicial conduct which ought to attend the disposition of a great issue.

The newspapers make a derivative claim under the First Amendment; they denominate this right as the public right-to-know; by implication, the *Times* asserts a sole trusteeship of that right by virtue of its journalist "scoop." The right is asserted as an absolute. Of course, the First Amendment right itself is not an absolute, as Justice Holmes so long ago pointed out in his aphorism concerning the right to shout "fire" in a crowded theater. There are other exceptions, some of which Chief Justice Hughes mentioned by way of example in *Near* v. *Minnesota*. There are no doubt other exceptions no one has had occasion to describe or discuss. Conceivably such exceptions may be lurking in these cases and would have been flushed had they been properly considered in the trial courts, free from unwarranted deadlines and frenetic pressures. A great issue of this kind should be tried in a judicial atmosphere conducive to thoughtful, reflective deliberation, especially when haste, in terms of hours, is unwarranted in light of the long period the *Times,* by its own choice, deferred publication.

It is not disputed that the *Times* has had unauthorized possession of the documents for three to four months, during which it has had its expert analysts studying them, presumably digesting them and preparing the material for publication. . . . But why should the United States Government, from whom this information was illegally acquired by someone, along with all the counsel, trial judges, and appellate judges be placed under needless pressure? After these months of deferral, the alleged right-to-know has somehow and suddenly become a right that must be vindicated instanter.

MR. JUSTICE HARLAN, with whom THE CHIEF JUSTICE and MR. JUSTICE BLACKMUN join, dissenting.

Forced as I am to reach the merits of these cases, I dissent from the opinion and judgments of the Court.

It is plain to me that the scope of the judicial function in passing upon the activities of the Executive Branch of the Government in the field of foreign affairs is very narrowly restricted. This view is, I think, dictated by the concept of separation of powers upon which our constitutional system rests.

In a speech on the floor of the House of Representatives, Chief Justice John Marshall, then a member of that body, stated:

> The President is the sole organ of the nation in its external relations, and its sole representative with foreign nations. Annals, 6th Cong., col. 613 (1800).

From that time, shortly after the founding of the Nation, to this, there has been no substantial challenge to this description of the scope of executive power. See *United States* v. *Curtiss-Wright Export Corp.,* . . . (1936), collecting authorities.

The power to evaluate the "pernicious influence" of premature disclosure is not, however, lodged in the Executive alone. I agree that, in performance of its duty to protect the values of the First Amendment against political pressures, the judiciary must review the initial Executive determination to the point of satisfying itself that the subject matter of the dispute does lie within the proper compass of the President's foreign relations power. Constitutional considerations forbid "a complete abandonment of judicial control." . . . Moreover, the judiciary may properly insist that the determination that disclosure of the subject matter would irreparably impair the national security be made by the head of the Executive Department concerned — here the Secretary of State or the Secretary of Defense — after actual personal consideration by the officer. This safeguard is required in the analogous area of executive claims of privilege for secrets of state. . . .

But in my judgment the judiciary may not properly go beyond these two inquiries and redetermine for itself the probable impact of disclosure on the national security.

> [T]he very nature of executive decisions as to foreign policy is political, not judicial. Such decisions are wholly confined by our

Constitution to the political departments of the government, Executive and Legislative. They are delicate, complex, and involve large elements of prophecy. They are and should be undertaken only by those directly responsible to the people whose welfare they advance or imperil. They are decisions of a kind for which the Judiciary has neither aptitude, facilities nor responsibility and which has long been held to belong in the domain of political power not subject to judicial intrusion or inquiry. *Chicago & Southern Air Lines* v. *Waterman Steamship Corp.*, . . . (1948) (Jackson, J.).

Even if there is some room for the judiciary to override the executive determination, it is plain that the scope of review must be exceedingly narrow. I can see no indication in the opinions of either the District Court or the Court of Appeals in the *Post*

litigation that the conclusions of the Executive were given even the deference owing to an administrative agency, much less that owing to a co-equal branch of the Government operating within the field of its constitutional prerogative.

MR. JUSTICE BLACKMUN, dissenting.

The First Amendment, after all, is only one part of an entire Constitution. Article II of the great document vests in the Executive Branch primary power over the conduct of foreign affairs and places in that branch the responsibility for the Nation's safety. Each provision of the Constitution is important, and I cannot subscribe to a doctrine of unlimited absolutism for the First Amendment at the cost of downgrading other provisions. First Amendment absolutism has never commanded a majority of this Court. [E]ven the newspapers concede that there are times where restraint is in order and is constitutional. . . .

CHAPTER 3

The Problems of Yesteryear: National Authority over Commerce and Taxation

Historically, national regulatory power rested largely on the commerce power and the power to tax and spend for the general welfare. The power to regulate commerce may be the basis for direct control of a subject matter, or it may be the basis for the congressional prohibition of travel of goods or persons in interstate commerce not conforming to a congressional policy. Similarly, taxes can be assessed at high or low rates to encourage or discourage behavior. For example, via special lower tax rates, the federal government encourages factories producing strategic goods to locate outside major metropolitan areas. It can accomplish the same thing via subsidies or direct payments, by spending as well as taxing.

The commerce and taxing powers are both provided for in the grant of powers to Congress and are functionally quite distinct. The impact of commerce power regulation on state power is obviously more subtle and complex than the question of coexistence of state and federal taxes. Yet, because the commerce and tax powers mark the major boundaries of the relation between nation and state, the interpretation of their scope has been remarkably parallel.

Marshall found commerce and tax powers wide in scope, though a suggestion of limits appeared in his later decisions. These limits became more and more prominent. As the post–Civil War court developed the notion of "dual federalism"—the idea of equal and opposite levels of government—it also gradually developed two contradictory lines of decisions for both commerce and tax cases that gave the Court policy control over outcomes. With the New Deal challenge the dual line of precedent ended entirely in commerce cases, and largely with respect to taxing and spending cases.

Today the national government has almost unqualified constitutional power to deal with national problems through use of these powers. The problems of yesteryear have largely disappeared.

The Commerce Clause in History

The Commerce Power in Marshall's Grand Design

The need for national policies to promote trade, plus the too-visible presence of state burdens upon that trade, were the major impetus for the Annapolis meeting to reform the Articles of Confederation. The resulting call for a more extensive meeting in Philadelphia was also clearly motivated by a desire to create what we would now call a "common market" in the United States — to end tax and other barriers between states and to promote commercial growth throughout the country.

The Commerce Clause, which attempts to create that market, is one of the great accomplishments of the Constitution. Some of our most thoughtful justices have considered it the heart of that document. It has also been a major instrument in achieving national power in many areas of policy, some having little obvious connection with commerce. Until the Fourteenth Amendment became a mini-Constitution in its own right — a development of the second quarter of the twentieth century — the Commerce Clause was the major single source of constitutional litigation, both in defining national power and, as we shall see in detail in the next chapter, in circumscribing state power over commerce.

"The great Commerce Clause" is simple and elegant, conferring upon Congress "power to regulate commerce with foreign nations and among the several states, and with the Indian tribes." It has been argued that what was intended was a massive grant of authority over internal trade, as comprehensive as with foreign countries. Concerns expressed at the Convention that the national government would create monopolies support such an interpretation. But the Federalists quickly denied such a scope in order to quiet the opposition. The boundary of the power has been left to litigation, and most generalists have found slightly, and at

times greatly, different answers to this question of interpretation.

Many of Marshall's great decisions were expositions of the Commerce Clause. They have usually been seen as triumphs for national power, though at least one commentator — Crosskey — sees them as ignoble retreats from a truly simple and strong national system. Marshall rephrased "commerce among the states" to "that commerce which concerns more states than one," and this in turn has become the more familiar "interstate commerce." While it is obvious that the connotations of each of these successive rubrics are increasingly restrictive of national power, it remains an object of controversy as to which notion most accurately captures the intent of the Founding Fathers. In any event, by the twentieth century the development of a national economy helped diminish almost any difference in nuance between those standards for national power.

In contrast, when a subject is found to be within national authority but also of concern to the states, Marshall's answers are clear and without ambiguity. "This power is complete in itself," he wrote with verbal power of his own, ". . . may be exercised to its utmost, and acknowledges no limitations, other than are prescribed in the constitution . . . vested in congress as absolutely as it would be in a single government having in its constitution the same restrictions." Marshall's majestic view of the Commerce Clause as a supreme and absolute grant of a major — though bounded — power has remained the touchstone of national authority. Judicial quotations from GIBBONS V. OGDEN (1824) [as in other areas from McCULLOCH V. MARYLAND (1819)] are virtual tip-offs that national power will be vindicated.

Marshall's grand design, because it has re-emerged in our time as dominant doctrine, seems so clear and clean. But it was obscured for about a century. His interpretation was neither denied nor overruled but, through a series of turgid

Court decisions, turned on its head and effectively used for opposite purposes. The technique used to subvert Marshall's view was to oppose to the Commerce Clause some provision of the Constitution, particularly the Tenth Amendment, and to suggest that the Constitution established "dual sovereigns." The implications of federalism prevailed even over clear constitutional assignment of authority. The "plenary" nature of the Commerce Clause was subordinated to an unspecified division of power between states and nation.

The gradual retreat from Marshall's "plenary power" theory of the Commerce Clause was roughly completed by the last decade of the nineteenth century. The high-water mark was the decision in the E. C. KNIGHT case (1895). There the Court held that, though Congress could prohibit conspiracies as to shipping commodities in interstate commerce (upholding the Sherman Antitrust Act), it could not prohibit a sugar refiner from buying out all its competitors, because stock sales are local in nature and, under the Tenth Amendment, can be regulated only by the state governments. Of course, ownership is the most complete form of monopolization.

Even as the Court announced this controversial decision, it began to find new application for Marshall's broad view of national authority. Recognizing the impracticability of regulating stockyards and other meat-producing facilities by states, it found federal authority to inhere in "the stream of commerce," notwithstanding the fact that animals were generally brought to a stockyard from outside a state's borders and subsequently shipped out as meat to still other states [*Swift* v. *U.S.* (1905); *Stafford* v. *Wallace* (1922)]. It recognized that national authority over railroad rates had to extend to local rates for genuine regulation [SHREVEPORT CASE (1914)].

While the Court gradually returned to Marshallian notions in the twentieth century, it did so generally in broad regulatory areas. Where the interests of labor were concerned, the Court was rigidly "dual federalist" and sharply curtailed the national government. National regulations on child labor or adult wages and hours were rejected under reasoning ignored in other areas of commerce legislation. (The Court also hemmed in the states under the Fourteenth Amendment, but with a bit more flexibility, particularly where women's employment was involved.)

The climax came with the invalidation of major parts of the New Deal in 1935–36, and in the sweeping vote of confidence the country gave the President in the landslide of 1936. With new appointments to the Court, and subtle but significant shifts in emphasis by the "swing justices," Hughes and Roberts, the Court abandoned its odd stance and accepted the Marshallian view of the Commerce Clause. Labor regulations were no longer somehow different. Just as prison-made goods and stolen automobiles were within Congress' power to exclude from interstate commerce, so were products produced by children, or in violation of federal wages and hours regulations.

From National Power to Shared Power

Marshall's decision in GIBBONS remains a masterpiece, the basic discussion of legal construction of the Commerce Clause, and a broad charter for national power. Its sweep goes in many directions. It suggests an untrammeled power unlimited by reservations radiating from the Tenth Amendment. It also provides a broad definition of "commerce," itself an undefined term in the Constitution.

What is unusual is that all of this was done in a case not overtly or even necessarily to be decided on federal grounds. The State of New York had granted a monopoly to operate steamboats in its waters to business interests affiliated with Robert Fulton and the influential Livingston family. Instead of striking down (or sustaining) that grant under standards of *state* limits to regulate commerce, Marshall found a direct conflict between the New York monopoly and the licensing of

Gibbons by the federal government. The case then hinged on the constitutionality of the *federal* regulations and the effect of a conflict. A potentially negative limit on the states was turned into a rhapsody for positive affirmation of federal authority.

The federal power to deal with commerce was found to embrace navigation; commerce was more than the simple act of trade. "It describes the Commercial intercourse between nations," explained Marshall, who also concluded that "All America understands and has uniformly understood the word 'commerce' to comprehend navigation"; since the licensing of steamboat pilots was within that authority, Congress' action was comprehensive, "complete in itself," and within the rights of the national government, and therefore supreme. The apparent logic suggests Marshall also would have ruled that manufacture was—like navigation—a part of commerce, but no such ruling occurred.

If Marshall had served as a justice longer, perhaps he would have attempted to find a boundary line *prior* to trade and shipment with respect to national power. More reasonably, a majority on his Court might have forced him to do so. Marshall, almost to his last, persuaded his fellow justices to speak usually unanimously, and we know from Justice Story that he even wrote opinions where he disagreed with the majority-dictated outcome. But his logic suggests such a boundary line was up to Congress, not the Court. He did, however, limit national power by attempting to draw a boundary line at the other end. He suggested "commerce among the states" ended when an object of commerce was removed from the "original package"; at that point, the object was absorbed into the mass of state-regulated objects, its federally regulated journey over.

Whether this decision in BROWN V. MARYLAND (1827) was truly Marshallian in origin or was thrust upon him by others, it spawned rather weird and inept decisions and, though never abandoned totally, is not taken very seriously today.

But the problem it raises—whether there is no boundary to what the federal government may regulate—has remained on the prime agenda of the Court.

It was characteristic of the Taney Court to move only interstitially in altering Marshallian doctrines. In an age of "states' rights" dominance, few initiatives in federal regulation provided new tests of national power. Rather, tiny expansion of such doctrines as the "original package" test nibbled at the fringes of federal authority. More dramatic was its enlargement of state power to legislate where Marshall might have found federal monopoly. This, however, is the subject of Chapter 4.

It was in the last decades of the nineteenth century that federal regulation of business emerged as a response to a national economy. When such regulatory agencies as the ICC (1887) were created, and such economic programs as the Sherman Antitrust Act (1890) were enacted, the limits of federal authority to control policy directly were tested.

The Supreme Court did not directly contest the principal effort or power. What it did was to limit severely the scope of permissible regulation by assuming a very restrictive view of interstate commerce, emphasizing the need for movement and transport of goods. In the E. C. KNIGHT case (1895), conspiracy to purchase stock and so establish a monopoly was not held to be "interstate," since such transactions take place in one locale at a time. Control over the total company was obviously a permitted evasion of the national policy against monopolization of trade; it was also the simplest and most common method of achieving just that kind of monopoly. [By a vote of 5 to 4, the Court retreated from this reasoning in *Northern Securities Co.* v. *U.S.* (1904).]

Similarly, some businesses were held unregulatable almost by nature. Insurance was found to involve local transactions in spite of the network of interstate reinsurance arrangements, national distribution of agents, and the wide flow of paid premiums. These aspects were found to be incidental to the essence of the business. Theatrical productions were also held to be local in nature — ironically, just at the time show business began to be dominated by a string of national chains and a small number of agencies. On this basis, too, baseball was declared inherently local and exempt from federal antitrust regulation.

Yet, a quite different line of reasoning emerged from other cases, where the legislation or actions had no class bias or did not seem to represent social legislation. In a truly Marshallian decision the Supreme Court held, in the SHREVEPORT CASE, that a purely local railroad could be regulated by the ICC to protect interstate commerce. In this instance, the Texas Commission had set rates so that shipment of goods within Texas cost much less than transportation to outside areas — a clearly autarchic policy and a violation of the nondiscrimination interpretations of state power. While this played an important role in the Court's thinking, Hughes' opinion emphasizes the positive power of the national government to protect against burdens on interstate commerce.

Again, in cases involving federal regulation of stockyards, an expansive view of national commerce power was developed. Though slaughtering physically takes place entirely in one locale, the Court found stockyards were part of a nationwide system; they were "throats" or conduits in the "flow of commerce." The regulations establishing sanitary and humane butchering conditions were allowable in the light of such an interstate progress — perhaps, it has been suggested, because justices must also eat.

But when faced with regulation of industrial arrangements, the Court refused to accept analogies with meatpacking. "Commerce succeeds to manufacture, but is not part of it." Faced by evidence of the nationwide nature of enterprises other than meatpacking, the Court found the situation a threat to the constitutional fabric. To find all nationwide enterprises regulatable by the national government seemed to the justices to destroy local government. The truth that business was increasingly interstate was the basis for their keenness to *prevent its being seen as "commerce."*

To buttress this dual line of reasoning, the conservative justices — led by Sutherland and Van Devanter — formulated a notion of "direct" and "indirect" effects. Those matters held to directly affect interstate commerce could be regulated, either at all times or when the level of consequence was great enough. Other matters were intrinsically "indirect," and no matter how intensely their effect was felt — even if it were absolutely dominant — it could not establish a federal authority to intervene. Thus, in SCHECHTER POULTRY CORP. V. U.S. (1935), trivial goods reaching their final point of sale — chickens slaughtered at the end rather than the middle of the stream — were not regulatable. Nor was continued production of coal — a major national good necessary for significant production of most major products — regulatable, since it was at the beginning of the process, anticipating commerce, rather than being part of it. (The justices rejected arguments that goods *are* brought into a coal mine, tools and other means being part of a flow.)

Obviously, the justices' concern was that, precisely because American industry had become nationwide, the national government was in a position to supplant the states as chief regulator of economic policy. Less-than-friendly critics also saw this as a device to maintain nonregulation of business and enshrinement of laissez-faire and the economics of Adam Smith as a constitutional faith. They noted that many of the regulations held unconstitutional, as exceeding national power under the Commerce Clause, were also forbidden when enacted by the states as violations of the Due Process Clause of the Fourteenth Amendment. Having created a dual federalism concept of balanced sovereigns, they now seemed to use this system as the basis for creating a "twilight zone" of unregulatable activity for business while following a different line of precedents when logically analogous regulations (relating, for example, to cleaner food) were involved. The same picture was to emerge elsewhere, causing even more severe criticism. (We shall deal later with regulation through taxation, for example.)

A second use of the federal commerce power to deal with labor or social relations was to exclude from interstate commerce materials deemed objectionable. In many instances this effectively dried up supplies or markets; in others it merely diminished them. In either case, the regulation could often discourage conduct or production, as was intended by Congress. As early as *Cohens* v. *Virginia* (1821), Marshall had upheld federal power to allow or deny shipment of lottery tickets to states not permitting lotteries. The courts have always rejected the argument that the power to regulate interstate commerce was only to foster and encourage it. The power could be exercised to diminish or abolish it. "Regulate" meant just that, in positive and negative terms.

Through the years the national government has used the commerce power to forbid shipment of gambling paraphernalia, colored margarine, machine guns, explosives, and liquor over state boundaries. The Mann Act forbids transportation of women across state lines for immoral purposes, and it is even illegal to commit "unlawful flight to avoid arrest" by moving from one state to another.

Still, the use of a clearly granted federal power to regulate labor conditions proved a red flag to the justices. In HAMMER V. DAGENHART (1918), a federal effort to prohibit interstate shipment of goods produced by child labor was declared unconstitutional. In the face of a long line of cases, over a century old, the justices were forced to explain why "ruined lives" was not a proper basis of regulation while, say, prohibition of "adulterative fraud" through sale of colored oleo was constitutional.

In previous cases, the majority suggested, what was prohibited were goods themselves harmful or themselves the means of doing the harm. Explosives were not only dangerous to interstate commerce itself, they—like immoral women—could create problems at their destination.

But the evil of child labor precedes transportation, and the prohibition is an instrument of pre-transport "regulation." "The goods shipped are of themselves harmless." Holmes' classic dissent contemptuously rejected the newly derived formula. "The notion that prohibition is any less prohibition when applied to things now thought evil I do not understand. But if there is any matter upon which civilized nations have agreed . . . it is the evil of premature and excessive child labor."

Again, the distinction the majority created was applied only to federal regulations at variance with laissez-faire views. And once again a different line of reasoning was developed to prevent states from dealing with the same problems also found outside federal control. The Taft Court, only seven years after HAMMER V. DAGENHART, found that the federal government could prohibit shipment of stolen automobiles in interstate commerce, though stolen cars, once stolen, would seem as usable as purchased ones [*Brooks* v. *U.S.* (1925)]. And an anti-New Deal Court, in 1937, upheld prohibition of shipment in interstate commerce of prison-made goods (*Kentucky Whip and Collar* v. *Illinois Central Railway Co.*).

With Commerce Clause and Taxing Clause cases a major issue, the Court fight of 1937 brought these matters to a head. The justices had systematically found all major avenues to regulation of such matters as unionization, minimum wages, and hours (except for women) outside of governmental authority. Now the Court was eyeball-to-eyeball with President Roosevelt. The Court blinked even as it gave the President a political thrashing.

At first the decisions of the Hughes Court seemed to reflect some flexibility in the face of a paralyzing economic depression. Over objections of McReynolds, who announced in open court that "the Constitution is dead," the majority acknowledged a governmental right to leave the gold standard and control its fiscal policies. State regulations on mortgage moratoria, and some careful drafting of wages and hours legislation, were sustained in the early 1930s.

But by 1935 the Court's impatience with the "collectivist New Deal" was clear. The Commerce

Clause was constrained by the PANAMA REFINING Co. case (1935) and the SCHECHTER case (1935), finding "delegation run riot" and lack of proper limits to executive authority, but also finding the effort to use the commerce power to control competition in business beyond federal power. The "indirect" nature of the harm the regulated activities were deemed to have done, and the critical role Congress and the President argued they assumed in contributing to the depression, were irrelevant, even if provable. "Local" matters could not become "interstate," no matter how conclusive or cumulative their impact. Similarly, labor relations in the coal industry and production in coal mines could never become a constitutionally national issue.

Even Justice Brandeis became impatient with the direction and inefficiency of the New Deal. Abandoning his usual discretion, he told two reporters that the day in May, 1935, when three New Deal measures were invalidated, was "the most important day in the history of the Court, and the most beneficial." He summoned Thomas Corcoran, the New Deal brain-truster and Frankfurter protege, backstage, to the robing room, after the SCHECHTER decision. Corcoran described Brandeis as a black-clothed Fury, who told him, "this is the end of this business. . . . Go back and tell the President that we're not going to let this government centralize everything."[1]

With Roosevelt's smashing reelection, he was emboldened to challenge the Court. His remedy was to embrace a proposal made years earlier by Justice McReynolds, when he was serving as Attorney General under Wilson. It proposed that an additional appointment to the Court could be made if a justice chose not to retire at age 70. All of the justices were over 60, and six were then over 70. But one of those was Brandeis (in his eighties),

the most liberal sitting justice, who was personally affronted.

An overt alliance between the American Bar Association and key members of the Senate Judiciary Committee now emerged, in opposition to the President's plan. Senator Burton Wheeler, a Progressive, who had been La Follette's Vice Presidential candidate in 1924, became the public spokesman, to soften claims the opposition was simply Republican or conservative, the groups badly beaten in the 1936 election. Behind the scenes, Chief Justice Hughes and Justice Brandeis cooperated to provide Wheeler with a document in answer to his queries and the President's arguments. The Court, he said, was not behind in its docket, as alleged by Roosevelt. A larger number of justices would slow down matters, and the suggestion the Court could hear cases in smaller panels would violate the constitutional requirement of "one Supreme Court." Knowing that some of the justices would object, if not to the substantive part of the letter, then certainly to his "ruling" on constitutionality of a bill, Hughes consulted only Brandeis before releasing the letter.

Roosevelt was outmaneuvered throughout the campaign for his bill. The public outcry about his "not liking the call, so he was trying to change the umpire" surprised and overwhelmed him. But the Court came up with a series of flexible decisions. Justice Van Devanter resigned, the first of what was to prove a series of quick resignations and rapid changes in personnel. The Senate, relieved, saw no possible need for tinkering with a Court reforming itself. A set of preliminary votes in the Senate went badly for the President, and he agreed to a face-saving maneuver, gutting the bill as it applied to the Supreme Court, and preserving only its name.

Roosevelt, the master politician, had lost the political battle, but won a sweeping constitutional victory.

[1] Arthur Schlesinger, Jr., *The Politics of Upheaval* (New York: Houghton Mifflin, 1960), 280.

The Commerce Clause Today

The year 1937 was a watershed. Seldom has constitutional change emerged so clearly and so quickly. Precisely because many of the doctrines of the Taft and Hughes Courts were so strained and at variance with the historical line of precedents — even as their dual line of decision preserved most of them — rapid elimination of jerry-built obstacles to social regulation was legally easy. It was back to Marshall, back to the Constitution, and commentators spoke of "an old masterpiece restored." Simplicity replaced involuted distinctions.

The most important single decision was upholding the constitutionality of the National Labor Relations Act, the rockbed of industrial peace today. It recognizes the right of unionization, and empowers the National Labor Relations Board to supervise management and labor interaction, on the argument that industrial strife would deleteriously affect interstate commerce. Since labor troubles precede commerce, it was feared the Court might once more be a stumbling block, by holding that they were not part of the flow.

Chief Justice Hughes, in NLRB v. JONES & LAUGHLIN (1937), went a long way toward acknowledging broad national power, in an opinion that was more reminiscent of his SHREVEPORT opinion than cases he had been writing or had joined in while Chief Justice. Noting that the legislation was "narrowly" written, Hughes suggested the proviso that only labor relations "affecting commerce" would be affected by the Act, together with the definition given in the statute, guaranteed that the program would be kept within constitutional bounds. With this assurance that the reach of the federal government was not unlimited, he interred "direct and indirect effects." "Although activities may be intrastate in character when considered separately, if they have such a close and substantial relation to interstate commerce . . . that their control is essential or appropriate . . . Congress cannot be denied the power to exercise that control. . . . *The question is necessarily one of degree"* (emphasis added). Now, in dissent, McReynolds et al. argued that the question remained a question of kind, not alterable by circumstances or degree. While the Chief Justice insisted the decision represented no retreat or change, because it involved the nation's largest steel company, the Court simultaneously approved NLRB authority over a clothing manufacturer and a hat maker, on authority of the JONES & LAUGHLIN decision. The new tests of "affecting commerce" were not onerous ones.

In rapid succession, clear and emphatic authority was conceded to Congress to deal with commerce as need raised any issue to their attention. In WICKARD V. FILBURN (1942), the Commerce Clause was held to permit regulation of 269 bushels of wheat, though none of it left the farm, all of it being fed to the farmer's pigs. This minimal amount, the Court reasoned, was a constituent part of a category of grain that had a significant effect on the total supply. By what commentators called a "multiplier effect," something as trivial as these bushels was held to meet Hughes' standards. Jackson's opinion belittles any distinction at all between "production" and "marketing," explicitly repudiating "direct" and "indirect" arguments. The lack of movement of the wheat was irrelevant; other wheat would have been shipped if those over-quota bushels had not been grown and used. No actual transport was required. As Justice Jackson wrote in another case, "If it is interstate commerce that feels the pinch, it does not matter how local the operation that applies the squeeze."

The bar to federal prohibition established in DAGENHART was lifted with the decision in U.S. V. DARBY (1941), in words that virtually drove a stake through the heart of the notion that Congress could prohibit only goods "evil in themselves." Justice Stone noted, with obvious malicious joy, that the distinction, "novel when made and unsupported by any provision of the Constitution, has long since been abandoned...it should be and now is overruled."

In point of fact, today the commerce power is the most precisely defined, judgment-proof section of the Constitution, precisely because its tangled history of litigation now provides strong precedents for broad use. Thus, when the 1960s and the civil rights movement produced a demand for protection for citizens of any race as they traveled throughout the country, the primary constitutional basis was the Commerce Clause. While some felt it was demeaning to use a provision dealing with commodities to deal with a moral issue, and wished to base the protection upon enforcement provisions of the Fourteenth Amendment and the Privileges and Immunities Clauses, the administration strongly urged use of the Commerce Clause for prudential reasons. The Court had little difficulty sustaining these provisions, in HEART OF ATLANTA MOTEL V. U.S. (1964), as to hotels and inns, and in *Katzenbach* v. *McClung* (1964), as to restaurants. In the modern world, the involvement in interstate commerce for supplies, out-of-town reservations, or sales makes federal regulation possible in virtually every conceivable circumstance. The limitations are essentially those stated by Marshall in GIBBONS and MCCULLOCH — the political and administrative realities that make Congress cautious about taking over areas administered by the states. Local complaints and financial costs, the political controversy, will be risked only when there is a need sufficient to pass muster in a constitutional case. The authoritative compendium of constitutional law compiled by the Legislative Reference Service concluded, "the unmistakable lesson of recent cases is that the preservation of our federal system depends today mainly on Congress" (edition 2, p. 205).

The legal limits are a few bare-knuckle collisions with strong constitutional rights. Congress may not use the Commerce Clause to regulate and establish presumptions of guilt or intent that violate the Fifth Amendment. (We shall see analogous rulings that the taxing power cannot be used to compel "confession through registration.") A combination of Congress' war power and commerce power was not sufficient to justify invasion of First Amendment rights in several 1970s cases involving union leaders and alleged communism. And, in a fascinating and seemingly anomalous case, NATIONAL LEAGUE OF CITIES V. USERY (1976), the Supreme Court took the position that the commerce power cannot be used to undermine the very workings of state government. Minimum wage regulations could not be applied to state government employees themselves, since that would give the federal government direct control over costs of state government. Even this decision to keep some legalistic federalism, to try to keep the Court as protector of the states, is seen by many commentators as out of step with modern doctrine. The decision by Justice Rehnquist (with four justices dissenting) was hailed as a decisive move back when announced in 1976, but the Court quickly re-reversed itself.

Still, the great lesson of post-1937 Supreme Court decision making is how fast and how sweeping constitutional change can come. The flow of commerce decisions has therefore provided usually fine illustrations of dilemmas created by changing interpretations of the fixed, basic, fundamental Constitution. When laws are passed, they come in a context of existing interpretations of the Constitution. Changes in those interpretations may render a statute meaningless or drastically altered.

What happens when that underlying provision is reinterpreted — in Charles Lyon's words, when "old statutes" are reinvigorated by "new constitutions"? Sometimes whole industries are built in reliance on such constitutional decisions, which endure for decades but are altered overnight.

An example was the threatened application of the Antitrust Act to baseball. In 1923, as noted above, the Supreme Court had ruled that baseball was a local business and thus outside federal authority. Yet under current doctrine, statutes such as the Sherman Act would logically cover such an impressive enterprise built around national competition, travel, and television. In a remarkable decision, without easy parallel, the Court in effect refused to modernize the FEDERAL BASEBALL CLUB decision and left it to Congress to adjust the balance. In subsequent decisions other sports were not permitted exemption from antitrust laws, suggesting the justices were "soft on baseball." (Congress has since acted to adjust the situation somewhat.)

In other instances, Congress has recognized problems created by sudden application of regulations to an industry, and has moved to mitigate such occurrences. There are often practical problems in radical alteration of legal decisions, but the courts also have considerable leeway in implementing sweeping new decisions. In the field of national power and the Commerce Clause, these lie largely in the past. But in the areas of criminal law and civil rights this type of dilemma plagues the courts constantly.

National Power: Taxing and Spending, and Regulating Through Taxing and Spending

Federalism and Taxation

Like the regulation of commerce, producing and spending revenue have been historic powers of the national government. The pattern of the bulk of cases in this section follows closely that of the Commerce Clause cases. That parallelism indicates dramatically the force of the political and legal climate on interpretation of legal provisions, especially where constitutional law is involved. Different sections of the Constitution, with different problems, were treated identically, based upon a theory of federalism which prevailed over all other aspects.

Again, the constitutional provision dealing with taxes is deceptively simple. Congress is authorized "to lay and collect Taxes, Duties, Imposts and Excises, to pay the Debts and provide for the Common Defense and General Welfare of the United States," provided the "Duties, Imposts and Excises are uniform throughout the United States." It is the first power of Congress enumerated, and is the heart of congressional control over the executive. Historically, legislatures have been able to maintain or expand their powers by controlling revenue. Naturally, a provision dealing directly with money has attracted more than its share of ingenious legal arguments and litigation by brilliant advocates.

The central constitutional question here, as with the Commerce Clause, has been the degree to which the existence of the states limits the granted or enumerated powers of the national government—a problem even more obtrusive than with the Commerce Clause. The question also arises as to whether the Taxing and Spending Clause is in any event an independent power at all, or, like the "Necessary and Proper" Clause, a means or method of carrying out other powers.

The somewhat curious flourish of authorizing taxing and spending for national defense and the general welfare—language not debated in the Constitutional Convention and added by the Committee on Style—raises additional questions. Hamilton suggested the intent was clearly to add to national power. Congress could already tax and spend for stated purposes of the Constitution as "necessary and proper" to carry them out. In addition, it could "tax and spend"—but not directly legislate—for other purposes they deemed to be of general welfare.

A still more extreme form of this argument is that the General Welfare Clause is per se an independent power, allowing even direct regulation by the national government. Though popularly advanced during the Populist and Progressive eras, and having considerable scholarly support, drawing also upon the language of the Preamble, this view has never even been considered seriously by the courts. At a minimum it requires wrenching the language out of its setting in a provision dealing with fiscal matters only. It would also make unnecessary the enumeration of the list of other granted powers.

Madison's view was that in point of fact the language of "General Welfare" was a further restriction of the national power. Again, paralleling arguments about the "Necessary and Proper" Clause, he argued that not only was taxing and spending limited to purposes traceable to the enumerated powers, but those must be utilized only for the "General Welfare."

The issue was not resolved until 1936—in a curious double take, at that—in favor of the Hamiltonian view. See the discussion in U.S. V. BUTLER (1936). But Congress has throughout our history assumed an expansive view of the spending provision—witness the Louisiana Purchase, an expenditure not directly authorized by any other provision.

A more vexing problem has been the use of taxing as a regulatory device in areas not conferred upon the national government and using expenditures to reward (if you will, bribe) compliance when direct legislation would be impermissible. This aspect of the Hamiltonian-Madisonian debate has been answered in different terms in history, along the dual federalism lines noted in Commerce Clause cases.

The ultimate example is to be found in the question of whether the states and the national government could enact taxes upon each other. This was, of course, a controlling issue in the MCCULLOCH decision, where Marshall emphatically ruled that a state could not tax the nation. Further, he argued at length that the U.S. *could* enact taxes upon the states: "But the two cases are not on the same reason. . . . The difference is that which always exists and must exist between the action of the whole on a part, and the action of a part on the whole." A state could unfairly enrich itself at the expense of the rest of the country, but the national government would be constrained by

the fact the states were its very backbone. Only the national government can be trusted not to take unfair advantage of its right to tax.

The issue of federal taxation of states was not at issue in MCCULLOCH, so Marshall's statements on the question do not constitute a precedent. They are obiter dicta—statements made in passing—that are of historic interest only. Subsequent judges did not have to overrule MCCULLOCH to create a "separate but equal" dual federalist protectionism for state governments. What is amusing is that they always solemnly announced they were *carrying out* Marshall's logic as announced in MCCULLOCH.

The erection of the principles of mutual non-taxation of governments became an elaborate structure of complex rules and subrules. Not only were the governments themselves found exempt, but various agencies and, subsequently, employees and even contractors engaged in tasks for the governments, where those government contracts were fairly clearly demarcated, were exempt. Intricate contract arrangements were contrived, and esoteric rulings were the product of such doctrine.

The reaction in the 1930s was not merely to strengthen the national power to tax. It reflected a desire by the judges to sweep away the spider's web of decisions that prevented states and the nation from being able to tax uniformly whole classes of revenue. Indeed, the first step was to rule that federal employees were subject to state income taxes, so long as those fell uniformly on all residents and the taxes weren't—as they were in MCCULLOCH—a form of discrimination: GRAVES V. NEW YORK EX REL. O'KEEFE (1939).

Subsequently, Congress' right to collect taxes from state employees was similarly vindicated. And in NEW YORK V. UNITED STATES (1946), business taxes were held collectible from a state, where the state had gone into the business of selling bottled geyser water. The Court was so badly divided in that case that no opinion speaks for a majority. But it was suggested that, short of a tax applying only to states—e.g., based on value of the capitols — Congress could enact taxes even on the state governments. Earlier and later decisions have made emphatic this return to the MᴄCᴜʟʟᴏᴄʜ logic. Congress is seen as trustworthy, as a second "umpire to the federal system." It can immunize national instrumentalities from state taxing and tax the states almost — but, as we shall see, maybe not quite — at will. The Supremacy Clause is taken at maximum meaning.

The parallel history of the Commerce Clause and the Taxing and Spending Clause leads to federal supremacy. Those questions have been decisively settled in nationalistic terms. In Robert Stern's phrase, these are "questions of yesteryear." With negligible exceptions those powers are indeed regarded as "complete in themselves," and they can be employed by Congress as though states were not there.

However, the history of litigation in those clauses is not merely of antiquarian interest. To be sure, they contain the history of the chief social battles waged in the constitutional arena and are illuminating in understanding our constitutional history. But: (1) They also are important in explaining aspects of our current law otherwise inexplicable. (2) The doctrines from the past emphatically rejected after being dominant for decades are not likely to be restructured, but minor doctrines given little attention are often reusable. (Justice O'Connor seems determined to restore some Tenth Amendment cases.) (3) Finally, even when constitutional law has been altered, political realities may force retention of a situation no longer constitutionally mandated.

We can illustrate only briefly the above propositions. Baseball's anomalous situation with exemption from antitrust laws was a product of an early 1920 decision made under old constitutional doctrine. Our national minimum wage laws are generally written to cover fewer workers than current notions of the extent of national power. The original acts were drafted to avoid constitutional challenges based upon narrower views prevailing in the late 1930s, and this continues to have a dwindling influence. Municipal and state bonds are largely exempt from federal taxation, not because the courts would invalidate a national tax, but because Congress is reluctant to change the status quo. To end the exemption would raise local costs of financing and bring pressure on the national government to increase state and local aid. Finally, such unusual and unexpected decisions as Nᴀᴛɪᴏɴᴀʟ Lᴇᴀɢᴜᴇ ᴏғ Cɪᴛɪᴇs ᴠ. Usᴇʀʏ (1976) — which held the minimum wage could not be enforced against state and local employees — utilize reasoning obviously borrowed from old intergovernmental immunity cases. Usᴇʀʏ, in turn, was to be repudiated quickly, as such dual federalist decisions usually have been. As Holmes tells us, "Historic continuity with the past is not a duty, it is only a necessity."

Taxing and Spending: Special Issues

There are, however, some considerations exclusive to the problem of taxation. Of these the requirement that no "capitation or other direct tax" could be levied except in accordance with the census is the most intriguing. In *Hylton v. U.S.* (1796), the Court gave us the best early reading of that requirement. (In order to reach an amount at issue sufficient to justify a hearing on a tax assessed at $16 a carriage, Hylton alleged he owned 125 carriages, a patently absurd claim for the times.) Hylton argued that a tax on carriages constituted a "direct" tax, which should be assessed by population.

The justices rejected such a claim, and three of the five sitting justices ventured opinions. (Individual opinion followed from British practice. After Marshall became Chief Justice, he persuaded his colleagues that a single unified voice had more authority, and that remains the Court's objective.) All opinions emphasized that the effect of apportioning by population would be to make the tax unequal, since there were different densities of carriages in the states. A tax based on population might result in a state with few carriages, relative to population, requiring an owner to pay many times the tax elsewhere. In any event, this was a tax not on the person but on use of the carriage, and therefore an "excise." Chase and Paterson both suggested, without deciding, that direct taxes included only capitation taxes ("head" or "poll" taxes at so much per person) or taxes on land.

All of this set the scene for the peculiar drama that occurred in 1894 and 1895, in POLLOCK V. FARMERS' LOAN AND TRUST CO. (1895), which dealt with the constitutionality of the Income Tax Act of 1894. At its first hearing, the Court ruled that the tax was unconstitutional as applied to land and income from land. It was divided on whether taxes on other property or income were constitutional. Justice Jackson rejoined the Court to dissent in the 1895 decision, which by 5 to 4 decided all taxes based on personal property, as well as income property, were direct taxes. Since the Court had unanimously sustained a Civil War Income Tax in *Springer* v. *U.S.* (1881), the decision came as a shock.

The nullification of the Income Tax Act in POLLOCK was undone eighteen years later by the Sixteenth Amendment. However, given the peculiarities of the vote, historians have been perplexed as to who changed his mind from the 4 to 4 division in 1894. The broad expansion of the concept of direct taxation made this a most controversial decision indeed. In lectures on the Supreme Court during the interlude between his two periods of service on the Court, Charles Evans Hughes singled it out, along with the DRED SCOTT decision, as among the most egregious of "self-inflicted wounds," historically damaging to Court authority. Worse yet, it occurred in the same year in which the E. C. KNIGHT CO. case severely limited the use of antitrust power, while the breaking of the Pullman strike by President Cleveland's calling out the National Guard in order to maintain the flow of mail was sustained by the Court in *In re Debs*.

The Court backed away from the POLLOCK decision almost as the ink dried. After adoption of the Sixteenth Amendment, the first decision under the Amendment suggested POLLOCK was decided wrongly: "The Sixteenth Amendment conferred no new power of taxation but simply prohibited the previous complete and plenary power of income taxation possessed by Congress from the beginning from being taken out of the category of indirect taxation to which it inherently belonged."

This picture of erratic and class-oriented behavior emerged, too, from the history of regulatory taxation. While McCULLOCH had suggested the national government could tax state instrumentalities—the two were not of the same footing—the courts, in a series of cases culminating in COLLECTOR V. DAY (1871), established a dual federalist notion that state and nation were on a par. Sovereigns could not tax sovereigns. Further limitations on taxing for social purposes nipped at the fringes of national power.

In BAILEY V. DREXEL FURNITURE CO. (1922), an effort to tax products of child labor was challenged. The statute was passed after HAMMER V. DAGENHART (1918) had invalidated efforts to regulate child labor under the Commerce Clause. The law provided that an employer who knowingly used child labor would be assessed 10 percent of net income.

Chief Justice Taft acknowledged a long series of cases in which prohibitive taxes were assessed on matters not necessarily directly within federal cognizance—state bank notes, oleo, narcotics. What was different, he argued cogently, was that the statute in question was, on its face, not a tax but a regulation with a penalty attached. "Scienter is associated with penalties not with taxes." The "tax" was also not apportioned to any rate of use; it was the same for one day's employment for one employee or the use of children for the entire work force. (Interestingly, Holmes and Brandeis did *not* dissent.)

The principle of BAILEY is that, where a tax directly discriminates between compliant and noncompliant behavior—whether defined by federal or state law—it is valid only where Congress has regulatory power and the tax has not been repudiated, unlike the parallel doctrine in the Commerce Clause area. (However, unconditional taxation may go beyond Congress' other powers, as suggested by Taft.) More important and more apropos are the rulings on regulation through expenditure.

The taxing and spending power was given strained construction in U.S. v. BUTLER (1936). This involved the first Agricultural Adjustment Act (AAA), a leading New Deal measure. Faced with the choice between the Hamiltonian and Madisonian theories of taxing and spending, the Court majority for the first time unqualifiedly approved the Hamiltonian view — that it was an additional grant of power. But it then held the augmentation could not involve an infringement of the Tenth Amendment, a position which is logically compatible only with the Madisonian theory. If the national government could tax and/or spend beyond its granted powers, it had to spill over into "reserved powers" of the states. In later decisions, Roberts' broad endorsement of the national right to spend has been taken at face value, while the invalidation of the AAA is generally ignored in embarrassment.

In MULFORD V. SMITH (1939), the revised AAA was upheld as a regulation of interstate commerce. Warehousemen who sold tobacco for a producer in excess of allotted quotas were assessed a penalty that could be deducted from the payment to the producer. (In the original AAA, processors were assessed a tax and then complying farmers given a subsidy from the resulting fund.) Justice Roberts, who wrote both opinions, insisted the difference in results was not merely a product of the constitutional revolution that took place between 1936 and 1939. He emphasized the absence of a specified fund, which made the control system somewhat like that in the BAILEY case. But he also noted that there was no effort to directly control the acreage of farmers' by giving them back their own money. Rather, this was a regulation of interstate shipments.

In STEWARD MACHINE CO. V. DAVIS (1937), the power of taxing and spending was given an unambiguous endorsement for the first time, as the Social Security System was held constitutional. Though it constitutes a "comprehensive" program, dealing with matters not provided for by other congressional authority, the taxing and spending power was found to cover the matter. The fact that states could choose not to comply — even though it was made financially very advantageous for the citizens of most states if the states did cooperate — made the scheme constitutional.

By 1953, the power to tax was taken sufficiently for granted that it was utilized as a means for indirect regulation. In the light of hearings on organized crime, legislation was passed requiring professional gamblers to register and pay a tax. Since gambling was illegal in all states but Nevada, it was argued that this was "confession by taxation," and Black and Douglas dissented on the grounds it violated the Fifth Amendment. Reed's opinion noted the Fifth Amendment protects past, not contemplated, violations of the law, and emphasized the broad authority of Congress on the taxing power. Jackson, concurring, suggested the measure went "to the very edge" of the power. Frankfurter, dissenting, pointed to the Brandeis-Holmes participation in the second child labor case, and found this gambling tax on its face a similar "oblique" use for other purposes.

Though they failed in 1951, the dissenters were vindicated in subsequent decisions. In MARCHETTI V. U. S. (1968), the pattern established on its face — not merely the tax, but the requirement on conspicuous posting and similar aspects — was held to constitute a violation of the Fifth Amendment.

Still, the endorsement of the Hamiltonian view of taxing and spending has given the national government an important and major weapon for regulation. "Money talks." Congressional taxation can be an effective tool to direct or inhibit behavior, though this has limits, as the BAILEY case indicates. But legislation may reward desired behavior through "grants-in-aid," "matching funds," or other inducement, even in areas where Congress cannot act directly. Much of the "cooperative federalism" of our day — the welfare programs of the Great Society and the "safety nets" still operative — rest on the constitutional authorizations of these cases.

Federalism Again: The Basic Relationship Between the Nation and States

The relationship between nation and state has been, as we have seen, a changing one. The dramatic changes have been in the domain of the commerce power. While other relationships have stayed constant legally, or moved more slowly or been altered by events, they nevertheless condition the manner in which the national government impinges upon states. (The reciprocal relation of states is treated in the next chapter.)

The great statement on the indissoluble partnership of these sovereigns is found in TEXAS V. WHITE (1869). During the Civil War, the Texas legislature authorized a change in conditions by which U.S. bonds owned by Texas could be paid to private persons. In 1867, the Reconstruction Government of Texas, still not permitted by Congress to send Representatives to Washington, sued to recover some of those bonds, bringing the matter directly to the Supreme Court, under its original jurisdiction to hear cases brought by one state against the citizens of another state.

But was Texas a state in a constitutional sense? In THE PRIZE CASES (1863), the Court had sustained the constitutionality of President Lincoln's declaration of a blockade, an act of belligerency, against any claim that one cannot blockade a constituent part of one's own country. Presumably Texas was an enemy. Now, Chief Justice Chase suggested that aspects of statehood were suspendable, but not the fact of statehood. "The Constitution in all its provisions looks to an indestructible union, composed of indestructible states." The Congress recognized a Reconstruction Government. This qualified that government to be a juridical entity, but that did not preclude denying full-scale political status as part of a postrebellion situation. "Texas," however, existed as a state, even when a full-scale government might not be in operation.

In other cases, the Court has extended both this notion of permanent building blocks as well as the difference between political and legal authority. Congress can require a prospective state to meet conditions of various sorts. Once in the Union, its rights are full and equal to others. Oklahoma was admitted to the Union with a proviso that it would not move its capitol from the City of Guthrie for at least six years. When it chose to do so, the Supreme Court held the issue was not a constitutional matter. Once Oklahoma became a state it was as free to choose its capitol as any other commonwealth. There are no second-class states with special obligations. Utah was required to include monogamy in its state constitution as a price for admission. Clearly, it could repeal that provision, though authorization of once-traditional plural marriage would evoke strong challenges, including one under the Equal Protection Clause. (The Mormon Church also now strongly forbids plural marriages.)

We have already adverted to the Supremacy Clause many times. Direct collision of federal and state laws is easily disposed of. But a major problem is what to do when Congress is not explicit in an attempt to displace state action. We have already seen Marshall's use of a federal licensing statute to establish a conflict with the New York steamship monopoly — a perhaps strained effort to find a contradiction. A more usual form of such inferred conflict is illustrated in PENNSYLVANIA V. NELSON (1956). The Court there found that the scheme to control sedition established by Congress was so comprehensive it must have been intended to preclude state action. This inference is based on what the courts sometimes call "occupation of the field," or "supersedure," or "preemption." The PENNSYLVANIA case, coming during the Cold War period, was politically sensitive and attracted wide comment. But such decisions take place often in such areas as labor relations, where the federal statutes are complicated and extensive, usually without controversy. Currently the degree to which federal environmental control and federal nuclear development programs are "preemptive" are major issues. Environmentalist groups and anti–nuclear-power activists advocate states' rights, to press for more stringent regulations, since they have been having some notable successes at the local levels. Litigation has been proceeding at a fairly brisk clip.

Federal authority is not limited to exercise of the Commerce and Tax Clauses (though it sometimes seems that way), or even to the grants of power of Article 1, Section 8. *Katzenbach* v. *Morgan* (1966) and SOUTH CAROLINA V. KATZENBACH (1966) are examples involving the power of Congress to act under the authority of the neglected Enforcement Clause of the Fifteenth Amendment. That Amendment prohibits discrimination in voting by race and was largely ignored in the South. The 1965 Voting Rights Act was based on the provision that Congress had "the power to enforce this article by appropriate legislation." The SOUTH CAROLINA case tested the effort of the federal government to control "literacy tests" and other devices to limit black voting. If a state had such rules and less than 50 percent of its voting-age population registered or voted, the Attorney General was empowered to suspend tests and appoint federal registrars and poll-watchers.

Those provisions were unanimously sustained by the Court. However, Justice Black dissented over requirements of approval by the Attorney General, or the Federal District Court of Appeals of the District of Columbia, of any new legal tests. Black argued such a step did not involve a "case or controversy," but, more significantly, objected to such approval as placing the state legislative power in tutelage to the national government in an improper way. States could no longer legislate freely.

In *Katzenbach* v. *Morgan,* the challenge was to Congress' determination that New York could not deny those Puerto Ricans completing sixth grade or more the right to vote, on the basis of illiteracy in English. Harlan and Stewart dissented, arguing this was an arbitrary judgment by Congress.

Brennan's majority opinion found that the context of the Act's passage suggested due care, and thus upheld Congress' authority under the Fourteenth and Fifteenth Amendments to enforce voting guarantees. Those actions were all functions of specifically allocated power. In 1982, Congress renewed those decisions, in much the same form, by an overwhelming vote.

A final issue involves the national power to affect state operations. This issue has come up in two guises, both discussed earlier in this chapter. The Supreme Court developed the notion of "dual immunity" to taxation to protect the national government from being exploited by a state, and, as the nineteenth century unfolded, extended the reasoning to national taxation of states, in the face of Marshall's repudiation of that step in McCULLOCH. Both immunities were elaborately expanded and made complex, against objections by Holmes, Brandeis, and Stone. In the late 1930s, the Court began to sustain nondiscriminatory taxes applying to government employees, both state and federal, where their assessments were in common with similarly situated nonpublic earners. Led by Chief Justice Stone, the Court returned to the logic of McCULLOCH and generally permitted federal determination of what the limits of state immunity were to be. In NEW YORK V. U.S. (1946), the question faced was whether there are any limits to Congress' power to tax state instruments, even including, say, a state capitol. While the majority seemed to agree there are limits, it is not clear what they were suggesting as appropriate limits.

The problem also surfaced as to federal control of wages under the Commerce Clause. The principles upheld in the JONES & LAUGHLIN decision were expanded in later legislation and upheld in *Maryland* v. *Wirtz* (1968). The amendments involved accepted the "whole company" notion of application of federal standards to all employees of a company engaged in interstate commerce, rather than those employees directly affecting commerce — an interesting footnote to Chief Justice Hughes' efforts to minimize the significance of the NLRB case by emphasizing the wording that was no longer deemed vital. The Act also, for the first time, was applied to public employees and was sustained as it applied to hospital workers. In *Fry* v. *U.S.* (1975), President Nixon's wage-freeze policy was upheld as it applied to state employees as well. Like tax immunity, it appeared that wage policies could be dictated by the national government to the states, so long as the policy was a general and nondiscriminatory program.

It was, therefore, a surprise—bordering on shock—when the Supreme Court in 1976, only a year later, invalidated application of the Fair Employment Labor Standards Act to state and local governments. The Act, which had been sustained in U.S. v. DARBY, originally had an exemption for governmental employees, but the exemption was repealed in 1974, and it was this action that was directly at issue. In a 5-to-4 decision in NATIONAL LEAGUE OF CITIES V. USERY (1976), Justice Rehnquist noted the effects, not merely of minimum wages, but also of overtime provisions, on the costs of state governments. The effect might well be to control policies over such matters as police and fire functions. As such, it could be said to impair the independence of those governments.

Blackmun's was the fifth vote, and his concurring opinion went out of its way to note that the federal government's power to regulate the environment was not impaired by the decision. It was clear he was voicing deep misgivings over the reasoning itself.

While some writers, such as Laurence Tribe, hailed the decision for keeping federalism alive, the Court began the retreat almost immediately. In *Hodel* v. *Surface Mining* (1981), the Court unanimously echoed Blackmun's concurrence in USERY, distinguishing between a state as an operative entity and a state as a regulator. Two years later, Blackmun silently shifted his position, providing the crucial vote to sustain application of the federal law prohibiting age-based discrimination to state employees [*Equal Employment Opportunity Commission* v. *Wyoming* (1983).] In concurring, Justice Stevens denounced USERY as on a par with HAMMER V. DAGENHART and E. C. KNIGHT as confused efforts to thwart the Supremacy Clause. Only outright overruling could avoid sophistry and incoherence.

By 1985, Justice Blackmun was sufficiently convinced to author the opinion in GARCIA V. SAN ANTONIO METROPOLITAN AUTHORITY (1985), which overruled USERY and applied minimum wage laws to municipal and state workers. Dissenters indicated that they were not giving up and that they were indeed waiting for a fifth vote. Until then, federal supremacy seems unchallenged.

Cases

Gibbons v. Ogden

9 Wheaton 1 (1824)
Vote: 7–0, but Johnson concurred.

This magnificently written opinion draws heavily on the brief of Daniel Webster and the work of other great legal and political figures, as it was one of the most hotly debated cases of its time. It is to Commerce Clause cases what McCULLOCH V. MARYLAND is to tax and spending—a broad positive assertion of federal power.

New York had assigned exclusive rights of steamboats to sail in its waters to financial interests associated with Robert Fulton and the very prominent Livingston family. Ogden had a license from those interests to sail between New York and New Jersey. Gibbons operated without such authorization.

While Marshall's interpretation of the commerce power is expansive, he rests the national power on Congress' authorization of Gibbons' right to be a pilot and finds a conflict between the two levels of government. Note Johnson's concurring opinion, which would have found New York's law an infringement on commerce in its own right. Is his argument more sensible than Marshall's argument that a license to be a pilot means a license to do business everywhere? The State of New Jersey and other states were in the process of fighting New York's extravagant claim to control not only its own waters but its part of rivers that were shared with other states. Would a "license war" have made Johnson's opinion more attractive to his fellow judges? Was Marshall's finding of conflict between congressional legislation and the New York law another sample of his judicial sleight-of-hand, similar to MARBURY?

MR. CHIEF JUSTICE MARSHALL delivered the opinion of the Court, and, after stating the case, proceeded as follows:

The appellant contends that this decree is erroneous, because the laws which purport to give the exclusive privilege it sustains, are repugnant to the constitution and laws of the United States.

They are said to be repugnant —

1st. To that clause in the constitution which authorizes Congress to regulate commerce.

2d. To that which authorizes Congress to promote the progress of science and useful arts. . . .

As preliminary to the very able discussions of the constitution, which we have heard from the bar, and as having some influence on its construction, reference has been made to the political situation of these States, anterior to its formation. It has been said, that they were sovereign, were completely independent, and were connected with each other only by a league. This is true. But, when these allied sovereigns converted their league into a government, when they converted their Congress of Ambassadors, deputed to deliberate on their common concerns, and to recommend measures of general utility, into a Legislature, empowered to enact laws on the most interesting subjects, the whole character in which the States appear, underwent a change, the extent of which must be determined by a fair consideration of the instrument by which that change was effected.

This instrument contains an enumeration of powers expressly granted by the people to their government. It has been said, that these powers ought to be construed strictly. But why ought they to be so construed? Is there one sentence in the constitution which gives countenance to this rule? In the last of the enumerated powers, that which grants, expressly, the means for carrying all others into execution, Congress is authorized "to make all laws which shall be necessary and proper" for the purpose. But this limitation on the means which may be used, is not extended to the powers which are conferred; nor is there one sentence in the constitution, which has been pointed out by the gentlemen of the bar, or which we have been able to discern, that prescribes this rule. We do not, therefore, think ourselves justified in adopting it. What do gentlemen mean, by a strict construction? If they contend only against that enlarged construction, which would extend words beyond their natural and obvious import, we might question the application of the term, but should not controvert the principle. If they contend for that narrow construction which, in support of some theory not to be found in the constitution, would deny to the government those powers which the words of the grant, as usually understood, import, and which are consistent with the general views and objects of the instrument; for that narrow construction, which would cripple the government, and render it unequal to the object for which it is declared to be instituted, and to which the powers given, as fairly understood, render it competent; then we cannot perceive the propriety of this strict construction, nor adopt it as the rule by which the constitution is to be expounded. . . . We know of no rule for construing the extent of such powers, other than is given by the language of the instrument which confers them, taken in connexion with the purposes for which they were conferred.

The words are, "Congress shall have power to regulate commerce with foreign nations, and among the several States, and with the Indian tribes."

The subject to be regulated is commerce; and our constitution being, as was aptly said at the bar, one of enumeration, and not of definition, to ascertain the extent of the power, it becomes necessary to settle the meaning of the word. The counsel for the appellee would limit it to traffic, to buying and selling, or the interchange of commodities, and do not admit that it comprehends navigation. This would restrict a general term, applicable to many objects, to one of its significations. Commerce, undoubtedly, is traffic, but it is something more: it is intercourse. It describes the commercial intercourse between nations, and parts of nations, in all its branches, and is regulated by prescribing rules for carrying on that intercourse. The mind can scarcely conceive a system for regulating commerce between nations, which shall exclude all laws concerning navigation, which shall be silent on the admission of the vessels of the one nation into the ports of the other, and be confined to prescribing rules for the conduct of individuals, in the actual employment of buying and selling, or of barter.

If commerce does not include navigation, the government of the Union has no direct power over that subject, and can make no law prescribing what shall constitute American vessels, or requiring that they shall be navigated by American seamen. Yet this power has been exercised from the commencement of the government, has been exercised with the consent of all, and has been understood by all to be a commercial regulation. All America understands, and has uniformly understood, the word "commerce," to comprehend navigation. It was so understood, and must have been so understood, when the constitution was framed. The power over commerce, including navigation, was one of the primary objects for which the people of America adopted their government, and must have been contemplated in forming it. The convention must have used the word in that sense, because all have understood it in that sense; and the attempt to restrict it comes too late. . . .

The word used in the constitution, then, comprehends, and has been always understood to comprehend, navigation within its meaning; and a power to regulate navigation, is as expressly granted, as if that term had been added to the word "commerce." . . .

It has, we believe, been universally admitted, that these words comprehend every species of commercial intercourse between the United States and foreign nations. No sort of trade can be carried on between this country and any other, to which this power does not extend. It has been truly said, that commerce, as the word is used in the constitution, is a unit, every part of which is indicated by the term. . . .

The subject to which the power is next applied, is to commerce "among the several States." The word "among" means intermingled with. A thing which is among others, is intermingled with them. Commerce among the States, cannot stop at the external boundary line of each State, but may be introduced into the interior.

It is not intended to say that these words comprehend that commerce, which is completely internal, which is carried on between man and man in a State, or between different parts of the same State, and which does not extend to or affect other States. Such a power would be inconvenient, and is certainly unnecessary.

Comprehensive as the word "among" is, it may very properly be restricted to that commerce which concerns more States than one. The phrase is not one which would probably have been selected to indicate the completely interior traffic of a State, because it is not an apt phrase for that purpose; and the enumeration of the particular classes of commerce, to which the power was to be extended, would not have been made, had the intention been to extend the power to every description. . . . The genius and character of the whole government seem to be, that its action is to be applied to all the external concerns of the nation, and to those internal concerns which affect the States generally; but not to those which are completely within a particular State, which do not affect other States, and with which it is not necessary to interfere, for the purpose of executing some of the general powers of the government. The completely internal commerce of a State, then, may be considered as reserved for the State itself.

But, in regulating commerce with foreign nations, the power of Congress does not stop at the jurisdictional lines of the several States. It would be a very useless power, if it could not pass those lines. The commerce of the United States with foreign nations, is that of the whole United States. Every district has a right to participate in it. The deep streams which penetrate our country in every direction, pass through the interior of almost every State in the Union, and furnish the means of exercising this right. If Congress has the power to regulate it, that power must be exercised whenever the subject exists. If it exists within the States, if a foreign voyage may commence or terminate at a port within a State, then the power of Congress may be exercised within a State.

This principle is, if possible, still more clear, when applied to commerce "among the several States." They either join each other, in which case they are separated by a mathematical line, or they are remote from each other, in which case other States lie between them. What is commerce "among" them; and how is it to be conducted? Can a trading expedition between two adjoining States, commence and terminate outside of each? And if the trading intercourse be between two States remote from each other, must it not commence in one, terminate in the other, and probably pass through a third? Commerce among the States must, of necessity, be commerce with the States. . . .

We are now arrived at the inquiry — What is this power?

It is the power to regulate; that is, to prescribe

the rule by which commerce is to be governed. This power, like all others vested in Congress, is complete in itself, may be exercised to its utmost extent, and acknowledges no limitations, other than are prescribed in the constitution. These are expressed in plain terms, and do not affect the questions which arise in this case, or which have been discussed at the bar. If, as has always been understood, the sovereignty of Congress, though limited to specified objects, is plenary as to those objects, the power over commerce with foreign nations, and among the several States, is vested in Congress as absolutely as it would be in a single government, having in its constitution the same restrictions on the exercise of the power as are found in the constitution of the United States. The wisdom and the discretion of Congress, their identity with the people, and the influence which their constituents possess at elections, are, in this, as in many other instances, as that, for example, of declaring war, the sole restraints on which they have relied, to secure them from its abuse. They are the restraints on which the people must often rely solely, in all representative governments. . . .

But it has been urged with great earnestness, that, although the power of Congress to regulate commerce with foreign nations, and among the several States, be co-extensive with the subject itself, and have no other limits than are prescribed in the constitution, yet the States may severally exercise the same power, within their respective jurisdictions. In support of this argument, it is said, that they possessed it as an inseparable attribute of sovereignty, before the formation of the constitution, and still retain it, except so far as they have surrendered it by that instrument; that this principle results from the nature of the government, and is secured by the tenth amendment; that an affirmative grant of power is not exclusive, unless in its own nature it be such that the continued exercise of it by the former possessor is inconsistent with the grant, and that this is not of that description.

The appellant, conceding these postulates, except the last, contends, that full power to regulate a particular subject, implies the whole power, and leaves no residuum; that a grant of the whole is incompatible with the existence of a right in another to any part of it. . . .

In discussing the question, whether this power is still in the States, in the case under consideration, we may dismiss from it the inquiry, whether it is surrendered by the mere grant to Congress, or is retained until Congress shall exercise the power. We may dismiss that inquiry, because it has been exer-

cised, and the regulations which Congress deemed it proper to make, are now in full operation. . . .

But, the inspection laws are said to be regulations of commerce, and are certainly recognised in the constitution, as being passed in the exercise of a power remaining with the States.

That inspection laws may have a remote and considerable influence on commerce, will not be denied; but that a power to regulate commerce is the source from which the right to pass them is derived, cannot be admitted. . . . They form a portion of that immense mass of legislation, which embraces everything within the territory of a State, not surrendered to the general government: all which can be most advantageously exercised by the States themselves. Inspection laws, quarantine laws, health laws of every description, as well as laws for regulating the internal commerce of a State, and those which respect turnpike roads, ferries, &c., are component parts of this mass.

No direct general power over these objects is granted to Congress; and, consequently, they remain subject to State legislation. If the legislative power of the Union can reach them, it must be for national purposes; it must be where the power is expressly given for a special purpose, or is clearly incidental to some power which is expressly given. . . . All experience shows, that the same measures, or measures scarcely distinguishable from each other, may flow from distinct powers; but this does not prove that the powers themselves are identical. Although the means used in their execution may sometimes approach each other so nearly as to be confounded, there are other situations in which they are sufficiently distinct to establish their individuality.

It has been said, that the act of August 7, 1789, acknowledges a concurrent power in the States to regulate the conduct of pilots, and hence is inferred an admission of their concurrent right with Congress to regulate commerce with foreign nations, and amongst the States. But this inference is not, we think, justified by the fact.

Although Congress cannot enable a State to legislate, Congress may adopt the provisions of a State on any subject. When the government of the Union was brought into existence, it found a system for the regulation of its pilots in full force in every State. The act which has been mentioned, adopts this system, and gives it the same validity as if its provisions had been specially made by Congress. But the act, it may be said, is prospective also, and the adoption of laws to be made in future, presupposes the right in the maker to legislate on the subject.

The act unquestionably manifests an intention to

leave this subject entirely to the States, until Congress should think proper to interpose; but the very enactment of such a law indicates an opinion that it was necessary; that the existing system would not be applicable to the new state of things, unless expressly applied to it by Congress. But this section is confined to pilots within the "bays, inlets, rivers, harbours, and ports of the United States," which are, of course, in whole or in part, also within the limits of some particular state. . . .

In argument, however, it has been contended, that if a law passed by a State, in the exercise of its acknowledged sovereignty, comes into conflict with a law passed by Congress in pursuance of the constitution, they affect the subject, and each other, like equal opposing powers.

But the framers of our constitution foresaw this state of things, and provided for it, by declaring the supremacy not only of itself, but of the laws made in pursuance of it. The nullity of any act, inconsistent with the constitution, is produced by the declaration, that the constitution is the supreme law. The appropriate application of that part of the clause which confers the same supremacy of laws and treaties, is to such acts of the State Legislatures as do not transcend their powers, but, though enacted in the execution of acknowledged State powers, interfere with, or are contrary to the laws of Congress, made in pursuance of the constitution, or some treaty made under the authority of the United States. In every such case, the act of Congress, or the treaty, is supreme; and the law of the State, though enacted in the exercise of powers not controverted, must yield to it. . . .

But we will proceed briefly to notice those sections which bear more directly on the subject.

The first section declares, that vessels enrolled by virtue of a previous law, and certain other vessels, enrolled as described in that act, and having a license in force, as is by the act required, "and no others, shall be deemed ships or vessels of the United States, entitled to the privileges of ships or vessels employed in the coasting trade."

The word "license," means permission, or authority; and a license to do any particular thing, is a permission or authority to do that thing; and if granted by a person having power to grant it, transfers to the grantee the right to do whatever it purports to authorize. It certainly transfers to him all the right which the grantor can transfer, to do what is within the terms of the license.

It has been denied that these words authorize a voyage from New Jersey to New York. It is true, that no ports are specified; but it is equally true, that the words used are perfectly intelligible, and do confer such authority as unquestionably, as if the ports had been mentioned. The coasting trade is a term well understood. The law has defined it; and all know its meaning perfectly. The act describes, with great minuteness, the various operations of a vessel engaged in it; and it cannot, we think, be doubted, that a voyage from New-Jersey to New-York, is one of those operations.

But, if the license be a permit to carry on the coasting trade, the respondent denies that these boats were engaged in that trade, or that the decree under consideration has restrained them from prosecuting it. The boats of the appellant were, we are told, employed in the transportation of passengers; and this is no part of that commerce which Congress may regulate.

If the power reside in Congress, as a portion of the general grant to regulate commerce, then acts applying that power to vessels generally, must be construed as comprehending all vessels. If none appear to be excluded by the language of the act, none can be excluded by construction. Vessels have always been employed to a greater or less extent in the transportation of passengers, and have never been supposed to be, on that account, withdrawn from the control or protection of Congress.

If, then, it were even true, that the Bellona and the Stoudinger were employed exclusively in the conveyance of passengers between New-York and New-Jersey, it would not follow that this occupation did not constitute a part of the coasting trade of the United States, and was not protected by the license annexed to the answer. . . .

But all inquiry into this subject seems to the Court to be put completely at rest, by the act already mentioned, entitled, "An act for the enrolling and licensing of steam boats."

This act authorizes a steam boat employed, or intended to be employed, only in a river or bay of the United States, owned wholly or in part by an alien, resident within the United States, to be enrolled and licensed as if the same belonged to a citizen of the United States.

This act demonstrates the opinion of Congress, that steam boats may be enrolled and licensed, in common with vessels using sails. . . . and the act of a State inhibiting the use of either to any vessel having a license under the act of Congress, comes, we think, in direct collision with that act.

Powerful and ingenious minds, taking, as postulates, that the powers expressly granted to the government of the Union, are to be contracted by construction, into the narrowest possible compass, and that the original powers of the States are retained, if any possible construction will retain them, may, by a course of well digested, but refined and metaphysical reasoning, founded on these premises, explain away the constitution of our country, and leave it, a magnificent structure, indeed, to look at, but totally unfit for use. They may so entangle and perplex the understanding, as to obscure principles, which were before thought quite plain, and induce doubts where, if the mind were to pursue its own course, none would be perceived. In such a case, it is peculiarly necessary to recur to safe and fundamental principles to sustain those principles, and, when sustained, to make them the tests of the arguments to be examined.

MR. JUSTICE JOHNSON.

The grant to Livingston and Fulton, interferes with the freedom of intercourse among the States; and on this principle its constitutionality is contested.

When speaking of the power of Congress over navigation, I do not regard it as a power incidental to that of regulating commerce; I consider it as the thing itself; inseparable from it as vital motion is from vital existence. . . .

It is impossible, with the views which I entertain of the principle on which the commercial privileges of the people of the United States, among themselves, rests, to concur in the view which this Court takes of the effect of the coasting license in this cause. I do not regard it as the foundation of the right set up in behalf of the appellant. If there was any one object riding over every other in the adoption of the constitution, it was to keep the commercial intercourse among the States free from all invidious and partial restraints. And I cannot overcome the conviction that if the licensing act was repealed tomorrow, the rights of the appellant to a reversal of the decision complained of, would be as strong as it is under this license. . . .

Brown v. Maryland

12 Wheaton 419 (1827)
Vote: 6–1

The problem in *Brown* v. *Maryland* is a recurrent problem in commerce and taxing situations — drawing a boundary between federal and state authority. At stake was a Maryland statute that required importers to pay a license fee or be fined $100. Brown sold a package of foreign dry goods without a license. In appeals in Maryland courts, he filed a demurrer (the legal "so what?"), admitting the facts but arguing that Maryland's licensing was an invasion of national power over foreign commerce. Losing in the state courts, Brown appealed on a writ of error in the United States Supreme Court.

MR. CHIEF JUSTICE MARSHALL delivered the opinion of the Court.

The cause depends entirely on the question, whether the legislature of a State can constitutionally require the importer of foreign articles to take out a license from the State, before he shall be permitted to sell a bale or package so imported.

An impost or duty on imports, is a custom or a tax levied on articles brought into a country, and is most usually secured, before the importer is allowed to exercise his rights of ownership over them, because evasions of the law can be prevented more certainly by executing it while the articles are in its custody. It would not, however, be less an impost or duty on the articles, if it were to be levied on them, after they were landed. The policy and consequent practice of levying or securing the duty before, or on entering the port, does not limit the power to that state of things, nor, consequently, the prohibition, unless the true meaning of the clause so confines it. What, then, are "imports?" The lexicons inform us, they are "things imported." If we appeal to usage for the meaning of the word, we shall receive the same answer. They are the articles themselves which are brought into the country. "A duty on imports," then, is not merely a duty on the act of importation, but is a duty on the thing imported.

From the vast inequality between the different States of the confederacy, as to commercial advantages, few subjects were viewed with deeper interest, or excited more irritation, than the manner in which the several States exercised, or seemed disposed to exercise, the power of laying duties on imports. From motives which were deemed sufficient by the statesmen of that day, the general power of taxation, indispensably necessary as it was, and jealous as the States were of any encroachment on it, was so far abridged as to forbid them to touch imports or exports, with the single exception which has been noticed. Why are they restrained from imposing these duties? Plainly, because, in the general opinion, the interest of all would be best promoted by placing that whole subject under the control of

Congress. Whether the prohibition to "lay imposts, or duties on imports or exports," proceeded from an apprehension that the power might be so exercised as to disturb that equality among the States which was generally advantageous, or that harmony between them which it was desirable to preserve, or to maintain unimpaired our commercial connexions with foreign nations, or to confer this source of revenue on the government of the Union, or whatever other motive might have induced the prohibition, it is plain, that the object would be as completely defeated by a power to tax the article in the hands of the importer the instant it was landed, as by a power to tax it while entering the port. There is no difference, in effect, between a power to prohibit the sale of an article, and a power to prohibit its introduction into the country. The one would be a necessary consequence of the other. No goods would be imported if none could be sold. No object of any description can be accomplished by laying a duty on importation, which may not be accomplished with equal certainty by laying a duty on the thing being imported in the hands of the importer. It is obvious, that the same power which imposes a light duty, can impose a very heavy one, one which amounts to a prohibition. Questions of power do not depend on the degree to which it may be exercised. If it may be exercised at all, it must be exercised at the will of those in whose hands it is placed. If the tax may be levied in this form by a State, it may be levied to an extent which will defeat the revenue by impost, so far as it is drawn from importations into the particular State. We are told, that such wild and irrational abuse of power is not to be apprehended, and is not to be taken into view when discussing its existence. All power may be abused; and if the fear of its abuse is to constitute an argument against its existence, it might be urged against the existence of that which is universally acknowledged, and which is indispensable to the general safety. The States will never be so mad as to destroy their own commerce, or even to lessen it.

We do not dissent from these general propositions. We do not suppose any State would act so unwisely. But we do not place the question on that ground. . . . Conceding, to the full extent which is required, that every State would, in its legislation on this subject, provide judiciously for its own interests, it cannot be conceded, that each would respect the interests of others. A duty on imports is a tax on the article which is paid by the consumer. The great importing States would thus levy a tax on the non-importing States, which would not be less a tax because their interest would afford ample security

against its ever being so heavy as to expel commerce from their ports. This would necessarily produce countervailing measures on the part of those States whose situation was less favourable to importation. For this, among other reasons, the whole power of laying duties on imports was, with a single and slight exception, taken from the States. When we are inquiring whether a particular act is within this prohibition, the question is not, whether the State may so legislate as to hurt itself, but whether the act is within the words and mischief of the prohibitory clause. It has already been shown, that a tax on the article in the hands of the importer, is within its words; and we think it too clear for controversy, that the same tax is within its mischief. We think it unquestionable, that such a tax has precisely the same tendency to enhance the price of the article, as if imposed upon it while entering the port.

The counsel for the State of Maryland insist, with great reason, that if the words of the prohibition be taken in their utmost latitude, they will abridge the power of taxation, which all admit to be essential to the States, to an extent which has never yet been suspected, and will deprive them of resources which are necessary to supply revenue, and which they have heretofore been admitted to possess. These words must, therefore, be construed with some limitation; and, if this be admitted, they insist, that entering the country is the point of time when the prohibition ceases, and the power of the State to tax commences. . . . [T]here must be a point of time when the prohibition ceases, and the power of the State to tax commences; we cannot admit that this point of time is the instant that the articles enter the country. It is, we think, obvious, that this construction would defeat the prohibition.

The constitutional prohibition on the States to lay a duty on imports, a prohibition which a vast majority of them must feel an interest in preserving, may certainly come in conflict with their acknowledged power to tax persons and property within their territory. The power, and the restriction on it, though quite distinguishable when they do not approach each other, may yet, like the intervening colours between white and black, approach so nearly as to perplex the understanding, as colours perplex the vision in marking the distinction between them. Yet the distinction exists, and must be marked as the cases arise. Till they do arise, it might be premature to state any rule as being universal in its application. It is sufficient for the present to say, generally, that when the importer has so acted upon the thing imported, that it has become incorporated and mixed up with the mass of property in the country, it has, perhaps, lost its distinctive character as an import, and has become subject to the taxing power of the State; but while remaining the property of the importer, in his warehouse, in the original form or package in which it was imported, a tax upon it is too plainly a duty on imports to escape the prohibition in the constitution.

U.S. v. E.C. Knight Co.

156 U.S. 1 (1895)
Vote: 7–1

The Sherman Antitrust Act has been a bulwark of U.S. business policy since its passage in 1890. It makes it unlawful to monopolize or to restrain interstate commerce. The American Sugar Co. bought the stock and acquired control of its major competitors. The issue presented was whether congressional control of commerce, by the standards then prevailing, extended to business transactions that had subsequent consequences for commerce. The standards were quite different from those of Marshall's broad approach, and the *Knight* case represents probably the most restrictive view of the commerce power.

It was the basis of the anti–New Deal decision in the SCHECHTER case (1935), and these two cases are the high-water marks of judicial control over and limitation of the federal commerce power.

A historical note should be added: We know that Attorney General Olney strongly disapproved of the Sherman Antitrust Act. While some critics have claimed the Justice Department was less diligent than it should have been, it is not evident that the decision was influenced by Olney's predilections.

MR. CHIEF JUSTICE FULLER, after stating the case, delivered the opinion of the court.

By the purchase of the stock of the four Philadelphia refineries, with shares of its own stock, the American Sugar Refining Company acquired nearly complete control of the manufacture of refined sugar within the United States. The bill charged that the contracts under which these purchases were made constituted combinations in restraints of trade, and that in entering into them the defendants combined and conspired to restrain the trade and commerce in refined sugar among the several States and with foreign nations, contrary to the act of Congress of July 2, 1890.

The fundamental question is, whether conceding that the existence of a monopoly in manufacture is established by the evidence, that monopoly can be directly suppressed under the act of Congress in the mode attempted by this bill. . . . The relief of the citizens of each State from the burden of monopoly and the evils resulting from the restraint of trade among such citizens was left with the States to deal with, and this court has recognized their possession of that power even to the extent of holding that an employment or business carried on by private individuals, when it becomes a matter of such public interest and importance as to create a common charge or burden upon the citizen; in other words, when it becomes a practical monopoly, to which the citizen is compelled to resort and by means of which a tribute can be exacted from the community, is subject to regulation by state legislative power. On the other hand, the power of Congress to regulate commerce among the several States is also exclusive. The Constitution does not provide that interstate commerce shall be free, but, by the grant of this exclusive power to regulate it, it was left free except as Congress might impose restraints. . . . That which belongs to commerce is within the jurisdiction of the United States, but that which does not belong to commerce is within the jurisdiction of the police power of the State.

The argument is that the power to control the manufacture of refined sugar is a monopoly over a necessary of life, to the enjoyment of which by a large part of the population of the United States interstate commerce is indispensable, and that, therefore, the general government in the exercise of the power to regulate commerce may repress such monopoly directly and set aside the instruments which have created it. But this argument cannot be confined to necessaries of life merely, and must include all articles of general consumption. Doubtless the power to control the manufacture of a given thing involves in a certain sense the control of its disposition, but this is a secondary and not the primary sense; and although the exercise of that power may result in bringing the operation of commerce into play, it does not control it, and affects it only incidentally and indirectly. Commerce succeeds to manufacture, and is not a part of it. The power to regulate commerce is the power to prescribe the rule by which commerce shall be governed, and is a power independent of the power to suppress monopoly.

But it may operate in repression of monopoly whenever that comes within the rules by which commerce is governed or whenever the transaction is itself a monopoly of commerce.

It is vital that the independence of the commercial power and of the police power, and the delimitation between them, however sometimes perplexing, should always be recognized and observed, for while the one furnishes the strongest bond of union, the other is essential to the preservation of the autonomy of the States as required by our dual form of government....

Contracts to buy, sell, or exchange goods to be transported among the several States, the transportation and its instrumentalities, and articles bought, sold, or exchanged for the purposes of such transit among the States, or put in the way of transit, may be regulated, but this is because they form part of interstate trade or commerce. The fact that an article is manufactured for export to another State does not of itself make it an article of interstate commerce, and the intent of the manufacturer does not determine the time when the article or product passes from the control of the State and belongs to commerce. This was so ruled in *Coe* v. *Errol*....

Contracts, combinations, or conspiracies to control domestic enterprise in manufacture, agriculture, mining, production in all its forms, or to raise or lower prices or wages, might unquestionably tend to restrain external as well as domestic trade, but the restraint would be an indirect result, however inevitable and whatever its extent, and such result would not necessarily determine the object of the contract, combination, or conspiracy.

It was in the light of well-settled principles that the act of July 2, 1890, was framed. Congress did not attempt thereby to assert the power to deal with monopoly directly as such; or to limit and restrict the rights of corporations created by the States or the citizens of the States in the acquisition, control, or disposition of property.... What the law struck at was combinations, contracts, and conspiracies to monopolize trade and commerce among the several States or with foreign nations; but the contracts and acts of the defendants related exclusively to the acquisition of the Philadelphia refineries and the business of sugar refining in Pennsylvania, and bore no direct relation to commerce between the States or with foreign nations. The object was manifestly private gain in the manufacture of the commodity, but not through the control of interstate or foreign commerce. It is true that the bill alleged that the products of these refineries were sold and distributed among the several States, and that all the companies were engaged in trade or commerce with the several States and with foreign nations; but this was no more than to say that trade and commerce served manufacture to fulfill its function.... [I]t does not follow that an attempt to monopolize, or the actual monopoly of, the manufacture was an attempt, whether executory or consummated, to monopolize commerce, even though, in order to dispose of the product, the instrumentality of commerce was necessarily invoked. There was nothing in the proofs to indicate any intention to put a restraint upon trade or commerce, and the fact, as we have seen, that trade or commerce might be indirectly affected was not enough to entitle complainants to a decree. The subject-matter of the sale was shares of manufacturing stock... yet the act of Congress only authorized the Circuit Courts to proceed by way of preventing and restraining violations of the act in respect of contracts, combinations, or conspiracies in restraint of interstate or international trade or commerce.

MR. JUSTICE HARLAN, dissenting.

The fundamental inquiry in this case is, What, in a legal sense, is an unlawful restraint of trade?... Under the power with which it is invested, Congress may remove unlawful obstructions, of whatever kind, to the free course of trade among the States. In so doing it would not interfere with the "autonomy of the States," because the power thus to protect interstate commerce is expressly given by the people of all the States.... Any combination, therefore, that disturbs or unreasonably obstructs freedom in buying and selling articles manufactured to be sold to persons in other States or to be carried to other States — a freedom that cannot exist if the right to buy and sell is fettered by unlawful restraints that crush out competition — affects, not incidentally, but directly, the people of all the States; and the remedy for such an evil is found only in the exercise of powers confided to a government which, this court has said, was the government of all, exercising powers delegated by all, representing all, acting for all. *McCulloch* v. *Maryland*.... It is said that manufacture precedes commerce and is not a part of it. But it is equally true that when manufacture ends, that which has been manufactured becomes a subject of commerce; that buying and selling succeed manufacture, come into existence after the process of manufacture is completed, precede transportation, and are as much commercial intercourse, where articles are bought *to be* carried from one State to another, as is the manual transportation of such articles after they have been so purchased. The distinction was recognized by this court in *Gibbons* v. *Ogden,* where the principal question was whether commerce included navigation. Both the court and counsel recognized buying and selling or barter *as included in commerce.*

. . . Whatever improperly obstructs the free course of interstate intercourse and trade, as involved in the buying and selling of articles to be carried from one State to another, may be reached by Congress, under its authority to regulate commerce among the States. The exercise of that authority so as to make trade among the States, in all recognized articles of commerce, absolutely free from unreasonable or illegal restrictions imposed by combinations, is justified by an express grant of power to Congress and would redound to the welfare of the whole country.

It is said that there are no proofs in the record which indicate an *intention* upon the part of the American Sugar Refining Company and its associates to put a restraint upon trade or commerce. Was it necessary that formal proof be made that the persons engaged in this combination admitted, in words, that they intended to restrain trade or commerce? Did any one expect to find in the written agreements which resulted in the formation of this combination a distinct expression of a purpose to restrain interstate trade or commerce? Men who form and control these combinations are too cautious and wary to make such admissions orally or in writing. Why, it is conceded that the object of this combination was to obtain control of the business of making and selling refined sugar throughout the entire country. Those interested in its operations will be satisfied with nothing less than to have the whole population of America pay tribute to them. That object is disclosed upon the very face of the transactions described in the bill. And it is proved — indeed, is conceded — that that object has been accomplished to the extent that the American Sugar Refining Company now controls ninety-eight per cent of all the sugar refining business in the country, and therefore controls the price of that article everywhere. Now, the *mere existence* of a combination having such an object and possessing such extraordinary power is itself, under settled principles of law — there being no adjudged case to the contrary in this country — a direct restraint of trade in the article for the control

of the sales of which in this country that combination was organized.

Hammer v. Dagenhart

> 247 U.S. 251 (1918)
> Vote: 5–4

⟨The federal government sought to control the incidence of child labor by forbidding interstate transportation of such goods.⟩ Was prohibition of interstate channels by Congress used as a means of effecting a policy (local labor conditions) not directly under congressional power a constitutional use of the commerce power? The government thought a set of previous decisions — for example, the decision in *Champion* v. *Ames* (1903) upholding congressional prohibition of lottery tickets — constituted ample precedent. The mill in which Reuben Dagenhart (aged seven, but described in the Court opinion as "under the age of fourteen years") worked did not think so and helped his father sue on "his" behalf.

Notice the severe language criticizing *Hammer* v. *Dagenhart* in U.S. V. DARBY (1941). Is this justified by *Hammer*'s being unusually cavalier with precedent, or is it simply that child labor is an emotional issue?

MR. JUSTICE DAY delivered the opinion of the court.

A bill was filed in the United States District Court for the Western District of North Carolina by a father in his own behalf and as next friend of his two minor sons, one under the age of fourteen years and the other between the ages of fourteen and sixteen years, employees in a cotton mill at Charlotte, North Carolina, to enjoin the enforcement of the act of Congress intended to prevent interstate commerce in the products of child labor. . . .

The District Court held the act unconstitutional and entered a decree enjoining its enforcement. This appeal brings the case here.

The attack upon the act rests upon three propositions: First: It is not a regulation of interstate and foreign commerce; Second: It contravenes the Tenth

All Local

Amendment to the Constitution; Third: It conflicts with the Fifth Amendment to the Constitution.

The controlling question for decision is: Is it within the authority of Congress in regulating commerce among the States to prohibit the transportation in interstate commerce of manufactured goods, the product of a factory in which, within thirty days prior to their removal therefrom, children under the age of fourteen have been employed or permitted to work, or children between the ages of fourteen and sixteen years have been employed or permitted to work more than eight hours in any day, or more than six days in any week, or after the hour of seven o'clock P.M. or before the hour of 6 o'clock A.M.?

The power essential to the passage of this act, the Government contends, is found in the commerce clause of the Constitution which authorizes Congress to regulate commerce with foreign nations and among the States. . . . [T]he power is one to control the means by which commerce is carried on, which is directly the contrary of the assumed right to forbid commerce from moving and thus destroy it as to particular commodities. But it is insisted that adjudged cases in this court establish the doctrine that the power to regulate given to Congress incidentally includes the authority to prohibit the movement of ordinary commodities and therefore that the subject is not open for discussion. The cases demonstrate the contrary. They rest upon the character of the particular subjects dealt with and the fact that the scope of governmental authority, state or national, possessed over them is such that the authority to prohibit is as to them but the exertion of the power to regulate.

The first of these cases is _Champion v. Ames_, 188 U.S. 321, the so-called _Lottery Case_, in which it was held that Congress might pass a law having the effect to keep the channels of commerce free from use in the transportation of tickets used in the promotion of lottery schemes. In _Hipolite Egg Co. v. United States_, 220 U.S. 45, this court sustained the power of Congress to pass the Pure Food and Drug Act which prohibited the introduction into the States by means of interstate commerce of impure foods and drugs. In _Hoke v. United States_, 227 U.S. 308, this court sustained the constitutionality of the so-called "White Slave Traffic Act" whereby the transportation of a woman in interstate commerce for the purpose of prostitution was forbidden.

In each of these instances the use of interstate transportation was necessary to the accomplishment of harmful results. In other words, although the power over interstate transportation was to regulate, that could only be accomplished by prohibiting

the use of the facilities of interstate commerce to effect the evil intended.

This element is wanting in the present case. The thing intended to be accomplished by this statute is the denial of the facilities of interstate commerce to those manufacturers in the States who employ children within the prohibited ages. The act in its effect does not regulate transportation among the States, but aims to standardize the ages at which children may be employed in mining and manufacturing within the States. The goods shipped are of themselves harmless. The act permits them to be freely shipped after thirty days from the time of their removal from the factory. When offered for shipment, and before transportation begins, the labor of their production is over, and the mere fact that they were intended for interstate commerce transportation does not make their production subject to federal control under the commerce power. . . .

Over interstate transportation, or its incidents, the regulatory power of Congress is ample, but the production of articles, intended for interstate commerce, is a matter of local regulation. . . .

It is further contended that the authority of Congress may be exerted to control interstate commerce in the shipment of child-made goods because of the effect of the circulation of such goods in other States where the evil of this class of labor has been recognized by local legislation, and the right to thus employ child labor has been more rigorously restrained than in the State of production. In other words, that the unfair competition, thus engendered, may be controlled by closing the channels of interstate commerce to manufacturers in those States where the local laws do not meet what Congress deems to be the more just standard of other States.

There is no power vested in Congress to require the States to exercise their police power so as to prevent possible unfair competition. Many causes may coöperate to give one State, by reason of local laws or conditions, an economic advantage over others. The Commerce Clause was not intended to give to Congress a general authority to equalize such conditions. . . .

It may be desirable that such laws be uniform, but our Federal Government is one of enumerated powers; "this principle," declared Chief Justice Marshall in _McCulloch v. Maryland_, 4 Wheat. 316, "is universally admitted."

A statute must be judged by its natural and reasonable effect. _Collins v. New Hampshire_, 171 U.S. 30, 33, 34. The control by Congress over interstate commerce cannot authorize the exercise of authority not entrusted to it by the Constitution. _Pipe Line_

Congress Has Power

Cases, 234 U.S. 548, 560. The maintenance of the authority of the States over matters purely local is as essential to the preservation of our institutions as is the conservation of the supremacy of the federal power in all matters entrusted to the Nation by the Federal Constitution.

In interpreting the Constitution it must never be forgotten that the Nation is made up of States to which are entrusted the powers of local government. And to them and to the people the powers not expressly delegated to the National Government are reserved. *Lane County* v. *Oregon,* 7 Wall. 71, 76. The power of the States to regulate their purely internal affairs by such laws as seem wise to the local authority is inherent and has never been surrendered to the general government. *New York* v. *Miln,* 11 Pet. 102, 139; *Slaughter House Cases,* 16 Wall. 36, 63; *Kidd* v. *Pearson, supra.* To sustain this statute would not be in our judgment a recognition of the lawful exertion of congressional authority over interstate commerce, but would sanction an invasion by the federal power of the control of a matter purely local in its character, and over which no authority has been delegated to Congress in conferring the power to regulate commerce among the States.

... [I]f Congress can thus regulate matters entrusted to local authority by prohibition of the movement of commodities in interstate commerce, all freedom of commerce will be at an end, and the power of the States over local matters may be eliminated, and thus our system of government be practically destroyed.... [T]his law exceeds the constitutional authority of Congress.

Affirmed.

MR. JUSTICE HOLMES, dissenting.

... The objection urged against the power is that the States have exclusive control over their methods of production and that Congress cannot meddle with them, and taking the proposition in the sense of direct intermeddling I agree to it and suppose that no one denies it. But if an act is within the powers specifically conferred upon Congress, it seems to me that it is not made any less constitutional because of the indirect effects that it may have, however obvious it may be that it will have those effects, and that we are not at liberty upon such grounds to hold it void.

The first step in my argument is to make plain what no one is likely to dispute — that the statute in question is within the power expressly given to Congress if considered only as to its immediate effects and that if invalid it is so only upon some collateral ground. The statute confines itself to prohibiting the carriage of certain goods in interstate or foreign commerce. Congress is given power to regulate such commerce in unqualified terms. It would not be argued today that the power to regulate does not include the power to prohibit. Regulation means the prohibition of something, and when interstate commerce is the matter to be regulated I cannot doubt that the regulation may prohibit any part of such commerce that Congress sees fit to forbid. At all events it is established by the *Lottery Case* and others that have followed it that a law is not beyond the regulative power of Congress merely because it prohibits certain transportation out and out.

... I should have thought that the most conspicuous decisions of this Court had made it clear that the power to regulate commerce and other constitutional powers could not be cut down or qualified by the fact that it might interfere with the carrying out of the domestic policy of any State.

The manufacture of oleomargarine is as much a matter of state regulation as the manufacture of cotton cloth. Congress levied a tax upon the compound when colored so as to resemble butter that was so great as obviously to prohibit the manufacture and sale. In a very elaborate discussion the present Chief Justice excluded any inquiry into the purpose of an act which apart from that purpose was within the power of Congress....

... And to come to cases upon interstate commerce, notwithstanding *United States* v. *E. C. Knight Co.,* 156 U.S. 1, the Sherman Act has been made an instrument for the breaking up of combinations in restraint of trade and monopolies, using the power to regulate commerce as a foothold, but not proceeding because that commerce was the end actually in mind. The objection that the control of the States over production was interfered with was urged again and again but always in vain.

The notion that prohibition is any less prohibition when applied to things now thought evil I do not understand. But if there is any matter upon which civilized countries have agreed — far more unanimously than they have with regard to intoxicants and some other matters over which this country is now emotionally aroused — it is the evil of premature and excessive child labor. I should have thought that if we were to introduce our own moral conceptions where in my opinion they do not belong, this was preëminently a case for upholding the exercise of all its powers by the United States.

But I had thought that the propriety of the exercise of a power admitted to exist in some cases was for the consideration of Congress alone and that this Court always had disavowed the right to intrude its judgment upon questions of policy or morals. It is not for this Court to pronounce when prohibition is necessary to regulation if it ever may be necessary — to say that it is permissible as against strong drink but not as against the product of ruined lives.

The act does not meddle with anything belonging to the States. They may regulate their internal affairs and their domestic commerce as they like. But when they seek to send their products across the state line they are no longer within their rights. If there were no Constitution and no Congress their power to cross the line would depend upon their neighbors. Under the Constitution such commerce belongs not to the States but to Congress to regulate.

The Shreveport Case:
Houston E. & W. Texas Railway Co. v. U.S.

> 234 U.S. 342 (1914)
> Vote: 7–2

In accordance with rates set by the Texas Railroad Commission, the Texas Railroad charged up to three times as much per mile for goods shipped out of state as for the same goods shipped within state. This had great commercial effect on Shreveport, Louisiana, just across the Texas border. On complaint from the Louisiana Railroad Commission, the Interstate Commerce Commission, which had found the railroad's interstate rates to be reasonable, issued an order that the railroads charge at the same rate from Shreveport to Dallas as from Dallas eastward for equal distances. The U.S. Commerce Court dismissed petitions to set aside the ICC order and rejected the railroad's claim that the ICC had no jurisdiction over local rates.

MR. JUSTICE HUGHES delivered the opinion of the court.

These suits were brought in the Commerce Court by the Houston, East & West Texas Railway Company, and the Houston & Shreveport Railroad Company, and by the Texas & Pacific Railway Company, respectively, to set aside an order of the Interstate Commerce Commission, dated March 11, 1912,

upon the ground that it exceeded the Commission's authority.

The order of the Interstate Commerce Commission was made in a proceeding initiated in March, 1911, by the Railroad Commission of Louisiana. The complaint was that the appellants, and other interstate carriers, maintained unreasonable rates from Shreveport, Louisiana, to various points in Texas, and, further, that these carriers in the adjustment of rates over their respective lines unjustly discriminated in favor of traffic within the State of Texas and against similar traffic between Louisiana and Texas. . . .

The gravamen of the complaint, said the Interstate Commerce Commission, was that the carriers made rates out of Dallas and other Texas points into eastern Texas which were much lower than those which they extended into Texas from Shreveport. The situation may be briefly described: Shreveport, Louisiana, is about 40 miles from the Texas state line, and 231 miles from Houston, Texas, on the line of the Houston, East & West Texas and Houston & Shreveport Companies (which are affiliated in interest); it is 189 miles from Dallas, Texas, on the line of the Texas & Pacific. Shreveport competes with both cities for the trade of the intervening territory. The rates on these lines from Dallas and Houston, respectively, eastward to intermediate points in Texas were much less, according to distance, than from Shreveport westward to the same points. It is undisputed that the difference was substantial and injuriously affected the commerce of Shreveport. It appeared, for example, that a rate of 60 cents carried first class traffic a distance of 160 miles to the eastward from Dallas, while the same rate would carry the same class of traffic only 55 miles into Texas from Shreveport. The first class rate from Houston to Lufkin, Texas, 118.2 miles, was 50 cents per 100 pounds, while the rate from Shreveport to the same point, 112.5 miles, was 69 cents. The rate on wagons from Dallas to Marshall, Texas, 147.7 miles, was 36.8 cents, and from Shreveport to Marshall, 42 miles, 56 cents. The rate on furniture from Dallas to Longview, Texas, 124 miles, was 24.8 cents, and that from Shreveport to Longview, 65.7 miles, was 35 cents. These instances of differences in rates are merely illustrative; they serve to indicate the character of the rate adjustment.

The Interstate Commerce Commission found that the interstate class rates out of Shreveport to named Texas points were unreasonable, and it established maximum class rates for this traffic. These rates, we understand, were substantially the same as the class rates fixed by the Railroad Commission of Texas, and charged by the carriers, for transportation for similar distances in that State.

The point of the objection to the order is that, as the discrimination found by the Commission to be unjust arises out of the relation of intrastate rates, maintained under state authority, to interstate rates that have been upheld as reasonable, its correction was beyond the Commission's power. Manifestly the order might be complied with, and the discrimination avoided, either by reducing the interstate rates from Shreveport to the level of the competing intrastate rates, or by raising these intrastate rates to the level of the interstate rates, or by such reduction in the one case and increase in the other as would result in equality. But it is urged that, so far as the interstate rates were sustained by the Commission as reasonable, the Commission was without authority to compel their reduction in order to equalize them with the lower intrastate rates. . . . The invalidity of the order in this aspect is challenged upon two grounds:

(1) That Congress is impotent to control the intrastate charges of an interstate carrier even to the extent necessary to prevent injurious discrimination against interstate traffic; and

(2) That, if it be assumed that Congress has this power, still it has not been exercised, and hence the action of the Commission exceeded the limits of the authority which has been conferred upon it.

First. It is unnecessary to repeat what has frequently been said by this court with respect to the complete and paramount character of the power confided to Congress to regulate commerce among the several States. It is of the essence of this power that, where it exists, it dominates. Interstate trade was not left to be destroyed or impeded by the rivalries of local governments. The purpose was to make impossible the recurrence of the evils which had overwhelmed the Confederation and to provide the necessary basis of national unity by insuring 'uniformity of regulation against conflicting and discriminating state legislation.' By virtue of the comprehensive terms of the grant, the authority of Congress is at all times adequate to meet the varying exigencies that arise and to protect the national interest by securing the freedom of interstate commercial intercourse from local control. . . .

Congress is empowered to regulate, — that is, to provide the law for the government of interstate commerce; to enact 'all appropriate legislation' for its 'protection and advancement' (*The Daniel Ball*, 10 Wall. 557, 564); to adopt measures 'to promote its growth and insure its safety' (*County of Mobile* v. *Kimball, supra*); 'to foster, protect, control and

restrain' (*Second Employers' Liability Cases, supra*). . . . As it is competent for Congress to legislate to these ends, unquestionably it may seek their attainment by requiring that the agencies of interstate commerce shall not be used in such manner as to cripple, retard or destroy it. The fact that carriers are instruments of intrastate commerce, as well as of interstate commerce, does not derogate from the complete and paramount authority of Congress over the latter or preclude the Federal power from being exerted to prevent the intrastate operations of such carriers from being made a means of injury to that which has been confided to Federal care. Wherever the interstate and intrastate transactions of carriers are so related that the government of the one involves the control of the other, it is Congress, and not the State, that is entitled to prescribe the final and dominant rule, for otherwise Congress would be denied the exercise of its constitutional authority and the State, and not the Nation, would be supreme within the national field.

The use of the instrument of interstate commerce in a discriminatory manner so as to inflict injury upon that commerce, or some part thereof, furnishes abundant ground for Federal intervention. Nor can the attempted exercise of state authority alter the matter, where Congress has acted, for a State may not authorize the carrier to do that which Congress is entitled to forbid and has forbidden.

It is also to be noted — as the Government has well said in its argument in support of the Commission's order — that the power to deal with the relation between the two kinds of rates, as a relation, lies exclusively with Congress. It is manifest that the State cannot fix the relation of the carrier's interstate and intrastate charges without directly interfering with the former, unless it simply follows the standard set by Federal authority. . . . Congress is entitled to maintain its own standard as to these rates and to forbid any discriminatory action by interstate carriers which will obstruct the freedom of movement of interstate traffic over their lines in accordance with the terms it establishes.

Having this power, Congress could provide for its execution through the aid of a subordinate body; and we conclude that the order of the Commission now in question cannot be held invalid upon the ground that it exceeded the authority which Congress could lawfully confer.

The decree of the Commerce Court is affirmed in each case.

Affirmed.

MR. JUSTICE LURTON and MR. JUSTICE PITNEY dissent.

Panama Refining Co. v. Ryan

> 293 U.S. 388 (1935)
> Vote: 8–1

Schechter Poultry Corp. v. U.S.

> 295 U.S. 495 (1935)
> Vote: 9–0

Carter v. Carter Coal Co.

> 298 U.S. 238 (1936)
> Vote: 5–1–3

These New Deal cases are landmarks of the final struggle of the Supreme Court to retain its dual line of Commerce Clause cases, leading to a confrontation with President Franklin Roosevelt. In each of these cases the major issue was the scope of the Commerce Clause, but, to various degrees, delegation of legislative power was also at stake, complicating the issue. In addition the emergency nature of New Deal legislation, with sloppy drafting and execution, was a subtle factor.

Panama Refining was a key case that moved Brandeis into an anti–New Deal position, crystallizing his faith in small-scale industry into a repudiation of New Deal mass-regulation efforts. In this case (known also as the "Hot Oil" case), in contest was Congress' delegation of discretion to the President to prohibit as much or as little as he chose of oil produced in excess of state-authorized levels. Section 9(c) of the National Industrial Recovery Act (NIRA) was at issue, and, though the decision hinged on delegation, the outcome was ominous for the entire program.

The major test of the NIRA came in *Schechter*. The Act had been passed in 1933 and was a comprehensive plan to control the Great Depression through cooperation by government, business, and unions in the control of production and distribution. Agreements called "codes" were drafted and enforced. (This effort resembled some programs in Mussolini's Italy, and had been called "fascist.") The trade associations entrusted with proposing the codes were to be representative of the industry involved; in approving or disapproving the codes the President was enjoined not to encourage industry monopoly, but was otherwise free of guidelines.

The *Schechter* case involved a small kosher poultry establishment that was accused of violating wages-and-hours requirements and sanitation requirements, as well as the poultry code provision that ordered "live-kill" poultry dealers to sell the chicken first grabbed from a coop rather than giving purchasers a choice. The Schechter brothers challenged the constitutionality of such a scheme, arguing they did not constitute part of "interstate commerce" and that there was improper delegation of legislative power.

Carter v. *Carter Coal* involved the Bituminous Coal Conservation Act of 1935, "The Guffey Act," which established by legislation for the troubled mining industry a code similar to that invalidated with others in *Schechter*. Labor relations were controlled and regulated. (This portion of the Act was in many ways a model for the Wagner Act of 1935.) All coal producers were to be taxed, and those who accepted the code received a 90 percent rebate.

James Carter brought "suit" against his own company to prevent their complying with the statute. The Department of Justice defended the statute on behalf of the United States. A District of Columbia Court held the labor provisions unconstitutional but sustained the rest of the Act. Other cases were consolidated when the Supreme Court granted certiorari.

At issue was the sweep of the federal commerce power to extend to production preceding manufacture (goods were shipped regularly to enable mining) and the delegation power of Congress.

PANAMA REFINING CO. v. RYAN
MR. CHIEF JUSTICE HUGHES delivered the opinion of the Court.

On July 11, 1933, the President, by Executive Order, prohibited "the transportation in interstate and foreign commerce of petroleum and the products thereof produced or withdrawn from storage in excess of the amount permitted to be produced or withdrawn from storage by any State law or valid regulation or order prescribed thereunder, by any board, commission, officer, or other duly authorized agency of a State." This action was based on §9(c) of Title I of the National Industrial Recovery Act of June 16, 1933.

On July 15, 1933, the Secretary of the Interior issued regulations to carry out the President's orders of July 11 and 14, 1933. . . . The *Panama Refining Company,* as owner of an oil refining plant in Texas, and its co-plaintiff, a producer having oil and gas leases in Texas, sued to restrain the defendants, who were federal officials, from enforcing Regulations IV, V and VII prescribed by the Secretary of the Interior under §9(c) of the National Industrial Recovery Act. Plaintiffs attacked the validity of §9(c) as an unconstitutional delegation of the President of legislative power and as transcending the authority of the Congress under the commerce clause. . . . Section 9(c) is assailed upon the ground that it is an unconstitutional delegation of legislative power. The section purports to authorize the President to pass a prohibitory law. The subject to which this authority relates is defined. It is the transportation in interstate and foreign commerce of petroleum products which are produced or withdrawn from storage in excess of the amount permitted by state authority.

Section 9(c) is brief and unambiguous. It does not attempt to control the production of petroleum and petroleum products within a State. It does not seek to lay down rules for the guidance of state legislatures or state officers. It leaves to the States and to their constituted authorities the determination of what production shall be permitted. It does not qualify the President's authority by reference to the basis, or extent, of the State's limitation of production. Section 9(c) does not state whether, or in what circumstances or under what conditions, the President is to prohibit the transportation of the amount of petroleum or petroleum products produced in excess of the State's permission. It establishes no criterion to govern the President's course. It does not require any finding by the President as a condition of his action. The Congress in §9(c) thus declares no policy as to the transportation of the excess production. So far as this section is concerned, it gives to the President an unlimited authority to determine the policy and to lay down the prohibition, or not to lay it down, as he may see fit. And disobedience to his order is made a crime punishable by fine and imprisonment.

. . . It is declared to be the policy of Congress "to remove obstructions to the free flow of interstate and foreign commerce which tend to diminish the amount thereof"; "to provide for the general welfare by promoting the organization of industry for the purpose of coöperative action among trade groups"; "to induce and maintain united action of labor and management under adequate governmental sanctions and supervision"; "to eliminate unfair competitive practices, to promote the fullest possible utilization of the present productive capacity of industries, to avoid undue restriction of production (except as may be temporarily required), to increase the consumption of industrial and agricultural products by increasing purchasing power, to reduce and relieve unemployment, to improve standards of labor, and otherwise to rehabilitate industry and to conserve natural resources."

This general outline of policy contains nothing as to the circumstances or conditions in which transportation of petroleum or petroleum products should be prohibited, —nothing as to the policy of prohibiting, or not prohibiting, the transportation of production exceeding what the States allow. . . . It is manifest that this broad outline is simply an introduction of the Act, leaving the legislative policy as to particular subjects to be declared and defined, if at all, by the subsequent sections.

It is no answer to insist that deleterious consequences follow the transportation of "hot oil," —oil exceeding state allowances. The Congress did not prohibit that transportation. The Congress did not undertake to say that the transportation of "hot oil" was injurious. The Congress did not say that transportation of that oil was "unfair competition." The Congress did not declare in what circumstances that transportation should be forbidden, or require the President to make any determination as to any facts or circumstances. Among the numerous and diverse objectives broadly stated, the President was not required to choose. The President was not required to ascertain and proclaim the conditions prevailing in the industry which made the prohibition necessary.

. . . If the Congress can make a grant of legislative authority of the sort attempted by §9(c), we find nothing in the Constitution which restricts the Congress to the selection of the President as grantee. The Congress may vest the power in the officer of its choice or in a board or commission such as it may select or create for the purpose. Nor, with respect to such a delegation, is the question concerned merely with the transportation of oil, or of oil produced in excess of what the State may allow. If legislative power may thus be vested in the President, or other grantee, as to that excess of production, we see no reason to doubt that it may similarly be vested with respect to the transportation of oil without reference to the State's requirements. That reference simply defines the subject of the prohibition which the President is authorized to enact, or not to enact, as he pleases. And if that legislative power may be given to the President or other grantee, it would seem to follow that such power may similarly be conferred with respect to the transportation of other commodities in interstate commerce with or without reference to state action, thus giving to the grantee of the power the determination of what is a wise policy as to that transportation, and authority to permit or prohibit it, as the person, or board or commission, so chosen, may think desirable. . . .

The Constitution provides that "All legislative powers herein granted shall be vested in a Congress of the United States, which shall consist of a Senate and House of Representatives." Art I, §1. And the Congress is empowered "To make all laws which shall be necessary and proper for carrying into execution" its general powers. Art. I, §8, par. 18. The Congress manifestly is not permitted to abdicate, or to transfer to others, the essential legislative functions with which it is thus vested. Undoubtedly legislation must often be adapted to complex conditions involving a host of details with which the national legislature cannot deal directly. The Constitution has never been regarded as denying to the Congress the necessary resources of flexibility and practicality, which will enable it to perform its function in laying down policies and establishing standards, while leaving to selected instrumentalities the making of subordinate rules within prescribed limits and the determination of facts to which the policy as declared by the legislature is to apply. . . . But the constant recognition of the necessity and validity of such provisions, and the wide range of administrative authority which has been developed by means of them, cannot be allowed to obscure the limitations of the authority to delegate, if our constitutional system is to be maintained.

. . . Authorizations given by Congress to selected instrumentalities for the purpose of ascertaining the existence of facts to which legislation is directed, have constantly been sustained. Moreover, the Congress may not only give such authorizations to determine specific facts but may establish primary standards, devolving upon others the duty to carry out the declared legislative policy, that is, as Chief Justice Marshall expressed it, "to fill up

the details" under the general provisions made by the legislature.

So, also, from the beginning of the Government, the Congress has conferred upon executive officers the power to make regulations, — "not for the government of their departments, but for administering the laws which did govern." *United States* v. *Grimaud*, 220 U.S. 506, 517. Such regulations become, indeed, binding rules of conduct, but they are valid only as subordinate rules and when found to be within the framework of the policy which the legislature has sufficiently defined. . . .

In every case in which the question has been raised, the Court has recognized that there are limits of delegation which there is no constitutional authority to transcend. We think that §9(c) goes beyond those limits. As to the transportation of oil production in excess of state permission, the Congress has declared no policy, has established no standard, has laid down no rule. . . .

Both §9(c) and the Executive Order are in notable contrast with historic practice (as shown by many statutes and proclamations we have cited in the margin) by which declarations of policy are made by the Congress and delegations are within the framework of that policy and have relation to facts and conditions to be found and stated by the President in the appropriate exercise of the delegated authority.

We see no escape from the conclusion that the Executive Orders of July 11, 1933, and July 14, 1933, and the Regulations issued by the Secretary of the Interior thereunder, are without constitutional authority.

Reversed.

MR. JUSTICE CARDOZO, dissenting.

My point of difference with the majority of the court is narrow. I concede that to uphold the delegation there is need to discover in the terms of the act a standard reasonably clear whereby discretion must be governed. I deny that such a standard is lacking in respect of the prohibitions permitted by this section when the act with all its reasonable implications is considered as a whole. What the standard is becomes the pivotal inquiry.

As to the nature of the *act* which the President is authorized to perform there is no need for implication. . . . He is not left to roam at will among all the possible subjects of interstate transportation, picking and choosing as he pleases. I am far from asserting now that delegation would be valid if accompanied by all that latitude of choice. In the laying of his interdict he is to confine himself to a particular commodity, and to that commodity when produced or withdrawn from storage in contravention of the policy and statutes of the states. He has choice, though within limits, as to the occasion, but none whatever as to the means. The means have been prescribed by Congress. . . .

His act being thus defined, what else must he ascertain in order to regulate his discretion and bring the power into play? The answer is not given if we look to §9(c) only, but it comes to us by implication from a view of other sections where the standards are defined. The prevailing opinion concedes that a standard will be as effective if imported into §9(c) by reasonable implication as if put there in so many words. If we look to the whole structure of the statute, the test is plainly this, that the President is to forbid the transportation of the oil when he believes, in the light of the conditions of the industry as disclosed from time to time, that the prohibition will tend to effectuate the declared policies of the act. . . .

I am persuaded that a reference, express or implied, to the policy of Congress as declared in §1 is a sufficient definition of a standard to make the statute valid. . . . [T]he separation of powers between the Executive and Congress is not a doctrinaire concept to be made use of with pedantic rigor. There must be sensible approximation, there must be elasticity of adjustment, in response to the practical necessities of government, which cannot foresee today the developments of tomorrow in their nearly infinite variety.

From a host of precedents available, both legislative and judicial, I cite a few as illustrations. By an act approved June 4, 1794, during the administration of Washington (1 Stat. 372; *Field* v. *Clark,* 143 U.S. 649, 683) Congress authorized the President, when Congress was not in session, and for a prescribed period "whenever, in his opinion, the public safety shall so require, to lay an embargo . . . and to continue or revoke the same, whenever he shall think proper." By an act of September 21, 1922 (42 Stat. 858, 941, 945), sustained in *Hampton & Co.* v. *United States, supra,* the President was empowered to increase or decrease tariff duties so as to equalize the differences between the costs of production at home and abroad, and empowered, by the same means, to give redress for other acts of discrimination or unfairness "when he finds that the public interest will be served thereby." The President was not required either by the Constitution or by any statute to state the reasons that had induced him to exercise the granted power. It is enough that the

grant of power had been made and that pursuant to that grant he had signified the will to act. The will to act being declared, the law presumes that the declaration was preceded by due inquiry and that it was rooted in sufficient grounds. Such, for a hundred years and more, has been the doctrine of this court.

SCHECHTER CORP. v. UNITED STATES

MR. CHIEF JUSTICE HUGHES delivered the opinion of the Court.

Petitioners in No. 854 were convicted in the District Court of the United States for the Eastern District of New York on eighteen counts of an indictment charging violations of what is known as the "Live Poultry Code," and on an additional count for conspiracy to commit such violations. By demurrer to the indictment and appropriate motions on the trial, the defendants contended (1) that the Code had been adopted pursuant to an unconstitutional delegation by Congress of legislative power; (2) that it attempted to regulate intrastate transactions which lay outside the authority of Congress; and (3) that in certain provisions it was repugnant to the due process clause of the Fifth Amendment.

New York City is the largest live-poultry market in the United States. Ninety-six percent of the live poultry there marketed comes from other states. . . . A. L. A. Schechter Poultry Corporation and Schechter Live Poultry Market are corporations conducting wholesale poultry slaughterhouse markets in Brooklyn, New York City. . . .

Defendants ordinarily purchase their live poultry from commission men at the West Washington Market in New York City or at the railroad terminals serving the City, but occasionally they purchase from commission men in Philadelphia. They buy the poultry for slaughter and resale. . . . Defendants do not sell poultry in interstate commerce.

The "Live Poultry Code" was promulgated under §3 of the National Industrial Recovery Act. That section . . . authorizes the President to approve "codes of fair competition." Such a code may be approved for a trade or industry, upon application by one or more trade or industrial associations or groups, if the President finds (1) that such associations or groups "impose no inequitable restrictions on admission to membership therein and are truly representative," and (2) that such codes are not designed "to promote monopolies or to eliminate or oppress small enterprises and will not operate to discriminate against them, and will tend to effectuate the policy" of Title I of the Act. . . .

The "Live Poultry Code" was approved by the President on April 13, 1934. . . .

The Code fixes the number of hours for workdays. It provides that no employee, with certain exceptions, shall be permitted to work in excess of forty (40) hours in any one week, and that no employee, save as stated, "shall be paid in any pay period less than at the rate of fifty (50) cents per hour." The article containing "general labor provisions" prohibits the employment of any person under sixteen years of age, and declares that employees shall have the right of "collective bargaining," and freedom of choice with respect to labor organizations, in the terms of §7(a) of the Act. The minimum number of employees, who shall be employed by slaughterhouse operators, is fixed, the number being graduated according to the average volume of weekly sales.

Provision is made for administration through an "industry advisory committee," to be selected by trade associations and members of the industry, and a "code supervisor" to be appointed, with the approval of the committee, by agreement between the Secretary of Agriculture and the Administrator for Industrial Recovery. The expenses of administration are to be borne by the members of the industry proportionately upon the basis of volume of business, or such other factors as the advisory committee may deem equitable, "subject to the disapproval of the Secretary and/or Administrator."

Of the eighteen counts of the indictment upon which the defendants were convicted, aside from the count for conspiracy, two counts charged violation of the minimum wage and maximum hour provisions of the Code, and ten counts were for violation of the requirement (found in the "trade practice provisions") of "straight killing." This requirement was really one of "straight" selling. The term "straight killing" was defined in the Code as "the practice of requiring persons purchasing poultry for resale to accept the run of any half coop, coop, or coops, as purchased by slaughterhouse operators, except for culls." The charges in the ten counts, respectively, were that the defendants in selling to retail dealers and butchers had permitted "selections of individual chickens taken from particular coops and half coops."

. . . We are told that the provision of the statute authorizing the adoption of codes must be viewed in the light of the grave national crisis with which Congress was confronted. Undoubtedly, the conditions to which power is addressed are always to be considered when the exercise of power is challenged. Extraordinary conditions may call for extraordinary remedies. But the argument necessarily stops short of an attempt to justify action which lies outside the sphere of constitutional authority. Extraordinary conditions do not create or enlarge constitutional power. The Constitution established a national government with powers deemed to be adequate, as they have proved to be both in war and peace, but these powers of the national government are limited by the constitutional grants. Those who act under these grants are not at liberty to transcend the imposed limits because they believe that more or different power is necessary. . . .

The further point is urged that the national crisis demanded a broad and intensive coöperative effort by those engaged in trade and industry, and that this necessary coöperation was sought to be fostered by permitting them to initiate the adoption of codes. But the statutory plan is not simply one for voluntary effort. It does not seek merely to endow voluntary trade or industrial associations or groups with privileges or immunities. It involves the coercive exercise of the law-making power. The codes of fair competition which the statute attempts to authorize are codes of laws. If valid, they place all persons within their reach under the obligation of positive law, binding equally those who assent and those who do not assent. . . .

Second. The question of the delegation of legislative power. We recently had occasion to review the pertinent decisions and the general principles which govern the determination of this question. *Panama Refining Co.* v. *Ryan,* 293 U.S. 388. . . . The Congress is not permitted to abdicate or to transfer to others the essential legislative functions with which it is thus vested. We have repeatedly recognized the necessity of adapting legislation to complex conditions involving a host of details with which the national legislature cannot deal directly. . . . But we said that the constant recognition of the necessity and validity of such provisions, and the wide range of administrative authority which has been developed by means of them, cannot be allowed to obscure the limitations of the authority to delegate, if our constitutional system is to be maintained. . . . As to the "codes of fair competition," under §3 of the Act, the question is more fundamental. It is whether there is any adequate definition of the subject to which the codes are to be addressed.

The question, then, turns upon the authority which §3 of the Recovery Act vests in the President to approve or prescribe. If the codes have standing as penal statutes, this must be due to the effect of the executive action. But Congress cannot delegate legislative power to the President to exercise an unfettered discretion to make whatever laws he thinks may be needed or advisable for the rehabilitation and expansion of trade or industry.

To summarize and conclude upon this point: Section 3 of the Recovery Act is without precedent. It supplies no standards for any trade, industry or activity. It does not undertake to prescribe rules of conduct to be applied to particular states of fact determined by appropriate administrative procedure. Instead of prescribing rules of conduct, it authorizes the making of codes to prescribe them. For that legislative undertaking, §3 sets up no standards, aside from the statement of the general aims of rehabilitation, correction and expansion described in section one. In view of the scope of that broad declaration, and of the nature of the few restrictions that are imposed, the discretion of the President in approving or prescribing codes, and thus enacting laws for the government of trade and industry throughout the country, is virtually unfettered. We think that the code-making authority thus conferred is an unconstitutional delegation of legislative power.

(1) Were these transactions *"in"* interstate commerce? Much is made of the fact that almost all the poultry coming to New York is sent there from other States. But the code provisions, as here applied, do not concern the transportation of the poultry from other States to New York, or the transactions of the commission men or others to whom it is consigned, or the sales made by such consignees to defendants. When defendants had made their purchases, whether at the West Washington Market in New York City or at the railroad terminals serving the City, or elsewhere, the poultry was trucked to their slaughterhouses in Brooklyn for local disposition. The interstate transactions in relation to that poultry then ended.

The undisputed facts thus afford no warrant for the argument that the poultry handled by defendants at their slaughterhouse markets was in a *"current"* or *"flow"* of interstate commerce and was thus subject to congressional regulation. The mere fact that there may be a constant flow of commodities into a State does not mean that the flow continues after the property has arrived and has become commingled with the mass of property within the State and is there held solely for local disposition and use. So far as the poultry here in question is concerned, the flow in interstate commerce had ceased. The poultry had come to a permanent rest within the State. . . . Hence, decisions which deal with a stream of interstate commerce — where goods come to rest within a State temporarily and are later to go forward in interstate commerce — and with the regulations of

transactions involved in that practical continuity of movement, are not applicable here.

(2) Did the defendants' transactions directly *"affect"* interstate commerce so as to be subject to federal regulation? The power of Congress extends not only to the regulation of transactions which are part of interstate commerce, but to the protection of that commerce from injury. It matters not that the injury may be due to the conduct of those engaged in intrastate operations. Thus, Congress may protect the safety of those employed in interstate transportation "no matter what may be the source of the dangers which threaten it." *Southern Ry. Co.* v. *United States,* 222 U.S. 20, 27. We said in *Second Employers' Liability Cases,* 223 U.S. 1, 51, that it is the "effect upon interstate commerce," not "the source of the injury," which is "the criterion of congressional power."

In determining how far the federal government may go in controlling intrastate transactions upon the ground that they "affect" interstate commerce, there is a necessary and well-established distinction between direct and indirect effects. The precise line can be drawn only as individual cases arise, but the distinction is clear in principle. Direct effects are illustrated by the railroad cases we have cited, as *e.g.,* the effect of failure to use prescribed safety appliances on railroads which are the highways of both interstate and intrastate commerce, injury to an employee engaged in interstate transportation by the negligence of an employee engaged in an intrastate movement, the fixing of rates for intrastate transportation which unjustly discriminate against interstate commerce. But where the effect of intrastate transactions upon interstate commerce is merely indirect, such transactions remain within the domain of state power. If the commerce clause were construed to reach all enterprises and transactions which could be said to have an indirect effect upon interstate commerce, the federal authority would embrace practically all the activities of the people and the authority of the State over its domestic concerns would exist only by sufferance of the federal government. . . . The persons employed in slaughtering and selling in local trade are not employed in interstate commerce. Their hours and wages have no direct relation to interstate commerce.

The argument of the Government proves too much. If the federal government may determine the wages and hours of employees in the internal commerce of a State, because of their relation to cost and prices and their indirect effect upon interstate commerce, it would seem that a similar control might be exerted over other elements of cost, also affecting prices, such as the number of employees, rents, advertising, methods of doing business, etc. All the processes of production and distribution that enter into cost could likewise be controlled. . . .

The Government also makes the point that efforts to enact state legislation establishing high labor standards have been impeded by the belief that unless similar action is taken generally, commerce will be diverted from the States adopting such standards . . . of wages and hours. The apparent implication is that the federal authority under the commerce clause should be deemed to extend to the establishment of rules to govern wages and hours in intrastate trade and industry generally throughout the country, thus overriding the authority of the States to deal with domestic problems. . . .

It is not the province of the Court to consider the economic advantages or disadvantages of such a centralized system. It is sufficient to say that the Federal Constitution does not provide for it. . . . The authority of the federal government may not be pushed to such an extreme as to destroy the distinction, which the commerce clause itself establishes, between commerce "among the several States" and the internal concerns of a State.

On both the grounds we have discussed, the attempted delegation of legislative power, and the attempted regulation of intrastate transactions which affect interstate commerce only indirectly, we hold the code provisions here in question to be invalid and that the judgment of conviction must be reversed.

MR. JUSTICE CARDOZO, concurring.

The delegated power of legislation which has found expression in this code is not canalized within banks that keep it from overflowing. It is unconfined and vagrant, if I may borrow my own words in an earlier opinion. . . .

This court has held that delegation may be unlawful though the act to be performed is definite and single, if the necessity, time and occasion of performance have been left in the end to the discretion of the delegate. *Panama Refining Co.* v. *Ryan, supra.* I thought that ruling went too far. . . . Here in effect is a roving commission to inquire into evils and upon discovery correct them. . . . If that conception shall prevail, anything that Congress may do within the limits of the commerce clause for the betterment of business may be done by the President upon the recommendation of a trade association by calling it a code. . . .

I am authorized to state that MR. JUSTICE STONE joins in this opinion.

CARTER v. CARTER COAL CO.

MR. JUSTICE SUTHERLAND delivered the opinion of the Court.

The purposes of the "Bituminous Coal Conservation Act of 1935," involved in these suits, as declared by the title, are to stabilize the bituminous coal-mining industry and promote its interstate commerce:

By the terms of the act, every producer of bituminous coal within the United States is brought within its provisions. . . . The act confers the power to fix the minimum price of coal at each and every coal mine in the United States, with such price variations as the board may deem necessary and proper. There is also a provision authorizing the commission, when deemed necessary in the public interest, to establish maximum prices in order to protect the consumer against unreasonably high prices. Certain recitals contained in the act plainly suggest that its makers were of opinion that its constitutionality could be sustained under some general federal power, thought to exist, apart from the specific grants of the Constitution. The fallacy of that view will be apparent when we recall fundamental principles which, although hitherto often expressed in varying forms of words, will bear repetition whenever their accuracy seems to be challenged. The recitals to which we refer are contained in §1 (which is simply a preamble to the act), and, among others, are to the effect that the distribution of bituminous coal is of national interest, affecting the health and comfort of the people and the general welfare of the nation. . . . These affirmations — and the further ones that the production and distribution of such coal "directly affect interstate commerce," do not constitute an exertion of the *will* of Congress which is legislation, but a recital of considerations which in the *opinion* of that body existed and justified the expression of its will in the present act. Nevertheless, this preamble may not be disregarded. On the contrary it is important, because it makes clear, except for the pure assumption that the conditions described "directly" affect interstate commerce, that the powers which Congress undertook to exercise are not specific but of the most general character.

Whether the end sought to be attained by an act of Congress is legitimate is wholly a matter of constitutional power and not at all of legislative discretion. Legislative congressional discretion begins with the choice of means and ends with the adoption of methods and details to carry the delegated powers into effect. . . . It may be said that to a constitutional end many ways are open; but to an end not within the terms of the Constitution, all ways are closed.

The proposition, often advanced and as often discredited, that the power of the federal government inherently extends to purposes affecting the nation as a whole with which the states severally cannot deal or cannot adequately deal, and the related notion that Congress, entirely apart from those powers delegated by the Constitution, may enact laws to promote the general welfare, have never been accepted but always definitely rejected by this court. . . . Since the validity of the act depends upon whether it is a regulation of interstate commerce, the nature and extent of the power conferred upon Congress by the commerce clause becomes the determinative question. . . .

As used in the Constitution, the word "commerce" is the equivalent of the phrase "intercourse for the purposes of trade," and includes transportation, purchase, sale, and exchange of commodities between the citizens of the different states. And the power to regulate commerce embraces the instruments by which commerce is carried on.

That commodities produced or manufactured within a state are intended to be sold or transported outside the state does not render their production or manufacture subject to federal regulation under the commerce clause. . . . Plainly, the incidents leading up to and culminating in the mining of coal do not constitute such intercourse. The employment of men, the fixing of their wages, hours of labor and working conditions, the bargaining in respect of these things — whether carried on separately or collectively — each and all constitute intercourse for the purposes of production, not of trade. The latter is a thing apart from the relation of employer and employee, which in all producing occupations is purely local in character. Extraction of coal from the mine is the aim and the completed result of local activities. Commerce in the coal mined is not brought into being by force of these activities, but by negotiations, agreements, and circumstances entirely apart from production. Mining brings the subject matter of commerce into existence. Commerce disposes of it.

. . . Everything which moves in interstate commerce has had a local origin. Without local production somewhere, interstate commerce, as now carried on, would practically disappear. Neverthe-

less, the local character of mining, of manufacturing and of crop growing is a fact, and remains a fact, whatever may be done with the products.

Certain decisions of this court, superficially considered, seem to lend support to the defense of the act now under review. But upon examination, they will be seen to be inapposite.

Another group of cases, of which *Swift & Co.* v. *United States,* 196 U.S. 375, is an example, rest upon the circumstance that the acts in question constituted direct interferences with the "flow" of commerce among the states. In the *Swift* case, livestock was consigned and delivered to stockyards — not as a place of final destination, but, as the court said in *Stafford* v. *Wallace,* 258 U.S. 495, 516, "a throat through which the current flows." The sales which ensued merely changed the private interest in the subject of the current without interfering with its continuity.

The restricted field covered by the *Swift* and kindred cases is illustrated by the *Schechter* case, *supra,* p. 543. There the commodity in question, although shipped from another state, had come to rest in the state of its destination, and, as the court pointed out, was no longer in a current or flow of interstate commerce. The *Swift* doctrine was rejected as inapposite. In the *Schechter* case the flow had ceased. Here it had not begun. The difference is not one of substance. The applicable principle is the same.

Whether the effect of a given activity or condition is direct or indirect is not always easy to determine. The word "direct" implies that the activity or condition invoked or blamed shall operate proximately — not mediately, remotely, or collaterally — to produce the effect. It connotes the absence of an efficient intervening agency or condition. And the extent of the effect bears no logical relation to its character. The distinction between a direct and an indirect effect turns, not upon the magnitude of either the cause or the effect, but entirely upon the manner in which the effect has been brought about. If the production by one man of a single ton of coal intended for interstate sale and shipment, and actually so sold and shipped, affects interstate commerce indirectly, the effect does not become direct by multiplying the tonnage, or increasing the number of men employed, or adding to the expense or complexities of the business, or by all combined. It is quite true that rules of law are sometimes qualified by considerations of degree, as the government argues. But the matter of degree has no bearing upon the question here, since that question is not — What is the *extent* of the local activity or condition, or the *extent* of the effect produced upon interstate commerce? but — What is the *relation* between the activity or condition and the effect?

Much stress is put upon the evils which come from the struggle between employers and employees over the matter of wages, working conditions, the right of collective bargaining, etc., and the resulting strikes, curtailment and irregularity of production and effect on prices; and it is insisted that interstate commerce is *greatly* affected thereby. But, in addition to what has just been said, the conclusive answer is that the evils are all local evils over which the federal government has no legislative control. . . . Such effect as they may have upon commerce, however extensive it may be, is secondary and indirect. An increase in the greatness of the effect adds to its importance. It does not alter its character.

. . . The conclusion is unavoidable that the price-fixing provisions of the code are so related to and dependent upon the labor provisions as conditions, considerations or compensations, as to make it clearly probable that the latter being held bad, the former would not have been passed. The fall of the latter, therefore, carries down with it the former. . . .

The price-fixing provisions of the code are thus disposed of without coming to the question of their constitutionality.

Separate opinion of MR. CHIEF JUSTICE HUGHES.

I do not think that the question of separability should be determined by trying to imagine what Congress would have done if certain provisions found to be invalid were excised. That, if taken broadly, would lead us into a realm of pure speculation.

MR. JUSTICE CARDOZO (dissenting in Nos. 636, 649 and 650, and in No. 651 concurring in the result).

My conclusions compendiously stated are these:

(a) Part II of the statute sets up a valid system of price-fixing as applied to transactions in interstate commerce and to those in intrastate commerce where interstate commerce is directly or intimately affected. The prevailing opinion holds nothing to the contrary.

. . . Mining and agriculture and manufacture are not interstate commerce considered by themselves, yet their relation to that commerce may be such that for the protection of the one there is need to regulate the other. *Schechter Poultry Corp.* v. *United States,* 295 U.S. 495, 544, 545, 546. Sometimes it is said that the relation must be "direct" to bring that power into play. In many circumstances such a de-

scription will be sufficiently precise to meet the needs of the occasion. But a great principle of constitutional law is not susceptible of comprehensive statement in an adjective. The underlying thought is merely this, that "the law is not indifferent to considerations of degree." *Schechter Poultry Corp.* v. *United States, supra,* concurring opinion, p. 554. It cannot be indifferent to them without an expansion of the commerce clause that would absorb or imperil the reserved powers of the states. A survey of the cases shows that the words have been interpreted with suppleness of adaptation and flexibility of meaning. The power is as broad as the need that evokes it.

One of the most common and typical instances of a relation characterized as direct has been that between interstate and intrastate rates for carriers by rail where the local rates are so low as to divert business unreasonably from interstate competitors. In such circumstances Congress has the power to protect the business of its carriers against disintegrating encroachments. *Shreveport Case,* 234 U.S. 342, 351, 352. . . . To be sure, the relation even then may be characterized as indirect if one is nice or over-literal in the choice of words. Strictly speaking, the intrastate rates have a primary effect upon the intrastate traffic and not upon any other, though the repercussions of the competitive system may lead to secondary consequences affecting interstate traffic also.

What has been said in this regard is said with added certitude when complainants' business is considered in the light of the statistics exhibited in the several records. In No. 636, the Carter case, the complainant has admitted that "substantially all" (over 97½%) of the sales of the Carter Company are made in interstate commerce.

My vote is for affirmance.

I am authorized to state that MR. JUSTICE BRANDEIS and MR. JUSTICE STONE join in this opinion.

NLRB v. Jones & Laughlin Steel Corp.

301 U.S. 1 (1937)
Vote: 5–4

The National Labor Relations Act (the Wagner Act) was passed in 1935 to replace the labor provisions of the invalidated NIRA, and it remains the basis for U.S. labor relations today. It recognized a right of workers to organize, and prohibited specified unfair practices for employers engaged in interstate commerce. The National Labor Relations Board found the Jones & Laughlin Steel Corporation, the fourth largest steel producer in the country, in violation of the Act. It petitioned a U.S. circuit court of appeals (as specified in the statute) to order compliance with its findings. The court held the Act unconstitutional and the Board appealed.

MR. CHIEF JUSTICE HUGHES delivered the opinion of the Court.

In a proceeding under the National Labor Relations Act of 1935, the National Labor Relations Board found that the respondent, Jones & Laughlin Steel Corporation, had violated the Act by engaging in unfair labor practices affecting commerce. The proceeding was instituted by the Beaver Valley Lodge No. 200, affiliated with the Amalgamated Association of Iron, Steel and Tin Workers of America, a labor organization. The unfair labor practices charged were that the corporation was discriminating against members of the union with regard to hire and tenure of employment, and was coercing and intimidating its employees in order to interfere with their self-organization. The discriminatory and coercive action alleged was the discharge of certain employees.

The National Labor Relations Board, sustaining the charge, ordered the corporation to cease and desist from such discrimination and coercion, to offer reinstatement to ten of the employees named, to make good their losses in pay, and to post for thirty days notices that the corporation would not discharge or discriminate against members, or those desiring to become members, of the labor union. As the corporation failed to comply, the Board petitioned the Circuit Court of Appeals to enforce the order. The court denied the petition, holding that the order lay beyond the range of federal power. 83 F. (2d) 998. We granted certiorari.

The scheme of the National Labor Relations Act — which is too long to be quoted in full — may be briefly stated. The first section sets forth findings with respect to the injury to commerce resulting from the denial by employers of the right to employees to organize and from the refusal of employers to accept the procedure of collective bargaining. There follows a declaration that it is the policy of the United States to eliminate these causes of obstruction to the free flow of commerce. The Act then defines the terms it uses, including the terms "commerce" and "affecting commerce." §2. It creates the National Labor Rela-

tions Board and prescribes its organization. §§3–6. It sets forth the right of employees to self-organization and to bargain collectively through representatives of their own choosing. §7. It defines "unfair labor practices." §8. It lays down rules as to the representation of employees for the purpose of collective bargaining. §9. The Board is empowered to prevent the described unfair labor practices affecting commerce and the Act prescribes the procedure to that end. The Board is authorized to petition designated courts to secure the enforcement of its orders.

The facts as to the nature and scope of the business of the Jones & Laughlin Steel Corporation have been found by the Labor Board and, so far as they are essential to the determination of this controversy, they are not in dispute. The Labor Board has found: The corporation is organized under the laws of Pennsylvania and has its principal office at Pittsburgh. It is engaged in the business of manufacturing iron and steel in plants situated in Pittsburgh and nearby Aliquippa, Pennsylvania. It manufactures and distributes a widely diversified line of steel and pig iron, being the fourth largest producer of steel in the United States. With its subsidiaries — nineteen in number — it is a completely integrated enterprise, owning and operating ore, coal and limestone properties, lake and river transportation facilities and terminal railroads located at its manufacturing plants. It owns or controls mines in Michigan and Minnesota. It operates four ore steamships on the Great Lakes, used in the transportation of ore to its factories. It owns coal mines in Pennsylvania. It operates towboats and steam barges used in carrying coal to its factories. It owns limestone properties in various places in Pennsylvania and West Virginia. It owns the Monongahela connecting railroad which connects the plants of the Pittsburgh works and forms an interconnection with the Pennsylvania, New York Central and Baltimore and Ohio Railroad systems. . . . Much of its product is shipped to its warehouses in Chicago, Detroit, Cincinnati and Memphis, — to the last two places by means of its own barges and transportation equipment. In Long Island City, New York, and in New Orleans it operates structural steel fabricating shops in connection with the warehousing of semi-finished materials sent from its works. . . .

Respondent points to evidence that the Aliquippa plant, in which the discharged men were employed, contains complete facilities for the production of finished and semi-finished iron and steel products from raw materials. . . .

First. The scope of the Act. — The Act is challenged in its entirety as an attempt to regulate all industry, thus invading the reserved powers of the States over their local concerns. . . . The authority of the federal government may not be pushed to such an extreme as to destroy the distinction, which the commerce clause itself establishes, between commerce "among the several States" and the internal concerns of a State. That distinction between what is national and what is local in the activities of commerce is vital to the maintenance of our federal system. *Id.*

But we are not at liberty to deny effect to specific provisions, which Congress has constitutional power to enact, by superimposing upon them inferences from general legislative declarations of an ambiguous character, even if found in the same statute. The cardinal principle of statutory construction is to save and not to destroy. We have repeatedly held that as between two possible interpretations of a statute by one of which it would be unconstitutional and by the other valid, our plain duty is to adopt that which will save the act. Even to avoid a serious doubt the rule is the same.

We think it clear that the National Labor Relations Act may be construed so as to operate within the sphere of constitutional authority. The jurisdiction conferred upon the Board, and invoked in this instance, is found in §10(a), which provides:

"SEC. 10(a). The Board is empowered, as hereinafter provided, to prevent any person from engaging in any unfair labor practice (listed in section 8) affecting commerce."

The critical words of this provision, prescribing the limits of the Board's authority in dealing with the labor practices, are "affecting commerce." . . . This definition is one of exclusion as well as inclusion. The grant of authority to the Board does not purport to extend to the relationship between all industrial employees and employers. Its terms do not impose collective bargaining upon all industry regardless of effects upon interstate or foreign commerce. It purports to reach only what may be deemed to burden or obstruct that commerce and, thus qualified, it must be construed as contemplating the exercise of control within constitutional bounds. . . . Whether or not particular action does affect commerce in such a close and intimate fashion as to be subject to federal control, and hence to lie within the authority conferred upon the Board, is left by the statute to be determined as individual cases arise. We are thus to inquire whether in the instant case the constitutional boundary has been passed.

Second. The unfair labor practices in question. —
. . . The statute goes no further than to safeguard the right of employees to self-organization and to select representatives of their own choosing for collec-

tive bargaining or other mutual protection without restraint or coercion by their employer.

That is a fundamental right. Employees have as clear a right to organize and select their representatives for lawful purposes as the respondent has to organize its business and select its officers and agents. Discrimination and coercion to prevent the free exercise of the right of employees to self-organization and representation is a proper subject for condemnation by competent legislative authority.

Third. The application of the Act to employees engaged in production. — The principle involved. —
Respondent says that whatever may be said of employees engaged in interstate commerce, the industrial relations and activities in the manufacturing department of respondent's enterprise are not subject to federal regulation. The argument rests upon the proposition that manufacturing in itself is not commerce.

The Government distinguishes these cases. The various parts of respondent's enterprise are described as interdependent and as thus involving "a great movement of iron ore, coal and limestone along well-defined paths to the steel mills, thence through them, and thence in the form of steel products into the consuming centers of the country — a definite and well-understood course of business." It is urged that these activities constitute a "stream" or "flow" of commerce, of which the Aliquippa manufacturing plant is the focal point, and that industrial strife at that point would cripple the entire movement. Reference is made to our decision sustaining the Packers and Stockyards Act. *Stafford* v. *Wallace,* 258 U.S. 495. The Court found that the stockyards were but a "throat" through which the current of commerce flowed and the transactions which there occurred could not be separated from that movement.

We do not find it necessary to determine whether these features of defendant's business dispose of the asserted analogy to the "stream of commerce" cases. The instances in which the metaphor has been used are but particular, and not exclusive, illustrations of the protective power which the Government invokes in support of the present Act. The congressional authority to protect interstate commerce from burdens and obstructions is not limited to transactions which can be deemed to be an essential part of a "flow" of interstate or foreign commerce. Burdens and obstructions may be due to injurious action springing from other sources. The fundamental principle is that the power to regulate commerce is the power to enact "all appropriate legislation" for "its protection and advancement." That power is plenary and may be exerted to protect interstate com-

as a "necessary and proper" implementation of the power of Congress over interstate commerce.

The Government's concern lest the Act be held to be a regulation of production or consumption, rather than of marketing, is attributable to a few dicta and decisions of this Court which might be understood to lay it down that activities such as "production," "manufacturing," and "mining" are strictly "local" and, except in special circumstances which are not present here, cannot be regulated under the commerce power because their effects upon interstate commerce are, as matter of law, only "indirect."

We believe that a review of the course of decision under the Commerce Clause will make plain, however, that questions of power of Congress are not to be decided by reference to any formula which would give controlling force to nomenclature such as "production" and "indirect" and foreclose consideration of the actual effects of the activity in question upon interstate commerce.

At the beginning Chief Justice Marshall described the federal commerce power with a breadth never yet exceeded. *Gibbons* v. *Ogden,* 9 Wheat 1, 194–195. He made emphatic the embracing and penetrating nature of this power by warning that effective restraints on its exercise must proceed from political rather than judicial processes. *Id.* at 197.

In the *Shreveport Rate Cases,* 234 U.S. 342, the Court held that railroad rates of an admittedly intrastate charcter and fixed by authority of the state might, nevertheless, be revised by the Federal Government because of the economic effects which they had upon interstate commerce.

The Court's recognition of the relevance of the economic effects in the application of the Commerce Clause, exemplified by this statement, has made the mechanical application of legal formulas no longer feasible. Once an economic measure of the reach of the power granted to Congress in the Commerce Clause is accepted, questions of federal power cannot be decided simply by finding the activity in question to be "production," nor can consideration of its economic effects be foreclosed by calling them "indirect."

Whether the subject of the regulation in question was "production," "consumption," or "marketing" is, therefore, not material for purposes of deciding the question of federal power before us. That an activity is of local character may help in a doubtful case to determine whether Congress intended to reach it. The same consideration might help in determining whether in the absence of Congressional action it would be permissible for the state to exert its power

on the subject matter, even though in so doing it to some degree affected interstate commerce. But even if appellee's activity be local and though it may not be regarded as commerce, it may still, whatever its nature, be reached by Congress if it exerts a substantial economic effect on interstate commerce, and this irrespective of whether such effect is what might at some earlier time have been defined as "direct" or "indirect."

. . . That appellee's own contribution to the demand for wheat may be trivial by itself is not enough to remove him from the scope of federal regulation where, as here, his contribution, taken together with that of many others similarly situated, is far from trivial. . . . It can hardly be denied that a factor of such volume and variability as home-consumed wheat would have a substantial influence on price and market conditions. This may arise because being in marketable condition such wheat overhangs the market and, if induced by rising prices, tends to flow into the market and check price increases. But if we assume that it is never marketed, it supplies a need of the man who grew it which would otherwise be reflected by purchases in the open market. Home-grown wheat in this sense competes with wheat in commerce. The stimulation of commerce is a use of the regulatory function quite as definitely as prohibitions or restrictions thereon. This record leaves us no doubt that Congress may properly have considered that wheat consumed on the farm where grown, if wholly outside the scheme of regulation, would have a substantial effect in defeating and obstructing its purpose to stimulate trade therein at increased prices.

It is said, however, that this Act, forcing some farmers into the market to buy what they could provide for themselves, is an unfair promotion of the markets and prices of specializing wheat growers. It is of the essence of regulation that it lays a restraining hand on the self-interest of the regulated and that advantages from the regulation commonly fall to others. The conflicts of economic interest between the regulated and those who advantage by it are wisely left under our system to resolution by the Congress under its more flexible and responsible legislative process. Such conflicts rarely lend themselves to judicial determination. And with the wisdom, workability, or fairness, of the plan of regulation we have nothing to do.

Appellee's claim that the Act works a deprivation of due process . . . is not persuasive. Appellee's claim is not that his quota represented less than a fair share of the national quota, but that the Fifth

Amendment requires that he be free from penalty for planting wheat and disposing of his crop as he sees fit.

We do not agree. In its effort to control total supply, the Government gave the farmer a choice which was, of course, designed to encourage coöperation and discourage non-coöperation. The farmer who planted within his allotment was in effect guaranteed a minimum return above what his wheat would have brought if sold on a world market basis. . . . It is hardly lack of due process for the Government to regulate that which it subsidizes.

That appellee is the worse off for the aggregate of this legislation does not appear; it only appears that, if he could get all that the Government gives and do nothing that the Government asks, he would be better off than this law allows. To deny him this is not to deny him due process of law. . . .

Reversed.

Heart of Atlanta Motel v. U.S.

379 U.S. 241 (1964)
Vote: 9–0

In 1964, Congress acted to end segregation in hotel and restaurant establishments in the United States. Acting on advice from the Department of Justice, the Civil Rights Act of 1964 grounded these aims in the Commerce Clause, finding that racial and other arbitrary denials of food and facilities discouraged vulnerable minorities from undertaking interstate travel. A three-judge federal court ordered the motel to admit blacks, and the motel appealed.

In a companion case, *Katzenbach* v. *McClung* (1964), the Attorney General appealed a three-judge district court holding that McClung's Barbecue was not regulatable, though over half the food served there had moved in interstate commerce. Justice Clark held that direct evidence linking discrimination in service with any flow of interstate food was not necessary to sustain the legislation. It was enough that Congress could rationally conclude that discrimination affect commerce generally, and to establish that the restaurant fell within the constitutional and statutory definitions of regulatable establishments.

MR. JUSTICE CLARK delivered the opinion of the Court.

This is a declaratory judgment action, 28 U.S.C. §2201 and §2202 (1958 ed.), attacking the constitutionality of Title II of the Civil Rights Act of 1964.

The case comes here on admissions and stipulated facts. Appellant owns and operates the Heart of Atlanta Motel which has 216 rooms available to transient guests. . . . Appellant solicits patronage from outside the State of Georgia through various national advertising media, including magazines of national circulation; it maintains over 50 billboards and highway signs within the State, soliciting patronage for the motel; it accepts convention trade from outside Georgia and approximately 75% of its registered guests are from out of State. Prior to passage of the Act the motel had followed a practice of refusing to rent rooms to Negroes, and it alleged that it intended to continue to do so. In an effort to perpetuate that policy this suit was filed.

The appellant contends that Congress in passing this Act exceeded its power to regulate commerce under Art. I, §8, cl. 3, of the Constitution of the United States; that the Act violates the Fifth Amendment because appellant is deprived of the right to choose its customers and operate its business as it wishes, resulting in a taking of its liberty and property without due process of law and a taking of its property without just compensation; and, finally, that by requiring appellant to rent available rooms to Negroes against its will, Congress is subjecting it to involuntary servitude in contravention of the Thirteenth Amendment.

Since Title II is the only portion under attack here, we confine our consideration to those public accommodation provisions. There are listed in §201(b) four classes of business establishments, each of which "serves the public" and "is a place of public accommodation" within the meaning of §201(a) "if its operations affect commerce, or if discrimination or segregation by it is supported by State action." The covered establishments are:

"(1) any inn, hotel, motel, or other establishment which provides lodgings to transient guests, other than an establishment located within a building which contains not more than five rooms for rent or hire and which is actually occupied by the proprietor of such establishment as his residence;

"(2) any restaurant, cafeteria. . . [not here involved];

"(3) any motion picture house... [not here involved];

"(4) any establishment... which is physically located within the premises of any establishment otherwise covered by this subsection, or... within the premises of which is physically located any such covered establishment... [not here involved]."

Section 201(c) defines the phrase "affect commerce" as applied to the above establishments. It first declares that "any inn, hotel, motel, or other establishment which provides lodgings to transient guests," affects commerce *per se.*

It is admitted that the operation of the motel brings it within the provisions of §201(a) of the Act and that appellant refused to provide lodging for transient Negroes because of their race or color and that it intends to continue that policy unless restrained.

The sole question posed is, therefore, the constitutionality of the Civil Rights Act of 1964 as applied to these facts. The legislative history of the Act indicates that Congress based the Act on §5 and the Equal Protection Clause of the Fourteenth Amendment as well as its power to regulate interstate commerce under Art. I, §8, cl. 3, of the Constitution.

The Senate Commerce Committee made it quite clear that the fundamental object of Title II was to vindicate "the deprivation of personal dignity that surely accompanies denials of equal access to public establishments." At the same time, however, it noted that such an objective has been and could be readily achieved "by congressional action based on the commerce power of the Constitution." S. Rep. No. 872, *supra,* at 16–17. Our study of the legislative record, made in the light of prior cases, has brought us to the conclusion that Congress possessed ample power in this regard, and we have therefore not considered the other grounds relied upon. This is not to say that the remaining authority upon which it acts was not adequate, a question upon which we do not pass, but merely that since the commerce power is sufficient for our decision here we have considered it alone.

In light of our ground for decision, it might be well at the outset to discuss the *Civil Rights Cases, supra,* which declared provisions of the Civil Rights Act of 1875 unconstitutional.... Unlike Title II of the present legislation, the 1875 Act broadly proscribed discrimination in "inns, public conveyances on land or water, theaters, and other places of public amusement," without limiting the categories of affected businesses to those impinging upon interstate commerce. The sheer increase in volume of interstate traffic alone would give discriminatory practices which inhibit travel a far larger impact upon the Nation's commerce than such practices had on the economy of another day. Finally, there is language in the *Civil Rights Cases* which indicates that the Court did not fully consider whether the 1875 Act could be sustained as an exercise of commerce power.

While the Act as adopted carried no congressional findings the record of its passage through each house is replete with evidence of the burdens that discrimination by race or color places upon interstate commerce.

The power of Congress to deal with these obstructions depends on the meaning of the Commerce Clause. Its meaning was first enunciated 140 years ago by the great Chief Justice John Marshall in *Gibbons v. Ogden,* 9 Wheat. 1 (1824)....

It is said that the operation of the motel here is of a purely local character. But, assuming this to be true, "[i]f it is interstate commerce that feels the pinch, it does not matter how local the operation which applies the squeeze." *United States* v. *Women's Sportswear Mfrs. Assn.*

Thus the power of Congress to promote interstate commerce also includes the power to regulate the local incidents thereof, including local activities in both the States of origin and destination, which might have a substantial and harmful effect upon that commerce.... Congress may—as it has—prohibit racial discrimination by motels serving travelers, however "local" their operations may appear.

Nor does the Act deprive appellant of liberty or property under the Fifth Amendment. The commerce power invoked here by Congress is a specific and plenary one authorized by the Constitution itself. The only questions are: (1) whether Congress had a rational basis for finding that racial discrimination by motels affected commerce, and (2) if it had such a basis, whether the means it selected to eliminate that evil are reasonable and appropriate. If they are, appellant has no "right" to select its guests as it sees fit, free from governmental regulation.

There is nothing novel about such legislation. Thirty-two States now have it on their books either by statute or executive order and many cities provide such regulation. Some of these Acts go back four-score years. It has been repeatedly held by this Court that such laws do not violate the Due Process Clause of the Fourteenth Amendment....

We find no merit in the remainder of appellant's contentions, including that of "involuntary servitude." As we have seen, 32 States prohibit racial discrimination in public accommodations. These laws but codify the common-law innkeeper rule which long predated the Thirteenth Amendment. It is difficult to believe that the Amendment was intended to abrogate this principle. . . . It may be argued that Congress could have pursued other methods to eliminate the obstructions it found in interstate commerce caused by racial discrimination. But this is a matter of policy that rests entirely with the Congress, not with the courts. How obstructions in commerce may be removed—what means are to be employed—is within the sound and exclusive discretion of the Congress. It is subject only to one caveat—that the means chosen by it must be reasonably adapted to the end permitted by the Constitution. We cannot say that its choice here was not so adapted. The Constitution requires no more.

Adapted.

MR. JUSTICE BLACK, concurring.

The choice of policy is of course within the exclusive power of Congress; but whether particular operations affect interstate commerce sufficiently to come under the constitutional power of Congress to regulate them is ultimately a judicial rather than a legislative question, and can be settled finally only by this Court. I agree that as applied to this motel and this restaurant the Act is a valid exercise of congressional power, in the case of the motel because the record amply demonstrates that its practice of discrimination tended directly to interfere with interstate travel, and in the case of the restaurant because Congress had ample basis for concluding that a widespread practice of racial discrimination by restaurants buying as substantial a quantity of good shipped from other States as this restaurant buys could distort or impede interstate trade. I recognize that every remote, possible, speculative effect on commerce should not be accepted as an adequate constitutional ground to uproot and throw into discard all our traditional distinctions between what is purely local, and therefore controlled by state laws, and what affects the national interest and is therefore subject to control by federal laws. I recognize too that some isolated and remote lunchroom which sells only to local people and buys almost all its supplies in the locality may possibly be beyond the reach of the power of Congress to regulate commerce, just as such an establishment is not covered by the present Act. But in deciding the constitutional power of Congress in cases like the two before us we do not consider the effect on interstate commerce of only one isolated, individual, local event, without regard to the fact that this single local event when added to many others of a similar nature may impose a burden on interstate commerce by reducing its volume or distorting its flow.

MR. JUSTICE DOUGLAS, concurring. *[handwritten: Right to Travel – Due Process]*

Though I join the Court's opinions, I am somewhat reluctant here, as I was in *Edwards* v. *California,* 314 U.S. 160, 177, to rest solely on the Commerce Clause. My reluctance is not due to any conviction that Congress lacks power to regulate commerce in the interest of human rights. It is rather my belief that the right of people to be free of state action that discriminates against them because of race, like the "right of persons to move freely from State to State" (*Edwards* v. *California, supra,* at 177), "occupies a more protected position in our constitutional system than does the movement of cattle, fruit, steel and coal across state lines."

Hence I would prefer to rest on the assertion of legislative power contained in §5 of the Fourteenth Amendment which states: "The Congress shall have power to enforce, by appropriate legislation, the provisions of this article"—a power which the Court concedes was exercised at least in part in this Act.

A decision based on the Fourteenth Amendment would have a more settling effect, making unnecessary litigation over whether a particular restaurant or inn is within the commerce definitions of the Act or whether a particular customer is an interstate traveler. Under my construction, the Act would apply to all customers in all the enumerated places of public accommodation. And that construction would put an end to all obstructionist strategies and finally close one door on a bitter chapter in American history.

MR. JUSTICE GOLDBERG, concurring.

Federal Baseball Club v. National League

259 U.S. 200 (1922)
Vote: 9–0

This case plays much the same role in the baseball cases as *Paul* v. *Virginia* does for insurance (see Chapter 4). A private party—the Federal Baseball Club—sued for damages under the Sherman Antitrust Act, only to be told that baseball was not "commerce," and that the statute did not cover activities in that "game." Subsequent broader decisions on the Commerce Clause made the *Federal* decisions obsolete, and the Court's curious response should be contrasted with its cleaner work in the SOUTHEAST UNDERWRITERS Case (Chapter 4). Though the latter was controversial at that time, its effects are now generally accepted, in a way that the baseball cases are not.

MR. JUSTICE HOLMES delivered the opinion of the court.

This is a suit for threefold damages brought by the plaintiff in error under the Anti-Trust Acts of July 2, 1890, c. 647, §7, 26 Stat. 209, 210, and of October 15, 1914, c. 323, §4, 38 Stat. 730, 731.

A summary statement of the nature of the business involved will be enough to present the point. The clubs composing the Leagues are in different cities and for the most part in different States. The end of the elaborate organizations and sub-organizations that are described in the pleadings and evidence is that these clubs shall play against one another in public exhibitions for money, one or the other club crossing a state line in order to make the meeting possible. When as the result of these contests one club has won the pennant of its League and another club has won the pennant of the other League, there is a final competition for the world's championship between these two. Of course the scheme requires constantly repeated travelling on the part of the clubs, which is provided for, controlled and disciplined by the organizations, and this it is said means commerce among the States. But we are of opinion that the Court of Appeals was right.

The business is giving exhibitions of baseball, which are purely state affairs. It is true that, in order to attain for these exhibitions the great popularity that they have achieved, competitions must be arranged between clubs from different cities and States. But the fact that in order to give the exhibitions the Leagues must induce free persons to cross state lines and must arrange and pay for their doing so is not enough to change the character of the business. According to the distinction insisted upon in *Hooper* v. *California,* 155 U.S. 648, 655, the transport is a mere incident, not the essential thing. That to which it is incident, the exhibition, although made for money, would not be called trade or commerce in the commonly accepted use of those words. As it is put by the defendants, personal effort, not related to production, is not a subject of commerce. That which

in its consummation is not commerce does not become commerce among the States because the transportation that we have mentioned takes place. To repeat the illustrations given by the Court below, a firm of lawyers sending out a member to argue a case, or the Chautauqua lecture bureau sending out lecturers, does not engage in such commerce because the lawyer or lecturer goes to another State.

If we are right the plaintiff's business is to be described in the same way and the restrictions by contract that prevented the plaintiff from getting players to break their bargains and the other conduct charged against the defendants were not an interference with commerce among the States.

Judgment affirmed.

Toolson v. New York Yankees

346 U.S. 356 (1953)
Vote: 7–2

The logic of SOUTHEASTERN UNDERWRITERS would seem to dictate that the change of Commerce Clause concepts would result in the Antitrust Act's being applied to baseball. This would have ended the "reserve clause" and the baseball draft by which clubs obtain exclusive rights to deal with a player. Such an arrangement obviously violated the letter and spirit of the Sherman Act. The judges clearly were influenced by the fact that vital arrangements of the exclusive draft were directly threatened by a ruling that made baseball subject to antitrust laws. Is this a logical basis for a Supreme Court decision? Why should football, whose institutions also were created subsequent to, and in reliance on, FEDERAL BASEBALL CLUB, be treated differently? Does this suggest stare decisis is a highly limited and variable concept?

In *Flood* v. *Kuhn* (1972), Justice Blackmun solemnly "explained" that the exemption of the "national pastime" from rules applied to other sports (e.g., football and boxing) and live theater was an "established aberration." "It is an aberration that has been with us now for half a century; one heretofore deemed fully entitled to the benefit of stare decisis and one that has survived the Court's expanding concept of interstate commerce. It rests on a recognition and an acceptance of baseball's unique characteristics and needs."

PER CURIAM

In *Federal Baseball Club of Baltimore* v. *National League of Professional Baseball Clubs,* 259 U.S. 200 (1922), this Court held that the business of providing public baseball games for profit between clubs of professional baseball players was not within the scope of the federal antitrust laws. Congress has had the ruling under consideration but has not seen fit to bring such business under these laws by legislation having prospective effect. The business has thus been left for thirty years to develop, on the understanding that it was not subject to existing antitrust legislation. The present cases ask us to overrule the prior decision and, with retrospective effect, hold the legislation applicable. We think that if there are evils in this field which now warrant application to it of the antitrust laws it should be by legislation. Without reexamining the underlying issues, the judgments below are affirmed on the authority of *Federal Baseball Club of Baltimore* v. *National League of Professional Baseball Clubs, supra,* so far as that decision determines that Congress had no intention of including the business of baseball within the scope of the federal antitrust laws.

Affirmed.

MR. JUSTICE BURTON, with whom MR. JUSTICE REED concurs, dissenting.

Whatever may have been the situation when the *Federal Baseball Club* case was decided in 1922, I am not able to join in today's decision which, in effect, announces that organized baseball, in 1953, still is not engaged in interstate trade or commerce. In the light of organized baseball's well-known and widely distributed capital investments used in conducting competitions between teams constantly traveling between states, its receipts and expenditures of large sums transmitted between states, its numerous purchases of materials in interstate commerce, the attendance at its local exhibitions of large audiences often traveling across state lines, its radio and television activities which expand its audience beyond state lines, its sponsorship of interstate advertising, and its highly organized "farm system" of minor league baseball clubs, coupled with restrictive contracts and understandings between individuals

and among clubs or leagues playing for profit throughout the United States, and even in Canada, Mexico and Cuba, it is a contradiction in terms to say that the defendants in the cases before us are not now engaged in interstate trade or commerce as those terms are used in the Constitution of the United States and in the Sherman Act.

In the *Federal Baseball Club* case the Court did not state that even if the activities of organized baseball amounted to interstate commerce those activities were exempt from the Sherman Act. The Court acted on its determination that the activities before it did not amount to interstate commerce. The Court of Appeals for the District of Columbia, in that case, in 1920, described a major league baseball team as "local in its beginning and its end."

That the Court realized that the then incidental interstate features of organized baseball might rise to a magnitude that would compel recognition of them independently is indicated by the statement made in 1923 by Mr. Justice Holmes, the writer of the Court's opinion in the *Federal Baseball Club* case. In 1923, in considering a bill in equity alleging a violation of the Sherman Act by parties presenting local exhibitions on an interstate vaudeville circuit, the Court held that the bill should be considered on its merits and, in writing for the Court, Mr. Justice Holmes said "The bill was brought before the decision of the *Baseball Club Case,*" and it may be that what in general is incidental, in some instances may rise to a magnitude that requires it to be considered independently.

Conceding the major asset which baseball is to our Nation, the high place it enjoys in the hearts of our people and the possible justification of special treatment for organized sports which are engaged in interstate trade or commerce, the authorization of such treatment is a matter within the discretion of Congress. Congress, however, has enacted no express exemption of organized baseball from the Sherman Act, and no court has demonstrated the existence of an implied exemption from the Act of any sport that is so highly organized as to amount to an interstate monopoly or which restrains interstate trade or commerce. In the absence of such an exemption, the present popularity of organized baseball increases, rather than diminishes, the importance of its compliance with standards of reasonableness comparable with those now required by law of interstate trade or commerce. It is interstate trade or commerce and, as such, it is subject to the Sherman Act until exempted.

Pollock v. Farmers' Loan and Trust Co.

158 U.S. 601 (1895)
Vote: 5–4

Congress provided for an income tax in 1894. Pollock sued the Farmers' Loan and Trust, of which he was a shareholder, to prevent their compliance. He challenged the tax on real estate, state and local bonds, and the general principle of an income tax based upon total income and providing for exemptions at lower income levels. The tax was upheld by a U.S. circuit court, but the Supreme Court found the first two objections compelling. It was evenly divided on the principle objection, Justice Howell Jackson being ill. It therefore set the case for rehearing the following year. The issue was whether such an income tax constituted a "direct" tax, requiring apportionment by population by Article I, Section 9 of the Constitution. As Justice Jackson dissented in this rehearing, and the lineup of the 4 to 4 split in the original was never announced, an intriguing question remains: How close a vote (or change of a vote) still qualifies under Marshall's notion that unconstitutionality will be declared only in a "clear case."

MR. CHIEF JUSTICE FULLER delivered the opinion of the court.

[T]he Constitution divided Federal taxation into two great classes, the class of direct taxes, and the class of duties, imposts, and excises; and prescribed two rules which qualified the grant of power as to each class.

The power to lay direct taxes apportioned among the several States in proportion to their representation in the popular branch of Congress, a representation based on population as ascertained by the census, was plenary and absolute; but to lay direct taxes without apportionment was forbidden. The power to lay duties, imposts, and excises was subject to the qualification that the imposition must be uniform throughout the United States. . . .

. . . .

We are now permitted to broaden the field of inquiry, and to determine to which of the two great classes a tax upon a person's entire income, whether derived from rents, or products, or otherwise, of real estate, or from bonds, stocks, or other forms of personal property, belongs; and we are unable to conclude that the enforced subtraction from the yield of all the owner's real or personal property, in the manner prescribed, is so different from a tax upon the property itself, that it is not a direct, but an indirect tax, in the meaning of the Constitution.

. . . .

Admitting that this act taxes the income of property irrespective of its source, still we cannot doubt that such a tax is necessarily a direct tax in the meaning of the Constitution.

. . . .

[I]n light of the circumstances to which we have referred, is it not an evasion of that prohibition to hold that a general unapportioned tax, imposed upon all property owners as a body for or in respect of their property, is not direct, in the meaning of the Constitution, because confined to the income therefrom?

Whatever the speculative views of political economists or revenue reformers may be, can it be properly held that the Constitution, taken in its plain and obvious sense, and with due regard to the circumstances attending the formation of the government, authorizes a general unapportioned tax on the products of the farm and the rents of real estate, although imposed merely because of ownership and with no possible means of escape from payment, as belonging to a totally different class from that which includes the property from whence the income proceeds?

There can be but one answer, unless the constitutional restriction is to be treated as utterly illusory and futile, and the object of its framers defeated. . . .

. . . .

The stress of the argument is thrown, however, on the assertion that an income tax is not a property tax at all; that it is not a real estate tax, or a crop tax, or a bond tax; that it is an assessment upon the taxpayer on account of his money-spending power as shown by his revenue for the year preceding the assessment; that rents received, crops harvested, interest collected, have lost all connection with their origin, and although once not taxable have become transmuted in their new form into taxable subject-matter; in other words, that income is taxable irrespective of the source from whence it is derived.

. . . .

Our conclusions may, therefore, be summed up as follows:

First. We adhere to the opinion already announced, that, taxes on real estate being indisputably direct taxes, taxes on the rents or income of real estate are equally direct taxes.

Second. We are of the opinion that taxes on personal property, or the income of personal property, are likewise direct taxes.

Third. The tax imposed by sections twenty-seven to thirty-seven, inclusive, of the act of 1894, so far as it falls on the income of real estate and of personal property, being a direct tax within the meaning of the Constitution, and, therefore, unconstitutional and void because not apportioned according to representation, all those sections, constituting one entire scheme of taxation, are necessarily invalid.

MR. JUSTICE HARLAN, dissenting.

At the convention of 1787, Rufus King asked what was the precise meaning of *direct* taxation, and no one answered. Madison Papers, 5 Elliott's Debates, 451. The debates of that now famous body do not show that any delegate attempted to give a clear, succinct definition of what, in his opinion, was a direct tax. Indeed, the report of those debates, upon the question now before us, is very meagre and unsatisfactory. . . .

If the question propounded by Rufus King had been answered in accordance with the interpretation now given, it is not at all certain that the Constitution, in its present form, would have been adopted by the convention, nor, if adopted, that it would have been accepted by the requisite number of States.

. . . .

In the judgment of the members of this court as constituted when the *Hylton case* was decided — all of whom were statesmen and lawyers of distinction, two, Wilson and Paterson, being recognized as great leaders in the convention of 1787 — the only taxes that could certainly be regarded as direct taxes, within the meaning of the Constitution, were capitation taxes and taxes on lands;

. . . .

[F]rom the foundation of the government, until 1861, Congress, following the declarations of the judges of the *Hylton case,* restricted direct taxation to real estate and slaves, and in 1861 to real estate exclusively, and has never, in any statute, indicated its belief that personal property, however assessed or valued, was the subject of "direct taxes" to be apportioned among the States; . . .

. . . .

[I]n 1861 and subsequent years Congress imposed, without apportionment among the States on the basis of numbers, but by the rule of uniformity, duties on *income* derived *from every kind of property, real and personal,* including income derived from *rents,* and from trades, professions, and employments, etc.; and, lastly, That upon every action when it has considered the question . . . this court has, *without a dissenting voice,* determined it in the negative, always proceeding on the ground that capitation taxes and taxes on land were the only direct taxes contemplated by the framers of the Constitution.

. . . .

. . . No such apportionment can possibly be made without doing gross injustice to the many for the benefit of the favored few in particular States. Any attempt upon the part of Congress to apportion among the States, upon the basis simply of their population, taxation of personal property or of incomes, would tend to arouse such indignation among the freemen of America that it would never be repeated. When, therefore, this court adjudges, as it does now adjudge, that Congress cannot impose a duty or tax upon personal property, or upon income arising either from rents of real estate or from personal property, including invested personal property, bonds, stocks, and investments of all kinds, except by apportioning the sum to be so raised among the States according to population, it *practically* decides that, *without an amendment of the Constitution —* two-thirds of both Houses of Congress and three-fourths of the States concurring — such property and income can never be made to contribute to the support of the national government.

MR. JUSTICE BROWN dissenting.

. . . .

So also, whenever this court has been called upon to give a construction to this clause of the Constitution, it has universally held the words "direct taxes" applied only to the capitation taxes and taxes upon the land. In the five cases most directly in point it was held that the following taxes were not direct, but rather in the nature of duty or excise, viz., a tax upon carriages, *Hylton v. United States,* a tax upon the business of insurance companies, *Pacific Insurance Co. v. Soule,* a tax of ten per cent upon the notes of state banks held by national banks, *Veazie v. Fenno,* a tax upon the devolution of real estate, *Scholey v. Rew,* and, finally, a general income tax was broadly upheld in *Springer v. United States.* These cases, consistent and undeviating as they are, and extending over nearly a century of our national life, seem to me to establish a canon of interpretation, which it is now too late to overthrow, or even to question. If there be any weight at all to be given to the doctrine of *stare decisis,* it surely ought to apply to a theory of constitutional construction, which has received the deliberate sanction of this court in five cases, and upon the faith of which Congress has enacted two income taxes at times when, it its judgment, extraordinary sources of revenue were necessary to be made available.

Bailey v. Drexel Furniture Co.

259 U.S. 20 (1922)
Vote: 8–1

In 1919, Congress enacted a tax on factory, mill, and mine owners who employed underage workers or employed children of specified ages in excess of eight hours a day or six days a week. Drexel Furniture employed a child under fourteen and sued to recover the tax paid. The government obtained a writ of error appealing a district court judgment that the Child Labor Tax Act was invalid.

MR. CHIEF JUSTICE TAFT delivered the opinion of the court.

This case presents the question of the constitutional validity of the Child Labor Tax Law. The plaintiff below, the Drexel Furniture Company, is engaged in the manufacture of furniture in the Western District of North Carolina. On September 20, 1921, it received a notice from Bailey, United States Collector of Internal Revenue for the District, that it had been assessed $6,312.79 for having during the taxable year 1919 employed and permitted to work in its factory a boy under fourteen years of age, thus incurring the tax of ten per cent on its net profits for that year. The Company paid the tax under protest, and after rejection of its claim for a refund, brought this suit.

The law is attacked on the ground that it is a regulation of the employment of child labor in the States — an exclusively state function under the Federal Constitution and within the reservations of the Tenth Amendment. It is defended on the ground that it is a mere excise tax levied by the Congress of the United States under its broad power of taxation conferred by §8, Article I, of the Federal Constitution. We must construe the law and interpret the intent and meaning of Congress from the language of the act. The words are to be given their ordinary meaning unless the context shows that they are differently used. Does this law impose a tax with only that incidental restraint and regulation which a tax must inevitably involve? Or does it regulate by the use of the so-called tax as a penalty? If a tax, it is clearly an excise. It it were an excise on a commodity or other thing of value we might not be permitted under previous decisions of this court to infer solely from its heavy burden that the act intends a prohibition instead of a tax. But this act is more. It provides a heavy exaction for a departure from a detailed and specific course of conduct in business. That course of business is that employers shall employ in mines and quarries, children of an age greater than sixteen years; in mills and factories, children of an age greater than fourteen years, and shall prevent children of less than sixteen years in mills and factories from working more than eight hours a day or six days a week. If an employer departs from this prescribed course of business, he is to pay to the Government one-tenth of his entire net income in the business for a full year. The amount is not to be proportioned in any degree to the extent or frequency of the departures, but is to be paid by the employer in full measure whether he employs five hundred children for a year, or employs only one for a day. Moreover, if he does not know the child is within the named age limit, he is not to pay; that is to say, it is only where he knowingly departs from the prescribed course that payment is to be exacted. Scienter is associated with penalties, not with taxes. The employer's factory is to be subject to inspection at any time not only by the taxing officers of the Treasury, the Department normally charged with the collection of taxes, but also by the Secretary of Labor and his subordinates whose normal function is the advancement and protection of the welfare of the workers. In the light of these features of the act, a court must be blind not to see that the so-called tax is imposed to stop the employment of children within the age limits prescribed. Its prohibitory and regulatory effect and purpose are palpable. All others can see and understand this. How can we properly shut our minds to it? . . .

Out of a proper respect for the acts of a coördinate branch of the Government, this court has gone far to sustain taxing acts as such, even though there has been ground for suspecting from the weight of the tax it was intended to destroy its subject. But, in the act before us, the presumption of validity cannot prevail, because the proof of the contrary is found on the very face of its provisions. Grant the validity of this law, and all that Congress would need to do, hereafter, in seeking to take over to its control any one of the great numbers of subjects of public interest, jurisdiction of which the States have never parted with, and which are reserved to them by the Tenth Amendment, would be to enact a detailed measure of complete regulation of the subject and enforce it by a so-called tax upon departures from it. To give such magic to the word "tax" would be to break down all constitutional limitations of the powers of Congress and completely wipe out the sovereignty of the States.

. . . Although Congress does not invalidate the contract of employment or expressly declare that the employment within the mentioned ages is illegal, it does exhibit its intent practically to achieve the latter result by adopting the criteria of wrongdoing and imposing its principal consequence on those who transgress its standard.

The analogy of the *Dagenhart Case* is clear. The congressional power over interstate commerce is, within its proper scope, just as complete and unlimited as the congressional power to tax, and the legislative motive in its exercise is just as free from judicial suspicion and inquiry. Yet when Congress threatened to stop interstate commerce in ordinary and necessary commodities, unobjectionable as subjects of transportation, and to deny the same to the people of a State in order to coerce them in compliance with Congress's regulation of state concerns, the court said this was not in fact a regulation of interstate commerce, but rather that of State concerns and was invalid. So here the so-called tax is a penalty to coerce people of a State to act as Congress wishes them to act in respect of a matter completely the business of the state government under the Federal Constitution.

. . . .

For the reasons given, we must hold the Child Labor Tax Law invalid and the judgment of the District Court is

Affirmed.

MR. JUSTICE CLARKE dissents.

U.S. v. Butler

297 U.S. 1 (1936)
Vote: 6–3

The New Deal effort to control the Great Depression was the Agricultural Adjustment Act of 1933. It levied a tax on processors, based on the difference, for the appropriate crop, between current prices and those prevailing during the base period, 1909–1914. This money was then used to pay farmers who agreed to reduce their crops. Butler refused to pay the tax, lost his case in the district court, but prevailed in the court of appeals. The government appealed to the Supreme Court.

MR. JUSTICE ROBERTS delivered the opinion of the Court.

In this case we must determine whether certain provisions of the Agricultural Adjustment Act, 1933, conflict with the Federal Constitution.

Title I of the statute is captioned "Agricultural Adjustment." Section 1 recites that an economic emergency has arisen, due to disparity between the prices of agricultural and other commodities, with consequent destruction of farmers' purchasing power and breakdown in orderly exchange, which, in turn, have affected transactions in agricultural commodities with a national public interest and burdened and obstructed the normal currents of commerce, calling for the enactment of legislation.

First. At the outset the United States contends that the respondents have no standing to question the validity of the tax. . . . *Massachusetts* v. *Mellon,* 262 U.S. 447, is claimed to foreclose litigation by the respondents or other taxpayers, as such, looking to restraint of the expenditure of government fund. That case might be an authority in the petitioners' favor if we were here concerned merely with a suit by a taxpayer to restrain the expenditure of the public moneys. But here the respondents who are called upon to pay moneys as taxes, resist the exaction as a step in an unauthorized plan. This circumstance clearly distinguishes the case. The Government in substance and effect asks us to separate the Agricultural Adjustment act into two statutes, the one levying an excise on processors of certain commodities, the other appropriating the public moneys independently of the first. Passing the novel suggestion that two statutes enacted as parts of a single scheme should be tested as if they were distinct and unrelated, we think the legislation now before us is not susceptible of such separation and treatment.

The tax can only be sustained by ignoring the avowed purpose and operation of the act, and holding it a measure merely laying an excise upon processors to raise revenue for the support of government.

The tax plays an indispensable part in the plan of regulation. As stated by the Agricultural Adjustment Administrator, it is "the heart of the law"; a means of "accomplishing one or both of two things intended to help farmers attain parity prices and purchasing power." A tax automatically goes into effect for a commodity when the Secretary of Agriculture determines that rental or benefit payments are to be made for reduction of production of that commodity. The tax is to cease when rental or benefit payments cease. The rate is fixed with the purpose of bringing about crop-reduction and price-raising.

It is inaccurate and misleading to speak of the exaction from processors prescribed by the challenged act as a tax, or to say that as a tax is subject to no infirmity. A tax, in the general understanding of the term, and as used in the Constitution, signifies an exaction for the support of the Government. The word has never been thought to connote the expropriation of money from one group for the benefit of another.

We conclude that the act is one regulating agricultural production; that the tax is mere incident of such regulation and that the respondents have standing to challenge the legality of the exaction.

It does not follow that as the act is not an exertion of the taxing power and the exaction not a true tax, the statute is void or the exaction uncollectible.

There should be no misunderstanding as to the function of this court in such a case. It is sometimes said that the court assumes a power to overrule or control the action of the people's representatives. This is a misconception. The Constitution is the supreme law of the land ordained and established by the people. All legislation must conform to the principles it lays down. When an act of Congress is appropriately challenged in the courts as not conforming to the constitutional mandate the judicial branch of the Government had only one duty, — to lay the article of the Constitution which is invoked beside the statute which is challenged and to decide whether the latter squares with the former. All the court does, or can do, is to announce its considered judgment upon the question. The only power it has,

if such it may be called, is the power of judgment. This court neither approves nor condemns any legislative policy. Its delicate and difficult office is to ascertain and declare whether the legislation is in accordance with, or in contravention of, the provisions of the Constitution; and, having done that, its duty ends.

The question is not what power the Federal Government ought to have but what powers in fact have been given by the people. It hardly seems necessary to reiterate that ours is a dual form of government; that in every state there are two governments, — the state and the United States. Each State has all governmental powers save such as the people, by their Constitution, have conferred upon the United States, denied to the States, or reserved to themselves. The federal union is a government of delegated powers. It has only such as are expressly conferred upon it and such as are reasonably implied from those granted. In this respect we differ radically from nations where all legislative power, without restriction or limitation, is vested in a parliament or other legislative body subject to no restrictions except the discretion of its members.

The clause thought to authorize the legislation, — the first, — confers upon the Congress power "to lay and collect Taxes, Duties, Imposts and Excises, to pay the Debts and provide for the common Defense and general Welfare of the United States. . . ." It is not contended that this provision grants power to regulate agricultural production upon the theory that such legislation would promote the general welfare. The Government concedes that the phrase "to provide for the general welfare" qualifies the power "to lay and collect taxes." The view that the clause grants power to provide for the general welfare, independently of the taxing power, has never been authoritatively accepted. Mr. Justice Story points out that if it were adopted "it is obvious that under color of the generality of the words, to 'provide for the common defence and general welfare,' the government of the United States is, in reality, a government of general and unlimited powers, notwithstanding the subsequent enumeration of specific powers." The true construction undoubtedly is that the only thing granted is the power to tax for the purpose of providing funds for payment of the nation's debts and making provision for the general welfare.

Nevertheless the Government asserts that warrant is found in this clause for the adoption of the Agricultural Adjustment Act. The argument is that Congress may appropriate and authorize the spending of moneys for the "general welfare"; that the phrase should be liberally construed to cover anything conducive to national welfare; that decision as to what will promote such welfare rests with Congress alone, and the courts may not review its determinations; and finally that the appropriation under attack was in fact for the general welfare of the United States.

The Congress is expressly empowered to lay taxes to provide for the general welfare. Funds in the Treasury as a result of taxation may be expended only through appropriation. (Art. I, §9, cl. 7.) They can never accomplish the objects for which they were collected unless the power to appropriate is as broad as the power to tax. The necessary implication from the terms of the grant is that the public funds may be appropriated "to provide for the general welfare of the United States." These words cannot be meaningless, else they would not have been used. The conclusion must be that they were intended to limit and define the granted power to raise and to expend money. How shall they be construed to effectuate the intent of the instrument?

Since the foundation of the Nation sharp differences of opinion have persisted as to the true interpretation of the phrase. Madison asserted it amounts to no more than a reference to the other powers enumerated in the subsequent clauses of the same section; that, as the United States is a government of limited and enumerated powers, the grant of power to tax and spend for the general national welfare must be confined to the enumerated legislative fields committed to the Congress. In this view the phrase is mere tautology, for taxation and appropriation are or may be necessary incidents of the exercise of any of the enumerated legislative powers. Hamilton, on the other hand, maintained the clause confers a power separate and distinct from those later enumerated, is not restricted in meaning by the grant of them, and Congress consequently has a substantive power to tax and to appropriate, limited only by the requirement that it shall be exercised to provide for the general welfare of the United States. Each contention has had the support of those whose views are entitled to weight. This court has noticed the question, but has never found it necessary to decide which is the true construction. Mr. Justice Story, in his Commentaries, espouses the Hamiltonian position. . . . Study of all these leads us to conclude that the reading advocated by Mr. Justice Story is the correct one. While, therefore, the power to tax is not unlimited, its confines are set in the clause which confers it, and not in those of §8

which bestow and define the legislative powers of the Congress. It results that the power of Congress to authorize the expenditure of public moneys for public purposes is not limited by the direct grants of legislative power found in the Constitution.

But the adoption of the broader construction leaves the power to spend subject to limitations. . . . Story says that if the tax be not proposed for the common defence or general welfare, but for other objects wholly extraneous, it would be wholly indefensible.

We are not now required to ascertain the scope of the phrase "general welfare of the United States" or to determine whether an appropriation in aid of agriculture falls within it. Wholly apart from that question, another principle embedded in our Constitution prohibits the enforcement of the Agricultural Adjustment Act. The act invades the reserved rights of the states. It is a statutory plan to regulate and control agricultural production, a matter beyond the powers delegated to the federal government. The tax, the appropriation of the funds raised, and the direction for their disbursement, are but parts of the plan. They are but means to an unconstitutional end.

From the accepted doctrine that the United States is a government of delegated powers, it follows that those not expressly granted, or reasonably to be implied from such as are conferred, are reserved to the states or to the people. To forestall any suggestion to the contrary, the Tenth Amendment was adopted. The same proposition, otherwise stated, is that powers not granted are prohibited. None to regulate agricultural production is given, and therefore legislation by Congress for that purpose is forbidden.

It is an established principle that the attainment of a prohibited end may not be accomplished under the pretext of the exertion of powers which are granted.

Third. If the taxing power may not be used as the instrument to enforce a regulation of matters of state concern with respect to which the Congress has no authority to interfere, may it, as in the present case, be employed to raise the money necessary to purchase a compliance which the Congress is powerless to command? The Government asserts that whatever might be said against the validity of the plan if compulsory, it is constitutionally sound because the end is accomplished by voluntary cooperation. There are two sufficient answers to the contention. The regulation is not in fact voluntary. The farmer, of course, may refuse to comply, but the price of such refusal is the loss of benefits. The amount offered is intended to be sufficient to exert pressure on him to agree on the proposed regulation. The power to confer or withhold unlimited benefits is the power to coerce or destroy. If the cotton grower elects not to accept the benefits, he will receive less for his crops; those who receive payments will be able to undersell him. The results may well be financial ruin. The coercive purpose and intent of the statute is not obscured by the fact that it has not been perfectly successful. It is pointed out that, because there still remained a minority whom the rental and benefit payment were insufficient to induce to surrender their independence of action, the Congress has gone further and, in the Bankhead Cotton Act, used the taxing power in a more directly minatory fashion to compel submission. This progression only serves more fully to expose the coercive purpose of the so-called tax imposed by the present act.

Congress has no power to enforce its commands on the farmer to the ends sought by the Agricultural Adjustment Act. It must follow that it may not indirectly accomplish those ends by taxing and spending to purchase compliance. The Constitution and the entire plan of our government negative any such use of the power to tax and to spend as the act undertakes to authorize. It does not help to declare that local conditions throughout the nation have created a situation of national concern; for this is but to say that whenever there is a widespread similarity of local conditions, Congress may ignore constitutional limitations upon its own powers and usurp those reserved to the states. If, in lieu of compulsory regulation of subjects within the states' reserved jurisdiction, which is prohibited, the Congress could invoke the taxing and spending power as a means to accomplish the same end, clause 1 of §8 of Article I would become the instrument for total subversion of the governmental powers reserved to the individual states.

If the act before us is a proper exercise of the federal taxing power, evidently the regulation of all industry throughout the United States may be accomplished by similar exercises of the same power.

Until recently no suggestion of the existence of any such power in the Federal Government has been advanced. The expressions of the framers of the Constitution, the decisions of this court interpreting that instrument, and the writings of great commentators will be searched in vain for any suggestion that there exists in the clause under discussion or elsewhere in the Constitution, the authority whereby every provision and every fair implication from that instrument may be subverted, the independence of the individual states obliterated, and the United States converted into a central government exercising uncontrolled police power in every state of the Union, superseding all local control or regulation of the affairs or concerns of the states.

Affirmed.

MR. JUSTICE STONE, dissenting.

I think the judgment should be reversed.

The present stress of widely held and strongly expressed differences of opinion and the wisdom of the Agricultural Adjustment Act makes it important, in the interest of clear thinking and sound result, to emphasize at the outset certain propositions which should have controlling influence in determining the validity of the Act. They are:

1. The power of courts to declare a statute unconstitutional is subject to two guiding principles of decision which ought never to be absent from judicial consciousness. One is that courts are concerned only with the power to enact statutes, not with their wisdom. The other is that while unconstitutional exercise of power by the executive and legislative branches of the government is subject to judicial restraint, the only check upon our own exercise of power is our own sense of self-restraint. For the removal of unwise laws from the statute books appeal lies not to the courts but to the ballot and to the processes of democratic government.

2. The constitutional power of Congress to levy an excise tax upon the processing of agricultural products is not questioned. The present levy is held invalid, not for any want of power in Congress to lay such a tax to defray public expenditures, including those for the general welfare, but because the use to which its proceeds are put is disapproved.

3. As the present depressed state of agriculture is nation wide in its extent and effects, there is no basis for saying that the expenditure of public money in aid of farmers is not within the specifically granted power of Congress to levy taxes to "provide for the . . . general welfare." The opinion of the Court does not declare otherwise.

. . . The suggestion of coercion finds no support in the record or in any data showing the actual operation of the Act. Threat of loss, not hope of gain, is the essence of economic coercion. Members of a long depressed industry have undoubtedly been tempted to curtail acreage by the hope of resulting better prices and by the proffered opportunity to obtain needed ready money. But there is nothing to indicate that those who accepted benefits were impelled by fear of lower prices if they did not accept.

. . . The presumption of constitutionality of a statute is not to be overturned by an assertion of its coercive effect which rests on nothing more substantial than groundless speculation.

The Constitution requires that public funds shall be spent for a defined purpose, the promotion of the general welfare. Their expenditure usually involves payment on terms which will insure use by the selected recipients within the limits of their constitutional purpose. Expenditures would fail of their purpose and thus lose their constitutional sanction if the terms of payment were not such that by their influence on the action of the recipients the permitted end would be attained. The power of Congress to spend is inseparable from persuasion to action over which Congress has no legislative control. . . .

The spending power of Congress is in addition to the legislative power and not subordinate to it. . . . It is a contradiction in terms to say that there is power to spend for the national welfare, while rejecting any power to impose conditions reasonably adapted to the attainment of the end which alone would justify the expenditure.

The limitation now sanctioned must lead to absurd consequences. The government may give seeds to farmers, but may not condition the gift upon their being planted in places where they are most needed or even planted at all. The government may give money to the unemployed, but may not ask that those who get it shall give labor in return, or even use it to support their families. It may give money to sufferers from earthquake, fire, tornado, pestilence or flood, but may not impose conditions — health precautions designed to prevent the spread of disease, or induce the movement of population to safer or more sanitary areas. All that, because it is purchased regulation infringing state powers, must be left for the states, who are unable or unwilling to supply the necessary relief. . . .

That the governmental power of the purse is a great one is not now for the first time announced. Every student of the history of government and economics is aware of its magnitude and of its existence in every civilized government. Both were well understood by the framers of the Constitution when they sanctioned the grant of the spending power to the federal government, and both were recognized by Hamilton and Story, whose views of the spending power as standing on parity with the other powers specifically granted, have hitherto been generally accepted.

The suggestion that it must now be curtailed by judicial fiat because it may be abused by unwise use hardly rises to the dignity of argument. So may judicial power be abused.

A tortured construction of the Constitution is not to be justified by recourse to extreme examples of reckless congressional spending which might occur if courts could not prevent — expenditures which, even if they could be thought to effect any national purpose, would be possible only by action of a legislature lost to all sense of public responsibility. Such suppositions are addressed to the mind accustomed to believe that it is the business of courts to sit in judgment on the wisdom of legislative action. Courts are not the only agency of government that must be assumed to have capacity to govern. Congress and the courts both unhappily may falter or be mistaken in the performance of their constitutional duty. But interpretation of our great charter of government which proceeds on any assumption that the responsibility for the preservation of our institutions is the exclusive concern of any one of the three branches of government, or that it alone can save them from destruction is far more likely, in the long run, "to obliterate the constitutent members" of "an indestructible union of indestructible states" than the frank recognition that language, even of a constitution, may mean what it says: that the power to tax and spend includes the power to relieve a nationwide economic maladjustment by conditional gifts of money.

MR. JUSTICE BRANDEIS and MR. JUSTICE CARDOZO join in this opinion.

Steward Machine Co. v. Davis

301 U.S. 548 (1937)
Vote: 5–4

The Social Security Act created the complex scheme known by that name, which was based upon contributions or taxes assessed as a percentage of workers' wages. Perhaps because of the BUTLER ruling, the sums were not put into a fund, a failing that was to come back to haunt the system in the 1980s. The Act was drafted with eleven different titles and programs to avoid the possibility of a ruling on unconstitutionality endangering other programs. Three main programs were developed: (1) old-age and survivor's insurance, federally administered; (2) aid to dependent children, the blind, and other handicapped persons, based upon grants-in-aid; (3) unemployment compensation plans, financed by employer contributions. The Act encouraged states to have plans, by giving employers federal tax write-offs if the state had an approved plan. By involving the states, through federal subsidy to them and their taxpayers, the drafters were seeking to avoid Tenth Amendment issues.

Steward Machine challenged the unemployment aspects of Social Security, which taxed employers of eight or more employees. It paid $46.11 and sued for recovery. The district court and circuit court rejected their claim; the Supreme Court granted certiorari.

MR. JUSTICE CARDOZO delivered the opinion of the Court.

The Social Security Act (Act of August 14, 1935, c. 531, 49 Stat. 620, 42 U.S.C., c. 7 (Supp.)) is divided into eleven separate titles, of which only Titles IX and III are so related to this case as to stand in need of summary.

The caption of Title IX is "Tax on Employers of Eight or More." Every employer (with stated exceptions) is to pay for each calendar year "an excise tax, with respect to having individuals in his employ," the tax to be measured by prescribed percentages of the total wages payable by the employer during the calendar year with respect to such employment. §901. One is not, however, an "employer" within the meaning of the act unless he employs eight persons or more. . . .

The assault on the statute proceeds on an extended front. Its assailants take the ground that the tax is not an excise; that it is not uniform throughout the United States as excises are required to be; that its exceptions are so many and arbitrary as to violate the Fifth Amendment; that its purpose was not revenue, but an unlawful invasion of the reserved powers of the states; and that the states in submitting to it have yielded to coercion and have abandoned governmental functions which they are not permitted to surrender. . . .

First. The tax, which is described in the statute as an excise, is laid with uniformity throughout the United States as a duty, an impost or an excise upon the relation of employment.

1. We are told that the relation of employment is one so essential to the pursuit of happiness that it may not be burdened with a tax. Appeal is made to history. From the precedents of the colonial days we

are supplied with illustrations of excises common in the colonies. They are said to have been bound up with the enjoyment of particular commodities. Appeal is also made to principle or the analysis of concepts. An excise, we are told, imparts a tax upon a privilege; employment, it is said, is a right, not a privilege, from which it follows that employment is not subject to an excise. Neither the one appeal nor the other leads to the desired goal.

As to the argument from history: Doubtless there were many exercises in colonial days and later that were associated, more or less intimately, with the enjoyment or the use of property. This would not prove, even if no others were then known, that the forms then accepted were not subject to enlargement.

. . . .

But in truth other excises *were* known, and known since early times. Thus in 1695 (6 & 7 Wm. III, c. 6), Parliament passed an act which granted "to His Majesty certain Rates and Duties upon Marriage, Births and Burials," all for the purpose of "carrying on the War against France with Vigour." See *Opinion of the Justices,* 196 Mass. 603, 609; 85 N.E. 545. No commodity was affected there. The industry of counsel has supplied us with an apter illustration where the tax was not different in substance from the one now challenged as invalid. In 1777, before our Constitutional Convention, Parliament laid upon employers an annual "duty" of 21 shillings for "every male Servant" employed in stated forms of work.

The historical prop failing, the prop or fancied prop of principle remains. We learn that employment for lawful gain is a "natural" or "inherent" or "inalienable" right, and not a "privilege" at all. But natural rights, so called, are as much subject to taxation as rights of less importance. An excise is not limited to vocations or activities that may be prohibited altogether. . . . "Business is as legitimate an object of the taxing powers as property." *Newton* v. *Atchison,* 31 Kan. 151, 154 (per Brewer, J.); 1 Pac. 288. Indeed, ownership itself, as we had occasion to point out the other day, is only a bundle of rights and privileges invested with a single name. *Henneford* v. *Silas Mason Co.,* 300 U.S. 577. "A state is at liberty, if it pleases, to tax them all collectively, or to separate the faggots and lay the charge distributively." *Ibid.* Employment is a business relation, if not iself a business. It is a relation without which business could seldom be carried on effectively. The power to tax the activities and relations that constitute a calling considered as a unit is the power to tax any of them. The whole includes the parts.

The subject matter of taxation open to the power of the Congress is as comprehensive as that open to the power of the states, though the method of apportionment may at times be different.... Together, these classes include every form of tax appropriate to sovereignty.... The statute books of the states are strewn with illustrations of taxes laid on occupations pursued of common right. We find no basis for a holding that the power in that regard which belongs by accepted practice to the legislatures of the states, has been denied by the Constitution to the Congress of the nation.

2. The tax being an excise, its imposition must conform to the canon of uniformity. There has been no departure from this requirement. According to the settled doctrine the uniformity exacted is geographical, not intrinsic....

Second. The excise is not invalid under the provisions of the Fifth Amendment by force of its exemptions.

The Fifth Amendment unlike the Fourteenth has no equal protection clause.... If this latitude of judgment is lawful for the states, it is lawful, *a fortiori,* in legislation by the Congress, which is subject to restraints less narrow and confining....

The classifications and exemptions directed by the statute now in controversy have support in considerations of policy and practical convenience that cannot be condemned as arbitrary. The classifications and exemptions would therefore be upheld if they had been adopted by a state and the provisions of the Fourteenth Amendment were invoked to annul them....

Third. The excise is not void as involving the coercion of the States in contravention of the Tenth Amendment or of restrictions implicit in our federal form of government.... The case for the petitioner is built on the contention that here an ulterior aim is wrought into the very structure of the act, and what is even more important that the aim is not only ulterior, but essentially unlawful. In particular, the 90 percent credit is relied upon as supporting that conclusion. But before the statute succumbs to an assault upon these lines, two propositions must be made out by the assailant. *Cincinnati Soap C.* v. *United States, supra.* There must be a showing in the first place that separated from the credit the revenue provisions are incapable of standing by themselves. There must be a showing in the second place that the tax and the credit in combination are weapons of coercion, destroying or impairing the autonomy of the states. The truth of each proposition being essential to the success of the assault, we pass for convenience to a consideration of the sec-

ond, without pausing to inquire whether there has been a demonstration of the first.

... The assailants of the statute say that its dominant end and aim is to drive the state legislatures under the whip of economic pressure into the enactment of unemployment compensation laws at the bidding of the central goverment. Supporters of the statute say that its operation is not constraint, but the creation of a larger freedom, the states and the nation joining in a coöperative endeavor to avert a common evil. Before Congress acted, unemployment compensation insurance was still, for the most part, a project and no more....

The Social Security Act is an attempt to find a method by which all these public agencies may work together to a common end. Every dollar of the new taxes will continue in all likelihood to be used and needed by the nation as long as states are unwilling, whether through timidity or for other motives, to do what can be done at home. At least the inference is permissible that Congress so believed, though retaining undiminished freedom to spend the money as it pleased. On the other hand fulfillment of the home duty will be lightened and encouraged by crediting the taxpayer upon his account of the Treasury of the nation to the extent that his contributions under the laws of the locality have simplified or diminished the problem of relief and the probable demand upon the resources of the fisc. Duplicated taxes, or burdens that approach them, are recognized hardships that government, state or national, may properly avoid.

Who then is coerced through the operation of this statute? Not the taxpayer. He pays in fulfillment of the mandate of the local legislature. Not the state. Even now she does not offer a suggestion that in passing the unemployment law she was affected by duress. See *Carmichael* v. *Southern Coal & Coke Co.,* and *Carmichael* v. *Gulf State Paper Corp., supra.* For all that appears she is satisfied with her choice, and would be sorely disappointed if it were now to be annuled. The difficulty with the petitioner's contention is that it confuses motive with coercion. "Every tax is in some measure regulatory. To some extent it interposes an economic impediment to the activity taxed as compared with others not taxed." *Sonzinsky* v. *United States, supra.* In like manner every rebate from a tax when conditioned upon conduct is in some measure a temptation. But to hold that motive or temptation is equivalent to coercion is to plunge the law in endless difficulties. The outcome of such a doctrine is the acceptance of a philosophical determinism by which choice becomes impossible. Till now the law has been guided by a robust common sense which assumes the freedom of the will as a working hypothesis in the solution of its problems. The wisdom of the hypothesis has illustration in this case. Nothing in the case suggests the exertion of a power akin to undue influence, if we assume that such a concept can ever be applied with fitness to the relations between state and nation. Even on that assumption the location of the point at which pressure turns into compulsion, and ceases to be inducement, would be a question of degree, — at times, pehaps, of fact. The point had not been reached when Alabama made her choice. We cannot say that she was acting, not of her unfettered will, but under the strain of a persuasion equivalent to undue influence, when she chose to have relief administered under laws of her own making, by agents of her own selection, instead of under federal laws, administered by federal officers, with all the ensuing evils, at least to many minds, of federal patronage and power. There would be a strange irony, indeed, if her choice were now to be annulled on the basis of an assumed duress in the enactment of a statute which her courts have accepted as a true expression of her will. . . .

In ruling as we do, we leave many questions open. We do not say that a tax is valid, when imposed by act of Congress, if it is laid upon the condition that a state may escape its operation through the adoption of a statute unrelated in subject matter to activities fairly within the scope of national policy and power. No such question is before us. . . .

United States v. *Butler, supra,* is cited by petitioner as a decision to the contrary. . . . The decision was by a divided court, a minority taking the view that the objections were untenable. None of them is applicable to the situation here developed.

(a) The proceeds of the tax in controversy are not earmarked for a special group.

(b) The unemployment compensation law which is a condition of the credit has had the approval of the state and could not be a law without it.

(c) The condition is not linked to an irrevocable agreement, for the state at its pleasure may repeal its unemployment law . . . terminate the credit, and place itself where it was before the credit was accepted.

(d) The condition is not directed to the attainment of an unlawful end, but to an end, the relief of unemployment, for which nation and state may lawfully coöperate.

Fourth. The statute does not call for a surrender by the states of powers essential to their quasi-sovereign existence. . . . The states are at liberty, upon obtaining the consent of Congress, to make agreements with one another. Constitution, Art. I, §10, par. 3. *Poole* v. *Fleeger,* 11 Pet. 185, 209; *Rhode Island* v. *Massachusetts,* 12 Pet. 657, 725. We find no room for doubt that they may do the like with Congress if the essence of their statehood is maintained without impairment.

Affirmed.

Separate opinion of MR. JUSTICE MCREYNOLDS.

No defense is offered for the legislation under review upon the basis of emergency. The hypothesis is that hereafter it will continuously benefit unemployed members of a class. Forever, so far as we can see, the States are expected to function under federal direction concerning an internal matter. By the sanction of this adventure, the door is open for progressive inauguration of others of like kind under which it can hardly be expected that the States will retain genuine independence of action. And without independent States a Federal Union as contemplated by the Constitution becomes impossible.

Ordinarily, I must think, a denial that the challenged action of Congress and what has been done under it amount to coercion and impair freedom of government by the people of the State would be regarded as contrary to practical experience. Unquestionably our federate plan of government confronts an enlarged peril.

Separate opinion of MR. JUSTICE SUTHERLAND.

With most of what is said in the opinion just handed down, I concur.

But the question with which I have difficulty is whether the administrative provisions of the act invade the governmental administrative powers of the several states reserved by the Tenth Amendment. A state may enter into contracts; but a state cannot, by contract or statute, surrender the execution, or a share in the execution, of any of its governmental powers either to a sister state or to the federal government, any more than the federal government can surrender the control of any of its governmental powers to a foreign nation. The power to tax is vital and fundamental and, in the highest degree, governmental in character. Without it, the state could not exist. Fundamental also, and no less important, is the governmental power to expend the moneys realized from taxation, and exclusively to administer the laws in respect of the character of the tax and methods of laying and collecting it and expending the proceeds.

By these various provisions of the act, the federal agencies are authorized to supervise and hamper the administrative powers of the state to a degree which not only does not comport with the dignity of a quasi-sovereign state — a matter with which we are not judicially concerned — but which denies to it that supremacy and freedom from external interference in respect of its affairs which the Constitution contemplates — a matter of very definite judicial concern.

MR. JUSTICE VAN DEVANTER joins in this opinion.

MR. JUSTICE BUTLER, dissenting.

Obviously the Act creates the peril of federal tax not to raise revenue but to persuade. Of course, each State was free to reject any measure so proposed. But, if it failed to adopt a plan acceptable to federal authority, the full burden of the federal tax would be exacted. And, as federal demands similarly conditioned may be increased from time to time as Congress shall determine, possible federal pressure in that field is without limit.

Mulford v. Smith

307 U.S. 39 (1939)
Vote 7–2

Taking its cues from the BUTLER opinion, Congress passed the Second Agricultural Adjustment Act of 1938, to replace the program struck down by the Supreme Court. Instead of creating a fund from processors' taxes, it assessed a penalty on those who exceeded quotas. In addition to the technical differences that closely follow some of the objections in BUTLER, the climate of Supreme Court decisions on commerce and taxation had changed by 1939. The case began in a Georgia superior court, with tobacco growers suing warehousemen to prevent deduction of the penalty. The case was removed by defendants to a three-person federal court, the government joining as intervenor. The court dismissed the bill, and the farmers appealed directly to the Supreme Court.

MR. JUSTICE ROBERTS delivered the opinion of the Court.

The appellants, producers of flue-cured tobacco, assert that the Agricultural Adjustment Act of 1938, is unconstitutional as it affects their 1938 crop.

The portions of the statute involved are those included in Title III, providing marketing quotas for flue-cured tobacco. The Act directs that when the supply is found to exceed the level defined in the Act as the "reserve supply level" a national marketing quota shall become effective which will permit enough flue-cured tobacco to be marketed during the ensuing marketing year to maintain the supply at the reserve supply level. The quota is to be apportioned to the farms on which tobacco is grown. Penalties are to be paid by tobacco auction warehousemen for marketing tobacco from a farm in excess of its quota.

Section 311 is a finding by the Congress that the marketing of tobacco is a basic industry which directly affects interstate and foreign commerce; that stable conditions in such marketing are necessary to the general welfare; that tobacco is sold on a national market and it and its products move almost wholly in interstate and foreign commerce; that without federal assistance the farmers are unable to bring about orderly marketing, with the consequence that abnormally excessive supplies are produced and dumped indiscriminately on the national market; that this disorderly marketing of excess supply burdens and obstructs interstate and foreign commerce, causes reduction in prices and consequent injury to commerce, creates disparity between the prices of tobacco in interstate and foreign commerce and the prices of industrial products in such commerce, and diminishes the volume of interstate commerce in industrial products; and that the establishment of quotas as provided by the Act is necessary and appropriate to promote, foster and obtain an orderly flow of tobacco in interstate and foreign commerce. . . .

The Act provides for the apportionment of the state allotment amongst the farms which produced tobacco in the current year or have produced previously in one or more of the four preceding years. Apportionment to these farms is to be made on the basis of past marketing, after due allowance for drought, flood, hail, and other abnormal weather conditions, plant bed and other diseases, land, labor, and equipment available for the production of tobacco, crop-rotation practices, and soil and other physical factors affecting production. A limit is fixed below which the adjustment may not reduce the production of a given farm. Allotment to new tobacco farms is to be made on a slightly different basis.

Apportionment of the quota amongst individual farms is to be by local committees of farmers according to standards prescribed in the Act, amplified by regulations and instructions issued by the Secretary. Each farmer is to be notified of his marketing quota and the quotas of individual farms are to be kept available for public inspection in the country or district where the farm is located. If the farmer is dissatisfied with his allotment he may have his quota reviewed by a local review committee, and, if dissatisfied with the determination of that committee, he may obtain judicial review.

Section 314 provides that if tobacco in excess of the quota for the farm on which the tobacco is produced is marketed through a warehouseman, the latter must pay to the Secretary a penalty equal to fifty per cent of the market price of the excess, and may deduct an amount equivalent to the penalty from the price paid the producer.

The appellants plant themselves upon three propositions: (1) that the Act is a statutory plan to control agricultural production and, therefore, beyond the powers delegated to Congress; (2) that the standard for calculating farm quotas is uncertain, vague, and indefinite, resulting in an unconstitutional delegation of legislative power to the Secretary; (3) that, as applied to appellants' 1939 crop, the Act takes their property without due process of law.

First. The statute does not purport to control production. It sets no limit upon the acreage which may be planted or produced and imposes no penalty for the planting and producing of tobacco in excess of the marketing quota. It purports to be solely a regulation of interstate commerce, which it reaches and affects at the throat where tobacco enters the stream of commerce, — the marketing warehouse. The record discloses that at least two-thirds of all flue-cured tobacco sold at auction warehouses is sold for immediate shipment to an interstate or foreign destination. In Georgia nearly one hundred per cent of the tobacco so sold is purchased by extra-state purchasers. In markets where tobacco is sold to both interstate and intrastate purchasers it is not known, when the grower places his tobacco on the warehouse floor for sale, whether it is destined for interstate or intrastate commerce. Regulation to be effective, must, and therefore may constitutionally, apply to all sales.

The provisions of the Act under review constitute a regulation of interstate and foreign commerce within the competency of Congress under the power delegated to it by the Constitution.

Second. The appellants urge that the standard for allotting farm quotas is so uncertain, vague, and indefinite that it amounts to a delegation of legislative power to an executive officer and thus violates the Constitutional requirement that laws shall be enacted by the Congress.

What has been said in summarizing the provisions of the Act sufficiently discloses that definite standards are laid down for the government of the Secretary, first, in fixing quota and, second, in its allotment

amongst states and farms. He is directed to adjust the allotments so as to allow for specified factors which have abnormally affected the production of the state or the farm in question in the test years.

The decree is *Affirmed.*

MR. JUSTICE BUTLER, dissenting.

In *United States* v. *Butler*... we held the federal government without power to control farm production. We condemned the statutory plan there sought to be enforced as repugnant to the Tenth Amendment. That scheme was devised and put in effect under the guise of exertion of power to tax. We held it to be in excess of the powers delegated to the federal government; found the tax, the appropriation of the money raised, and the directions for its disbursement, to be but the means to an unconstitutional end; showed that the Constitution confers no power to regulate production and that therefore legislation for that purpose is forbidden;

After failure of that measure, Congress, assuming power under the commerce clause, enacted the provisions authorizing the quotas and penalties the validity of which is questioned in this case. Plaintiffs contend that the Act is a plan to control agricultural production and therefore beyond the powers delegated to Congress. The Court impliedly concedes that such a plan would be beyond congressional power, but says that the provisions do not purport to control production, set no limit upon the acreage which may be planted or produced and impose no penalty upon planting and production in excess of marketing quota. Mere inspection of the statute and Secretary's regulations unmistakably discloses purpose to raise price by lessening production. Whatever may be its declared policy or appearance, the enactment operates to control quantity raised by each farmer. It is wholly fallacious to say that the penalty is not imposed upon production. The farmer raises tobacco only for sale. Punishment for selling is the exact equivalent of punishment for raising the tobacco. The Act is therefore invalid.

Marchetti v. U.S.

390 U.S. 39 (1968)
Vote: 7–1; Marshall not participating.

In *U.S.* v. *Kahriger* (1953), federal power to help states regulate gambling was condoned. But by 1967 the tide of individual liberty generated by the Warren Court made the decision anomalous. In *Marchetti,* the tide of other decisions on incrimination all but forced reversal. Ironically, Chief Justice Warren dissented alone, and the opinion was written by Justice Harlan, normally the spokesperson for judicial restraint.

MR. JUSTICE HARLAN delivered the opinion of the Court.

Petitioner was convicted in the United States District Court for the District of Connecticut under two indictments which charged violations of the federal wagering tax statutes. . . . The Court of Appeals for the Second Circuit affirmed, 352 F. 2d 848, on the authority of *United States* v. *Kahriger,* 345 U.S. 22, and *Lewis* v. *United States,* 348 U.S. 419.

We granted certiorari to re-examine the constitutionality under the Fifth Amendment of the pertinent provisions of the wagering tax statutes, and more particularly to consider whether *Kahriger* and *Lewis* still have vitality. 383 U.S. 942. For reasons which follow, we have concluded that these provisions may not be employed to punish criminally those persons who have defended a failure to comply with their requirements with a proper assertion of the privilege against self-incrimination. The judgment below is accordingly reversed.

The issue before us is *not* whether the United States may tax activities which a State or Congress has declared unlawful. The Court has repeatedly indicated that the unlawfulness of an activity does not prevent its taxation, and nothing that follows is intended to limit or diminish the vitality of those cases. The issue is instead whether the methods employed by Congress in the federal wagering tax statutes are, in this situation, consistent with the limitations created by the privilege against self-incrimination guaranteed by the Fifth Amendment. We must for this purpose first examine the implications of these statutory provisions.

The laws of every State, except Nevada, include broad prohibitions against gambling, wagering, and associated activities. . . . Information obtained as a consequence of the federal wagering tax laws is readily available to assist the efforts of state and federal authorities to enforce . . . penalties.

Evidence of the possession of a federal wagering tax stamp, or of payment of the wagering taxes, has often been admitted at trial in state and federal prosecutions for gambling offenses; such evidence has doubtless proved useful even more frequently to lead prosecuting authorities to other evidence upon which convictions have subsequently been obtained. Finally, we are obliged to notice that a former Commissioner of Internal Revenue has acknowledged that the Service "makes available" to law enforcement agencies the names and addresses of those who have paid the wagering taxes, and that it is in "full cooperation" with the efforts of the Attorney General of the United States to suppress organized gambling. Caplin, The Gambling Business and Federal Taxes, 8 Crime & Delin. 371, 372, 377.

In these circumstances, it can scarcely be denied that the obligations to register and to pay the occupational tax created for petitioner "real and appreciable," and not merely "imaginary and unsubstantial," hazards of self-incrimination. . . . Petitioner was confronted by a comprehensive system of federal and state prohibitions against wagering activities; he was required, on pain of criminal prosecution, to provide information which he might reasonably suppose would be available to prosecuting authorities, and which would surely prove a significant "link in a chain" of evidence tending to establish his guilt.

Nonetheless, this Court has twice concluded that the privilege against self-incrimination may not appropriately be asserted by those in petitioner's circumstances.

. . . .

The Court held in both *Kahriger* and *Lewis* that the registration and occupational tax requirements are entirely prospective in their application, and that the constitutional privilege, since it offers protection only as to past and present acts, is accordingly unavailable. This reasoning appears to us twice deficient: first, it overlooks the hazards here of incrimination as to past or present acts; and second, it is hinged upon an excessively narrow view of the scope of the constitutional privilege, satisfaction of those requirements increases the likelihood that any past or present gambling offenses will be discovered and successfully prosecuted. . . .

. . . .

There is a second, and more fundamental, deficiency in the reasoning of *Kahriger* and *Lewis.* Its linchpin is plainly the premise that the privilege is entirely inapplicable to prospective acts; . . .

We see no warrant for so rigorous a constraint upon the constitutional privilege. History, to be sure, offers no ready illustrations of the privilege's application to prospective acts, but the occasions on which such claims might appropriately have been made must necessarily have been very infrequent. . . .

[W]e can only conclude, under the wagering tax system as presently written, that petitioner properly asserted the privilege against self-incrimination, and that his assertion should have provided a complete defense to this prosecution. This defense should have reached both the substantive counts for failure to register and to pay the occupational tax, and the count for conspiracy to evade payment of the tax. We emphasize that we do not hold that these wagering tax provisions are as such constitutionally impermissible; we hold only that those who properly assert the constitutional privilege as to these provisions may not be criminally punished for failure to comply with their requirements. If, in different circumstances, a taxpayer is not confronted by substantial hazards of self-incrimination, or if he is otherwise outside the privilege's protection, nothing we decide today would shield him from the various penalties prescribed by the wagering tax statutes.

The judgment of the Court of Appeals is

Reversed.

MR. JUSTICE MARSHALL took no part in the consideration or decision of this case.

MR. JUSTICE STEWART, concurring.

MR. JUSTICE BRENNAN, concurring.

MR. CHIEF JUSTICE WARREN, dissenting.

I cannot agree with the Court's conclusion on the constitutional questions presented, and I would affirm the convictions in these two cases on the authority of *Kahriger* and *Lewis*.

In addition to being in disagreement with the Court on the result it reaches in these cases, I am puzzled by the reasoning process which leads it to that result. The Court professes to recognize and accept the power of Congress legitimately to impose taxes on activities which have been declared unlawful by federal or state statutes. Yet, by its sweeping declaration that the congressional scheme for enforcing and collecting the taxes imposed on wagers and gamblers is unconstitutional, the Court has stripped from Congress the power to make its taxing scheme effective.

What seems to trouble the Court is not that registration is required but that information obtained through the registration requirement is turned over by federal officials, under the statutory compulsion of 26 U.S.C. §6107, to state prosecutors to aid them in the enforcement of state gambling laws.

Conceding that the statutory scheme is intended to assist law enforcement, the fact that taxes in the sum of $115,000,000 have flowed from the wagering tax scheme to the Treasury in the past several years

is convincing evidence of a legitimate tax purpose. The congressional intent to assist law enforcement should not be the excuse for frustrating the revenue purpose of the statutes before the Court. Regardless of legislative intent, this Court has in the past refused "to formulate a rule of constititonal law broader than is required."

Selective Service System v. Minnesota Public Interest Research Group

104 S.Ct. 3348 (1984)
Vote: 5–1–2

The power of Congress to secure compliance with its policies through its power over taxing and spending was further tested in this recent case. Congress linked federal aid to college students to draft registration by requiring male applicants for federal college aid to certify that they had registered as required under the Military Selective Service Act. Students raised the MARCHETTI issue — the problem of "confession by application" — in challenging the statute.

Is the result really different from, say, WICKARD V. FILBURN?

CHIEF JUSTICE BURGER delivered the opinion of the Court.

Appellees are anonymous individuals who were required to register before September 1, 1982. On September 8, Congress enacted the Department of Defense Authorization Act of 1983, Publ. L. 97–252, 96 Stat. 718. Section 1113(f)(1) provides that any peson who is required to register and fails to do so "in accordance with any proclamation" issued under the Military Selective Service Act "shall be ineligible for any form of assistance or benefit provided under title IV of the Higher Education Act of 1965." Section 1113(f)(2) requires applicants for Title IV assistance to file with their institutions of higher education a statement attesting to their compliance with the draft registration law and regulations issued under it. Sections 1113(f)(3) and (4) require the Secretary of Education, in agreement with the Director of Selective Service, to prescribe methods for verifying such statements of compliance and to issue implementing regulations.

....

In November 1982 the Minnesota Public Interest Research Group filed a complaint in the United States District Court for the District of Minnesota seeking to enjoin the operation of §1113. The District court dismissed the Minnesota Group for lack of standing but allowed three anonymous students to intervene as plaintiffs.... This suit was informally consolidated with a separate action brought by three other anonymous students making essentially the same allegations as the intervenors.

In March 1983 the District Court granted a preliminary injunction.... First, the District Court thought it likely that §1113 was a Bill of Attainder. The court interpreted the statutory bar to student aid as applicable to students who registered late. Thus interpreted, the statute "clearly singles out an ascertainable group based on past conduct" and "legislatively determines the guilt of this ascertainable group."... Second, the District Court found it likely that §1113 violated appellees' Fifth Amendment privilege against compelled self-incrimination. In the District Court's view, the statement of compliance required by §1113 compels students who have not registered for the draft and need financial aid to confess to the fact of nonregistration, which is a crime. 50 U.S.C. §462.

On June 16, 1983, the District Court entered a permanent, nationwide injunction against the enforcement of §1113.... To understand the District Court's analysis, it is necessary to turn to its construction of the statute.... In the court's view, the language of §1113, coupled with the Proclamation's 30-day registration requirement, precluded late registrants from qualifying for Title IV aid. Having construed §1113 as precluding late registration, the District Court read the statute to be retrospective, in that it denies financial assistance to an identifiable group—nonregistrants—based on their past conduct....

We reject the District Court's view that §1113 requires registration within the time fixed by Proclamation No. 4771. That view is plainly inconsistent with the structure of §1113 and with the legislative history.... The statute clearly gives nonregistrants 30 days after receiving notice that they are ineligible for Title IV aid to register for the draft and qualify for aid....

....

Because it allows late registration, §1113 is clearly distinguishable from the provisions struck down in *Cummings* and *Garland*. *Cummings* and *Garland*

dealt with absolute barriers to entry into certain professions for those who could not file the required loyalty oaths; no one who had served the Confederacy could possibly comply, for his status was irreversible. By contrast, §1113's requirements, far from irreversible, can be met readily by either timely or late filing. "Far from attaching to...past and ineradicable actions," ineligibility for Title IV benefits "is made to turn upon continuingly contemporaneous fact" which a student who wants public assistance can correct....

....

In deciding whether a statute inflicts forbidden punishment, we have recognized three necessary inquiries: (1) whether the challenged statute falls within the historical meaning of legislative punishment; (2) whether the statute, "viewed in terms of the type and severity of burdens imposed, reasonably can be said to further nonpunitive legislative purposes"; and (3) whether the legislative record "evinces a congressional intent to punish."

....

...A statute that leaves open perpetually the possibility of qualifying for aid does not fall within the historical meaning of forbidden legislative punishment.

....

The legislative history reflects that §1113 represents the considered congressional decision to further nonpunitive legislative goals. Congress was well aware that more than half a million young men had failed to comply with the registration requirement. The legislators emphasized that one of the primary purposes of §1113 was to encourage those required to register to do so.

Conditioning receipt of Title IV aid on registration is plainly a rational means to improve compliance with the registration requirement. Since the group of young men who must register for the draft overlaps in large part with the group of students who are eligible for Title IV aid, Congress reasonably concluded that §1113 would be a strong tonic to many nonregistrants.

Section 1113 also furthers a fair allocation of scarce federal resources by limiting Title IV aid to those who are willing to meet their responsibilities to the United States by registering with the Selective Service when required to do so....

....

Appellees assert that §1113 violates the Fifth Amendment by compelling nonregistrants to acknowledge that they have failed to register timely when confronted with certifying to their schools that they have complied with the registration law. Pointing to the fact that the willful failure to register within the time fixed by Proclamation No. 4771 is a criminal offense punishable under 50 U.S.C. App. §462, they contend that §1113 requires them — since in fact they have not registered — to confess to a criminal act and that this is "compulsion" in violation of their Fifth Amendment rights.

However, a person who has not registered clearly is under no compulsion to seek financial aid; if he has not registered, he is simply ineligible for aid. Since a nonregistrant is bound to know that his application for federal aid would be denied, he is in no sense under any "compulsion" to seek that aid. He has no reason to make any statement to anyone as to whether or not he has registered.

If appellees decide to register late, they could, of course, obtain Title IV aid without providing any information to their school that would incriminate them, since the statement to the school by the applicant is simply that he is in compliance with the registration law; it does not require him to disclose whether he was a timely or a late registrant. . . . A late registrant is therefore not required to disclose any incriminating information in order to become eligible for aid.

Although an applicant who registers late need not disclose that fact in his application for financial aid, the Government concedes that a late registrant must disclose that his action is untimely when he makes a late registration with the Selective Service; the draft registration card must be dated and contain the registrant's date of birth. . . . This raises the question whether §1113 violates appellees' Fifth Amendment rights because they must register late in order to get aid and thus reveal to the Selective Service the failure to comply timely with the registration law. . . .

. . . .

None of these appellees has registered and thus none of them has been confronted with a need to assert a Fifth Amendment privilege when asked to disclose his date of birth. . . . [T]hese appellees have not been denied the opportunity to register and in no sense have they been disqualified for financial aid "for asserting a constitutional privilege."

. . . .

We conclude that §1113 does not violate the proscription against Bills of Attainder. Nor have appellees raised a cognizable claim under the Fifth Amendment. . . .

JUSTICE BLACKMUN took no part in the decision of this case.

JUSTICE POWELL, concurring in part and concurring in the judgment.

I do not disagree with the holding or, indeed, with most of the Court's opinion. As I view this case, however, the Bill of Attainder issue can and should be disposed of solely on the ground that §1113 of the Defense Authorization Act of 1983 is not *punitive* legislation.

JUSTICE BRENNAN, dissenting.

JUSTICE MARSHALL, dissenting.

. . . .

The *Marchetti-Grosso* Court based its holding in part on the fact that the information-gathering scheme was directed at those "inherently suspect of criminal activities." Here, it is fair to say that the Government does not expect that most registrants will be in violation of the Selective Service laws. At first blush, the required information might therefore seem less like the *Marchetti-Gross* inquiries and more like income tax returns, "neutral on their face and directed at the public at large." . . .

. . . .

To adopt this analogy, however, is to ignore the actual case or controversy before the Court. When Congress passed §1113, its focus was assuredly *not* prospective. As the majority explains, Congress forged the link between education aid and Selective Service registration in order to bring into compliance with the law the 674,000 existing nonregistrants, including the six appellees in these cases. Although as a general matter it is correct to say that registration is like income tax (neutral on its face and directed to the (male) population at large), §1113-compelled *late* registration is directed to a group inherently suspect of criminal activity, squarely presenting a *Marchetti* issue.

In my view, therefore, young men who have failed to register with Selective Service, and at whom §1113 was substantially aimed, are entitled to the same "claim by silence" as Marchetti and Grosso. But these students are compelled to forgo that right under this statutory scheme. The defect in §1113 is that it denies students seeking federal aid the freedom to withhold their identities from the Federal Government. If appellees assert their Fifth Amendment privilege by their silence, they are penalized for exercising a constitutional right by the withholding of education aid. If they succumb to the economic coercion either by registering, or by registering but claiming the privilege as to particular disclosures, they have incriminated themselves.

Thus, I cannot accept the majority's view that appellee's Fifth Amendment claims are not ripe for review. . . .

Texas v. White

7 Wallace 700 (1869)
Vote: (5–2)–1

This case presents, in two different guises, the constitutional problem of what a state is. Both grow out of Texas' role in the Civil War.

In 1851, Texas received U.S. bonds as settlement for some boundary claims. The legislature provided that the bonds could be redeemed only if endorsed by the governor. After secession, the rebel legislature repealed that provision, and unendorsed bonds were used to pay White and Chiles to provide supplies for the war. Thus the first question was whether the State of Texas existed during the war, so as to change its rules with respect to the bonds, so as to effect transfer to White and Chiles.

Additionally, the Reconstruction governor asked for an injunction forbidding sale of the bonds and asking for their return. Texas, as a state, went directly to the U.S. Supreme Court, under that body's original jurisdiction. Chiles, however, argued that the Reconstruction governments were not restored to statehood and could not sue, just as they still were not seated in Congress.

In effect, Texas argued that its power had lapsed during the Civil War, so its legislation was not effective, but it was now again a state and could sue. Chiles, in effect, argued that Texas' actions were legal during the war, but it at some point lost the right to sue as a state, and it was still in limbo.

MR. CHIEF JUSTICE CHASE delivered the opinion of the court:

This is an original suit in this court, in which the State of Texas, claiming certain bonds of the United States as her property, asks an injunction to restrain the defendants from receiving payment from the National Government, and to compel the surrender of the bonds to the State.

It appears from the bill, answers and proofs, that the United States, by Act of September 9, 1850, offered to the State of Texas, in compensation of her claims connected with the settlement of her boundary $10,000,000 in five per cent. bonds, each for the sum of $1,000; and that this offer was accepted by Texas.

. . . They were received in behalf of the State by the Comptroller of Public Accounts, under authority of an Act of the Legislature, which, besides giving that authority, provided that no bond should be available in the hands of any holder until after indorsement by the Governor of the State.

After the breaking out of the Rebellion, the insurgent Legislature of Texas, on the 11th of January, 1862, repealed the Act requiring the indorsement of the Governor. . . .

. . . On the 12th of March, 1865, White and Chiles received from the Military Board one hundred and thirty-five of these bonds, none of which were indorsed by any Governor of Texas. Afterward, in the course of the years 1865 and 1866, some of the same bonds came into the possession of others of the defendants, by purchase, or as security for advances of money.

. . . It is not to be questioned that this court has original jurisdiction of suits by States against citizens of other States, or that the States entitled to invoke this jurisdiction must be States of the Union. But, it is equally clear that no such jurisdiction has been conferred upon this court of suits by any other political communities than such States.

If, therefore, it is true that the State of Texas was not at the time of filing this bill, or is not now, one of the United States, we have no jurisdiction of this suit and it is our duty to dismiss it.

The Republic of Texas was admitted into the Union, as a State, on the 27th of December, 1845. By this Act the new State, and the people of the new State, were invested with all the rights, and became subject to all the responsibilities and duties of the original States under the Constitution.

From the date of admission, until 1861, the State was represented in the Congress of the United States by her Senators and Representatives, and her relations as a member of the Union remained unimpaired. In that year, acting upon the theory that the rights of a State under the Constitution might be renounced, and her obligations thrown off at pleasure, Texas undertook to sever the bond thus formed, and to break up her constitutional relations with the United States.

The representatives of the State in the Congress of the United States were withdrawn, and as soon as the seceded States became organized under a constitution, Texas sent Senators and Representatives to the Confederate Congress.

In all respects, so far as the object could be accomplished by ordinances of the Convention, by

Acts of the Legislature, and by votes of the citizens, the relations of Texas to the Union were broken up, and new relations to a new government were established for them. . . .

Did Texas, in consequence of these Acts, cease to be a State? Or, if not, did the State cease to be a member of the Union?

It is needless to discuss, at length, the question whether the right of a State to withdraw from the Union for any cause, regarded by herself as sufficient, is consistent with the Constitution of the United States.

The Union of the States never was a purely artificial and arbitrary relation. It began among the Colonies, and grew out of common origin, mutual sympathies, kindred principles, similar interests and geographical relations. It was confirmed and strengthened by the necessities of war, and received definite form, and character, and sanction from the Articles of Confederation. By these the Union was solemnly declared to "be perpetual." And when these articles were found to be inadequate to the exigencies of the country, the Constitution was ordained "to form a more perfect Union." It is difficult to convey the idea of indissoluble unity more clearly than by these words. What can be indissoluble if a perpetual Union, made more perfect, is not?

But the perpetuity and indissolubility of the Union by no means implies the loss of distinct and individual existence, or of the right of self government by the States. Under the Articles of Confederation each State retained its sovereignty, freedom and independence, and every power, jurisdiction and right not expressly delegated to the United States. Under the Constitution, though the powers of the States were much restricted, still, all powers not delegated to the United States, nor prohibited to the States, are reserved to the States respectively to the people. And we have already had occasion to remark at this term, that "the people of each State compose a State, having its own government, and endowed with all the functions essential to separate and independent existence," and that "without the States in union, there could be no such political body as the United States." *Lane Co.* v. *Oregon* [*infra*, 101]. Not only, therefore, can there be no loss of separate and independent autonomy to the States, through their union under the Constitution, but it may be not unreasonably said that the preservation of the States, and the maintenance of their governments, are as much within the design and care of the Constitution as the preservation of the Union and the maintenance of the National Government. The Constitution, in all its provisions, looks to an in-

destructible Union, composed of indestructible States. . . .

Considered, therefore, as transactions under the Constitution, the Ordinance of Secession, adopted by the convention and ratified by a majority of the citizens of Texas, and all the Acts of her Legislature intended to give effect to that ordinance, were absolutely null. They were utterly without operation in law. The obligations of the State as a member of the Union, and of every citizen of the State, as a citizen of the United States, remained perfect and unimpaired. It certainly follows that the State did not cease to be a State, nor her citizens to be citizens of the Union. If this were otherwise, the State must have become foreign, and her citizens foreigners. The war must have ceased to be a war for the suppression of rebellion, must have become a war for conquest and subjugation.

But in order to the exercise, by a State, of the right to sue in this court, there needs to be a State Government, competent to represent the State in its relations with the National Government, so far at least as the institution and prosecution of a suit is concerned.

And it is by no means a logical conclusion, from the premises which we have endeavored to establish, that the governmental relations of Texas to the Union remained unaltered. Obligations often remain unimpaired, while relations are greatly changed. The obligations of allegiance to the State, and obedience to her laws, subject to the Constitution of the United States, are binding upon all citizens, whether faithful or unfaithful to them; but the relations which subsist while these obligations are performed, are essentially different from those which arise when they are disregarded and set at nought. And the same must necessarily be true of the obligations and relations of States and citizens to the Union. No one has been bold enough to contend that, while Texas was controlled by a government hostile to the United States, and in affiliation with a hostile confederation, waging war upon the United States, Senators chosen by her Legislature, or Representatives elected by her citizens, were entitled to seats in Congress; or that any suit, instituted in her name, could be entertained in this court. All admit that, during this condition of civil war, the rights of the State as a member, and of her people as citizens of the Union, were suspended. The government and the citizens of the State, refusing to recognize their constitutional obligations, assumed the character of enemies, and incurred the consequences of rebellion.

These new relations imposed new duties upon the United States. The first was that of suppressing the Rebellion. The next was that of re-establishing the broken relations of the State with the Union. The first of these duties having been performed, the next necessarily engaged the attention of the National Government.

The authority for the performance of the first had been found in the power to suppress insurrection and carry on war; for the performance of the second, authority was derived from the obligation of the United States to guarantee to every State in the Union a republican form of government. The latter, indeed, in the case of a rebellion which involves the government of a State, and for the time excludes the national authority from its limits, seems to be a necessary complement to the former.

Of this, the case of Texas furnishes a striking illustration. When the war closed there was no government in the State except that which had been organized for the purpose of waging war against the United States. That government immediately disappeared. . . .

There being, then, no government in Texas in constitutional relations with the Union, it became the duty of the United States to provide for the restoration of such a government. But the restoration of the government which existed before the rebellion, without a new election of officers, was obviously impossible; and before any such election could be properly held, it was necessary that the old Constitution should receive such amendments as would conform its provisions to the new conditions created by emancipation, and afford adequate security to the people of the State.

In the exercise of the power conferred by the guaranty clause, as in the exercise of every other constitutional power, a discretion in the choice of means is necessarily allowed. It is essential only that the means must be necessary and proper for carrying into execution the power conferred, through the restoration of the State to its constitutional relations, under a republican form of government, and that no acts be done, and no authority exerted, which is either prohibited or unsanctioned by the Constitution.

What has thus been said generally describes, with sufficient accuracy, the situation of Texas. A provisional Governor of the State was appointed by the President in 1865; in 1866 a Governor was elected by the people under the constitution of that year; at a subsequent date a Governor was appointed by the commander of the district. Each of the three exercised executive functions and actually represented the State in the Executive Department.

In the case before us each has given his sanction to the prosecution of the suit, and we find no difficulty, without investigating the legal title of either to the executive office, in holding that the sanction thus given sufficiently warranted the action of the solicitor and counsel in behalf of the State. The necessary conclusion is that the suit was instituted and is prosecuted by competent authority.

In this case, however, it is said that the restriction imposed by the Act of 1851 was repealed by the Act of 1862. And this is true if the Act of 1862 can be regarded as valid. But was it valid?

The Legislature of Texas, at the time of the repeal, constituted one of the departments of a State Government, established in hostility to the Constitution of the United States. It cannot be regarded, therefore, in the courts of the United States, as a lawful Legislature, or its Acts as lawful Acts. And yet it is an historical fact that the Government of Texas, then in full control of the State, was its only actual government; and certainly if Texas had been a separate State and not one of the United States, the new government, having displaced the regular authority, and having established itself in the customary seats of power and in the exercise of the ordinary functions of administration, would have constituted, in the strictest sense of the words, a *de facto* government, and its acts, during the period of its existence as such, would be effectual and, in almost all respects, valid. And, to some extent, this is true of the actual government of Texas, though unlawful and revolutionary as to the United States.

It is not necessary to attempt any exact definitions, within which the Acts of such a state Government must be treated as valid, or invalid. It may be said, perhaps with sufficient accuracy, that Acts necessary to peace and good order among citizens, such, for example, as Acts sanctioning and protecting marriage and the domestic relations, governing the course of descents, regulating the conveyance and transfer of property, real and personal, and providing remedies for injuries to person and estate, and other similar Acts, which would be valid if emanating from a lawful government, must be regarded, in general, as valid when proceeding from an actual, though unlawful government; and that Acts in furtherance or support of rebellion against the United States, or intended to defeat the just rights of citizens, and other Acts of like nature, must, in general, be regarded as invalid and void.

What, then, tried by these general tests, was the character of the contract of the military Board with White and Chiles?

That Board, as we have seen, was organized, not for the defense of the State against a foreign invasion, or for its protection against domestic violence, within the meaning of these words as used in the

National Constitution, but for the purpose, under the name of defense, of levying war against the United States. This purpose was, undoubtedly, unlawful, for the Acts which it contemplated are, within the express definition of the Constitution, treasonable.

On the whole case, therefore, our conclusion is that the State of Texas is entitled to the relief sought by her bill, and a decree must be made accordingly.

MR. JUSTICE GRIER, dissenting, delivered the following opinion:

Is Texas one of these United States? Or was she such at the time this bill was filed, or since?

This is to be decided as a political fact, not as a legal fiction. This court is bound to know and notice the public history of the nation.

If I regard the truth of history for the last eight years, I cannot discover the State of Texas as one of these United States.

Is Texas a State, now represented by members chosen by the people of that State and received on the floor of Congress? Has she two Senators to represent her as a State in the Senate of the United States? Has her voice been heard in the late election of President? Is she not now held and governed as a conquered province by military force? The Act of Congress of March 28th, 1867, declares Texas to be a "Rebel State," and provides for its government until a legal and republican State Government could be legally established. It constituted Louisiana and Texas the 5th military district, and made it subject, not to the civil authority, but to the "military authorities of the United States."

It is true that no organized rebellion now exists there, and the courts of the United States now exercise jurisdiction over the people of that province. But this is no test of the State's being in the Union; Dakota is no State, and yet the courts of the United States administer justice there as they do in Texas. I do not consider myself bound to express any opinion judicially as to the constitutional right of Texas to exercise the rights and privileges of a State of this Union, or the power of Congress to govern her a conquered province, to subject her to military domination, and keep her in pupilage. I can only submit to the fact as decided by the political position of the government; and I am not disposed to join in any essay to prove Texas to be a State of the Union, when Congress have decided that she is not. It is a question of fact, I repeat, and of fact only. Politically, Texas is not a State in this Union. Whether rightfully out of it or not is a question not before the court.

But conceding the fact to be as judicially assumed by my brethren, the next question is, whether she has a right to repudiate her contracts. Before proceeding to answer this question, we must notice a fact in this case that was forgotten in the argument. I mean that the United States are no party to this suit, and refusing to pay the bonds because the money paid would be used to advance the interests of the rebellion. It is a matter of utter insignificance to the Government of the United States to whom she makes the payment of these bonds. They are payable to the bearer. The government is not bound to inquire into the *bona fides* of the holder, nor whether the State of Texas has parted with the bonds wisely or foolishly.

MR. JUSTICE SWAYNE delivered the following opinion:

I concur with my brother GRIER as to the incapacity of the State of Texas, in her present condition, to maintain an original suit in this court. . . .

Upon the merits of the case, I agree with the majority of my brethren.

I am authorized to say that my brother MILLER unites with me in these views.

Coyle v. Smith

221 U.S. 559 (1911)
Vote: 7–2

The power of Congress to admit states also involves making judgments and imposing conditions. Clearly Congress has an obligation to require the "republican form of government" guaranteed by the Constitution. The most famous example was the requirement that Utah include in its constitution a prohibition of polygamy. But what other requirements can be imposed? In this case a requirement with respect to location of the state capitol was involved.

Does *Coyle* v. *Smith* suggest that if the Mormon Church returned to polygamy such conditions could be swept aside? If Congress requires special protection through amendable or difficult-to-amend clauses, are those subject to change by simple majorities with Court approval according to this decision? Is the logic of *Coyle* v. *Smith* more important today than its practical import, since few new states are likely to be created in the near future?

MR. JUSTICE LURTON delivered the opinion of the court.

The question reviewable under this writ of error, if any there be, arises under the claim set up by the petitioners, and decided against them, that the Oklahoma act of December 29, 1910, providing for the immediate location of the capital of the State of Oklahoma City was void as repugnant to the Enabling Act of Congress of June 16, 1906, under which the State was admitted to the Union. 34 Stat. 267, c. 3335. The act referred to is entitled "An act to enable the people of Oklahoma and the Indian Territory to form a constitution and state government and be admitted into the Union on an equal footing with the original States," etc. . . . The second section is lengthy and deals with the organization of a constitutional convention and concludes in these words: "The capital of said State shall temporarily be at the city of Guthrie, and shall not be changed therefrom previous to Anno Domini 1913." . . .

The power to locate its own seat of government and to determine when and how it shall be changed from one place to another, and to appropriate its own public funds for that purpose, are essentially and peculiarly state powers. That one of the original thirteen States could now be shorn of such powers by an act of Congress would not be for a moment entertained. The question then comes to this: Can a State be placed upon a plane of inequality with its sister States in the Union if the Congress chooses to impose conditions which so operate, at the time of its admission? The argument is, that while Congress may not deprive a State of any power which it *possesses,* it may, as a condition to the admission of a new State, constitutionally restrict its authority, to the extent at least, of suspending its powers for a definite time in respect to the location of its seat of government. This contention is predicated upon the constitutional power of admitting new States to this Union, and the constitutional duty of guaranteeing to "every State in this Union a republican form of government." The position of counsel for the appellants is substantially this: That the power of Congress to admit new States and to determine whether or not its fundamental law is republican in form, are political powers, and as such, uncontrollable by the courts. That Congress may in the exercise of such power impose terms and conditions upon the admission of the proposed new State, which, if accepted, will be obligatory, although they operate to deprive the State of powers which it would otherwise possess, and, therefore, not admitted upon "an equal footing with the original States."

The power of Congress in respect to the admission of new States is found in the third section of the fourth Article of the Constitution. That provision is that, "new States may be admitted by the Congress into this Union." The only expressed restriction upon this power is that no new State shall be formed within the jurisdiction of any other State, nor by the junction of two or more States, or parts of States, without the consent of such States, as well as of the Congress.

But what is this power? It is not to admit political organizations which are less or greater, or different in dignity or power, from those political entities which constitute the Union. It is, as strongly put by counsel, a "power to admit States." . . .

"This Union" was and is a union of States, equal in power, dignity and authority, each competent to exert that residuum of sovereignty not delegated to the United States by the Constitution itself. To maintain otherwise would be to say that the Union, through the power of Congress to admit new States, might come to be a union of States unequal in power, as including States whose powers were restricted only by the Constitution, with others whose powers had been further restricted by an act of Congress accepted as a condition of admission. Thus it would result, first, that the powers of Congress would not be defined by the Constitution alone, but in respect to new States, enlarged or restricted by the conditions imposed upon new States by its own legislation admitting them into the Union; and, second, that such new States might not exercise all of the powers which had not been delegated by the Constitution, but only such as had not been further bargained away as conditions of admission.

The argument that Congress derives from the duty of "guaranteeing to each State in this Union a republican form of government," power to impose restrictions upon a new State which deprives it of equality with other members of the Union, has no merit. It may imply the duty of such new State to provide itself with such state government, and impose upon Congress the duty of seeing that such form is not changed to one anti-republican, — *Minor v. Happersett,* 21 Wall, 162, 174, 175, — but it obviously does not confer power to admit a new State which shall be any less a State than those which compose the Union.

We come now to the question as to whether there is anything in the decisions of this court which sanctions the claim that Congress may by the imposition of conditions in an enabling act deprive a new State of any of those attributes essential to its equality in dignity and power with other States. In considering the decisions of this court bearing upon the question, we must distinguish, first, between provisions which are fulfilled by the admission of the State; second, between compacts or affirmative legislation intended to operate *in futuro,* which are within the scope of the conceded powers of Congress over the subject; and third, compacts or affirmative legislation which operates to restrict the powers of such new States in respect of matters which would otherwise be exclusively within the sphere of state power.

As to requirements in such enabling acts as relate only to the contents of the constitution for the proposed new State, little needs to be said. The constitutional provision concerning the admission of new States is not a mandate, but a power to be exercised with discretion. From this alone it would follow that Congress may require, under penalty of denying admission, that the organic laws of a new State at the time of admission shall be such as to meet its approval. A constitution thus supervised by Congress would, after all, be a constitution of a State, and as such subject to alteration and amendment by the State after admission. Its force would be that of a state constitution, and not that of an act of Congress. . . .

Has Oklahoma been admitted upon an equal footing with the original States? If she has, she by virtue of her jurisdictional sovereignty as such a State may determine for her own people the proper location of the local seat of government. She is not equal in power to them if she cannot.

In *Texas* v. *White* [1869] Chief Justice Chase said in strong and memorable language that, "the Constitution, in all of its provisions looks to an indestructible Union, composed of indestructible States."

To this we may add that the constitutional equality of the States is essential to the harmonious operation of the scheme upon which the Republic was organized. When that equality disappears we may remain a free people, but the Union will not be the Union of the Constitution.

Judgment affirmed.

MR. JUSTICE MCKENNA and MR. JUSTICE HOLMES dissent.

The Collector v. Day

11 Wallace 113 (1871)
Vote: 8–1

The Civil War forced the federal government to turn to an income tax as a source of revenue. Day, a Massachusetts local judge, chal-

lenged the tax. The circuit court held in his favor and the government appealed.

MR. JUSTICE NELSON delivered the opinion of the court.

The case presents the question whether or not it is competent for Congress, under the Constitution of the United States, to impose a tax upon the salary of a judicial officer of a State?

In *Dobbins* v. *The Commissioners of Erie County,* it was decided that it was not competent for the legislature of a State to levy a tax upon the salary or emoluments of an officer of the United States. The decision was placed mainly upon the ground that the officer was a means or instrumentality employed for carrying into effect some of the legitimate powers of the government, which could not be interfered with by taxation or otherwise by the States, and that the salary or compensation for the service of the officer was inseparably connected with the office; that if the officer, as such, was exempt, the salary assigned for his support or maintenance while holding the office was also, for like reasons, equally exempt.

It is a familiar rule of construction of the Constitution of the Union, that the sovereign powers vested in the State governments by their respective constitutions, remained unaltered and unimpaired, except so far as they were granted to the government of the United States. That the intention of the framers of the Constitution in this respect might not be misunderstood, this rule of interpretation is expressly declared in the tenth article of the amendments. . . .

The general government, and the States, although both exist within the same territorial limits, are separate and distinct sovereignties, acting separately and independently of each other, within their respective spheres. The former in its appropriate sphere is supreme; but the States within the limits of their powers not granted, or, in the language of the tenth amendment, "reserved," are as independent of the general government as that government within its sphere is independent of the States.

The relations existing between the two governments are well stated by the present Chief Justice in the case of *Lane County* v. *Oregon.* "Both the States and the United States," he observed, "existed before the Constitution. The people, through that instrument, established a more perfect union, by substituting a National government, acting with ample powers directly upon the citizens, instead of the Confederate government, which acted with powers greatly restricted, only upon the States. But, in many of the articles of the Constitution, the necessary existence of the States, and within their proper spheres, the independent authority of the States, are distinctly recognized. To them nearly the whole charge of interior regulation is committed or left; to them, and to the people, all powers, not expressly delegated to the National government, are reserved." Upon looking into the Constitution it will be found that but a few of the articles in that instrument could be carried into practical effect without the existence of the States.

The supremacy of the general government, therefore, so much relied on in the argument of the counsel for the plaintiff in error, in respect to the question before us, cannot be maintained. The two governments are upon an equality, and the question is whether the power "to lay and collect taxes" enables the general government to tax the salary of a judicial officer of the State, which officer is a means or instrumentality employed to carry into execution one of its most important functions, the administration of the laws, and which concerns the exercise of a right reserved to the States?

We do not say the mere circumstance of the establishment of the judicial department, and the appointment of officers to administer the laws, being among the reserved powers of the State, disables the general government from levying the tax, as that depends upon the express power "to lay and collect taxes," but it shows that it is an original inherent power never parted with, and, in respect to which, the supremacy of that government does not exist, and is of no importance in determining the question; and further, that being an original and reserved power, and the judicial officers appointed under it being a means or instrumentality employed to carry it into effect, the right and necessity of its unimpaired exercise, and the exemption of the officer from taxation by the general government stand upon as solid a ground, and are maintained by principles and reasons as cogent as those which led to the exemption of the Federal officer in *Dobbins* v. *The Commissioners of Erie* from taxation by the State; for, in this respect, that is, in respect to the reserved powers, the State is as sovereign and independent as the general government. And if the means and instrumentalities employed by that government to carry into operation the powers granted to it are, necessarily, and, for the sake of self-preservation, exempt from taxation by the States, why are not those of the States depending upon their reserved powers, for like reasons, equally exempt from Federal taxation? Their unimpaired existence in the one case is as essential as in the other. It is admitted that there is no express provision in the Constitution that prohibits the general government from taxing the means and instrumentalities of the States, nor is there any prohibiting the States from taxing the means and instrumentalities of that government. In both cases the exemption rests upon necessary implication, and is upheld by the great law of self-preservation; as any government, whose means employed in conducting its operations, if subject to the control of another and distinct government, can exist only at the mercy of that government.

Judgment Affirmed.

MR. JUSTICE BRADLEY, dissenting.

In my judgment, the limitation of the power of taxation in the general government, which the present decision establishes, will be found very difficult of control. Where are we to stop in enumerating the functions of the State governments which will be interfered with by Federal taxation? If a State incorporates a railroad to carry out its purposes of internal improvement, or a bank to aid its financial arrangements, reserving, perhaps, a percentage on the stock or profits, for the supply of its own treasury, will the bonds or stock of such an institution be free from Federal taxation? How can we now tell what the effect of this decision will be? I cannot but regard it as founded on a fallacy, and that it will lead to mischievous consequences.

Graves v. New York ex rel. O'Keefe

306 U.S. 466 (1939)
Vote: 7–2

This case effectively overturned THE COLLECTOR V. DAY and ended the proliferation of intergovernmental tax immunity.

O'Keefe was an employee of the Home Owners' Loan Corporation, a federal instrumentality. Graves, the New York State Tax Collector, tried to collect state tax. The New York Courts, feeling bound by previous constitutional decisions, held O'Keefe was exempt from taxation. The U.S. Supreme Court granted certiorari. The Solicitor General appeared as amicus curiae ("friend of the Court," a nonlitigating party) to argue against O'Keefe, and to urge the Supreme Court to limit the immunity doctrine.

MR. JUSTICE STONE delivered the opinion of the Court.

We are asked to decide whether the imposition by the State of New York of an income tax on the salary of an employee of the Home Owners' Loan Corporation places an unconstitutional burden upon the federal government.

The single question with which we are now concerned is whether the tax laid by the state upon the salary of respondent, employed by a corporate instrumentality of the federal government, imposes an unconstitutional burden upon that government. The theory of the tax immunity of either government, state or national, and its instrumentalities, from taxation by the other, has been rested upon an implied limitation on the taxing power of each, such as to forestall undue interference, through the exercise of that power, with the governmental activities of the other. That the two types of immunity may not, in all respects, stand on a parity has been recognized from the beginning, *McCulloch v. Maryland.*

So far as now relevant, those differences have been thought to be traceable to the fact that the federal government is one of delegated powers in the exercise of which Congress is supreme; so that every agency which Congress can constitutionally create is a governmental agency. And since the power to create the agency includes the implied power to do whatever is needful or appropriate, if not expressly prohibited, to protect the agency, there has been attributed to Congress some scope, the limits of which it is not now necessary to define, for granting or withholding immunity of federal agencies from state taxation. . . .

Congress has declared in §4 of the Act that the Home Owners' Loan Corporation is an instrumentality of the United States and that its bonds are exempt, as to principal and interest, from federal and state taxation, except surtaxes, estate, inheritance and gift taxes. . . . But Congress has given no intimation of any purpose either to grant or withhold immunity from state taxation of the salary of the corporation's employees, and the Congressional intention is not to be gathered from the statute by implication.

It is true that the silence of Congress, when it has authority to speak, may sometimes give rise to an implication as to the Congressional purpose. . . . But there is little scope for the application of that doctrine to the tax immunity of governmental instrumentalities. . . . [I]f it appears that there is no ground for implying a constitutional immunity, there is equally a want of any ground for assuming any purpose on the part of Congress to create an immunity.

The present tax is a non-discriminatory tax on income applied to salaries at a specified rate. It is not in form or substance a tax upon the Home Owners' Loan Corporation or its property or income, nor is it paid by the corporation or the government from their funds. It is measured by income which becomes the property of the taxpayer when received as compensation for his services; and the tax laid upon the privilege of receiving it is paid from his private funds and not from the funds of the government, either directly or indirectly. The theory, which once won a qualified approval, that a tax on income is legally or economically a tax on its source, is no longer tenable, and the only possible basis for implying a constitutional immunity from state income tax of the salary of an employee of the national government or of a governmental agency is that the economic burden of the tax is in some way passed on so as to impose a burden on the national government tantamount to an interference by one government with the other in the performance of its functions.

In the four cases in which this Court has held that the salary of an officer or employee of one government or its instrumentality was immune from taxation by the other, it was assumed, without discussion, that the immunity of a government or its instrumentality extends to the salaries of its officers and employees. . . .

The ultimate repudiation in *Helvering* v. *Mountain Producers Corp., supra,* of the doctrine that a tax on the income of a lessee derived from a lease of government owned or controlled lands is a forbidden interference with the activities of the government concerned led to the reexamination by this Court, in the *Gerhardt* case, of the theory underlying the asserted immunity from taxation by one government of salaries of employees of the other. It was there pointed out that the implied immunity of one government and its agencies from taxation by the other should, as a principle of constitutional construction, be narrowly restricted. For the expansion of the immunity of the one government correspondingly curtails the sovereign power of the other to tax, and where that immunity is invoked by the private citizen it tends to operate for his benefit at the expense of the taxing government and without corresponding benefit to the government in whose name the immunity is claimed.

The conclusion reached in the *Gerhardt* case that in terms of constitutional tax immunity a federal income tax on the salary of an employee is not a prohibited burden on the employer makes it imperative that we should consider anew the immunity here claimed for the salary of an employee of a federal instrumentality. As already indicated, such differences as there may be between the implied tax immunity of a state and the corresponding immunity of the national government and its instrumentalities may be traced to the fact that the national government is one of delegated powers, in the exercise of which it is supreme. Whatever scope this may give to the national government to claim immunity from state taxation of all instrumentalities which it may constitutionally create, and whatever authority Congress may possess as incidental to the exercise of its delegated powers to grant or withhold immunity from state taxation, Congress has not sought in this case to exercise such power. Hence these distinctions between the two types of immunity cannot affect the question with which we are now concerned. The burden on government of a nondiscriminatory income tax applied to the salary of the employee of a government or its instrumentality is the same, whether a state or national government is concerned.

. . . In no case is there basis for the assumption that any such tangible or certain economic burden is imposed on the government concerned as would justify a court's declaring that the taxpayer is clothed with the implied constitutional tax immunity of the government by which he is employed. . . . *Collector* v. *Day, supra,* and *New York ex rel. Rogers* v. *Graves, supra,* are overruled so far as they recognize an implied constitutional immunity from income taxation of the salaries of officers or employees of the national or a state government or their instrumentalities.

Reversed.

MR. CHIEF JUSTICE HUGHES concurs in the result.

MR. JUSTICE FRANKFURTER, concurring:

The judicial history of this doctrine of immunity is a striking illustration of an occasional tendency to encrust unwarranted interpretations upon the Constitution and thereafter to consider merely what has been judicially said about the Constitution, rather than to be primarily controlled by a fair conception of the Constitution. Judicial exegesis is unavoidable with reference to an organic act like our Constitution, drawn in many particulars with purposed vagueness so as to leave room for the unfolding future. But the ultimate touchstone of constitutionality is the Constitution itself and not what we have said about it. . . . Whether Congress may, by express legislation, relieve its functionaries from their civic obligations to pay for the benefits of the State governments under which they live is matter for another day.

MR. JUSTICE BUTLER, dissenting:

MR. JUSTICE MCREYNOLDS and I are of opinion that the Home Owners' Loan Corporation, being an instrumentality of the United States heretofore deemed immune from state taxation, "it necessarily results," as held in *New York ex rel. Rogers* v. *Graves* (1937), "that fixed salaries and compensation paid to its officers and employees in their capacity as such are likewise immune"; and that the judgment of the state court, unquestionably required by that decision, should be affirmed.

Appraisal of lurking or apparent implications of the Court's opinion can serve no useful end for, should occasion arise, they may be ignored or given direction differing from that at first seemingly intended. But safely it may be said that presently marked for destruction is the doctrine of reciprocal immunity that by recent decisions here has been so much impaired.

New York v. U.S.

326 U.S. 572 (1946)
Vote: 6–2; Jackson not participating.

The State of New York sold Saratoga Springs mineral water for profit, and refused to pay a federal tax, claiming exemption. A federal district court supported the IRS claim, and the decision was affirmed by the court of appeals. The Supreme Court granted certiorari.

With growing efforts by states to find income supplements, the case loomed as a major one. Note that as a result of some odd bargaining an "Opinion of the Court" is announced with considerably less support than the concurrence, which actually has plurality status, since Jackson recused himself.

MR. JUSTICE FRANKFURTER announced the judgment of the Court and delivered an opinion in which MR. JUSTICE RUTLEDGE joined.

Section 615 (a) (5) of the 1932 Revenue Act, 47 Stat. 169, 264, imposed a tax on mineral waters. The United States brought this suit to recover taxes assessed against the State of New York on the sale of mineral waters taken from Saratoga Springs, New York. The State claims immunity from this tax on the ground that "in the bottling and sale of the said waters the defendant State of New York was engaged in the exercise of a usual, traditional and essential governmental function."

On the basis of authority the case is quickly disposed of. When States sought to control the liquor traffic by going into the liquor business, they were denied immunity from federal taxes upon the liquor business. *South Carolina* v. *United States*. . . . And in rejecting a claim of immunity from federal taxation when Massachusetts took over the street railways of Boston, this Court a decade ago said: "We see no reason for putting the operation of a street railway [by a State] in a different category from the sale of liquors." *Helvering* v. *Powers*. . . . We certainly see no reason for putting soft drinks in a different constitutional category from hard drinks. . . .

One of the greatest sources of strength of our law is that it adjudicates concrete cases and does not pronounce principles in the abstract. But there comes a time when even the process of empiric adjudication calls for a more rational disposition than that the immediate case is not different from preceding cases. The argument pressed by New York and the forty-five other States who, as *amici curiae,* have joined her deserves an answer.

. . . [T]he fact that ours is a federal constitutional system, as expressly recognized in the Tenth Amendment, carries with it implications regarding the taxing power as in other aspects of government. . . . Thus, for Congress to tax State activities while leaving untaxed the same activities pursued by private persons would do violence to the presuppositions derived from the fact that we are a Nation composed of States.

But the fear that one government may cripple or obstruct the operations of the other early led to the assumption that there was a reciprocal immunity of the instrumentalities of each from taxation by the other. It was assumed that there was an equivalence in the implications of taxation by a State of the governmental activities of the National Government and the taxation by the National Government of State instrumentalities. This assumed equivalence was nourished by the phrase of Chief Justice Marshall that "the power to tax involves the power to destroy." *McCulloch* v. *Maryland*. . . . To be sure, it was uttered in connection with a tax of Maryland which plainly discriminated against the use by the United States of the Bank of the United States as one of its instruments. What he said may not have been irrelevant in its setting. But Chief Justice Marshall spoke at a time when social complexities did not so clearly reveal as now the practical limitations of a rhetorical absolute.

To press a juristic principle designed for the practical affairs of government to abstract extremes is neither sound logic nor good sense. And this Court is under no duty to make law less than sound logic and good sense. When this Court for the first time relieved State officers from a non-discriminatory Congressional tax, not because of anything said in the Constitution but because of the supposed implications of our federal system, Mr. Justice Bradley pointed out the invalidity of the notion of reciprocal intergovernmental immunity. The considerations bearing upon taxation by the States of activities or agencies of the federal government are not correlative with the considerations bearing upon federal taxation of State agencies or activities. The federal government is the government of all the States, and all the States share in the legislative process by which a tax of general applicability is laid. . . . Since then we have moved away from the theoretical assumption that the National Government is burdened if its functionaries, like other citizens, pay for the upkeep of their State governments, and we have denied the implied constitutional immunity of federal officials from State taxes.

In the meantime, cases came here, as we have already noted, in which States claimed immunity from a federal tax imposed generally on enterprises in which the State itself was also engaged. This problem did not arise before the present century, partly because State trading did not actively emerge until relatively recently, and partly because of the narrow scope of federal taxation. To rest the federal taxing power on what is "normally" conducted by private enterprise in contradiction to the "usual" governmental functions is too shifting a basis for determining constitutional power and too entangled in expediency to serve as a dependable legal criterion. The essential nature of the problem cannot be hidden by an attempt to separate manifestations of indivisible governmental powers. . . .

The present case illustrates the sterility of such an attempt. New York urges that in the use it is making of Saratoga Springs it is engaged in the disposition of its natural resources. And so it is. But in doing so it is engaged in an enterprise in which the State sells mineral waters in competition with private waters, the sale of which Congress has found necessary to tap as a source of revenue for carrying on the National Government. To say that the States cannot be taxed for enterprises generally pursued, like the sale of mineral water, because it is somewhat connected with a State's conservation policy, is to invoke an irrelevance to the federal taxing power. Liquor control by a State certainly concerns the most important of a State's natural resources — the health and well-being of its people. See *Mugler* v. *Kansas*. . . . If in its wisdom a State engages in the liquor business and may be taxed by Congress as others engaged in the liquor business are taxed, so also Congress may tax the States when they go into the business of bottling water as others in the mineral water business are taxed even though a State's sale of its mineral waters has relation to its conservation policy.

In the older cases, the emphasis was on immunity from taxation. The whole tendency of recent cases reveals a shift in emphasis to that of limitation upon immunity. They also indicate an awareness of the limited rôle of courts in assessing the relative weight of the factors upon which immunity is based. Any implied limitation upon the supremacy of the federal power to levy a tax like that now before us, in the absence of discrimination against State activities, brings fiscal and political factors into play. The problem cannot escape issues that do not lend themselves to judgment by criteria and methods of reasoning that are within the professional training and special competence of judges.

. . . There are, of course, State activities and State-owned property that partake of uniqueness from the point of view of intergovernmental relations. These inherently constitute a class by themselves. Only a State can own a Statehouse; only a State can get income by taxing. These could not be included for purposes of federal taxation in any abstract category of taxpayers without taxing the State as a State. But so long as Congress generally taps a source of revenue by whomsoever earned and not uniquely capable of being earned only by a State, the Constitution of the United States does not forbid it merely because its incidence falls also on a State. If Congress desires, it may of course leave untaxed enterprises pursued by States for the public good while it taxes like enterprises organized for private ends.

The process of Constitutional adjudication does not thrive on conjuring up horrible possibilities that never happen in the real world and devising doctrines sufficiently comprehensive in detail to cover the remotest contingency. Nor need we go beyond what is required for a reasoned disposition of the kind of controversy now before the Court.

Judgment affirmed.

Mr. Justice Jackson took no part in the consideration or decision of this case.

Mr. Justice Rutledge, concurring.

. . . If the way were open, I would add a further restricting factor, not of constitutional import, but of construction. . . . I should think two considerations well might be taken to require that, before a federal tax can be applied to activities carried on directly by the states, the intention of Congress to tax them should be stated expressly and not drawn merely from general wording of the statute applicable ordinarily to private sources of revenue.

Nevertheless, since *South Carolina* v. *United States, supra,* such a rule of construction seems not to have been thought required. Accordingly, although I gravely doubt that when Congress taxed every "person" it intended also to tax every state, the ruling has been made and I therefore acquiesce in this case.

Mr. Chief Justice Stone, concurring.

Mr. Justice Reed, Mr. Justice Murphy, Mr. Justice Burton and I concur in the result.

Concededly a federal tax discriminating against a State would be an unconstitutional exertion of power over a coexisting sovereignty within the same framework of government. But our difficulty with the formula, now first suggested as offering a new solution for an old problem, is that a federal tax which is not discriminatory as to the subject matter may nevertheless so affect the State, merely because it is a State that is being taxed, as to interfere unduly with the State's performance of its sovereign functions of government. . . . This is not because the tax can be regarded as discriminatory but because a sovereign government is the taxpayer, and the tax, even though non-discriminatory, may be regarded as infringing its sovereignty.

A State may, like a private individual, own real property and receive income. But in view of our former decisions we could hardly say that a general non-discriminatory real estate tax (apportioned), or an income tax laid upon citizens and States alike could be constitutionally applied to the State's capitol, its State-house, its public school houses, public parks, or its revenues from taxes or school lands, even though all real property and all income of the citizen is taxed. . . . Obviously Congress, in taxing property or income generally, is not taxing a State "as a State" because the State happens to own real estate or receive income. Whether a State or an individual is taxed, in each instance the taxable occasion is the same. The tax reaches the State because of the Congressional purpose to lay the tax on the subject matter chosen, regardless of who pays it. To say that the tax fails because the State happens to be the taxpayer is only to say that the State, to some extent undefined, is constitutionally immune from federal taxation. Only when and because the subject of taxation is State property or a State activity must we consider whether such a non-discriminatory tax unduly interferes with the performance of the State's functions of government. If it does, then the fact that the tax is non-discriminatory does not save it. . . .

It is enough for present purposes that the immunity of the State from federal taxation would, in this case, accomplish a withdrawal from the taxing power of the nation a subject of a nature which has been traditionally within that power from the beginning. Its exercise now, by a non-discriminatory tax, does not curtail the business of the state government more than it does the like business of the citizen. . . . The nature of the tax immunity requires that it be so construed as to allow to each government reasonable scope for its taxing power. . . .

The problem is not one to be solved by a formula, but we may look to the structure of the Constitution as our guide to decision. "In a broad sense, the taxing power of either government, even when exercised in a manner admittedly necessary and proper, unavoidably has some effect upon the other. The burden of federal taxation necessarily sets an economic limit to the practical operation of the taxing power of the states, and *vice versa*. Taxation by either the state or the federal government affects in some measure the cost of operation of the other.

Since all taxes must be laid by general, that is, workable, rules, the effect of the immunity on the national taxing power is to be determined not quantitatively but by its operation and tendency in withdrawing taxable property or activities from the reach of federal taxation. Not the extent to which a particular State engages in the activity, but the nature and extent of the activity by whomsoever performed is the relevant consideration.

Regarded in this light we cannot say that the Constitution either requires immunity of the State's mineral water business from federal taxation, or denies to the federal government power to lay the tax.

MR. JUSTICE DOUGLAS, with whom MR. JUSTICE BLACK concurs, dissenting.

I

If *South Carolina* v. *United States,* 199 U.S. 437, is to stand, the present judgment would have to be affirmed. For I agree that there is no essential difference between a federal tax on South Carolina's liquor business and a federal tax on New York's mineral water business. Whether *South Carolina* v. *United States* reaches the right result is another matter. . . . [A]s Mr. Justice White said in his dissent in *South Carolina* v. *United States,* any activity in which a State engages within the limits of its police power is a legitimate governmental activity. Here a State is disposing of some of its natural resources. Tomorrow it may issue securities, sell power from its public power project, or manufacture fertilizer. Each is an exercise of its power of sovereignty. Must it pay the federal government for the privilege of exercising that inherent power? If the Constitution grants it immunity from a tax on the issuance of securities, on what grounds can it be forced to pay a tax when it sells power or disposes of other natural resources?

II

One view, just announced, purports to reject the distinction which *South Carolina* v. *United States* drew between those activities of a State which are and those which are not strictly governmental, usual, or traditional. But it is said that a federal tax on a State will be sustained so long as Congress "does not attempt to tax a State because it is a State." Yet if that means that a federal real estate tax of general application (apportioned) would be valid if applied to a power dam owned by a State but invalid if applied to a Statehouse, the old doctrine has merely been poured into a new container. If, on the other hand, any federal tax on any state activity were sustained unless it discriminated against the State, then a constitutional rule would be fashioned which would undermine the sovereignty of the States as it has been understood throughout our history. Any such change should be accomplished only by constitutional amendment.

To say the present tax will be sustained because it does not impair the State's functions of government is to conclude either that the sale by the State of its mineral water is not a function of government or that the present tax is so slight as to be no burden. The former obviously is not true. The latter overlooks the fact that the power to tax lightly is the power to tax severely.

The notion that the sovereign position of the States must find its protection in the will of a transient majority of Congress is foreign to and a negation of our constitutional system. . . .

The immunity of the States from federal taxation is no less clear because it is implied. The States on entering the Union surrendered some of their sovereignty. It was further curtailed as various Amendments were adopted. But the Tenth Amendment provides that "The powers not delegated to the United States by the Constitution, nor prohibited by it to the States, are reserved to the States respectively, or to the people." The Constitution is a compact between sovereigns. The power of one sovereign to tax another is an innovation so startling as to require explicit authority if it is to be allowed. If the power of the federal government to tax the States is conceded, the reserved power of the States guaranteed by the Tenth Amendment does not give them the independence which they have always been assumed to have. They are relegated to a more servile status. . . .

There is no showing whatsoever that an expanding field of state activity even faintly promises to cripple the federal government in its search for needed revenues. If the truth were known, I suspect it would show that the activity of the States in the fields of housing, public power and the like have increased the level of income of the people and have raised the standards of marginal or sub-marginal groups. Such conditions affect favorably, not adversely, the tax potential of the federal government.

Pennsylvania v. Nelson

350 U.S. 497 (1956)
Vote: 6–3

The Pennsylvania Sedition Act punished sedition against the national as well as state governments. Nelson was convicted of violating the statute for expressions as to the national government. The Pennsylvania Supreme Court declared the Act in conflict with the Smith Act of 1940, holding that federal statute dealing with sedition "occupied the field," "superseded," or "preempted" state action. The concept of comprehensive federal action preempting by implication state legislation had until that time been used in Commerce Clause cases but not in civil liberties areas. The U.S. Supreme Court granted certiorari.

MR. CHIEF JUSTICE WARREN delivered the opinion of the Court.

The respondent Steve Nelson, an acknowledged member of the Communist Party, was convicted in the Court of Quarter Sessions of Allegheny County, Pennsylvania, of a violation of the Pennsylvania Sedition Act and sentenced to imprisonment for twenty years and to a fine of $10,000 and to costs of prosecution in the sum of $13,000. The Superior Court affirmed the conviction. 172 Pa. Super. 125, 92 A. 2d 431. The Supreme Court of Pennsylvania, recognizing but not reaching many alleged serious trial errors and conduct of the trial court infringing upon respondent's right to due process of law, decided the case on the narrow issue of supersession of the state law by the Federal Smith Act. In its opinion, the court stated:

> And, while the Pennsylvania statute proscribes sedition against either the Government of the United States or the Government of Pennsylvania, it is only alleged sedition against the United States with which the instant case is concerned. Out of all the voluminous testimony, we have not found, nor has anyone pointed to, a single word indicating a seditious act or even utterance directed against the Government of Pennsylvania.

The precise holding of the court, and all that is before us for review, is that the Smith Act of 1940, as amended in 1948, which prohibits the knowing advocacy of the overthrow of the Government of the United States by force and violence, supersedes the enforceability of the Pennsylvania Sedition Act which proscribes the same conduct. . . .

It should be said at the outset that the decision in this case does not affect the right of States to enforce their sedition laws at times when the Federal Government has not occupied the field and is not protecting the entire country from seditious conduct. The distinction between the two situations was clearly recognized by the court below. Nor does it limit the jurisdiction of the States where the Constitution and Congress have specifically given them concurrent jurisdiction, as was done under the Eighteenth Amendment and the Volstead Act. . . . Neither does it limit the right of the State to protect itself at any time against sabotage or attempted violence of all kinds.

Where, as in the instance case, Congress has not stated specifically whether a federal statute has occupied a field in which the States are otherwise free to legislate, different criteria have furnished touchstones for decision. . . .

In this case, we think that each of several tests of supersession is met.

First, "[t]he scheme of federal regulation [is] so pervasive as to make reasonable the inference that Congress left no room for the States to supplement it."

We examine these Acts only to determine the congressional plan. Looking to all of them in the aggregate, the conclusion is inescapable that Congress has intended to occupy the field of sedition. Taken as a whole, they evince a congressional plan which makes it reasonable to determine that no room has been left for the States to supplement it. . . .

Second, the federal statutes "touch a field in which the federal interest is so dominant that the federal system [must] be assumed to preclude enforcement of state laws on the same subject." . . . Congress declared that these steps were taken "to provide for the common defense, to preserve the sovereignty of the United States as an independent nation, and to guarantee to each State a republican form of government. . . ." Congress having thus treated seditious conduct as a matter of vital national concern, it is in no sense a local enforcement problem.

Third, enforcement of state sedition acts presents a serious danger of conflict with the administration of the federal program. Since 1939, in order to avoid a hampering of uniform enforcement of its program by sporadic local prosecutions, the Federal Government has urged local authorities not to intervene in such matters, but to turn over to the federal authorities immediately and unevaluated all information concerning subversive activities. . . .

Since we find that Congress has occupied the field to the exclusion of parallel state legislation, that the dominant interest of the Federal Government precludes state intervention, and that administration of state Acts would conflict with the operation of the federal plan, we are convinced that the decision of the Supreme Court of Pennsylvania is unassailable.

The judgment of the Supreme Court of Pennsylvania is

Affirmed.

MR. JUSTICE REED, with whom MR. JUSTICE BURTON and MR. JUSTICE MINTON join, dissenting.

Congress has not, in any of its statutes relating to sedition, specifically barred the exercise of state power to punish the same Acts under state law. And, we read the majority to assume for this case that, absent federal legislation, there is no constitutional bar to punishment of sedition against the United States by both a State and the Nation. The majority limits to the federal courts the power to try charges of sedition against the Federal Government.

First, the Court relies upon the pervasiveness of the antisubversive legislation embodied in the Smith Act of 1940, . . . the Internal Security Act of 1950, . . . and the Communist Control Act of 1954. . . . It asserts that these Acts in the aggregate mean that Congress has occupied the "field of sedition" to the exclusion of the States. The "occupation of the field" argument has been developed by this Court for the Commerce Clause and legislation thereunder to prevent partitioning of this country by locally erected trade barriers. In those cases this Court has ruled that state legislation is superseded when it conflicts with the comprehensive regulatory scheme and purpose of a federal plan. . . .

We cannot agree that the federal criminal sanctions against sedition directed at the United States are of such a pervasive character as to indicate an intention to void state action.

Secondly, the Court states that the federal sedition statutes touch a field "in which the federal interest is so dominant" they must preclude state laws on the same subject. This concept is suggested in a comment on *Hines* v. *Davidowitz,* 312 U.S. 52, in the *Rice* case, at 230. The Court in *Davidowitz* ruled that federal statutes compelling alien registration preclude enforcement of state statutes requiring alien registration. We read *Davidowitz* to teach nothing more than that, when the Congress provided a single nationwide integrated system of regulation so complete as that for aliens' registration (with fingerprinting, a scheduling of activities, and continuous information as to their residence), the Act bore so directly on our foreign relations as to make it evident that Congress intended only one uniform national alien registration system.

We look upon the Smith Act as a provision for controlling incitements to overthrow by force and violence the Nation, or any State, or any political subdivision of either. Such an exercise of federal police power carries, we think, no such dominancy over similar state powers as might be attributed to continuing federal regulations concerning foreign affairs or coinage, for example. In the responsibility of national and local governments to protect themselves against sedition, there is no "dominant interest."

Thirdly, the Court finds ground for abrogating Pennsylvania's antisedition statute because, in the Court's view, the State's administration of the Act may hamper the enforcement of the federal law. Quotations are inserted from statements of President Roosevelt and Mr. Hoover, the Director of the Federal Bureau of Investigation, to support the Court's position. But a reading of the quotations leads us to conclude that their purpose was to gain prompt knowledge of evidence of subversive activities so that the federal agency could be fully advised.

We find no suggestion from any official source that state officials should be less alert to ferret out or punish subversion. . . .

Finally, and this one point seems in and of itself decisive, there is an independent reason for reversing the Pennsylvania Supreme Court. The Smith Act appears in Title 18 of the United States Code, which Title codifies the federal criminal laws. Section 3231 of that Title provides:

> Nothing in this title shall be held to take away or impair the jurisdiction of the courts of the several States under the laws thereof.

That declaration springs from the federal character of our Nation. It recognizes the fact that maintenance of order and fairness rests primarily with the States. The section was first enacted in 1825 and has appeared successively in the federal criminal laws since that time. This Court has interpreted the section to mean that States may provide concurrent legislation in the absence of explicit congressional intent to the contrary. *Sexton* v. *California*, 189 U.S. 319, 324–325. The majority's position in this case cannot be reconciled with that clear authorization of Congress. . . .

South Carolina v. Katzenbach

383 U.S. 301 (1966)
Vote: 8–1, but Black dissenting only
  in part.

The Constitution leaves to the states the primary definition of the right to vote, but Amendments XIV and XV limit racial discrimination generally and, with respect to voting, specifically. Section 5 of Amendment XIV and Section 2 of Amendment XV authorize Congress "by appropriate legislation" to enforce the prohibitions of the Amendments.

Congress enacted the 1965 Voting Rights Act, which applied to any state or subdivision that employed a literacy test, as determined by the Attorney General, and was found to have less than 50 percent of its voting-age residents registered or voting. In such states, tests were suspended and federal registrars and poll-watchers were to be appointed to prevent racial discrimination. Furthermore, these states could change their laws on voting only if approved by the Attorney General of the U.S. or, failing that, by judgment from the U.S. District Court of the District of Columbia.

In a companion case, *Katzenbach* v. *Morgan* (1966), the Supreme Court upheld a provision of the Act that provides that Puerto Ricans who had completed sixth grade in Puerto Rico could not be denied the right to vote because of their inability to read or write English. The determination by Congress that literacy in another language was adequate for exercise of the franchise was held (Harlan and Stewart dissenting) to be a reasonable exercise of Congress' Fourteenth and Fifteenth Amendment powers.

While both voting rights cases involve the possible limits of national authority over state voting power, the South Carolina case also involves the issue raised by Black's dissent (in part) over the *continuing* supervisory power over state action exercised by organs of the national government. Would it be fair to say that the Attorney General was granted a veto over state legislation? Does this conflict with *Coyle* v. *Smith?*

MR. CHIEF JUSTICE WARREN delivered the opinion of the Court.

By leave of the Court, 382 U.S. 898, South Carolina has filed a bill of complaint, seeking a declaration that selected provisions of the Voting Rights Act of 1965 violate the Federal Constitution, and asking for an injunction against enforcement of these provisions by the Attorney General. Original jurisdiction is founded on the presence of a controversy between a State and a citizen of another State under Art. III, §2, of the Constitution.

Recognizing that the questions presented were of urgent concern to the entire country, we invited all of the States to participate in this proceeding as friends of the Court. A majority responded by submitting or joining in briefs on the merits, some supporting South Carolina and others the Attorney General. Seven of these States also requested and received permission to argue the case orally at our hearing. Without exception, despite the emotional overtones of the proceeding, the briefs and oral arguments were temperate, lawyerlike and constructive. All viewpoints on the issues have been fully developed, and this additional assistance has been most helpful to the Court.

The Voting Rights Act was designed by Congress to banish the blight of racial discrimination in voting, which has infected the electoral process in parts of our country for nearly a century. The Act creates stringent new remedies for voting discrimination where it persists on a pervasive scale, and in addition the statute strengthens existing remedies for pockets of voting discrimination elsewhere in the country. Congress assumed the power to prescribe these remedies from §2 of the Fifteenth Amendment, which authorizes the National Legislature to effectuate by "appropriate" measures the constitutional prohibition against racial discrimination in voting. We hold that the sections of the Act which are properly before us are an appropriate means for carrying out Congress' constitutional responsibilities and are consonant with all other provisions of the Constitution.

The Fifteenth Amendment to the Constitution was ratified in 1870. Promptly thereafter Congress passed the Enforcement Act of 1870, which made it a crime for public officers and private persons to obstruct exercise of the right to vote. The statute was amended in the following year to provide for detailed federal supervision of the electoral process, from registration to the certification of returns. As the years passed and fervor for racial equality waned, enforcement of the laws became spotty and ineffective, and most of their provisions were repealed in 1894....

Meanwhile, beginning in 1890, the States of Alabama, Georgia, Louisiana, Mississippi, North Carolina, South Carolina, and Virginia enacted tests still in use which were specifically designed to prevent Negroes from voting. Typically, they made the ability to read and write a registration qualification and also required completion of a registration form.

In recent years, Congress has repeatedly tried to cope with the problem of facilitating case-by-case litigation against voting discrimination.

Despite the earnest efforts of the Justice Department and of many federal judges, these new laws have done little to cure the problem of voting discrimination. According to estimates by the Attorney General during hearings on the Act, registration of voting-age Negroes in Alabama rose only from 14.2% to 19.4% between 1958 and 1964; in Louisiana it barely inched ahead from 31.7% to 31.8% between 1956 and 1965; and in Mississippi it increased only from 4.4% to 6.4% between 1954 and 1964. In each instance, registration of voting-age whites ran roughly 50 percentage points or more ahead of Negro registration.

The Voting Rights Act of 1965 reflects Congress' firm intention to rid the country of racial discrimination in voting. The heart of the Act is a complex scheme of stringent remedies aimed at areas where voting discrimination has been most flagrant. Section 4(a)–(d) lays down a formula defining the States and political subdivisions to which these new remedies apply. The first of the remedies, contained in §4(a), is the suspension of literacy tests and similar voting qualifications for a period of five years from the last occurrence of substantial voting discrimination. Section 5 prescribes a second remedy, the suspension of all new voting regulations pending review by federal authorities to determine whether their use would perpetuate voting discrimination. The third remedy, covered in §§6(b), 7, 9, and 13(a), is the assignment of federal examiners on certification by the Attorney General to list qualified applicants who are thereafter entitled to vote in all elections.

Other provisions of the Act prescribe subsidiary cures for persistent voting discrimination.

COVERAGE FORMULA

The remedial sections of the Act assailed by South Carolina automatically apply to any State, or to any separate political subdivision such as a county or parish, for which two findings have been made: (1) the Attorney General has determined that on November 1, 1964, it maintained a "test or device," and (2) the Director of the Census has determined that less than 50% of its voting-age residents were registered on November 1, 1964, or voted in the presidential election of November 1964. These findings are not reviewable in any court and are final upon publication in the Federal Register....

REVIEW OF NEW RULES   *exceptionaly conditions*

In a State or political subdivision covered by §4(b) of the Act, no person may be denied the right to vote in any election because of his failure to comply with a voting qualification or procedure different from those in force on November 1, 1964. This suspension of new rules is terminated, however, under either of the following circumstances: (1) if the area has submitted the rules to the Attorney General, and he has not interposed an objection within 60 days, or (2) if the area has obtained a declaratory judgment from the District Court for the District of Columbia, determining that the rules will not abridge the franchise on racial grounds.

These provisions of the Voting Rights Act of 1965 are challenged on the fundamental ground that they exceed the powers of Congress and encroach on an area reserved to the States by the Constitution. South Carolina and certain of the *amici curiae* also attack specific sections of the Act for more particular reasons. They argue that the coverage formula prescribed in §4(a)–(d) violates the principle of the equality of States, denies due process by employing an invalid presumption and by barring judicial review of administrative findings, constitutes a forbidden bill of attainder, and impairs the separation of powers by adjudicating guilt through legislation.

The ground rules for resolving this question are clear. The language and purpose of the Fifteenth Amendment, the prior decisions construing its several provisions, and the general doctrines of constitutional interpretation, all point to one fundamental principle. As against the reserved powers of the States, Congress may use any rational means to effectuate the constitutional prohibition of racial discrimination in voting. . . .

Section 1 of the Fifteenth Amendment declares that "[t]he right of citizens of the United States to vote shall not be denied or abridged by the United States or by any State on account of race, color, or previous condition of servitude." This declaration has always been treated as self-executing and has repeatedly been construed, without further legislative specification, to invalidate state voting qualifications or procedures which are discriminatory on their face or in practice. The gist of the matter is that the Fifteenth Amendment supersedes contrary exertions of state power. "When a State exercises power wholly within the domain of state interest, it is insulated from federal judicial review. But such insulation is not carried over when state power is used as an instrument for circumventing a federally protected right." . . .

South Carolina contends that the cases cited above are precedents only for the authority of the judiciary to strike down state statutes and procedures — that to allow an exercise of this authority by Congress would be to rob the courts of their rightful constitutional role. On the contrary, §2 of the Fifteenth Amendment expressly declares that "Congress shall have power to enforce this article by appropriate legislation." By adding this authorization, the Framers indicated that Congress was to be chiefly responsible for implementing the rights created in §1. "It is the power of Congress which has been enlarged. Congress is authorized to *enforce* the prohibitions by appropriate legislation. Some legislation is contemplated to make the [Civil War] amendments fully effective." *Ex parte Virginia,* 100 U.S. 339, 345. . . .

Congress has repeatedly exercised these powers in the past, and its enactments have repeatedly been upheld. . . . On the rare occasions when the Court has found an unconstitutional exercise of these powers, in its opinion Congress had attacked evils not comprehended by the Fifteenth Amendment. . . .

Congress exercised its authority under the Fifteenth Amendment in an inventive manner when it enacted the Voting Rights Act of 1965. First: The measure prescribes remedies for voting discrimination which go into effect without any need for prior adjudication. This was clearly a legitimate response to the problem, for which there is ample precedent under other constitutional provisions. See *Katzenbach* v. *McClung,* 379 U.S. 294, 302–304: *United States* v. *Darby,* 312 U.S. 100, 120–121. Congress had found that case-by-case litigation was inadequate to combat widespread and persistent discrimination in voting, because of the inordinate amount of time and energy required to overcome the obstructionist tactics invariably encountered in these lawsuits. After enduring nearly a century of systematic resistance to the Fifteenth Amendment, Congress might well decide to shift the advantage of time and inertia from the perpetrators of the evil to its victims. . . .

Second: The Act intentionally confines these remedies to a small number of States and political subdivisions which in most instances were familiar to Congress by name. This, too, was a permissible method of dealing with the problem. Congress had learned that substantial voting discrimination presently occurs in certain sections of the country, and it knew no way of accurately forecasting whether the evil might spread elsewhere in the future. In acceptable legislative fashion, Congress chose to limit its attention to the geographic areas where immediate action seemed necessary. . . . The doctrine of the equality of States, invoked by South Carolina, does not bar this approach, for that doctrine applies only to the terms upon which States are admitted to the Union, and not to the remedies for local evils which have subsequently appeared.

COVERAGE FORMULA

We now consider the related question of whether the specific States and political subdivisions within §4(b) of the Act were an appropriate target for the new remedies. South Carolina contends that the coverage formula is awkwardly designed in a number of respects and that it disregards various local conditions which have nothing to do with racial discrimination. These arguments, however, are largely beside the point. Congress began work with reliable evidence of actual voting discrimination in a great majority of the States and political subdivisions affected by the new remedies of the Act. The formula eventually evolved to describe these areas was relevant to the problem of voting discrimination, and Congress was therefore entitled to infer a significant danger of the evil in the few remaining States and political subdivisions covered by §4(b) of the Act. No more was required. . . .

Tests and devices are relevant to voting discrimination because of their long history as a tool for perpetrating the evil; a low voting rate is pertinent for the obvious reason that widespread disenfranchisement must inevitably affect the number of actual voters. Accordingly, the coverage formula is rational in both practice and theory. It was therefore permissible to impose the new remedies on the few remaining States and political subdivisions covered by the formula, at least in the absence of proof that they have been free of substantial voting discrimination in recent years. Congress is clearly not bound by the rules relating to statutory presumptions in criminal cases when it prescribes civil remedies against other organs of government.

It is irrelevant that the coverage formula excludes certain localities which do not employ voting tests and devices but for which there is evidence of voting discrimination by other means. Congress had learned that widespread and persistent discrimination in voting during recent years has typically entailed the misuse of tests and devices, and this was the evil for which the new remedies were specifically designed. At the same time, through §§3, 6(a), and 13(b) of the Act, Congress strengthened existing remedies for voting discrimination in other areas of the country. Legislation need not deal with all phases of a problem in the same way, so long as the distinctions drawn have some basis in practical experience.

REVIEW OF NEW RULES

The Act suspends new voting regulations pending scrutiny by federal authorities to determine whether their use would violate the Fifteenth Amendment. This may have been an uncommon exercise of congressional power, as South Carolina contends, but the Court has recognized that exceptional conditions can justify legislative measures not otherwise appropriate. . . . Congress knew that some of the States covered by §4(b) of the Act had resorted to the extraordinary stratagem of contriving new rules of various kinds for the sole purpose of perpetuating voting discrimination in the face of adverse federal court decrees. Congress had reason to suppose that

these States might try similar maneuvers in the future in order to evade the remedies for voting discrimination contained in the Act itself. Under the compulsion of these unique circumstances, Congress responded in a permissibly decisive manner.

FEDERAL EXAMINERS

The Act authorizes the appointment of federal examiners to list qualified applicants who are thereafter entitled to vote, subject to an expeditious challenge procedure. This was clearly an appropriate response to the problem, closely related to remedies authorized in prior cases.

After enduring nearly a century of widespread resistance to the Fifteenth Amendment, Congress has marshalled an array of potent weapons against the evil, with authority in the Attorney General to employ them effectively. Many of the areas directly affected by this development have indicated their willingness to abide by any restraints legitimately imposed upon them. We here hold that the portions of the Voting Rights Act properly before us are a valid means for carrying out the commands of the Fifteenth Amendment. Hopefully, millions of non-white Americans will now be able to participate for the first time on an equal basis in the government under which they live. We may finally look forward to the day when truly "[t]he right of citizens of the United States to vote shall not be denied or abridged by the United States or by any State on account of race, color, or previous condition of servitude."

The bill of complaint is

Dismissed.

Mr. Justice Black, concurring and dissenting.

I agree with substantially all of the Court's opinion sustaining the power of Congress under §2 of the Fifteenth Amendment to suspend state literacy tests and similar voting qualifications and to authorize the Attorney General to secure the appointment of federal examiners to register qualified voters in various sections of the country.

. . . I have no doubt whatever as to the power of Congress under §2 to enact the provisions of the Voting Rights Act of 1965 dealing with the suspension of state voting tests that have been used as notorious means to deny and abridge voting rights on racial grounds. This same congressional power necessarily exists to authorize appointment of federal examiners.

Though, as I have said, I agree with most of the Court's conclusions, I dissent from its holding that every part of §5 of the Act is constitutional.

Section 4(a), to which §5 is linked, suspends for five years all literacy tests and similar devices in those States coming within the formula of §4(b). Section 5 goes on to provide that a State covered by §4(b) can in no way amend its constitution or laws relating to voting without first trying to persuade the Attorney General of the United States or the Federal District Court for the District of Columbia that the new proposed laws do not have the purpose and will not have the effect of denying the right to vote to citizens on account of their race or color. I think this section is unconstitutional on at least two grounds.

(a) The Constitution gives federal courts jurisdiction over cases and controversies only. If it can be said that any case or controversy arises under this section which gives the District Court for the District of Columbia jurisdiction to approve or reject state laws or constitutional amendments, then the case or controversy must be between a State and the United States Government. But it is hard for me to believe that a justiciable controversy can arise in the constitutional sense from a desire by the United States Government or some of its officials to determine in advance what legislative provisions a State may enact or what constitutional amendments it may adopt.

(b) My second and more basic objection to §5 is that Congress has here exercised its power under §2 of the Fifteenth Amendment through the adoption of means that conflict with the most basic principles of the Constitution. As the Court says, the limitations of the power granted under §2 are the same as the limitations imposed on the exercise of any of the powers expressly granted Congress by the Constitution. . . . Section 5, by providing that some of the States cannot pass state laws or adopt state constitutional amendments without first being compelled to beg federal authorities to approve their policies, so distorts our constitutional structure of government as to render any distinction drawn in the Constitution between state and federal power almost meaningless. One of the most basic premises upon which our structure of government was founded was that the Federal Government was to have certain specific and limited powers and no others, and all other power was to be reserved either "to the States respectively, or to the people." Certainly if all the provisions of our Constitution which limit the power of the Federal Government and reserve other power to the States are to mean anything, they mean at least that the States have power to pass laws and amend their constitutions without first sending their officials hundreds of miles away to beg federal authorities to

approve them. Moreover, it seems to me that §5 which gives federal officials power to veto state laws they do not like is in direct conflict with the clear command of our Constitution that "The United States shall guarantee to every State in this Union a Republican Form of Government."

. . . And if one law concerning voting can make the States plead for this approval by a distant federal court or the United States Attorney General, other laws on different subjects can force the States to seek the advance approval not only of the Attorney General but of the President himself or any other chosen members of his staff. It is inconceivable to me that such a radical degradation of state power was intended in any of the provisions of our Constitution or its Amendments. Of course I do not mean to cast any doubt whatever upon the indisputable power of the Federal Government to invalidate a state law once enacted and operative on the ground that it intrudes into the area of supreme federal power. But the Federal Government has heretofore always been content to exercise this power to protect federal supremacy by authorizing its agents to bring lawsuits against state officials once an operative state law has created an actual case and controversy. A federal law which assumes the power to compel the States to submit in advance any proposed legislation they have for approval by federal agents approaches dangerously near to wiping the States out as useful and effective units in the government of our country. I cannot agree to any constitutional interpretation that leads inevitably to such a result.

National League of Cities v. Usery

426 U.S. 833 (1976)
Vote: (4–1)–4

In 1974, the Congress extended the minimum wage to state and local employees. The National League of Cities, a clearinghouse association, the National Governors' Conference, and various states and municipalities challenged the new measures. A three-judge district court found for the national government. The League and its cohorts appealed. The result clearly emphasizes limits on federal power over state government — limits that Black worried about in several cases, especially the HEART OF ATLANTA MOTEL and

SOUTH CAROLINA V. KATZENBACH cases, and which Rehnquist argued for earlier in *Fry* v. *U.S.* (1975).

What rule, if any, emerges? Is it significant that Rehnquist speaks of "dual sovereignty"? On what basis would environmental regulation be different from wages and hours of public employees, as suggested by Blackmun in his concurrence (not reproduced below)?

MR. JUSTICE REHNQUIST delivered the opinion of the Court.

Nearly 40 years ago Congress enacted the Fair Labor Standards Act, and required employers covered by the Act to pay their employees a minimum hourly wage and to pay them at one and one-half times their regular rate of pay for hours worked in excess of 40 during a workweek. . . . This Court unanimously upheld the Act as a valid exercise of congressional authority under the commerce power in *United States* v. *Darby* (1941), observing:

> Whatever their motive and purpose, regulations of commerce which do not infringe some constitutional prohibition are within the plenary power conferred on Congress by the Commerce Clause.

The original Fair Labor Standards Act passed in 1938 specifically excluded the States and their political subdivisions from its coverage. In 1974, however, Congress enacted the most recent of a series of broadening amendments to the Act. By these amendments Congress has extended the minimum wage and maximum hour provisions to almost all public employees employed by the States and by their various political subdivisions. Appellants in these cases include individual cities and States, the National League of Cities, and the National Governors' Conference. . . . The gist of their complaint was not that the conditions of employment of such public employees were beyond the scope of the commerce power had those employees been employed in the private sector but that the established constitutional doctrine of intergovernmental immunity consistently recognized in a long series of our cases affirmatively prevented the exercise of this authority in the manner which Congress chose in the 1974 amendments. . . .

Challenging these 1974 amendments in the District Court, appellants sought both declaratory and injunctive relief against the amendment's application to them, and a three-judge court was accordingly convened.

. . . The District Court stated it was "troubled" by appellants' contentions that the amendments would intrude upon the States' performance of essential governmental functions. The court went on to say that it considered their contentions

> substantial and that it may well be that the Supreme Court will feel it appropriate to draw back from the far-reaching implications of [*Maryland* v. *Wirtz, supra*]; but that is a decision that only the Supreme Court can make, and as a Federal district court we feel obliged to apply the Wirtz opinion as it stands. . . .

When considering the validity of asserted applications of this power to wholly private activity, the Court has made it clear that

> [e]ven activity that is purely intrastate in character may be regulated by Congress, where the activity, combined with like conduct by others similarly situated, affects commerce among the States or with foreign nations. *Fry* v. *United States* . . . (1975).

Congressional power over areas of private endeavor, even when its exercise may pre-empt express state-law determinations contrary to the result which has commended itself to the collective wisdom of Congress, has been held to be limited only by the requirement that "the means chosen by [Congress] must be reasonably adapted to the end permitted by the Constitution." *Heart of Atlanta Motel* v. *United States* . . . (1964).

Appellants in no way challenge these decisions establishing the breadth of authority granted Congress under the commerce power. Their contention, on the contrary, is that when Congress seeks to regulate directly the activities of States as public employers, it transgresses an affirmative limitation on the exercise of its power akin to other commerce power affirmative limitations contained in the Constitution.

This Court has never doubted that there are limits upon the power of Congress to override state sovereignty, even when exercising its otherwise plenary powers to tax or to regulate commerce which are conferred by Art. I of the Constitution. In *Wirtz,* for example, the Court took care to assure the appellants that it had "ample power to prevent . . . 'the utter destruction of the State as a sovereign political entity,'" which they feared. . . . Appellee Secretary in this case, both in his brief and upon oral argument, has agreed that our federal system of government imposes definite limits upon the authority of Congress to regulate the activities of the States as States by means of the commerce power.

The expressions in these more recent cases trace back to earlier decisions of this Court recognizing the essential role of the States in our federal system of government. Mr. Chief Justice Chase, perhaps because of the particular time at which he occupied that office, had occasion more than once to speak for the Court on this point. In *Texas* v. *White* . . . (1869), he declared that "[t]he Constitution, in all its provisions, looks to an indestructible Union, composed of indestructible States."

Appellee Secretary argues that the cases in which this Court has upheld sweeping exercises of authority by Congress, even though those exercises preempted state regulation of the private sector, have already curtailed the sovereignty of the States quite as much as the 1974 amendments to the Fair Labor Standards Act. We do not agree. It is one thing to recognize the authority of Congress to enact laws regulating individual businesses necessarily subject to the dual sovereignty of the government of the Nation and of the State in which they reside. It is quite another to uphold a similar exercise of congressional authority directed, not to private citizens, but to the States as States.

One undoubted attribute of state sovereignty is the States' power to determine the wages which shall be paid to those whom they employ in order to carry out their governmental functions, what hours those persons will work, and what compensation will be provided where these employees may be called upon to work overtime. The question we must resolve here, then, is whether these determinations are "'functions essential to separate and independent existence,'" . . . so that Congress may not abrogate the States' otherwise plenary authority to make them.

. . . .

Quite apart from the substantial costs imposed upon the States and their political subdivisions, the Act displaces state policies regarding the manner in which they will structure delivery of those governmental services which their citizens require. The Act, speaking directly to the States *qua* States, requires that they shall pay all but an extremely limited minority of their employees the minimum wage rates currently chosen by Congress. It may well be that as a matter of economic policy it would be desirable that States, just as private employers, comply with these minimum wage requirements. But it cannot be gainsaid that the federal requirement directly supplants the considered policy choices of the States' elected officials and administrators as to how they

wish to structure pay scales in state employment. The State might wish to employ persons with little or no training, or those who wish to work on a casual basis, or those who for some other reason do not possess minimum employment requirements, and pay them less than the federally prescribed minimum wage. It may wish to offer parttime or summer employment to teenagers at a figure less than the minimum wage, and if unable to do so may decline to offer such employment at all. But the Act would forbid such choices by the States. The only "discretion" left to them under the Act is either to attempt to increase their revenue to meet the additional financial burden imposed upon them by paying congressionally prescribed wages to their existing complement of employees, or to reduce that complement to a number which can be paid the federal minimum wage without increasing revenue.

This dilemma presented by the minimum wage restrictions may seem not immediately different from that faced by private employers. The difference, however, is that a State is not merely a factor in the "shifting economic arrangements" of the private sector of the economy, *Kovacs* v. *Cooper* . . . (1949) (Frankfurter, J., concurring), but is itself a coordinate element in the system established by the Framers for governing our Federal Union.

This congressionally imposed displacement of state decisions may substantially restructure traditional ways in which the local governments have arranged their affairs.

. . . Congress has sought to wield its power in a fashion that would impair the States' "ability to function effectively in a federal system," *Fry,* 7. This exercise of congressional authority does not comport with the federal system of government embodied in the Constitution. We hold that insofar as the challenged amendments operate to directly displace the States' freedom to structure integral operations in areas of traditional governmental functions, they are not within the authority granted Congress by Art. I, §8, cl. 3.

One final matter requires our attention. Appellee has vigorously urged that we cannot, consistently with the Court's decisions in *Maryland* v. *Wirtz* . . . (1968), and *Fry, supra,* rule against him here. It is important to examine this contention so that it will be clear what we hold today, and what we do not.

With regard to *Fry,* we disagree with appellee. . . . The Court expressly noted that the degree of intrusion upon the protected area of state sovereignty was in that case even less than that worked by the amendments to the FLSA which were before the Court in *Wirtz*. The Court recognized that the

Economic Stabilization Act was "an emergency measure to counter severe inflation that threatened the national economy." . . .

We think our holding today quite consistent with *Fry*. The enactment at issue there was occasioned by an extremely serious problem which endangered the well-being of all the component parts of our federal system and which only collective action by the National Government might forestall. The means selected were carefully drafted so as not to interfere with the States' freedom beyond a very limited, specific period of time. The effect of the across-the-board freeze authorized by that Act, moreover, displaced no state choices as to how governmental operations should be structured, nor did it force the States to remake such choices themselves. Instead, it merely required that the wage scales and employment relationships which the States themselves had chosen be maintained during the period of the emergency.

With respect to the Court's decision in *Wirtz*, we reach a different conclusion. Both appellee and the District Court thought that decision required rejection of appellants' claims. Appellants, in turn, advance several arguments by which they seek to distinguish the facts before the Court in *Wirtz* from those presented by the 1974 amendments to the Act. There are undoubtedly factual distinctions between the two situations, but in view of the conclusions expressed earlier in this opinion we do not believe the reasoning in *Wirtz* may any longer be regarded as authoritative.

Wirtz relied heavily on the Court's decision in *United States* v. *California* . . . (1936). The opinion quotes the following language from that case:

> '[We] look to the activities in which the states have traditionally engaged as marking the boundary of the restriction upon the federal taxing power. But there is no such limitation upon the plenary power to regulate commerce. The state can no more deny the power if its exercise has been authorized by Congress than can an individual. . . .'

But we have reaffirmed today that the States as States stand on a quite different footing from an individual or a corporation when challenging the exercise of Congress' power to regulate commerce. We think the dicta from *United States* v. *California*, simply wrong. . . . While there are obvious differences between the schools and hospitals involved in *Wirtz*, and the fire and police departments affected here, each provides an integral portion of those governmental services which the States and their political subdivisions have traditionally afforded their citizens. We are therefore persuaded that *Wirtz* must be overruled.

MR. JUSTICE BLACKMUN, concurring.

MR. JUSTICE BRENNAN, with whom MR. JUSTICE WHITE and MR. JUSTICE MARSHALL join, dissenting.

It must therefore be surprising that my Brethren should choose this bicentennial year of our independence to repudiate principles governing judicial interpretation of our Constitution settled since the time of Mr. Chief Justice John Marshall, discarding his postulate that the Constitution contemplates that restraints upon exercise by Congress of its plenary commerce power lie in the political process and not in the judicial process. . . . "[It] is not a controversy between equals" when the Federal Government "is asserting its sovereign power to regulate commerce. . . . [T]he interests of the nation are more important than those of any State." *Sanitary District* v. *United States* . . . (1925). The commerce power "is an affirmative power commensurate with the national needs." *North American Co.* v. *SEC* . . . (1946). The Constitution reserves to the States "only . . . that authority which is consistent with and not opposed to the grant to Congress. There is no room in our scheme of government for the assertion of state power in hostility to the authorized exercise of Federal power." *The Minnesota Rate Cases,* . . . (1913). "The framers of the Constitution never intended that the legislative power of the nation should find itself incapable of disposing of a subject matter specifically committed to its charge." *In re Rahrer* . . . (1891).

My Brethren thus have today manufacturered an abstraction without substance, founded neither in the words of the Constitution nor on precedent. An abstraction having such profoundly pernicious consequences is not made less so by characterizing the 1974 amendments as legislation directed against the "States *qua* States."

The reliance of my Brethren upon the Tenth Amendment as "an express declaration of [a state sovereignty] limitation," *ante,* at 842, not only suggests that they overrule governing decisions of this Court that address this question but must astound scholars of the Constitution.

My Brethren purport to find support for their novel state-sovereignty doctrine in the concurring opinion of Mr. Chief Justice Stone in *New York* v. *United States* . . . (1946). That reliance is plainly misplaced. That case presented the question whether the Constitution either required immunity of New

York State's mineral water business from federal taxation or denied to the Federal Government power to lay the tax. The Court sustained the federal tax. But the Chief Justice was addressing not the question of a state-sovereignty restraint upon the exercise of the commerce power but rather the principle of implied immunity of the States and Federal Government from taxation by the other: "The counterpart of such undue interference has been recognized since Marshall's day as the implied immunity of each of the dual sovereignties of our constitutional system from taxation by the other." *Ibid.*

That no precedent justifies today's result is particularly clear from the awkward extension of the doctrine of state immunity from federal taxation— an immunity conclusively distinguished by Mr. Justice Stone in *California,* and an immunity that is "narrowly limited" because "the people of all the states have created the national government and are represented in Congress." *Helvering* v. *Gerhardt* . . . (1938) (Stone, J.)—to fashion a judicially enforceable restraint on Congress' exercise of the commerce power that the Court has time and again rejected as having no place in our constitutional jurisprudence. I cannot recall another instance in the Court's history when the reasoning of so many decisions covering so long a span of time has been discarded in such a roughshod manner. That this is done without any justification not already often advanced and consistently rejected, clearly renders today's decision an *ipse dixit* reflecting nothing but displeasure with a congressional judgment.

My Brethren do more than turn aside longstanding constitutional jurisprudence that emphatically rejects today's conclusion. More alarming is the startling restructuring of our federal system, and the role they create therein for the federal judiciary. This Court is simply not at liberty to erect a mirror of its own conception of a desirable governmental structure. . . .

We are left then with a catastrophic judicial body blow at Congress' power under the Commerce Clause. . . . [T]here is an ominous portent of disruption of our constitutional structure implicit in today's mischievous decision. I dissent.

MR. JUSTICE STEVENS, dissenting.

The Federal Government may, I believe, require the State to act impartially when it hires or fires the janitor, to withhold taxes from his paycheck, to observe safety regulations when he is performing his job, to forbid him from burning too much soft coal in the capitol furnace, from dumping untreated refuse in an adjacent waterway, from overloading a state-owned garbage truck, or from driving either the truck or the Governor's limousine over 55 miles an hour. Even though these and many other activities of the capital janitor are activities of the State *qua* State, I have no doubt that they are subject to federal regulation.

. . . As far as the complexities of adjusting police and fire departments to this sort of federal control are concerned, I presume that appropriate tailor-made regulations would soon solve their most pressing problems. After all, the interests adversely affected by this legislation are not without political power.

My disagreements with the wisdom of this legislation may not, of course, affect my judgment with respect to its validity. . . . Since I am unable to identify a limitation on that federal power that would not also invalidate federal regulation of state activities that I consider unquestionably permissible, I am persuaded that this statute is valid.

Garcia v. San Antonio Metropolitan Authority

469 U.S. 528 (1985)
Vote: 5–4

With Blackmun "not untroubled" by the NATIONAL LEAGUE OF CITIES V. USERY decision, the Court tried to clarify and limit its implications in *Hodel* v. *Virginia Surface Mining and Reclamation Association* (1981). But the *Hodel* standards, described in the *Garcia* opinion, were not sufficient to allay his fears. Blackmun, without explanation, supported the majority in *E.E.O.C.* v. *Wyoming* (1983), upholding the application of federal age-discrimination provisions to prevent forced retirement of a state-employed game warden. Stevens' concurrence in that case virtually demanded that the Court drop the other shoe and overrule USERY.

Precisely that result occurred two years later in *Garcia*. Conservatives and the local government associations—such as the National League of Cities—denounced the decision. Fueling their concern was a conviction that Congress had developed a habit of pronouncing national standards and rights while imposing the bill on local governments.

Notice Powell's criticism of overruling a decision of only nine years' standing. Does the fact that USERY (1976) overruled *Maryland* v. *Wirtz* (1968) suggest that the sacredness of stare decisis depends on whether you like only the previous decision? Note that both Rehnquist and O'Connor suggest their day will come again. Are they not bound by stare decisis?

Note: The transit agency involved had its name changed during the period covered by Justice Blackmun's history.

JUSTICE BLACKMUN delivered the opinion of the Court.

We revisit in these cases an issue raised in *National League of Cities* v. *Usery* (1976). In that litigation, this Court, by a sharply divided vote, ruled that the Commerce Clause does not empower Congress to enforce the minimum-wage and overtime provisions of the Fair Labor Standards Act (FLSA) against the States "in areas of traditional governmental functions." . . . Although *National League of Cities* supplied some examples of "traditional governmental functions," it did not offer a general explanation of how a "traditional" function is to be distinguished from a "nontraditional" one. Since then, federal and state courts have struggled with the task thus imposed of identifying a traditional function for purposes of state immunity under the Commerce Clause.

In the present cases, a Federal District Court concluded that municipal ownership and operation of a mass-transit system is a traditional governmental function and thus, under *National League of Cities,* is exempt from the obligations imposed by the FLSA. Faced with the identical question, three Federal Courts of Appeals and one state appellate court have reached the opposite conclusion.

Our examination of this "function" standard applied in these and other cases over the last eight years now persuades us that the attempt to draw the boundaries of state regulatory immunity in terms of "traditional governmental function" is not only unworkable but is inconsistent with established principles of federalism and, indeed, with those very federalism principles on which *National League of Cities* purported to rest. That case, accordingly, is overruled.

When the FLSA was enacted in 1938, its wage and overtime provisions did not apply to local mass-

transit employees or, indeed, to employees of state and local governments. . . . In 1961, Congress extended minimum-wage coverage to employees of any private mass-transit carrier whose annual gross revenue was not less than $1 million. . . . Five years later, Congress extended FLSA coverage to state and local-government employees for the first time. . . .

The FLSA obligations of public mass-transit systems like SATS were expanded in 1974 when Congress provided for the progressive repeal of the surviving overtime exemption for mass-transit employees. . . . SATS complied with the FLSA's overtime requirements until 1976, when this Court, in *National League of Cities* . . . overruled *Maryland* v. *Wirtz*. . . . Four months after *National League of Cities* was handed down, SATS informed its employees that the decision relieved SATS of its overtime obligations under the FLSA.

Matters rested there until September 17, 1979, when the Wage and Hour Administration of the Department of Labor issued an opinion that SAMTA's operations "are not constitutionally immune from the application of the Fair Labor Standards Act." . . . On November 21 of that year, SAMTA filed this action against the Secretary of Labor. . . .

. . . Were SAMTA a privately owned and operated enterprise, it could not credibly argue that Congress exceeded the bounds of its Commerce Clause powers in prescribing minimum wages and overtime rates for SAMTA's employees. Any constitutional exemption from the requirements of the FLSA therefore must rest on SAMTA's status as a governmental entity rather than on the "local" nature of its operations.

The prerequisites for governmental immunity under *National League of Cities* were summarized by this Court in *Hodel, supra.* Under that summary, four conditions must be satisfied before a state activity may be deemed immune from a particular federal regulation under the Commerce Clause. First, it is said that the federal statute at issue must regulate "the 'States as States.'" Second, the statute must "address matters that are indisputably 'attribute[s]' of state sovereignty.'" Third, state compliance with the federal obligation must "directly impair [the States'] ability 'to structure integral operations in areas of traditional governmental functions.'" Finally, the relation of state and federal interests must not be such that "the nature of the federal interest . . . justifies state submission." . . .

The controversy in the present cases has focused on the third *Hodel* requirement — that the challenged federal statute trench on "traditional governmental functions." . . . Just how troublesome the task has been is revealed by the results reached in other federal cases. Thus, courts have held that regulating ambulance services, . . . operating a municipal airport, . . . and operating a highway authority . . . are functions *protected* under *National League of Cities.* At the same time, courts have held that issuance of industrial development bonds, . . . regulation of intrastate natural gas sales, . . . regulation of traffic on public roads, . . . regulation of air transportation, . . . operation of a telephone system, . . . leasing and sale of natural gas, . . . operation of a mental health facility, . . . and provision of in-house domestic services for the aged and handicapped . . . are *not* entitled to immunity. We find it difficult, if not impossible, to identify an organizing principle that places each of the cases in the first group on one side of a line and each of the cases in the second group on the other side. The constitutional distinction between licensing drivers and regulating traffic, for example, or between operating a highway authority and operating a mental health facility, is elusive at best.

Thus far, this Court itself has made little headway in defining the scope of the governmental functions deemed protected under *National League of Cities.* . . . The only other case in which the Court has had occasion to address the problem is *Long Island.* . . . We relied in large part there on "the *historical reality* that the operation of railroads is not among the functions *traditionally* performed by state and local governments," but we simultaneously disavowed "a static historical view of state functions generally immune from federal regulation.". . . [W]e did not offer an explanation of what makes one state function a "basic prerogative" and another function not basic. . . .

Many constitutional standards involve "undoubte[d] . . . gray areas,". . . and, despite the difficulties that this Court and other courts have encountered so far, it normally might be fair to venture the assumption that case-by-case development would lead to a workable standard for determining whether a particular governmental function should be immune from federal regulation under the Commerce Clause. A further cautionary note is sounded, however, by the Court's experience in the related field of state immunity from federal taxation. In *South Carolina v. United States* . . . (1905), the Court held for the first time that the state tax immunity recognized in *Collector* v. *Day,* . . . (1870), extended only to the "ordinary" and "strictly governmental" instrumentalities of state governments and not to instrumentalities "used by the State in the carrying on of an ordinary private business.". . . While the Court applied the distinction outlined in

South Carolina for the following 40 years, at no time during that period did the Court develop a consistent formulation of the kinds of governmental functions that were entitled to immunity. . . .

. . . It was this uncertainty that led the Court shortly thereafter, in *New York* v. *United States* . . . (1964), unanimously to conclude that the distinction between "governmental" and "proprietary" functions was "untenable" and must be abandoned. . . .

The distinction the Court discarded as unworkable in the field of tax immunity has proved no more fruitful in the field of regulatory immunity under the Commerce Clause. Neither do any of the alternative standards that might be employed to distinguish between protected and unprotected governmental functions appear manageable. We rejected the possibility of making immunity turn on a purely historical standard of "tradition" in *Long Island,* and properly so. The most obvious defect of a historical approach to state immunity is that it prevents a court from accommodating changes in the historical functions of States, changes that have resulted in a number of once-private functions like education being assumed by the States and their subdivisions. At the same time, the only apparent virtue of a rigorous historical standard, namely, its promise of a reasonably objective measure for state immunity, is illusory. Reliance on history as an organizing principle results in line-drawing of the most arbitrary sort; the genesis of state governmental functions stretches over a historical continuum from before the Revolution to the present, and courts would have to decide by fiat precisely how long-standing a pattern of state involvement had to be for federal regulatory authority to be defeated.

. . . .

We believe, however, that there is a more fundamental problem at work here, a problem that explains why the Court was never able to provide a basis for the governmental/proprietary distinction in the intergovernmental tax immunity cases and why an attempt to draw similar distinctions with respect to federal regulatory authority under *National League of Cities* is unlikely to succeed regardless of how the distinctions are phrased. The problem is that neither the government/proprietary distinction nor any other that purports to separate out important governmental functions can be faithful to the role of federalism in a democratic society. The essence of our federal system is that within the realm of authority left open to them under the Constitution, the States must be equally free to engage in any activity that their citizens choose for the common weal, no matter how unorthodox or unnecessary anyone else—including the judiciary—deems state involvement to be. Any rule of state immunity that looks to the "traditional," "integral," or "necessary" nature of governmental functions inevitably invites an unelected federal judiciary to make decisions about which state policies it favors and which ones it dislikes. "The science of government...is the science of experiment," *Anderson v. Dunn,* 6 Wheat. 204, 226 (1821), and the States cannot serve as laboratories for social and economic experiment, see *New State Ice Co.* v. *Liebmann,* 285 U.S. 262, 311 (1932) (Brandeis, J., dissenting), if they must pay an added price when they meet the changing needs of their citizenry by taking up functions that an earlier day and a different society left in private hands....

...Any such rule leads to inconsistent results at the same time that it disserves principles of democratic self-governance, and it breeds inconsistency precisely because it is divorced from those principles. If there are to be limits on the Federal Government's power to interfere with state functions—as undoubtedly there are—we must look elsewhere to find them. We accordingly return to the underlying issue that confronted this Court in *National League of Cities*—the manner in which the Constitution insulates States from the reach of Congress' power under the Commerce Clause.

We doubt that courts ultimately can identify principled constitutional limitations on the scope of Congress' Commerce Clause powers over the States merely by relying on *a priori* definitions of state sovereignty. In part, this is because of the elusiveness of objective criteria for "fundamental" elements of state sovereignty, a problem we have witnessed in the search for "traditional governmental functions." There is, however, a more fundamental reason: the sovereignty of the States is limited by the Constitution itself. A variety of sovereign powers, for example, are withdrawn from the States by Article I, Sec. 10. Section 8 of the same Article works an equally sharp contraction of state sovereignty by authorizing Congress to exercise a wide range of legislative powers and (in conjunction with the Supremacy Clause of Article VI) to displace contrary state legislation.... By providing for final review of questions of federal law in this Court, Article III curtails the sovereign power of the States' judiciaries to make authoritative determinations of law.... Finally, the developed application, through the Fourteenth Amendment, of the greater part of the Bill of Rights to the States limits the sovereign authority that States otherwise would possess to legislate with respect to their citizens and to conduct their own affairs.

The States unquestionably do "retai[n] a significant measure of sovereign authority."...They do so, however, only to the extent that the Constitution has not divested them of their original powers and transferred those powers to the Federal Government....

When we look for the States' "residuary and inviolable sovereignty,"...in the shape of the constitutional scheme rather than in predetermined notions of sovereign power, a different measure of state sovereignty emerges. Apart from the limitation on federal authority inherent to the delegated nature of Congress' Article I powers, the principal means chosen by the Framers to ensure the role of the States in the federal system lies in the structure of the Federal Government itself. It is no novelty to observe that the composition of the Federal Government was designed in large part to protect the States from overreaching by Congress....

...Madison placed particular reliance on the equal representation of the States in the Senate, which he saw as "at once a constitutional recognition of the portion of sovereignty remaining in the individual States, and an instrument for preserving that residuary sovereignty."...He further noted that "the residuary sovereignty of the States [is] implied *and secured* by that principle of representation in one branch of the [federal] legislature" (emphasis added)....

We realize that changes in the structure of the Federal Government have taken place since 1789, not the least of which has been the substitution of popular election of Senators by the adoption of the Seventeenth Amendment in 1913, and that these changes may work to alter the influence of the States in the federal political process. Nonetheless, against this background, we are convinced that the fundamental limitation that the constitutional scheme imposes on the Commerce Clause to protect the "States as States" is one of process rather than one of result. Any substantive restraint on the exercise of Commerce Clause powers must find its justification in the procedural nature of this basic limitation, and it must be tailored to compensate for possible failings in the national political process rather than to dictate a "sacred province of state autonomy."...

This analysis makes clear that Congress' action in affording SAMTA employees the protections of the wage and hour provisions of the FLSA contravened no affirmative limit on Congress' power under the Commerce Clause. The judgment of the District Court therefore must be reversed.

Though the separate concurrence providing the fifth vote in *National League of Cities* was "not untroubled by certain possible implications" of the decision, . . . the Court in that case attempted to articulate affirmative limits on the Commerce Clause power in terms of core governmental functions and fundamental attributes of state sovereignty. But the model of democratic decision making the Court there identified underestimated, in our view, the solicitude of the national political process for the continued vitality of the States. Attempts by other courts since then to draw guidance from this model have proved it both impracticable and doctrinally barren. In sum, in *National League of Cities* the Court tried to repair what did not need repair.

. . . .

It is so ordered.

Justice Powell, with whom The Chief Justice, Justice Rehnquist, and Justice O'Connor join, dissenting.

. . . Because I believe this decision substantially alters the federal system embodied in the Constitution, I dissent.

I

There are, of course, numerous examples over the history of this Court in which prior decisions have been reconsidered and overruled. There have been few cases, however, in which the principles of *stare decisis* and the rationale of recent decisions were ignored as abruptly as we now witness. The reasoning of the Court in *National League of Cities,* and the principle applied there, have been reiterated consistently over the past eight years. Since its decision in 1976, *National League of Cities* has been cited and quoted in opinions joined by every member of the present Court. . . .

To leave no doubt about its intention, the Court renounces its decision in *National League of Cities* because it "inevitably invites an unelected federal judiciary to make decisions about which state policies it favors and which ones it dislikes." In other words, the extent to which the States may exercise their authority, when Congress purports to act under the Commerce Clause, henceforth is to be determined from time to time by political decisions made by members of the federal government, decisions the Court says will not be subject to judicial review. I note that it does not seem to have occurred to the Court that it — an unelected majority of five justices — today rejects almost 200 years of the understanding of the constitutional status of federalism. . . .

. . . In finding the test to be unworkable, the Court begins by mischaracterizing *National League of Cities* and subsequent cases. . . .

A

Much of the Court's opinion is devoted to arguing that it is difficult to define *a priori* "traditional governmental functions." *National League of Cities* neither engaged in, nor required, such a task. The Court discusses and condemns as standards "traditional governmental function(s)," "purely historical" functions, "'uniquely' governmental functions," and "'necessary' governmental services." But nowhere does it mention that *National League of Cities* adopted a familiar type of balancing test for determining when the Commerce Clause enactments transgress constitutional limitations imposed by the federal nature of our system of government. This omission is noteworthy, since the author of today's opinion joined *National League of Cities* and concurred separately to point out that the Court's opinion in that case "adopt[s] a balancing approach [that] does not outlaw federal power in areas . . . where the federal interest is demonstrably greater and where state . . . compliance with imposed federal standards would be essential." . . .

Moreover, the statute at issue in this case, the FLSA, is the identical statute that was at issue in *National League of Cities*. Although Justice Blackmun's concurrence noted that he was "not untroubled by certain possible implications of the Court's opinion" in *National League of Cities,* it also stated that "the result with respect to the statute under challenge here [the FLSA] is *necessarily correct*." . . . His opinion for the Court today does not discuss the statute, nor identify any changed circumstances that warrant the conclusion today that *National League of Cities* is *necessarily wrong*.

. . . .

In our federal system, the States have a major role that cannot be preempted by the national government. As contemporaneous writings and the debates at the ratifying conventions make clear, the States' ratifications of the Constitution was predicated on this understanding of federalism. Indeed, the Tenth Amendment was adopted specifically to ensure that the important role promised the States by the proponents of the Constitution was realized.

This history, which the Court simply ignores, documents the integral role of the Tenth Amendment in our constitutional theory. It exposes as well, I believe, the fundamental character of the Court's error today. Far from being "unsound in principle,"... judicial enforcement of the Tenth Amendment is essential to maintaining the federal system so carefully designed by the Framers and adopted in the Constitution.

Thus, the harm to the States that results from federal overreaching under the Commerce Clause is not simply a matter of dollars and cents.... Nor is it a matter of the wisdom or folly of certain policy choices.... Rather, by usurping functions traditionally performed by the States, federal overreaching under the Commerce Clause undermines the constitutionally mandated balance of power between the States and the federal government, a balance designed to protect our fundamental liberties.

....

In contrast, the Court today propounds a view of federalism that pays only lip service to the role of the States. Although it says that the States "unquestionably do 'retai[n] a significant measure of sovereign authority,'"... it fails to recognize the broad, yet specific areas of sovereignty that the Framers intended the States to retain. Indeed, the Court barely acknowledges that the Tenth Amendment exists. The Amendment states explicitly that "[t]he powers not delegated to the United States... are reserved to the States."... The Court recasts this language to say that the States retain their sovereign powers only to the extent that the Constitution has not divested them of their original powers and transferred those powers to the Federal Government. ... This rephrasing is not a distinction without a difference; rather, it reflects the Court's unprecedented view that Congress is free under the Commerce Clause to assume a State's traditional sovereign power, and to do so without judicial re-

view of its action. Indeed, the Court's view of federalism appears to relegate the States to precisely the trivial role that opponents of the Constitution feared they would occupy.

JUSTICE REHNQUIST, dissenting.

I join both JUSTICE POWELL's and JUSTICE O'CONNOR's thoughtful dissents.

... I do not think it incumbent on those of us in dissent to spell out further the fine points of a principle that will, I am confident, in time again command the support of a majority of the Court.

JUSTICE O'CONNOR, with whom JUSTICE POWELL and JUSTICE REHNQUIST join, dissenting.

The Court today surveys the battle scene of federalism and sounds a retreat. Like JUSTICE POWELL, I would prefer to hold the field and, at the very least, render a little aid to the wounded. I join JUSTICE POWELL's opinion. I also write separately to note my fundamental disagreement with the majority's view of federalism and the duty of this Court.

In my view, federalism cannot be reduced to the weak "essence" distilled by the majority today. There is more to federalism than the nature of the constraints that can be imposed on the States in "the realm of authority left open to them by the Constitution." The central issue of federalism, of course, is whether any realm *is* left open to the States by the Constitution — whether any area remains in which a State may act free of federal interference. "The issue... is whether the federal system has any *legal* substance, any core of constitutional right that courts will enforce." C. Black, *Perspectives in Constitutional Law* 30 (1963). The true "essence" of federalism is that the states *as States* have legitimate interests which the National Government is bound to respect even though its laws are supreme....

CHAPTER 4

The Other Side of Federalism:
State Powers over Commerce and Taxation

Striking down state laws affecting commerce is something the Supreme Court has done almost from its beginning. But nowhere in the Constitution is such a function alluded to. Justice Jackson has suggested that the authorization comes from one of "the great silences" of the Constitution — a curious and dangerous way of justifying Court power. More often the power is seen as a derivative of the grant of authority over commerce to Congress. The positive authorization of national power is seen as requiring negative limitation of state authority.

This is the essence of GIBBONS V. OGDEN (1824). In finding that the power of licensing was federal, Marshall ruled the states could not regulate; the commerce power, when exercised, prevented state regulation. Marshall also suggests much more in GIBBONS — that, probably even without the existence of the Federal Coastal Licensing Act, the Commerce Clause itself is a bar to state action.

But how much and to what degree? Marshall did not answer fully, either in GIBBONS or in *Willson* v. *Blackbird Creek Marsh Co.* (1829), where his opinion permitted state regulation of a back-water pond. However, it is clear from these decisions that Marshall was wrestling with both sides of the question: the sweep of national power and what it left for state authority.

At one extreme was the "exclusive power" notion that the mere existence of the federal grant precluded any and all use of state power. This was implicitly rejected in GIBBONS and more directly in *Willson*. At the other extreme was the position that a federal grant had no effect on state power, a concept also rejected in both GIBBONS and BROWN V. MARYLAND (1827), which some have read as indicating Marshall's total abandonment of exclusive federal power. Indeed, BROWN can be read as containing all the elements urged by Webster in GIBBONS, including the "selective exclusivity" approach — exclusivity only where Congress or logic required it — which was ultimately to prevail in COOLEY V. BOARD OF WARDENS (1852). This opinion seems to suggest the primacy of congressional action or lack of action, and emphasis on the "police power" of the states. Yet, relying on the flow of events and assurances on Marshall's views by his close associate, Justice Story, Frankfurter concludes in his authoritative book on the Commerce Clause that Marshall continued to cling to "dormant power," exclusive federal notions. In *Willson v. Blackbird Creek Marsh Co.,* the basic point is that the state was exercising "police power," and there was no exercise of commerce power involved. What was at stake was a Deleware authorization to the company to build a dam, which was deliberately breached by Willson, who then continued to navigate the creek. Marshall upheld the state action but did not develop a convincing discussion of police power.

Marshall's other opinions seem to suggest a basic affinity for the "dormant power" theory, the notion that the commerce power was nationalized. Whether used by Congress or left dormant (sleeping), the power was beyond the state. But Marshall often temporized. In GIBBONS, Johnson's concurring opinion clearly rests on the dormant-power approach, while Marshall's majority opinion is primarily a national-supremacy-when-laws-conflict decision.

To make the dormant-power theory workable it was necessary to distinguish sharply the commerce power from permissible state action. BROWN V. MARYLAND, therefore, attempted to suggest commerce was the bringing of goods into the commonwealth, and that commerce ceased when goods were taken out of the "original package" and sold in smaller units. This mechanical test has not stood the strain of time for both factual reasons and conceptual ones. It must be understood as a heroic attempt to buttress the dormant-power approach.

In *Willson v. Blackbird Creek Marsh Co.,* Marshall drafted an enigmatic, murky opinion:

> The value of the property on its banks must be enhanced by excluding the water from the marsh, and the health of the inhabitants probably improved. Measures calculated to produce these objects, provided they do not come into collision with the powers of the general government, are undoubtedly within those which are reserved to the states. . . .
>
> The counsel for the plaintiffs in error insist that it comes in conflict with the power of the United States "to regulate commerce . . . among the several states." If Congress had passed any act which bore upon the case; any act in execution of the power to regulate commerce, the object of which was to control state legislation over those small navigable

> creeks into which the tide flows, and which abound throughout the lower country of the middle and southern states, we should feel not much difficulty in saying that a state law coming in conflict with such act would be void. But Congress has passed no such act. . . .
>
> We do not think, that the act empowering the Blackbird Creek Marsh Company to place a dam across the creek, can, under all the circumstances of the case, be considered as repugnant to the power to regulate commerce in its dormant state.

There is no guidance here as to when the "police powers" do or do not impinge on the regulation of commerce. And experience was to demonstrate the lack of such a boundary. To use a more modern analogy, Marshall was clinging to the notion that the federal government could regulate commerce along the highways, while the state government could regulate speed and other safety regulations, and the courts could easily distinguish between the two.

It was one of the great accomplishments of the Taney Court to clarify this situation and to sort out the remaining middle ground on the division of power between the levels of government. This was accomplished only after considerable confusion and badly split opinions. When the dust settled, the Court had agreed upon the argument of "selective exclusiveness," which Daniel Webster argued for in GIBBONS, and toward which Marshall might well have been veering.

In *New York v. Miln* (1837), the Taney Court dealt with state legislation to keep indigents from coming into New York by requiring masters of a ship to file a list of passengers and, on demand, to post bonds against their going on welfare roles. The Court, by an 8 to 1 vote, decided this was not a regulation of commerce, but an exercise of the police power of the state — a power which remained in the hands of the people. Justice Story alone dissented, on the grounds that it was a regulation of commerce. (He also mentioned in passing that Marshall, after hearing the arguments, had felt New York's action unconstitutional.) Story argued for the dormant-power approach, but also noted that Congress had regulated passengers:

"full power to regulate a particular subject implies the whole power and leaves no residuary, and a grant of the whole to one is incompatible with a grant to another of a part."

Substantively *New York* v. *Miln* was an anomaly. It was effectively overruled in *Henderson* v. *New York* (1876) and referred to derogatorily in EDWARDS V. CALIFORNIA (1941) and SHAPIRO V. THOMPSON (1969). Certainly its reference to immigrants who were potential paupers as a "moral pestilence" grates on our ears and clashes with wording on the Statute of Liberty.

Its positive significance was in a clear defense of some state authority to deal with local matters under the rubric "the police power." We now acknowledge that the term — defined as the state power to legislate for the "health, safety and morals" of its citizenry — is simply a label. But it was a useful device to counter "dormant power," exclusive authority, and nationalism. Without such realistic acknowledgment of local needs and national inadequacy to deal with all aspects of commerce, American federalism might well have floundered.

That the police power was an inadequate conception of the problem, a result rather than a tool of analysis, was made clear by Taney:

[W]hat are the police powers of a State? They are nothing more or less than the powers of government inherent in every sovereignty to the extent of its dominions. And whether a State passes a quarantine law, or a law to punish offenses, or to establish courts of justice, or requiring certain instruments to be recorded, or to regulate commerce within its own limits, in every case it exercises the same powers. . . . And when the validity of a State law making regulations of commerce is drawn into question in a judicial tribunal, the authority to pass it cannot be made to depend upon the motives that may be supposed to have influenced the legislature, nor can the court inquire whether it was intended to guard the citizens of the State from pestilence and disease, or to make regulations of commerce for the interests and convenience of trade.

Upon this question the object and motive of the State are of no importance, and cannot influence the decision. It is a question of power. Are the States absolutely prohibited by the Constitution from mak-

ing any regulations of foreign commerce? If they are, then such regulations are null and void, whatever may have been the motive of the State, or whatever the real object of the law; and it requires no law of Congress to control or annul them.

This analysis demonstrates the untenability of Marshall's attempt at boundaries. And the Taney Court, in refusing to follow its states' rights Chief Justice — Taney never voted to hold a single state regulation invalid because of the dormant power of the Commerce Clause — demonstrated the unworkability of the police power escape hatch, precisely as he predicted.

For all its states' rights impulses, the Taney Court still found it comforting to cling to the dormant-power simplicity. In the *License Cases* (1847), the Court embraced this notion, although there was no Opinion of the Court because of continuing disagreement.

The problem arose again only two years later. In the *Passenger Cases* (1849), the Court faced the issue of local taxes on passengers disembarking at ports of entry. Webster argued the unconstitutionality of the statutes, and secured a 5 to 4 victory. Eight separate opinions were written, indicating the inability of the Court to cope with the problem of drawing up any rules of interpretation. Two of the majority justices argued exclusive national power, while three found the state act conflicted with congressional action.

The Court resolved these elements in the leading case of COOLEY V. BOARD OF WARDENS (1852), aided by the advent of Benjamin Curtiss. One of the most gifted jurists to sit on the Court, he was able to build upon Webster's arguments and the weariness of the justices with their own disagreements to weave a consistent pattern. With this decision "selective exclusion" became the dominant approach to the position of the states.

The elements of the approach are clear, though the balance between the elements is frankly left wide open.

1. Some matters requiring a single national rule are foreclosed from state regulation by force of the

constitutional provision alone. (Securing Taney's acquiescence to this point, even in principle, was possible only because no particulars were specified.)

2. Where a matter does not inherently require a single rule, a determination by Congress that the subject should be either national or state will generally decide the issue. In a sense, the Court simply endorses Congress' judgment that a matter does or does not require a national rule.

3. In the absence of congressional determination, state regulations still may not overtly discriminate against or overly burden interstate commerce.

4. Where state regulations do not violate the above rules, the Courts will balance the state's need for regulation as against its intrusion into the domain of commerce. This last rule, implicit in *Willson* v. *Blackbird Creek Marsh Co.,* has quite generally been refined through the years and is represented most explicitly in SOUTHERN PACIFIC CO. V. ARIZONA (1945). In applying the rule, the courts subjectively assess the needs for regulation and its appropriateness. The frankness of Chief Justice Stone's opinion underlines the essential legislative nature of the Court's function in this area.

Justice Black was critical of any extensive use of Court power where a state regulation was not overtly discriminatory against commerce from outside the state, and it took a great deal to convince Black a measure was discriminatory. (He dissented, for example, in *Dean Milk Co.* v. *Madison* (1951), where Wisconsin prohibited sale of milk, as one critic quite accurately put it, "not pasteurized within sight of the state capitol.") Black emphasized the "leave it to Congress" approach, suggesting national legislation could cure state encroachments.

Both on and off the bench — especially as Attorney General — the leading defender of a vigorous legal protection for interstate commerce was Robert Jackson. Jackson argued that letting states add little burdens to the flow of goods would lead to Balkanization, and would jeopardize the free, nationwide market the Founding Fathers provided us. Waiting for Congress to act was unrealistic; the individual burdens enacted by the states are generally too small to justify scarce congressional time. But to wait until they accumulate enough to attract congressional attention would be to invite a political compromise solution.

The Court has never sharply opted for one approach or the other. Rather, it has preserved its options and varied in its friendliness to state regulations, depending on circumstances and Court membership.

We may paraphrase Thomas Reed Powell's summary of the Commerce Clause: "Congress may regulate interstate commerce. The states may also regulate interstate commerce, but not too much. How much is too much is up to the courts."

"Negative Implications" of the Commerce Clause

The Commerce Clause limits on the states are, as interpreted, highly flexible. Judicial use for purposes of broader policy parallels developments in interpretation of national power, but in a much more pallid fashion.

This is almost certainly because there were other clauses the justices found more convenient — the Contract Clause in the first half of the nineteenth century, and the Due Process Clause of the Fourteenth Amendment in the twentieth. Perhaps the lack of definitive wording has operated to limit negative applications of the Commerce Clause to its primary usage, precisely because judicial action using this power has no explicit foundation.

Certainly it is not because justices are reluctant

to strike down state legislation. The most authoritative listing of invalidations of federal and state legislation lists almost nine times as many state as federal laws. Of the state invalidations, the Commerce Clause was the basis of about 10 percent in the period through the 1870s, fully 25 percent from the 1880s to 1940, and about 5 percent in the past decades. Certainly the willingness to use the Commerce Clause has paralleled the degree of judicial concern with protection of laissez-faire. Still, most of the commerce cases invalidating state legislation were pure and simple efforts to prevent tariff and other barriers between states — precisely what the Court regards as one of the major goals of the Constitution, and one of the historical reasons for its own existence.

Still, the Court's role as arbiter with broad conceptual goals, but little in the way of operating rules, has allowed the justices to follow their predilections along different paths. Virtually the same Court that decided states could not prohibit importation of liquor, LEISY V. HARDIN (1890), later decided the states could prohibit importation of colored margarine, PLUMLEY V. MASSACHUSETTS (1894). The course of American history has eliminated the ban on yellow margarine and produced nationwide prohibition and later repeal, both by constitutional amendment. But the repeal amendment specified that states could exercise prohibition not merely of production, but also of importation of alcoholic beverages. SOUTHERN PACIFIC V. ARIZONA also illustrates in its deep division how much these decisions are legislative in character.

The problem of state regulation of commerce is not merely one affecting the flow of goods. It also relates to the partnership of nation and state. When Congress acts to reinforce state action, the conjoint powers are at maximum. PARKER V. BROWN (1943) involved the right of California, under federal authorization, to encourage its farmers to join in a cartel that would have been a clear violation of antitrust regulation if done independent of government sponsorship. But under the aegis of state and nation, the farmers' cooperative becomes an entity blessed not just by nature and the sun, but also by the maximum of both national and state power.

An even more complex pattern is represented by U.S. V. SOUTHEASTERN UNDERWRITERS (1944). Insurance had been held to be local in nature, and thus not part of interstate commerce, in *Paul* v. *Virginia* (1869). Regulation of the industry had been by the states, and a complex pattern for protection of the insured had been worked out in the various commonwealths. As early as 1906, Arthur Bentley noted that the decision was anomalous and predicted reversal — a prediction that took four decades to achieve. The Supreme Court decided SOUTHEASTERN UNDERWRITERS at a time when it was short-handed and a majority of four prevailed, finding insurance, by contemporary standards, to be involved in interstate commerce. The dissenters, not understanding the position Justice Black was espousing, thought of the decision as precluding state regulation. With his "leave it to Congress" approach, Black clearly conceived of price-fixing's being outlawed by the federal government without eliminating general regulation by states. After all, most regulation of corporations remains state regulation. For fear the dissenters were right legally, Congress immediately passed the McCarran Act, specifically authorizing state regulation of insurance. This logical action under the COOLEY doctrine was seen by Black as clarifying but not really necessary. The act was upheld in PRUDENTIAL INSURANCE CO. V. BENJAMIN (1946).

The example of SOUTHEASTERN was highly educational for the Court. Since then, it has pursued a highly permissive stance toward state regulation, where the only objective is alleged infringement on national prerogatives rather than discriminatory burden on interstate commerce. In such a permissive atmosphere, both levels of government are permitted to regulate, with Congress asserting supremacy when needed. As PARKER suggests, this allows a considerable degree of governmental regulation, even of basic economic relationships, forcing the electorate to make these choices, rather than depending on judges to define them.

The general attitude of the courts today is to tread lightly, even where state action is somewhat restrictive of commerce. But where the overt purpose is stated to be local preference, especially with regard to keeping out competition, the Court maintains a line of precedent, including, among others, HOOD V. DUMOND (1949) and *Dean Milk Co. v. Madison*. These cases involved, respectively, efforts to keep milk within New York (to keep prices down) and attempts to keep milk out of Wisconsin (presumably to keep prices up). Both purposes were held invalid over Justice Black's objections.

A state, then, may not as a regulator or government favor its own citizens. But what of the state as a commercial actor—buying, selling, contracting—or as an employer? The Burger court, in effect, decided the Commerce Clause was not intended to prevent partiality by a state to its "stockholders," meaning the citizens who sustain the business venture.

In 1976, the Court easily upheld a bounty for Maryland cars turned into scrap as a conservation measure, even though the regulations favored in-state reprocessors. In *Reeves, Inc.* v. *Stake* (1981), a state-run cement manufacturing enterprise was allowed to prefer its local customers when cement became scarce. But the Court suggested this was because of the state's role as a company, since the enterprise was organized primarily to benefit its own citizens. The Court divided badly, with four justices agreeing with the lower courts that this was precisely the sort of state action forbidden by HOOD V. DUMOND.

In 1983, the Court expanded the state-as-business approach in WHITE V. MASSACHUSETTS COUNCIL (1983), upholding an executive order of the Mayor of Boston requiring contractors receiving local subsidies to employ at least half their work force from city inhabitants. Only two justices found this pattern of preferential employment objectionable, even though it would have been clearly a restriction of interstate commerce if promulgated as a regulatory, financial policy.

In MINNESOTA V. CLOVER LEAF CREAMERY CO. (1981), the Court upheld a Minnesota law prohibiting the use of nonreturnable plastic milk bottles. This case suggests another modern dilemma. Environmental regulations, such as the Minnesota law, clearly have an impact on business, both interstate and intrastate. The outlawing of a particular type of milk container necessarily aids some businesses and hurts others. The Minnesota courts, in fact, ruled that this was the real purpose of the legislation and hence an unconstitutional limit on commerce. Reflecting the currently lenient federal approach, the U.S. Supreme Court ruled that the Minnesota regulation was an intrinsically legislative matter and not a burden on interstate commerce. Stevens' interesting dissent asked why local courts could not have a different philosophy about legislative and judicial roles, even with respect to the Commerce Clause, but such a complex notion must have sent a shudder up the spines of lawyers who already find Commerce Clause cases difficult enough.

After an expensive judicial process, the Minnesota statute was vindicated, but complaints had grown and the legislature repealed the statute before implementation. This ironic development allows people to draw from the story the moral of their choice. Yet it does illustrate the Supreme Court's attitude toward the "negative implications" of the Commerce Clause; namely, the commerce power should control only in the minimum of reasonably obvious instances of interstate favoritism, and not be expanded to limit other regulatory efforts by the states.

State Taxation in the Federal System

The realities and contradictions of two sovereign taxing powers were more evident from the beginning than the mysteries of sharing of the commerce and police powers. The Constitution indirectly recognizes that the states can impose taxes by attempting to define limits on that authority. If the states were to exist, income had to be forthcoming.

A continuation of the effort to find an exact limit on state taxation is reflected in BROWN V. MARYLAND (1827), a case involving products imported from abroad. As we have noted, the Marshall Court had few opportunities to test its approach to these problems. The Taney Court from the beginning refused to apply a stringent limit on the states and generally was dismissive of BROWN V. MARYLAND. But the Court realized that the tax power of the states could not be permitted to completely control the flow of people in the *Passenger Cases* and the *License Cases*. As the "original package" notion has been weakened by lack of acceptance in other areas, the Court finally freed itself almost completely of the doctrine as applied to nondiscriminatory tax rates in *Michelin Tire Co.* v. *Wages* (1976). The major survival of the doctrine involves imported liquor in the original package, which cannot be taxed (*Department of Revenue* v. *James B. Beam Co.*, 1964).

Goods actually in transit are not taxable by states but become taxable upon reaching their terminal point (*State Freight Tax Case,* 1873). The problem of being in transit is a complex one, dependent on intent. This is beautifully illustrated by the case of *Coe* v. *Errol* (1886), holding that logs shipped down a river and destined for interstate commerce purposes were not taxable, even if frozen in for a long winter in the middle of their trip.

A basic point, sometimes treated as a due process problem, is that states may not tax goods not in the state. However, an income tax on residents may be based on total income. (Nonresidents, conversely, may be taxed on money earned within the state.)

Robbins v. *Shelby County District* (1887) established the principle that a state may not apply a sales tax to goods purchased in other states, even when shipped to the purchaser. This created a loophole encouraging the purchase of goods in states with no or lower sales tax. In recent decades, states have established "use" taxes, which are equivalent to sales taxes, and give credit for sales taxes paid elsewhere. This was upheld in *Henneford* v. *Silas Mason Co.* (1937).

The major problem is to permit state taxation to exact a reasonable share from interstate commerce without permitting states to cleverly favor local business or gain income from outside the state. The balancing of these principles — "paying its way" as opposed to avoiding Balkanization — is historically one of the major purposes of the Constitution and the functions of the Supreme Court.

The dimensions of this approach were vigorously explored in the Stone and Vinson Courts. The major proponents took positions similar to their views on state regulation. Jackson, fearing Balkanization, above all else, opted for maximum Court intervention as to state regulations. Black strongly advocated leniency for both state and national legislation, ultimately relying on Congress to eliminate problems if the states encroached too badly on commerce. Frankfurter, Stone, and Rutledge developed their notions of balancing, in taxation as elsewhere.

All three philosophies now play a role in the interesting amalgam that has resulted from vigorous debate brilliantly expressed. In general, balancing is the mode, but deference to legislation is apparent. Preventing overt or covert discrimination against interstate commerce nonetheless is avowedly a special duty of the courts and such discrimination is, per se, to be struck down.

The current framework was crystallized in the Court's four-pronged approach of *Complete Auto Transit Inc.* v. *Brady* (1977). Specifically, the Court suggested a state tax was not in violation of the Commerce Clause, provided it "is applied to an activity with a substantial nexus with the taxing state, is fairly apportioned, does not discriminate against interstate commerce, and is fairly related to the services provided by the state."

The principle that a state must have substantial authority over goods or activities prior to taxation is derived from the federal system as well as the notion of due process. If states could tax to the hilt every transaction — say, for example, on the basis of casual phone calls — every state could tax most people and businesses in the U.S. The question arises each time in the cases below, but most clearly in BRANIFF AIRWAYS V. NEBRASKA BOARD OF EQUALIZATION (1954), which dealt with the problem of state taxation of an airline landing in several airports in the state but otherwise having its principal places of business elsewhere. To the majority of justices, the question whether a plane was more like a train or an ocean vessel was clear, and taxation was therefore permitted.

The Court had already wrestled with the fact that a generous definition of "nexus" creates the danger that many states will have such a connection. This involves the requirement of apportionment. In BRANIFF, Nebraska's tax was based on the assets of the corporation, but a formula was used to reflect Nebraska's involvement with the business. As Jackson pointed out, this did not resolve every possible issue involved in the problem of "multiple burdens," the possible evil of different state formulas cumulatively overwhelming a business. Still, the Court has felt reasonable apportionments should be sustained, or interstate businesses will be undertaxed, which, realistically, is a more likely danger.

That interstate commerce per se should not be taxed seems apparent. Still, some taxes may reasonably fall only on interstate commerce. Small charges on passengers leaving or coming to an airport have been upheld so long as the funds are for the facility itself.

Taxes that discriminate against interstate commerce are forbidden in principle, but this is in fact one of the most difficult tests to enforce, though it is perhaps conceptually the clearest.

A close examination of COMMONWEALTH EDISON V. MONTANA (1981) and MARYLAND V. LOUISIANA (1981) will indicate some of the problems. The Montana severance tax on coal was estimated to fall almost entirely on non-Montanans. The legislators who drastically increased the rate of that tax in 1979, during the height of the energy crisis, were avowedly aiming at getting more revenue from non-Montanans. But the rates were the same for the 10 percent of the coal used locally, and that was sufficient to allow the Court to sustain the tax.

In the LOUISIANA case, the "first use" tax had the same rates for in-state and out-of-state consumers, but the complex system of credits connected with the tax gave considerable economic advantages to local users, and the Court invalidated the statute. But it is not irrelevant that the Master who first heard the case for the Supreme Court found the advantages might balance off, and on net were not obviously one-sided. (The case had come under the Court's original jurisdiction, so the Master made findings and recommendations, much as a lower court would have.)

The fourth standard, of the tax's being "fairly apportioned to the services provided," currently divides the Court rather sharply. In the simple case of a user's fee (say, a fishing license) the process is a simple one that creates no perplexity. But what of a general revenue tax? The services provided in return for the income tax, for example, are not at all easily enumerated; most administrators prefer to fall back on Holmes' observation that he did not mind paying taxes. "They're the price I pay for civilization." "What price civilization?" is not easily handled in a court proceeding.

Still, to some justices the *Auto* test means what it says—the Court is obligated to see that the tax rates affecting interstate commerce are not out of line with the states' reciprocal activities, and that in some rough way judges should weigh these two. To the majority in the MONTANA case, the *Auto* decision calls for a much simpler scan, one which is already largely covered in the "nexus" and "reasonable apportionment" concepts. Courts simply can see if there is a strong enough basis for the tax's existence. To pass upon the rate of taxation, they argue, is to assume legislative power.

The *Complete Auto* standards were made more flexible in *Goldberg* v. *Sweet* (109 S.Ct. 582, 1989). The Court unanimously upheld the right of Illinois to tax long-distance calls billed to an Illinois number even if initiated out of state. Three different opinions as to why the apportionment was defensible were filed by the justices.

Emerging in recent years is an implicit recognition that states can hoard resources by tax burdens which reduce external demand. While regulations achieving this are vulnerable to Court review, judicial methods to deal with tax measures are not yet perfected. It is obvious that state taxation of interstate commerce is hardly a matter fully settled, even in principle, but the operating rules are clearer than in the past.

Intergovernmental Complexities and Mixed Puzzles

An "indestructible union of indestructible states" involves levels of relationships, including the mutual relationships of these units. Some of these relationships are fixed in constitutional terms; some have evolved or been legislated. A family of relationships has been given the name *interstate comity.*

The right of persons to travel freely among the states is perhaps the most firmly embedded right in the scheme of federalism. To paraphrase an old advertisement, if a hog could be shipped across state borders, people could travel, too. Even without reference to a clear textual reference, *Crandall* v. *Nevada* (1868) held unconstitutional a tax on vehicles leaving the state. This was underscored in EDWARDS V. CALIFORNIA (1941), invalidating that state's effort to keep out indigents. (That case also completed the repudiation of *New York* v. *Miln,* regarding indigent immigrants, which was effectively rejected in the *Passenger Cases* and *License Cases.*)

The importance of the right to travel resulted in the striking down of waiting periods for welfare recipients, which would discourage welfare families from changing residence. SHAPIRO V. THOMPSON (1969) held the right to travel "fundamental" and the residency requirement not related to a compelling state interest. Similarly, residency for voting was struck down in *Dunn* v. *Blumstein* (1973).

However, one-year residency for in-state tuition was upheld in *Sturgis* v. *Washington* (1974) without discussion of impact on interstate travel. Still, a requirement that students registered as out-of-state in their first year should pay out-of-state tuition thereafter was invalidated in *Vlandis* v. *Kline* (1973).

An interesting application of this principle occurred in 1982, when the effort of the Alaskan government to pay its citizens a sum of money based upon the number of years spent in the state was declared unconstitutional. The ample funds produced by oil revenues have virtually eliminated taxes but still provide surpluses, leading to the state's "rebate" program. But it was the Court's decision that such a measure would impede interstate travel. Alaska promptly enacted a flat rebate, unrelated to years of residency, to meet these objections.

Interstate Privileges and Immunities

The Constitution (art. IV, §2) provides that "The citizens of each state shall be entitled to all privileges and immunities of citizens in the several states." This is one of the worst drafted of all constitutional provisions, providing no guidance as to what is a "privilege or immunity" of "citizens of the several states" or as to where these privileges are cognizable — in one's home state or in others. The provision has not been used extensively by fastidious judges.

Justice Bushrod Washington, in the leading case of *Corfield* v. *Coryell* (1823), interpreted the provision to apply to out-of-staters and to require a state to provide visitors "fundamental" rights such as recourse to the courts and no discriminatory taxes. He held it did not cover minor discrepancies, as in the case before him, where New Jersey prohibited gathering of oysters by nonresidents. This type of limitation is probably not now permissible. However, *Toomer* v. *Witsell* (1948) (upholding higher hunting fees for out-of-state residents) and other cases since then establish the right of a state to charge reasonably higher fees for nonresidents if they are based upon considerations such as the fact that residents already pay taxes for some aspects of the state service.

Interstate Rendition

The Constitution strongly provides that "fugitives," when located in another state, shall be returned to the state from which the escape took place on demand of the executive of that state. But the leading case, *Kentucky* v. *Dennison* (1861), took place on the eve of the Civil War and involved a black freeman accused of assisting a slave to escape in Kentucky. The governor of Ohio refused to return the accused, much as abolitionist states had refused to return slaves under the Fugitive Slave Law. Chief Justice Taney found Ohio had an obligation to return the accused, but the federal government could not coerce the governor. In practice, most requests are honored, but *Dennison* permits some leeway.

Interstate Compacts

States are forbidden to enter into agreements except with consent of Congress. The courts have been generous in interpreting congressional consent, even inferring approval from inaction. Because of the national involvement in the agreement, such agreements are enforceable in federal courts and cannot be unilaterally discounted, as reasoned by the leading case of *West Virginia ex rel. Dyer* v. *Sims* (1951). It is clear that constitutional limits apply to compacts as they do to foreign treaties and presidential agreements.

Full Faith and Credit

Article IV, Section 1 of the Constitution requires each state to grant "full faith and credit" to official acts of other states. This requirement allows travelers and businesspersons to proceed with the full expectation that matters settled in one part of the country are not reopenable in each of the other states. Congress has acted to enforce this provision. Most matters are handled easily and present no problem, although the issue of divorce has provided perplexities now believed resolved.

In general, a challenge to a completed legal proceeding in another state can be pursued only by proving lack of jurisdiction. But the problems in the divorce area were particularly pronounced in the era when most states had very strict laws. For example, New York permitted divorce only on grounds of adultery, and couples mutually willing to divorce would arrange "discovery" of an "incriminating incident." An alternative was to go to a state with lax residence and divorce requirements. Nevada competed for this trade, and Reno became known as the divorce capitol of America.

After some initial floundering between full enforcement and concern whether states might sell wealthy clients exemption from home state regulations, the Court managed to complicate matters thoroughly in *Williams* v. *North Carolina* (1942). North Carolina tried to invalidate the union of a divorced man who returned from Reno with a new wife, on the grounds that proper service of papers to the first Mrs. Williams had not taken place. This

argument was rejected by the Supreme Court. But North Carolina proceeded to try Williams a second time, arguing that the residence and divorce were a sham. This time, WILLIAMS V. NORTH CAROLINA (1945), a badly divided Supreme Court accepted the argument, raising problems about double jeopardy. Even more distressing was the possibility that all divorces of this type were illegal, and that remarriages once thought legal would be reclassified as bigamous.

The Supreme Court subsequently worked its way out of the problem by creating the concept of divisible divorce. While the marriage is dissolved definitely in such proceedings, estate and custody matters may be relitigated in the home state, so that the motivation to use the process of another state is reduced. The development of easier divorce throughout the country has done even more to defuse the issue.

Cases

Cooley v. Board of Wardens

> 12 Howard 299 (1852)
> Vote: (6–1)–2

This rich opinion has influenced virtually every later approach to the Commerce Clause and remains the leading case on state power in commerce.

A Pennsylvania law of 1803 required ships using the Port of Philadelphia to employ a local pilot or pay an amount equal to one-half the fee set by the Board to a pension fund for the pilots. Exceptions were made for ships under 75 tons and certain vessels plying local waters.

Congress, in 1789, had authorized state laws on pilotage. Cooley, however, argued this was a tax on commerce, not a regulation of navigation.

A Pennsylvania local court and the State Supreme Court sustained the state law and Cooley

appealed to the U.S. Supreme Court under writ of error.

MR. JUSTICE CURTIS delivered the opinion of the court.

These cases are brought here by writ of error to the Supreme Court of the Commonwealth of Pennsylvania.

They are actions to recover half-pilotage fees under the 29th section of the act of the Legislature of Pennsylvania, passed on the second day of March, 1803. The plaintiff in error alleges that the highest court of the State has decided against a right claimed by him under the Constitution of the United States. That right is to be exempted from the payment of the sums of money demanded, pursuant to the State law above referred to, because that law contravenes several provisions of the Constitution of the United States.

We think this particular regulation concerning half-pilotage fees, is an appropriate part of a general system of regulations of this subject. Testing it by the practice of commercial States and countries legislating on this subject, we find it has usually been deemed necessary to make similar provisions. Numerous laws of this kind are cited in the learned argument of the counsel for the defendant in error; and their fitness, as a part of a system of pilotage, in many places, may be inferred from their existence in so many different States and countries. . . . They rest upon the propriety of securing lives and property exposed to the perils of a dangerous navigation, by taking on board a person peculiarly skilled to encounter or avoid them; upon the policy of discouraging the commanders of vessels from refusing to receive such persons on board at the proper times and places; and upon the expediency, and even intrinsic justice, of not suffering those who have incurred labor, and expense, and danger, to place themselves in a position to render important service generally necessary, to go unrewarded, because the master of a particular vessel either rashly refuses their proffered assistance, or, contrary to the general experience, does not need it.

It is urged that the second section of the act of the Legislature of Pennsylvania, of the 11th of June, 1832, proves that the State had other objects in view than the regulation of pilotage. That section is as follows:

"And be it further enacted, by the authority aforesaid, that from and after the first day of July next, no health-fee or half-pilotage shall be charged on any vessel engaged in the Pennsylvania coal trade."

It must be remembered, that the fair objects of a law imposing half-pilotage when a pilot is not received, may be secured, and at the same time some classes of vessels exempted from such charge. Thus the very section of the act of 1803, now under consideration, does not apply to coasting vessels of less burden than seventy-five tons, nor to those bound to, or sailing from, a port in the river Delaware.

We do not perceive any thing in the nature or extent of this particular discrimination in favor of vessels engaged in the coal trade, which would enable us to declare it to be other than a fair exercise of legislative discretion, acting upon the subject of the regulation of the pilotage of this port of Philadelphia, with a view to operate upon the masters of those vessels, who, as a general rule, ought to take a pilot, and with the further view of relieving from the charge of half-pilotage, such vessels as from their size, or the nature of their employment, should be exempted from contributing to the support of pilots, except so far as they actually receive their services.

It is further objected, that this law is repugnant to the fifth clause of the ninth section of the first article of the Constitution, viz. — "No preference shall be given by any regulation of commerce or revenue, to the ports of one State over those of another; nor shall vessels, to or from one State, be obliged to enter, clear, or pay duties in another."

But, as already stated, pilotage-fees are not duties within the meaning of the Constitution; and, certainly, Pennsylvania does not give a preference to the port of Philadelphia, by requiring the masters, owners, or consignees of vessels sailing to or from that port, to pay the charges imposed by the twentyninth section of the act of 1803. . . .

The opinion of the court is, that the law now in question is not repugnant to either of the abovementioned clauses of the Constitution.

It remains to consider the objection, that it is repugnant to the third clause of the eighth section of the first article. "The Congress shall have power to regulate commerce with foreign nations and among the several States, and with the Indian tribes."

That the power to regulate commerce includes the regulation of navigation, we consider settled. And when we look to the nature of the service performed by pilots, to the relations which that service and its compensations bear to navigation between the several States, and between the ports of the United States and foreign countries, we are brought to the conclusion, that the regulation of the qualifications of pilots, of the modes and times of offering and rendering their services, of the responsibilities which shall rest upon them, of the powers they shall possess, of the compensation they may demand, and of the penalties by which their rights and duties may be enforced, do constitute regulations of navigation, and consequently of commerce, within the just meaning of this clause of the Constitution.

The power to regulate navigation is the power to prescribe rules in conformity with which navigation must be carried on. It extends to the persons who conduct it, as well as to the instruments used. Accordingly, the first Congress assembled under the Constitution passed laws, requiring the masters of ships and vessels of the United States to be citizens of the United States, and established many rules for the government and regulation of officers and seamen. 1 Stat. at Large, 55, and 131. These have been from time to time added to and changed, and we are not aware that their validity has been questioned. . . . And if Congress has power to regulate the seamen who assist the pilot in the management of the vessel, a power never denied, we can perceive no valid reason why the pilot should be beyond the reach of the same power. . . . And a majority of the court are of opinion, that a regulation of pilots is a regulation of commerce, within the grant to Congress of the commercial power, contained in the third clause of the eighth section of the first article of the Constitution.

It becomes necessary, therefore, to consider whether this law of Pennsylvania, being a regulation of commerce, is valid.

The act of Congress of the 7th of August, 1789, sect. 4, is as follows:

"That all pilots in the bays, inlets, rivers, harbors, and ports of the United States shall continue to be regulated in conformity with the existing laws of the States, respectively, wherein such pilots may be, or with such laws as the States may respectively hereafter enact for the purpose, until further legislative provision shall be made by Congress."

If the law of Pennsylvania, now in question, had been in existence at the date of this act of Congress, we might hold it to have been adopted by Congress, and thus made a law of the United States, and so valid. Because this act does, in effect, give the force of an act of Congress, to the then existing State laws on this subject, so long as they should continue unrepealed by the State which enacted them.

But the law on which these actions are founded was not enacted till 1803. What effect then can be attributed to so much of the act of 1789, as declares, that pilots shall continue to be regulated in conformity, "with such laws as the States may respectively hereafter enact for the purpose, until further legislative provision shall be made by Congress"?

If the States were divested of the power to legislate on this subject by the grant of the commercial power to Congress, it is plain this act could not confer upon them power thus to legislate. If the Constitution excluded the States from making any law regulating commerce, certainly Congress cannot regrant, or in any manner reconvey to the States that power. And yet this act of 1789 gives its sanction only to laws enacted by the States. This necessarily implies a constitutional power to legislate; for only a rule created by the sovereign power of a State acting in its legislative capacity, can be deemed a law, enacted by a State; and if the State has so limited its sovereign power that it no longer extends to a particular subject, manifestly it cannot, in any proper sense, be said to enact laws thereon. Entertaining these views we are brought directly and unavoidably to the consideration of the question, whether the grant of the commercial power to Congress, did *per se* deprive the States of all power to regulate pilots. This question has never been decided by this court, nor, in our judgment, has any case depending upon all the considerations which must govern this one, come before this court. The grant of commer-

cial power to Congress does not contain any terms which expressly exclude the States from exercising an authority over its subject-matter. If they are excluded it must be because the nature of the power, thus granted to Congress, requires that a similar authority should not exist in the States. If it were conceded on the one side, that the nature of this power, like that to legislate for the District of Columbia, is absolutely and totally repugnant to the existence of similar power in the States, probably no one would deny that the grant of the power to Congress, as effectually and perfectly excludes the States from all future legislation on the subject, as if express words had been used to exclude them. And on the other hand, if it were admitted that the existence of this power in Congress, like the power of taxation, is compatible with the existence of a similar power in the States, then it would be in conformity with the contemporary exposition of the Constitution (Federalist, No. 32), and with the judicial construction, given from time to time by this court, after the most deliberate consideration, to hold that the mere grant of such a power to Congress, did not imply a prohibition on the States to exercise the same power; that it is not the mere existence of such a power, but its exercise by Congress, which may be incompatible with the exercise of the same power by the States, and that the States may legislate in the absence of congressional regulations. . . .

Now the power to regulate commerce embraces a vast field, containing not only many, but exceedingly various subjects, quite unlike in their nature; some imperatively demanding a single uniform rule, operating equally on the commerce of the United States in every port; and some, like the subject now in question, as imperatively demanding that diversity, which alone can meet the local necessities of navigation.

Either absolutely to affirm, or deny that the nature of this power requires exclusive legislation by Congress, is to lose sight of the nature of the subjects of this power, and to assert concerning all of them, what is really applicable but to a part. Whatever subjects of this power are in their nature national, or admit only of one uniform system, or plan of regulation, may justly be said to be of such a nature as to require exclusive legislation by Congress. That this cannot be affirmed of laws for the regulation of pilots and pilotage is plain. The act of 1789 contains a clear and authoritative declaration by the first Congress, that the nature of this subject is such, that until Congress should find it necessary to exert its power, it should be left to the legislation of the States; that it is local and not national; that it is likely to be the best provided for, not by one system, or plan of regulations, but by as many as the legislative discretion of the several States should deem applicable to the local peculiarities of the ports within their limits.

How then can we say, that by the mere grant of power to regulate commerce, the States are deprived of all the power to legislate on this subject, because from the nature of the power the legislation of Congress must be exclusive. This would be to affirm that the nature of the power is in any case, something different from the nature of the subject to which, in such case, the power extends, and that the nature of the power necessarily demands, in all cases, exclusive legislation by Congress, while the nature of one of the subjects of that power, not only does not require such exclusive legislation, but may be best provided for by many different systems enacted by the States, in conformity with the circumstances of the ports within their limits.

It is the opinion of a majority of the court that the mere grant to Congress of the power to regulate commerce did not deprive the States of power to regulate pilots, and that although Congress has legislated on this subject, its legislation manifests an intention, with a single exception, not to regulate this subject, but to leave its regulation to the several States. To these precise questions, which are all we are called on to decide, this opinion must be understood to be confined. It does not extend to the question what other subjects, under the commercial power, are within the exclusive control of Congress, or may be regulated by the States in the absence of all congressional legislation; nor to the general question how far any regulation of a subject by Congress may be deemed to operate as an exclusion of all legislation by the States upon the same subject.

We have not adverted to the practical consequences of holding that the States possess no power to legislate for the regulation of pilots, though in our apprehension these would be of the most serious importance.

If the grant of commercial power in the Constitution has deprived the States of all power to legislate for the regulation of pilots, if their laws on this subject are mere usurpations upon the exclusive power of the general government, and utterly void, it may be doubted whether Congress could, with propriety, recognize them as laws, and adopt them as its own acts; and how are the legislatures of the States to proceed in future, to watch over and amend these laws, as the progressive wants of a growing commerce will require, when the members of those legislatures are made aware that they cannot legislate on this subject without violating the oaths they have

taken to support the Constitution of the United States?

MR. JUSTICE MCLEAN and MR. JUSTICE WAYNE dissented; and MR. JUSTICE DANIEL, although he concurred in the judgment of the court, yet dissented from its reasoning.

MR. JUSTICE MCLEAN.

Why did Congress pass the act of 1789, adopting the pilot-laws of the respective States? Laws they unquestionably were, having been enacted by the States before the adoption of the Constitution. But were they laws under the Constitution? If they had been so considered by Congress, they would not have been adopted by a special act. There is believed to be no instance in the legislation of Congress, where a State law has been adopted, which, before its adoption, applied to federal powers. To suppose such a case, would be an imputation of ignorance as to federal powers, least of all chargeable against the men who formed the Constitution and who best understood it.

Congress adopted the pilot-laws of the States, because it was well understood, they could have had no force, as regulations of foreign commerce or of commerce among the States, if not so adopted. By their adoption they were made acts of Congress, and ever since they have been so considered and enforced. But it is said that Congress is incompetent to legislate on this subject. Is this so? Did not Congress, in 1789, legislate on the subject by adopting the State laws, and may it not do so again? Was not that a wise and politic act of legislation? This is admitted. But it is said that Congress cannot legislate on this matter in detail. The act of 1789 shows that it is unnecessary for Congress so to legislate. A single section covers the whole legislation of the States, in regard to pilots. Where, then, is the necessity of recognizing this power to exist in the States? There is no such necessity; and if there were, it would not make the act of the State constitutional; for it is admitted that the power is in Congress.

That a State may regulate foreign commerce, or commerce among the States, is a doctrine which has been advanced by individual judges of this court; but never before, I believe, has such a power been sanctioned by the decision of this court. In this case, the power to regulate pilots is admitted to belong to the commercial power of Congress; and yet it is held, that a State, by virtue of its inherent power, may regulate the subject, until such regulation shall be annulled by Congress. This is the principle established by this decision. Its language is guarded, in order to apply the decision only to the case before the court. But such restrictions can never operate, so as to render the principle inapplicable to other cases. And it is in this light that the decision is chiefly to be regretted.

But the present case goes further than this. Congress regulated pilots by the act of 1789, which made the acts of the State, on that subject, the acts of Congress. In 1803, Pennsylvania passed the law in question, which materially modified the act adopted by Congress; and this act of 1803 is held to be constitutional. This, then, asserts the right of a State, not only to regulate foreign commerce, but to modify, and, consequently, to repeal a prior regulation of Congress. Is there a mistake in this statement? There is none, if an adopted act of a State is thereby made an act of Congress, and if the regulation of pilots, in regard to foreign commerce, be a regulation of commerce.

I think the charge of half-pilotage is correct under the circumstances, and I only object to the power of the State to pass the law. Congress, to whom the subject peculiarly belongs, should have been applied to, and no doubt it would have adopted the act of the State.

MR. JUSTICE DANIEL.

The true question here is, whether the power to enact pilot-laws is appropriate and necessary, or rather most appropriate and necessary to the State or the federal governments. It being conceded that this power has been exercised by the States from their very dawn of existence; that it can be practically and beneficially applied by the local authorities only; it being conceded, as it must be, that the power to pass pilot-laws, as such, has not been in any express terms delegated to Congress, and does not necessarily conflict with the right to establish commercial regulations, I am forced to conclude that this is an original and inherent power in the States, and not one to be merely tolerated, or held subject to the sanction of the federal government.

Southern Pacific Co. v. Arizona

325 U.S. 761 (1945)
Vote: (6–1)–2

The Arizona Train Limit Act of 1912 limited passenger trains to fourteen cars and freight trains to seventy cars. The Southern Pacific Company exceeded both limits. The State Trial Court found for the company, but the Arizona Supreme Court upheld the statute. The railroad appealed to the U.S. Supreme Court, arguing, among other claims, a violation of the Commerce Clause.

MR. CHIEF JUSTICE STONE delivered the opinion of the Court.

The Arizona Train Limit Law of May 16, 1912, Arizona Code Ann., 1939, §69–119, makes it unlawful for any person or corporation to operate within the state a railroad train of more than fourteen passenger or seventy freight cars, and authorizes the state to recover a money penalty for each violation of the Act. The questions for decision are whether Congress has, by legislative enactment, restricted the power of the states to regulate the length of interstate trains as a safety measure and, if not, whether the statute contravenes the commerce clause of the Federal Constitution.

In 1940 the State of Arizona brought suit in the Arizona Superior Court against appellant, the Southern Pacific Company, to recover the statutory penalties for operating within the state two interstate trains, one a passenger train of more than fourteen cars, and one a freight train of more than seventy cars. Appellant answered, admitting the train operations, but defended on the ground that the statute offends against the commerce clause and the due process clause of the Fourteenth Amendment and conflicts with federal legislation. After an extended trial, without a jury, the court made detailed findings of fact on the basis of which it gave judgment for the railroad company. The Supreme Court of Arizona reversed and directed judgment for the state.

The Supreme Court left undisturbed the findings of the trial court and made no new findings. It held that the power of the state to regulate the length of interstate trains had not been restricted by Congressional action. It sustained the Act as a safety measure to reduce the number of accidents attributed to the operation of trains of more than the statutory maximum length, enacted by the state legislature in the exercise of its "police power."

Purporting to act under §1, paragraphs 10–17 of the Interstate Commerce Act, 24 Stat. 379 as amended (49 U.S.C. §1 *et seq.*), the Interstate Commerce Commission, as of September 15, 1942, promulgated as an emergency measure Service Order No. 85, 7 Fed. Reg. 7258, suspending the operation of state train limit laws for the duration of the war. . . .

The Commission's order was not in effect in 1940 when the present suit was brought for violations of the state law in that year, and the Commission's order is inapplicable to the train operations here charged as violations. Hence the question here is not of the effect of the Commission's order, which we assume for purposes of decision to be valid, but whether the grant of power to the Commission operated to supersede the state act before the Commission's order. We are of opinion that, in the absence of administrative implementation by the Commission, §1 does not of itself curtail state power to regulate train lengths. The provisions under which the Commission purported to act, phrased in broad and general language, do not in terms deal with that subject. We do not gain either from their words or from the legislative history any hint that Congress in enacting them intended, apart from Commission action, to supersede state laws regulating train lengths. We can hardly suppose that Congress, merely by conferring authority on the Commission to regulate car service in an "emergency," intended to restrict the exercise, otherwise lawful, of state power to regulate train lengths before the Commission finds an "emergency" to exist.

Congress, in enacting legislation within its constitutional authority over interstate commerce, will not be deemed to have intended to strike down a state statute designed to protect the health and safety of the public unless its purpose to do so is clearly manifested.

For a hundred years it has been accepted constitutional doctrine that the commerce clause, without the aid of Congressional legislation, thus affords some protection from state legislation inimical to the national commerce, and that in such cases, where Congress has not acted, this Court, and not the state legislature, is under the commerce clause the final arbiter of the competing demands of state and national interests. . . .

[I]n general Congress has left it to the courts to formulate the rules thus interpreting the commerce clause in its application, doubtless because it has appreciated the destructive consequences to the commerce of the nation if their protection were withdrawn . . . and has been aware that in their application state laws will not be invalidated without the support of relevant factual material which will "afford a sure basis" for an informed judgment.

There has thus been left to the states wide scope for the regulation of matters of local state concern, even though it in some measure affects the commerce, provided it does not materially restrict the free flow of commerce across state lines, or interfere with it in matters with respect to which uniformity of regulation is of predominant national concern.

The findings show that the operation of long trains, that is trains of more than fourteen passenger and more than seventy freight cars, is standard practice over the main lines of the railroads of the United States, and that, if the length of trains is to be regulated at all, national uniformity in the regulation adopted, such as only Congress can prescribe, is practically indispensable to the operation of an efficient and economical national railway system.

In Arizona, approximately 93% of the freight traffic and 95% of the passenger traffic is interstate. Because of the Train Limit Law appellant is required to haul over 30% more trains in Arizona than would otherwise have been necessary. . . . The additional cost of operation of trains complying with the Train Limit Law in Arizona amounts for the two railroads traversing that state to about $1,000,000 a year.

The unchallenged findings leave no doubt that the Arizona Train Limit Law imposes a serious burden on the interstate commerce conducted by appellant. . . . Compliance with a state statute limiting train lengths requires interstate trains of a length lawful in other states to be broken up and reconstituted as they enter each state according as it may impose varying limitations upon train lengths. The alternative is for the carrier to conform to the lowest train limit restriction of any of the states through which its trains pass, whose laws thus control the carriers' operations both within and without the regulating state.

If one state may regulate train lengths, so may all the others, and they need not prescribe the same maximum limitation. The practical effect of such regulation is to control train operations beyond the boundaries of the state exacting it because of the necessity of breaking up and reassembling long trains at the nearest terminal points before entering and after leaving the regulating state.

The trial court found that the Arizona law had no reasonable relation to safety, and made train operation more dangerous. Examination of the evidence and the detailed findings makes it clear that this conclusion was rested on facts found which indicate that such increased danger of accident and personal injury as may result from the greater length of trains is more than offset by the increase in the number of accidents resulting from the larger number of trains when train lengths are reduced.

The principal source of danger of accident from increased length of trains is the resulting increase of "slack action" of the train. Slack action is the amount of free movement of one car before it transmits its motion to an adjoining coupled car. . . .

. . . Loose coupling is necessary to enable the train to proceed freely around curves and is an aid in starting heavy trains, since the application of the locomotive power to the train operates on each car in the train successively, and the power is thus utilized to start only one car at a time.

As the trial court found, reduction of the length of trains also tends to increase the number of accidents because of the increase in the number of trains. . . . And the record amply supports the trial court's conclusion that the frequency of accidents is closely related to the number of trains run. The number of accidents due to grade crossing collisions between trains and motor vehicles and pedestrians, and to collisions between trains, which are usually far more serious than those due to slack action, and accidents due to locomotive failures, in general vary with the number of trains.

We think, as the trial court found, that the Arizona Train Limit Law, viewed as a safety measure, affords at most slight and dubious advantage, if any, over unregulated train lengths.

Appellees especially rely on the full train crew cases. . . . While the full train crew laws undoubtedly placed an added financial burden on the railroads in order to serve a local interest, they did not obstruct interstate transportation or seriously impede it. . . . In sustaining those laws the Court considered the restriction a minimal burden on the commerce comparable to the law requiring the licensing of engineers as a safeguard against those of reckless and intemperate habits. . . .

South Carolina Highway Dept. v. *Barnwell Bros.,* *supra,* was concerned with the power of the state to regulate the weight and width of motor cars passing interstate over its highways, a legislative field over which the state has a far more extensive control than over interstate railroads. . . . [T]here are few subjects of state regulation affecting interstate commerce which are so peculiarly of local concern as is the use of the state's highways. Unlike the railroads local highways are built, owned and maintained by the state or its municipal subdivisions.

The contrast between the present regulation and the full train crew laws in point of their effects on the commerce, and the like contrast with the highway safety regulations, in point of the nature of the subject of regulation and the state's interest in it, illustrate and emphasize the considerations which enter into a determination of the relative weights of state and national interests where state regulation affecting interstate commerce is attempted. Here examination of all the relevant factors makes it plain that the state interest is outweighed by the interest of the nation in an adequate, economical and efficient railway transportation service, which must prevail.

Reversed.

MR. JUSTICE RUTLEDGE concurs in the result.
MR. JUSTICE BLACK, dissenting.

Before the state trial court finally determined that the dangers found by the legislature in 1912 no longer existed, it heard evidence over a period of 5½ months which appears in about 3,000 pages of the printed record before us. It then adopted findings of fact submitted to it by the railroad, which cover 148 printed pages, and conclusions of law which cover 5 pages. We can best understand the nature of this "trial" by analogizing the same procedure to a defendant charged with violating a state or national safety appliance act, where the defendant comes into court and admits violation of the act. In such cases, the ordinary procedure would be for the court to pass upon the constitutionality of the act, and either discharge or convict the defendants. The procedure here, however, would justify quite a different trial method. Under it, a defendant is permitted to offer voluminous evidence to show that a legislative body has erroneously resolved disputed facts in finding a danger great enough to justify the passage of the law. This new pattern of trial procedure makes it necessary for a judge to hear all the evidence offered as to why a legislature passed a law and to make findings of fact as to the validity of those reasons. If under today's ruling a court does make findings, as to a danger contrary to the findings of the legislature, and the evidence heard "lends support" to those findings, a court can then invalidate the law. In this respect, the Arizona County Court acted, and this Court today is acting, as a "super-legislature."

When we finally get down to the gist of what the Court today actually decides, it is this: Even though more railroad employees will be injured by "slack action" movements on long trains than on short trains, there must be no regulation of this danger in the absence of "uniform regulations." That means that no one can legislate against this danger except the Congress; and even though the Congress is perfectly content to leave the matter to the different state legislatures, this Court, on the ground of "lack of uniformity," will require it to make an express avowal of the fact before it will permit a state to guard against that admitted danger.

We are not left in doubt as to why, as against the potential peril of injuries to employees, the Court tips the scales on the side of "uniformity." . . . The "burden" on commerce reduces itself to mere cost because there was no finding, and no evidence to support a finding, that by the expenditure of sufficient sums of money, the railroads could not enable themselves to carry goods and passengers just as quickly and efficiently with short trains as with long trains. . . . It may be that offsetting dangers are possible in the operation of short trains. The balancing of these probabilities, however, is not in my judgment a matter for judicial determination, but one which calls for legislative consideration. Representatives elected by the people to make their laws, rather than judges appointed to interpret those laws, can best determine the policies which govern the people. That at least is the basic principle on which our democratic society rests. . . .

MR. JUSTICE DOUGLAS, dissenting.

Leisy v. Hardin

135 U.S. 100 (1890)
Vote: 6–3

Iowa adopted a prohibition forbidding the manufacture or sale of alcoholic beverages except where licensed for medicinal and other specified purposes. Leisy, an Illinois brewer, shipped beer in the original barrels for sale. Hardin, a local constable, seized the barrels. Local courts held for Leisy, but the Iowa Supreme Court upheld the statute. Leisy brought a writ of error to the U.S. Supreme Court.

MR. CHIEF JUSTICE FULLER delivered the opinion of the court.

The power vested in Congress "to regulate commerce with foreign nations, and among the several States, and with the Indian tribes," is the power to prescribe the rule by which that commerce is to be governed, and is a power complete in itself, acknowledging no limitations other than those prescribed in the Constitution. It is co-extensive with the subject on which it acts and cannot be stopped at the external boundary of a State, but must enter its interior and must be capable of authorizing the disposition of those articles which it introduces, so that they may become mingled with the common mass of property within the territory entered. *Gibbons* v. *Ogden,* 9 Wheat. 1; *Brown* v. *Maryland,* 12 Wheat. 419.

And while, by virtue of its jurisdiction over persons and property within its limits, a State may provide for the security of the lives, limbs, health and comfort of persons and the protection of property so situated, yet a subject matter which has been confided exclusively to Congress by the Constitution is not within the jurisdiction of the police power of the State, unless placed there by congressional ac-

tion. . . . The power to regulate commerce among the States is a unit, but if particular subjects within its operation do not require the application of a general or uniform system, the States may legislate in regard to them with a view to local needs and circumstances until Congress otherwise directs; but the power thus exercised by the States is not identical in its extent with the power to regulate commerce among the States. . . .

[W]here, in relation to the subject matter, different rules may be suitable for different localities, the States may exercise powers which, though they may be said to partake of the nature of the power granted to the general government, are strictly not such, but are simply local powers, which have full operation until or unless circumscribed by the action of Congress in effectuation of the general power. *Cooley* v. *Port Wardens of Philadelphia,* 12 How. 299.

That ardent spirits, distilled liquors, ale and beer are subjects of exchange, barter and traffic, like any other commodity in which a right of traffic exists, and are so recognized by the usages of the commercial world, the laws of Congress and the decisions of courts, is not denied. Being thus articles of commerce, can a State, in the absence of legislation on the part of Congress, prohibit their importation from abroad or from a sister State? or when imported prohibit their sale by the importer?

In *Brown* v. *Maryland* (*supra*) the act of the state legislature drawn in question was held invalid as repugnant to the prohibition of the Constitution upon the States to lay any impost or duty upon imports or exports, and to the clause granting the power to regulate commerce. . . . [T]he point of time when the prohibition ceases and the power of the State to tax commences, is not the instant when the article enters the country, but when the importer has so acted upon it that it has become incorporated and mixed up with the mass of property in the country, which happens when the original package is no longer such in his hands.

. . . [W]here the subject is national in its character, and admits and requires uniformity of regulation, affecting alike all the States, such as transportation between the States, including the importation of goods from one State into another, Congress can alone act upon it and provide the needed regulations. The absence of any law of Congress on the subject is equivalent to its declaration that commerce in that matter shall be free. Thus the absence of regulations as to interstate commerce with reference to any particular subject is taken as a declaration that the importation of that article into the States shall be unrestricted. It is only after the importation is completed, and the property imported has mingled with and become a part of the general property of the State, that its regulations can act upon it, except so far as may be necessary to insure safety in the disposition of the import until thus mingled.

The conclusion follows that, as the grant of the power to regulate commerce among the States, so far as one system is required, is exclusive, the States cannot exercise that power without the assent of Congress, and, in the absence of legislation, it is left for the courts to determine when state action does or does not amount to such exercise, or, in other words, what is or is not a regulation of such commerce. When that is determined, controversy is at an end.

. . . Undoubtedly, it is for the legislative branch of the state governments to determine whether the manufacture of particular articles of traffic, or the sale of such articles, will injuriously affect the public, and it is not for Congress to determine what measures a State may properly adopt as appropriate or needful for the protection of the public morals, the public health or the public safety; but notwithstanding it is not vested with supervisory power over matters of local administration, the responsibility is upon Congress, so far as the regulation of interstate commerce is concerned, to remove the restriction upon the State in dealing with imported articles of trade within its limits, which have not been mingled with the common mass of property therein, if in its judgment the end to be secured justifies and requires such action.

Prior to 1888 the statutes of Iowa permitted the sale of foreign liquors imported under the laws of the United States, provided the sale was by the importer in the original casks or packages, and in quantities not less than those in which they were required to be imported. . . . But that provision of the statute was repealed in 1888, and the law so far amended that we understand it now to provide that, whether imported or not, wine cannot be sold in Iowa except for sacramental purposes, nor alcohol except for specified chemical purposes, nor intoxicating liquors, including ale and beer, except for pharmaceutical and medicinal purposes, and not at all except by citizens of the State of Iowa, who are registered pharmacists and have permits obtained as prescribed by the statute, a permit being also grantable to one discreet person in any township where a pharmacist does not obtain it.

The plaintiffs in error are citizens of Illinois, are not pharmacists, and have no permit, but import into Iowa beer, which they sell in original packages, as described. Under our decision in *Bowman* v. *Chi-*

cago &c. *Railway Co., supra,* they had the right to import this beer into that State, and in the view which we have expressed they had the right to sell it, by which act alone it would become mingled in the common mass of property within the State. Up to that point of time, we hold that in the absence of congressional permission to do so, the State had no power to interfere by seizure, or any other action, in prohibition of importation and sale by the foreign or non-resident importer. Whatever our individual views may be as to the deleterious or dangerous qualities of particular articles, we cannot hold that any articles which Congress recognizes as subjects of interstate commerce are not such, or that whatever are thus recognized can be controlled by state laws amounting to regulations, while they retain that character; although, at the same time, if directly dangerous in themselves, the State may take appropriate measures to guard against injury before it obtains complete jurisdiction over them. To concede to a State the power to exclude, directly or indirectly, articles so situated, without congressional permission, is to concede to a majority of the people of a State, represented in the state legislature, the power to regulate commercial intercourse between the States.

MR. JUSTICE GRAY, with whom concurred MR. JUSTICE HARLAN and MR. JUSTICE BREWER, dissenting.

The police power extends not only to things intrinsically dangerous to the public health, such as infected rags or diseased meat, but to things which, when used in a lawful manner, are subjects of property and of commerce, and yet may be used so as to be injurious or dangerous to the life, the health or the morals of the people. Gunpowder, for instance, is a subject of commerce and of lawful use, yet, because of its explosive and dangerous quality, all admit that the State may regulate its keeping and sale. And there is no article, the right of the State to control or to prohibit the sale or manufacture of which within its limits is better established, than intoxicating liquors. . . .

An intention on the part of Congress that commerce shall be free from the operation of laws passed by a State in the exercise of its police power cannot be inferred from the mere fact of there being no national legislation upon the subject, unless in matters as to which the power of Congress is exclusive. Where the power of Congress is exclusive, the States have, of course, no power to legislate; and it may be said that Congress, by not legislating, manifests an intention that there should be no legislation on the subject. But in matters over which the power of Congress is paramount only, and not exclusive, the power of the States is not excluded until Congress has legislated.

Plumley v. Massachusetts

155 U.S. 461 (1894)
Vote: 6–3

Massachusetts prohibited the manufacture and sale of oleo, if colored to resemble butter. Plumley, who was an agent of an out-of-state producer, was convicted of sales violating the act. The Supreme Judicial Court affirmed, and Plumley brought a writ of error. Four new justices had come to the Court since LEISY, and all were in the new majority with Harlan and Gray, who had dissented in LEISY.

MR. JUSTICE HARLAN delivered the opinion of the court.

Plumley, the plaintiff in error, was convicted in the Municipal Court of Boston upon the charge of having sold in that city on the 6th day of October, 1891, in violation of the law of Massachusetts, a certain article, product and compound known as oleomargarine, made partly of fats, oils and oleaginous substances and compounds thereof, not produced from unadulterated milk or cream but manufactured in imitation of yellow butter produced from pure unadulterated milk and cream.

The petitioner claimed that the statute of Massachusetts was repugnant to the clause of the Constitution providing that the Congress shall have power to regulate commerce among the several States; to the clause declaring that the citizens of each State shall be entitled to all the privileges and immunities of citizens in the several States; to the clause providing that no State shall make or enforce any law which shall abridge the privileges or immunities of citizens of the United States, nor deprive any person of life, liberty, or property without due process of law, nor deny to any person within its jurisdiction the equal protection of the laws; to the clause declaring that private property shall not be taken for public purposes; and to the act of Congress of August 2, 1886, c. 840, entitled "An act defining butter, also imposing a tax upon and regulating the manufacture, sale, importation, and exportation of oleomargarine." . . . But there is no ground to suppose that

Congress intended in that enactment to interfere with the exercise by the States of any authority they could rightfully exercise over the sale within their respective limits of the article defined as oleomargarine. The statute imposed certain special taxes upon manufacturers of oleomargarine, as well as upon wholesale and retail dealers in that compound. Section 3243 of the Revised Statutes is in these words: "The payment of any tax imposed by the internal revenue laws for carrying on any trade or business shall not be held to exempt any person from any penalty or punishment provided by the laws of any State for carrying on the same within such State, or in any manner to authorize the commencement or continuance of such trade or business contrary to the laws of such State or in places prohibited by municipal law."

It will be observed that the statute of Massachusetts which is alleged to be repugnant to the commerce clause of the Constitution does not prohibit the manufacture or sale of all oleomargarine, but only such as is colored in imitation of yellow butter produced from pure unadulterated milk or cream of such milk. If free from coloration or ingredient that "causes it to look like butter," the right to sell it "in a separate and distinct form, and in such manner as will advise the consumer of its real character," is neither restricted nor prohibited. It appears, in this case, that oleomargarine, in its natural condition, is of "a light-yellowish color," and that the article sold by the accused was artificially colored "in imitation of yellow butter." Now, the real object of coloring oleomargarine so as to make it look like genuine butter is that it may appear to be what it is not, and thus induce unwary purchasers, who do not closely scrutinize the label upon the package in which it is contained, to buy it as and for butter produced from unadulterated milk or cream from such milk. The suggestion that oleomargarine is artificially colored so as to render it more palatable and attractive can only mean that customers are deluded, by such coloration, into believing that they are getting genuine butter. If any one thinks that oleomargarine, not artificially colored so as to cause it to look like butter, is as palatable or as wholesome for purposes of food as pure butter, he is, as already observed, at liberty under the statute of Massachusetts to manufacture it in that State or to sell it there in such manner as to inform the customer of its real character. He is only forbidden to practice, in such matters, a fraud upon the general public. The statute seeks to suppress false pretenses and to promote fair dealing in the sale of an article of food. It compels the sale of oleomargarine for what it really is, by preventing its sale for what it is not. Can it be that the Constitution of the United States secures to any one the privilege of manufacturing and selling an article of food in such manner as to induce the mass of people to believe that they are buying something which, in fact, is wholly different from that which is offered for sale? Does the freedom of commerce among the States demand a recognition of the right to practice a deception upon the public in the sale of any articles, even those that may have become the subject of trade in different parts of the country?

If there be any subject over which it would seem the States ought to have plenary control, and the power to legislate in respect to which it ought not to be supposed was intended to be surrendered to the general government, it is the protection of the people against fraud and deception in the sale of food products. Such legislation may, indeed, indirectly or incidentally affect trade in such products transported from one State to another State. But that circumstance does not show that laws of the character alluded to are inconsistent with the power of Congress to regulate commerce among the States.

It is sufficient to say of *Leisy* v. *Hardin* that it did not in form or in substance present the particular question now under consideration. . . . So far as the record disclosed, and so far as the contentions of the parties were concerned, the article there in question was what it appeared to be, namely, genuine beer, and not a liquid or drink colored artificially so as to cause it to look like beer.

We are not unmindful of the fact—indeed, this court has often had occasion to observe—that the acknowledged power of the States to protect the morals, the health, and safety of their people by appropriate legislation, sometimes touches, in its exercise, the line separating the respective domains of national and state authority. . . . [T]he judiciary of the United States should not strike down a legislative enactment of a State—especially if it has direct connection with the social order, the health, and the morals of its people—unless such legislation plainly and palpably violates some right granted or secured by the national Constitution or encroaches upon the authority delegated to the United States for the attainment of objects of national concern. . . .

MR. JUSTICE JACKSON, now absent, was present at the argument and participated in the decision of this case. He concurs in this opinion.

Judgment affirmed.

MR. CHIEF JUSTICE FULLER, with whom concurred MR. JUSTICE FIELD and MR. JUSTICE BREWER, dissenting.

[O]leomargarine is conceded to be a wholesome, palatable, and nutritious article of food, in no way deleterious to the public health or welfare. . . .

I deny that a State may exclude from commerce legitimate subjects of commercial dealings because of the possibility that their appearance may deceive purchasers in regard to their qualities.

Parker v. Brown

317 U.S. 341 (1943)
Vote: 9–0

Some cases present issues of state power over commerce as opposed to national regulation. This case tests the limits of state authority when its exercise is encouraged by national legislation.

The California Agriculture Prorate Act of 1933 developed a system of restricting production and marketing of selected agricultural products. Brown, a raisin grower, was permitted to sell only a portion of his crop. He argued that California was fostering an illegal monopoly in restraint of trade, violating the Sherman Antitrust Act and acting in conflict with the Second AAA (1938). Further, since 95 percent of all raisins in California ended in interstate commerce, he argued, the restrictions were an unconstitutional burden on interstate commerce.

Brown won his case in the district court, and the three-judge appellate court affirmed. Parker, the State Director of Agriculture, then appealed to the U.S. Supreme Court.

MR. CHIEF JUSTICE STONE delivered the opinion of the Court.

The California Agricultural Prorate Act authorizes the establishment, through action of state officials, of programs for the marketing of agricultural commodities produced in the state, so as to restrict competition among the growers and maintain prices in the distribution of their commodities to packers.

Upon the petition of ten producers for the establishment of a prorate marketing plan for any commodity within a defined production zone (§8), and after a public hearing (§9), and after making prescribed economic findings (§10) showing that the institution of a program for the proposed zone will prevent agricultural waste and conserve agricultural wealth of the state without permitting unreasonable profits to producers, the Commission is authorized to grant the petition.

The seasonal proration marketing program for raisins, with which we are now concerned, became effective on September 7, 1940. . . . The committee is required to establish receiving stations within the zone to which every producer must deliver all raisins which he desires to market. The raisins are graded at these stations. All inferior raisins are to be placed in the "inferior raisin pool," to be disposed of by the committee "only for assured by-product and other diversion purposes." All substandard raisins, and at least 20 percent of the total standard and substandard raisins produced, must be placed in a "surplus pool." Raisins in this pool may also be disposed of only for "assured by-product and other diversion purposes," except that under certain circumstances the program committee may transfer standard raisins from the surplus pool to the stabilization pool. Fifty percent of the crop must be placed in a "stabilization pool." . . .

Appellee's bill of complaint challenges the validity of the proration program as in violation of the Commerce Clause and the Sherman Act; in support of the decree of the district court he also urges that it conflicts with and is superseded by the Federal Agricultural Marketing Agreement Act of 1937. The complaint alleges that he is engaged within the marketing zone both in producing and in purchasing and packing raisins for sale and shipment interstate; that before the adoption of the program he had entered into contracts for the sale of 1940 crop raisins; that, unless enjoined, appellants will enforce the program against appellee by criminal prosecutions and will prevent him from marketing his 1940 crop, from fulfilling his sales contracts, and from purchasing for sale and selling in interstate commerce raisins of that crop.

Section 1 of the Sherman Act, 15 U.S.C. §1, makes unlawful "every contract, combination . . . or conspiracy, in restraint of trade or commerce among the several States." And §2, 15 U.S.C. §2, makes it unlawful to "monopolize, or attempt to monopolize, or combine or conspire with any other person or persons, to monopolize any part of the trade or commerce among the several States." We may assume for present purposes that the California prorate program would violate the Sherman Act if it were organized and made effective solely by virtue of a contract, combination or conspiracy of private persons, individual or corporate. We may assume also, without deciding, that Congress could, in the

exercise of its commerce power, prohibit a state from maintaining a stabilization program like the present because of its effect on interstate commerce. Occupation of a legislative "field" by Congress in the exercise of a granted power is a familiar example of its constitutional power to suspend state laws.

But it is plain that the prorate program here was never intended to operate by force of individual agreement or combination. It derived its authority and its efficacy from the legislative command of the state and was not intended to operate or become effective without that command. We find nothing in the language of the Sherman Act or in its history which suggests that its purpose was to restrain a state or its officers or agents from activities directed by its legislature. In a dual system of government in which, under the Constitution, the states are sovereign, save only as Congress may constitutionally subtract from their authority, an unexpressed purpose to nullify a state's control over its officers and agents is not lightly to be attributed to Congress.

The Sherman Act makes no mention of the state as such, and gives no hint that it was intended to restrain state action or official action directed by a state.

We may assume that the powers conferred upon the Secretary would extend to the control of surpluses in the raisin industry through a pooling arrangement such as was promulgated under the California Prorate Act in the present case. . . . We may assume also that a stabilization program adopted under the Agricultural Marketing Agreement Act would supersede the state act. But the federal act becomes effective only if a program is ordered by the Secretary.

. . . From this and the whole structure of the Act, it would seem that it contemplates that its policy may be effectuated by a state program either with or without the promulgation of a federal program by order of the Secretary. Cf. *United States* v. *Rock Royal Co-op., supra*. It follows that the adoption of an adequate program by the state may be deemed by the Secretary a sufficient ground for believing that the policies of the federal act will be effectuated without the promulgation of an order.

It is evident, therefore, that the Marketing Act contemplates the existence of state programs at least until such time as the Secretary shall establish a federal marketing program, unless the state program in some way conflicts with the policy of the federal act. The Act contemplates that each sovereign shall operate "in its own sphere but can exert its authority in conformity rather than in conflict with that of the other."

The question is thus presented whether in the absence of Congressional legislation prohibiting or regulating the transactions affected by the state program, the restrictions which it imposes upon the sale within the state of a commodity by its producer to a processor who contemplates doing, and in fact does, work upon the commodity before packing and shipping it in interstate commerce, violate the Commerce Clause.

The governments of the states are sovereign within their territory save only as they are subject to the prohibitions of the Constitution or as their action in some measure conflicts with powers delegated to the National Government, or with Congressional legislation enacted in the exercise of those powers. This Court has repeatedly held that the grant of power to Congress by the Commerce Clause did not wholly withdraw from the states the authority to regulate the commerce with respect to matters of local concern, on which Congress has not spoken. . . . A fortiori there are many subjects and transactions of local concern not themselves interstate commerce or a part of its operations which are within the regulatory and taxing power of the states, so long as state action serves local ends and does not discriminate against the commerce, even though the exercise of those powers may materially affect it. Whether we resort to the mechanical test sometimes applied by this Court in determining when interstate commerce begins with respect to a commodity grown or manufactured within a state and then sold and shipped out of it — or whether we consider only the power of the state in the absence of Congressional action to regulate matters of local concern, even though the regulation affects or in some measure restricts the commerce — we think the present regulation is within state power.

In applying the mechanical test to determine when interstate commerce begins and ends . . . this Court has frequently held that for purposes of local taxation or regulation "manufacture" is not interstate commerce even though the manufacturing process is of slight extent. . . .

All of these cases proceed on the ground that the taxation or regulation involved, however drastically it may affect interstate commerce, is nevertheless not prohibited by the Commerce Clause where the regulation is imposed before any operation of interstate commerce occurs. Applying that test, the regulation here controls the disposition, including the sale and purchase, of raisins before they are processed and packed preparatory to interstate sale and shipment. The regulation is thus applied to transactions wholly intrastate before the raisins are ready for shipment in interstate commerce.

When Congress has not exerted its power under the Commerce Clause, and state regulation of matters of local concern is so related to interstate commerce that it also operates as a regulation of that commerce, the reconciliation of the power thus granted with that reserved to the state is to be attained by the accommodation of the competing demands of the state and national interests involved.

In comparing the relative weights of the conflicting local and national interests involved, it is significant that Congress, by its agricultural legislation, has recognized the distressed condition of much of the agricultural production of the United States, and has authorized marketing procedures, substantially like the California prorate program, for stabilizing the marketing of agricultural products. Acting under this legislation the Secretary of Agriculture has established a large number of market stabilization programs for agricultural commodities moving in interstate commerce in various parts of the country, including seven affecting California crops. All involved attempts in one way or another to prevent over-production of agricultural products and excessive competition in marketing them, with price stabilization as the ultimate objective. Most if not all had a like effect in restricting shipments and raising or maintaining prices of agricultural commodities moving in interstate commerce.

It thus appears that whatever effect the operation of the California program may have on interstate commerce, it is one which it has been the policy of Congress to aid and encourage through federal agencies in conformity to the Agricultural Marketing Agreement Act, and §302 of the Agricultural Adjustment Act. Nor is the effect on the commerce greater than or substantially different in kind from that contemplated by the stabilization programs authorized by federal statutes. As we have seen, the Agricultural Marketing Agreement Act is applicable to raisins only on the direction of the Secretary of Agriculture who, instead of establishing a federal program has, as the statute authorizes, cooperated in promoting the state program and aided it by substantial federal loans. Hence we cannot say that the effect of the state program on interstate commerce is one which conflicts with Congressional policy or is such as to preclude the state from this exercise of its reserved power to regulate domestic agricultural production.

We conclude that the California prorate program for the 1940 raisin crop is a regulation of state industry of local concern which, in all the circumstances of this case which we have detailed, does not impair national control over the commerce in a manner or to a degree forbidden by the Constitution.

Reversed.

U.S. v. Southeastern Underwriters

322 U.S. 533 (1944)
Vote: 4–1–2; only seven justices
sitting because of vacancies.

Under older concepts of the Commerce Clause, the insurance industry had been held completely regulatable by state governments. But modern developments brought the national industry closer together. In any event, the logic of recent commerce decisions suggested insurance was as regulatable as, say, the securities business. In *Southeastern,* the U.S. sought to apply the Sherman antitrust statute to an industry which was, at the time of the law's adoption, not included. What should happen when concepts of the reach of federal law are expanded? In a sense, the real argument here is not over the antitrust statute at all. It is over the consequence to state regulation if the federal government is held to have newly permitted constitutional authority. Those who saw coexistent regulation possible, or approved of congressional power to authorize state action, saw no great issue. Justice Black even saw no need for congressional action, and therefore no problem at all.

MR. JUSTICE BLACK delivered the opinion of the Court.

For seventy-five years this Court has held, whenever the question has been presented, that the Commerce Clause of the Constitution does not deprive the individual states of power to regulate and tax specific activities of foreign insurance companies which sell policies within their territories. Each state has been held to have this power even though negotiation and execution of the companies' policy contracts involved communications of information and

movements of persons, moneys, and papers across state lines. Not one of all these cases, however, has involved an Act of Congress which required the Court to decide the issue of whether the Commerce Clause grants to Congress the power to regulate insurance transactions stretching across state lines. Today for the first time in the history of the Court that issue is squarely presented and must be decided.

Appellees — the Southeastern Underwriters Association (S.E.U.A.), and its membership of nearly 200 private stock fire insurance companies, and 27 individuals — were indicted in the District Court for alleged violations of the Sherman Anti-Trust Act. The indictment alleges two conspiracies. The first, in violation of §1 of the Act, was to restrain interstate trade and commerce by fixing and maintaining arbitrary and non-competitive premium rates on fire and specified "allied lines" of insurance in Alabama, Florida, Georgia, North Carolina, South Carolina, and Virginia; the second, in violation of §2, was to monopolize trade and commerce in the same lines of insurance in and among the same states.

The kind of interference with the free play of competitive forces with which the appellees are charged is exactly the type of conduct which the Sherman Act has outlawed for American "trade or commerce" among the states. Appellees have not argued otherwise. Their defense, set forth in a demurrer, has been that they are not required to conform to the standards of business conduct established by the Sherman Act because "the business of fire insurance is not commerce." Sustaining the demurrer, the District Court held that "the business of insurance is not commerce, either intrastate or interstate."

Ordinarily courts do not construe words used in the Constitution so as to give them a meaning more narrow than one which they had in the common parlance of the times in which the Constitution was written. To hold that the word "commerce" as used in the Commerce Clause does not include a business such as insurance would do just that. Whatever other meanings "commerce" may have included in 1787, the dictionaries, encyclopedias, and other books of the period show that it included trade: business in which persons bought and sold, bargained and contracted. And this meaning has persisted to modern times. Surely, therefore, a heavy burden is on him who asserts that the plenary power which the Commerce Clause grants to Congress to regulate "Commerce among the several States" does not include the power to regulate trading in insurance to the same extent that it includes power to regulate other trades or businesses conducted across state lines.

The modern insurance business holds a commanding position in the trade and commerce of our Nation. Built upon the sale of contracts of indemnity, it has become one of the largest and most important branches of commerce. Its total assets exceed $37,000,000,000, or the approximate equivalent of the value of all farm lands and buildings in the United States. Its annual premium receipts exceed $6,000,000,000, more than the average annual revenue receipts of the United States Government during the last decade. Included in the labor force of insurance are 524,000 experienced workers, almost as many as seek their livings in coal mining or automobile manufacturing. Perhaps no modern commercial enterprise directly affects so many persons in all walks of life as does the insurance business. Insurance touches the home, the family, and the occupation or the business of almost every person in the United States.

This business is not separated into 48 district territorial compartments which function in isolation from each other. Interrelationship, interdependence, and integration of activities in all the states in which they operate are practical aspects of the insurance companies' methods of doing business. A large share of the insurance business is concentrated in a comparatively few companies located, for the most part, in the financial centers of the East. Premiums collected from policyholders in every part of the United States flow into these companies for investment. As policies become payable, checks and drafts flow back to the many states where the policyholders reside. The result is a continuous and indivisible stream of intercourse among the states composed of collections of premiums, payments of policy obligations, and the countless documents and communications which are essential to the negotiation and execution of policy contracts. Individual policyholders living in many different states who own policies in a single company have their separate interests blended in one assembled fund of assets upon which all are equally dependent for payment of their policies. The decisions which that company makes at its home office — the risks it insures, the premiums it charges, the investments it makes, the losses it pays — concern not just the people of the state where the home office happens to be located. They concern people living far beyond the boundaries of that state. . . .

Despite all of this, despite the fact that most persons, speaking from common knowledge, would instantly say that of course such a business is engaged in trade and commerce, the District Court felt compelled by decisions of this Court to conclude that the insurance business can never be trade or commerce within the meaning of the Commerce Clause. We must therefore consider these decisions.

In 1869 this Court held, in sustaining a statute of Virginia which regulated foreign insurance companies, that the statute did not offend the Commerce Clause because "issuing a policy of insurance is not a transaction of commerce." *Paul v. Virginia*. . . . Since then, in similar cases, this statement has been repeated, and has been broadened. . . .

In all cases in which the Court has relied upon the proposition that "the business of insurance is not commerce," its attention was focused on the validity of state statutes — the extent to which the Commerce Clause automatically deprived states of the power to regulate the insurance business. Since Congress had at no time attempted to control the insurance business, invalidation of the state statutes would practically have been equivalent to granting insurance companies engaged in interstate activities a blanket license to operate without legal restraint. As early as 1866 the insurance trade, though still in its infancy, was subject to widespread abuses. To meet the imperative need for correction of these abuses the various state legislatures, including that of Virginia, passed regulatory legislation. *Paul v. Virginia* upheld one of Virginia's statutes. To uphold insurance laws of other states, including tax laws, *Paul v. Virginia's* generalization and reasoning have been consistently adhered to.

Today, however, we are asked to apply this reasoning, not to uphold another state law, but to strike down an Act of Congress which was intended to regulate certain aspects of the methods by which interstate insurance companies do business; and, in so doing, to narrow the scope of the federal power to regulate the activities of a great business carried on back and forth across state lines. But past decisions of this Court emphasize that legal formulae devised to uphold state power cannot uncritically be accepted as trustworthy guides to determine Congressional power under the Commerce Clause. Furthermore, the reasons given in support of the generalization that "the business of insurance is not commerce" and can never be conducted so as to constitute "Commerce among the States" are inconsistent with many decisions of this Court which have upheld federal statutes regulating interstate commerce under the Commerce Clause. . . .

One reason advanced for the rule in the *Paul* case has been that insurance policies "are not commodities to be shipped or forwarded from one State to another." But both before and since *Paul* v. *Virginia* this Court has held that Congress can regulate traffic though it consists of intangibles. . . .

Another reason advanced to support the result of the cases which follow *Paul* v. *Virginia* has been that, if any aspects of the business of insurance be treated as interstate commerce, "then all control over it is taken from the States and the legislative regulations which this Court has heretofore sustained must be declared invalid." Accepted without qualification, that broad statement is inconsistent with many decisions of this Court. It is settled that, for Constitutional purposes, certain activities of a business may be intrastate and therefore subject to state control, while other activities of the same business may be interstate and therefore subject to federal regulation. And there is a wide range of business and other activities which, though subject to federal regulation, are so intimately related to local welfare that, in the absence of Congressional action, they may be regulated or taxed by the states. In marking out these activities the primary test applied by the Court is not the mechanical one of whether the particular activity affected by the state regulation is part of interstate commerce, but rather whether, in each case, the competing demands of the state and national interests involved can be accommodated. And the fact that particular phases of an interstate business or activity have long been regulated or taxed by states has been recognized as a strong reason why, in the continued absence of conflicting Congressional action, the state regulatory and tax laws should be declared valid.

The real answer to the question before us is to be found in the Commerce Clause itself and in some of the great cases which interpret it. Many decisions make vivid the broad and true meaning of that clause.

The precise boundary between national and state power over commerce has never yet been, and doubtless never can be, delineated by a single abstract definition. The most widely accepted general description of that part of commerce which is subject to the federal power is that given in 1824 by Chief Justice Marshall in *Gibbons* v. *Ogden*. . . . "Commerce, undoubtedly, is traffic, but it is something more: it is intercourse. It describes the commercial intercourse between nations, and parts of nations, in all its branches. . . ." Commerce is interstate, he said, when it "concerns more States than one." . . . No decision of this Court has ever questioned this as too comprehensive a description of the subject matter of the Commerce Clause. To accept a description less comprehensive, the Court has recog-

nized, would deprive the Congress of that full power necessary to enable it to discharge its Constitutional duty to govern commerce among the states.

Our basic responsibility in interpreting the Commerce Clause is to make certain that the power to govern intercourse among the states remains where the Constitution placed it. That power, as held by this Court from the beginning, is vested in the Congress, available to be exercised for the national welfare as Congress shall deem necessary. No commercial enterprise of any kind which conducts its activities across state lines has been held to be wholly beyond the regulatory power of Congress under the Commerce Clause. We cannot make an exception of the business of insurance.

We come then to the contention, earnestly pressed upon us by appellees, that Congress did not intend in the Sherman Act to exercise its power over the interstate insurance trade.

Certainly the Act's language affords no basis for this contention. Declared illegal in §1 is "every contract, combination in the form of trust or otherwise, or conspiracy, in restraint of trade or commerce among the several States. . . ."

Appellees argue that the Congress knew, as doubtless some of its members did, that this Court had prior to 1890 said that insurance was not commerce and was subject to state regulation, and that therefore we should read the Act as though it expressly exempted that business. But neither by reports nor by statements of the bill's sponsors or others was any purpose to exempt insurance companies revealed. And we fail to find in the legislative history of the Act an expression of a clear and unequivocal desire of Congress to legislate only within that area previously declared by this Court to be within the federal power. . . . We have been shown not one piece of reliable evidence that the Congress of 1890 intended to freeze the proscription of the Sherman Act within the mold of then current judicial decisions defining the commerce power. On the contrary, all the acceptable evidence points the other way. That Congress wanted to go to the utmost extent of its Constitutional power in restraining trust and monopoly agreements such as the indictment here charges admits of little, if any, doubt.

Appellees further argue that, quite apart from what the Sherman Act meant in 1890, the succeeding Congresses have accepted and approved the decisions of this Court that the business of insurance is not commerce. They call attention to the fact that at various times since 1890 Congress has refused to enact legislation providing for federal regulation of the insurance business, and that several resolutions proposing to amend the Constitution specifically to authorize federal regulation of insurance have failed of passage. In addition they emphasize that, although the Sherman Act has been amended several times, no amendments have been adopted which specifically bring insurance within the Act's proscription.

The most that can be said of all this evidence considered together is that it is inconclusive as to any point here relevant. By no means does it show that the Congress of 1890 specifically intended to exempt insurance companies from the all-inclusive scope of the Sherman Act. Nor can we attach significance to the omission of Congress to include in its amendments to the Act an express statement that the Act covered insurance. From the beginning Congress has used language broad enough to include all businesses, and never has amended the Act to define these businesses with particularity.

Finally it is argued at great length that virtually all the states regulate the insurance business on the theory that competition in the field of insurance is detrimental both to the insurers and the insured, and that if the Sherman Act be held applicable to insurance much of this state regulation will be destroyed. The first part of this argument is buttressed by opinions expressed by various persons that unrestricted competition in insurance results in financial chaos and public injury. Whether competition is a good thing for the insurance business is not for us to consider. Having power to enact the Sherman Act, Congress did so; if exceptions are to be written into the Act, they must come from the Congress, not this Court.

The argument that the Sherman Act necessarily invalidates many state laws regulating insurance we regard as exaggerated. Few states go so far as to permit private insurance companies, without state supervision, to agree upon and fix uniform insurance rates. Cf. *Parker v. Brown.* . . . No states authorize combinations of insurance companies to coerce, intimidate, and boycott competitors and consumers in the manner here alleged, and it cannot be that any companies have acquired a vested right to engage in such destructive business practices.

Reversed.

MR. JUSTICE ROBERTS and MR. JUSTICE REED took no part in the consideration or decision of this case.

MR. CHIEF JUSTICE STONE, dissenting:

The conclusion seems inescapable that the formation of insurance contracts, like many others, and the business of so doing, is not, without more, commerce within the protection of the commerce clause of the Constitution and thereby, in large measure, excluded from state control and regulation. . . . This conclusion seems, upon analysis, not only correct on principle and in complete harmony with the uniform rulings by which this Court has held that the formation of all types of contract which do not stipulate for the performance of acts of interstate commerce, are likewise not interstate commerce, but it has the support of an unbroken line of decisions of this Court beginning with *Paul v. Virginia,* seventy-five years ago, and extending down to the present time.

To give blind adherence to a rule or policy that no decision of this Court is to be overruled would be itself to overrule many decisions of the Court which do not accept that view. But the rule of *stare decisis* embodies a wise policy because it is often more important that a rule of law be settled than that it be settled right. This is especially so where, as here, Congress is not without regulatory power. . . . The question then is not whether an earlier decision should ever be overruled, but whether a particular decision ought to be. And before overruling a precedent in any case it is the duty of the Court to make certain that more harm will not be done in rejecting than in retaining a rule of even dubious validity. . . .

From what has been said it seems plain that our decisions that the business of insurance is not commerce are not unsound in principle, and involve no inconsistency or lack of harmony with accepted doctrine. They place no field of activity beyond the control of both the national and state governments as did *Hammer v. Dagenhart,* 247 U.S. 251, overruled three years ago by a unanimous Court in *United States v. Darby,* 312 U.S. 100, 117. On the contrary the ruling that insurance is not commerce, and is therefore unaffected by the restrictions which the commerce clause imposes on state legislation, removed the most serious obstacle to regulation of that business by the states. Through their plenary power over domestic and foreign corporations which are not engaged in interstate commerce, the states have developed extensive and effective systems of regulation of the insurance business, often solving regulatory problems of a local character with which it would be impractical or difficult for Congress to deal through the exercise of the commerce power. And in view of the broad powers of the federal government to regulate matters which, though not themselves commerce, nevertheless affect interstate commerce, *Wickard v. Filburn,* 317 U.S. 111; *Polish Alliance v. Labor Board, supra,* there can be no doubt of the power of Congress if it so desires to regulate many aspects of the insurance business mentioned in this indictment.

But the immediate and only practical effect of the decision now rendered is to withdraw from the states, in large measure, the regulation of insurance and to confer it on the national government, which has adopted no legislative policy and evolved no scheme of regulation with respect to the business of insurance. . . .

MR. JUSTICE FRANKFURTER:

I join in the opinion of the Chief Justice.

[T]he evidence is overwhelming that the inapplicability of the Sherman Act, in its contemporaneous setting, to insurance transactions such as those charged by this indictment has been confirmed and not modified by Congressional attitude and action in the intervening fifty years. There is no Congressional warrant therefore for bringing about the far-reaching dislocations which the opinions of the Chief Justice and Mr. Justice Jackson adumbrate.

MR. JUSTICE JACKSON, dissenting in part:

The doctrine that insurance business is not commerce always has been criticized as unrealistic, illogical, and inconsistent with other holdings of the Court. I am unable to make any satisfactory distinction between insurance business as now conducted and other transactions that are held to constitute interstate commerce. Were we considering the question for the first time and writing upon a clean slate, I would have no misgivings about holding that insurance business is commerce and where conducted across state lines is interstate commerce and therefore that congressional power to regulate prevails over that of the states. I have little doubt that if the present trend continues federal regulation eventually will supersede that of the states.

The question therefore for me settles down to this: What role ought the judiciary to play in reversing the trend of history and setting the nation's feet on a new path of policy?

Instead of overruling our repeated decisions that insurance is not commerce, the Court could apply to this case the principle that even if it is not commerce the antitrust laws prohibit its manipulation to restrain interstate commerce, just as we hold that the National Labor Relations Act prohibits insurance companies, even if not in commerce, from engaging in unfair labor practices which affect commerce. . . . This would require the Government to show that any acts it sought to punish affect something more than insurance and substantially affect interstate transportation or interstate commerce in some commodity. Whatever problems of reconciliation between state and federal authority this would present— and it would not avoid them all—it would leave the basis of state regulation unimpaired.

The majority of the sitting Justices insist that we follow the more drastic course. Abstract logic may support them, but the common sense and wisdom of the situation seem opposed. It may be said that practical consequences are no concern of a court, that it should confine itself to legal theory. Of course, in cases where a constitutional provision or a congressional statute is clear and mandatory, its wisdom is not for us. But the Court now is not following, it is overruling, an unequivocal line of authority reaching over many years. We are not sustaining an act of Congress against attack on its constitutionality, we are making unprecedented use of the Act to strike down the constitutional basis of state regulation. I think we not only are free, but are duty bound, to consider practical consequences of such a revision of constitutional theory. . . .

The orderly way to nationalize insurance supervision, if it be desirable, is not by court decision but through legislation. Judicial decision operates on the states and the industry retroactively. We cannot anticipate, and more than likely we could not agree, what consequences upon tax liabilities, refunds, liabilities under state law to states or to individuals, and even criminal liabilities will follow this decision. Such practical considerations years ago deterred the Court from changing its doctrine as to insurance. Congress, on the other hand, if it thinks the time has come to take insurance regulation into the federal system, may formulate and announce the whole scope and effect of its action in advance, fix a future effective date, and avoid all the confusion, surprise, and injustice which will be caused by the action of the Court.

Prudential Insurance Co. v. Benjamin

328 U.S. 408 (1946)
Vote: (7–1)–0

After SOUTHEASTERN UNDERWRITERS ruled that insurance was commerce, reversing *Paul* v. *Virginia,* lawyers seized upon the new situation to open up formerly closed questions. Congress, in the interim, had acted to avert such a sweeping reevaluation by specifically authorizing state regulation of the insurance industry. But here Prudential argued that Congress may not authorize what the Commerce Clause forbids.

MR. JUSTICE RUTLEDGE delivered the opinion of the Court.

This case and *Robertson* v. *California* . . . bring not unexpected sequels to *United States* v. *Southeastern Underwriters Assn.* . . . In cycle reminiscent conversely of views advanced there and in *Paul* v. *Virginia,* claims are put forward on the basis of the *Southeastern* decision to sustain immunity from state taxation and, in the *Robertson* case, from state regulation of the business of insurance.

The specific effect asserted in this case is that South Carolina no longer can collect taxes from Prudential, a New Jersey corporation, which for years prior to 1945 the state had levied and the company had paid.

Prudential insists that the tax discriminates against interstate commerce and in favor of local business, since it is laid only on foreign corporations and is measured by their gross receipts from premiums derived from business done in the state, regardless of its interstate or local character. Accordingly it says the tax cannot stand consistently with many decisions of this Court outlawing state taxes which discriminate against interstate commerce. South Carolina denies that the tax is discriminatory or has been affected by the *Southeastern* decision. But in any event it maintains that the tax is valid, more particularly in view of the McCarran Act, by which it is claimed Congress has consented to continuance of this form of taxation and thus has removed any possible constitutional objection which otherwise might exist. This Prudential asserts Congress has not done and could not do.

The State Supreme Court has held the continued exaction of the tax not to be in violation of the commerce clause or affected by the ruling made in the *Southeastern* case.

The versatility with which argument inverts state and national power, each in alternation to ward off the other's incidence, is not simply a product of protective self-interest. It is a recurring manifestation of the continuing necessity in our federal system for accommodating the two great basic powers it comprehends. For this Court's part, from *Gibbons* v. *Ogden,* no phase of that process has been more continuous or at times perplexing than reconciling the paramount national authority over commerce, created by Article I, §8 of the Constitution, with appropriate exercise of the states' reserved powers touching the same or related subject matter.

No phase has had a more atypical history than regulation of the business of insurance. This fact is important for the problems now presented. They have origin in that history.

Whether *Paul* v. *Virginia* represented in its day an accommodation with or a departure from the pre-existing evolution of commerce clause law and whether its ruling, together with later ones adhering to it, remained consonant with the subsequent general development of that law, may still be debated. But all may concede that the *Paul* case created for the business of insurance a special, if not a wholly unique, way of thinking and acting in the regulation of business done across state lines.

. . . [F]rom *Paul* to *Southeastern* the states took over exclusively the function of regulating the insurance business in its specific legislative manifestations. Congress legislated only in terms applicable to commerce generally, without particularized reference to insurance. At the same time, on the rationalization that insurance was not commerce, yet was business affected with a vast public interest, the states developed comprehensive regulatory and taxing systems. . . .

Meanwhile the business of insurance experienced a nation-wide expansion graphically depicted not only in the facts of the situation presented in the *Southeastern* case but also in the operations of Prudential as described by its advocates in this cause. These divergent facts, legal and economic, necessarily were reflected in state legislation. States grappling with nation-wide, but nationally unregulated, business inevitably exerted their powers to limits and in ways not sought generally to be applied to other business held to be within the reach of the commerce clause's implied prohibition.

Now we are told many of these statutes no longer can stand. The process of readjustment began affirmatively with *Southeastern*. Since the commerce clause is a two-edged instrument, the indicated next step, indeed the constitutionally required one, as the argument runs, is to apply its negatively cutting edge. Conceptions so developed with reference to other commerce must now be extended to the commerce of insurance in completion of the readjustment. This, it is confidently asserted, will require striking down much of the state legislation enacted and effective prior to the *Southeastern* decision. Particularly will this be true of all discriminatory state taxes, of which it is said South Carolina's is one. Moreover, those results must follow regardless of the McCarran Act's provisions. For by that Act, in Prudential's assessment, Congress neither intended to, nor could, validate such taxes.

Prudential's misconception relates not to the necessity for applying, but to the nature and scope of the negative function of the commerce clause. It is not the simple, clean-cutting tool supposed. . . . [I]ts implied negative operation on state power has been uneven, at times highly variable. More often than not, in matters more governable by logic and less by experience, the business of negative implication is slippery.

That the clause imposes some restraint upon state power has never been doubted. For otherwise the grant of power to Congress would be wholly ineffective. But the limitation not only is implied. It is open to different implications of meaning. And this accounts largely for variations in this field continuing almost from the beginning until now. . . .

Moreover, the parallel encompasses the latest turn in the long-run trend. For, concurrently with the broadening of the scope for permissible application of federal authority, the tendency also has run toward sustaining state regulatory and taxing measures formerly regarded as inconsonant with Congress' unexercised power over commerce, and to doing so by a new, or renewed, emphasis on facts and practical considerations rather than dogmatic logistics. . . . [I]t will be helpful to note the exact effects of Prudential's argument.

Fundamentally it maintains that the commerce clause "of its own force" and without reference to any action by Congress, whether through its silence or otherwise, forbids discriminatory state taxation of interstate commerce. This is to say, in effect, that neither Congress acting affirmatively nor Congress and the states thus acting coordinately can validly impose any regulation which the Court has found or would find to be forbidden by the commerce clause, if laid only by state action taken while Congress' power lies dormant. In this view the limits of state power to regulate commerce in the absence of affirmative action by Congress are also the limits of Congress' permissible action in this respect, whether taken alone or in coordination with state legislation.

Merely to state the position in this way compels its rejection. So conceived, Congress' power over commerce would be nullified to a very large extent. For in all the variations of commerce clause theory it has never been the law that what the states may do in the regulation of commerce, Congress being silent, is the full measure of its power. Much less has this boundary been thought to confine what Congress and the states acting together may accomplish. . . .

The commerce clause is in no sense a limitation upon the power of Congress over interstate and foreign commerce. On the contrary, it is, as Marshall declared in *Gibbons* v. *Ogden,* a grant to Congress of plenary and supreme authority over those subjects. The only limitation it places upon Congress' power is in respect to what constitutes commerce, including

whatever rightly may be found to affect it sufficiently to make congressional regulation necessary or appropriate. . . . The one is concerned with defining commerce, with fixing the outer boundary of the field over which the authority granted shall govern. The other relates only to matters within the field of commerce, once this is defined, including whatever may fall within the "affectation" doctrine. The one limitation bounds the power of Congress. The other confines only the powers of the states.

Prudential . . . has posed an enigma. It is, if the commerce clause "by its own force" forbids discriminatory state taxation, or other measures, how is it that Congress by expressly consenting can give that action validity?

The answer need not be labored. Prudential in this case makes no contention that commerce is not involved. Its argument is exactly the opposite. Its contention founded on the commerce clause is one wholly of implied prohibition within the field of commerce.

This it regards as operative not only in Congress' silence, but in the face of its positive expression by the McCarran Act that the continued regulation and taxation by the states of the business of insurance is in accord with Congress' policy. That expression raises questions concerning its own validity and also concerning whether the policy stated extends to the kind of state legislation which is immediately in issue. But those questions are not answered, as Prudential seeks to have them answered, by any conception that Congress' declaration of policy adds nothing to the validity of what the states have done within the area covered by the declaration. . . . [W]e are not required to determine whether South Carolina's tax would be valid in the dormancy of Congress' power. For Congress has expressly stated its intent and policy in the Act. And, for reasons to be stated, we think that the declaration's effect is clearly to sustain the exaction and that this can be done without violating any constitutional provision.

It is not necessary to spend much time with interpreting the McCarran Act. . . .

Obviously Congress' purpose was broadly to give support to the existing and future state systems for regulating and taxing the business of insurance.

Moreover, in taking this action Congress must have had full knowledge of the nation-wide existence of state systems of regulation and taxation. . . .

It would serve no useful purpose now to inquire whether or how far this effort was necessary, in view of the explicit reservations made in the majority opinion in the *Southeastern* case. Nor is it necessary to conclude that Congress, by enacting the

McCarran Act, sought to validate every existing state regulation or tax. And we agree with Prudential that there can be no inference that Congress intended to circumvent constitutional limitations upon its own power.

Congress intended to declare, and in effect declared, that uniformity of regulation, and of state taxation, are not required in reference to the business of insurance by the national public interest, except in the specific respects otherwise expressly provided for. This necessarily was a determination by Congress that state taxes, which in its silence might be held invalid as discriminatory, do not place on interstate insurance business a burden which it is unable generally to bear or should not bear in the competition with local business.

That judgment was one of policy and reflected long and clear experience.... In view of all these considerations, we would be going very far to rule that South Carolina no longer may collect her tax. To do so would flout the expressly declared policies of both Congress and the state.

Affirmed.

Hood v. DuMond

336 U.S. 525 (1949)
Vote: 5–4

This case is the high-water mark of Court protection of interstate commerce. The 5 to 4 decision by Jackson invalidated a New York regulation that attempted to keep milk within the state and prevent excessive local competition. Without balancing interests, the majority suggest it is improper for a state to attempt to isolate its economy, either to exclude competing out-of-state commodities or to keep local goods within. Vigorous dissents by Black (with Murphy) and Frankfurter (with Rutledge) go in quite different directions. Black found this an arrogation of control by judges who were creating a new kind of "no-man's zone" where business could escape any regulation. Frankfurter urged "balancing" and the need for more evidence.

Hood v. *DuMond* did not produce the calamities predicted by Black, nor has it been overruled. It

stands as a separate standard normally applied only to clear and direct assertions of local preference. As the Court has proven more tolerant of both federal and state regulation, it stands as a paradigmatic statement of the very purpose of the Commerce Clause.

MR. JUSTICE JACKSON delivered the opinion of the Court.

This case concerns the power of the State of New York to deny additional facilities to acquire and ship milk in interstate commerce where the grounds of denial are that such limitation upon interstate business will protect and advance local economic interests.

H. P. Hood & Sons, Inc., a Massachusetts corporation, has long distributed milk and its products to inhabitants of Boston.... The area in which Hood has been denied an additional license to make interstate purchases has been developed as a part of the Boston milkshed from which both the Hood Company and a competitor have shipped to Boston.

The state courts have held and it is conceded here that Hood's entire business in New York, present and proposed, is interstate commerce. This Hood has conducted for some time by means of three receiving depots, where it takes raw milk from farmers. The milk is not processed in New York but is weighed, tested and, if necessary, cooled and on the same day shipped as fluid milk to Boston. These existing plants have been operated under license from the State and are not in question here as the State has licensed Hood to continue them. The controversy concerns a proposed additional plant for the same kind of operation at Greenwich, New York.

Article 21 of the Agriculture and Markets Law of New York forbids a dealer to buy milk from producers unless licensed to do so by the Commissioner of Agriculture and Markets....

The Commissioner's denial was based on further provisions of this section which require him to be satisfied "that the issuance of the license will not tend to a destructive competition in a market already adequately served, and that the issuance of the license is in the public interest."

Upon the hearing pursuant to the statute, milk dealers competing with Hood as buyers in the area opposed licensing the proposed Greenwich plant. They complained that Hood, by reason of conditions under which it sold in Boston, had competitive advantages under applicable federal milk orders, Boston health regulations, and OPA ceiling prices. There was also evidence of a temporary shortage of supply in the Troy, New York market during the fall and winter of 1945–46. The Commissioner was urged not to allow Hood to compete for additional supplies of milk or to take on producers then delivering to other dealers.

. . . .

In denying the application for expanded facilities, the Commissioner states his grounds as follows:

> If applicant is permitted to equip and operate another milk plant in this territory, and to take on producers now delivering to plants other than those which it operates, it will tend to reduce the volume of milk received at the plants which lose those producers, and will tend to increase the cost of handling milk in those plants.
>
> If applicant takes producers now delivering milk to local markets such as Troy, it will have a tendency to deprive such markets of a supply needed during the short season.

. . . .

Our decision in a milk litigation most relevant to the present controversy deals with the converse of the present situation. *Baldwin* v. *Selig*, 294 U.S. 511. In that case, New York placed conditions and limitations on the local sale of milk imported from Vermont designed in practical effect to exclude it, while here its order proposes to limit the local facilities for purchase of additional milk so as to withhold milk from export. The State agreed then, as now, that the Commerce Clause prohibits it from directly curtailing movement of milk into or out of the State. But in the earlier case, it contended that the same result could be accomplished by controlling delivery, bottling and sale after arrival, while here it says it can do so by curtailing facilities for its purchase and receipt before it is shipped out. In neither case is the measure supported by health or safety considerations but solely by protection of local economic interests, such as supply for local consumption and limitation of competition. This Court unanimously rejected the State's contention in the *Seelig* case and held that the Commerce Clause, even in the absence of congressional action, prohibits such regulations for such ends.

. . . .

The Constitution, said Mr. Justice Cardozo for the unanimous Court, "was framed upon the theory that the peoples of the several states must sink or swim together, and that in the long run prosperity and salvation are in union and not division." He reiterated that the economic objective, as distinguished from

any health, safety and fair-dealing purpose of the regulation, was the root of its invalidity. The action of the State would "neutralize the economic consequences of free trade among the states." "Such a power, if exerted, will set a barrier to traffic between one state and another as effective as if customs duties, equal to the price differential, had been laid upon the thing transported.". . .

. . . .

The desire of the Forefathers to federalize regulation of foreign and interstate commerce stands in sharp contrast to their jealous preservation of the state's power over its internal affairs. No other federal power was so universally assumed to be necessary, no other state power was so readily relinquished. . . .

. . . .

The Commerce Clause is one of the most prolific sources of national power and an equally prolific source of conflict with legislation of the state. While the Constitution vests in Congress the power to regulate commerce among the states, it does not say what the states may or may not do in the absence of congressional action, nor how to draw the line between what is and what is not commerce among the states. Perhaps even more than by interpretation of its written word, this Court has advanced the solidarity and prosperity of this Nation by the meaning it has given to these great silences of the Constitution.

. . . .

This principle that our economic unit is the Nation, which alone has the gamut of powers necessary to control of the economy, including the vital power of erecting customs barriers against foreign competition, has as its corollary that the states are not separable economic units. . . .

. . . .

. . . We need only consider the consequences if each of the states that produce copper, lead, high-grade iron ore, timber, cotton, oil or gas should decree that industries located in that state shall have priority. What fantastic rivalries and dislocations and reprisals would ensue if such practices were begun. . . .

. . . .

The State, however, contends that such restraint or obstruction as its order imposes on interstate commerce does not violate the Commerce Clause because the State regulation coincides with, supplements and is part of the federal regulatory scheme. This contention that Congress has taken possession of "the field" but shared it with the State, it is to be noted, reverses the contention usually made in comparable cases, which is that Congress has not fully occupied the field and hence the State may fill the void.

. . . .

But no federal approval or responsibility for the challenged features of this order appears in any of these provisions or arrangements. . . .

. . . We have no doubt that Congress in the national interest could prohibit or curtail shipments of milk in interstate commerce, unless and until local demands are met. Nor do we know of any reason why Congress may not, if it deems it in the national interest, authorize the states to place similar restraints on movement of articles of commerce. . . .

. . . [W]e can hardly assume that the challenged provisions of this order advance the federal scheme of regulation because Congress forbids inclusion of such a policy in a federal milk order. . . .

. . . .

Since the statute as applied violates the Commerce Clause and is not authorized by federal legislation pursuant to that Clause, it cannot stand. The judgment is reversed and the case remanded for proceedings not inconsistent with this opinion.

It is so ordered.

MR. JUSTICE BLACK, dissenting:

In this case the Court sets up a new constitutional formula for invalidation of state laws regulating local phases of interstate commerce. I believe the New York law is invulnerable to constitutional attack under constitutional rules which the majority of this Court have long accepted. . . . All local activities that fall within the scope of this new formula will be free from any regulatory control whatever. For it is inconceivable that Congress could pass uniform national legislation capable of adjustment and application to all the local phases of interstate activities that take place in the 48 states. . . .

. . . .

Gibbons v. *Ogden,* decided in 1824, held invalid a New York statute regulating commerce which conflicted with an Act of Congress. The Court there left undecided the question strongly urged that the commerce clause of itself forbade New York to regulate commerce. In 1847 this undecided question was discussed by Chief Justice Taney. His view was that the commerce clause of itself did no more than grant power to Congress to regulate commerce among the states; that until Congress acted states could regulate the commerce; and that this Court was without power to strike down state regulations unless they conflicted with a valid federal law. . . .

In 1852 this Court rejected in part the Taney interpretation of the commerce clause. *Cooley* v. *Board of Wardens.* . . . The opinion there stated that the commerce clause *per se* forbade states to regulate commerce under some circumstances but left them free to do so under other circumstances. The dividing line was not precisely drawn, but the Court outlined broad principles to guide future determinations of the side of the line on which commercial transactions would be held to fall. . . . Numerous cases, for example *Parker* v. *Brown,* which made judicial appraisals under the *Cooley* rule, are gently laid to rest. . . . The vacancy left by the *Cooley* principle will be more than filled, however, by the new formula which without balancing interests, automatically will relieve many businesses from state regulation.

. . . .

It requires more than invocation of the spectre of "Balkanization" and eulogy of the Constitution's framers to prove that there is a gnat's heel difference in the burdens imposed on commerce by the two laws. It cannot even be said that one regulation was "on commerce" and one was not (whatever "on commerce" means), for both affected the capacity of dealers to buy milk for interstate sales.

. . . .

The Court now steps in where Congress wanted it to stay out. The Court puts itself in the position of guardian of interstate trade in the milk industry. Congress, with full constitutional power to do so, selected the Secretary of Agriculture to do this job. Maybe this Court would be a better guardian, but it may be doubted that authority for the Court to undertake the task can be found in the Constitution—even in its "great silences." At any rate, I had supposed that this Court would not find conflict where Congress explicitly has commanded cooperation.

. . . .

. . . While I have doubt about the wisdom of this New York law, I do not conceive it to be the function of this Court to revise that state's economic judgments. . . .

MR. JUSTICE MURPHY joins in this opinion.

MR. JUSTICE FRANKFURTER, with whom MR. JUSTICE RUTLEDGE joins, dissenting.

If the Court's opinion has meaning beyond deciding this case in isolation, its effect is to hold that no matter how important to the internal economy of a State may be the prevention of destructive competition, and no matter how unimportant the interstate commerce affected, a State cannot as a means of preventing such competition deny an applicant access to a market within the State if that applicant happens to intend the out-of-state shipment of the product that he buys. I feel constrained to dissent because I cannot agree in treating what is essentially a problem of striking a balance between competing interests as an exercise in absolutes. . . .

White v. Massachusetts Council

460 U.S. 204 (1983)
Vote: 7–2

The states may not use their sovereign power to thwart the free flow of people and goods protected by the Commerce Clause. But governments are not merely regulators of commerce. Increasingly, they are purchasers of goods and manufacturers of products as well. Are the states bound to foster free trade in these roles as well? A decade of Supreme Court decisions establishes that when operating as a commercial enterprise, the state may favor its citizens. Defining when a state is operating in these different roles — commercial versus regulatory — is not always easy. (Compare this problem with the intergovernmental tax case NEW YORK V. U.S., 1946).

Note the unanimous agreement of the justices that Congress may authorize states to discriminate in interstate commerce. Is that surprising, considering the flow of decisions on Congress' plenary authority over commerce since the 1960s?

JUSTICE REHNQUIST delivered the opinion of the Court.

In 1979 the mayor of Boston, Massachusetts, issued an executive order which required that all construction projects funded in whole or in part by city funds, or funds which the city had authority to administer, should be performed by a work force consisting of at least half *bona fide* residents of Boston. The Supreme Judicial Court of Massachusetts decided that the order was unconstitutional, observing that the Commerce Clause "presents a clear obstacle to the city's order." . . . We granted certiorari to decide whether the Commerce Clause of the United States Constitution, Art. I, §8, cl. 3, prevents the city from giving effect to the mayor's

order. . . . We now conclude that it does not and reverse.

I

We were first asked in *Hughes* v. *Alexandria Scrap Corp.*, . . . (1976), to decide whether state and local governments are restrained by the Commerce Clause when they seek to effect commercial transactions not as "regulators" but as "market participants." In that case, the Maryland legislature, in an attempt to encourage the recycling of abandoned automobiles, offered a bounty for every Maryland-titled automobile converted into scrap if the scrap processor supplied documentation of ownership. An amendment to the Maryland statute imposed more exacting documentation requirements on out-of-state than in-state processors, who in turn demanded more exacting documentation from those who sold the junked automobiles for scrap. As a result, it became easier for those in possession of the automobiles to sell to in-state processors. . . . In upholding the Maryland statute in the face of a Commerce Clause challenge, we said that "[n]othing in the purpose animating the Commerce Clause prohibits a State, in the absence of congressional action, from participating in the market and exercising the right to favor its own citizens over others." . . .

We faced the question again in *Reeves, Inc.* v. *Stake*, 447 U.S. 429 (1980), when confronted with a South Dakota policy to confine the sales of cement by a state-operated cement plant to residents of South Dakota. We underscored the holding of *Hughes* v. *Alexandria Scrap Corp.*, saying:

> The basic distinction drawn in *Alexandria Scrap* between States as market participants and States as market regulators makes good sense and sound law. As that case explains, the Commerce Clause responds principally to state taxes and regulatory measures impeding free private trade in the national marketplace. [Citation omitted]. There is no indication of a constitutional plan to limit the ability of the States themselves to operate freely in the free market.

Alexandria Scrap and *Reeves*, therefore, stand for the proposition that when a state or local government enters the market as a participant it is not subject to the restraints of the Commerce Clause. As we said in *Reeves*, in this kind of case there is "a single inquiry: whether the challenged 'program con-

stituted direct state participation in the market.'"
We reaffirm that principle now.

The Supreme Judicial Court of Massachusetts concluded that the City of Boston is not participating in the market in the sense described in *Alexandria Scrap Corp.* and *Reeves* because the order applies where the city is acting in a nonproprietary capacity, has a significant impact on interstate commerce, is more sweeping than necessary to achieve its objectives, and applies to funds the city receives from federal grants. For the same reasons the court found that the city is not a market participant, it concluded that the executive order violated the substantive restraints of the Commerce Clause.

II

. . . .

The Supreme Judicial Court of Massachusetts expressed reservations as to the application of the "market participation" principle to the city here, reasoning that "the implementation of the mayor's order will have a significant impact on those firms which engage in specialized areas of construction and employ permanent work crews composed of out-of-state residents.". . . to the inquiry of whether the city is participating in the marketplace when it provides city funds for building construction. If the city is a market participant, then the Commerce Clause establishes no barrier to conditions such as these which the city demands for its participation. Impact on out-of-state residents figures in the equation only after it is decided that the city is regulating the market rather than participating in it, for only in the former case need it be determined whether any burden on interstate commerce is permitted by the Commerce Clause.

The same may be said of the Massachusetts court's finding that the executive order sweeps too broadly, creating more burden than is necessary to accomplish its stated objectives. While relevant if the Commerce Clause imposes restraints on the city's activity, this characterization is of no help in deciding whether those restraints apply. . . .

In *Hicklin* we considered an Alaska statute which required employment in all work connected with oil and gas leases to which the State was a party to be offered first to "qualified" Alaska residents in preference to non-residents. The State sought to justify the "Alaska Hire" law on the ground that the underlying oil and gas were owned by the State itself. Analyzing the case under the Privileges and Immunities Clause of Art. IV, §2, cl. 1, we held that mere ownership of a natural resource did not in all cir-cumstances render a state regulation such as the "Alaska Hire" law immune from attack under that clause. We summarized our view of the Alaska statute in these words:

> In sum, the Act is an attempt to force virtually all businesses that benefit in some way from the economic ripple effect of Alaska's decision to develop its oil and gas resources to bias their employment practices in favor of the State's residents.

Even though respondents no longer press the Privileges and Immunities Clause holding of *Hicklin* in support of their Commerce Clause argument, we note that on the record before us the application of the mayor's executive order to contracts involving only city funds does not represent the sort of "attempt to force virtually all businesses that benefit in some way from the economic ripple effect" of the city's decision to enter into contracts for construction projects "to bias their employment practices in favor of the [city's] residents."

The Supreme Judicial Court of Massachusetts also observed that "a significant percentage of the funds affected by the order are received from Federal sources.". . .

But all of this proves too much. The Commerce Clause is a grant of authority to Congress, and not a restriction on the authority of that body. See *American Power & Light Co.* v. *SEC* (1946); *Gibbons* v. *Ogden* (1824). Congress, unlike a state legislature authorizing similar expenditures, is not limited by any negative implications of the Commerce Clause in the exercise of its spending power. Where state or local government action is specifically authorized by Congress, it is not subject to the Commerce Clause even if it interferes with interstate commerce. *Southern Pacific Co.* v. *Arizona.* . . . Thus, if the restrictions imposed by the city on construction projects financed in part by federal funds are directed by Congress then no dormant Commerce Clause issue is presented.

III

Insofar as the city expended only its own funds in entering into construction contracts for public projects, it was a market participant and entitled to be treated as such under the rule of *Hughes* v. *Alexandria Scrap Corp., supra.* Insofar as the mayor's executive order was applied to projects funded in part with funds obtained from the federal programs described above, the order was affirmatively sanctioned by the pertinent regulations of those programs....

It is so ordered.

JUSTICE BLACKMUN, with whom JUSTICE WHITE joins, concurring in part and dissenting in part.

I am in agreement with the Court's conclusion that Congress, in creating the grant programs in question, specifically authorized "the type of parochial favoritism expressed in the order." As the Court holds, Congress unquestionably has the power to authorize state or local discrimination against interstate commerce that otherwise would violate the dormant aspect of the Commerce Clause. *Prudential Ins. Co.* v. *Benjamin* (1946).

II

I do not agree, however, with the Court's holding that the executive order is immune from Commerce Clause scrutiny insofar as it applies to city activities undertaken *without* specific congressional authorization.

....

In *Alexandria Scrap,* the effect of the Maryland statute was to offer a subsidy only to scrap processors located within the State....

In *Reeves,* South Dakota refused to sell cement to out-ot-state consumers until the orders of all in-state customers were filled. The Court held that the Commerce Clause is not implicated when a State prefers its own residents as direct purchasers of state-produced goods. Neither *Reeves* nor *Alexandria Scrap,* however, went beyond ensuring that the States enjoy "'the long recognized right of trader or manufacturer, engaged in an entirely private business, freely to exercise his own independent discretion as to parties with whom he will deal.'"...

Boston's executive order goes much further. The city has not attempted merely to choose the "parties with whom [it] will deal." Instead, it has imposed as a condition of obtaining a public construction contract the requirement that *private firms* hire only Boston residents for 50% of specified jobs. Thus, the order directly restricts the ability of private employers to hire nonresidents, and thereby curtails nonresidents' access to jobs with private employers. I had thought it well established that, under the Commerce Clause, States and localities cannot impose restrictions granting their own residents either the exclusive right, or a priority, to private sector economic opportunities....

Minnesota v. Clover Leaf Creamery Co.

449 U.S. 456 (1981)
Vote: 6–2; Rehnquist not participating.

Environmental groups and commercial interests combined to enact a state statute forbidding use of nonreturnable plastic milk bottles in retail sales. The local court and State Supreme Court found this policy was not sustainable by evidence of the comparative effects on the environment of paperboard cartons, the most common mode of milk sale. The local court also ruled this a violation of the Commerce Clause, and a clear effort by the paper carton industry to keep out competition.

Ironically, the U.S. Supreme Court reversed the Minnesota courts and, in the opinion below, found the issues to be legislative in nature. The Minnesota legislature, apparently convinced by the evidence, repealed the statute before it even went into effect.

Does this anticlimactic result justify or call into question the U.S. Supreme Court's judgment that the questions were in the realm of political and legislative judgment?

JUSTICE BRENNAN delivered the opinion of the Court:
In 1977, the Minnesota Legislature enacted a statute banning the retail sale of milk in plastic nonreturnable, nonrefillable containers, but permitting such sale in other nonreturnable, nonrefillable containers, such as paperboard milk cartons....

....

Proponents of the legislation argued that it would promote resource conservation, ease solid waste disposal problems, and conserve energy. Relying on the results of studies and other information, they stressed the need to stop introduction of the plastic nonreturnable container before it became entrenched in the market. Opponents of the Act, also presenting empirical evidence, argued that the Act would not promote the goals asserted by the proponents, but would merely increase the costs of retail milk products and prolong the use of ecologically undesirable paperboard milk cartons.

After the Act was passed, respondents filed suit in Minnesota District Court, seeking to enjoin its enforcement. The Court conducted extensive evidentiary hearings into the Act's probable consequences, and found the evidence "in sharp conflict."... Nevertheless, finding itself, "as factfinder... obliged to weigh and evaluate this evidence," *ibid.*, the Court resolved the evidentiary conflicts in favor of respondents, and concluded that the Act "would not succeed in effecting the Legislature's published policy goals...."... The Court further found that, contrary to the statement of purpose in §1, the "actual basis" for the Act "was to promote the economic interests of certain segments of the local dairy and pulpwood industries at the expense of the economic interests of other segments of the dairy industry and the plastics industry."... The Court therefore declared the Act "null, void, and unenforceable" and enjoined its enforcement, basing the judgment on substantive due process under the Fourteenth Amendment to the United States Constitution and Art. I, §7, of the Minnesota Constitution; equal protection under the Fourteenth Amendment; and prohibition of unreasonable burdens on interstate commerce....

Justice Stevens's dissenting opinion argues that the Minnesota Supreme Court when reviewing a challenge to a Minnesota statute on equal protection grounds is not bound by the limits applicable to federal courts, but may independently reach conclusions, contrary to those of the legislature concerning legislative facts bearing on the wisdom or utility of the legislation. This argument, though novel, is without merit. A state court may, of course, apply a more stringent standard of review as a matter of state law under the State's equivalent to the Equal Protection or Due Process Clauses....

The State appealed to the Supreme Court of Minnesota, which affirmed the District Court on the federal equal protection and due process grounds, without reaching the Commerce Clause or state law issues....

The parties agreed that the standard of review applicable to this case under the Equal Protection Clause is the familiar "rational basis" test....

....

Although parties challenging legislation under the Equal Protection Clause may introduce evidence supporting their claim that it is irrational, *United States* v. *Carolene Products Co.* (1938), they cannot prevail so long as "it is evident from all the considerations presented to [the legislature], and those of which we may take judicial notice, that the question is at least debatable." Where there was evidence be-fore the legislature reasonably supporting the classification, litigants may not procure invalidation of the legislation merely by tendering evidence in court that the legislature was mistaken.

The District Court candidly admitted that the evidence was "in sharp conflict," but resolved the conflict in favor of respondents and struck down the statute. The Supreme Court of Minnesota, however, did not reverse on the basis of this patent violation of the principles governing rationality analysis under the Equal Protection Clause. Rather, the Court analyzed the statute afresh under the Equal Protection Clause, and reached the conclusion that the statute is constitutionally invalid. The State contends that in this analysis the Court impermissibly substituted its judgment for that of the legislature. We turn now to that argument.

The State identifies four reasons why the classification between plastic and nonplastic nonreturnables is rationally related to the articulated statutory purposes. If any one of the four substantiates the State's claim, we must reverse the Minnesota Supreme Court, and sustain the Act.

First, the State argues that elimination of the popular plastic milk jug will encourage the use of environmentally superior containers.... Citing evidence that the plastic jug is the most popular, and the gallon paperboard carton the most cumbersome and least well regarded package in the industry, the State argues that the ban on plastic nonreturnables will buy time during which environmentally preferable alternatives may be further developed and promoted.

....

The Minnesota Supreme Court dismissed this asserted state interest as "speculative and illusory."...

We find the State's approach fully supportable under our precedents. This Court has made clear that a legislature need not "strike at all evils at the same time or in the same way."... Whether in fact the Act will promote more environmentally desirable milk packaging is not the question: the Equal Protection Clause is satisfied by our conclusion that the Minnesota Legislature could rationally have decided that its ban on plastic nonreturnable milk jugs might foster greater use of environmentally desirable alternatives.

Second, the State argues that its ban on plastic nonreturnable milk containers will reduce the economic dislocation foreseen from the movement toward greater use of environmentally superior containers....

....

Thus, by banning the plastic container while continuing to permit the paperboard container, the State was able to prevent the industry from becoming reliant on the new container, while avoiding severe economic dislocation.

The Minnesota Supreme Court did not directly address this justification, but we find it supported by our precedents as well. . . .

Third, the State argues that the Act will help to conserve energy. It points out that plastic milk jugs are made from plastic resin, an oil and natural gas derivative, whereas paperboard milk cartons are primarily composed of pulpwood, which is a renewable resource. . . .

The Minnesota Supreme Court held, in effect, that the legislature misunderstood the facts. The Court admitted that the results of a reliable study support the legislature's conclusion that less energy is consumed in the production of paperboard containers than in the production of plastic nonreturnables, but, after crediting the contrary testimony of respondents' expert witness and altering certain factual assumptions, the Court concluded that "production of plastic nonrefillables requires less energy than production of paper containers." . . .

The Minnesota Supreme Court may be correct that the Act is not a sensible means of conserving energy. But we reiterate that "it is up to legislatures, not courts, to decide on the wisdom and utility of legislation." *Ferguson v. Skrupa* . . . (1963). Since in view of the evidence before the legislature, the question clearly is "at least debatable," . . . the Minnesota Supreme Court erred in substituting its judgment for that of the legislature.

. . . .

We therefore conclude that the ban on plastic nonreturnable milk containers bears a rational relation to the State's objectives, and must be sustained under the Equal Protection Clause.

The District Court also held that the Minnesota statute is unconstitutional under the Commerce Clause because it imposes an unreasonable burden on interstate commerce. We cannot agree.

When legislating in areas of legitimate local concern, such as environmental protection and resource conservation, States are nonetheless limited by the Commerce Clause. . . . If a state law purporting to promote environmental purposes is in reality "simple economic protectionism," we have applied a "virtually *per se* rule of invalidity." Even if a statute regulates "even-handedly," and imposes only "incidental" burdens on interstate commerce, the courts must nevertheless strike it down if "the burden imposed on such commerce is clearly excessive in relation to the putative local benefits." . . .

Minnesota's statute does not effect "simple protectionism," but "regulates even-handedly" by prohibiting all milk retailers from selling their products in plastic, nonreturnable milk containers, without regard to whether the milk, the containers, or the sellers are from outside the State. This statute is therefore unlike statutes discriminating against interstate commerce, which we have consistently struck down. . . .

Since the statute does not discriminate between interstate and intrastate commerce, the controlling question is whether the incidental burden imposed on interstate commerce by the Minnesota Act is "clearly excessive in relation to the putative local benefits." . . . We conclude that it is not.

The burden imposed on interstate commerce by the statute is relatively minor. Milk products may continue to move freely across the Minnesota border, and since most dairies package their products in more than one type of containers, the inconvenience of having to conform to different packaging requirements in Minnesota and the surrounding States should be slight. . . . Within Minnesota, business will presumably shift from manufacturers of plastic nonreturnable containers to producers of paperboard cartons, refillable bottles, and plastic pouches, but there is no reason to suspect that the gainers will be Minnesota firms, or the losers out-of-state firms. Indeed, two of the three dairies, the sole milk retailer, and the sole milk container producer challenging the statute in this litigation are Minnesota firms.

. . . .

Even granting that the out-of-state plastics industry is burdened relatively more heavily than the Minnesota pulpwood industry, we find that this burden is not "clearly excessive" in light of the substantial state interest in promoting conservation of energy and other natural resources and easing solid waste disposal problems, which we have already reviewed in the context of equal protection analysis. We find these local benefits ample to support Minnesota's decision under the Commerce Clause. Moreover, we find that no approach with "a lesser impact on interstate activities," *Pike* v. *Bruce Church, Inc.*, . . . is available. . . .

". . . [T]he Commerce Clause protects the interstate market, not particular interstate firms, from prohibitive or burdensome regulations." . . . A nondiscriminatory regulation serving substantial state purposes is not invalid simply because it causes some business to shift from a predominantly out-of-state industry to a predominantly in-state industry. Only if the burden on interstate commerce clearly outweighs the State's legitimate purposes does such a regulation violate the Commerce Clause.

The judgment of the Minnesota Supreme Court is *Reversed.*

JUSTICE REHNQUIST took no part in the consideration or decision of this case.

JUSTICE POWELL, concurring in part and dissenting in part.

. . . I concur in the view that the statute survives equal protection challenge, and therefore join the judgment of reversal on this ground. . . .

I would not, however, reach the Commerce Clause issue, but would remand it for consideration by the Supreme Court of Minnesota. . . .

. . . In drawing its conclusions, the court included no discussion whatever of the Commerce Clause issue and, certainly, no rejection of the trial court's express and repeated findings concerning the legislature's actual purpose.

I conclude therefore that this Court has no basis for *inferring* a rejection of the quite specific fact findings by the trial court. The Court's decision today, holding that Chapter 268 does not violate the Commerce Clause, is flatly contrary to the only relevant specific findings of fact. Although we are not *barred* from reaching the Commerce Clause issue, in doing so we also act without the benefit of a decision by the highest court of Minnesota on the question. In these circumstances, it is both unnecessary—and in my opinion inappropriate—for this Court to decide the Commerce Clause issue. . . .

JUSTICE STEVENS, dissenting.

While the Court in this case seems to do nothing more than apply well-established equal protection and Commerce Clause principles to a particular state statute, in reality its reversal of the Minnesota Supreme Court is based upon a newly discovered principle of federal constitutional law. According to this principle, which is applied but not explained by the majority, the Federal Constitution defines, not only the relationship between Congress and the federal courts, but also the relationship between state legislatures and state courts. Because I can find no support for this novel constitutional doctrine in either the language of the Federal Constitution or the prior decisions of this Court, I respectfully dissent.

The keystone of the Court's equal protection analysis is its pronouncement that "it is not the function of the courts to substitute their evaluation of legislative facts for that of the legislature." If the pronouncement concerned the function of *federal*

courts, it would be amply supported by reason and precedent. For federal tribunals are courts of limited jurisdiction, whose powers are confined by the Federal Constitution, by statute, and by the decisions of this Court. It is not surprising, therefore, that the Court's pronouncement is supported by citation only to precedents dealing with the function that a *federal* court may properly perform when it is reviewing the constitutionality of a law enacted by Congress or by a state legislature.

But what is the source—if indeed there be one—of this Court's power to make the majestic announcement that it is not the function of a *state court* to substitute its evaluation of legislative facts for that of a state legislature? I should have thought the allocation of functions within the structure of a state government would be a matter for the State to determine. I know of nothing in the Federal Constitution that prohibits a State from giving lawmaking power to its courts. Nor is there anything in the Federal Constitution that prevents a state court from reviewing factual determinations made by a state legislature or any other state agency. . . .

Braniff Airways v. Nebraska Board of Equalization

347 U.S. 590 (1954)
Vote: 7–2

The problem of "multiple burdens" and the potential for excessive taxation of interstate commerce vies with the possibility that it will escape taxation altogether. A classic example is that of the airline industry. The problem is not in agreeing that interstate commerce should pay its own way, but, as Justice Frankfurter states in this case, in figuring out what the "way" is, and how it can be apportioned. Airlines, by nature, present particular problems in regulation, with their nexus in so many states.

In *Northwest Airlines* v. *Minnesota* (1944), by a 5 to 4 decision, Minnesota was permitted to base the airline's taxes upon the total worth of the airline's assets, in the absence of any evidence of other states' claims. The majority was weakened by disparate concurrences by Black and Jackson, but even so the case underscored the potential for multiple-state taxation. (Jackson explicitly argued that *only* the home state might tax an airline, while Black called for congressional resolution of the issue.)

Congress began to study the problem but was unable to resolve the matter. However, a Civil Aeronautics Board report recommended an allocative formula, which was also recommended by the Council of State Governments. Nebraska enacted such a law, which assessed the value of airplanes to be taxed by averaging three ratios: (1) the ratio of the line's arrivals and departures within the state to its total arrivals and departures; (2) tonnage handled by planes in state airports compared to tonnage carried by the airline; and (3) the ratio of the airline's in-state revenues to those of the whole line. It was Nebraska's assessment of Braniff's tax that led to this case.

MR. JUSTICE REED delivered the opinion of the Court.

The question presented by this appeal from the Supreme Court of Nebraska is whether the Constitution bars the State of Nebraska from levying an apportioned ad valorem tax on the flight equipment of appellant, an interstate air carrier. . . . Such flight equipment is employed as a part of a system of interstate air commerce operating over fixed routes and landing on and departing from airports within Nebraska on regular schedules. . . .

The home port registered with the Civil Aeronautics Authority and the overhaul base for the aircraft in question is the Minneapolis-St. Paul Airport, Minnesota. All of the aircraft not undergoing overhaul fly regular schedules upon a circuit ranging from Minot, North Dakota, to New Orleans, Louisiana, with stops in fourteen states. . . . The Nebraska stops are of short duration since utilized only for the discharge and loading of passengers, mail, express, and freight, and sometimes for refueling. Appellant neither owns nor maintains facilities for repairing, reconditioning, or storing its flight equipment in Nebraska, but rents depot space and hires other services as required. . . .

It is stipulated that the tax in question is assessed only against regularly scheduled air carriers and is not applied to carriers who operate only intermittently in the state. . . .

The statute uses the allocation formula of the "proposed uniform statute to provide for an equitable method of state taxation of air carriers" adopted by the Council of State Governments upon the recommendation of the National Association of Tax Administrators in 1947. Use of a uniform allocation formula to apportion air-carrier taxes among the states follows the recommendation of the Civil Aeronautics Board in its report to Congress.

Required reports filed by Mid-Continent for 1950 show that about 9% of its revenue and 11½% of the total system tonnage originated in Nebraska and about 9% of its total stops were made in that state. From these figures, using the statutory formula, the Tax Commissioner arrived at a valuation of $118,901 allocable to Nebraska, resulting in a tax of $4,280.44. . . .

Appellant argues that federal statutes governing air commerce enacted under the commerce power preempt the field of regulation of such air commerce and preclude this tax. . . .

. . . Federal Acts regulating air commerce are bottomed on the commerce power of Congress, not on national ownership of the navigable air space, as distinguished from sovereignty. . . . The commerce power, since *Gibbons v. Ogden,* 9 Wheat. 1, 193, has comprehended navigation of streams. Its breadth covers all commercial intercourse. But the federal commerce power over navigable streams does not prevent state action consistent with that power. . . . Federal regulation of interstate land and water carriers under the commerce power has not been deemed to deny all state power to tax the property of such carriers. We conclude that existent federal air-carrier regulation does not preclude the Nebraska tax challenged here.

Nor has appellant demonstrated that the Commerce Clause otherwise bars this tax as a burden on interstate commerce. We have frequently reiterated that the Commerce Clause does not immunize interstate instrumentalities from all state taxation, but that such commerce may be required to pay a nondiscriminatory share of the tax burden. And appellant does not allege that this Nebraska statute discriminates against it nor, as noted above, does it challenge the reasonableness of the apportionment prescribed by the statute.

The argument upon which appellant depends ultimately, however, is that its aircraft never "attained a taxable situs within Nebraska" from which it argues that the Nebraska tax imposes a burden on interstate commerce. In relying upon the Commerce Clause on this issue and in not specifically claiming protection under the Due Process Clause of the Fourteenth Amendment, appellant names the wrong constitutional clause to support its position. While the question of whether a commodity en route to market is sufficiently settled in a state for purpose of subjection to a property tax has been determined by this Court as a Commerce Clause question, the bare question whether an instrumentality of commerce has tax situs in a state for the purpose of subjection to a property tax is one of due process. . . .

Appellant relies upon cases involving ocean-going vessels to support its contention that its aircraft attained no tax situs in Nebraska. . . . A closer analogy exists between planes flying interstate and boats that ply the inland waters. We perceive no logical basis for distinguishing the constitutional power to impose a tax on such aircraft from the power to impose taxes on river boats. . . .

Thus the situs issue devolves into the question of whether eighteen stops per day by appellant's aircraft is sufficient contact with Nebraska to sustain that state's power to levy an apportioned ad valorem tax on such aircraft. We think such regular contact is sufficient to establish Nebraska's power to tax even though the same aircraft do not land every day and even though none of the aircraft is continuously within the state. . . . This leaves it in the position of other carriers such as rails, boats and motors that pay for the use of local facilities so as to have the opportunity to exploit the commerce, traffic, and trade that originates in or reaches Nebraska. Approximately one-tenth of appellant's revenue is produced by the pickup and discharge of Nebraska freight and passengers. Nebraska certainly affords protection during such stops and these regular landings are clearly a benefit to appellant.

. . . .

Appellant urges that *Northwest Airlines* v. *Minnesota*, 322 U.S. 292, precludes this tax unless that case is to be overruled. In that case Minnesota, as the domicile of the air carrier and its "home port," was permitted to tax the entire value of the fleet ad valorem although it ranged by fixed routes through eight states. While no one view mustered a majority of this Court, it seems fair to say that without the position stated in the Conclusion and Judgment which announced the decision of this Court, the result would have been the reverse. That position was that it was not shown "that a defined part of the domiciliary corpus has acquired a permanent location, *i.e.,* a taxing situs, elsewhere. . . ." When *Standard Oil Co.* v. *Peck,* 342 U.S. 382, 384, was here, the Court interpreted the *Northwest Airlines* case to permit states other than those of the corporate domicile to tax boats in interstate commerce on the apportionment basis in accordance with their use in the taxing state. We adhere to that interpretation.

Affirmed.

MR. JUSTICE BLACK concurs in the result.

MR. JUSTICE JACKSON dissents for the reasons stated in his concurring opinion in *Northwest Airlines* v. *Minnesota,* 322 U.S. 292, 302.

MR. JUSTICE DOUGLAS, concurring.

My understanding of our decisions is that the power to lay an ad valorem tax turns on the permanency of the property in the State. All the property may be there or only a fraction of it. Property in transit, whether a plane discharging passengers or an automobile refueling, is not subject to an ad valorem tax. Property in transit may move so regularly and so continuously that part of it is always in the State. Then the fraction, but no more, may be taxed ad valorem.

. . . .

I do not think the Court takes a position contrary to what I have said. But there are passages in the opinion which blur the constitutional issues as they are blurred and confused in the interesting report of the Civil Aeronautics Board, entitled Multiple Taxation of Air Commerce. Hence I have joined in the judgment of the Court but not in the opinion.

MR. JUSTICE FRANKFURTER, dissenting.

. . . The differences in result and the conflict even among those who agreed in result in *Northwest Airlines* v. *Minnesota* . . . demonstrate not the contrariness or caprice of different minds but the inherent perplexities of the law's adjustment to such novel problems as the exercise of the taxing power over commercial aviation in a federal system. The problems canvassed in that case were unprecedented, and perhaps the most important thing that was there decided was the refusal of the Court to apply to air transportation the doctrines that had been enunciated with regard to land and water transportation.

The plain intimation of the case — that these novel problems, affecting the taxing power of the States and the Nation, call for the comprehensive powers of legislation possessed by Congress — found response in a resolution of Congress directing the Civil Aeronautics Board to develop the "means for eliminating and avoiding, as far as practicable, multiple taxation of persons engaged in air commerce . . . which has the effect of unduly burdening or unduly impeding the development of air commerce." 58 Stat. 723. The inquiry thus set afoot produced an illuminating report. See H.R. Doc. No. 141, 79th Cong., 1st Sess., which analyzed the difficulties and also made concrete proposals. The gist of these proposals was that Congress make an apportionment of taxes among the States over which air carriers fly, based upon relevant factors and in appropriate ratios. The basis of taxation by Nebraska, here under review, substantially reflects the factors which the Civil Aeronautics Board recommended to the Congress. It is one thing, however, for the individual States to determine what factors should be taken into account and how they should be weighted. It is quite another for Congress to devise, as the Civil Aeronautics Board recommended it should, a scheme of apportionment binding on all the States. Until that time, Nebraska may rely on one scheme of apportionment; other States on other schemes. And each State may, from time to time, modify the relevant factors.

. . . .

The appealing phrase that "interstate business must pay its way" can be invoked only when we know what the "way" is for which interstate business must pay. Of course, the appellant must pay for the use of airports and other services it enjoys in Nebraska. . . .

. . . Not unless Nebraska can show that appellant has airplanes that have a substantially permanent presence in Nebraska can Nebraska exert its taxing power on their presence. I do not believe that planes which pause for a few moments can be made the basis for the exercise of such power. If Nebraska can tax without such a tie, every other State through which the planes fly or in which they alight for a few minutes can tax. Surely this is an obvious inroad upon the Commerce Clause and as such is barred by the Constitution.

It cannot be said that for airplanes, flying regularly scheduled flights, to alight, stop over for a short time and then take off is so tenuously related to Nebraska that it would deny due process for that State to seize on these short stopovers as the basis of an ad valorem tax. But the incidence of a tax may offend the Commerce Clause, even though it must satisfy the Due Process Clause.

Commonwealth Edison Co. v. Montana

101 S.Ct. 2946 (1981)
Vote: (5–1)–3

By the 1980s, the Supreme Court had developed a fairly satisfactory approach to state taxation built around the "four-pronged" approach of the *Complete Auto Transit* case. It had also ap-proved of "severance taxes"—taxes built around the principle that depletion of mineral and other exhaustible supplies created financial burdens for a state. Montana, a great mineral exporter, drastically increased its severance on coal, about 90 percent of which goes to out-of-state users. The electric company wished to argue in detail that the severance tax exceeded reasonable charges associated with state provision of services. This case essentially defines the "fairly related to services provided" test of state power where there is no discrimination in tax rates as between local or interstate users.

As commodities, such as energy sources, become more scarce, it is anticipated that more severance taxes will be enacted. To what degree should reasonableness be determined by the federal courts and to what degree by Congress?

JUSTICE MARSHALL delivered the opinion of the Court.

Montana, like many other States, imposes a severance tax on mineral production in the State. In this appeal, we consider whether the tax Montana levies on each ton of coal mined in the State violates the Commerce and Supremacy Clauses of the United States Constitution.

I

Buried beneath Montana are large deposits of low-sulfur coal, most of it on federal land. Since 1921, Montana has imposed a severance tax on the output of Montana coal mines, including coal mined on federal land.

The tax is levied at varying rates depending on the value, energy content, and method of extraction of the coal, and may equal, at a maximum, 30% of the "contract sale price." . . .

Appellants, four Montana coal producers and 11 of their out-of-state utility company customers, filed these suits in Montana state court in 1978. They sought refunds of over $5.4 million in severance taxes paid under protest, a declaration that the tax is invalid under the Supremacy and Commerce Clauses, and an injunction against further collection of the tax. Without receiving any evidence the court upheld the tax and dismissed the complaints.

. . . The Supreme Court held that the tax is not subject to scrutiny under the Commerce Clause because it is imposed on the severance of coal, which the court characterized as an intrastate activity preceding entry of the coal into interstate commerce. In this regard, the Montana court relied on this Court's decisions, . . . which employed similar reasoning in upholding state severance taxes against Commerce Clause challenges. As an alternative basis for its resolution of the Commerce Clause issue, the Montana court held, as a matter of law, that the tax survives scrutiny under the four-part test articulated by this Court in *Complete Auto Transit, Inc.* v. *Brady,* (1977). . . .

II

As an initial matter, appellants assert that the Montana Supreme Court erred in concluding that the Montana tax is not subject to the strictures of the Commerce Clause. In appellants' view, *Heisler's* "mechanical" approach, which looks to whether a state tax is levied on goods prior to their entry into interstate commerce, no longer accurately reflects the law. . . .

We agree that *Heisler's* reasoning has been undermined by more recent cases. The *Heisler* analysis evolved at a time when the Commerce Clause was thought to prohibit the States from imposing any direct taxes on interstate commerce. . . . Consequently, the distinction between intrastate activities and interstate commerce was crucial to protecting the States' taxing power.

The Court has, however, long since rejected any suggestion that a state tax or regulation affecting interstate commerce is immune from Commerce Clause scrutiny because it attaches only to a "local" or intrastate activity. . . . Correspondingly, the Court has rejected the notion that state taxes levied on interstate commerce are *per se* invalid. . . . We conclude that the same "practical" analysis should apply in reviewing Commerce Clause challenges to state severance taxes.

In the first place, there is no real distinction — in terms of economic effects — between severance taxes and other types of state taxes that have been subjected to Commerce Clause scrutiny. . . . State taxes levied on a "local" activity preceding entry of the goods into interstate commerce may substantially affect interstate commerce, and this effect is the proper focus of Commerce Clause inquiry.

Second, this Court has acknowledged that "a State has a significant interest in exacting from interstate commerce its fair share of the cost of state government." . . .

We therefore hold that a state severance tax is not immunized from Commerce Clause scrutiny by a claim that the tax is imposed on goods prior to their entry into the stream of interstate commerce. Any contrary statements in *Heisler* and its progeny are disapproved. We agree with appellants that the Montana tax must be evaluated under *Complete Auto Transit's* four-part test. Under that test, a state tax does not offend the Commerce Clause if it "is applied to an activity with a substantial nexus with the taxing State, is fairly apportioned, does not discriminate against interstate commerce, and is fairly related to services provided by the State."

Appellants do not dispute that the Montana tax satisfies the first two prongs of the *Complete Auto Transit* test. As the Montana Supreme Court noted, "there can be no argument here that a substantial, in fact, the only nexus of the severance of coal is established in Montana." . . . Nor is there any question here regarding apportionment or potential multiple taxation, for as the state court observed, "the severance can occur in no other state" and "no other state can tax the severance." . . .

Appellants assert that the Montana tax "discriminate[s] against interstate commerce" because 90% of Montana coal is shipped to other States under contracts that shift the tax burden primarily to non-Montana utility companies and thus to citizens of other States. But the Montana tax is computed at the same rate regardless of the final destination of the coal, and there is no suggestion here that the tax is administered in a manner that departs from this even-handed formula. We are not, therefore, confronted here with the type of differential tax treatment of interstate and intrastate commerce that the Court has found in other "discrimination" cases. . . .

Instead, the gravamen of appellants' claim is that a state tax must be considered discriminatory for purposes of the Commerce Clause if the tax burden is borne primarily by out-of-state consumers. Appellants do not suggest that this assertion is based on any of this Court's prior discriminatory tax cases. . . .

The premise of our discrimination cases is that "[t]he very purpose of the Commerce Clause was to create an area of free trade among the several States." . . . Consequently, to accept appellants' theory and invalidate the Montana tax solely because most of Montana's coal is shipped across the very state borders that ordinarily are to be considered irrelevant would require a significant, and, in our view, unwarranted departure from the rationale of our prior discrimination cases.

Furthermore, appellants' assertion that Montana may not "exploit" its "monopoly" position by exporting tax burdens to other States, cannot rest on a claim that there is need to protect the out-of-state consumers of Montana coal from discriminatory tax treatment. As previously noted, there is no real discrimination in this case; the tax burden is borne according to the amount of coal consumed and not according to any distinction between in-state and out-of-state consumers. Rather, appellants assume that the Commerce Clause gives residents of one State a right of access at "reasonable" prices to resources located in another State that is richly endowed with such resources, without regard to whether and on what terms residents of the resource-rich State have access to the resources. We are not convinced that the Commerce Clause, of its own force, gives the residents of one State the right to control in this fashion the terms of resource development and depletion in a sister State.

In any event, appellants' discrimination theory ultimately collapses into their claim that the Montana tax is invalid under the fourth prong of the *Complete Auto Transit* test: that the tax is not "fairly related to the services provided by the State." Because appellants concede that Montana may impose *some* severance tax on coal mined in the State, the only remaining foundation for their discrimination theory is a claim that the tax burden borne by the out-of-state consumers of Montana coal is excessive....

... [T]heir only complaint is that the *amount* the State receives in taxes far exceeds the value of the services provided to the coal mining industry. In objecting to the tax on this ground, appellants may be assuming that the Montana tax is, in fact, intended to reimburse the State for the cost of specific services furnished to the coal mining industry. Alternatively, appellants could be arguing that a State's power to tax an activity connected to interstate commerce cannot exceed the value of the services specifically provided to the activity. Either way, the premise of appellants' argument is invalid. Furthermore, appellants have completely misunderstood the nature of the inquiry under the fourth prong of the *Complete Auto Transit* test.

The Montana Supreme Court held that the coal severance tax is "imposed for the general support of the government."... Consequently, in reviewing appellants' contentions, we put to one side those cases in which the Court reviewed challenges to "user" fees or "taxes" that were designed and defended as a specific charge imposed by the State for the use of state-owned or state-provided transportation or other facilities and services.... This Court has indicated that States have considerable latitude in imposing general revenue taxes. The court has, for example, consistently rejected claims that the Due Process Clause of the Fourteenth Amendment

stands as a barrier against taxes that are "unreasonable" or "unduly burdensome."...

....

There is no reason to suppose that this latitude afforded the States under the Due Process Clause is somehow divested by the Commerce Clause merely because the taxed activity has some connection to interstate commerce; particularly when the tax is levied on an activity conducted within the State.... To accept appellants' apparent suggestion that the Commerce Clause prohibits the States from requiring an activity connected to interstate commerce to contribute to the general cost of providing governmental services, as distinct from those costs attributable to the taxed activity, would place such commerce in a privileged position. But as we recently reiterated, " '[i]t was not the purpose of the commerce clause to relieve those engaged in interstate commerce from their just share of state tax burden even though it increases the cost of doing business.' "...

The entire value of the coal, before transportation, originates in the State, and mining of coal depletes the resource base and wealth of the State, thereby diminishing a future source of taxes and economic activity. In many respects, a severance tax is like a real property tax, which has never been doubted as a legitimate means of raising revenue by the situs State (quite apart from the right of that or any other State to tax income derived from use of the property).... When, as here, a general revenue tax does not discriminate against interstate commerce and is apportioned to activities occurring within the State, the State "is free to pursue its own fiscal policies, unembarrassed by the Constitution, if by the practical operation of a tax the state has exerted its power in relation to opportunities which it has given, to protection which it has afforded, to benefits which it has conferred by the fact of being an orderly civilized society."... This assertion reveals that appellants labor under a misconception about a court's role in cases such as this. The simple fact is that the appropriate level or rate of taxation is essentially a matter for legislative, and not judicial, resolution....

In the first place, it is doubtful whether any legal test could adequately reflect the numerous and competing economic, geographic, demographic, social, and political considerations that must inform a decision about an acceptable rate or level of state taxation, and yet be reasonably capable of application in a wide variety of individual cases. But even apart from the difficulty of the judicial undertaking, the nature of the factfinding and judgment that would be required of the courts merely reinforces the conclusion that questions about the appropriate level of state taxes must be resolved through the political process. Under our federal system, the determination is to be made by state legislatures in the first instance and, if necessary, by Congress, when particular state taxes are thought to be contrary to federal interests.

Furthermore, the reference in the cases to police and fire protection and other advantages of civilized society is not, as appellants suggest, a disingenuous incantation designed to avoid a more searching inquiry into the relationship between the *value* of the benefits conferred on the taxpayer and the *amount* of taxes it pays. Rather, when the measure of a tax is reasonably related to the taxpayer's activities or presence in the State — from which it derives some benefit such as the substantial privilege of mining coal — the taxpayer will realize, in proper proportion to the taxes it pays, "[t]he only benefit to which it is constitutionally entitled. . . [:] that derived from his enjoyment of the privileges of living in an organized society." . . .

As the Montana Legislature foresaw, the imposition of this severance tax has generated enormous revenues for the State. . . .

. . . In 1972, the then current flat rate severance tax on coal provided only 0.4% of Montana's total tax revenue; in contrast, in the year following the 1975 amendment, the coal severance tax supplied 11.4% of the State's total tax revenue.

So ordered.

JUSTICE WHITE, concurring.

This is a very troublesome case for me, and I join the Court's opinion with considerable doubt and with the realization that Montana's levy on consumers in other States may in the long run prove to be an intolerable and unacceptable burden on commerce. Indeed, there is particular force in the argument that the tax is here and now unconstitutional. Montana collects most of its tax from coal lands owned by the Federal Government and hence by all of the people of this country, while at the same time sharing equally and directly with the Federal Government all of the royalties reserved under the leases the United States has negotiated on its land in the State of Montana. This share is intended to compensate the State for the burdens that coal mining may impose upon it. . . . In addition, there is statutory provision for federal grants to areas affected by increased coal production.

But this very fact gives me pause and counsels withholding our hand, at least for now. Congress has the power to protect interstate commerce from intolerable or even undesirable burdens. It is also very much aware of the Nation's energy needs, of the Montana tax and of the trend in the energy-rich States to aggrandize their position and perhaps lessen the tax burdens on their own citizens by imposing unusually high taxes on mineral extraction. Yet, Congress is so far content to let the matter rest, and we are counseled by the Executive Branch through the Solicitor General not to overturn the Montana tax as inconsistent with either the Commerce Clause or federal statutory policy in the field of energy or otherwise. . . .

JUSTICE BLACKMUN, with whom JUSTICE POWELL and JUSTICE STEVENS join, dissenting.

In *Complete Auto Transit, Inc.* v. *Brady* (1977), a unanimous Court observed: "A tailored tax, however accomplished, must receive the careful scrutiny of the courts to determine whether it produces a forbidden effect upon interstate commerce." . . . Appellants further alleged that the tax bears no reasonable relationship to the services or protection provided by the State. The issue here, of course, is whether they are entitled to a trial on that claim, not whether they will succeed on the merits. It should be noted, however, that Montana imposes numerous other taxes upon coal mining. In addition, because 70% to 75% of the coal-bearing land in Montana is owned by the Federal Government, Montana derives a large amount of coal mining revenue from the United States as well. In light of these circumstances, the Interstate and Foreign Commerce Committee of the United States House of Representatives concluded that Montana's coal severance tax results in revenues "far in excess of the direct and indirect impact costs attributable to the coal production." . . .

This Court's Commerce Clause cases have been marked by tension between two competing concepts: the view that interstate commerce should enjoy a "free trade" immunity from state taxation . . . and the view that interstate commerce may be required to "'pay its way,'" . . . In *Complete Auto Transit,* the Court resolved that tension by unanimously reaffirming that interstate commerce is not immune from state taxation. . . . But at the same time the Court made clear that not all state taxation of interstate commerce is valid. . . .

I cannot agree, however, with the Court's application of that test to the facts of the present case. . . . The Court also correctly observes that Montana's severance tax is facially neutral. It does not automatically follow, however, that the Montana severance tax does not unduly burden or interfere with interstate commerce. The gravamen of appellants' complaint is that the severance tax does not satisfy the fourth prong of the *Complete Auto Transit* test because it is tailored to, and does, force interstate commerce to pay *more* than its way. Under our established precedents, appellants are entitled to a trial on this claim.

The Court's conclusion to the contrary rests on the premise that the relevant inquiry under the fourth prong of the *Complete Auto Transit* test is simply whether the *measure* of the tax is fixed as a percentage of the value of the coal taken.... This interpretation emasculates the fourth prong. No trial will ever be necessary on the issue of fair relationship so long as a State is careful to impose a proportional rather than a flat tax rate; thus, the Court's rule is no less "mechanical" than the approach entertained in *Heisler* v. *Thomas Colliery Co.*... (1922), disapproved today....

The Court has never suggested, however, that interstate commerce may be required to pay *more* than its own way. The Court today fails to recognize that the Commerce Clause does impose limits upon the State's power to impose even facially neutral and properly apportioned taxes....

As a number of commentators have noted, state severance taxes upon minerals are particularly susceptible to "tailoring." "Like a tollgate lying athwart a trade route, a severance or processing tax conditions access to natural resources."...

It is true that a trial in this case would require "complex factual inquiries" into whether economic conditions are such that Montana is in fact able to export the burden of its severance tax.... I do not believe, however, that this threshold inquiry is beyond judicial competence. If the trial court were to determine that the tax is exported, it would then have to determine whether the tax is "fairly related," within the meaning of *Complete Auto Transit.* The Court to the contrary, this would not require the trial court "to second-guess legislative decisions about the amount or disposition of tax revenues."... If the tax is in fact a legitimate general revenue measure identical or roughly comparable to taxes imposed upon similar industries, a court's inquiry is at an end; on the other hand, if the tax singles out this particular interstate activity and charges it with a grossly disproportionate share of the general costs of government, the court must determine whether there is some reasonable basis for the legislative judgment that the tax is necessary to compensate the State for the particular costs imposed by the activity.

This case poses extremely grave issues that threaten both to "polarize the Nation,"... and to reawaken "the tendencies toward economic Balkanization" that the Commerce Clause was designed to remedy.... Perhaps even more than by its interpretation of the written word, this Court has advanced the solidarity and prosperity of this Nation by the meaning it has given to these great silences of the Constitution. *H. P. Hood & Sons, Inc.* v. *DuMond* ... (1949). I would not lightly abandon that role. Because I believe that appellants are entitled to an opportunity to prove that, in Holmes' words, Montana's severance tax "embodies what the Commerce Clause was meant to end," I dissent.

Maryland v. Louisiana

100 S.Ct. 2114 (1981)
Vote: 7–1; Powell not participating.

Questions on permissible state taxes on commerce are often highly technical. This case, which must be contrasted with COMMONWEALTH EDISON CO. V. MONTANA (1981), involved Louisiana's attempt to tax natural gas derived from off-shore fields leased from the federal government but refined in Louisiana. Approximately 98 percent of the gas, it is estimated, was sold via interstate commerce. The "first use" tax was substantially a severance tax, even though the territory involved was federal land by sovereignty, in contrast to Montana, where the federal government was essentially only a landowner under state law. The case also turns on: (1) construction of state policy in respect to stated policies and authority of the Federal Energy Regulatory Commission, a supremacy issue; and (2) differences in treatment of Louisiana consumers and out-of-state consumers, a Commerce Clause question. All three of these matters (including the sovereignty issue) distinguish the case from the Montana decision.

JUSTICE WHITE delivered the opinion of the Court.
In this original action, several States, joined by the United States and a number of pipeline companies, challenge the constitutionality of Louisiana's "First Use Tax" imposed on certain uses of natural gas brought into Louisiana, principally from the outer continental shelf (OCS), as violative of the Supremacy Clause and the Commerce Clause of the United States Constitution.

I

The lands beneath the Gulf of Mexico have large reserves of oil and natural gas. Initially, these reserves could not be developed due to technological difficulties associated with off-shore drilling.... With the advent of new technologies, offshore drilling has become commonplace.... [T]he Court applied the principle of its holding in *United States* v. *California* ... (1947) — that the United States possesses paramount rights to lands beneath the Pacific Ocean seaward of California's low-water mark — to the off-shore areas adjacent to Louisiana. In 1953, Congress passed the Submerged Lands Act, 43 U.S.C. §§1301–1315, ceding any federal interest in the lands within three miles of the coast, while confirming the Federal Government's interest in the area seaward of the three-mile limit.

. . . .

In 1978, the Louisiana Legislature enacted a tax of 7 cents per thousand cubic feet of natural gas on the "first use" of any gas imported into Louisiana which was not previously subjected to taxation by another State or the United States.... The Tax imposed is precisely equal to the severance tax the State imposes on Louisiana gas producers. The Tax is owed by the owner of the gas at the time the first taxable "use" occurs within Louisiana.... About 85% of the OCS gas brought ashore is owned by the pipeline companies, the rest by the producers. Since most States impose their own severance tax, it is acknowledged that the primary effect of the First-Use Tax will be on gas produced in the federal OCS area and then piped to processing plants located within Louisiana....

The stated purpose of the First-Use Tax was to reimburse the people of Louisiana for damages to the State's waterbottoms, barrier islands, and coastal areas resulting from the introduction of natural gas into Louisiana from areas not subject to state taxes as well as to compensate for the costs incurred by the State in protecting those resources....

The Act itself, as well as provisions found elsewhere in the state statutes, provided a number of exemptions from and credits for the First-Use Tax....

II

Louisiana asserts that this case should be dismissed for want of standing because the Tax is imposed on the pipeline companies and not directly on the ultimate consumers. Under its view, the alleged interests of the plaintiff States do not fall within the type of "sovereignty" concerns justifying exercise of our original jurisdiction. Standing to sue, however, exists for constitutional purposes if the injury alleged "fairly can be traced to the challenged action of the defendant, and not injury that results from the independent action of some third party not before the court.''... This is clearly the case here. The plaintiff States are substantial consumers of natural gas.... Thus, the Special Master properly determined that "although the tax is collected from the pipelines, it is really a burden on consumers.''... It is clear that the plaintiff States, as major purchasers of natural gas whose cost has increased as a direct result of Louisiana's imposition of the First-Use Tax, are directly affected in a "substantial and real" way so as to justify their exercise of this Court's original jurisdiction.

Jurisdiction is also supported by the State's interest as *parens patriae*. A State is not permitted to enter a controversy as a nominal party in order to forward the claims of individual citizens.... But it may act as the representative of its citizens in original actions where the injury alleged affects the general population of a State in a substantial way....

... For the reasons stated above, we reject Louisiana's exceptions to the Report of the Special Master, and accept the recommendation that we deny Louisiana's motion to dismiss.

III

On the merits, plaintiffs argue that the First-Use Tax violates the Supremacy Clause because it interferes with federal regulation of the transportation and sale of natural gas in interstate commerce.... Consideration under the Supremacy Clause starts with the basic assumption that Congress did not intend to displace state law....

. . . .

In 1938, Congress enacted the Gas Act to assure that consumers of natural gas receive a fair price and also to protect against the economic power of the interstate pipelines....

As part of the First-Use Tax, Louisiana has directed that the amount of the Tax should be "deemed a cost associated with uses made by the owner in preparation of marketing of the natural gas.''... The Act further provides that an owner shall not have an enforceable right to seek reimbursement for payment of the Tax from any third party other than a purchaser of the gas....

The effect of §1303 C is to interfere with the FERC's authority to regulate the determination of the proper allocation of costs associated with the sale of natural gas to consumers. The unprocessed gas obtained at the wellhead contains extractable hydrocarbons which are most often owned and sold separately from the "dried" gas. The FERC normally allocates part of the processing costs between these related products, and insists that the owners of the liquefiable hydrocarbons bear a fair share of the expense associated with processing.... By specifying that the First-Use Tax is a processing cost to be either borne by the pipeline or other owner without compensation, an unlikely event in light of the large sums involved, or passed on to purchasers, Louisiana has attempted a substantial usurpation of the authority of the FERC by dictating to the pipelines the allocation of processing costs for the interstate shipment of natural gas....

Plaintiffs also argue that the First-Use Tax violates the Commerce Clause of the United States Constitution which provides that "[t]he Congress shall have Power... [t]o regulate Commerce... among the several States...." Art. I, §8, cl. 3. Prior case law has established that a state law is not *per se* invalid because it burdens interstate commerce since interstate commerce may constitutionally be made to pay its way. *Complete Auto Transit, Inc.* v. *Brady....* The State's right to tax interstate is limited, however, and no state tax may be sustained unless the tax: (1) has a substantial nexus with the State; (2) is fairly apportioned; (3) does not discriminate against interstate commerce; and (4) is fairly related to the services provided by the State.... One of the fundamental principles of Commerce Clause jurisprudence is that no State, consistent with the Commerce Clause, may "impose a tax which discriminates against interstate commerce... by providing a direct commercial advantage to local business." *Northwestern States Portland Cement Co.* v. *Minnesota....* This antidiscrimination principle follows inexorably from the basic purpose of the Clause to prohibit the multiplication of preferential trade areas destructive of the free commerce anticipated by the Constitution....

. . . .

The common thread running through the cases upholding compensatory taxes is the equality of treatment between local and interstate commerce.... As already demonstrated, however, the pattern of credits and exemptions allowed under the Louisiana statute undeniably violates this principle of equality....

It may be true that further hearings would be required to provide a precise determination of the extent of the discrimination in this case, but this is an insufficient reason for not now declaring the Tax unconstitutional and eliminating the discrimination....

JUSTICE POWELL took no part in the consideration or decision of this case.

CHIEF JUSTICE BURGER, concurring.

JUSTICE REHNQUIST, dissenting.

It has been a consistent and dominant theme in decisions of this Court that our original jurisdiction should be exercised with considerable restraint and only after searching inquiry into the necessity for doing so. As we noted in *Illinois* v. *Milwaukee*, "[i]t has long been this Court's philosophy that 'our original jurisdiction should be invoked sparingly.'"...

None of these concerns are adequately answered by the expedient of employing a Special Master to conduct hearings, receive evidence, and submit recommendations for our review....

The Court accepts original jurisdiction in this case for two separate reasons: because the plaintiff States are injured in their capacity as purchasers of natural gas, *ante*, at 2123–2124, and because the plaintiff States may sue as *parens patriae, ante,* at 2124–2125. In ruling that jurisdiction exists because of the plaintiff States' own purchases of natural gas, the Court does not even purport to consider the nature or essential quality of the States' claim or whether it is of sufficient "seriousness and dignity" to justify invoking our "delicate and grave" original jurisdiction. The Court recognizes that "unique concerns of federalism" form the basis of our original jurisdiction... but does not explain how such concerns are implicated simply because one State levies a tax on an item which is eventually passed on to consumers, one of which happens to be another State....

I would hold that, as a general rule, when a State's claim is indistinguishable from the claim of any other private consumer it is insufficient to invoke our original jurisdiction....

The facts that States now purchase countless varieties of items for their own use which were not purchased 50 or even 25 years ago suggests that concern for our own limited resources is not the only factor which should motivate us in allowing our original jurisdiction to be invoked sparingly. With the greatly increased litigation dockets in most state and federal trial courts, there will be the strongest temptation for various interest groups within the State to attempt to persuade the Attorney General of that State to bring an action in the name of the State in order to make an end run around the barriers of time and delay which would confront them if they were merely private litigants. . . .

The basic problem with the Court's opinion, in my view, is that it articulates no limiting principles that would prevent this Court from being deluged by original actions brought by States simply in their role as consumers or on behalf of groups of their citizens as consumers. . . .

A state tax must be assessed in light of its actual effect considered in conjunction with other provisions of a State's tax scheme. . . . In this case, the Louisiana First-Use Tax unquestionably discriminates against interstate commerce in favor of local interests as the necessary result of various tax credits and exclusions. No further hearings are necessary to sustain this conclusion. Under the specific provision of the First-Use Tax, OCS gas used for certain purposes within Louisiana is exempted from the Tax. OCS gas consumed in Louisiana for (1) producing oil, natural gas, or sulphur; (2) processing natural gas for the extraction of liquefiable hydrocarbons; or (3) manufacturing fertilizer and anhydrous ammonia, is exempt from the First-Use Tax. Competitive users in other States are burdened with the Tax. Other Louisiana statutes, enacted as part of the First-Use Tax package, provide important tax credits favoring local interests. Under the Severance Tax Credit, an owner paying the First-Use Tax on OCS gas receives an equivalent tax credit on any state severance tax owed in connection with production in Louisiana. . . . The obvious economic effect of this Severance Tax Credit is to encourage natural gas owners involved in the production of OCS gas to invest in mineral exploration and development within Louisiana rather than to invest in further OCS development or in production in other States. . . .

Edwards v. California

314 U.S. 160 (1941)
Vote: (5–3–1)–0

As GIBBONS so eloquently suggested, the Commerce Clause was intended to foster not merely trade, but navigation and traffic. The free flow of individuals was part of that concept. In the *Passenger Cases* (1849), an inspection fee for passengers coming into New York Harbor was invalidated though defended as a police power regulation with the fee being a way to defray the cost of the service. In *Crandall* v. *Nevada* (1868), the right to travel freely within the U.S. was asserted as an attribute of national citizenship, necessary for political effectiveness, but also implied by the Constitution as a benefit of the world's first "common market." A tax on travel was struck down as interfering with that freedom. The issue was enlarged upon in *Edwards* v. *California,* when, during the Great Depression, California tried to enforce an antivagrancy statute to prevent migrants from impoverished areas from entering its more prosperous borders. The so-called "anti-Okie" regulations were quickly challenged in state courts and then appealed to the Supreme Court.

MR. JUSTICE BYRNES delivered the opinion of the Court.

The facts of this case are simple and are not disputed. Appellant is a citizen of the United States and a resident of California. In December, 1939, he left his home in Marysville, California, for Spur, Texas, with the intention of bringing back to Marysville his wife's brother, Frank Duncan, a citizen of the United States and a resident of Texas. When he arrived in Texas, appellant learned that Duncan had last been employed by the Works Progress Administration. Appellant thus became aware of the fact that Duncan was an indigent person and he continued to be aware of it throughout the period involved in this case. . . .

In Justice Court a complaint was filed against appellant under §2615 of the Welfare and Institutions Code of California, which provides: "Every person, firm or corporation or officer or agent thereof that brings or assists in bringing into the State any indigent person who is not a resident of the State, knowing him to be an indigent person, is guilty of a misdemeanor." On demurrer to the complaint, appellant urged that the Section violated several provisions of the Federal Constitution. The demurrer was overruled, the cause was tried, appellant was convicted and sentenced to six months imprisonment in the county jail, and sentence was suspended.

. . . The appellee claims for the Section a very limited scope. It urges that the term "indigent person" must be taken to include only persons who are presently destitute of property and without resources to obtain the necessities of life, and who have no relatives or friends able and willing to support them. It is conceded, however, that the term is not confined to those who are physically or mentally incapacitated.

While the generality of the language of the Section contains no hint of these limitations, we are content to assign to the term this narrow meaning.

Article I, §8 of the Constitution delegates to the Congress the authority to regulate interstate commerce. And it is settled beyond question that the transportation of persons is "commerce," within the meaning of that provision. It is nevertheless true, that the States are not wholly precluded from exercising their police power in matters of local concern even though they may thereby affect interstate commerce. *California v. Thompson,* 313 U.S. 109, 113. The issue presented in this case, therefore, is whether the prohibition embodied in §2615 against the "bringing" or transportation of indigent persons into California is within the police power of that State. We think that it is not, and hold that it is an unconstitutional barrier to interstate commerce. . . . The State asserts that the huge influx of migrants into California in recent years has resulted in problems of health, morals, and especially finance, the proportions of which are staggering. It is not for us to say that this is not true. We have repeatedly and recently affirmed, and we now reaffirm, that we do not conceive it our function to pass upon "the wisdom, need, or appropriateness" of the legislative efforts of the States to solve such difficulties.

But this does not mean that there are no boundaries to the permissible area of State legislative activity. There are. And none is more certain than the prohibition against attempts on the part of any single State to isolate itself from difficulties common to all of them by restraining the transportation of persons and property across its borders. It is frequently the case that a State might gain a momentary respite from the pressure of events by the simple expedient of shutting its gates to the outside world. But, in the words of Mr. Justice Cardozo: "The Constitution was framed under the dominion of a political philosophy less parochial in range. It was framed upon the theory that the peoples of the several States must sink or swim together, and that in the long run prosperity and salvation are in union and not division."

It is difficult to conceive of a statute more squarely in conflict with this theory than the Section challenged here. Its express purpose and inevitable effect is to prohibit the transportation of indigent persons across the California border. The burden upon interstate commerce is intended and immediate; it is the plain and sole function of the statute. Moreover, the indigent non-residents who are the real victims of the statute are deprived of the opportunity to exert political pressure upon the California legislature in order to obtain a change in policy. *South Carolina Highway Dept.* v. *Barnwell Bros.* . . . We think this statute must fail under any known test of the validity of State interference with interstate commerce.

. . . Moreover, and unlike the relief problem, this phenomenon does not admit of diverse treatment by the several States. The prohibition against transporting indigent non-residents into one State is an open invitation to retaliatory measures, and the burdens upon the transportation of such persons become cumulative. . . .

Whether an able-bodied but unemployed person like Duncan is a "pauper" within the historical meaning of the term is open to considerable doubt. . . . But assuming that the term is applicable to him and to persons similarly situated, we do not consider ourselves bound by the language referred to. *City of New York* v. *Miln* was decided in 1837. Whatever may have been the notion then prevailing, we do not think that it will now be seriously contended that because a person is without employment and without funds he constitutes a "moral pestilence." Poverty and immorality are not synonymous.

. . . In the view we have taken it is unnecessary to decide whether the Section is repugnant to other provisions of the Constitution.

Reversed.

Mr. Justice Douglas, concurring:

. . . I am of the opinion that the right of persons to move freely from State to State occupies a more protected position in our constitutional system than does the movement of cattle, fruit, steel and coal across state lines. While the opinion of the Court expresses no view on that issue, the right involved is so fundamental that I deem it appropriate to indicate the reach of the constitutional question which is present.

The right to move freely from State to State is an incident of *national* citizenship protected by the privileges and immunities clause of the Fourteenth Amendment against state interference. Mr. Justice Moody, in *Twining* v. *New Jersey* . . . [1908], stated, "Privileges and immunities of citizens of the United States . . . are only such as arise out of the nature and essential character of the National Government, or are specifically granted or secured to all citizens or persons by the Constitution of the United States." And he went on to state that one of those rights of *national* citizenship was "the right to pass freely from State to State." . . . Now it is apparent that this right is not specifically granted by the Constitution. Yet before the Fourteenth Amendment it was recognized as a right fundamental to the national character of our Federal government. It was so decided in 1867 by *Crandall* v. *Nevada* . . . [1868]. . . . In that case this Court struck down a Nevada tax "upon every person leaving the State" by common carrier. Mr. Justice Miller writing for the Court held that the right to move freely throughout the nation was a right of *national* citizenship. That the right was implied did not make it any the less "guaranteed" by the Constitution. . . .

The conclusion that the right of free movement is a right of *national* citizenship stands on firm historical ground. If a state tax on that movement, as in the *Crandall* case, is invalid, *a fortiori* a state statute which obstructs or in substance prevents that movement must fall. That result necessarily follows unless perchance a State can curtail the right of free movement of those who are poor or destitute. But to allow such an exception to be engrafted on the rights of *national* citizenship would be to contravene every conception of national unity. It would also introduce a caste system utterly incompatible with the spirit of our system of government. . . . Since the state statute here challenged involves such consequences, it runs afoul of the privileges and immunities clause of the Fourteenth Amendment.

MR. JUSTICE BLACK and MR. JUSTICE MURPHY join in this opinion.

MR. JUSTICE JACKSON, concurring:

While instances of valid "privileges or immunities" must be but few, I am convinced that this is one. I do not ignore or belittle the difficulties of what has been characterized by this Court as an "almost forgotten" clause. But the difficulty of the task does not excuse us from giving these general and abstract words whatever of specific content and concreteness they will bear as we mark out their application, case by case. That is the method of the common law, and it has been the method of this Court with other no less general statements in our fundamental law. This Court has not been timorous about giving concrete meaning to such obscure and vagrant phrases as "due process," "general welfare," "equal protection," or even "commerce among the several States." But it has always hesitated to give any real meaning to the privileges and immunities clause lest it improvidently give too much.

This Court should, however, hold squarely that it is a privilege of citizenship of the United States, protected from state abridgment, to enter any state of the Union, either for temporary sojourn or for the establishment of permanent residence therein and for gaining resultant citizenship thereof.

If national citizenship means less than this, it means nothing. . . .

Any measure which would divide our citizenry on the basis of property into one class free to move from state to state and another class that is poverty-bound to the place where it has suffered misfortune is not only at war with the habit and custom by which our country has expanded, but is also a short-sighted blow at the security of property itself. Property can have no more dangerous, even if unwitting, enemy than one who would make its possession a pretext for unequal or exclusive civil rights. Where those rights are derived from national citizenship no state may impose such a test, and whether the Congress could do so we are not called upon to inquire. . . . Rich or penniless, Duncan's citizenship under the Constitution pledges his strength to the defense of California as a part of the United States, and his right to migrate to any part of the land he must defend is something she must respect under the same instrument. Unless this Court is willing to say that citizenship of the United States means at least this much to the citizen, then our heritage of constitutional privileges and immunities is only a promise to the ear to be broken to the hope, a teasing illusion like a munificent bequest in a pauper's will.

Shapiro v. Thompson

> 394 U.S. 618 (1969)
> Vote: 6–3

Thompson, an unwed mother, moved to Connecticut and was denied welfare under the Aid to Dependent Children program. She had not resided in the State of Connecticut for the required year. The federal district court invalidated the requirement, and Shapiro, the State Welfare Commissioner, appealed to the Supreme Court. Similar cases involving residence requirements in Pennsylvania and the District of Columbia were consolidated.

Query: Is a residence requirement for in-state tuition on the same footing as one for welfare payments?

MR. JUSTICE BRENNAN delivered the opinion of the Court.

These three appeals were restored to the calendar for reargument. 392 U.S. 920 (1968). Each is an appeal from a decision of a three-judge District Court holding unconstitutional a State or District of Columbia statutory provision which denies welfare assistance to residents of the State or District who have not resided within their jurisdictions for at least one year immediately preceding their applications for such assistance. We affirm the judgments of the District Courts in the three cases. . . .

There is no dispute that the effect of the waiting-period requirement in each case is to create two classes of needy resident families indistinguishable from each other except that one is composed of residents who have resided a year or more, and the second of residents who have resided less than a year, in the jurisdiction. On the basis of this sole difference the first class is granted and the second class is denied welfare aid upon which may depend the ability of the families to obtain the very means to subsist — food, shelter, and other necessities of life. In each case, the District Court found that appellees met the test for residence in their jurisdictions, as well as all other eligibility requirements except the requirement of residence for a full year prior to their applications. On reargument, appellees' central contention is that the statutory prohibition of benefits to residents of less than a year creates a classification which constitutes an invidious discrimination denying them equal protection of the laws. We agree. The interests which appellants assert are promoted by the classification either may not constitutionally be promoted by government or are not compelling governmental interests.

Primarily, appellants justify the waiting-period requirement as a protective device to preserve the fiscal integrity of state public assistance programs. It is asserted that people who require welfare assistance during their first year of residence in a State are likely to become continuing burdens on state welfare programs. Therefore, the argument runs, if such people can be deterred from entering the jurisdiction by denying them welfare benefits during the first year, state programs to assist long-time residents will not be impaired by a substantial influx of indigent newcomers.

There is weighty evidence that exclusion from the jurisdiction of the poor who need or may need relief was the specific objective of these provisions.
. . . .

We do not doubt that the one-year waiting-period device is well suited to discourage the influx of poor families in need of assistance. An indigent who desires to migrate, resettle, find a new job, and start a new life will doubtless hesitate if he knows that he must risk making the move without the possibility of falling back on state welfare assistance during his first year of residence, when his need may be most acute. But the purpose of inhibiting migration by needy persons into the State is constitutionally impermissible.

This Court long ago recognized that the nature of our Federal Union and our constitutional concepts of personal liberty unite to require that all citizens be free to travel throughout the length and breadth of our land uninhibited by statutes, rules, or regulations which unreasonably burden or restrict this movement. That proposition was early stated by Chief Justice Taney in the *Passenger Cases* . . . (1849). . . .

Thus, the purpose of deterring the in-migration of indigents cannot serve as justification for the classification created by the one-year waiting period, since that purpose is constitutionally impermissible. If a law has "no other purpose . . . than to chill the assertion of constitutional rights by penalizing those who choose to exercise them, then it [is] patently unconstitutional." *United States* v. *Jackson* . . . (1968). . . . [A] State may no more try to fence out those indigents who seek higher welfare benefits than it may try to fence out indigents generally. Implicit in any such distinction is the notion that indigents who enter a State with the hope of securing higher welfare benefits are somehow less deserving than indigents who do not take this consideration into account. But we do not perceive why a mother who is seeking to make a new life for herself and her children should be regarded as less deserving because she considers, among other factors, the level of a State's public assistance. Surely such a mother is no less deserving than a mother who moves into a particular State in order to take advantage of its better educational facilities.

Appellants argue further that the challenged classification may be sustained as an attempt to distinguish between new and old residents on the basis of the contribution they have made to the community through the payment of taxes. We have difficulty seeing how long-term residents who qualify for welfare are making a greater present contribution to the State in taxes than indigent residents who have recently arrived. If the argument is based on contributions made in the past by the long-term residents, there is some question, as a factual matter, whether this argument is applicable in Pennsylvania where the record suggests that some 40% of those denied public assistance because of the waiting period had lengthy prior residence in the State. But we need not rest on the particular facts of these cases. Appellants' reasoning would logically permit the State to bar new residents from schools, parks, and libraries or deprive them of police and fire protection. Indeed it would permit the State to apportion all benefits and services according to the past tax contributions of its citizens. The Equal Protection Clause prohibits such an apportionment of state services.

We recognize that a State has a valid interest in preserving the fiscal integrity of its programs. It may legitimately attempt to limit its expenditures, whether for public assistance, public education, or any other program. But a State may not accomplish such a purpose by invidious distinctions between classes of its citizens. It could not, for example, reduce expenditures for education by barring indigent children from its schools. Similarly, in the cases before us, appellants must do more than show that denying welfare benefits to new residents saves money. The saving of welfare costs cannot justify an otherwise invidious classification. . . .

The argument that the waiting-period requirement facilitates budget predictability is wholly unfounded. The records in all three cases are utterly devoid of evidence that either State or the District of Columbia in fact uses the one-year requirement as a means to predict the number of people who will require assistance in the budget year. None of the appellants takes a census of new residents or collects any other data that would reveal the number of newcomers in the State less than a year. Nor are new residents required to give advance notice of their need for welfare assistance. . . .

The argument that the waiting period serves as an administratively efficient rule of thumb for determining residency similarly will not withstand scrutiny. . . .

Similarly, there is no need for a State to use the one-year waiting period as a safeguard against fraudulent receipt of benefits; for less drastic means are available, and are employed, to minimize that hazard.

Pennsylvania suggests that the one-year waiting period is justified as a means of encouraging new residents to join the labor force promptly. But this logic would also require a similar waiting period for long-term residents of the State. . . . Since the classification here touches on the fundamental right of interstate movement, its constitutionality must be judged by the stricter standard of whether it promotes a *compelling* state interest. Under this standard, the waiting-period requirement clearly violates the Equal Protection Clause.

Connecticut and Pennsylvania argue, however, that the constitutional challenge to the waiting-period requirements must fail because Congress expressly approved the imposition of the requirement by the States as part of the jointly funded AFDC program.

Section 402(b) of the Social Security Act of 1935, as amended, 42 U.S.C. §602(b), provides that:

> The Secretary shall approve any [state assistance] plan which fulfills the conditions specified in subsection (a) of this section, except that he shall not approve any plan which imposes as a condition of eligibility for aid to families with dependent children, a residence requirement which denies aid with respect to any child residing in the State (1) who has resided in the State for one year immediately preceding the application for such aid, or (2) who was born within one year immediately preceding the application, if the parent or other relative with whom the child is living has resided in the State for one year immediately preceding the birth.

On its face, the statute does not approve, much less prescribe, a one-year requirement. It merely directs the Secretary of Health, Education, and Welfare not to disapprove plans submitted by the States because they include such a requirement. The suggestion that Congress enacted that directive to encourage state participation in the AFDC program is completely refuted by the legislative history of the section. That history discloses that Congress enacted the directive to curb hardships resulting from lengthy residence requirements. Rather than constituting an approval or a prescription of the requirement in state plans, the directive was the means chosen by Congress to deny federal funding to any State which persisted in stipulating excessive residence requirements as a condition of the payment of benefits.

Finally, even if it could be argued that the constitutionality of §402(b) is somehow at issue here, it follows from what we have said that the provision, insofar as it permits the one-year waiting-period requirement, would be unconstitutional. Congress may not authorize the States to violate the Equal Protection Clause.

The waiting-period requirement in the District of Columbia Code involved in No. 33 is also unconstitutional even though it was adopted by Congress as an exercise of federal power. In terms of federal power, the discrimination created by the one-year requirement violates the Due Process Clause of the Fifth Amendment. "[W]hile the Fifth Amendment contains no equal protection clause, it does forbid discrimination that is 'so unjustifiable as to be violative of due process.'" *Schneider* v. *Rusk* . . . (1964); *Bolling* v. *Sharpe* . . . (1954).

Affirmed.

MR. JUSTICE STEWART, concurring.

In joining the opinion of the Court, I add a word in response to the dissent of my Brother Harlan, who, I think, has quite misapprehended what the Court's opinion says.

The Court today does *not* "pick out particular human activities, characterize them as 'fundamental,' and give them added protection. . . ." "[T]he right to travel freely from State to State finds constitutional protection that is quite independent of the Fourteenth Amendment.". . . As we made clear in *Guest,* it is a right broadly assertable against private interference as well as governmental action. Like the right of association, *NAACP* v. *Alabama* . . . [1958], it is a virtually unconditional personal right, guaranteed by the Constitution to us all.

The Court today, therefore, is not conceiving new constitutional principles. It is deciding these cases under the aegis of established constitutional law.

MR. CHIEF JUSTICE WARREN, with whom MR. JUSTICE BLACK joins, dissenting.

In my opinion the issue before us can be simply stated: May Congress, acting under one of its enumerated powers, impose minimal nationwide residence requirements or authorize the States to do so? Since I believe that Congress does have this power and has constitutionally exercised it in these cases, I must dissent.

The Court insists that §402(b) of the Social Security Act "does not approve, much less prescribe, a one-year requirement.". . . From its reading of the legislative history it concludes that Congress did not intend to authorize the States to impose residence requirements. An examination of the relevant legislative materials compels, in my view, the opposite conclusion, *i.e.,* Congress intended to authorize state residence requirements of up to one year.

Congress has imposed a residence requirement in the District of Columbia and authorized the States to impose similar requirements. The issue before us must therefore be framed in terms of whether Congress may create minimal residence requirements, not whether the States, acting alone, may do so. See *Prudential Insurance Co.* v. *Benjamin* . . . (1946); *In re Rahrer* . . . (1891). Appellees insist that a congressionally mandated residence requirement would violate their right to travel. The import of their con-

tention is that Congress, even under its "plenary" power to control interstate commerce, is constitutionally prohibited from imposing residence requirements. I reach a contrary conclusion for I am convinced that the extent of the burden on interstate travel when compared with the justification for its imposition requires the Court to uphold this exertion of federal power.

The Court's decision reveals only the top of the iceberg. Lurking beneath are the multitude of situations in which States have imposed residence requirements including eligibility to vote, to engage in certain professions or occupations or to attend a state-supported university. Although the Court takes pains to avoid acknowledging the ramifications of its decision, its implications cannot be ignored. I dissent.

MR. JUSTICE HARLAN, dissenting.

The Court today holds unconstitutional Connecticut, Pennsylvania, and District of Columbia statutes which restrict certain kinds of welfare benefits to persons who have lived within the jurisdiction for at least one year immediately preceding their applications. The Court has accomplished this result by an expansion of the comparatively new constitutional doctrine that some state statutes will be deemed to deny equal protection of the laws unless justified by a "compelling" governmental interest, and by holding that the Fifth Amendment's Due Process Clause imposes a similar limitation on federal enactments. Having decided that the "compelling interest" principle is applicable, the Court then finds that the governmental interests here asserted are either wholly impermissible or are not "compelling." For reasons which follow, I disagree both with the Court's result and with its reasoning.

In upholding the equal protection argument, the Court has applied an equal protection doctrine of relatively recent vintage: the rule that statutory classifications which either are based upon certain "suspect" criteria or affect "fundamental rights" will be held to deny equal protection unless justified by a "compelling" governmental interest. . . .

The "compelling interest" doctrine, which today is articulated more explicitly than ever before, constitutes an increasingly significant exception to the long-established rule that a statute does not deny equal protection if it is rationally related to a legitimate governmental objective. The "compelling interest" doctrine has two branches. The branch which requires that classifications based upon "suspect" criteria be supported by a compelling interest apparently had its genesis in cases involving racial classifications, which have, at least since *Korematsu* v. *United States* ... (1944), been regarded as inherently "suspect." The criterion of "wealth" apparently was added to the list of "suspects" as an alternative justification for the rationale in *Harper* v. *Virginia Bd. of Elections* ... (1966), in which Virginia's poll tax was struck down. The criterion of political allegiance may have been added in *Williams* v. *Rhodes* ... (1968). Today the list apparently has been further enlarged to include classifications based upon recent interstate movement, and perhaps those based upon the exercise of *any* constitutional right.

I think that this branch of the "compelling interest" doctrine is sound when applied to racial classifications, for historically the Equal Protection Clause was largely a product of the desire to eradicate legal distinctions founded upon race. However, I believe that the more recent extensions have been unwise. For the reasons stated in my dissenting opinion in *Harper* v. *Virginia Bd. of Elections* ... I do not consider wealth a "suspect" statutory criterion.

In my view, it is playing ducks and drakes with the statute to argue, as the Court does... that Congress did not mean to *approve* these state residence requirements.... I think that by any fair reading this section must be regarded as conferring congressional approval upon any plan containing a residence requirement of up to one year.

Nor do I find it credible that Congress intended to refrain from expressing approval of state residence requirements because of doubts about their constitutionality or their compatibility with the Act's beneficient purposes. With respect to constitutionality, a similar residence requirement was already in effect for the District of Columbia, and the burdens upon travel which might be caused by such requirements must, even in 1935, have been regarded as within the competence of Congress under its commerce power. If Congress had thought residence requirements entirely incompatible with the aims of the Act, it could simply have provided that state assistance plans containing such requirements should not be approved at all, rather than having limited approval to plans containing residence requirements of less than one year.

The Commerce Clause can be of no assistance to these appellees, since that clause grants plenary power to Congress, and Congress either enacted or approved all of the residence requirements here challenged.... On the authority of *Crandall* v. *Nevada*, (1868), those privileges and immunities have repeatedly been said to include the right to travel from State to State, presumably for the reason assigned in *Crandall*: that state restrictions on travel might interfere with intercourse between the Federal Government and its citizens. This kind of objection to state welfare residence requirements would seem necessarily to vanish in the face of congressional authorization, for except in those instances when its authority is limited by a constitutional provision binding upon it (as the Fourteenth Amendment is not), Congress has full power to define the relationship between citizens and the Federal Government.... I cannot find that the burden imposed by residence requirements upon ability to travel outweighs the governmental interests in their continued employment. Nor do I believe that the period of residence required in these cases — one year — is so excessively long as to justify a finding of unconstitutionality on that score.

I conclude with the following observations. Today's decision, it seems to me, reflects to an unusual degree the current notion that this Court possesses a peculiar wisdom all its own whose capacity to lead this Nation out of its present troubles is contained only by the limits of judicial ingenuity in contriving new constitutional principles to meet each problem as it arises. For anyone who, like myself, believes that it is an essential function of this Court to maintain the constitutional divisions between state and federal authority and among the three branches of the Federal Government, today's decision is a step in the wrong direction.

Williams v. North Carolina (Williams II)

325 U.S. 226 (1945)
Vote: 6–3

This surprising case caused grief to many, including the justices. In *Williams I* the Supreme Court had held that North Carolina must accept as valid a Nevada divorce even though the first Mrs. Williams had not had notice of the proceeding. The state persevered by bringing a charge of bigamy, this time arguing the divorce was invalid because Mr. Williams had only pretended to establish residency in Nevada.

As is apparent, the Court was disturbed by the possibility of evading family responsibility by jurisdiction shopping. As we noted, the Court eventually solved this by the concept of "divisible divorce."

A marriage could be ended anywhere, but the state where the family was rooted could control financial and custody arrangements.

MR. JUSTICE FRANKFURTER delivered the opinion of the Court.

This case is here to review judgments of the Supreme Court of North Carolina, affirming convictions for bigamous cohabitation, assailed on the ground that full faith and credit, as required by the Constitution of the United States, was not accorded divorces decreed by one of the courts of Nevada. *Williams* v. *North Carolina* . . . [1942] decided an earlier aspect of the controversy. It was there held that a divorce granted by Nevada, on a finding that one spouse was domiciled in Nevada, must be respected in North Carolina, where Nevada's finding of domicil was not questioned, though the other spouse had neither appeared nor been served with process in Nevada and though recognition of such a divorce offended the policy of North Carolina. The record then before us did not present the question whether North Carolina had the power "to refuse full faith and credit to Nevada divorce decrees because, contrary to the findings of the Nevada court, North Carolina finds that no *bona fide* domicil was acquired in Nevada." . . . This is the precise issue which has emerged after retrial of the cause following our reversal. Its obvious importance brought the case here. . . .

Under our system of law, judicial power to grant a divorce — jurisdiction, strictly speaking — is founded on domicil. . . . Divorce, like marriage, is of concern not merely to the immediate parties. It affects personal rights of the deepest significance. It also touches basic interests of society. Since divorce, like marriage, creates a new status, every consideration of policy makes it desirable that the effect should be the same wherever the question arises.

It is one thing to reopen an issue that has been settled after appropriate opportunity to present their contentions has been afforded to all who had an interest in its adjudication. . . . The State of domiciliary origin should not be bound by an unfounded, even if not collusive, recital in the record of a court of another State. As to the truth or existence of a fact, like that of domicil, upon which depends the power to exert judicial authority, a State not a party to the exertion of such judicial authority in another State but seriously affected by it has a right, when asserting its own unquestioned authority, to ascertain the truth or existence of that crucial fact. . . . In short, the decree of divorce is a conclusive adjudication of everything except the jurisdictional facts upon which it is founded, and domicil is a jurisdictional fact. To permit the necessary finding of domicil by one State to foreclose all States in the protection of their social institutions would be intolerable.

But to endow each State with controlling authority to nullify the power of a sister State to grant a divorce based upon a finding that one spouse had acquired a new domicil within the divorcing State would, in the proper functioning of our federal system, be equally indefensible. No State court can assume comprehensive attention to the various and potentially conflicting interests that several States may have in the institutional aspects of marriage. The necessary accommodation between the right of one State to safeguard its interest in the family relation of its own people and the power of another State to grant divorces can be left to neither State.

The problem is to reconcile the reciprocal respect to be accorded by the members of the Union to their adjudications with due regard for another most important aspect of our federalism whereby "the domestic relations of husband and wife . . . were matters reserved to the States."

What is immediately before us is the judgment of the Supreme Court of North Carolina. We have authority to upset it only if there is want of foundation for the conclusion that that Court reached. The conclusion it reached turns on its finding that the spouses who obtained the Nevada decrees were not domiciled there. The fact that the Nevada court found that they were domiciled there is entitled to respect, and more. The burden of undermining the verity which the Nevada decrees import rests heavily upon the assailant. But simply because the Nevada court found that it had power to award a divorce decree cannot, we have seen, foreclose reexamination by another State. Otherwise, as was pointed out long ago, a court's record would establish its power and the power would be proved by the record. Such circular reasoning would give one State a control over all the other States which the Full Faith and Credit Clause certainly did not confer.

When this case was first here, North Carolina did not challenge the finding of the Nevada court that petitioners had acquired domicils in Nevada. . . . Against the charge of bigamous cohabitation under §14–183 of the North Carolina General Statutes, petitioners stood on their Nevada divorces and offered exemplified copies of the Nevada proceedings. The trial judge charged that the State had the burden of proving beyond a reasonable doubt that (1) each petitioner was lawfully married to one person; (2) thereafter each petitioner contracted a second marriage with another person outside North Carolina; (3) the spouses of petitioners were living at the time of this second marriage; (4) petitioners cohabited with one another in North Carolina after the second marriage. The burden, it was charged, then developed upon petitioners "to satisfy the trial jury, not beyond a reasonable doubt nor by the greater weight of the evidence, but simply to satisfy" the jury from all the evidence, that petitioners were domiciled in Nevada at the time they obtained their divorces. The court further charged that "the recitation" of *bona fide* domicil in the Nevada decree was "prima facie evidence" sufficient to warrant a finding of domicil in Nevada but not compelling "such an inference." . . .

The scales of justice must not be unfairly weighted by a State when full faith and credit is claimed for a sister-State judgment. But North Carolina has not so dealt with the Nevada decrees. She has not raised unfair barriers to their recognition. North Carolina did not fail in appreciation or application of federal standards of full faith and credit.

It would be highly unreasonable to assert that a jury could not reasonably find that the evidence demonstrated that petitioners went to Nevada solely for the purpose of obtaining a divorce and intended all along to return to North Carolina.

In seeking a decree of divorce outside the State in which he has theretofore maintained his marriage, a person is necessarily involved in the legal situation created by our federal system whereby one State can grant a divorce of validity in other States only if the applicant has a *bona fide* domicil in the State of the court purporting to dissolve a prior legal marriage. The petitioners therefore assumed the risk that this Court would find that North Carolina justifiably concluded that they had not been domiciled in Nevada. Since the divorces which they sought and received in Nevada had no legal validity in North Carolina and their North Carolina spouses were still alive, they subjected themselves to prosecution for bigamous cohabitation under North Carolina law. . . . Mistaken notions about one's legal rights are not sufficient to bar prosecution for crime.

As for the suggestion that *Williams* v. *North Carolina, supra,* foreclosed the Supreme Court of North Carolina from ordering a second trial upon the issue of domicil, it suffices to refer to our opinion in the earlier case.

Affirmed.

MR. JUSTICE MURPHY, concurring.

No justifiable purpose is served by imparting constitutional sanctity to the efforts of petitioners to establish a false and fictitious domicil in Nevada. Such a result would only tend to promote wholesale disre-gard of North Carolina's divorce laws by its citizens, thus putting an end to "the existence of all efficacious power on the subject of divorce." Certainly no policy of Nevada dictates lending the full faith and credit clause to protect actions grounded in deceit. . . .

There are no startling or dangerous implications in the judgment reached by the Court in this case. All of the uncontested divorces that have ever been granted in the forty-eight states are as secure today as they were yesterday or as they were before our previous decision in this case. Those based upon fraudulent domicils are now and always have been subject to later reexamination with possible serious consequences.

Nor are any issues of civil liberties at stake here. It is unfortunate that the petitioners must be imprisoned for acts which they probably committed in reliance upon advice of counsel and without intent to violate the North Carolina statute. But there are many instances of punishment for acts whose criminality was unsuspected at the time of their occurrence.

The CHIEF JUSTICE and MR. JUSTICE JACKSON join in these views.

MR. JUSTICE RUTLEDGE, dissenting.

Once again the ghost of "unitary domicil" returns on its perpetual round, in the guise of "jurisdictional fact," to upset judgments, marriages, divorces, undermine the relations founded upon them, and make this Court the unwilling and uncertain arbiter between the concededly valid laws and decrees of sister states. From *Bell* and *Andrews* to *Davis* to *Haddock* to *Williams* and now back to *Haddock* and *Davis* through *Williams* again — is the maze the Court has travelled in a domiciliary wilderness, only to come out with no settled constitutional policy where one is needed most.

Nevada's judgment has not been voided. It could not be, if the same test applies to sustain it as upholds the North Carolina convictions. It stands, with the marriages founded upon it, unimpeached. For all that has been determined or could be, unless another change is in the making, petitioners are lawful husband and wife in Nevada. . . . They may be such everywhere outside North Carolina. Lawfully wedded also, in North Carolina, are the divorced spouse of one and his wife, taken for all we know in reliance upon the Nevada decree. That is, unless another jury shall find they too are bigamists for their reliance. No such jury has been impanelled. But were one called, it could pronounce the Nevada decree valid upon the identical evidence from which the jury in this case drew the contrary conclusion. That jury or it and another, if petitioners had been tried separately, could have found one guilty, the other innocent, upon that evidence unvaried by a hair. And, by the Court's test, we could do nothing but sustain the contradictory findings in all these cases.

I do not believe the Constitution has thus confided to the caprice of juries the faith and credit due the laws and judgments of sister states. Nor has it thus made that question a local matter for the states themselves to decide. Were all judgments given the same infirmity, the full faith and credit clause would be only a dead constitutional letter.

I agree it is not the Court's business to determine policies of divorce. But precisely its function is to lay the jurisdictional foundations upon which the states' determinations can be made effective, within and without their borders. For in the one case due process, in the other full faith and credit, commands of equal compulsion upon the states and upon us, impose that duty.

I do not think we perform it, we rather abdicate, when we confide the ultimate decision to the states or to their juries. This we do when, for every case that matters, we make their judgment conclusive.

What, exactly, are the effects of the decision? The Court is careful not to say that Nevada's judgment is not valid in Nevada. To repeat, the Court could not so declare it, unless a different test applies to sustain that judgment than supports North Carolina's. Presumably the same standard applies to both; and each state accordingly is free to follow its own policy, wherever the evidence, whether the same or different, permits conflicting inferences of domicil, as it always does when the question becomes important. The Constitution does not mention domicil. Nowhere does it posit the powers of the states or the nation upon that amorphous, highly variable common-law conception. Judges have imported it. The importation, it should be clear by now, has failed in creating a workable constitutional criterion for this delicate region.

MR. JUSTICE BLACK, dissenting.

. . . These petitioners have been sentenced to prison because they were unable to prove their innocence to the satisfaction of the State of North Carolina. They have been convicted under a statute so uncertain in its application that not even the most learned member of the bar could have advised them in advance as to whether their conduct would violate the law. In reality the petitioners are being deprived of their freedom because the State of Nevada,

through its legislature and courts, follows a liberal policy in granting divorces. They had Nevada divorce decrees which authorized them to remarry. Without charge or proof of fraud in obtaining these decrees, and without holding the decrees invalid under Nevada law, this Court affirms a conviction of petitioners, for living together as husband and wife. I cannot reconcile this with the Full Faith and Credit Clause and with Congressional legislation passed pursuant to it. . . . Even more, the Court's opinion today will cast a cloud over the lives of countless numbers of the multitude of divorced persons in the United States. . . . This Court today affirms those sentences without a determination that the Nevada marriage was invalid under that state's laws. This holding can be supported, if at all, only on one of two grounds: (1) North Carolina has extra-territorial power to regulate marriages within Nevada's territorial boundaries, or, (2) North Carolina can punish people who live together in that state as husband and wife even though they have been validly married in Nevada.

A further consequence is to subject people to criminal prosecutions for adultery and bigamy merely because they exercise their constitutional right to pass from a state in which they were validly married into another state which refuses to recognize their marriage. Such a consequence runs counter to the basic guarantees of our federal union. *Edwards* v. *California,* 314 U.S. 160. It is true that persons validly married under the laws of one state have been convicted of crime for living together in other states. But those state convictions were not approved by this Court. And never before today has this Court decided a case upon the assumption that men and women validly married under the laws of one state could be sent to jail by another state for conduct which involved nothing more than living together as husband and wife. . . . None of the parties to the marriage, although formally notified of the Nevada divorce proceedings, made any protest before or after the decrees were rendered. The state did not sue here to protect any North Carolinian's property rights or to obtain support for the families which had been deserted. The result of all this is that the right of the state to attack the validity of these decrees in a criminal proceeding is today sustained, although the state's citizens, on whose behalf it purports to act, could not have done so at the time of the conviction in a civil proceeding. . . . While the doctrine that "Ignorance of the law excuses no man" has sometimes been applied with harsh consequences, American courts have not been in the habit of making ignorance of law the crucial and controlling element in a penitentiary offense. . . . It is quite a different thing, however, to send people to prison for lacking the clairvoyant gift of prophesying when one judge or jury will upset the findings of fact made by another.

MR. JUSTICE DOUGLAS joins in this dissent.

Part II

CHAPTER 5

Property, the Constitution, and the States

Constitutional Protection of Property

Chapters 3 and 4 showed how both the taxing and spending powers of the national government and the structure of federalism have been used to shape American economic policies. Indeed the history of American constitutional law is in large part the history of the Court's review of government involvement in the economy. This chapter examines still other constitutional provisions that have shaped this history, those provisions in the Fourteenth Amendment that have been used to protect liberty and property rights. It completes our exploration of the rise and fall of the Supreme Court's effort to write laissez-faire economic theory into the Constitution during the period of "dual federalism," roughly from the 1880s to the New Deal. During this period the Court struck down national powers by narrowly construing the commerce clause and taxing powers of Congress, and then went on to strike down nearly 200 state regulations as violations of the Due Process and Equal Protection provisions in the Fourteenth Amendment. Together these limits on the national and state governments created a zone of economic activity that was virtually exempt

from meaningful regulation by any government, national or state.

There are, however, important differences in the history of the Court's treatment of national and state economic policies. The fear of many of the Framers of the Constitution was not that the national government would become too powerful, but that it would be too weak because powerful states would cripple it. Thus their central concern was to create a strong national government, with power to protect liberty, including private property, and to stimulate economic activity. They sought to ensure the right of property holders to be secure in their possessions and free to do business, and to this end wanted weak state governments and a strong national government to foster commerce and industry. During the period immediately following the Revolutionary War, economically hard-hit farmers and small businessmen prevailed upon their state legislative assemblies to help cope with their plight by abrogating debts and overturning court judgments against them. The Federalists, supported as they were by the "vested interests" — large property holders and financial institutions — sought to nullify these practices by inserting provisions in the new Constitution that would limit the powers of the states to undercut property rights. Various provisions were suggested for inclusion in the Constitution, only to be rejected. Alexander Hamilton, a leading architect of the Federalists' philosophy, argued for a Senate composed of the "rich and well born," who would hold office for life. Others argued for property qualifications for voters and office-holders.

Although these proposals failed, other Federalist ideas were adopted. James Madison led the successful effort to obtain two very important concessions for property rights. Article I, Section 10 provides that "No State shall... pass any... *ex post facto* law," and "[no] laws impairing the obligation of contracts." While the first provision was quickly interpreted away by the Supreme Court, in CALDER V. BULL (1798), the Contract Clause became a powerful limit on state power and continues to exert an influence; see, for example, UNITED STATES TRUST CO. OF NEW YORK V. STATE OF NEW JERSEY (1977).

The concerns of the Federalists were obvious. Having accumulated property, they wanted to keep it. They were concerned lest the democratic masses would use their numerical strength to advantage in the state legislatures, as they had under the Articles of Confederation, to abrogate debts, circumscribe commerce, and tax industry excessively. Thus they sought to provide for constitutional limitations upon state encroachments on property.

The protections of property as against the national government were adopted four years later in the Bill of Rights. This expanded concern with protecting property is seen most clearly in the Fifth Amendment, sections of which provide that "No person shall... be deprived of life, liberty, or property, without due process of law; nor shall private property be taken for public use, without just compensation." A concern with the link between liberty and property also informs the Fourth Amendment's prohibition against unreasonable searches and seizures and its admonition

about the "right of the people to be secure in their persons, houses, papers, and effects." And a concern with protecting property is central to an understanding of the Seventh Amendment's provision that courts shall operate "according to the rules of the common law," a clear reference to the conceptions of property then embedded in the common law.

Later, the Fourteenth Amendment provided that "No state shall make or enforce any law which shall abridge the privileges or immunities of citizens of the United States"; and, echoing the Fifth Amendment, continued, "nor shall any State deprive any person of life, liberty, or property without due process of law"; and concluded, "nor deny to any person within its jurisdiction the equal protection of the laws."

Still other constitutional provisions have emerged to protect "property interests." The First Amendment's safeguards for speech and the press have protected one type of property interest, the publishing and broadcasting industries, and have been extended to cover some forms of advertising and commercial expression. Libel law has been extended to protect "corporate" as well as "individual" reputations. When each of these several provisions is added to the long-standing legal fiction that a corporation is a person, one can begin to appreciate the extent to which American corporate and business activity is accorded a sweeping array of constitutional protections.

In this Chapter we examine those provisions in Article I, Section 10, and in the Fourteenth Amendment that most directly and explicitly are aimed at protecting property against encroachment by government. The Framers' concerns with property notwithstanding, these provisions must be understood in the context of competing claims against which property interests have always been balanced. Even the most ardent Federalists recognized the long-standing interest of government, one which is often considered an *inherent* power — indeed the very reason for the existence of government — to act to promote public health, safety, and welfare. The problem, of course, is that property rights and the inherent power of government to regulate in the public interest can come into conflict. Within the American constitutional framework, this collision has been found time and again between property rights, protected by expansive interpretations of the Contract Clause and the Fifth and Fourteenth Amendments' Due Process Clauses, and what have come to be known as the states' inherent police powers to regulate in the interests of promoting public health, safety, and welfare. Thus here, as with most other important constitutional provisions, we find contrary sentiments producing tensions that the Supreme Court is called upon to resolve.

In the nearly two hundred years since the adoption of the Constitution, the Court has come to favor the state police power as against property interests, although the development of this position has not been steady, nor is it without important limitations. The relative weight of the two interests, as they have made themselves felt in Court decisions, has shifted from time to time, and reflects changes in economic and social realities and shifts in public sentiments. Thus, to follow the development of constitutional doctrine in this area is in many respects to trace changing public acceptance of government involvement in the economy and the growth of the modern welfare state.

But to say that the governmental role in the economy and state police power has received an expansive interpretation in recent years is not to say that the Court's concern with "vested rights" or property interests has been entirely abandoned. While the relative importance of the two sets of interests has shifted dramatically, the tension between them still exists, and from time to time the Court is still called upon to balance these contending concerns. Also, in as much as the relative power of the two sets of interests reflects public sentiment and political expression, there is no reason to believe that the Court will not continue to wrestle with the problem, readjusting the balance between its concerns for property rights and state police powers. The cases presented will give you an appreciation for the historical shift in the Court's position on the issues, as well as present the current nature of this continuing debate.

Even as we review these shifts in the Court's treatment of the "rights of property," it is important to be aware of what has remained unchanged, and is so well ingrained in our legal and constitutional history that, despite its importance, is often ignored in discussions of constitutional law. In both common and constitutional law the corporation has assumed the legal status of a person. While this fiction has yielded a host of benefits — it was developed in part to aid accumulation of capital and stimulate investment, and to facilitate recovery of damages by those injured — it has also erected a constitutional wall around business enterprises that helps to provide American business far greater autonomy and constitutional protection than business in other countries. When the United States government attempts to regulate business it must follow constitutional principles that extend to the business concern many of the same constitutional protections available to individuals. Indeed, a number of commentators have noted the affinity between the American constitutional framework and capitalism. Marxists have criticized this connection, while advocates of free-market economies, like Milton Friedman and James Buchanan, have celebrated it as the genius of American politics.

Ex Post Facto Laws and the Contract Clause

Article I, §10, reads in part: "No State shall... pass any... *ex post facto* Law, or Law impairing the obligation of contracts." The first of these provisions, the prohibition against *ex post facto* laws, was almost immediately restricted to criminal law when it first appeared before the Supreme Court in 1798. In CALDER, the Court held that the provision did *not* apply to legislation dealing with property and contractual obligations, and following Blackstone held, that it was aimed solely as a limit on criminal laws. No case since CALDER has attempted to resurrect this provision as a bulwark against state encroachment on economic liberty, and, in effect, time has all but written it out of the Constitution as such a protection.

If the Federalists lost in their first battle to use the *ex post facto* provision as a bulwark against state encroachment on property, they won significant early victories with their other weapon, the Contract Clause. We have already seen that in interpreting the rights of the national as against the state government to regulate interstate commerce, the Supreme Court under Chief Justice Marshall construed the powers of the states to regulate commercial interests very narrowly, while at the same time giving the national government wide latitude. A similar judicial expansiveness prevailed in efforts to breathe meaning into the Contract Clause as well.

Fletcher v. *Peck* (1810) revealed the ingenuity and aggressiveness with which John Marshall pursued his task. Challenged with what appeared to be an insuperable obstacle — an "arranged" (rather than a "real") controversy in a case that involved what was probably the largest land scandal to date in the nation's history — Marshall turned the case to advantage, and wrote an opinion that paved the way for an extraordinarily broad interpretation of the Constitution's Contract Clause as a defense of property and a limit on state power.

In 1795, a corrupt Georgia legislature approved the sale of vast portions of the state (what is now the greater part of Alabama and Mississippi) to a group of speculators, doing business as the Yazoo Land Companies, for a ridiculously low price. Once it was found that almost all members of the Georgia legislature held interest in these companies and stood to reap windfall profits, they were voted out of office. The new legislature repealed the statute authorizing the sale, and the case — "arranged" by the land companies and people who had repurchased the land from them so as to clarify title — came before the Court.

In *Fletcher*, Marshall held that the repeal of the act by the Georgia legislature constituted an unconstitutional impairment of obligation of contract. Typically, Marshall sought to justify the Court's decision on several different grounds. Remaining wholly silent on the issue of the corrupt legislature that authorized the sale, Marshall argued that repeal of the statute violated vested rights and as such went contrary to the fundamental principles of organized government. He went on to argue that the Contract Clause applied to executed contracts as well as executory contracts, and that it applied to public as well as private arrangements. This latter point is important, since the most obvious meaning of the Contract Clause is that contracting parties are to be bound to their agreement under the law, and here it was the law itself that had been changed. The spirit of Marshall's effort is nicely summarized in the last paragraph of his opinion, where he concluded that the Georgia legislature's repeal was intolerable "either by general principles that are common to our free institutions, or by particular provision of the Constitution."

Seven years later (1819), Marshall wrote an even more sweeping opinion on the Contract Clause, expanding still further the protections of economic interests as against the states. In this case, TRUSTEES OF DARTMOUTH COLLEGE V. WOODWARD (1819), Marshall extended the Contract Clause to protect corporate charters as well as public grants. Under the common law, a corporation of whatever sort existed solely at the discretion of the government, and its charter, i.e., the official recognition of its existence and authorization to do business, could be rescinded at will by the government. The effect of the DARTMOUTH decision was to make all contracts and charters — to profit-making institutions as well as nonprofit schools such as the college — in perpetuity, thus placing them beyond the control of legislatures. Although state legislatures subsequently circumvented the sweeping consequences of this decision by adopting standard "reservation clauses" (which explicitly permitted states to alter or repeal a charter) in government documents chartering organizations, the effect of Marshall's decision was to elevate property rights to a privileged position, to something of a "natural" right worthy of "absolute" constitutional protections as against government.

But even as the Marshall Court boldly pronounced this preferred position of property, it began to acknowledge that there was another set of considerations that limits the rights of property. This competing concern was state police power, a power nowhere mentioned in the Constitution but widely acknowledged as the states' legitimate power to regulate for the health, safety, and welfare of their citizens. In GIBBONS V. OGDEN (1824), for instance, Marshall observed that the inherent police power of a state enabled it to regulate commerce "to a considerable extent." Thus, despite Marshall's sweeping language in *Fletcher* and in DARTMOUTH, he too recognized the need for some limits on commerce and the legitimate interests of states to regulate property. Still, under Marshall the spirit of *Fletcher* and DARTMOUTH held sway, informing the decisions of state courts (particularly in commercial centers) and causing state courts and legislatures to adopt narrow conceptions of their roles.

The election of Andrew Jackson in 1828 changed much of this. It signaled the end of the Federalist era and marked a significant expansion of democracy. With the election came renewed enthusiasm for legislative sovereignty and renewed challenges to the exalted position of entrenched interests that sought governmental creation of monopolies, exclusive state charters, and other forms of protection. These shifts in political mood made themselves felt on the Supreme Court as well, although adherence to precedent and the longevity of the justices caused the Court to lag. With respect to the relationship between the preferred position of vested interests and state police power, the shift in balance did not begin until 1836, two years after Roger Taney succeeded John Marshall as Chief Justice. In the famous case CHARLES RIVER BRIDGE CO. V. WARREN BRIDGE CO. (1837), the Court, with Taney writing for the majority, held that state police power allowed states to amend and abrogate governmentally created privilege.

In many respects CHARLES RIVER BRIDGE signaled the beginning of the end of the Contract Clause as a significant constitutional protector of commercial interests and limitation on state powers. Cases since then have simultaneously narrowed the scope of coverage of the Contract Clause and widened the meaning of legitimate state police power. In HOME BUILDING AND LOAN ASSOCIATION V. BLAISDELL (1934), decided in the midst of the Depression, the Supreme Court all but eliminated the Contract Clause as a protection of business interests. In announcing its 5 to 4 decision, the majority took cognizance of the "national emergency" created by the Depression, and went on to uphold a Minnesota statute that liberalized the terms of mortgage contracts in an effort to help farmers and homeowners retain possession of their property even though they had defaulted on their mortgage payments. Placing great emphasis on the distinction between an obligation to contract and the remedy in event of failure to meet that obligation, Chief Justice Charles Evans Hughes argued that the state law did not impair the obligation, only the remedy. The dissenters argued vigorously that this distinction is specious and that the majority all but eliminated the Contract Clause as a significant constitutional protection. However, more recent decisions suggest that the Contract Clause is not yet moribund.

The Court's 1965 decision in *El Paso* v. *Simmons*, 379 U.S. 497, suggests that the warning of these dissenters in BLAISDELL may not have been too far off the mark, but more recent decisions suggest that the Court has not yet "balanced away" all limits of the Contract Clause. In UNITED STATES TRUST COMPANY OF NEW YORK V. STATE OF NEW JERSEY (1977), a divided Supreme Court held that New York and New Jersey had violated the Constitution's Contract Clause when they retroactively repealed a statutory covenant between the two states that limited the power of the Port Authority of New York and New Jersey. Thus the vitality of the Contract Clause remains, and although now diminished, it may yet emerge as a significant restriction on government.

The Rise and Fall (and Rise?) of Substantive Due Process

The Constitution reflects the pluralism of American politics. Just as interests make themselves felt in many different ways and forms, so are they pursued and protected under different provisions of the Constitution. Indeed, even as the sun was beginning to set on an expansive interpretation of the Contract Clause, other provisions contained in the Fifth Amendment, as well as in the Fourteenth Amendment adopted in the aftermath of the Civil War, were emerging as a protection of economic interests. So far as we are concerned here, the key provisions of the Fourteenth Amendment are found in the first of its five sections, which provides that "No State shall make or enforce any law which shall abridge the privileges or immunities of citizens of the United States; nor shall any State deprive any person of life, liberty, or property, without due process of law; nor deny to any person within its jurisdiction the equal protection of the laws." While the proximate purpose of these provisions was the protection of the newly freed slaves, this did not preclude others from urging broader scope to their meaning.

Events prior to the Civil War provided the basis for this broader economic reading of the Fourteenth Amendment. Prior to adoption of the Fourteenth Amendment the Supreme Court had recognized the legal fiction that a corporation is a citizen under the law. Designed in large part to facilitate corporate accountability and legal liability, the fiction was taken literally and urged as a rationale to guarantee that commercial entities be accorded the same type and degree of rights and liberties as individuals. Thus, the specific protections accorded citizens in the Fourteenth

Amendment were also put forward as protections for commercial enterprises against state encroachment.

In 1873, in BUTCHERS' BENEVOLENT ASSOC. V. CRESCENT CITY LIVESTOCK LANDING AND SLAUGHTERHOUSE CO. (known as the SLAUGHTERHOUSE CASES) (1873), the Supreme Court was urged to use the Privileges and Immunities Clause of the newly adopted Fourteenth Amendment to overturn legislation that granted a single slaughterhouse exclusive franchise for the entire city. Designed to curb pollution and subsequent contamination of the water supply of New Orleans, the statute had the effect of displacing a number of butchers, who were forced either to cease operations or move to the new slaughterhouse. In upholding the Louisiana Supreme Court's decision favoring the state-created monopoly, the Supreme Court went on to give a very narrow interpretation of the Privileges and Immunities Clause. It has never emerged as a guarantee of any substance, standing as something of a dead letter in the Constitution.

This denial of economic claims did not, however, put an end to the movement to protect economic interests under the Fourteenth Amendment. Rather, the locus of attention intensified around another provision, the Due Process Clause, perhaps made all the more desirable because it explicitly protected "liberty" and "property" and because of a short history of an expansive interpretation of the due process concept in a handful of widely heralded state Supreme Court decisions just prior to the Civil War. See, for example, *Wynehamer* v. *New York Court of Appeals of New York,* 13 N.Y. 378 (1856), in which the Court held that state legislation limiting commercial activities violated due process under the state constitution.

The Court did not embrace this new economic or "substantive" due process doctrine immediately. In the SLAUGHTERHOUSE opinion, it explicitly rejected an economic application of the Fourteenth Amendment's Privileges and Immunities Clause, and gave even shorter shrift to the due process argument that was advanced. A short time later, in MUNN V. ILLINOIS (1877), the Court upheld a state statute regulating grain elevators, which had been challenged on grounds that it deprived owners of income, and hence liberty and property, without due process.

But even as they rejected the claims that the Fourteenth Amendment's Due Process Clause limited the substance of state legislation in these cases, the justices sowed the seeds for the Court's eventual acceptance of the doctrine. Both the SLAUGHTERHOUSE and MUNN decisions occasioned fervent dissents. Four justices dissented in the SLAUGHTERHOUSE CASES, arguing, in the words of Justice Bradley, that "a law which prohibits a large class of citizens from adopting a lawful employment or from following a lawful employment previously adopted, does deprive them of liberty as well as property, without due process of law." In MUNN, Justice Field issued a strong dissent, arguing that the Illinois statute violated due process. Perhaps most important in MUNN, the majority defended the statute because the *special* nature of the grain business was "affected with a public interest," and thus in their view was a legitimate subject for state regulation. So even as the Court endorsed a broad concept of state powers to regulate economic interests, it perhaps unwittingly opened the door to substantive due process when it relied so heavily on the distinction between business with and without a "public interest." By insisting so definitely that government could regulate private property if it is "clothed with a public interest," the opinion implied that if the business was not so clothed, states could not regulate, because to do so would deprive businesses of "liberty of contract" or "property" without due process of law.

MUNN reasserted the common law doctrine that governments can regulate businesses "affected with a public interest," and in subsequent cases the Court was called upon to identify businesses that were not so affected. In retrospect, the Court's effort to classify enterprises, and in so doing to permit or prohibit state "interference," appears arbitrary and chaotic. Yet at the time and for a period of fifty years, the Court earnestly pursued such an endeavor. It upheld state regulation of grain elevators, railroads, gas and electric companies, and other so-called public utilities, but overturned regulation of insurance (ALLEGYAR V. LOUISIANA, 1905); meatpacking businesses (*Wolff Packing Co.* v. *Industrial Court,* 1923); businesses selling theater tickets (*Tyson and Brother* v. *Banton,* 1927); gasoline prices (*Williams* v. *Standard Oil Co.* 1929); and the business of selling ice (*New State Ice Co.* v. *Liebmann,* 1932). It overturned state laws regulating the number of hours bakers could work, but upheld a law limiting the number of hours women could be employed.

But even where the Court found that the business was "affected with a public interest," it did not always defer to the legislature. The Court became a regulatory agency in that it sought to identify those conditions that would have to go into the establishment of a *reasonable* rate. Within a decade after MUNN, the Court became entangled in a long series of cases in which it was asked by railroads to void state laws that regulated rates they could charge customers. While the Court did not hold that regulation per se constituted an impairment of due process, it did insist on reviewing the regulations to determine if their substance was unreasonable. In effect, the Court and not the legislatures became the determiners of what a "fair return" was, and between the 1880s and the 1930s, one of the Court's major tasks was to supervise the rate-making authority of states, a task that involved developing "reasonable" formulas for determining the value of property, cost of operations, market value, replacement costs, likely effects from competition, and so forth. In *Smyth v. Ames,* 169 U.S. 466 (1898), the Court held that a regulated rate had to bring in a "fair return on fair valuation" of property, and in subsequent decisions it attempted to determine what a fair return was. In 1909, it indicated that 6 percent was fair, although subsequent decisions suggested that fair return would vary depending upon circumstances, competition, how property was valued, and the like.

Throughout this chapter of the Court's history, there remained a determined minority which, to paraphrase Justice Holmes, one of the most vigorous dissenters, argued that the Founding Fathers had not written any particular economic philosophy into the Constitution. The major argument of the dissenters during this period was that the Court's involvement in the area ran counter to democratic principles in that it only served to frustrate the views of the public as expressed through legislative majorities that had adopted such regulations. Additionally, these dissenters argued, the courts were not equipped to set rates, make intelligent decisions about reasonableness in setting prices, or judge what were acceptable returns on investments. These issues involved political judgments and technical knowledge best left to the political process and the experts called upon by the legislatures and regulatory commissions.

The cases included in this chapter only illustrate the approach and range of considerations faced by the Court during this important period in its history. The sweeping language of MUNN demonstrates that at one time (1877) the Court was prepared to give great deference to state legislatures and had no intention of breathing "substance" into the Fourteenth Amendment's Due Process Clause.

We have included two of the dozens of cases in which the Supreme Court invoked "liberty of contract" and "property rights" in holding that the Fourteenth Amendment's prohibition against denial of "life, liberty, or property without due process" had been violated by state regulations. In ALLGEYAR V. LOUISIANA, 165 U.S. 578 (1897), the Court invoked "liberty of contract" for the first time and used it to overturn a state law specifying conditions to be met before insurance companies could do business in the state and providing a penalty for those who did business with noncomplying out-of-state companies.

LOCHNER V. NEW YORK (1905) is perhaps the single best case to illustrate the Court's philosophy of substantive due process. It is particularly suited for this task because its dissenting opinion, authored by Justice Oliver Wendell Holmes, contains an eloquent expression of the opposing view. As you read these cases, contrast the views expressed by Holmes in dissent in LOCHNER with the majority's views in MUNN, decided twenty-eight years earlier, prior to the advent of substantive due process.

Contrast these two cases with the subsequent majority opinion in WEST COAST HOTEL CO. V. PARRISH (1937), an important case that announced the Court's intention of withdrawing from the enterprise of trying to assess the reasonableness of the substance of state regulation. This case, in effect, announced the Court's intention of granting legislative assemblies great leeway in pursuing the regulatory function.

MULLER V. OREGON (1908) is presented for several reasons. It is one of the small handful of pre-1937 cases in which the Court upheld a state regulation, here limitations on the number of hours women could work in a laundry. It was in this case that Louis Brandeis, then a Boston lawyer arguing in support of Oregon's regulation, marshalled evidence on the employment and health of women in the United States and abroad, to produce what has come to be known as the "Brandeis brief," the use of social science evidence to support a particular argument before the Court. Brandeis was successful here; the Court upheld the Oregon statute, and MULLER stands as something of an anomaly during this period. Can you distinguish the situation in LOCHNER from that in MULLER? Return to MULLER after you have read the cases in Chapter 11, and ask yourself whether the Court's reasoning in MULLER is any more or less enlightened than it is in LOCHNER.

We see in the period stretching from MUNN in 1877 to WEST COAST HOTEL in 1937 the rise and fall of the doctrine of substantive due process.

State Power and the Rise and Fall of Substantive Due Process

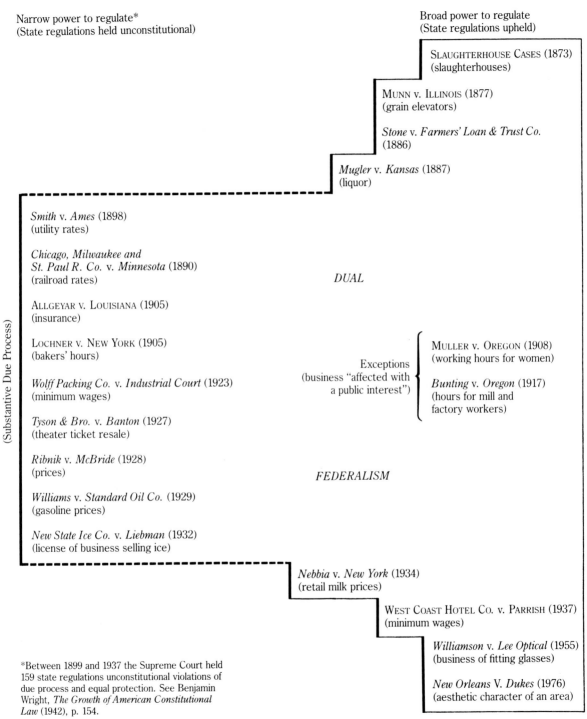

Narrow power to regulate*
(State regulations held unconstitutional)

Broad power to regulate
(State regulations upheld)

SLAUGHTERHOUSE CASES (1873)
(slaughterhouses)

MUNN v. ILLINOIS (1877)
(grain elevators)

Stone v. *Farmers' Loan & Trust Co.*
(1886)

Mugler v. *Kansas* (1887)
(liquor)

Smith v. *Ames* (1898)
(utility rates)

*Chicago, Milwaukee and
St. Paul R. Co.* v. *Minnesota* (1890)
(railroad rates)

ALLGEYAR v. LOUISIANA (1905)
(insurance)

LOCHNER v. NEW YORK (1905)
(bakers' hours)

Wolff Packing Co. v. *Industrial Court* (1923)
(minimum wages)

Tyson & Bro. v. *Banton* (1927)
(theater ticket resale)

Ribnik v. *McBride* (1928)
(prices)

Williams v. *Standard Oil Co.* (1929)
(gasoline prices)

New State Ice Co. v. *Liebman* (1932)
(license of business selling ice)

(Substantive Due Process)

DUAL

Exceptions
(business "affected with
a public interest")

MULLER v. OREGON (1908)
(working hours for women)

Bunting v. *Oregon* (1917)
(hours for mill and
factory workers)

FEDERALISM

Nebbia v. *New York* (1934)
(retail milk prices)

WEST COAST HOTEL CO. v. PARRISH (1937)
(minimum wages)

Williamson v. *Lee Optical* (1955)
(business of fitting glasses)

New Orleans V. *Dukes* (1976)
(aesthetic character of an area)

*Between 1899 and 1937 the Supreme Court held
159 state regulations unconstitutional violations of
due process and equal protection. See Benjamin
Wright, *The Growth of American Constitutional
Law* (1942), p. 154.

Constitutional Protection of Property **335**

While the Fourteenth Amendment and its Due Process Clause were adopted in 1868, the concept of due process is ancient, and in earlier cases (e.g., BARRON V. BALTIMORE, 1833), the Court had explicitly rejected the use of the Fifth Amendment's Due Process Clause as a limit on the substance of government regulation of business. This same position was repeated in 1877, in MUNN V. ILLINOIS. Thus the period in which the Court embraced the doctrine of substantive due process, roughly between 1880 and the sweeping decision in WEST COAST HOTEL CO., in 1937, can accurately be characterized as a period of deviation, a period in which the Court breathed novel and expansive meaning into traditional doctrine in an effort to curb mounting public pressure to restrain and regulate growing business enterprises. This period is charted on page 335.

To say that the Court has retreated from its concern with substantive due process does not mean that it has withdrawn entirely from the arena. Justifications for state regulation of business are couched in terms of state police power to regulate in the interests of the health, safety, and welfare of the public. And even though the Court has expanded on these categories to include aesthetics (in 1976, it upheld the authority of the City of New Orleans to regulate street vendors in the French Quarter in connection with its efforts to foster an aesthetic environment and attract tourists, *City of New Orleans* v. *Dukes*, 427 U.S. 297), these police powers remain as limitations or confining boundaries on state power to regulate business. The Court also continues to be concerned with reasonableness of such regulation, even if in a limited way. Thus, for instance, the Court is willing to overturn regulations if they are not reasonably related to the professed goals of the regulation, if they entail "invidious discrimination," or if they are "wholly arbitrary." See, for example, *Morey* v. *Doud*, 354 U.S. 457 (1957). What this suggests is that the concepts *substance* and *procedure* are neither hard and fast nor mutually exclusive. When they blend together, the

Court may be willing to inquire, although it is safe to say that the Court is extremely reluctant to sit as a superior legislature and judge the wisdom and desirability of legislative policy that affects the local economic sphere.

One must also understand the rise and fall of substantive due process in the context of the times and in light of the Supreme Court's work in other areas. The interested student is invited to trace the histories of shifts in the Court's interpretation of the Constitution's interstate commerce and taxing and spending provisions, presented in Chapters 3 and 4, to examine the parallels with the history of the Court's interpretations of the Due Process Clause in the Fourteenth Amendment.

Despite the Court's announced retreat from reviewing the substance of state legislation affecting property, the economy, and social welfare, the Court has never wholly abandoned its willingness to scrutinize carefully the substance of legislation. Indeed, in the 1930s even as the Court was announcing its deference to other branches, it was laying the groundwork for an activist stance with respect to reviewing legislation affecting individual rights and liberties. The explicit provisions in the Bill of Rights, which in the 1930s were being nationalized (see Chapter 6), helped spur this process. But this activism was given an independent base as the Court developed a philosophy of protecting "insular minorities" and other groups that owing to unpopularity and small numbers could not be expected to successfully pursue their cases with sufficient vigor in the electoral arena. These developments are charted in Chapters 10 and 11.

The Court's deference to the legislature when property and economic "interests" are involved led it to develop what is known as the "rational relation" test. Under it, the Court starts with the assumption that legislation bears some rational relation to a state's legitimate powers and places the burden on opponents to prove there is no conceivable rational relationship between the statute or regulation and a legitimate function of government. Not surprisingly, since 1937 almost all such challenges have failed.

In contrast in the area of individual rights and liberties, the Court has developed other tests that make it far easier to successfully challenge state action as unconstitutional. "Strict scrutiny" or "heightened scrutiny" tests are applied when legislation classifies people by race or impinges on "fundamental rights" such as those protected in the Bill of Rights. These tests assume that such regulations are impermissible and place the burden on the state to defend their use. If it cannot show a compelling reason, the provisions must fail. Few provisions can withstand this scrutiny.

This restraint in one area and activism in another has led many to complain that the Court has a double standard. In Chapters 10 and 11 we explore this issue at some length, including several theories that defend this double standard. Here, however, we want to note features of this complex issue that bear directly on the powers of states to exercise their police powers. There are those who argue that the distinction between economic or property interests on one hand and civil rights and liberties on the other is untenable and is more confusing than illuminating because it breaks down so often.

During the past fifty years most of the justices have defended this double standard, and none has advocated adoption of a firm single standard by which the constitutionality of *all* legislation could be assessed. As you will see in Chapters 10 and 11, the double standard remains intact, though surrounded with controversy. In recent years, and particularly with the advent of the Rehnquist Court, there has been some evidence that the Court is contracting its standards of review of "individual" rights and expanding its standards of review of governmental activities affecting economic policies and property interests. One such indication is a 1985 case, CITY OF CLEBURNE V. CLEBURNE LIVING CENTER, which involved a challenge to a city zoning ordinance that required a special use permit before a group home for the mentally

retarded could be established. Rejecting the argument that the mentally retarded are a "quasi-suspect class" in need of the protection of "heightened scrutiny," the Court treated the issue as a standard regulatory matter that should be judged by the "rationality" test. Using this test, it overturned the zoning ordinance, causing some to say that the decision paves the way for a return to substantive due process in economic and regulatory issues. Other recent developments (see the discussion of the "Takings" cases, below) indicate that the Court is becoming more concerned about protecting property interests. It remains to be seen how far these arguments will be carried.

The preceding discussion has assumed the distinction between individual rights and economic or property rights, one that is often made by both the Court and commentators. For the most part this distinction is asserted but not analyzed. However, Justice Stewart questioned the distinction and found it wanting in LYNCH V. HOUSEHOLD FINANCE CORP. (1972). After reading LYNCH, reread LOCHNER, ALLGEYAR, and the SLAUGHTERHOUSE CASES. And keep Justice Stewart's discussion in mind as you consider the issues raised in Chapters 7–11. Can you see how the logic in LYNCH might be extended in ways that would lead to a rethinking of issues thought settled since the 1930s? Is CLEBURNE a step in this direction?

A Note on the Takings Clause of the Fifth Amendment

The last clause of the Fifth Amendment, known as the Takings Clause or the Just Compensation Clause, states that private property shall not "be taken for public use, without just compensation." Governments have long been recognized to have the power of *eminent domain,* that is, to be able to take private property for public use. The Fifth Amendment acknowledges that power, but qualifies it. When title to property is transferred under the state's power of eminent domain, there is little question that this constitutes a "taking," although there may be continuing issues as to what constitutes "just compensation." In such instances, the Supreme Court has required that the decision be referred to a disinterested body and that owners have an opportunity to present arguments in behalf of their position.

However, there are many situations in which it is problematic whether in fact a taking has occurred. The issue is more problematic when we consider regulations that limit the use and may depreciate the value of property. If a legislature institutes price or rent controls, or similarly, if government builds a highway that affects property values, is the state, under the Takings Clause, required to compensate those who lose out? Generally, the Court has said no, that regulations affecting property values, even significantly, are not Fifth Amendment "takings." Indeed, the Court has held that the government may even designate a building as a "historic landmark" and impose on owners use and maintenance restrictions that affect the value of the property (*Penn Central Transportation Co.* v. *New York,* 438 U.S. 104, 1978).

However, the Court has recognized limits, and at times has ruled that even though title has not changed, government regulations amount to "takings" under the Fifth Amendment and require compensation. In addition to the *Penn Central* case, it has ruled that when airports have expanded their operations in ways that made adjacent land no longer suitable for its current use, this constitutes a taking that requires compensation.

Recently the Rehnquist Court has been even more aggressive in protecting property rights under the Takings Clause. During the October 1986 term, the Court handed down two major decisions broadening the meaning and scope of this provision. In *First English Evangelical Lutheran Church of Glendale* v. *Los Angeles,* 107 S.Ct. 2378 (1987), Justice Rehnquist, writing for the majority, gave a broad reading to the clause and upheld a church's claim that it had a right to sue for compensation after a "temporary" county ordinance

aimed at flood control had prohibited use of its property as a campground.

In another 1987 ruling, the Court overturned a condition imposed by the California Coastal Commission on the owners of a seafront lot who wanted to build a home (*Nollan* v. *California Coastal Commission,* 107 S.Ct. 3141, 1987). The Nollan's owned a slip of land between two public beaches, and as a condition of building a home on it the Commission required that they and other adjacent homeowners allow a public easement on their beachfront property to connect the two beaches. The Court held that this restriction on private property constituted a "taking" under the Fifth Amendment, and as the Nollan's were uncompensated it was unconstitutional. The Court began by noting that a government has the authority under its police powers to restrict land use, so long as the restrictions "substantially advance... legitimate state interests." It then reviewed a number of possible state interests, such as protecting the public's ability to view the seashore, access to the beaches from the highway, and preventing congestion on the beaches, and concluded that the walkway connecting the two beaches did not serve any of them. It went on to state that "it is quite impossible to understand how a requirement that people already on the public beaches be able to walk across the [Nollan's] property reduces any obstacles to viewing the beach created by the new house. It is also impossible to understand how it lowers any psychological barrier to using the public beaches, or how it helps to remedy any additional congestion on them caused by construction of the new houses." In short, the Court held that conditions cannot be placed on building permits unless the conditions advance the same interests that are affected by the construction being restricted. It is not enough that the condition simply advance *a* legitimate state interest. It must advance the *same* interest that the building affects. Since zoning ordinances and building permits have long been used to advance a variety of public interests, this decision is likely to have far-reaching ramifications for developers and municipal and state governments. Coupled with *Lutheran Church* v. *Los Angeles,* this decision will make it more costly for governments to regulate land use and correspondingly easier for developers to build.

In a 1989 case, *Allegheny Pittsburgh Coal Co.* v. *County Commission of Webster County,* 57 LW 4095, the Court ruled in favor of a company which claimed that a county's tax assessment practices violated the Equal Protection Clause. The county had assessed some property on the basis of its recent purchase price while it made only minor modifications to assessed values of property which had not been recently transferred. The result was gross disparity in assessments and taxes. The consequence, a unanimous Court held, was "intentional" and "systematic undervaluation" that "denies petitioner the equal protection of the law." Although the Court emphasized the gross and long-standing nature of the disparities and the fact that the local assessor's policies did not conform to state law, this case nevertheless opens the possibility that the Court may be willing to consider a host of other tax schemes under an equal protection analysis.

In CLEBURNE, *Lutheran Church,* and *Nollan Allegheny* we may be witnessing a return to the functional equivalent of substantive due process in economic regulation. Perhaps one reason these cases have been greeted with a somewhat subdued reaction is that in each instance they have involved "sympathetic" petitioners, who have challenged government regulations, supporters of the mentally retarded in CLEBURNE, and a church, a homeowner, and a company discriminated against by a cantankerous tax assessor in the other three cases. Still, these decisions have precedential ramifications well beyond these types of parties; together they constitute a significant step by the Court to strengthen the protections of property interests, which in an era of large-scale organizations means large corporations as well as homeowners and small businesses, against the power of the government to regulate and tax. This concern, it appears, may be the mission of the Court as it moves toward the turn of the century.

Cases

Calder v. Bull

3 Dallas 386 (1798)
Vote: Unanimous

Article I of the Constitution contains two prohibitions against *ex post facto* laws. The first, in Section 9, is a general statement applicable only to the national government. The second, in Section 10, is an express prohibition against the states' enacting *ex post facto* laws. At the time of the adoption of the Constitution, and during the period immediately after, many Federalists viewed these provisions as protections of economic interests against governmental interference. *Calder* v. *Bull* is the first important case involving the *ex post facto* provision, and the Court's interpretation here has remained intact since. As a consequence, the prohibition against *ex post facto* laws never emerged as defenses of property.

This case arose from a dispute between the Calder and Bull families over the interpretation of the will of Normand Morrison. Mr. Morrison's will was rejected by the Probate Court of Hartford, Connecticut, with the consequence that property the Bulls expected to receive was awarded to Calder and his wife. The Bulls continued to contest this action.

In the meantime, in 1795, the Connecticut legislature enacted a law dealing with issues raised in this controversy. Among other things, the new law allowed a new hearing to take place in such types of disputes. At the new hearing, which would not have been allowed under the old law, the probate court disregarded the earlier court decision and awarded the property to Bull rather than Calder. Calder brought suit and eventually took the case to the United States Supreme Court. He argued that the provision against *ex post facto* laws prohibited the court from holding a new hearing in this controversy because it had arisen *before* adoption of the new procedures. The Court rejected his position and allowed the new hearing.

The upshot of this case is that the *ex post facto* provision, in effect, is restricted only to criminal statutes.

[JUSTICE CHASE writing.]

The effect of the resolution or law of Connecticut above stated, is to revise a decision of one of its inferior courts, called the court of probate for Hartford, and to direct a new hearing of the case by the same court of probate that passed the decree against the will of Normand Morrison. By the existing law of Connecticut, a right to recover certain property had vested in Calder and wife (the appellants) in consequence of a decision of a court of justice, but, in virtue of a subsequent resolution or law, and the new hearing thereof, and the decision in consequence, this right to recover certain property was divested, and the right to the property declared to be in Bull and wife, the appellees. The sole inquiry is, whether this resolution or law of Connecticut, having such operation, is an *ex post facto* law, within the prohibition of the federal constitution?

. . . .

All the restrictions contained in the constitution of the United States on the power of the state legislatures, were provided in favor of the authority of the federal government. The prohibition against their making any *ex post facto* laws was introduced for greater caution, and very probably arose from the knowledge that the parliament of Great Britain claimed and exercised a power to pass such laws, under the denomination of bills of attainder, or bills of pains and penalties; the first inflicting capital, and the other less punishment. These acts were legislative judgments; and an exercise of judicial power. . . . With very few exceptions, the advocates of such laws were stimulated by ambition, or personal resentment and vindictive malice. To prevent such, and similar acts of violence and injustice, I believe, the

federal and state legislatures were prohibited from passing any bill of attainder, or any *ex post facto* law.

. . . .

I shall endeavor to show what law is to be considered an *ex post facto* law, within the words and meaning of the prohibition in the federal constitution. The prohibition, "that no State shall pass any *ex post facto* law," necessarily requires some explanation; for naked and without explanation it is unintelligible, and means nothing. Literally it is only that a law shall not be passed concerning, and after the fact, or thing done, or action committed. I would ask, what fact; of what nature or kind; and by whom done? That Charles I., king of England, was beheaded; that Oliver Cromwell was protector of England; that Louis XVI., late king of France, was guillotined; are all facts that have happened, but it would be nonsense to suppose that the States were prohibited from making any law after either of these events, and with reference thereto. The prohibition in the letter is not to pass any law concerning and after the fact, but the plain and obvious meaning and intention of the prohibition is this, that the legislatures of the several States shall not pass laws after a fact done by a subject, or citizen, which shall have relation to such fact, and shall punish him for having done it. The prohibition, considered in this light, is an additional bulwark in favor of the personal security of the subject, to protect his person from punishment by legislative acts, having a retrospective operation. I do not think it was inserted to secure the citizen in his private rights, of either property or contracts. The prohibitions not to make any thing but gold and silver coin a tender in payment of debts, and not to pass any law impairing the obligation of contracts, were inserted to secure private rights; but the restriction not to pass any *ex post facto* law, was to secure the person of the subject from injury or punishment, in consequence of such law. If the prohibition against making *ex post facto* laws was intended to secure personal rights from being affected or injured by such laws, and the prohibition is sufficiently extensive for that object, the other restraints I have enumerated were unnecessary, and therefore improper, for both of them are retrospective.

I will state what laws I consider *ex post facto* laws, within the words and the intent of the prohibition. 1st. Every law that makes an action done before the passing of the law, and which was innocent when done, criminal; and punishes such action. 2d. Every law that aggravates a crime, or makes it greater than it was, when committed. 3d. Every law that changes the punishment, and inflicts a greater punishment than the law annexed to the crime, when committed. 4th. Every law that alters the legal rules of evidence, and receives less or different testimony than the law required at the time of the commission of the offence, in order to convict the offender. All these and similar laws are manifestly unjust and oppressive. In my opinion, the true distinction is between *ex post facto* laws and retrospective laws. Every *ex post facto* law must necessarily be retrospective, but every retrospective law is not an *ex post facto* law; the former only are prohibited. Every law that takes away or impairs rights vested, agreeably to existing laws, is retrospective, and is generally unjust, and may be oppressive; and it is a good general rule that a law should have no retrospect; but there are cases in which laws may justly, and for the benefit of the community, and also of individuals, relate to a time antecedent to their commencement; as statutes of oblivion, or of pardon. They are certainly retrospective, and literally both concerning, and after, the facts committed. But I do not consider any law *ex post facto*, within the prohibition, that mollifies the rigor of the criminal law; but only those that create, or aggravate, the crime; or increase the punishment, or change the rules of evidence, for the purpose of conviction. Every law that is to have an operation before the making thereof, as to commence at an antecedent time, or to save time from the statute of limitations, or to excuse acts which were unlawful, and before committed, and the like, is retrospective. But such laws may be proper or necessary, as the case may be. There is a great and apparent difference between making an unlawful act lawful, and the making an innocent action criminal, and punishing it as a crime. The expressions *"ex post facto* laws" are technical; they had been in use long before the Revolution, and had acquired an appropriate meaning, by legislators, lawyers, and authors. The celebrated and judicious Sir William Blackstone, in his Commentaries, considers an *ex post facto* law precisely in the same light I have done. His opinion is confirmed by his successor, Mr. Wooddeson, and by the author of the Federalist, whom I esteem superior to both, for his extensive and accurate knowledge of the true principles of government.

I also rely greatly on the definition, or explanation of *ex post facto* laws, as given by the conventions of Massachusetts, Maryland, and North Carolina, in their several constitutions, or forms of government.

. . . .

I am of the opinion that the decree of the supreme court of errors of Connecticut be affirmed, with costs.

Judgement Affirmed.

[JUSTICES PATERSON, IREDELL, and CUSHING each wrote separate concurring opinions.]

Trustees of Dartmouth College v. Woodward

4 Wheaton 518 (1819)
Vote: 6–1

It was generally understood at the drafting of the Constitution that Article I's prohibition against "impairing the obligation of contracts" applied to personal, private agreements. Yet the first important cases dealing with this provision to reach the Supreme Court did not involve controversies over private business contracts but changes in conditions of legislative grants. In the case of *Fletcher* v. *Peck,* 6 Cranch 87 (1810), a case involving allegations of the corruption of a legislature, the Supreme Court held that a grant of land by a state legislature, once made, could not later be rescinded by that state's legislature. In his opinion for the Court, Chief Justice Marshall completely ignored claims that the grant arrangements had been effected through corrupt means. He wrote that when "a law is in its nature a contract, when absolute rights have vested under that contract, a repeal of the law cannot divest those rights."

This expansion of the meaning of the term *contract* and the absolutist interpretation given to it is seen even more clearly in *Dartmouth College.* Dartmouth College was chartered by the English Crown in 1769. The charter also created a Board of Trustees and authorized them to select a president and fill vacancies on the Board. During the early 1800s a rift grew between the college president, John Wheelock, and the Board of Trustees. The controversy came to a head in 1815, when the Federalist-oriented trustees removed Wheelock as president. In the following year, the Republican backers of the deposed president gained control of the New Hampshire legislature and enacted legislation that altered the conditions of the royal charter governing the administration of the college. Among other things, the new provisions gave the governor authority to appoint a majority of the Board that controlled the college. This new organization promptly reappointed Wheelock as president. The old trustees refused to accede to these new conditions and brought suit against the "new" university, in the form of a case against President Wheelock, the secretary and the treasurer of Dartmouth, who had sided with him, and the new trustees, all of whom had refused to relinquish college documents to the new Board.

The case worked its way up to the Supreme Court, where the young Daniel Webster, an alumnus of Dartmouth, argued against the reorganization imposed by the New Hampshire legislature, on the grounds that the new state reorganization constituted an unconstitutional abridgement of the right to contract. In its decision, written by Chief Justice Marshall, the Court held that a corporate charter is a contract that may not be altered by legislative enactment.

. . . The opinion of the court was delivered by MARSHALL, CH. JUSTICE.

. . . .

It can require no argument to prove, that the circumstances of this case constitute a contract. An application is made to the crown for a charter to incorporate a religious and literary institution. In the application, it is stated, that large contributions have been made for the object, which will be conferred on the corporation, as soon as it shall be created. The charter is granted, and on its faith the property is conveyed. Surely, in this transaction every ingredient of a complete and legitimate contract is to be found. The points for consideration are, 1. Is this contract protected by the constitution of the United States? 2. Is it impaired by the acts under which the defendant holds?

. . . .

. . . Dartmouth College is an eleemosynary institution, incorporated for the purpose of perpetuating the application of the bounty of the donors, to the specified objects of that bounty; that its trustees or governors were originally named by the founder, and invested with the power of perpetuating themselves; that they are not public officers, nor is it a civil institution, participating in the administration of government; but a charity-school, or a seminary of education, incorporated for the preservation of its property, and the perpetual application of that property to the objects of its creation.

Yet a question remains to be considered, of more real difficulty, on which more doubt has been entertained, than on all that have been discussed. The founders of the college, at least, those whose contributions were in money, have parted with the property bestowed upon it, and their representatives have no interest in that property. The donors of land are equally without interest, so long as the corporation shall exist. Could they be found, they are unaffected by any alteration in its constitution, and probably regardless of its form, or even of its existence. The students are fluctuating, and no individual among our youth has a vested interest in the institution, which can be asserted in a court of justice. Neither the founders of the college, nor the youth for whose benefit it was founded, complain of the alteration made in its charter, or think themselves injured by it. The trustees alone complain, and the trustees have no beneficial interest to be protected. Can this be such a contract, as the constitution intended to withdraw from the power of state legislation? Contracts, the parties to which have a vested beneficial interest, and those only, it has been said, are the objects about which the constitution is solicitous, and to which its protection is extended.

The court has bestowed on this argument the most deliberate consideration, and the result will be stated. Dr. Wheelock [the founder], acting for himself, and for those who, at his solicitation, had made contributions to his school, applied for this charter, as the instrument which should enable him, and them, to perpetuate their beneficent intention. It was granted. An artificial, immortal being, was created by the crown, capable of receiving and distributing forever, according to the will of the donors, the donations which should be made to it. On this being, the contributions which had been collected were immediately bestowed. These gifts were made, not indeed to make a profit for the donors, or their posterity, but for something, in their opinion, of inestimable value; for something which they deemed a full equivalent for the money with which it was purchased. The consideration for which they stipulated, is the perpetual application of the fund to its object, in the mode prescribed by themselves. Their descendants may take no interest in the preservation of this consideration. But in this respect their descendants are not their representatives; they are represented by the corporation. The corporation is the assignee of their rights, stands in their place, and distributes their bounty, as they would themselves have distributed it, had they been immortal. So, with respect to the students who are to derive learning from this source; the corporation is a trustee for them also. Their potential rights, which, taken distributively, are imperceptible, amount collectively to a most important interest. These are, in the aggregate, to be exercised, asserted and protected, by the corporation. They were as completely out of the donors, at the instant of their being vested in the corporation, and as incapable of being asserted by the students, as at present.

According to the theory of the British constitution, their parliament is omnipotent. To annul corporate rights might give a shock to public opinion, which that government has chosen to avoid; but its power is not questioned. Had parliament, immediately after the emanation of this charter, and the execution of those conveyances which followed it, annulled the instrument, so that the living donors would have witnessed the disappointment of their hopes, the perfidy of the transaction would have been universally acknowledged. Yet, then, as now, the donors would have no interest in the property; then, as now, those who might be students would have had no rights to be violated; then, as now, it might be said, that the trustees, in whom the rights of all were combined, possessed no private, individual, beneficial interests in the property confided to their protection. Yet the contract would, at that time, have been deemed sacred by all. What has since occurred, to strip it of its inviolability? Circumstances have not changed it. In reason, in justice, and in law, it is now, what it was in 1769.

This is plainly a contract to which the donors, the trustees and the crown (to whose rights and obligations New Hampshire succeeds) were the original parties. It is a contract made on a valuable consideration. It is a contract for the security and disposition of property. It is a contract, on the faith of which, real and personal estate has been conveyed to the corporation. It is, then, a contract within the letter of the constitution, and within its spirit also, unless the fact, that the property is invested by the donors in trustees, for the promotion of religion and education, for the benefit of persons who are perpetually changing, though the objects remain the same, shall create a particular exception, taking this case out of the prohibition contained in the constitution.

It is more than possible, that the preservation of rights of this description was not particularly in the view of the framers of the constitution, when the clause under consideration was introduced into that instrument. It is probable, that interferences of more frequent occurrence, to which the temptation was stronger, and of which the mischief was more extensive, constituted the great motive for imposing this restriction on the state legislatures. But although a particular and a rare case may not, in itself, be of sufficient magnitude to induce a rule, yet it must be governed by the rule, when established, unless some plain and strong reason for excluding it can be given. It is not enough to say, that this particular case was not in the mind of the convention, when the article was framed, nor of the American people, when it was adopted. It is necessary to go further, and to say that, had this particular case been suggested, the language would have been so varied,

as to exclude it, or it would have been made a special exception. The case being within the words of the rule, must be within its operation likewise, unless there be something in the literal construction, so obviously absurd or mischievous, or repugnant to the general spirit of the instrument, as to justify those who expound the constitution in making it an exception.

On what safe and intelligible ground, can this exception stand? There is no expression in the constitution, no sentiment delivered by its contemporaneous expounders, which would justify us in making it. In the absence of all authority of this kind, is there, in the nature and reason of the case itself, that which would sustain a construction of the constitution, not warranted by its words? Are contracts of this description of a character to excite so little interest, that we must exclude them from the provisions of the constitution, as being unworthy of the attention of those who framed the instrument? Or does public policy so imperiously demand their remaining exposed to legislative alteration, as to compel us, or rather permit us, to say, that these words, which were introduced to give stability to contracts, and which in their plain import comprehend this contract, must yet be so construed as to exclude it?

Almost all eleemosynary corporations, those which are created for the promotion of religion, of charity or of education, are of the same character. The law of this case is the law of all. . . .

The opinion of the court, after mature deliberation, is, that this is a contract, the obligation of which cannot be impaired, without violating the constitution of the United States. This opinion appears to us to be equally supported by reason, and by the former decisions of this court.

2. We next proceed to the inquiry, whether its obligation has been impaired by those acts of the legislature of New Hampshire, to which the special verdict refers?

. . . .

It has been already stated, that the act "to amend the charter, and enlarge and improve the corporation of Dartmouth College," increases the number of trustees to twenty-one, gives the appointment of the additional members to the executive of the state, and creates a board of overseers, to consist of twenty-five persons, of whom twenty-one are also appointed by the executive of New Hampshire, who have power to inspect and control the most important acts of the trustees.

On the effect of this law, two opinions cannot be entertained. Between acting directly, and acting through the agency of trustees and overseers, no essential difference is perceived. The whole power of governing the college is transferred from trustees, appointed according to the will of the founder, expressed in the charter, to the executive of New Hampshire. The management and application of the funds of this eleemosynary institution, which are placed by the donors in the hands of trustees named in the charter, and empowered to perpetuate themselves, are placed by this act under the control of the government of the state. The will of the state is substituted for the will of the donors, in every essential operation of the college. This is not an immaterial change. The founders of the college contracted, not merely for the perpetual application of the funds which they gave, to the objects for which those funds were given; they contracted also, to secure that application by the constitution of the corporation. They contracted for a system, which should, so far as human foresight can provide, retain forever the government of the literary institution they had formed, in the hands of persons approved by themselves. This system is totally changed. The charter of 1769 exists no longer. It is re-organized; and re-organized in such a manner, as to convert a literary institution, moulded according to the will of its founders, and placed under the control of private literary men, into a machine entirely subservient to the will of government. This may be for the advantage of this college in particular, and may be for the advantage of literature in general; but it is not according to the will of the donors, and is subversive of that contract, on the faith of which their property was given.

. . . .

It results from this opinion, that the acts of the legislature of New Hampshire, which are stated in the special verdict found in this cause, are repugnant to the constitution of the United States; and that the judgment on this special verdict ought to have been for the plaintiffs. The judgment of the state court must, therefore, be reversed.

[JUSTICES WASHINGTON and JOHNSON wrote separate concurring opinions. JUSTICE DUVALL dissented.]

Charles River Bridge Co. v. Warren Bridge Co.

11 Peters 420 (1837)
Vote: 4–3

In 1785 the Massachusetts legislature enacted a statute that incorporated the Charles River Bridge Co. and authorized the company to build and maintain a toll bridge for profit on condition that it pay Harvard College a fixed term per annum in return for the college's agreeing not to insist on its exclusive right to operate a ferry at the same location, which had been granted to Harvard in 1650. In 1792 these conditions were extended for seventy years. However, in 1828 the Massachusetts legislature incorporated the Warren Bridge Co. and authorized construction of a second bridge near the first. This bridge was to charge tolls until the costs of its construction were recouped; then it was to become a free bridge. This clearly would have meant financial ruin for the Charles River Bridge Co. The Charles River Bridge Co. asked a court to issue an injunction prohibiting construction of the second bridge. It lost, and as the bridge was being built the case wound its way to the Supreme Court, where attorneys for the Charles River Bridge Co. urged the court to consider the charters of 1785 and 1792 in light of the royal charter of 1650, which had given Harvard College exclusive right to maintain a ferry "in that line of travel."

TANEY, C. J., delivered the opinion of the court.

The questions involved in this case are of the gravest character, and the court have given to them the most anxious and deliberate consideration. . . .

. . . .

. . . [U]pon what ground can the plaintiffs in error contend that the ferry rights of the college have been transferred to the proprietors of the bridge? If they have been thus transferred, it must be by some mode of transfer known to the law; and the evidence relied on to prove it can be pointed out in the record. How was it transferred? It is not suggested that there ever was, in point of fact, a deed of conveyance executed by the college to the bridge company. . . . The ferry, with all its privileges was intended to be forever at an end, and a compensation in money was given in lieu of it. The college acquiesced in this arrangement, and there is proof, in the record, that it was all done with their consent. Can a deed of assignment to the bridge company which would keep alive the ferry rights in their hands, be presumed under such circumstances? . . .

This brings us to the act of the legislature of Massachusetts, of 1785, by which the plaintiffs were incorporated by the name of "The Proprietors of the Charles River Bridge," and it is here, and in the law of 1792, prolonging their charter, that we must look for the extent and nature of the franchise conferred upon the plaintiffs. . . .

 . . . .

 . . . The object and end of all government is to promote the happiness and prosperity of the community by which it is established; and it can never be assumed, that the government intended to diminish its power of accomplishing the end for which it was created. And in a country like ours, free, active, and enterprising, continually advancing in numbers and wealth, new channels of communication are daily found necessary, both for travel and trade; and are essential to the comfort, convenience, and prosperity of the people. A State ought never to be presumed to surrender this power, because, like the taxing power, the whole community have an interest in preserving it undiminished. And when a corporation alleges, that a State has surrendered for seventy years, its power of improvement and public accommodation, in a great and important line of travel, along which a vast number of its citizens must daily pass; the community have a right to insist, in the language of this court above quoted, "that its abandonment ought not to be presumed, in a case, in which the deliberate purpose of the State to abandon it does not appear." The continued existence of a government would be of no great value, if by implications and presumptions, it was disarmed of the powers necessary to accomplish the ends of its creation; and the functions it was designed to perform, transferred to the hands of privileged corporations. The rule of construction announced by the court, was not confined to the taxing power; nor is it so limited in the opinion delivered. On the contrary, it was distinctly placed on the ground that the interests of the community were concerned in preserving, undiminished, the power then in question; and whenever any power of the State is said to be surrendered or diminished, whether it be the taxing power or any other affecting the public interest, the same principle applies, and the rule of construction must be the same. No one will question that the interests of the great body of the people of the State, would, in this instance, be affected by the surrender of this great line of travel to a single corporation, with the right to exact toll, and exclude competition for seventy years. While the rights of private property are sacredly guarded, we must not forget that the community also have rights, and that the happiness and well being of every citizen depends on their faithful preservation.

Adopting the rule of construction above stated as the settled one, we proceed to apply it to the charter of 1785, to the proprietors of the Charles River Bridge. This act of incorporation is in the usual form, and the privileges such as are commonly given to corporations of that kind. It confers on them the ordinary faculties of a corporation, for the purpose of building the bridge; and establishes certain rates of toll, which the company are authorized to take. This is the whole grant. There is no exclusive privilege given to them over the waters of Charles River, above or below their bridge. No right to erect another bridge themselves, nor to prevent other persons from erecting one. No engagement from the State that another shall not be erected; and no undertaking not to sanction competition, nor to make improvements that may diminish the amount of its income.

Upon all these subjects the charter is silent; and nothing is said in it about a line of travel, so much insisted on in the argument, in which they are to have exclusive privileges. No words are used, from which an intention to grant any of these rights can be inferred. If the plaintiff is entitled to them, it must be implied, simply, from the nature of the grant; and cannot be inferred from the words by which the grant is made.

The relative position of the Warren Bridge has already been described. It does not interrupt the passage over the Charles River Bridge, nor make the way to it or from it less convenient. None of the faculties or franchises granted to that corporation have been revoked by the legislature, and its right to take the tolls granted by the charter remains unaltered. In short, all the franchises and rights of property enumerated in the charter, and there mentioned to have been granted to it, remain unimpaired. But its income is destroyed by the Warren Bridge; which, being free, draws off the passengers and property which would have gone over it, and renders their franchise of no value. This is the gist of the complaint. For it is not pretended that the erection of the Warren Bridge would have done them any injury, or in any degree affected their right of property, if it had not diminished the amount of their tolls. In order then to entitle themselves to relief, it is necessary to show that the legislature contracted not to do the act of which they complain, and that they impaired, or, in other words, violated that contract by the erection of the Warren Bridge.

The inquiry then is, Does the charter contain such a contract on the part of the State? Is there any such stipulation to be found in that instrument? It must be admitted on all hands that there is none, — no words that even relate to another bridge, or to the diminution of their tolls, or to the line of travel. If a contract on that subject can be gathered from the charter, it must be by implication, and cannot be found in the words used. Can such an agreement be implied? The rule of construction before stated is an answer to the question. In charters of this description, no rights are taken from the public, or given to the corporation, beyond those which the words of the charter, by their natural and proper construction, purport to convey. There are no words which import such a contract as the plaintiffs in error contend for, and none can be implied. . . . The whole community are interested in this inquiry, and they have a right to require that the power of promoting their comfort and convenience, and of advancing the public prosperity, by providing safe, convenient, and cheap ways for the transportation of produce and the purposes of travel, shall not be construed to have been surrendered or diminished by the State, unless it shall appear by plain words that it was intended to be done.

. . . .

Indeed, the practice and usage of almost every State in the Union old enough to have commenced the work of internal improvement, is opposed to the doctrine contended for on the part of the plaintiffs in error. Turnpike roads have been made in succession on the same line of travel; the later ones interfering materially with the profits of the first. These corporations have, in some instances, been utterly ruined by the introduction of newer and better modes of transportation and travelling. In some cases, railroads have rendered the turnpike roads on the same line of travel so entirely useless, that the franchise of the turnpike corporation is not worth preserving. Yet in none of these cases have the corporation supposed that their privileges were invaded, or any contract violated on the part of the State. . . .

And what would be the fruits of this doctrine of implied contracts on the part of the States, and of property in a line of travel by a corporation, if it should now be sanctioned by this court? . . . We shall be thrown back to the improvements of the last century, and obliged to stand still. . . . This court are not prepared to sanction principles which must lead to such results.

. . . .

The judgment of the supreme judicial court of the commonwealth of Massachusetts, dismissing the plaintiffs' bill, must, therefore, be affirmed, with costs.

[JUSTICES McLEAN, STORY, and THOMPSON dissented.]

Home Building and Loan Association v. Blaisdell

290 U.S. 398 (1934)
Vote: 5–4

We saw in the CHARLES RIVER BRIDGE case a limit on the Court's willingness to expand the scope of coverage of the Contract Clause. In his opinion, Justice Taney relied primarily on the argument that contracts required a strict reading and that the Court would not accept provisions that were only implied. This led him to conclude that the Charles River Bridge Co. was not entitled to the monopoly it sought. There was another thrust to Taney's argument as well. He also raised the issue of public concern, arguing that the Court must interpret ambiguous provisions of charters and contracts in such a manner as to benefit the community rather than private parties. This dictum, recognizing as it does a need for state police power, was seized and enlarged upon by subsequent decisions, most notably in *Stone* v. *Mississippi*, 101 U.S. 814 (1879), in which the Supreme Court upheld a section in the new Mississippi constitution that prohibited lotteries, a provision in direct conflict with a law authorizing the creation of a lottery two years earlier, prior to adoption of the new constitution. In its opinion the Supreme Court upheld the antilottery provision of the new constitution on the grounds that no legislature can bargain away the future police power of a state. Thus the basis for state authority to rescind prior contractual arrangements it had entered into was expanded.

In the case included below, the Supreme Court goes still further and appears to drive a stake through the heart of the Contract Clause in so far as it is meant to serve as a limit on state police powers. Handed down in the midst of the Great Depression, this decision upheld the state's authority to enact a law providing for a two-year moratorium on the foreclosure of real estate mortgages, in an effort to protect homeowners and owners of small businesses. Still, the Court went out of its way to note the extreme circumstances that prevailed at the time and the limited nature of the relief, suggesting that it would not automatically uphold all legislation that altered conditions of contracts.

This controversy arose as a result of the Minnesota Moratorium Law of 1933, which provided that owners of homes and small businesses who were unable to pay a mortgage could petition the court for a moratorium from foreclosure for a period of up to two years. Blaisdell, who had a mortgage with the Home Building and Loan Association, was unable to meet his mortgage payment. As a consequence, the association foreclosed on him and prepared to sell his land. Blaisdell sought to prevent this under the provision of the Mortgage Moratorium Law. The Minnesota Supreme Court upheld his claim, and the Home Building and Loan Association appealed to the U.S. Supreme Court.

MR. CHIEF JUSTICE HUGHES delivered the opinion of the Court.

Appellant contests the validity of . . . the Minnesota Mortgage Moratorium Law, as being repugnant to the contract clause (article 1, §10) and the due process and equal protection clauses of the Fourteenth Amendment of the Federal Constitution. The statute was sustained by the Supreme Court of Minnesota . . . and the case comes here on appeal.

The act provides that, during the emergency declared to exist, relief may be had through authorized judicial proceedings with respect to foreclosures of mortgages, and execution sales, of real estate; that sales may be postponed and periods of redemption may be extended. The act does not apply to mortgages subsequently made nor to those made previously which shall be extended for a period ending more than a year after the passage of the act (part 1, §8). There are separate provisions in part 2 relating to homesteads, but these are to apply "only to cases not entitled to relief under some valid provision of Part One." The act is to remain in effect "only during the continuance of the emergency and in no event beyond May 1, 1935." No extension of the period for redemption and no postponement of sale is to be allowed which would have the effect of extending the period of redemption beyond that date. . . . We are here concerned with the provisions of part 1, §4,

authorizing the district court of the county to extend the period of redemption from foreclosure sales "for such additional time as the court may deem just and equitable," subject to the above-described limitation. The extension is to be made upon application to the court, on notice, for an order determining the reasonable value of the income on the property involved in the sale, or, if it has no income, then the reasonable rental value of the property, and directing the mortgagor "to pay all or a reasonable part of such income or rental value, in or toward the payment of taxes, insurance, interest, mortgage . . . indebtedness at such times and in such manner" as shall be determined by the court. . . .

. . . Appellees applied to the district court of Hennepin county for an order extending the period of redemption from a foreclosure sale. Their petition stated that they owned a lot in Minneapolis which they had mortgaged to appellant; that the mortgage contained a valid power of sale by advertisement, and that by reason of their default the mortgage had been foreclosed and sold to appellant on May 2, 1932 for $3700.98; that appellant was the holder of the sheriff's certificate of sale; that, because of the economic depression, appellees had been unable to obtain a new loan or to redeem, and that, unless the period of redemption were extended, the property would be irretrievably lost; and that the reasonable value of the property greatly exceeded the amount due on the mortgage, including all liens, costs, and expenses.

. . . [T]he court found that the time to redeem would expire on May 2, 1933, under the laws of the state as they were in effect when the mortgage was made and when it was foreclosed. . . .

The court entered its judgment extending the period of redemption to May 1, 1935, subject to the condition that the appellees should pay to the appellant $40 a month through the extended period from May 2, 1933; that is, that in each of the months of August, September, and October, 1933, the payments should be $80, in two installments, and thereafter $10 a month, all these amounts to go to the payment of taxes, insurance, interest, and mortgage indebtedness. It is this judgment, sustained by the Supreme Court of the state on the authority of its former opinion, which is here under review.

The state court upheld the statute as an emergency measure. Although conceding that the obligations of the mortgage contract were impaired, the court decided that what it thus described as an impairment was, notwithstanding the contract clause of the Federal Constitution, within the police power of the state as that power was called into exercise by the public economic emergency which the Legislature had found to exist. . . .

. . . .

In determining whether the provision for this temporary and conditional relief exceeds the power of the state by reason of the clause in the Federal Constitution prohibiting impairment of the obligations of contracts, we must consider the relation of emergency to constitutional power, the historical setting of the contract clause, the development of the jurisprudence of this Court in the construction of that clause, and the principles of construction which we may consider to be established.

Emergency does not create power. Emergency does not increase granted power or remove or diminish the restrictions imposed upon power granted or reserved. The Constitution was adopted in a period of grave emergency. Its grants of power to the federal government and its limitations of the power of the States were determined in the light of emergency, and they are not altered by emergency. What power was thus granted and what limitations were thus imposed are questions which have always been, and always will be, the subject of close examination under our constitutional system.

While emergency does not create power, emergency may furnish the occasion for the exercise of power. "Although an emergency may not call into life a power which has never lived, nevertheless emergency may afford a reason for the exertion of a living power already enjoyed." *Wilson* v. *New,* 243 U.S. 332 [1917]. . . . The constitutional question presented in the light of an emergency is whether the power possessed embraces the particular exercise of it in response to particular conditions. Thus, the war power of the federal government is not created by the emergency of war, but it is a power given to meet that emergency. It is a power to wage war successfully, and thus it permits the harnessing of the entire energies of the people in a supreme cooperative effort to preserve the nation. But even the war power does not remove constitutional limitations safeguarding essential liberties. When the provisions of the Constitution, in grant or restriction, are specific, so particularized as not to admit of construction, no question is presented. Thus, emergency would not permit a state to have more than two Senators in the Congress, or permit the election of President by a general popular vote without regard to the number of electors to which the States are respectively entitled, or permit the States to "coin money" or to "make anything but gold and silver coin a tender in payment of debts." But, where constitutional grants and limitations of power are set forth in general clauses, which afford a broad outline, the process of construction is essential to fill in the details. That is true of the contract clause. . . .

. . . .

Not only is the constitutional provision qualified by the measure of control which the state retains over remedial processes, but the state also continues to possess authority to safeguard the vital interests of its people. . . . Not only are existing laws read into contracts in order to fix obligations as between the parties, but the reservation of essential attributes of sovereign power is also read into contracts as a postulate of the legal order. The policy of protecting contracts against impairment presupposes the maintenance of a government by virtue of which contractual relations are worthwhile, — a government which retains adequate authority to secure the peace and good order of society. This principle of harmonizing the constitutional prohibition with the necessary residuum of state power has had progressive recognition in the decisions of this Court.

While the charters of private corporations constitute contracts, a grant of exclusive privilege is not to be implied as against the state. *Charles River Bridge* v. *Warren Bridge,* [1837]. And all contracts are subject to the right of eminent domain. *West River Bridge* v. *Dix,* [1848]. The reservation of this necessary authority of the state is deemed to be a part of the contract. In the case last cited, the Court answered the forcible challenge of the state's power by the following statement of the controlling principle, a statement reiterated by this Court speaking through Mr. Justice Brewer, nearly fifty years later, in *Long Island Water Supply Co.* v. *Brooklyn,* [1897]. "But into all contracts, whether made between states and individuals or between individuals only, there enter conditions which arise, not out of the literal terms of the contract itself. They are superinduced by the pre-existing and higher authority of the laws of nature, of nations, or of the community to which the parties belong. They are always presumed, and must be presumed, to be known and recognized by all, are binding upon all, and need never, therefore, be carried into express stipulation, for this could add nothing to their force. Every contract is made in subordination to them, and must yield to their control, as conditions inherent and paramount, wherever a necessity for their execution shall occur."

. . . .

The argument is pressed that in the cases we have cited the obligation of contracts was affected only incidentally. This argument proceeds upon a misconception. The question is not whether the legislative action affects contracts incidentally, or directly or indirectly, but whether the legislation is addressed to a legitimate end and the measures taken are reasonable and appropriate to that end. Another argument, which comes more closely to the point, is that the state power may be addressed directly to the prevention of the enforcement of contracts only when these are of a sort which the Legislature in its discretion may denounce as being in themselves hostile to public morals, or public health, safety, or welfare, or where the prohibition is merely of injurious practices; that interference with the enforcement of other and valid contracts according to appropriate legal procedure, although the interference is temporary and for a public purpose, is not permissible. This is but to contend that in the latter case the end is not legitimate in the view that it cannot be reconciled with a fair interpretation of the constitutional provision.

Undoubtedly, whatever is reserved of state power must be consistent with the fair intent of the constitutional limitation of that power. The reserved power cannot be construed so as to destroy the limitation, nor is the limitation to be construed to destroy the reserved power in its essential aspects. They must be construed in harmony with each other. This principle precludes a construction which would permit the state to adopt as its policy the repudiation of debts or the destruction of contracts or the denial of means to enforce them. But it does not follow that conditions may not arise in which a temporary restraint of enforcement may be consistent with the spirit and purpose of the constitutional provision and thus be found to be within the range of the reserved power of the state to protect the vital interests of the community. It cannot be maintained that the constitutional prohibition should be so construed as to prevent limited and temporary interpositions with respect to the enforcement of contracts if made necessary by a great public calamity such as fire, flood, or earthquake. . . . The reservation of state power appropriate to such extraordinary conditions may be deemed to be as much a part of all contracts as is the reservation of state power to protect the public interest in the other situations to which we have referred. And, if state power exists to give temporary relief from the enforcement of contracts in the presence of disasters due to physical causes such as fire, flood, or earthquake, that power cannot be said to be nonexistent when the urgent public need demanding such relief is produced by other and economic causes.

. . . .

It is manifest from this review of our decisions that there has been a growing appreciation of public needs and of the necessity of finding ground for a rational compromise between individual rights and public welfare. The settlement and consequent contraction of the public domain, the pressure of a constantly increasing density of population, the interrelation of the activities of our people and the complexity of our economic interests, have inevitably led to an increased use of the organization of society in order to protect the very bases of individual opportunity. Where, in earlier days, it was thought that only the concerns of individuals or of classes were involved, and that those of the state itself were touched only remotely, it has later been found that the fundamental interests of the state are directly affected; and that the question is no longer merely that of one party to a contract as against another, but of the use of reasonable means to safeguard the economic structure upon which the good of all depends.

It is no answer to say that this public need was not apprehended a century ago, or to insist that what the provision of the Constitution meant to the vision of that day it must mean to the vision of our time. If by the statement that what the Constitution meant at the time of its adoption it means today, it is intended to say that the great clauses of the Constitution must be confined to the interpretation which the framers, with the conditions and outlook of their time, would have placed upon them, the statement carries its own refutation. It was to guard against such a narrow conception that Chief Justice Marshall uttered the memorable warning: "We must never forget, that it is a *constitution* we are expounding" (*McCulloch* v. *Maryland,* 4 Wheat. 316, [1819]); "a constitution intended to endure for ages to come, and, consequently, to be adapted to the various *crises* of human affairs." . . . The case before us must be considered in the light of our whole experience and not merely in that of what was said a hundred years ago."

Nor is it helpful to attempt to draw a fine distinction between the intended meaning of the words of the Constitution and their intended application. . . . The vast body of law which has been developed was unknown to the fathers, but it is believed to have preserved the essential content and the spirit of the Constitution. With a growing recognition of public needs and the relation of individual right to public security, the court has sought to prevent the perversion of the clause through its use as an instrument to throttle the capacity of the states to protect their fundamental interests. This development is a growth from the seeds which the fathers planted. . . .

Applying the criteria established by our decisions, we conclude:

1. An emergency existed in Minnesota which furnished a proper occasion for the exercise of the reserved power of the state to protect the vital interests of the community. The declarations of the existence of this emergency by the Legislature and by the Supreme Court of Minnesota cannot be regarded as a subterfuge or as lacking in adequate basis. . . . The finding of the Legislature and state court has support in the facts of which we take judicial notice. . . .

2. The legislation was addressed to a legitimate end; that is, the legislation was not for the mere advantage of particular individuals but for the protection of a basic interest of society.

3. In view of the nature of the contracts in question — mortgages of unquestionable validity — the relief afforded and justified by the emergency. . . .

4. The conditions upon which the period of redemption is extended do not appear to be unreasonable. . . .

5. The legislation is temporary in operation. It is limited to the exigency which called it forth. . . .

Judgment affirmed.

[JUSTICE SUTHERLAND wrote a dissent in which JUSTICES VAN DEVANTER, MCREYNOLDS, and BUTLER concurred.]

United States Trust Co. of New York v. State of New Jersey

431 U.S. 1 (1977)
Vote: 4–3; two not participating.

Since the Court's decision in HOME BUILDING AND LOAN ASSOCIATION V. BLAISDELL (1934), the so-called *Minnesota Moratorium* case, it has commonly been assumed that the Contract Clause no longer stood as any serious limitation on the power of government, and this view has been reinforced by several Supreme Court opinions since. Yet constitutional provisions have long lives, and doctrines once out of favor have ways of reasserting themselves. Something of this sort appears to be occurring with respect to the Contract Clause. Once thought to be all but dead, recent court decisions and renewed academic interest in the topic suggests that it may emerge once again as a meaningful provision of the Constitution.

In a 1965 case, *El Paso* v. *Simmons,* the Court upheld a state law modifying conditions of a purchase agreement, but went on to note that "the power of a State to modify or affect the obligation of contract is not without limit." That decision occasioned a vigorous dissent by Justice Black, who argued,

I have previously had a number of occasions to dissent from judgments of this Court balancing away the First Amendment's unequivocally guaranteed rights of free speech, press, assembly and petition. In this case I am compelled to dissent from the Court's balancing away the plain guarantee of Article I, §10, that "No State shall . . . pass any . . . Law impairing the Obligation of Contracts . . . ," a balancing which results in the State of Texas taking a man's private property for public use without compensation in violation of the equally plain guarantee of the Fifth Amendment, made applicable to the States by the Fourteenth, that ". . . private property [shall not] be taken for public use, without just compensation."

Justice Black's dissent may have gained some supporters among new members of the Court, for in 1977, in the case reprinted below, the Court, with four justices appointed since *El Paso* siding all together in the majority, found a violation of the Contract Clause. If the Court's opinion did not embrace Justice Black's absolutist language, it did serve to remind us that the Contract Clause is still alive, and in so doing suggest that it *may* once again become a protean force in American constitutional law.

The circumstances giving rise to this case are as follows: In 1921 the states of New York and New Jersey established the Port Authority of New York and New Jersey by bistate compact in order "to effectuate a better coordination of facilities of commerce in the Port of New York." Since then it has engaged in numerous projects and public works. In 1962 both states enacted laws authorizing the Authority to build and acquire a railroad. A provision of these laws specified that so long as any bonds issued by the Authority to finance this project remained outstanding and unpaid, neither state nor the Authority could use for other than well-defined and permitted purposes any revenue pledged as security for those bonds without the consent of all holders of the bonds.

In 1973 and 1974 both states enacted legislation which in effect repealed the 1962 covenant, as part of the Port Authority's wide-ranging new program to deal with the energy crisis and conserve fuel. Among those provisions affected was the prohibition against using revenue pledged as surety without prior approval. As a consequence, a holder of Port Authority bonds, the United States Trust Co. of New York, brought suit in a New Jersey state court challenging the constitutionality of that state's new law repealing the 1962 covenant. The trial court upheld the New Jersey law, and this was reaffirmed by the Supreme Court of New Jersey, whereupon United States Trust appealed to the U.S. Supreme Court.

MR. JUSTICE BLACKMUN delivered the opinion of the Court.

This case presents a challenge to a New Jersey statute . . . as violative of the Contract Clause of the United States Constitution. That statute, together with a concurrent and parallel New York statute, . . . repealed a statutory covenant made by the two States in 1962 that had limited the ability of The Port Authority of New York and New Jersey to subsidize rail passenger transportation from revenues and reserves.

. . . .

II

At the time the Constitution was adopted, and for nearly a century thereafter, the Contract Clause was one of the few express limitations on state power. The many decisions of this Court involving the Contract Clause are evidence of its important place in our constitutional jurisprudence. Over the last century, however, the Fourteenth Amendment has assumed a far larger place in constitutional adjudication concerning the States. We feel that the present role of the Contract Clause is largely illuminated by two of this Court's decisions. In each, legislation was sustained despite a claim that it had impaired the obligations of contracts.

Home Building & Loan Assn. v. *Blaisdell,* . . . (1934), is regarded as the leading case in the modern era of Contract Clause interpretation. At issue was the Minnesota Mortgage Moratorium Law, enacted in 1933, during the depth of the Depression and when that State was under severe economic stress, and appeared to have no effective alternative. The statute was a temporary measure that allowed judicial extension of the time for redemption; a mortgagor who remained in possession during the extension period was required to pay a reasonable income or rental value to the mortgagee. A closely divided Court, in an opinion by Mr. Chief Justice Hughes, observed that "emergency may furnish the occasion for the exercise of power" and that the "constitutional question presented in the light of an emergency is whether the power possessed embraces the particular exercise of it in response to particular conditions." . . . It noted that the debates in the Constitutional Convention were of little aid in the construction of the Contract Clause, but that the general purpose of the Clause was clear: to encourage trade and credit by promoting confidence in the stability of contractual obligations. . . . Nevertheless, a State "continues to possess authority to safeguard the vital interests of its people. . . . This principle of harmonizing the constitutional prohibition with the necessary residuum of state power has had progressive recognition in the decisions of this Court." . . . The great clauses of the Constitution are to be considered in the light of our whole experience, and not merely as they would be interpreted by its Framers in the conditions and with the outlook of their time. . . .

This Court's most recent Contract Clause decision is *El Paso* v. *Simmons,* 379 U.S. 497 (1965). That case concerned a 1941 Texas statute that limited to a 5-year period the reinstatement rights of an interest-defaulting purchaser of land from the State. For many years prior to the enactment of that statute, such a defaulting purchaser, under Texas law, could have reinstated his claim to the land upon written request and payment of delinquent interest, unless rights of third parties had intervened. This Court held that "it is not every modification of a contractual promise that impairs the obligation of contract under federal law." . . . It observed that the State "has the 'sovereign right . . . to protect the . . . general welfare of the people'" and "'we must respect the "wide discretion on the part of the legislature in determining what is and what is not necessary,"'" . . . quoting *East New York Savings Bank* v. *Hahn,* 326 U.S. 230 . . . (1945). The Court recognized that "the power of a State to modify or affect the obligation of contract is not without limit," but held that "the objects of the Texas statute make abundantly clear that it impairs no protected right under the Contract Clause."...

Both of these cases eschewed a rigid application of the Contract Clause to invalidate state legislation. Yet neither indicated that the Contract Clause was without meaning in modern constitutional jurisprudence, or that its limitation on state power was illusory. Whether or not the protection of contract rights comports with current views of wise public policy, the Contract Clause remains a part of our written Constitution. We therefore must attempt to apply that constitutional provision to the instant case with due respect for its purpose and the prior decisions of this Court.

III

We first examine appellant's general claim that repeal of the 1962 covenant impaired the obligation of the States' contract with the bondholders. It long has been established that the Contract Clause limits the power of the States to modify their own contracts as well as to regulate those between private parties.... Yet the Contract Clause does not prohibit the States from repealing or amending statutes generally, or from enacting legislation with retroactive effects. Thus, as a preliminary matter, appellant's claim requires a determination that the repeal has the effect of impairing a contractual obligation. [The Court then reviewed the history of the 1962 legislative covenant and the effects of the 1973 repeal and, agreeing with the trial court, concluded that the "repeal impaired a contractual obligation of the states...."]

IV

. . . .

The States must possess broad power to adopt general regulatory measures without being concerned that private contracts will be impaired, or even destroyed, as a result. Otherwise, one would be able to obtain immunity from state regulation by making private contractual arrangements. This principle is summarized in Mr. Justice Holmes' well-known dictum: "One whose rights, such as they are, are subject to state restriction, cannot remove them from the power of the State by making a contract about them."...

Yet private contracts are not subject to unlimited modification under the police power. The Court in *Blaisdell* recognized that laws intended to regulate existing contractual relationships must serve a legitimate public purpose.... A State could not "adopt as

its policy the repudiation of debts or the destruction of contracts or the denial of means to enforce them."... Legislation adjusting the rights and responsibilities of contracting parties must be upon reasonable conditions and of a character appropriate to the public purpose justifying its adoption.... As is customary in reviewing economic and social regulation, however, courts properly defer to legislative judgment as to the necessity and reasonableness of a particular measure....

When a State impairs the obligation of its own contract, the reserved-powers doctrine has a different basis. The initial inquiry concerns the ability of the State to enter into an agreement that limits its power to act in the future. As early as *Fletcher v. Peck,* the Court considered the argument that "one legislature cannot abridge the powers of a succeeding legislature." 6 Cranch, at 135. It is often stated that "the legislature cannot bargain away the police power of a State." *Stone* v. *Mississippi*... (1880). This doctrine requires a determination of the State's power to create irrevocable contract rights in the first place, rather than an inquiry into the purpose or reasonableness of the subsequent impairment. In short, the Contract Clause does not require a State to adhere to a contract that surrenders an essential attribute of its sovereignty.

In deciding whether a State's contract was invalid *ab initio* under the reserved-powers doctrine, earlier decisions relied on distinctions among the various powers of the State. Thus, the police power and the power of eminent domain were among those that could not be "contracted away," but the State could bind itself in the future exercise of the taxing and spending powers. Such formalistic distinctions perhaps cannot be dispositive, but they contain an important element of truth. Whatever the propriety of a State's binding itself to a future course of conduct in other contexts, the power to enter into effective financial contracts cannot be questioned. Any financial obligation could be regarded in theory as a relinquishment of the State's spending power, since money spent to repay debts is not available for other purposes. Similarly, the taxing power may have to be exercised if debts are to be repaid. Notwithstanding these effects, the Court has regularly held that the States are bound by their debt contracts.

The instant case involves a financial obligation and thus as a threshold matter may not be said automatically to fall within the reserved powers that cannot be contracted away. Not every security provision, however, is necessarily financial. For example, a revenue bond might be secured by the State's promise to continue operating the facility in question; yet such a promise surely could not validly be construed to bind the State never to close the facility for health or safety reasons. The security provision at issue here, however, is different: The States promised that revenues and reserves securing the bonds would not be depleted by the Port Authority's operation of deficit-producing passenger railroads beyond the level of "permitted deficits." Such a promise is purely financial and thus not necessarily a compromise of the State's reserved powers.

Of course, to say that the financial restrictions of the 1962 covenant were valid when adopted does not finally resolve this case. The Contract Clause is not an absolute bar to subsequent modification of a State's own financial obligations. As with laws impairing the obligations of private contracts, an impairment may be constitutional if it is reasonable and necessary to serve an important public purpose. In applying this standard, however, complete deference to a legislative assessment of reasonableness and necessity is not appropriate because the State's self-interest is at stake. A governmental entity can always find a use for extra money, especially when taxes do not have to be raised. If a State could reduce its financial obligations whenever it wanted to spend the money for what it regarded as an important public purpose, the Contract Clause would provide no protection at all.

V

Mass transportation, energy conservation, and environmental protection are goals that are important and of legitimate public concern. Appellees contend that these goals are so important that any harm to bondholders from repeal of the 1962 covenant is greatly outweighed by the public benefit.... We can only sustain the repeal of the 1962 covenant if that impairment was both reasonable and necessary to serve the admittedly important purposes claimed by the State.

The more specific justification offered for the repeal of the 1962 covenant was the States' plan for encouraging users of private automobiles to shift to public transportation. The States intended to discourage private automobile use by raising bridge and tunnel tolls and to use the extra revenue from those tolls to subsidize improved commuter railroad service. Appellees contend that repeal of the 1962 covenant was necessary to implement this plan because the new mass transit facilities could not possibly be self-supporting and the covenant's "permitted deficits" level had already been exceeded. We reject

this justification because the repeal was neither necessary to achievement of the plan nor reasonable in light of the circumstances.

The determination of necessity can be considered on two levels. First, it cannot be said that total repeal of the covenant was essential; a less drastic modification would have permitted the contemplated plan without entirely removing the covenant's limitations on the use of Port Authority revenues and reserves to subsidize commuter railroads. Second, without modifying the covenant at all, the States could have adopted alternative means of achieving their twin goals of discouraging automobile use and improving mass transit. Appellees contend, however, that choosing among these alternatives is a matter for legislative discretion. But a State is not completely free to consider impairing the obligations of its own contracts on a par with other policy alternatives. Similarly, a State is not free to impose a drastic impairment when an evident and more moderate course would serve its purposes equally well. In *El Paso* v. *Simmons, supra,* the imposition of a five-year statute of limitations on what was previously a perpetual right of redemption was regarded by this Court as "quite clearly necessary" to achieve the State's vital interest in the orderly administration of its school lands program. ... In the instant case the State has failed to demonstrate that repeal of the 1962 covenant was similarly necessary.

We also cannot conclude that repeal of the covenant was reasonable in light of the surrounding circumstances. In this regard a comparison with *El Paso* v. *Simmons, supra,* again is instructive. There a 19th century statute had effects that were unforeseen and unintended by the legislature when originally adopted. As a result speculators were placed in a position to obtain windfall benefits. The Court held that adoption of a statute of limitation was a reasonable means to "restrict a party to those gains reasonably to be expected from the contract" when it was adopted....

By contrast, in the instant case the need for mass transportation in the New York metropolitan area was not a new development, and the likelihood that publicly owned commuter railroads would produce substantial deficits was well known. As early as 1922, over a half century ago, there were pressures to involve the Port Authority in mass transit. It was with full knowledge of these concerns that the 1962 covenant was adopted. Indeed, the covenant was specifically intended to protect the pledged revenues and reserves against the possibility that such concerns would lead the Port Authority into greater involvement in deficit mass transit.

During the 12-year period between adoption of the covenant and its repeal, public perception of the importance of mass transit undoubtedly grew because of increased general concern with environmental protection and energy conservation. But these concerns were not unknown in 1962, and the subsequent changes were of degree and not of kind. We cannot say that these changes caused the covenant to have a substantially different impact in 1974 than when it was adopted in 1962. And we cannot conclude that the repeal was reasonable in the light of changed circumstances.

We therefore hold that the Contract Clause of the United States Constitution prohibits the retroactive repeal of the 1962 covenant. The judgment of the Supreme Court of New Jersey is reversed.

It is so ordered.

JUSTICES STEWART and POWELL took no part in the decision of this case. MR. CHIEF JUSTICE BERGER wrote a brief concurring opinion.

MR. JUSTICE BRENNAN, with whom MR. JUSTICE WHITE and MR. JUSTICE MARSHALL join, dissenting.

Decisions of this Court for at least a century have construed the Contract Clause largely to be powerless in binding a State to contracts limiting the authority of successor legislatures to enact laws in furtherance of the health, safety, and similar collective interests of the polity. In short, those decisions established the principle that lawful exercises of a State's police powers stand paramount to private rights held under contract. Today's decision... rejects this previous understanding and remolds the Contract Clause into a potent instrument for overseeing important policy determinations of the state legislature. At the same time, by creating a constitutional safe haven for property rights embodied in a contract, the decision substantially distorts modern constitutional jurisprudence governing regulation of private economic interests. I might understand, though I could not accept, this revival of the Contract Clause were it in accordance with some coherent and constructive view of public policy. But elevation of the Clause to the status of regulator of the municipal bond market at the heavy price of frustration of sound legislative policy-making is as demonstrably unwise as it is unnecessary. The justification for today's decision, therefore, remains a mystery to me, and I respectfully dissent.

I

The Court holds that New Jersey's repeal of the 1962 covenant constitutes an unreasonable invasion of contract rights and hence an impairment of contract. The formulation of the legal standard by which the Court would test asserted impairments of contracts is, to me, both unprecedented and most troubling.... In my view, the Court's casual consideration both of the substantial public policies that prompted New Jersey's repeal of the 1962 covenant, and of the relatively inconsequential burdens that resulted for the Authority's creditors, belies its conclusion that the State acted unreasonably in seeking to relieve its citizens from the strictures of this earlier legislative policy.

. . . .

Whether the 1962 New Jersey Legislature acted wisely in accepting this new restriction is, for me, quite irrelevant. What is important is that the passage of the years conclusively demonstrated that this effective barrier to the development of rapid transit in the port region squarely conflicts with the legitimate needs of the New York metropolitan community, and will persist in doing so into the next century. In the Urban Mass Transportation Assistance Act of 1970,... Congress found that "within urban areas ... the ability of all citizens to move quickly and at a reasonable cost [has become] an urgent national problem." Concurrently, the Clean Air Act ... advocated the curtailment of air pollution through the development of transportation-control strategies that place heavy emphasis on rapid transit alternatives to the automobile. For northern New Jersey in particular, with ambient air-quality levels among the worst in the Nation, the Clean Air Act has led to new regulations premised on [a policy of the development of large-scale mass transit facilities].... Finally, the Court itself cites the Emergency Petroleum Allocation Act ... [1970] which signaled "a national energy crisis which is a threat to the public health, safety, and welfare," and sought to stimulate further initiatives toward the development of public transportation and similar programs.

It was in response to these societal demands that the New Jersey and New York Legislatures repealed the 1962 covenant....

The Court's consideration of this factual background is, I believe, most unsatisfactory. The Court never explicitly takes issue with the core of New Jersey's defense of the repeal: that the State was faced with serious and growing environmental, energy, and transportation problems, and the covenant worked at cross-purposes with efforts at remedying these concerns. Indeed, the Court candidly concedes that the State's purposes in effectuating the 1974 repeal were "admittedly important." ...

Instead, the Court's analysis focuses upon related, but peripheral, matters.

For example, several hypothetical alternative methods are proposed whereby New Jersey might hope to secure funding for public transportation, and these are made the basis for a holding that repeal of the covenant was not "necessary.". . . Setting aside the propriety of this surprising legal standard, the Court's effort at fashioning its own legislative program for New York and New Jersey is notably unsuccessful. In fact, except for those proffered alternatives which also amount to a repeal or substantial modification of the 1962 covenant, none of the Court's suggestions is compatible with the basic antipollution and transportation-control strategies that are crucial to metropolitan New York. . . . The Court's various alternative proposals, while perhaps interesting speculations, simply are not responsive to New York's and New Jersey's real environmental and traffic problems, and, in any event, intrude the Court deeply into complex and localized policy matters that are for the States' legislatures and not the judiciary to resolve.

Equally unconvincing is the Court's contention that repeal of the 1962 covenant was unreasonable because the environmental and energy concerns that prompted such action "were not unknown in 1962, and the subsequent changes were of degree and not of kind." . . . Nowhere are we told why a state policy, no matter how responsive to the general welfare of its citizens, can be reasonable only if it confronts issues that previously were absolutely unforeseen. Indeed, this arbitrary perspective seems peculiarly inappropriate in a case like this where at least three new and independent congressional enactments between the years 1962 and 1974 summoned major urban centers like New York and New Jersey to action in the environmental, energy, and transportation fields. In short, on this record, I can neither understand nor accept the Court's characterization of New Jersey's action as unreasonable.

If the Court's treatment of New Jersey's legitimate policy interests is inadequate, its consideration of the countervailing injury ostensibly suffered by the appellant is barely discernible at all. . . .

. . . .

In brief, only by disregarding the detailed factual findings of the trial court in a systematic fashion is the Court today able to maintain that repeal of the 1962 covenant was anything but a minimal interference with the realistic economic interests of the bond-holders. The record in this case fairly establishes that we are presented with a relatively incon-sequential infringement of contract rights in the pursuit of substantial and important public ends. Yet, this meager record is seized upon by the Court as the vehicle for resuscitation of long discarded Contract Clause doctrine — a step out of line with both the history of Contract Clause jurisprudence and with constitutional doctrine generally in its attempt to delineate the reach of the lawmaking power of state legislatures in the face of adverse claims by property owners.

II

The Court today dusts off the Contract Clause and thereby undermines the bipartisan policies of two States that manifestly seek to further the legitimate needs of their citizens. The Court's analysis, I submit, fundamentally misconceives the nature of the Contract Clause guarantee.

One of the fundamental premises of our popular democracy is that each generation of representatives can and will remain responsive to the needs and desires of those whom they represent. [The opinion goes on to review the Court's prior interpretations of the Contract Clause.]

. . . .

It need hardly be said that today's decision is markedly out of step with this deferential philosophy. The Court's willingness to uphold an impairment of contract — no matter how "technical" the injury — only on a showing of "necessity," is particularly distressing, for this Court always will be able to devise abstract alternatives to the concrete action actually taken by a State. For example, in virtually every decided Contract Clause case, the government could have exercised the Court's "lesser alternative" of resorting to its powers of taxation as a substitute for modifying overly restrictive contracts. . . .

By the same token, if unforeseeability is the key to a "reasonable" decision, as the Court now contends, . . . almost all prior cases again must be repudiated. . . .

. . . Given that this is the first case in some 40 years in which this Court has seen fit to invalidate purely economic and social legislation on the strength of the Contract Clause, one may only hope that it will prove a rare phenomenon, turning on the Court's particularized appraisal of the facts before it. But there also is reason for broader concern. . . . If today's case signals a return to substantive constitutional review of States' policies, and a new resolve to protect property owners whose interest or circumstances may happen to appeal to Members of this Court, then more than the citizens of New Jersey and New York will be the losers.

III

I would not want to be read as suggesting that the States should blithely proceed down the path of repudiating their obligations, financial or otherwise. Their credibility in the credit market obviously is highly dependent on exercising their vast lawmaking powers with self-restraint and discipline, and I, for one, have little doubt that few, if any, jurisdictions would choose to use their authority "so foolish[ly] as to kill a goose that lays golden eggs for them." But in the final analysis, there is no reason to doubt that appellant's financial welfare is being adequately policed by the political processes and the bond marketplace itself. The role to be played by the Constitution is at most a limited one. For this Court should have learned long ago that the Constitution — be it through the Contract or Due Process Clause — can actively intrude into such economic and policy matters only if my Brethren are prepared to bear enormous institutional and social costs. Because I consider the potential dangers of such judicial interference to be intolerable, I dissent.

Butchers' Benevolent Assoc. v. Crescent City Livestock Handling and Slaughterhouse Co. (The Slaughterhouse Cases)

16 Wall 36 (1873)
Vote: 5–4

The City of New Orleans responded to a long-standing health problem by granting a monopoly to a group of butchers that agreed to operate a slaughterhouse in a specified location, in a specified manner, and with set fees. This arrangement was the result of an effort by the city to deal with contamination of the Mississippi River due to the dumping of animal carcasses by a number of slaughterhouses. Several butchers were put out of business by this action. They organized into the Butchers' Benevolent Association and challenged the law under the recently enacted Civil War

Amendments, claiming that the law deprived them of the "right" to practice their profession. Specifically, they argued that the law imposed a form of "involuntary servitude" in violation of the Thirteenth Amendment, and that it deprived them of their privileges and immunities of citizenship, their liberty and property without due process, and their right to equal protection of the laws.

In this first major decision on the issue, the Court gives short shrift to the Privileges and Immunities clause. And although there have been periodic efforts to revive this provision, it has not figured significantly in the history of constitutional law. For purposes of this chapter, what is most revealing is Justice Miller's sweeping analysis of state police powers and his understanding of the scope of both the Due Process and Equal Protection Clauses. Contrast his position on these provisions with those in the LOCHNER, ALLGEYAR, and CLEBURNE cases later in this chapter. The decision in this case was 5 to 4. Note Justice Field's dissent. As you will see, this position was soon to gain additional support, and would hold sway on the Court until the 1930s.

MR. JUSTICE MILLER delivered the opinion of the Court.

. . . The wisdom of the monopoly granted by the legislature may be open to question, but it is difficult to see a justification for the assertion that the butchers are deprived of the right to labor in their occupation, or the people of their daily service in preparing food, or how this statute, with the duties and guards imposed upon the company, can be said to destroy the business of the butcher, or seriously interfere with its pursuit.

The power here exercised by the legislature of Louisiana is, in its essential nature, one which has been, up to the present period in the constitutional history of this country, always conceded to belong to the States, however it may *now* be questioned in some of its details.

. . . .

. . . This [police] power is, and must be from its very nature, incapable of any exact definition or limitation. Upon it depends the security of social order, the life and health of the citizen, the comfort of an existence in a thickly populated community, the enjoyment of private and social life, and the beneficial use of property.

. . . The regulation of the place and manner of conducting the slaughtering of animals, and the business of butchering within a city, and the inspection of the animals to be killed for meat, and of the meat afterwards, are among the most necessary and frequent exercises of this power.

. . . [T]he authority of the legislature of Louisiana to pass the present statute is ample, unless some restraint in the exercise of that power is found in the constitution of that State or in the amendments to the Constitution of the United States, adopted since the date of the decisions we have already cited.

. . . The plaintiffs in error accepting this issue, allege that the statute is a violation of the Constitution of the United States in these several particulars:

That it creates an involuntary servitude forbidden by the thirteenth article of amendment;

That it abridges the privileges and immunities of citizens of the United States;

That it denies to the plaintiffs the equal protection of the laws; and,

That it deprives them of their property without due process of law; contrary to the provisions of the first section of the fourteenth article of amendment.

This court is thus called upon for the first time to give construction to these articles. . . .

The most cursory glance at these articles discloses a unity of purpose, when taken in connection with the history of the times, which cannot fail to have an important bearing on any question of doubt concerning their true meaning. . . . [O]n the most casual examination of the language of these amendments, no one can fail to be impressed with the one pervading purpose found in them all, lying at the foundation of each, and without which none of them would have been even suggested; we mean the freedom of the slave race, the security and firm establishment of that freedom, and the protection of the newly-made freeman and citizen from the oppressions of those who had formerly exercised dominion over him. . . .

We do not say that no one else but the negro can share in this protection. Both the language and the spirit of these articles are to have their fair and just weight in any question of construction. . . . But what we do say, and what we wish to be understood, is, that in any fair and just construction of any section or phrase of these amendments, it is necessary to look to the purpose which we have said was the pervading spirit of them all, the evil which they were designed to remedy, and the process of continued addition to the Constitution, until that purpose was

supposed to be accomplished, as far as constitutional law can accomplish it.

. . . .

. . . [T]he distinction between citizenship of the United States and citizenship of a state is clearly recognized and established. Not only may a man be a citizen of the United States without being a citizen of a state, but an important element is necessary to convert the former into the latter. He must reside within the state to make him a citizen of it, but it is only necessary that he should be born or naturalized in the United States to be a citizen of the Union.

It is quite clear, then, that there is a citizenship of the United States, and a citizenship of a state, which are distinct from each other and which depend upon different characteristics or circumstances in the individual.

We think this distinction and its explicit recognition in this Amendment of great weight in this argument, because the next paragraph of this same section, which is the one mainly relied on by the plaintiffs in error, speaks only of privileges and immunities of citizens of the United States, and does not speak of those of citizens of the several states. The argument, however, in favor of the plaintiffs, rests wholly on the assumption that the citizenship is the same and the privileges and immunities guaranteed by the clause are the same.

The language is: "No state shall make or enforce any law which shall abridge the privileges or immunities of citizens of the United States." It is a little remarkable, if this clause was intended as a protection to the citizen of a state against the legislative power of his own state, that the words "citizen of the state" should be left out when it is so carefully used, and used in contradistinction to "citizens of the United States" in the very sentence which precedes it. It is too clear for argument that the change in phraseology was adopted understandingly and with a purpose.

Of the privileges and immunities of the citizens of the United States, and of the privileges and immunities of the citizen of the state, and what they respectively are, we will presently consider; but we wish to state here that it is only the former which are placed by this clause under the protection of the Federal Constitution, and that the latter, whatever they may be, are not intended to have any additional protection by this paragraph of the Amendment.

If, then, there is a difference between the privileges and immunities belonging to a citizen of the United States as such, and those belonging to the citizen of the state as such, the latter must rest for their security and protection where they have heretofore rested; for they are not embraced by this paragraph of the Amendment.

. . . .

[The] sole purpose [of the privileges and immunities clause] was to declare to the several states, that whatever those rights, as you grant or establish them to your own citizens, or as you limit or qualify, or impose restrictions on their exercise, the same, neither more nor less, shall be the measure of the rights of citizens of other states within your jurisdiction.

. . . .

The argument has not been much pressed in these cases that the defendant's charter deprives the plaintiffs of their property without due process of law. . . . The first of these paragraphs has been in the Constitution since the adoption of the 5th Amendment, as a restraint upon the Federal power. It is also to be found in some form of expression in the constitutions of nearly all the states. . . .

We are not without judicial interpretation, therefore, both state and national, of the meaning of this clause. And it is sufficient to say that under no construction of that provision that we have ever seen, or any that we deem admissable, can the restraint imposed by the state of Louisiana upon the exercise of their trade by the butchers of New Orleans be held to be a deprivation of property within the meaning of that provision.

"Nor shall any state deny to any person within its jurisdiction the equal protection of the laws."

In the light of the history of these amendments, and the pervading purpose of them, . . . it is not difficult to give a meaning to this clause. The existence of laws in the states where the newly emancipated negroes resided, which discriminated with gross injustice and hardship against them as a class, was the evil to be remedied by this clause, and by it such laws are forbidden.

. . . We doubt very much whether any action of a state not directed by way of discrimination against the negroes as a class, or on account of their race, will ever be held to come within the purview of this provision. It is so clearly a provision for that race and that emergency, that a strong case would be necessary for its application to any other. But as it is a state that is to be dealt with, and not alone the validity of its laws, we may safely leave that matter until Congress shall have exercised its power, or some case of state oppression, by denial of equal justice in its courts, shall have claimed a decision at our hands. We find no such case in the one before us, and do not deem it necessary to go over the argument again, as it may have relation to this particular clause of the Amendment. . . .

The judgments of the Supreme Court of Louisiana in these cases are affirmed.

MR. JUSTICE FIELD, with whom MR. CHIEF JUSTICE CHASE, MR. JUSTICE SWAYNE, and MR. JUSTICE BRADLEY concurred, dissented, saying in part:

The Amendment does not attempt to confer any new privileges or immunities upon citizens or to enumerate or define those already existing. It assumes that there are such privileges and immunities which belong of right to citizens as such, and ordains that they shall not be abridged by state legislation. If this inhibition has no reference to privileges and immunities of this character, but only refers, as held by the majority of the court in their opinion, to such privileges and immunities as were before its adoption specially designated in the Constitution or necessarily implied as belonging to citizens of the United States, it was a vain and idle enactment, which accomplished nothing, and most unnecessarily excited Congress and the people on its passage. With privileges and immunities thus designated no state could ever have interfered by its laws, and no new constitutional provision was required to inhibit such interference. The supremacy of the Constitution and the laws of the United States always controlled any state legislation of that character. But if the Amendment refers to the natural and inalienable rights which belong to all citizens, the inhibition has a profound significance and consequence. . . .

MR. JUSTICE SWAYNE AND MR. JUSTICE BRADLEY filed separate dissenting opinions.

Munn v. Illinois

94 U.S. 133 (1877)
Vote: 7–2

14th Amendment Due Process Clause

A number of cases have dealt with efforts to protect economic interests through provisions in the Constitution. In CALDER V. BULL (1798), the Court refused to interpret the prohibition against *ex post facto* laws to apply to noncriminal laws. However, in DARTMOUTH COLLEGE (1819), the Court upheld claims of "vested interests" against legislative encroachment, giving hope to those who wanted to use the Contract Clause as a reign against state legislatures. This desire was short-lived, as was seen in CHARLES RIVER BRIDGE Co. v. WARREN BRIDGE Co. (1837), where Chief Justice Taney's opinion provides ample support for an expansive interpretation of state police powers, a view subsequently reinforced by other cases. Thus neither the *ex post facto* provision nor the Contract Clause became vehicles for protecting economic interests, as some Federalists once hoped.

But even as the Contract Clause was faltering in this effort, another Constitutional provision was being urged as a defense of property against governmental encroachment. In BARRON V. BALTIMORE (1833), the Court was asked to use the Due Process Clause of the Fifth Amendment to protect a property owner against state actions that had undercut the value of his property. The Court rejected this claim, holding that the Fifth Amendment applied only to the national and not a state government. However, it should be noted that in his opinion for the Court, Marshall said that historically the guarantee of due process had provided that government, when acting, would abide by its own established procedures or rules. In this dictum, he went on to say that the courts would consider challenges to due process only to ensure that governments would follow their own established procedures, not to scrutinize the wisdom and substance of governmental actions.

Despite this, the Court continued to be asked to consider the substance of legislation when it sought to regulate "property." Reacting to the wave of state regulatory actions spurned by the expanded Jacksonian democracy prior to the Civil War, attorneys for vested interests conducted a vigorous campaign in state courts, speeches, articles, and elsewhere for an interpretation of due process that would protect property against state regulatory action. These efforts eventually paid off. In at least one state high court, in New York, a state law regulating business matters was overturned as being in violation of the state's constitutional guarantee of due process (*Wynhammer* v. *New York,* 1856). Adoption of the Fourteenth Amendment, with its own due process provision made expressly applicable to the states, filled this campaign for substantive due process with renewed vigor.

Still, the Supreme Court was initially reluctant to embrace substantive due process as protection of propertied interests against legislative regulation. As we saw in the SLAUGHTERHOUSE CASES, the Court upheld the state's power to regulate. While the Court focused on the privileges and immunities provision in the Fourteenth Amendment, it also dismissed the idea that that Amendment's due process provision was a protection against state regulation.

However, cases continued to raise the issue, and even as the Court continued to reject the claim in particular cases, it was unwittingly laying the ground for recognition of substantive due process. This shift is seen in the case below, one of a large number of cases that upheld state police power to regulate railroads and warehouses in an effort to control entrepreneurs and monopolies as they expanded railroads and shipping in the west.

In this case, Munn, the operator of a grain elevator in Chicago, brought suit against Illinois, arguing that recent legislation requiring grain elevators to be leased by the state and fixing the maximum price they could charge for storage was an unreasonable interference with business and as such violated the due process provision of the Fourteenth Amendment. Munn lost his appeal in the Illinois Supreme Court and brought the case to the United States Supreme Court. Note with care the reasoning in this case, as well as the argument of the two dissenting justices. Although the majority rejects Munn's claim, do they in fact reject the argument for a substantive economic interpretation of the Due Process Clause?

MR. CHIEF JUSTICE WAITE delivered the opinion of the court.

Every statute is presumed to be constitutional. The courts ought not to declare one to be unconstitutional, unless it is clearly so. If there is doubt, the expressed will of the legislature should be sustained.

The Constitution contains no definition of the word "deprive," as used in the Fourteenth Amendment. To determine its signification, therefore, it is necessary to ascertain the effect which usage has given it, when employed in the same or a like connection.

While this provision of the amendment is new in the Constitution of the United States, as a limitation upon the powers of the States, it is old as a principle of civilized government. It is found in Magna Charta, and, in substance if not in form, in nearly or quite all the constitutions that have been from time to time adopted by the several States of the Union. . . .

When one becomes a member of society, he necessarily parts with some rights or privileges which, as an individual not affected by his relations to others, he might retain. "A body politic," as aptly defined in the preamble of the Constitution of Massachusetts, "is a social compact by which the whole people covenants with each citizen, and each citizen with the whole people, that all shall be governed by certain laws for the common good." This does not confer power upon the whole people to control rights which are purely and exclusively private, . . . but it does authorize the establishment of laws requiring each citizen to so conduct himself, and so use his own property, as not unnecessarily to injure another. This is the very essence of government. . . .

From this it is apparent that, down to the time of the adoption of the Fourteenth Amendment, it was not supposed that statutes regulating the use, or even the price of the use, of private property necessarily deprived an owner of his property without due process of law. Under some circumstances they may, but not under all. The amendment does not change the law in this particular; it simply prevents the States from doing that which will operate as such a deprivation.

This brings us to inquire as to the principles upon which this power of regulation rests, in order that we may determine what is within and what without its operative effect. Looking, then, to the common law, from whence came the right which the Constitution protects, we find that when private property is "affected with a public interest, it ceases to be *juris privati* only." This was said by Lord Chief Justice Hale more than two hundred years ago, . . . and has been accepted without objection as an essential element in the law of property ever since. Property does become clothed with a public interest when used in a manner to make it of public consequence, and affect the community at large. When, therefore, one devotes his property to a use in which the public has an interest, he, in effect, grants to the public an interest in that use, and must submit to be controlled by the public for the common good, to the extent of the interest he has thus created. He may

withdraw his grant by discontinuing the use; but, so long as he maintains the use, he must submit to the control.

. . . .

But we need not go further. Enough has already been said to show that, when private property is devoted to a public use, it is subject to public regulation. It remains only to ascertain whether the warehouses of these plaintiffs in error, and the business which is carried on there, come within the operation of this principle.

For this purpose we accept as true the statements of fact contained in the elaborate brief of one of the counsel of the plaintiffs in error. . . . The quantity [of grain] received in Chicago has made it the greatest grain market in the world. This business has created a demand for means by which the immense quantity of grain can be handled or stored, and these have been found in grain warehouses, which are commonly called elevators. . . . The grain warehouses or elevators in Chicago are immense structures, holding from 300,000 to 1,000,000 bushels at one time, according to size. . . . It has been found impossible to preserve each owner's grain separate, and this has given rise to a system of inspection and grading, by which the grain of different owners is mixed, and receipts issued for the number of bushels which are negotiable, and redeemable in like kind, upon demand. . . . The railways have found it impracticable to own such elevators, and public policy forbids the transaction of such business by the carrier; the ownership has, therefore, been by private individuals, who have embarked their capital and devoted their industry to such business as a private pursuit.

In this connection it must also be borne in mind that, although in 1874 there were in Chicago fourteen warehouses adapted to this particular business, and owned by about thirty persons, nine business firms controlled them, and that the prices charged and received for storage were such "as have been from year to year agreed upon and established by the different elevators or warehouses in the city of Chicago, and which rates have been annually published. . . . Thus it is apparent that all the elevating facilities . . . may be a "virtual" monopoly.

Under such circumstances it is difficult to see why, if the common carrier, or the miller, or the ferryman, or the innkeeper, or the wharfinger, or the baker, or the cartman, or the hackney-coachman, pursues a public employment and exercises "a sort of public office," these plaintiffs in error do not. . . . Certainly, if any business can be clothed "with a public interest, and cease to be *juris privati* only," this has been. It may not be made so by the operation of the Constitution of Illinois of this statute, but it is by the facts.

We also are not permitted to overlook the fact that, for some reason, the people of Illinois, when they revised their Constitution in 1870, saw fit to make it the duty of the general assembly to pass laws "for the protection of producers, shippers, and receivers of grain and produce," art. 13, sec. 7; and by sect. 5 of the same article, to require all railroad companies receiving and transporting grain in bulk or otherwise to deliver the same at any elevator to which it might be consigned, that could be reached by any track that was or could be used by such company, and that all railroad companies should permit connections to be made with their tracks, so that any public warehouse, &c, might be reached by the cars on their railroads. This indicates very clearly that during the twenty years in which this peculiar business had been assuming its present "immense proportions," something had occurred which led the whole body of the people to suppose that remedies such as are usually employed to prevent abuses by virtual monopolies might not be inappropriate here. For our purposes we must assume that, if a state of facts could exist that would justify such legislation, it actually did exist when the statute now under consideration was passed. For us the question is one of power, not of expediency. If no state of circumstances could exist to justify such a statute, then we may declare this one void, because in excess of the legislative power of the State. But if it could, we must presume it did. Of the propriety of legislative interference within the scope of legislative power, the legislature is the exclusive judge.

Neither is it a matter of any moment that no precedent can be found for a statute precisely like this. It is conceded that the business is one of recent origin, that its growth has been rapid, and that it is already of great importance. And it must also be conceded that it is a business in which the whole public has a direct and positive interest. It presents, therefore, a case for the application of a long-known and well-established principle in social science, and this statute simply extends the law so as to meet this new development of commercial progress. There is no attempt to compel these owners to grant the public an interest in their property, but to declare their obligations, if they use it in this particular manner.

It matters not in this case that these plaintiffs in error had built their warehouses and established their business before the regulations complained of were adopted. What they did was from the beginning subject to the power of the body politic to require them to conform to such regulations as might be established by the proper authorities for the common good. . . .

It is insisted, however, that the owner of property is entitled to a reasonable compensation for its use, even though it be clothed with a public interest, and that what is reasonable is a judicial and not a legislative question.

As has already been shown, the practice has been otherwise. In countries where the common law prevails, it has been customary from time immemorial for the legislature to declare what shall be a reasonable compensation under such circumstances, or, perhaps more properly speaking, to fix a maximum beyond which any charge made would be unreasonable. . . .

We know that this is a power which may be abused; but that is no argument against its existence. For protection against abuses by legislatures the people must resort to the polls, not to the courts.

. . . .

. . . We do not say that a case may not arise in which it will be found that a State, under the form of regulating its own affairs, has encroached upon the exclusive domain of Congress in respect to interstate commerce, but we do say that, upon the facts as they are represented to us in this record, that has not been done.

Judgment affirmed.

[JUSTICE FIELD wrote a dissent in which MR. JUSTICE STRONG concurred.]

I am compelled to dissent from the decision of the court in this case, and from the reasons upon which that decision is founded. The principle upon which the opinion of the majority proceeds is, in my judgment, subversive of the rights of private property, heretofore believed to be protected by constitutional guaranties against legislative interference, and is in conflict with the authorities cited in its support.

. . . .

The same liberal construction which is required for the protection of life and liberty, in all particulars in which life and liberty are of any value, should be applied to the protection of private property. If the legislature of a State, under pretence of providing for the public good, or for any other reason, can determine, against the consent of the owner, the uses to which private property shall be devoted, or the prices which the owner shall receive for its uses, it can deprive him of the property as completely as by a special act for its confiscation or destruction. . . .

. . . .

There is nothing in the character of the business of the defendants as warehousemen which called for the interference complained of in this case. Their buildings are not nuisances; their occupation of receiving and storing grain infringes upon no rights of others, disturbs no neighborhood, infects not the air, and in no respect prevents others from using and enjoying their property as to them may seem best. The legislation in question is nothing less than a bold assertion of absolute power by the State. . . .

. . . .

. . . No prerogative or privilege of the crown to establish warehouses was ever asserted at the common law. The business of a warehouseman was, at the common law, a private business, and is so in its nature. It has no special privileges connected with it, nor did the law ever extend to it any greater protection than it extended to all other private business. No reason can be assigned to justify legislation interfering with the legitimate profits of that business, that would not equally justify an intermeddling with the business of every man in the community, so soon, at least, as his business became generally useful.

I am of opinion that the judgment of the Supreme Court of Illinois should be reversed.

Allgeyar v. Louisiana

165 U.S. 578 (1897)
Vote: 9–0

Based on what it thought was its police power to enact regulations to protect the public from questionable practices of insurance companies, Louisiana passed a law that said, in part, "No foreign [insurance] corporation shall do any business in this state without having one or more known places of business and an authorized agent or agents in the state upon whom process may be served." The statute went on to provide a penalty for those who obtained an insurance policy from companies that were not in compliance with the act. Allgeyar, a Louisiana company, maintained, by mail, a policy with a noncomplying New York company, and in a test case was charged with violating the act when it sought to ship 100 pounds of

cotton insured by the noncomplying company. In overturning the state law, the Court held that it violated "liberty of contract," a term first used by the Court here and nowhere to be found in the Constitution. It came to be used with great frequency between 1880 and 1937.

Contrast the Court's view of Louisiana's police powers and the concept of "liberty" in this case with its treatment of another Louisiana law twenty years earlier in the SLAUGHTERHOUSE CASES.

MR. JUSTICE PECKHAM delivered the opinion of the Court.

. . . .

. . . [W]e think the statute is a violation of the fourteenth amendment of the federal constitution, in that it deprives the defendants of their liberty without due process of law. The statute which forbids such act does not become due process of law, because it is inconsistent with the provisions of the constitution of the Union. The "liberty" mentioned in that amendment means, not only the right of the citizen to be free from the mere physical restraint of his person, as by incarceration, but the term is deemed to embrace the right of the citizen to be free in the enjoyment of all his faculties; to be free to use them in all lawful ways; to live and work where he will; to earn his livelihood by any lawful calling; to pursue any livelihood or avocation; and for that purpose to enter into all contracts which may be proper, necessary, and essential to his carrying out to a successful conclusion the purposes above mentioned.

. . . To deprive the citizen of such a right as herein described without due process of law is illegal. Such a statute as this in question is not due process of law, because it prohibits an act which under the federal constitution the defendants had a right to perform. This does not interfere in any way with the acknowledged right of the state to enact such legislation in the legitimate exercise of its police or other powers as it may seem proper. In the exercise of such right, however, care must be taken not to infringe upon those other rights of the citizen which are protected by the federal constitution.

In the privilege of pursuing an ordinary calling or trade, and of acquiring, holding, and selling property, must be embraced the right to make all proper contracts in relation thereto; and although it may be conceded that this right to contract in relation to persons or property or to do business within the jurisdiction of the state may be regulated, and sometimes prohibited, when the contracts or business conflict with the policy of the state as contained in its statutes, yet the power does not and cannot extend to prohibiting a citizen from making contracts of the nature involved in this case outside of the limits and jurisdiction of the state, and which are also to be performed outside of such jurisdiction; nor can the state legally prohibit its citizens from doing such an act as writing this letter of notification, even though the property which is the subject of the insurance may at the time when such insurance attaches be within the limits of the state. The mere fact that a citizen may be within the limits of a particular state does not prevent his making a contract outside its limits while he himself remains within it. . . . The contract in this case was thus made. It was a valid contract, made outside of the state, to be performed outside of the state, although the subject was property temporarily within the state. As the contract was valid in the place where made and where it was to be performed, the party to the contract, upon whom is devolved the right or duty to send the notification in order that the insurance provided for by the contract may attach to the property specified in the shipment mentioned in the notice, must have the liberty to do that act and to give that notification within the limits of the state, any prohibition of the state statute to the contrary notwithstanding. The giving of the notice is a mere collateral matter. It is not the contract itself, but is an act performed pursuant to a valid contract, which the state had no right or jurisdiction to prevent its citizen from making outside the limits of the state.

For these reasons we think the statute in question was a violation of the federal constitution, and afforded no justification for the judgment awarded by that court against the plaintiffs in error. That judgment must therefore be reversed. . . .

Lochner v. New York

198 U.S. 45 (1905)
Vote: 5–4

The New York Labor Law of 1897 provided that no employee should be "required or permitted to work in a biscuit, bread, or cake bakery or confectionary establishment more than sixty hours in any one week or more than ten hours in any one day unless for the purpose of

making a shorter day on the last day of the week." This provision was adopted after the legislature heard expert testimony that prolonged exposure to flour dust by bakers constituted a health hazard, affecting the lungs in much the same way that coal dust injures the lungs of coal miners.

Lochner, the owner of a bakery, was convicted of violating a related provision of this law, which subjected an employer to a criminal sanction for permitting an employee to exceed these hours. He was convicted and fined $5000. His conviction was upheld upon appeal by the two state appellate courts, and on his petition the case was brought to the United States Supreme Court upon a writ of error.

This case clearly illustrates the political and economic theory that was enshrined as constitutional doctrine during this period. The dissenting opinions, particularly that of Holmes, is remembered as one of the strongest statements in opposition to this doctrine, a position that was finally embraced by a majority on the Supreme Court in WEST COAST HOTEL CO. V. PARRISH (1937).

JUSTICE PECKHAM delivered the opinion of the Court.

The statute necessarily interferes with the right of contract between the employer and employees, concerning the number of hours in which the latter may labor in the bakery of the employer. The general right to make a contract in relation to his business is part of the liberty of the individual protected by the 14th Amendment of the Federal Constitution. . . . Under that provision no state can deprive any person of life, liberty, or property without due process of law. The right to purchase or sell labor is part of the liberty protected by this amendment, unless there are circumstances which exclude the right. There are, however, certain powers, existing in the sovereignty of each state in the Union, somewhat vaguely termed police powers, the exact description and limitation of which have not been attempted by the courts. Those powers, broadly stated, and without, at present, any attempt at a more specific limitation, relate to the safety, health, morals, and general welfare of the public. Both property and liberty are held on such reasonable conditions as may be imposed by the governing power of the state in the exercise of those powers, and with such conditions the 14th Amendment was not designed to interfere. . . .

The state, therefore, has power to prevent the individual from making certain kinds of contracts, and in regard to them the Federal Constitution offers no protection. If the contract be one which the state, in the legitimate exercise of its police power, has the right to prohibit, it is not prevented from prohibiting it by the 14th Amendment. Contracts in violation of a statute, either of the Federal or state government, or a contract to let one's property for immoral purposes, or to do any other unlawful act, could obtain no protection from the Federal Constitution, as coming under the liberty of person or of free contract. Therefore, when the state, by its legislature, in the assumed exercise of its police powers, has passed an act which seriously limits the right to labor or the right of contract in regard to their means of livelihood between persons who are *sui juris* (both employer and employee), it becomes of great importance to determine which shall prevail, — the right of the individual to labor for such time as he may choose, or the right of the state to prevent the individual from laboring, or from entering into any contract to labor, beyond a certain time prescribed by the state.

. . . .

It must, of course, be conceded that there is a limit to the valid exercise of the police power by the state. There is no dispute concerning this general proposition. Otherwise the 14th Amendment would have no efficacy and the legislatures of the states would have unbounded power, and it would be enough to say that any piece of legislation was enacted to conserve the morals, the health, or the safety of the people; such legislation would be valid, no matter how absolutely without foundation the claim might be. The claim of the police power would be a mere pretext, — become another and delusive name for the supreme sovereignty of the state to be exercised free from constitutional restraint. This is not contended for. In every case that comes before this court, therefore, where legislation of this character is concerned, and where the protection of the Federal Constitution is sought, the question necessarily arises: Is this a fair, reasonable, and appropriate exercise of the police power of the state, or is it an unreasonable, unnecessary, and arbitrary interference with the right of the individual to his personal liberty, or to enter into those contracts in relation to labor which may seem to him appropriate or necessary for the support of himself and his family? Of course the liberty of contract relating to labor includes both parties to it. The one has as much right to purchase as the other to sell labor.

This is not a question of substituting the judgment of the court for that of the legislature. If the act be within the power of the state it is valid, although the judgment of the court might be totally opposed to the enactment of such a law. But the question would still remain: Is it within the police power of the state? and that question must be answered by the court.

The question whether this act is valid as a labor law, pure and simple, may be dismissed in a few words. There is no reasonable ground for interfering with the liberty of person or the right of free contract, by determining the hours of labor, in the occupation of a baker. There is no contention that bakers as a class are not equal in intelligence and capacity to men in other trades or manual occupations, or that they are not able to assert their rights and care for themselves without the protecting arm of the state, interfering with their independence of judgment and of action. They are in no sense wards of the state. Viewed in the light of a purely labor law, with no reference whatever to the question of health, we think that a law like the one before us involves neither the safety, the morals, nor the welfare of the public, and that the interest of the public is not in the slightest degree affected by such an act. The law must be upheld, if at all, as a law pertaining to the health of the individual engaged in the occupation of a baker. It does not affect any other portion of the public than those who are engaged in that occupation. Clean and wholesome bread does not depend upon whether the baker works but ten hours per day or only sixty hours a week. The limitation of the hours of labor does not come within the police power on that ground.

It is a question of which of two powers or rights shall prevail, — the power of the state to legislate or the right of the individual to liberty of person and freedom of contract. The mere assertion that the subject relates, though but in a remote degree, to the public health, does not necessarily render the enactment valid. The act must have a more direct relation, as a means to an end, and the end itself must be appropriate and legitimate, before an act can be held to be valid which interferes with the general right of an individual to be free in his person and in his power to contract in relation to his own labor.

. . . .

We think the limit of the police power has been reached and passed in this case. There is, in our judgment, no reasonable foundation for holding this to be necessary or appropriate as a health law to safeguard the public health, or the health of the individuals who are following the trade of a baker. If this statute be valid, and if, therefore, a proper case is made out in which to deny the right of an individual, *sui juris,* as employer or employee, to make contracts for the labor of the latter under the protection of the provisions of the Federal Constitution, there would seem to be no length to which legislation of this nature might not go. . . .

We think that there can be no fair doubt that the trade of a baker, in and of itself, is not an unhealthy one to that degree which would authorize the legislature to interfere with the right to labor, and with the right of free contract on the part of the individual, either as employer or employee. In looking through statistics regarding all trades and occupations, it may be true that the trade of a baker does not appear to be as healthy as some other trades, and is also vastly more healthy than still others. To the common understanding the trade of a baker has never been regarded as an unhealthy one. . . .

It is also urged, pursuing the same line of argument, that it is to the interest of the state that its population should be strong and robust, and therefore any legislation which may be said to tend to make people healthy must be valid as health laws, enacted under the police power. If this be a valid argument and a justification of this kind of legislation, it follows that the protection of the Federal Constitution from undue interference with liberty of person and freedom of contract is visionary, wherever the law is sought to be justified as a valid exercise of the police power. Scarcely any law but might find shelter under such assumptions, and conduct, properly so called, as well as contract, would come under the restrictive sway of the legislature. . . .

. . . .

. . . It seems to us that the real object and purpose were simply to regulate the hours of labor between the master and his employees (all being men, *sui juris*), in a private business, not dangerous in any degree to morals, or in any real and substantial degree to the health of the employees. Under such circumstances the freedom of master and employee to contract with each other in relation to their employment, and in defining the same, cannot be prohibited or interfered with, without violating the Federal Constitution.

The judgment . . . must be reversed.

MR. JUSTICE HOLMES, dissenting:

This case is decided upon an economic theory which a large part of the country does not entertain.

If it were a question whether I agreed with that theory, I should desire to study it further and long before making up my mind. But I do not conceive that to be my duty, because I strongly believe that my agreement or disagreement has nothing to do with the right of a majority to embody their opinions in law. It is settled by various decisions of this court that state constitutions and state laws may regulate life in many ways which we as legislators might think as injudicious, or if you like as tyrannical, as this, and which, equally with this, interfere with the liberty to contract. Sunday laws and usury laws are ancient examples. A more modern one is the prohibition of lotteries. The liberty of the citizen to do as he likes so long as he does not interfere with the liberty of others to do the same, which has been a shibboleth for some well-known writers, is interfered with by school laws, by the Postoffice, by every state or municipal institution which takes his money for purposes thought desirable, whether he likes it or not. The 14th Amendment does not enact Mr. Herbert Spencer's Social Statics. The other day we sustained the Massachusetts vaccination law. *Jacobson* v. *Massachusetts* . . . [1905]. United States and state statutes and decisions cutting down the liberty to contract by way of combination are familiar to this court. *Northern Securities Co.* v. *United States* . . . [1904]. Two years ago we upheld the prohibition of sales of stock on margins, or for future delivery, in the Constitution of California. *Otis* v. *Parker* . . . [1903]. The decision sustaining an eight-hour law for miners is still recent. *Holden* v. *Hardy* . . . [1898]. Some of these laws embody convictions or prejudices which judges are likely to share. Some may not. But a Constitution is not intended to embody a particular economic theory, whether of paternalism and the organic relation of the citizen to the state or of *laissez faire*. It is made for people of fundamentally differing views, and the accident of our finding certain opinions natural and familiar, or novel and even shocking, ought not to conclude our judgment upon the question of whether statutes embodying them conflict with the Constitution of the United States.

General propositions do not decide concrete cases. The decision will depend on a judgment or intuition more subtle than any articulate major premise. But I think that the proposition just stated, if it is accepted, will carry us far toward the end. Every opinion tends to become a law. I think that the word "liberty," in the 14th Amendment, is perverted when it is held to prevent the natural outcome of a dominant opinion, unless it can be said that a rational and fair man necessarily would admit that the statute proposed would infringe fundamental principles as they have been understood by the traditions of our people and our law. It does not need research to show that no such sweeping condemnation can be passed upon the statute before us. A reasonable man might think it a proper measure on the score of health. Men whom I certainly could not pronounce unreasonable would uphold it as a first installment of a general regulation of the hours of work. Whether in the latter aspect it would be open to the charge of inequality I think it unnecessary to discuss.

MR. JUSTICE HARLAN (with whom MR. JUSTICE WHITE and MR. JUSTICE DAY concurred) also wrote a dissenting opinion.

Muller v. Oregon

208 U.S. 412 (1908)
Vote: 9–0

A 1903 Oregon statute provided in part that "no female shall be employed in any mechanical establishment, or factory, or laundry in this state more than ten hours during any one day," and went on to make it a misdemeanor subject to a fine for employers to violate this law.

Muller, the owner of a laundry, was subsequently charged and convicted of violating this provision. He appealed on the grounds that the Oregon statute limited his contracting ability and thus violated the Fourteenth Amendment's equal protection and due process provisions.

This case, decided just three years after LOCHNER, provided the origins of the Brandeis Brief, the marshalling of sociological facts and data to support a position. In this case, as you will see from the opinion, Louis Brandeis, then a Boston lawyer, introduced a lengthy brief in support of the Oregon regulation, attempting to show that the need for limiting women's working hours was great.

Can you reconcile the Court's decision here with LOCHNER? with the Court's rulings on women's rights in the 1970s and 1980s (see Chapters 10 and 11)?

MR. JUSTICE BREWER delivered the opinion of the court:

. . . In patent cases counsel are apt to open the argument with a discussion of the state of the art. It may not be amiss, in the present case, before examining the constitutional question, to notice the course of legislation, as well as expressions of opinion from other than judicial sources. In the brief filed by Mr. Louis D. Brandeis for the defendant in error is a very copious collection of all these matters, an epitome of which is found in the [footnote].[†]
. . . .

The legislation and opinions referred to in the [footnote] may not be, technically speaking, authorities, and in them is little or no discussion of the constitutional question presented to us for determination, yet they are significant of a widespread belief that woman's physical structure, and the functions she performs in consequence thereof, justify special legislation restricting or qualifying the conditions under which she should be permitted to toil. Constitutional questions, it is true, are not settled by even a consensus of present public opinion, for it is the peculiar value of a written constitution that it places in unchanging form limitations upon legislative action, and thus gives a permanence and stability to popular government which otherwise would be lacking. At the same time, when a question of fact is debated and debatable, and the extent to which a special constitutional limitation goes is affected by the truth in respect to that fact, a widespread and long-continued belief concerning it is worthy of consideration. We take judicial cognizance of all matters of general knowledge.

It is undoubtedly true, as more than once declared by this court, that the general right to contract in relation to one's business is part of the liberty of the individual, protected by the 14th Amendment to the Federal Constitution; yet it is equally well settled that this liberty is not absolute and extending to all contracts, and that a state may, without conflicting

[†]The following . . . states impose restrictions in some form or another upon the hours of labor that may be required of women: Massachusetts, . . . Rhode Island, . . . Louisiana, . . . Connecticut, . . . Maine, . . . New Hampshire, . . . Maryland, . . . Virginia, . . . Pennsylvania, . . . New York, . . . Nebraska, . . . Washington, . . . Colorado, . . . New Jersey, . . . Oklahoma, . . . North Dakota, . . . South Dakota, . . . Wisconsin, . . . South Carolina.
Mr. Brandeis calls attention to [similar legislation in] Great Britain, . . . France, . . . Switzerland, . . . Austria, . . . Holland, . . . Italy, . . . and Germany.

with the provisions of the 14th Amendment, restrict in many respects the individual's power of contract. . . .

That woman's physical structure and the performance of maternal functions place her at a disadvantage in the struggle for subsistence is obvious. This is especially true when the burdens of motherhood are upon her. Even when they are not, by abundant testimony of the medical fraternity continuance for a long time on her feet at work, repeating this from day to day, tends to injurious effects upon the body, and, as healthy mothers are essential to vigorous offspring, the physical well-being of woman becomes an object of public interest and care in order to preserve the strength and vigor of the race.

Still again, history discloses the fact that woman has always been dependent upon man. He established his control at the outset by superior physical strength, and this control in various forms, with diminishing intensity, has continued to the present. . . . She will still be where some legislation to protect her seems necessary to secure a real equality of right. Doubtless there are individual exceptions, and there are many respects in which she has an advantage over him; but looking at it from the viewpoint of the effort to maintain an independent position in life, she is not upon an equality. Differentiated by these matters from the other sex, she is properly placed in a class by herself, and legislation designed for her protection may be sustained, even when like legislation is not necessary for men, and could not be sustained. It is impossible to close one's eyes to the fact that she still looks to her brother and depends upon him. Even though all restrictions on political, personal, and contractual rights were taken away, and she stood, so far as statutes are concerned, upon an absolutely equal plane with him, it would still be true that she is so constituted that she will rest upon and look to him for protection; that her physical structure and a proper discharge of her maternal functions — having in view not merely her own health, but the well-being of the race — justify legislation to protect her from the greed as well as the passion of man. The limitations which this statute places upon her contractual powers, upon her right to agree with her employer as to the time she shall labor, are not imposed solely for her benefit, but also largely for the benefit of all. Many words cannot make this plainer. The two sexes differ in structure of body, in the functions to be performed by each, in the amount of physical strength, in the capacity for long continued labor, particularly when done standing, the influence of vigorous health upon the future well-being of the race, the self-reliance which enables one to assert full rights, and in the capacity to maintain the struggle for subsistence. This difference* justifies a difference in legislation, and upholds that which is designed to compensate for some of the burdens which rest upon her.

We have not referred in this discussion to the denial of the elective franchise in the state of Oregon, for while that may disclose a lack of political equality in all things with her brother, that is not of itself decisive. The reason runs deeper, and rests in the inherent difference between the two sexes, and in the different functions in life which they perform.

For these reasons, and without questioning in any respect the decision in *Lochner* v. *New York,* we are of the opinion that it cannot be adjudged that the act in question is in conflict with the Federal Constitution, so far as it respects the work of a female in a laundry, and the judgment of the Supreme Court of Oregon is affirmed.

West Coast Hotel Co. v. Parrish

300 U.S. 379 (1937)
Vote: 5–4

Elsie Parrish was employed by the West Coast Hotel Co., where she was paid a weekly wage below the minimum set for women and minors, as established by the Industrial Welfare

*Then follow extracts from over ninety reports of committees, bureaus of statistics, commissioners of hygiene, inspectors of factories, both in this country and in Europe, to the effect that long hours of labor are dangerous for women primarily because of their special physical organization. The matter is discussed in these reports in different aspects, but all agree to the danger. It would, of course, take too much space to give these reports in detail. Following them are extracts from similar reports discussing the general benefits of short hours from an economic aspect of the question. In many of these reports individual instances are given tending to support the general conclusion. Perhaps the general scope and character of all these reports may be summed up in what an inspector for Hanover says: "The reasons for the reduction of the working day to ten hours — (a) the physical organization of women, (b) her maternal functions, (c) the rearing and education of the children, (d) the maintenance of the home — are all so important and so far reaching that the need for such reduction need hardly be discussed."

Commission under its authority under a 1913 statute. Ms. Parrish sued to recover the difference between the established minimum wage and what she had been paid. The hotel company claimed that this regulation was a limitation of liberty in violation of the Fourteenth Amendment. The state trial court found for the company, but the Washington Supreme Court upheld the statute and Ms. Parrish's claim, whereupon the case was appealed to the United States Supreme Court.

The Washington statute was in all crucial respects identical to a provision adopted by the Congress for the District of Columbia, which had been struck down by the Court in 1923, in *Adkins* v. *Children's Hospital,* 261 U.S. 525. Writing for the majority of five in that case, Justice Sutherland relied heavily on LOCHNER and all but ignored MULLER V. OREGON, which increasingly had become something of a neglected exception.

It should be noted that this current case was handed down in the midst of the battle over President Franklin Roosevelt's famous court-packing plan. It is one of the cases that precipitated the saying "A switch in time saves nine."

CHIEF JUSTICE HUGHES deliverd the opinion of the Court.

. . . The principle which must control our decision is not in doubt. The constitutional provision invoked is the due process clause of the Fourteenth Amendment governing the states, as the due process clause invoked in the Adkins Case governed Congress. In each case the violation alleged by those attacking minimum wage regulation for women is deprivation of freedom of contract. What is this freedom? The Constitution does not speak of freedom of contract. It speaks of liberty and prohibits the deprivation of liberty without due process of law. In prohibiting that deprivation, the Constitution does not recognize an absolute and uncontrollable liberty. Liberty in each of its phases has its history and connotation. But the liberty safeguarded is liberty in a social organization which requires the protection of law against the evils which menace the health, safety, morals, and welfare of the people. Liberty under the Constitution is thus necessarily subject to the restraints of due process, and regulation which is reasonable in relation to its subject and is adopted in the interests of the community is due process.

This essential limitation of liberty in general governs freedom of contract in particular. More than twenty-five years ago we set forth the applicable principle in these words, after referring to the cases where the liberty guaranteed by the Fourteenth Amendment had been broadly described.

"But it was recognized in the cases cited, as in many others, that freedom of contract is a qualified, and not an absolute, right. There is no absolute freedom to do as one wills or to contract as one chooses. The guaranty of liberty does not withdraw from legislative supervision that wide department of activity which consists of the making of contracts, or deny to government the power to provide restrictive safeguards. Liberty implies the absence of arbitrary restraint, not immunity from reasonable regulations and prohibitions imposed in the interests of the community." *Chicago, Burlington & Quincy R. Co.* v. *McGuire,* . . . [1911].

This power under the Constitution to restrict freedom of contract has had many illustrations. That it may be exercised in the public interest with respect to contracts between employer and employee is undeniable. Thus statutes have been sustained limiting employment in underground mines and shelters to eight hours a day, . . . requiring redemption in cash of store orders or other evidences of indebtedness issued in the payment of wages, . . . forbidding the payment of seamen's wages in advance, . . . making it unlawful to contract to pay miners employed at quantity rates upon the basis of screened coal instead of the weight of the coal as originally produced in the mine, . . . prohibiting contracts limiting liability for injuries to employees, . . . limiting hours of work of employees in manufacturing establishments, . . . and in maintaining workmen's compensation laws. . . . In dealing with the relation of employer and employed, the Legislature has necessarily a wide field of discretion in order that there may be suitable protection of health and safety, and that peace and good order may be promoted through regulations designed to insure wholesome conditions of work and freedom from oppression. . . .

The point that has been strongly stressed that adult employees should be deemed competent to make their own contracts was decisively met nearly forty years ago in *Holden* v. *Hardy,* [1898], where we pointed out the inequality in the footing of the parties.

. . . .

It is manifest that this established principle is peculiarly applicable in relation to the employment of women in whose protection the state has a special interest. That phase of the subject received elaborate consideration in *Muller* v. *Oregon* (1908)..., where the constitutional authority of the state to limit the working hours of women was sustained. We emphasized the consideration that "woman's physical structure and the performance of maternal functions place her at a disadvantage in the struggle for subsistence" and that her physical well-being "becomes an object of public interest and care in order to preserve the strength and vigor of the race." We emphasized the need of protecting women against oppression despite her possession of contractual rights. We said that "though limitations upon personal and contractual rights may be removed by legislation, there is that in her disposition and habits of life which will operate against a full assertion of those rights. She will still be where some legislation to protect her seems necessary to secure a real equality of right." Hence she was "properly placed in a class by herself, and legislation designed for her protection may be sustained, even when like legislation is not necessary for men, and could not be sustained." We concluded that the limitations which the statute there in question "places upon her contractual powers, upon her right to agree with her employer, as to the time she shall labor" were "not imposed solely for her benefit, but also largely for the benefit of all."...

This array of precedents and the principles they applied were thought by the dissenting Justices in the Adkins Case to demand that the minimum wage statute be sustained. The validity of the distinction made by the Court between a minimum wage and a maximum of hours in limiting liberty of contract was especially challenged.... That challenge persists and is without any satisfactory answer....

....

We think that... the decision in the Adkins Case was a departure from the true application of the principles governing the regulation by the state of the relation of employer and employed....

With full recognition of the earnestness and vigor which characterize the prevailing opinion in the Adkins Case, we find it impossible to reconcile that ruling with these well-considered declarations. What can be closer to the public interest than the health of women and their protection from unscrupulous and overreaching employers? And if the protection of women is a legitimate end of the exercise of state power, how can it be said that the requirement of the payment of a minimum wage fairly fixed in order to meet the very necessities of existence is not an admissible means to that end? The Legislature of the state was clearly entitled to consider the situation of women in employment, the fact that they are in the class receiving the least pay, that their bargaining power is relatively weak, and that they are the ready victims of those who would take advantage of their necessitous circumstances. The Legislature was entitled to adopt measures to reduce the evils of the "sweating system," the exploiting of workers at wages so low as to be insufficient to meet the bare cost of living, thus making their very helplessness the occasion of a most injurious competition. The Legislature had the right to consider that its minimum wage requirements would be an important aid in carrying out its policy of protection. The adoption of similar requirements by many states evidences a deepseated conviction both as to the presence of the evil and as to the means adopted to check it. Legislative response to that conviction cannot be regarded as arbitrary or capricious and that is all we have to decide. Even if the wisdom of the policy be regarded as debatable and its effects uncertain, still the Legislature is entitled to its judgment.

There is an additional and compelling consideration which recent economic experience has brought into a strong light. The exploitation of a class of workers who are in an unequal position with respect to bargaining power and are thus relatively defenseless against the denial of a living wage is not only detrimental to their health and well-being, but casts a direct burden for their support upon the community. What these workers lose in wages the taxpayers are called upon to pay. The bare cost of living must be met. We may take judicial notice of the unparalleled demands for relief which arose during the recent period of depression and still continue to an alarming extent despite the degree of economic recovery which has been achieved. It is unnecessary to cite official statistics to establish what is of common knowledge through the length and breadth of the land. While in the instant case no factual brief has been presented, there is no reason to doubt that the state of Washington has encountered the same social problem that is present elsewhere. The community is not bound to provide what is in effect a subsidy for unconscionable employers. The community may direct its law-making power to correct the abuse which springs from their selfish disregard of the public interest. The argument that the legislation in question constitutes an arbitrary discrimination, because it does not extend to men, is unavailing. This Court has frequently held that the legislative authority, acting within its proper field, is not bound to extend its regulation to all cases which it might possibly reach. The Legislature "is free to recognize degrees of harm and it may confine its restrictions to those classes of cases where the need is deemed to be clearest." If "the law presumably hits the evil where it is most felt, it is not to be overthrown because there are also other instances to which it might have been applied." There is no "doctrinaire requirement" that the legislation should be couched in all-embracing terms. . . .

Our conclusion is that the case of *Adkins* v. *Children's Hospital* should be, and it is, overruled. The judgment of the Supreme Court of the state of Washington is affirmed.

Affirmed.

[MR. JUSTICE SUTHERLAND dissented in an opinion in which JUSTICES VAN DEVANTER, MCREYNOLDS, and BUTLER concurred.]

City of Cleburne v. Cleburne Living Center

105 S.Ct. 3249 (1985)
Vote: 9–0

The Cleburne Living Center (CLC) wanted to operate a group home for the mildly mentally retarded, but was prohibited from doing so by the city. In the neighborhood where the home was to be located, zoning regulations permitted the establishment of nursing homes, homes for convalescents and the aged, and sanitariums and hospitals, but prohibited "hospitals for the feeble-minded" unless granted a special use permit. After a hearing the city denied CLC a special use permit. CLC challenged the city ordinance, alleging that the ordinance, on its face and as applied, violated the equal protection rights of CLC and its potential residents. The District Court upheld the city, but the Court of Appeals reversed, holding that mental retardation is a "quasi-suspect" classification requiring "heightened scrutiny," rather than the standard "rational relation" test, to determine if the ordinance is valid. (See Chapter 11 for extended treatment of this issue.) Using the stricter "heightened scrutiny" test the Court of Appeals ruled the ordinance invalid on its face and as applied.

The city challenged this decision, and in the opinion below the Supreme Court upholds the

judgment of the Court of Appeals but alters the reason for doing so. Employing the lesser standard of scrutiny, the "rational relation" test, the majority holds that the ordinance as applied is a violation of the Equal Protection Clause.

We consider this case here, and again in Chapter 11, because it may pave the way for a more vigorous life for the "rational relation" test and because it is a link between individual and economic substantive due process. In earlier cases in this chapter we traced the rise and fall of substantive due process and changes in the Court's willingness to second-guess the rationale of legislatures. Modern "rational relation" tests, as WEST COAST HOTEL indicates, are exceedingly deferential to the political process, and only rarely when employing this test has the Court invalidated governmental actions. *Cleburne* is one of those rare exceptions, and as such it may signify an increased willingness of the Court to review a wide variety of governmental regulations and practices that differentially affect businesses. If this case is understood as a "property" rights issue rather than a "civil" rights issue, it could signal a return to substantive due process and substantive equal protection in the realm of economic regulation. If so, it has more in common with the activism of LOCHNER than the deference of WEST COAST HOTEL. Alternatively, the decision may be an anomaly: Faced with an instance of blatant discrimination against the mentally retarded, the Court may have wanted to extend its sympathy without granting still one more group a special-pleading status.

JUSTICE WHITE delivered the opinion of the Court.
. . . .
. . . The general rule is that legislation is presumed to be valid and will be sustained if the classification drawn by the statute is rationally related to a legitimate state interest. . . . When social or economic legislation is at issue, the Equal Protection Clause allows the states wide latitude, . . . and the Constitution presumes that even improvident decisions will eventually be rectified by the democratic processes.
The general rule gives way, however, when a statute classifies by race, alienage or national origin.

These factors are so seldom relevant to the achievement of any legitimate state interest that laws grounded in such considerations are deemed to reflect prejudice and antipathy—a view that those in the burdened class are not as worthy or deserving as others. For these reasons and because such discrimination is unlikely to be soon rectified by legislative means, these laws are subjected to strict scrutiny and will be sustained only if they are suitably tailored to serve a compelling state interest. . . .

Legislative classifications based on gender also call for a heightened standard of review. That factor generally provides no sensible ground for differential treatment. . . .

We have declined, however, to extend heightened review to differential treatment based on age. . . .

Against this background, we conclude for several reasons that the Court of Appeals erred in holding mental retardation a quasi-suspect classification calling for a more exacting standard of judicial review than is normally accorded economic and social legislation. . . .

. . . .

Doubtless, there have been and there will continue to be instances of discrimination against the retarded that are in fact invidious, and that are properly subject to judicial correction under constitutional norms. But the appropriate method of reaching such instances is not to create a new quasi-suspect classification and subject all governmental action based on that classification to more searching evaluation. Rather, we should look to the likelihood that governmental action premised on a particular classification is valid as a general matter, not merely to the specifics of the case before us. Because mental retardation is a characteristic that the government may legitimately take into account in a wide range of decisions, and because both state and federal governments have recently committed themselves to assisting the retarded, we will not presume that any given legislative action, even one that disadvantages retarded individuals, is rooted in considerations that the Constitution will not tolerate.

Our refusal to recognize the retarded as a quasi-suspect class does not leave them entirely unprotected from invidious discrimination. To withstand equal protection review, legislation that distinguishes between the mentally retarded and others must be rationally related to a legitimate governmental purpose. This standard, we believe, affords government the latitude necessary both to pursue policies designed to assist the retarded in realizing their full potential, and to freely and efficiently engage in activities that burden the retarded in what is essen-

tially an incidental manner. The State may not rely on a classification whose relationship to an asserted goal is so attenuated as to render the distinction arbitrary or irrational. . . .

. . . .

The constitutional issue is clearly posed. The City does not require a special use permit in an R–3 zone for apartment houses, multiple dwellings, boarding and lodging houses, fraternity or sorority houses, dormitories, apartment hotels, hospitals, sanitariums, nursing homes for convalescents or the aged (other than for the insane or feeble-minded or alcoholics or drug addicts), private clubs or fraternal orders, and other specified uses. It does, however, insist on a special permit for the Featherston home, and it does so, as the District Court found, because it would be a facility for the mentally retarded. May the city require the permit for this facility when other care and multiple dwelling facilities are freely permitted?

It is true, as already pointed out, that the mentally retarded as a group are indeed different from others not sharing their misfortune, and in this respect they may be different from those who would occupy other facilities that would be permitted in an R–3 zone without a special permit. But this difference is largely irrelevant unless the Featherston home and those who would occupy it would threaten legitimate interests of the city in a way that other permitted uses such as boarding houses and hospitals would not. Because in our view the record does not reveal any rational basis for believing that the Featherston home would pose any special threat to the city's legitimate interests, we affirm the judgment below insofar as it holds the ordinance invalid as applied in this case.

The District Court found that the City Council's insistence on the permit rested on several factors. First, the Council was concerned with the negative attitude of the majority of property owners located within 200 feet of the Featherston facility, as well as with the fears of elderly residents of the neighborhood. But mere negative attitudes, or fear, unsubstantiated by factors which are properly cognizable in a zoning proceeding, are not permissible bases for treating a home for the mentally retarded differently from apartment houses, multiple dwellings, and the like. . . .

Second, the Council had two objections to the location of the facility. It was concerned that the facility was across the street from a junior high school, and it feared that the students might harass the occupants of the Featherston home. But the school itself is attended by about 30 mentally retarded students, and denying a permit based on such vague, undifferentiated fears is again permitting some portion of the community to validate what would otherwise be an equal protection violation. The other objection to the home's location was that it was located on "a five hundred year flood plain." This concern with the possibility of flood, however, can hardly be based on a distinction between the Featherston home and, for example, nursing homes, homes for convalescents or the aged, or sanitariums or hospitals, any of which could be located on the Featherston site without obtaining a special use permit. . . .

Fourth, the Council was concerned with the size of the home and the number of people that would occupy it. The District Court found, and the Court of Appeals repeated, that "[i]f the potential residents of the Featherston Street home were not mentally retarded, but the home was the same in all other respects, its use would be permitted under the city's zoning ordinance." . . . Given this finding, there would be no restrictions on the number of people who could occupy this home as a boarding house, nursing home, family dwelling, fraternity house, or dormitory. The question is whether it is rational to treat the mentally retarded differently. It is true that they suffer disability not shared by others; but why this difference warrants a density regulation that others need not observe is not at all apparent. At least this record does not clarify how, in this connection, the characteristics of the intended occupants of the Featherston home rationally justify denying to those occupants what would be permitted to groups occupying the same site for different purposes. Those who would live in the Featherston home are the type of individuals who, with supporting staff, satisfy federal and state standards for group housing in the community; and there is no dispute that the home would meet the federal square-footage-per-resident requirement for facilities of this type. . . .

. . . .

The short of it is that requiring the permit in this case appears to us to rest on an irrational prejudice against the mentally retarded, including those who would occupy the Featherston facility and who would live under the closely supervised and highly regulated conditions expressly provided for by state and federal law.

The judgment of the Court of Appeals is affirmed insofar as it invalidates the zoning ordinance as applied to the Featherston home. . . .

[JUSTICE STEVENS, with whom THE CHIEF JUSTICE joined, wrote a concurring opinion.]

JUSTICE MARSHALL, with whom JUSTICE BRENNAN and JUSTICE BLACKMUN join, concurring in the judgment in part and dissenting in part.

. . . .

I cannot agree . . . with the way in which the Court reaches its results or with the narrow, as-applied remedy it provides for the City of Cleburne's equal protection violation. The Court holds the ordinance invalid on rational basis grounds and disclaims that anything special, in the form of heightened scrutiny, is taking place. Yet Cleburne's ordinance surely would be valid under the traditional rational basis test applicable to economic and commercial regulation. . . .

At the outset, two curious and paradoxical aspects of the Court's opinion must be noted. First, because the Court invalidates Cleburne's zoning ordinance on rational basis grounds, the Court's wideranging discussion of heightened scrutiny is wholly superfluous to the decision of this case. . . .

Second, the Court's heightened scrutiny discussion is even more puzzling given that Cleburne's ordinance is invalidated only after being subjected to precisely the sort of probing inquiry associated with heightened scrutiny. To be sure, the Court does not label its handiwork heightened scrutiny, and perhaps the method employed must hereafter be called "second order" rational basis review rather than "heightened scrutiny." But however labelled, the rational basis test invoked today is most assuredly not the rational basis test of *Williamson* v. *Lee Optical,* 348 U.S. 483, . . . (1955), *Allied Stores* v. *Bowers,* 358 U.S. 522, . . . (1959), and their progeny.

The Court, for example, concludes that legitimate concerns for fire hazards or the serenity of the neighborhood do not justify singling out respondents to bear the burdens of these concerns, for analogous permitted uses appear to pose similar threats. Yet under the traditional and most minimal version of the rational basis test, "reform may take one step at a time, addressing itself to the phase of the problem which seems most acute to the legislative mind." *Williamson* v. *Lee Optical Co.* . . . The "record" is said not to support the ordinance's classifications, . . . but under the traditional standard we do not sift through the record to determine whether policy decisions are squarely supported by a firm factual foundation. . . . Finally, the Court further finds it "difficult to believe" that the retarded present different or special hazards than other groups. In normal circumstances, the burden is not on the legislature to convince the Court that the lines it has drawn are sensible; legislation is presumptively constitutional, and a State "is not required to resort to close distinctions or to maintain a precise, scientific uniformity with reference" to its goals. . . .

I share the Court's criticisms of the overly broad lines that Cleburne's zoning ordinance has drawn. But if the ordinance is to be invalidated for its imprecise classification, it must be pursuant to more powerful scrutiny than the minimal rational-basis test used to review classifications affecting only economic and commercial matters. The same imprecision in a similar ordinance that required opticians but not optometrists to be licensed to practice, see *Williamson* v. *Lee Optical Co.*, ... or that excluded new but not old businesses from parts of a community, see *New Orleans* v. *Dukes*, ... would hardly be fatal to the statutory scheme.

The refusal to acknowledge that something more than minimum rationality review is at work here is, in my view, unfortunate in at least two respects. The suggestion that the traditional rational basis test allows this sort of searching inquiry creates precedent for this Court and lower courts to subject economic and commercial classifications to similar and searching "ordinary" rational basis review—a small and regrettable step back toward the days of *Lochner* v. *New York*, 198 U.S. 45... (1905). Moreover, by failing to articulate the factors that justify today's "second order" rational basis review, the Court provides no principled foundation for determining when more searching inquiry is to be invoked....

Lynch v. Household Finance Corp.

405 U.S. 538 (1972)
Vote: 4–3

In 1969 Household Finance Corp. sued Dorothy Lynch in a state court for $525, alleging nonpayment of a loan. Before she was served with process, Household Finance garnished her savings account under provisions in a Connecticut statute authorizing summary prejudicial garnishment at the behest of attorneys for alleged creditors. Lynch challenged the Connecticut garnishment law, claiming that it did not provide for prior notice of the garnishment and that she had no opportunity to be heard. Specifically, she claimed that the law violated the Equal Protection and Due Process Clauses of the Fourteenth Amendment and sought declaratory relief under 42 U.S.C., section 1983, which provides a cause of action against those who under color of law deprive persons of their civil rights, and section 1343(3), which grants

federal district courts original jurisdiction for hearing such suits. Claiming that Household Finance acting under the authority of Connecticut law had deprived her of her civil rights, Lynch sought an injunction prohibiting state court proceedings to enforce the garnishment statute. The District Court dismissed Ms. Lynch's complaint, holding "that 1343(3) applies only if 'personal' rights as opposed to 'property' rights are impaired."

Although Justice Stewart's discussion of the distinction is in terms of sections 1983 and 1343(3) jurisprudence, it has wider ramifications. If, as he suggests, the distinction is impossible to make, might not someone whose employment or business, as opposed to savings account, is jeopardized by a regulation have a legitimate complaint? More generally, might not *Lynch* provide a basis for rethinking the Court's traditional deference towards legislatures when reviewing actions affecting economic regulation and property interests?

MR. JUSTICE STEWART delivered the opinion of the Court.

....

This Court has never adopted the distinction between personal liberties and proprietary rights as a guide to the contours of §1343(3) jurisdiction. Today we expressly reject that distinction.

Neither the words of §1343(3) nor the legislative history of that provision distinguishes between personal and property rights. In fact, the Congress that enacted the predecessor of §§1983 and 1343(3) seems clearly to have intended to provide a federal judicial forum for the redress of wrongful deprivations of property by persons acting under color of state law.

This Court has traced the origin of §1983 and its jurisdictional counterpart to the Civil Rights Act of 1866, 14 Stat. 27.... That Act guaranteed "broad and sweeping... protection" to basic civil rights.... Acquisition, enjoyment, and alienation of property were among those rights....

....

The broad concept of civil rights embodied in the 1866 Act and in the Fourteenth Amendment is unmistakably evident in the legislative history of §1 of the Civil Rights Act of 1871, 17 Stat. 13, the direct lineal ancestor of §§1983 and 1343(3).... [T]he 1871 Act was passed for the express purpose of "enforc[ing] the Provisions of the Fourteenth Amendment."... And the rights that Congress sought to protect in the Act of 1871 were described by the chairman of the House Select Committee that drafted the legislation as "the enjoyment of life and liberty, with the right to acquire and possess property of every kind, and to pursue and obtain happiness and safety."...That the protection of property as well as personal rights was intended is also confirmed by President Grant's message to Congress urging passage of the legislation, and by the remarks of many members of Congress during the legislative debates.

....

A final, compelling reason for rejecting a "personal liberties" limitation upon §1343(3) is the virtual impossibility of applying it. The federal courts have been particularly bedeviled by "mixed" cases in which both personal and property rights are implicated, and the line between them has been difficult to draw with any consistency or principled objectivity. The case before us presents a good example of the conceptual difficulties created by the test.

Such difficulties indicate that the dichotomy between personal liberties and property rights is a false one. Property does not have rights. People have rights. The right to enjoy property without unlawful deprivation, no less than the right to speak or the right to travel, is in truth, a "personal" right, whether the "property" in question be a welfare check, a home, or a savings account. In fact, a fun-

damental interdependence exists between the personal right to liberty and the personal right in property. Neither could have meaning without the other. That rights in property are basic civil rights has long been recognized. J. Locke, Of Civil Government 82–85 (1924); J. Adams, A Defence of the Constitutions of Government of the United States of America, in F. Coker, Democracy, Liberty, and Property 121–132 (1942); 1 W. Blackstone, Commentaries. Congress recognized these rights in 1871 when it enacted the predecessor of §§1983 and 1343(3). We do no more than reaffirm the judgment of Congress today.

....

We conclude, therefore, that the District Court had jurisdiction to entertain the appellant's suit for an injunction under §1983. Accordingly, the judgment before us is reversed, and the case remanded for further proceedings consistent with this opinion.

It is so ordered.

Judgment reversed and case remanded.

Mr. Justice Powell and Mr. Justice Rehnquist took no part in the consideration or decision of this case.

[Mr. Justice White, with whom The Chief Justice and Mr. Justice Blackmun joined, wrote a dissenting opinion.]

CHAPTER 6

Nationalization of the Bill of Rights: A Policy in Search of a Theory

An overriding concern in the debates at the Constitutional Convention — and one evidenced in the Constitution itself — was the protection of various private interests against government. But different people envisioned different types of possible governmental encroachment. Alexander Hamilton and the Federalists were concerned primarily about the tyranny of state legislatures. They sought to protect commercial and property interests by means of a strong national government and those constitutional provisions examined in the previous chapter. Thomas Jefferson was the spokesman for those who viewed a strong national government as a threat to liberty and sought to preserve individual liberties by circumscribing the powers of the national government. The result was a two-part compromise in constitutional structure. The first three Articles of the Constitution *enumerate* the powers of the national government, with the intent of limiting its powers to only those powers specified. Second was inclusion of a Bill of Rights explicitly aimed at protecting individual rights by expressly limiting the general government from enacting laws abridging a number of specified freedoms.

One argument against explicitly limiting the powers of the national government was that it was

unnecessary. Some held that the protections against governmental infringement on expression and allied actions expressly prohibited in the Bill of Rights were inalienable natural rights, self-evident and unnecessary to spell out. Indeed, Madison argued that trying to define these protections with precision would lead to their narrowing. Others argued that such explicit prohibitions were unnecessary because the Constitution was written so that powers not expressly granted to the national government were retained by the states and individuals. Hence a provision granting specific rights and liberties to individuals as against the national government was superfluous and perhaps even an invitation not to take the theory of enumerated powers seriously.

Still, to many at the Convention, these assurances were not enough. Throughout the Constitutional Convention, they continued to insist on inclusion of a bill of rights, and while this proposal was not acted upon at the Convention, it became a condition of their support for ratification. In 1791, four years after ratification of the Constitution, the first ten Amendments were adopted.

These Amendments, the first eight of which are known as the Bill of Rights, are cherished as important protections of individual liberty from infringement by government. While these Amendments have come to be seen as important safeguards for individual liberty against *government,* they did not begin that way. The Bill of Rights is not written in a way to protect individual rights against all government, but as a limitation on *congressional* power. The First Amendment unequivocally sets the tone: "Congress shall make no law . . ." The first eight Amendments are wholly silent on the powers of the states.

But even as applied to the national government, the Bill of Rights had little meaning breathed into it by the Supreme Court. Reviewing Supreme Court cases with respect to political freedom to 1933, Judge Henry Edgerton wrote, in 1938, that he found not one single case involving speech, press, and assembly that resulted in its protection.* While others have disputed his review of relevant case law, there is little disagreement among constitutional scholars that the Bill of Rights lay more or less dormant until well into the twentieth century.

Needless to say, there was even less activity in respect to cases involving challenges of state infringements of liberties identified in the Bill of Rights. In an early and important case, BARRON V. BALTIMORE (1833), the Supreme Court refused to hear the claim of a merchant who argued that the Fifth Amendment's due process provision protected him against arbitrary actions of local (and by extension, state) government. In rejecting his claim, the Supreme Court held that "These amendments demanded security against the apprehended encroachments of the general government — not against those of the local governments."

Technically, Marshall's ruling in BARRON still holds today, although subsequent events have all but overruled it. With the adoption of the Fourteenth Amendment in 1868, Barron's effort to make the Bill of Rights applicable to state as well as the "general" government was revived. This time the argument was that the Fourteenth Amendment's privileges and immunities and due process provisions, designed to protect individuals against *state* actions, should mean that the provisions of the Bill of Rights were applicable to the states as well as the national government. Although the Court specifically considered and rejected this contention in the SLAUGHTERHOUSE CASES in 1873, and has continued to reject *full* incorporation of the Bill of Rights into the Fourteenth Amendment, over the years it has "nationalized" various provisions of the Bill of Rights. This process of "selective incorporation," as the process has come to be called, constitutes one of the most important chapters of the Court's history, and coincides with the Court's resolve to breathe substantive meaning into these provisions as well. Indeed, in a great many instances, the Court's first bold moves to give significant interpretation to provisions in the Bill of Rights involved cases that simultaneously extended their coverage to the states.

Section 1 of the Fourteenth Amendment contains two provisions that were used to try to get the Court to expand individual liberties. The first provides in part that "No State shall make or enforce any law which shall abridge the privileges or immunities of citizens of the United States." Urged to give broad meaning to the Privileges and Immunities Clause in 1873, the Supreme Court responded with a narrow interpretation. Writing for a majority of five, Justice Miller argued that this clause did not confer any substantive rights on state citizenship. It simply meant, he asserted, that states could not discriminate among people within its borders, regardless of their place of residence. This decision, and the Court's subsequent and continued acquiescence to it, in effect rendered the Privileges and Immunities Clause worthless as a meaningful protection of individual liberty.

However, the second provision in Section 1 of the Fourteenth Amendment, the Due Process Clause, has suffered no such fate. Recall from Chapter 5 that it emerged as a protection of prop-

*Henry Edgerton, "The Incidence of Judicial Control Over Congress," in *Selected Essays in Constitutional Law* (Brooklyn: Foundation Press, 1938), pp. 793–97.

erty and business interests beginning in the 1800s and continuing into the 1930s. Similarly, as the Court embraced substantive economic protections into the Fourteenth Amendment's Due Process Clause, it also began to breathe substantive meaning into its implications for civil rights as well.

Here, too, its history of involvement is uneven. Initially, the Court rejected such claims. Speaking for an eight-man majority in HURTADO V. CALIFORNIA, 110 U.S. 516 (1884), Justice Miller upheld the constitutionality of a California law that provided for indictment by information rather than by grand jury, which is a right in federal criminal proceedings guaranteed by the Fifth Amendment. He argued that the Fourteenth Amendment's Due Process Clause was a *general* guarantee of fairness that prohibited arbitrary governmental power but does not prohibit experimentation with "new and various experiences." Subsequently, two more decisions reinforced the Court's reluctance to bring the Bill of Rights within the meaning of the Fourteenth Amendment's Due Process Clause. In MAXWELL V. DOW (1900), the Court upheld a Utah law that provided for an eight-man jury in a criminal trial, despite the traditional federal requirement that the "right to jury trial" meant a jury of twelve. Eight years later, in TWINING V. STATE OF NEW JERSEY (1908), the Court upheld the constitutionality of a state trial court judge's comment that drew attention to the fact that the defendants had refused to testify in their own behalf, an act which had it taken place in federal court might have been a violation of the Fifth Amendment's prohibition against self-incrimination.

But even as it was rejecting these particular claims, the Supreme Court was laying the groundwork for a substantive interpretation of due process as applied to civil rights and liberties. These decisions suggest that due process of law provides for "fundamental fairness," a standard that must be viewed in light of the entire process surrounding a criminal proceeding rather than any single practice by itself. Thus the stage was set for a substantive interpretation of the Due Process Clause, one that could consider specific protec-

tions included in the Bill of Rights, even if it did not embrace them and Supreme Court cases interpreting them word for word.

Three distinct theories as to the scope and substance of the Fourteenth Amendment's Due Process Clause vis-à-vis the substantive provisions of the Bill of Rights have emerged: (1) the "fundamental fairness" standard first enunciated by Justice Miller in HURTADO, which later found fuller expression in the opinions of Justices Cardozo, Frankfurter, and Harlan (the second); (2) the "total incorporation" position first propounded by Justice Harlan (the first) but most closely associated with Justice Hugo Black, which holds that the term *liberty* in the Due Process Clause of the Fourteenth Amendment is shorthand for incorporation of the Bill of Rights into the Fourteenth Amendment; and, (3) the "total incorporation plus implied and evolving rights" position, associated most closely with Justice William O. Douglas, which holds that the Fourteenth Amendment not only incorporates *all* of the Bill of Rights but also protects other rights not explicitly enunciated in them.

Since HURTADO, the Court has dramatically expanded the meaning of the Fourteenth Amendment's Due Process Clause, so that now most of the provisions of the Bill of Rights are applicable to the states, although the rationale for doing so has remained subject to considerable controversy and debate. It is important, then, to understand the role each of these theories has had in shaping their proponents' views and affecting the development of the Fourteenth Amendment'a Due Process Clause. The cases in this chapter were selected to illustrate these theories, and to demonstrate that the debate over them remains alive and well, if somewhat muted.

The due-process-as-fairness position, first suggested by Justice Miller in 1883, in HURTADO, was given a boost by Justice Sanford in GITLOW V. NEW YORK (1925) when he casually observed that "For present purposes we may and do assume that freedom of speech and press... are among the fundamental personal rights and 'liberties' protected by the due process clause of the Fourteenth Amendment from impairment by the States." Twelve years later a more elaborate defense of the "fundamental rights" position was developed by Justice Cardozo in his majority opinion in PALKO V. CONNECTICUT (1937). This position found its most eloquent advocate in Justice Frankfurter, in *Betts* v. *Brady,* 316 U.S. 455 (1942), ADAMSON V. CALIFORNIA, 332 U.S. 46 (1947), *Wolf* v. *Colorado,* 338 U.S. 25 (1949), and ROCHIN V. CALIFORNIA, 342 U.S. 165 (1952). In PALKO, Justice Cardozo wrote that the Fourteenth Amendment's Due Process Clause protected those rights that were of the "essence of a scheme of ordered liberty," and went on to argue that while some of the provisions in the Bill of Rights (the First Amendment, in particular) met this test and were to be included within the scope of the Fourteenth Amendment, not all of them did. Like Justice Miller in HURTADO, Cardozo was willing to allow the states considerable leeway to experiment and deviate from federal requirements, in areas that they deemed were not crucial and were still consistent with a concept of ordered liberty. The scope of coverage and meaning, their position implied, would have to be determined on a case-by-case basis, as the interests of the individual were balanced against the interests of the community and as notions of fairness evolved.

Because this position includes at least some of the provisions of the Bill of Rights within the scope of the Fourteenth Amendment's Due Process Clause, it has at times been termed the "selective incorporation" position. This term, however, is something of a misnomer, for even though this view holds that some of the specific guarantees in the Bill of Rights might also be deemed "of the essence of a scheme of ordered liberty," under the test advocated by its proponents, the provisions in the Bill of Rights only provide guidance, and those Fourteenth Amendment limitations informed by the Bill of Rights need not be given identical meaning in the two jurisdictions. For instance, while the Supreme Court has ruled in *Duncan* v. *Louisiana,* 391 U.S. 145 (1968), that the Sixth Amendment's right to jury trial is appli-

cable to the states, the Court has also allowed the states to adopt jury rules providing for nonunanimous verdicts, something a majority of the Court would not permit in federal courts (APODACA V. OREGON, 406 U.S. 404, 1972). The Court also allows states to have fewer than twelve jurors in criminal trials, again something that a majority would not permit in federal courts (*Williams* v. *Florida,* 399 U.S. 78, 1970). In short, there is a different and "lesser" right to a jury in state courts under the Fourteenth Amendment than there is in federal courts under the Sixth Amendment. However, for most other provisions in the Bill of Rights that are also "applicable" to the states through the Fourteenth Amendment, this distinction has evolved to be more formal than real.

An extended justification of the selective incorporation position is found in Justice Frankfurter's concurring opinion in ADAMSON V. CALIFORNIA, where the Court refused to extend Fifth Amendment protections applicable in federal courts to the states. Another facet of this position — the "independent effect" of due process — is seen in Frankfurter's opinion for the Court in ROCHIN V. CALIFORNIA (1952), where actions of local police were held to violate "due process," although no single provision in the Bill of Rights was identified as the repository of the Court's concern. The most recent extensive restatement of the selective incorporation position is found in Justice Harlan's dissenting opinion in *Duncan v. Louisiana,* where he argued that while valuable, the Sixth Amendment's guarantee of a right to jury is not a principle "fundamental to ordered liberty" and therefore should not be incorporated into the Fourteenth Amendment in an "absolutist" way.

The total incorporation theory of the relation between the Fourteenth Amendment and the Bill of Rights is much simpler than the fundamental-fairness–selective-incorporation position. First enunciated by Justice John Harlan, Jr., in his lone dissent in HURTADO V. CALIFORNIA (1884), it holds that the term "liberty" in the Fourteenth Amendment's Due Process Clause means those protections enumerated in the Bill of Rights, and that one of the aims of the framers of the Fourteenth Amendment was to extend the prohibitions to the states so that individuals' rights and liberties would be protected against *all* government. In this view the substantive meaning of the Due Process Clause in the Fourteenth Amendment means nothing more or less than giving full and equal application of the protections in the Bill of Rights to the states and the national government.

The modern proponent of this total incorporation position was Justice Hugo Black, who like Justice Harlan, Jr., argued that his views derived from the intent of the framers of the Fourteenth Amendment. While the weight of scholarly evidence suggests that Justice Black misinterpreted, perhaps purposefully, the intent of the framers, his most appealing argument was not history, but parsimony. An unrelenting critic of what he sarcastically referred to as Frankfurter's "accordian-like" approach to due process, Black argued that there was need to give the term fixed and precise content. To him all the provisions in the Bill of Rights were fundamental — that's why they were there! — and he ridiculed Frankfurter's efforts to separate them into two categories, those which are essential to a scheme of ordered liberty and therefore applicable to the states, and those which are merely important and hence are not applicable as protections against state government actions or are applicable according to lesser standards. Justice Black forcefully articulates his position in dissent in ADAMSON and in his concurring opinion in ROCHIN.

The third position, "full incorporation plus implied and evolving rights," is something of an amalgam of both Frankfurter's evolutionary approach to due process and Black's position on total incorporation. Associated most clearly with Justices Murphy and Rutledge, and later Justice Douglas, this position holds that the Due Process Clause of the Fourteenth Amendment not only nationalizes *all* the provisions of the Bill of Rights but also protects other rights necessary for a "scheme of ordered liberty" that are not enumerated there. See, for example, Murphy's brief concurring opinion in ADAMSON V. CALIFORNIA. A more recent variation of this position was seen in the majority opinion in GRISWOLD V. CONNECTICUT (1965), in which Justice Douglas referred to privacy as a right "older than the Bill of Rights" and one created and protected by the penumbra of the "specific guarantees in the Bill of Rights, formed by emanations from those guarantees that help give them life and substance."

The debate among proponents of these various positions on the scope of the Fourteenth Amendment's Due Process Clause has never been resolved by the Court. The history of what the Court actually has done and said in its majority opinions is a mixture of each of the three positions. It has been said that Justice Frankfurter won the battles while Justice Black won the war. There is much in this. Never has a majority of justices on the Court held a total incorporation position; thus, technically, Frankfurter's position has prevailed. Yet over the years, majorities on the Court have held that almost all of the provisions of the Bill of Rights are "essential to a scheme of ordered liberty," thereby incorporating selectively and piecemeal what Black wanted to do in a single swoop, and in so doing destroying the value of the categories Frankfurter so painstakingly constructed. Furthermore, with but few exceptions, the Court has come to give identical interpretations to these provisions as they apply to state and national governments. Thus, using Frankfurter's language and tests, the Court has with but minor exceptions reached the end sought by Black. The Court's decision in *Duncan,* incorporating the right to trial by jury, constituted the final step in this journey that began with the setbacks in MAXWELL over eighty years earlier. The table on pp. 382–383 lists the provisions of the Bill of Rights and the leading cases in which they were "incorporated" into the Fourteenth Amendment.

Viewed in still another light, it might be argued that the incorporation-plus position has won the day. Like Justice Black, Justice Douglas argued that all the provisions of the Bill of Rights should be made applicable to the states in the same way they are to the national government. However, unlike Black, whose argument rested on an absolutist approach, Douglas advocated an evolutionary or flexibile approach to the Fourteenth Amendment's Due Process Clause. In this sense, he embraced a view something like Frankfurter's, namely, that the Fourteenth Amendment was designed to protect "fundamental" rights. But unlike Frankfurter's, Douglas' approach was expansive. When protecting the rights of individuals as against government, Douglas accorded little deference to the principles of federalism, gave less weight to the interests of the state when balancing competing claims, and was willing to create new rights that "emanated" in the penumbra of the several enumerated provisions in the Bill of Rights. Without formally acknowledging it, a majority has embraced this position, as seen in the Court's decision in GRISWOLD, where the Court in effect found new rights in the "penumbra" of the Bill of Rights and held that they were applicable to the states.

So far, this discussion has focused on the *extension* of the various provisions in the Bill of Rights to the states, and the various theories of their application. There is also another dimension to this issue — their *breadth* of coverage. How broadly or narrowly shall the provisions in the Bill of Rights be interpreted? And, excepting Black's position of equal applicability and interpretation, even if extended to the states, do they apply in the same way as against the national government?

Although logically distinct from the issue of nationalization considered above, answers to these questions are intimately connected with the various positions on incorporation. This is because in a great many instances the Court in one and the same case was faced with considering the incorporation question and with breathing meaning into the provisions of the Bill of Rights. The various positions on incorporation supplied guidance on how to interpret the Bill of Rights.

Justice Frankfurter's fundamental-fairness-and-selective-incorporation approach stemmed from his view of the judicial task as one of "balancing interests" among competing claims and his deference to federalism. Thus his test for giving content to provisions of the Bill of Rights was to weigh the competing claims and strike a balance, permitting the states as much leeway as possible.

Justice Black's total incorporation approach stemmed from his belief that this was the intent of the framers of the Fourteenth Amendment. In interpreting the several provisions of the Bill of Rights, Black also, was a "literalist" and "absolutist," who argued that the Court's task was to apply the obvious intent of the words in the provisions. The Bill of Rights, he argued, was framed in plain and simple terms. To him, "no law" meant *no* law, and certainly did not mean some laws, as determined by balancing of competing interests. He ridiculed Justice Frankfurter's flexibility and evolutionary approach, arguing that the provisions in the Bill of Rights had absolute fixed and permanent meaning not amenable to balancing or evolutionary adjustment "in light of new circumstances."

The majorities on the Court during the formative years of interpretation of the Bill of Rights — say, roughly from the 1920s to the 1960s — adopted something of a hybrid approach. Rejecting an absolutist approach, the Court nevertheless often took an expansive view of the Bill of Rights and in so doing was not always deferential to legislative majorities. Still, it has rarely spoken in absolutist language.

We noted above that in most respects the debate over incorporation has been settled. All the major provisions have been incorporated, and for the most part the tests devised by the Court apply equally to the national and state governments. Still the debate is not fully resolved, as the Court's ruling in APODACA V. OREGON indicates. That case revealed a majority of five (Justice Powell in his concurring opinion and the four dissenters), who believed that the Sixth Amendment required a rule of jury unanimity in federal courts, while at the same time a majority of five (Justice Powell and the four other justices who together constituted the majority in this case) held that the jury requirement as applied to the states did not require unanimous verdicts. The four justices whom

Powell joined in *result* were of the opinion that the Sixth Amendment did not require unanimous verdicts on federal courts. Thus, although only one justice was of the opinion that the Sixth and the Fourteenth Amendments' jury requirements permit different standards, given the division among the other eight justices (who did not share this view), the effect of the Court's result is contrary and upholds different constitutional requirements.

Although these various positions were made in reference to the right to jury trial, they have implications for other provisions in the Bill of Rights as well. Recall that a Court majority has never embraced the full and complete incorporation view of Justice Black. One might argue that the standards the Court has developed — usually implicitly — for other provisions of the Bill of Rights are matters of *convenience,* not high *principles* of constitutional law. If so, APODACA might be a harbinger for justifying "lesser" standards for the states in other, presumably "incorporated" positions as well. As we will see, this remains a serious objective of several current justices who want the Court to rethink its interpretation of the Fourth Amendment's prohibition against unreasonable searches and seizures, although there the issue is further complicated by the debate as to whether the "exclusionary rule" — that is, the exclusion of evidence obtained by unconstitutional means — is a principle of constitutional law or a convenient court rule.

A variation of this "double standard," with lesser requirements for states, is also found in the Court's reapportionment decisions. Since 1973, the Supreme Court has tolerated ever-increasing variations in population for state legislative districts though not for congressional districts.

In the mid-1980s, continuing controversy over incorporation and what it means was reopened by then Attorney General Edwin Meese. In a series of speeches, he challenged the soundness of each of the three prevailing theories, claiming that they all lacked a solid historical basis and all encroached on the autonomy of the states, undercutting the federal system. While he mounted a sweeping attack on incorporation, his more proximate concern may have been the Supreme Court's rulings affecting rights of criminal suspects, and particularly the exclusionary rule adopted in MAPP V. OHIO (1961). Under the Reagan and Bush Administrations, the Department of Justice has pressed the Court to reconsider MAPP and other landmark rulings in this area. This campaign has taken many forms, one of which is the claim that the Due Process Clause of the Fourteenth Amendment allows for lower and different standards for assessing state practices dealing with search warrants, search and seizure, right to counsel, and right to silence than do the Bill of Rights' provisions, which apply to federal officials. As you will see in Chapter 9, there is growing support for this view. However, there is even more support for lowering requirements for all law enforcement officials, federal as well as state. These new directions are seen in a pair of cases reprinted in Chapter 9, MICHIGAN V. LONG (1983), which broadened the search-and-seizure powers of police officers, and UNITED STATES V. LEON (1984), which created a "good faith" exception for the exclusionary rule.

The bold arguments challenging standard theories of incorporation have had additional impact. It is noteworthy that the federal District Court judge in WALLACE V. JAFFREE (1985) upheld Alabama's statute prescribing a "moment of silence" in the state's public schools at the outset of each school day on the grounds that the First Amendment does not apply to the states. Although the Court of Appeals and the Supreme Court made short shrift of the argument, that the ruling was made at all may say something about the temper of the times.

The Process of Nationalizing the Bill of Rights

Year	Amendment	Provision	Case(s)
1896–7	Fifth	Public use and "just compensation" in the taking of private property or property by government	*Missouri Pacific Railway Co.* v. *Nebraska,* 164 U.S. 403; *Chicago, Burlington & Quincy Railway Co.* v. *Chicago,* 166 U.S. 226
1927	First	Free speech	*Gilbert* v. *Minnesota,* 254 U.S. 325 (dicta); GITLOW V. NEW YORK, 268 U.S. 652 (dicta); *Fiske* v. *Kansas,* 274 U.S. 380
1931	First	Free press	NEAR V. MINNESOTA, 283 U.S. 697
1932	Sixth*	Fair trial and right to counsel in capital cases	*Powell* v. *Alabama,* 287 U.S. 45
1937	First*	Freedom of assembly and association (implied)	*DeJonge* v. *Oregon,* 299 U.S. 352
1940	First	Free exercise of religion	*Cantwell* v. *Connecticut,* 310 U.S. 296
1947	First	Right against establishment of religion	*Everson* v. *Board of Education,* 330 U.S. 1
1948	Sixth*	Right to public trial	*In re Oliver,* 333 U.S. 25
1949	Fourth	Right against unreasonable searches and seizures	*Wolf* v. *Colorado,* 338 U.S. 25
1961	Fourth	Exclusionary rule; re evidence from unreasonable searches and seizures	*Mapp* v. *Ohio,* 367 U.S. 643
1962	Eighth	Prohibition of cruel and unusual punishments	*Robinson* v. *California,* 370 U.S. 660
1963	Sixth	Right to counsel in felony cases	GIDEON V. WAINWRIGHT, 372 U.S. 335
1964	Fifth	Right against self-incrimination	*Malloy* v. *Hogan,* 378 U.S. 1; *Murphy* v. *Waterfront Commission,* 378 U.S. 52
1965	Sixth	Right to confront witnesses	*Pointer* v. *Texas,* 380 U.S. 400
1965	First, Fourth, Ninth	Right to privacy	GRISWOLD V. CONNECTICUT, 381 U.S. 479
1966	Sixth	Right to impartial jury	*Parker* v. *Gladden,* 385 U.S. 213
1967	Sixth	Right to speedy trial	*Klopfer* v. *North Carolina,* 386 U.S. 213
1967	Sixth	Right to compel witnesses to appear	*Washington* v. *Texas,* 388 U.S. 14
1968	Sixth	Right to trial by jury	*Duncan* v. *Louisiana,* 391 U.S. 145
1969	Fifth	Right against double jeopardy	*Benton* v. *Maryland,* 395 U.S. 784
1972	Sixth	Right to counsel in all criminal cases with jail terms	*Argersinger* v. *Hamlin,* 407 U.S. 25

*The First Amendment's right of petition and the Sixth Amendment's right to be informed of the nature and cause of criminal accusation are generally regarded to have been made applicable to the states in light of the incorporation of other related provisions.

Provisions not applied to the states

Second	All provisions
Third	All provisions
Fifth	Right to indictments by grand jury
Seventh	All provisions
Eighth	Right against excessive bail
	Right against excessive fines

Cases

Barron v. Baltimore

7 Peters 243 (1833)
Vote: Unanimous

John Barron, the owner of a wharf in Baltimore harbor, sued the city of Baltimore, alleging that streams diverted as part of a street construction project had caused "large masses of sand and earth" to build up near his wharf. The result was that the water became too shallow to allow boats to use his facilities, which in turn meant financial ruin for his business.

Barron sought recourse in the courts, claiming that the state's actions violated the guarantee of the Fifth Amendment's provision that private property shall not be "taken for public use, without just compensation." The trial court held for Barron and awarded him $45,000, but this decision was reversed by the state's appellate court, whereupon Barron petitioned the United States Supreme Court to bring up this case upon writ of error.

MR. CHIEF JUSTICE MARSHALL delivered the opinion of the court.

The question thus presented is, we think, of great importance, but not of much difficulty.

The Constitution was ordained and established by the people of the United States for themselves, for their own government, and not for the government of the individual States. Each State established a constitution for itself, and in that constitution provided such limitations and restrictions on the powers of its particular government as its judgment dictated. The people of the United States framed such a government for the United States as they supposed best adapted to their situation, and best calculated to promote their interests. The powers they conferred on this government were to be exercised by itself; and the limitations on power, if expressed in general terms, are naturally, and, we think, necessarily applicable to the government created by the instrument. They are limitations of power granted in the instrument itself; not of distinct governments, framed by different persons and for different purposes.

If these propositions be correct, the fifth amendment must be understood as restraining the power of the general government, not as applicable to the States. In their several constitutions they have imposed such restrictions on their respective governments as their own wisdom suggested; such as they deemed most proper for themselves. It is a subject on which they judge exclusively, and with which others interfere no farther than they are supposed to have a common interest.

. . . .

We are of opinion that the provision in the fifth amendment to the Constitution, declaring that private property shall not be taken for public use without just compensation, is intended solely as a limitation on the exercise of power by the government of the United States, and is not applicable to the legislation of the States. We are therefore of opinion that there is no repugnancy between the several acts of the General Assembly of Maryland, given in evidence by the defendants at the trial of this cause in the court of that State, and the Constitution of the United States.

This court, therefore, has no jurisdiction of the cause, and is dismissed.

Hurtado v. California

110 U.S. 516 (1884)
Vote: 7–1

Soon after the Civil War, the Supreme Court was asked to interpret the provisions of the Fourteenth Amendment. In the SLAUGHTERHOUSE CASES, the Court all but wrote the privileges and immunities provision out of the Constitution, although it eventually gave expansive interpretation to the Fourteenth Amendment's two other key provisions: the Due Process Clause and the Equal Protection Clause.

The Due Process Clause was the first of these two provisions to be given substantive interpretation. Once this occurred, a process for urging still broader interpretation was set in motion that continues to this day.

In *Hurtado,* Barron's basic claim that provisions in the Bill of Rights were *general* protections of liberty against *all* government was revived. This time it was argued that the Due Process Clause of the Fourteenth Amendment included in its scope the protections enumerated in the Bill of Rights. This position was urged for some time by various scholars and lawyers. The Supreme Court's first decision dealing squarely with the issue is the case before us.

Joseph Hurtado was charged with and convicted of murder in a California court. He appealed his conviction, claiming that he had been denied due process. Specifically, Hurtado argued that by being charged by means of an "information" rather than by grand jury indictment, as provided for in the Fifth Amendment, he had been denied his constitutional rights and was entitled to a new trial.

MR. JUSTICE MATTHEWS delivered the opinion of the court.

The proposition of law we are asked to affirm is that an indictment or presentment by a grand jury, as known to the common law of England, is essential to that "due process of law," when applied to prosecutions for felonies, which is secured and guaranteed by this provision of the Constitution of the United States, and which accordingly it is forbidden to the States respectively to dispense with in the administration of criminal law.

. . . .

. . . [I]t is maintained on behalf of the plaintiff in error that the phrase "due process of law" is equivalent to "law of the land," as found in the 20th chapter of Magna Charta; that by immemorial usage it has acquired a fixed, definite, and technical meaning; that it refers to and includes, not only the general principles of public liberty and private right, which lie at the foundation of all free government, but the very institutions which, venerable by time and custom, have been tried by experience and found fit and necessary for the preservation of those principles, and which, having been the birthright and inheritance of every English subject, crossed the Atlantic with the colonists and were transplanted and established in the fundamental laws of the State; that, having been originally introduced into the Constitution of the United States as a limitation upon the powers of the government, brought into being by that instrument, it has now been added as an additional security to the individual against oppression by the States themselves; that one of these institutions is that of the grand jury, an indictment or presentment by which against the accused in cases of alleged felonies is an essential part of due process of law, in order that he may not be harassed or destroyed by prosecutions founded only upon private malice or popular fury.

. . . .

It is urged upon us, however, in argument, that the claim made in behalf of the plaintiff in error is supported by the decision of this court in *Murray's Lessee* v. *Hoboken Land & Improvement Company,* 18 How. 272. There Mr. Justice Curtis, delivering the opinion of the court, after showing . . . that due process of law must mean something more than the actual existing law of the land, for otherwise it would be no restraint upon legislative power, proceeds as follows:

To what principle, then, are we to resort to ascertain whether this process, enacted by Congress, is due process? To this the answer must be twofold. We must examine the Constitution itself to see whether this process be in conflict with any of its provisions. If not found to be so, we must look to those settled usages and modes of proceeding existing in the common and statute law of England before the emigration of our ancestors, and which are shown not to have been unsuited to their civil and political condition by having been acted on by them after the settlement of this country.

This, it is argued, furnishes an indispensable test of what constitutes "due process of law;" that any proceeding otherwise authorized by law, which is not thus sanctioned by usage, or which supersedes and displaces one that is, cannot be regarded as due process of law.

But this interference is unwarranted. The real syllabus of the passage quoted is, that a process of law, which is not otherwise forbidden, must be taken to be due process of law, if it can show the sanction of settled usage both in England and in this country; but it by no means follows that nothing else can be due process of law. The point in the case cited arose in reference to a summary proceeding, questioned on that account, as not due process of law. The answer was: however exceptional it may be, as tested by definitions and principles of ordinary procedure, nevertheless, this, in substance, has been immemorially the actual law of the land, and, therefore, is due process of law. But to hold that such a characteristic is essential to due process of law, would be to deny every quality of the law but its age, and to render it incapable of progress or improvement. It would be to stamp upon our jurisprudence the unchangeableness attributed to the laws of the Medes and Persians.

. . . .

When we add to this that the primitive grand jury heard no witnesses in support of the truth of the charges to be preferred, but presented upon their own knowledge, or indicated upon common fame and general suspicion, we shall be ready to acknowledge that it is better not to go too far back into antiquity for the best securities for our "ancient liberties." It is more consonant to the true philosophy of our historical legal institutions to say that the spirit of personal liberty and individual right, which they embodied, was preserved and developed by a progressive growth and wise adaptation to new circumstances and situations of the forms and processes found fit to give, from time to time, new expression and greater effect to modern ideas of self-government.

. . . .

The Constitution of the United States was ordained, it is true, by descendants of Englishmen, who inherited the traditions of English law and history; but it was made for an undefined and expanding future, and for a people gathered and to be gathered from many nations and of many tongues. And while we take just pride in the principles and institutions of the common law, we are not to forget that in lands where other systems of jurisprudence prevail, the ideas and processes of civil justice are also not unknown. Due process of law, in spite of the absolutism of continental governments, is not alien to that code which survived the Roman Empire as the foundation of modern civilization in Europe, and which has given us that fundamental maxim of distributive justice — *suum cuique tribuere*. There is nothing in Magna Charta, rightly construed as a broad charter of public right and law, which ought to exclude the best ideas of all systems and of every age; and as it was the characteristic principle of the common law to draw its inspiration from every fountain of justice, we are not to assume that the sources of its supply have been exhausted. On the contrary, we should expect that the new and various experiences of our own situation and system will mould and shape it into new and not less useful forms.

. . . .

We are to construe this phrase in the Fourteenth Amendment by the *usus loquendi* of the Constitution itself. The same words are contained in the Fifth Amendment. That article makes specific and express provision for perpetuating the institution of the grand jury, so far as relates to prosecutions for the more aggravated crimes under the laws of the United States.

. . . .

According to a recognized canon of interpretation, especially applicable to formal and solemn instruments of constitutional law, we are forbidden to assume without clear reason to the contrary, that any part of this most important amendment is superfluous. The natural and obvious inference is, that in the sense of the Constitution, "due process of law" was not meant or intended to include, *ex vi termini,* the institution and procedure of a grand jury in any case. The conclusion is equally irresistible, that when the same phrase was employed in the Fourteenth Amendment to restrain the action of the States, it was used in the same sense and with no greater extent; and that if in the adoption of that amendment it had been part of its purpose to perpetuate the institution of the grand jury in all the States, it would have embodied, as did the Fifth Amendment, express declarations to that effect. Due process of law in the latter refers to that law of the land which derives its authority from the legislative powers conferred upon Congress by the Constitution of the United States, exercised within the limits therein prescribed, and interpreted according to the principles of the common law. In the Fourteenth Amendment, by parity of reason, it refers to that law of the land in each State, which derives its authority from the inherent and reserved powers of the State, exerted within the limits of those fundamental principles of liberty and justice which lie at the base of all our civil and political institutions, and the greatest security for which resides in the right of the people to make their own laws, and alter them at their pleasure.

. . . .

But it is not to be supposed that these legislative powers are absolute and despotic, and that the amendment prescribing due process of law is too vague and indefinite to operate a practical restraint. It is not every act, legislative in form, that is law. Law is something more than mere will exerted as an act of power. It must be not a special rule for a particular person or a particular case, but, in the language of Mr. Webster, in his familiar definition, "the general law, a law which hears before it condemns, which proceeds upon inquiry, and renders judgment only after trial," so "that every citizen shall hold his life, liberty, property and immunities under the protection of the general rules which govern society," and thus excluding, as not due process of law, acts of attainder, bills of pains and penalties, acts of confiscation, acts reversing judgments, and acts directly transferring one man's estate to another, legislative judgments and decrees, and other similar special, partial and arbitrary exertions of power under the forms of legislation. Arbitrary power, enforcing its edicts to the injury of the persons and property of its subjects, is not law, whether manifested as the decree of a personal monarch or of an impersonal multitude. And the limitations imposed by our constitutional law upon the action of the governments, both the State and national are essential to the preservation of public and private rights, notwithstanding the representative character of our political institutions. . . .

It follows that any legal proceeding enforced by public authority, whether sanctioned by age and custom, or newly devised in the discretion of the legislative power, in furtherance of the general public good, which regards and preserves these principles of liberty and justice, must be held to be due process of law.

. . . .

Tried by these principles, we are unable to say that the substitution for a presentment or indictment by a grand jury of the proceeding by information, after examination and commitment by a magistrate, certifying to the probable guilt of the defendant, with the right on his part to the aid of counsel, and to the cross-examination of the witnesses produced for the prosecution, is not due process of law. It is, as we have seen, an ancient proceeding at common law, which might include every case of an offence of less grade than a felony, except misprision of treason; and in every circumstance of its administration, as authorized by the statute of California, it carefully considers and guards the substantial interest of the prisoner. It is merely a preliminary proceeding, and can result in no final judgment, except as the consequence of a regular judicial trial, conducted precisely as in cases of indictments.

. . . .

For these reasons, finding no error therein, the judgment of the Supreme Court of California is

Affirmed.

MR. JUSTICE HARLAN, dissenting.

. . . .

The phrase "due process of law" is not new in the constitutional history of this country or of England. It antedates the establishment of our institutions. Those who had been driven from the mother country by oppression and persecution brought with them, as their inheritance, which no government could rightfully impair or destroy, certain guaranties of the rights of life and liberty, and property, which had long been deemed fundamental in Anglo-Saxon institutions. . . .

". . . The article is a restraint on the legislative as well as on the executive and judicial powers of the government, and cannot be so construed as to leave Congress free to make any process 'due process of law' by its mere will. To what principles are we to resort to ascertain whether this process enacted by Congress is due process? To this the answer must be two-fold. We must examine the Constitution itself to see whether this process be in conflict with any of its provisions. If not found to be so, we must look *to those settled usages and modes of proceeding existing in the common and statute law of England before the emigration of our ancestors, and which are shown not to have been unsuited to their civil and political condition by having been acted on by them after the settlement of this country.*"

[Justice Harlan then proceeds to review a number of authorities whose works, he concludes,] prove that, according to the settled usages and modes of proceeding existing under the common and statute law of England at the settlement of this country, information in capital cases was not consistent with the "law of the land," or with "due process of law." Such was the understanding of the patriotic men who established free institutions upon this continent. Almost the identical words of Magna Charta were incorporated into most of the State Constitutions before the adoption of our national Constitution. When they declared, in substance, that no person should be deprived of life, liberty, or property, except by the judgment of his peers or the law of the land, they intended to assert his right to the same guaranties that were given in the mother country by the great charter and the laws passed in furtherance of its fundamental principles.

My brethren concede that there are principles of liberty and justice, lying at the foundation of our civil and political institutions, which no State can violate consistently with that due process of law required by the Fourteenth Amendment in proceedings involving life, liberty, or property. Some of these principles are enumerated in the opinion of the court. But, for reasons which do not impress my mind as satisfactory, they exclude from that enumeration the exemption from prosecution, by information, for a public offence involving life. By what authority is that exclusion made? Is it justified by the settled usages and modes of procedure existing under the common and statute law of England at the emigration of our ancestors, or at the foundation of our government? Does not the fact that the people of the original States required an amendment of the national Constitution, securing exemption from prosecution, for a capital offence, except upon the indictment or presentment of a grand jury, prove that, in their judgment, such an exemption was essential to protection against accusation and unfounded prosecution, and, therefore, was a fundamental principle in liberty and justice? . . .

. . . [I]t is said that the framers of the Constitution did not suppose that due process of law necessarily required for a capital offence the institution and procedure of a grand jury, else they would not in the same amendment prohibiting the deprivation of life, liberty, or property, without due process of law, have made specific and express provision for a grand jury where the crime is capital or otherwise infamous; therefore, it is argued, the requirement by the Fourteenth Amendment of due process of law in all proceedings involving life, liberty, and property, without specific reference to grand juries in any case whatever, was not intended as a restriction upon the power which it is claimed the States previously had, so far as the express restrictions of the national Constitution are concerned, to dispense altogether with grand juries.

This line of argument, it seems to me, would lead to results which are inconsistent with the vital principles of republican government. If the presence in the Fifth Amendment of a specific provision for grand juries in capital cases, alongside the provision for due process of law in proceedings involving life, liberty, or property, is held to prove that "due process of law" did not, in the judgment of the framers of the Constitution, necessarily require a grand jury in capital cases, inexorable logic would require it to be, likewise, held that the right not to be put twice in jeopardy of life and limb for the same offence, nor compelled in a criminal case to testify against one's self — rights and immunities also specifically recognized in the Fifth Amendment — were not protected by that due process of law required by the settled usages and proceedings existing under the common and statute law of England at the settlement of this country. More than that, other amendments of the Constitution proposed at the same time, expressly recognize the right of persons to just compensation for private property taken for public use; their right, when accused of crime, to be informed of the nature and cause of the accusation against them, and to a speedy and public trial, by an impartial jury of the State and district wherein the crime was committed; to be confronted by the witnesses against them; and to have compulsory process for obtaining witnesses in their favor. Will it be claimed that these rights were not secured by the "law of the land" or by "due process of law," as declared and established at the foundation of our government? Are they to be excluded from the enumeration of the fundamental principles of liberty and justice, and, therefore, not embraced by "due process of law"? If the argument of my brethren be sound, those rights — although universally recognized at the establishment of our institutions as secured by that due process of law which for centuries had been the foundation of Anglo-Saxon liberty — were not deemed by our fathers as essential in the due process of law prescribed by our Constitution; because, — such seems to be the argument — had they been regarded as involved in due process of law they would not have been specifically and expressly provided for, but left to the protection given by the general clause forbidding the deprivation of life, liberty, or property without due process of law. . . .

. . . .

It is said by the court that the Constitution of the United States was made for an undefined and expanding future, and that its requirement of due process of law in proceedings involving life, liberty and property, must be so interpreted as not to deny to the law the capacity of progress and improvement; that the greatest security for the fundamental principles of justice resides in the right of the people to make their own laws and alter them at pleasure. It is difficult, however, to perceive anything in the system of prosecuting human beings for their lives, by information, which suggests that the State which adopts it has entered upon an era of progress and improvement in the law of criminal procedure.

Maxwell v. Dow

176 U.S. 581 (1900)
Vote: 8–1

In 1898, Maxwell was charged by the State of Utah with the crime of robbery. He was tried before a jury composed of eight jurors and convicted. Upon appeal, Maxwell sought to have his conviction overturned on the bases that he had been prosecuted under an information rather than indictment by a grand jury and that he had been tried by a jury of eight rather than twelve, in violation of his constitutional rights as protected by the Fifth, Sixth, and Fourteenth Amendments.

MR. JUSTICE PECKHAM delivered the opinion of the court.

The . . . question is, whether in denying the right of an individual, in all criminal cases not capital, to have a jury composed of twelve jurors, the State deprives him of life, liberty or property, without due process of law.

This question is, as we believe, substantially answered by the reasoning of the opinion in the *Hurtado case, supra*. The distinct question was there presented whether it was due process of law to prosecute a person charged with murder by an information under the state constitution and law. It was held that it was, and that the Fourteenth Amendment did not prohibit such a procedure. In our opinion the right to be exempt from prosecution for an infamous crime, except upon a presentment by a grand jury, is of the same nature as the right to a petit jury of the number fixed by the common law. If

the State have the power to abolish the grand jury and the consequent proceeding by indictment, the same course of reasoning which establishes that right will and does establish the right to alter the number of the petit jury from that provided by the common law. . . .

Trial by jury has never been affirmed to be a necessary requisite of due process of law. . . .

It appears to us that the questions whether a trial in criminal cases not capital shall be by a jury composed of eight instead of twelve jurors, and whether in case of an infamous crime a person shall only be liable to be tried after presentment or indictment of a grand jury, are eminently proper to be determined by the citizens of each State for themselves, and do not come within the clause of the amendment under consideration, so long as all persons within the jurisdiction of the State are made liable to be proceeded against by the same kind of procedure and to have the same kind of trial, and the equal protection of the laws is secured to them. . . . It is emphatically the case of the people by their organic law, providing for their own affairs, and we are of opinion they are much better judges of what they ought to have in these respects than any one else can be. The reasons given in the learned and most able opinion of Mr. Justice Matthews, in the *Hurtado case,* for the judgment therein rendered, apply with equal force in regard to a trial by a jury of less than twelve jurors. The right to be proceeded against only by indictment, and the right to a trial by twelve jurors, are of the same nature, and are subject to the same judgment, and the people in the several States have the same right to provide by their organic law for the change of both or either. . . . There is no reason to doubt their willingness or their ability to do so, and when providing in their constitution and legislation for the manner in which civil or criminal actions shall be tried, it is in entire conformity with the character of the Federal Government that they should have the right to decide for themselves what shall be the form and character of the procedure in such trials, whether there shall be an indictment or an information only, whether there shall be a jury of twelve or a less number, and whether the verdict must be unanimous or not. These are matters which have no relation to the character of the Federal Government. . . . [T]he State has full control over the procedure in its courts, both in civil and criminal cases, subject only to the qualification that such procedure must not work a denial of fundamental rights or conflict with specific and applicable provisions of the Federal Constitution. The legislation in question is not, in our opinion, open to either of these objectives.

Affirmed.

Mr. Justice Harlan dissented.

Twining v. New Jersey

211 U.S. 78 (1908)
Vote: 8–1

Albert Twining and a colleague were indicted for fraud. At their trial, they neither called witnesses in their behalf nor took the stand in their own defense. In his charge to the jury the trial judge noted that the jury had "a right to consider the fact that [the defendant] does not go upon the stand where a direct accusation is made against him." Twining and his codefendant were subsequently convicted and sentenced. Their conviction was upheld in the state's highest appellate court, whereupon they brought the case before the United States Supreme Court, claiming that their right against self-incrimination, as specifically provided for in the Fifth Amendment, had been denied them by the judge's comments to the jury.

Mr. Justice Moody . . . delivered the opinion of the court.

[The court considered and rejected plaintiffs' claim that the lower court had not protected their rights under the Privileges and Immunities Clause of the Fourteenth Amendment.]

The defendants, however, do not stop here. They appeal to another clause of the Fourteenth Amendment, and insist that the self-incrimination, which they allege the instruction to the jury compelled, was a denial of due process of law. This contention requires separate consideration, for it is possible that some of the personal rights safeguarded by the first eight Amendments against National action may also be safeguarded against state action, because a denial of them would be a denial of due process of law. . . . If this is so, it is not because those rights are enumerated in the first eight Amendments, but because they are of such a nature that they are included in the conception of due process of law. Few

phrases of the law are so elusive of exact apprehension as this. Doubtless the difficulties of ascertaining its connotation have been increased in American jurisprudence, where it has been embodied in constitutions and put to new uses as a limit on legislative power. This court has always declined to give a comprehensive definition of it, and has preferred that its full meaning should be gradually ascertained by the process of inclusion and exclusion in the course of the decisions of cases as they arise. There are certain general principles well settled, however, which narrow the field of discussion and may serve as helps to correct conclusions. . . . From the consideration of the meaning of the words in the light of their historical origin this court has drawn the following conclusions:

First. What is due process of law may be ascertained by an examination of those settled usages and modes of proceedings existing in the common and statute law of England before the emigration of our ancestors, and shown not to have been unsuited to their civil and political condition by having been acted on by them after the settlement of this country. . . .

Second. It does not follow, however, that a procedure settled in English law at the time of the emigration, and brought to this country and practiced by our ancestors, is an essential element of due process of law. If that were so the procedure of the first half of the seventeenth century would be fastened upon the American jurisprudence like a straightjacket, only to be unloosed by constitutional amendment. . . .

Third. But, consistently with the requirements of due process, no change in ancient procedure can be made which disregards those fundamental principles, to be ascertained from time to time by judicial action, which have relation to process of law and protect the citizen in his private right, and guard him against the arbitrary action of government. . . .

The question under consideration may first be tested by the application of these settled doctrines of this court. If the statement of Mr. Justice Curtis, as elucidated in *Hurtado* v. *California,* is to be taken literally, that alone might almost be decisive. For nothing is more certain, in point of historical fact, than that the practice of compulsory self-incrimination in the courts and elsewhere existed for four hundred years after the granting of Magna Carta, continued throughout the reign of Charles I (though then beginning to be seriously questioned), gained at least some foothold among the early colonists of this country, and was not entirely omitted at trials in England until the eighteenth century. . . .

. . . .

... But without repudiating or questioning the test proposed by Mr. Justice Curtis for the court, or rejecting the inference drawn from English law, we prefer to rest our decision on broader grounds, and inquire whether the exemption from self-incrimination is of such a nature that it must be included in the conception of due process. Is it a fundamental principle of liberty and justice which inheres in the very idea of free government and is the inalienable right of a citizen of such a government? If it is, and if it is of a nature that pertains to process of law, this court has declared it to be essential to due process of law. In approaching such a question it must not be forgotten that in a free representative government nothing is more fundamental than the right of the people through their appointed servants to govern themselves in accordance with their own will, except so far as they have restrained themselves by constitutional limits specifically established, and that in our peculiar dual form of government nothing is more fundamental than the full power of the State to order its own affairs and govern its own people, except so far as the Federal Constitution expressly or by fair implication has withdrawn that power.... The question before us is the meaning of a constitutional provision which forbids the States to deny to any person due process of law. In the decision of this question we have the authority to take into account only those fundamental rights which are expressed in that provision, not the rights fundamental in citizenship, state or National, for they are secured otherwise, but the rights fundamental in due process, and therefore an essential part of it. We have to consider whether the right is so fundamental in due process that a refusal of the right is a denial of due process.... [W]e find nothing to show that it was then thought to be other than a just and useful principle of law. None of the great instruments in which we are accustomed to look for the declaration of the fundamental rights made reference to it....

Even if the historical meaning of due process of law and the decisions of this court did not exclude the privilege from [being essential to due process], it would be going far to rate it as an immutable principle of justice which is the inalienable possession of every citizen of a free government. Salutary as the principle may seem to the great majority, it cannot be ranked with the right to hearing before condemnation, the immunity from arbitrary power not acting by general laws, and the inviolability of private property. The wisdom of the exemption has never been universally assented to since the days of Bentham; many doubt it to-day, and it is best defended not as an unchangeable principle of universal justice but as a law proved by experience to be expedient.... It has no place in the jurisprudence of civilized and free countries outside the domain of the common law, and it is nowhere observed among our own people in the search for truth outside the administration of the law....

We have assumed only for the purpose of discussion that what was done in the case at bar was an infringement of the privilege against self-incrimination. We do not intend, however, to lend any countenance to the truth of that assumption....

Judgment affirmed.

MR. JUSTICE HARLAN dissented.

Palko v. Connecticut

> 302 U.S. 319 (1937)
> Vote: 8–1

In the three preceding cases, we saw the Court reject the argument that provisions of the Bill of Rights were included within the meaning of the Fourteenth Amendment's Due Process Clause. But even as it was rejecting the specific claims, the Court was laying the groundwork for incorporating *some* of the Bill of Rights' provisions. By rejecting the claims of Hurtado, Twining, and Maxwell because they did not deal with "fundamental" rights, the Court was creating a category of rights that presumably would be subject to incorporation.

This reasoning invited continual litigation on the issue and a separate consideration of virtually each provision in the first eight amendments to the Constitution. It also led to the articulation of distinct "theories of incorporation," each of which had its own fierce and articulate advocates. The three major positions, selective incorporation based upon fundamental fairness, total incorporation, and incorporation plus are seen in the majority, minority, and concurring opinions in the following cases.

While the debate over incorporation is general and applies to the overall relationship between the Fourteenth and the first eight Amendments, at first glance it appears to be primarily a debate over criminal procedure. This is because the incorporation of some of the most important provisions in the Bill of Rights — those contained in the First Amendment — were never seriously contested by advocates of any of the positions and were incorporated without controversy (although there remains considerable controversy over the meaning and scope of coverage of these provisions.) The arguments became heated, however, when issues of criminal procedure were considered. Thus the various philosophies of incorporation were spelled out in cases involving the rights of the criminally accused, where state practices historically diverged from constitutional (and federal) standards.

In the case below, Justice Cardozo, for the majority of eight, articulates a position that was later seized upon and refined by Justice Frankfurter. He also catalogues those provisions in the Bill of Rights that were already accepted by the Court as rights "implicit in the concept of ordered liberty."

Palko was tried in a Connecticut court for first degree murder, but the jury found him guilty of second degree murder and sentenced him to life imprisonment. The state appealed Palko's conviction on the grounds that the trial court had made an error of law prejudicial to the prosecution. Connecticut's State Supreme Court of Errors held that such an appeal was permitted under state law. It also upheld the claim of prejudicial error to the state and ordered a new trial. At the second trial, additional evidence and a different set of instructions were presented to the jury, which returned a verdict of first degree murder and sentenced Palko to death. Palko challenged this conviction, claiming that the retrial amounted to double jeopardy in violation of the Fifth and Fourteenth Amendments.

MR. JUSTICE CARDOZO delivered the opinion of the Court.

The argument for appellant is that whatever is forbidden by the Fifth Amendment is forbidden by the Fourteenth also. The Fifth Amendment, which is not directed to the states, but solely to the federal government, creates immunity for double jeopardy. No person shall be "subject for the same offense to be twice put in jeopardy of life or limb." The Fourteenth Amendment ordains, "nor shall any State deprive any person of life, liberty, or property, without due process of law." To retry a defendant, though under one indictment and only one, subjects him, it is said, to double jeopardy in violation of the Fifth Amendment, if the prosecution is one on behalf of the United States. From this consequence is said to follow that there is a denial of life or liberty without due process of law, if the prosecution is one on behalf of the People of a State. . . .

. . . .

We have said that in appellant's view the Fourteenth Amendment is to be taken as embodying the prohibitions of the Fifth. His thesis is even broader. Whatever would be a violation of the original bill of rights (Amendments I and VIII) if done by the federal government is now equally unlawful by force of the Fourteenth Amendment if done by a state. There is no such general rule.

The Fifth Amendment provides, among other things, that no person shall be held to answer for a capital or otherwise infamous crime unless on presentment or indictment of a grand jury. This court has held that, in prosecutions by a state, presentment or indictment by a grand jury may give way to informations at the instance of a public officer. *Hurtado* v. *California*. . . . The Fifth Amendment provides also that no person shall be compelled in any criminal case to be a witness against himself. This court has said that, in prosecutions by a state, the exemption will fail if the state elects to end it. *Twining* v. *New Jersey*. . . . The Sixth Amendment calls for a jury trial in criminal cases and the Seventh for a jury trial in civil cases at common law where the value in controversy shall exceed twenty dollars. This court has ruled that consistently with those amendments trial by jury may be modified by a state or abolished altogether. . . .

On the other hand, the due process clause of the Fourteenth Amendment may make it unlawful for a state to abridge by its statutes the freedom of speech which the First Amendment safeguards against encroachment by the Congress . . . or the like freedom of the press . . . or the free exercise of religion . . . or the right of peaceable assembly, without which speech would be unduly trammeled . . . or the right of one accused of crime to the benefit of counsel. . . . In these and other situations immunities that are valid as against the federal government by force of the specific pledges of particular amendments have been found to be implicit in the concept of ordered liberty, and thus, through the Fourteenth Amendment, become valid as against the states.

The line of division may seem to be wavering and broken if there is a hasty catalogue of the cases on the one side and the other. Reflection and analysis will induce a different view. There emerges the perception of a rationalizing principle which gives to discrete instances a proper order and coherence. The right to trial by jury and the immunity from prosecution except as the result of an indictment may have value and importance. Even so, they are not of the very essence of a scheme of ordered liberty. To abolish them is not to violate a "principle of justice so rooted in the traditions and conscience of our people as to be ranked as fundamental." . . . Few would be so narrow or provincial as to maintain that a fair and enlightened system of justice would be impossible without them. What is true of jury trials and indictments is true also, as the cases show, of the immunity from compulsory self-incrimination. . . . This too might be lost, and justice still be done. Indeed, today as in the past there are students of our penal system who look upon the immunity as a mischief rather than a benefit, and who would limit its scope, or destroy it altogether. No doubt there would remain the need to give protection against torture, physical or mental. . . . Justice, however, would not perish if the accused were subject to a duty to respond to orderly inquiry. The exclusion of these immunities and privileges from the privileges and immunities protected against the action of the states has not been arbitrary or casual. It has been dictated by a study and appreciation of the meaning, the essential implications, of liberty itself.

We reach a different plane of social and moral values when we pass to the privileges and immunities that have been taken over from the earlier articles of the federal bill of rights and brought within the Fourteenth Amendment by a process of absorption. These in their origin were effective against the federal government alone. If the Fourteenth Amendment has absorbed them, the process of absorption has had its source in the belief that neither liberty nor justice would exist if they were sacrificed. . . . This is true, for illustration, of freedom of thought, and speech. Of that freedom one may say that it is the matrix, the indispensable condition, of nearly every other form of freedom. With rare aberrations a pervasive recognition of that truth can be traced in our history, political and legal. So it has come about that the domain of liberty, withdrawn by the Fourteenth Amendment from encroachment by the states, has been enlarged by latter-day judgments to include liberty of the mind as well as liberty of action. The extension became, indeed, a logical imperative when once it was recognized, as long ago it was, that liberty is something more than exemption from physical restraint, and that even in the field of substantive rights and duties the legislative judgment, if oppressive and arbitrary, may be overridden by the courts. . . . Fundamental too in the concept of due process, and so in that of liberty, is the thought that condemnation shall be rendered only after trial. . . . The hearing, moreover, must be a real one, not a sham or a pretense. . . . For that reason, ignorant defendants in a capital case were held to have been condemned unlawfully when in truth, though not in form, they were refused the aid of consel. . . . The decision did not turn upon the fact that the benefit of counsel would have been guaranteed to the defendants by the provisions of the Sixth Amendment if they had been prosecuted in a federal court. The decision turned upon the fact that in the particular situation laid before us in the evidence the benefit of counsel was essential to the substance of a hearing.

Our survey of the cases serves, we think, to justify the statement that the dividing line between them, if not unfaltering throughout its course, has been true for the most part to a unifying principle. On which side of the line the case made out by the appellant has appropriate location must be the next inquiry and the final one. Is that kind of double jeopardy to which the statute has subjected him a hardship so acute and shocking that our polity will not endure it? Does it violate those "fundamental principles of liberty and justice which lie at the base of all our civil and political institutions"? . . . The answer surely must be "no." What the answer would have to be if the state were permitted after a trial free from error to try the accused over again or to bring another case against him, we have no occasion to consider. We deal with the statute before us and no other. The state is not attempting to wear the accused out by a multitude of cases with accumulated trials. It asks no more than this, that the case against him shall go on until there be a trial free from the corrosion of substantial legal error. . . . This is not cruelty at all, nor even vexation in any immoderate degree. If the trial had been infected with error adverse to the accused, there might have been review at his instance, and as often as necessary to purge the vicious taint. A reciprocal privilege, subject at all times to the discretion of the presiding judge, . . . has now been granted to the state. There is here no seismic innovation. The edifice of justice stands, its symmetry, to many, greater than before.

The judgment is

Affirmed.

[MR. JUSTICE BUTLER dissented without opinion.]

Adamson v. California

332 U.S. 46 (1947)
Vote: 5–4

The various opinions in *Adamson* contain all three of the major positions on incorporation, and this is the primary historical importance of this case. Indeed, for historical purposes Reed's opinion for the Court may be the least important of the four opinions spawned by this case. Much more telling are Frankfurter's concurring opinion, which outlines his fundamental-fairness position; Black's dissent, which succinctly restates his total incorporation position; and Justice Murphy's brief separate dissenting opinion, which outlines the incorporation-plus philosophy later developed by Justice Douglas as well.

The issues that gave rise to this case are as follows: At his trial for first degree murder, Adamson declined to take the stand in his own defense. Acting in accordance with California law, both the prosecution and the judge commented in an adverse way upon this failure of the defendant. Adamson, whose prior convictions for burglary, larceny, and robbery would have been revealed had he taken the stand, appealed his conviction, claiming that the California law permitting such adverse comments put him in a double bind. If he took the stand, his prior record would be revealed to the jury, but if he did not, the prosecutor and court could remark on his failure to take the stand so as to prejudice him. Specifically, Adamson argued that the California law that permitted this type of adverse commentary was in violation of the Fifth Amendment's provision that no person "shall be compelled in any criminal case to be a witness against himself," which was made applicable to the states through the Fourteenth Amendment's Due Process Clause and Privileges and Immunities Clause. (The court also raised but quickly and firmly rejected this latter contention.)

At the time, commentary on the defendant's failure to take the stand by either the prosecutor or the judge was prohibited in the federal courts and in the vast majority of state courts.

MR. JUSTICE REED delivered the opinion of the Court.

[A]ppellant relies upon the due process of law clause of the Fourteenth Amendment to invalidate the provisions of the California law, . . . and as applied (a) because comment on failure to testify is permitted, (b) because appellant was forced to forego testimony in person because of danger to disclosure of his past convictions through cross-examination, and (c) because the presumption of innocence was infringed by the shifting of the burden of proof to appellant in permitting comment on his failure to testify.
. . . .

Appellant . . . contends that if the privilege against self-incrimination is not a right protected by the privileges and immunities clause of the Fourteenth Amendment against state action [in a section of the opinion not reprinted here, the Court rejected the privileges and immunities argument]; this privilege, to its full scope under the Fifth Amendment, inheres in the right to a fair trial. A right to a fair trial is a right admittedly protected by the due process clause of the Fourteenth Amendment. Therefore, appellant argues, the due process clause of the Fourteenth Amendment protects his privilege against self-incrimination. The due process clause of the Fourteenth Amendment, however, does not draw all the rights of the federal Bill of Rights under its protection. That contention was made and rejected in *Palko* v. *Connecticut.* . . . It was rejected with citation of the cases excluding several of the rights, protected by the Bill of Rights, against infringement by the National Government. Nothing has been called to our attention that either the framers of the Fourteenth Amendment or the states that adopted intended its due process clause to draw within its scope the earlier amendments to the Constitution. *Palko* held that such provisions of the Bill of Rights as were "implicit in the concept of ordered liberty," . . . became secure from state interference by the clause. But it held nothing more.

Specifically, the due process clause does not protect, by virtue of its mere existence, the accused's freedom from giving testimony by compulsion in state trials that is secured to him against federal interference by the Fifth Amendment. . . . For a state to require testimony from an accused is not necessarily a breach of a state's obligation to give a fair trial. Therefore, we must examine the effect of the

California law applied in this trial to see whether the comment on failure to testify violates the protection against state action that the due process clause does grant to an accused. The due process clause forbids compulsion to testify by fear of hurt, torture or exhaustion. It forbids any other type of coercion that falls within the scope of due process.... So our inquiry is directed, not at the broad question of the constitutionality of compulsory testimony from the accused under the due process clause, but to the constitutionality of the provision of the California law that permits comment upon his failure to testify....

Generally, comment on the failure of an accused to testify is forbidden in American jurisdictions.... California, however, is one of the few states that permit limited comment upon a defendant's failure to testify. That permission is narrow.... This does not involve any presumption, rebuttable or irrebuttable, either of guilt or of truth of any fact, that is offered in evidence.... It allows inferences to be drawn from proven facts. Because of this clause, the court can direct the jury's attention to whatever evidence there may be that a defendant could deny and the prosecution can argue as to inferences that may be drawn from the accused's failure to testify.... There is here no lack of power in the trial court to adjudge and no denial of a hearing. California has prescribed a method for advising the jury in the search for truth. However sound may be the legislative conclusion that an accused should not be compelled in any criminal case to be a witness against himself, we see no reason why comment should not be made upon his silence. It seems quite natural that when a defendant has opportunity to deny or explain facts and determines not to do so, the prosecution should bring out the strength of the evidence by commenting upon defendant's failure to explain or deny it. The prosecution evidence may be of facts that may be beyond the knowledge of the accused. If so, his failure to testify would have little if any weight. But the facts may be such as are necessarily in the knowledge of the accused. In that case a failure to explain would point to an inability to explain.

Affirmed.

MR. JUSTICE FRANKFURTER, concurring.

. . . .

For historical reasons a limited immunity from the common duty to testify was written into the Federal Bill of Rights, and I am prepared to agree that, as part of that immunity, comment on the failure of an accused to take the witness stand is forbidden in federal prosecutions. It is so, of course, by explicit act of Congress.... But to suggest that such a limitation can be drawn out of "due process" in its protection of ultimate decency in a civilized society is to suggest that the Due Process Clause fastened fetters of unreason upon the States....

Between the incorporation of the Fourteenth Amendment into the Constitution and the beginning of the present membership of the Court—a period of seventy years—the scope of that Amendment was passed upon by forty-three judges. Of all these judges, only one, who may respectfully be called an eccentric exception, ever indicated the belief that the Fourteenth Amendment was a shorthand summary of the first eight Amendments theretofore limiting only the Federal Government, and that due process incorporated those eight Amendments as restrictions upon the powers of the States. Among these judges were not only those who would have to be included among the greatest in the history of the Court, but—it is especially relevant to note—they included those whose services in the cause of human rights and the spirit of freedom are the most conspicuous in our history. It is not invidious to single out Miller, Davis, Bradley, Waite, Matthews, Gray, Fuller, Holmes, Brandeis, Stone and Cardozo (to speak only of the dead) as judges who were alert in safeguarding and promoting the interests of liberty and human dignity through law. But they were also judges mindful of the relation of our federal system to a progressively democratic society and therefore duly regardful of the scope of authority that was left to the States even after the Civil War. And so they did not find that the Fourteenth Amendment, concerned as it was with matters fundamental to the pursuit of justice, fastened upon the States procedural arrangements which, in the language of Mr. Justice Cardozo, only those who are "narrow or provincial" would deem essential to "a fair and enlightened system of justice."... To suggest that it is inconsistent with a truly free society to begin prosecutions without an indictment, to try petty civil cases without the paraphernalia of a common law jury, to take into consideration that one who has full opportunity to make a defense remains silent is, in de Tocqueville's phrase, to confound the familiar with the necessary.

The short answer to the suggestion that the provision of the Fourteenth Amendment, which ordains "nor shall any State deprive any person of life, liberty, or property, without due process of law," was a way of saying that every State must thereafter initiate prosecutions through indictment by a grand jury, must have a trial by a jury of twelve in criminal cases, and must have trial by such a jury in common law suits where the amount in controversy exceeds twenty dollars, is that it is a strange way of saying it. It would be extraordinarily strange for a Constitution to convey such specific commands in such a roundabout and inexplicit way. After all, an amendment to the Constitution should be read in a "sense most obvious to the common understanding at the time of its adoption.... For it was for public adoption that it was proposed."... Those reading the English language with the meaning which it ordinarily conveys, those conversant with the political and legal history of the concept of due process, those sensitive to the relations of the States to the central government as well as the relation of some of the provisions of the Bill of Rights to the process of justice, would hardly recognize the Fourteenth Amendment as a cover for the various explicit provisions of the first eight Amendments. Some of these are enduring reflections of experience with human nature, while some express the restricted views of Eighteenth-Century England regarding the best methods for the ascertainment of facts. The notion that the Fourteenth Amendment was a covert way of imposing upon the States all the rules which it seemed important to Eighteenth Century statesmen to write into the Federal Amendments, was rejected by judges who were themselves witnesses of the process by which the Fourteenth Amendment became part of the Constitution. Arguments that may not be adduced to prove that the first eight Amendments were concealed within the historic phrasing of the Fourteenth Amendment were not unknown at the time of its adoption. A surer estimate of their bearing was possible for judges at the time than distorting distance is likely to vouchsafe. Any evidence of design or purpose not contemporaneously known could hardly have influenced those who ratified the Amendment. Remarks of a particular proponent of the Amendment, no matter how influential, are not to be deemed part of the Amendment. What was submitted for ratification was his proposal, not his speech. Thus, at the time of the ratification of the Fourteenth Amendment the constitutions of nearly half of the ratifying States did not have the rigorous requirements of the Fifth Amendment for instituting criminal proceedings through a grand jury. It could hardly have occurred to these States that by ratifying the Amendment they uprooted their established methods for prosecuting crime and fastened upon themselves a new prosecutorial system.

Indeed, the suggestion that the Fourteenth Amendment incorporates the first eight Amendments as such is not unambiguously urged. Even the boldest innovator would shrink from suggesting to more than half the States that they may no longer initiate prosecutions without indictment by grand jury, or that thereafter all the States of the Union must furnish a jury of twelve for every case involving a claim above twenty dollars. There is suggested merely a selective incorporation of the first eight Amendments into the Fourteenth Amendment. Some are in and some are out, but we are left in the dark as to which are in and which are out. Nor are we given the calculus for determining which go in and which stay out. If the basis of selection is merely that those provisions of the first eight Amendments are incorporated which commend themselves to individual justices as indispensable to the dignity and happiness of a free man, we are thrown back to a merely subjective test....

... The Due Process Clause of the Fourteenth Amendment has an independent potency, precisely as does the Due Process Clause of the Fifth Amendment in relation to the Federal Government.... It ought not to require argument to reject the notion that due process of law meant one thing in the Fifth Amendment and another in the Fourteenth. The Fifth Amendment specifically prohibits prosecution of an "infamous crime" except upon indictment; it forbids double jeopardy; it bars compelling a person to be a witness against himself in any criminal case; it precludes deprivation of life, liberty, or property, without due process of law...." Are Madison and his contemporaries in the framing of the Bill of Rights to be charged with writing into it a meaningless clause? To consider "due process of law" as merely a shorthand statement of other specific clauses in the same amendment is to attribute to the authors and proponents of this Amendment ignorance of, or indifference to, a historic conception which was one of the great instruments in the arsenal of constitutional freedom which the Bill of Rights was to protect and strengthen.

MR. JUSTICE BLACK, with whom MR. JUSTICE DOUGLAS concurs, dissenting.

This decision reasserts a constitutional theory spelled out in *Twining* v. *New Jersey*, 211 U.S. 78, that this Court is endowed by the Constitution with boundless power under "natural law" periodically to expand and contract constitutional standards to conform to the Court's conception of what at a particular time constitutes "civilized decency" and "fundamental liberty and justice." Invoking this *Twining* rule, the Court concludes that although comment upon testimony in a federal court would violate the Fifth Amendment, identical comment in a state court does not violate today's fashion in civilized decency and fundamentals and is therefore not prohibited by the Federal Constitution as amended.

. . . I would not reaffirm the *Twining* decision. I think that decision and the "natural law" theory of the Constitution upon which it relies degrade the constitutional safeguards of the Bill of Rights and simultaneously appropriate for this Court a broad power which we are not authorized by the Constitution to exercise. . . .

The first ten amendments were proposed and adopted largely because of fear that Government might unduly interfere with prized individual liberties. The people wanted and demanded a Bill of Rights written into their Constitution. The amendments embodying the Bill of Rights were intended to curb all branches of the Federal Government in the fields touched by the amendments — Legislative, Executive, and Judicial. The Fifth, Sixth, and Eighth Amendments were pointedly aimed at confining exercise of power by courts and judges within precise boundaries, particularly in the procedure used for the trial of criminal cases. . . .

. . . .

My study of the historical events that culminated in the Fourteenth Amendment, and the expressions of those who sponsored and favored, as well as those who opposed its submission and passage, persuades me that one of the chief objects that the provisions of the Amendment's first section, separately, and as a whole, were intended to accomplish was to make the Bill of Rights applicable to the states. With full knowledge of the import of the *Barron* decision, the framers and backers of the Fourteenth Amendment proclaimed its purpose to be to overturn the constitutional rule that case had announced. . . .

. . . .

I cannot consider the Bill of Rights to be an outworn 18th Century "strait jacket" as the *Twining* opinion did. Its provisions may be thought outdated abstractions by some. And it is true that they were designed to meet ancient evils. But they are the same kind of human evils that have emerged from century to century wherever excessive power is sought by the few at the expense of the many. . . . In my judgment the people of no nation can lose their liberty so long as a Bill of Rights like ours survives and its basic purposes are conscientiously interpreted, enforced and respected so as to afford continuous protection against old, as well as new, devices and practices which might thwart those purposes. I fear to see the consequences of the Court's practice of substituting its own concepts of decency and fundamental justice for the language of the Bill of

Rights as its point of departure in interpreting and enforcing that Bill of Rights. If the choice must be between the selective process of the *Palko* decision applying some of the Bill of Rights to the States, or the *Twining* rule applying none of them, I would choose the *Palko* selective process. But rather than accept either of these choices, I would follow what I believe was the original purpose of the Fourteenth Amendment — to extend to all the people of the nation the complete protection of the Bill of Rights. To hold that this Court can determine what, if any, provisions of the Bill of Rights will be enforced, and if so to what degree, is to frustrate the great design of a written Constitution.

Conceding the possibility that this Court is now wise enough to improve on the Bill of Rights by substituting natural law concepts for the Bill of Rights, I think the possibility is entirely too speculative to agree to take that course. I would therefore hold in this case that the full protection of the Fifth Amendment's proscription against compelled testimony must be afforded by California. This I would do because of reliance upon the original purpose of the Fourteenth Amendment.

MR. JUSTICE MURPHY, with whom MR. JUSTICE RUTLEDGE concurs, dissenting.

While in substantial agreement with the views of Mr. Justice Black, I have one reservation and one addition to make.

I agree that the specific guarantees of the Bill of Rights should be carried over intact into the first section of the Fourteenth Amendment. But I am not prepared to say that the latter is entirely and necessarily limited by the Bill of Rights. Occasions may arise where a proceeding falls so short of conforming to fundamental standards of procedure as to warrant constitutional condemnation in terms of a lack of due process despite the absence of a specific provision in the Bill of Rights.

Rochin v. California

342 U.S. 165 (1952)
Vote: 8–0

The relevant facts of the case are summarized at the beginning of the Court's opinion.

MR. JUSTICE FRANKFURTER delivered the opinion of the Court.

Having "some information that [the petitioner here] was selling narcotics," three deputy sheriffs of the County of Los Angeles, on the morning of July 1, 1949, made for the two-story dwelling house in which Rochin lived with his mother, common-law wife, brothers and sisters. Finding the outside door open, they entered and then forced open the door to Rochin's room on the second floor. Inside they found petitioner sitting partly dressed on the side of the bed, upon which his wife was lying. On a "night stand" beside the bed the deputies spied two capsules. When asked "Whose stuff is this?" Rochin seized the capsules and put them in his mouth. A struggle ensued, in the course of which the three officers "jumped upon him" and attempted to extract the capsules. The force they applied proved unavailing against Rochin's resistance. He was handcuffed and taken to a hospital. At the direction of one of the officers a doctor forced an emetic solution through a tube into Rochin's stomach against his will. This "stomach pumping" produced vomiting. In the vomited matter were found two capsules which proved to contain morphine.

Rochin was brought to trial [at which time the capsules were introduced as evidence, and he was convicted]. . . .

On appeal, the District Court of Appeal affirmed the conviction, despite the finding that the officers "were guilty of unlawfully breaking into and entering defendant's room and were guilty of unlawfully assaulting and battering defendant while in the room," and "were guilty of unlawfully assaulting, battering, torturing and falsely imprisoning the defendant at the alleged hospital.". . . One of the three judges, while finding that "the record in this case reveals a shocking series of violations of constitutional rights," concurred only because he felt bound by decisions of his Supreme Court. . . .

This Court granted certiorari. . . .

. . . Regard for the requirements of the Due Process Clause "inescapably imposes upon this Court an exercise of judgment upon the whole course of the proceedings [resulting in a conviction] in order to ascertain whether they offend those canons of decency and fairness which express the notions of justice of English-speaking peoples even toward those charged with the most heinous offenses." *Malinski v. New York*. These standards of justice are not authoritatively formulated anywhere as though they were specifics. Due process of law is a summarized constitutional guarantee of respect for those personal immunities which, as Mr. Justice Cardozo twice wrote for the Court, are "so rooted in the traditions and conscience of our people as to be ranked as fundamental," *Snyder v. Massachusetts*, . . . or are "implicit in the concept of ordered liberty." *Palko v. Connecticut*. . . .

The Court's function in the observance of this settled conception of the Due Process Clause does not leave us without adequate guides in subjecting State criminal procedures to constitutional judgment. In dealing not with the machinery of government but with human rights, the absence of formal exactitude, or want of fixity of meaning, is not an unusual or even regrettable attribute of constitutional provisions. Words being symbols do not speak without a gloss. On the one hand the gloss may be the deposit of history, whereby a term gains technical content. Thus the requirements of the Sixth and Seventh Amendments for trial by jury in the federal courts have a rigid meaning. No changes or chances can alter the content of the verbal symbol of "jury" — a body of twelve men who must reach a unanimous conclusion if the verdict is to go against the defendant. On the other hand, the gloss of some of the verbal symbols of the Constitution does not give them a fixed technical content. It exacts a continuing process of application.

When the gloss has thus not been fixed but is a function of the process of judgment, the judgment is bound to fall differently at different times and differently at the same time through different judges. Even more specific provisions, such as the guaranty of freedom of speech and the detailed protection against unreasonable searches and seizures, have inevitably evoked as sharp divisions in this Court as the least specific and most comprehensive protection of liberties, the Due Process Clause.

The vague contours of the Due Process Clause do not leave judges at large. We may not draw on our merely personal and private notions and disregard the limits that bind judges in their judicial function. Even though the concept of due process of law is not final and fixed, these limits are derived from considerations that are fused in the whole nature of our judicial process. See Cardozo, The Nature of the Judicial Process; The Growth of the Law; The Paradoxes of Legal Science. These are considerations deeply rooted in reason and in the compelling traditions of the legal profession. The Due Process Clause places upon this Court the duty of exercising a judgment, within the narrow confines of judicial power in reviewing State convictions, upon interests of society pushing in opposite directions.

Due process of law thus conceived is not to be derided as resort to a revival of "natural law." To believe that this judicial exercise of judgment could be avoided by freezing "due process of law" at some fixed stage of time or thought is to suggest that the most important aspect of constitutional adjudication is a function for inanimate machines and not for judges, for whom the independence safeguarded by Article III of the Constitution was designed and who are presumably guided by established standards of judicial behavior. Even cybernetics has not yet made that haughty claim. To practice the requisite detachment and to achieve sufficient objectivity no doubt demands of judges the habit of self-discipline and self-criticism, incertitude that one's own views are incontestable and alert tolerance toward views not shared. But these are precisely the presuppositions of our judicial process. They are precisely the qualities society has a right to expect from those entrusted with ultimate judicial power.

Restraints on our jurisdiction are self-imposed only in the sense that there is from our decisions no immediate appeal short of impeachment or constitutional amendment. But that does not make due process of law a matter of judicial caprice. The faculties of the Due Process Clause may be indefinite and vague, but the mode of their ascertainment is not self-willed. In each case "due process of law" requires an evaluation based on a disinterested inquiry pursued in the spirit of science, on a balanced order of facts exactly and fairly stated, on the detached consideration of conflicting claims, . . . on a judgment not *ad hoc* and episodic but duly mindful of reconciling the needs both of continuity and of change in a progressive society.

Applying these general considerations to the circumstances of the present case, we are compelled to conclude that the proceedings by which this conviction was obtained do more than offend some fastidious squeamishness or private sentimentalism about combatting crime too energetically. This is conduct that shocks the conscience. Illegally breaking into the privacy of the petitioner, the struggle to open his mouth and remove what was there, the forcible extraction of his stomach's contents — this course of proceeding by agents of government to obtain evidence is bound to offend even hardened sensibilities. They are methods too close to the rack and the screw to permit of constitutional differentiation.

It has long since ceased to be true that due process of law is heedless of the means by which otherwise relevant and credible evidence is obtained. This was not true even before the series of recent cases enforced the constitutional principle that the State may not base convictions upon confessions, however much verified, obtained by coercion. These deci-

sions are not arbitrary exceptions to the comprehensive right of States to fashion their own rules of evidence for criminal trials. They are not sports in our constitutional law but applications of a general principle. They are only instances of the general requirement that States in their prosecutions respect certain decencies of civilized conduct. Due process of law, as a historic and generative principle, precludes defining, and thereby confining, these standards of conduct more precisely than to say that convictions cannot be brought about by methods that offend "a sense of justice." . . . It would be a stultification of the responsibility which the course of constitutional history has cast upon this Court to hold that in order to convict a man the police cannot extract by force what is in his mind but can extract what is in his stomach.

To attempt in this case to distinguish what lawyers call "real evidence" from verbal evidence is to ignore the reasons for excluding coerced confessions. Use of involuntary verbal confessions in State criminal trials is constitutionally obnoxious not only because of their unreliability. They are inadmissible under the Due Process Clause even though statements contained in them may be independently established as true. Coerced confessions offend the community's sense of fair play and decency. So here, to sanction the brutal conduct which naturally enough was condemned by the court whose judgment is before us, would be to afford brutality the cloak of law. Nothing would be more calculated to discredit law and thereby to brutalize the temper of a society.

In deciding this case we do not heedlessly bring into question decisions in many States dealing with essentially different, even if related, problems. We therefore put to one side cases which have arisen in the State courts through use of modern methods and devices for discovering wrongdoers and bringing them to book. It does not fairly represent these decisions to suggest that they legalize force so brutal and so offensive to human dignity in securing evidence from a suspect as is revealed by this record. Indeed the California Supreme Court has not sanctioned this mode of securing a conviction. It merely exercised its discretion to decline a review of the conviction. All the California judges who have expressed themselves in this case have condemned the conduct in the strongest language.

We are not unmindful that hypothetical situations can be conjured up, shading imperceptibly from the circumstances of this case and by gradations producing practical differences despite seemingly logical extensions. But the Constitution is "intended to preserve practical and substantial rights, not to maintain theories."...

On the facts of this case the conviction of the petitioner has been obtained by methods that offend the Due Process Clause. The judgment below must be

Reversed.

MR. JUSTICE MINTON took no part in the consideration or decision of this case.

MR. JUSTICE BLACK, concurring.

Adamson v. *California* ... sets out reasons for my belief that state as well as federal courts and law enforcement officers must obey the Fifth Amendment's command that "No person ... shall be compelled in any criminal case to be a witness against himself." I think a person is compelled to be a witness against himself not only when he is compelled to testify, but also when as here, incriminating evidence is forcibly taken from him by contrivance of modern science....

In the view of a majority of the Court, however, the Fifth Amendment imposes no restraint of any kind on the states. They nevertheless hold that California's use of this evidence violated the Due Process Clause of the Fourteenth Amendment. Since they hold as I do in this case, I regret my inability to accept their interpretation without protest. But I believe that faithful adherence to the specific guarantees in the Bill of Rights insures a more permanent protection of individual liberty than that which can be afforded by the nebulous standards stated by the majority.

What the majority hold is that the Due Process Clause empowers this Court to nullify any state law if its application "shocks the conscience," offends "a sense of justice" or runs counter to the "decencies of civilized conduct." The majority emphasize that these statements do not refer to their own consciences or to their senses of justice and decency. For we are told that "we may not draw on our merely personal and private notions"; our judgment must be grounded on "considerations deeply rooted in reason and in the compelling traditions of the legal profession." We are further admonished to measure the validity of state practices, not by our reason, or by the traditions of the legal profession, but by "the community's sense of fair play and decency"; by the "traditions and conscience of our people"; or by "those canons of decency and fairness which express the notions of justice of English-speaking peoples." These canons are made necessary, it is said, be-

cause of "interests of society pushing in opposite directions."

If the Due Process Clause does vest this Court with such unlimited power to invalidate laws, I am still in doubt as to why we should consider only the notions of English-speaking peoples to determine what are immutable and fundamental principles of justice. Moreover, one may well ask what avenues of investigation are open to discover "canons" of conduct so universally favored that this Court should write them into the Constitution? All we are told is that the discovery must be made by an "evaluation based on a disinterested inquiry pursued in the spirit of science, on a balanced order of facts."

Some constitutional provisions are stated in absolute and unqualified language such, for illustration, as the First Amendment stating that no law shall be passed prohibiting the free exercise of religion or abridging the freedom of speech or press. Other constitutional provisions do require courts to choose between competing policies, such as the Fourth Amendment which, by its terms, necessitates a judicial decision as to what is an "unreasonable" search or seizure. There is, however, no express constitutional language granting judicial power to invalidate *every* state law of *every* kind deemed "unreasonable" or contrary to the Court's notion of civilized decencies; yet the constitutional philosophy used by the majority has, in the past, been used to deny a state the right to fix the price of gasoline, *Williams* v. *Standard Oil Co.* ... and even the right to prevent bakers from palming off smaller for larger loaves of bread, *Jay Burns Baking Co.* v. *Bryan.* ... These cases, and others, show the extent to which the evanescent standards of the majority's philosophy have been used to nullify state legislative programs passed to suppress evil economic practices. What paralyzing role this same philosophy will play in the future economic affairs of this country is impossible to predict. Of even graver concern, however, is the use of the philosophy to nullify the Bill of Rights. I long ago concluded that the accordion-like qualities of this philosophy must inevitably imperil all the individual liberty safeguards specifically enumerated in the Bill of Rights. Reflection and recent decisions of this Court sanctioning abridgment of the freedom of speech and press have strengthened this conclusion.

MR. JUSTICE DOUGLAS, concurring.

. . . .

As an original matter it might be debatable whether the provision in the Fifth Amendment that no person "shall be compelled in any criminal case to be a witness against himself" serves the ends of justice. Not all civilized legal procedures recognize it. But the choice was made by the Framers, a choice which sets a standard for legal trials in this country. The Framers made it a standard of due process for prosecutions by the Federal Government. If it is a requirement of due process for a trial in the federal courthouse, it is impossible for me to say it is not a requirement of due process for a trial in the state courthouse. That was the issue recently surveyed in *Adamson* v. *California,* 332 U.S. 46. The Court rejected the view that compelled testimony should be excluded and held in substance that the accused in a state trial can be forced to testify against himself. I disagree. Of course an accused can be compelled to be present at the trial, to stand, to sit, to turn this way or that, and to try on a cap or a coat. . . . But I think that words taken from his lips, capsules taken from his stomach, blood taken from his veins are all inadmissible provided they are taken from him without his consent. They are inadmissible because of the command of the Fifth Amendment.

That is an unequivocal, definite and workable rule of evidence for state and federal courts. But we cannot in fairness free the state courts from that command and yet excoriate them for flouting the "decencies of civilized conduct" when they admit the evidence. That is to make the rule turn not on the Constitution but on the idiosyncrasies of the judges who sit here.

Apodaca v. Oregon

406 U.S. 404 (1972)
Vote: 6–3

In *Duncan* v. *Louisiana,* 391 U.S. 145 (1968), the Supreme Court held that the Sixth Amendment's right to jury trial was applicable to the states in cases of serious crime. However, *Duncan* did not fully resolve the issue of the right to a jury trial. Several questions remained: How large must the jury be? How representative must the jury be? Must it be unanimous? What is a "serious" case? Are state juries subjected to the same requirements as federal juries? In a series of cases since *Duncan,* the Court has begun to address these and related issues.

The case below addresses one of these issues, the difference between state and federal provisions regarding jury unanimity. It reveals that the issues of incorporation and the questions of fundamental fairness are not fully settled.

Apodaca and several similarly situated petitioners were found guilty of felony offenses by less-than-unanimous jury verdicts that were permitted under Oregon law. They appealed their convictions, claiming that the Oregon law violated their constitutional right to a trial by jury. (They raised other issues about the representativeness of the nonunanimous jury, but these issues need not concern us here.) The Oregon Supreme Court upheld their conviction, and they petitioned the United States Supreme Court to bring the case up on a writ of certiorari.

MR. JUSTICE WHITE announced the judgment of the Court and an opinion in which THE CHIEF JUSTICE, MR. JUSTICE BLACKMUN, and MR. JUSTICE REHNQUIST joined.

Like the requirement that juries consist of 12 men, the requirement of unanimity arose during the Middle Ages and had become an accepted feature of the common-law jury by the 18th century. But, as we observed in *Williams,* "the relevant constitutional history casts considerable doubt on the easy assumption . . . that if a given feature existed in a jury at common law in 1789, then it was necessarily preserved in the Constitution." . . .

Our inquiry must focus upon the function served by the jury in contemporary society. . . . As we said in *Duncan,* the purpose of trial by jury is to prevent oppression by the Government by providing a "safeguard against the corrupt or overzealous prosecutor and against the compliant, biased, or eccentric judge." . . . "Given this purpose, the essential feature of a jury obviously lies in the interposition between the accused and his accuser of the commonsense judgment of a group of laymen. . . ." A requirement of unanimity, however, does not materially contribute to the exercise of this commonsense judgment. . . . In terms of this function we perceive no difference between juries required to act unanimously and those permitted to convict or acquit by votes of 10 to two or 11 to one. . . .

Petitioners nevertheless argue that unanimity serves other purposes constitutionally essential to the continued operation of the jury system. Their principal contention is that a Sixth Amendment "jury trial" made mandatory on the States by virtue of the Due Process Clause of the Fourteenth Amendment, *Duncan* v. *Louisiana*, . . . should be held to require a unanimous jury verdict in order to give substance to the reasonable-doubt standard otherwise mandated by the Due Process Clause. . . .

We are quite sure, however, that the Sixth Amendment itself has never been held to require proof beyond a reasonable doubt in criminal cases. The reasonable-doubt standard developed separately from both the jury trial and the unanimous verdict. As the Court noted in the *Winship* case, the rule requiring proof of crime beyond a reasonable doubt did not crystallize in this country until after the Constitution was adopted. . . . And in that case, which held such a burden of proof to be constitutionally required, the Court purported to draw no support from the Sixth Amendment.

Petitioners' argument that the Sixth Amendment requires jury unanimity in order to give effect to the reasonable-doubt standard thus founders on the fact that the Sixth Amendment does not require proof beyond a reasonable doubt at all. . . .

Petitioners also cite quite accurately a long line of decisions of this Court upholding the principle that the Fourteenth Amendment requires jury panels to reflect a cross section of the community. . . . They then contend that unanimity is a necessary precondition for effective application of the cross-section requirement, because a rule permitting less than unanimous verdicts will make it possible for convictions to occur without the acquiescence of minority elements within the community.

There are two flaws in this argument. One is petitioners' assumption that every distinct voice in the community has a right to be represented on every jury and a right to prevent conviction of a defendant in any case. All that the Constitution forbids, however, is systematic exclusion of identifiable segments of the community from jury panels and from the juries ultimately drawn from those panels; a defendant may not, for example, challenge the makeup of a jury merely because no members of his race are on the jury, but must prove that his race has been systematically excluded. . . .

We also cannot accept petitioners' second assumption — that minority groups, even when they are represented on a jury, will not adequately represent the viewpoint of those groups simply because they may be outvoted in the final result. They will be present during all deliberations, and their views will be heard. We cannot assume that the majority of the jury will refuse to weigh the evidence and reach a decision upon rational grounds, just as it must now do in order to obtain unanimous verdicts, or that a majority will deprive a man of his liberty on the basis of prejudice when a minority is presenting a reasonable argument in favor of acquittal. We simply find no proof for the notion that a majority will disregard its instructions and cast its votes for guilt or innocence based on prejudice rather than the evidence.

We accordingly affirm the judgment of the Court of Appeals of Oregon.

[MR. JUSTICE POWELL concurred in the judgment; a section of his opinion in a companion case is directed at *Apodaca* and is presented below.]

. . . I concur in the plurality opinion in this case insofar as it concludes that a defendant in a state court may constitutionally be convicted by less than a unanimous verdict, but I am not in accord with a major premise upon which that judgment is based. Its premise is that the concept of jury trial, as applicable to the States under the Fourteenth Amendment, must be identical in every detail to the concept required in federal courts by the Sixth Amendment. I do not think that all of the elements of jury trial within the meaning of the Sixth Amendment are necessarily embodied in or incorporated into the Due Process Clause of the Fourteenth Amendment. . . .

In an unbroken line of cases reaching back into the late 1800's, the Justices of this Court have recognized, virtually without dissent, that unanimity is one of the indispensable features of *federal* jury trial. . . . In these cases, the Court has presumed that unanimous verdicts are essential in federal jury trials, not because unanimity is necessarily fundamental to the function performed by the jury, but because that result is mandated by history. The reasoning that runs throughout this Court's Sixth Amendment precedents is that, in amending the Constitution to guarantee the right to jury trial, the framers desired to preserve the jury safeguard as it was known to them at common law. At the time the Bill of Rights was adopted, unanimity had long been established as one of the attributes of a jury conviction at common law. It therefore seems to me, in accord both with history and precedent, that the Sixth Amendment requires a unanimous jury verdict to convict in a federal criminal trial.

But it is the Fourteenth Amendment, rather than the Sixth, that imposes upon the States the requirement that they provide jury trials to those accused of serious crimes. This Court has said, in cases decided when the intention of that Amendment was not as clouded by the passage of time, that due process does not require that the States apply the federal jury-trial right with all its gloss. . . .

The question, therefore, that should be addressed in this case is whether unanimity is in fact so fundamental to the essentials of jury trial that this particular requirement of the Sixth Amendment is necessarily binding on the States under the Due Process Clause of the Fourteenth Amendment. An affirmative answer . . . would give unwarranted and unwise scope to the incorporation doctrine as it applies to the due process right of state criminal defendants to trial by jury.

. . . .

Moreover, in holding that the Fourteenth Amendment has incorporated "jot-for-jot and case-for-case" every element of the Sixth Amendment, the Court derogates principles of federalism that are basic to our system. In the name of uniform application of high standards of due process, the Court has embarked upon a course of constitutional interpretation that deprives the States of freedom to experiment with adjudicatory processes different from the fed-

eral model. At the same time, the Court's understandable unwillingness to impose requirements that it finds unnecessarily rigid . . . has culminated in the dilution of federal rights that were, until these decisions, never seriously questioned. . . .

While the Civil War Amendments altered substantially the balance of federalism, it strains credulity to believe that they were intended to deprive the States of all freedom to experiment with variations in jury-trial procedure. In an age in which empirical study is increasingly relied upon as a foundation for decision-making, one of the more obvious merits of our federal system is the opportunity it affords each State, if its people so choose, to become a "laboratory" and to experiment with a range of trial and procedural alternatives. Although the need for the innovations that grow out of diversity has always been great, imagination unimpeded by unwarranted demands for national uniformity is of special importance at a time when serious doubt exists as to the adequacy of our criminal justice system. . . .

[JUSTICE STEWART wrote a dissent with which JUSTICES BRENNAN and MARSHALL concurred.]

CHAPTER 7

Freedom of Religion

The Establishment Clause

The early history of the founding of the American colonies is in large part a history of the quest for freedom to worship. Several of the early colonies in New England and later in the mid-Atlantic region were founded by religious groups seeking to escape persecution in England and on the continent. Later, in part as a result of bitter strife within the American colonies, there emerged within the colonies a movement for religious tolerance. Indeed, Pennsylvania was founded as a settlement without an official religion as a haven of tolerance for those who had found difficulty worshiping in other settlements. Religious tolerance later found an eloquent spokesman in Thomas Jefferson, and in part through his persistence the two protections of religious freedom were included in the First Amendment.

These provisions are the "Congress shall make no law respecting the establishment of religion, or prohibiting the free exercise thereof." Taken together their purpose is clear. In order to assure freedom of worship, Congress is prohibited from establishing an official state church. But even as the general purpose is clear, these provisions are open to various interpretations, and if given broad enough scope they begin to collide with one another. Further, in a modern, complex, and secular society there is considerable difficulty in drawing the boundary between religious and secular activity and beliefs.

One of the continuing issues for the Court in the 1980s has been to balance and reconcile free exercise and establishment provisions when they collide, and to draw workable distinctions between religious and secular beliefs, activities, and purposes.

Historically, the Establishment Clause has been interpreted in two quite different ways. One school of thought holds that the prohibition against the establishment of religion was a reaction to a standard practice in Europe at the time of the Revolution, and simply bars Congress from establishing an *official* national church supported at public expense. Such an interpretation, presumably, would permit the states to support religious institutions (which was the case in some of the colonies at the time of the Revolution and which continued for some time in a few states after adoption of the constitution). This interpretation would also allow for governmental aid to religious institutions so long as it is nonpreferential.

An alternative interpretation of the Establishment Clause was held by Thomas Jefferson, the primary advocate of the Bill of Rights. His view was that the First Amendment built a "wall of separation between Church and State," and it is this view and this phrase that has come to be accepted by history and the Court. Still, it is something of a porous wall, in that *complete* separation is all but impossible and at times might even have to be purchased at the expense of free exercise of religion.

Historically, there have never been any clearcut theories of the Free Exercise Clause, although it too has aroused considerable controversy. Here the issues involve efforts by the state to force people to *behave* in ways inconsistent with their religious beliefs. This has forced the court to wrestle with the distinction between *belief* and *action,* and to consider how to reconcile valid secular policies when they conflict with religious scruples. While the Court has consistently stressed the importance of the freedom of religious *beliefs,* it has been less tolerant of those whose actions based upon religious beliefs begin to collide with conduct proscribed or prescribed by the state. Considerations of these issues constitute the major theme in Supreme Court cases involving the Free Exercise Clause.

Recall that the First Amendment begins, *"Congress* shall make no law . . . ." Despite the express mention of Congress, once the process of selective incorporation of the Bill of Rights was set in motion, there was relatively little controversy over nationalization of the First Amendment, including its two freedom of religion clauses. Under any of the theories of incorporation, the First Amendment apparently seems to have been nationalized. This was first suggested in the free speech case GITLOW V. NEW YORK (1925), in the dicta of Justice Holmes, although it was not until 1940, in *Cantwell* v. *Connecticut,* that the Free Exercise Clause was formally incorporated, and not until 1947, in *Everson* v. *Board of Education,* that the Establishment Clause was nationalized via the Due Process Clause of the Fourteenth Amendment.

Although there were a handful of nineteenth- and early twentieth-century Supreme Court decisions interpreting the two freedom of religion provisions, the bulk of the constitutional law on the subject is of relatively recent vintage, and like so many other Bill of Rights issues deals largely with actions involving states, not the national government. Still, some of these earlier decisions are worth mentioning because they set the stage for the issues that arose later. In an 1899 case, *Bradfield* v. *Roberts,* 175 U.S. 291, the Supreme Court upheld a District of Columbia provision to finance a hospital to be run by a religious organization. In 1938, it allowed Louisiana to furnish textbooks for students in parochial schools (*Cochran* v. *Louisiana State Board of Education,* 281 U.S. 370). In these and a handful of other cases the Court defended governmental actions on grounds that they were valid exercises of police powers in pursuit of legitimate state interests.

However, beginning with *Everson* v. *Board of Education,* 330 U.S. 1 (1947), the Court began to scrutinize the connection between government and religious institutions and practices more closely. In this case, which also formally brought the Establishment Clause under the protection of the Fourteenth Amendment, the Court upheld public financing of free transportation of students attending parochial schools. Even as Justice Black penned an eloquent defense of the separation of church and state, he defended the state's free transportation on grounds that it served a valid *secular* purpose. This decision occasioned a sharp dissent by Justice Rutledge, which was joined by three other justices, including Justice Frankfurter, who argued that state aid for students in parochial schools, for whatever purpose or in whatever amount, breeched the wall of separation of church and state. The *Everson* opinions raised the issues that form the heart of a debate that continues on the Court to this day.

In 1948, in *McCollum* v. *Illinois,* 333 U.S. 203, the Court delcared unconstitutional a practice in the Champaign, Illinois, public schools that permitted released time for students to attend weekly religious classes on school premises. But four years later it upheld as constitutional a plan that permitted release of public school students for attendance at religion classes *off* school property, even though students not attending were required to remain on campus (ZORACH V. CLAUSON, 1952). Writing for the majority of six in ZORACH, Justice Douglas said, "We are a religious people whose institutions presuppose a Supreme Being. . . . When the state encourages religious instruction or cooperates with religious authorities by adjusting the schedule of public events to sectarian needs, it follows the best of our traditions."

McCollum and ZORACH show just how difficult it is to draw a line between *acceptable cooperation* between church and state and *unconstitutional establishment.* One key — but by no means exclusive — ingredient in this distinction is agreed upon by both the majority and the dissenters: the element of *coercion.* But while all agree that the use of the coercive powers of the state in behalf of any or all religious activity is unacceptable, they cannot agree on a test or framework by which to measure state coercion. Each position seizes upon different factors.

While released-time schemes did not continue to come before the Supreme Court, cases involving related issues and the recurring problem of coercion did.

If, in these three cases under Chief Justice Vinson, the Court appeared halting and *inconsistent* in its first serious encounter with the Establishment Clause, during the 1960s under Chief Justice Warren it spoke with a much bolder voice. In a series of important decisions beginning in 1962, which occasioned bitter and sustained public outcry, the Court held invalid a variety of practices in public school classrooms and government subsidies to students in parochial schools. In *Engel* v. *Vitale,* 370 U.S. 421 (1962), the Court, with only Justice Stewart dissenting, held that recitation of a state-composed prayer in public school classrooms violated the Establishment Clause. The following

year, in two companion cases, ABINGTON SCHOOL DISTRICT V. SCHEMPP and *Murray* v. *Curlett* (1963), the Court prohibited prayer and Bible-reading devotions in public school classrooms. In each of these cases, the majority held that the state was unconstitutionally placing the weight of its authority and prestige behind clearly religious exercises. Justice Stewart continued to stress that separation did not prohibit cooperation and argued that the practices in question were voluntary — those wishing to could be excused — and noncoercive. As if in response to Justice Stewart, some members of the Court went to great length to stress the youthfulness of the students involved and the *likelihood* of informal, although perhaps unwitting, coercion at such a tender and impressionable age. This issue may be relevant in cases we will consider later and which involve challenges of government support for activities in church-related colleges.

Reaction to the Court's ban on Bible reading and prayer in the public schools was both intense and sustained. Religious groups mobilized to introduce devotionals in public schools in direct defiance of the Court. Members of Congress introduced, and continue to do so to this day, proposed amendments to the Constitution and plans to strip the Court of its appellate jurisdiction over such issues. It became a salient issue in the presidential election of 1964, when the Republican nominee, Barry Goldwater, campaigned against the Court on several issues, including those decisions that had "taken God out of the classroom." The same issue emerged again in the elections of the 1980s, when the Moral Majority campaigned for successful presidential candidate Ronald Reagan and mobilized public support for a so-called "school prayer amendment." While some might argue that the school prayer and Bible-reading cases involve symbolic issues with little substantial consequences, the Court has been confronted with a set of issues that have direct, substantial, and immediate financial consequences. These cases involve use of public funds to support selected activities of parochial schools, where conceivably an expansive interpretation of a ban on state aid could spell an end to parochial schools. Here the Burger and Rehnquist Courts have modified but not rejected the basic course set by the Warren Court.

Recall that in *Everson* the Court upheld free bus transportation for students in parochial schools, justifying it as a legitimate state function that primarily benefited school children and their parents and only incidentally benefited religious-sponsored schools. Twenty-one years later, in 1968, in *Board of Education* v. *Allen,* 392 U.S. 236, the Court upheld by a margin of 5 to 4 a similar scheme that provided free textbooks for *secular* subjects for students in parochial schools, and in so doing reiterated the "child benefit" theory of *Everson.* The four dissenters each wrote separate opinions warning against the likely consequences of state involvement in this enterprise. They worried that the distinctive features of religious education would be diluted.

Encouraged by their victory in *Allen,* supporters of public aid for parochial school students in those states with substantial numbers of such pupils sought to take advantage of the child benefit theory by urging other types of public support to relieve parents of some of the cost of sending their children to parochial schools.

Legislatures in a number of states enacted statutes that, in effect, provided for state subsidies for teachers, materials, buildings, and other items and activities used for "secular" purposes at parochial schools and church colleges and universities. Congress approved government grants to church colleges and universitites for the construction of buildings and to buy equipment (usually very expensive scientific laboratories) for "secular" uses. Some states also passed laws granting tax relief to parents who paid parochial school tuition. This flurry of legislative activity precipitated a series of cases before the Supreme Court.

At this same time a significant transformation was taking place on the Court. Beginning with President Nixon's appointment of Warren Burger as Chief Justice in 1969, five new appointments were made by Presidents Nixon and Ford between 1969 and 1976. For the most part this meant the replacement of known liberals with unknown justices appointed by avowedly "strict constructionist" presidents. Thus in the 1970s a largely new Court faced a new set of issues in light of overwhelming public support for "bringing God back into the classroom," and in the face of conflicting and confusing precedents in the area of public support for parochial school students.

In light of the public positions of Presidents Nixon, Ford, and Reagan, it is testimony to the independence of the judiciary and evidence of the weight of precedent and the complexity of the issues that the new Court did not swiftly come to embrace closer relationships between church and state. Between 1971 and 1976, the Supreme Court handed down nine important full opinions involving government aid to parochial schools and dealt with a number of other issues summarily. While not openly rejecting past doctrines, the majority in these cases shifted focus away from the student to the nature of the school itself. In so doing the Court appeared to be paving the way to direct grants to schools rather than only to students or parents, as provided in the earlier version of the child-benefit test.

The first of these cases was LEMON V. KURTZMAN (1971), which was handed down with a companion case, *Tilton* v. *Richardson,* 403 U.S. 672 (1971). In LEMON, the Court invalidated state legislation that provided state funds for the payment of salaries of teachers of secular subjects in private elementary and secondary schools, and in *Tilton* the Court upheld a federal statute (Title I of the Higher Educational Facilities Act of 1963) that provided for grants to church-related colleges and universities for the construction of buildings to be used for secular purposes.

LEMON is important for the three-part test espoused by Chief Justice Burger in his opinion for the Court's majority, in which he said a grant to parochial schools could stand only if (1) it had a valid secular purpose; (2) its primary effect neither advanced nor inhibited religion; and (3) it did not foster excessive government entanglement with religion. While in this and a companion case the Court went on to find that the statutes in question did not pass muster, seen in light of the earlier statements by the Court, the *neutrality* provisions of the second part and the *excessive* prohibition of the third are significant qualifications of the earlier test, and were seen by some as a Court retreat in the face of vociferous criticism of its earlier actions.

Since it was first announced by Chief Justice Burger the three-part test in LEMON has become the vehicle for examining Establishment Clause issues. While some justices reject the test, on the grounds that it distorts the intention of the framers of the First Amendment, it commands wide acceptance from most of them and remains as the framework for defining issues. Perhaps one of the reasons it has endured is its flexibility. Far from neatly disposing of issues, as its architect Chief Justice Burger may have hoped it would, it has proven to be flexible enough to encourage a great many proponents of greater government support for religion to press their claims. They have won frequently enough before the Court to reinforce their optimism. Since LEMON the Court has been inundated with Establishment Clause cases. Outcomes have been close and mixed; many cases have been decided 5 to 4 or 6 to 3. Some have upheld government support; others have ruled it unconstitutional.

Initially, those seeking state aid to support elementary and secondary parochial schools found LEMON to be an insurmountable obstacle. In *Committee for Public Education* v. *Nyquist,* 413 U.S. 756 (1973), the Court overturned New York and Pennsylvania tuition "grant" statutes. It also overturned New York's tax credit statute and a program authorizing state funds for the repair and maintenance of private school buildings. Even when, as in the case of the tuition grant and credit programs, state money went to parents, the Court rejected the child-benefit theory underlying the statutes and held that they ran afoul of the LEMON test because they had the "effect" of advancing

religion. But *Nyquist* may have been the high-water mark of the LEMON test. Since then the Court has retreated. In *Meek* v. *Pittinger,* 421 U.S. 349 (1975), and in *Wolman* v. *Walter,* 433 U.S. 429 (1977), the Court did uphold some of the provisions of Pennsylvania and Ohio statutes that authorized state payment for secular books, standardized testing and scoring, diagnostic services, and therapeutic and remedial services, even though it invalidated others involving state payments for instructional materials, equipment, and field trips.

The continuing task for the Court is to sort out what types of activities and aid are permissible, what types are not, and why. For instance, the Court has permitted state purchase of secular books but denied state purchase of tape recorders. As the entries in both the permissible and the impermissible categories grow, there will be a tendency to develop a rationale for what has emerged somewhat haphazardly; and if none can be found, there will be pressure to shift one way or the other, either broadening or narrowing the categories, until a sharper and acceptable *principle* is defined. To date, the Court's decisions remain primarily a jurisprudence of fact rather than principle.

Recently, the divisions on the Court have become more sharply focused as an emergent majority led by Chief Justice Rehnquist and Justice Scalia has further relaxed the LEMON test. In MUELLER V. ALLEN (1983), a narrowly divided Court upheld a Minnesota statute allowing parents of children to deduct expenses incurred in providing "tuition, textbooks and transportation" for their children attending elementary and secondary schools. Justice Rehnquist, for a majority of five, distinguished the Minnesota program from those struck down in *Nyquist* on the grounds that Minnesota provided for tax deductions for various educational expenses rather than direct grants or tax credits for private school tuition; further, the Minnesota law applied to parents of *all* school-age children, not just those attending *private* schools. Citing LEMON's and *Nyquist*'s emphases on "effects," the dissent argued that there is no conceptual difference between a tax credit and a tax deduction and pointed out that over 95 percent of all the deductions in Minnesota were for tuition in parochial schools. The following term, the Court appeared to broaden its relaxation of the LEMON test still further. In an expansive opinion in LYNCH V. DONNELLEY (1984), Justice Burger, for a majority of six, upheld a long-standing practice of Pawtucket, Rhode Island, to supply, maintain, and erect a crèche in a Christmas display in a downtown (nonpublic) park. Here, too, the dissenters, in a biting opinion by Justice Marshall, accused the majority of purposely misreading the Court's prior rulings.

In 1989 a highly fragmented Court handed down its most important religious display case since *Lynch*. This complicated case involved two government-sponsored displays a few hundred feet from each other; one featuring a crèche for Christmas, and the other a menorah for Chanukah. *Allegheny* v. *American Civil Liberties Union,* 57 LW 5045. In a plurality opinion Justice Blackmun argued that the crèche ran afoul of the endorsement prong of the *Lemon* test while the menorah did not. He distinguished the crèche here from the one approved in *Lynch* on the grounds that in the former the religious content of the display was "framed" and was labeled as being sponsored by the Roman Catholic Church. In contrast he emphasized that the menorah in another display down the street was placed next to a Christmas tree and other secular items, and as such did not constitute an endorsement of religion. However, three justices believed that both displays violated the First Amendment, and four justices, in an opinion by Justice Kennedy, indicated that neither display did. In his sweeping opinion, which was joined by the Chief Justice and Justices White and Scalia, Justice Kennedy condemned the majority's use of the *Lemon* test, and endorsed a new approach that would be much more consistent with our "nation's history" of "accommodation to religion." His proposed new test would draw the line at government "proselytization," a much lower threshold of establishment than is suggested in any of the Court's previous Establishment Clause cases. It should be noted that his proposed new approach

had the unqualified support of three other justices. In contrast the other five justices were divided among themselves in at least three different ways.

In the 1984 term, prayer in the public schools resurfaced, and in WALLACE V. JAFFREE (1985) a divided Court held unconstitutional an Alabama statute that provided for public school students a one-minute period of silence for meditation. However, in his opinion for the Court, Justice Stevens emphasized the statute's legislative history, which was saturated with the avowedly religious intentions of its chief sponsor. The impact of the opinion was to invite similar statutes without such clear legislative pedigrees.

In recent years the Court also has continued its effort to distinguish between permissible and impermissible aid to public schools. In *Grand Rapids School District* v. *Ball,* 105 S.Ct. 3216 (1985), it declared unconstitutional a school district's "shared time" program taught as an overload by full-time public school employees and a "community education program" taught as an overload by private-school teachers. These programs, which involved primarily religious school teachers, provided tax funds to support after-school remedial and enrichment classes to private-school students in private-school classrooms. In a companion case, Justice Brennan, writing for the majority, struck down a New York program that sent public-school teachers and other professionals to religious schools to provide remedial instruction and guidance in secular subjects (*Aguilar* v. *Felton,* 105 S.Ct. 3232, 1985).

Public aid to church-sponsored colleges and universities has been less problematic than aid to elementary and secondary schools. In *Tilton* v. *Richardson,* 403 U.S. 672 (1971), the Court upheld federal funds for buildings for church-supported colleges and universities, and in the three important college-aid cases since *Tilton,* a majority has upheld other types of public support to private colleges and universities. The most significant of these decisions is *Roemer* v. *Maryland Public Works Board,* 426 U.S. 736 (1976). Here, Justice Blackmun, writing for a plurality of three (White and Rehnquist concurred in result only), and in light of four separate and sharp dissents, upheld a Maryland provision for annual noncategorical grants to state-accredited private colleges, including church colleges, provided only that those funds not be used for sectarian purposes and that the recipient institutions not award only seminarian or theological degrees.

This apparent distinction between public aid to primary and secondary schools versus aid to colleges and universities suggests the presence of an unarticulated principle lurking beneath all these cases; namely, that the age and the impressionability of the students involved is a key concern.

Although hinted at from time to time in the Court's opinions, the "psychological" fact, if that is what it is, has not been squarely acknowledged, let alone supported by social science evidence. Furthermore, despite the greater tolerance for state aid to church colleges, the Court continues to look to the three-part test in LEMON as its test for *all* financial aid cases. The Constitution, after all, does not distinguish between religious establishment within various types of public institutions, but prohibits any and all establishment. Yet here, it appears, the age of those directly benefiting from public support is decisive.

Continuing Establishment Clause Issues

As we have seen, the Court has been extremely reluctant to permit use of public funds to support church-related institutions, and whenever it has upheld the expenditure of public funds, it has emphasized the child-benefit theory or some other "secular" justification. But even as the Court has taken this test seriously and wrestled with ways to develop a set of workable principles of separation, others have argued that the single greatest form of public subsidy has been in the form of tax exemptions for church property, exemptions estimated to result in the loss of hundreds of millions of dollars annually to public treasuries. Some proponents of strict separation have argued that there is no real difference between government subsidy and tax exemptions, and that the logic that compels prohibition of the former type of support is equally applicable to the latter. But as Holmes once suggested, the development of law is found in history, not logic.

Given the Court's positions in the school prayer decisions in the 1960s and the school aid cases of the late 1960s and early 1970s, as well as the expanded opportunity for taxpayers' suits, it was perhaps inevitable that the Court would eventually accept a case that directly challenged laws exempting churches from paying property taxes. That case was WALZ V. TAX COMMISSION (1970), in which Chief Justice Warren Burger, writing for the majority (only Justice Douglas dissented), upheld New York's (and by extension all other states') provisions for tax exemptions for religious institutions, and at least for the present put a stop to any hopes for an end to this type of public support for religious institutions.

The 1960s and early 1970s witnessed American involvement in an unpopular war in Vietnam, an activity that for the first time in American history led to large numbers of young men trying to avoid military service. Countless thousands took advantage of their status as college students to gain exemptions, thousands of others went abroad to avoid military induction, and still others sought to avoid induction by taking advantage of exemptions for conscientious objectors (CO) under the Selective Service Act. Historically, those who have been granted CO status have belonged to conventional religious groups whose doctrines prohibit the shedding of blood, even in the defense of home and country, and whose history give evidence of this tradition. The Vietnam war, however, produced applications for CO status that did *not* rest upon conventional religious beliefs by members of well-established religious groups. Instead, many CO applications were made by nonaffiliated individuals whose "philosophical" and ethical views forbade participation in *selected* wars. Met with refusal by local draft boards and courts, some of these objectors pursued their positions to the Supreme Court, arguing that accepting only a "narrow" religious basis for CO status, as the Selective Service Act appeared to have in mind, was violative of the Establishment Clause. In a series of cases, the Supreme Court side-stepped the constitutional issues by giving wide latitude in its interpretation of the statutes in question. One of the most important of these cases is *Gillette* v. *United States,* 401 U.S. 437 (1971). In its decision, the Court upheld the CO provisions in the Selective Service Act of 1967 but construed them broadly to include philosophical beliefs.

There are many other types of establishment issues that federal and state courts have dealt with in recent years. Most of them are cognates or derivatives of the important decisions included in this volume. For instance, the Court's ban on religious exercises in the public schools precipitated a host of other suits challenging traditional school practices such as "select devotionals"; school baccalaureate services; Christmas celebrations, symbols and carols in school; opening prayers at football games; distribution of free Bibles to school children by religious organizations; and the like. In general, the Supreme Court has refused to hear such cases, preferring to let the lower courts sort out the issues. No doubt another reason is the desire to avoid the public abuse that decisions in these cases would provoke. But recently, a slim but firm majority has been more willing to act and to accommodate to religion. In *Widmar* v. *Vincent* (1981), the Court upheld a policy that allowed religious programs on a campus because the same forum was "neutrally open to a broad class of nonreligious as well as religious speakers." And in *Marsh* v. *Chambers* (1983), the Court saw no conflict with the Establishment Clause when Nebraska employed members of the clergy as official legislative chaplains. Here as elsewhere the new majority reveals that official "neutrality" can tolerate a variety of accommodations.

The issue of evolution has simmered for years, and occasionally has come before the Court. Responding to Christian fundamentalists who believe in the literal interpretation of the creation story in the Bible, many school districts have been caught in a dilemma, either refusing to teach theories of evolution altogether or teaching them and running the risk of engaging the wrath of fundamentalists. In 1968, a unanimous court struck down an Arkansas law that prohibited public schools from teaching "the theory or doctrine that mankind ascended or descended from lower-order animals," or "to adopt or use in any such institution a textbook that teaches [evolution]" (*Epperson* v. *Arkansas,* 393 U.S. 97, 1968).

Reacting to this defeat, believers in the biblical account of creation embraced the language of science and mounted an effort to develop a plausible scientific and historical case for the biblical account of creation. One element of this strategy was to have the biblical account of creation renamed "creation science," and to put it forward on an equal footing with traditional scientific accounts. Supporters argued that "creation science" was a legitimate scientific theory deserving of equal treatment with other theories, and that it should be accorded equal space in textbooks and equal time in the classroom.

In response to this movement, Louisiana adopted a "Balanced Treatment Act" that forbade the teaching of the theory of evolution in public schools unless accompanied by instruction in "creation science." The act was challeneged as a violation of the Establishment Clause, and when the case reached the Supreme Court, it was ruled unconstitutional (*Edwards* v. *Aguillard* 107 S.Ct. 2573, 1987). In a lengthy opinion for the Court, Justice Brennan held that the act violated the LEMON test in that it promoted a religious purpose and had no clear secular purpose. Notwithstanding the term *creation science,* the purpose of the act, he argued, was to "advance the religious viewpoint that a supernatural being created humankind," and that in so doing it "advances a religious doctrine by requiring either the banishment of the theory of evolution from public school classrooms or the presentation of a religious viewpoint that rejects evolution in its entirety."

In a biting dissent joined by Chief Justice Rehnquist, Justice Scalia argued that "it would be extraordinary to invalidate the Balanced Treatment Act for lack of a valid secular purpose." Taking the stated purpose of the act at face value and arguing that the Court should defer to the elected representatives of the people, Justice Scalia wrote that "the legislature wanted to ensure that students would be free to decide for themselves how life began, based upon a fair and balanced presentation of the scientific evidence." Conceding that some legislators were probably motivated by religious sensitivities, he argued that "this alone would not suffice to invalidate the Act, so long as there was a genuine secular purpose as well."

The Court has also faced numerous related non-school issues, such as challenges of the expenditure of tax funds to pay for chaplains in the armed forces, holding religious services on U.S. military bases and in buildings built by public funds expressly for that purpose, recitation of prayers at public functions (e.g., the opening of the U.S. Congress), insertion of "under God" in the pledge of allegiance, inclusion of "In God we trust" on our coins and currency, and the like. Other cases with more direct and immediate consequences include challenges to provisions requiring consideration of religion or inclusion of religious advisors in matters of adoption, divorce, and child custody. Here too the Supreme Court has attempted to avoid these types of cases, preferring to let lower court decisions stand, even though to date the various lower court decisions have not yielded any consistent pattern.

Free Exercise of Religion

In 1879, in perhaps its first significant free-exercise case, the Supreme Court upheld a federal statute outlawing polygamy, a provision aimed at curbing a Mormon practice in the Territory of Utah (*Reynolds* v. *United States,* 98 U.S. 145, 1879). In doing so, the Court made a distinction between religious *beliefs* and *practices,* implying that the Free Exercise Clause applied only to the former and that Congress could regulate the latter. This distinction has taken root and continues to be used by the Court. In 1905, the Court upheld a Massachusetts law that required vaccinations when it was challenged by parents of a child who claimed their religious beliefs prohibited inoculations (*Jacobson* v. *Massachusetts,* 97 U.S. 11, 1905). In its opinion, the Court reiterated the belief/action distinction, and found that the statute was aimed at a "valid secular policy," well within its police powers. But in 1925, the Court did invalidate an Oregon law that prohibited parochial schools (*Pierce* v. *Society of Sisters,* 268 U.S. 510, 1925), arguing that the Oregon statute violated the Fourteenth Amendment's prohibition against the denial of liberty without due process. Here too it did not directly confront the First Amendment's Free Exercise Clause.

In fact, although the Court suggested that all the First Amendment freedoms were applied to the states via the Fourteenth Amendment in GITLOW V. NEW YORK (1925), it was not until 1940 that the Court explicitly nationalized the first of the two religious freedom provisions. In that case, *Cantwell* v. *Connecticut,* 310 U.S. 296, the Court overturned the conviction of a Jehovah's Witness for failure to apply for and receive a state permit before soliciting money for a religious purpose. In his opinion for a unanimous court, Justice Roberts held that such a provision constituted an impermissible censorship of religious expression.

Cantwell was the first of a long series of important cases beginning in the 1940s involving the Jehovah's Witnesses that dealt with challenges to state practices alleged to circumscribe the free exercise of religion. Indeed, it is fair to say that the Court's basic position on free exercise was framed in response to challenges by Jehovah's Witnesses, who in the 1940s persisted in exercising their religious obligations as they saw them in the face of vociferous community opposition. In upholding their right to proselytize, sell and distribute literature (*Murdock* v. *Pennsylvania,* 319 U.S. 105, 1943), hold meetings during a time of war in public places (*Cantwell*), and engage in such seemingly unpatriotic practices as refusing to salute and pledge allegiance to the flag (WEST VIRGINIA STATE BOARD OF EDUCATION V. BARNETTE, 1943), the Court paved the way for a broad interpretation of not only the Free Exercise Clause but freedom of expression (including speech and assembly) generally. And in so doing, the Court began to rethink the simple dichotomy of belief and action it had so confidently asserted in the early *Reynolds* case. This rethinking is witnessed in WISCONSIN V. YODER (1972).

The development of constitutional law in this area has not been easy nor without controversy. Although during the 1940s the Court consistently struck down registration laws that worked to limit door-to-door soliciting for religious purposes, its reaction to other types of government requirements in conflict with the scruples of the Jehovah's Witnesses met with mixed reactions. Indeed, one of the most celebrated about-faces in the Court's history involved two nearly identical pairs of cases, each handed down within a short period of each other. In the first, *Minersville School District* v. *Gobitis,* 310 U.S. 586 (1940), the Supreme Court upheld a state provision compelling school children to salute and pledge allegiance to the flag even if it violated their religious scruples. In a 4 to 3 decision (two justices not sitting), Justice Frankfurter for the majority relied on the belief/action distinction and upheld the law. But three years later, the full Court, with new justices, agreed to hear a nearly identical case, and in it overruled *Gobitis*. This case, WEST VIRGINIA STATE BOARD OF EDUCATION V. BARNETTE (1943), was decided by a vote of 6 to 3, with one of the *Gobitis* majority switching his position and voting with recently appointed justices to overrule *Gobitis*.

The second, but less dramatic, switch occurred in 1943 in *Murdock* v. *Pennsylvania,* 319 U.S. 105, when the Court voted 5 to 4 to overrule an equally close decision on just one year's standing, *Jones* v. *Opelika,* 316 U.S. 584 (1942), and upheld a Jehovah's Witness' claim that a law requiring that people selling religious material had to register

and pay a licensing tax constituted an unconstitutional censorship of religious liberty.

The Court has dealt with a variety of other free-exercise issues as well, and in so doing has not always supported the claim of religious freedom. In pursuing its task, the Court has been guided by dicta in the Mormon polygamy case, *Reynolds* v. *U.S.,* 98 U.S. 145 (1879), in which the Court observed that free exercise of religion does not permit conduct "in violation of social duties or subversive to good order." The flag salute and solicitation cases discussed above were ultimately decided as they were because after weighing the claim of religious freedom with the state's claims of the need for order, the Court found the latter claims relatively weak. No substantial social ills, the Court seemed to be saying, would follow from permitting the Jehovah's Witnesses their wishes in these situations.

In contrast, the Court has upheld a number of other types of state regulations that conflict with the religious practices of some people. While lower courts have upheld the right of ill and injured people to refuse blood transfusions and operations that would save their lives, as a rule the Supreme Court has not done so when these claims have involved children or pregnant women. Similarly, the Court upheld the convictions on fraud of members of a religious group who had solicited funds through the mail based upon claims of having supernaturally healed hundreds of people, *United States* v. *Ballard,* 322 U.S. 78 (1944).

More recently the courts have been faced with an array of cases involving claims by members of new or nontraditional groups claiming protection under the Free Exercise Clause. These issues include claims to constitutional protection for the use of hallucinogenics in religious services, the handling of poisonous snakes (*State ex rel. Swann* v. *Pack,* 527 S.W. 2d 99, 1975), refusal to join labor unions, and freedom of adult children to remain in sects generally thought to brainwash their members. (This latter controversy involves a clash between adult members of the Unification Church — called "Moonies," after the founder, Reverend

Moon — and their parents, who have sought to be appointed guardians as a first step towards forcefully removing their children from the cult's facilities and influence.) In the most important of these cases, the courts have upheld the rights to association with the "Moonies" (*Katz* v. *Supreme Court,* 73 Cal. App. 3d 952, 141 Cal. Rptr. 234, 1977). But in *Heffron* v. *International Society for Krisha Consciousness* (452 U.S. 640, 1981), the Supreme Court upheld, in the face of a challenge by members of the Krishna Movement, a Minnesota state law, applicable to charitable, nonprofit, and commercial organizations alike, limiting the time, place, and manner in which sales, solicitations, and literature distribution could take place at the state fair. Rejecting the claim that the law suppressed a member's free speech — the Society did not develop a separate free exercise argument — the Court found the rule to be "evenhanded" and "nondiscriminatory." Four justices dissented in part, arguing that the Minnesota law was too broad and restrictive. They would have upheld the ban on the sale of literature and the solicitation of funds but overturned the prohibition against distribution of the religious literature.

So far we have considered the two religious clauses as separate and distinct provisions. But if either is pursued in vigorous, absolutist fashion it can quickly come into conflict with the other. For instance, the Supreme Court has struck down a Tennessee law prohibiting members of the clergy from holding elective public office. Although presumably enacted as a measure to avoid entanglement between church and state, the Court held that it was an unconstitutional infringement on free exercise.

The major and most difficult issues, however, involve state efforts to accommodate to the religious views of some. These issues were raised in certain of the so-called Sunday-closing cases of 1961, although the Court side-stepped the confrontation between the two clauses in the most important of these cases, McGOWAN V. MARYLAND (1961), by upholding the Sunday closure on secular, not religious freedom, grounds. But the issue

quickly surfaced in different form. In *Braunfeld* v. *Brown* (366 U.S. 599, 1961), the Court upheld the application of Pennsylvania's Sunday-closing laws as they applied to Jews whose religious principles prohibited work on Saturday and who thereby were forced to close for two days or abandon their principles, in contrast to Gentile competitors who were confronted with only one day's closure. Writing for a bare majority, Chief Justice Warren defended the practice as serving a valid secular purpose, and expressed fear at having the state make "inquiry into the sincerity of the individual's religious beliefs," a practice which would itself run afoul of the spirit of the constitutionally protected guarantees. These decisions have led opponents of closing laws and the various exemptions to attack them, on due process grounds, a tactic that has proven highly successful in some states.

Similar concerns have arisen in connection with other issues, including state refusal to grant unemployment benefits to someone who refused for religious reasons to work on Saturday when employment was available (SHERBER, V. VERNER, 1963), and various challenges to provisions that facilitate religious exercise in such public facilities as prisons and military bases. In the Selective Service draft exemption cases, the Court gave a broad interpretation to "religious beliefs" for purposes of draft exemption for conscientious objection; see, for example, *United States* v. *Seeger,* 380 U.S. 180 (1965), and *Gillette* v. *United States,* 401 U.S. 437 (1971).

Three cases handed down in the 1980s illustrate the continuing issues faced by the Court in its effort to balance the protection of religious freedom with other social interests. In *Thornton* v. *Caldor,* 105 S.Ct. 2914 (1985), the Court struck down a Connecticut law that provided sabbath observers who requested it with an absolute and unqualified right not to work on their sabbath. The Court found that the statute imposed upon employers an absolute duty to conform their business practices to the particular religious practices of each of their employees, and as such concluded that "this unyielding weighting in favor of Sabbath observers over all other interests contravenes a fundamental principle of the Religious Clauses."

The following year the Court, in a 5 to 4 vote, upheld a military regulation that required that only authorized headgear could be worn by military personnel (*Goldman* v. *Weinberger,* 106 S.Ct. 1310, 1986). This case arose when an air force officer, an orthodox Jew who wore a yarmulke, challenged the provision as applied on grounds that it violated his religious freedom. In his opinion for the Court, Chief Justice Rehnquist stressed the Court's need to defer to the legislative process and the military's need to impose discipline through uniformity of dress.

In *Frazee* v. *Illinois Department of Employment Security,* 57 LW 4397 (1989), a unanimous Court overturned an interpretation of an Illinois law that denied unemployment benefits to a man who, on the basis of religious beliefs, refused to work on Sundays. Illinois had rejected his argument because he was not a member of any religious organization, but the Supreme Court held that if there is evidence—as there was in this case—of "sincere religious belief," denial of benefits for failure to accept Sunday employment violates the Free Exercise Clause.

One of the most agonizing controversies has involved the competing claims of the state to insist upon attendance at publicly certified schools (usually to age 16) and the firm religious beliefs of those in sects who wish to "shun" modern society. While this conflict has long simmered in American history, it became increasingly problematic after World War II, as states adopted higher-minimum-age school attendance laws and upgraded accreditation standards, and developed the capacity to enforce both. Although open conflict and court battles are often avoided by ad hoc accommodation by local officials, it was inevitable that the issue would sooner or later be ruled on by the Supreme Court. That case was WISCONSIN V. YODER (1972). Here, Chief Justice Warren Burger, writing for the majority, held for a group of Amish parents who sought exemption from portions of the state's school attendance laws. While the decision was a victory for the Amish, some supporters of expanded freedom for religious practices have greeted the Court's opinion with serious reservations because it emphasized so heavily the long history of this sect's beliefs. By the Court's own logic, it is not clear that newer and less socially acceptable sects would find such sympathy before the Court. After reading the case, ask yourself if the Court would have been so sympathetic to similar claims by a religious group based in California and founded in 1968.

A variation on this issue was raised in *Lyng* v. *Indian Cemetery Protective Association,* 56 L.W. 4292 (1988). There the Court, in a 6 to 3 decision, turned aside claims of the Hoppa Valley Indians, who had sought to prevent the construction of a forest service road through, and limit other uses of, a government-owned wilderness area that historically had been used by Indians for religious rituals that depend upon privacy, silence, and an undisturbed natural setting. The dissenters, in an opinion by Justice Brennan, took the majority to task for its "narrow formulation of religious burdens" and its unwillingness to determine if the "interests served by the . . . road are in any way compelling."

Conclusion

There is something of a paradox in the short history of the Court's concern with the two religious freedom provisions in the First Amendment. In its earliest cases, the Court tended to uphold the authority of government, even as it used impressive language to express a commitment to religious freedom. By contrast, in the important cases of the 1970s and 1980s, the Court tended to uphold the claims of religious freedom but did so using cautious language. No firm doctrines or clear principles have been forthcoming, so it is not surprising that in both periods there have been vigorous dissents. In the earlier period, dissenters found their views were eventually accepted by majorities, and there is no reason to believe that dissenters in the current period may not find their views acceptable to a new majority in the future.

These concerns are made all the more problematic as the types of issues likely to come before the Court involve situations that pit free exercise against establishment claims. This tension is seen in a 1989 case, *Texas Monthly* v. *Bullock,* 57 LW 4168, in which a sharply divided Court held unconstitutional a Texas statute that exempted subscribers to religious periodicals from having to pay sales tax. The Court rejected the state's argument that the exemption was designed to facilitate the free exercise of religion and had been adopted in light of the famous 1943 decision, *Murdock* v. *Pennsylvania,* in which the Court, in an expansive opinion, had relied upon the Free Exercise Clause to exempt missionaries, who sold religious tracts door to door, from having to pay salespeople's license fees. In overturning the Texas law, the Court distanced itself from some of the "sweeping dicta" in *Murdock,* and held that, WALZ notwithstanding, the Texas exemption collided with the secular purpose prong of LEMON'S Establishment Clause test.

Cases

Zorach v. Clauson

343 U.S. 306 (1952)
Vote: 6–3

Between 1947 and 1952, the Supreme Court handed down three important decisions involving religious exercises and the public schools. The first of these, *Everson* v. *Board of Education,* 330 U.S. 1 (1947), upheld a New Jersey statute that permitted local school districts to reimburse parents of school children for costs incurred in using public transportation to send their children to school, including the parents of children who attended parochial schools. In upholding this practice over four vigorous dissents, the majority invoked the child-benefit doctrine the Court had relied on from time to time in the past.

The next year, in *Illinois ex rel. McCollum* v. *Board of Education,* 333 U.S. 20 (1948), the Court confronted another challenge, this time a so-called "released time" program operating in champaign, Illinois, which provided for religious instruction in public-school classrooms during regular school hours but taught by outside teachers. The Court balked at this type of "cooperation," finding that the teachers had to be approved by the public-school authorities, records of attendance were maintained, indirect costs of the program were borne by the public, and that there was a close integration of religious education and compulsory powers of the state. Under these circumstances, the Court held, the arrangement violated the Establishment Clause of the First Amendment.

The case below grew out of a conscious effort to overcome the Court's objections to the released-time program in Champaign. The facts thought to distinguish the two types of programs are set forth at the beginning of Justice Douglas' opinion for the majority.

MR. JUSTICE DOUGLAS delivered the opinion of the Court.

New York City has a program which permits its public schools to release students during the school day so that they may leave the school buildings and school grounds and go to religious centers for religious instruction or devotional exercises. A student is released on written request of his parents. Those not released stay in the classrooms. The churches make weekly reports to the schools, sending a list of children who have been released from public school but who have not reported for religious instruction.

This "released time" program involves neither religious instruction in public school classrooms nor the expenditure of public funds. All costs, including the application blanks, are paid by the religious organizations. The case is therefore unlike *McCollum* v. *Board of Education.* . . .

Appellants, who are taxpayers and residents of New York City and whose children attend its public schools, challenge the present law, contending it is in essence not different from the one involved in the McCollum case. Their argument, stated elaborately in various ways, reduces itself to this: the weight and influence of the school is put behind a program for religious instruction; public school teachers police it, keeping tab on students who are released; the classroom activities come to a halt while the students who are released for religious instruction are on leave; the school is a crutch on which the churches are leaning for support in their religious training; without the cooperation of the schools this "released time" program, like the one in the McCollum case, would be futile and ineffective. . . .

. . . Our problem reduces itself to whether New York by this system has either prohibited the "free exercise" of religion or has made a law "respecting an establishment of religion" within the meaning of the First Amendment.

It takes obtuse reasoning to inject any issue of the "free exercise" of religion into the present case. No one is forced to go to the religious classroom and no religious exercise or instruction is brought to the classrooms of the public schools. A student need not take religious instruction. He is left to his own desires as to the manner or time of his religious devotions, if any.

There is a suggestion that the system involved the use of coercion to get public school students into religious classrooms. There is no evidence in the record before us that supports that conclusion. The present record indeed tells us that the school authorities are neutral in this regard and do no more than release students whose parents so request. If in fact coercion were used, if it were established that any one or more teachers were using their office to persuade or force students to take the religious instruction, a wholly different case would be presented. Hence we put aside that claim of coercion both as respects the "free-exercise" of religion and "an establishment of religion" within the meaning of the First Amendment.

Moreover, apart from that claim or coercion, we do not see how New York by this type of "released time" program has made a law respecting an establishment of religion within the meaning of the First Amendment. There is much talk of the separation of Church and State in the history of the Bill of Rights and in the decisions clustering around the First Amendment. . . . There cannot be the slightest doubt that the First Amendment reflects the philosophy that Church and State should be separated. And so far as interference with the "free exercise" of religion and an "establishment" of religion are concerned, the separation must be complete and unequivocal. The First Amendment within the scope of its coverage permits no exception; the prohibition is absolute. The First Amendment, however, does not say that in every and all respects there shall be a separation of Church and State. Rather, it studiously defines the manner, the specific ways, in which there shall be no concert or union or dependency one on the other That is the common sense of the matter. Otherwise the state and religion would be aliens to each other — hostile, suspicious, and even unfriendly. Churches could not be required to pay even property taxes. Municipalities would not be permitted to render police or fire protection to religious groups. Policemen who helped parishioners into their places of worship would violate the constitution. Prayers in our legislative halls; the appeals to the Almighty in the messages of the Chief Executive; the proclamations making Thanksgiving Day a holiday; "so help me God" in our courtroom oaths — these and all other references to the Almighty that run through our laws, our public rituals, our ceremonies would be flouting the First Amendment. A fastidious atheist or agnostic could even object to the supplication with which the Court opens each session: "God save the United States and this Honorable Court."

We would have to press the concept of separation of Church and State to these extremes to condemn the present law on constitutional grounds. The nullification of this law would have wide and profound effects. A Catholic student applies to his teacher for permission to leave the school during hours on a Holy Day of Obligation to attend a mass. A Jewish student asks his teacher for permission to be excused for Yom Kippur. A Protestant wants the afternoon off for a family baptismal ceremony. In each case the teacher requires parental consent in writing. In each case the teacher, in order to make sure the student is not a truant, goes further and requires a report from the priest, the rabbi, or the minister. The teacher in other words cooperates in a religious program to the extent of making it possible for her students to participate in it. Whether she does it occasionally for a few students, regularly for one, or pursuant to a systematized program designed to further the religious needs of all the students does not alter the character of the act.

We are a religious people whose institutions presuppose a Supreme Being. We guarantee the freedom to worship as one chooses. We make room for as wide a variety of beliefs and creeds as the spiritual needs of man deem necessary. We sponsor an attitude on the part of government that shows no partiality to any one group and that lets each flourish according to the zeal of its adherents and the appeal of its dogma. When the state encourages religious instruction or cooperates with religious authorities by adjusting the schedule of public events to sectarian needs, it follows the best of our traditions. For it then respects the religious nature of our people and accommodates the public service to their spiritual needs. To hold that it may not would be to find in the Constitution a requirement that the government show a callous indifference to religious groups. That would be preferring those who believe in no religion over those who do believe. Government may not finance religious groups nor undertake religious instruction nor blend secular and sectarian education nor use secular institutions to force one or some religion on any person. But we find no constitutional requirement which makes it necessary for government to be hostile to religion and to throw its weight against efforts to widen the effective scope of religious influence. The government must be neutral when it comes to competition between sects. It may not thrust any sect on any person. It may not make a religious observance compulsory. It may not coerce anyone to attend church, to observe a religious holiday, or to take religious instruction. But it can close its doors or suspend its operations as to those who want to repair to their religious sanctuary for worship or instruction. No more than that is undertaken here. . . .

. . . .

In the McCollum case the classrooms were used for religious instruction and the force of the public school was used to promote that instruction. Here, as we have said, the public schools do no more than accommodate their schedules to a program of outside religious instruction. We follow the McCollum case. But we cannot expand it to cover the present released time program unless separation of Church and State means that public institutions can make no adjustments of their schedules to accommodate the religious needs of the people. We cannot read into the Bill of Rights such a philosophy of hostility to religion.

Affirmed.

MR. JUSTICE BLACK, dissenting.

Illinois ex rel. McCollum v. *Board of Education* . . . held invalid as an "establishment of religion" an Illinois system under which school children, compelled by law to go to public schools, were freed from some hours of required school work on condition that they attend special religious classes held in the school buildings. Although the classes were taught by sectarian teachers neither employed nor paid by the state, the state did use its power to further the program by releasing some of the children from regular class work, insisting that those released attend the religious classes, and requiring that those who remained behind do some kind of academic work while the others received their religious training. . . .

I see no significant difference between the invalid Illinois system and that of New York here sustained. Except for the use of the school buildings in Illinois, there is no difference between the systems which I consider even worthy of mention. In the New York program, as in that of Illinois, the school authorities release some of the children on the condition that they attend the religious classes, get reports on whether they attend, and hold the other children in the school building until the religious hour is over. As we attempted to make categorically clear, the McCollum decision would have been the same if the religious classes had not been held in the school buildings. . . .

. . . McCollum thus held that Illinois could not constitutionally manipulate the compelled classroom hours of its compulsory school machinery so as to channel children into sectarian classes. Yet that is exactly what the Court holds New York can do.

. . . .

Difficulty of decision in the hypothetical situations mentioned by the Court, but not now before us, should not confuse the issues in this case. Here the sole question is whether New York can use its compulsory education laws to help religious sects get attendants presumably too unenthusiastic to go unless moved to do so by the pressure of this state machinery. That this is the plan, purpose, design and consequence of the New York program cannot be denied. The state thus makes religious sects beneficiaries of its power to compel children to attend secular schools. Any use of such coercive power by the state to help or hinder some religious sects or to prefer all religious sects over nonbelievers or vice versa is just what I think the First Amendment forbids. In considering whether a state has entered this forbidden field the question is not whether it has entered too far but whether it has entered at all. New York is manipulating its compulsory education laws to help religious sects get pupils. This is not separation but combination of Church and State.

The Court's validation of the New York system rests in part on its statement that Americans are "a religious people whose institutions presuppose a Supreme Being." This was at least as true when the First Amendment was adopted; and it was just as true when eight Justices of the Court invalidated the released time system in McCollum on the premise that a state can no more "aid all religions" than it can aid one. It was precisely because Eighteenth Century Americans were a religious people divided into many fighting sects that we were given the constitutional mandate to keep Church and State completely separate. Colonial history had already shown that, here as elsewhere, zealous sectarians entrusted with governmental power to further their causes would sometimes torture, maim and kill those they branded "heretics," "atheists" or "agnostics." The First Amendment was therefore to insure that no one powerful sect or combination of sects could use political or governmental power to punish dissenters whom they could not convert to their faith. Now as then, it is only by wholly isolating the state from the religious sphere and compelling it to be completely neutral, that the freedom of each and every denomination and of all nonbelievers can be maintained. It is this neutrality the Court abandons today when it treats New York's coercive system as a program which *merely* "encourages religious instruction or co-operates with religious authorities." The abandonment is all the more dangerous to liberty because of the Court's legal exaltation of the orthodox and its derogation of unbelievers.

Under our system of religious freedom, people have gone to their religious sanctuaries not because they feared the law but because they loved their God. The choice of all has been as free as the choice of those who answered the call to worship moved only by the music of the old Sunday morning church bells. The spiritual mind of man has thus been free to believe, disbelieve, or doubt, without repression, great or small, by the heavy hand of government. Statutes authorizing such repression have been stricken. Before today, our judicial opinions have refrained from drawing invidious distinctions between those who believe in no religion and those who do believe. The First Amendment has lost much if the religious follower and the atheist are no longer to be judicially regarded as entitled to equal justice under law.

State help to religion injects political and party prejudices into a holy field. It too often substitutes force for prayer, hate for love, and persecution for persuasion. Government should not be allowed, under cover of the soft euphemism of "co-operation," to steal into the sacred area of religious choice.

MR. JUSTICE FRANKFURTER, dissenting.

The Court tells us that in the maintenance of its public schools, "[The State government] can close its doors or suspend its operations" so that its citizens may be free for religious devotions or instruction. If that were the issue, it would not rise to the dignity of a constitutional controversy. Of course a State may provide that the classes in its schools shall

be dismissed, for any reason, or no reason, on fixed days, or for special occasions. The essence of this case is that the school system did not "close its doors" and did not "suspend its operations." There is all the difference in the world between letting the children out of school and letting some of them out of school into religious classes. If every one is free to make what use he will of time wholly unconnected from schooling required by law — those who wish sectarian instruction devoting it to that purpose, those who have ethical instruction at home, to that, those who study music, to that — then of course there is no conflict with the Fourteenth Amendment.

The pith of the case is that formalized religious instruction is substituted for other school activity which those who do not participate in the released-time program are compelled to attend. The school system is very much in operation during this kind of released time. If its doors are closed, they are closed upon those students who do not attend the religious instruction, in order to keep them within the school. That is the very thing which raises the constitutional issue. It is not met by disregarding it. Failure to discuss this issue does not take it out of the case.

Again, the Court relies upon the absence from the record of evidence of coercion in the operation of the system. "If in fact coercion were used," according to the Court, "if it were established that any one or more teachers were using their office to persuade or force students to take the religious instruction, a wholly different case would be presented." Thus, "coercion" in the abstract is acknowledged to be fatal. But the Court disregards the fact that as the case comes to us, there could be no proof of coercion, for the appellants were not allowed to make proof of it. Appellants alleged that "The operation of the released time program has resulted and inevitably results in the exercise of pressure and coercion upon parents and children to secure attendance by the children for religious instruction." This allegation — that coercion was in fact present and is inherent in the system, no matter what disavowals might be made in the operating regulations — was denied by respondents. Thus were drawn issues of fact which cannot be determined, on any conceivable view of judicial notice, by judges out of their own knowledge or experience. Appellants sought an opportunity to adduce evidence in support of these allegations at an appropriate trial. And though the courts below cited the concurring opinion in McCollum . . . to "emphasize the importance of detailed analysis of the facts to which the Constitutional test of Separation is to be applied," they denied that opportunity on the ground that such proof was irrelevant to the issue of constitutionality. . . . I cannot see how a finding that coercion was absent, deemed critical by this Court in sustaining the practice, can be made here, when appellants were prevented from making a timely showing of coercion because the courts below thought it irrelevant.

. . . .

The deeply devisive controversy aroused by the attempts to secure public school pupils for sectarian instruction would promptly end if the advocates of such instruction were content to have the school "close its doors or suspend its operations" — that is, dismiss classes in their entirety, without discrimination — instead of seeking to use the public schools as the instrument for securing attendance at denominational classes. The unwillingness of the promoters of this movement to dispense with such use of the public schools betrays a surprising want of confidence in the inherent power of the various faiths to draw children to outside sectarian classes — an attitude that hardly reflects the faith of the greatest religious spirits.

MR JUSTICE JACKSON, dissenting.

This released time program is founded upon a use of the State's power of coercion, which, for me, determines its unconstitutionality. Stripped to its essentials, the plan has two stages, first, that the State compel each student to yield a large part of his time for public secular education and, second, that some of it be "released" to him on condition that he devote it to sectarian religious purposes.

No one suggests that the Constitution would permit the State directly to require this "released" time to be spent, "under the control of a duly constituted religious body." This program accomplishes that forbidden result by indirection. If public education were taking so much of the pupil's time as to injure the public or the students' welfare by encroaching upon their religious opportunity, simply shortening everyone's school day would facilitate voluntary and optional attendance at Church classes. But the suggestion is rejected upon the ground that if they are made free many students will not go to the Church. Hence, they must be deprived of freedom for this period, with Church attendance put to them as one of the two permissible ways of using it.

The greater effectiveness of this system over voluntary attendance after school hours is due to the truant officer who, if the youngster fails to go to the Church school, dogs him back to the public schoolroom. Here schooling is more or less suspended during the "released time" so the nonreligious attendants will not forge ahead of the churchgoing absentees. But it serves as a temporary jail for a pupil who will not go to Church. It takes more subtlety of mind than I possess to deny that this is governmental constraint in support of religion. It is as unconstitutional, in my view, when exerted by indirection as when exercised forthrightly.

As one whose children, as a matter of free choice, have been sent to privately supported Church schools, I may challenge the Court's suggestion that opposition to this plan can only be antireligious, atheistic, or agnostic. My evangelistic brethren confuse an objection to compulsion with an objection to religion. It is possible to hold a faith with enough confidence to believe that what should be rendered to God does not need to be decided and collected by Caesar.

The day that this country ceases to be free for irreligion it will cease to be free for religion — except for the sect that can win political power. The same epithetical jurisprudence used by the Court today to beat down those who oppose pressuring children into some religion can devise as good epithets tomorrow against those who object to pressuring them into a favored religion. And, after all, if we concede to the State power and wisdom to single out "duly constituted religious" bodies as exclusive alternatives for compulsory secular instruction, it would be logical to also uphold the power and wisdom to choose the true faith among those "duly constituted." We start down a rough road when we begin to mix compulsory public education with compulsory godliness.

. . . The distinction attempted between [McCollum] and this is trivial, almost to the point of cynicism, magnifying its nonessential details and disparaging compulsion which was the underlying reason for invalidity. A reading of the Court's opinion in that case along with its opinion in this case will show such difference of overtones and undertones as to make clear that the McCollum case has passed like a storm in a teacup. The wall which the Court was professing to erect between Church and State has become even more warped and twisted than I expected. Today's judgment will be more interesting to students of psychology and of the judicial processes than to students of constitutional law.

Abington School District v. Schempp

474 U.S. 203 (1963)

[handwritten: 379]

Vote: 8–1

Millions of Americans grew up taking part in morning devotionals over a schoolwide public address system in school classrooms at the outset of each day. These services varied. Some involved recitation of prayers, singing a hymn or two, listening to a brief inspirational talk, a Bible reading, or some combination of these activities. They generally lasted for five to ten minutes and were followed by general announcements about school activities.

In *Engel* v. *Vitale,* 370 U.S. 421 (1962), the Court, by an 8 to 1 vote, called a halt to recitation of an officially composed and prescribed prayer as part of an organized devotional. In this case, the Court considers a challenge to similar but even more traditional practices: Bible reading and public recitation of the Lord's Prayer.

The practices in question in this case grew out of separate suits by parents and school children in two states, which subsequently were considered together by the United States Supreme Court.

In *Abington* v. *Schempp,* the parents of Roger and Donna Schempp challenged a Pennsylvania law requiring that "at least ten verses from the Holy Bible shall be read, without comment, at the opening of each public school on each school day. Any child shall be excused from such Bible readings... upon the written request of his parents or guardian." The Schempps, who did not want their children to participate in this exercise, were not satisfied with the provision made for those wishing to be excused, claiming that absence from the room during the service would unfairly single out their children, and that they would miss the school announcements that often immediately followed the Bible reading. Accordingly, they brought suit in federal district court challenging the constitutionality of the state's provision. The district court held that the state provision violated the First and Fourteenth Amendments, whereupon the state appealed the decision to the United States Supreme Court.

The Maryland suit, *Murray* v. *Curlett,* 374 U.S. 203 (1963), involved a challenge by Madalyn Murray and her son, William, both professed atheists, to a rule adopted by the Board of School Commissioners of Baltimore pursuant to a state law which provided for the "reading, without comment, of a chapter in the Holy Bible and/or the use of the Lord's Prayer." Although the rule was amended at the Murrays' insistence to permit children to be excused from the exercise on request of a parent, the Murrays were unsuccessful in their efforts to get the school board to rescind the rule entirely. As a consequence, they filed suit in a Maryland district court on the grounds that the rule, even as amended to permit excused absences, was violation of their First and Fourteenth Amendment rights. Both the trial court and the Maryland court of appeals, by a divided vote of 4 to 3, sustained the rule, holding that it was not in violation of the First and Fourteenth Amendments. Upon petition by the Murrays, the United States Supreme Court granted certiorari.

MR. JUSTICE CLARK delivered the opinion of the Court.

. . . .

It is true that religion has been closely identified with our history and government. As we said in *Engel* v. *Vitale,* "The history of man is inseparable from the history of religion. And... since the beginning of that history many people have devoutly believed that 'More things are wrought by prayer than this world dreams of.'" In *Zorach* v. *Clauson* . . . (1952), we gave specific recognition to the proposition that "[w]e are a religious people whose institutions presuppose a Supreme Being." The fact that the Founding Fathers believed devoutly that there was a God and that the unalienable rights of man were rooted in Him is clearly evidenced in their writings, from the Mayflower Compact to the Constitution itself. This background is evidenced today in our public life through the continuance in our oaths of office from the Presidency to the Alderman of the final supplication, "So help me God." Likewise each House of Congress provides through its Chaplain an opening prayer, and the sessions of this Court are declared open by the crier in a short ceremony, the final phrase of which invokes the grace of God. Again, there are such manifestations in our military forces, where those of our citizens who are under the restrictions of military service wish to engage in voluntary worship. Indeed, only last year an official survey of the country indicated that 64% of our people have church membership. . . . It can be truly said, therefore, that today, as in the beginning, our national life reflects a religious people. . . .

This is not to say, however, that religion has been so identified with our history and government that religious freedom is not likewise as strongly inbedded in our public and private life. Nothing but the most telling of personal experiences in religious persecution suffered by our forebears . . . could have planted our belief in liberty of religious opinion any more deeply in our heritage. It is true that this liberty frequently was not realized by the colonists, but this is readily accountable by their close ties to the Mother Country. However, the views of Madison and Jefferson, preceded by Roger Williams, came to be incorporated not only in the Federal Constitution but likewise in those of most of our States. This freedom to worship was indispensable in a country whose people came from the four quarters of the earth and brought with them a diversity of religious opinion. . . .

Almost a hundred years ago in *Minor* v. *Board of Education of Cincinnati,* Judge Alphonso Taft, father of the revered Chief Justice, in an unpublished opinion stated the ideal of our people as to religious freedom as one of

> absolute equality before the law, of all religious opinions and sects. . . .
>
> The government is neutral, and, while pretecting all, it perfers none, and it *disparages* none.

. . . .

The wholesome "neutrality" of which this Court's cases speak thus stems from a recognition of the teachings of history that powerful sects or groups might bring about a fusion of governmental and religious functions or a concert or dependency of one upon the other to the end that official support of the State or Federal Government would be placed behind the tenets of one or of all orthodoxies. This the Establishment Clause prohibits. And a further reason for neutrality is found in the Free Exercise Clause, which recognizes the value of religious training, teaching and observance and, more particularly, the right of every person to freely choose his own course with reference thereto, free of compulsion from the state. This the Free Exercise Clause guarantees. . . . [T]he Establishment Clause has been directly considered by the Court eight times in the past score of years and, with only one Justice dissenting on the point, it has consistently held that the clause withdrew all legislative power respecting religious belief or the expression thereof. The test may be stated as follows: what are the purpose and the primary effect of the enactment? If either is the advancement or inhibition of religion, then the enactment exceeds the scope of legislative power as circumscribed by the Constitution. That is to say that to withstand the strictures of the Establishment Clause there must be a secular legislative purpose and a primary effect that neither advances nor inhibits religion. . . . The Free Exercise Clause, likewise considered many times here, withdraws from legislative power, state and federal, the exertion of any restraint on the free exercise of religion. Its purpose is to secure religious liberty in the individual by prohibiting any invasions thereof by civil authority. Hence it is necessary in a free exercise case for one to show the coercive effect of the enactment as it operates against him in the practice of his religion. The distinction between the two clauses is apparent — a violation of the Free Exercise Clause is predicated on coercion while the Establishment Clause violation need not be so attended.

Applying the Establishment Clause principles to the cases at bar we find that the States are requiring the selection and reading at the opening of the school day of verses from the Holy Bible and the recitation of the Lord's Prayer by the students in unison. These exercises are prescribed as part of the curricular activities of students who are required by law to attend school. They are held in the school buildings under the supervision and with the participation of teachers employed in those schools. None of these factors, other than compulsory school attendance, was present in the program upheld in *Zorach* v. *Clauson*. . . .

. . . .

The conclusion follows that in both cases the laws require religious exercises and such exercises are being conducted in direct violation of the rights of the appellees and petitioners. Nor are these required exercises mitigated by the fact that individual students may absent themselves upon parental request, for that fact furnishes no defense to a claim of unconstitutionality under the Establishment Clause. See *Engel* v. *Vitale, supra.* Further, it is no defense to urge that the religious practices here may be relatively minor encroachments on the First Amendment. The breach of neutrality that is today a trickling stream may all too soon become a raging torrent and, in the words of Madison, it is proper to take alarm at the first experiment on our liberties." . . .

. . . Nothing we have said here indicates that such study of the Bible or of religion, when presented objectively as part of a secular program of education, may not be effected consistently with the First Amendment. But the exercises here do not fall into those categories. They are religious exercises, required by the States in violation of the command of the First Amendment that the government maintain strict neutrality, neither aiding nor opposing religion.

Finally, we cannot accept that the concept of neutrality, which does not permit a State to require a religious exercise even with the consent of the majority of those affected, collides with the majority's right to free exercise of religion. While the Free Exercise Clause clearly prohibits the use of state action to deny the rights of free exercise to *anyone*, it has never meant that a majority could use the machinery of the State to practice its beliefs. . . .

The place of religion in our society is an exalted one, achieved through a long tradition of reliance on the home, the church and the inviolable citadel of the individual heart and mind. We have come to recognize through bitter experience that it is not within the power of government to invade that citadel, whether its purpose or effect be to aid or oppose, to advance or retard. In the relationship between man and religion, the State is firmly committed to a position of neutrality. Though the application of that rule requires interpretation of a delicate sort, the rule itself is clearly and concisely stated in the words of the First Amendment. Applying that rule to the facts of these cases, we affirm the judgment in [*Abington v. Schempp*]. In [*Murray v. Curlett*], the judgment is reversed and the cause remanded to the Maryland Court of Appeals for further proceedings consistent with this opinion.

MR. JUSTICE DOUGLAS, concurring.

. . . .

These regimes violate the Establishment Clause in two different ways. In each case the State is conducting a religious exercise; and, as the Court holds, that cannot be done without violating the "neutrality" required of the State by the balance of power between individual, church and state that has been struck by the First Amendment. But the Establishment Clause . . . also forbids the State to employ its facilities or funds in a way that gives any church, or all churches, greater strength in our society than it would have by relying on its members alone. Thus, the present regimes must fall under that clause for the additional reason that public funds, though small in amount, are being used to promote a religious exercise. Through the mechanism of the State, all of the people are being required to finance a religious exercise that only some of the people want and that violates the sensibilities of others.

Such contributions may not be made by the State even in a minor degree without violating the Establishment Clause. It is not the amount of public funds expended; as this case illustrates, it is the use to which public funds are put that is controlling. For the First Amendment does not say that some forms of establishment are allowed; it says that "no law respecting an establishment of religion" shall be made. What may not be done directly may not be done indirectly lest the Establishment Clause become a mockery.

[JUSTICE BRENNAN wrote a concurring opinion. JUSTICE GOLDBERG, with whom JUSTICE HARLAN joined, wrote a concurring opinion. JUSTICE STEWART dissented.]

Lemon v. Kurtzman

403 U.S. 642 (1971)
Vote: 8–1

In *Everson v. Board of Education,* 330 U.S. 1 (1947), the Court upheld a program providing free transportation for students, including those students attending parochial schools. In *Board of Education v. Allen* 392 U.S. 236 (1968), the Court upheld the expenditure of public funds for secular books to be used in parochial schools. In both situations the practices under challenge were justified by the Court as having a valid secular purpose which might only incidentally (and nonpreferentially) benefit religious institutions.

With a suggested test for drawing the dividing line in these cases, it was inevitable that supporters of parochial schools would attempt to obtain still more support under the "child benefit" or "valid secular legislative purpose" theory suggested by the Court. Thus during the late 1960s and 1970s a Court undergoing rapid change of membership was confronted with a new generation of school aid cases. One of the earliest of these cases was *Lemon v. Kurtzman,* and in his opinion below, the Chief Justice reviews prior holdings and tries to restate the principles distinguishing acceptable from unacceptable aid. In doing so, however, he may have significantly expanded these principles.

The *Lemon* case involved challenges to Pennsylvania and Rhode Island statutes that provided various types of aid to students at parochial schools and also provided for a built-in system of surveillance to see that this aid went only for valid secular purposes. This case was one of several considered together by some of the justices and treated separately by others. In a companion case, *Tilton v. Richardson,* 403 U.S. 672 (1971), the Court upheld federal funding for buildings at church-supported colleges and universities.

In Pennsylvania, Alton Lemon brought a tax-payer's suit against David Kurtzman, State Superintendent of Public Instruction, seeking an injunction prohibiting him from spending state funds for reimbursement to nonpublic schools for the cost of teachers salaries, textbooks, and instructional materials in secular subjects. The Rhode Island cases, also treated in *Lemon,* arose when taxpayers challenged state provisions that paid up to a 15 percent salary supplement to nonpublic school teachers for their secular teaching.

MR. CHIEF JUSTICE BURGER delivered the opinion of the Court.

In *Everson* v. *Board of Education* . . . (1947), this Court upheld a state statute that reimbursed the parents of parochial school children for bus transportation expenses. There Mr. Justice Black, writing for the majority, suggested that the decision carried to "the verge" of forbidden territory under the Religion Clauses. . . . Candor compels acknowledgment, moreover, that we can only dimly perceive the lines of demarcation in this extraordinarily sensitive area of constitutional law.

The language of the Religion Clauses of the First Amendment is at best opaque, particularly when compared with other portions of the Amendment. Its authors did not simply prohibit the establishment of a state church or state religion, an area history shows they regarded as very important and fraught with great dangers. Instead they commanded that there should be "no law *respecting* an establishment of religion." A law may be one "respecting" the forbidden objective while falling short of its total realization. A law "respecting" the proscribed result, that is, the establishment of religion, is not always easily identifiable as one violative of the Clause. A given law might not *establish* a state religion but nevertheless be one "respecting" that end in the sense of being a step that could lead to such establishment and hence offend the First Amendment.

In the absence of precisely stated constitutional prohibitions, we must draw lines with reference to the three main evils against which the Establishment Clause was intended to afford protection: "sponsorship, financial support, and active involvement of the sovereign in religious activity." *Walz* v. *Tax Commission* . . . (1970).

Every analysis in this area must begin with consideration of the cumulative criteria developed by the Court over many years. Three such tests may be gleaned from our cases. First, the statute must have a secular legislative purpose; second, its principal or primary effect must be one that neither advances nor inhibits religion, *Board of Education* v. *Allen* . . . (1968); finally, the statute must not foster "an excessive government entanglement with religion." *Walz* (1970). . . .

Inquiry into the legislative purposes of the Pennsylvania and Rhode Island statutes affords no basis for a conclusion that the legislative intent was to advance religion. On the contrary, the statutes themselves clearly state that they are intended to enhance the quality of the secular education in all schools covered by the compulsory attendance laws. There is no reason to believe the legislatures meant anything else. A State always has a legitimate concern for maintaining minimum standards in all schools it allows to operate. As in *Allen,* we find nothing here that undermines the stated legislative intent; it must therefore be accorded appropriate deference.

In *Allen* the Court acknowledged that secular and religious teachings were not necessarily so intertwined that secular textbooks furnished to students by the State were in fact instrumental in the teaching of religion. . . . The legislatures of Rhode Island and Pennsylvania have concluded that secular and religious education are identifiable and separable. In the abstract we have no quarrel with this conclusion.

The two legislatures, however, have also recognized that church-related elementary and secondary schools have a significant religious mission and that a substantial portion of their activities is religiously oriented. They have therefore sought to create statutory restrictions designed to guarantee the separation between secular and religious educational functions and to ensure that State financial aid supports only the former. All these provisions are precautions taken in candid recognition that these programs approached, even if they did not intrude upon, the forbidden areas under the Religion Clauses. We need not decide whether these legislative precautions restrict the principal or primary effect of the programs to the point where they do not offend the Religion Clauses, for we conclude that the cumulative impact of the entire relationship arising under the statutes in each state involves excessive entanglement between government and religion.

. . . .

Our prior holdings do not call for total separation between church and state; total separation is not possible in an absolute sense. Some relationship between government and religious organizations is inevitable. *Zorach* v. *Clauson* . . . (1952); *Sherbert* v. *Verner* . . . (1963). . . . Fire inspections, building and zoning regulations, and state requirements under compulsory school-attendance laws are examples of necessary and permissible contacts. Indeed, under the statutory exemption before us in *Walz,* the State had a continuing burden to ascertain that the exempt property was in fact being used for religious worship. Judicial caveats against entanglement must recognize that the line of separation, far from being a "wall," is a blurred, indistinct, and variable barrier depending on all the circumstances of a particular relationship.

In order to determine whether the government entanglement with religion is excessive, we must examine the character and purposes of the institutions that are benefited, the nature of the aid that the State provides, and the resulting relationship between the government and the religious authority.... Here we find that both statutes foster an impermissible degree of entanglement.

(a) RHODE ISLAND PROGRAM

The District Court made extensive findings on the grave potential for excessive entanglement that inheres in the religious character and purpose of the Roman Catholic elementary schools of Rhode Island, to date the sole beneficiaries of the Rhode Island Salary Supplement Act.

The church schools involved in the program are located close to parish churches. This understandably permits convenient access for religious exercises since instruction in faith and morals is part of the total educational process. The school buildings contain identifying religious symbols such as crosses on the exterior and crucifixes, and religious paintings and statues either in the classrooms or hallways. Although only approximately 30 minutes a day are devoted to direct religious instruction, there are religiously oriented extracurricular activities. Approximately two-thirds of the teachers in these schools are nuns of various religious orders. Their dedicated efforts provide an atmosphere in which religious instruction and religious vocations are natural and proper parts of life in such schools. Indeed, as the District Court found, the role of teaching nuns in enhancing the religious atmosphere has led the parochial school authorities to attempt to maintain a one-to-one ratio between nuns and lay teachers in all schools rather than to permit some to be staffed almost entirely by lay teachers.

. . . .

... [T]he considerable religious activities of these schools led the legislature to provide for careful governmental controls and surveillance by state authorities in order to ensure that state aid supports only secular education.

The schools are governed by the standards set forth in a "Handbook of School Regulations," which has the force of synodal law in the diocese. It em-phasizes the role and importance of the teacher in parochial schools: "The prime factor for the success or the failure of the school is the spirit and personality, as well as the professional competency, of the teacher." The Handbook also states that: "Religious formation is not confined to formal courses; nor is it restricted to a single subject area." Finally, the Handbook advises teachers to stimulate interest in religious vocations and missionary work. Given the mission of the church school, these instructions are consistent and logical.

Several teachers testified, however, that they did not inject religion into their secular classes. And the District Court found that religious values did not necessarily affect the content of the secular instruction. But what has been recounted suggests the potential if not actual hazards of this form of state aid....

. . . .

... An eligible recipient must teach only those courses that are offered in the public schools and use only those texts and materials that are found in the public schools. In addition the teacher must not engage in teaching any course in religion.

A comprehensive, discriminating, and continuing state surveillance will inevitably be required to ensure that these restrictions are obeyed and the First Amendment otherwise respected. Unlike a book, a teacher cannot be inspected once so as to determine the extent and intent of his or her personal beliefs and subjective acceptance of the limitations imposed by the First Amendment. These prophylactic contacts will involve excessive and enduring entanglement between state and church.

There is another area of entanglement in the Rhode Island program that gives concern. The statute excludes teachers employed by nonpublic schools whose average per-pupil expenditures on secular education equal or exceed the comparable figures for public schools. In the event that the total expenditures of an otherwise eligible school exceed this norm, the program requires the government to examine the school's records in order to determine how much of the total expenditures is attributable to secular education and how much to religious activity. This kind of state inspection and evaluation of the religious content of a religious organization is fraught with the sort of entanglement that the Constitution forbids. It is a relationship pregnant with dangers of excessive government direction of church schools and hence of churches.... [W]e cannot ignore here the danger that pervasive modern governmental power will ultimately intrude on religion and thus conflict with the Religion Clauses.

. . . .

... Ordinarily political debate and division, however vigorous or even partisan, are normal and healthy manifestations of our democratic system of government, but political division along religious lines was one of the principal evils against which the First Amendment was intended to protect.... It conflicts with our whole history and tradition to permit questions of the Religion Clauses to assume such importance in our legislatures and in our elections that they could divert attention from the myriad issues and problems that confront every level of government. The highways of church and state relationships are not likely to be one-way streets, and the Constitution's authors sought to protect religious worship from the pervasive power of government. The history of many countries attests to the hazards of religion's intruding into the political arena or of political power intruding into the legitimate and free exercise of religious belief.

....

The potential for political divisiveness related to religious beliefs and practice is aggravated in these two statutory programs by the need for continuing annual appropriations and the likelihood of larger and larger demands as costs and populations grow....

....

... [M]odern governmental programs have self-perpetuating and self-expanding propensities. These internal pressures are only enhanced when the schemes involve institutions whose legitimate needs are growing and whose interests have substantial political support. Nor can we fail to see that in constitutional adjudication some steps, which when taken were thought to approach "the verge," have become the platform for yet further steps. A certain momentum develops in constitutional theory and it can be a "downhill thrust" easily set in motion but difficult to retard or stop. Development by momentum is not invariably bad; indeed, it is the way the common law has grown, but it is a force to be recognized and reckoned with. The dangers are increased by the difficulty of perceiving in advance exactly where the "verge" of the precipice lies. As well as constituting an independent evil against which the Religion Clauses were intended to protect, involvement or entanglement between government and religion serves as a warning signal.

Finally, nothing we have said can be construed to disparage the role of church-related elementary and secondary schools in our national life. Their contribution has been and is enormous. Nor do we ignore their economic plight in a period of rising costs and expanding need. Taxpayers generally have been spared vast sums by the maintenance of these educational institutions by religious organizations, largely by the gifts of faithful adherents.

The merit and benefits of these schools, however, are not the issue before us in these cases. The sole question is whether state aid to these schools can be squared with the dictates of the Religion Clauses. Under our system the choice has been made that government is to be entirely excluded from the area of religious instruction and churches excluded from the affairs of government. The Constitution decrees that religion must be a private matter of the individual, the family, and the institutions of private choice, and that while some involvement and entanglement are inevitable, lines must be drawn.

The judgment of the Rhode Island District Court... is affirmed. The judgment of the Pennsylvania District Court... is reversed, and the case is remanded for further proceedings consistent with this opinion.

[JUSTICE DOUGLAS, with whom JUSTICE BLACK joined, concurred. JUSTICE WHITE concurred in part and dissented in part.]

Wallace v. Jaffree

105 472 U.S. 38 (1985)
Vote: 6–3

In 1978 the Alabama legislature enacted a statute, Sec. 16-1-20, that authorized a one-minute period of silence in all public schools "for meditation"; in 1981, in Sec. 16-1-20.1, it authorized a period of silence "for meditation or voluntary prayer"; and in 1982, in Sec. 16-1-20.2, it authorized teachers to lead "willing students" in a prescribed prayer to "Almighty God... the Creator and Supreme Judge of the world." These provisions were challenged, and in an earlier case the Supreme Court unanimously declared Sec. 16-1-20.2, authorizing a prescribed prayer, to be unconstitutional. In the case below petitioners did *not* challenge Sec. 16-1-20, and the only issue before the Court was whether Sec. 16-1-20.1, authorizing a period of silence for "meditation or voluntary prayer," was constitutional.

Some commentators on the outcome of this case have argued that the "establishment opponents" have "won the battle but lost the war."

Others have observed that the battle has been won, and this case demonstrates that "there are only skirmishes left." How would you assess the Court's decision?

JUSTICE STEVENS delivered the opinion of the Court.
. . . .
. . . [T]he narrow question for decision is whether Sec. 16-1-20.1, which authorizes a period of silence for "meditation or voluntary prayer," is a law respecting the establishment of religion within the meaning of the First Amendment.
. . . .
In applying the purpose [portion of the *Lemon*] test, it is appropriate to ask "whether the government's actual purpose is to endorse or disapprove of religion." In this case, the answer to that question is dispositive. For the record not only provides us with an unambiguous affirmative answer, but it also reveals that the enactment of Sec. 16-1-20.1 was not motivated by any clearly secular purpose—indeed, the statute had *no* secular purpose.
. . . .
The legislative intent to return prayer to public schools is, of course, quite different from merely protecting every student's right to engage in voluntary prayer during an appropriate moment of silence during the school day. The 1978 statute already protected that right, containing nothing that prevented any student from engaging in voluntary prayer during a silent minute of meditation. Appellants have not identified any secular purpose that was not fully served by Sec. 16-1-20 before the enactment of Sec. 16-1-20.1. Thus, only two conclusions are consistent with the text of Sec. 16-1-20.1: (1) the statute was enacted to convey a message of State endorsement and promotion of prayer; or (2) the statute was enacted for no purpose. No one suggests that the statute was nothing but a meaningless or irrational act.

We must, therefore, conclude that the Alabama Legislature . . . enacted Sec. 16-1-20.1 despite the existence of Sec. 16-1-20 for the sole purpose of expressing the State's endorsement of prayer activities for one minute at the beginning of each school day. The addition of "or voluntary prayer" indicates that the State intended to characterize prayer as a favored practice. Such an endorsement is not consistent with the established principle that the government must pursue a course of complete neutrality toward religion.

The importance of that principle does not permit us to treat this as an inconsequential case involving nothing more than a few words of symbolic speech on behalf of the political majority. For whenever the State itself speaks on a religious subject, one of the questions that we must ask is "whether the Government intends to convey a message of endoresemnt or disapproval of religion." The well-supported concurrent findings of the District Court and the Court of Appeals—that Sec. 16-1-20.1 was intended to convey a message of State-approval of prayer activities in the public schools—make it unnecessary, and indeed inappropriate, to evaluate the practical significance of the addition of the words "or voluntary prayer" to the statute. Keeping in mind, as we must, "both the fundamental place held by the Establishment Clause in our constitutional scheme and the myriad, subtle ways in which Establishment Clause values can be eroded," we conclude that Sec. 16-1-20.1 violates the First Amendment.

The judgment of the Court of Appeals is

Affirmed.

[JUSTICES POWELL and O'CONNOR each wrote separate concurring opinions.]

JUSTICE REHNQUIST, dissenting.
[After a lengthy review of the history of the First Amendment's provisions protecting religious freedom and establishment and a review of the problems the Court has faced in using the *Lemon* test, JUSTICE REHNQUIST concluded with the following observations.]

If a constitutional theory has no basis in the history of the amendment it seeks to interpret, is difficult to apply and yields unprincipled results, I see little use in it. The "crucible of litigation" . . . has produced only consistent unpredictability and today's effort is just a continuation of "the sisyphean task of trying to patch together the 'blurred, indistinct and variable barrier' described in *Lemon* v. *Kurtzman.*" . . . We have done much straining since 1947, but still we admit that we can only "dimly perceive" the *Everson* wall. . . . Our perception has been clouded not by the Constitution but by the mist of an unnecessary metaphor.

The true meaning of the Establishment Clause can only be seen in its history. . . . As drafters of our Bill of Rights, the Framers inscribed the principles that control today. Any deviation from their intentions frustrates the permanence of that Charter and will only lead to the type of unprincipled decision making that has plagued our Establishment Clause cases since *Everson*.

The Framers intended the Establishment Clause to prohibit the designation of any church as a "national" one. The Clause was also designed to stop the Federal Government from asserting a preference for one religious denomination or sect over others. Given the "incorporation" of the Establishment Clause as against the States via the Fourteenth Amendment in *Everson,* States are prohibited as well from establishing a religion or discriminating between sects. As its history abundantly shows, however, nothing in the Establishment Clause requires government to be strictly neutral between religion and irreligion, nor does that Clause prohibit Congress or the States from pursuing legitimate secular ends through nondiscriminatory sectarian means.

The Court strikes down the Alabama statute . . . because the state wished to "endorse prayer as a favored practice." . . . It would come as much of a shock to those who drafted the Bill of Rights as it will to a large number of thoughtful Americans today to learn that the Constitution, as construed by the majority, prohibits the Alabama Legislature from "endorsing" prayer. George Washington himself, at the request of the very Congress which passed the Bill of Rights, proclaimed a day of "public thanksgiving and prayer, to be observed by acknowledging with grateful hearts the many and signal favors of Almighty God." History must judge whether it was the father of his country in 1789, or a majority of the Court today, which has strayed from the meaning of the Establishment Clause.

The State surely has a secular interest in regulating the manner in which public schools are conducted. Nothing in the Establishment Clause of the First Amendment, properly understood, prohibits any such generalized "endorsement" of prayer. I would therefore reverse the judgment of the Court of Appeals in *Wallace* v. *Jaffree.*

[CHIEF JUSTICE BURGER and JUSTICE WHITE each wrote separate dissenting opinions.]

Walz v. Tax Commission

397 U.S. 664 (1970)
Vote: 8–1

Petitioner Walz, a New York City lawyer, purchased a 22 × 29-foot plot of land in New York's Staten Island in order to qualify as a taxpayer for purposes of challenging New York City's tax exemption for churches and synagogues. He refused to pay his assessed tax of $5.24, arguing that a portion of his tax would go to support the city's churches and synagogues, which paid no taxes.

The case arose when the city brought an action against Mr. Walz seeking to recover back taxes. The lower courts, relying in part upon a 1966 Supreme Court decision not to review the Maryland high court decision upholding that state's property tax exemptions for religious institutions, held for the state tax commissioner and ordered Mr. Walz to pay his back taxes, whereupon he appealed to the Supreme Court.

In 1989 a closely divided Court declared unconstitutional a Texas law that exempted subscribers to *religious periodicals* from having to pay sales tax, *Texas Monthly* v. *Bullock,* 57 LW 4168. In that case three dissenters argued that *Walz* should be controlling and the Texas law upheld. How would you distinguish the law upheld in *Walz* from the Texas law overturned in the 1989 case?

MR. CHIEF JUSTICE BURGER delivered the opinion of the Court.

The Court has struggled to find a neutral course between the two Religion Clauses, both of which are cast in absolute terms, and either of which, if expanded to logical extreme, would tend to clash with the other. . . .

. . . .

The course of constitutional neutrality in this area cannot be an absolutely straight line; rigidity could well defeat the basic purpose of these provisions, which is to insure that no religion be sponsored or favored, none commanded, and none inhibited. The general principle deducible from the First Amendment and all that has been said by the Court is this: that we will not tolerate either governmentally established religion or governmental interference with religion. Short of those expressly proscribed governmental acts there is room for play in the joints productive of a benevolent neutrality which will permit religious exercise to exist without sponsorship and without interference.

. . . .

The legislative purpose of the property tax exemption is neither the advancement nor the inhibition of religion; it is neither sponsorship nor hostility. New York, in common with the other States, has determined that certain entities that exist in a harmonious relationship to the community at large, and that foster its "moral or mental improvement," should not be inhibited in their activities by property taxation or the hazard of loss of those properties for nonpayment of taxes. It has not singled out one particular church or religious group or even churches as such; rather, it has granted exemption to all houses of religious worship within a broad class of property owned by non-profit, quasi-public corporations which include hospitals, libraries, playgrounds, scientific, professional, historical, and patriotic groups. The State has an affirmative policy that considers these groups as beneficial and stabilizing influences in community life and finds this classification useful, desirable, and in the public interest. Qualification for tax exemption is not perpetual or immutable; some tax-exempt groups lose that status when their activities take them outside the classification and new entities can come into being and qualify for exemption.

Governments have not always been tolerant of religious activity, and hostility toward religion has taken many shapes and forms—economic, political, and sometimes harshly oppressive. Grants of exemption historically reflect the concern of authors of constitutions and statutes as to the latent dangers inherent in the imposition of property taxes; exemption constitutes a reasonable and balanced attempt to guard against those dangers. The limits of permissible state accommodation to religion are by no means coextensive with the noninterference mandated by the Free Exercise Clause. To equate the two would be to deny a national heritage with roots in the Revolution itself. . . . We cannot read New York's statute as attempting to establish religion; it is simply sparing the exercise of religion from the burden of property taxation levied on private profit institutions.

We find it unnecessary to justify the tax exemption on the social welfare services or "good works" that some churches perform for parishioners and others—family counselling, aid to the elderly and the infirm, and to children. Churches vary substantially in the scope of such services; programs expand or contract according to resources and need. As public-sponsored programs enlarge, private aid from the church sector may diminish. The extent of social services may vary, depending on whether the church serves an urban or rural, a rich or poor constituency. To give emphasis to so variable an aspect of the work of religious bodies would introduce an element of governmental evaluation and standards as to the worth of particular social welfare programs, thus producing a kind of continuing day-to-day relationship which the policy of neutrality seeks to minimize. . . .

. . . .

Granting tax exemptions to churches necessarily operates to afford an indirect economic benefit and also gives rise to some, but yet a lesser, involvement than taxing them. In analyzing either alternative the questions are whether the involvement is excessive, and whether it is a continuing one calling for official and continuing surveillance leading to an impermissible degree of entanglement. Obviously a direct money subsidy would be a relationship pregnant with involvement and, as with most governmental grant programs, could encompass sustained and detailed administrative relationships for enforcement of statutory or administrative standards, but that is not this case. The hazards of churches supporting government are hardly less in their potential than the hazards of government supporting churches; each relationship carries some involvement rather than the desired insulation and separation. We cannot ignore the instances in history when church support of government led to the kind of involvement we seek to avoid.

The grant of a tax exemption is not sponsorship since the government does not transfer part of its revenue to churches but simply abstains from demanding that the church support the state. No one has ever suggested that tax exemption has converted libraries, art galleries, or hospitals into arms of the state or put employees "on the public payroll." There is no genuine nexus between tax exemption and establishment of religion. . . . The exemption creates only a minimal and remote involvement between church and state and far less than taxation of churches. It restricts the fiscal relationship between church and state, and tends to complement and reinforce the desired separation insulating each from the other.

Separation in this context cannot mean absence of all contact; the complexities of modern life inevitably produce some contact and the fire and police protection received by houses of religious worship are no more than incidental benefits accorded all persons or institutions within a State's boundaries, along with many other exempt organizations. The appellant has not established even an arguable quantitative correlation between the payment of an ad valorem property tax and the receipt of these municipal benefits.

. . . .

Nothing in this national attitude toward religious tolerance and two centuries of uninterrupted freedom from taxation has given the remotest sign of leading to an established church or religion and on the contrary it has operated affirmatively to help guarantee the free exercise of all forms of religious belief. Thus, it is hardly useful to suggest that tax exemption is but the "foot in the door" or the "nose of the camel in the tent" leading to an established church. If tax exemption can be seen as this first step toward "establishment" of religion, as MR. JUS-TICE DOUGLAS fears, the second step has been long in coming. Any move that realistically "establishes" a church or tends to do so can be dealt with "while this Court sits."

. . . .

The argument that making "fine distinctions" between what is and what is not absolute under the Constitution is to render us a government of men, not laws, gives too little weight to the fact that it is an essential part of adjudication to draw distinctions, including fine ones, in the process of interpreting the Constitution. We must frequently decide, for example, what are "reasonable" searches and seizures under the Fourth Amendment. Determining what acts of government tend to establish or interfere with religion falls well within what courts have long been called upon to do in sensitive areas.

[JUSTICES BRENNAN and HARLAN wrote concurring opinions.]

MR. JUSTICE DOUGLAS, dissenting.

. . . The question in the case therefore is whether believers — organized in church groups — can be made exempt from real estate taxes, merely because they are believers, while nonbelievers, whether organized or not, must pay the real estate taxes.

. . . .

In *Torcaso* v. *Watkins* . . . we held that a State could not bar an atheist from public office in light of the freedom of belief and religion guaranteed by the First and Fourteenth Amendments. Neither the State nor the Federal Government, we said, "can constitutionally pass laws or impose requirements which aid all religions as against non-believers, and neither can aid those religions based on a belief in the existence of God as against those religions founded on different beliefs.". . .

That principle should govern this case.

. . . .

In affirming this judgment the Court largely overlooks the revolution initiated by the adoption of the Fourteenth Amendment. That revolution involved the imposition of new and far-reaching constitutional restraints on the States. Nationalization of many civil liberties has been the consequence of the Fourteenth Amendment, reversing the historic position that the foundations of those liberties rested largely in state law.

The process of the "selective incorporation" of various provisions of the Bill of Rights into the Fourteenth Amendment, although often provoking lively disagreement at large as well as among the members of this Court, has been a steady one. . . .

Those developments in the last 30 years have had unsettling effects. It was, for example, not until 1962 that state-sponsored, sectarian prayers were held to violate the Establishment Clause. . . . That decision brought many protests, for the habit of putting one sect's prayer in public schools had long been practiced. . . .

Hence the question in the present case makes irrelevant the "two centuries of uninterrupted freedom from taxation," referred to by the Court. . . . If history be our guide, then tax exemption of church property in this country is indeed highly suspect, as it arose in the early days when the church was an agency of the state. . . .

With all due respect the governing principle is not controlled by *Everson* v. *Board of Education. Everson* involved the use of public funds to bus children to parochial as well as to public schools. Parochial schools teach religion; yet they are also educational institutions offering courses competitive with public schools. They prepare students for the professions and for activities in all walks of life. Education in the secular sense was combined with religious indoctrination at the parochial schools involved in *Everson.* Even so, the *Everson* decision was five to four and though one of the five, I have since had grave doubts about it, because I have become convinced that grants to institutions teaching a sectarian creed violate the Establishment Clause. . . .

This case, however, is quite different. Education is not involved. The financial support rendered here is to the church, the place of worship. A tax exemption is a subsidy. Is my Brother BRENNAN correct in saying that we would hold that state or federal grants to churches, say, to construct the edifice itself would be unconstitutional? What is the difference between that kind of subsidy and the present subsidy?

Mueller v. Allen

463 U.S. 388 (1983)
Vote: 5–4

Applying the "effect" prong of the three-part LEMON test, the Supreme Court, in *Committee for Public Education* v. *Nyquist,* 413 U.S. 756 (1973), held invalid a New York statute that in part granted financial incentives in the form of tuition grants and tax credits to parents of children attending private schools. Writing for a majority opinion of six in *Nyquist,* Justice Powell found no distinction between the direct grants and the tax credits, and observed: "Special tax benefits . . . cannot be squared with the principle of neutrality established by the decisions of this Court. To the contrary, insofar as such benefits render assistance to parents who send their children to sectarian schools, their purpose and inevitable effect are to aid and advance those religious institutions."

Despite this ruling and what appears to be broad language prohibiting use of "special tax benefits," Minnesota devised another scheme to assist parents of children in private schools. Section 290.99(22) of the Minnesota code allows taxpayers to deduct expenses incurred in providing "tuition, textbooks and transportation" for their children attending an elementary or secondary school. Note differences between the New York provision struck down in *Nyquist* and this provision. The New York statute applied only to parents with children in *private* schools, while the Minnesota law covers expenses and tuition in *all* schools. This is a distinction the majority seized upon, but given that all states provide free public schooling, and other expenses are minimal, is it a meaningful distinction? In fact, are there any significant differences between the two schemes?

In his dissent in *Nyquist,* Justice White reiterated his disapproval of the outcome in LEMON: "I am quite unreconciled to the Court's decision in LEMON V. KURTZMAN. I thought then, and I think now, that the Court's conclusion there was not required . . . and is contrary to the long-range interests of the country." In the case below, Justice White is part of the majority (along with Chief Justice Burger, who authored the majority opinion in LEMON). Although the opinion below does not disavow and, in fact, reaffirms the Court's commitment to LEMON, has Justice White won the day?

JUSTICE REHNQUIST delivered the opinion of the Court.

. . . .

The general nature of our inquiry in this area has been guided . . . by the "three-part" test laid down in [*Lemon*]. . . .

Little time need be spent on the question of whether the Minnesota tax deduction has a secular purpose. . . .

. . . .

. . . [Several] justifications are readily available to support §290.09(22), and each is sufficient to satisfy the secular purpose inquiry of *Lemon.*

We turn therefore to the more difficult but related question whether the Minnesota statute has "the primary effect of advancing the sectarian aims of the nonpublic schools." . . . In concluding that it does not, we find several features of the Minnesota tax deduction particularly significant. First, an essential feature of Minnesota's arrangement is the fact that §290.09(22) is only one among many deductions — such as those for medical expenses . . . and charitable contributions . . . — available under the Minnesota tax laws. Our decisions consistently have recognized that traditionally "[l]egislatures have especially broad latitude in creating classifications and distinctions in tax statutes," . . . in part because the "familiarity with local conditions" enjoyed by legislators especially enables them to "achieve an equitable distribution of the tax burden." . . . Under our prior decisions, the Minnesota legislature's judgment that a deduction for educational expenses fairly equalizes the tax burden of its citizens and encourages desirable expenditures for educational purposes is entitled to substantial deference.

Other characteristics of §290.09(22) argue equally strongly for the provision's constitutionality. Most importantly, the deduction is available for educational expenses incurred by *all* parents, including those whose children attend public schools and those whose children attend non-sectarian private schools or sectarian private schools. Just as in *Widmar* v. *Vincent* . . . (1981), where we concluded that the state's provision of a forum neutrally "open to a broad class of nonreligious as well as religious speakers" does not "confer any imprimatur of State approval," so here: "the provision of benefits to so broad a spectrum of groups is an important index of secular effect."

In this respect, as well as others, this case is vitally different from the scheme struck down in *Nyquist.* There, public assistance amounting to tuition grants, was provided only to parents of children in *nonpublic* schools.... Unlike the assistance at issue in *Nyquist,* §290.09(22) permits *all* parents — whether their children attend public school or private — to deduct their childrens' educational expenses. As *Widmar* and our other decisions indicate, a program, like §290.09(22), that neutrally provides state assistance to a broad spectrum of citizens is not readily subject to challenge under the Establishment Clause.

We also agree with the Court of Appeals that, by channeling whatever assistance it may provide to parochial schools through individual parents, Minnesota has reduced the Establishment Clause objections to which its action is subject. It is true, of course, that financial assistance provided to parents ultimately has an economic effect comparable to that of aid given directly to the schools attended by their children. It is also true, however, that under Minnesota's arrangement public funds become available only as a result of numerous, private choices of individual parents of school-age children. For these reasons, we recognized in *Nyquist* that the means by which state assistance flows to private schools is of some importance: we said that "the fact aid is disbursed to parents rather than to ... schools" is a material consideration in Establishment Clause analysis, albeit "only one among many to be considered." ... It is noteworthy that all but one of our recent cases invalidating state aid to parochial schools have involved the direct transmission of assistance from the state to the schools themselves. The exception, of course, was *Nyquist,* which, as discussed previously, is distinguishable from this case on other grounds. Where, as here, aid to parochial schools is available only as a result of decisions of individual parents, no "imprimatur of State approval" ... can be deemed to have been conferred on any particular religion, or on religion generally.

We find it useful, in the light of the foregoing characteristics of §290.09(22), to compare the attenuated financial benefits flowing to parochial schools from the section to the evils against which the Establishment Clause was designed to protect. These dangers are well-described by our statement that "what is at stake as a matter of policy [in Establishment Clause cases] is preventing that kind and degree of government involvement in religious life that, as history teaches us, is apt to lead to strife and frequently strain a political system to the breaking point." ... The Establishment Clause of course extends beyond prohibition of a state church or payment of state funds to one or more churches. We do not think, however, that its prohibition extends to the type of tax deduction established by Minnesota. The historic purposes of the clause simply do not encompass the sort of attenuated financial benefit, ultimately controlled by the private choices of individual parents, that eventually flows to parochial schools from the neutrally available tax benefit at issue in this case.

Petitioners argue that, notwithstanding the facial neutrality of §290.09(22), in application the statute primarily benefits religious institutions. Petitioners rely, as they did below, on a statistical analysis of the type of persons claiming the tax deduction. They contend that most parents of public school children incur no tuition expenses, see Minn. Stat. §120.06, and that other expenses deductible under §290.09(22) are negligible in value; moreover, they claim that 96% of the children in private schools in 1978–1979 attended religiously-affiliated institutions. Because of all this, they reason, the bulk of deductions taken under §290.09(22) will be claimed by parents of children in sectarian schools. Respondents reply that petitioners have failed to consider the impact of deductions for items such as transportation, summer school tuition, tuition paid by parents whose children attended schools outside the school districts in which they resided, rental or purchase costs for a variety of equipment, and tuition for certain types of instruction not ordinarily provided in public schools.

We need not consider these contentions in detail. We would be loath to adopt a rule grounding the constitutionality of a facially neutral law on annual reports reciting the extent to which various classes of private citizens claimed benefits under the law. Such an approach would scarcely provide the certainty that this field stands in need of, nor can we perceive principled standards by which such statistical evidence might be evaluated. Moreover, the fact that private persons fail in a particular year to claim the tax relief to which they are entitled — under a facially neutral statute — should be of little importance in determining the constitutionality of the statute permitting such relief.

Finally, private educational institutions, and parents paying for their children to attend these schools, make special contributions to the areas in which they operate. "Parochial schools, quite apart from their sectarian purpose, have provided an educational alternative for millions of young Americans; they often afford wholesome competition with our public schools; and in some States they relieve substantially the tax burden incident to the operation of public schools."... If parents of children in private schools choose to take especial advantage of the relief provided by §290.09(22), it is no doubt due to the fact that they bear a particularly great financial burden in educating their children. More fundamentally, whatever unequal effect may be attributed to the statutory classification can fairly be regarded as a rough return for the benefits, discussed above, provided to the state and all taxpayers by parents sending their children to parochial schools. In the light of all this, we believe it wiser to decline to engage in the type of empirical inquiry into those persons benefited by state law which petitioners urge.

Thus, we hold that the Minnesota tax deduction for educational expenses satisfies the primary effect inquiry of our Establishment Clause cases.

Turning to the third part of the *Lemon* inquiry, we have no difficulty in concluding that the Minnesota statute does not "excessively entangle" the state in religion. The only plausible source of the "comprehensive, discriminating, and continuing state surveillance"... necessary to run afoul of this standard would lie in the fact that state officials must determine whether particular textbooks qualify for a deduction. In making this decision, state officials must disallow deductions taken from "instructional books and materials used in the teaching of religious tenets, doctrines or worship, the purpose of which is to inculcate such tenets, doctrines or worship." Minn. Stat. §290.09(22). Making decisions such as this does not differ substantially from making the types of decisions approved in earlier opinions of this Court. In *Board of Education* v. *Allen* ... (1968), for example, the Court upheld the loan of secular textbooks to parents of children attending nonpublic schools; though state officials were required to determine whether particular books were or were not secular, the system was held not to violate the Establishment Clause.... The same result follows in this case.

For the foregoing reasons, the judgment of the Court of Appeals is

Affirmed.

JUSTICE MARSHALL, with whom JUSTICE BRENNAN, JUSTICE BLACKMUN and JUSTICE STEVENS join, dissenting.

The Establishment Clause of the first Amendment prohibits a State from subsidizing religious education, whether it does so directly or indirectly. In my view, this principle of neutrality forbids not only the tax benefits struck down in *Committee for Public Education* v. *Nyquist* ... (1973), but any tax benefit, including the tax deduction at issue here, which subsidizes tuition payments to sectarian schools. I also believe that the Establishment Clause prohibits the tax deductions that Minnesota authorizes for the cost of books and other instructional materials used for sectarian purposes.

I

. . . .

Like the law involved in *Nyquist,* the Minnesota law can be said to serve a secular purpose: promoting pluralism and diversity among the State's public and nonpublic schools. But the Establishment Clause requires more than that legislation have a secular purpose.... "[T]he propriety of a legislature's purposes may not immunize from further scrutiny a law which ... has a primary effect that advances religion."... Moreover, even if one " 'primary' effect [is] to promote some legitimate end under the State's police power," the legislation is not "immune from further examination to ascertain whether it also has the direct and immediate effect of advancing religion."...

As we recognized in *Nyquist,* direct government subsidization of parochial school tuition is impermissible because "the effect of the aid is unmistakably to provide desired financial support for nonpublic, sectarian institutions."... "[A]id to the educational function of [parochial] schools ... necessarily results in aid to the sectarian enterprise as a whole" because "[t]he very purpose of those schools is to provide an integrated secular and religious education."... For this reason, aid to sectarian schools must be restricted to ensure that it may be not used to further the religious mission of those schools.... While "services such as police and fire protection, sewage disposal, highways, and sidewalks" may be provided to parochial schools in common with other institutions, because this type of assistance is clearly " 'marked off from the religious function' " of those schools, ... unrestricted financial assistance, such as grants for the maintenance and construction of parochial schools, may not be provided.... "In the absence of an effective means of guaranteeing that the state aid derived from public funds will be used exclusively for secular, neutral, and nonideological purposes, it is clear from our cases that direct aid in whatever form is invalid."

Indirect assistance in the form of financial aid to parents for tuition payments is similarly impermissible because it is not "subject to ... restrictions" which " 'guarantee the separation between secular and religious educational functions and ensure that

State financial aid supports only the former.'"... By ensuring that parents will be reimbursed for tuition payments they make, the Minnesota statute requires that taxpayers in general pay for the cost of parochial education and extends a financial "incentive to parents to send their children to sectarian schools."...

That parents receive a reduction of their tax liability, rather than a direct reimbursement, is of no greater significance here than it was in *Nyquist*. "[F]or purposes of determining whether such aid has the effect of advancing religion," it makes no difference whether the qualifying "parent receives an actual cash payment [or] is allowed to reduce... the sum he would otherwise be obliged to pay over to the State."... It is equally irrelevant whether a reduction in taxes takes the form of a tax "credit," a tax "modification," or a tax "deduction."... What is of controlling significance is not the form but the "substantive impact" of the financial aid.... "[I]nsofar as such benefits render assistance to parents who send their children to *sectarian* schools, their purpose and inevitable effect are to aid and advance those religious institutions."...

The majority attempts to distinguish *Nyquist* by pointing to two differences between the Minnesota tuition-assistance program and the program struck down in *Nyquist*. Neither of these distinctions can withstand scrutiny.

The majority first attempts to distinguish *Nyquist* on the ground that Minnesota makes all parents eligible to deduct up to $500 or $700 for each dependent, whereas the New York law allowed a deduction only for parents whose children attended nonpublic schools. Although Minnesota taxpayers who send their children to local public schools may not deduct tuition expenses because they incur none, they may deduct other expenses, such as the cost of gym clothes, pencils, and notebooks, which are shared by all parents of school-age children. This, in the majority's view, distinguishes the Minnesota scheme from the law at issue in *Nyquist*.

That the Minnesota statute makes some small benefit available to all parents cannot alter the fact that the most substantial benefit provided by the statute is available only to those parents who send their children to schools that charge tuition. It is simply undeniable that the single largest expense that may be deducted under the Minnesota statute is tuition. The statute is little more than a subsidy of tuition masquerading as a subsidy of general educational expenses. The other deductible expenses are *de minimis* in comparison to tuition expenses.

Contrary to the majority's suggestion, ... the bulk of the tax benefits afforded by the Minnesota scheme are enjoyed by parents of parochial school children not because parents of public school children fail to claim deductions to which they are entitled, but because the latter are simply *unable* to claim the largest tax deduction that Minnesota authorizes. Fewer than 100 of more than 900,000 school-age children in Minnesota attend public schools that charge a general tuition. Of the total number of taxpayers who are eligible for the tuition deduction, approximately 96% send their children to religious schools. Parents who send their children to free public schools are simply ineligible to obtain the full benefit of the deduction except in the unlikely event that they buy $700 worth of pencils, notebooks, and bus rides for their school-age children. Yet parents who pay at least $700 in tuition to nonpublic, sectarian schools can claim the full deduction even if they incur no other educational expenses.

That this deduction has a primary effect of promoting religion can easily be determined without any resort to the type of "statistical evidence" that the majority fears would lead to constitutional uncertainty.... The only factual inquiry necessary is the same as that employed in *Nyquist* and *Sloan* v. *Lemon*... (1973): whether the deduction permitted for tuition expenses primarily benefits those who send their children to religious schools. In *Nyquist* we unequivocally rejected any suggestion that, in determining the effect of a tax statute, this Court should look exclusively to what the statute on its face purports to do and ignore the actual operation of the challenged provision. In determining the effect of the New York statute, we emphasized that "virtually all" of the schools receiving direct grants for maintenance and repair were Roman Catholic schools, ... that reimbursements were given to parents "who send their children to nonpublic schools, the bulk of which is concededly sectarian in orientation," that "it is precisely the function of New York's law to provide assistance to private schools, the great majority of which are sectarian," and that "tax reductions authorized by this law flow primarily to the parents of children attending sectarian, nonpublic schools."...

In this case, it is undisputed that well over 90% of the children attending tuition-charging schools in Minnesota are enrolled in sectarian schools. History and experience likewise instruct us that any generally available financial assistance for elementary and secondary school tuition expenses mainly will further religious education because the majority of the schools which charge tuition are sectarian.... Because Minnesota, like every other State, is committed to providing free public education, tax assistance for tuition payments inevitably redounds to the benefit of nonpublic, sectarian schools and parents who send their children to those schools.

....

II

In my view, Minnesota's tax deduction for the cost of textbooks and other instructional materials is also constitutionally infirm. The majority is simply mistaken in concluding that a tax deduction, unlike a tax credit or a direct grant to parents, promotes religious education in a manner that is only "attenuated."... A tax deduction has a primary effect that advances religion if it is provided to offset expenditures which are not restricted to the secular activities of parochial schools.

The instructional materials which are subsidized by the Minnesota tax deduction plainly may be used to inculcate religious values and belief. In *Meek* v. *Pittenger*... we held that even the use of "wholly neutral, secular instructional material and equipment" by church-related schools contributes to religious instruction because "'[t]he secular education those schools provide goes hand in hand with the religious mission that is the only reason for the schools' existence.'" In *Wolman* v. *Walter*... we concluded that precisely the same impermissible effect results when the instructional materials are loaned to the pupil or his parent, rather than directly to the schools. We stated that "it would exalt form over substance if this distinction were found to justify a result different from that in *Meek.*" It follows that a tax deduction to offset the cost of purchasing instructional materials for use in sectarian schools, like a loan of such materials to parents, "necessarily results in aid to the sectarian school enterprise as a whole" and is therefore a "substantial advancement of religious activity" that "constitutes an impermissible establishment of religion."

There is no reason to treat Minnesota's tax deduction for textbooks any differently. Secular textbooks, like other secular instructional materials, contribute to the religious mission of the parochial schools that use those books. Although this Court upheld the loan of secular textbooks to religious schools in *Board of Education* v. *Allen,* the Court believed at that time that it lacked sufficient experience to determine "based solely on judicial notice" that "the processes of secular and religious training are so intertwined that secular textbooks furnished to students by the public [will always be] instrumental in the teaching of religion." This basis for distinguishing secular instructional materials and secular textbooks is simply untenable, and is inconsistent with many of our more recent decisions concerning state aid to parochial schools....

In any event, the Court's assumption in *Allen* that the textbooks at issue there might be used only for secular education was based on the fact that those very books had been chosen by the State for use in the public schools.... In contrast, the Minnesota statute does not limit the tax deduction to those books which the State has approved for use in public schools. Rather, it permits a deduction for books that are chosen by the parochial schools themselves. Indeed, under the Minnesota statutory scheme, textbooks chosen by parochial schools but not used by public schools are likely to be precisely the ones purchased by parents for their children's use. Like the law upheld in *Board of Education* v. *Allen*... (1968), Minn. Stat. §§123.932 and 123.933 authorize the state board of education to provide textbooks used in public schools to nonpublic school students. Parents have little reason to purchase textbooks that can be borrowed under this provision.

III

There can be little doubt that the State of Minnesota intended to provide, and has provided, "[s]ubstantial aid to the educational function of [church-related] schools," and that the tax deduction for tuition and other educational expenses "necessarily results in aid to the sectarian school enterprise as a whole."... It is beside the point that the State may have legitimate secular reasons for providing such aid. In focusing upon the contributions made by church-related schools, the majority has lost sight of the issue before us in this case....

In my view, the lines drawn in *Nyquist* were drawn on a reasoned basis with appropriate regard for the principles of neutrality embodied by the Establishment Clause. I do not believe that the same can be said of the lines drawn by the majority today. For the first time, the Court has upheld financial support for religious schools without any reason at all to assume that the support will be restricted to the secular functions of those schools and will not be used to support religious instruction. This result is flatly at odds with the fundamental principle that a State may provide no financial support whatsoever to promote religion. As the Court stated in *Everson*...

> No tax in any amount, large or small, can be levied to support any religious activities or institutions, whatever they may be called, or whatever form they may adopt to teach or practice religion.

I dissent.

Lynch v. Donnelly

465 U.S. 668 (1984)
Vote: 5–4

Each Christmas for over forty years, the City of Pawtucket, Rhode Island, in cooperation with downtown merchants has erected a display as part of its observance of the holiday season. The display is situated in a park owned by a nonprofit organization and located in the heart of the shopping district. The display comprises many of the figures and decorations traditionally associated with Christmas, including a Santa Claus house, reindeer pulling Santa's sleigh, candy-striped poles, a Christmas tree, carolers, circus figures, colored lights, and a crèche consisting of traditional figures, including the infant Jesus, Mary and Joseph, angels, shepherds, kings, and animals. All components of the display, including the crèche, are owned by the city and erected at the city's expense. The erection and dismantling of the crèche cost the city about $20 per year and no money has been expended in maintaining it for the past twenty years.

Representatives of the Rhode Island affiliate of the American Civil Liberties Union brought suit in federal District Court challenging the city's inclusion of the crèche in the display. The District Court held that "erection of the crèche has the real and substantial effect of affiliating Pawtucket with the Christian beliefs that the crèche represents," and as such violated the Establishment Clause. The Court of Appeals affirmed this decision. The Supreme Court granted certiorari.

In 1989 a badly fragmented Court held that a more overtly religious display of a crèche than the one in *Lynch* was unconstitutional, but upheld the display of a menorah that was set next to a Christmas tree. *Allegheny* v. *American Civil Liberties Union* 57 LW 5045. Perhaps most telling in this case was Justice Kennedy's sweeping dissent, joined by three other justices, which called for abandoning the *Lemon* test and replacing it with a "proselytization" test that would permit "accomodation" and "recognition" of our nation's religious heritage (see p. 408).

CHIEF JUSTICE BURGER delivered the opinion of the Court.

This Court has explained that the purpose of the Establishment and Free Exercise Clauses of the First Amendment is

> to prevent, as far as possible, the intrusion of either [the church or the state] into the precincts of the other. *Lemon* v. *Kurtzman*

At the same time, however, the Court has recognized that

> total separation is not possible in an absolute sense. Some relationship between government and religious organizations is inevitable.

In every Establishment Clause case, we must reconcile the inescapable tension between the objective of preventing unnecessary intrusion of either the church or the state upon the other, and the reality that, as the Court has so often noted, total separation of the two is not possible.

The Court has sometimes described the Religion Clauses as erecting a "wall" between church and state.... The concept of a "wall" of separation is a useful figure of speech probably deriving from views of Thomas Jefferson. The metaphor has served as a reminder that the Establishment Clause forbids an established church or anything approaching it. But the metaphor itself is not a wholly accurate description of the practical aspects of the relationship that in fact exists between church and state.

No significant segment of our society and no institution within it can exist in a vacuum or in total or absolute isolation from all the other parts, much less from government. "It has never been thought either possible or desirable to enforce a regime of total separation...." Nor does the Constitution require complete separation of church and state; it affirmatively mandates accommodation, not merely tolerance, of all religions, and forbids hostility toward any.... Anything less would require the "callous indifference" we have said was never intended by the Establishment Clause.... Indeed, we have observed, such hostility would bring us into "war with our national tradition as embodied in the First Amendment's guaranty of the free exercise of religion."...

The Court's interpretation of the Establishment Clause has comported with what history reveals was the contemporaneous understanding of its guarantees....

....

Our history is replete with official references to the value and invocation of Divine guidance in deliberations and pronouncements of the Founding Fathers and contemporary leaders. Beginning in the early colonial period long before Independence, a day of Thanksgiving was celebrated as a religious holiday to give thanks for the bounties of Nature as gifts from God. President Washington and his successors proclaimed Thanksgiving, with all its religious overtones, a day of national celebration and Congress made it a National Holiday more than a century ago. . . . That holiday has not lost its theme of expressing thanks for Divine aid any more than has Christmas lost its religious significance.

Executive Orders and other official announcements of Presidents and of the Congress have proclaimed both Christmas and Thanksgiving National Holidays in religious terms. And, by Acts of Congress, it has long been the practice that federal employees are released from duties on these National Holidays, while being paid from the same public revenues that provide the compensation of the Chaplains of the Senate and the House and the military services. . . . Thus, it is clear that Government has long recognized — indeed it has subsidized — holidays with religious significance.

Other examples of reference to our religious heritage are found in the statutorily prescribed national motto "In God We Trust," . . . which Congress and the President mandated for our currency, . . . and in the language "One nation under God," as part of the Pledge of Allegiance to the American flag. That pledge is recited by thousands of public school children — and adults — every year.

Art galleries supported by public revenues display religious paintings of the 15th and 16th centuries, predominantly inspired by one religious faith. The National Gallery in Washington, maintained with Government support, for example, has long exhibited masterpieces with religious messages, notably the Last Supper, and paintings depicting the Birth of Christ, the Crucifixion, and the Resurrection, among many others with explicit Christian themes and messages. The very chamber in which oral arguments on this case were heard is decorated with a notable and permanent — not seasonal — symbol of religion: Moses with Ten Commandments. Congress has long provided chapels in the Capitol for religious worship and meditation.

There are countless other illustrations of the Government's acknowledgment of our religious heritage and governmental sponsorship of graphic manifestations of that heritage. . . .

This history may help explain why the Court consistently has declined to take a rigid, absolutist view of the Establishment Clause. We have refused "to construe the Religion Clauses with a literalness that would undermine the ultimate constitutional objective *as illuminated by history.*" . . . In our modern, complex society, whose traditions and constitutional underpinnings rest on and encourage diversity and pluralism in all areas, an absolutist approach in applying the Establishment Clause is simplistic and has been uniformly rejected by the Court.

Rather than mechanically invalidating all governmental conduct or statutes that confer benefits or give special recognition to religion in general or to one faith — as an absolutist approach would dictate — the Court has scrutinized challenged legislation or official conduct to determine whether, in reality, it establishes a religion or religious faith, or tends to do so. . . .

In each case, the inquiry calls for line drawing; no fixed, *per se* rule can be framed. The Establishment Clause like the Due Process Clauses is not a precise, detailed provision in a legal code capable of ready application. The purpose of the Establishment Clause "was to state an objective, not to write a statute." . . . The line between permissible relationships and those barred by the Clause can no more be straight and unwavering than due process can be defined in a single stroke or phrase or test. The Clause erects a "blurred, indistinct, and variable barrier depending on all the circumstances of a particular relationship." . . .

In the line-drawing process we have often found it useful to inquire whether the challenged law or conduct has a secular purpose, whether its principal or primary effect is to advance or inhibit religion, and whether it creates an excessive entanglement of government with religion. But, we have repeatedly emphasized our unwillingness to be confined to any single test or criterion in this sensitive area. . . .

. . . .

The narrow question is whether there is a secular purpose for Pawtucket's display of the crèche. The display is sponsored by the city to celebrate the Holiday and to depict the origins of that Holiday. These are legitimate secular purposes. The District Court's inference, drawn from the religious nature of the crèche, that the city has no secular purpose was, on this record, clearly erroneous.

The District Court found that the primary effect of including the crèche is to confer a substantial and impermissible benefit on religion in general and on the Christian faith in particular. Comparisons of the relative benefits to religion of different forms of governmental support are elusive and difficult to make. But to conclude that the primary effect of including the crèche is to advance religion in violation of the Establishment Clause would require that we view it as more beneficial to and more an endorsement of religion, for example, than expenditure of large sums of public money for textbooks supplied throughout the country to students attending church-sponsored schools, . . . expenditure of public funds for transportation of students to church-sponsored schools, . . . federal grants for college buildings of church-sponsored institutions of higher education combining secular and religious education, . . . noncategorical grants to church-sponsored colleges and universities, . . . and the tax exemptions for church properties sanctioned in *Walz.* It would also require that we view it as more of an endorsement of religion than the Sunday Closing Laws upheld in *McGowan* v. *Maryland* . . . (1961), the release time program for religious training in *Zorach,* and the legislative prayers upheld in *Marsh.* . . .

The dissent asserts some observers may perceive that the city has aligned itself with the Christian faith by including a Christian symbol in its display and that this serves to advance religion. We can assume, *arguendo,* that the display advances religion in a sense; but our precedents plainly contemplate that on occasion some advancement of religion will result from governmental action. The Court has made it abundantly clear, however, that "not every law that confers an 'indirect,' 'remote,' or 'incidental' benefit upon [religion] is, for that reason alone, constitutionally invalid." . . . Here, whatever benefit to one faith or religion, or to all religions, is indirect, remote and incidental; display of the crèche is no more an advancement or endorsement of religion than the Congressional and Executive recognition of the origins of the Holiday itself as "Christ's Mass," or the exhibition of literally hundreds of religious paintings in governmentally supported museums.

The District Court found that there had been no administrative entanglement between religion and state resulting from the city's ownership and use of the crèche. . . . But it went on to hold that some political divisiveness was engendered by this litigation. Coupled with its finding of an impermissible sectarian purpose and effect, this persuaded the court that there was "excessive entanglement." The Court of Appeals expressly declined to accept the District Court's finding that inclusion of the crèche has caused political divisiveness along religious lines, and noted that this Court has never held that political divisiveness alone was sufficient to invalidate government conduct.

Entanglement is a question of kind and degree. In this case, however, there is no reason to disturb the District Court's finding on the absence of administrative entanglement. There is no evidence of contact with church authorities concerning the content or

design of the exhibit prior to or since Pawtucket's purchase of the crèche. No expenditures for maintenance of the crèche have been necessary; and since the city owns the crèche, now valued at $200, the tangible material it contributes is *de minimis.* In many respects the display requires far less ongoing, day-to-day interaction between church and state than religious paintings in public galleries. There is nothing here, of course, like the "comprehensive, discriminating, and continuing state surveillance" or the "enduring entanglement" present in *Lemon.*

The Court of Appeals correctly observed that this Court has not held that political divisiveness alone can serve to invalidate otherwise permissible conduct. And we decline to so hold today. This case does not involve a direct subsidy to church-sponsored schools or colleges, or other religious institutions, and hence no inquiry into potential political divisiveness is even called for, *Mueller* v. *Allen* . . . (1983). In any event, apart from this litigation there is no evidence of political friction or divisiveness over the crèche in the 40-year history of Pawtucket's Christmas celebration. The District Court stated that the inclusion of the crèche for the 40 years has been "marked by no apparent dissension" and that the display has had a "calm history." . . . Curiously, it went on to hold that the political divisiveness engendered by this lawsuit was evidence of excessive entanglement. A litigant cannot, by the very act of commencing a lawsuit, however, create the appearance of divisiveness and then exploit it as evidence of entanglement.

We are satisfied that the city has a secular purpose for including the crèche, that the city has not impermissibly advanced religion, and that including the crèche does not create excessive entanglement between religion and government.

. . . .

We hold that, notwithstanding the religious significance of the crèche, the City of Pawtucket has not violated the Establishment Clause of the First Amendment. Accordingly, the judgment of the Court of Appeals is reversed.

[JUSTICE O'CONNOR wrote a concurring opinion.]

JUSTICE BRENNAN, with whom JUSTICE MARSHALL, JUSTICE BLACKMUN and JUSTICE STEVENS join, dissenting.

. . . .

Applying the three-part [*Lemon*] test to Pawtucket's crèche, I am persuaded that the city's inclusion of the crèche in its Christmas display simply does not reflect a "clearly secular purpose." Unlike the typical case in which the record reveals some contemporaneous expression of a clear purpose to advance religion... or, conversely, a clear secular purpose, here we have no explicit statement of purpose by Pawtucket's municipal government accompanying its decision to purchase, display and maintain the crèche. Governmental purpose may nevertheless be inferred.... In the present case, the City claims that its purposes were exclusively secular. Pawtucket sought, according to this view, only to participate in the celebration of a national holiday and to attract people to the downtown area in order to promote pre-Christmas retail sales and to help engender the spirit of goodwill and neighborliness commonly associated with the Christmas season....

Despite these assertions, two compelling aspects of this case indicate that our generally prudent "reluctance to attribute unconstitutional motives" to a governmental body... should be overcome. First... all of Pawtucket's "valid secular objectives can be readily accomplished by other means."* Plainly, the city's interest in celebrating the holiday and in promoting both retail sales and goodwill are fully served by the elaborate display of Santa Claus, reindeer, and wishing wells that are already a part of Pawtucket's annual Christmas display. More importantly, the nativity scene, unlike every other element of the Hodgson Park display, reflects a sectarian exclusivity that the avowed purposes of celebrating the holiday season and promoting retail commerce simply do not encompass. To be found constitutional, Pawtucket's seasonal celebration must at least be non-denominational and not serve to promote religion. The inclusion of a distinctly religious element like the crèche, however, demonstrates that a narrower sectarian purpose lay behind the decision to include a nativity scene. That the crèche retained this religious character for the people and municipal government of Pawtucket is suggested by the Mayor's testimony at trial in which he stated that for him, as well as others in the City, the effort to eliminate the nativity scene from Pawtucket's Christmas celebration "is a step towards establishing another religion, non-religion that it may

*I find it puzzling, to say the least, that the Court today should find "irrelevant," the fact that the City's secular objectives can be readily and fully accomplished without including the crèche, since only last Term in *Larkin* v. *Grendel's Den,* (1983), the Court relied upon precisely the same point in striking down a Massachusetts statute which vested in church governing bodies the power to veto applications for liquor licenses. It seems the Court is willing to alter its analysis from Term to Term in order to suit its preferred results.

be." Plainly, the city and its leaders understood that the inclusion of the crèche in its display would serve the wholly religious purpose of "keep[ing] 'Christ in Christmas.'"... From this record, therefore, it is impossible to say with the kind of confidence that was possible in *McGowan* v. *Maryland*,... (1961), that a wholly secular goal predominates.

The "primary effect" of including a nativity scene in the City's display is, as the District Court found, to place the government's imprimatur of approval on the particular religious beliefs exemplified by the crèche. Those who believe in the message of the nativity receive the unique and exclusive benefit of public recognition and approval of their views. For many, the City's decision to include the crèche as part of its extensive and costly efforts to celebrate Christmas can only mean that the prestige of the government has been conferred on the beliefs associated with the crèche, thereby providing "a significant symbolic benefit to religion...." The effect on minority religious groups, as well as on those who may reject all religion, is to convey the message that their views are not similarly worthy of public recognition nor entitled to public support. It was precisely this sort of religious chauvinism that the Establishment Clause was intended forever to prohibit. In this case, as in *Engel* v. *Vitale,* "[w]hen the power, prestige and financial support of government is placed behind a particular religious belief, the indirect coercive pressure upon religious minorities to conform to the prevailing officially approved religion is plain." Our decision in *Widmar* v. *Vincent*,... (1981), rests upon the same principle. There the Court noted that a state university policy of "equal access" for both secular and religious groups would "not confer any imprimatur of State approval" on the religious groups permitted to use the facilities because "a broad spectrum of groups" would be served and there was no evidence that religious groups would dominate the forum. Here, by contrast, Pawtucket itself owns the crèche and instead of extending similar attention to a "broad spectrum" of religious and secular groups, it has singled out Christianity for special treatment.

Finally, it is evident that Pawtucket's inclusion of a crèche as part of its annual Christmas display does pose a significant threat of fostering "excessive entanglement." As the Court notes, the District Court found no administrative entanglement in this case, primarily because the city had been able to administer the annual display without extensive consultation with religious officials.... Of course, there is no reason to disturb that finding, but it is worth noting that after today's decision, administrative entanglements may well develop. Jews and other non-Christian groups, prompted perhaps by the Mayor's remark that he will include a Menorah in future displays, can be expected to press government for inclusion of their symbols, and faced with such requests, government will have to become involved in accommodating the various demands.... More importantly, although no political divisiveness was apparent in Pawtucket prior to the filing of respondents' lawsuit, that act, as the District Court found, unleashed powerful emotional reactions which divided the city along religious lines. The fact that calm had prevailed prior to this suit does not immediately suggest the absence of any division on the point for, as the District Court observed, the quiescence of those opposed to the crèche may have reflected nothing more than their sense of futility in opposing the majority. Of course, the Court is correct to note that we have never held that the potential for divisiveness alone is sufficient to invalidate a challenged governmental practice; we have, nevertheless, repeatedly emphasized that "too close a proximity" between religious and civil authorities... may represent a "warning signal" that the values embodied in the Establishment Clause are at risk.... Furthermore, the Court should not blind itself to the fact that because communities differ in religious composition, the controversy over whether local governments may adopt religious symbols will continue to fester. In many communities, non-Christian groups can be expected to combat practices similar to Pawtucket's; this will be so especially in areas where there are substantial non-Christian minorities.

In sum, considering the District Court's careful findings of fact under the three-part analysis called for by our prior cases, I have no difficulty concluding that Pawtucket's display of the crèche is unconstitutional.

The Court advances two principal arguments to support its conclusion that the Pawtucket crèche satisfies the *Lemon* test. Neither is persuasive.

First. The Court, by focusing on the holiday "context" in which the nativity scene appeared, seeks to explain away the clear religious import of the crèche and the findings of the District Court that most observers understood the crèche as both a symbol of Christian beliefs and a symbol of the city's support for those beliefs.... Thus, although the Court concedes that the city's inclusion of the nativity scene plainly serves "to depict the origins" of Christmas as a "significant historical religious event," and that the crèche "is identified with one religious faith," we are nevertheless expected to believe that Pawtucket's use of the crèche does not signal the city's support for the sectarian symbolism that the nativity scene evokes. The effect of the crèche, of course, must be gauged not only by its inherent religious significance but also by the overall setting in which it appears. But it blinks reality to claim, as the Court does, that by including such a distinctively religious object as the crèche in its Christmas display, Pawtucket has done no more than make use of a "traditional" symbol of the holiday, and has thereby purged the crèche of its religious content and conferred only an "incidental and indirect" benefit on religion.

The Court's struggle to ignore the clear religious effect of the crèche seems to me misguided for several reasons. In the first place, the city has positioned the crèche in a central and highly visible location within the Hodgson Park display....

Moreover, the city has done nothing to disclaim government approval of the religious significance of the crèche, to suggest that the crèche represents only one religious symbol among many others that might be included in a seasonal display truly aimed at providing a wide catalogue of ethnic and religious celebrations, or to disassociate itself from the religious content of the crèche....

Third, we have consistently acknowledged that an otherwise secular setting alone does not suffice to justify a governmental practice that has the effect of aiding religion....

Finally, and most importantly, even in the context of Pawtucket's seasonal celebration, the crèche retains a specifically Christian religious meaning. I refuse to accept the notion implicit in today's decision that non-Christians would find that the religious content of the crèche is eliminated by the fact that it appears as part of the city's otherwise secular celebration of the Christmas holiday. The nativity scene is clearly distinct in its purpose and effect from the rest of the Hodgson Park display for the simple reason that it is the only one rooted in a biblical account of Christ's birth. It is the chief symbol of the characteristically Christian belief that a divine Savior was brought into the world and that the purpose of this miraculous birth was to illuminate a path toward salvation and redemption. For Christians, that path is exclusive, precious and holy. But for those who do not share these beliefs, the symbolic re-enactment of the birth of a divine being who has been miraculously incarnated as a man stands as a dramatic reminder of their differences with Christian faith. When government appears to sponsor such religiously inspired views, we cannot say that the practice is "'so separate and so indisputably marked off from the religious function,' that [it] may fairly be viewed as reflect[ing] a neutral posture toward religious institutions."... To be so excluded on religious grounds by one's elected government is an insult and an injury that, until today, could not be countenanced by the Establishment Clause.

Second. The Court also attempts to justify the crèche by entertaining a beguilingly simple, yet faulty syllogism. The Court begins by noting that government may recognize Christmas day as a public holiday; the Court then asserts that the crèche is nothing more than a traditional element of Christmas celebrations; and it concludes that the inclusion of a crèche as part of a government's annual Christmas celebration is constitutionally permissible.... The Court apparently believes that once it finds that the designation of Christmas as a public holiday is constitutionally accepted, it is then free to conclude that virtually every form of governmental association with the celebration of the holiday is also constitutional. The vice of this dangerously superficial argument is that it overlooks the fact that the Christmas holiday in our national culture contains both secular and sectarian elements. To say that government may recognize the holiday's traditional, secular elements of gift-giving, public festivities and community spirit, does not mean that government may indiscriminately embrace the distinctively sectarian aspects of the holiday. Indeed, in its eagerness to approve the crèche, the Court has advanced a rationale so simplistic that it would appear to allow the Mayor of Pawtucket to participate in the celebration of a Christmas mass, since this would be just another unobjectionable way for the city to "celebrate the holiday." As is demonstrated below, the Court's logic is fundamentally flawed both because it obscures the reason why public designation of Christmas day as a holiday is constitutionally acceptable, and blurs the distinction between the secular aspects of Christmas and its distinctively religious character, as exemplified by the crèche.

When government decides to recognize Christmas day as a public holiday, it does no more than accommodate the calendar of public activities to the plain fact that many Americans will expect on that day to spend time visiting with their families, attending religious services, and perhaps enjoying some respite from pre-holiday activities. The Free Exercise Clause, of course, does not necessarily compel the government to provide this accommodation, but neither is the Establishment Clause offended by such a step.... Because it is clear that the celebration of Christmas has both secular and sectarian elements, it may well be that by taking note of the holiday, the government is simply seeking to serve the same

kinds of wholly secular goals — for instance, promoting goodwill and a common day of rest — that were found to justify Sunday Closing laws in *McGowan.* If public officials go further and participate in the *secular* celebration of Christmas — by, for example, decorating public places with such secular images as wreaths, garlands or Santa Claus figures — they move closer to the limits of their constitutional power but nevertheless remain within the boundaries set by the Establishment Clause. But when those officials participate in or appear to endorse the distinctively religious elements of this otherwise secular event, they encroach upon First Amendment freedoms. For it is at that point that the government brings to the forefront the theological content of the holiday, and places the prestige, power and financial support of a civil authority in the service of a particular faith.

The inclusion of a crèche in Pawtucket's otherwise secular celebration of Christmas clearly violates these principles. Unlike such secular figures as Santa Claus, reindeer and carolers, a nativity scene represents far more than a mere "traditional" symbol of Christmas. The essence of the crèche's symbolic purpose and effect is to prompt the observer to experience a sense of simple awe and wonder appropriate to the contemplation of one of the central elements of Christian dogma — that God sent His son into the world to be a Messiah. Contrary to the Court's suggestion, the crèche is far from a mere representation of a "particular historic religious event." It is, instead, best understood as a mystical re-creation of an event that lies at the heart of Christian faith. To suggest, as the Court does, that such a symbol is merely "traditional" and therefore no different from Santa's house or reindeer is not only offensive to those for whom the crèche has profound significance, but insulting to those who insist for religious or personal reasons that the story of Christ is in no sense a part of "history" nor an unavoidable element of our national "heritage."

For these reasons, the crèche in this context simply cannot be viewed as playing the same role that an ordinary museum display does.

. . . .

Intuition tells us that some official "acknowledgment" is inevitable in a religious society if government is not to adopt a stilted indifference to the religious life of the people.... It is equally true, however, that if government is to remain scrupulously neutral in matters of religious conscience, as our Constitution requires, then it must avoid those overly broad acknowledgments of religious practices that may imply governmental favoritism toward one set of religious beliefs. . . .

Despite [a] body of case law, the Court has never comprehensively addressed the extent to which government may acknowledge religion by, for example, incorporating religious references into public ceremonies and proclamations, and I do not presume to offer a comprehensive approach. Nevertheless, it appears from our prior decisions that at least three principles — tracing the narrow channels which government acknowledgments must follow to satisfy the Establishment Clause — may be identified. First, although the government may not be compelled to do so by the Free Exercise Clause, it may, consistently with the Establishment Clause, act to accommodate to some extent the opportunities of individuals to practice their religion. . . . That is the essential meaning, I submit, of this Court's decision in *Zorach v. Clauson* . . . (1952), finding that government does not violate the Establishment Clause when it simply chooses to "close its doors or suspend its operations as to those who want to repair to their religious sanctuary for worship or instruction." And for me that principle would justify government's decision to declare December 25th a public holiday.

Second, our cases recognize that while a particular governmental practice may have derived from religious motivations and retain certain religious connotations, it is nonetheless permissible for the government to pursue the practice when it is continued today solely for secular reasons. As this Court noted with reference to Sunday Closing Laws in *McGowan* v. *Maryland,* the mere fact that a governmental practice coincides to some extent with certain religious beliefs does not render it unconstitutional. . . .

Finally, we have noted that government cannot be completely prohibited from recognizing in its public actions the religious beliefs and practices of the American people as an aspect of our national history and culture. . . . While I remain uncertain about these questions, I would suggest that such practices as the designation of "In God We Trust" as our national motto, or the references to God contained in the Pledge of Allegiance can best be understood, in Dean Rostow's apt phrase, as a form a "ceremonial deism," protected from Establishment Clause scrutiny chiefly because they have lost through rote repetition any significant religious content. . . . Moreover, these references are uniquely suited to serve such wholly secular purposes as solemnizing public occasions, or inspiring commitment to meet some national challenge in a manner that simply could not be fully served in our culture if government were limited to purely non-religious phrases. . . . The practices by which the government has long acknowledged religion are therefore probably necessary to serve certain secular functions, and that necessity, coupled with their long history, gives those practices an essentially secular meaning.

The crèche fits none of these categories. Inclusion of the crèche is not necessary to accommodate individual religious expression. This is plainly not a case in which individual residents of Pawtucket have claimed the right to place a crèche as part of a wholly private display on public land. . . . Nor is the inclusion of the crèche necessary to serve wholly secular goals: it is clear that the city's secular purposes of celebrating the Christmas holiday and promoting retail commerce can be fully served without the crèche. . . . And the crèche, because of its unique association with Christianity, is clearly more sectarian than those references to God that we accept in ceremonial phrases or in other contexts that assure neutrality. The religious works on display at the National Gallery, Presidential references to God during an Inaugural Address, or the national motto present no risk of establishing religion. To be sure, our understanding of these expressions may begin in contemplation of some religious element, but it does not end there. Their message is dominantly secular. In contrast, the message of the crèche begins and ends with reverence for a particular image of the divine.

By insisting that such a distinctively sectarian message is merely an unobjectionable part of our "religious heritage," the Court takes a long step backwards to the days when Justice Brewer could arrogantly declare for the Court that "this is a Christian nation." . . . Those days, I had thought, were forever put behind us by the Court's decision in *Engel* v. *Vitale.* . . .
. . . .

Under our constitutional scheme, the role of safeguarding our "religious heritage" and of promoting religious beliefs is reserved as the exclusive prerogative of our nation's churches, religious institutions and spiritual leaders. Because the Framers of the Establishment Clause understood that "religion is too personal, too sacred, too holy to permit its 'unhallowed perversion' by civil [authorities]," the clause demands that government play no role in this effort. The Court today brushes aside these concerns by insisting that Pawtucket has done nothing more than include a "traditional" symbol of Christmas in its celebration of this national holiday, thereby muting the religious content of the crèche. But the city's action should be recognized for what it is: a coercive, though perhaps small, step toward establishing the sectarian preferences of the majority at the expense of the minority, accomplished by placing public facilities and funds in support of the religious symbolism and theological tidings that the crèche conveys. As Justice Frankfurter, writing in *McGowan v. Maryland,* observed, the Establishment Clause "withdr[aws] from the sphere of legitimate legislative concern and competence a specific, but comprehensive area of human conduct: man's belief or disbelief in the verity of some transcendental idea and man's expression in action of that belief or disbelief." That the Constitution sets this realm of thought and feeling apart from the pressures and antagonisms of government is one of its supreme achievements. Regrettably, the Court today tarnishes that achievement.

I dissent.

JUSTICE BLACKMUN, with whom JUSTICE STEVENS joins, dissenting.

. . . If [*Lemon*] and its guidelines mean anything, the presence of Pawtucket's crèche in a municipally sponsored display must be held to be a violation of the First Amendment.

Not only does the Court's resolution of this controversy make light of our precedents, but also, ironically, the majority does an injustice to the crèche and the message it manifests. While certain persons, including the Mayor of Pawtucket, undertook a crusade to "keep Christ in Christmas," the Court today has declared that presence virtually irrelevant. The majority urges that the display, "with or without a crèche," "recall[s] the religious nature of the Holiday," and "engenders a friendly community spirit of good will in keeping with the season." Before the District Court, an expert witness for the city made a similar, though perhaps more candid, point, stating that Pawtucket's display invites people "to participate in the Christmas spirit, brotherhood, peace, and let loose with their money." . . . The crèche has been relegated to the role of a neutral harbinger of the holiday season, useful for commercial purposes, but devoid of any inherent meaning and incapable of enhancing the religious tenor of a display of which it is an integral part. The city has its victory—but it is a Pyrrhic one indeed.

The import of the Court's decision is to encourage use of the crèche in a municipally sponsored display, a setting where Christians feel constrained in acknowledging its symbolic meaning and non-Christians feel alienated by its presence. Surely, this is a misuse of a sacred symbol. Because I cannot join the Court in denying either the force of our precedents or the sacred message that is at the core of the crèche, I dissent and join JUSTICE BRENNAN'S opinion.

West Virginia State Board of Education v. Barnette

319 U.S. 624 (1943)
Vote: 6–3

This case was one of several highly publicized Supreme Court cases in the 1940s that involved the Jehovah's Witnesses, a religious sect whose beliefs are at times at odds with majority sentiment and practice. One doctrine of the Jehovah's Witnesses prohibits saluting or pledging allegiance to a flag, on grounds that this would be a violation of the First Commandment's injunction not to bow down before graven images. Always a source of tension between the Jehovah's Witnesses and their neighbors, this refusal became a burning issue during the late 1930s and 1940s, a period of enhanced patriotic fervor.

In response to the Jehovah's Witnesses a number of states passed laws compelling school children to salute and pledge allegiance to the flag upon penalty of expulsion. This requirement met with resistance from Jehovah's Witnesses and soon resulted in a highly publicized Supreme Court decision, *Minersville School District* v. *Gobitis,* 310 U.S. 586 (1940), in which the Court, by an 8 to 1 vote, upheld the validity of West Virginia's compulsory flag salute requirement for school children. Justice Stone wrote a stinging dissent.

In subsequent decisions that considered other state laws challenged by Jehovah's Witnesses, some of which were certainly enacted to spite the Jehovah's Witnesses, some members of the *Gobitis* majority indicated a change of heart, and when Justice Rutledge was appointed to replace Justice Byrnes, a member of the *Gobitis* majority, it was clear that most members of the Court no longer subscribed to their own ruling. *West Virginia* v. *Barnette* raised essentially the same issues that had been treated three years earlier in *Gobitis.* Here, however, the Court came to a quite different conclusion.

MR. JUSTICE JACKSON delivered the opinion of the Court.

This case calls upon us to reconsider a precedent decision, as the Court throughout its history often has been required to do. Before turning to the *Gobitis* case, however, it is desirable to notice certain characteristics by which this controversy is distinguished.

The freedom asserted by these appellees does not bring them into collision with rights asserted by any other individual. It is such conflicts which most frequently require intervention of the State to determine where the rights of one end and those of another begin. But the refusal of these persons to participate in the ceremony does not interfere with or deny rights of others to do so. Nor is there any question in this case that their behavior is peaceable and orderly. The sole conflict is between authority and rights of the individual. The State asserts power to condition access to public education on making a prescribed sign and profession and at the same time to coerce attendance by punishing both parent and child. The latter stand on a right of self-determination in matters that touch individual opinion and personal attitude.

As the present CHIEF JUSTICE said in dissent in the *Gobitis* case, the State may "require teaching by instruction and study of all in our history and in the structure and organization of our government, including the guaranties of civil liberty, which tend to inspire patriotism and love of country."... Here, however, we are dealing with a compulsion of students to declare a belief. They are not merely made acquainted with the flag salute so that they may be informed as to what it is or even what it means. The issue here is whether this slow and easily neglected route to aroused loyalties constitutionally may be short-cut by substituting a compulsory salute and slogan....

There is no doubt that, in connection with the pledges, the flag salute is a form of utterance....

It is also to be noted that the compulsory flag salute and pledge requires affirmation of a belief and an attitude of mind. It is not clear whether the regulation contemplates that pupils forego any contrary convictions of their own and become unwilling converts to the prescribed ceremony or whether it will be acceptable if they simulate assent by words without belief and by a gesture barren of meaning. It is now a commonplace that censorship or suppression of expression of opinion is tolerated by our Constitution only when the expression presents a clear and present danger of action of a kind the State is empowered to prevent and punish. It would seem that involuntary affirmation could be commanded only on even more immediate and urgent grounds than silence. But here the power of compulsion is invoked without any allegation that remaining passive during a flag salute ritual creates a clear and present danger that would justify an effort even to muffle expression. To sustain the compulsory flag salute we are required to say that a Bill of Rights which guards the individual's right to speak his own mind, left it open to public authorities to compel him to utter what is not in his mind.

. . . .

Nor does the issue as we see it turn on one's possession of particular religious views or the sincerity with which they are held. While religion supplies appellees' motive for enduring the discomforts of making the issue in this case, many citizens who do not share these religious views hold such a compulsory rite to infringe constitutional liberty of the individual. It is not necessary to inquire whether non-conformist beliefs will exempt from the duty to salute unless we first find power to make the salute a legal duty.

The *Gobitis* decision, however, *assumed*, as did the argument in that case and in this, that power exists in the State to impose the flag salute discipline upon school children in general. The Court only examined and rejected a claim based on religious beliefs of immunity from an unquestioned general rule. The question which underlies the flag salute controversy is whether such a ceremony so touching matters of opinion and political attitude may be imposed upon the individual by official authority under powers committed to any political organization under our Constitution. We examine rather than assume existence of this power and, against this broader definition of issues in this case, reexamine specific grounds assigned for the *Gobitis* decision.

. . . .

. . . The *Gobitis* opinion reasoned that this is a field "where courts possess no marked and certainly no controlling competence," that it is committed to the legislatures as well as the courts to guard cherished liberties and that it is constitutionally appropriate to "fight out the wise use of legislative authority in the forum of public opinion and before legislative assemblies rather than to transfer such a contest to the judicial arena," since all the "effective means of inducing political changes are left free."...

The very purpose of a Bill of Rights was to withdraw certain subjects from the vicissitudes of political controversy, to place them beyond the reach of majorities and officials and to establish them as legal principles to be applied by the courts. One's right to life, liberty, and property, to free speech, a free press, freedom of worship and assembly, and other fundamental rights may not be submitted to vote; they depend on the outcome of no elections.

. . . .

. . . *Gobitis* reasons that "National unity is the basis of national security," that the authorities have "the right to select appropriate means for its attainment," and hence reaches the conclusion that such compulsory measures toward "national unity" are constitutional. Upon the verity of this assumption depends our answer in this case.

National unity as an end which officials may foster by persuasion and example is not in question. The problem is whether under our Constitution compulsion as here employed is a permissible means for its achievement.

Struggles to coerce uniformity of sentiment in support of some end thought essential to their time and country have been waged by many good as well as by evil men. Nationalism is a relatively recent phenomenon but at other times and places the ends have been racial or territorial security, support of a dynasty or regime, and particular plans for saving souls. As first and moderate methods to attain unity have failed, those bent on its accomplishment must resort to an ever-increasing severity. As governmental pressure toward unity becomes greater, so strife becomes more bitter as to whose unity it shall be. Probably no deeper division of our people could proceed from any provocation than from finding it necessary to choose what doctrine and whose program public educational officials shall compel youth to unite in embracing. Ultimate futility of such attempts to compel coherence is the lesson of every such effort from the Roman drive to stamp out Christianity as a disturber of its pagan unity, the Inquisition, as a means to religious and dynastic unity, the Siberian exiles as a means to Russian unity, down to the fast failing efforts of our present totalitarian enemies. Those who begin coercive elimination of dissent soon find themselves exterminating dissenters. Compulsory unification of opinion achieves only the unanimity of the graveyard.

It seems trite but necessary to say that the First Amendment to our Constitution was designed to avoid these ends by avoiding these beginnings. There is no mysticism in the American concept of the State or of the nature or origin of its authority. We set up government by consent of the governed, and the Bill of Rights denies those in power any legal opportunity to coerce that consent. Authority here is to be controlled by public opinion, not public opinion by authority.

The case is made difficult not because the principles of its decision are obscure but because the flag involved is our own. Nevertheless, we apply the limitations of the Constitution with no fear that freedom to be intellectually and spiritually diverse or even contrary will disintegrate the social organization. To believe that patriotism will not flourish if patriotic ceremonies are voluntary and spontaneous instead of a compulsory routine is to make an unflattering estimate of the appeal of our institutions to free minds. We can have intellectual individualism and the rich cultural diversities that we owe to exceptional minds only at the price of occasional eccentricity and abnormal attitudes. When they are so harmless to others or to the State as those we deal with here, the price is not too great. But freedom to differ is not limited to things that do not matter much. That would be a mere shadow of freedom. The test of its substance is the right to differ as to things that touch the heart of the existing order.

If there is any fixed star in our constitutional constellation, it is that no official, high or petty, can prescribe what shall be orthodox in politics, nationalism, religion, or other matters of opinion or force citizens to confess by word or act their faith therein. If there are any circumstances which permit an exception, they do not now occur to us.

We think the action of the local authorities in compelling the flag salute and pledge transcends constitutional limitations on their power and invades the sphere of intellect and spirit which is the purpose of the First Amendment to our Constitution to reserve from all official control.

The decision of this Court in *Minersville School District* v. *Gobitis* and the holdings of those few *per curiam* decisions which preceded and foreshadowed it are overruled, and the judgment enjoining enforcement of the West Virginia Regulation is

Affirmed.

[JUSTICES BLACK and DOUGLAS concurred. JUSTICE MURPHY concurred. JUSTICES ROBERTS and REED dissented.]

MR. JUSTICE FRANKFURTER, dissenting:

One who belongs to the most vilified and persecuted minority in history is not likely to be insensible to the freedoms guaranteed by our Constitution. Were my purely personal attitude relevant I should wholeheartedly associate myself with the general libertarian views in the Court's opinion, representing as they do the thought and action of a lifetime. But as judges we are neither Jew nor Gentile, neither Catholic nor agnostic. We owe equal attachment to the Constitution and are equally bound by our judicial obligations whether we derive our citizenship from the earliest or the latest immigrants to these shores. As a member of this Court I am not justified in writing my private notions of policy into the Constitution, no matter how deeply I may cherish them or how mischievous I may deem their disregard. The duty of a judge who must decide which of two claims before the Court shall prevail, that of a State to enact and enforce laws within its general competence or that of an individual to refuse obedience because of the demands of his conscience, is not that of the ordinary person. It can never be emphasized too much that one's own opinion about the wisdom or evil of a law should be excluded altogether when one is doing one's duty on the bench. The only opinion of our own even looking in that direction that is material is our opinion whether legislators could in reason have enacted such a law. In the light of all the circumstances, including the history of this question in this Court, it would require more daring than I possess to deny that reasonable legislators could have taken the action which is before us for review. Most unwillingly, therefore, I must differ from my brethren with regard to legislation like this. I cannot bring my mind to believe that the "liberty" secured by the Due Process Clause gives this Court authority to deny to the State of West Virginia the attainment of that which we all recognize as a legitimate legislative end, namely, the promotion of good citizenship, by employment of the means here chosen.

. . . .

We are not reviewing merely the action of a local school board. The flag salute requirement in this case comes before us with the full authority of the State of West Virginia. We are in fact passing judgment on "the power of the State as a whole." . . . Practically we are passing upon the political power of each of the forty-eight states. Moreover, since the First Amendment has been read into the Fourteenth, our problem is precisely the same as it would be if we had before us an Act of Congress for the District of Columbia. To suggest that we are here concerned with the heedless action of some village tyrants is to distort the augustness of the constitutional issue and the reach of the consequences of our decision.

Under our constitutional system the legislature is charged solely with civil concerns of society. If the avowed or intrinsic legislative purpose is either to promote or to discourage some religious community or creed, it is clearly within the constitutional restrictions imposed on legislatures and cannot stand. But it by no means follows that legislative power is wanting whenever a general non-discriminatory civil regulation in fact touches conscientious scruples or religious beliefs of an individual or a group. Regard for such scruples or beliefs undoubtedly presents one of the most reasonable claims for the exertion of legislative accommodation. It is, of course, beyond our power to rewrite the State's requirement, by providing exemptions for those who do not wish to participate in the flag salute or by making some other accommodations to meet their scruples. That wisdom might suggest the making of such accommodations and that school administration would not find it too difficult to make them and yet maintain the ceremony for those not refusing to conform, is outside our province to suggest. Tact, respect, and generosity toward variant views will always commend themselves to those charged with the duties of legislation so as to achieve a maximum of good will and to require a minimum of unwilling submission to a general law. But the real question is, who is to make such accommodations, the courts or the legislature?

This is no dry, technical matter. It cuts deep into one's conception of the democratic process — it concerns no less the practical differences between the means for making these accommodations that are open to courts and to legislatures. . . .

The constitutional protection of religious freedom terminated disabilities, it did not create new privileges. It gave religious equality, not civil immunity. Its essence is freedom from conformity to religious dogma, not freedom from conformity to law because of religious dogma. Religious loyalties may be exercised without hindrance from the state, not the state may not exercise that which except by leave of religious loyalties is within the domain of temporal power. Otherwise each individual could set up his own censor against obedience to laws conscientiously deemed for the public good by those whose business it is to make laws.

. . . .

The essence of the religious freedom guaranteed by our Constitution is therefore this: no religion shall either receive the state's support or incur its hostility. Religion is outside the sphere of political government. This does not mean that all matters on which religious organizations or beliefs may pronounce are outside the sphere of government. Were this so, instead of the separation of church and state, there would be the subordination of the state on any matter deemed within the sovereignty of the religious conscience. Much that is the concern of temporal authority affects the spiritual interests of men. But it is not enough to strike down a non-discriminatory law that it may hurt or offend some dissident view. It would be too easy to cite numerous prohibitions and injunctions to which laws run counter if the variant interpretations of the Bible were made the tests of obedience to law. The validity of secular laws cannot be measured by their conformity to religious doctrines. It is only in a theocratic state that ecclesiastical doctrines measure legal right or wrong.

An act compelling profession of allegiance to a religion, no matter how subtly or tenuously promoted, is bad. But an act promoting good citizenship and national allegiance is within the domain of governmental authority and is therefore to be judged by the same considerations of power and of constitutionality as those involved in the many claims of immunity from civil obedience because of religious scruples.

. . . .

Law is concerned with external behavior and not with the inner life of man. It rests in large measure upon compulsion. Socrates lives in history partly because he gave his life for the conviction that duty of obedience to secular law does not presuppose consent to its enactment or belief in its virtue. The consent upon which free government rests is the consent that comes from sharing in the process of making and unmaking laws. The state is not shut out from a domain because the individual conscience may deny the state's claim. The individual conscience may profess what faith it chooses. It may affirm and promote that faith — in the language of the Constitution, it may "exercise" it freely — but it cannot thereby restrict community action through political organs in matters of community concern, so long as the action is not asserted in a discriminatory way either openly or by stealth. One may have the right to practice one's religion and at the same time owe the duty of formal obedience to laws that run counter to one's beliefs. . . .

We are told that a flag salute is a doubtful substitute for adequate understanding of our institutions. . . . We may deem it a foolish measure, but the point is that this Court is not the organ of government to resolve doubts as to whether it will fulfill its purpose. Only if there be no doubt that any reasonable mind could entertain can we deny to the states the right to resolve doubts their way and not ours.

. . . .

Of course patriotism can not be enforced by the flag salute. But neither can the liberal spirit be enforced by judicial invalidation of illiberal legislation. Our constant preoccupation with the constitutionality of legislation rather than with its wisdom tends to preoccupation of the American mind with a false value. The tendency of focussing attention on constitutionality is to make constitutionality synonymous with wisdom, to regard a law as all right if it is constitutional. Such an attitude is a great enemy of liberalism. Particularly in legislation affecting freedom of thought and freedom of speech much which should offend a free-spirited society is constitutional. Reliance for the most precious interests of civilization, therefore, must be found outside of their vindication in courts of law. Only a persistent positive translation of the faith of a free society into the convictions and habits and actions of a community is the ultimate reliance against unabated temptations to fetter the human spirit.

McGowan v. Maryland

366 U.S. 420 (1961)
Vote: 8–1

In the case below, the appellants, all employees of a large department store in Anne Arundel County, Maryland, were convicted and fined for selling a loose-leaf binder, a can of floor wax, a stapler, staples, and a toy, in violation of a state statute prohibiting sale on Sunday of all merchandise except tobacco products, confectionaries, milk, bread, fruit, gasoline, oils, grease, drugs, medicines, newspapers, and periodicals. The provisions were part of a set of state laws that prohibited a variety of activities on Sunday.

Appellants argued that the prohibitions in question here violated the Equal Protection Clause and the Due Process Clause of the Fourteenth Amendment and the Establishment Clause of the First Amendment made applicable to the states via the Fourteenth Amendment. In one portion of the opinion, not reprinted below, the Court considered and rejected appellants' equal protection and due process arguments, before turning to consider the establishment argument, which is reproduced below.

This case arrived at the United States Supreme Court upon appeal from the Maryland Court of Appeals, which had sustained the trial court's conviction and fine.

McGowan was one of four Sunday closing cases handed down by the Supreme Court on the same day. In the companion cases, *Braunfeld* v. *Brown,* 366 U.S. 599 (1961), and *Gallagher* v. *Crown Kosher Market,* 366 U.S. 617 (1961), the Court considered Sunday closing ordinances as they affected Jewish merchants. In these cases merchants challenged the Sunday closing laws on free exercise as well as establishment of religion grounds, contending that the Sunday closing laws put them at an economic disadvantage because they had to close as well on Saturdays for religious observance. Despite the additional claim of free exercise, the Court, this time by a vote of 6 to 3, upheld the Sunday closing laws that did not permit exceptions for those who had to close on other days for religious reasons. The Court reasoned, "To strike, without the most critical scrutiny, legislation which imposes only an indirect burden on the exercise of religion, i.e., legislation which does not make unlawful the religious practice itself, would radically restrict the operating latitude of the legislature." Justice Douglas' dissent in *McGowan* was also written to cover the court's ruling in *Braunfeld* and *Crown Kosher Market.*

If the legislature was willing to make "free exercise" exceptions and allow Sunday openings for those with a "free exercise" reason, what language would it use to define the exceptions? How would it, or the courts, validate these claims? What reasons can you think of for the Court's not wanting to open the door to such an issue? How might equal protection and due process arguments be used to deal with at least some Sunday closing laws?

MR. CHIEF JUSTICE WARREN delivered the opinion of the Court.

The issues in this case concern the constitutional validity of Maryland criminal statutes, commonly known as Sunday Closing Laws or Sunday Blue Laws. These statutes, with exceptions to be noted hereafter, generally proscribe all labor, business and other commercial activities on Sunday. The questions presented are whether the classifications within the statutes bring about a denial of equal protection of the law, whether the laws are so vague as to fail to give reasonable notice of the forbidden conduct and therefore violate due process, and whether the statutes are laws respecting an establishment of religion or prohibiting the free exercise thereof.

Appellants are seven employees of a large discount department store located on a highway in Anne Arundel County, Maryland. They were indicted for the Sunday sale of a three-ring loose-leaf binder, a can of floor wax, a stapler and staples, and a toy submarine in violation of Md. Ann. Code, Art. 27, §521. Generally, this section prohibited, throughout the State, the Sunday sale of all merchandise except the retail sale of tobacco products, confectionaries, milk, bread, fruits, gasoline, oils, greases, drugs and medicines, and newspapers and periodicals. Recently amended, this section also now excepts from the general prohibition the retail sale in Anne Arundel County of all foodstuffs, automobile and boating accessories, flowers, toilet goods, hospital supplies and souvenirs. It now further provides that any retail establishment in Anne Arundel County which does not employ more than one person other than the owner may operate on Sunday.

Although appellants were indicted only under §521, in order properly to consider several of the broad constitutional contentions, we must examine the whole body of Maryland Sunday laws. Several sections of the Maryland statutes are particularly relevant to evaluation of the issues presented. Section 492 of Md. Ann. Code, Art. 27, forbids all persons from doing any work or bodily labor on Sunday and forbids permitting children or servants to work on that day or to engage in fishing, hunting and unlawful pastimes or recreations. The section excepts all works of necessity and charity. Section 522 of Md. Ann. Code, Art. 27, disallows the opening or use of any dancing saloon, opera house, bowling alley or barber shop on Sunday. However, in addition to the exceptions noted above, Md. Ann. Code, Art. 27, §509, exempts, for Anne Arundel County, the Sunday operation of any bathing beach, bathhouse, dancing saloon and amusement park, and activities incident thereto and retails sales of merchandise customarily sold at, or incidental to, the operation of the aforesaid occupations and businesses. Section 90 of Md. Ann. Code, Art. 2B, makes generally unlawful the sale of alcoholic beverages on Sunday. However, this section, and immediately succeeding ones, provide various immunities for the Sunday sale of different kinds of alcoholic beverages, at different hours during the day, by vendors holding different types of licenses, in different political divisions of the State — particularly in Anne Arundel County. See Md. Ann. Code, Art. 2B, §28(a).

The remaining statutory sections concern a myriad of exceptions for various counties, districts of counties, cities and towns throughout the State. Among the activities allowed in certain areas on Sunday are such sports as football, baseball, golf, tennis, bowling, croquet, basketball, lacrosse, soccer, hockey, swimming, softball, boating, fishing, skating, horseback riding, stock car racing and pool or billiards. Other immunized activities permitted in some regions of the State include group singing or playing of musical instruments; the exhibition of motion pictures; dancing; the operation of recreation centers, picnic grounds, swimming pools, skating rinks and miniature golf courses. The taking of oysters and the hunting or killing of game is generally forbidden, but shooting conducted by organized rod and gun clubs is permitted in one county. In some of the subdivisions within the State, the exempted Sunday activities are sanctioned throughout the day; in others, they may not commence until early afternoon or evening; in many, the activities may only be conducted during the afternoon and late in the evening. Certain localities do not permit the allowed Sunday activity to be carried on within one hundred yards of any church where religious services are being held. Local ordinances and regulations concerning certain limited activities supplement the State's statutory scheme. In Anne Arundel County, for example, slot machines, pinball machines and bingo may be played on Sunday.

Among other things, appellants contended at the trial that the Maryland statutes under which they were charged were contrary to the Fourteenth Amendment for the reasons stated at the outset of this opinion. Appellants were convicted and each was fined five dollars and costs. The Maryland Court of Appeals affirmed....

The essence of appellants' "establishment" argument is that Sunday is the Sabbath day of the predominant Christian sects; that the purpose of the enforced stoppage of labor on that day is to facilitate and encourage church attendance; that the purpose of setting Sunday as a day of universal rest is to induce people with no religion or people with marginal religious beliefs to join the predominant Christian sects; that the purpose of the atmosphere of tranquility created by Sunday closing is to aid the conduct of church services and religious observance of the sacred day.... There is no dispute that the original laws which dealt with Sunday labor were motivated by religious forces. But what we must decide is whether present Sunday legislation, having undergone extensive changes from the earliest forms, still retains its religious character.

. . . .

But, despite the strongly religious origin of these laws, beginning before the eighteenth century non-religious arguments for Sunday closing began to be

heard more distinctly and the statutes began to lose some of their totally religious flavor....

More recently, further secular justifications have been advanced for making Sunday a day of rest, a day when people may recover from the labors of the week just passed and may physically and mentally prepare for the week's work to come....

The proponents of Sunday closing legislation are no longer exclusively representatives of religious interests....

Throughout the years, state legislatures have modified, deleted from and added to their Sunday statutes. As evidenced by the New Jersey laws mentioned above, current changes are commonplace. Almost every State in our country presently has some type of Sunday regulation and over forty possess a relatively comprehensive system.... Thus have Sunday laws evolved from the wholly religious sanctions that originally were enacted....

In light of the evolution of our Sunday Closing Laws through the centuries, and of their more or less recent emphasis upon secular considerations, it is not difficult to discern that as presently written and administered, most of them, at least, are of a secular rather than of a religious character, and that presently they bear no relationship to establishment of religion as those words are used in the Constitution of the United States.

Throughout this century and longer, both the federal and state governments have oriented their activities very largely toward improvement of the health, safety, recreation and general well-being of our citizens. Numerous laws affecting public health, safety factors in industry, laws affecting hours and conditions of labor of women and children, week-end diversion at parks and beaches, and cultural activities of various kinds, now point the way toward the good life for all. Sunday Closing Laws, like those before us, have become part and parcel of this great governmental concern wholly apart from their original purposes or connotations. The present purpose and effect of most of them is to provide a uniform day of rest for all citizens; the fact that this day is Sunday, a day of particular significance for the dominant Christian sects, does not bar the State from achieving its secular goals. To say that the States cannot prescribe Sunday as a day of rest for those purposes solely because centuries ago such laws had their genesis in religion would give a constitutional interpretation of hostility to the public welfare rather than one of mere separation of church and State.

. . . .

Considering the language and operative effect of the current statutes, we no longer find the blanket prohibition against Sunday work or bodily labor. . . . These provisions, along with those which permit various sports and entertainments on Sunday, seem clearly to be fashioned for the purpose of providing a Sunday atmosphere of recreation, cheerfulness, repose and enjoyment. Coupled with the general proscription against other types of work, we believe that the air of the day is one of relaxation rather than one of religion.

. . . .

But this does not answer all of appellants' contentions. We are told that the State has other means at its disposal to accomplish its secular purpose, other courses that would not even remotely or incidentally give state aid to religion. . . . It is true that if the State's interest were simply to provide for its citizens a periodic respite from work, a regulation demanding that everyone rest one day in seven, leaving the choice of the day to the individual, would suffice.

However, the State's purpose is not merely to provide a one-day-in-seven work stoppage. In addition to this, the State seeks to set one day apart from all others as a day of rest, repose, recreation and tranquility — a day which all members of the family and community have the opportunity to spend and enjoy together, a day on which there exists relative quiet and disassociation from the everyday intensity of commercial activities, a day on which people may visit friends and relatives who are not available during working days.

Finally, we should make clear that this case deals only with the constitutionality of §521 of the Maryland statute before us. We do not hold that Sunday legislation may not be a violation of the "Establishment" Clause if it can be demonstrated that its purpose — evidenced either on the face of the legislation, in conjunction with its legislative history, or in its operative effect — is to use the State's coercive power to aid religion.

Accordingly, the decision is

Affirmed.

[JUSTICES HARLAN and FRANKFURTER concurred.]

MR. JUSTICE DOUGLAS, dissenting.

The question is not whether one day out of seven can be imposed by a State as a day of rest. The question is not whether Sunday can by force of custom and habit be retained as a day of rest. The question is whether a State can impose criminal sanctions on those who, unlike the Christian majority that makes up our society, worship on a different day or do not share the religious scruples of the majority.

. . . .

The institutions of our society are founded on the belief that there is an authority higher than the authority of the State; that there is a moral law which the State is powerless to alter; that the individual possesses rights, conferred by the Creator, which government must respect. . . .

. . . .

But those who fashioned the First Amendment decided that if and when God is to be served, His service will not be motivated by coercive measures of government. . . .

The First Amendment commands government to have no interest in theology or ritual; it admonishes government to be interested in allowing religious freedom to flourish — whether the result is to produce Catholics, Jews, or Protestants, or to turn the people toward the path of Buddha, or to end in a predominantly Moslem nation, or to produce in the long run atheists or agnostics. On matters of this kind government must be neutral. . . . The "establishment" clause protects citizens also against any law which selects any religious custom, practice, or ritual, puts the force of government behind it, and fines, imprisons, or otherwise penalizes a person for not observing it. The Government plainly could not join forces with one religious group and decree a universal and symbolic circumcision. Nor could it require all children to be baptized or give tax exemptions only to those whose children were baptized.

Could it require a fast from sunrise to sunset throughout the Moslem month of Ramadan? I should think not. Yet why then can it make criminal the doing of other acts, as innocent as eating, during the day that Christians revere?

. . . .

The Court balances the need of the people for rest, recreation, late sleeping, family visiting and the like against the command of the First Amendment that no one need bow to the religious beliefs of another. There is in this realm no room for balancing. I see no place for it in the constitutional scheme. . . .

The State can, of course, require one day of rest a week: one day when every shop or factory is closed. Quite a few States make that requirement. Then the "day of rest" becomes purely and simply a health measure. But the Sunday laws operate differently. They force minorities to obey the majority's religious feelings of what is due and proper for a Christian community; they provide a coercive spur to the "weaker brethren," to those who are indifferent to the claims of a Sabbath through apathy or scruple. Can there be any doubt that Christians, now aligned vigorously in favor of these laws, would be as strongly opposed if they were prosecuted under a Moslem law that forbade them from engaging in secular activities on days that violated Moslem scruples?

There is an "establishment" of religion in the constitutional sense if any practice of any religious group has the sanction of law behind it. There is an interference with the "free exercise" of religion if what in conscience one can do or omit doing is required because of the religious scruples of the community. Hence I would declare each of those laws unconstitutional as applied to the complaining parties, whether or not they are members of a sect which observes as its Sabbath a day other than Sunday.

Sherbert v. Verner

374 U.S. 398 (1963)
Vote: 7–2

Adell Sherbert, a member of the Seventh-Day Adventist Church, was discharged by her employer because she would not work on Saturday, the Sabbath Day of her faith. She was not able to obtain other employment in the area for this same reason. Subsequently, she filed for unemployment compensation. However, the South Carolina Employment Security Commission denied her application, ruling that she was ineligible for compensation due to a provision in the applicable law providing that one who refuses suitable work when it is offered cannot receive unemployment benefits.

Sherbert then filed suit against Verner and other members of the South Carolina Employment Security Commission, challenging the ruling. The Commission's position was upheld by a trial court and the South Carolina Supreme Court, whereupon Sherbert appealed to the United States Supreme Court.

Sherbert was reaffirmed and expanded in a 1989 case in which a unanimous Court held that persons who refuse to work on Sundays because of their "sincere religious beliefs" are eligible for unemployment benefits even though they are not members of any religious sect or organization. *Frazee v. Illinois Department of Employment Security,* 57 LW 4397.

Sherbert was handed down two years after the Supreme Court's ruling in *Braunfeld* v. *Brown,* 366 U.S. 599 (1961), in which the Court upheld a 1959 Pennsylvania statute forbidding the retail sale on Sundays of various commodities. In that case, Braunfeld and other merchants, all Jews who for religious reasons did not conduct business on Saturday, claimed that the law as interpreted violated the establishment of religion and free exercise provisions of the First Amendment in that the law forced them to abandon religious principle or suffer the economic hardship of a two-day closure. In the current case, the majority opinion takes great pains to distinguish Sherbert's situation from Braunfeld's. Is it convincing?

MR. JUSTICE BRENNAN delivered the opinion of the Court.

. . . If . . . the decision of the South Carolina Supreme Court is to withstand appellant's constitutional challenge, it must be either because her disqualification as a beneficiary represents no infringement by the State of her constitutional rights of free exercise, or because any incidental burden on the free exercise of appellant's religion may be justified by a "compelling state interest in the regulation of a subject within the State's constitutional power to regulate. . . ."

We turn first to the question whether the disqualification for benefits imposes any burden on the free exercise of appellant's religion. We think it is clear that it does. . . . The ruling forces her to choose between following the precepts of her religion and forfeiting benefits, on the one hand, and abandoning one of the precepts of her religion in order to accept work, on the other hand. Governmental imposition of such a choice puts the same kind of burden upon the free exercise of religion as would a fine imposed against appellant for her Saturday worship.

Nor may the South Carolina court's construction of the statute be saved from constitutional infirmity on the ground that unemployment compensation benefits are not appellant's "right" but merely a "privilege." It is too late in the day to doubt that the liberties of religion and expression may be infringed by the denial of or placing of conditions upon a benefit or privilege. . . . [T]o condition the availability of benefits upon this appellant's willingness to violate a cardinal principle of her religious faith effectively penalizes the free exercise of her constitutional liberties.

. . . .

We must next consider whether some compelling state interest enforced in the eligibility provisions of the South Carolina statute justifies the substantial infringement of appellant's First Amendment right. It is basic that no showing merely of a rational relationship to some colorable state interest would suffice; in this highly sensitive constitutional area, "[o]nly the gravest abuses, endangering paramount interests, give occasion for permissible limitation."... No such abuse or danger has been advanced in the present case. The appellees suggest no more than a possibility that the filing of fraudulent claims by unscrupulous claimants feigning religious objections to Saturday work might not only dilute the unemployment compensation fund but also hinder the scheduling by employers of necessary Saturday work....

In these respects, then, the state interest asserted in the present case is wholly dissimilar to the interests which were found to justify the less direct burden upon religious practices in *Braunfeld* v. *Brown*.... The Court recognized that the Sunday closing law which that decision sustained undoubtedly served "to make the practice of [the Orthodox Jewish merchants']... religious beliefs more expensive."... But the statute was nevertheless saved by a countervailing factor which finds no equivalent in the instant case—a strong state interest in providing one uniform day of rest for all workers. That secular objective could be achieved, the Court found, only by declaring Sunday to be that day of rest. Requiring exemptions for Sabbatarians, while theoretically possible, appeared to present an administrative problem of such magnitude, or to afford the exempted class so great a competitive advantage, that such a requirement would have rendered the entire statutory scheme unworkable. In the present case no such justifications underlie the determination of the state court that appellant's religion makes her ineligible to receive benefits.

The judgment of the South Carolina Supreme Court is reversed and the case is remanded for further proceedings not inconsistent with this opinion.

It is so ordered.

[MR. JUSTICE DOUGLAS wrote a concurring opinion.]

MR. JUSTICE STEWART, concurring in the result.

... This case presents a double-barreled dilemma, which in all candor I think the Court's opinion has not succeeded in papering over. The dilemma ought to be resolved.

. . . .

I am convinced that no liberty is more essential to the continued vitality of the free society which our Constitution guarantees than is the religious liberty protected by the Free Exercise Clause explicit in the First Amendment and imbedded in the Fourteenth. And I regret that on occasion, and specifically in *Braunfeld* v. *Brown*, ... the Court has shown what

has seemed to me a distressing insensitivity to the appropriate demands of this constitutional guarantee. By contrast I think that the Court's approach to the Establishment Clause has on occasion, and specifically in *Engel, Schempp* and *Murray,* been not only insensitive, but positively wooden, and that the Court has accorded to the Establishment Clause a meaning which neither the words, the history, nor the intention of the authors of that specific constitutional provision even remotely suggests.

... And the result is that there are many situations where legitimate claims under the Free Exercise Clause will run into head-on collision with the Court's insensitive and sterile construction of the Establishment Clause. The controversy now before us is clearly such a case.

Because the appellant refuses to accept available jobs which would require her to work on Saturdays, South Carolina has declined to pay unemployment compensation benefits to her. Her refusal to work on Saturdays is based on the tenets of her religious faith. The Court says that South Carolina cannot under these circumstances declare her to be not "available for work" within the meaning of its statute because to do so would violate her constitutional right to the free exercise of her religion.

Yet what this Court has said about the Establishment Clause must inevitably lead to a diametrically opposite result. If the appellant's refusal to work on Saturdays were based on indolence, or on a compulsive desire to watch the Saturday television programs, no one would say that South Carolina could not hold that she was not "available for work" within the meaning of its statute. That being so, the Establishment Clause as construed by this Court not only *permits* but affirmatively *requires* South Carolina equally to deny the appellant's claim for unemployment compensation when her refusal to work on Saturdays is based upon her religious creed....

To require South Carolina to so administer its laws as to pay public money to the appellant under the circumstances of this case is thus clearly to require the State to violate the Establishment Clause as construed by this Court. This poses no problem for me, because I think the Court's mechanistic concept of the Establishment Clause is historically unsound and constitutionally wrong. I think the process of constitutional decision in the area of the relationships between government and religion demands considerably more than the invocation of broadbrushed rhetoric of the kind I have quoted. And I think that the guarantee of religious liberty embodied in the Free Exercise Clause affirmatively requires government to create an atmosphere of hospitality and accommodation to individual belief or disbelief.

In short, I think our Constitution commands the positive protection by government of religious freedom — not only for a minority, however small — not only for the majority, however large — but for each of us.

. . . .

The impact upon the appellant's religious freedom in the present case is considerably less onerous [than in *Braunfeld*]. We deal here not with a criminal statute, but with the particularized administration of South Carolina's Unemployment Compensation Act. Even upon the unlikely assumption that the appellant could not find suitable non-Saturday employment, the appellant at the worst would be denied a maximum of 22 weeks of compensation payments. I agree with the Court that the possibility of that denial is enough to infringe upon the appellant's constitutional right to the free exercise of her religion. But it is clear to me that in order to reach this conclusion the Court must explicitly reject the reasoning of *Braunfeld* v. *Brown*. I think the *Braunfeld* case was wrongly decided and should be overruled, and accordingly I concur in the result reached by the Court in the case before us.

MR. JUSTICE HARLAN, whom MR. JUSTICE WHITE joins, dissenting.

Today's decision is disturbing both in its rejection of existing precedent and in its implications for the future. . . . What the Court is holding is that if the State chooses to condition unemployment compensation on the applicant's availability for work, it is constitutionally compelled to *carve out an exception* — and to provide benefits — for those whose unavailability is due to their religious convictions. Such a holding has particular significance in two respects.

First, despite the Court's protestations to the contrary, the decision necessarily overrules *Braunfeld* v. *Brown,* which held that it did not offend the "Free Exercise" Clause of the Constitution for a State to forbid a Sabbatarian to do business on Sunday. The secular purpose of the statute before us today is even clearer than that involved in *Braunfeld.* And just as in *Braunfeld* — where exceptions to the Sunday closing laws for Sabbatarians would have been inconsistent with the purpose to achieve a uniform day of rest and would have required case-by-case inquiry into religious beliefs — so here, an exception to the rules of eligibility based on religious convictions would necessitate judicial examination of those convictions and would be at odds with the limited purpose of the statute to smooth out the economy during periods of industrial instability. Finally, the in-

direct financial burden of the present law is far less than that involved in *Braunfeld.* . . .

Wisconsin v. Yoder

406 U.S. 205 (1972)
Vote: 6–1

Jonas Yoder and Wallace Miller, both members of the Old Order Amish religion, and Adin Yutzy, a member of the Conservative Amish Mennonite Church, were convicted of violating Wisconsin's compulsory school-attendance law (which requires school attendance until age 16) for refusing to send their children to public or private school after they had graduated from the eighth grade. This decision was based upon their belief that high school attendance was contrary to the Amish religion and way of life. The Amish shun modern culture, and the parents believed that the sustained exposure to the secular world that their children would receive in high school would endanger their own salvation and that of their children. Evidence at trial showed that the Amish provide continuing informal vocational education to their children that is designed to prepare them for life in the rural Amish community.

Wisconsin officials acknowledged the sincerity of the parents' beliefs, but argued that there was a compelling state interest in compulsory high school attendance. Yoder, Miller, and Yutzy contended that as applied to them, the law violated the free exercise provision of the First Amendment as made applicable to the states through the Fourteenth Amendment. The Wisconsin Supreme Court sustained this claim, whereupon the state successfully petitioned the United States Supreme Court for a writ of certiorari.

MR. CHIEF JUSTICE BURGER delivered the opinion of the Court.

. . . The trial testimony showed that respondents believed, in accordance with the tenets of Old Order Amish communities generally, that their children's attendance at high school, public or private, was contrary to the Amish religion and way of life. They believed that by sending their children to high school, they would not only expose themselves to the danger of the censure of the church community, but, as found by the county court, also endanger their own salvation and that of their children. The State stipulated that respondents' religious beliefs were sincere.

. . . .

There is no doubt as to the power of a State, having a high responsibility for education of its citizens, to impose reasonable regulations for the control and duration of basic education. See, *e.g., Pierce* v. *Society of Sisters* (1925). Providing public schools ranks at the very apex of the function of a State. Yet even this paramount responsibility was, in *Pierce,* made to yield to the right of parents to provide an equivalent education in a privately operated system. There the Court held that Oregon's statute compelling attendance in a public school from age eight to age 16 unreasonably interfered with the interest of parents in directing the rearing of their offspring, including their education in church-operated schools. As that case suggests, the values of parental direction of the religious upbringing and education of their children in their early and formative years have a high place in our society. . . . Thus, a State's interest in universal education, however highly we rank it, is not totally free from a balancing process when it impinges on fundamental rights and interests, such as those specifically protected by the Free Exercise Clause of the First Amendment, and the traditional interest of parents with respect to the religious upbringing of their children so long as they, in the words of *Pierce,* "prepare [them] for additional obligations." . . .

It follows that in order for Wisconsin to compel school attendance beyond the eighth grade against a claim that such attendance interferes with the practice of a legitimate religious belief, it must appear either that the State does not deny the free exercise of religious belief by its requirement, or that there is a state interest of sufficient magnitude to override the interest claiming protection under the Free Exercise Clause. . . .

The essence of all that has been said and written on the subject is that only those interests of the highest order and those not otherwise served can overbalance legitimate claims to the free exercise of religion. We can accept it as settled, therefore, that, however strong the State's interest in universal compulsory education, it is by no means absolute to the exclusion or subordination of all other interests. . . .

We come then to the quality of the claims of the respondents concerning the alleged encroachment of Wisconsin's compulsory school-attendance statute on their rights and the rights of their children to the free exercise of the religious beliefs they and their forebears have adhered to for almost three centuries. In evaluating those claims we must be careful to determine whether the Amish religious faith and their mode of life are, as they claim, inseparable and interdependent. A way of life, however virtuous and admirable, may not be interposed as a barrier to reasonable state regulation of education if it is based on purely secular considerations; to have the protection of the Religion Clauses, the claims must be rooted in religious belief. Although a determination of what is a "religious" belief or practice entitled to constitutional protection may present a most delicate question, the very concept of ordered liberty precludes allowing every person to make his own standards on matters of conduct in which society as a whole has important interests. Thus, if the Amish asserted their claims because of their subjective evaluation and rejection of the contemporary secular values accepted by the majority, much as Thoreau rejected the social values of his time and isolated himself at Walden Pond, their claims would not rest on a religious basis. Thoreau's choice was philosophical and personal rather than religious, and such belief does not rise to the demands of the Religion Clauses.

Giving no weight to such secular considerations, however, we see that the record in this case abundantly supports the claim that the traditional way of life of the Amish is not merely a matter of personal preference, but one of deep religious conviction, shared by an organized group, and intimately related to daily living. . . .

The impact of the compulsory-attendance law on respondents' practice of the Amish religion is not only severe, but inescapable, for the Wisconsin law affirmatively compels them, under threat of criminal sanction, to perform acts undeniably at odds with fundamental tenets of their religious beliefs. . . . Nor is the impact of the compulsory-attendance law confined to grave interference with important Amish religious tenets from a subjective point of view. It carries with it precisely the kind of objective danger to the free exercise of religion that the First Amendment was designed to prevent. As the record shows, compulsory school attendance to age 16 for Amish children carries with it a very real threat of undermining the Amish community and religious practice as they exist today; they must either abandon belief and be assimilated into society at large, or be forced to migrate to some other and more tolerant region.

In sum, the unchallenged testimony of acknowledged experts in education and religious history, almost 300 years of consistent practice, and strong evidence of a sustained faith pervading and regulating respondents' entire mode of life support the claim that enforcement of the States' requirement of compulsory formal education after the eighth grade would gravely endanger if not destroy the free exercise of respondents' religious beliefs.

. . . .

[This case cannot] be disposed of on the grounds that Wisconsin's requirement for school attendance to age 16 applies uniformly to all citizens of the State and does not, on its face, discriminate against religions or a particular religion, or that it is motivated by legitimate secular concerns. A regulation neutral on its face may, in its application, nonetheless offend the constitutional requirement for governmental neutrality if it unduly burdens the free exercise of religion. *Sherbert* v. *Verner* [1963]; *Walz* v. *Tax Commission* (1970). The Court must not ignore the danger that an exception from a general obligation of citizenship on religious grounds may run afoul of the Establishment Clause, but that danger cannot be allowed to prevent any exception no matter how vital it may be to the protection of values promoted by the right of free exercise. . . .

The State advances two primary arguments in support of its system of compulsory education. It notes, as Thomas Jefferson pointed out early in our history, that some degree of education is necessary to prepare citizens to participate effectively and intelligently in our open political system if we are to preserve freedom and independence. Further, education prepares individuals to be self-reliant and self-sufficient participants in society. We accept these propositions.

. . . .

The State attacks respondents' position as one fostering "ignorance" from which the child must be protected by the State. No one can question the State's duty to protect children from ignorance but this argument does not square with the facts disclosed in the record. Whatever their idiosyncrasies as seen by the majority, this record strongly shows that the Amish community has been a highly successful social unit within our society, even if apart from the conventional "mainstream." Its members are productive and very law-abiding members of society; they reject public welfare in any of its usual modern forms. The Congress itself recognized their self-sufficiency by authorizing exemption of such groups as the Amish from the obligation to pay social security taxes.

The State, however, supports its interest in providing an additional one to two years of compulsory high school education to Amish children because of the possibility that some such children will choose to leave the Amish community, and that if this occurs they will be ill-equipped for life. The State argues that if Amish children leave their church they should not be in the position of making their way in the world without the education available in the one or two additional years the State requires. However, on this record, that argument is highly speculative. There is no specific evidence of the loss of Amish adherents by attrition, nor is there any showing that upon leaving the Amish community Amish children, with their practical agricultural training and habits of industry and self-reliance, would become burdens on society because of educational shortcomings. . . .

There is nothing in this record to suggest that the Amish qualities of reliability, self-reliance, and dedication to work would fail to find ready markets in today's society. Absent some contrary evidence supporting the State's position, we are unwilling to assume that persons possessing such valuable vocational skills and habits are doomed to become burdens on society should they determine to leave the Amish faith, nor is there any basis in the record to warrant a finding that an additional one or two years of formal school education beyond the eighth grade would serve to eliminate any such problem that might exist.

Insofar as the State's claim rests on the view that a brief additional period of formal education is imperative to enable the Amish to participate effectively and intelligently in our democratic process, it must fall. The Amish alternative to formal secondary school education has enabled them to function effectively in their day-to-day life under self-imposed limitations on relations with the world, and to survive and prosper in contemporary society as a separate, sharply identifiable and highly self-sufficient community for more than 200 years in this country. In itself this is strong evidence that they are capable of fulfilling the social and political responsibilities of citizenship without compelled attendance beyond the eighth grade at the price of jeopardizing their free exercise of religious belief. . . .

. . . The independence and successful social functioning of the Amish community for a period approaching almost three centuries and more than 200 years in this country are strong evidence that there is at best a speculative gain, in terms of meeting the duties of citizenship, from an additional one or two years of compulsory formal education.

Against this background it would require a more particularized showing from the State on this point to justify the severe interference with religious freedom such additional compulsory attendance would entail.

. . . .

The requirement of compulsory schooling to age 16 must therefore be viewed as aimed not merely at providing educational opportunities for children, but as an alternative to the equally undesirable consequence of unhealthful child labor displacing adult workers, or, on the other hand, forced idleness. The two kinds of statutes — compulsory school attendance and child labor laws — tend to keep children of certain ages off the labor market and in school; this regimen in turn provides opportunity to prepare for a livelihood of a higher order than that which children could pursue without education and protects their health in adolescence.

In these terms, Wisconsin's interest in compelling the school attendance of Amish children to age 16 emerges as somewhat less substantial than requiring such attendance for children generally. For, while agricultural employment is not totally outside the legitimate concerns of the child labor laws, employment of children under parental guidance and on the family farm from age 14 to age 16 is an ancient tradition that lies at the periphery of the objectives of such laws. There is no intimation that the Amish employment of their children on family farms is in any way deleterious to their health or that Amish parents exploit children at tender years. . . .

Finally, the State, on authority of *Prince* v. *Massachusetts,* argues that a decision exempting Amish children from the State's requirement fails to recognize the substantive right of the Amish child to a secondary education, and fails to give due regard to the power of the State as *parens patriae* to extend the benefit of secondary education to children regardless of the wishes of their parents. . . .

This case, of course, is not one in which any harm to the physical or mental health of the child or to the public safety, peace, order, or welfare has been demonstrated or may be properly inferred. The record is to the contrary, and any reliance on that theory would find no support in the evidence.

Contrary to the suggestion of the dissenting opinion of MR. JUSTICE DOUGLAS, our holding today in no degree depends on the assertion of the religious interest of the child as contrasted with that of the parents. It is the parents who are subject to prosecution here for failing to cause their children to attend school, and it is their right of free exercise, not that of their children, that must determine Wisconsin's power to impose criminal penalties on the parent. The dissent argues that a child who expresses a desire to attend public high school in conflict with the wishes of his parents should not be prevented from doing so. There is no reason for the Court to consider that point since it is not an issue in the case. The children are not parties to this litigation. The State has at no point tried this case on the theory that respondents were preventing their children from attending school against their expressed desires, and indeed the record is to the contrary. The State's position from the outset has been that it is empowered to apply its compulsory-attendance law to Amish parents in the same manner as to other parents — that is, without regard to the wishes of the child. That is the claim we reject today.

Our holding in no way determines the proper resolution of possible competing interests of parents, children, and the State in an appropriate state court proceeding in which the power of the State is asserted on the theory that Amish parents are preventing their minor children from attending high school despite their expressed desires to the contrary. . . .

In the face of our consistent emphasis on the central values underlying the Religion Clauses in our constitutional scheme of government, we cannot accept a *parens patriae* claim of such all-encompassing scope and with such sweeping potential for broad and unforeseeable application as that urged by the State.

. . . . Our disposition of this case, however, in no way alters our recognition of the obvious fact that courts are not school boards or legislatures, and are ill-equipped to determine the "necessity" of discrete aspects of a State's program of compulsory education. This should suggest that courts must move with great circumspection in performing the sensitive and delicate task of weighing a State's legitimate social concern when faced with religious claims for exemption from generally applicable educational requirements. It cannot be overemphasized that we are not dealing with a way of life and mode of education by a group claiming to have recently discovered some "progressive" or more enlightened process for rearing children for modern life.

Aided by a history of three centuries as an identifiable religious sect and a long history as a successful and self-sufficient segment of American society, the Amish in this case have convincingly demonstrated the sincerity of their religious beliefs, the interrelationship of belief with their mode of life, the vital role that belief and daily conduct play in the continued survival of Old Order Amish communities and their religious organization, and the hazards presented by the State's enforcement of a statute generally valid as to others. Beyond this, they have carried the even more difficult burden of demonstrating the adequacy of their alternative mode of continuing informal vocational education in terms of precisely those overall interests that the State advances in support of its program of compulsory high school education. In light of this convincing showing, one that probably few other religious groups or sects could make, and weighing the minimal difference between what the State would require and what the Amish already accept, it was incumbent on the State to show with more particularity how its admittedly strong interest in compulsory education would be adversely affected by granting an exemption to the Amish. *Sherbert* v. *Verner, supra.*

Nothing we hold is intended to undermine the general applicability of the State's compulsory school-attendance statutes or to limit the power of the State to promulgate reasonable standards that, while not impairing the free exercise of religion, provide for continuing agricultural vocational education under parental and church guidance by the Old Order Amish or others similarly situated. The States have had a long history of amicable and effective relationships with church-sponsored schools, and there is no basis for assuming that, in this related context, reasonable standards cannot be established concerning the content of the continuing vocational education of Amish children under parental guidance, provided always that state regulations are not inconsistent with what we have said in this opinion.

Affirmed.

MR. JUSTICE POWELL and MR. JUSTICE REHNQUIST took no part in the consideration or decision of this case.

[JUSTICES STEWART, WHITE, and BRENNAN concurred.]

MR. JUSTICE DOUGLAS, dissenting in part.

I agree with the Court that the religious scruples of the Amish are opposed to the education of their children beyond the grade schools, yet I disagree with the Court's conclusion that the matter is within the dispensation of parents alone. The Court's analysis assumes that the only interests at stake in the case are those of the Amish parents on the one hand, and those of the State on the other. The difficulty with this approach is that, despite the Court's claim, the parents are seeking to vindicate not only their own free exercise claims, but also those of their high-school-age children.

It is argued that the right of the Amish children to religious freedom is not presented by the facts of the case, as the issue before the Court involves only the Amish parents' religious freedom to defy a state criminal statute imposing upon them an affirmative duty to cause their children to attend high school.

First, respondents' motion to dismiss in the trial court expressly asserts, not only the religious liberty of the adults, but also that of the children, as a defense to the prosecutions. It is, of course, beyond question that the parents have standing as defendants in a criminal prosecution to assert the religious interests of their children as a defense. Although the lower courts and a majority of this Court assume an identity of interest between parent and child, it is clear that they have treated the religious interest of the child as a factor in the analysis.

Second, it is essential to reach the question to decide the case, not only because the question was squarely raised in the motion to dismiss, but also because no analysis of religious-liberty claims can take place in a vacuum. If the parents in this case are allowed a religious exemption, the inevitable effect is to impose the parents' notions of religious duty upon their children. Where the child is mature enough to express potentially conflicting desires, it would be an invasion of the child's rights to permit such an imposition without canvassing his views. As in *Prince* v. *Massachusetts,* . . . it is an imposition resulting from this very litigation. As the child has no other effective forum, it is in this litigation that his rights should be considered. And, if an Amish child desires to attend high school, and is mature enough to have that desire respected, the State may well be able to override the parents' religiously motivated objections.

. . . .

These children are "persons" within the meaning of the Bill of Rights. We have so held over and over again. In *Haley* v. *Ohio,* 332 U.S. 596, we extended the protection of the Fourteenth Amendment in a state trial of a 15-year-old boy. In *In re Gault,* 387 U.S. 1, 13, we held that "neither the Fourteenth Amendment nor the Bill of Rights is for adults alone." In *In re Winship,* 397 U.S. 358, we held that a 12-year-old boy, when charged with an act which would be a crime if committed by an adult, was entitled to procedural safeguards contained in the Sixth Amendment.

In *Tinker* v. *Des Moines School District,* we dealt with 13-year-old, 15-year-old, and 16-year-old students who wore armbands to public schools and were disciplined for doing so. . . .

On this important and vital matter of education, I think the children should be entitled to be heard.

While the parents, absent dissent, normally speak for the entire family, the education of the child is a matter on which the child will often have decided views. He may want to be a pianist or an astronaut or an oceanographer. To do so he will have to break from the Amish tradition.

It is the future of the student, not the future of the parents, that is imperiled by today's decision. . . .

The views of the two children in question were not canvassed by the Wisconsin courts. The matter should be explicitly reserved so that new hearings can be held on remand of the case.

CHAPTER 8

Freedom of Expression in America's First 150 Years: A Meager History

Freedom of Expression in America's First 150 Years

The First Amendment looms so large in contemporary constitutional law that we have a tendency to project the same centrality onto our entire history. In fact, almost all of the litigation and political discussion of the Amendment took place in the twentieth century. Even the philosophy of its interpretation is principally a product of the past half-century or so.

The Amendment was part of a package introduced as the last compromise of the Constitution. Led by Madison, a member of the first House of Representatives, the Jeffersonians packaged the reservations attached to the Constitution by the various state conventions, and Congress presented them as prospective amendments. Two did not survive the state process of ratification, while the First Amendment quite accidentally survived at the top of the list.

How far did the Founders intend to go with provisions in the Bill of Rights? To what degree did they expect the judiciary to sit in judgment on laws alleged to violate freedom of speech and press? As with other aspects of judicial review, we can only guess. But Jefferson, then ambassador to France, urged Madison to labor for a Bill of Rights precisely because of "the legal check it puts in the hands of the Judiciary."

Zechariah Chafee, Jr., the author of the first attempt at delineating the history of freedom of the press, concluded that the Founders intended to change radically the common law on this question. More recent scholarship, particularly Leonard Levy's magisterial *Legacy of Suppression*, has rendered that conclusion most doubtful. The pre-Revolutionary period was a transitional one for British law; still on the books were requirements for governmental approval before publication of any printed material. (Indeed, the British government's last effort to suppress a book for not having a license was aimed at Thomas Paine's *Rights of Man* in 1792.) According to Blackstone, the classic legal writer looked upon as authority for legal terms, freedom of the press meant simply the absence of licensing. Examining all kinds of discussions, Levy finds no evidence that leaders, thinkers, and lawyers wanted to go beyond this step — the elimination of censorship, "prior restraint" — and his research shows that subsequent punishment was left to the discretion of the legislature. Levy's historical evidence is impressive and, on the whole, convincing.

But there remains a vital problem. The draftsman of the First Amendment paralleled freedom of the press with freedom of speech. The latter was an even murkier concept. Certainly "prior restraint," or licensing, has no meaning in the context of speech. If the Founders really intended to be conservative, they somehow missed the mark. Furthermore, as Levy emphasizes in his second edition, the practice of editors in Colonial America as well as under the Republic was to permit robust discussion.

The offhand adoption of the First Amendment was followed rather quickly by one of the more intense periods of exploration of its meaning. The emergence of political parties challenged the Founders' sense of democratic governance. Federalists in control of the national government enacted the Alien and Sedition Acts, designed to hamper and imprison their Democratic opponents. Jeffersonians in control of state governments prosecuted Federalist editors who criticized "democracy." Levy's *Legacy of Suppression* argues that it is the failure of mutual suppression that taught us tolerance. As NEW YORK TIMES CO. V. SULLIVAN (1964) suggests: "This is the lesson to be drawn from the great controversy over the Sedition Act of 1798 (1 Stat. 596) which first crystallized a national awareness of the central meaning of the First Amendment."

Though trials were held under the Alien and Sedition Acts, the constitutional issue was fought out in the political arena, not the judicial. Holmes, in his dissent in *Abrams,* suggested that Congress

had inferentially declared the Acts unconstitutional by remitting the fines involved, a judgment echoed in NEW YORK TIMES V. SULLIVAN, the first opinion of the Supreme Court that ever indicated the Alien and Sedition Acts violated the First Amendment.

Debate over major issues in our history did spill over into First Amendment concerns throughout the nineteenth century, but, as with the Alien and Sedition Acts, controversy was largely confined to congressional and political dispute. The slavery controversy, in particular, provided legal quandaries of considerable moment. For example, Congress refused even to receive Abolitionist petitions. John Quincy Adams, a former president who accepted service in the House of Representatives, pressed the issue within Congress. But no one in those times would have thought it reasonable to coerce Congress through litigation to obey the clear mandate of the First Amendment, which guarantees the right of petition. Another issue was the right of postmasters to prohibit "incendiary" material, forbidden by states, in the U.S. Mail. This essentially anti-Abolitionist regulation was debated largely on the question of governmental authority over the mails, rather than on First Amendment grounds. The "freedom" argument was weakened in that the federal government was making no judgment about the materials. That judgment was made by state governments, which, under BARRON V. BALTIMORE (1833), had no First Amendment limitations. (In 1878 and in 1892 the Court sustained similar legislation involving the use of the mails for lottery information.)

Civil War cases also had no important First Amendment ramifications. They centered on the issues of military authority over civilians and the suspension of the writ of habeas corpus.

Some turn-of-the-century Syndicalist trials could have been free speech cases by modern standards. The notion of preventing the overthrow of the government was so ingrained as to make the opinions cursory. Many of them involved the question of whether states were bound by the Fourteenth Amendment to grant political freedoms. The answer here was uniform. As late as 1922, only three years before its complete about-face, the Court reasserted that "neither the Fourteenth Amendment nor any other provision... imposes on the States any restrictions about 'freedom of speech' or the 'liberty of silence'" (*Prudential Insurance* v. *Cheek*, 1922).

It was, then, on a largely blank slate that the Court was forced to write its First Amendment philosophy when World War I witnessed extensive federal efforts to enforce regulations designed to prevent opposition to conscription. In its first cases, the Court turned to Justice Holmes as spokesman and embraced his formula, "clear and present danger," as providing adequate protection for *both* expression and defense of law and order.

Adapting a similar formulation from his important lectures *The Common Law,* Holmes noted the problem in classic terms. Words are the vehicles of expression and, as such, to be protected. But they are also the "triggers to action." They can be precipitants or "components of crimes." As pure expression, they are protected. As triggers or part of action, they are regulatable. But the boundary zone is poorly demarcated. The boundary problems could be solved if the dangers from words were manifest and imminent — "clear and present" — providing margins of safety for both speakers and society. The test has proven less clear and less persuasive, both for the justices and for others, than when it was beguilingly presented by Holmes. Interestingly, however, the Supreme Court in the 1980s has come back to it for many purposes, after many detours and byways.

So long as Holmes and Brandeis joined in holding that the clear-and-present-danger test justified punishment, the conservative majority followed their leadership. But when, in *Abrams* v. *U.S.* (1919), Holmes and Brandeis felt the test pointed to release of the defendants, the majority went their own way. Here, and in WHITNEY V. CALIFORNIA (1927), the majority mechanically found the statute involved constitutional rights without much articulation of standards.

But in GITLOW V. NEW YORK (1925), the Court's majority made two antithetical contributions. By far the most important aspect of the case is its remarkable and stunningly casual announcement that for "present purposes we may and do assume that freedom of speech and of the press" were protected by federal courts, as limits on state governments. Why the majority so sharply shifted from the language of *Prudential* v. *Cheek* has never been explained, and this remarkable event, which has sharply changed constitutional law and even our whole society, has never been adequately given its historical due.

Justice Sanford also formulated what has been labelled the "bad tendency" test. Speech may be suppressed if it presents a serious danger or has a tendency to create evils. Words, he suggested, can ignite future, as well as present, dangers. The state should not be compelled to balance things nicely in "a jeweler's scale." The rational possibility of a spark's igniting a flame of rebellion was sufficient justification for legislative action. The tendency to provoke evil, even distant evil, justified suppression.

Holmes' dissents in *Abrams* and GITLOW, and Brandeis' concurrence in WHITNEY, challenged the bad-tendency test, pointing out, as Holmes said, that "every idea is an incitement." The test was one of fear alone, said Brandeis, and fear was not much of a test; men feared witches and should not cripple speech by irrational fear. While legal opinion heavily favored the Holmes-Brandeis test, the Taft Court did not alter the bad-tendency test.

But the advent of Chief Justice Hughes brought a new tone to civil liberties decisions. In NEAR V. MINNESOTA (1931), the Chief Justice spoke for a Court divided 5 to 4 in invalidating a Minnesota statute that permitted the state to padlock papers judged a "public nuisance." Hughes emphasized the conclusion that this was effectively "prior restraint," that is, censorship. Carefully noting that even prior restraint was not absolutely forbidden (e.g., prohibition of troop ship departure dates in wartime), Hughes emphasized the desire of the

Founders to end licensing, and suggested this was a core concept to understanding and defending the First Amendment.

By 1937, the Court had grown stronger in its commitment to liberty. In *Herndon* v. *Lowry,* a Georgia conviction of a Communist organizer under its anti-Syndicalist statute was reversed. The jury, Justice Roberts emphasized, had not been instructed to examine whether the organizer's activities amounted to "a clear and present danger of forcible obstruction of a particular State function." Not only were Holmes and Brandeis vindicated; for the first time in our history the First Amendment had been used to defend an avowed critic of society. Furthermore, as in NEAR, First Amendment limitations had been applied to state enactments to exonerate defendants.

Other major opinions by the Hughes Court supporting freedom of expression include *Stromberg* v. *California* (1931); *Grosjean* v. *American Press Co.* (1936), involving punitive newspaper taxes; *Hague* v. *CIO* (1939), establishing a public right to use parks and streets for purposes of expression; *Lovell* v. *Griffin* (1938); and *Schneider* v. *Irvington* (1939), involving handbill distribution. A new productive era of First Amendment primacy had begun.

The Crisis of "Clear and Present Danger"

It was quickly evident that the simplicity of Holmes' test was delusive. Many free expression matters were not solved by it. Civil liberties advocates like Roger Baldwin, Founder of the American Civil Liberties Union, refused to accept it at all, feeling expression should always be exempt from control unless violence or other evil actually occurred—not because some danger seemed likely. In many areas, such as obscenity, film censorship, libel, and slander, the Court was not sure how far to apply its new concept. And in other areas it became obvious that the boundary between word and deed was inherently ambiguous. The liberal Stone Court that resulted from the post-1937 appointments quickly became fragmented on many of these issues. The Vinson Court was to fail entirely.

The first sign of trouble was the terribly divisive struggle over the flag-salute cases. Frankfurter, in both *Minersville School District* v. *Gobitis* and WEST VIRGINIA STATE BOARD OF EDUCATION V. BARNETTE (1943), persisted in treating the issue as a request for exemption from a regulation on religious freedom grounds, and Stone had essentially argued the children of Jehovah's Witnesses had such a right of conscience. Jackson, in BARNETTE, argued the flag salute was an invasion of the right of nonexpression, and that it could not be required at all. If that analysis were accepted, no clear and present danger was ascertainable, even with a high-powered microscope. Yet Frankfurter, wrapped in the Holmes-Brandeis tradition, was unyielding. Brandeis, still alive but retired to the side lines, held an enigmatic silence as his disciples tore at each other.

Again, the Vinson Court faced two classic cases involving hostile crowds and the problem of how far police could go to control them. Splitting the difference, they accepted the police evaluation in the case of an outdoor speaker (whose conviction for refusal to stand down when ordered by police was upheld by three New York Courts (FEINER V. NEW YORK, 1951), but rejected conviction of a racist demagogue accused of fomenting trouble by his speech (TERMINIELLO V. CHICAGO, 1949). Yet there was considerably more turmoil involved in the Chicago case, and, in effect, Feiner was not merely fined, but also prevented from speaking. The Court split badly in its interpretation of the formula, and non-Court commentary, even when it was friendly, was puzzled by the mode of interpretation.

In one area the Court found its analysis confounded by the clear-and-present-danger test, and worked its way through to a new approach. That area was peaceful picketing. In *Thornhill* v. *Alabama* (1940), Murphy proclaimed that "the facts of a labor dispute must be regarded as within that area of free discussion that is guaranteed by the Constitution."

But this was quickly followed by a case where the Court limited picketing because of previous violence, *Milk Wagon Drivers Union* v. *Meadowmoor Dairies* (1941). The following year, Justice Douglas rationalized the sustaining of greater restriction permitted in labor cases, pointing out that "picketing is more than free speech," since picketing involves occupation of physical space and often suggests or threatens physical action (*Bakery and Pastry Drivers* v. *Wohl,* 1942).

This recognition that speech could be wrapped in action, and not merely be a prelude thereto, was an analytic understanding that went beyond Holmes' original insight. It was to prove useful, especially to Justice Black in his quest for "absolutism," but also to the majority in dealing with "symbolic speech" and other more modern controversies.

The Stone and Vinson Courts largely sidestepped other issues that would probably not have survived examination under clear-and-present-danger regulation of obscenity and censorship of movies. In *Winters* v. *New York* (1948), the Court found New York's effort to modernize and limit older standards like "lewd" and "indecent" void for vagueness. *Burstyn* v. *Wilson* (1952) found movies within the orbit of the First Amendment and voided banning of the movie "The Miracle" under a standard prohibiting "sacrilege." By making these liberal but basically unobjectionable interpretations, the justices avoided coming to grips with the question of why control in these areas was exempt from the standards elsewhere. Commonsense distinction by areas was not merely used to weight the different considerations (e.g., a movie might be held to constitute a "clearer

danger" because of its graphic quality), but was rather a constitutional conclusion by which no weighting was done at all. Eventually this caught up with the Court, and was dealt with, yielding quite different results.

The most significant failure, however, was the Court's inability to develop reasonable protection for core values of freedom of expression during the Communist scare of the late 1940s and early 1950s — its failure, in any important way, to thwart what is now referred to as "McCarthyism." This disillusioned supporters such as Justice Black, who was to abandon the clear-and-present-danger test, and ultimately convert Justice Douglas, as well.

In the years 1950–1952, the Court had its opportunities to deal with antisubversion measures, and sustained virtually all of the major programs, no matter how far-reaching.

Loyalty oaths for state officials were sustained in a series of cases. These included a requirement of an oath that one was not a member of the Communist Party (*Garner* v. *Board of Public Works,* 1951), or not "subversive persons" (*Gerende* v. *Board of Supervisors,* 1951). An oath that one was not a member of any organization on the Attorney General's List of Subversive Organizations was invalidated because it did not exempt those who innocently joined the organization (*Wieman* v. *Updegraff,* 1952). It was not until the late 1960s and 1970s that the Court was to invalidate punishment for merely knowing affiliation, without a showing of individual disloyalty or illegality.

Similarly, the Court upheld state laws designed to remove public officials for membership in a Communist organization. The main targets were teachers who had taken political stands. This was upheld in *Adler* v. *Board of Education* (1952) on the grounds that teachers were in a sensitive position. (This case was overruled in 1967 in *Keyishian* v. *Board of Regents.*)

Invocation of the Fifth Amendment before a congressional committee investigating Communism was held to be an impermissible ground for dismissal. However, the employer's rights to ask about Communist affiliation and to discharge employees not answering were upheld in *Lerner* v. *Casey* and *Beilan* v. *Board of Public Education* (1958). In one case a school teacher was involved, and in the other a subway conductor, transit being solemnly declared by the Civil Service Commission to be a "security agency."

Only in NAACP V. ALABAMA (1958) and in *Shelton* v. *Tucker* (1960) was the Court, in these years, protective of rights of association. The NAACP, of course, is a fairly conservative civil rights organization, although in these years Deep South officials were convinced it was in league with Communists, if not the devil. In NAACP V. ALABAMA, the Court ruled the right of association was constitutionally protected, and the state's request for a full roster of its members had to be reasonably adjusted to the state's need to know. (Although the Court did not dwell on it, the likelihood of harassment of known members of the NAACP was great — by both private segregationists and state officials.) Applying these principles in *Shelton,* the justices held an Arkansas requirement that every teacher list all memberships every year was unconstitutional. Its "unlimited and excessive sweep" was not justified by any state need. (Together with later cases, such as *Elfbrandt* v. *Russell* (1966), *Shelton* casts strong doubt on the validity of most of the 1950s decisions we have just reviewed.)

At the federal level, the justices were, if anything, more deferential to congressionally enacted restrictions. In *ACA* v. *Douds* (1950), the Court dealt with the non-Communist oath requirements of the Taft-Hartley Act (1947). This modification of the Wagner National Labor Relations Act required leaders of a union to file an affidavit of non-membership in the Communist Party if the union wished to use the good offices of the National Labor Relations Board.

The Court sustained the statute. Admitting that it did constitute a limitation on free affiliation, the opinion by Chief Justice Vinson also noted that strikes by Communist unions were a common political tactic in other countries, and Congress might therefore move to limit Communist control.

The oath, in any event, proved ineffective; Communist unionists apparently resigned from the Party and signed or perjured themselves. It was repealed in 1959, and a new provision made it a crime for a Communist member to serve as a union leader. In *U.S.* v. *Brown* (1965), this was invalidated as a bill of attainder.

The ultimate issue was joined in DENNIS V. U.S. (1951). The case involved prosecution of eleven prominent leaders of the Communist Party for violation of the Smith Act of 1940. (Ironically, the Communist Party had helped promote that statute to hamper Trotskyite leaders of rival unions.) The leaders were indicted for (1) conspiring to organize a group to advocate overthrow, or (2) advocating and teaching the duty or desirability of overthrowing the government.

Admittedly, there were no overt acts other than conspiring, and organizing. The Government's case was that Communist parties *would* advocate overthrow, since this was Party doctrine. But no evidence that the Communist Party did so in contemporary terms was advanced.

Therefore, Judge Learned Hand restated the clear-and-present-danger test to allow serious evils to be less than imminent, and the majority opinion by Chief Justice Vinson accepted his modification. This test — the gravity of the evil discounted by its improbability — was not clearly distinguishable from the bad-tendency test and shattered any precision at all in the Holmes approach. Jackson's concurrence suggested that was a fact of life. Clear and *present* danger could be used to judge street-corner and other minor violations. For serious constitutional problems, such as the degree of danger from Communism, only popular opinion can be decisive. The judicial process simply is not adequate to a trial of such far-flung issues. As Edmund Cahn pointed out, Jackson's view is that judicial review of First Amendment violations is required, but when it is needed most, it will not be there.

The DENNIS decision was not well received and was quickly recognized as judicial surrender to a temporary public panic. In YATES V. U.S. (1957), the Court undid the damage, in a deft decision by Justice Harlan which, by technical construction of the statute, made it unusable as a vehicle for further prosecution of Communists for membership alone.

It also redefined the formula used to guide juries in such cases, contending that Judge Medina's charge in DENNIS V. U.S. was adequate, but that the charge in YATES had not adequately emphasized the need for "advocacy, for accomplishment."

What is striking is the absence of reference to clear and present danger or any of the familiar formulae. The standard had been inadequate to its most significant test. It was time for an agonizing reappraisal.

The Modern Era of First Amendment Litigation: Approaches

The Carolene Products Footnote

The modern approach to liberty and judicial intervention is easily traced to Justice Stone's remarkable footnote in the CAROLENE PRODUCTS case in 1938. The essence of the approach is in its partial answer to democratic doubts, the non-majoritarian nature of the judicial process. Judges, the footnote suggests, act when majority rule breaks down—for example, to preserve the democratic process itself when censorship or voting distortions tend to prevent majorities from ruling, or to protect minorities unable to vindicate themselves.

This appealing concept had behind it Stone's authority and Hughes' powerful backing. Only a year and a half later, in *Schneider* v. *Irvington* (1939), Roberts, speaking for the entire Court except McReynolds, suggested that "mere legislative preferences or beliefs respecting matters of public convenience may well support regulation directed at other personal activities, but be insufficient to justify such as diminishes the exercise of rights so vital to the maintenance of democratic institutions." Frankfurter concurred, and the Court seemed to be forging a new approach around a new consensus.

All of this broke down, probably as a result of the fight over the flag-salute cases. The more libertarian of the Roosevelt justices joined ranks under the banner of "preferred freedoms," while the others insisted the Constitution had no second-class provisions.

Preferred Freedoms: A Doctrine for a Decade, but an Enduring Idea

In dissenting in *Jones* v. *Opelika* (1942), Stone first employed the term "preferred freedoms," applying it to the First Amendment protections of speech and religion. When that decision was reversed in *Murdock* v. *Pennsylvania* (1943), the iteration of this point was also made in the majority opinion. In two dozen cases or so over the next twelve years, the term was to be used by seven different justices, and was dispositive of at least nine cases before the Court.

Yet Frankfurter, in *Kovacs* v. *Cooper* (1949), called the approach "mischievous" and denied that a majority had ever endorsed the doctrine. That statement was at best pettifogging, and objectively misleading. Why should Frankfurter have been so provoked by a formula so close to some of his own or of his idol, Brandeis? To this day it is hard to give a satisfactory answer.

The preferred freedoms concept was never a repudiation of the notion of clear and present danger, but was seen as giving its purposes a firmer base and texture—incorporating it much as Einsteinian physics incorporates Newtonian. Both operated on the assumption that the Constitution, in balancing the scales on legislation, had registered strong preference for freedom. In ordinary cases, legislation is assumed to be constitutional, with deference given to congressional wisdom. Less deference is given in the domain of civil liberties. In *St. Joseph Stockyards Co.* v. *U.S.* (1936), two years before the CAROLENE footnote, Brandeis had assembled a host of cases proving much the same point. Frankfurter acquiesced in the opinion in *Schneider* v. *Irvington;* he wrote of the need for the judiciary to look at measures affecting free speech with "a jealous eye," and spoke of the "momentum of respect lacking" for legislation attacking "indispensable conditions for an open society," as opposed to ordinary legislation. The difference seems almost to lie in the choice of metaphors.

The extent to which preferred freedoms is enmeshed in clear-and-present-danger notions is remarkably captured by what Herman Pritchett calls "perhaps the strongest statement" of this concept by Rutledge, in *Thomas* v. *Collins* (1945):

> Any attempt to restrict those liberties must be justified by clear public interest, threatened not doubtfully or remotely, but by clear and present danger. The rational connection between the remedy provided and the evil to be curbed, which in other contexts might support legislation against attack on due process grounds, will not suffice. These rights rest on firmer foundation. Accordingly, whatever occasion would restrain orderly discussion and persuasion, at appropriate time and place, must have clear support in public danger, actual or impending. Only the gravest abuses, endangering paramount interests, give occasion for permissible limitation.

Rising Court support for preferred freedoms drove Frankfurter to argue that Holmes did not really intend clear and present danger to be a test of legislative constitutionality, or a legal doctrine at all. And Jackson argued that preference would create a complicated hierarchy of rights — a contention given some credence by Murphy's suggestions (in dissent), in *Jones* v. *Opelika,* that religious freedom was to be preferred to all other preferred freedoms.

In the end, the problem seems to have been that the notion has no real bite and suggests no degree of preference. It is capable of being reconciled with a slightly more rigorous look at legislation, curbing rights, by viewing all such legislation as presumptively unconstitutional, or even the absolutist position where facts are irrelevant. When the DENNIS challenge came, the justices had to reiterate the clear-and-present-danger test and give their reasons for it. Given the anger the notion of preferred freedoms aroused in some justices, and its real lack of independent utility in difficult cases, its advocates came to conclude that the idea was not worth fighting for, since its basic ambiguity clung to it in applied situations as well. Preferred freedoms became something of a liability in the effort to expand the protection of free expression, since it engendered disagreement even where there was considerable consensus.

Absolutism in Scholarly Discussion: The Work of Alexander Meiklejohn

The only modern rival to the CAROLENE footnote is the work of a philosopher whose legal competence and historical competence were both questionable, though perhaps crucial. Alexander Meiklejohn, a philosopher and university administrator, in his work *Free Speech and its Relationship to Self-Government,* relied on the actual wording of the First Amendment, the functioning of discussion in the political system, analogies to the town meeting, and an analysis of the relationship of ruler and ruled in a democracy.

Meiklejohn placed great emphasis on the precise wording of the First Amendment. Congress was prohibited from any and all abridgements of freedom of speech. This was, he reasoned, intentional. Speech, press, and assembly, he argued, constituted political freedom, the process by which society makes up its mind. That process is in democracy unlimited, just as speakers in a town meeting may speak back and forth on any issue.

Meiklejohn also called attention to the wording, parallelism, and function of congressional immunity. What members of Congress say in their governmental capacity is exempt, so that they may exercise their authority to the hilt. So, too, said Meiklejohn, the citizens in their sovereign capacities must not be answerable or limited. Absolutism was required because it seeks to perfect the "thinking process of the community."

Initially, Meiklejohn distinguished sharply between public speech — on political issues — and private communication, cultural discussions, and personal matters. Political speech was protected absolutely under the First Amendment. Other speech was protected under the Fifth Amendment (for national purposes) and the Fourteenth (for state purposes), but was regulatable provided due process standards were met.

Meiklejohn was heavily criticized for eliminating intellectual freedom from first-class protection, and he subsequently decided academic thought also was "political freedom." This was reassuring to his fellow professors, but underscored the fact that Meiklejohn was spinning his own whole cloth.

Meiklejohn also had provided hope to libertarians that his "two-tier" approach to expression could permit broad protection for general communication while permitting pockets of more restriction by isolating less useful speech. The possibility was that obscenity regulation, libel laws, and even movie censorship might survive by finding these to be different in kind from other forms of expression. Meiklejohn's facile reassignment of academic freedom made it clear that the "boundary" between his vital speech and private speech was at least arbitrary and probably nonexistent. Justice Brennan almost certainly was influenced by Meiklejohn's notions of types or areas of speech in his majority opinion in Roth v. U.S. (1957), finding obscenity not free speech, just as Black and Douglas were influenced by his absolutism. Brennan's sixteen years with the notion of areas were to end with his confession that the approach was a failure. Both experience and argument seem to have demonstrated the two-tier approach cannot bear water.

There is also virtually no historical support for Meiklejohn's interesting speculation as to what the Founders would have believed had they been social utilitarians half a century ahead of their time. The legal framework is even creakier. And yet Meiklejohn's insight into democratic society is most instructive, and the social stake in free speech is clarified by his discussion. Finally, his term "political freedom" and the frame of thought that went with it has had considerable influence. Yet Meiklejohn would loom as an interesting, if irrelevant, thinker if Justice Black had not been captivated by his audacity.

Absolutism on the Supreme Court: The Black-Douglas Heresy

For Justice Black to embrace a "wild" theory was quite different from such a move by even a prominent philosopher. A judge's doctrinal whims directly affect the lives of others when applied to real cases. And other justices are less likely to follow a leader who takes them into blind alleys or dangerous intellectual territory. Black had been the dominant leader of the Court for a few years and was now in the temporary position of leading an embattled minority. His stand was important, and he tested his conversion to absolutism over a long period of cases — thinking through its ramifications before really going public only in 1962, in a lecture-interview with legal philosopher Edmond Cahn.

Black was particularly attracted to absolutism, because it so readily meshed with literalism. Black was a constitutional fundamentalist who carried a copy of the Constitution in his jacket pocket and whipped it out in discussion the way Bible buffs resort to scripture. He also preferred unfanciful readings. He could say: "I cannot read 'Congress shall make no law' to mean 'Congress can make reasonable laws' abridging freedom of speech."

Black simply argued that for whatever reasons — libertarian or federalist — the national government was excluded from any control or authority over the content of speech. And the Fourteenth Amendment had extended that same limit to the states. With these sweeping and unqualified statements, Black concluded that the law of libel was unconstitutional, and had been for a hundred years. Further, he argued that the jurisprudence of speech areas had to go. Regulation of obscenity, movies, television, or what have you — dealing in symbols — could in no event be regulated because of their content. It was improper for the justices to view stag movies in the Supreme Court screening room to mull over the question of film obscenity. If such movies could be regulated it had to be for reasons other than content.

But Black was aware of the Holmes challenge. A false shout of "Fire!" in a crowded theater *was* punishable, because it was not just words, but also involved action. The words "Your money or your life" could be examined, in the case of a person walking into a bank toward the end of the working day, keeping hands in pockets menacingly, as indicating intent to commit a crime. Just as in *Milk Wagon Drivers Union* v. *Meadowmoor Dairies* (312 U.S. 287, 1941), where the Court found action (mass picketing) to be "speech plus," different rules applied to "symbolic speech" than to pure speech. With legal proprieties considered as to circumstances, "pure speech" was unassailable, whatever its content.

Black's modification of absolutism included careful attention to time, manner, and place of expression. Perhaps in compensation for his acceptance of all content, his tolerance for situation for expression was often on the conservative side. Black's argument was again simple. One could express all thoughts in contexts where one had a right to be and to express any thought. But intrusions upon other people's property were not a form of First Amendment expression.

This led to a paradox. "Absolutist" Black often found against expressive participation his less absolutist colleagues upheld. In ADDERLEY V. FLORIDA (1966) and BROWN V. LOUISIANA (1966), we have good examples of this phenomenon as well as of the Court's more eclectic pattern. Perhaps even more extreme was Black's dissent in TINKER V. DES MOINES INDEPENDENT COMMUNITY SCHOOL DISTRICT (1969), involving students donning black armbands to protest the Vietnam war. Schools, he argued, could ban any form of expression, since students had access to schools to learn, not to politic or to teach. The majority reasoned that expression should be tolerated in the absence of any logical or empirical demonstration of disruption.

Black's campaign against libel bore important fruit in NEW YORK TIMES CO. V. SULLIVAN (1964), a landmark case. The absolutist argument is that libels can be answered and refuted. Experience, however, demonstrates that many people do not have reasonable media access. (Indeed, the Court's protection of "insular" groups, of which Black was a fervent advocate, rests on the assumption that whole segments of society have inadequate power to respond.) The lives of individuals may be drastically affected by reckless media coverage. As we shall see, the Court tried to distinguish between prominent public figures and others, and to retain varying protection through libel suits for each. In doing so, the Court has inched towards restoring greater latitude to libel suits, and away from absolutism. NEW YORK TIMES V. SULLIVAN strikes a satisfactory balance, with just a bit of later fine tuning.

In general, the Black position on libel, with its complete faith in speech-rebutting-speech in the marketplace of ideas, seems misplaced. Psychological studies show "corrections" do not displace erroneous charges, and may reinforce them. Ideas that eventually prevail do not have corporeal being and wait their turn. Bryant wrote that "Truth crushed to earth will rise again, the eternal years of God are hers." But real people may die before truth catches up on their behalf — and they may not rely even on that.

With Black and Douglas gone, no other absolutists have emerged. However much most other justices respect their aim, none of them has embraced it. Still, this extreme position served a valuable function, by forcing other justices to clarify their thinking and broaden their own defenses of free expression. Indeed, without the Black-Douglas absolutist critique, it is difficult to imagine the emergence of the SULLIVAN decision. But in all candor it is doubtful that a sensible balance would have been struck, as it was in SULLIVAN, if the absolutist position had been vigorously argued.

Justice Frankfurter's Balancing

To a large extent, Frankfurter's reactions were negative — in opposition to preferred freedoms, which he apparently regarded as a Trojan Horse for his real target, absolutism. Frankfurter was appalled by the crudity and oversimplification brought to bear upon complex issues by absolutism. But his counterattack seems never to have found a working formula that had a convincing ring. He and his ally, Justice Jackson, were rather effective at probing problems and weaknesses in their opponents' approach. But their talent at negative slogans led them into the same oversimplifications they had sought to avoid.

Essentially, the balancing approach suggests, as Frankfurter often asserted, that the judges' function was not truly different from one part of the Constitution to the next. A judge weighed considerations that were dissimilar in a factual and experiential way in, say, Commerce Clause and First Amendment cases, but the process was similar in all cases. Further, he argued, deference to the legislature was not different from one type of case to another.

This argument is not fully convincing. Of course, all judges balance considerations in First Amendment cases. Preferred freedoms advocates argue that the Constitution has heavily weighted the scales against infringement, but balancing is in order. Even Black accepted balancing as the proper mode of analysis where action and expression were intertwined. But Frankfurter and Jackson argued fervently that judges had special mandates to enforce the Commerce Clause against state discrimination. HOOD V. DUMOND (1949) comes close to being an absolute ban against state preference for internal supplies. Frankfurter accepted the strong proposition of NEAR, that prior restraint is virtually interdicted by the First Amendment. And Black mocked his opponents by "writing" a burlesque opinion, purporting to uphold a bill of attainder, which is forbidden by the Constitution, since it was, on balance, only a slight infraction.

Since Frankfurter and Jackson in their votes were more libertarian than many of their colleagues on the Vinson Court, the balancing test seemed to vary from case to case. When they wished to sustain a statute, they utilized what Thomas Emerson (an off-Court admirer of Black and long-time protegé of Douglas) calls "ad-hoc balancing." The considerations of the particular case were evaluated closely. This meant they could speak of the low cost of the diminution of rights of individuals (or even all others affected by the restraint involved) as against the blockbuster danger to society, if restraint were not imposed. This, plus deference to legislatures, would make an impeccable case.

When they wished to invalidate, balancing was done on a more analytic basis. The social need said to justify repression was balanced against the social stake in free expression. This recognizes the contagion of repression, its ability to justify further incursion. When that consideration is involved, the First Amendment's provisions are almost automatically invoked, and balancing becomes a fraternal, if not identical, twin of "preference."

Where the Court Stands Today

The Rehnquist Court, like the Burger Court before it, is a lawyers' Court, not a philosopher's seminar or even an assemblage of statesmen. The justices are pragmatic and generally go to arms over concrete issues, not abstract approaches. They disagree about what to do about smut, rather than the nature of the judicial process. They prefer complex "three- or four-pronged tests," with sliding scales and distinctive vectors for each fact situation. They are more at home deciding cases than propounding principles. This obviously has costs as well as strengths.

In the domain of freedom of expression, they can live off the rich philosophic heritage of the Roosevelt and Warren Courts. There is ample work to be done in applying principles already laid down in situations not anticipated, or in areas where controversy will not die, such as obscenity regulation.

There is relatively little generalized controversy, largely because Justice Brennan, in NEW YORK TIMES V. SULLIVAN (1964), accomplished for expression something like the synthesis of absolutism and balancing that COOLEY V. BOARD OF WARDENS (1852) accomplished for claims for national exclusivity vs. state prerogatives in commerce. NEW YORK TIMES V. SULLIVAN established both a narrow rule and a broad, pro-expression tone to First Amendment litigation that does not forget day-to-day judgment is often necessary. The approach has had ramifications far beyond libel law.

There are no absolutists on the Court as of this writing in 1988, although Brennan and Marshall are aware of the approach and its admonitions and come as close to absolutism as their consciences

permit. There are no straight-out balancers, although Rehnquist and O'Connor are more respectful of legislative enactments than their colleagues. There is a general acceptance of the proposition that the First Amendment states a preference for freedom. The language that is used to express that preference is "clear and present danger." For a long while this phrase was out of fashion and was — as Jackson suggested it should be — used only with respect to crowd situations or other explosive circumstances of the FEINER or *Abrams* type. But it has made a comeback, in a Court relatively content with the stock of guiding principles it is working with. And the current use of clear and present danger is quite consonant with the "tough minded" use of it by the advocates of preferred freedoms, both in the breadth of considerations and the degree to which the Court accepts the notion that liberty is the rule and infringement the exception.

This does not mean the Court is tranquil. There are deep and even nasty divisions in freedom cases, but they are in very specific and quite limited areas. Obscenity regulation is exceptionally divisive, as it has been for decades. Applying TIMES V. SULLIVAN is not trouble-free. The complex new questions of regulation of electoral contributions and expenditures, and the extent of First Amendment protection of commercial speech, churn emotions as they challenge judicial creativity.

The New Era: Seditious Libel and Political Freedom Since *New York Times* v. *Sullivan*

We have already discussed the basic outline of views on the First Amendment. More specifically, it was the contention of Zechariah Chafee, Jr., that the Founders wished to eliminate seditious libel. But the Court did not sustain that interpretation until 1964. It was NEW YORK TIMES V. SULLIVAN that found that the right to criticize pub-

lic officials constituted the "central meaning" of the First Amendment, and that libel awards based upon criticism of public officials were highly circumscribed.

This substantial modification of previous decisions, which had sustained similar awards without much ado, came in the context of Alabama's effort to avenge itself on Yankee media covering civil rights demonstrations. An ad appealing for funds that appeared in the *New York Times* contained some factual errors in its account of one civil rights demonstration. In SULLIVAN, and another suit arising out of the ad, awards were made of $500,000 each. Eleven other suits were outstanding, involving $5.6 million. It appeared Alabama had found a potent weapon to prevent unfavorable media coverage whenever public opinion was congealed enough to produce huge jury awards.

Brennan's opinion held that the crystallized meaning of the First Amendment commitment that "debate on public issues should be uninhibited, robust and wide-eyed" prevented such tactics. While truth was a defense, error in criticizing a public official was not sufficient to permit libel awards, since that would inhibit criticism. Such awards were permissible if they met the standard of "actual malice." (That legal term, oddly, is defined as "with knowledge that it was false or with reckless disregard of truth," rather than anything conveyed by its face wording.)

This was objected to by Black and Douglas, joined by Goldberg, who thought an absolute rule should be applied. Still, compared to previous decisions, NEW YORK TIMES V. SULLIVAN constituted a striking move toward the Meiklejohn approach.

The Court extended the NEW YORK TIMES rationale to "public figures" who thrust themselves into the news. Subsequently, candidates for office were treated as public officials, and the rationale for not making all libel laws confrom to the "malicious falsehood" standard was, quite simply, that a private person, who is neither an official nor a celebrity, is in a poor position to answer or question coverage.

The Court has found it hard to define a public figure and has created confusion thereby. Its current tendency is to limit the category and therefore to restore some of the domain of old libel law. In *Hutchinson* v. *Proxmire* (1979), a professor receiving federal grants for research was held not to be a public figure. Senator Proxmire's "Golden Fleece Award" ridiculed Hutchinson's research in a news release and on television, with the Senator

also claiming falsely that Hutchinson charged twice for the same work.

Similarly, an individual whose aunt and uncle pleaded guilty in 1958 to espionage charges was mentioned in a recent book as an "agent" who was indicted. In fact, he had never been indicted, but had once refused to appear at the Grand Jury investigation, and had received a suspended sentence. He had subsequently avoided publicity. The Court held he was not a public figure either. It is clear that the Court demands that a public figure take an active role in creating the publicity. Justice Brennan has become a lone dissenter in such matters.

The general effect of NEW YORK TIMES V. SULLIVAN was broadly to encourage wider freedom of the media. Investigative reporting has flourished, knowing that suits by public officials are unlikely since comments about them are almost verdict-proof. However, ambiguity about who is a public figure has encouraged greater litigation. Judging by comments of the justices, as well as their deeds, the Court feels it has overshot and would like to tinker. The media contend that increasing litigation costs make these threats more inhibiting than in the past.

The Court has also introduced a less restrictive standard that apparently applies only to public figures. In cases involving public figures, media can be sued where standards of coverage fall below normal standards. This was established in *Curtis Publishing Co.* v. *Butts* (1967). The *Saturday Evening Post* had accused the athletic director at the University of Georgia of cooperating with gamblers on the basis of testimony of a convicted perjurer, without checking either his record or the elements of his story, which were easily refuted.

"Normal professional standards" trials involve expert witnesses testifying as to what media people could reasonably be expected to do. Often, as in insanity cases, there are "equal and opposite experts." The "reckless disregard for truth" standard presents difficult problems of evidence, raising such questions as to how deeply a plaintiff may dig into reporters' notes and other materials.

senting, the majority noted that Puerto Rico could regulate gambling or totally prohibit advertising. Hence, it may be selective in its regulation. Stevens would have found the selective prohibition unconstitutional, while the other dissenters challenged the right to prohibit ads at all. It is clear the case impinges upon possible regulation of cigarette ads, but the close vote provides little guidance.

The Rehnquist Court seems to wish to reassess the full thrust of its "commercial speech" position.

In a 1989 decision (6–3) it remanded a case involving a "Tupperware" type party held by a student in a dorm, where the university forbade such ventures (*Board of Trustees of SUNY* v. *Todd Fox* 57 LW 5015). The majority rejected the claim that "the least restrictive means test" applied and distinguished sharply commercial and other forms of expression. Blackmun, Brennan, and Marshall would have found the regulation unconstitutional for overbreadth.

Free Press Versus Fair Trial

Aggressive reporting, firmer standards of what constitutes a fair trial, a greater opening of the courts to the media, and police attempts to use reporters to develop cases have produced court-media collisions unprecedented in our history.

Reporters' aggressive coverage of trials has made it more difficult to make sure juries come to a trial without information biasing the result. While juries can be sequestered during a trial, pretrial publicity can, consciously or unconsciously, affect juries not yet chosen, or make it difficult to get a jury listening to the case from scratch. Yet, with First Amendment emphasis so strong, the traditional power of judges to control the press through contempt proceedings has been largely eliminated.

Do the media have the right of access to court proceedings, particularly pretrial decisions? This is a question that has come up in several guises. States have experimented with opening court proceedings to television. The Supreme Court has ruled that televising by itself will not invalidate a trial. And in two cases, the Supreme Court, with a little help from its friends (as well as some enemies), decided a public trial was the rule and closed trials the exception under First Amendment doctrine (*Gannett Co.* v. *DePasquale*, 1979, and Richmond Newspapers v. Virginia, 1980).

In the 1989 case *Florida Star* v. *B.J.F.* (109 S.

Ct. 2603), the Rehnquist Court dealt with Florida statutes prohibiting printing of a rape victim's name. The police report had inadvertently included her name and it was correctly printed. Since the state could not punish a truthful publication absent a state interest "of the highest order" and due care by public officials would have withheld the name without censorship, the statute was held unconstitutional. White, Rehnquist, and O'Connor dissented claiming the majority was dooming "one of the most significant legal advances of this country," the tort of privacy.

In a series of cases, police have attempted to develop evidence through enlisting reporters. In Branzburg v. Hayes (1972), the Court decided there was no constitutional or common law privilege not to reveal sources. Since that time, state shield laws have multiplied, and Court decisions have been friendlier, at least on the state level. A police raid on a newspaper to try to gather evidence used in a story was sustained (*Zurcher* v. *Stanford Daily*, 1978), but Congress has since modified federal law to strictly limit such raids by federal agents.

No term of the Supreme Court goes by without an interesting case in this area. Usually, new rules of some importance emerge, indicating the justices have not yet resolved these matters to their own satisfaction.

Cases

Violate speech & press?
No

Schenck v. U.S.

Clear + present Danger

249 U.S. 47 (1919)
Vote: 9–0

During World War I, defendants mailed circulars directly to men eligible for the draft, urging them to resist conscription. They were tried in federal court for violation of the Espionage Act of 1917, which prohibited obstruction of recruiting. Holmes, for a unanimous Court, upheld the conviction. The case, however, is important for Holmes' unveiling of the clear-and-present-danger test.

In this case, as in *Frohwerk* v. *U.S.* (1919) and *Debs* v. *U.S.* (1919), the test was invoked to sustain convictions, which may explain the Court's readiness to accept the standard. In those cases the circumstances seemed to Holmes and Brandeis to support restraint of speech. But in *Abrams* v. *U.S.* (1919), some garment workers randomly threw out pamphlets opposing the American excursion in Russia. The majority affirmed their conviction, but Holmes and Brandeis dissented, in one of Holmes' finest opinions, noting little danger from this expression. The majority in *Abrams* was unable to offer a coherent theory or explain why the progenitor of clear and present danger found none there. The formulation of a rival approach came in GITLOW V. NEW YORK.

MR. JUSTICE HOLMES delivered the opinion of the court.

① This is an indictment in three counts. The first charges a conspiracy to violate the Espionage Act of June 15, 1917, c. 30, §3, 40 Stat. 217, 219, by causing and attempting to cause insubordination, &c., in the military and naval forces of the United States, and to obstruct the recruiting and enlistment service of the United States, when the United States was at war with the German Empire, to-wit, that the defendants wilfully conspired to have printed and circulated to men who had been called and accepted for military service under the Act of May 18, 1917, a document set forth and alleged to be calculated to cause such insubordination and obstruction.... The

defendants were found guilty on all the counts. They set up the First Amendment to the Constitution forbidding Congress to make any law abridging the freedom of speech, or of the press, and bringing the case here on that ground have argued some other points also of which we must dispose....

The document in question upon its first printed side recited the first section of the Thirteenth Amendment, said that the idea embodied in it was violated by the Conscription Act and that a conscript is little better than a convict. In impassioned language it intimated that conscription was despotism in its worst form and a monstrous wrong against humanity in the interest of Wall Street's chosen few. It said "Do not submit to intimidation," but in form at least confined itself to peaceful measures such as a petition for the repeal of the act. The other and later printed side of the sheet was headed "Assert Your Rights." It stated reasons for alleging that any one violated the Constitution when he refused to recognize "your right to assert your opposition to the draft," and went on "If you do not assert and support your rights, you are helping to deny or disparage rights which it is the solemn duty of all citizens and residents of the United States to retain."... Of course the document would not have been sent unless it had been intended to have some effect, and we do not see what effect it could be expected to have upon persons subject to the draft except to influence them to obstruct the carrying of it out. The defendants do not deny that the jury might find against them on this point.

But it is said, suppose that that was the tendency of this circular, it is protected by the First Amendment to the Constitution. Two of the strongest expressions are said to be quoted respectively from well-known public men. It well may be that the prohibition of laws abridging the freedom of speech is not confined to previous restraints, although to prevent them may have been the main purpose, as intimated in *Patterson* v. *Colorado*, 205 U.S. 454, 462. We admit that in many places and in ordinary times the defendants in saying all that was said in the circular would have been within their constitutional rights. But the character of every act depends upon the circumstances in which it is done. *Aikens* v. *Wisconsin*, 195 U.S. 194, 205, 206. The most stringent protection of free speech would not protect a man in falsely shouting fire in a theatre and causing a panic. It does not even protect a man from an injunction against uttering words that may have all the effect

① Diss. People's call to resist draft

② Using mail to distribute non-mailable matter under Espionage Act

③ Unlawful use of mail,

of force. *Gompers* v. *Bucks Stove & Range Co.,* 221 U.S. 418, 439. The question in every case is whether the words used are used in such circumstances and are of such a nature as to create a clear and present danger that they will bring about the substantive evils that Congress has a right to prevent. It is a question of proximity and degree. When a nation is at war many things that might be said in time of peace are such a hindrance to its effort that their utterance will not be endured so long as men fight and that no Court could regard them as protected by any constitutional right. It seems to be admitted that if an actual obstruction of the recruiting service were proved, liability for words that produced that effect might be enforced. The statute of 1917 in §4 punishes conspiracies to obstruct as well as actual obstruction. If the act, (speaking, or circulating a paper,) its tendency and the intent with which it is done are the same, we perceive no ground for saying that success alone warrants making the act a crime.

Judgments affirmed.

Gitlow v. New York

268 U.S. 652 (1925)
Vote: 7–2

This momentous decision marked the real beginning of "incorporation" of civil rights (as opposed to property protection) and the alteration of the Supreme Court's place in the American system. The casualness of Sanford's statement that "for present purposes we may and do assume" freedom of press and speech are protected by the Fourteenth Amendment should not obscure the fact that it was a historical turning point. Research has not established how or why it came about. Perhaps the majority justices, in the process of redefining and replacing the clear-and-present-danger test in this case, were concerned to move in a pro-liberties way as compensatory. Holmes' dissent restates clear and present danger and riddles the majority's approach, which was labelled the "evil (or bad) tendency" test and which the Court abandoned without discussion in the 1930s.

Gitlow was tried in a New York Court for violating the state's criminal anarchy statute by publishing a *Left Wing Manifesto*, referred to below. There was no evidence of any consequences from

the publication, only an analysis of words deemed "anarchistic." Gitlow attacked the constitutionality of the statute. Upon conviction, he appealed to the New York court of appeals, which affirmed the decision. His case was then appealed to the U.S. Supreme Court. The case was originally argued in that court in April of 1923, and argued again in November, 1923, but not decided until June of 1925, indicating legal difficulty not suggested by the vote.

MR. JUSTICE SANFORD delivered the opinion of the Court.

. . . The defendant is a member of the Left Wing Section of the Socialist Party, a dissenting branch or faction of that party formed in opposition to its dominant policy of "moderate Socialism." . . . The Left Wing Section was organized nationally at a conference in New York City in June, 1919. The conference elected a National Council, of which the defendant was a member, and left to it the adoption of a "Manifesto." This was published in The Revolutionary Age, the official organ of the Left Wing. . . .

. . . [Coupled with a review of the rise of Socialism, it] condemned the dominant "moderate Socialism" for its recognition of the necessity of the democratic parliamentary state; repudiated its policy of introducing Socialism by legislative measures; and advocated, in plain and unequivocal language, the necessity of accomplishing the "Communist Revolution" by a militant and "revolutionary Socialism," based on "the class struggle" and mobilizing the "power of the proletariat in action," through mass industrial revolts. . . .

At the outset of the trial the defendant's counsel objected to the introduction of any evidence under the indictment on the grounds that, as a matter of law, the Manifesto "is not in contravention of the statute," and that "the statute is in contravention of" the due process clause of the Fourteenth Amendment. . . .

The court, among other things, charged the jury, in substance, that they must determine what was the intent, purpose and fair meaning of the Manifesto; that its words must be taken in their ordinary meaning, as they would be understood by people whom it might reach; that a mere statement or analysis of social and economic facts and historical incidents, in the nature of an essay, accompanied by prophecy as to the future course of events, but with no teaching, advice or advocacy of action, would not constitute the advocacy, advice or teaching of a doctrine for the overthrow of government within the meaning of the statute; that a mere statement that

Gitlow v. New York **477**

unlawful acts might accomplish such a purpose would be insufficient, unless there was a teaching, advising and advocacy of employing such unlawful acts for the purpose of overthrowing government; and that if the jury had a reasonable doubt that the Manifesto did teach, advocate or advise the duty, necessity or propriety of using unlawful means for the overthrowing of organized government, the defendant was entitled to an acquittal. . . . The sole contention here is, essentially, that as there was no evidence of any concrete result flowing from the publication of the Manifesto or of circumstances showing the likelihood of such result, the statute as construed and applied by the trial court penalizes the mere utterance, as such, of "doctrine" having no quality of incitement, without regard either to the circumstances of its utterance or to the likelihood of unlawful sequences; and that, as the exercise of the right of free expression with relation to government is only punishable "in circumstances involving likelihood of substantive evil," the statute contravenes the due process clause of the Fourteenth Amendment. The argument in support of this contention rests primarily upon the following propositions: 1st, That the "liberty" protected by the Fourteenth Amendment includes the liberty of speech and of the press; and 2nd, That while liberty of expression "is not absolute," it may be restrained "only in circumstances where its exercise bears a causal relation with some substantive evil, consummated, attempted or likely," and as the statute "takes no account of circumstances," it unduly restrains this liberty and is therefore unconstitutional.

The statute does not penalize the utterance or publication of abstract "doctrine" or academic discussion having no quality of incitement to any concrete action. It is not aimed against mere historical or philosophical essays. It does not restrain the advocacy of changes in the form of government by constitutional and lawful means. . . .

. . . .

For present purposes we may and do assume that freedom of speech and of the press — which are protected by the First Amendment from abridgment by Congress — are among the fundamental personal rights and "liberties" protected by the due process clause of the Fourteenth Amendment from impairment by the States. . . .

It is a fundamental principle, long established, that the freedom of speech and of the press which is secured by the Constitution, does not confer an absolute right to speak or publish, without responsibility, whatever one may choose. . . .

By enacting the present statute the State has determined, through its legislative body, that utter-
ances advocating the overthrow of organized government by force, violence and unlawful means, are so inimical to the general welfare and involve such danger of substantive evil that they may be penalized in the exercise of its police power. That determination must be given great weight. Every presumption is to be indulged in favor of the validity of the statute. . . . That utterances inciting to the overthrow of organized government by unlawful means, present a sufficient danger of substantive evil to bring their punishment within the range of legislative discretion, is clear. Such utterances, by their very nature, involve danger to the public peace and to the security of the State. They threaten breaches of the peace and ultimate revolution. And the immediate danger is none the less real and substantial, because the effect of a given utterance cannot be accurately foreseen. The State cannot reasonably be required to measure the danger from every such utterance in the nice balance of a jeweler's scale. A single revolutionary spark may kindle a fire that, smouldering for a time, may burst into a sweeping and destructive conflagration. It cannot be said that the State is acting arbitrarily or unreasonably when in the exercise of its judgment as to the measures necessary to protect the public peace and safety, it seeks to extinguish the spark without waiting until it has enkindled the flame or blazed into the conflagration. It cannot reasonably be required to defer the adoption of measures for its own peace and safety until the revolutionary utterances lead to actual disturbances of the public peace or imminent and immediate danger of its own destruction; but it may, in the exercise of its judgment, suppress the threatened danger in its incipiency. In *People* v. *Lloyd*, *supra*, p. 35, it was aptly said: "Manifestly, the legislature has authority to forbid the advocacy of a doctrine designed and intended to overthrow the government without waiting until there is a present and imminent danger of the success of the plan advocated. If the State were compelled to wait until the apprehended danger became certain, then its right to protect itself would come into being simultaneously with the overthrow of the government. . . ."

. . . .

MR. JUSTICE HOLMES, dissenting.

MR. JUSTICE BRANDEIS and I are of opinion that this judgment should be reversed. The general principle of free speech, it seems to me, must be taken to be included in the Fourteenth Amendment, in view of the scope that has been given to the word "liberty" as there used, although perhaps it may be accepted with a somewhat larger latitude of interpretation than is allowed to Congress. . . . If what I think the correct test is applied, it is manifest that there was no present danger of an attempt to overthrow the government by force on the part of the admittedly small minority who shared the defendant's views. It is said that this manifesto was more than a theory, that it was an incitement. Every idea is an incitement. It offers itself for belief and if believed it is acted on unless some other belief outweighs it or some failure of energy stifles the movement at its birth. The only difference between the expression of an opinion and an incitement in the narrower sense is the speaker's enthusiasm for the result. Eloquence may set fire to reason. But whatever may be thought of the redundant discourse before us it had no chance of starting a present conflagration. . . .

. . . .

Whitney v. California

274 U.S. 357 (1927)
Vote: (7–2)–0

Ms. Whitney was convicted under the California Anti-Syndicalism Act for being involved with people who advocated violent means to effect change. Justice Sanford wrote the majority opinion along the lines of his GITLOW "remote tendency" doctrine.

Brandeis' concurrence notes the failure of Whitney to invoke clear and present danger as grounds for invalidity of the statute. Therefore, he concludes the conviction cannot be set aside. But he does attempt to further develop the logic of the clear-and-present-danger test. The legislature can only make a presumption along those lines; it is for the judge or jury to weigh the full measure of the danger. (Incidentally, Brandeis' opinion suggests he was opposed to "incorporation" of the First Amendment and accepts it only because of precedent.)

Professor Pritchett's summary of the early history of clear and present danger is mordant, and only a bit unfair: "From 1919 to 1927 its successive statements were eloquent. But it kept no one out of jail." (*The American Constitution,* 3rd ed. New York: McGraw-Hill, 1977, p. 304.)

The Hughes Court ignored or distinguished *Whitney* in several cases: *Stromberg* v. *California* (1931), *DeJonge* v. *Oregon* (1937), and *Herndon* v. *Lowry* (1937). All insisted on the principle of personal guilt. *DeJonge* included the right of assembly as a right protected against the states, and suggests an individual lawfully participating in an assembly cannot be convicted for the unlawful intent of others.

In *Brandenburg* v. *Ohio* (1969), a conviction under the Ohio Criminal-Syndicalism Act of 1919 was overturned in a per curiam opinion. Noting that the Ohio and California statutes were substantially similar, the Court said that "*Whitney* has been discredited by later decisions" that prevent punishment of mere advocacy.

MR. JUSTICE SANFORD delivered the opinion of the Court.

. . . [T]he freedom of speech which is secured by the Constitution does not confer an absolute right to speak, without responsibility, whatever one may choose, or an unrestricted and unbridled license giving immunity for every possible use of language and preventing the punishment of those who abuse this freedom; and that a State in the exercise of its police power may punish those who abuse this freedom by utterances inimical to the public welfare, tending to incite to crime, disturb the public peace, or endanger the foundations of organized government and threaten its overthrow by unlawful means, is not open to question. *Gitlow* v. *New York,* 268 U.S. 652, 666–668, and cases cited.

By enacting the provisions of the Syndicalism Act the State has declared, through its legislative body, that to knowingly be or become a member of or assist in organizing an association to advocate, teach or aid and abet the commission of crimes or unlawful acts of force, violence or terrorism as a means of accomplishing industrial or political changes, involves such danger to the public peace and the security of the State, that these acts should be penalized in the exercise of its police power. That determination must be given great weight. Every presumption is to be indulged in favor of the validity of the statute, *Mugler* v. *Kansas,* 123 U.S. 623, 661; and it may not be declared unconstitutional unless it is an arbitrary or unreasonable attempt to exercise the authority vested in the State in the public interest. *Great Northern Railway* v. *Clara City,* 246 U.S. 434, 439.

The essence of the offense denounced by the Act is the combining with others in an association for the accomplishment of the desired ends through the advocacy and use of criminal and unlawful methods. It partakes of the nature of a criminal conspiracy. See *People* v. *Steelik, supra,* 376. That such united and joint action involves even greater danger to the public peace and security than the isolated utterances and acts of individuals, is clear. We cannot hold that, as here applied, the Act is an unreasonable or arbitrary exercise of the police power of the State, unwarrantably infringing any right of free speech, assembly or association, or that those persons are protected from punishment by the due process clause who abuse such rights by joining and furthering an organization thus menacing the peace and welfare of the State.

MR. JUSTICE BRANDEIS, concurring.

The felony which the statute created is a crime very unlike the old felony of conspiracy or the old misdemeanor of unlawful assembly. The mere act of assisting in forming a society for teaching syndicalism, of becoming a member of it, or of assembling with others for that purpose is given the dynamic quality of crime. There is guilt although the society may not contemplate immediate promulgation of the doctrine. Thus the accused is to be punished, not for contempt, incitement or conspiracy, but for a step in preparation, which, if it threatens the public order at all, does so only remotely. The novelty in the prohibition introduced is that the statute aims, not at the practice of criminal syndicalism, nor even directly at the preaching of it, but at association with those who propose to preach it.

Despite arguments to the contrary which had seemed to me persuasive, it is settled that the due process clause of the Fourteenth Amendment applies to matters of substantive law as well as to matters of procedure. Thus all fundamental rights comprised within the term liberty are protected by the Federal Constitution from invasion by the States. The right of free speech, the right to teach and the right of assembly are, of course, fundamental rights. . . . These may not be denied or abridged. But, although the rights of free speech and assembly are fundamental, they are not in their nature absolute. Their exercise is subject to restriction, if the particular restriction proposed is required in order to protect the State from destruction or from serious injury, political, economic or moral. That the necessity which is essential to a valid restriction does not exist unless speech would produce, or is intended to produce, a clear and imminent danger of some substantive evil which the State constitutionally may seek to prevent has been settled. See *Schenck* v. *United States*. . . .

It is said to be the function of the legislature to determine whether at a particular time and under the particular circumstances the formation of, or assembly with, a society organized to advocate criminal syndicalism constitutes a clear and present danger of substantive evil; and that by enacting the law here in question the legislature of California determined that question in the affirmative. Compare *Gitlow* v. *New York*. The legislature must obviously decide, in the first instance, whether a danger exists which calls for a particular protective measure. But where a statute is valid only in case certain conditions exist, the enactment of the statute cannot alone establish the facts which are essential to its validity. Prohibitory legislation has repeatedly been held invalid, because unnecessary, where the denial of liberty involved was that of engaging in a particular business. The power of the courts to strike down an offending law is no less when the interests involved are not property rights, but the fundamental personal rights of free speech and assembly.

Those who won our independence believed that the final end of the State was to make men free to develop their faculties; and that in its government the deliberative forces should prevail over the arbitrary. They valued liberty both as an end and as a means. They believed liberty to be the secret of happiness and courage to be the secret of liberty. They believed that freedom to think as you will and to speak as you think are means indispensable to the discovery and spread of political truth; that without free speech and assembly discussion would be futile; that with them, discussion affords ordinarily adequate protection against the dissemination of noxious doctrine; that the greatest menace to freedom is an inert people; that public discussion is a political duty; and that this should be a fundamental principle of the American government. They recognized the risks to which all human institutions are subject. But they knew that order cannot be secured merely through fear of punishment for its infraction; that it is hazardous to discourage thought, hope and imagination; that fear breeds repression; that repression breeds hate; that hate menaces stable government; that the path of safety lies in the opportunity to discuss freely supposed grievances and proposed remedies; and that the fitting remedy for evil counsels is good ones. Believing in the power of reason as applied through public discussion, they eschewed silence coerced by law — the argument of force in its worst form. Recognizing the occasional tyrannies of governing majorities, they amended the Constitution so that free speech and assembly should be guaranteed.

Fear of serious injury cannot alone justify suppression of free speech and assembly. Men feared witches and burnt women. It is the function of speech to free men from the bondage of irrational fears. To justify suppression of free speech there must be reasonable ground to fear that serious evil will result if free speech is practiced. There must be reasonable ground to believe that the danger apprehended is imminent. There must be reasonable ground to believe that the evil to be prevented is a serious one. Every denunciation of existing law tends in some measure to increase the probability that there will be violation of it.

Those who won our independence by revolution were not cowards. They did not fear political change. They did not exalt order at the cost of liberty. To courageous, self-reliant men, with confidence in the power of free and fearless reasoning applied through the processes of popular government, no danger flowing from speech can be deemed clear and present, unless the incidence of the evil apprehended is so imminent that it may befall before there is opportunity for full discussion. If there be time to expose through discussion the falsehood and fallacies, to avert the evil by the processes of education, the remedy to be applied is more speech, not enforced silence. Only an emergency can justify repression. Such must be the rule if authority is to be reconciled with freedom. Such, in my opinion, is the command of the Constitution. It is therefore always open to Americans to challenge a law abridging free speech and assembly by showing that there was no emergency justifying it.

Moreover, even imminent danger cannot justify resort to prohibition of these functions essential to effective democracy, *unless* the evil apprehended is relatively serious. Prohibition of free speech and assembly is a measure so stringent that it would be inappropriate as the means for averting a relatively trivial harm to society. A police measure may be unconstitutional merely because the remedy, although effective as means of protection, is unduly harsh or oppressive. It is hardly conceivable that this Court would hold constitutional a statute which punished as a felony the mere voluntary assembly with a society formed to teach that pedestrians had the moral right to cross unenclosed, unposted, waste lands and to advocate their doing so, even if there was imminent danger that advocacy would lead to a trespass.

Whether in 1919, when Miss Whitney did the things complained of, there was in California such clear and present danger of serious evil, might have been made the important issue in the case. She might have required that the issue be determined either by the court or the jury. She claimed below that the statute as applied to her violated the Federal Constitution; but she did not claim that it was void because there was no clear and present danger of serious evil, nor did she request that the existence of these conditions of a valid measure thus restricting the rights of free speech and assembly be passed upon by the court or a jury. On the other hand, there was evidence on which the court or jury might have found that such danger existed. I am unable to assent to the suggestion in the opinion of the Court that assembling with a political party, formed to advocate the desirability of a proletarian revolution by mass action at some date necessarily far in the future, is not a right within the protection of the Fourteenth Amendment. In the present case, however, there was other testimony which tended to establish the existence of a conspiracy, on the part of members of the International Workers of the World, (sic) to commit present serious crimes; and likewise to show that such a conspiracy would be furthered by the activity of the society of which Miss Whitney was a member. Under these circumstances the judgment of the state court cannot be disturbed.

Near v. Minnesota

283 U.S. 697 (1931)
Vote: 5–4

This landmark case signaled a new approach by the Supreme Court to First Amendment issues, reflecting the advent of Chief Justice Hughes. It also established an important beginning for the Court's exploration of the problem of "prior restraint," meaning governmental authority to censor material in advance.

A Minnesota statute of 1925 provided that a Court, upon finding a newspaper, magazine, or periodical "malicious, scandalous or defamatory," could enjoin temporary or permanent publication, with a penalty for violation of the injunction of a $1000 fine or a year in jail. Near was editor of a newspaper accused of such scurrilous publication. He defended with a demurrer—the legal equivalent of "so what?"—arguing unconstitutionality of the statute. The district court certified the question of constitutionality to the state supreme court, which sustained the statute. The paper was then found a nuisance by the district court, and this was affirmed by the state supreme court. Near appealed to the U.S. Supreme Court.

MR. CHIEF JUSTICE HUGHES delivered the opinion of the Court.
. . . .
The County Attorney of Hennepin County brought this action to enjoin the publication of what was described as a "malicious, scandalous and defamatory

newspaper, magazine and periodical," known as "The Saturday Press," published by the defendants in the city of Minneapolis. The complaint alleged that the defendants, on September 24, 1927, and on eight subsequent dates in October and November, 1927, published and circulated editions of that periodical which were "largely devoted to malicious, scandalous and defamatory articles."...

...[T]he articles charged in substance that a Jewish gangster was in control of gambling, bootlegging and racketeering in Minneapolis, and that law enforcing officers and agencies were not energetically performing their duties. Most of the charges were directed against the Chief of Police; he was charged with gross neglect of duty, illicit relations with gangsters, and with participation in graft. The County Attorney was charged with knowing the existing conditions and with failure to take adequate measures to remedy them. The Mayor was accused of inefficiency and dereliction. One member of the grand jury was stated to be in sympathy with the gangsters.

....

The defendants demurred to the complaint upon the ground that it did not state facts sufficient to constitute a cause of action, and on this demurrer challenged the constitutionality of the statute. The District Court overruled the demurrer and certified the question of constitutionality to the Supreme Court of the State. The Supreme Court sustained the statute... over the objection that it violated not only the state constitution but also the Fourteenth Amendment of the Constitution of the United States.

....

The District Court made findings of fact, which followed the allegations of the complaint and found in general terms that the editions in question were "chiefly devoted to malicious, scandalous and defamatory articles," concerning the individuals named.... Judgment was thereupon entered adjudging that "the newspaper, magazine, and periodical known as The Saturday Press," as a public nuisance, "be and is hereby abated." The judgment perpetually enjoined the defendants "from producing, editing, publishing, circulating, having in their possession, selling or giving away any publication whatsoever which is a malicious, scandalous or defamatory newspaper, as defined by law," and also "from further conducting said nuisance under the name and title of said The Saturday Press or any other name or title."

The defendant Near appealed from this judgment to the Supreme Court of the State, again asserting his right under the Federal Constitution, and the judgment was affirmed upon the authority of the former decision....

From the judgment as thus affirmed, the defendant Near appeals to this Court.

This statute, for the suppression as a public nuisance of a newspaper or periodical, is unusual, if not unique, and raises questions of grave importance transcending the local interests involved in the particular action. It is no longer open to doubt that the liberty of the press, and of speech, is within the liberty safeguarded by the due process clause of the Fourteenth Amendment from invasion by state action.... Liberty of speech, and of the press, is also not an absolute right, and the State may punish its abuse. *Whitney* v. *California.* Liberty, in each of its phases, has its history and connotation and, in the present instance, the inquiry is as to the historic conception of the liberty of the press and whether the statute under review violates the essential attributes of that liberty.

....

The statute is not aimed at the redress of individual or private wrongs. Remedies for libel remain available and unaffected. The statute, said the state court, "is not directed at threatened libel but at an existing business which, generally speaking, involves more than libel." It is aimed at the distribution of scandalous matter as "detrimental to public morals and to the general welfare," tending "to disturb the peace of the community" and "to provoke assaults and the commission of crime."... The court sharply defined the purpose of the statute, bringing out the precise point, in these words: "There is no constitutional right to publish a fact merely because it is true. It is a matter of common knowledge that prosecutions under the criminal libel statutes do not result in efficient repression or suppression of the evils of scandal.... This law is not for the protection of the person attacked nor to punish the wrongdoer. It is for the protection of the public welfare."

The statute not only operates to suppress the offending newspaper or periodical but to put the publisher under an effective censorship. When a newspaper or periodical is found to be "malicious, scandalous and defamatory," and is suppressed as such, resumption of publication is punishable as a contempt of court by fine or imprisonment. Thus, where a newspaper or periodical has been suppressed because of the circulation of charges against public officers of official misconduct, it would seem to be clear that the renewal of the publication of such charges would constitute a contempt and that the judgment would lay a permanent restraint upon the publisher, to escape which he must satisfy the court as to the character of a new publication. Whether he would be permitted again to publish matter deemed to be derogatory to the same or other public officers would depend upon the court's ruling....

If we cut through mere details of procedure, the operation and effect of the statute in substance is that public authorities may bring the owner or publisher of a newspaper or periodical before a judge upon a charge of conducting a business of publishing scandalous and defamatory matter — in particular that the matter consists of charges against public officers of official dereliction — and unless the owner or publisher is able and disposed to bring competent evidence to satisfy the judge that the charges are true and are published with good motives and for justifiable ends, his newspaper or periodical is suppressed and further publication is made punishable as a contempt. This is of the essence of censorship.

The question is whether a statute authorizing such proceedings in restraint of publication is consistent with the conception of the liberty of the press as historically conceived and guaranteed. In determining the extent of the constitutional protection, it has been generally, if not universally, considered that it is the chief purpose of the guaranty to prevent previous restraints upon publication. The struggle in England, directed against the legislative power of the licenser, resulted in renunciation of the censorship of the press. The liberty deemed to be established was thus described by Blackstone: "The liberty of the press is indeed essential to the nature of a free state; but this consists in laying no *previous* restraints upon publication, and not in freedom from censure for criminal matter when published."...

The criticism upon Blackstone's statement has not been because immunity from previous restraint upon publication has not been regarded as deserving of special emphasis, but chiefly because that immunity cannot be deemed to exhaust the conception of the liberty guaranteed by state and federal constitutions. The point of criticism has been "that the mere exemption from previous restraints cannot be all that is secured by the constitutional provisions"; and that "the liberty of the press might be rendered a mockery and a delusion, and the phrase itself a by-word, if, while every man was at liberty to publish what he pleased, the public authorities might nevertheless punish him for harmless publications."...

The objection has also been made that the principle as to immunity from previous restraint is stated too broadly, if every such restraint is deemed to be prohibited. That is undoubtedly true; the protection even as to previous restraint is not absolutely unlimited. But the limitation has been recognized only in exceptional cases: "When a nation is at war many things that might be said in time of peace are such a hindrance to its effort that their utterance will not be endured so long as men fight and that no Court could regard them as protected by any constitutional right." *Schenck* v. *United States*.... No one would

question but that a government might prevent actual obstruction to its recruiting service or the publication of the sailing dates of transports or the number and location of troops. On similar grounds, the primary requirements of decency may be enforced against obscene publications. The security of the community life may be protected against incitements to acts of violence and the overthrow by force of orderly government. The constitutional guaranty of free speech does not "protect a man from an injunction against uttering words that may have all the effect of force...." *Schenck* v. *United States*.... These limitations are not applicable here. Nor are we now concerned with questions as to the extent of authority to prevent publications in order to protect private rights according to the principles governing the exercise of the jurisdiction of courts of equity.

. . . .

The fact that for approximately one hundred and fifty years there has been almost an entire absence of attempts to impose previous restraints upon publications relating to the malfeasance of public officers is significant of the deep-seated conviction that such restraints would violate constitutional right. Public officers, whose character and conduct remain open to debate and free discussion in the press, find their remedies for false accusations in actions under libel laws providing for redress and punishment, and not in proceedings to restrain the publication of newspapers and periodicals. The general principle that the constitutional guaranty of the liberty of the press gives immunity from previous restraints has been approved in many decisions under the provisions of state constitutions.

. . . .

The statute in question cannot be justified by reason of the fact that the publisher is permitted to show, before injunction issues, that the matter published is true and is published with good motives and for justifiable ends. If such a statute, authorizing suppression and injunction on such basis, is constitutionally valid, it would be equally permissible for the legislature to provide that at any time the publisher of any newspaper could be brought before a court, or even an administrative officer (as the constitutional protection may not be regarded as resting on mere procedural details) and required to produce proof of the truth of his publication, or of what he intended to publish, and of his motives, or stand enjoined. If this can be done, the legislature may provide machinery for determining in the complete exercise of its discretion what are justifiable ends and restrain publication accordingly. And it would be but a step to a complete system of censorship. The recognition of authority to impose previous restraint upon publication in order to protect the community against the circulation of charges of misconduct, and especially of official misconduct, necessarily would carry with it the admission of the authority of the censor against which the constitutional barrier was erected....

Equally unavailing is the insistence that the statute is designed to prevent the circulation of scandal which tends to disturb the public peace and to provoke assaults and the commission of crime. Charges of reprehensible conduct, and in particular of official malfeasance, unquestionably create a public scandal, but the theory of the constitutional guaranty is that even a more serious public evil would be caused by authority to prevent publication....

. . . .

. . . The fact that the public officers named in this case, and those associated with the charges of official dereliction, may be deemed to be impeccable, cannot affect the conclusion that the statute imposes an unconstitutional restraint upon publication.

Judgment reversed.

MR. JUSTICE BUTLER, dissenting.

The decision of the Court in this case declares Minnesota and every other State powerless to restrain by injunction the business of publishing and circulating among the people malicious, scandalous and defamatory periodicals that in due course of judicial procedure has been adjudged to be a public nuisance. It gives to freedom of the press a meaning and a scope not heretofore recognized and construes "liberty" in the due process clause of the Fourteenth Amendment to put upon the States a federal restriction that is without precedent.

. . . .

It is well known, as found by the state supreme court, that existing libel laws are inadequate effectively to suppress evils resulting from the kind of business and publications that are shown in this case. The doctrine that measures such as the one before us are invalid because they operate as previous restraints to infringe freedom of press exposes the peace and good order of every community and the business and private affairs of every individual to the constant and protracted false and malicious assaults of any insolvent publisher who may have purpose and sufficient capacity to contrive and put into effect a scheme or program for oppression, blackmail or extortion.

The judgment should be

Affirmed.

MR. JUSTICE VAN DEVANTER, MR. JUSTICE MCREYNOLDS, and MR. JUSTICE SUTHERLAND concur in this opinion.

Terminiello v. Chicago

337 U.S. 1 (1949)
Vote: 5–(1–3)

Terminiello delivered a rabble-rousing speech in an auditorium with a hostile mob outside. He was convicted of breach of the peace, under a charge to the jury that called for conviction if behavior "stirs the public to anger." Regarding such instructions as controlling, the majority found its duty clear. There was no need to determine whether Terminiello was in fact disruptive and to weigh it as against the obligation of the police to protect expression. The narrow 5 to 4 decision saw the dissenters focus on the unsavory, racial, and religious slurs in Terminiello's remarks.

MR. JUSTICE DOUGLAS delivered the opinion of the Court.

Petitioner after jury trial was found guilty of disorderly conduct in violation of a city ordinance of Chicago and fined. The case grew out of an address he delivered in an auditorium in Chicago under the auspices of the Christian Veterans of America. The meeting commanded considerable public attention. The auditorium was filled to capacity with over eight hundred persons present. Others were turned away. Outside of the auditorium a crowd of about one thousand persons gathered to protest against the meeting. A cordon of policemen was assigned to the meeting to maintain order; but they were not able to prevent several disturbances. The crowd outside was angry and turbulent.

Petitioner in his speech condemned the conduct of the crowd outside and vigorously, if not viciously, criticized various political and racial groups whose activities he denounced as inimical to the nation's welfare.

The trial court charged that "breach of the peace" consists of any "misbehavior which violates the public peace and decorum"; and that the "misbehavior may constitute a breach of the peace if it stirs the public to anger, invites dispute, brings about a condition of unrest, or creates a disturbance, or if it molests the inhabitants in the enjoyment of peace and quiet by arousing alarm." Petitioner did not take exception to that instruction. But he maintained at all times that the ordinance as applied to his conduct violated his right of free speech under the Federal Constitution....

The vitality of civil and political institutions in our society depends on free discussion. As Chief Justice Hughes wrote in *De Jonge* v. *Oregon,* 299 U.S. 353, 365, it is only through free debate and free exchange of ideas that government remains responsive to the will of the people and peaceful change is effected. The right to speak freely and to promote diversity of ideas and programs is therefore one of the chief distinctions that sets us apart from totalitarian regimes.

Accordingly a function of free speech under our system of government is to invite dispute. It may indeed best serve its high purpose when it induces a condition of unrest, creates dissatisfaction with conditions as they are, or even stirs people to anger. Speech is often provocative and challenging. It may strike at prejudices and preconceptions and have profound unsettling effects as it presses for acceptance of an idea. That is why freedom of speech, though not absolute, *Chaplinsky* v. *New Hampshire, supra,* pp. 571–572, is nevertheless protected against censorship or punishment, unless shown likely to produce a clear and present danger of a serious substantive evil that rises far above public inconvenience, annoyance, or unrest. See *Bridges* v. *California,* 314 U.S. 252, 262; *Craig* v. *Harney,* 331 U.S. 367, 373. There is no room under our Constitution for a more restrictive view. For the alternative would lead to standardization of ideas either by legislatures, courts, or dominant political or community groups.

The ordinance as construed by the trial court seriously invaded this province. It permitted conviction of petitioner if his speech stirred people to anger, invited public dispute, or brought about a condition of unrest. A conviction resting on any of those grounds may not stand.

The fact that petitioner took no exception to the instruction is immaterial. No exception to the instructions was taken in *Stromberg* v. *California,* 283 U.S. 359. But a judgment of conviction based on a general verdict under a state statute was set aside in that case, because one part of the statute was unconstitutional. . . .

But it is said that throughout the appellate proceedings the Illinois courts assumed that the only conduct punishable and punished under the ordinance was conduct constituting "fighting words." That emphasizes, however, the importance of the rule of the *Stromberg* case. Petitioner was not convicted under a statute so narrowly construed. For all anyone knows he was convicted under the parts of the ordinance (as construed) which, for example, make it an offense merely to invite dispute or to bring about a condition of unrest. We cannot avoid that issue by saying that all Illinois did was to mea-sure petitioner's conduct, not the ordinance, against the Constitution. Petitioner raised both points — that his speech was protected by the Constitution; that the inclusion of his speech within the ordinance was a violation of the Constitution.

Reversed.

MR. CHIEF JUSTICE VINSON, dissenting.

It will not do to say that, because the Illinois appellate courts affirmed the petitioner's conviction in the face of a constitutional attack, they necessarily must have approved the interpretation of the Chicago ordinance contained in the unnoticed instruction. The fact is that the Illinois courts construed the ordinance as punishing only the use of "fighting words." Their opinions plainly show that they affirmed because they thought that the petitioner's speech had been found by the jury to come within that category.

MR. JUSTICE FRANKFURTER, dissenting.

Reliance on *Stromberg* v. *California,* 283 U.S. 359, for what is done today is wholly misplaced. Neither expressly nor by implication has that decision any bearing upon the issue which the Court's opinion in this case raises, namely, whether it is open for this Court to reverse the highest court of a State on a point which was not brought before that court, did not enter into the judgment rendered by that Court, and at no stage of the proceedings in this Court was invoked as error by the State court whose reversal is here sought. The *Stromberg* case presented precisely the opposite situation. In that case the claim which here prevailed was a ground of unconstitutionality urged before the California court; upon its rejection by that court it was made the basis of appeal to this Court; it was here urged as the decisive ground for the reversal of the California judgment. . . . All that the case holds is that where the validity of a statute is successfully assailed as to one of three clauses of a statute and all three clauses were submitted to the jury, the general verdict has an infirmity because it cannot be assumed that the jury convicted on the valid portions of the statute and not on the invalid. There was no question in that case of searching the record for an alleged error that at no time was urged against the State judgment brought here for review.

Freedom of speech undoubtedly means freedom to express views that challenge deep-seated, sacred beliefs and to utter sentiments that may provoke resentment. But those indulging in such stuff as that to which this proceeding gave rise are hardly so deserving as to lead this Court to single them out as beneficiaries of the first departure from the restrictions that bind this Court in reviewing judgments of State courts. Especially odd is it to bestow such favor not for the sake of life or liberty, but to save a small amount of property — $100, the amount of the fine imposed upon the petitioner in a proceeding which is civil, not criminal, under the laws of Illinois, and thus subject only to limited review. . . .

MR. JUSTICE JACKSON, dissenting.

The Court reverses this conviction by reiterating generalized approbations of freedom of speech with which, in the abstract, no one will disagree. Doubts as to their applicability are lulled by avoidance of more than passing reference to the circumstances of Terminiello's speech and judging it as if he had spoken to persons as dispassionate as empty benches, or like a modern Demosthenes practicing his Philippics on a lonely seashore.

But the local court that tried Terminiello was not indulging in theory. It was dealing with a riot and with a speech that provoked a hostile mob and incited a friendly one, and threatened violence between the two.

An old proverb warns us to take heed lest we "walk into a well from looking at the stars." I think the Court is in some danger of doing just that, I must bring these deliberations down to earth by a long recital of facts. . . .

As this case declares a nation-wide rule that disables local and state authorities from punishing conduct which produces conflicts of this kind, it is unrealistic not to take account of the nature, methods and objectives of the forces involved. This was not an isolated, spontaneous and unintended collision of political, racial or ideological adversaries. . . . Increasingly, American cities have to cope with it. One faction organizes a mass meeting, the other organizes pickets to harass it; each organizes squads to counteract the other's pickets; parade is met with counterparade. Each of these mass demonstrations has the potentiality, and more than a few the purpose, of disorder and violence. . . . Terminiello's theoretical right to speak free from interference would have no reality if Chicago should withdraw its officers to some other section of the city, or if the men assigned to the task should look the other way when the crowd threatens Terminiello. Can society be expected to keep these men at Terminiello's service if it has nothing to say of his behavior which may force them into dangerous action? . . .

In considering abuse of freedom by provocative utterances it is necessary to observe that the law is more tolerant of discussion than are most individuals or communities.

Certain practical reasons reinforce the legal view that cities and states should be sustained in the power to keep their streets from becoming the battleground for these hostile ideologies to the destruction and detriment of public order.

This Court has gone far toward accepting the doctrine that civil liberty means the removal of all restraints from these crowds and that all local attempts to maintain order are impairments of the liberty of the citizen. The choice is between order and liberty. It is between liberty with order and anarchy without either. There is danger that, if the Court does not temper its doctrinaire logic with a little practical wisdom, it will convert the constitutional Bill of Rights into a suicide pact.

I would affirm the conviction.

MR. JUSTICE BURTON joins in this opinion.

Feiner v. New York

340 U.S. 315 (1951)
Vote: (5–1)–(1–2)

Paralleling Terminiello, this case involved a soapbox orator haranguing a crowd and making provocative comments. Policemen, detecting "restlessness" and danger from the crowd, asked the speaker to desist, and when he failed to do so arrested him. His conviction was affirmed in two state court appeal processes. Over dissents by Black, Douglas, and Murphy, the Supreme Court upheld the decision of the New York courts. Emphasis was placed upon the careful review of the New York courts, but it was clear the Court was giving broad authority to "the cop on the beat" to deal with free expression.

In *Edwards* v. *South Carolina* (1963), a decade of First Amendment thought and civil rights conflict combined to bring a different result. Students attempting to demonstrate at a state capitol were ordered to disperse. The Court found the meeting to have been peaceable and therefore legal. In *Cox* v. *Louisiana* (1956) much the same result was arrived at.

While the principle in *Feiner* — that there are limits to the capacities of the police to protect unpopular speakers — still is operative, more recent cases illustrate renewed emphasis that the first duty of the police is to control disrupters, not interfere with free expression. So in 1978, the courts ordered the Chicago suburb of Skokie, Illinois, to issue a permit to demonstrate to the American Nazi Party, even though the town had a rather large group of residents who were survivors of concentration camps. No one was compelled to attend the demonstration, so the anguish the camp survivors might feel could not justify infringement on expression. Neither did threats of counter-demonstrations or riots.

[Opinion of CHIEF JUSTICE VINSON]

On the evening of March 8, 1949, petitioner Irving Feiner was addressing an open-air meeting at the corner of South McBride and Harrison Streets, in the City of Syracuse. At approximately 6:30 p.m., the police received a telephone complaint concerning the meeting, and two officers were detailed to investigate. One of these officers went to the scene immediately, the other arriving some twelve minutes later. They found a crowd of about seventy-five or eighty people, both Negro and white, filling the sidewalk and spreading out into the street. Petitioner, standing on a large wooden box on the sidewalk, was addressing the crowd through a loud-speaker system attached to an automobile. . . . [H]e was making derogatory remarks concerning President Truman, the American Legion, the Mayor of Syracuse, and other local political officials.

The police officers made no effort to interfere with petitioner's speech, but were first concerned with the effect of the crowd on both pedestrian and vehicular traffic. They observed the situation from the opposite side of the street, noting that some pedestrians were forced to walk in the street to avoid the crowd. Since traffic was passing at the time, the officers attempted to get the people listening to petitioner back on the sidewalk. The crowd was restless and there was some pushing, shoving and milling around.

At this time, petitioner was speaking in a "loud, high-pitched voice." He gave the impression that he was endeavoring to arouse the Negro people against the whites, urging that they rise up in arms and fight for equal rights. The statements before such a mixed audience "stirred up a little excitement." Some of the onlookers made remarks to the police about their inability to handle the crowd and at least one threatened violence if the police did not act. There were others who appeared to be favoring pe-

titioner's arguments. Because of the feeling that existed in the crowd both for and against the speaker, the officers finally "stepped in to prevent it from resulting in a fight." One of the officers approached the petitioner, not for the purpose of arresting him, but to get him to break up the crowd. He asked petitioner to get down off the box, but the latter refused to accede to his request and continued talking. The officer waited for a minute and then demanded that he cease talking. Although the officer had thus twice requested petitioner to stop over the course of several minutes, petitioner not only ignored him but continued talking. During all this time, the crowd was pressing closer around petitioner and the officer. Finally, the officer told petitioner he was under arrest and ordered him to get down from the box, reaching up to grab him. Petitioner stepped down, announcing over the microphone that "the law has arrived, and I suppose they will take over now." In all, the officer had asked petitioner to get down off the box three times over a space of four or five minutes. Petitioner had been speaking for over a half hour. . . .

We are not faced here with blind condonation by a state court of arbitrary police action. Petitioner was accorded a full, fair trial. The trial judge heard testimony supporting and contradicting the judgment of the police officers that a clear danger of disorder was threatened. After weighing this contradictory evidence, the trial judge reached the conclusion that the police officers were justified in taking action to prevent a breach of the peace.

We are well aware that the ordinary murmurings and objections of a hostile audience cannot be allowed to silence a speaker, and are also mindful of the possible danger of giving overzealous police officials complete discretion to break up otherwise lawful public meetings. "A State may not unduly suppress free communication of views, religious or other, under the guise of conserving desirable conditons." (*Cantwell* v. *Connecticut*)

. . . But we are not faced here with such a situation. It is one thing to say that the police cannot be used as an instrument for the suppression of unpopular views, and another to say that, when as here the speaker passes the bounds of argument or persuasion and undertakes incitement to riot, they are powerless to prevent a breach of the peace. Nor in this case can we condemn the considered judgment of three New York courts approving the means which the police, faced with a crisis, used in the exercise of their power and duty to preserve peace and order. The findings of the state courts as to the existing situation and the imminence of greater disorder coupled with petitioner's deliberate defiance of the police officers convince us that we should not reverse this conviction in the name of free speech.

Affirmed.

MR. JUSTICE BLACK, dissenting.

The Court's opinion apparently rests on this reasoning: The policeman, under the circumstances detailed, could reasonably conclude that serious fighting or even riot was imminent; therefore he could stop petitioner's speech to prevent a breach of peace; accordingly, it was "disorderly conduct" for petitioner to continue speaking in disobedience of the officer's request. As to the existence of a dangerous situation on the street corner, it seems far-fetched to suggest that the "facts" show any imminent threat of riot or uncontrollable disorder. It is neither unusual nor unexpected that some people at public street meetings mutter, mill about, push, shove, or disagree, even violently, with the speaker. Indeed, it is rare where controversial topics are discussed that an outdoor crowd does not do some or all of these things. Nor does one isolated threat to assault the speaker forebode disorder. Especially should the danger be discounted where, as here, the person threatening was a man whose wife and two small children accompanied him and who, so far as the record shows, was never close enough to petitioner to carry out the threat.

Moreover, assuming that the "facts" did indicate a critical situation, I reject the implication of the Court's opinion that the police had no obligation to protect petitioner's constitutional right to talk. The police of course have power to prevent breaches of the peace. But if, in the name of preserving order, they ever can interfere with a lawful public speaker, they first must make all reasonable efforts to protect him. Here the policemen did not even pretend to try to protect petitioner. According to the officers' testimony, the crowd was restless but there is no showing of any attempt to quiet it. . . .

Finally, I cannot agree with the Court's statement that petitioner's disregard of the policeman's unexplained request amounted to such "deliberate defiance" as would justify an arrest or conviction for disorderly conduct. On the contrary, I think that the policeman's action was a "deliberate defiance" of ordinary official duty as well as of the constitutional right of free speech. For at least where time allows, courtesy and explanation of commands are basic elements of good official conduct in a democratic society. Here petitioner was "asked" then "told" then "commanded" to stop speaking, but a man making a lawful address is certainly not required to be silent merely because an officer directs it. . . .

[MR. JUSTICE DOUGLAS and MR. JUSTICE MINTON also dissented.]

Dennis v. U.S.

341 U.S. 494 (1951)

Vote: (4–1–1)–(2); Clark not participating.

The Smith Act of 1940 made it unlawful to "knowingly or willfully advocate, abet, advise or teach" the desirability of overthrowing the government or to "organize" for that purpose. In 1948 the eleven top leaders of the Communist Party were indicted on grounds of conspiracy to organize to advocate and conspiracy to teach the desirability of overthrow of the government. A raucous and prolonged trial resulted in the conviction of the leaders, and this was affirmed by the court of appeals. The court of appeals' opinion by the very prestigious Judge Learned Hand suggested that clear and present danger should also take into account the seriousness of the event to be guarded against: "the gravity of the 'evil' discounted by its improbability." Danger to the government being highly grave, the probability or "presentness" of the danger could be low. Certiorari was granted.

Clark, a recent Attorney General, recused himself. The Chief Justice could mobilize only three others in the plurality opinion, while Frankfurter and Jackson concurred. Black and Douglas dissented vigorously.

MR. CHIEF JUSTICE VINSON announced the judgment of the Court and an opinion in which MR. JUSTICE REED, MR. JUSTICE BURTON and MR. JUSTICE MINTON join.

Petitioners were indicted in July, 1948, for violation of the conspiracy provisions of the Smith Act, 54 Stat. 671, 18 U.S.C. (1964 ed.) §11, during the period of April, 1945, to July, 1948. The pretrial motion to quash the indictment on the grounds, *inter alia,* that the statute was unconstitutional was denied... and the case was set for trial on January 17, 1949. A verdict of guilty as to all the petitioners was returned by the jury on October 14, 1949. The Court of Appeals affirmed the convictions. 183 F. 2d 201. We granted certiorari, 340 U.S. 863, limited to the following two questions: (1) Whether either §2 or §3 of the Smith Act, inherently or as construed and applied in the instant case, violates the First Amendment and other provisions of the Bill of Rights; (2) whether either §2 or §3 of the Act, inherently or as construed and applied in the instant case, violates the First and Fifth Amendments because of indefiniteness.

Sections 2 and 3 of the Smith Act, 54 Stat. 671, 18 U.S.C. (1946 ed.) §§10, 11 (see present 18 U.S.C. §2385), provide as follows:

> SEC. 2. (a) It shall be unlawful for any person—
> "(1) to knowingly or willfully advocate, abet, advise, or teach the duty, necessity, desirability, or propriety of overthrowing or destroying any government in the United States by force or violence, or by the assassination of any officer of any such government; ...
> "(3) to organize or help to organize any society, group, or assembly of persons who teach, advocate, or encourage the overthrow or destruction of any government in the United States by force or violence; or to be or become a member of, or affiliate with, any such society, group, or assembly of persons, knowing the purposes thereof." ...

The indictment charged the petitioners with wilfully and knowingly conspiring (1) to organize as the Communist Party of the United States of America a society, group, and assembly of persons who teach and advocate the overthrow and destruction of the Government of the United States by force and violence, and (2) knowingly and wilfully to advocate and teach the duty and necessity of overthrowing and destroying the Government of the United States by force and violence....

The trial of the case extended over nine months, six of which were devoted to the taking of evidence, resulting in a record of 16,000 pages....

....

The obvious purpose of the statute is to protect existing Government, not from change by peaceable, lawful and constitutional means, but from change by violence, revolution and terrorism. That it is within the *power* of the Congress to protect the Government of the United States from armed rebellion is a proposition which requires little discussion. Whatever theoretical merit there may be to the argument that there is a "right" to rebellion against dictatorial governments is without force where the existing structure of the government provides for peaceful and orderly change. We reject any principle of governmental helplessness in the face of preparation for revolution, which principle, carried to its logical conclusion, must lead to anarchy. No one could conceive that it is not within the power of Congress to prohibit acts intended to overthrow the Government by force and violence. The question with which we are concerned here is not whether Congress has such *power,* but whether the *means* which it has employed conflict with the First and Fifth Amendments to the Constitution.

One of the bases for the contention that the means which Congress has employed are invalid takes the form of an attack on the face of the statute on the grounds that by its terms it prohibits academic discussion of the merits of Marxism-Leninism, that it stifles ideas and is contrary to all concepts of a free speech and a free press. . . .

The very language of the Smith Act negates the interpretation which petitioners would have us impose on that Act. It is directed at advocacy, not discussion. Thus, the trial judge properly charged the jury that they could not convict if they found that petitioners did "no more than pursue peaceful studies and discussions or teaching and advocacy in the realm of ideas." He further charged that it was not unlawful "to conduct in an American college or university a course explaining the philosophical theories set forth in the books which have been placed in evidence." Such a charge is in strict accord with the statutory language, and illustrates the meaning to be placed on those words. Congress did not intend to eradicate the free discussion of political theories, to destroy the traditional rights of Americans to discuss and evaluate ideas without fear of governmental sanction. Rather Congress was concerned with the very kind of activity in which the evidence showed these petitioners engaged.

But although the statute is not directed at the hypothetical cases which petitioners have conjured, its application in this case has resulted in convictions for the teaching and advocacy of the overthrow of the Government by force and violence, which, even though coupled with the intent to accomplish that overthrow, contains an element of speech. For this reason, we must pay special heed to the demands of the First Amendment marking out the boundaries of speech.

We pointed out in *Douds, supra,* that the basis of the First Amendment is the hypothesis that speech can rebut speech, propaganda will answer propaganda, free debate or ideas will result in the wisest governmental policies. It is for this reason that this Court has recognized the inherent value of free discourse. An analysis of the leading cases in this Court which have involved direct limitations on speech, however, will demonstrate that both the majority of the Court and the dissenters in particular cases have recognized that this is not an unlimited, unqualified right, but that the societal value of speech must, on occasion, be subordinated to other values and considerations.

. . . .

In this case we are squarely presented with the application of the "clear and present danger" test, and must decide what that phrase imports. We first note that many of the cases in which this Court has reversed convictions by use of this or similar tests have been based on the fact that the interest which the State was attempting to protect was itself too insubtantial to warrant restriction of speech. . . . Overthrow of the Government by force and violence is certainly a substantial enough interest for the Government to limit speech. Indeed, this is the ultimate value of any society, for if a society cannot protect its very structure from armed internal attack, it must follow that no subordinate value can be protected. If, then, this interest may be protected, the literal problem which is presented is what has been meant by the use of the phrase "clear and present danger" of the utterances bringing about the evil within the power of Congress to punish.

Obviously, the words cannot mean that before the Government may act, it must wait until the *putsch* is about to be executed, the plans have been laid and the signal is awaited. If Government is aware that a group aiming at its overthrow is attempting to indoctrinate its members and to commit them to a course whereby they will strike when the leaders feel the circumstances permit, action by the Government is required. The argument that there is no need for Government to concern itself, for Government is strong, it possesses ample powers to put down a rebellion, it may defeat the revolution with ease needs no answer. For that is not the question. Certainly an attempt to overthrow the Government by force, even though doomed from the outset because of inadequate numbers or power of the revolutionists, is

a sufficient evil for Congress to prevent. The damage which such attempts create both physically and politically to a nation makes it impossible to measure the validity in terms of the probability of success, or the immediacy of a successful attempt. In the instant case the trial judge charged the jury that they could not convict unless they found that petitioners intended to overthrow the Government "as speedily as circumstances would permit." This does not mean, and could not properly mean, that they would not strike until there was certainty of success. What was meant was that the revolutionists would strike when they thought the time was ripe. We must therefore reject the contention that success or probability of success is the criterion.

The situation in which Justices Holmes and Brandeis were concerned in *Gitlow* was a comparatively isolated event, bearing little relation in their minds to any substantial threat to the safety of the community. Such also is true of cases like *Fiske* v. *Kansas,* 274 U.S. 380, 71 L ed 1108, 47 S Ct 655 (1927), and *De Jonge* v. *Oregon,* 299 U.S. 353, 81 L ed 278, 57 S Ct 255 (1937); but cf. *Lazar* v. *Pennsylvania,* 286 U.S. 532, 76 L ed 1272, 52 S Ct 639 (1932). They were not confronted with any situation comparable to the instant one — the development of an apparatus designed and dedicated to the overthrow of the Government, in the context of world crisis after crisis.

Chief Judge Learned Hand, writing for the majority below, interpreted the phrase as follows: "In each case [courts] must ask whether the gravity of the 'evil,' discounted by its improbability, justifies such invasion of free speech as is necessary to avoid the danger." 183 F. 2d at 212. We adopt this statement of the rule. As articulated by Chief Judge Hand, it is as succinct and inclusive as any other we might devise at this time. It takes into consideration those factors which we deem relevant, and relates their significances. More we cannot expect from words. . . .

. . . [T]here remains the problem of whether the trial judge's treatment of the issue was correct. He charged the jury, in relevant part, as follows:

> I find as matter of law that there is sufficient danger of a substantive evil that the Congress has a right to prevent to justify the application of the statute under the First Amendment of the Constitution.

It is thus clear that he reserved the question of the existence of the danger for his own determination, and the question becomes whether the issue is of such a nature that it should have been submitted to the jury.

. . . .

Petitioners' reliance upon Justice Brandeis' language in his concurrence in *Whitney, supra,* is misplaced. In that case Justice Brandeis pointed out that the defendant could have made the existence of the requisite danger the important issue at her trial, but that she had not done so. In discussing this failure, he stated that the defendant could have had the issue determined by the court *or* the jury. No realistic construction of this disjunctive language could arrive at the conclusion that he intended to state that the question was *only* determinable by the jury. . . .

. . . .

We hold that §§2(a)(1), 2(a)(3) and 3 of the Smith Act do not inherently, or as construed or applied in the instant case, violate the First Amendment and other provisions of the Bill of Rights, or the First and Fifth Amendments because of indefiniteness. . . .

Affirmed.

MR. JUSTICE CLARK took no part in the consideration or decision of this case.

MR. JUSTICE FRANKFURTER, concurring in affirmance of the judgment.

. . . The demands of free speech in a democratic society as well as the interest in national security are better served by candid and informed weighing of the competing interests, within the confines of the judicial process, than by announcing dogmas too inflexible for the non-Euclidian problems to be solved.

But how are competing interests to be assessed? Since they are not subject to quantitative ascertainment, the issue necessarily resolves itself into asking, who is to make the adjustment? — who is to balance the relevant factors and ascertain which interest is in the circumstances to prevail? Full responsibility for the choice cannot be given to the courts. Courts are not representative bodies. They are not designed to be a good reflex of a democratic society. Their judgment is best informed, and therefore most dependable, within narrow limits. Their essential quality is detachment, founded on independence. History teaches that the independence of the judiciary is jeopardized when courts become embroiled in the passions of the day and assume primary responsibility in choosing between competing political, economic and social pressures.

Primary responsibility for adjusting the interests which compete in the situation before us of necessity belongs to the Congress. The nature of the power to be exercised by this Court has been delineated in decisions not charged with the emotional appeal of situations such as that now before us. We are to set aside the judgment of those whose duty it is to legislate only if there is no reasonable basis for it. . . .

. . . In reviewing statutes which restrict freedoms protected by the First Amendment, we have emphasized the close relation which those freedoms bear to maintenance of a free society. See *Kovacs* v. *Cooper . . .* (concurring). Some members of the Court — and at times a majority — have done more. They have suggested that our function in reviewing statutes restricting freedom of expression differs sharply from our normal duty in sitting in judgment on legislation. It has been said that such statutes "must be justified by clear public interest, threatened not doubtfully or remotely, but by clear and present danger. The rational connection between the remedy provided and the evil to be curbed, which in other contexts might support legislation against attack on due process grounds, will not suffice." *Thomas* v. *Collins. . . .* It has been suggested, with the casualness of a footnote, that such legislation is not presumptively valid, see *United States* v. *Carolene Products Co. . . .* and it has been weightily reiterated that freedom of speech has a "preferred position" among constitutional safeguards. . . .

The precise meaning intended to be conveyed by these phrases need not now be pursued. It is enough to note that they have recurred in the Court's opinions, and their cumulative force has, not without justification, engendered belief that there is a constitutional principle, expressed by those attractive but imprecise words, prohibiting restriction upon utterance unless it creates a situation of "imminent" peril against which legislation may guard. It is on this body of the Court's pronouncements that the defendants' argument here is based. . . .

The defendants have been convicted of conspiring to organize a party of persons who advocate the overthrow of the Government by force and violence. The jury has found that the object of the conspiracy is advocacy as "a rule or principle of action," "by language reasonably and ordinarily calculated to incite persons to such action," and with the intent to cause the overthrow "as speedily as circumstances would permit."

On any scale of values which we have hitherto recognized, speech of this sort ranks low.

. . . .

It is not for us to decide how we would adjust the clash of interests which this case presents were the primary responsibility for reconciling it ours. Congress has determined that the danger created by advocacy of overthrow justifies the ensuing restriction on freedom of speech. The determination was made after due deliberation, and the seriousness of the congressional purpose is attested by the volume of legislation passed to effectuate the same ends.

Can we then say that the judgment Congress exercised was denied it by the Constitution? Can we establish a constitutional doctrine which forbids the elected representatives of the people to make this choice? Can we hold that the First Amendment deprives Congress of what it deemed necessary for the Government's protection?

To make validity of legislation depend on judicial reading of events still in the womb of time — a forecast, that is, of the outcome of forces at best appreciated only with knowledge of the topmost secrets of nations — is to charge the judiciary with duties beyond its equipment. We do not expect courts to pronounce historic verdicts on bygone events. Even historians have conflicting views to this day on the origins and conduct of the French Revolution, or, for that matter, varying interpretations of "the glorious Revolution" of 1688. It is as absurd to be confident that we can measure the present clash of forces and their outcome as to ask us to read history still enveloped in clouds of controversy.

. . . .

MR. JUSTICE JACKSON, concurring.

The Communists have no scruples against sabotage, terrorism, assassination, or mob disorder; but violence is not with them, as with the anarchists, an end in itself. The Communist Party advocates force only when prudent and profitable. Their strategy of stealth precludes premature or uncoordinated outbursts of violence, except, of course, when the blame will be placed on shoulders other than their own. They resort to violence as to truth, not as a principle but as an expedient. Force or violence, as they would resort to it, may never be necessary, because infiltration and deception may be enough. . . .

The "clear and present danger" test was an innovation by Mr. Justice Holmes in the *Schenck* case, reiterated and refined by him and Mr. Justice Brandeis in later cases, all arising before the era of World War II revealed the subtlety and efficacy of modernized revolutionary techniques used by totalitarian parties. . . .

I would save it, unmodified, for application as a "rule of reason" in the kind of case for which it was devised. When the issue is criminality of a hot-headed speech on a street corner, or circulation of a few incendiary pamphlets, or parading by some zealots behind a red flag, or refusal of a handful of school children to salute our flag, it is not beyond the capacity of the judicial process to gather, compre-

hend, and weigh the necessary materials for decision whether it is a clear and present danger of substantive evil or a harmless letting off of steam. . . .

. . . .

I think reason is lacking for applying that test to this case.

If we must decide that this Act and its application are constitutional only if we are convinced that petitioner's conduct creates a "clear and present danger" of violent overthrow, we must appraise imponderables, including international and national phenomena which baffle the best informed foreign offices and our most experienced politicians. We would have to foresee and predict the effectiveness of Communist propaganda, opportunities for infiltration, whether, and when, a time will come that they consider propitious for action, and whether and how fast our existing government will deteriorate. And we would have to speculate as to whether an approaching Communist *coup* would not be anticipated by a nationalistic fascist movement. No doctrine can be sound whose application requires us to make a prophecy of that sort in the guise of a legal decision. The judicial process simply is not adequate to a trial of such far-flung issues. The answers given would reflect our own political predilections and nothing more.

The authors of the clear and present danger test never applied it to a case like this, nor would I. If applied as it is proposed here, it means that the Communist plotting is protected during its period of incubation; its preliminary stages of organization and preparation are immune from the law; the Government can move only after imminent action is manifest, when it would, of course, be too late.

. . . .

What really is under review here is a conviction of conspiracy, after a trial for conspiracy, on an indictment charging conspiracy, brought under a statute outlawing conspiracy. With due respect to my colleagues, they seem to me to discuss anything under the sun except the law of conspiracy. One of the dissenting opinions even appears to chide me for "invoking the law of conspiracy." As that is the case before us, it may be more amazing that its reversal can be proposed without even considering the law of conspiracy.

The Constitution does not make conspiracy a civil right. The Court has never before done so and I think it should not do so now. . . .

. . . .

. . . The Communist Party realistically is a state within a state, an authoritarian dictatorship within a republic. It demands these freedoms, not for its members, but for the organized party. It denies to its own members at the same time the freedom to dissent, to debate, to deviate from the party line, and enforces its authoritarian rule by crude purges, if nothing more violent.

The law of conspiracy has been the chief means at the Government's disposal to deal with the growing problems created by such organizations. I happen to think it is an awkward and inept remedy, but I find no constitutional authority for taking this weapon from the Government. There is no constitutional right to "gang up" on the Government.

While I think there was power in Congress to enact this statute and that, as applied in this case, it cannot be held unconstitutional, I add that I have little faith in the long-range effectiveness of this conviction to stop the rise of the Communist movement. Communism will not go to jail with these Communists. No decision by this Court can forestall revolution whenever the existing government fails to command the respect and loyalty of the people and sufficient distress and discontent is allowed to grow up among the masses. Many failures by fallen governments attest that no government can long prevent revolution by outlawry. Corruption, ineptitude, inflation, oppressive taxation, militarization, injustice, and loss of leadership capable of intellectual initiative in domestic or foreign affairs are allies on which the Communists count to bring opportunity knocking to their door. . . .

MR. JUSTICE BLACK, dissenting.

At the outset I want to emphasize what the crime involved in this case is, and what it is not. These petitioners were not charged with an attempt to overthrow the Government. They were not charged with overt acts of any kind designed to overthrow the Government. They were not even charged with saying anything or writing anything designed to overthrow the Government. The charge was that they agreed to assemble and to talk and publish certain ideas at a later date: The indictment is that they conspired to organize the Communist Party and to use speech or newspapers and other publications in the future to teach and advocate the forcible overthrow of the Government. No matter how it is worded, this is a virulent form of prior censorship of speech and press, which I believe the First Amendment forbids. I would hold §3 of the Smith Act authorizing this prior restraint unconstitutional on its face and as applied.

. . . .

Public opinion being what it now is, few will protest the conviction of these Communist petitioners.

There is hope, however, that in calmer times, when present pressures, passions and fears subside, this or some later Court will restore the First Amendment liberties to the high preferred place where they belong in a free society.

MR. JUSTICE DOUGLAS, dissenting.

. . . .

Yates v. U.S.

354 U.S. 298 (1957)
Vote: 4–2–1; Brennan and Whittaker not participating.

Six years after the DENNIS decision, the climate of opinion was rapidly changing. The Court's opinion in that case was subjected to devastating analyses indicating that the clear-and-probable-danger test was as inadequate as the old bad-tendency standard.

The Department of Justice had proceeded after DENNIS to indict fourteen "second-tier" Communist leaders. Yates and his colleagues were convicted and the court of appeals affirmed. The Supreme Court granted certiorari.

Justice Harlan's opinion in this case is often cited as an example of how a judge may use technical skills to defuse an issue without challenging legislative authority or calling attention to the scope of the decision. There are two important facets to his opinion, both of major importance to civil liberties: (1) The word "organize" is narrowly construed to mean form or establish; the federal statute of limitations, therefore, barred further prosecution for mere creation of the Communist Party. (2) DENNIS was "explained" as requiring "advocacy of action" and "advocacy of overthrow" for conviction.

This judgment was agreed to by all but Clark, (though Black and Douglas wanted all the defendants acquitted). The Department of Justice decided shortly afterwards that the evidence against the nine not discharged by the Supreme Court was inadequate to meet *Yates* standards. The Red Scare of the 1950s was largely over.

MR. JUSTICE HARLAN delivered the opinion of the Court.

These 14 petitioners stand convicted, after a jury trial in the United States District Court for the Southern District of California, upon a single count indictment charging them with conspiring (1) to advocate and teach the duty and necessity of overthrowing the Government of the United States by force and violence, and (2) to organize, as the Communist Party of the United States, a society of persons who so advocate and teach, all with the intent of causing the overthrow of the Government by force and violence as speedily as circumstances would permit.

. . . .

Petitioners claim that "organize" means to "establish," "found," or "bring into existence," and that in this sense the Communist Party was organized by 1945 at the latest. On this basis petitioners contend that this part of the indictment, returned in 1951, was barred by the three-year statute of limitations. The Government, on the other hand, says that "organize" connotes a continuing process which goes on throughout the life of an organization, and that, in the words of the trial court's instructions to the jury, the term includes such things as "the recruiting of new members and the forming of new units, and the regrouping or expansion of existing clubs, classes and other units of any society, party, group or other organization." The two courts below accepted the Government's position. . . . Stated most simply, the problem is to choose between two possible answers to the question: when was the Communist Party "organized"? Petitioners contend that the only natural answer to the question is the formation date — in this case, 1945. The Government would have us answer the question by saying that the Party today is still not completely "organized"; that "organizing" is a continuing process that does not end until the entity is dissolved. . . . While the legislative history of the Smith Act does show that concern about communism was a strong factor leading to this legislation, it also reveals that the statute, which was patterned on state anti-sedition laws directed not against Communists but against anarchists and syndicalists, was aimed equally at all groups falling within its scope. . . . In these circumstances we should follow the familiar rule that criminal statutes are to be strictly construed and give to "organize" its narrow meaning, that is, that the word refers only to acts entering into the creation of a new organization, and not to acts thereafter performed in carrying on its activities, even though such acts may loosely be termed "organizational."

We conclude, therefore, that since the Communist Party came into being in 1945, and the indictment was not returned until 1951, the three-year statute of limitations had run on the "organizing" charge, and required the withdrawal of that part of the indictment from the jury's consideration.

In failing to distinguish between advocacy of forcible overthrow as an abstract doctrine and advocacy of action to that end, the District Court appears to have been led astray by the holding in *Dennis* that advocacy of violent action to be taken at some future time was enough. It seems to have considered that, since "inciting" speech is usually thought of as something calculated to induce immediate action, and since *Dennis* held advocacy of action for future overthrow sufficient, this meant that advocacy, irrespective of its tendency to generate action, is punishable, provided only that it is uttered with a specific intent to accomplish overthrow. In other words, the District Court apparently thought that *Dennis* obliterated the traditional dividing line between advocacy of abstract doctrine and advocacy of action.

This misconceives the situation confronting the Court in *Dennis* and what was held there. Although the jury's verdict, interpreted in light of the trial court's instructions, did not justify the conclusion that the defendant's advocacy was directed at, or created any danger of, immediate overthrow, it did establish that the advocacy was aimed at building up a seditious group and maintaining it in readiness for action at a propitious time. In such circumstances, said Chief Justice Vinson, the Government need not hold its hand "until the *putsch* is about to be executed, the plans have been laid and the signal is awaited. If Government is aware that a group aiming at its overthrow is attempting to indoctrinate its members and to commit them to a course whereby they will strike when the leaders feel the circumstances permit, action by the Government is required." 341 U.S., at 509. The essence of the *Dennis* holding was that indoctrination of a group in preparation for future violent action, as well as exhortation to immediate action, by advocacy found to be directed to "action for the accomplishment" of forcible overthrow, to violence as "a rule or principle of action," and employing "language of incitement," *id.*, at 511–512, is not constitutionally protected when the group is of sufficient size and cohesiveness, is sufficiently oriented towards action, and other circumstances are such as reasonably to justify apprehension that action will occur. This is quite a different thing from the view of the District Court here that mere doctrinal justification of forcible overthrow, if engaged in with the intent to accomplish overthrow, is punishable *per se* under the Smith Act. That sort of advocacy, even though uttered with the hope that it may ultimately lead to violent revolution, is too remote from concrete action to be regarded as the kind of indoctrination preparatory to action which was condemned in *Dennis*.

In light of the foregoing we are unable to regard the District Court's charge upon this aspect of the case as adequate. The jury was never told that the Smith Act does not denounce advocacy in the sense of preaching abstractly the forcible overthrow of the Government. We think that the trial court's statement that the proscribed advocacy must include the "urging," "necessity," and "duty" of forcible overthrow, and not merely its "desirability" and "propriety," may not be regarded as a sufficient substitute for charging that the Smith Act reaches only advocacy of action for the overthrow of government by force and violence. The essential distinction is that those to whom the advocacy is addressed must be urged to *do* something, now or in the future, rather than merely to *believe* in something.

The determinations already made require a reversal of these convictions. Nevertheless, in the exercise of our power under 28 U.S.C. §2106 to "direct the entry of such appropriate judgment . . . as may be just under the circumstances," we have conceived it to be our duty to scrutinize this lengthy record with care, in order to determine whether the way should be left open for a new trial of all or some of these petitioners. Such a judgment, we think, should, on the one hand, foreclose further proceedings against those of the petitioners as to whom the evidence of this record would be palpably insufficient upon a new trial, and should, on the other hand, leave the Government free to retry the other petitioners under proper legal standards, especially since it is by no means clear that certain aspects of the evidence against them could not have been clarified to the advantage of the Government had it not been under a misapprehension as to the burden cast upon it by the Smith Act.

On this basis we have concluded that the evidence against petitioners Connelly, Kusnitz, Richmond, Spector, and Steinberg is so clearly insufficient that their acquittal should be ordered. . . . [A]part from the inadequacy of the evidence to show, at best, more than the abstract advocacy and teaching of forcible overthrow by the Party, it is difficult to perceive how the requisite specific intent to accomplish such overthrow could be deemed proved by a showing of mere membership or the holding of office in the Communist Party. We therefore think that as to these petitioners the evidence was entirely too mea-

gre to justify putting them to a new trial, and that their acquittal should be ordered.

As to the nine remaining petitioners, we consider that a different conclusion should be reached. There was testimony from the witness Foard, and other evidence, tying Fox, Healey, Lambert, Lima, Schneiderman, Stack, and Yates to Party classes conducted in the San Francisco area during the year 1946, where there occurred what might be considered to be the systematic teaching and advocacy of illegal action which is condemned by the statute.

As to these nine petitioners, then, we shall not order an acquittal.

It is so ordered.

MR. JUSTICE BURTON, concurring in the result.

I agree with the result reached by the Court, and with the opinion of the Court except as to its interpretation of the term "organize" as used in the Smith Act. As to that, I agree with the interpretation given it by the Court of Appeals.

MR. JUSTICE BLACK, with whom MR. JUSTICE DOUGLAS joins, concurring in part and dissenting in part.

I would reverse every one of these convictions and direct that all the defendants be acquitted.

The kind of trials conducted here are wholly dissimilar to normal criminal trials. Ordinarily these "Smith Act" trials are prolonged affairs lasting for months. In part this is attributable to the routine introduction in evidence of massive collections of books, tracts, pamphlets, newspapers, and manifestoes discussing Communism, Socialism, Capitalism, Feudalism and governmental institutions in general, which, it is not too much to say, are turgid, diffuse, abstruse, and just plain dull. . . . Guilt or innocence may turn on what Marx or Engels or someone else wrote or advocated as much as a hundred years ago. . . . When the propriety of obnoxious or unorthodox views about government is in reality made the crucial issue, as it must be in cases of this kind, prejudice makes conviction inevitable except in the rarest circumstances.

First. — I agree with Part I of the Court's opinion that deals with the statutory term, "organize," and holds that the organizing charge in the indictment was barred by the three-year statute of limitations.

Second. — I also agree with the Court insofar as it holds that the trial judge erred in instructing that persons could be punished under the Smith Act for teaching and advocating forceful overthrow as an abstract principle.

Under the Court's approach, defendants could still be convicted simply for agreeing to talk as distinguished from agreeing to act. I believe that the First Amendment forbids Congress to punish people for talking about public affairs, whether or not such discussion incites to action, legal or illegal.

MR. JUSTICE CLARK, dissenting.

The conspiracy includes the same group of defendants as in the *Dennis* case though petitioners here occupied a lower echelon in the party hierarchy. They, nevertheless, served in the same army and were engaged in the same mission. . . .

. . . In its long history I find no case in which an acquittal has been ordered by this Court solely on the *facts*. It is somewhat too late to start in now usurping the function of the jury, especially where new trials are to be held covering the same charges. . . . I notice however that to the majority "The essence of the *Dennis* holding was that indoctrination of a group in preparation for future violent actions, as well as exhortation to immediate action, by advocacy found to be directed to 'action for the accomplishment' of forcible overthrow, to violence 'as a rule or principle of action,' and employing 'language of incitement,' *id.*, at 511–512, is not constitutionally protected when the group is of sufficient size and cohesiveness, is sufficiently oriented towards action, and other circumstances are such as reasonably to justify apprehension that action will occur." I have read this statement over and over but do not seem to grasp its meaning for I see no resemblance between it and what the respected Chief Justice wrote in *Dennis*, nor do I find any such theory in the concurring opinions.

NAACP v. Alabama

357 U.S. 449 (1958)
Vote: 9–0

The Constitution guarantees freedom of speech, assembly, and petition, but, as an eighteenth-century document, it does not guarantee political organization or the right of association, in express terms.

Shortly after BROWN V. BOARD OF EDUCATION (1955), southern states began to harass potential litigators, including such organizations as the NAACP. In Alabama, the attorney general argued the NAACP was a "business," not a nonprofit association, and secured a court order asking, among other things, for full membership lists to ascertain whether it was an interstate business with registration requirements. The NAACP provided all records except those involving names of members, and offered to register if that would resolve the matter. They argued that providing individual names under prevailing conditions in the deep south would subject members to harassment, perhaps even danger. It would have, in any event, a "chilling effect" on new membership and, they argued, would be an unconstitutional exercise of state authority.

The state circuit court refused to accept any of this as compliance, found the NAACP in contempt, and fined it $100,000. The contempt finding had the effect of freezing further lower court proceedings until the NAACP purged itself by supplying its lists. Thus it could not have a hearing on the main issue.

Prior to being found in contempt the NAACP sought a stay from the Alabama Supreme Court. It refused to anticipate such a contempt citation, and the justices suggested that the correct remedy in Alabama was, after the citation for contempt, to return and seek certiorari from them. The NAACP returned to the Alabama Supreme Court, which refused to hear the case, stating the proper remedy was mandamus. It did, however, rule on the membership issue, holding the organization had no Fifth Amendment rights, only the members did, and, as a matter of state law, was therefore not privileged.

The U.S. Supreme Court granted certiorari.

The State of Alabama argued no review was possible, since the state supreme court had held the NAACP used the wrong procedure in bringing the case, and the decision therefore rested on a nonfederal basis.

In a portion of the opinion omitted because of its technical nature, the U.S. Supreme Court considered this claim by Alabama. It noted that the nonfederal ground does not defeat federal authority if it is "without any fair or substantial support." Reviewing this and previous similar procedural issues before the Alabama high court, the Supreme Court concluded: "We are unable to reconcile the procedural holding of the Alabama Supreme Court in the present case with its past unambiguous holdings as to the scope of review available upon a writ of certiorari addressed to a contempt judgment." In effect, the U.S. Supreme Court found the Alabama court to be faking a rule in an attempt to thwart federal jurisdiction. It, therefore, held the matter was properly before them.

MR. JUSTICE HARLAN delivered the opinion of the Court.

The question presented is whether Alabama, consistently with the Due Process Clause of the Fourteenth Amendment, can compel petitioner to reveal to the State's Attorney General the names and addresses of all its Alabama members and agents, without regard to their positions or functions in the Association. . . .

Alabama has a statute similar to those of many other States which requires a foreign corporation, except as exempted, to qualify before doing business by filing its corporate charter with the Secretary of State and designating a place of business and an agent to receive service of process. . . . The National Association for the Advancement of Colored People is a nonprofit membership corporation organized under the laws of New York. Its purposes, fostered on a nationwide basis, are those indicated by its name, and it operates through chartered affiliates which are independent unincorporated associations, with membership therein equivalent to membership in petitioner. . . . The Association has never complied with the qualification statute, from which it considered itself exempt.

. . . .

The Association both urges that it is constitutionally entitled to resist official inquiry into its membership lists, and that it may assert, on behalf of its members, a right personal to them to be protected from compelled disclosure by the State of their affiliation with the Association as revealed by the membership lists. We think that petitioner argues more appropriately the rights of its members, and that its nexus with them is sufficient to permit that it act as their representative before this Court. In so concluding, we reject respondent's argument that the Association lacks standing to assert here constitu-

tional rights pertaining to the members, who are not of course parties to the litigation.

To limit the breadth of issues which must be dealt with in particular litigation, this Court has generally insisted that parties rely only on constitutional rights which are personal to themselves. . . . This rule is related to the broader doctrine that constitutional adjudication should where possible be avoided. See *Ashwander* v. *Tennessee Valley Authority* . . . (concurring opinion). The principle is not disrespected where constitutional rights of persons who are not immediately before the Court could not be effectively vindicated except through an appropriate representative before the Court. . . .

If petitioner's rank-and-file members are constitutionally entitled to withhold their connection with the Association despite the production order, it is manifest that this right is properly assertable by the Association. To require that it be claimed by the members themselves would result in nullification of the right at the very moment of its assertion. Petitioner is the appropriate party to assert these rights, because it and its members are in every practical sense identical. The Association, which provides in its constitution that "[a]ny person who is in acccordance with [its] principles and policies . . ." may become a member, is but the medium through which its individual members seek to make more effective the expression of their own views. . . .

. . . Petitioner argues that in view of the facts and circumstances shown in the record, the effect of compelled disclosure of the membership lists will be to abridge the rights of its rank-and-file members to engage in lawful association in support of their common beliefs. It contends that governmental action which, although not directly suppressing association, nevertheless carries this consequence, can be justified only upon some overriding valid interest of the State.

Effective advocacy of both public and private points of view, particularly controversial ones, is undeniably enhanced by group association, as this Court has more than once recognized by remarking upon the close nexus between the freedoms of speech and assembly. *De Jonge* v. *Oregon*, . . . *Thomas* v. *Collins*. . . . It is beyond debate that freedom to engage in association for the advancement of beliefs and ideas is an inseparable aspect of the "liberty" assured by the Due Process Clause of the Fourteenth Amendment, which embraces freedom of speech. . . . Of course, it is immaterial whether the beliefs sought to be advanced by association pertain to political, economic, religious or cultural matters, and state action which may have the effect of curtailing the freedom to associate is subject to the closest scrutiny.

The fact that Alabama, so far as is relevant to the validity of the contempt judgment presently under review, has taken no direct action, cf. *De Jonge* v. *Oregon, supra; Near* v. *Minnesota,* . . . to restrict the right of petitioner's members to associate freely, does not end inquiry into the effect of the production order. . . . In the domain of these indispensable liberties, whether of speech, press, or association, the decisions of this Court recognize that abridgment of such rights, even though unintended, may inevitably follow from varied forms of governmental action. Thus in *Douds,* the Court stressed that the legislation there challenged, which on its face sought to regulate labor unions and to secure stability in interstate commerce, would have the practical effect "of discouraging" the exercise of constitutionally protected political rights, 339 U.S., at 393, and it upheld the statute only after concluding that the reasons advanced for its enactment were constitutionally sufficient to justify its possible deterrent effect upon such freedoms. . . . The governmental action challenged may appear to be totally unrelated to protected liberties. Statutes imposing taxes upon rather than prohibiting particular activity have been struck down when perceived to have the consequence of unduly curtailing the liberty of freedom of press assured under the Fourteenth Amendment. . . .

It is hardly a novel perception that compelled disclosure of affiliation with groups engaged in advocacy may constitute as effective a restraint on freedom of association as the forms of governmental action in the cases above were thought likely to produce upon the particular constitutional rights there involved. This Court has recognized the vital relationship between freedom to associate and privacy in one's associations. . . .

. . . Petitioner has made an uncontroverted showing that on past occasions revelation of the identity of its rank-and-file members has exposed these members to economic reprisal, loss of employment, threat of physical coercion, and other manifestations of public hostility. Under these circumstances, we think it apparent that compelled disclosure of petitioner's Alabama membership is likely to affect adversely the ability of petitioner and its members to pursue their collective effort to foster beliefs which they admittedly have the right to advocate, in that it may induce members to withdraw from the Association and dissuade others from joining it because of fear of exposure of their beliefs shown through their associations and of the consequences of this exposure.

It is not sufficient to answer, as the State does here, that whatever repressive effect compulsory disclosure of names of petitioner's members may have upon participation by Alabama citizens in petitioner's activities follows not from *state* action but from *private* community pressures. The crucial factor is the interplay of governmental and private action, for it is only after the initial exertion of state power represented by the production order that private action takes hold.

We turn to the final question whether Alabama has demonstrated an interest in obtaining the disclosures it seeks from petitioner which is sufficient to justify the deterrent effect which we have concluded these disclosures may well have on the free exercise by petitioner's members of their constitutionally protected right of association. . . .

It is important to bear in mind that petitioner asserts no right to absolute immunity from state investigation, and no right to disregard Alabama's laws. As shown by its substantial compliance with the production order, petitioner does not deny Alabama's right to obtain from it such information as the State desires concerning the purposes of the Association and its activities within the State. Petitioner has not objected to divulging the identity of its members who are employed by or hold official positions with it. It has urged the rights solely of its ordinary rank-and-file members. This is therefore not analogous to a case involving the interest of a State in protecting its citizens in their dealing with paid solicitors or agents of foreign corporations by requiring identification. . . .

Whether there was "justification" in this instance turns solely on the substantiality of Alabama's interest in obtaining the membership lists. During the course of a hearing before the Alabama Circuit Court on a motion of petitioner to set aside the production order, the State Attorney General presented at length, under examination by petitioner, the State's reason for requesting the membership lists. The exclusive purpose was to determine whether petitioner was conducting intrastate business in violation of the Alabama foreign corporation registration statute, and the membership lists were expected to help resolve this question. The issues in the litigation commenced by Alabama by its bill in equity were whether the character of petitioner and its activities in Alabama had been such as to make petitioner subject to the registration statute, and whether the extent of petitioner's activities without qualifying suggested its permanent ouster from the State. Without intimating the slightest view upon the merits of these issues, we are unable to perceive that the disclosure of the names of petitioner's rank-and-file members has a substantial bearing on either of them. . . .

New York Times Co. v. Sullivan

376 U.S. 254 (1964)
Vote: (6–3)–0

Civil rights activists took an advertisement in the *New York Times* presenting their view of events in Montgomery, where a major confrontation had taken place. Sullivan, one of three commissioners of the city, sued signers and the *New York Times,* claiming he had been libeled. Although Sullivan was not named in the advertisement, and only 394 copies of the paper were distributed in the whole state, the jury awarded $500,000 in damages. The Alabama Supreme court affirmed the verdict and the U.S. Supreme Court granted certiorari.

MR. JUSTICE BRENNAN delivered the opinion of the Court.

Respondent's complaint alleged that he had been libeled by statements in a full-page advertisement that was carried in the New York Times on March 29, 1960. Entitled "Heed Their Rising Voices," the advertisement began by stating that "As the whole world knows by now, thousands of Southern Negro students are engaged in widespread non-violent demonstrations in positive affirmation of the right to live in human dignity as guaranteed by the U.S. Constitution and the Bill of Rights." It went on to charge that "in their efforts to uphold these guarantees, they are being met by an unprecedented wave of terror by those who would deny and negate that document which the whole world looks upon as setting the pattern for modern freedom. . . ." Succeeding paragraphs purported to illustrate the "wave of terror" by describing certain alleged events. The text concluded with an appeal for funds for three purposes: support of the student movement, "the struggle for the right-to-vote," and the legal defense of Dr. Martin Luther King, Jr., leader of the movement, against a perjury indictment then pending in Montgomery.

. . . .

Of the 10 paragraphs of text in the advertisement, the third and a portion of the sixth were the basis of respondent's claim of libel. . . .

. . . .

It is uncontroverted that some of the statements contained in the two paragraphs were not accurate descriptions of events which occurred in Montgomery. Although Negro students staged a demonstration on the State Capitol steps, they sang the National Anthem and not "My Country, 'Tis of Thee." Although nine students were expelled by the State Board of Education, this was not for leading the demonstration at the Capitol, but for demanding service at a lunch counter in the Montgomery County Courthouse on another day. Not the entire student body, but most of it, had protested the expulsion, not by refusing to register, but by boycotting classes on a single day; virtually all the students did register for the ensuing semester. The campus dining hall was not padlocked on any occasion, and the only students who may have been barred from eating there were the few who had neither signed a preregistration application nor requested temporary meal tickets. Although the police were deployed near the campus in large numbers on three occasions, they did not at any time "ring" the campus, and they were not called to the campus in connection with the demonstration on the State Capitol steps, as the third paragraph implied. Dr. King had not been arrested seven times, but only four; and although he claimed to have been assaulted some years earlier in connection with his arrest for loitering outside a courtroom, one of the officers who made the arrest denied that there was such an assault.

On the premise that the charges in the sixth paragraph could be read as referring to him, respondent was allowed to prove that he had not participated in the events described. . . .

Respondent made no effort to prove that he suffered actual pecuniary loss as a result of the alleged libel. . . .

The cost of the advertisement was approximately $4800, and it was published by the Times upon an order from a New York advertising agency acting for the signatory Committee. . . . The manager of the Advertising Acceptability Department testified that he had approved the advertisement for publication because he knew nothing to cause him to believe that anything in it was false, and because it bore the endorsement of "a number of people who are well known and whose reputation" he "had no reason to question." . . .

Alabama law denies a public officer recovery of punitive damages in a libel action brought on account of a publication concerning his official conduct unless he first makes a written demand for a public retraction and the defendant fails or refuses to comply. Alabama Code, Tit. 7, §914. Respondent served such a demand upon each of the petitioners. None of the individual petitioners responded to the demand, primarily because each took the position that he had not authorized the use of his name on the advertisement and therefore had not published the statements that respondent alleged had libeled him. The Times did not publish a retraction in response to the demand, but wrote respondent a letter stating, among other things, that "we . . . are somewhat puzzled as to how you think the statements in any way reflect on you," and "you might, if you desire, let us know in what respect you claim that the statements in the advertisement reflect on you." Respondent filed this suit a few days later without answering the letter. . . .

The trial judge submitted the case to the jury under instructions that the statements in the advertisement were "libelous pe se" and were not privileged, so that petitioners might be held liable if the jury found that they had published the advertisement and that the statements were made "of and concerning" respondent. . . . An award of punitive damages—as distinguished from "general" damages, which are compensatory in nature—apparently requires proof of actual malice under Alabama law, and the judge charged that "mere negligence or carelessness is not evidence of actual malice or malice in fact, and does not justify an award of exemplary or punitive damages." He refused to charge, however, that the jury must be "convinced" of malice, in the sense of "actual intent" to harm or "gross negligence and recklessness," to make such an award. . . .

In affirming the judgment, the Supreme Court of Alabama sustained the trial judge's rulings and instructions in all respects. . . .

Because of the importance of the constitutional issues involved, we granted the separate petitions for certiorari of the individual petitioners and of the Times. 371 U.S. 946. We reverse the judgment. We hold that the rule of law applied by the Alabama courts is constitutionally deficient for failure to provide the safeguards for freedom of speech and of the press that are required by the First and Fourteenth Amendments in a libel action brought by a public official against critics of his official conduct.

. . . .

Respondent relies heavily, as did the Alabama courts, on statements of this Court to the effect that the Constitution does not protect libelous publications. Those statements do not foreclose our inquiry here. None of the cases sustained the use of libel laws to impose sanctions upon expression critical of the official conduct of public officials. . . . In *Beauharnais* v. *Illinois,* the Court sustained an Illinois criminal libel statute as applied to a publication held to be both defamatory of a racial group and "liable to cause violence and disorder." But the Court was careful to note that it "retains and exercises authority to nullify action which encroaches on freedom of utterance under the guise of punishing libel"; for "public men are, as it were, public property," and "discussion cannot be denied and the right, as well as the duty, of criticism must not be stifled." . . .

. . . .

Thus we consider this case against the background of a profound national commitment to the principle that debate on public issues should be uninhibited, robust, and wide-open, and that it may well include vehement, caustic, and sometimes unpleasantly sharp attacks on government and public officials. See *Terminiello* v. *Chicago,* . . . *De Jonge* v. *Oregon.* . . . The present advertisement, as an expression of grievance and protest on one of the major public issues of our time, would seem clearly to qualify for the constitutional protection. The question is whether it forfeits that protection by the falsity of some of its factual statements and by its alleged defamation of respondent.

Authoritative interpretations of the First Amendment guarantees have consistently refused to recognize an exception for any test of truth, whether administered by judges, juries, or administrative officials—and especially not one that puts the burden of proving truth on the speaker. Cf. *Speiser* v. *Randall.* . . . The constitutional protection does not turn upon "the truth, popularity, or social utility of the ideas and beliefs which are offered." *NAACP* v. *Button.* . . . As Madison said, "Some degree of abuse is inseparable from the proper use of every thing; and in no instance is this more true than in that of the press."

Just as factual error affords no warrant for repressing speech that would otherwise be free, the same is true of injury to official reputation. Where judicial officers are involved, this Court has held that concern for the dignity and reputation of the courts does not justify the punishment as criminal contempt of criticism of the judge or his decision. *Bridges* v. *California.* . . . This is true even though the utterance contains "half-truths" and "misinformation." . . . Such repression can be justified, if at all, only by a clear and present danger of the obstruction of justice. See also *Craig* v. *Harney, Wood* v. *Georgia.* . . .

If neither factual error nor defamatory content suffices to remove the constitutional shield from criticism of official conduct, the combination of the two elements is no less inadequate. This is the lesson to be drawn from the great controversy over the Sedition Act of 1798, 1 Stat. 596, which first crystallized a national awareness of the central meaning of the First Amendment. See Levy, Legacy of Suppression (1960)....

....

Although the Sedition Act was never tested in this Court, the attack upon its validity has carried the day in the court of history. Fines levied in its prosecution were repaid by Act of Congress on the ground that it was unconstitutional....

There is no force in respondent's argument that the constitutional limitations implicit in the history of the Sedition Act apply only to Congress and not to the States.... [T]his distinction was eliminated with the adoption of the Fourteenth Amendment and the application to the States of the First Amendment's restrictions. See, *e.g., Gitlow* v. *New York*....

....

...A rule compelling the critic of official conduct to guarantee the truth of all his factual assertions — and to do so on pain of libel judgments virtually unlimited in amount — leads to a comparable "self-censorship." Allowance of the defense of truth, with the burden of proving it on the defendant, does not mean that only false speech will be deterred....

The constitutional guarantees require, we think, a federal rule that prohibits a public official from recovering damages for a defamatory falsehood relating to his official conduct unless he proves that the statement was made with "actual malice" — that is, with knowledge that it was false or with reckless disregard of whether it was false or not.

....

Such a privilege for criticism of official conduct is appropriately analogous to the protection accorded a public official when *he* is sued for libel by a private citizen. In *Barr* v. *Matteo,* this Court held the utterance of a federal official to be absolutely privileged if made "within the outer perimeter" of his duties. The States accord the same immunity to statements of their highest officers, although some differentiate their lesser officials and qualify the privilege they enjoy. But all hold that all officials are protected unless actual malice can be proved....

We hold today that the Constitution delimits a State's power to award damages for libel in actions brought by public officials against critics of their official conduct. Since this is such an action, the rule requiring proof of actual malice is applicable....

....

Applying these standards, we consider that the proof presented to show actual malice lacks the con-

vincing clarity which the constitutional standard demands, and hence that it would not constitutionally sustain the judgment for respondent under the proper rule of law....

....

...There is no legal alchemy by which a State may thus create the cause of action that would otherwise be denied for a publication which, as respondent himself said of the advertisement, "reflects not only on me but on the other Commissioners and the community." Raising as it does the possibility that a goodfaith critic of government will be penalized for his criticism, the proposition relied on by the Alabama courts strikes at the very center of the constitutionally protected area of free expression. We hold that such a proposition may not constitutionally be utilized to establish that an otherwise impersonal attack on governmental operations was a libel of an official responsible for those operations....

Reversed and remanded.

MR. JUSTICE BLACK, with whom MR. JUSTICE DOUGLAS joins, concurring.

...An unconditional right to say what one pleases about public affairs is what I consider to be the minimum guarantee of the First Amendment.

I regret that the Court has stopped short of this holding indispensable to preserve our free press from destruction.

MR. JUSTICE GOLDBERG, with whom MR. JUSTICE DOUGLAS joins, concurring in the result.

....

...I strongly believe that the Constitution accords citizen and press an unconditional freedom to criticize official conduct. It necessarily follows that in a case such as this, where all agree that the allegedly defamatory statements relate to official conduct, the judgments for libel cannot constitutionally be sustained.

Herbert v. Lando

441 U.S. 153 (1979)
Vote: 6–1–2

The decision in NEW YORK TIMES V. SULLIVAN inevitably left a number of problems in its wake: defining a public figure; clarifying the new (but legally old) standard of "actual malice" in a new setting; and eventually problems about these issues.

The *Herbert* case is an example of the third issue. The "actual malice" or "reckless disregard for truth" standard involves some inquiry into the state of mind of the commentator. Herbert, alleging he had been libelled, wished to examine the cut-film and other work products of the "Sixty Minutes" staff relating to their coverage of him, to bolster his case. Reporters are sensitive to rummaging through their work and claim "reporter's privilege" similar to the privileges the media usually oppose for anyone else.

Herbert filed suit under New York Law in federal district court, under a diversity jurisdiction. The judge ordered Lando to permit discovery on work product, and he appealed this order. The court of appeals panel, by a divided vote, held the reporter's privilege was absolute. The Supreme Court granted certiorari.

MR. JUSTICE WHITE delivered the opinion of the Court.

By virtue of the First and Fourteenth Amendments, neither the Federal nor a State Government may make any law "abridging the freedom of speech, or of the press. . . ." The question here is whether those Amendments should be construed to provide further protection for the press when sued for defamation than has hitherto been recognized. More specifically, we are urged to hold for the first time that when a member of the press is alleged to have circulated damaging falsehoods and is sued for injury to the plaintiff's reputation, the plaintiff is barred from inquiring into the editorial processes of those responsible for the publication, even though the inquiry would produce evidence material to the proof of a critical element of his cause of action.

Petitioner, Anthony Herbert, is a retired Army officer who had extended wartime service in Vietnam and who received widespread media attention in 1969-1970 when he accused his superior officers of covering up reports of atrocities and other war crimes. Three years later, on February 4, 1973, respondent Columbia Broadcasting System, Inc. (CBS), broadcast a report on petitioner and his accusations. The program was produced and edited by respondent Barry Lando and was narrated by respondent Mike Wallace. Lando later published a related article in Atlantic Monthly magazine. Herbert then sued Lando, Wallace, CBS, and Atlantic Monthly for defamation in Federal District Court, basing jurisdiction on diversity of citizenship. In his complaint, Herbert alleged that the program and article falsely and maliciously portrayed him as a liar and a person who had made war-crimes charges to explain his relief from command, and he requested substantial damages for injury to his reputation and to the literary value of a book he had just published recounting his experiences.

Although his cause of action arose under New York State defamation law, Herbert conceded that because he was a "public figure" the First and Fourteenth Amendments precluded recovery absent proof that respondents had published a damaging falsehood "with 'actual malice' — that is, with knowledge that it was false or with reckless disregard of whether it was false or not." This was the holding of *New York Times Co.* v. *Sullivan,* 376 U.S. 254, 280 (1964), with respect to alleged libels of public officials, and extended to "public figures" by *Curtis Publishing Co.* v. *Butts,* 388 U.S. 130 (1967). Under this rule, absent knowing falsehood, liability requires proof of reckless disregard for truth, that is, that the defendant "in fact entertained serious doubts as to the truth of his publication." *St. Amant* v. *Thompson,* 390 U.S. 727, 731 (1968). Such "subjective awareness of probable falsity," *Gertz* v. *Robert Welch, Inc.,* 418 U.S. 323, 335 n. 6 (1974), may be found if "there are obvious reasons to doubt the veracity of the informant or the accuracy of his reports.". . .

In preparing to prove his case in light of these requirements, Herbert deposed Lando at length and sought an order to compel answers to a variety of questions to which response was refused on the ground that the First Amendment protected against inquiry into the state of mind of those who edit, produce, or publish, and into the editorial process. . . .

. . . [T]he District Court ruled that because the defendant's state of mind was of "central importance" to the issue of malice in the case, it was obvious that the questions were relevant and "entirely appropriate to Herbert's efforts to discover whether Lando had any reason to doubt the veracity of certain of his sources, or, equally significant, to prefer the veracity of one source over another."

A divided panel reversed the District Court. . . . Two judges, writing separate but overlapping opinions, concluded that the First Amendment lent sufficient protection to the editorial processes to protect Lando from inquiry about his thoughts, opinions, and conclusions with respect to the material gathered by him and about his conversations with his editorial colleagues. The privilege not to answer was held to be absolute. We granted certiorari because of the importance of the issue involved. 435 U.S. 922 (1978). We have concluded that the Court of Appeals misconstrued the First and Fourteenth Amendments and accordingly reverse its judgment. . . . Until *New York Times,* the prevailing jurisprudence was that "[l]ibelous utterances [are not] within the area of constitutionally protected speech. . . ." *New York Times* and *Butts* effected major changes in the standards applicable to civil libel actions. Under these cases public officials and public figures who sue for defamation must prove knowing or reckless falsehood in order to establish liability. Later, in *Gertz* v. *Robert Welch, Inc.,* 418 U.S. 323 (1974), the Court held that nonpublic figures must demonstrate some fault on the defendant's part and, at least where knowing or reckless untruth is not shown, some proof of actual injury to the plaintiff before liability may be imposed and damages awarded.

Given the required proof, however, damages liability for defamation abridges neither freedom of speech nor freedom of the press.

Nor did these cases suggest any First Amendment restriction on the sources from which the plaintiff could obtain the necessary evidence to prove the critical elements of his cause of action. On the contrary, *New York Times* and its progeny made it essential to proving liability that the plaintiff focus on the conduct and state of mind of the defendant.

Reliance upon such state-of-mind evidence is by no means a recent development arising from *New York Times* and similar cases. Rather, it is deeply rooted in the common-law rule, predating the First Amendment, that a showing of malice on the part of the defendant permitted plaintiffs to recover punitive or enhanced damages. . . .

It is nevertheless urged by respondents that the balance struck in *New York Times* should now be modified to provide further protections for the press when sued for circulating erroneous information damaging to individual reputation. It is not uncommon or improper, of course, to suggest the abandonment, modification, or refinement of existing constitutional interpretation, and notable developments in First Amendment jurisprudence have evolved from just such submissions. But in the 15 years since *New York Times,* the doctrine announced by that case, which represented a major development and which was widely perceived as essentially protective of press freedoms, has been repeatedly affirmed as the appropriate First Amendment standard applicable in libel actions brought by public officials and public figures.

As respondents would have it, the defendant's reckless disregard of the truth, a critical element, could not be shown by direct evidence through inquiry into the thoughts, opinions, and conclusions of the publisher, but could be proved only by objective evidence from which the ultimate fact could be inferred. It may be that plaintiffs will rarely be successful in proving awareness of falsehood from the mouth of the defendant himself, but the relevance of answers to such inquiries, which the District Court recognized and the Court of Appeals did not deny, can hardly be doubted. To erect an impenetrable barrier to the plaintiff's use of such evidence on his side of the case is a matter of some substance, particularly when defendants themselves are prone to assert their goodfaith belief in the truth of their publications, and libel plaintiffs are required to prove knowing or reckless falsehood with "convincing clarity." *New York Times Co.* v. *Sullivan.* . . .

Nevertheless, we are urged by respondents to override these important interests because requiring disclosure of editorial conversations and of a reporter's conclusions about the veracity of the material he has gathered will have an intolerable chilling effect on the editorial process and editorial decision-making. But if the claimed inhibition flows from the fear of damages liability for publishing knowing or reckless falsehoods, those effects are precisely what *New York Times* and other cases have held to be consistent with the First Amendment. Spreading false information in and of itself carries no First Amendment credentials. "[T]here is no constitutional value in false statements of facts." *Gertz* v. *Robert Welch, Inc., supra,* at 340.

Realistically, however, some error is inevitable; and the difficulties of separating fact from fiction convinced the Court in *New York Times, Butts, Gertz,* and similar cases to limit liability to instances where some degree of culpability is present in order to eliminate the risk of undue self-censorship and the suppression of truthful material. Those who publish defamatory falsehoods with the requisite culpability, however, are subject to liability, the aim being not only to compensate for injury but also to deter publication of unprotected material threatening injury to individual reputation. Permitting plaintiffs such as Herbert to prove their cases by direct as well as indirect evidence is consistent with the balance struck by our prior decisions. If such proof results in liability for damages which in turn discourages the publication of erroneous information known to be false or probably false, this is no more than what our cases contemplate and does not abridge either freedom of speech or of the press.

It is also urged that frank discussion among reporters and editors will be dampened and sound editorial judgment endangered if such exchanges, oral or written, are subject to inquiry by defamation plaintiffs. We do not doubt the direct relationship between consultation and discussion on the one hand and sound decisions on the other; but whether or not there is liability for the injury, the press has an obvious interest in avoiding the infliction of harm by the publication of false information, and it is not unreasonable to expect the media to invoke whatever procedures may be practicable and useful to that end.... Nor is there sound reason to believe that editorial exchanges and the editorial process are so subject to distortion and to such recurring misunderstanding that they should be immune from examination in order to avoid erroneous judgments in defamation suits. The evidentiary burden Herbert must carry to prove at least reckless disregard for the truth is substantial indeed, and we are unconvinced that his chances of winning an undeserved verdict are such that an inquiry into what Lando learned or said during editorial process must be foreclosed.

This is not to say that the editorial discussions or exchanges have no constitutional protection from casual inquiry. There is no law that subjects the editorial process to private or official examination merely to satisfy curiosity or to serve some general end such as the public interest; and if there were, it would not survive constitutional scrutiny as the First Amendment is presently construed. No such problem exists here, however, where there is a specific claim of injury arising from a publication that is alleged to have been knowingly or recklessly false.

... To this end, the requirement of Rule 26(b)(1) that the material sought in discovery be "relevant" should be firmly applied, and the district courts should not neglect their power to restrict discovery where "justice requires [protection for] a party or person from annoyance, embarrassment, oppression, or undue burden or expense...." Rule 26(c). With this authority at hand, judges should not hesitate to exercise appropriate control over the discovery process.

MR. JUSTICE POWELL, concurring.

... [W]hen a discovery demand arguably impinges on First Amendment rights a district court should measure the degree of relevance required in light of both the private needs of the parties and the public concerns implicated. On the one hand, as this Court has repeatedly recognized, the solicitude for First Amendment rights evidenced in our opinions reflects concern for the important public interest in a free flow of news and commentary.... On the other hand, there also is a significant public interest in according to civil litigants discovery of such matters as may be genuinely relevant to their lawsuit. Although the process of weighing these interests is hardly an

exact science, it is a function customarily carried out by judges in this and other areas of the law....

MR. JUSTICE BRENNAN, dissenting in part.

I agree with the Court that no such privilege insulates factual matters that may be sought during discovery, and that such a privilege should not shield respondents' "mental processes."... I would hold, however, that the First Amendment requires predecisional communication among editors to be protected by an editorial privilege, but that this privilege must yield if a public-figure plaintiff is able to demonstrate to the prima facie satisfaction of a trial judge that the publication in question constitutes defamatory falsehood.... To the extent coverage of such figures becomes fearful and inhibited, to the extent the accuracy, effectiveness, and thoroughness of such coverage is undermined, the social values protected by the First Amendment suffer abridgment.

I find compelling these justifications for the existence of an editorial privilege. The values at issue are sufficiently important to justify some incidental sacrifice of evidentiary material.

I fully concede that my reasoning is essentially paradoxical. For the sake of more accurate information, an editorial privilege would shield from disclosure the possible inaccuracies of the press; in the name of a more responsible press, the privilege would make more difficult of application the legal restraints by which the press is bound. The same paradox, however, inheres in the concept of an executive privilege: so as to enable the government more effectively to implement the will of the people, the people are kept in ignorance of the workings of their government. The paradox is unfortunately intrinsic to our social condition. Judgment is required to evaluate and balance these competing perspectives.

MR. JUSTICE STEWART, dissenting.

It seems to me that both the Court of Appeals and this Court have addressed a question that is not presented by the case before us. As I understand the constitutional rule of *New York Times Co.* v. *Sullivan,* inquiry into the broad "editorial process" is simply not relevant in a libel suit brought by a public figure against a publisher. And if such an inquiry is not relevant, it is not permissible. Fed. Rule Civ. Proc. 26(b).

Although I joined the Court's opinion in *New York Times,* I have come greatly to regret the use in that opinion of the phrase "actual malice." For the fact of the matter is that "malice" as used in the *New York Times* opinion simply does not mean malice as that word is commonly understood. In common understanding, malice means ill will or hostility, and the most relevant question in determining whether a person's action was motivated by actual malice is to ask "why." As part of the constitutional standard enunciated in the *New York Times* case, however, "actual malice" has nothing to do with hostility or ill will, and the question "why" is totally irrelevant.

The gravamen of such a lawsuit thus concerns that which was in fact published. What was *not* published has nothing to do with the case. And liability ultimately depends upon the publisher's state of knowledge of the falsity of what he published, not at all upon his motivation in publishing it — not at all, in other words, upon actual malice as those words are ordinarily understood.

MR. JUSTICE MARSHALL, dissenting.

The potential for abuse of liberal discovery procedures is of particular concern in the defamation context. As members of the bench and bar have increasingly noted, rules designed to facilitate expeditious resolution of civil disputes have too often proved tools for harassment and delay.

Not only is the risk of *in terrorem* discovery particularly pronounced in the defamation context, but the societal consequences attending such abuse are of special magnitude. Rather than submit to the intrusiveness and expense of protracted discovery, even editors confident of their ability to prevail at trial or on a motion for summary judgment may find it prudent to "'steer far wid[e] of the unlawful zone' thereby keeping protected discussion from public cognizance." . . . Faced with the prospect of escalating attorney's fees, diversion of time from journalistic endeavors, and exposure of potentially sensitive information, editors may well make publication judgments that reflect less the risk of liability than the expense of vindication.

If prepublication dialogue is freely discoverable, editors and reporters may well prove reluctant to air their reservations or to explore other means of presenting information and comment. The threat of unchecked discovery may well stifle the collegial discussion essential to sound editorial dynamics.

Brown et al. v. Louisiana

383 U.S. 131 (1966)
Vote: (3–1–1)–4

The civil rights movement, largely inspired by the Supreme Court's prophetic vision, presented its share of dilemmas for the Court's in-genuity. *Brown* v. *Louisiana* marked the high-water mark of Court support of demonstrations, and the division on the Court showed growing impatience with illegal demonstrations. Not only was the vote 5 to 4, but Justice Black defected in a testy opinion. Note that Brennan and White concurred only in the judgment; Brennan would have made further inroads on the Louisiana "breach of the peace" statute and, as his later vote in ADDERLEY V. FLORIDA confirmed, broadly shared the pro-demonstration attitude of Fortas, Warren, and Douglas. But White's concurrence was quite narrow, presaging the limits he as well as Fortas (author of the opinion below) thought were finally breached in ADDERLY, the case that follows.

This case originated when blacks protesting segregation entered a whites-only library and asked for a book. Informed that it was not available and asked to leave, they refused to depart; subsequently they were arrested and convicted of breach of peace. Under Louisiana law no further appeal was possible. The highest state court with jurisdiction having acted, defendants appealed to the U.S. Supreme Court.

MR. JUSTICE FORTAS announced the judgment of the Court and an opinion in which THE CHIEF JUSTICE and MR. JUSTICE DOUGLAS join.

This is the fourth time in little more than four years that this Court has reviewed convictions by the Louisiana courts for alleged violations, in a civil rights context, of that State's breach of the peace statute. In the three preceding cases the convictions were reversed.

The Audubon Regional Library is operated jointly by the Parishes of East Feliciana, West Feliciana, and St. Helena. It has three branches and two book-mobiles. The bookmobiles served 33 schools, both white and Negro, as well as "individuals." One of the bookmobiles was red, the other blue. The red bookmobile served only white persons. The blue bookmobile served only Negroes. It is a permissible inference that no Negroes used the branch libraries.

The registration cards issued to Negroes were stamped with the word "Negro." A Negro in possession of such a card was entitled to borrow books, but only from the blue bookmobile. A white person could not receive service from the blue bookmobile. He would have to wait until the red bookmobile came around, or would have to go to a branch library.

This tidy plan was challenged on Saturday, March 7, 1964, at about 11:30 a.m. Five young Negro males, all residents of East or West Feliciana Parishes, went into the adult reading or service room of the Audubon Regional Library at Clinton. The branch assistant, Mrs. Katie Reeves, was alone in the room. She met the men "between the tables" and asked if she "could help." Petitioner Brown requested a book, "The Story of the Negro" by Arna Bontemps. Mrs. Reeves checked the card catalogue, ascertained that the Branch did not have the book, so advised Mr. Brown, and told him that she would request the book from the State Library, that he would be notified upon its receipt and that "he could either pick it up or it would be mailed to him." She told him that "his point of service was a bookmobile or it could be mailed to him." Mrs. Reeves testified that she expected that the men would then leave; they did not, and she asked them to leave. They did not. Petitioner Brown sat down and the others stood near him. They said nothing; there was no noise or boisterous talking.

Neither Mrs. Reeves nor Mrs. Perkins had called the sheriff, but in "10 to 15 minutes" from the time of the arrival of the men at the library, the sheriff and deputies arrived. The sheriff asked the Negroes to leave. They said they would not. The sheriff then arrested them. The sheriff had been notified that morning that members of the Congress of Racial Equality "were going to sit-in" at the library.

The library obtained the requested book and mailed it to Mr. Brown on March 28, 1964. An accompanying card said, "You may return the book either by mail or to the Blue Bookmobile." The reference to the color of the vehicle was obviously not designed to facilitate identification of the library vehicle. The blue bookmobile is for Negroes and for Negroes only.

In the course of argument before this Court, counsel for both the State and petitioners stated that the Clinton Branch was closed after the incident of March 7. Counsel for the State also advised the court that the use of cards stamped "Negro" continues to be the practice of the regional library.

On March 25, 1964, Mr. Brown and his four companions were tried and found guilty.

Under Louisiana law, these convictions were not appealable. See *Garner* v. *Louisiana*. . . . Petitioners sought discretionary review by the Louisiana Supreme Court, which denied their application, finding no error. This Court granted certiorari, 381 U.S. 901, and we reverse. . . . Without reference to the statute, it must be noted that the petitioners' presence in the library was unquestionably lawful. It was a public facility, open to the public. Negroes could not be denied access since white persons were welcome. . . . Petitioners' deportment while in the library was unexceptionable. They were neither loud, boisterous, obstreperous, indecorous nor impolite. There is no claim that, apart from the continuation — for ten or fifteen minutes — of their presence itself, their conduct provided a basis for the order to leave, or for a charge of breach of the peace.

We come, then, to the barebones of the problem. Petitioners, five adult Negro men, remained in the library room for a total of ten or fifteen minutes. The first few moments were occupied by a ritualistic request for service and a response. We may assume that the response constituted service, and we need not consider whether it was merely a gambit in the ritual. This ceremony being out of the way, the Negroes proceeded to the business in hand. They sat and stood in the room, quietly, as monuments of protest against the segregation of the library. They were arrested and charged and convicted of breach of the peace under a specific statute.

The argument of the State of Louisiana, however, is that the issue presented by this case is much simpler than our statement would indicate. The issue, asserts the State, is simply that petitioners were using the library room "as a place in which to loaf or make a nuisance of themselves." The State argues that the "test" — the permissible civil rights demonstration — was concluded when petitioners entered the library, asked for service and were served. Having satisfied themselves, the argument runs, that they could get service, they should have departed. . . . There is no dispute that the library system was segregated, and no possible doubt that these petitioners were there to protest this fact. But even if we were to agree with the State's ingenuous characterization of the events, we would have to reverse. There was no violation of the statute which petitioners are accused of breaching; no disorder, no intent to provoke a breach of the peace and no circumstances indicating that a breach might be occasioned by petitioners' actions. The sole statutory provision invoked by the State contains not a word about occupying the reading room of a public library for more than 15 minutes, any more than it purports to punish the bare refusal to obey an unexplained command to withdraw from a public street. . . .

But there is another and sharper answer which is called for. We are here dealing with an aspect of a basic constitutional right — the right under the First and Fourteenth Amendments guaranteeing freedom of speech and of assembly, and freedom to petition the Government for a redress of grievances. The Constitution of the State of Louisiana reiterates these guaranties. See Art. I, §§3, 5. As this Court has repeatedly stated, these rights are not confined to verbal expression. They embrace appropriate types of action which certainly include the right in a peaceable and orderly manner to protest by silent and reproachful presence, in a place where the protestant has every right to be, the unconstitutional segregation of public facilities. Accordingly, even if the accused action were within the scope of the statutory instrument, we would be required to assess the constitutional impact of its application, and we would have to hold that the statute cannot constitutionally be applied to punish petitioners' actions in the circumstances of this case. See *Edwards* v. *South Carolina*. . . . The statute was deliberately and purposefully applied solely to terminate the reasonable, orderly, and limited exercise of the right to protest the unconstitutional segregation of a public facility. Interference with this right, so exercised, by state action is intolerable under our Constitution. *Wright* v. *Georgia*. . . .

It is an unhappy circumstance that the locus of these events was a public library — a place dedicated to quiet, to knowledge, and to beauty. It is a sad commentary that this hallowed place in the Parish of East Feliciana bore the ugly stamp of racism. It is sad, too, that it was a public library which, reasonably enough in the circumstances, was the stage for a confrontation between those discriminated against and the representatives of the offending parishes. Fortunately, the circumstances here were such that no claim can be made that use of the library by others was disturbed by the demonstration. Perhaps the time and method were carefully chosen with this in mind. Were it otherwise, a factor not present in this case would have to be considered. Here, there was no disturbance of others, no disruption of library activities, and no violation of any library regulations.

Reversed.

MR. JUSTICE BRENNAN, concurring in the judgment.

. . . The overbreadth of the statute recognized in *Cox* therefore requires the reversal of these convictions.

MR. JUSTICE WHITE, concurring in the result.

In my view, the behavior of these petitioners and their use of the library building, even though it was for the purposes of a demonstration, did not depart significantly from what normal library use would contemplate. . . . The State arrested petitioners because they refused to leave the library but offers no convincing explanation for why they were asked to leave. On this record, it is difficult to avoid the conclusion that petitioners were asked to leave the library because they were Negroes. If they were, their convictions deny them equal protection of the laws.

MR. JUSTICE BLACK, with whom MR. JUSTICE CLARK, MR. JUSTICE HARLAN, and MR. JUSTICE STEWART join, dissenting.

I do not believe that any provision of the United States Constitution forbids any one of the 50 States of the Union, including Louisiana, to make it unlawful to stage "sit-ins" or "stand-ups" in their public libraries for the purpose of advertising objections to the State's public policies. That, however, is precisely what the Court or at least a majority of the Court majority here holds that all the States are forbidden to do by our Constitution. I dissent. . . .

It was not against the policy of the library to allow citizens with library registration cards to read if they cared to. But according to Mrs. Reeves' testimony at trial, "very few people read; if a book is there and they want it, they take it and go." . . .

[T]here simply was no racial discrimination practiced in this case. These petitioners were treated with every courtesy and granted every consideration to which they were entitled in the Audubon Regional Library. . . . [A]lthough the record shows without the slightest dispute that there was no discrimination of any kind or character practiced against these petitioners, in at least the prevailing opinion and that of my Brother White it is nevertheless implied at several places that the equal treatment given these petitioners was some kind of subterfuge or sham. . . .

The State's District Attorney, who argued the case before us, stated frankly and forthrightly that there would be no defense had Louisiana denied these petitioners equal service at its public libraries on account of their race. There was no such denial. . . . A tiny parish branch library, staffed by two women, is not a department store as in *Garner* v. *Louisiana, supra,* nor a bus terminal as in *Taylor* v. *Louisiana, supra,* nor a public thoroughfare as in *Edwards* v. *South Carolina, supra,* and *Cox.* Short of physical violence, petitioners could not have more completely upset the normal, quiet functioning of the Clinton branch of the Audubon Regional Library. The state courts below thought the disturbance created by petitioners constituted a violation of the statute. So far as the reversal here rests on a holding that the Louisiana statute was not violated, the Court simply substitutes its judgment for that of the Louisiana courts as to what conduct satisfies the requirements of that state statute.

... In this case this new constitutional principle means that even though these petitioners did not want to use the Louisiana public library for library purposes, they had a constitutional right nevertheless to stay there over the protest of the librarians who had lawful authority to keep the library orderly for the use of people who wanted to use its books, its magazines, and its papers. But the principle espoused also has a far broader meaning. It means that the Constitution (the First and the Fourteenth Amendments) requires the custodians and supervisors of the public libraries in this country to stand helplessly by while protesting groups advocating one cause or another, stage "sit-ins" or "stand-ups" to dramatize their particular views on particular issues. And it should be remembered that if one group can take over libraries for one cause, other groups will assert the right to do so for causes which, while wholly legal, may not be so appealing to this Court. The States are thus paralyzed with reference to control of their libraries for library purposes, and I suppose that inevitably the next step will be to paralyze the schools.

The prevailing opinion laments the fact that the place where these events took place was "a public library — a place dedicated to quiet, to knowledge, and to beauty." I too lament this fact, and for this reason I am deeply troubled with the fear that powerful private groups throughout the Nation will read the Court's action, as I do — that is, as granting them a license to invade the tranquillity and beauty of our libraries whenever they have quarrel with some state policy which may or may not exist. I would affirm.

Adderley v. Florida

> 385 U.S. 39 (1966)
> Vote: 5–4

The issues troubling the Court in BROWN were again before it in *Adderley,* only a year later. Students gathered at a jail to protest segregation and arrests of earlier demonstrators. They were convicted of trespass, and the decisions were upheld by state courts. There was just enough variation, both in terms of the legal basis of prosecution of the demonstrators and in the fact

that the location of the demonstration was a jail, to turn BROWN's 5 to 4 vote for the demonstrators to a 5 to 4 decision against them here. Black's vigorous defense of the state's right to limit use of public places is in accord with his philosophy but probably goes beyond Court doctrine, although Black equally vigorously notes that such denial cannot be discriminatory. The case suggested the Court had begun to weigh and examine demonstrators' rights, rather than straining continuously for new doctrines to protect them. Still, the key practical point here is that demonstrations in front of jails represent special problems for law enforcement.

MR. JUSTICE BLACK delivered the opinion of the Court.

Petitioners, apparently all students of the Florida A. & M. University in Tallahassee, had gone from the school to the jail about a mile away, along with many other students, to "demonstrate" at the jail their protests of arrests of other protesting students the day before, and perhaps to protest more generally against state and local policies and practices of racial segregation, including segregation of the jail. The county sheriff, legal custodian of the jail and jail grounds, tried to persuade the students to leave the jail grounds. When this did not work, he notified them that they must leave, that if they did not leave he would arrest them for trespassing, and that if they resisted he would charge them with that as well. Some of the students left, but others, including petitioners, remained and they were arrested.

Petitioners have insisted from the beginning of this case that it is controlled by and must be reversed because of our prior cases of *Edwards* v. *South Carolina* ... and *Cox* v. *Louisiana.* ... We cannot agree.

The *Edwards* case, like this one, did come up when a number of persons demonstrated on public property against their State's segregation policies. They also sang hymns and danced, as did the demonstrators in this case. But here the analogies to this case end. In *Edwards,* the demonstrators went to the South Carolina State Capitol grounds to protest. In this case they went to the jail. Traditionally, state capitol grounds are open to the public. Jails, built for security purposes, are not. The demonstrators at the South Carolina Capitol went in through a public driveway and as they entered they were told by state officials there that they had a right as citizens to go through the State House grounds as long as they were peaceful. Here the demonstrators entered the jail grounds through a driveway used only for jail purposes and without warning to or permission from the sheriff. More importantly, South Carolina sought to prosecute its State Capitol demonstrators by charging them with the common-law crime of breach of the peace. This Court in *Edwards* took pains to point out at length the indefinite, loose, and broad nature of this charge; indeed, this Court pointed out at p. 237, that the South Carolina Supreme Court had itself declared that the "breach of the peace" charge is "not susceptible of exact definition." South Carolina's power to prosecute, it was emphasized at p. 236, would have been different had the State proceeded under a "precise and narrowly drawn regulatory statute evincing a legislative judgment that certain specific conduct be limited or proscribed" such as, for example, "limiting the periods during which the State House grounds were open to the public. . . ."

The Florida trespass statute under which these petitioners were charged cannot be challenged on this ground. It is aimed at conduct of one limited kind, that is, for one person or persons to trespass upon the property of another with a malicious and mischievous intent. There is no lack of notice in this law, nothing to entrap or fool the unwary.

Petitioners seem to argue that the Florida trespass law is void for vagueness because it requires a trespass to be "with malicious and mischievous intent. . . ." But these words do not broaden the scope of trespass. . . . On the contrary, these words narrow the scope of the offense.

Petitioners in this Court invoke the doctrine of abatement announced by this Court in *Hamm* v. *City of Rock Hill*. . . . But that holding was that the Civil Rights Act of 1964, 78 Stat. 241, which made it unlawful for places of public accommodation to deny service to any persons because of race, effected an abatement of prosecutions of persons for seeking such services that arose prior to the passage of the Act. But this case in no way involves prosecution of petitioners for seeking service in establishments covered by the Act.

Under the foregoing testimony the jury was authorized to find that the State had proven every essential element of the crime, as it was defined by the state court. That interpretation is, of course, binding on us, leaving only the question of whether conviction of the state offense, thus defined, unconstitutionally deprives petitioners of their rights to freedom of speech, press, assembly or petition. We hold it does not. The sheriff, as jail custodian, had power, as the state courts have here held, to direct that this large crowd of people get off the grounds. There is not a shred of evidence in this record that this power was

exercised, or that its exercise was sanctioned by the lower courts, because the sheriff objected to what was being sung or said by the demonstrators or because he disagreed with the objectives of their protest. The record reveals that he objected only to their presence on that part of the jail grounds reserved for jail uses. There is no evidence at all that on any other occasion had similarly large groups of the public been permitted to gather on this portion of the jail grounds for any purpose. Nothing in the Constitution of the United States prevents Florida from even-handed enforcement of its general trespass statute against those refusing to obey the sheriff's order to remove themselves from what amounted to the curtilage of the jailhouse. The State, no less than a private owner of property, has power to preserve the property under its control for the use to which it is lawfully dedicated. For this reason there is no merit to the petitioners' argument that they had a constitutional right to stay on the property, over the jail custodian's objections, because this "area chosen for the peaceful civil rights demonstration was not only 'reasonable' but also particularly appropriate. . . ." Such an argument has as its major unarticulated premise the assumption that people who want to propagandize protests or views have a constitutional right to do so whenever and however and wherever they please. That concept of constitutional law was vigorously and forthrightly rejected in two of the cases petitioners rely on. . . . We reject it again.

Affirmed.

Mr. Justice Douglas, with whom The Chief Justice, Mr. Justice Brennan, and Mr. Justice Fortas concur, dissenting.

. . . [T]he Court errs in treating the case as if it were an ordinary trespass case or an ordinary picketing case.

The jailhouse, like an executive mansion, a legislative chamber, a courthouse, or the statehouse itself (*Edwards* v. *South Carolina, supra*) is one of the seats of government, whether it be the Tower of London, the Bastille, or a small county jail. And when it houses political prisoners or those who many think are unjustly held, it is an obvious center for protest. The right to petition for the redress of grievances has an ancient history and is not limited to writing a letter or sending a telegram to a congressman. . . . Conventional methods of petitioning may be, and often have been, shut off to large groups of our citizens. Legislators may turn deaf ears; formal complaints may be routed endlessly through a bureaucratic maze; courts may let the wheels of justice grind very slowly. Those who do not control television and radio, those who cannot afford to advertise in newspapers or circulate elaborate pamphlets may have only a more limited type of access to public officials. Their methods should not be condemned as tactics of obstruction and harassment as long as the assembly and petition are peaceable, as these were. . . . It is said that some of the group blocked part of the driveway leading to the jail entrance. The chief jailer, to be sure, testified that vehicles would not have been able to use the driveway. Never did the students locate themselves so as to cause interference with persons or vehicles going to or coming from the jail. Indeed, it is undisputed that the sheriff and deputy sheriff, in separate cars, were able to drive up the driveway to the parking places near the entrance and that no one obstructed their path. Further, it is undisputed that the entrance to the jail was not blocked. And whenever the students were requested to move they did so. . . .

[T]he jailhouse grounds were not marked with "NO TRESPASSING!" signs, nor does respondent claim that the public was generally excluded from the grounds. Only the sheriff's fiat transformed lawful conduct into an unlawful trespass. To say that a private owner could have done the same if the rally had taken place on private property is to speak of a different case, as an assembly and a petition for redress of grievances run to government, not to private proprietors.

The Court forgets that prior to this day our decisions have drastically limited the application of state statutes inhibiting the right to go peacefully on public property to exercise First Amendment rights. As Mr. Justice Roberts wrote in *Hague* v. *C.I.O.,*

> . . . Wherever the title of streets and parks may rest, they have immemorially been held in trust for the use of the public and, time out of mind, have been used for purposes of assembly, communicating thoughts between citizens, and discussing public questions.

. . . When we allow Florida to construe her "malicious trespass" statute to bar a person from going on property knowing it is not his own and to apply that prohibition to public property, we discard *Cox* and *Edwards.* Would the case be any different if, as is common, the demonstration took place outside a building which housed both the jail and the legislative body? . . . It is said that the sheriff did not make the arrests because of the views which petitioners espoused. That excuse is usually given, as we know from the many cases involving arrests of minority groups for breaches of the peace, unlawful assem-

blies, and parading without a permit. The charge against William Penn, who preached a nonconformist doctrine in a street in London, was that he caused "a great concourse and tumult of people" in contempt of the King and "to the great disturbance of his peace." 6 How. St. Tr. 951, 955. That was in 1670. In modern times, also, such arrests are usually sought to be justified by some legitimate function of government. Yet by allowing these orderly and civilized protests against injustice to be suppressed, we only increase the forces of frustration which the conditions of second-class citizenship are generating amongst us.

PruneYard Shopping Center v. Robins

447 U.S. 74 (1980)
Vote: 9–0

Students sought to circulate petitions in a private shopping center that had consistently barred public expressive behavior. On being excluded, they turned to the California Superior Court, which denied them an injunction. On appeal, the California Supreme Court held as a matter of California law that a shopping center was obliged to permit such political activity, rejecting the owner's argument that to compel such activity on private property violated his Fifth and First Amendment rights. The case came On Appeal to the United States Supreme Court.

As a matter of federal law the issue was confused, but seemingly against the petitioners. In labor picketing cases the Court had wavered. In *Food Employees* v. *Logan Valley* (1968), the right to picket in a privately owned shopping center was upheld where there was no alternative place to protest. But in *Lloyd Corp.* v. *Tanner* (1972), passing out handbills was held prohibitable since other means of expression, not involving invasion of private property, were easily available. And in *Hudgens* v. *NLRB* (1976), the majority clearly rejected another claim to so use a shopping center, but split on the question of whether *Tanner* overruled *Logan Valley.*

In an important related case, the Supreme Court overturned Florida's right-of-reply law. In

Miami Herald Publishing Co. v. *Tornillo* (1974), the Florida requirement that political candidates be permitted to reply to newspaper criticism was held a governmental intrusion upon press freedom.

PruneYard, however, was even more complex. Would these negative federal precedents justify overruling the state law as interpreted by the California Supreme Court? Was *that* interpretation forbidden by the Constitution? On this question all of the justices came to the same conclusion, though by different routes.

MR. JUSTICE REHNQUIST delivered the opinion of the Court.

Appellant PruneYard is a privately owned shopping center in the city of Campbell, Cal. It covers approximately 21 acres—5 devoted to parking and 16 occupied by walkways, plazas, sidewalks, and buildings that contain more than 65 specialty shops, 10 restaurants, and a movie theater. The PruneYard is open to the public for the purpose of encouraging the patronizing of its commercial establishments. It has a policy not to permit any visitor or tenant to engage in any publicly expressive activity, including the circulation of petitions, that is not directly related to its commercial purposes. This policy has been strictly enforced in a nondiscriminatory fashion. The PruneYard is owned by appellant Fred Sahadi.

Appellees are high school students who sought to solicit support for their opposition to a United Nations resolution against "Zionism." On a Saturday afternoon they set up a card table in a corner of PruneYard's central courtyard. They distributed pamphlets and asked passersby to sign petitions, which were to be sent to the President and Members of Congress. Their activity was peaceful and orderly and so far as the record indicates was not objected to by PruneYard's patrons.

Soon after appellees had begun soliciting signatures, a security guard informed them that they would have to leave because their activity violated PruneYard regulations. The guard suggested that they move to the public sidewalk at the PruneYard's perimeter. Appellees immediately left the premises and later filed this lawsuit in the California Superior Court of Santa Clara County. They sought to enjoin appellants from denying them access to the Prune-Yard for the purpose of circulating their petitions.

The Superior Court held that appellees were not entitled under either the Federal or California Constitution to exercise their asserted rights on the shopping center property. . . .

The California Supreme Court reversed, holding that the California Constitution protects "speech and petitioning, reasonably exercised, in shopping centers even when the centers are privately owned."

We initially conclude that this case is properly before us as an appeal. . . .

Appellants next contend that a right to exclude others underlies the Fifth Amendment guarantee against the taking of property without just compensation and the Fourteenth Amendment guarantee against the deprivation of property without due process of law.

Here the requirement that appellants permit appellees to exercise state-protected rights of free expression and petition on shopping center property clearly does not amount to an unconstitutional infringement of appellants' property rights under the Taking Clause. There is nothing to suggest that preventing appellants from prohibiting this sort of activity will unreasonably impair the value or use of their property as a shopping center. The PruneYard is a large commercial complex that covers several city blocks, contains numerous separate business establishments, and is open to the public at large. The decision of the California Supreme Court makes it clear that the PruneYard may restrict expressive activity by adopting time, place, and manner regulations that will minimize any interference with its commercial functions. Appellees were orderly, and they limited their activity to the common areas of the shopping center. In these circumstances, the fact that they may have "physically invaded" appellants' property cannot be viewed as determinative. In *Nebbia* v. *New York* . . . this Court stated:

> [N]either property rights nor contract rights are absolute. . . . Equally fundamental with the private right is that of the public to regulate it in the common interest. . . .
>
> . . . [T]he guaranty of due process, as has often been held, demands only that the law shall not be unreasonable, arbitrary or capricious, and that the means selected shall have a real and substantial relation to the objective sought to be attained.

Appellants have failed to provide sufficient justification for concluding that this test is not satisfied by the State's asserted interest in promoting more expansive rights of free speech and petition than conferred by the Federal Constitution.

Appellants finally contend that a private property owner has a First Amendment right not to be forced by the State to use his property as a forum for the speech of others. . . . Appellants also argue that their

First Amendment rights have been infringed in light of *West Virginia State Board of Education* v. *Barnette,* 319 U.S. 624 (1943), and *Miami Herald Publishing Co.* v. *Tornillo,* 418 U.S. 241 (1974). *Barnette* is inapposite because it involved the compelled recitation of a message containing an affirmation of belief. This Court held such compulsion unconstitutional because it "require[d] the individual to communicate by word and sign his acceptance" of government-dictated political ideas, whether or not he subscribed to them. 319 U.S., at 633. Appellants are not similarly being compelled to affirm their belief in any governmentally prescribed position or view, and they are free to publicly dissociate themselves from the views of the speakers or handbillers.

Tornillo struck down a Florida statute requiring a newspaper to publish a political candidate's reply to criticism previously published in that newspaper. It rests on the principle that the State cannot tell a newspaper what it must print. The Florida statute contravened this principle in that it "exact[ed] a penalty on the basis of the content of a newspaper." 418 U.S., at 256. There also was a danger in *Tornillo* that the statute would "dampe[n] the vigor and limi[t] the variety of public debate" by deterring editors from publishing controversial political statements that might trigger the application of the statute. *Id.,* at 257. Thus, the statute was found to be an "intrusion into the function of editors." *Id.,* at 258. These concerns obviously are not present here.

We conclude that neither appellants' federally recognized property rights nor their First Amendment rights have been infringed by the California Supreme Court's decision recognizing a right of appellees to exercise state-protected rights of expression and petition on appellants' property. The judgment of the Supreme Court of California is therefore

Affirmed.

MR. JUSTICE BLACKMUN joins the opinion of the Court except that sentence thereof, *ante,* at 84, which reads: "Nor as a general proposition is the United States, as opposed to the several States, possessed of residual authority that enables it to define 'property' in the first instance."

MR. JUSTICE MARSHALL, concurring.

I join the opinion of the Court, but write separately to make a few additional points.

I continue to believe that *Logan Valley* was rightly decided, and that both *Lloyd* and *Hudgens* were in-

correct interpretations of the First and Fourteenth Amendments. State action was present in all three cases. In all of them the shopping center owners had opened their centers to the public at large, effectively replacing the State with respect to such traditional First Amendment forums as streets, sidewalks, and parks. The State had in turn made its laws of trespass available to shopping center owners, enabling them to exclude those who wished to engage in expressive activity on their premises. Rights of free expression become illusory when a State has operated in such a way as to shut off effective channels of communication. I continue to believe, then, that "the Court's rejection of any role for the First Amendment in the privately owned shopping center complex stems... from an overly formalistic view of the relationship between the institution of private ownership of property and the First Amendment's guarantee of freedom of speech." *Hudgens* v. *NLRB.* . . . The California court concluded that its state "[c]onstitution broadly proclaims speech and petition rights. Shopping centers to which the public is invited can provide an essential and invaluable forum for exercising those rights." . . . Like the Court in *Logan Valley,* the California court found that access to shopping centers was crucial to the exercise of rights of free expression. And like the Court in *Logan Valley,* the California court rejected the suggestion that the Fourteenth Amendment barred the intrusion on the property rights of the shopping center owners. I applaud the court's decision, which is a part of a very healthy trend of affording state constitutional provisions a more expansive interpretation than this Court has given to the Federal Constitution.

MR. JUSTICE WHITE, concurring in part and concurring in the judgment.

[I]t bears pointing out that the Federal Constitution does not require that a shopping center permit distributions or solicitations on its property. Indeed, *Hudgens* v. *NLRB,* and *Lloyd Corp.* v. *Tanner,* . . . hold that the First and Fourteenth Amendments do not prevent the property owner from excluding those who would demonstrate or communicate on his property. Insofar as the Federal Constitution is concerned, therefore, a State may decline to construe its own constitution so as to limit the property rights of the shopping center owner.

MR. JUSTICE POWELL, with whom MR. JUSTICE WHITE joins, concurring in part and in the judgment.

U.S. v. O'Brien

391 U.S. 367 (1968)
Vote: 7–1; Marshall not participating.

O'Brien was convicted of burning a draft card, in violation of a statute punishing one who "knowingly destroys" such a card. The First Circuit's Court of Appeals panel unanimously declared the law unconstitutional as an infringement of First Amendment rights protecting "symbolic speech." To prohibit the burning of draft cards served no purpose not covered by the requirement the card be in possession of the draftee. But a similar panel in the Second Circuit held the law constitutional. To resolve the disagreement the Supreme Court granted certiorari.

MR. CHIEF JUSTICE WARREN delivered the opinion of the Court.

On the morning of March 31, 1966, David Paul O'Brien and three companions burned their Selective Service registration certificates on the steps of the South Boston Courthouse. . . . After he was advised of his right to counsel and to silence, O'Brien stated to FBI agents that he had burned his registration certificate because of his beliefs, knowing that he was violating federal law. He produced the charred remains of the certificate, which, with his consent, were photographed.

For this act, O'Brien was indicted, tried, convicted, and sentenced in the United States District Court for the District of Massachusetts. . . .

On appeal, the Court of Appeals for the First Circuit held the 1965 Amendment unconstitutional as a law abridging freedom of speech. . . . We granted the Government's petition to resolve the conflict in the circuits, and we also granted O'Brien's cross-petition. We hold that the 1965 Amendment is constitutional both as enacted and as applied. . . .

By the 1965 Amendment, Congress added to §12(b)(3) of the 1948 Act the provision here at issue, subjecting to criminal liability not only one who "forges, alters, or in any manner changes" but also one who "knowingly destroys, [or] knowingly mutilates" a certificate. We note at the outset that the 1965 Amendment plainly does not abridge free speech on its face, and we do not understand

O'Brien to argue otherwise. Amended §12(b)(3) on its face deals with conduct having no connection with speech. It prohibits the knowing destruction of certificates issued by the Selective Service System, and there is nothing necessarily expressive about such conduct. The Amendment does not distinguish between public and private destruction, and it does not punish only destruction engaged in for the purpose of expressing views. Compare *Stromberg* v. *California* . . . (1931). A law prohibiting destruction of Selective Service certificates no more abridges free speech on its face than a motor vehicle law prohibiting the destruction of drivers' licenses, or a tax law prohibiting the destruction of books and records.

O'Brien nonetheless argues that the 1965 Amendment is unconstitutional in its application to him, and is unconstitutional as enacted because what he calls the "purpose" of Congress was "to suppress freedom of speech." We consider these arguments separately.

O'Brien first argues that the 1965 Amendment is unconstitutional as applied to him because his act of burning his registration certificate was protected "symbolic speech" within the First Amendment. His argument is that the freedom of expression which the First Amendment guarantees includes all modes of "communication of ideas by conduct," and that his conduct is within this definition because he did it in "demonstration against the war and against the draft."

We cannot accept the view than an apparently limitless variety of conduct can be labeled "speech" whenever the person engaging in the conduct intends thereby to express an idea. However, even on the assumption that the alleged communicative element in O'Brien's conduct is sufficient to bring into play the First Amendment, it does not necessarily follow that the destruction of a registration certificate is constitutionally protected activity. This Court has held that when "speech" and "nonspeech" elements are combined in the same course of conduct, a sufficiently important governmental interest in regulating the nonspeech element can justify incidental limitations on First Amendment freedoms. To characterize the quality of the governmental interest which must appear, the Court has employed a variety of descriptive terms: compelling; substantial; subordinating; paramount; cogent; strong. Whatever imprecision inheres in these terms, we think it clear that a government regulation is sufficiently justified if it is within the constitutional power of the Government; if it furthers an important or substantial governmental interest; if the governmental interest is unrelated to the suppression of free expression; and if the incidental restriction on alleged First Amendment freedoms is no greater than is essential to the furtherance of that interest. We find that the 1965 Amendment to §12(b)(3) of the Universal Military Training and Service Act meets all of these requirements, and consequently that O'Brien can be constitutionally convicted for violating it.

The constitutional power of Congress to raise and support armies and to make all laws necessary and proper to that end is broad and sweeping. . . . The power of Congress to classify and conscript manpower for military service is "beyond question." *Lichter* v. *United States* . . . (1948). . . . Pursuant to this power, Congress may establish a system of registration for individuals liable for training and service. . . .

O'Brien's argument to the contrary is necessarily premised upon his unrealistic characterization of Selective Service certificates. He essentially adopts the position that such certificates are so many pieces of paper designed to notify registrants of their registration or classification, to be retained or tossed in the wastebasket according to the convenience or taste of the registrant. Once the registrant has received notification, according to this view, there is no reason for him to retain the certificates. O'Brien notes that most of the information on a registration certificate serves no notification purpose at all; the registrant hardly needs to be told his address and physical characteristics. We agree that the registration certificate contains much information on which the registrant needs no notification. This circumstance, however, does not lead to the conclusion that the certificate serves no purpose, but that, like the classification certificate, it serves purposes in addition to initial notification. Many of these purposes would be defeated by the certificates' destruction or mutilation. Among these are:

1. The registration certificate serves as proof that the individual described thereon has registered for the draft.

2. The information supplied on the certificates facilitates communication between registrants and local boards, simplifying the system and benefiting all concerned. To begin with, each certificate bears the address of the registrant's local board, an item unlikely to be committed to memory. Further, each card bears the registrant's Selective Service number, and a registrant who has his number readily available so that he can communicate it to his local board.

3. Both certificates carry continual reminders that the registrant must notify his local board of any change of address, and other specified changes in his status.

4. The regulatory scheme involving Selective Service certificates includes clearly valid prohibitions against the alteration, forgery, or similar deceptive misuse. . . .

The many functions performed by Selective Service certificates establish beyond doubt that Congress has a legitimate and substantial interest in preventing their wanton and unrestrained destruction and assuring their continuing availability by punishing people who knowingly and wilfully destroy or mutilate them. And we are unpersuaded that the pre-existence of the nonpossession regulations in any way negates this interest.

In the absence of a question as to multiple punishment, it has never been suggested that there is anything improper in Congress' providing alternative statutory avenues of prosecution to assure the effective protection of one and the same interest.

Equally important, a comparison of the regulations with the 1965 Amendment indicates that they protect overlapping but not identical governmental interests, and that they reach somewhat different classes of wrongdoers. The gravamen of the offense defined by the statute is the deliberate rendering of certificates unavailable for the various purposes which they may serve. Whether registrants keep their certificates in their personal possession at all times, as required by the regulations, is of no particular concern under the 1965 Amendment, as long as they do not mutilate or destroy the certificates so as to render them unavailable. . . .

O'Brien finally argues that the 1965 Amendment is unconstitutional as enacted because what he calls the "purpose" of Congress was "to suppress freedom of speech." We reject this argument because under settled principles the purpose of Congress, as O'Brien uses that term, is not a basis for declaring this legislation unconstitutional.

It is a familiar principle of constitutional law that this Court will not strike down an otherwise constitutional statute on the basis of an alleged illicit legislative motive. As the Court long ago stated:

> The decisions of this court from the beginning lend no support whatever to the assumption that the judiciary may restrain the exercise of lawful power on the assumption that a wrongful purpose or motive has caused the power to be exerted. *McCray* v. *United States,* 195 U.S. 27, 56 (1904).

Inquiries into congressional motives or purposes are a hazardous matter. When the issue is simply the interpretation of legislation, the Court will look to statements by legislators for guidance as to the purpose of the legislature, because the benefit to sound decision-making in just such a tax. Similarly, in

Gomillion, the Court sustained a complaint which, if true, established that the "inevitable effect"... of the redrawing of municipal boundaries was to deprive the petitioners of their right to vote for no reason other than that they were Negro. In these cases, the purpose of the legislation was irrelevant, because the inevitable effect — the "necessary scope and operation," *McCray* v. *United States* ... (1904) — abridged constitutional rights. The statute attacked in the instant case has no such inevitable unconstitutional effect, since the destruction of Selective Service certificates is in no respect inevitably or necessarily expressive. Accordingly, the statute itself is constitutional.

MR. JUSTICE HARLAN, concurring.

I wish to make explicit my understanding that this passage does not foreclose consideration of First Amendment claims in those rare instances when an "incidental" restriction upon expression, imposed by a regulation which furthers an "important or substantial" governmental interest and satisfies the Court's other criteria, in practice has the effect of entirely preventing a "speaker" from reaching a significant audience with whom he could not otherwise lawfully communicate. This is not such a case, since O'Brien manifestly could have conveyed his message in many ways other than by burning his draft card.

MR. JUSTICE DOUGLAS, dissenting.

The underlying and basic problem in this case, however, is whether conscription is permissible in the absence of a declaration of war. That question has not been briefed nor was it presented in oral argument; but it is, I submit, a question upon which the litigants and the country are entitled to a ruling....

The rule that this Court will not consider issues not raised by the parties is not inflexible and yields in "exceptional cases"... to the need correctly to decide the case before the court.

Tinker v. Des Moines Independent Community School District

393 U.S. 503 (1969)
Vote: 7–2

Students decided to wear black armbands in protest against the Vietnam war, persisting even though school principals adopted a regulation forbidding such activity. The Tinkers were suspended, and turned to the federal district court for reinstatement. The court dismissed their complaint, though recognizing the symbolic speech argument, because the judge nonetheless found the state interest in schooling outweighed the free speech considerations. The circuit court sitting en banc divided evenly, thus affirming, and the U.S. Supreme Court granted certiorari. The case thus presented questions of classroom rights and the dimensions of symbolic speech.

Without reversing *Tinker,* the Court has since modified its support for in-school rights, distinguishing the level of freedom students have, based on their age level and experience. High school newspapers issued under authority of the school are subject to regulation, at least in their comments on sexual behavior of specific individuals, and school authorities may also punish a student for explicit sexual innuendo in a school speech. These restrictions would not be applicable at the college level, where generally the autonomy granted students amounts to the creation of a public forum with guarantees of expression. (See *Bethel School District* v. *Fraser,* 1986, and *Hazelwood School District* v. *Kuhlmeir,* 1988.)

MR. JUSTICE FORTAS delivered the opinion of the court.

In December 1965, a group of adults and students in Des Moines held a meeting at the Eckhardt home. The group determined to publicize their objections to the hostilities in Vietnam and their support for a truce by wearing black armbands during the holiday season and by fasting on December 16 and New Year's Eve....

The principals of the Des Moines schools became aware of the plan to wear armbands. On December 14, 1965, they met and adopted a policy that any student wearing an armband to school would be asked to remove it, and if he refused he would be suspended until he returned without the armband. Petitioners were aware of the regulation that the school authorities adopted.

On December 16, Mary Beth and Christopher wore black armbands to their schools. John Tinker wore his armband the next day. They were all sent home and suspended from school until they would come back without their armbands. They did not return to school until after the planned period for wearing armbands had expired — that is, until after New Year's Day.

The District Court recognized that the wearing of an armband for the purpose of expressing certain views is the type of symbolic act that is within the Free Speech Clause of the First Amendment. See *West Virginia* v. *Barnette,* (1943). . . . As we shall discuss, the wearing of armbands in the circumstances of this case was entirely divorced from actually or potentially disruptive conduct by those participating in it. It was closely akin to "pure speech" which, we have repeatedly held, is entitled to comprehensive protection under the First Amendment. Cf. *Cox* v. *Louisiana*. . .; *Adderley* v. *Florida*. . . .

First Amendment rights, applied in light of the special characteristics of the school environment, are available to teachers and students. It can hardly be argued that either students or teachers shed their constitutional rights to freedom of speech or expression at the schoolhouse gate. This has been the unmistakable holding of this Court for almost 50 years. On the other hand, the Court has repeatedly emphasized the need for affirming the comprehensive authority of the States and of school officials, consistent with fundamental constitutional safeguards, to prescribe and control conduct in the schools. See *Epperson* v. *Arkansas*. . .; *Meyer* v. *Nebraska*. . . . Our problem lies in the area where students in the exercise of First Amendment rights collide with the rules of the school authorities.

The problem posed by the present case does not relate to regulation of the length of skirts or the type of clothing, to hair style, or deportment. . . . Our problem involves direct, primary First Amendment rights akin to "pure speech."

The school officials banned and sought to punish petitioners for a silent, passive expression of opinion, unaccompanied by any disorder or disturbance on the part of petitioners. There is here no evidence whatever of petitioners' interference, actual or nascent, with the schools' work or of collision with the rights of other students to be secure and to be let alone. Accordingly, this case does not concern speech or action that intrudes upon the work of the schools or the rights of other students.

Only a few of the 18,000 students in the school system wore the black armbands. Only five students were suspended for wearing them. There is no indication that the work of the schools or any class was disrupted. Outside the classrooms, a few students made hostile remarks to the children wearing armbands, but there were no threats or acts of violence on school premises.

The District Court concluded that the action of the school authorities was reasonable because it was based upon their fear of a disturbance from the wearing of the armbands. But, in our system, undifferentiated fear or apprehension of disturbance is not enough to overcome the right to freedom of expression. Any departure from absolute regimentation may cause trouble. Any variation from the majority's opinion may inspire fear. Any word spoken, in class, in the lunchroom, or on the campus, that deviates from the views of another person may start an argument or cause a disturbance. But our Constitution says we must take this risk, *Terminiello* v. *Chicago* . . . (1949); and our history says that it is this sort of hazardous freedom — this kind of openness — that is the basis of our national strength and of the independence and vigor of Americans who grow up and live in this relatively permissive, often disputatious, society.

On the contrary, the action of the school authorities appears to have been based upon an urgent wish to avoid the controversy which might result from the expression, even by the silent symbol of armbands, of opposition to this Nation's part in the conflagration in Vietnam. It is revealing, in this respect, that the meeting at which the school principals decided to issue the contested regulation was called in response to a student's statement to the journalism teacher in one of the schools that he wanted to write an article on Vietnam and have it published in the school paper. (The student was dissuaded.)

It is also relevant that the school authorities did not purport to prohibit the wearing of all symbols of political or controversial significance. The record shows that students in some of the schools wore buttons relating to national political campaigns, and some even wore the Iron Cross, traditionally a symbol of Nazism. The order prohibiting the wearing of armbands did not extend to these. Instead, a particular symbol — black armbands worn to exhibit opposition to this Nation's involvement in Vietnam — was singled out for prohibition. Clearly, the prohibition of expression of one particular opinion, at least without evidence that it is necessary to avoid material and substantial interference with schoolwork or discipline, is not constitutionally permissible.

In our system, state-operated schools may not be enclaves of totalitarianism. School officials do not possess absolute authority over their students. Students in school as well as out of school are "persons" under our Constitution. They are possessed of fundamental rights which the State must respect, just as they themselves must respect their obligations to the State. In our system, students may not be regarded as closed-circuit recipients of only that which the State chooses to communicate. They may not be confined to the expression of those sentiments that are officially approved. In the absence of a specific showing of constitutionally valid reasons to regulate their speech, students are entitled to freedom of expression of their views. . . .

Under our Constitution, free speech is not a right that is given only to be so circumscribed that it exists in principle but not in fact. Freedom of expression would not truly exist if the right could be exercised only in an area that a benevolent government has provided as a safe haven for crackpots. The Constitution says that Congress (and the States) may not abridge the right to free speech. This provision means what it says. We properly read it to permit reasonable regulation of speech-connected activities in carefully restricted circumstances. But we do not confine the permissible exercise of First Amendment rights to a telephone booth or the four corners of a pamphlet, or to supervised and ordained discussion in a school classroom.

If a regulation were adopted by school officials forbidding discussion of the Vietnam conflict, or the expression by any student of opposition to it anywhere on school property except as part of a prescribed classroom exercise, it would be obvious that the regulation would violate the constitutional rights of students, at least if it could not be justified by a showing that the students' activities would materially and substantially disrupt the work and discipline of the school. In the circumstances of the present case, the prohibition of the silent, passive "witness of the armbands," as one of the children called it, is no less offensive to the Constitution's guarantees.

MR. JUSTICE STEWART, concurring.

Although I agree with much of what is said in the Court's opinion, and with its judgment in this case, I cannot share the Court's uncritical assumption that, school discipline aside, the First Amendment rights of children are co-extensive with those of adults. . . .

MR. JUSTICE WHITE, concurring.

While I join the Court's opinion, I deem it appropriate to note, that the Court continues to recognize a distinction between communicating by words and communicating by acts or conduct which sufficiently impinges on some valid state interest. . . .

MR. Justice Black, dissenting.

The Court's holding in this case ushers in what I deem to be an entirely new era in which the power to control pupils by the elected "officials of state-supported public schools. . ." in the United States is in ultimate effect transferred to the Supreme Court. . . . Ordered to refrain from wearing the armbands in school by the elected school officials and the teachers vested with state authority to do so, apparently only seven out of the school system's 18,000 pupils deliberately refused to obey the order.

Assuming that the Court is correct in holding that the conduct of wearing armbands for the purpose of conveying political ideas is protected by the First Amendment, cf., e.g., Giboney v. Empire Storage & Ice Co. . . (1949), the crucial remaining questions are whether students and teachers may use the schools at their whim as a platform for the exercise of free speech—"symbolic" or "pure"—and whether the courts will allocate to themselves the function of deciding how the pupils' school day will be spent. While I have always believed that under the First and Fourteenth Amendments neither the State nor the Federal Government has any authority to regulate or censor the content of speech, I have never believed that any person has a right to give speeches or engage in demonstrations where he pleases and when he pleases. This Court has already rejected such a notion. In Cox v. Louisiana . . . (1965), for example, the Court clearly stated that the rights of free speech and assembly "do not mean that everyone with opinions or beliefs to express may address a group at any public place and at any time."

While the record does not show that any of these armband students shouted, used profane language, or were violent in any manner, detailed testimony by some of them shows their armbands caused comments, warnings by other students, the poking of fun at them, and a warning by an older football player that other, nonprotesting students had better let them alone. There is also evidence that a teacher of mathematics had his lesson period practically "wrecked" chiefly by disputes with Mary Beth Tinker, who wore her armband for her "demonstration." Even a casual reading of the record shows that this armband did divert students' minds from their regular lessons, and that talk, comments, etc., made John Tinker "self-conscious" in attending school with his armband. While the absence of obscene remarks or boisterous and loud disorder perhaps justifies the Court's statement that the few armband students did not actually "disrupt" the classwork, I think the record overwhelmingly shows that the armbands did exactly what the elected school officials and principals foresaw they would, that is, took the students' minds off their classwork and diverted them to thoughts about the highly emotional subject of the Vietnam war. And I repeat that if the time has come when pupils of state-supported schools, kindergartens, grammar schools, or high schools, can defy and flout orders of school officials to keep their minds on their own schoolwork, it is the beginning of a new revolutionary era of permissiveness in this country fostered by the judiciary. The next logical step, it appears to me, would be to hold unconstitutional laws that bar pupils under 21 or 18 from voting, or from being elected members of the boards of education.

... The truth is that a teacher of kindergarten, grammar school, or high school pupils no more carries into a school with him a complete right to freedom of speech and expression than an anti-Catholic or anti-Semite carries with him a complete freedom of speech and religion into a Catholic church or Jewish synagogue....

In my view, teachers in state-controlled public schools are hired to teach there. Although Mr. Justice McReynolds may have intimated to the contrary in *Meyer* v. *Nebraska, supra,* certainly a teacher is not paid to go into school and teach subjects the State does not hire him to teach as a part of its selected curriculum. Nor are public school students sent to the schools at public expense to broadcast political or any other views to educate and inform the public. The original idea of schools, which I do not believe is yet abandoned as worthless or out of date, was that children had not yet reached the point of experience and wisdom which enabled them to teach all of their elders. It may be that the Nation has outworn the old-fashioned slogan that "children are to be seen, not heard," but one may, I hope, be permitted to harbor the thought that taxpayers send children to school on the premise that at their age they need to learn, not teach....

Change has been said to be truly the law of life but sometimes the old and the tried and true are worth holding. The schools of this Nation have undoubtedly contributed to giving us tranquility and to making us a more law-abiding people. Uncontrolled and uncontrollable liberty is an enemy to domestic peace. We cannot close our eyes to the fact that some of the country's greatest problems are crimes committed by the youth, too many of school age. School discipline, like parental discipline, is an integral and important part of training our children to be good citizens — to be better citizens. Here a very small number of students have crisply and summarily refused to obey a school order designed to give pupils who want to learn the opportunity to do so. One does not need to be a prophet or the son of a prophet to know that af-

ter the Court's holding today some students in Iowa schools and indeed in all schools will be ready, able, and willing to defy their teachers on practically all orders. This is the more unfortunate for the schools since groups of students all over the land are already running loose, conducting break-ins, sit-ins, lie-ins, and smash-ins. Many of these student groups, as is all too familiar to all who read the newspapers and watch the television news programs, have already engaged in rioting, property seizures, and destruction. They have picketed schools to force students not to cross their picket lines and have too often violently attacked earnest but frightened students who wanted an education that the pickets did not want them to get. Students engaged in such activities are apparently confident that they know far more about how to operate public school systems than do their parents, teachers, and elected school officials. It is no answer to say that the particular students here have not yet reached such high points in their demands to attend classes in order to exercise their political pressures. Turned loose with lawsuits for damages and injunctions against their teachers as they are here, it is nothing but wishful thinking to imagine that young, immature students will not soon believe it is their right to control the schools rather than the right of the States that collect the taxes to hire the teachers for the benefit of the pupils.

Mr. Justice Harlan, dissenting.

... I would, in cases like this, cast upon those complaining the burden of showing that a particular school measure was motivated by other than legitimate school concerns — for example, a desire to prohibit the expression of an unpopular point of view, while permitting expression of the dominant opinion.

Chaplinsky v. New Hampshire

315 U.S. 568 (1942)
Vote: 9–0

This seemingly minor case has had enormous influence and is the legal source of the notion of "nonprotected," or "two-tiered," speech, sometimes called the "jurisprudence of areas." For example, the "fighting words" doctrine that emerges was heavily relied upon in the obscenity decisions.

A Jehovah's Witness encountering difficulties in addressing an audience asked a policeman to protect him. In the course of a disputed exchange with the policeman, Chaplinsky employed personal epithets, for which he was convicted of a state statute prohibiting such use in municipal court and in a trial de novo in superior court. (A de novo trial is a new proceeding with witnesses, disregarding the previous trial, not a review On Appeal with a frozen record from below. It is not uncommon for states to allow a new trial after proceedings in Justice-of-the-Peace or other cursory court structures.) The decision was affirmed by the state supreme court, and the U.S. Supreme Court granted certiorari.

MR. JUSTICE MURPHY delivered the opinion of the Court.

Appellant, a member of the sect known as Jehovah's Witnesses, was convicted in the municipal court of Rochester, New Hampshire, for violation of Chapter 378, §2, of the Public Laws of New Hampshire:

"No person shall address any offensive, derisive or annoying word to any other person who is lawfully in any street or other public place, nor call him by any offensive or derisive name, nor make any noise or exclamation in his presence and hearing with intent to deride, offend or annoy him, or to prevent him from pursuing his lawful business or occupation."

The complaint charged that appellant, "with force and arms, in a certain public place in said city of Rochester, to wit, on the public sidewalk on the easterly side of Wakefield Street, near unto the entrance of the City Hall, did unlawfully repeat, the words following, Addressed to the complainant, that is to say, 'You are a God damned racketeer' and 'a damned Fascist and the whole government of Rochester are Fascists or agents of Fascists,' the same being offensive, derisive and annoying words and names."

Upon appeal there was a trial de novo of appellant before a jury in the Superior Court. He was found guilty and the judgment of conviction was affirmed by the Supreme Court of the State.

There is no substantial dispute over the facts. . . .

Chaplinsky's version of the affair was slightly different. He testified that, when he met Bowering, he asked him to arrest the ones responsible for the disturbance. In reply, Bowering cursed him and told him to come along. Appellant admitted that he said the words charged in the complaint, with the exception of the name of the Deity.

Appellant assails the statute as a violation of all three freedoms, speech, press and worship, but only

an attack on the basis of free speech is warranted. The spoken, not the written, word is involved. And we cannot conceive that cursing a public officer is the exercise of religion in any sense of the term. But even if the activities of the appellant which preceded the incident could be viewed as religious in character, and therefore entitled to the protection of the Fourteenth Amendment, they would not cloak him with immunity from the legal consequences for concomitant acts committed in violation of a valid criminal statute. . . .

Allowing the broadest scope to the language and purpose of the Fourteenth Amendment, it is well understood that the right of free speech is not absolute at all times and under all circumstances. There are certain well-defined and narrowly limited classes of speech, the prevention and punishment of which have never been thought to raise any Constitutional problem. These include the lewd and obscene, the profane, the libelous, and the insulting or "fighting" words — those which by their very utterance inflict injury or tend to incite an immediate breach of the peace. It has been well observed that such utterances are no essential part of any exposition of ideas, and are of such slight social value as a step to truth that any benefit that may be derived from them is clearly outweighed by the social interest in order and morality.

On the authority of its earlier decisions, the state court declared that the statute's purpose was to preserve the public peace, no words being "forbidden except such as have a direct tendency to cause acts of violence by the persons to whom, individually, the remark is addressed. It was further said: "The word 'offensive' is not to be defined in terms of what a particular addressee thinks. . . . The test is what men of common intelligence would understand would be words likely to cause an average addressee to fight. . . . The English language has a number of words and expressions which by general consent are 'fighting words' when said without a disarming smile." . . .

We are unable to say that the limited scope of the statute as thus construed contravenes the Constitutional right of free expression. It is a statute narrowly drawn and limited to define and punish specific conduct lying within the domain of state power, the use in a public place of words likely to cause a breach of the peace. . . .

The refusal of the state court to admit evidence of provocation and evidence bearing on the truth or falsity of the utterances, is open to no Constitutional objection. Whether the facts sought to be proved by such evidence constitute a defense to the charge, or may be shown in mitigation, are questions for the state court to determine. . . .

Affirmed.

Texas v. Gregory Lee Johnson

517 LW 4770 (1989)
Vote: 5–4

During the 1984 Republican Convention, a group of about 100 protestors marched and staged "die-ins" to dramatize the threat of nuclear war. Johnson, a demonstrator, burned an American flag in front of the city hall. He was convicted of "desecration of a venerated object" and, under Texas law, sentenced to one year in prison and fined $2,000. The Texas Court of Criminal Appeals reversed the decision.

The case was decided in the aftermath of a presidential campaign criticizing a nominee for vetoing a flag salute law "merely" on the advice of the State Attorney General that the bill was unconstitutional. The flag burning decision unleashed a torrent of public criticism, record sales of flags, and President Bush's call for a constitutional amendment authorizing punishment of flag desecrators.

Note the unusual line-up of the Court's most liberal and most conservative members. Note also the strong, positive citation of *Chaplinsky.*

JUSTICE BRENNAN delivered the opinion of the Court.
. . . .

Acknowledging that this Court had not yet decided whether the Government may criminally sanction flag desecration in order to preserve the flag's symbolic value, the Texas court nevertheless concluded that our decision in *West Virginia Board of Education* v. *Barnette,* 319 U.S. 624 (1943), suggested that furthering this interest by curtailing speech was impermissible. "Recognizing that the right to differ is the centerpiece of our First Amendment freedoms," the court explained, "a government cannot mandate by fiat a feeling of unity in its citizens. Therefore, that very same government cannot carve out a symbol of unity and prescribe a set of approved messages to be associated with that symbol when it cannot mandate the status or feeling the symbol purports to represent." 755 S. W. 2d, at 97. Noting that the State had not shown that the flag was in "grave and imme-

diate danger," *Barnette, supra,* at 639, of being stripped of its symbolic value, the Texas court also decided that the flag's special status was not endangered by Johnson's conduct. 755 S. W. 2d, at 97.

As to the State's goal of preventing breaches of the peace, the court concluded that the flag-desecration statute was not drawn narrowly enough to encompass only those flag-burnings that were likely to result in a serious disturbance of the peace. . . .

. . . .

Johnson was convicted of flag desecration for burning the flag rather than for uttering insulting words. This fact somewhat complicates our consideration of his conviction under the First Amendment. We must first determine whether Johnson's burning of the flag constituted expressive conduct, permitting him to invoke the First Amendment in challenging his conviction. See, *e.g., Spence* v. *Washington,* 418 U.S. 405, 409–11 (1974). If his conduct was expressive, we next decide whether the State's regulation is related to the suppression of free expression. See, *e.g., United States* v. *O'Brien,* 391 U.S. 367, 377 (1968); *Spence, supra,* at 414, n. 8. If the State's regulation is not related to expression, then the less stringent standard we announced in *United States* v. *O'Brien* for regulations of noncommunicative conduct controls. . . .

. . . .

The First Amendment literally forbids the abridgement only of "speech," but we have long recognized that its protection does not end at the spoken or written word. While we have rejected "the view that an apparently limitless variety of conduct can be labeled 'speech' whenever the person engaging in the conduct intends thereby to express an idea," *United States* v. *O'Brien, supra,* at 376, we have acknowledged that conduct may be "sufficiently imbued with elements of communication to fall within the scope of the First and Fourteenth Amendments." *Spence, supra,* at 409.

In deciding whether particular conduct possesses sufficient communicative elements to bring the First Amendment into play, we have asked whether "[a]n intent to convey a particularized message was present, and [whether] the likelihood was great that the message would be understood by those who viewed it." 418 U.S., at 410–411. Hence, we have recognized the expressive nature of students' wearing of black armbands to protest American military involvement in Vietnam, *Tinker* v. *Des Moines Independent Community School Dist.,* 393 U.S. 503, 505 (1969); of a sit-in by blacks in a "whites only" area to protest segregation, *Brown* v. *Louisiana,* 383 U.S. 131, 141–142 (1966); of the wearing of American military uniforms in a dramatic presentation criticizing American involvement in Vietnam, *Schacht* v. *United States,* 398 U.S. 58 (1970); and of picketing about a wide variety of causes, see, *e.g., Food Employees* v. *Logan Valley Plaza, Inc.,* 391 U.S. 308, 313–314 (1968). . . .

. . . .

The State of Texas conceded for purposes of its oral argument in this case that Johnson's conduct was expressive conduct, . . . Johnson burned an American flag as part — indeed, as the culmination — of a political demonstration that coincided with the convening of the Republican Party and its renomination of Ronald Reagan for President. The expressive, overtly political nature of this conduct was both intentional and overwhelmingly apparent. . . .

. . . .

The Government generally has a freer hand in restricting expressive conduct than it has in restricting the written or spoken word. See *O'Brien,* 391 U.S. at 376–377; *Clark* v. *Community for Creative Non-Violence,* 468 U.S. 288, 293 (1984); *Dallas* v. *Stanglin,* 490 U.S. ___ , ___ (1989) (slip op., at 5–6). It may not, however, proscribe particular conduct *because* it has expressive elements. . . .

. . . .

Thus, although we have recognized that where "'speech' and 'nonspeech' elements are combined in the same course of conduct, a sufficiently important governmental interest in regulating the nonspeech element can justify incidental limitations on First Amendment freedoms," *O'Brien, supra,* at 376, we have limited the applicability of *O'Brien's* relatively lenient standard to those cases in which "the governmental interest is unrelated to the suppression of free expression." . . .

. . . .

. . . The State offers two separate interests to justify this conviction: preventing breaches of the peace, and preserving the flag as a symbol of nationhood and national unity. We hold that the first interest is not implicated on this record and that the second is related to the suppression of expression.

A

Texas claims that its interest in preventing breaches of the peace justifies Johnson's conviction for flag desecration. However, no disturbance of the peace actually occurred or threatened to occur because of Johnson's burning of the flag. Although the State stresses the disruptive behavior of the protestors during their march toward City Hall, Brief for Petitioner 34–36, it admits that "no actual breach of the peace occurred at the time of the flagburning or in response to the flagburning." *Id.,* at 34. The State's emphasis on the protestors' disorderly actions prior

to arriving at City Hall is not only somewhat surprising given that no charges were brought on the basis of this conduct, but it also fails to show that a disturbance of the peace was a likely reaction to *Johnson's* conduct. The only evidence offered by the State at trial to show the reaction to Johnson's actions was the testimony of several persons who had been seriously offended by the flag-burning. *Id.,* at 6–7.

The State's position, therefore, amounts to a claim that an audience that takes serious offense at particular expression is necessarily likely to disturb the peace and that the expression may be prohibited on this basis. Our precedents do not countenance such a presumption. On the contrary, they recognize that a principal "function of free speech under our system of government is to invite dispute. It may indeed best serve its high purpose when it induces a condition of unrest, creates dissatisfaction with conditions as they are, or even stirs people to anger." *Terminiello* v. *Chicago,* 337 U.S. 1, 4 (1949). . . .

. . . .

Nor does Johnson's expressive conduct fall within that small class of "fighting words" that are "likely to provoke the average person to retaliation, and thereby cause a breach of the peace." *Chaplinsky* v. *New Hampshire,* 315 U.S. 568, 574 (1942). No reasonable onlooker would have regarded Johnson's generalized expression of dissatisfaction with the policies of the Federal Government as a direct personal insult or an invitation to exchange fisticuffs. . . .

. . . .

B

The State also asserts an interest in preserving the flag as a symbol of nationhood and national unity. In *Spence,* we acknowledged that the Government's interest in preserving the flag's special symbolic value "is directly related to expression in the context of activity" such as affixing a peace symbol to a flag. 418 U.S., at 414, n. 8. We are equally presuaded that this interest is related to expression in the case of Johnson's burning of the flag. The State, apparently, is concerned that such conduct will lead people to believe either that the flag does not stand for nationhood and national unity, but instead reflects other, less positive concepts, or that the concepts reflected in the flag do not in fact exist, that is, we do not enjoy unity as a Nation. These concerns blossom only when a person's treatment of the flag communicates some message, and thus are related "to the suppression of free expression" within the meaning of *O'Brien.* We are thus outside of *O'Brien's* test altogether.

. . . .

Moreover, Johnson was prosecuted because he knew that his politically charged expression would cause "serious offense." If he had burned the flag as a means of disposing of it because it was dirty or torn, he would not have been convicted of flag desecration under this Texas law: federal law designates burning as the preferred means of disposing of a flag "when it is in such condition that it is no longer a fitting emblem for display," 36 U.S.C. §176(k), and Texas has no quarrel with this means of disposal. Brief for Petitioner 45. The Texas law is thus not aimed at protecting the physical integrity of the flag in all circumstances, but is designed instead to protect it only against impairments that would cause serious offense to others. . . .

. . . .

Texas' focus on the precise nature of Johnson's expression, moreover, misses the point of our prior decisions: their enduring lesson, that the Government may not prohibit expression simply because it disagrees with its message, is not dependent on the particular mode in which one chooses to express an idea. If we were to hold that a State may forbid flag-burning wherever it is likely to endanger the flag's symbolic role, but allow it wherever burning a flag promotes that role — as where, for example, a person ceremoniously burns a dirty flag — we would be saying that when it comes to impairing the flag's physical integrity, the flag itself may be used as a symbol — as a substitute for the written or spoken word or a "short cut from mind to mind" — only in one direction. We would be permitting a State to "prescribe what shall be orthodox" by saying that one may burn the flag to convey one's attitude toward it and its referents only if one does not endanger the flag's representation of nationhood and national unity.

. . . .

There is, moreover, no indication — either in the text of the Constitution or in our cases interpreting it — that a separate juridical category exists for the American flag alone. Indeed, we would not be surprised to learn that the persons who framed our Constitution and wrote the Amendment that we now construe were not known for their reverence for the Union Jack. The First Amendment does not guarantee that other concepts virtually sacred to our Nation as a whole — such as the principle that discrimination on the basis of race is odious and destructive — will go unquestioned in the marketplace of ideas. See *Brandenburg v. Ohio,* 395 U.S. 444 (1969). We decline, therefore, to create for the flag an exception to the joust of principles protected by the First Amendment.

It is not the State's ends, but its means, to which we object. It cannot be gainsaid that there is a special place reserved for the flag in this Nation, and thus we do not doubt that the Government has a legitimate interest in making efforts to "preserv[e] the national flag as an unalloyed symbol of our country." *Spence,* 418 U.S., at 412. We reject the suggestion, urged at oral argument by counsel for Johnson, that the Government lacks "any state interest whatsoever" in regulating the manner in which the flag may be displayed. Tr. of Oral Arg. 38. Congress has, for example, enacted precatory regulations describing the proper treatment of the flag, see 36 U.S.C. §§173–177, and we cast no doubt on the legitimacy of its interest in making such recommendations. To say that the Government has an interest in encouraging proper treatment of the flag, however, is not to say that it may criminally punish a person for burning a flag as a means of political protest. "National unity as an end which officials may foster by persuasion and example is not in question. The problem is whether under our Constitution compulsion as here employed is a permissible means for its achievement." *Barnette,* 319 U.S., at 640.

We are fortified in today's conclusion by our conviction that forbidding criminal punishment for conduct such as Johnson's will not endanger the special role played by our flag or the feeling it inspires. To paraphrase Justice Holmes, we submit that nobody can suppose that this one gesture of an unknown man will change our Nation's attitude towards its flag. . . .

. . . .

The way to preserve the flag's special role is not to punish those who feel differently about these matters. It is to persuade them that they are wrong.

. . . .

. . . We can imagine no more appropriate response to burning a flag than waving one's own, no better way to counter a flag-burner's message than by saluting the flag that burns, no surer means of preserving the dignity even of the flag that burned than by — as one witness here did — according its remains a respectful burial. We do not consecrate the flag by punishing its desecration, for in doing so we dilute the freedom that this cherished emblem represents.

. . . .

JUSTICE KENNEDY, concurring.

I write not to qualify the words JUSTICE BRENNAN chooses so well, for he says with power all that is necessary to explain our ruling. I join his opinion without reservation, but with a keen sense that this case, like others before us from time to time, exacts its personal toll. . . .

. . . .

The hard fact is that sometimes we must make decisions we do not like. We make them because they are right, right in the sense that the law and the Constitution, as we see them, compel the result. And so great is our commitment to the process that, except in the rare case, we do not pause to express distaste for the result, perhaps for fear of undermining a valued principle that dictates the decision. This is one of those rare cases.

Our colleagues in dissent advance powerful arguments why respondent may be convicted for his expression, reminding us that among those who will be dismayed by our holding will be some who have had the singular honor of carrying the flag in battle. And I agree that the flag holds a lonely place of honor in an age when absolutes are distrusted and simple truths are burdened by unneeded apologetics.

With all respect to those views, I do not believe the Constitution gives us the right to rule as the dissenting members of the Court urge, however painful this judgment is to announce. Though symbols often are what we ourselves make of them, the flag is constant in expressing beliefs Americans share, beliefs in law and peace and that freedom which sustains the human spirit. The case here today forces recognition of the costs to which those beliefs commit us. . . .

CHIEF JUSTICE REHNQUIST, with whom JUSTICE WHITE and JUSTICE O'CONNOR join, dissenting.

. . . For more than 200 years, the American flag has occupied a unique position as the symbol of our Nation, a uniqueness that justifies a governmental prohibition against flag burning in the way respondent Johnson did here.

At the time of the American Revolution, the flag served to unify the Thirteen Colonies at home, while obtaining recognition of national sovereignty abroad. Ralph Waldo Emerson's Concord Hymn describes the first skirmishes of the Revolutionary War in these lines:

> "By the rude bridge that arched the flood
>   Their flag to April's breeze unfurled,
> "Here once the embattled farmers stood
>   And fired the shot heard round the world."

. . . .

The American flag played a central role in our Nation's most tragic conflict, when the North fought against the South. The lowering of the American flag at Fort Sumter was viewed as the start of the war. . . .

. . . .

In the First and Second World Wars, thousands of our countrymen died on foreign soil fighting for the American cause. At Iwo Jima in the Second World War, United States Marines fought hand-to-hand against thousands of Japanese. By the time the Marines reached the top of Mount Suribachi, they raised a piece of pipe upright and from one end fluttered a flag. That ascent had cost nearly 6,000 American lives. The Iwo Jima Memorial in Arlington National Cemetery memorializes that event. . . .

. . . .

The flag symbolizes the Nation in peace as well as in war. It signifies our national presence on battleships, airplanes, military installations, and public buildings from the United States Capitol to the thousands of county courthouses and city halls throughout the country. Two flags are prominently placed in our courtroom. Countless flags are placed by the graves of loved ones each year on what was first called Decoration Day, and is now called Memorial Day. The flag is traditionally placed on the casket of deceased members of the Armed Forces, and it is later given to the deceased's family. 10 U.S.C. §§1481, 1482. Congress has provided that the flag be flown at half-staff upon the death of the President, Vice President, and other government officials "as a mark of respect to their memory." . . .

. . . .

The American flag, then, throughout more than 200 years of our history, has come to be the visible symbol embodying our Nation. It does not represent the views of any particular political party, and it does not represent any particular political philosophy. The flag is not simply another "idea" or "point of view" competing for recognition in the marketplace of ideas. Millions and millions of Americans regard it with an almost mystical reverence regardless of what sort of social, political, or philosophical beliefs they may have. I cannot agree that the First Amendment invalidates the Act of Congress, and the laws of 48 of the 50 States, which make criminal the public burning of the flag.

. . . .

But the Court insists that the Texas statute prohibiting the public burning of the American flag infringes on respondent Johnson's freedom of expression. Such freedom, of course, is not absolute. . . . In *Chaplinsky* v. *New Hampshire*, 315 U.S. 568 (1942), a unanimous Court . . . upheld Chaplinsky's conviction under a state statute that made it unlawful to "address any offensive, derisive or annoying word to any person who is lawfully in any street or other public place." . . .

. . . .

Here it may equally well be said that the public burning of the American flag by Johnson was no essential part of any exposition of ideas, and at the same time it had a tendency to incite a breach of the peace. Johnson was free to make any verbal denunciation of the flag that he wished; indeed, he was free to burn the flag in private. He could publicly burn other symbols of the Government or effigies of political leaders.

. . . .

The Court could not, and did not, say that Chaplinsky's utterances were not expressive phrases — they clearly and succinctly conveyed an extremely low opinion of the addressee. The same may be said of Johnson's public burning of the flag in this case; it obviously did convey Johnson's bitter dislike of his country. But his act, like Chaplinsky's provocative words, conveyed nothing that could not have been conveyed and was not conveyed just as forcefully in a dozen different ways. As with "fighting words," so with flag burning. . . .

. . . .

Our prior cases dealing with flag desecration statutes have left open the question that the Court resolves today. In *Street* v. *New York*, 394 U.S. 576, 579 (1969), the defendant burned a flag in the street, shouting "We don't need no damned flag" and, "[i]f they let that happen to Meredith we don't need an American flag." The Court ruled that since the defendant might have been convicted solely on the basis of his words, the conviction could not stand, but it expressly reserved the question of whether a defendant could constitutionally be convicted for burning the flag. *Id.,* at 581.

Chief Justice Warren, in dissent, stated: "I believe that the States and Federal Government do have the power to protect the flag from acts of desecration and disgrace. . . . [I]t is difficult for me to imagine that, had the Court faced this issue, it would have concluded otherwise." *Id.,* at 605 (Warren, C. J., dissenting). Justices Black and Fortas also expressed their personal view that a prohibition on flag burning did not violate the Constitution. . . .

. . . .

But the Court today will have none of this. The uniquely deep awe and respect for our flag felt by virtually all of us are bundled off under the rubric of "designated symbols," *ante,* at 19, that the First Amendment prohibits the government from "establishing." But the government has not "established" this feeling; 200 years of history have done that. The government is simply recognizing as a fact the profound regard for the American flag created by that history when it enacts statutes prohibiting the disrespectful public burning of the flag.

The Court concludes its opinion with a regrettably

patronizing civics lecture, presumably addressed to the Members of both Houses of Congress, the members of the 48 state legislatures that enacted prohibitions against flag burning, and the troops fighting under that flag in Vietnam who objected to its being burned: "The way to preserve the flag's special role is not to punish those who feel differently about these matters. It is to persuade them that they are wrong." *Ante,* at 21–22. The Court's role as the final expositor of the Constitution is well established, but its role as a platonic guardian admonishing those responsible to public opinion as if they were truant school children has no similar place in our system of government. . . .

. . . .

. . . The Court decides that the American flag is just another symbol, about which not only must opinions pro and con be tolerated, but for which the most minimal public respect may not be enjoined. The government may conscript men into the Armed Forces where they must fight and perhaps die for the flag, but the government may not prohibit the public burning of the banner under which they fight. I would uphold the Texas statute as applied in this case.

JUSTICE STEVENS, dissenting.

. . . [I]n my considered judgment, sanctioning the public desecration of the flag will tarnish its value — both for those who cherish the ideas for which it waves and for those who desire to don the robes of martyrdom by burning it. That tarnish is not justified by the trivial burden on free expression occasioned by requiring that an available, alternative mode of expression — including uttering words critical of the flag, see *Street* v. *New York*, 394 U.S. 576 (1969) — be employed.

. . . .

. . . The statute does not compel any conduct or any profession of respect for any idea or any symbol.

. . . .

. . . The concept of "desecration" does not turn on the substance of the message the actor intends to convey, but rather on whether those who view the *act* will take serious offense. Accordingly, one intending to convey a message of respect for the flag by burning it in a public square might nonetheless be guilty of desecration if he knows the others — perhaps simply because they misperceive the intended message — will be seriously offended. Indeed, even if the actor knows that all possible witnesses understand that he intends to send a message of respect, he might still be guilty of desecration if he also knows that this understanding does not lessen the offense taken by some of those witnesses. . . .

. . . .*

Cohen v. California

403 U.S. 15 (1971)

Vote: 5–(3– 1)

Cohen was sentenced to 30 days' imprisonment for going through a courthouse wearing a jacket with the words "Fuck the Draft" on it. He was convicted of disturbing the peace. The California Superior Court affirmed and the state supreme court declined review. The U.S. Supreme Court granted certiorari.

Query: Is there much left to the CHAPLINSKY precedent after this decision?

HARLAN, J., delivered the opinion of the Court, in which DOUGLAS, BRENNAN, STEWART, and MARSHALL, JJ., joined.

Appellant Paul Robert Cohen was convicted in the Los Angeles Municipal Court of violating that part of California Penal Code §415 which prohibits "maliciously and willfully disturb[ing] the peace or quiet of any neighborhood or person . . . by . . . offensive conduct. . . ." He was given 30 days' imprisonment. The facts upon which his conviction rests are detailed in the opinion of the Court of Appeal of California, Second Appellate District, as follows:

*The Court suggests that a prohibition against flag desecration is not content-neutral because this form of symbolic speech is only used by persons who are critical of the flag or the ideas it represents. In making this suggestion the Court does not pause to consider the far-reaching consequences of its introduction of disparate impact analysis into our First Amendment jurisprudence. It seems obvious that a prohibition against the desecration of a gravesite is content-neutral even if it denies some protesters the right to make a symbolic statement by extinguishing the flame in Arlington Cemetery where John F. Kennedy is buried while permitting others to salute the same flame by bowing their heads. Few would doubt that a protester who extinguishes the flame has desecrated the gravesite, regardless or whether he prefaces that act with a speech explaining that his purpose is to express deep admiration or unmitigated scorn for the late President. Likewise, few would claim that the protester who bows his head has desecrated the gravesite, even if he makes it clear that his purpose is to show disrespect. In such a case, as in a flag burning case, the prohibition against desecration has absolutely nothing to do with the content of the message that the symbolic speech is intended to convey.

On April 26, 1968, the defendant was observed in the Los Angeles County Courthouse in the corridor outside of division 20 of the municipal court wearing a jacket bearing the words 'Fuck the Draft' which were plainly visible. There were women and children present in the corridor. The defendant was arrested. The defendant testified that he wore the jacket knowing that the words were on the jacket as a means of informing the public of the depth of his feelings against the Vietnam War and the draft.

The defendant did not engage in, nor threaten to engage in, nor did anyone as the result of his conduct in fact commit or threaten to commit any act of violence. The defendant did not make any loud or unusual noise, nor was there any evidence that he uttered any sound prior to his arrest. 1 Cal. App. 3d 94, 97–98, 81 Cal. Rptr. 503, 505 (1969).

In affirming the conviction the Court of Appeal held that "offensive conduct" means "behavior which has a tendency to provoke *others* to acts of violence or to in turn disturb the peace," and that the State had proved this element because, on the facts of this case, "[i]t was certainly reasonably foreseeable that such conduct might cause others to rise up to commit a violent act against the person of the defendant or attempt to forceably remove his jacket." 1 Cal. App. 3d, at 99–100, 81 Cal. Rptr., at 506. The California Supreme Court declined review by a divided vote.

The conviction quite clearly rests upon the asserted offensiveness of the *words* Cohen used to convey his message to the public. The only "conduct" which the State sought to punish is the fact of communication. Thus, we deal here with a conviction resting solely upon "speech," cf. *Stromberg* v. *California,* 283 U.S. 359 (1931), not upon any separately identifiable conduct which allegedly was intended by Cohen to be perceived by others as expressive of particular views but which, on its face, does not necessarily convey any message and hence arguably could be regulated without effectively repressing Cohen's ability to express himself. Cf. *United States* v. *O'Brien,* 391 U.S. 367 (1968). Further, the State certainly lacks power to punish Cohen for the underlying content of the message the inscription conveyed. At least so long as there is no showing of an intent to incite disobedience to or disruption of the draft, Cohen could not, consistently with the First and Fourteenth Amendments, be punished for asserting the evident position on the inutility or immorality of the draft his jacket reflected.

Appellant's conviction, then, . . . can be justified, if at all, only as a valid regulation of the manner in which he exercised that freedom, not as a permissible prohibition on the substantive message it conveys. This does not end the inquiry, of course, for the First and Fourteenth Amendments have never been thought to give absolute protection to every individual to speak whenever or wherever he pleases, or to use any form of address in any circumstances that he chooses. In this vein, too, however, we think it important to note that several issues typically associated with such problems are not presented here.

In the first place, Cohen was tried under a statute applicable throughout the entire State. Any attempt to support this conviction on the ground that the statute seeks to preserve an appropriately decorous atmosphere in the courthouse where Cohen was arrested must fail in the absence of any language in the statute that would have put appellant on notice that certain kinds of otherwise permissible speech or conduct would nevertheless, under California law, not be tolerated in certain places.

In the second place, as it comes to us, this case cannot be said to fall within those relatively few categories of instances where prior decisions have established the power of government to deal more comprehensively with certain forms of individual expression simply upon a showing that such a form was employed. This is not, for example, an obscenity case.

This Court has also held that the States are free to ban the simple use, without a demonstration of additional justifying circumstances, of so-called "fighting words," those personally abusive epithets which, when addressed to the ordinary citizen, are, as a matter of common knowledge, inherently likely to provoke violent reaction. *Chaplinsky* v. *New Hampshire*, 315 U.S. 568 (1942). While the four-letter word displayed by Cohen in relation to the draft is not uncommonly employed in a personally provocative fashion, in this instance it was clearly not "directed to the person of the hearer." *Cantwell* v. *Connecticut*, 310 U.S. 296, 309 (1940). No individual actually or likely to be present could reasonably have regarded the words on appellant's jacket as a direct personal insult. Nor do we have here an instance of the exercise of the State's police power to prevent a speaker from intentionally provoking a given group to hostile reaction. Cf. *Feiner* v. *New York* . . . (1951). *Terminiello* v. *Chicago* . . . (1949).

Finally, in arguments before this Court much has been made of the claim that Cohen's distasteful mode of expression was thrust upon unwilling or unsuspecting viewers, and that the State might therefore legitimately act as it did in order to protect the sensitive from otherwise unavoidable exposure to appellant's crude form of protest. Of course, the mere presumed presence of unwitting listeners or viewers does not serve automatically to justify curtailing all speech capable of giving offense. . . . The ability of government, consonant with the Constitution, to shut off discourse solely to protect others from hearing it is, in other words, dependent upon a showing that substantial privacy interests are being invaded in an essentially intolerable manner. Any broader view of this authority would effectively empower a majority to silence dissidents simply as a matter of personal predilections.

In this regard, persons confronted with Cohen's jacket were in a quite different posture than, say, those subjected to the raucous emissions of sound trucks blaring outside their residences. Those in the Los Angeles courthouse could effectively avoid further bombardment of their sensibilities simply by averting their eyes. And, while it may be that one has a more substantial claim to a recognizable privacy interest when walking through a courthouse corridor than, for example, strolling through Central Park, surely it is nothing like the interest in being free from unwanted expression in the confines of one's own home. Cf. *Keefe, supra.* Given the subtlety and complexity of the factors involved, if Cohen's "speech" was otherwise entitled to constitutional protection, we do not think the fact that some unwilling "listeners" in a public building may have been briefly exposed to it can serve to justify this breach of the peace conviction where, as here, there was no evidence that persons powerless to avoid appellant's conduct did in fact object to it, and where that portion of the statute upon which Cohen's conviction rests evinces no concern, either on its face or as construed by the California courts, with the special plight of the captive auditor, but, instead, indiscriminately sweeps within its prohibitions all "offensive conduct" that disturbs "any neighborhood or person." Cf. *Edwards* v. *South Carolina*.

Against this background, the issue flushed by this case stands out in bold relief. It is whether California can excise, as "offensive conduct," one particular scurrilous epithet from the public discourse, either upon the theory of the court below that its use is inherently likely to cause violent reaction or upon a more general assertion that the States, acting as guardians of public morality, may properly remove this offensive word from the public vocabulary.

The rationale of the California court is plainly untenable. At most it reflects an "undifferentiated fear or apprehension of disturbance [which] is not enough to overcome the right to freedom of expression." *Tinker* v. *Des Moines Indep. Community School Dist.* . . . (1969).

At the outset, we cannot overemphasize that, in our judgment, most situations where the State has a justifiable interest in regulating speech will fall within one or more of the various established exceptions, discussed above but not applicable here, to the usual rule that governmental bodies may not prescribe the form or content of individual expression. . . . That the air may at times seem filled with verbal cacophony is, in this sense, not a sign of weakness but of strength. We cannot lose sight of the fact that, in what otherwise might seem a trifling and annoying instance of individual distasteful abuse of a privilege, these fundamental societal values are truly implicated. That is why "[w]holly neutral futilities . . . come under the protection of free speech as fully as do Keats' poems or Donne's sermons," *Winters* v. *New York* . . . (1948) . . . and why "so long as the means are peaceful, the communication need not meet standards of acceptability," *Organization for a Better Austin* v. *Keefe*, 402 U.S. . . . (1971).

. . . How is one to distinguish this from any other offensive work? Surely the State has no right to cleanse public debate to the point where it is grammatically palatable to the most squeamish among us. Yet no readily ascertainable general principle exists for stopping short of that result were we to affirm the judgment below. For, while the particular four-letter word being litigated here is perhaps more distasteful than most others of its genre, it is nonetheless often true that one man's vulgarity is another's lyric. Indeed, we think it is largely because governmental officials cannot make principled distinctions in this area that the Constitution leaves matters of taste and style so largely to the individual.

Additionally, we cannot overlook the fact, because it is well illustrated by the episode involved here, that much linguistic expression serves a dual communicative function: it conveys not only ideas capable of relatively precise, detached explication, but otherwise inexpressible emotions as well. In fact, words are often chosen as much for their emotive as their cognitive force.

Finally, and in the same vein, we cannot indulge the facile assumption that one can forbid particular words without also running a substantial risk of suppressing ideas in the process. Indeed, governments might soon seize upon the censorship of particular words as a convenient guise for banning the expression of unpopular views. We have been able, as noted above, to discern little social benefit that might result from running the risk of opening the door to such grave results.

Reversed.

MR. JUSTICE BLACKMUN, with whom THE CHIEF JUSTICE and MR. JUSTICE BLACK join, dissenting.

Cohen's absurd and immature antic, in my view, was mainly conduct and little speech. . . . As a consequence, this Court's agonizing over First Amendment values seems misplaced and unnecessary. [JUSTICE WHITE joined in a portion of the Blackmun dissent.]

Roth v. U.S.
Alberts v. California

354 U.S. 476 (1957)
Vote: 6–3 in *Roth*; 7–2 in *Alberts*

This was the first major attempt by the Supreme Court to deal with obscenity as a serious First Amendment problem. Rejecting the clear-and-present-danger test, the majority espoused what has been called "the jurisprudence of areas," which is really an attempt to define sectors of regulation, akin to Meiklejohn's early distinction between public and private speech. Justice Harlan's warning that "obscenity" would come to haunt the Court because it is not a genre has proven prophetic.

Roth was a bookdealer who sold and advertised erotica. He was indicted under a federal statute outlawing "obscene, lewd, lascivious or filthy" matter, or advertisements for them, in the mails. Acquitted as to the sale of nude photographs, he was found guilty of selling and advertising an obscene magazine. The decision was affirmed by the court of appeals.

Alberts was a dealer in posed photographs of nude or scantily dressed females. His conviction under California law was affirmed by a state superior court.

Chief Justice Warren's concurrence tries to deal with the Douglas-Black objection to regulation of content by claiming it is the pornographer's actions that are on trial, not the books. Is this convincing? In *Ginzburg* v. *U.S.* (1966), the Court essayed the "intent" of the seller as the basis for deciding what was obscene, and not only split 5 to 4, but earned only criticism and derision.

In later cases, Brennan insisted that *Roth* is a libertarian, highly limited exception to the First Amendment, for it outlaws materials that are utterly without socially redeeming merit. Only materials "utterly" without merit can be proscribed regardless of their lewdness. Is this the plain meaning of *Roth*? (See *Jacobellis* v. *Ohio*, 1964.)

MR. JUSTICE BRENNAN delivered the opinion of the Court.

The constitutionality of a criminal obscenity statute is the question in each of these cases. In *Roth*, the primary constitutional question is whether the federal obscenity statute violates the provision of the First Amendment that "Congress shall make no law . . . abridging the freedom of speech, or of the press. . . ." In *Alberts*, The primary constitutional question is whether the obscenity provisions of the California Penal Code invade the freedoms of speech and press as they may be incorporated in the liberty protected from state action by the Due Process Clause of the Fourteenth Amendment.

Roth conducted a business in New York in the publication and sale of books, photographs and magazines. He used circulars and advertising matter to solicit sales. He was convicted by a jury in the District Court for the Southern District of New York upon 4 counts of a 26-count indictment charging him with mailing obscene circulars and advertising, and an obscene book, in violation of the federal obscenity statute.

Alberts conducted a mail-order business from Los Angeles. He was convicted by the Judge of the Municipal Court of the Beverly Hills Judicial District (having waived a jury trial) under a misdemeanor complaint which charged him with lewdly keeping for sale obscene and indecent books, and with writing, composing and publishing an obscene advertisement of them, in violation of the California Penal Code.

The dispositive question is whether obscenity is utterance within the area of protected speech and press. Although this is the first time the question has been squarely presented to this Court, either under the First Amendment or under the Fourteenth Amendment, expressions found in numerous opinions indicate that this Court has always assumed that obscenity is not protected by the freedoms of speech and press. . . .

In light of this history, it is apparent that the unconditional phrasing of the First Amendment was not intended to protect every utterance. This phrasing did not prevent this Court from concluding that libelous utterances are not within the area of constitutionally protected speech. *Beauharnais* v. *Illinois,* 343 U.S. 250, 266. At the time of the adoption of the First Amendment, obscenity law was not as fully developed as libel law, but there is sufficiently contemporaneous evidence to show that obscenity, too, was outside the protection intended for speech and press.

All ideas having even the slightest redeeming social importance — unorthodox ideas, controversial ideas, even ideas hateful to the prevailing climate of opinion — have the full protection of the guaranties, unless excludable because they encroach upon the limited area of more important interests. But implicit in the history of the First Amendment is the rejection of obscenity as utterly without redeeming social importance.

This is the same judgement expressed by this court in *Chaplinsky* v. *New Hampshire.* "There are certain well-defined and narrowly limited classes of speech, the prevention of which have never been thought to raise any constitutional problem. *These include the lewd and obscene. . . . It has been well-observed that such utterances are no part of any exposition of ideas and are of such slight social value as a step to truth that any benefit that might be derived from them is clearly outweighed by the social interest in order and morality . . .*" [emphasis added].

. . . We hold that obscenity is not within the area of constitutionally protected speech or press.

It is strenuously urged that these obscenity statutes offend the constitutional guaranties because they punish incitation to impure sexual *thoughts,* not shown to be related to any overt antisocial conduct which is or may be incited in the persons stimulated to such *thoughts.*

. . . It is insisted that the constitutional guaranties are violated because convictions may be had without proof either that obscene material will perceptibly create a clear and present danger of antisocial conduct, or will probably induce its recipients to such conduct. But, in light of our holding that obscenity is not protected speech, the complete answer to this argument is in the holding of this Court in *Beauharnais* v. *Illinois.*

Libelous utterances not being within the area of constitutionally protected speech, it is unnecessary, either for us or for the State courts, to consider the issues behind the phrase 'clear and present danger.' Certainly no one would contend that obscene speech, for example, may be punished only upon a showing of such circumstances. Libel, as we have seen, is in the same class.

However, sex and obscenity are not synonymous. Obscene material is material which deals with sex in a manner appealing to prurient interest. The portrayal of sex, *e.g.*, in art, literature and scientific works, is not itself sufficient reason to deny material the constitutional protection of freedom of speech and press. Sex, a great and mysterious motive force in human life, has indisputably been a subject of absorbing interest to mankind through the ages; it is one of the vital problems of human interest and public concern. . . .

The early leading standard of obscenity allowed material to be judged merely by the effect of an isolated excerpt upon particularly susceptible persons. *Regina* v. *Hicklin* [1868]. . . . Some American courts adopted this standard but later decisions have rejected it and substituted this test, whether to the average person, applying contemporary community standards, the dominant theme of the material taken as a whole appeals to prurient interest. The *Hicklin* test, judging obscenity by the effect of isolated passages upon the most susceptible persons, might well encompass material legitimately treating with sex, and so it must be rejected as unconstitutionally restrictive of the freedoms of speech and press. On the other hand, the substituted standard provides safeguards adequate to withstand the charge of constitutional infirmity. . . .

Many decisions have recognized that these terms of obscenity statutes are not precise. This Court, however, has consistently held that lack of precision is not itself offensive to the requirements of due process. ". . . [T]he Constitution does not require impossible standards"; all that is required is that the language "conveys sufficiently definite warning as to the proscribed conduct when measured by common understanding and practices. . . ."

In summary, then, we hold that these statutes, applied according to the proper standard for judging obscenity, do not offend constitutional safeguards against convictions based upon protected material, or fail to give men in acting adequate notice of what is prohibited.

Affirmed.

MR. CHIEF JUSTICE WARREN, concurring in the result.

I agree with the result reached by the Court in these cases, but, because we are operating in a field of expression and because broad language used here may eventually be applied to the arts and sciences and freedom of communication generally, I would limit our decision to the facts before us and to the validity of the statutes in question as applied. . . . It is not the book that is on trial; it is a person. The conduct of the defendant is the central issue, not the obscenity of a book or picture. The nature of the materials is, of course, relevant as an attribute of the defendant's conduct, but the materials are thus placed in context from which they draw color and character. A wholly different result might be reached in a different setting.

The personal element in these cases is seen most strongly in the requirement of *scienter*. Under the California law, the prohibited activity must be done "wilfully and lewdly." The federal statute limits the crime to acts done "knowingly." In his charge to the jury, the district judge stated that the matter must be "calculated" to corrupt or debauch. The defendants in both these cases were engaged in the business of purveying textual or graphic matter openly advertised to appeal to the erotic interest of their customers. They were plainly engaged in the commercial exploitation of the morbid and shameful craving for materials with prurient effect. I believe that the State and Federal Governments can constitutionally punish such conduct.

MR. JUSTICE HARLAN, concurring in the result in [Alberts] and dissenting in [Roth].

I regret not to be able to join the Court's opinion. I cannot do so because I find lurking beneath its disarming generalizations a number of problems which not only leave me with serious misgivings as to the future effect of today's decisions, but which also, in my view, call for different results in these two cases. . . . The Court seems to assume that "obscenity" is a peculiar *genus* of "speech and press," which is as distinct, recognizable, and classifiable as poison ivy is among other plants. On this basis the *constitutional* question before us simply becomes, as the Court says, whether "obscenity," as an abstraction, is protected by the First and Fourteenth Amendments, and the question whether a *particular* book may be suppressed becomes a mere matter of classification, of "fact," to be entrusted to a factfinder and insulated from independent constitutional judgment.

My second reason for dissatisfaction with the Court's opinion is that the broad strides with which the Court has proceeded has led it to brush aside with perfunctory ease the vital constitutional considerations which, in my opinion, differentiate these two cases. It does not seem to matter to the Court that in one case we balance the power of a State in this field against the restrictions of the Fourteenth Amendment, and in the other the power of the Federal Government against the limitations of the First Amendment. I do not think it follows that state and federal powers in this area are the same, and that just because the State may suppress a particular utterance, it is automatically permissible for the Federal Government to do the same. I agree with Mr. Justice Jackson that the historical evidence does not bear out the claim that the Fourteenth Amendment "incorporates" the First in any literal sense. See *Beauharnais* v. *Illinois*. But laying aside any consequences which might flow from that conclusion, cf. Mr. Justice Holmes in *Gitlow* v. *New York*, . . . I prefer to rest my views about this case on broader and less abstract grounds.

The Constitution differentiates between those areas of human conduct subject to the regulation of the States and those subject to the powers of the Federal Government. The substantive powers of the two governments, in many instances, are distinct. And in every case where we are called upon to balance the interest in free expression against other interests, it seems to me important that we should keep in the forefront the question of whether those other interests are state or federal. . . .

MR. JUSTICE DOUGLAS, with whom MR. JUSTICE BLACK concurs, dissenting.

When we sustain these convictions, we make the legality of a publication turn on the purity of thought which a book or tract instills in the mind of the reader. I do not think we can approve that standard and be faithful to the command of the First Amendment, which by its terms is a restraint on Congress and which by the Fourteenth is a restraint on the States. . . .

The absence of dependable information on the effect of obscene literature on human conduct should make us wary. It should put us on the side of protecting society's interest in literature, except and unless it can be said that the particular publication has an impact on action that the government can control. . . . With the exception of *Beauharnais* v. *Illinois*, none of our cases has resolved problems of free speech and free press by placing any form of expression beyond the pale of the absolute prohibition of the First Amendment. Unlike the law of libel, wrongfully relied on in *Beauharnais*, there is no special historical evidence that literature dealing with sex was intended to be treated in a special manner by those who drafted the First Amendment. In fact, the first reported court decision in this country involving obscene literature was in 1821. . . .

Stanley v. Georgia

394 U.S. 557 (1969)
Vote: (5–1–3)–0

Searching for evidence of bookmaking, federal and state agents found film the state officials deemed obscene. After conviction and affirmance by the Georgia Supreme Court, an appeal was made to the U.S. Supreme Court.

The cumulative effect of previous obscenity decisions added up to disaster. The Court had developed its three-pronged test, but disagreed vehemently on application of each standard, and constantly was adding additional external criteria—for example, the pandering test in *Ginzburg* v. *U.S.* (1966) and the concept of narrow and specific audience in *Mishkin* v. *N.Y.* (1966) (involving sadomasochistic materials) or in *Ginsberg* v. *N.Y.* (1968) (involving juveniles). Efforts to redefine "hard-core pornography" were equally disastrous. In the interim, seven elderly men read questionable works or traipsed to their movie room to watch film and determine its erotic impact on audiences. (Black and Douglas refused to attend, since in their jurisprudence content was irrelevant to the issue of suppression.) Their reward was criticism on all sides, for too much leniency and excessive stringency.

Confessing their problems and inability to agree, the justices, in a remarkable per curiam opinion in *Redrup* v. *N.Y.* (1967), also suggested that pandering, obtrusive exposure of obscene material, and distribution to minors constituted a special set of circumstances that a state could continue to regulate. The central notion of this new approach was invasion of privacy. Obtrusive material was offensive and captive audiences had the right to object. Therefore Congress could pass a law allowing individuals to object to mailings they held obscene. After notification of a desire to be off a mailing list, a persisting firm could be prosecuted (*Rowan* v. *Post Office,* 1970). Juveniles could be specially protected, as thrusting of materials upon them intruded on the parental right to shape their children's morals (*Ginsberg* v. *N.Y.,* 1968). (This ruling, in turn, opened up the issue of who — for this purpose — is a juvenile.)

In *Stanley,* privacy was used in its obverse sense — to justify private use of materials. The Court quickly held, however, that this justification did not extend to any right to purchase publicly or receive materials (*U.S.* v. *Reidel; U.S.* v. *Thirty-Seven Photographs,* 1971). Is this logical? Was *Roth* good law? See the next episode!

MR. JUSTICE MARSHALL delivered the opinion of the Court.

An investigation of appellant's alleged bookmaking activities led to the issuance of a search warrant for appellant's home. Under authority of this warrant, federal and state agents secured entrance. They found very little evidence of bookmaking activity, but while looking through a desk drawer in an upstairs bedroom, one of the federal agents, accompanied by a state officer, found three reels of eight-millimeter film. Using a projector and screen found in an upstairs living room, they viewed the films. The state officer concluded that they were obscene and seized them. Since a further examination of the bedroom indicated that appellant occupied it, he was charged with possession of obscene matter and placed under arrest. He was later indicted for "knowingly hav[ing] possession of . . . obscene matter" in violation of Georgia law. Appellant was tried before a jury and convicted. The Supreme Court of Georgia affirmed. . . .

Appellant raises several challenges to the validity of his conviction. We find it necessary to consider only one. Appellant argues here, and argued below, that the Georgia obscenity statute, insofar as it punishes mere private possession of obscene matter, violates the First Amendment, as made applicable to the States by the Fourteenth Amendment. For reasons set forth below, we agree that the mere private possession of obscene matter cannot constitutionally be made a crime.

The court below saw no valid constitutional objection to the Georgia statute, even though it extends further than the typical statute forbidding commercial sales of obscene material. It held that "[i]t is not essential to an indictment charging one with possession of obscene matter that it be alleged that such possession was 'with intent to sell, expose or circulate the same.'" . . . The State and appellant both agree that the question here before us is whether "a statute imposing criminal sanctions upon the mere [knowing] possession of obscene matter" is constitutional. In this context, Georgia concedes that the present case appears to be one of "first impression . . . on this exact point," but contends that since "obscenity is not within the area of constitutionally protected speech or press," *Roth* v. *United States,* 354 U.S. 476, 485 (1957), the States are free, subject to the limits of other provisions of the Constitution, see, *e.g., Ginsberg* v. *New York,* 390 U.S. 629, 637–645 (1968), to deal with it any way deemed necessary, just as they may deal with possession of other things thought to be detrimental to the welfare of their citizens. If the State can protect the body of a citizen, may it not, argues Georgia, protect his mind?

It is true that *Roth* does declare, seemingly without qualification, that obscenity is not protected by the First Amendment. That statement has been repeated in various forms in subsequent cases. . . . However, neither *Roth* nor any subsequent decision of this Court dealt with the precise problem involved in the present case. . . . None of the statements cited by the Court in *Roth* for the proposition that "this Court has always assumed that obscenity is not protected by the freedoms of speech and press" were made in the context of a statute punishing mere private possession of obscene material. . . . Those cases dealt with the power of the State and Federal Governments to prohibit or regulate certain public actions taken or intended to be taken with respect to obscene matter. . . . In this context, we do not believe that this case can be decided simply by citing *Roth.* . . .

It is now well established that the Constitution protects the right to receive information and ideas.

These are the rights that appellant is asserting in the case before us. He is asserting the right to read or observe what he pleases — the right to satisfy his intellectual and emotional needs in the privacy of his own home. He is asserting the right to be free from state inquiry into the contents of his library. Georgia contends that appellant does not have these rights, that there are certain types of materials that the individual may not read or even possess. Georgia justifies this assertion by arguing that the films in the present case are obscene. But we think that mere categorization of these films as "obscene" is insufficient justification for such a drastic invasion of personal liberties guaranteed by the First and Fourteenth Amendments. Whatever may be the justifications for other statutes regulating obscenity, we do not think they reach into the privacy of one's own home. If the First Amendment means anything, it means that a State has no business telling a man, sitting alone in his own house, what books he may read or what films he may watch. Our whole constitutional heritage rebels at the thought of giving government the power to control men's minds. Nor is it relevant that obscene materials in general, or the particular films before the Court, are arguably devoid of any ideological content. The line between the transmission of ideas and mere entertainment is much too elusive for this Court to draw, if indeed such a line can be drawn at all. See *Winters* v. *New York*. Whatever the power of the state to control public dissemination of ideas inimical to the public morality, it cannot constitutionally premise legislation on the desirability of controlling a person's private thoughts.

Perhaps recognizing this, Georgia asserts that exposure to obscene materials may lead to deviant sexual behavior or crimes of sexual violence. There appears to be little empirical basis for that assertion. But more important, if the State is only concerned about printed or filmed materials inducing antisocial conduct, we believe that in the context of private consumption of ideas and information we should adhere to the view that "[a]mong free men, the deterrents ordinarily to be applied to prevent crime are education and punishment for violations of the law...." Given the present state of knowledge, the State may no more prohibit mere possession of obscene matter on the ground that it may lead to antisocial conduct than it may prohibit possession of chemistry books on the ground that they may lead to the manufacture of homemade spirits.

It is true that in *Roth* this Court rejected the necessity of proving that exposure to obscene material would create a clear and present danger of antisocial conduct or would probably induce its recipients to such conduct.... But that case dealt with public distribution of obscene materials and such distribution is subject to different objections. For example, there is always the danger that obscene material might fall into the hands of children, see *Ginsberg* v. *New York*, or that it might intrude upon the sensibilities or privacy of the general public. See *Redrup* v. *New York*... (1967). No such dangers are present in this case.

...*Roth* and the cases following that decision are not impaired by today's holding. As we have said, the States retain broad power to regulate obscenity; that power simply does not extend to mere possession by the individual in the privacy of his home....

It is so ordered.

MR. JUSTICE STEWART, with whom MR. JUSTICE BRENNAN and MR. JUSTICE WHITE join, concurring in the result.

In affirming the appellant's conviction, the Georgia Supreme Court specifically determined that the films had been lawfully seized. The appellant correctly contends that this determination was clearly wrong under established principles of constitutional law. But the Court today disregards this preliminary issue in its hurry to move on to newer constitutional frontiers. I cannot so readily overlook the serious inroads upon Fourth Amendment guarantees countenanced in this case by the Georgia courts.

Miller v. California

413 U.S. 15 (1973)
Vote: 5–4

Paris Adult Theatre I v. Slaton

413 U.S. 49 (1973)
Vote: 5–4

The Burger Court's decision in these two cases came in a pair of 5 to 4 decisions announced the same day. In *Miller* v. *California,* a dealer was convicted by a jury of mass mailings of advertisements that contained photographs and drawings which portrayed various sexual activities. The conviction was upheld without opinion by a California Superior Court. The issue here involved obtrusive behavior in that the recipients of the brochures had not requested them. The Supreme Court granted certiorari.

In *Paris Adult Theatre,* the District Attorney, Slaton, sought to enjoin the theater from exhibiting allegedly obscene material, under Georgia civil law. There was no prior restraint. The judge (in a jury-waived trial) viewed the films and dismissed, without expert testimony, on the grounds that exhibiting films to consenting adults was permissible. The Georgia Supreme Court reversed, holding that the films were "hard-core pornography."

The majority opinion of Mr. Justice Burger in *Miller* is reprinted below. *Paris Adult Theatre* was decided on the same grounds. The modified ROTH test was retained except that: (1) "contemporary community standards" were to be — as Chief Justice Warren had urged — based upon contemporary *local* standards; (2) "patent offensiveness" included matters such as sexual conduct offensively portrayed that were "specifically defined by the applicable state law"; and (3) the "utterly without redeeming social value" standard was replaced by "whether the work as a whole lacks serious literary, artistic, political or scientific value."

Brennan's dissent in *Paris Adult Theatre* (for Marshall and Stewart) is of great interest, for he concedes the failure of the ROTH approach and comes out forthrightly for the "privacy" notion immanent in STANLEY V. GEORGIA.

The majority opinion in *Paris Adult Theatre* and other dissents in *Miller* v. *California* are omitted. The division on the Court was identical in the two cases and the opinions also parallel each other.

MILLER v. CALIFORNIA

CHIEF JUSTICE BURGER delivered the opinion of the Court.

[S]ince the Court now undertakes to formulate standards more concrete than those in the past, it is useful for us to focus on two of the landmark cases in the somewhat tortured history of the Court's obscenity decisions. In *Roth* v. *United States,* 354 U.S. 476 (1957), the Court sustained a conviction under a federal statute punishing the mailing of "obscene, lewd, lascivious or filthy..." materials. The key to that holding was the Court's rejection of the claim that obscene materials were protected by the First Amendment.

Nine years later in *Memoirs* v. *Massachusetts,* 383 U.S. 413 (1966), the Court veered sharply away from the *Roth* concept and, with only three Justices in the plurality opinion, articulated a new test of obscenity....

While *Roth* presumed "obscenity" to be "utterly without redeeming social value," *Memoirs* required that to prove obscenity it must be affirmatively established that the material is *"utterly* without redeeming social value." Thus, even as they repeated the words of *Roth,* the *Memoirs* plurality produced a drastically altered test that called on the prosecution to prove a negative, *i.e.,* that the material was *"utterly* without redeeming social value" — a burden virtually impossible to discharge under our criminal standards of proof. Such considerations caused Justice Harlan to wonder if the *"utterly* without redeeming social value" test had any meaning at all.

Apart from the initial formulation in the *Roth* case, no majority of the Court has at any given time been able to agree on a standard to determine what constitutes obscene, pornographic material subject to

regulation under the States' police power. See, *e.g., Redrup* v. *New York,* 386 U.S. 767, 770–771 (1967). We have seen "a variety of views among the members of the Court unmatched in any other course of constitutional adjudication."

This much has been categorically settled by the Court, that obscene material is unprotected by the First Amendment.... We acknowledge, however, the inherent dangers of undertaking to regulate any form of expression. State statutes designed to regulate obscene materials must be carefully limited. See *Interstate Circuit, Inc.* v. *Dallas, supra,* 390 U.S., at 682–685 (1968). As a result, we now confine the permissible scope of such regulation to works which depict or describe sexual conduct. That conduct must be specifically defined by the applicable state law, as written or authoritatively construed. A state offense must also be limited to works which, taken as a whole, appeal to the prurient interest in sex, which portray sexual conduct in a patently offensive way, and which, taken as a whole, do not have serious literary, artistic, political, or scientific value.

The basic guidelines for the trier of fact must be: (a) whether "the average person, applying contemporary community standards" would find that the work, taken as a whole, appeals to the prurient interest,... (b) whether the work depicts or describes, in a patently offensive way, sexual conduct specifically defined by the applicable state law, and (c) whether the work, taken as a whole, lacks serious literary, artistic, political, or scientific value. We do not adopt as a constitutional standard the *"utterly without redeeming social value"* test of *Memoirs* v. *Massachusetts, supra,* 383 U.S., at 419 (1966); that concept has never commanded the adherence of more than three Justices at one time.... If a state law that regulates obscene material is thus limited, as written or construed, the First Amendment values applicable to the States through the Fourteenth Amendment are adequately protected by the ultimate power of appellate courts to conduct an independent review of constitutional claims when necessary.

We emphasize that it is not our function to propose regulatory schemes for the States. That must await their concrete legislative efforts. It is possible, however, to give a few plain examples of what a state statute could define for regulation under the second part (b) of the standard announced in this opinion, *supra:*

(a) Patently offensive representations or descriptions of ultimate sexual acts, normal or perverted, actual or simulated.

(b) Patently offensive representations or descriptions of masturbation, excretory functions, and lewd exhibition of the genitals.

Sex and nudity may not be exploited without limit by films or pictures exhibited or sold in places of public accommodation any more than live sex and nudity can be exhibited or sold without limit in such public places. At a minimum, prurient, patently offensive depiction or description of sexual conduct must have serious literary, artistic, political, or scientific value to merit First Amendment protection.... For example, medical books for the education of physicians and related personnel necessarily use graphic illustrations and descriptions of human anatomy. In resolving the inevitably sensitive questions of fact and law, we must continue to rely on the jury system, accompanied by the safeguards that judges, rules of evidence, presumption of innocence and other protective features provide, as we do with rape, murder and a host of other offenses against society and its individual members."

MR. JUSTICE BRENNAN, author of the opinions of the Court, or the plurality opinions in *Roth* v. *United States, supra, Jacobellis* v. *Ohio, supra, Ginzburg* v. *United States,* 383 U.S. 463 (1966), *Mishkin* v. *New York,* 383 U.S. 502 (1966), and *Memoirs* v. *Massachusetts, supra,* has abandoned his former positions and now maintains that no formulation of this Court, the Congress, or the States can adequately distinguish obscene material unprotected by the First Amendment from protected expression.... Paradoxically, MR. JUSTICE BRENNAN indicates that suppression of unprotected obscene material is permissible to avoid exposure to unconsenting adults, as in this case, and to juveniles, although he gives no indication of how the division between protected and nonprotected materials may be drawn with greater precision for these purposes than for regulation of commercial exposure to consenting adults only. Nor does he indicate where in the Constitution he finds the authority to distinguish between a willing "adult" one month past the state law age of majority and a willing "juvenile" one month younger.

Under the holdings announced today, no one will be subject to prosecution for the sale or exposure of obscene materials unless these materials depict or describe patently offensive "hard core" sexual conduct specifically defined by the regulating state law, as written or construed. We are satisfied that these specific prerequisites will provide fair notice to a dealer in such materials that his public and commercial activities may bring prosecution.

Under a national Constitution, fundamental First Amendment limitations on the powers of the States do not vary from community to community, but this does not mean that there are, or should or can be, fixed, uniform national standards of precisely what appeals to the "prurient interest" or is "patently offensive." These are essentially questions of fact, and our nation is simply too big and too diverse for this Court to reasonably expect that such standards could be articulated for all 50 States in a single formulation, even assuming the prerequisite consensus exists. When triers of fact are asked to decide whether "the average person, applying contemporary community standards" would consider certain materials "prurient," it would be unrealistic to require that the answer be based on some abstract formulation. The adversary system, with lay jurors as the usual ultimate fact-finders in criminal prosecutions, has historically permitted triers-of-fact to draw on the standards of their community, guided always by limiting instructions on the law. To require a State to structure obscenity proceedings around evidence of a *national* "community standard" would be an exercise in futility.

We conclude that neither the State's alleged failure to offer evidence of "national standards," nor the trial court's charge that the jury consider state community standards, were constitutional errors.... People in different States vary in their tastes and attitudes, and this diversity is not to be strangled by the absolutism of imposed uniformity.

The dissenting Justices sound the alarm of repression. But, in our view, to equate the free and robust exchange of ideas and political debate with commercial exploitation of obscene material demeans the grand conception of the First Amendment and its high purposes in the historic struggle for freedom.

There is no evidence, empirical or historical, that the stern 19th century American censorship of public distribution and display of material relating to sex, see *Roth* v. *United States, supra,* 354 U.S., at 482–485 (1957), in anyway limited or affected expression of serious literary, artistic, political, or scientific ideas. On the contrary, it is beyond any question that the era following Thomas Jefferson to Theodore Roosevelt was an "extraordinarily vigorous period" not just in economics and politics, but in *belles lettres* and in "the outlying fields of social and political philosophies." We do not see the harsh hand of censorship of ideas — good or bad, sound or unsound — and "repression" of political liberty lurking in every state regulation of commercial exploitation of human interest in sex.

MR. JUSTICE DOUGLAS, dissenting.

I do not think we, the judges, were ever given the constitutional power to make definitions of obscenity. If it is to be defined, let the people debate and decide by a constitutional amendment what they want to ban as obscene and what standards they want the legislatures and the courts to apply. Perhaps the people will decide that the path towards a mature, integrated society requires that all ideas competing for acceptance must have no censor. Perhaps they will decide otherwise. Whatever the choice, the courts will have some guidelines. Now we have none except our own predilections.

PARIS ADULT THEATRE I v. SLATON

MR. JUSTICE BRENNAN, with whom MR. JUSTICE STEWART and MR. JUSTICE MARSHALL join, dissenting.

... I am convinced that the approach initiated 16 years ago in *Roth* v. *United States,* 354 U.S. 476 (1957), and culminating in the Court's decision today, cannot bring stability to this area of the law without jeopardizing fundamental First Amendment values....

Our experience since *Roth* requires us not only to abandon the effort to pick out obscene materials on a case-by-case basis, but also to reconsider a fundamental postulate of *Roth:* that there exists a definable class of sexually oriented expression that may be totally suppressed by the Federal and State Governments. Assuming that such a class of expression does in fact exist, I am forced to conclude that the concept of "obscenity" cannot be defined with sufficient specificity and clarity to provide fair notice to persons who create and distribute sexually oriented materials, to prevent substantial erosion of protected speech as a byproduct of the attempt to suppress unprotected speech, and to avoid very costly institutional harms. Given these inevitable side effects of state efforts to suppress what is assumed to be *unprotected* speech, we must scrutinize with care the state interest that is asserted to justify the suppression. For in the absence of some very substantial interest in suppressing such speech, we can hardly condone the ill effects that seem to flow inevitably from the effort.

. . . .

Because we assumed — incorrectly, as experience has proved — that obscenity could be separated from other sexually oriented expression without significant costs either to the First Amendment or to the judicial machinery charged with the task of safeguarding First Amendment freedoms, we had no occasion in *Roth* to probe the asserted state interest in curtailing unprotected, sexually oriented speech. Yet, as we have increasingly come to appreciate the vagueness of the concept of obscenity, we have begun to recognize and articulate the state interests at stake. . . .

The opinions in *Redrup* and *Stanley* reflected our emerging view that the state interests in protecting children and in protecting unconsenting adults may stand on a different footing from the other asserted state interests. . . .

But, whatever the strength of the state interests in protecting juvenile and unconsenting adults from exposure to sexually oriented materials, those interests cannot be asserted in defense of the holding of the Georgia Supreme Court in this case. That court assumed for the purposes of its decision that the films in issue were exhibited only to persons over the age of 21 who viewed them willingly and with prior knowledge of the nature of their contents. And on that assumption the state court held that the films could still be suppressed. The justification for the suppression must be found, therefore, in some independent interest in regulating the reading and viewing habits of consenting adults.

. . . .

... Like the proscription of abortions, the effort to suppress obscenity is predicated on unprovable, although strongly held, assumptions about human behavior, morality, sex, and religion. The existence of these assumptions cannot validate a statute that substantially undermines the guarantes of the First Amendment, any more than the existence of similar assumptions on the issue of abortion can validate a statute that infringes the constitutionally protected privacy interests of a pregnant woman.

... For if a State, in an effort to maintain or create a particular moral tone, may prescribe what its citizens cannot read or cannot see, then it would seem to follow that in pursuit of that same objective a State could decree that its citizens must read certain books or must view certain films. . . .

In short, while I cannot say that the interests of the State — apart from the question of juveniles and unconsenting adults — are trivial or nonexistent, I am compelled to conclude that these interests cannot justify the substantial damage to constitutional rights and to this Nation's judicial machinery that inevitably results from state efforts to bar the distribution even of unprotected material to consenting adults....

... [T]he view I espouse today would introduce a large measure of clarity to this troubled area, would reduce the institutional pressure on this Court and the rest of the State and Federal Judiciary, and would guarantee fuller freedom of expression while leaving room for the protection of legitimate governmental interests. . . .

Central Hudson Gas v. Public Service Commission

447 U.S. 557 (1980)
Vote: (5–3)–1

As long as the Court generally adhered to the "jurisprudence of areas," advertising and other commercial speech could be treated as non-First Amendment cases. Even so, the boundary *was* blurred; as we know, the leading modern case, NEW YORK TIMES V. SULLIVAN, involved a political advertisement. But attention to the logic of ideas disseminated through advertising demonstrates that even purely economic communication involves ideas. Cigarette advertisements imply they should not be banned. In cases involving state prohibitions barring professionals (like lawyers) from advertising, there is not merely regulation involved, but a concept of how that profession should operate and might be changed. (The emergence of legal clinics or prepaid plans almost requires advertising, and advertising generates not only business but also support or opposition to the concept.)

Central Hudson is the watershed case, confronting the Court squarely with the issue of possible First Amendment protection of advertising. The Public Service Commission of New York, which has extensive rate-making and regulating authority over electric utilities, banned all advertisements to encourage additional use of electricity by consumers as an energy-saving and cost-efficient measure.

Three levels of New York courts sustained the regulation. The New York City Court of Appeals found little value in advertising "in the noncompetitive market in which electric corporations operate." From that court the matter came to the U.S. Supreme Court On Appeal.

MR. JUSTICE POWELL delivered the opinion of the Court.

In December 1973, the Commission, appellee here, ordered electric utilities in New York State to cease all advertising that "promot[es] the use of electricity." . . .

Three years later, when the fuel shortage had eased, the Commission requested comments from the public on its proposal to continue the ban on promotional advertising. Central Hudson Gas & Electric Corp., the appellant in this case, opposed the ban on First Amendment grounds. App. A10. After reviewing the public comments, the Commission extended the prohibition in a Policy Statement issued on February 25, 1977.

. . . The Commission declared all promotional advertising contrary to the national policy of conserving energy. It acknowledged that the ban is not a perfect vehicle for conserving energy. For example, the Commission's order prohibits promotional advertising to develop consumption during periods when demand for electricity is low. By limiting growth in "off-peak" consumption, the ban limits the "beneficial side effects" of such growth in terms of more efficient use of existing powerplants. . . .

The Commission's order restricts only commercial speech, that is, expression related solely to the economic interests of the speaker and its audience. . . . The First Amendment, as applied to the States through the Fourteenth Amendment, protects commercial speech from unwarranted governmental regulation. . . . In applying the First Amendment to this area, we have rejected the "highly paternalistic" view that government has complete power to suppress or regulate commercial speech. "[P]eople will perceive their own best interests if only they are well enough informed, and . . . the best means to that end is to open the channels of communication, rather than to close them. . . ." *Id.*, at 770; see *Linmark Associates, Inc.* v. *Willingboro*, 431 U.S. 85, 92 (1977). Even when advertising communicates only an incomplete version of the relevant facts, the First Amendment presumes that some accurate information is better than no information at all. . . .

Nevertheless, our decisions have recognized "the 'commonsense' distinction between speech proposing a commercial transaction, which occurs in an area traditionally subject to government regulation, and other varieties of speech." . . . The Constitution therefore accords a lesser protection to commercial speech than to other constitutionally guaranteed expression. . . . The protection available for particular commercial expression turns on the nature both of the expression and of the governmental interests served by its regulation.

The First Amendment's concern for commercial speech is based on the informational function of advertising. . . . Consequently, there can be no constitutional objection to the suppression of commercial messages that do not accurately inform the public about lawful activity. The government may ban forms of communication more likely to deceive the public than to inform it. . . .

If the communication is neither misleading nor related to unlawful activity, the government's power is more circumscribed. The State must assert a substantial interest to be achieved by restrictions on commercial speech. Moreover, the regulatory technique must be in proportion to that interest. The limitation on expression must be designed carefully to achieve the State's goal. Compliance with this requirement may be measured by two criteria. First, the restriction must directly advance the state interest involved; the regulation may not be sustained if it provides only ineffective or remote support for the government's purpose. Second, if the governmental interest could be served as well by a more limited restriction on commercial speech, the excessive restrictions cannot survive.

Under the first criterion, the Court has declined to uphold regulations that only indirectly advance the state interest involved. In both *Bates* and *Virginia Pharmacy Board,* the Court concluded that an advertising ban could not be imposed to protect the ethical or performance standards of a profession. . . .

The second criterion recognizes that the First Amendment mandates that speech restrictions be "narrowly drawn." . . . The regulatory technique may extend only as far as the interest it serves. The State cannot regulate speech that poses no danger to the asserted state interest, see *First National Bank of Boston* v. *Bellotti,* . . . nor can it completely suppress information when narrower restrictions on expression would serve its interest as well. For example, in *Bates* the Court explicitly did not "foreclose the possibility that some limited supplementation, by way of warning or disclaimer or the like, might be required" in promotional materials. . . .

In commercial speech cases, then, a four-part analysis has developed. At the outset, we must determine whether the expression is protected by the First Amendment. For commercial speech to come within that provision, it at least must concern lawful activity and not be misleading. Next, we ask whether the asserted governmental interest is substantial. If both inquiries yield positive answers, we must determine whether the regulation directly ad-

vances the governmental interest asserted, and whether it is not more extensive than is necessary to serve that interest.

. . . .

The Commission does not claim that the expression at issue either is inaccurate or relates to unlawful activity. . . . Appellant's monopoly position does not alter the First Amendment's protection for its commercial speech.

The Commission offers two state interests as justifications for the ban on promotional advertising. The first concerns energy conservation. . . . In view of our country's dependence on energy resources beyond our control, no one can doubt the importance of energy conservation. Plainly, therefore, the state interest asserted is substantial.

The Commission also argues that promotional advertising will aggravate inequities caused by the failure to base the utilities' rates on marginal cost. . . . The State's concern that rates be fair and efficient represents a clear and substantial governmental interest.

Next, we focus on the relationship between the State's interests and the advertising ban. Under this criterion, the Commission's laudable concern over the equity and efficiency of appellant's rates does not provide a constitutionally adequate reason for restricting protected speech. The link between the advertising prohibition and appellant's rate structure is, at most, tenuous. The impact of promotional advertising on the equity of appellant's rates is highly speculative. . . .

In contrast, the State's interest in energy conservation is directly advanced by the Commission order at issue here. There is an immediate connection between advertising and demand for electricity. Central Hudson would not contest the advertising ban unless it believed that promotion would increase its sales. Thus, we find a direct link between the state interest in conservation and the Commission's order.

We come finally to the critical inquiry in this case: whether the Commission's complete suppression of speech ordinarily protected by the First Amendment is no more extensive than necessary to further the State's interest in energy conservation. The Commission's order reaches all promotional advertising, regardless of the impact of the touted service on overall energy use. But the energy conservation rationale, as important as it is, cannot justify suppressing information about electric devices or services that would cause no net increase in total energy use. In addition, no showing has been made that a more limited restriction on the content of promotional advertising would not serve adequately the State's interests.

. . . .

. . . We accept without reservation the argument that conservation, as well as the development of alternative energy sources, is an imperative national goal. Administrative bodies empowered to regulate electric utilities have the authority — and indeed the duty — to take appropriate action to further this goal. When, however, such action involves the suppression of speech, the First and Fourteenth Amendments require that the restriction be no more extensive than is necessary to serve the state interest. . . .

Reversed.

MR. JUSTICE BLACKMUN, with whom MR. JUSTICE BRENNAN joins, concurring in the judgment.

. . . I do not agree, however, that the Court's four-part test is the proper one to be applied when a State seeks to suppress information about a product in order to manipulate a private economic decision that the State cannot or has not regulated or outlawed directly.

. . . .

. . . Permissible restraints on commercial speech have been limited to measures designed to protect consumers from fraudulent, misleading, or coercive sales techniques. Those designed to deprive consumers of information about products or services that are legally offered for sale consistently have been invalidated.

. . . .

If the First Amendment guarantee means anything, it means that, absent clear and present danger, government has no power to restrict expression because of the effect its message is likely to have on the public. . . .

. . . We have not suggested that the "common-sense differences" between commercial speech and other speech justify relaxed scrutiny of restraints that suppress truthful, nondeceptive, noncoercive commercial speech. The differences articulated by the Court, see *ante,* at 564, n. 6, justify a more permissive approach to regulation of the manner of commercial speech for the purpose of protecting consumers from deception or coercion, and these differences explain why doctrines designed to prevent "chilling" of protected speech are inapplicable to commercial speech. No differences between commercial speech and other protected speech justify suppression of commercial speech in order to influence public conduct through manipulation of the availability of information. . . .

MR. JUSTICE STEVENS, with whom MR. JUSTICE BRENNAN joins, concurring in the judgment.

This case involves a governmental regulation that completely bans promotional advertising by an electric utility. This ban encompasses a great deal more than mere proposals to engage in certain kinds of commercial transactions. It prohibits all advocacy of the immediate or future use of electricity. It curtails expression by an informed and interested group of persons of their point of view on questions relating to the production and consumption of electrical energy — questions frequently discussed and debated by our political leaders. . . .

In sum, I concur in the result because I do not consider this to be a "commercial speech" case. Accordingly, I see no need to decide whether the Court's four-part analysis, *ante,* at 566, adequately protects commercial speech — as properly defined — in the face of a blanket ban of the sort involved in this case.

MR. JUSTICE REHNQUIST, dissenting.

The Court's asserted justification for invalidating the New York law is the public interest discerned by the Court to underlie the First Amendment in the free flow of commercial information. . . . Given what seems to me full recognition of the holding of *Virginia Pharmacy Board* that commercial speech is entitled to some degree of First Amendment protection, I think the Court is nonetheless incorrect in invalidating the carefully considered state ban on promotional advertising in light of pressing national and state energy needs.

The Court's analysis in my view is wrong in several respects. Initially, I disagree with the Court's conclusion that the speech of a state-created monopoly, which is the subject of a comprehensive regulatory scheme, is entitled to protection under the First Amendment. I also think that the Court errs here in failing to recognize that the state law is most accurately viewed as an economic regulation and that the speech involved (if it falls within the scope of the First Amendment at all) occupies a significantly more subordinate position in the hierarchy of First Amendment values than the Court gives it today. Finally, the Court in reaching its decision improperly substitutes its own judgment for that of the State in deciding how a proper ban on promotional advertising should be drafted. With regard to this latter point, the Court adopts as its final part of a four-part test a "no more extensive than necessary" analysis that will unduly impair a state legislature's ability to adopt legislation reasonably designed to promote interests that have always been rightly thought to be of great importance to the State.

. . . .

. . . The test adopted by the Court thus elevates the protection accorded commercial speech that falls within the scope of the First Amendment to a level that is virtually indistinguishable from that of noncommercial speech. I think the Court in so doing has effectively accomplished the "devitalization" of the First Amendment that it counseled against in *Ohralik*. I think it has also by labeling economic regulation of business conduct as a restraint on "free speech" gone far to resurrect the discredited doctrine of cases such as *Lochner* and *Tyson & Brother* v. *Banton*. . . . New York's order here is in my view more akin to an economic regulation to which virtually complete deference should be accorded by this Court.

. . . .

The plethora of opinions filed in this case highlights the doctrinal difficulties that emerge from this Court's decisions granting First Amendment protection to commercial speech. . . .

The First Amendment, however, does not always require a clear and present danger to be present before the government may regulate speech. Although First Amendment protection is not limited to the "exposition of ideas" on public issues . . . both because the line between the informing and the entertaining is elusive and because art, literature, and the like may contribute to important First Amendment interests of the individual in freedom of speech — it is well established that the government may regulate obscenity even though its does not present a clear and present danger. Compare, *e.g., Paris Adult Theatre I* v. *Slaton*. . . with *Brandenburg* v. *Ohio*. . . . Indecent speech, at least when broadcast over the airwaves, also may be regulated absent a clear and present danger of the type described by Mr. Justice Brandeis and required by this Court in *Brandenburg. FCC* v. *Pacifica Foundation*. . . . And in a slightly different context this Court declined to apply the clear-and-present-danger test to a conspiracy among members of the press in violation of the Sherman Act because to do so would "degrade" that doctrine. *Associated Press* v. *United States*. . . . Nor does the Court today apply the clear-and-present-danger test in invalidating New York's ban on promotional advertising. . . .

. . . .

I remain of the view that the Court unlocked a Pandora's Box when it "elevated" commercial speech to the level of traditional political speech by according it First Amendment protection in *Virginia Pharmacy Board* v. *Virginia Citizens Consumer Council*. . . .

Metromedia v. San Diego

453 U.S. 490 (1981)
Vote: (4–2)–3

The City of San Diego banned billboards, unless covered by one of twelve specific exceptions. Metromedia, a billboard company, sued on constitutional grounds. The trial court found the ordinance an unconstitutional exercise of the police power, and an abridgement of First Amendment rights. The California Court of Appeals did not reach the First Amendment claim, but affirmed the decision. The California Supreme Court reversed, rejecting both arguments. It relied on past Supreme Court dismissal, "for want of a substantial federal question," of a previous case involving state regulation of billboards. The case came up On Appeal to the U.S. Supreme Court.

JUSTICE WHITE announced the judgment of the Court and delivered an opinion in which JUSTICE STEWART, JUSTICE MARSHALL and JUSTICE POWELL join.

I

Stating that its purpose was "to eliminate hazards to pedestrians and motorists brought about by distracting sign displays" and "to preserve and improve the appearance of the City," San Diego enacted an ordinance to prohibit "outdoor advertising display signs." . . .

. . . .

. . . The specific categories exempted from the prohibition include: government signs; signs located at public bus stops; signs manufactured, transported or stored within the city, if not used for advertising purposes; commemorative historical plaques; religious symbols; signs within shopping malls; for-sale and for-lease signs; signs on public and commercial vehicles; signs depicting time, temperature, and news; approved temporary, off-premises, subdivision directional signs; and "temporary political campaign signs." Under this scheme, onsite commercial advertising is permitted, but other commercial advertising and noncommercial communications using fixed-structure signs are everywhere forbidden unless permitted by one of the specified exceptions.

II

Early cases in this Court sustaining regulation of and prohibitions aimed at billboards did not involve First Amendment considerations. . . . [B]ecause it is designed to stand out and apart from its surroundings, the billboard creates a unique set of problems for land-use planning and development.

Billboards, then, like other media of communication, combine communicative and noncommunicative aspects. As with other media, the government has legitimate interests in controlling the noncommunicative aspects of the medium, *Kovacs* v. *Cooper, supra,* but the First and Fourteenth Amendments foreclose a similar interest in controlling the communicative aspects. Because regulation of the noncommunicative aspects of a medium often impinges to some degree on the communicative aspects, it has been necessary for the courts to reconcile the government's regulatory interests with the individual's right to expression. . . .

As construed by the California Supreme Court, the ordinance restricts the use of certain kinds of outdoor signs. That restriction is defined in two ways: first, by reference to the structural characteristics of the sign; second, by reference to the content, or message, of the sign. Thus, the regulation only applies to a "permanent structure constituting, or used for the display of, a commercial or other advertisement to the public." 164 Cal. Rptr., at 513, n. 2, 610 P.2d, at 410. Within that class, the only permitted signs are those (1) identifying the premises on which the sign is located, or its owner or occupant, or advertising the goods produced or services rendered on such property and (2) those within one of the specified exemptions to the general prohibition, such as temporary political campaign signs. To determine if any billboard is prohibited by the ordinance, one must determine how it is constructed, where it is located, and what message it carries.

Thus, under the ordinance (1) a sign advertising goods or services available on the property where the sign is located is allowed; (2) a sign on a building or other property advertising goods or services produced or offered elsewhere is barred; (3) noncommercial advertising, unless within one of the specific exceptions, is everywhere prohibited. The occupant of property may advertise his own goods or services; he may not advertise the goods or services of others, nor may he display most noncommercial messages.

. . . .

The extension of First Amendment protections to purely commercial speech is a relatively recent development in First Amendment jurisprudence. Prior to 1975, purely commercial advertisements of services or goods for sale were considered to be outside the protection of the First Amendment. . . . That construction of the First Amendment was severely cut back. . . . In *Virginia Pharmacy Board* v. *Virginia Consumer Council* . . . we plainly held that speech proposing no more than a commercial transaction enjoys a substantial degree of First Amendment protection: A state may not completely suppress the dissemination of truthful information about an entirely lawful activity merely because it is fearful of that information's effect upon its disseminators and its recipients. That decision, however, did not equate commercial and noncommercial speech for First Amendment purposes; indeed, it expressly indicated the contrary. . . .

Finally, in *Central Hudson* v. *Public Service Comm'n* . . . we held that: "The Constitution . . . accords a lesser protection to commercial speech than to other constitutionally guaranteed expression. The protection available for a particular commercial expression turns on the nature both of the expression and of the governmental interests served by its regulation." . . . We then adopted a four-part test for determining the validity of government restrictions on commercial speech as distinguished from more fully protected speech. (1) The First Amendment protects commercial speech only if that speech concerns lawful activity and is not misleading. A restriction on otherwise protected commercial speech is valid only if it (2) seeks to implement a substantial governmental interest, (3) directly advances that interest, and (4) reaches no farther than necessary to accomplish the given objective. . . .

Appellants agree that the proper approach to be taken in determining the validity of the restrictions on commercial speech is that which was articulated in *Central Hudson,* but assert that the San Diego ordinance fails that test. We do not agree.

There can be little controversy over the application of the first, second, and fourth criteria. There is no suggestion that the commercial advertising at issue here involves unlawful activity or is misleading. Nor can there be substantial doubt that the twin goals that the ordinance seeks to further — traffic safety and the appearance of the city — are substantial governmental goals. . . . Similarly, we reject appellants' claim that the ordinance is broader than necessary and, therefore, fails the fourth part of the *Central Hudson* test. If the city has a sufficient basis for believing that billboards are traffic hazards and are unattractive, than obviously the most direct and perhaps the only effective approach to solving the problems they create is to prohibit them. The city has gone no farther than necessary in seeking to meet its ends. Indeed, it has stopped short of fully accomplishing its ends: It has not prohibited all billboards, but allows on-site advertising and some other specifically exempted signs.

The more serious question, then, concerns the third of the *Central Hudson* criteria: Does the ordinance "directly advance" governmental interests in traffic safety and in the appearance of the city? . . . The California Supreme Court noted the meager record on this point but held "as a matter of law that an ordinance which eliminates billboards designed to be viewed from the streets and highways reasonably relates to traffic safety." . . .

We reach a similar result with respect to the second asserted justification for the ordinance — advancement of the city's esthetic interests. It is not speculative to recognize that billboards by their very nature, wherever located and however constructed, can be perceived an "esthetic harm." . . .

. . . In sum, insofar as it regulates commercial speech the San Diego ordinance meets the constitutional requirements of *Central Hudson, supra.*

 . . . .

V

It does not follow, however, that San Diego's general ban on signs carrying noncommercial advertising is also valid under the First and Fourteenth Amendments. The fact that the city may value commercial messages relating to on-site goods and services more than it values commercial communications relating to off-site goods and services does not justify prohibiting an occupant from displaying its own ideas or those of others.

As indicated above, our recent commercial speech cases have consistently accorded noncommercial speech a greater degree of protection than commercial speech. San Diego effectively inverts this judgment, by affording a greater degree of protection to commercial than to noncommercial speech. There is a broad exception for on-site commercial advertisements, but there is no similar exception for noncommercial speech. The use of on-site billboards to carry commercial messages related to the commercial use of the premises is freely permitted, but the use of otherwise identical billboards to carry noncommercial messages is generally prohibited. The city does not explain how or why noncommercial billboards located in places where commercial billboards are permitted would be more threatening to safe driving or would detract more from the beauty of the

city. Insofar as the city tolerates billboards at all, it cannot choose to limit their content to commercial messages; the city may not conclude that the communication of commercial information concerning goods and services connected with a particular site is of greater value than the communication of noncommercial messages.

VI

Despite the rhetorical hyperbole of The Chief Justice's dissent, there is a considerable amount of common ground between the approach taken in this opinion and that suggested by his dissent. Both recognize that each medium of communication creates a unique set of First Amendment problems, both recognize that the city has a legitimate interest in regulating the noncommunicative aspects of a medium of expression, and both recognize that the proper judicial role is to conduct "a careful inquiry into the competing concerns of the State and the interests protected by the guarantee of free expression." . . .

Because The Chief Justice misconceives the nature of the judicial function in this situation, he misunderstands the significance of the city's extensive exceptions to its billboard prohibition. He characterizes these exceptions as "essentially negligible," *post,* at 2920, and then opines that it borders on the frivolous to suggest that in "allowing such signs but forbidding noncommercial billboards, the city has infringed freedom of speech." . . .

There can be no question that a prohibition on the erection of billboards infringes freedom of speech: The exceptions do not create the infringement, rather the general prohibition does. But the exceptions to the general prohibition are of great significance in assessing the strength of the city's interest in prohibiting billboards. We conclude that by allowing commercial establishments to use billboards to advertise the products and services they offer, the city necessarily has conceded that some communicative interests, *e.g.,* on-site commercial advertising, are stronger than its competing interests in esthetics and traffic safety.

The Chief Justice . . . seems to argue that although the Constitution affords a greater degree of protection to noncommercial than to commercial speech, a legislature need not make the same choices. *Post,* at 2923. This position makes little sense even abstractly, and it surely is not consistent with our cases or with The Chief Justice's own argument that statutes challenged on First Amendment grounds must be evaluated in light of the unique facts and circumstances of the case. Governmental interests are only revealed and given concrete force by the steps taken to meet these interests. If the city has concluded that its official interests are not as strong as private interests in commercial communications, may it nevertheless claim that those same official interests outweigh private interests in noncommercial communications? Our answer, which is consistent with our cases, is in the negative.

JUSTICE BRENNAN, with whom JUSTICE BLACKMUN joins, concurring in the judgment.

Believing that "a total prohibition of outdoor advertising is not before us," *ante,* at 2896, n. 20, the plurality does not decide "whether such a ban would be consistent with the First Amendment," *ibid.* Instead, it concludes that San Diego may ban all billboards containing commercial speech messages without violating the First Amendment, thereby sending the signal to municipalities that bifurcated billboard regulations prohibiting commercial messages but allowing noncommercial messages would pass constitutional muster. *Id.,* at 2899, n. 25. I write separately because I believe this case in effect presents the total ban question, and because I believe the plurality's bifurcated approach itself raises serious First Amendment problems and relies on a distinction between commercial and noncommercial speech unanticipated by our prior cases.

. . . .

. . . As I read the ordinance, the content of the sign depends strictly on the identity of the owner or occupant of the premises. If the occupant is a commercial enterprise, the substance of a permissible identifying sign would be commercial. If the occupant is an enterprise usually associated with noncommercial speech, the substance of the identifying sign would be noncommercial. Just as a supermarket or barbershop could identify itself by name, so too could a political campaign headquarters or a public interest group. I would also presume that, if a barbershop could advertise haircuts, a political campaign headquarters could advertise "Vote for Brown," or "Vote for Proposition 13."

More importantly, I cannot agree with the plurality's view that an ordinance totally banning commercial billboards but allowing noncommercial billboards would be constitutional. For me, such an ordinance raises First Amendment problems at least as serious as those raised by a total ban, for it gives city officials the right — before approving a billboard — to determine whether the proposed message is "commercial" or "noncommercial." Of course the plurality is correct when it observes that "our cases have consistently distinguished between the constitutional protection afforded commercial as opposed to noncommercial speech," *ante,* at 2891, but it errs in assuming that a *governmental unit* may be put in the position in the first instance of deciding whether the proposed speech is commercial or noncommercial. . . .

. . . .

. . . May the city decide that a United Automobile Workers billboard with the message "Be a patriot — do not buy Japanese-manufactured cars" is "commercial" and therefore forbid it? What if the same sign is placed by Chrysler?

JUSTICE STEVENS, dissenting.

The principal question presented is, whether a city may prohibit this medium of communication. Instead of answering that question, the plurality focuses its attention on the exceptions from the total ban and, somewhat ironically, concludes that the ordinance is an unconstitutional abridgment of speech because it does not abridge enough speech.

. . . .

. . . [I]n my judgment the constitutionality of the prohibition of outdoor advertising involves two separate questions. First, is there any reason to believe that the regulation is biased in favor of one point of view or another, or that it is a subtle method of regulating the controversial subjects that may be placed on the agenda for public debate? Second, is it fair to conclude that the market which remains open for the communication of both popular and unpopular ideas is ample and not threatened with gradually increasing restraints?

In this case, there is not even a hint of bias or censorship in the city's actions. Nor is there any reason to believe that the overall communications market in San Diego is inadequate. . . .

If one is persuaded, as I am, that a wholly impartial total ban on billboards would be permissible, it is difficult to understand why the exceptions in San Diego's ordinance present any additional threat to the interests protected by the First Amendment. The plurality suggests that, because the exceptions are based in part on the subject matter of noncommercial speech, the city somehow is choosing the permissible subjects for public debate. See *ante,* at 2896. While this suggestion is consistent with some of the broad dictum in *Consolidated Edison Co.* v. *Public Service Commission . . .* it does not withstand analysis in this case.

. . . Although *Consolidated Edison* broadly identified regulations based on the subject matter of speech as impermissible content-based regulations, essential First Amendment concerns were implicated in that case because the government was attempting to limit discussion of controversial topics . . . and thus was shaping the agenda for public debate. The neutral exceptions in the San Diego ordinance do not present this danger.

CHIEF JUSTICE BURGER, dissenting.

Today the Court takes an extraordinary—even a bizarre—step by severely limiting the power of a city to act on risks it perceives to traffic safety and the environment posed by large, permanent billboards. Those joining the plurality opinion invalidate a city's effort to minimize these traffic hazards and eyesores simply because, in exercising rational legislative judgment, it has chosen to permit a narrow class of signs that serve special needs.

Relying on simplistic platitudes about content, subject matter, and the dearth of other means to communicate, the billboard industry attempts to escape the real and growing problems every municipality faces in protecting safety and preserving the environment in an urban area. . . . American cities desiring to mitigate the dangers mentioned must, as a matter of *federal constitutional law,* elect between two unsatisfactory options: (a) allowing all "noncommercial" signs, no matter how many, how dangerous, or how damaging to the environment; or (b) forbidding signs altogether. Indeed, lurking in the recesses of today's opinions is a not-so-veiled threat that the second option, too, may soon be withdrawn. This is the long arm and voracious appetite of federal power—this time judicial power—with a vengeance, reaching and absorbing traditional concepts local authority.

. . . .

. . . [T]his Court's duty is not to make the primary policy decisions but instead is to determine whether the legislative approach is essentially neutral to the messages conveyed and leaves open other adequate means of conveying those messages. This is the essence of both democracy and federalism, and we gravely damage both when we undertake to throttle legislative discretion and judgment at the "grass roots" of our system.

The plurality, in a remarkable *ipse dixit,* states that "[t]here can be no question that a prohibition on the erection of billboards infringes freedom of speech. . . ." *Ante,* at 2899. Of course the city has restricted one form of communication and this action implicates the First Amendment. But to say the ordinance presents a First Amendment *issue* is not necessarily to say that it constitutes a First Amendment violation. . . .

. . . San Diego has not attempted to suppress any particular point of view or any category of messages; it has not censored any information; it has not banned any thought. . . . Moreover, aside from a few narrow and essentially negligible exceptions, see *infra,* at 2922–2923, San Diego has not differentiated with regard to topic. . . .

The fatal flaw in the plurality's logic comes when they conclude that San Diego, by exempting on-site commercial signs, thereby has "afford[ed] a greater degree of protection to commercial than to noncommercial speech." *Ante,* at 2895. The "greater degree of protection" our cases have given noncommercial speech establishes a narrow range of constitutionally permissible regulation. To say commercial speech receives a greater degree of *constitutional* protection, however, does not mean that a legislature is forbidden to afford differing degrees of *statutory* protection when the restrictions on each form of speech—commercial and noncommercial—otherwise pass constitutional muster under the standards respectively applicable.

No case in this Court creates, as the plurality suggests, a hierarchy of types of speech in which, if one type is actually protected through legislative judgment, the Constitution compels that judgment be exercised in favor of all types ranking higher on the list. When a city chooses to impose looser restrictions in one area than it does in another analogous area—even one in which the Constitution more narrowly constrains legislative discretion—it neither undermines the constitutionality of its regulatory scheme nor renders its legislative choices *ipso facto* irrational. A city does not thereby "conced[e] that some communicative interests %y(e)27 are stronger than its competing interests in esthetics and traffic safety," *ante* at 2899; it has only declined, in one area, to exercise its powers to the full extent the Constitution permits. The Constitution does not require any governmental entity to reach the limit of permissible regulation solely because it has chosen to do so in a related area. . . .

. . . .

This Court has often faced the problem of applying the broad principles of the First Amendment to unique forums of expression. . . . Even a cursory reading of these opinions reveals that at times First Amendment values must yield to other societal interests. These cases support the cogency of Justice Jackson's remark in *Kovacs v. Cooper,* . . . (1949): Each method of communicating ideas is "a law unto itself" and that law must reflect the "differing natures, values, abuses and dangers" of each method. We deal here with the law of billboards.

JUSTICE REHNQUIST, dissenting.

. . . I regret even more keenly my contribution to

this judicial clangor, but find that none of the views expressed in the other opinions written in the case come close enough to mine to warrant the necessary compromise to obtain a Court opinion.

In my view, the aesthetic justification alone is sufficient to sustain a total prohibition of billboards within a community... regardless of whether the particular community is "a historic community such as Williamsburg" or one as unsightly as the older parts of many of our major metropolitan areas. Such areas should not be prevented from taking steps to correct, as best they may, mistakes of their predecessors. Nothing in my experience on the bench has led me to believe that a judge is in any better position than a city or county commission to make decisions in an area such as aesthetics. Therefore, little can be gained in the area of constitutional law, and much lost in the process of democratic decisionmaking, by allowing individual judges in city after city to second-guess such legislative or administrative determinations.

Nebraska Press Association v. Stuart

427 U.S. 539 (1976)
Vote: 9–0, but several concurrences.

Six members of a family were found murdered in their homes in a small town of some 850 people. Media coverage was immediate and extensive. The police gave reporters a description of a suspect, who was arrested and arraigned. The county attorney and defense attorney joined in requesting a court order forbidding publication of information about the pretrial proceedings. After deliberation the judge issued such an order. The process continued in open court, and the prosecutor altered the charges, based on the autopsies, to include the charge that the murders had occurred in the course of a sexual assault.

The Press Association mobilized four days later to request a Stay of the Order. They also applied to the Nebraska Supreme Court for a Writ of Mandamus, a Stay, and an expedited appeal on the matter. The Supreme Court modified the order, but sustained it against charges of unconstitutionality, and left in force the ban as to confessions made by the defendant.

The Supreme Court granted *certiorari* as to the issues raised in 1975, but refused to expedite the appeal. The defendant went to trial on January 7, 1976, and had been convicted and sentenced to death by the time the U.S. Supreme Court dealt with the issue.

By its own terms the gag order expired once the jury was empaneled. The Court, therefore, had to decide whether the issue was moot. It held that it could review if the underlying dispute is one "capable of repetition yet evading review," citing a 1911 case, *Southern Pacific Terminal* v. *ICC*. Since defendant's conviction was under appeal, he might be faced with another such order. More broadly, the Press Association might anticipate exclusions and prosecutors might seek such orders, and the short duration of such orders made judicial review difficult if not impossible.

In two highly publicized cases, *Estes* v. *Texas* (1965) and the sensational murder trial *Sheppard* v. *Maxwell* (1966), the Supreme Court had reversed, citing lack of courtroom control by the judge as a factor in its decision. This criticism looms as a background factor, and the Supreme Court is at some pains here to distinguish between the pretrial and trial stages.

MR. CHIEF JUSTICE BURGER delivered the opinion of the Court.

The respondent State District Judge entered an order restraining the petitioners from publishing or broadcasting accounts of confessions or admissions made by the accused or facts "strongly implicative" of the accused in a widely reported murder of six persons. We granted certiorari to decide whether the entry of such an order on the showing made before the state court violated the constitutional guarantee of freedom of the press.

. . . .

In the overwhelming majority of criminal trials, pretrial publicity presents few unmanageable threats to this important right. But when the case is a "sensational" one tensions develop between the right of the accused to trial by an impartial jury and the rights guaranteed others by the First Amendment. . . .

. . . .

In *Sheppard* v. *Maxwell* . . . (1966), the Court focused sharply on the impact of pretrial publicity and a trial court's duty to protect the defendant's constitutional right to a fair trial. With only Mr. Justice Black dissenting, and he without opinion, the Court ordered a new trial for the petitioner, even though the first trial had occurred 12 years before. Beyond doubt the press had shown no responsible concern for the constitutional guarantee of a fair trial; the community from which the jury was drawn had been inundated by publicity hostile to the defendant. But the trial judge "did not fulfill this duty to protect [the defendant] from the inherently prejudicial publicity which saturated the community and to control disruptive influences in the courtroom."...

. . . .

. . . Pretrial publicity — even pervasive, adverse publicity — does not inevitably lead to an unfair trial. The capacity of the jury eventually impaneled to decide the case fairly is influenced by the tone and extent of the publicity, which is in part, and often in large part, shaped by what attorneys, police, and other officials do to precipitate news coverage. The trial judge has a major responsibility. What the judge says about a case, in or out of the courtroom, is likely to appear in newspapers and broadcasts. More important, the measures a judge takes or fails to take to mitigate the effects of pretrial publicity — the measures described in *Sheppard* — may well determine whether the defendant receives a trial consistent with the requirements of due process. That this responsibility has not always been properly discharged is apparent from the decisions just reviewed.

. . . .

The state trial judge in the case before us acted responsibly, out of a legitimate concern, in an effort to protect the defendant's right to a fair trial. What we must decide is not simply whether the Nebraska courts erred in seeing the possibility of real danger to the defendant's rights, but whether in the circumstances of this case the means employed were foreclosed by another provision of the Constitution.

The First Amendment provides that "Congress shall make no law . . . abridging the freedom . . . of the press."... The Court has interpreted these guarantees to afford special protection against orders that prohibit the publication or broadcast of particular information or commentary — orders that impose a "previous" or "prior" restraint on speech....

. . . .

The thread running through all these cases is that prior restraints on speech and publication are the most serious and the least tolerable infringement on First Amendment rights. A criminal penalty or a judgment in a defamation case is subject to the whole panoply of protections afforded by deferring the impact of the judgment until all avenues of appel-

late review have been exhausted. Only after judgment has become final, correct or otherwise, does the law's sanction become fully operative.

A prior restraint, by contrast and by definition, has an immediate and irreversible sanction. If it can be said that a threat of criminal or civil sanctions after publication "chills" speech, prior restraint "freezes" it at least for the time.

. . . .

The authors of the Bill of Rights did not undertake to assign priorities as between First Amendment and Sixth Amendment rights, ranking one as superior to the other. In this case, the petitioners would have us declare the right of an accused subordinate to their right to publish in all circumstances. But if the authors of these guarantees, fully aware of the potential conflicts between them, were unwilling or unable to resolve the issue by assigning to one priority over the other, it is not for us to rewrite the Constitution by undertaking what they declined to do. It is unnecessary, after nearly two centuries, to establish a priority applicable in all circumstances. Yet it is nonetheless clear that the barriers to prior restraint remain high unless we are to abandon what the Court has said for nearly a quarter of our national existence and implied throughout all of it....

. . .

We turn now to the record in this case to determine whether, as Learned Hand put it, "the gravity of the 'evil,' discounted by its improbability, justifies such invasion of free speech as is necessary to avoid the danger."...

. . . .

Our review of the pretrial record persuades us that the trial judge was justified in concluding that there would be intense and pervasive pretrial publicity concerning this case. He could also reasonably conclude, based on common human experience, that publicity might impair the defendant's right to a fair trial. He did not purport to say more, for he found only "a clear and present danger that pre-trial publicity *could* impinge upon the defendant's right to a fair trial." (Emphasis added.)

We find little in the record that goes to another aspect of our task, determining whether measures short of an order restraining all publication would have insured the defendant a fair trial....

Most of the alternatives to prior restraint of publication in these circumstances were discussed with obvious approval in *Sheppard* v. *Maxwell*... (a) change of trial venue to a place less exposed to the intense publicity that seemed imminent in Lincoln County; (b) postponement of the trial to allow public attention to subside; (c) searching questioning of prospective jurors, as Mr. Chief Justice Marshall used in the *Burr* case, to screen out those with fixed opinions as to guilt or innocence; (d) the use of emphatic and clear instructions on the sworn duty of each juror to decide the issues only on evidence presented in open court. Sequestration of jurors is, of course, always available. Although that measure insulates jurors only after they are sworn, it also enhances the likelihood of dissipating the impact of pretrial publicity and emphasizes the elements of the jurors' oaths.

. . . .

. . . There is no finding that alternative measures would not have protected Simants' rights, and the Nebraska Supreme Court did no more than imply that such measures might not be adequate. Moreover, the record is lacking in evidence to support such a finding.

. . . .

Finally, we note that the events disclosed by the record took place in a community of 850 people. It is reasonable to assume that, without any news accounts being printed or broadcast, rumors would travel swiftly by word of mouth. One can only speculate on the accuracy of such reports, given the generative propensities of rumors; they could well be more damaging than reasonably accurate news accounts. But plainly a whole community cannot be restrained from discussing a subject intimately affecting life within it.

Given these practical problems, it is far from clear that prior restraint on publication would have protected Simants' rights.

MR. JUSTICE WHITE, concurring.

Technically there is no need to go farther than the Court does to dispose of this case, and I join the Court's opinion. I should add, however, that for the reasons which the Court itself canvasses there is grave doubt in my mind whether orders with respect to the press such as were entered in this case would ever be justifiable. . . . If the recurring result, however, in case after case is to be similar to our judgment today, we should at some point announce a more general rule and avoid the interminable litigation that our failure to do so would necessarily entail.

MR. JUSTICE POWELL, concurring.

In my judgment a prior restraint may issue only when it is shown to be necessary to prevent the dissemination of prejudicial publicity that otherwise poses a high likelihood of preventing, directly and irreparably, the impaneling of a jury meeting the Sixth Amendment requirement of impartiality. This re-

quires a showing that (i) there is a clear threat to the fairness of trial, (ii) such a threat is posed by the actual publicity to be restrained, and (iii) no less restrictive alternatives are available. . . .

I believe these factors are sufficiently addressed in the Court's opinion to demonstrate beyond question that the prior restraint here was impermissible.

MR. JUSTICE BRENNAN, with whom MR. JUSTICE STEWART and MR. JUSTICE MARSHALL join, concurring in the judgment.

. . . I would hold, however, that resort to prior restraints on the freedom of the press is a constitutionally impermissible method for enforcing that right; judges have at their disposal a broad spectrum of devices for ensuring that fundamental fairness is accorded the accused without necessitating so drastic an incursion on the equally fundamental and salutary constitutional mandate that discussion of public affairs in a free society cannot depend on the preliminary grace of judicial censors.

. . . .

The only exception that has thus far been recognized even in dictum to the blanket prohibition against prior restraints against publication of material which would otherwise be constitutionally shielded was the "military security" situation addressed in *New York Times Co. v. United States.* But unlike the virtually certain, direct, and immediate harm required for such a restraint under *Near* and *New York Times,* the harm to a fair trial that might otherwise eventuate from publications which are suppressed pursuant to orders such as that under review must inherently remain speculative.

. . . .

These are obviously only some examples of the problems that plainly would recur, not in the almost theoretical situation of suppressing disclosure of the location of troops during wartime, but on a regular basis throughout the courts of the land. Recognition of any judicial authority to impose prior restraints on the basis of harm to the Sixth Amendment rights of particular defendants, especially since that harm must remain speculative, will thus inevitably interject judges at all levels into censorship roles that are simply inappropriate and impermissible under the First Amendment. Indeed, the potential for arbitrary and excessive judicial utilization of any such power would be exacerbated by the fact that judges and committing magistrates might in some cases be determining the propriety of publishing information that reflects on their competence, integrity, or general performance on the bench.

Richmond Newspapers v. Virginia

448 U.S. 555 (1980)
Vote: 7–1; Powell not participating.

NEBRASKA PRESS ASSOCIATION V. STUART eliminated one possible solution to the "free coverage vs. fair trial dilemma." *Gannett Co.* v. *DePasquale* (1979) and *Richmond Newspapers* tackled another.

The *Gannett* case involved an apparent murder-robbery, with extensive coverage due to complications such as extradition proceedings being involved and failure to recover the drowned body. Defense lawyers requested closed proceedings on a pretrial motion to suppress evidence. The District Attorney did not object, and neither did a newspaper reporter present. The trial judge granted the motion.

The Gannett Company, a leading national newspaper chain, requested the transcript in a letter the next day. Judge DePasquale indicated he reserved decision as to when the transcript would be released. Petitioners therefore filed a motion to set aside the order, which the judge denied. They appealed to the Appellate Division, which held the order transgressed "the public's vital interest in open proceedings" and constituted prior restraint.

The New York Court of Appeals reversed this decision, ruling that the case was technically moot, since the defendants had agreed to a plea-bargained arrangement. It held, on the merits, that trials were presumptively open, but that this exclusion of the media was justifiable.

The U.S. Supreme Court granted certiorari. On the issue of mootness, it followed NEBRASKA PRESS ASSOCIATION V. STUART and cited *Weinstein* v. *Bradford* (1975), to define cases "capable of repetition yet evading review":

> (1) the challenged action was in its duration too short to be fully litigated prior to its cessation or expiration, and (2) there was a reasonable expectation that the same complaining party would be subjected to the same action again.

On the merits, Justice Stewart's opinion for the Court noted that the right of a public trial is mentioned solely in context of the rights of the accused. Acknowledging a public interest in open trials, and the minority opinion which detailed the history of open trials, Stewart nevertheless concluded that neither the public interest nor a common-law rule of open trials rose to the level of a constitutional right.

While the Chief Justice concurred to suggest limiting the decision to pretrial proceedings, Justice Rehnquist in a separate opinion noted that Stewart's language was comprehensive. Justice Powell, concurring, expressed the view that public access to trials was protected by the First and Fourteenth Amendments. Again, Rehnquist repudiated this view, and suggested that "the lower courts should not assume" they had to follow the restraints suggested by Powell or even follow the procedures employed by the trial court in Gannett. He invited the lower courts "to determine for themselves the question whether to open or close the proceedings."

Blackmun's dissent, for himself, Brennan, White, and Marshall, emphasized a public right to an open trial under the Sixth Amendment guarantee. It, like Powell's opinion, took potshots in the footnotes at Rehnquist, who again replied in kind.

By any standards, the *Gannett* case laid an egg. Seldom has professional and public condemnation been so uniform.

Worse yet was the reaction of lower court judges. Perhaps spurred on by Rehnquist's mischievous (and needlessly provocative) concurrence, lower courts closed proceedings at a rate many times any previously recorded. The media were insulted. Blackmun's demonstration that the *Gannett* case circumstance was neither luridly nor widely covered underscored how easy it would be for a judge to avoid trouble by closing a court to the public.

Seldom has the Court moved so fast to correct an error. Again, a murder trial was involved. There had been no less than three previous mistrials, based upon: (1) improperly admitted evidence; (2) withdrawal of a juror with no alternate available; and (3) a prospective juror reading about the case and informing others in the panel prior to the trial. Perhaps it was weariness that led to the judge's granting the motion to exclude the public, so witnesses could not learn what other witnesses said — a standard that presumably could apply to any trial, although the defense counsel stressed that this was a fourth effort on trial. The prosecution took no position, and the judge refused to vacate the order, when later the same day lawyers for plaintiff appeared and so moved. (The judge ruled the argument on this point was part of the trial, so reporters could not be present to hear the argument about their rights.) The Virginia Supreme Court denied the petition for appeal, sustaining the lower court. The case came to the U.S. Supreme Court On Appeal.

Powell recused himself. Seven justices found First Amendment privilege, but six opinions differ widely in nuance. Rehnquist's dissent is unrepentant and takes no notice of critiques of *Gannett* from outside the Court.

Query: Rehnquist aside, was there ever much *practical* distance between the other justices? If not, why couldn't they bury the hatchet and come up with an opinion of the Court in *Richmond?* Why did the dissenting phalanx in *Gannett* dissolve in *Richmond?* Why didn't it reach some understanding with Powell in *Gannett?*

MR. CHIEF JUSTICE BURGER announced the judgment of the Court and delivered an opinion, in which MR. JUSTICE WHITE and MR. JUSTICE STEVENS joined.

The narrow question presented in this case is whether the right of the public and press to attend criminal trials is guaranteed under the United States Constitution.

We begin consideration of this case by noting that the precise issue presented here has not previously been before this Court for decision. In *Gannett Co. v. DePasquale, supra,* the Court was not required to decide whether a right of access to *trials,* as distinguished from hearings on *pre*trial motions, was constitutionally guaranteed. The Court held that the Sixth Amendment's guarantee to the accused of a public trial gave neither the public nor the press an enforceable right of access to a *pre*trial suppression

hearing. One concurring opinion specifically emphasized that "a hearing on a motion before trial to suppress evidence is not a *trial....*" (BURGER, C. J., concurring). Moreover, the Court did not decide whether the First and Fourteenth Amendments guarantee a right of the public to attend trials; nor did the dissenting opinion reach this issue. (opinion of BLACKMUN, J.)

. . . .

As we have shown, and as was shown in both the Court's opinion and the dissent in *Gannett,...* the historical evidence demonstrates conclusively that at the time when our organic laws were adopted, criminal trials both here and in England had long been presumptively open....

. . . .

The First Amendment, in conjunction with the Fourteenth, prohibits governments from "abridging the freedom of speech, or of the press; or the right of the people peaceably to assemble, and to petition the Government for a redress of grievances." These expressly guaranteed freedoms share a common core purpose of assuring freedom of communication on matters relating to the functioning of government. Plainly it would be difficult to single out any aspect of government of higher concern and importance to the people than the manner in which criminal trials are conducted: as we have shown, recognition of this pervades the centuries-old history of open trials and the opinions of this Court....

The right of access to places traditionally open to the public, as criminal trials have long been, may be seen as assured by the amalgam of the First Amendment guarantees of speech and press; and their affinity to the right of assembly is not without relevance. From the outset, the right of assembly was regarded not only as an independent right but also as a catalyst to augment the free exercise of the other First Amendment rights with which it was deliberately linked by the draftsmen.

The State argues that the Constitution nowhere spells out a guarantee for the right of the public to attend trials, and that accordingly no such right is protected....

But arguments such as the State makes have not precluded recognition of important rights not enumerated. Notwithstanding the appropriate caution against reading into the Constitution rights not explicitly defined, the Court has acknowledged that certain unarticulated rights are implicit in enumerated guarantees. For example, the rights of association and of privacy, the right to be presumed innocent, and the right to be judged by a standard of proof beyond a reasonable doubt in a criminal trial, as well as the right to travel, appear nowhere in the Constitution or Bill of Rights. Yet these important but unarticulated rights have nonetheless been found to share constitutional protection in common with explicit guarantees. . . .

We hold that the right to attend criminal trials is implicit in the guarantees of the First Amendment; without the freedom to attend such trials, which people have exercised for centuries, important aspects of freedom of speech and "of the press could be eviscerated." . . .

MR. JUSTICE POWELL took no part in the consideration or decision in this case.

MR. JUSTICE WHITE, concurring.

This case would have been unnecessary had *Gannett Co.* v. *DePasquale* . . . construed the Sixth Amendment to forbid excluding the public from criminal proceedings except in narrowly defined circumstances. But the Court there rejected the submission of four of us to this effect, thus requiring that the First Amendment issue involved here be addressed. On this issue, I concur in the opinion of The Chief Justice.

MR. JUSTICE STEVENS, concurring.

This is a watershed case. Until today the Court has accorded virtually absolute protection to the dissemination of information or ideas, but never before has it squarely held that the acquisition of newsworthy matter is entitled to any constitutional protection whatsoever. . . .

. . . I explained at length why MR. JUSTICE BRENNAN, MR. JUSTICE POWELL, and I were convinced that "[a]n official prison policy of concealing . . . knowledge from the public by arbitrarily cutting off the flow of information at its source abridges the freedom of speech and of the press protected by the First and Fourteenth Amendments to the Constitution." . . .

It is somewhat ironic that the Court should find more reason to recognize a right of access today than it did in *Houchins*. For *Houchins* involved the plight of a segment of society least able to protect itself, an attack on a longstanding policy of concealment, and an absence of any legitimate justification for abridging public access to information about how government operates. In this case we are protecting the interests of the most powerful voices in the community, we are concerned with an almost unique exception to an established tradition of openness in the conduct of criminal trials, and it is likely that the closure order was motivated by the judge's desire to protect the individual defendant from the burden of a fourth criminal trial.

MR. JUSTICE BRENNAN, with whom MR. JUSTICE MARSHALL joins, concurring in the judgment.

The Court's approach in right-of-access cases simply reflects the special nature of a claim of First Amendment right to gather information. Customarily, First Amendment guarantees are interposed to protect communication between speaker and listener. . . . But the First Amendment embodies more than a commitment to free expression and communicative interchange for their own sakes; it has a *structural* role to play in securing and fostering our republican system of self-government. . . .

However, because "the stretch of this protection is theoretically endless," . . . it must be invoked with discrimination and temperance. . . .

. . . With regard to the case at hand, our ingrained tradition of public trials and the importance of public access to the broader purposes of the trial process tip the balance strongly toward the rule that trials be open. What countervailing interests might be sufficiently compelling to reverse this presumption of openness need not concern us now, for the statute at stake here authorizes trial closures at the unfettered discretion of the judge and parties. . . .

MR. JUSTICE STEWART, concurring in the judgment.

MR. JUSTICE BLACKMUN, concurring in the judgment.

It is gratifying, first, to see the Court now looking to and relying upon legal history in determining the fundamental public character of the criminal trial. *Ante,* at 564–569, 572–574, and n. 9. The partial dissent in *Gannett* . . . took great pains in assembling—I believe adequately—the historical material and in stressing its importance to this area of the law. . . .

The Court's return to history is a welcome change in direction.

It is gratifying, second, to see the Court wash away at least some of the graffiti that marred the prevailing opinions in *Gannett*. No fewer than 12 times in the primary opinion in that case, the Court (albeit in what seems now to have become clear dicta) observed that its Sixth Amendment closure ruling applied to the *trial* itself. The author of the first concurring opinion was fully aware of this and would have restricted the Court's observations and ruling to the suppression hearing. . . . Nonetheless, he *joined* the Court's opinion, *ibid.,* with its multiple references to the trial itself; the opinion was not a mere concurrence in the Court's judgment. . . .

. . . I remain convinced that the right to a public trial is to be found where the Constitution explicitly placed it — in the Sixth Amendment.

The Court, however, has eschewed the Sixth Amendment route. The plurality turns to other possible constitutional sources and invokes a veritable potpourri of them—the Speech Clause of the First Amendment, the Press Clause, the Assembly Clause, the Ninth Amendment, and a cluster of penumbral guarantees recognized in past decisions. This course is troublesome, but it is the route that has been selected and, at least for now, we must live with it. . . .

. . . I do not believe that either the First or Sixth Amendment, as made applicable to the States by the Fourteenth, requires that a State's reasons for denying public access to a trial, where both the prosecuting attorney and the defendant have consented to an order of closure approved by the judge, are subject to any additional constitutional review at our hands. And I most certainly do not believe that the Ninth Amendment confers upon us any such power to review orders of state trial judges closing trials in such situations. . . .

. . . [O]ur authority to reverse a decision by the highest court of the State is limited to only those occasions when the state decision violates some provision of the United States Constitution. And that authority should be exercised with a full sense that the judges whose decisions we review are making the same effort as we to uphold the Constitution. As said by Mr. Justice Jackson, concurring in the result in *Brown v. Allen* . . . , "we are not final because we are infallible, but we are infallible only because we are final."

Branzburg v. Hayes

> 408 U.S. 665 (1972)
> Vote: 5–4

Reporters who had written articles covering possible crimes refused to divulge their sources to grand juries and were found in contempt. In one instance the reporter wrote an article on his witnessing hashish being produced from marijuana; he refused to name the producers. In the other, reporters who had developed contacts with the Black Panthers refused to give information to federal courts.

In the aftermath of these cases, an effort was made to draft a federal "shield law" for reporters, but legal and practical problems thwarted this. However, many states now recognize various forms of reporter's privilege, and some federal rights are implicit in the decision in HERBERT V. LANDO (1979).

Opinion of the Court by MR. JUSTICE WHITE, announced by the CHIEF JUSTICE.

Petitioners Branzburg and Pappas and respondent Caldwell press First Amendment claims that may be simply put: that to gather news it is often necessary to agree either not to identify the source of information published or to publish only part of the facts revealed, or both; that if the reporter is nevertheless forced to reveal these confidences to a grand jury, the source so identified and other confidential sources of other reporters will be measurably deterred from furnishing publishable information, all to the detriment of the free flow of information protected by the First Amendment. Although petitioners do not claim an absolute privilege against official interrogation in all circumstances, they assert that the reporter should not be forced either to appear or to testify before a grand jury or at trial until and unless sufficient grounds are shown for believing that the reporter possesses information relevant to a crime the grand jury is investigating, that the information the reporter has is unavailable from other sources, and that the need for the information is sufficiently compelling to override the claimed invasion of First Amendment interests occasioned by the disclosure. . . . We do not question the significance of free speech, press or assembly to the country's welfare. Nor is it suggested that news gathering does not qualify for First Amendment protection; without some protection for seeking out the news, freedom of the press could be eviscerated. But this case involves no intrusions upon speech or assembly, no prior restraint or restriction on what the press may publish, and no express or implied command that the press publish what it prefers to withhold. No exaction or tax for the privilege of publishing, and no penalty, civil or criminal, related to the content of published material is at issue here. The use of confidential sources by the press is not forbidden or restricted; reporters remain free to seek news from any source by means within the law. No attempt is made to require the press to publish its sources of information or indiscriminately to disclose them on request.

The sole issue before us is the obligation of reporters to respond to grand jury subpoenas as other citizens do and to answer questions relevant to an investigation into the commission of crime. Citizens generally are not constitutionally immune from grand jury subpoenas; and neither the First Amendment nor other constitutional provision protects the average citizen from disclosing to a grand jury information that he has received in confidence. The claim is, however, that reporters are exempt from these obligations because if forced to respond to subpoenas and identify their sources or disclose other confidences, their informants will refuse or be reluctant to furnish newsworthy information in the future. This asserted burden on news gathering is said to make compelled testimony from newsmen constitutionally suspect and to require a privileged position for them.

It is clear that the First Amendment does not invalidate every incidental burdening of the press that may result from the enforcement of civil or criminal statutes of general applicability. Under prior cases, otherwise valid laws serving substantial public interests may be enforced against the press as against others, despite the possible burden that may be imposed. . . . [T]he Associated Press, a news-gathering and disseminating organization, was not exempt from the requirements of the National Labor Relations Act. . . . Likewise, a newspaper may be subjected to nondiscriminatory forms of general taxation. . . .

It has generally been held that the First Amendment does not guarantee the press a constitutional right of special access to information not available to the public generally. . . .

. . . .

. . . Hence the grand jury's authority to subpoena witnesses is not only historic, but essential to its task. Although the powers of the grand jury are not unlimited and are subject to the supervision of a judge, the long-standing principle that "the public has a right to every man's evidence," except for those persons protected by a constitutional, common law, or statutory privilege. *United States* v. *Bryan*, (1950). . . .

A number of States have provided newsmen a statutory privilege of varying breadth, but the majority have not done so, and none has been provided by federal statute. Until now the only testimonial privilege for unofficial witnesses that is rooted in the Federal Constitution is the Fifth Amendment privilege against compelled self-incrimination. We are asked to create another by interpreting the First Amendment to grant newsmen a testimonial privilege that other citizens do not enjoy. This we decline to do. Fair and effective law enforcement aimed at

providing security for the person and property of the individual is a fundamental function of government, and the grand jury plays an important, constitutionally mandated role in this process. On the records now before us, we perceive no basis for holding that the public interest in law enforcement and in ensuring effective grand jury proceedings is insufficient to override the consequential, but uncertain, burden on news gathering which is said to result from insisting that reporters, like other citizens, respond to relevant questions put to them in the course of a valid grand jury investigation or criminal trial.

This conclusion itself involves no restraint on what newspapers may publish or on the type or quality of information reporters may seek to acquire, nor does it threaten the vast bulk of confidential relationships between reporters and their sources. Grand juries address themselves to the issues of whether crimes have been committed and who committed them. Only where news sources themselves are implicated in crime or possess information relevant to the grand jury's task need they or the reporter be concerned about grand jury subpoenas. Nothing before us indicates that a large number or percentage of *all* confidential news sources fall into either category and would in any way be deterred by our holding that the Constitution does not, as it never has, exempt the newsman from performing the citizen's normal duty of appearing and furnishing information relevant to the grand jury's task.

. . . .

The argument that the flow of news will be diminished by compelling reporters to aid the grand jury in a criminal investigation is not irrational, nor are the records before us silent on the matter. But we remain unclear how often and to what extent informers are actually deterred from furnishing information when newsmen are forced to testify before a grand jury. . . .

Accepting the fact, however, that an undetermined number of informants not themselves implicated in crime will nevertheless, for whatever reason, refuse to talk to newsmen if they fear identification by a reporter in an official investigation, we cannot accept the argument that the public interest in possible future news about crime from undisclosed, unverified sources must take precedence over the public interest in pursuing and prosecuting those crimes reported to the press by informants and in thus deterring the commission of such crimes in the future.

. . . .

We are admonished that refusal to provide a First Amendment reporter's privilege will undermine the freedom of the press to collect and disseminate news. But this is not the lesson history teaches us. As noted previously, the common law recognized no such privilege, and the constitutional argument was not even asserted until 1958. . . .

. . . .

The requirements of those cases, see n. 18, *supra,* which hold that a State's interest must be "compelling" or "paramount" to justify even an indirect burden on First Amendment rights, are also met here. As we have indicated, the investigation of crime by the grand jury implements a fundamental governmental role of securing the safety of the person and property of the citizen, and it appears to us that calling reporters to give testimony in the manner and for the reasons that other citizens are called "bears a reasonable relationship to the achievement of the governmental purpose asserted as its justification." If the test is that the Government "convincingly show a substantial relation between the information sought and a subject of overriding and compelling state interest," *Gibson* v. *Florida Investigation Committee,* (1963), it is quite apparent (1) that the State has the necessary interest in extirpating the traffic in illegal drugs, in forestalling assassination attempts on the President, and in preventing the community from being disrupted by violent disorders endangering both persons and property; and (2) that, based on the stories Branzburg and Caldwell wrote and Pappas' admitted conduct, the grand jury called these reporters as they would others — because it was likely that they could supply information to help the Government determine whether illegal conduct had occurred and, if it had, whether there was sufficient evidence to return an indictment.

. . . .

. . . The administration of a constitutional newsman's privilege would present practical and conceptual difficulties of a high order. Sooner or later, it would be necessary to define those categories of newsmen who qualified for the privilege, a questionable procedure in light of the traditional doctrine that liberty of the press is the right of the lonely pamphleteer who uses carbon paper or a mimeograph just as much as of the large metropolitan publisher who utilizes the latest photo-composition methods. . . . Freedom of the press is a "fundamental personal right" which "is not confined to newspapers and periodicals. It necessarily embraces pamphlets and leaflets. . . . The press in its historic connotation

comprehends every sort of publication which affords a vehicle of information and opinion." . . . The informative function asserted by representatives of the organized press in the present cases is also performed by lecturers, political pollsters, novelists, academic researchers, and dramatists. Almost any author may quite accurately assert that he is contributing to the flow of information to the public, that he relies on confidential sources of information, and that these sources will be silenced if he is forced to make disclosures before a grand jury. . . .

. . . .

At the federal level, Congress has freedom to determine whether a statutory newsman's privilege is necessary and desirable and to fashion standards and rules as narrow or broad as deemed necessary to address the evil discerned and, equally important, to re-fashion those rules as experience from time to time may dictate. There is also merit in leaving state legislatures free, within First Amendment limits, to fashion their own standards in light of the conditions and problems with respect to the relations between law enforcement officials and press in their own areas. . . .

MR. JUSTICE POWELL, concurring in the opinion of the Court.

As indicated in the concluding portion of the opinion, the Court states that no harassment of newsmen will be tolerated. If a newsman believes that the grand jury investigation is not being conducted in good faith he is not without remedy. Indeed, if the newsman is called upon to give information bearing only a remote and tenuous relationship to the subject of the investigation, or if he has some other reason to believe that his testimony implicates confidential source relationships without a legitimate need of law enforcement, he will have access to the Court on a motion to quash and an appropriate protective order may be entered. . . .

MR. JUSTICE DOUGLAS, dissenting.

Sooner or later any test which provides less than blanket protection to beliefs and associations will be twisted and relaxed so as to provide virtually no protection at all. . . . A compelling interest test may prove as pliable as did the clear and present danger test. Perceptions of the worth of state objectives will change with the composition of the Court and with the intensity of the politics of the times. . . .

. . . Forcing a reporter before a grand jury will have two retarding effects upon the ear and the pen of the press. Fear of exposure will cause dissidents to communicate less openly to trusted reporters. And, fear of accountability will cause editors and critics to write with more restrained pens.

I see no way of making mandatory the disclosure of a reporter's confidential source of the information on which he bases his news story.

The press has a preferred position in our constitutional scheme not to enable it to make money, not to set newsmen apart as a favored class, but to bring fulfillment to the public's right to know. The right to know is crucial to the governing powers of the people, to paraphrase Alexander Meiklejohn. Knowledge is essential to informed decisions.

. . . .

The intrusion of government into this domain is symptomatic of the disease of this society. As the years pass the power of government becomes more and more pervasive. It is a power to suffocate both people and causes. Those in power, whatever their politics, want only to perpetuate it. Now that the fences of the law and the tradition that has protected the press are broken down, the people are the victims. The First Amendment, as I read it, was designed precisely to prevent that tragedy.

MR. JUSTICE STEWART, with whom MR. JUSTICE BRENNAN and MR. JUSTICE MARSHALL join, dissenting.

The Court's crabbed view of the First Amendment reflects a disturbing insensitivity to the critical role of an independent press in our society. . . . While MR. JUSTICE POWELL's enigmatic concurring opinion gives some hope of a more flexible view in the future, the Court in these cases holds that a newsman has no First Amendment right to protect his sources when called before a grand jury. The Court thus invites state and federal authorities to undermine the historic independence of the press by attempting to annex the journalistic profession as an investigative arm of government. . . .

. . . .

It is obvious that informants are necessary to the news-gathering process as we know it today. If it is to perform its constitutional mission, the press must do far more than merely print public statements or publish prepared handouts. Familiarity with the people and circumstances involved in the myriad background activities that result in the final product called "news" is vital to complete and responsible journalism, unless the press is to be a captive mouthpiece of "newsmakers."

. . . .

After today's decision, the potential informant can never be sure that his identity or off-the-record communications will not subsequently be revealed through the compelled testimony of a newsman. A public-spirited person inside government, who is not implicated in any crime, will now be fearful of revealing corruption or other governmental wrongdoing, because he will now know he can subsequently be identified by use of compulsory process. The potential source must, therefore, choose between risking exposure by giving information or avoiding the risk by remaining silent.

. . . .

The impairment of the flow of news cannot, of course, be proven with scientific precision, as the Court seems to demand. Obviously, not every news-gathering relationship requires confidentiality. And it is difficult to pinpoint precisely how many relationships do require a promise or understanding of nondisclosure. But we have never before demanded that First Amendment rights rest on elaborate empirical studies demonstrating beyond any conceivable doubt that deterrent effects exist; we have never before required proof of the exact number of people potentially affected by governmental action who would actually be dissuaded from engaging in First Amendment activity.

. . . .

Accordingly, when a reporter is asked to appear before a grand jury and reveal confidences, I would hold that the government must (1) show that there is probable cause to believe that the newsman has information which is clearly relevant to a specific probable violation of law; (2) demonstrate that the information sought cannot be obtained by alternative means less destructive of First Amendment rights; and (3) demonstrate a compelling and overriding interest in the information.

. . . .

The crux of the Court's rejection of any newsman's privilege is its observation that only "where news sources themselves are implicated in crime or possess information *relevant* to the grand jury's task need they or the reporter be concerned about grand jury subpoenas." But this is a most misleading construct. For it is obviously not true that the only persons about whom reporters will be forced to testify will be those "confidential informants involved in actual criminal conduct" and those having "information suggesting illegal conduct by others." As noted above, given the grand jury's extraordinarily broad investigative powers and the weak standards of relevance and materiality that apply during such inquiries, reporters, if they have no testimonial privilege, will be called to give information about informants who have neither committed crimes nor have information about crime. . . .

Both the "probable cause" and "alternative means" requirements would thus serve the vital function of mediating between the public interest in the administration of justice and the constitutional protection of the full flow of information. These requirements would avoid a direct conflict between these competing concerns, and they would generally provide adequate protection for newsmen. . . .

CHAPTER 9

Rights in the Criminal Justice System and Fair Procedure in the Administrative Process

Searches, Seizures, and the Warrant Requirement

The Fourth Amendment contains two important provisions designed to protect citizens suspected of crimes from government officials. The first is contained in the phrase "the right of the people to be secure in their persons, houses, papers, and effects against unreasonable searches and seizures, shall not be violated." The second provides that "no warrants shall issue, but upon probable cause, supported by oath or affirmation, and particularly describing the place to be searched, and the person or thing to be seized." The general purpose of these two provisions is clear: to prevent arbitrary action by public officials and to subject the arrest to due process and oversight by neutral officials. But while the broad aim of the Amendment is clear, there is considerable leeway in interpreting it. And like so many other provisions in the Bill of Rights, the process of breathing meaning into it began relatively recently and occurred nearly simultaneously with its application to the states via incorporation through the Due Process Clause of the Fourteenth Amendment.

Aside from the issue of the application to the states, the Fourth Amendment raises three sets of issues. First, these provisions provide no remedy for their violation. So one can reasonably ask, what happens when citizens are deprived of their rights protected by this Amendment? The Court's answer to this question — the so-called exclusionary rule — remains as perhaps the most controversial of all the Court's rulings. Second, the prohibition against *unreasonable* searches and seizures means that some searches and seizures can be reasonable and hence acceptable. Thus the Court must fashion a set of principles that can distinguish reasonable from unreasonable searches and seizures, an effort that, as you will see, has involved the Court in a detailed assessment of the facts of cases. So far no clear set of rules has been developed. Not surprisingly, this result is frustrating to law enforcement officials, defense attorneys, and trial judges alike. Third, in confronting the reality of criminal conduct and the needs of the police in a modern society, the Court has come to acknowledge a number of exceptions to the general rule requiring a search warrant.

Often these three sets of issues arise simultaneously and in combination in cases presented to the Court. Perhaps more than in any other major area of constitutional law, the Court's thinking in this area is unsettled and in flux. One indication of this is the frequency of narrowly divided decisions in the leading cases. More important are recent decisions that have cut significant inroads into the landmark rulings of the 1960s.

The Exclusionary Rule

However broadly or narrowly the Court chooses to interpret the Fourth Amendment, it must still face the question of what to do when one of its provisions is violated. For this reason, we take up the issue of the exclusionary rule first.

During most of our history, the Fourth Amendment applied only to the national government and law enforcement was primarily a matter for the states, with the states developing their own procedures for obtaining evidence. Furthermore, during most of our history both the United States Supreme Court and state courts embraced the long-standing rule of common law that permitted the introduction of illegally obtained evidence at trial. But in 1914, in *Weeks* v. *United States,* 232 U.S. 383, the Supreme Court ruled that evidence seized by federal officials in violation of the Fourth Amendment could *not* be admitted as evidence in *federal* courts. The Court came to this decision with some reluctance and misgiving, recognizing that one consequence would be to allow some factually guilty people to escape conviction. Still, it reasoned, "if letters and private documents can thus be seized and held and used in evidence against a citizen accused of an offense, the protection of the Fourth Amendment, declaring his right to be secure against such searches and seizures, is of no value, and, so far as those thus placed are concerned, might as well be stricken from the Constitution." Additionally, the Court reasoned,

the use of such "tainted" evidence by judges compromises the integrity of the judicial process.

The Court's bold ruling in *Weeks,* however, was tempered by its scope; *Weeks* applied only to *federal* courts, while the vast majority of criminal cases were handled by local law enforcement officials who took their cases to state court, where the old common law rule permitting introduction of unreasonably seized evidence still held sway.

It is hardly surprising that early in the incorporation controversy the Court was urged to extend the *Weeks* ruling to the states. Given the implications for local law enforcement and the emotions attached to crime policy in general, it also is not surprising that such a proposal met with fierce resistance. The Court first squarely addressed the issue of extending the exclusionary rule to the states in 1949, in *Wolf* v. *Colorado,* 338 U.S. 25. Writing for the majority, Justice Felix Frankfurter held that the Fourth Amendment's prohibition against unreasonable search and seizure was "implicit in a concept of ordered liberty" and therefore enforceable against the states through the Due Process Clause of the Fourteenth Amendment. But, he continued, the exclusionary rule itself was not. He reasoned that it is merely one of several practical ways to try to enforce this right, and went on to note that most of the English-speaking world did not subscribe to an exclusionary rule. The implication from Frankfurter's opinion is that the exclusionary rule in *Weeks* stemmed from the Court's supervisory, or common-law making, powers, not from the Constitution. However, *Weeks* was not explicit about this, and other justices disagreed with Frankfurter. This issue continues to be debated today. Three dissenters in *Wolf*—Justices Douglas, Murphy, and Rutledge—argued for extending the exclusionary rule to the states and lamented the "double standard" the Court had created. ROCHIN V. CALIFORNIA (1952), although not directly a Fourth Amendment case, presents this dilemma in sharp relief.

The differences in standards governing federal and state courts created still another problem, which came to be known as the "silver platter" doctrine, so-called because unconstitutionally seized evidence by *state* officials could be turned over to federal officials to be used in federal courts. This was outlawed by the Court in *Elkins v. United States,* 364 U.S. 206 (1960).

The Court also continued to consider the gap created by *Weeks* and *Wolf.* Finally, in MAPP V. OHIO (1961), this gap was closed. In MAPP, the Court reviewed the experience with *Wolf* and concluded that the states had not developed any other remedy besides the exclusionary rule with which to enforce Fourth Amendment rights. The Court was especially impressed that a number of states — most notably California — had adopted the exclusionary rule on their own. Thus, while not especially enthusiastic about the extension and not in agreement as to reasons, a majority on the Court nevertheless concluded that the exclusionary rule was the only viable way at its disposal to try to give efficacy to these important rights.

Save for the desegregation cases, perhaps no other Supreme Court decision in modern times has engendered as much political controversy as MAPP. While recent empirical work suggests that the impact of excluding unconstitutionally seized evidence in both state and federal courts is minimal, the symbolic effect of suppressing this evidence imposes what one scholar has called "a self-inflicted wound" on society's defense against crime. MAPP has been fiercely resisted both by officials in the criminal process and by scholars.

In the years since MAPP, a growing number of justices favor overruling it and voiding the exclusionary rule. Although total victory has not been achieved, the emerging conservative majority has enjoyed significant successes. It has successfully diminished its applicability and is poised for a direct attack on the rule. The Court's doctrinal assault has moved along three fronts:

1. A majority has clearly characterized the rule as a "judicially contrived doctrine," a rule of thumb rather than a principle rooted in the Constitution itself. (In MAPP, only a plurality of four justices found a constitutional basis for the rule;

three justices found exclusion rooted in the Fourth Amendment itself, while Justice Black, concurring, located it in the meeting of the Fourth Amendment with the Fifth Amendment prohibition on compelled self-incrimination.)

2. A majority believes that the purpose of the rule is to deter police violation of the Fourth Amendment by denying them the fruits of unconstitutional searches or seizures. An alternative purpose — preserving the integrity of the courts — which was emphasized by the Court when the rule was first adopted in *Weeks* and stressed in MAPP, has receded into the background.

3. In its analysis of the exclusionary rule (and, as we shall see, in its substantive interpretation of the Fourth Amendment as well) the Court has increasingly utilized a balancing test to weigh the costs and benefits of excluding evidence in particular contexts. As in most balancing tests, the interests of the state tend to predominate.

All three of these developments interact. Having characterized the exclusionary rule as a judicially contrived enforcement device, the Court has legitimated the use of a cost/benefit balancing test, an approach usually deemed inappropriate where basic Constitutional rights are at stake. The balancing test naturally complements a view that deterrence of police violations is the central purpose of excluding evidence, since deterrence is readily measurable and murky notions like "integrity" are not. Conversely, placed on the balancing test, deterrence provides little support for extending the exclusionary rule, since the costs are readily ascertainable while the benefits are difficult to measure. Also, if no obvious deterrent effects can be shown, the rule's rationale is undermined.

While MAPP has not (yet?) been overruled, a solid majority has used the more subtle art of interpretation to significantly diminish its scope in two important ways. First, the *range* of legal proceedings for which evidence obtained in violation of the Fourth Amendment is inadmissible has been restricted to the prosecution's case-in-chief, leaving such evidence to be admitted at other stages of the criminal process, such as grand jury proceedings, cross examinations when defendants testify, and in proceedings not formally defined as criminal trials (e.g., parole revocation hearings or deportation hearings for illegal immigrants).

Second, in 1984 the Court took a giant step when it carved out an *exception* to the exclusionary rule. In UNITED STATES v. LEON (1984), the Court held that evidence gathered by police who relied in "good faith" on a warrant approved by a magistrate but later found to be defective need not be excluded. By itself this exception is significant, but it has even more far-reaching implications for cutting back on MAPP. There is nothing in the logic of the Court's opinion in LEON that would not apply to warrantless searches as well. Thus we can reasonably expect a move for a general good faith exception, one that applies to warrant and warrantless arrests alike. Given that the overwhelming majority of arrests are without warrants, an extension of the good faith exception will represent still another major incursion into the MAPP ruling.

At first blush a good faith exception is appealing. After all, if the police believe they are acting within the confines of the Fourth Amendment, i.e., in good faith compliance with the Constitution, the exclusionary rule is not likely to be a deterrent. But, we might also ask, would not an exclusionary rule serve as an incentive to police officers to learn Fourth Amendment law, and in its absence won't there be less of an incentive to learn the law? And returning to the Court's original emphasis in *Weeks*, doesn't it undermine the integrity of the judicial process if a court in upholding the law relies upon illegal actions of public officials?

What other policy to enforce the Fourth Amendment might replace the exclusionary rule? An alternative, championed by Chief Justice Burger and more recently by Chief Justice Rehnquist and other justices, is for victims of police violations of the Fourth Amendment to seek monetary damages through tort law. This method has the attraction of providing a remedy for those against whom no evidence has been found to suppress, i.e., the factually innocent. On the other hand, scholars have long questioned whether criminal defendants would have the resources to bring such suits, whether compensation would be large enough to motivate lawyers to take such cases, and whether judges and juries would treat criminal suspects — and, in some instances, convicted criminals — fairly in such a suit against police officers. Even now there is nothing to preclude Fourth Amendment victims from bringing tort suits, yet the evidence to date does not suggest that a tort approach will serve as a significant deterrent to police misconduct. Still, we can expect to see this approach tested more fully in the near future.

Since it was announced in 1984, the LEON exception has been reaffirmed and expanded. In a companion case, *Massachusetts* v. *Sheppard,* 468 U.S. 981 (1984), the Court held that evidence excluded because of a technical defect in a warrant should have been introduced at trial, and in *INS* v. *Lopez-Mendoza,* 468 U.S. 1032 (1984), it ruled that illegally seized evidence could be introduced at a deportation hearing, since it was not a criminal proceeding. In 1987, the Court further extended the good faith exception to apply to statutes, holding that the exclusionary rule does not apply to evidence obtained by police who acted in "objectively reasonable reliance" upon a statute authorizing warrantless administrative searches that later was found to violate the Fourth Amendment (*Illinois* v. *Krull,* 480 U.S. 340, 1987).

In another recent case, *Murray* v. *U.S.*, 108 S.Ct. 2529 (1988), the Court drew on the "inevitable discovery" doctrine announced in *Nix* v. *Williams* (1984) to justify another exception to the Fourth Amendment's exclusionary rule. In *Nix,* the court held that evidence obtained in violation of the Sixth Amendment is admissible if inevitably it would have been discovered anyway. In *Murray,* the Court held that the an "independent source" exception to the exclusionary rule permits the introduction of evidence that is obtained in an illegal search if that evidence is *rediscovered* during a valid search. This independent-source doctrine holds that illegally obtained evidence may be used if it has a lawful source that is independent of the illegal source. Writing for the majority, Justice Scalia argued that the rationale for this doctrine is that the police should not be worse off than they would have been in the absence of the initial illegal conduct. Justice Marshall, for a minority that included Justices O'Connor and Stevens, argued that the majority's position further undermines the deterrent effect of the Fourth Amendment. "The police," he wrote, ". . . have little to lose and much to gain by foregoing the bother of obtaining a warrant and undertaking an illegal search."

Unreasonable Searches and Seizures and Warrants

We now turn to the task of giving scope and substantive content to the Fourth Amendment. Although the Amendment contains two separate provisions—the prohibition against unreasonable searches and seizures and the requirement of a warrant based upon probable cause—the two are so interwoven that they must be considered together. The dominant trend of both judicial and scholarly interpretation in modern times has been to read the second clause into the first. "Reasonable" searches and seizures, by this view, are ones carried out under a warrant properly issued on probable cause. As we shall see, there are numerous exceptions to this definition of reasonable that allow police to forego the warrant requirement, but for the most part police are required to meet the probable cause standard. However, a second strand of Fourth Amendment interpretation has argued that the two clauses should not be viewed as wedded.

Both the Warren and Burger Courts consistently maintained that the "probable cause" standard (the heart of the warrant clause) is required for a search or arrest to be reasonable. Yet a line of cases started under Warren, and considerably expanded under Burger and Rehnquist, have defined certain forms of detention and search as different enough from formal arrest or search to be reasonable without either warrants or probable cause. These include less obtrusive criminal actions and administrative actions in which the Court has balanced social needs against a minimum of intrusion upon people's privacy. The Court's willingness to broaden this balancing test to include a wider range of more serious criminal matters has caused some scholars to speculate that the Court will eventually separate the two clauses and evaluate the reasonableness of all police searches and detentions by balancing state and individual interests without reference to the warrant requirement or probable cause standard. (See, for example, R. Wasserman, "The Incredible Shrinking Fourth Amendment," *Georgetown Law Journal,* 1984.)

The Warrant Requirement

A casual reading of the Fourth Amendment could leave the impression that almost all arrests are made on warrant. But nothing would be further from the truth. The overwhelming majority of arrests—for both misdemeanors and felonies—are made without warrants. Long ago the Court recognized the realities of law enforcement and granted exceptions to the general rule for warrants. Many of the cases included in this section spell out these exceptions. Others deal with the borderline question of the so-called stop and frisk practice, referring to when the police stop and accost citizens in the absence of probable cause.

There are five generally acknowledged exceptions to the warrant rule: (1) when the right has been waived and consent has been given; (2) when the search is incidental to a valid arrest; (3) when the search is in a motor vehicle that is easily *movable* from the jurisdiction; (4) immediately following "hot pursuit" of a suspect; and (5) when the object seized is in plain sight. Two other exceptions are more difficult to place in an analytic category as they involve a case-by-case consideration of the "totality of the circumstances." Some police searches or seizures that do not fit easily into the above categories are justified without a warrant on the grounds of "exigent circumstances." Also, both the warrant and probable cause requirements have been waived for certain less obtrusive searches and seizures sometimes called "stop and frisk." Given that all of the established exceptions rely heavily on the context and facts of an individual case, it may be that this last emerging exception will come to serve as a general category that replaces the other exceptions.

While the Court has always allowed citizens to waive their rights under the Constitution, the question remains as to what constitutes an *informed* waiver, meaning informed consent to allow the police to conduct a search without a warrant. The interested student is urged to consult *Schneckloth* v. *Bustamonte,* 412 U.S. 218 (1973), on this topic.

The need for authority to conduct a search without a warrant incident to a valid arrest is obvious in certain situations, namely, as a protective measure to disarm a suspect who might use a weapon to resist being taken into custody, and to obtain evidence of the crime which led to the arrest. Still there are questions. How broad and thorough can the search be? Can arrest for a minor and nonviolent offense serve as an excuse for a full-scale invasion of one's body? car? home? Furthermore, in the absence of limits on searches conducted incident to a valid arrest, by arranging to arrest someone at home or at their place of business — with or without a warrant, but with probable cause — do law enforcement officials have the authority under this exception to conduct a fishing expedition for evidence relating to other possible crimes? This issue is raised squarely in CHIMEL V. CALIFORNIA (1969). There the Court overturned a conviction based upon evidence obtained by police who, while possessing a valid arrest warrant, had waited to effect the arrest at the suspect's home so that they could conduct a lengthy and thorough search of the premises "incident to the arrest." This broad search, the Court reasoned, stretched the exception beyond its limits, especially since the officers could easily have arrested the suspect earlier and obtained a separate warrant to search his house.

The framers of the Fourth Amendment were concerned primarily with official invasion of the privacy of people's homes and places of business, and the Amendment was written with these situations in mind. But the mobility and technology of modern life, and especially the automobile, complicates this notion of privacy. A car is something like a house in that it is closed and contained, but unlike a house in that it is easily movable. This fact has not been lost on the Court, which has generally been more tolerant of warrantless searches of automobiles than of buildings. The case that first acknowledged the special nature of automobiles was *Carroll* v. *United States,* 267 U.S. 132 (1925), in which the Court appeared to exempt automobiles entirely from Fourth Amendment privacy. The Court, in *Carroll,* suggested that both a lesser privacy interest in and the inherent difficulties of dealing with highly mobile property like automobiles justified waiver of the warrant requirement. Forty-five years later, in *Chambers* v. *Maroney,* 399 U.S. 42 (1970), which upheld a warrantless car search where the car was at the police station and the driver was in custody, the Court appeared to reinforce this categorical exception for automobile searches. But in a case decided in the next year, COOLIDGE V. NEW HAMPSHIRE (1971), the Court began to circumscribe the exception where police flagrantly avoided seeking a valid warrant when more than enough time was available.

For a time the Court struggled with setting the precise parameters of a warrantless car search, but today police are fairly secure in searching a car without a warrant at the time of or soon after they develop probable cause. After a number of tortuous twists and turns (see *United States* v. *Robinson,* 414 U.S. 218 (1973), and *United States* v. *Chadwick,* 433 U.S. 1 (1977)), the Court finally drew a "bright line" rule allowing search of the entire car and every object inside the car capable of containing the sought-after evidence or contraband without a warrant, provided the police have probable cause (*United States* v. *Ross,* 456 U.S. 798, 1982). This exception was extended still further when, in a 5 to 4 decision, the Court ruled that a warrantless search of a motor home, based on probable cause to believe that narcotics were being stored and sold there, was not unreasonable under the "car search" exception (*California* v. *Carney*, 471 U.S. 386, 1985).

The hot pursuit exception for a warrantless arrest again rests on an appeal to the obvious: police in hot pursuit of a suspect whom they have probable cause to believe guilty of a crime do not have to halt in their tracks and apply for a warrant if that person disappears into a building. Rather, the police can enter immediately. While the general principle behind the exception is universally accepted, its particular applications are not. The issues become increasingly problematic as the length of time between sighting the suspect and warrantless entry increases, or if it is unlikely that the suspect will evade apprehension or destroy evidence if there is a delay necessitated by obtaining a warrant. The issue might be put as follows: the exception for hot pursuit depends on how hot the pursuit is — as it cools, the need for a warrant increases. But this issue, too, merges into the general problem of the "totality of the circumstances" and as such does not easily lend itself to clear rules. See, for example, *United States* v. *Santana*, 427 U.S. 38 (1976).

A fifth exception to the general warrant requirement is the plain sight rule. Here, too, the wisdom of the general principle is undeniable. The Court has reasoned that there is no obligation for an official to ignore what is plainly evident to him or her, and has gone on to uphold convictions based upon evidence so obtained. The general issues in this exception are discussed by the Court in CHIMEL V. CALIFORNIA (1969), a case in which a warrant had been issued but whose facts under the circumstances also raise plain-sight issues. Similarly, the Court's discussion in the motor vehicle exception case, COOLIDGE V. NEW HAMPSHIRE (1971), also raises these issues.

A much more difficult set of facts is presented in *Cupp* v. *Murphy*, 412 U.S. 291 (1973), in which the Court upheld the conviction of a man whose fingernails had been forcibly scraped when he was being questioned by the police, and which were later found to reveal incriminating evidence.

There the Court reasoned that the police officer's belief that the stains on the suspect's fingernails, which were in plain sight, constituted a reasonable basis for the seizure, so the evidence was admissible under the plain-sight exception.

A number of other exceptions are justified under the emerging "exigent circumstances" doctrine — understood roughly as an emergency situation under the totality of circumstances.

Most of the above exceptions accord with intuitively valid insights concerning the need for safety and effectiveness in police work. Indeed, cases exist that exemplify the purposes of each exception. But there are numerous other cases that defy easy placement and blur the lines of exceptions or push the exceptions to their limits. This expanding number of exceptions invokes the fear in some scholars and dissenters on the Court that the clear intent of the Fourth Amendment to prohibit arbitrary police interference may get lost in a blizzard of small rules or be overwhelmed with a sweeping but amorphous totality of the circumstances rule that employs an ad hoc balancing test whose effect will be fatal to the Fourth Amendment. Can police officers conduct a full-scale body search (including vaginal searches) of suspects under arrest for petty nonviolent offenses? Can a police officer subject *all* the occupants and the automobile to a thorough search when the driver has been stopped for an offense? a petty traffic offense? Can a car be casually searched in connection with a random drivers license or motor vehicle safety check? thoroughly searched? What standards must govern routine auto safety and drivers license checks? Can evidence of a crime that is in plain sight be seized when a car is stopped in connection with a routine check?

A final exception to the warrant requirement is the so-called "stop and frisk" practice of police. Because such cases involve elimination of both the warrant and the probable cause standard, they deserve careful consideration. While the earliest cases endorsing this standard were coupled with the Court's emphasis on the danger inherent in the situation and the limited nature of the exception, recent decisions have dramatically expanded the standard to new areas in which danger is not a central element of concern.

The leading stop and frisk case is TERRY V. OHIO (1968), in which the Court upheld the conviction of an individual who had been approached and frisked by a police officer who thought the man's behavior suspicious, but for whom there was no probable cause for arrest. The frisk revealed a gun, which was subsequently introduced into evidence at his trial. The Court upheld use of this evidence, reasoning that under the circumstances the police officer's behavior was reasonable.

The particular facts in TERRY — an unfolding street encounter with potentially armed suspects — were compelling enough to convince the Court to create an exception to the probable cause requirement. But more recent decisions have given broad sweep to this limited exception, and the Court now reads TERRY as permitting brief seizures of persons and things and unobtrusive searches even in the absence of the likelihood of danger and for reasons other than protecting officers' safety. This trend has invoked bitter commentary among dissenters, who fear that the unambiguous probable cause requirement has been eroded, leaving police actions to be judged on a case-by-case basis or alternatively opening up the possibility of sweeping new powers for the police and a radical new approach to the Fourth Amendment.

This continuing tension is revealed in a number of cases in which the Court has validated searches and seizures despite the lack of probable cause or the possibility of imminent danger. A number of these cases have involved stops by border patrol agents in the southwest as part of their effort to stem the influx of illegal aliens. In these cases the Court has upheld some types of detentions on grounds that they further a valid public policy and are not overly intrusive or burdensome. In several recent criminal cases the rationale for detentions in the absence of probable cause has been expanded. In MICHIGAN V. SUMMERS, 452 U.S. 692 (1981), the Court held that the police did not violate a suspect's Fourth Amendment rights when, without probable cause, they detained him as he

was leaving a house they were about to search under valid warrant. The police held Summers until the search was completed, at which time they arrested him for narcotics found in the house. The Court reasoned that Summers' detention (seizure) was a minimal intrusion when balanced against the government's interest in facilitating the search.

The Court has extended this independent principle of reasonableness as a basis for upholding police actions to searches as well as seizures, and in so doing has approved of practices that go far beyond the brief frisk or pat-down of outer clothing that it had approved in TERRY. In *United States v. Robinson,* 414 U.S. 218 (1973), the Court upheld a full body search after arrest on a custodial but relatively minor traffic offense. In *Michigan v. Long,* 463 U.S. 1032 (1983), the Court upheld a body frisk and an interior search of an automobile after police had stopped to check on a driver who had suddenly swerved off a road and on whose automobile floorboard they saw a hunting knife.

What these cases suggest is the possibility of a radical transformation of the Fourth Amendment. The Court may be changing the Fourth Amendment, originally conceived of and long regarded as a device to protect individuals accused or suspected of crimes, into a positive grant of expanded powers of law enforcement officials, allowing them to justify their behavior as "reasonable" on public policy grounds wholly independent of their limited law enforcement concerns of investigating and solving crimes. If this assessment is too sweeping, at a minimum it is clear that the Court is erasing the distinction it made in TERRY between primary criminal investigation functions of law enforcement officials and additional public safety concerns, and in so doing is merging and expanding both concepts. This process is being facilitated by TERRY and its progeny, which have separated the reasonableness standard from the probable cause requirement. With an independent life of its own, reasonableness permits a limitless array of public concerns to be put forward to offset intrusion into the privacy of individuals. To the extent this continues, it will lead to a replacement of principled rights analysis with a balancing approach in which social interests can easily come to outweigh individual privacy rights.

Recent cases involving drugs indicate that this development is well under way. Relying on TERRY and the discussion of the expectation of privacy in U.S. v. KATZ (1967), a unanimous Court in U.S. v. PLACE, 462 U.S. 696 (1983), held that a seizure of a passenger's luggage for 90 minutes following a "sniff test" by a trained airport security dog did not constitute a "seizure" in violation of the Fourth Amendment. And writing for a majority of six, Chief Justice Rehnquist relied upon TERRY to uphold a sixteen-hour detention of a woman suspected of smuggling cocaine in her alimentary canal (*United States* v. *Montoya de Hernandez,* 473 U.S. 531, 1985). Based upon a "risk profile" developed to spot smugglers, customs agents detained Ms. Montoya de Hernandez and offered her the choice of leaving the country immediately, submitting to an X-ray exam, or waiting in custody until a bowel movement determined whether their suspicions were borne out. Later, in the course of her court-ordered examination, cocaine was discovered, which was introduced into evidence. In *United States* v. *Sokolow,* 57 LW 4401 (1989), by a vote of seven to two, the Court articulated a full-fledged rationale for an expanded "investigative detention" exception as it applies to the war on drugs. In so doing it upheld the search of an airline passenger who fit a "drug courier profile" and had been stopped because he had embarked from Miami for a brief trip, paid for his ticket by cash, brought only carry-on luggage, had his phone listed in another person's name, was dressed in a black jumpsuit, and wore gold jewelry. In still another case in which the Court sought to balance the expectations of privacy against "the operational realities of the workplace," a highly fragmented Court upheld the search of a doctor's office by hospital officials following allegations of improprieties against him (*O'Connor* v. *Ortega,* 480 U.S. 709, 1987).

The fullest expression of this emerging power of an independent "reasonableness" standard to govern searches and seizures is seen in NEW JERSEY V. T.L.O., 469 U.S. 325 (1985), in which the Court upheld a search of a high school student's purse even though officials lacked a warrant or probable cause.

It is unclear how far this line of cases will be carried to broaden the power of state officials to undertake searches and seizures in the absence of probable cause. However, it is clear that an important new framework has been established and that a growing number of justices on the Rehnquist Court embrace it. In light of the continuing "war on drugs," there will certainly be increased pressure to expand still further this new approach.

Modern Surveillance: What Does the Fourth Amendment Protect?

However salutory the warrant requirement and the probable cause standard — with or without the TERRY exception and the exclusionary rule — they come into play only when law enforcement officials intrude into an area covered by the Fourth Amendment. Thus we must consider its scope of coverage. While literally applicable only to things — persons, houses, and papers — modern developments in sophisticated tools for electronic surveillance, changing life-styles in mobile society, and new methods in modern law enforcement have transformed the once simple issue of scope into a real and immensely complicated issue. We have already gained some appreciation of these problems in the Court's cases wrestling with the automobile exception. But the list of problem areas is much longer and the issues even more confusing.

One of the central challenges for the Court has been to fashion a Fourth Amendment response to the development of electronic surveillance, a problem obviously not contemplated by the Framers of the Fourth Amendment. This twentieth-century issue first appeared before the Court in *Olmstead* v. *U.S.,* 277 U.S. 438 (1928), a case that involved a wiretap of a telephone line, an issue which has since come before the Court on numerous occasions.

In *Olmstead,* Chief Justice Taft writing for a bare majority upheld the conviction of individuals under the National Prohibition Act on the basis of evidence obtained from a warrantless wiretap of a telephone line between their homes and offices. Taft dealt with the matter in a formal way — the Fourth Amendment speaks to the privacy of *persons, papers,* and *homes,* not public telephone lines. The dissenters, including both Justice Holmes and Brandeis, were not satisfied with this formalism. They argued that although it was expressed in language of the eighteenth-century, the Fourth Amendment also speaks to the challenges to privacy that new technology might raise. Brandeis' succinct dissent, in which Justice Holmes and Stone joined, stands out as a powerful indictment of legal literalism and contains a compelling argument for the need to subject government officials to the scrutiny of law if liberty is to be preserved. It contains some of Brandeis' most often quoted language.

The majority's view in *Olmstead* made privacy roughly parallel to a property interest. While this interpretation might well be true to the Framers' original understanding, it left a gap in protection for people living in a mobile environment. It left exposed significant portions of social and business life conducted in public or semipublic places as well as private messages which move through electronic communications systems.

While the *Olmstead* Court refused to invoke the Constitution against electronic surveillance, it did recognize this issue as serious. Its solution was to suggest that Congress set policy in this area. Six years later, Congress acted, adopting a provision that barred persons unauthorized by the sender from intercepting and making public communications over telephones. Subsequent Court decisions held that this prohibition extended to government officials as well as to private individuals. The effect of this joint enterprise was to exclude wiretap evidence and derivative "fruits" of such evidence from trial. Still, executive officials continued to argue well into the 1960s that they were free to wiretap without obtaining warrants if the information obtained was not made public (at trial or else-where). This policy was modified by the Omnibus Crime Control and Safe Streets Act in 1968 and President Johnson's subsequent order to halt warrantless electronic surveillance except in instances of national security, where prior approval of the executive was required.

Olmstead and subsequent congressional policy did nothing, however, to affect the states; in the absence of state restrictions, state and local officials remained free to tap telephone lines and to introduce with impunity evidence obtained thereby. This separate policy for state and federal officials also led to a close form of cooperation between these officials, as state and local police were free to pass along wiretap information to federal officials, who could honestly claim that *they* had not obtained it in violation of federal laws. These loopholes were eventually closed as Court rulings and congressional action eroded *Olmstead.*

Finally, in two cases in 1967, the Court effectively overruled *Olmstead* and extended Fourth Amendment coverage, at both the state and national levels, to wiretaps and other forms of electronic surveillance devices. In so doing, it enlarged the capacity of the Fourth Amendment to deal with the technological challenge first posed by *Olmstead.* In *Berger* v. *New York,* 388 U.S. 41, the Court held unconstitutional a New York statute outlining procedures for issuing warrants for wiretap on the grounds that it was not specific enough to meet Fourth Amendment standards.

In the watershed case, KATZ V. UNITED STATES (1967), the Court overturned a conviction based upon evidence obtained as a result of a bug placed on the outside of a *public* telephone booth that was used regularly by an individual suspected of placing illegal bets over the phone. In this case, the Court expressly overruled *Olmstead* and brought telephones — even public pay telephones — under the protection of the Fourth Amendment. In so doing it finally caught up with the prophecy Holmes and Brandeis had issued in dissent forty years earlier.

At first reading the decision in KATZ may appear only to extend the coverage of the Fourth Amendment to a new locale, the public telephone booth.

But the majority did much more. Its emphasis on protecting what a person "seeks to preserve as private" regardless of place, precipitated a fundamentally new methodology for determining coverage by the Fourth Amendment. Instead of rooting the Fourth Amendment in the traditional inquiry of people, places, objects, KATZ involves the Court in defining and protecting *expectations* of privacy.

The operative standard which has emerged from the KATZ opinion, including Justice Harlan's important concurrence, involves a two-step analysis. First, was there an actual "expectation of privacy" by the person concerned? Second, does society accept this expectation as legitimate?

KATZ invites the justices to become robed sociologists inquiring into the realm of mores and norms. The test devised in it allows the constitutional protection of privacy to accommodate changing social values and practices. At the same time it increases the sensitivity of the Fourth Amendment to changing political currents on the Court. At the time it was handed down, KATZ suggested the possibility of a rapid expansion of Fourth Amendment coverage. Yet now the case stands as the high-water mark of Fourth Amendment coverage. With the considerable political shift brought on by the Nixon and Reagan appointees, the Court has declined to extend protection to a number of areas of surveillance, electronic or otherwise, and has cut back considerably on the coverage envisioned in KATZ itself.

With respect to surveillance by government agents who infiltrate the company of those contemplating or undertaking criminal conduct, the Court has continued to find no Fourth Amendment protection under KATZ's expectations test, just as it had not under the traditional analysis of privileged places. In *United States* v. *White,* 401 U.S. 745 (1971), the Court upheld evidence obtained without a warrant by a government secret agent. The Court reasoned that since another person, friend or otherwise, might on his or her own volition reveal what someone had confided, there was no legitimate privacy expectation in information entrusted to others even under deceptive conditions. See also *Hoffa* v. *United States,* 385 U.S. 293 (1966).

On the same reasoning the Court has upheld warrantless installation and use of a pen register (a monitoring device that records numbers dialed on a telephone but does not record conversations). Since the telephone company may voluntarily reveal those numbers, the Court held, a person can have no legitimate privacy expectation under the Fourth Amendment that will prohibit use of such information by the police (*Smith* v. *Maryland,* 442 U.S. 735, 1979).

Likewise in *United States* v. *Knotts,* 460 U.S. 276 (1983), the Court held that the use of a tracking beeper in a container of chloroform that the police suspected would be used to manufacture illicit drugs did not constitute a search under the Fourth Amendment. In this case the police had placed a tracking beeper in an order of chemicals Knotts was to pick up in order to facilitate their tailing him to his suspected — correctly — destination, an illegal drug manufacturing center. The Court argued that the police or anyone else who cared could have followed Knotts along public roads from the chloroform manufacturer to his destination, so that there was no expectation of privacy in such movements. So, the Court concluded, the use of the beeper to facilitate such tracking raised no Fourth Amendment problem. However, the Court did leave open the question of whether the original placement of the beeper constituted a Fourth Amendment violation. In effect, the cases above nullify privacy interests and expectations when persons reveal or take the risk of revealing their actions or words to others.

Using this same interpretation of the KATZ doctrine, the Court has also declined to extend coverage to surveillance techniques that are used to detect only unlawful possessions such as narcotics while remaining blind to whatever else a person might possess. In UNITED STATES V. PLACE, 462 U.S. 696 (1983), the Court suppressed cocaine discovered by police dogs in a suitcase of a suspected drug courier in an airport luggage rack because the police had held it for too long, but it went on to suggest in dicta that such dog sniffs that only intrude upon illegal possessions are not searches for Fourth Amendment purposes. This line of reasoning was embraced more directly in *United States* v. *Jacobsen,* 466 U.S. 109 (1984), in which the Court held that a chemical test that revealed whether or not a white powder was cocaine but revealed nothing else was not a search under the Fourth Amendment.

While these last cases would appear to pose no threat to the privacy of those not carrying contraband, they leave open the possibility suggested by Justice Brennan, in his dissent in *Jacobsen,* that with further advances in technology the police might be able to subject everyone to secret monitoring for contraband, thereby effectively avoiding any Fourth Amendment regulation, even as they engaged in what might be total surveillance. What if, for instance, we had a device that could detect and record remote conversations but would instantaneously erase all conversations unless triggered by a preprogrammed series of words that indicated the speakers were involved with known drug dealers or the like? Or imagine other issues: Can the police use parabolic microphones capable of listening to conversations two thousand feet away to monitor conversations of those they suspect of illegal activities? Can the government secretly install X-ray machines on random street corners to detect possession of illegal knives and guns?

With respect to the domain of privacy that it will protect, the KATZ test is a double-edged sword. While it has brought some forms of advanced technology under the Fourth Amendment, it still leaves wide discretion to the police in the use of this technology. As you read KATZ and the other cases in this section, consider the problem posed by Justice Harlan in his dissent in *United States* v. *White,* 401 U.S. 745 (1971). While KATZ invites the Court to protect those individual privacy expectations which society takes as legitimate, Harlan also pointed out that:

> Our expectations, and the risks we assume, are in large part a reflection of laws that translate into rules the customs and values of the past and present.

> Since it is the task of the law to form and project as well as mirror and reflect, we should not, as judges, merely recite the expectations and risks without examining the desirability of saddling them upon society.

In recent years the courts have been undertaking the type of assessment that Harlan anticipated, and have produced a growing number of decisions restricting privacy, upholding mandatory drug tests for employees, probationers, and parolees, and permitting various forms of sophisticated surveillance by law enforcement officers. Several such issues already have come before the Supreme Court and received its blessing. NEW JERSEY V. T.L.O. (1985) and UNITED STATES V. PLACE (1983) suggest the new directions likely to be followed by the Court under the KATZ test.

Other, more recent cases reinforce this trend. In *California* v. *Ciraolo,* 476 U.S. 207 (1986), the Court upheld introduction of evidence obtained through air-borne surveillance. Acting on a tip that Ciraolo was growing marijuana in his backyard, which was surrounded by a high fence, police hired a commercial pilot to fly over Ciraolo's backyard and obtain visual and photographic evidence of marijuana cultivation. Only then did they pursue a warrant to conduct a full search. Writing for the Court, Chief Justice Burger found the case an easy application of the KATZ requirements that there be a subjective expectation of privacy and that the expectation be one society considers legitimate. Although he conceded that with the building of the high fence Ciraolo had manifest an expectation of privacy with respect to ground intruders, whose vision he had blocked, this expectation was not reasonably extended to air-borne observers.

In a companion case, the Court affirmed a lower court decision dismissing a suit brought by Dow Chemical Company against the Environmental Protection Agency (EPA) seeking to halt warrantless aerial photographing of Dow's facilities. Using a highly specialized camera that could record information not obtainable by the naked eye, EPA agents flew over Dow's plant and took photographs aimed at establishing possible violations of the Clean Air Act. Rejecting Dow's argument that this form of search violated its Fourth Amendment right of privacy, the Court held that this form of "enhancement of human vision by technology . . . does not give rise to constitutional problems." In dissent, Justice Powell took issue with the majority's cavalier dismissal of the technology question, and warned that in an age of satellites the Court might easily render the Fourth Amendment useless unless the Court began to take more seriously the issue of technology.

Ciraolo was reaffirmed and extended in a January 1989 case, *Florida* v. *Riley,* 109 S.Ct. 693. In *Ciraolo* the police flew over a field at 1000 feet; in *Riley* the Court lowered the altitude when it permitted evidence obtained by means of a helicopter hovering at 400 feet. We can expect further cases to decrease this still further. Back on the ground, the police received the Court's approval for warrantless inspection of a suspect's garbage left at curbside (*California* v. *Greenwood,* 486 U.S. 35, 1988).

In the wake of KATZ, Congress, in Title III of the Crime Control and Safe Streets Act of 1968, authorized electronic surveillance under varying conditions. Title III provides for presidential authorization of surveillance to obtain information about foreign intelligence operations without the need for prior judicial approval. It also provides for surveillance warrants in a variety of situations involving only felonies, national security, and organized crime, but requires that they be issued only after a showing of probable cause. The life of a warrant is limited to thirty days, when reapplication to a court must be made for an extension. Title III also requires states to adopt similar procedures if their officials are to use surveillance equipment. Finally, Title III makes it a criminal offense to undertake electronic surveillance outside the procedures established by the Act.

The national security exception provided for in Title III has been the source of considerable controversy. The Nixon Administration took a broad view of its provisions, contending that they acknowledged an inherent power in the executive to authorize without judicial supervision surveillance

of domestic groups whose activities threatened the American political system. This issue came to head in *United States* v. *United States District Court,* 407 U.S. 297 (1972), in which the Supreme Court held that the executive had exceeded its powers when the Attorney General authorized without judicial approval wiretaps of members of antiwar activist groups in Ann Arbor, Michigan. The opinion acknowledges the executive's power to authorize warrantless wiretaps in situations involving foreign agents and national security, but found that these issues were not involved in the case before it. More important, it reaffirmed judicial authority to determine whether or not any particular wiretap involved issues of national security that were exempted by statute from the normal warrant requirement.

While Title III authorizes surreptitious electronic surveillance, it is silent on how the equipment to gather such information is to be located. This was the issue in DALIA V. UNITED STATES, 441 U.S. 238 (1979), where the Court, over vigorous dissent, concluded that "the Fourth Amendment does not require that a Title III electronic surveillance order include a specific authorization to enter covertly the premises described in the order."

Search, Seizure, and the Administrative State

Although we have focused on the practices of law enforcement officials as they pertain *directly* to persons suspected of crimes, the Fourth Amendment is not framed as a limitation on police. Rather, it is a general protection against unwarranted intrusions, a broad guarantee of privacy. The Court has come to recognize this by extending the coverage of the Fourth Amendment to include a variety of other situations and circumstances not directly involved with police work.

In these cases the Court has attempted to balance the "expectation of privacy" implied in the Fourth Amendment with the need of officials to search and seize private things. In balancing those

In these cases the Court has attempted to balance the "expectation of privacy" implied in the factors the Court reflected on the expectations of privacy in such places as homes, automobiles, offices, coatracks, and toilet stalls in public restrooms. It has reviewed the authority of welfare and safety inspectors to enter homes, security officials to search luggage in airports, the border patrol to stop automobiles in search of illegal aliens, and, as we have seen in NEW JERSEY V. T.L.O., school officials to search students' purses. This enterprise has yielded mixed results. While the Court has clearly construed the Fourth Amendment's protections to cover public places where a modicum of privacy can be expected, and extended its coverage to activities other than traditional law enforcement concerns, it has generally adopted a more tolerant view towards encroaching on privacy in quasi-public places and by public officials other than law enforcement officials. As a general rule the Court appears to be saying that the particular circumstances and situations and special needs of public institutions all work together to generate a lower set of expectations of privacy. Two cases illustrate this variable approach to Fourth Amendment privacy. The first is WYMAN V. JAMES (1971), and the other is *Almeda-Sanchez* v. *United States,* 413 U.S. 266 (1973).

Historically, administrative inspections of homes for safety and health purposes were not subject to Fourth Amendment restrictions. The Court began to chart a new direction in *Camara* v. *Municipal Court,* 387 U.S. 523 (1967), when it overturned the conviction of a person who had refused to allow a municipal employee to inspect his premises for possible housing code violations. But four years later, in WYMAN V. JAMES (1971), the court withdrew from this new path when it upheld the suspension of welfare benefits for a woman who refused to allow a social worker to inspect her home. Since then, this withdrawal has accelerated, as increasingly the Court has deferred to the interests of the state in efficiency and collective safety.

The Court has also been tolerant of warrantless searches by the border patrol. While it continues to grant customs officials the right to inspect luggage and persons upon entering the country — as part of the inherent right of the sovereign — it has begun to exercise oversight into other types of searches conducted away from the border. The issue has taken on significant dimensions in the southwest, where the Border Patrol has become quite active in seeking to stem the influx of illegal aliens entering the United States from Mexico.

Using a balancing test, the Court has created a continuum along which less intrusive customs inspections are permitted to operate under less stringent requirements of particularity and suspicion. In *Almeda-Sanchez* v. *United States,* 413 U.S. 266 (1973), the Court held that roving patrols in the general area of the border could stop and search vehicles for illegal aliens without consent only if there was probable cause to believe that the particular car contained such aliens. In *United States* v. *Brignoni-Ponce,* 422 U.S. 873 (1975), the Court held that roving patrol units could stop cars in the border vicinity for brief questioning concerning residence status on the basis of "specific articulable facts." Finally, in *United States* v. *Martinez-Fuerte,* 428 U.S. 543 (1976), the Court allowed that permanent check points set up near the border could briefly stop and question drivers, with no particular suspicion at all.

The student should remember that the balancing test is a flexible method that weighs the individual's privacy interest against the public's legitimate policy goals. If the immigration issue continues to increase in perceived economic and political significance, then near the border or in areas of alien concentration, the balance may move even further against individual privacy.

The student is invited to consider circumstances more closely related to his or her own experience. Does the Fourth Amendment prohibit university officials from conducting warrantless searches of school lockers? dormitory rooms? Would it make a difference whether such searches were at public or private schools? at high schools or universities? Or if the searches yield evidence that leads to dismissal from school versus criminal prosecution? Can college newspaper offices be searched by the police to locate evidence that could be used for the criminal conviction of third parties whose personal belongings are not on the premises? See *Zurcher v. Stanford Daily,* 436 U.S. 547 (1978). Moving further afield, is a patient's right to privacy violated by a warrantless search of his psychiatrist's office, even when it is defended in the interests of national security? This is the issue in *United States v. Erlichman,* 376 F. Supp. 29 (1974).

In the 1980s, inexpensive tests for the presence of drugs and alcohol in the urine were developed, and they came to be widely employed in the criminal justice system as a condition of probation and parole, and in both the private and public sectors as a condition of employment. They were immediately challenged on both statutory and Fourth Amendment and privacy grounds. Traditionally, criminal justice officials have had vast discretionary powers to set conditions for parole and probation, so it was relatively easy for the courts to dispose of the Fourth Amendment objections to urine tests in those situations. The law is less settled with respect to other situations. Thus, drug testing requirements for athletes, students, truck drivers, and government employees produced a host of suits alleging abridgment of constitutional privacy rights.

The future of these challenges is suggested by a pair of decisions handed down by the Supreme Court in March 1989. By a vote of 7 to 2 the Supreme Court upheld a federal regulation that subjected all crew members of trains involved in serious accidents to mandatory blood and urine testing for drug use. Writing for the majority, which rejected a lower court requirement of "particularized suspicion," Justice Kennedy held that the regulation was a reasonable and effective way to serve the government's "surpassing safety interests" in protecting both the traveling public and rail workers from the dangers of equipment being operated under the influence of illegal substances (*Skinner v. Railway Labor Executives,* 109 S. Ct. 1402, 1989).

In a second, and potentially more far-reaching, decision, the Court, by a vote of 5 to 4, upheld a mandatory test that applies to employees who work in the drug division of the U.S. Customs Service. Again for the majority, Justice Kennedy wrote that the government's interest in safeguarding the national borders and protecting public safety outweighed privacy interests (*National Treasury Employees* v. *Von Raab,* 109 S. Ct. 1384, 1989). Dissenting in both cases, Justice Marshall accused the Court of being "swept away" by the nation's concern about drugs, adding that "history teaches that grave threats to liberty often come in times of urgency, when constitutional rights seem too extravagant to endure." "There is no drug exception to the Constitution," he concluded. In a somewhat surprising move, Justice Scalia dissented in the Customs Service case, castigating the requirement as "a kind of immolation of privacy and human dignity in symbolic opposition to drug use." Noting that tests revealed that only five of the 3600 employees tested had used drugs, Scalia observed, "Symbolism, even symbolism for so worthy a cause as the abolition of unlawful drugs, cannot validate an otherwise unreasonable search."

Throughout the 1990s the Court is sure to hear more such cases. These decisions suggest that it is willing to grant considerable deference to the government. It remains to be seen just where it will draw the line in deference to governmental interests. For instance, do state universities have a strong enough interest to require athletes to produce urine specimans on demand? Can they require all students to submit to such tests? What about private colleges? private employers? Would it matter that they received large amounts of public funds?

The Future of Search and Seizure

Be aware that the search and seizure decisions considered in this volume were handed down by a sharply divided Court, and that the most recent cases still involve sharp divisions accompanied by numerous opinions containing caustic comments on other opinions. More significantly, many of the Court's rulings depend upon the facts and context of the search and seizure in question, an indication that the Court is in the midst of a confusing situation.

Here, too, the distinct trend of the Court is to narrow the scope of the Fourth Amendment guarantees, or at least not to extend them broadly in newly litigated areas, as had been done in the past. But this tendency is retarded by adherence to precedent. One result is the creative search for factors that distinguish current from prior cases, in order to narrow the scope of the earlier cases. This is done by emphasizing distinctive features

and facts among the cases, a long-standing judicial technique, but one that if carried to the extreme undercuts the Court's ability to fashion rules that can serve as workable and understandable guides for public officials charged with enforcing the law. Without attempting to predict how rapidly the Court will move in the near future, it is safe to say that the constitutional law in this area is unstable and in flux. The justices are likely to feel compelled to move in ways that clarify and simplify the current bewildering patchwork quilt of rulings.

Cases

Mapp v. Ohio

367 U.S. 643 (1961) Vote: 6–3

In May 1957, Dollree Mapp's home was raided by police officers who thought a fugitive was hiding out there. Miss Mapp refused admittance to the officers when she found they did not have a search warrant. Despite her protest and her effort to physically resist, the police forceably entered her apartment, restrained her, and proceeded to conduct a thorough search of the home.

Although the police did not find their suspect, they discovered obscene materials in the bottom of a closed dresser drawer. This evidence was later used to convict Mapp under the Ohio laws prohibiting possession of obscene materials. Mapp appealed her conviction, relying primarily on an argument that Ohio's obscenity law was violative of the First Amendment. Only an amicus brief filed by the American Civil Liberties Union argued that the Court's 1949 decision in *Wolf* v. *Colorado,* refusing to extend the exclusionary rule to the states, should be overturned, and that the evidence against Mapp should be excluded for having

been seized in violation of the Fourth Amendment. It was this issue that preoccupied the Court.

MR. JUSTICE CLARK delivered the opinion of the Court.

In 1949, 35 years after *Weeks* was announced, this Court, in *Wolf* v. *Colorado,* . . . again for the first time, discussed the effect of the Fourth Amendment upon the States through the operation of the Due Process Clause of the Fourteenth Amendment. It said:

> [W]e have no hesitation in saying that were a State affirmatively to sanction such police incursion into privacy it would run counter to the guaranty of the Fourteenth Amendment. At p. 28.

Nevertheless, after declaring that the "security of one's privacy against arbitrary intrusion by the police" is "implicit in 'the concept of ordered liberty'" and as such enforceable against the States through the Due Process Clause," . . . and announcing that it "stoutly adhere[d]" to the *Weeks* decision, the Court decided that the *Weeks* exclusionary rule would not then be imposed upon the States as "an essential ingredient of the right.". . . The Court's reasons for not considering essential to the right to privacy, as a curb imposed upon the States by the Due Process Clause, that which decades before had been posited as part and parcel of the Fourth Amendment's limitation upon federal encroachment of individual privacy, were bottomed on factual considerations.

While they are not basically relevant to a decision that the exclusionary rule is an essential ingredient of the Fourth Amendment as the right it embodies is vouchsafed against the States by the Due Process Clause, we will consider the current validity of the factual grounds upon which *Wolf* was based.

The Court in *Wolf* first stated that "[t]he contrariety of views of the States" on the adoption of the exclusionary rule of *Weeks* was "particularly impressive"... and, in this connection, that it could not "brush aside the experience of States which deem the incidence of such conduct by the police too slight to call for a deterrent remedy... by overriding the [States'] relevant rules of evidence."... While in 1949, prior to the *Wolf* case, almost two-thirds of the States were opposed to the use of the exclusionary rule, now, despite the *Wolf* case, more than half of those since passing upon it, by their own legislative or judicial decision, have wholly or partly adopted or adhered to the *Weeks* rule.... (1960). Significantly, among those now following the rule is California, which, according to its highest court, was "compelled to reach that conclusion because other remedies have completely failed to secure compliance with the constitutional provisions...." In connection with this California case, we note that the second basis elaborated in *Wolf* in support of its failure to enforce the exclusionary doctrine against the States was that "other means of protection" have been afforded "the right to privacy."... The experience of California that such other remedies have been worthless and futile is buttressed by the experience of other States. The obvious futility of relegating the Fourth Amendment to the protection of other remedies has, moreover, been recognized by this Court since *Wolf*....

Indeed, we are aware of no restraint, similar to that rejected today, conditioning the enforcement of any other basic constitutional right. The right to privacy, no less important than any other right carefully and particularly reserved to the people, would stand in marked contrast to all other rights declared as "basic to a free society."... This Court has not hesitated to enforce as strictly against the States as it does against the Federal Government the rights of free speech and of a free press, the rights to notice and to a fair, public trial, including, as it does, the right not to be convicted by use of a coerced confession, however logically relevant it be, and without regard to its reliability. *Rogers* v. *Richmond*... (1961). And nothing could be more certain than that when a coerced confession is involved, "the relevant rules of evidence" are overridden without regard to

"the incidence of such conduct by the police," slight or frequent. Why should not the same rule apply to what is tantamount to coerced testimony by way of unconstitutional seizure of goods, papers, effects, documents, etc.?

... [O]ur holding that the exclusionary rule is an essential part of both the Fourth and Fourteenth Amendments is not only the logical dictate of prior cases, but it also makes very good sense. There is no war between the Constitution and common sense. Presently, a federal prosecutor may make no use of evidence illegally seized, but a State's attorney across the street may, although he supposedly is operating under the enforceable prohibitions of the same Amendment. Thus the State, by admitting evidence unlawfully seized, serves to encourage disobedience to the Federal Constitution which it is bound to uphold.... [T]he double standard recognized until today hardly put such a thesis into practice. In nonexclusionary States, federal officers, being human, were by it invited to and did, as our cases indicate, step across the street to the State's attorney with their unconstitutionally seized evidence. Prosecution on the basis of that evidence was then had in a state court in utter disregard of the enforceable Fourth Amendment. If the fruits of an unconstitutional search had been inadmissible in both state and federal courts, this inducement to evasion would have been sooner eliminated....

Federal-state cooperation in the solution of crime under constitutional standards will be promoted, if only by recognition of their now mutual obligation to respect the same fundamental criteria in their approaches.... Denying shortcuts to only one of two cooperating law enforcement agencies tends naturally to breed legitimate suspicion of "working arrangements" whose results are equally tainted....

There are those who say, as did Justice (then Judge) Cardozo, that under our constitutional exclusionary doctrine "[t]he criminal is to go free because the constable has blundered."... In some cases this will undoubtedly be the result. But, as was said in *Elkins,* "there is another consideration — the imperative of judicial integrity."... The criminal goes free, if he must, but it is the law that sets him free. Nothing can destroy a government more quickly than its failure to observe its own laws, or worse, its disregard of the charter of its own existence.... Nor can it lightly be assumed that, as a practical matter, adoption of the exclusionary rule fetters law enforcement....

The ignoble shortcut to conviction left open to the State tends to destroy the entire system of constitutional restraints on which the liberties of the people rest. Having once recognized that the right to privacy embodied in the Fourth Amendment is enforceable against the States, and that the right to be secure against rude invasions of privacy by state officers is, therefore, constitutional in origin, we can no longer permit that right to remain an empty promise. Because it is enforceable in the same manner and to like effect as other basic rights secured by the Due Process Clause, we can no longer permit it to be revocable at the whim of any police officer who, in the name of law enforcement itself, chooses to suspend its enjoyment. Our decision, founded on reason and truth, gives to the individual no more than that which the Constitution guarantees him, to the police officer no less than that to which honest law enforcement is entitled, and, to the courts, that judicial integrity so necessary in the true administration of justice.

The judgment of the Supreme Court of Ohio is reversed and the cause remanded for further proceedings not inconsistent with this opinion.

Reversed and remanded.

MR. JUSTICE BLACK, concurring.

I am still not persuaded that the Fourth Amendment, standing alone, would be enough to bar the introduction into evidence against an accused of papers and effects seized from him in violation of its commands. For the Fourth Amendment does not itself contain any provision expressly precluding the use of such evidence, and I am extremely doubtful that such a provision could properly be inferred from nothing more than the basic command against unreasonable searches and seizures. Reflection on the problem, however, in the light of cases coming before the Court since *Wolf*, has led me to conclude that when the Fourth Amendment's ban against unreasonable searches and seizures is considered together with the Fifth Amendment's ban against compelled self-incrimination, a constitutional basis emerges which not only justifies but actually requires the exclusionary rule.

U.S. v. Leon

468 U.S. 897 (1984) Vote: 6–3

Leon is one of three cases handed down in July 1984 dealing with challenges to the exclusionary rule. In *Segura* v. *United States*, 468 U.S. 796, Chief Justice Burger, writing for a majority of five, held that the exclusionary rule does not apply if the connection between illegal police conduct and the discovery and seizure of evidence is "so attenuated as to dissipate the taint," for example, where, the police had an independent source for discovery of the evidence and would not have been dependent upon the warrant. In *Massachusetts* v. *Sheppard*, 468 U.S. 981, the Court, building on *Leon*, which it had just decided, held that the exclusionary rule should not be applied when an officer conducting a search relied in good faith on a warrant issued by a magistrate. Here a judge had noted a fatal but correctable defect in the warrant at the warrant hearing and indicated to the officer that he would make the necessary changes before issuing it. However, the judge neglected to do so and the officer failed to notice it. While the Supreme Court agreed that an error of constitutional dimensions had been committed, it held that the judge and not the police officer was at fault. Suppressing evidence because the judge had made a "clerical" mistake, while the officer had acted in good faith, it reasoned, would not serve the deterrent function the exclusionary rule was designed to achieve.

However, it was *Leon* in which the Court chose to reach out and elaborate on its rationale for this new and significant exception to the exclusionary rule. As you read the Court's opinion, consider what other types of exceptions the Court might be willing to make. Are these cases only the first step towards overruling MAPP V. OHIO?

The relevant facts in *Leon* are as follows. A confidential informant of unproven reliability informed Rombach, a Burbank, California, police officer, that two persons he knew were selling large quantities of cocaine and methaqualone from their residence, and that he had witnessed a drug sale at that residence several months before. This same informant also provided other information about the pair's drug dealing. Acting on this information, police initiated a drug-trafficking investigation and surveillance of the residence. During this surveillance, the police identified several people with histories of drug arrests entering the residence and leaving with small packages. During the investigation, the police connected those frequenting the house with several other people, including Alberto Leon, all of whom had histories of drug arrests. Leon was identified as a major supplier.

Based on this information and additional observations, Rombach, an officer with considerable experience and training as a narcotics investigator, prepared an application for a search warrant of the residences and automobiles of several of those under surveillance. This application was reviewed by several deputy district attorneys before it was submitted to a state superior court judge, who then issued it. The ensuing searches produced large quantities of drugs, and Leon and others were subsequently indicted and charged on federal drug offenses. They filed motions to suppress the evidence seized pursuant to the warrant on grounds that the affidavit attached to the warrant application was insufficient to establish probable cause because some of the evidence on which it was founded was fatally stale and the warrant application failed to establish the informant's credibility. The trial court found these defects were neither cured nor corroborated by the officers' independent investigation and, as a consequence, it ruled that some of the evidence seized as a result of the improperly issued warrant should be excluded.

Although explicitly acknowledging that Officer Rombach had acted in "good faith," the district court rejected the government suggestion that the exclusionary rule should not apply where evidence is seized in reasonable, good faith reliance on a search warrant. As it reached the Supreme Court, the government's petition for certiorari presented only the question whether a good faith exception to the Fourth Amendment exclusionary rule should be recognized.

JUSTICE WHITE delivered the opinion of the Court.
. . . .
. . . Language in opinions of this Court and of individual Justices has sometimes implied that the exclusionary rule is a necessary corollary of the Fourth Amendment, . . . or that the rule is required by the conjunction of the Fourth and Fifth Amendments. . . . These implications need not detain us long. The Fifth Amendment theory has not withstood critical analysis or the test of time, . [. and the Fourth Amendment "has never been interpreted to proscribe the introduction of illegally seized evidence in all proceedings or against all persons." . . .]

. . . .

. . . Whether the exclusionary sanction is appropriately imposed in a particular case, our decisions make clear, is "an issue separate from the question whether the Fourth Amendment rights of the party seeking to invoke the rule were violated by police conduct." . . . Only the former question is currently before us, and it must be resolved by weighing the costs and benefits of preventing the use in the prosecution's case-in-chief of inherently trustworthy tangible evidence obtained in reliance on a search warrant issued by a detached and neutral magistrate that ultimately is found to be defective.

The substantial social costs exacted by the exclusionary rule for the vindication of Fourth Amendment rights have long been a source of concern. "Our cases have consistently recognized that unbending application of the exclusionary sanction to enforce ideals of governmental rectitude would impede unacceptably the truth-finding functions of judge and jury." . . . An objectionable collateral consequence of this interference with the criminal justice system's truth-finding function is that some guilty defendants may go free or receive reduced sentences as a result of favorable plea bargains. Particularly when law enforcement officers have acted in objective good faith or their transgressions have been minor, the magnitude of the benefit conferred on such guilty defendants offends basic concepts of the criminal justice system. . . . Indiscriminate application of the exclusionary rule, therefore, may well "generat[e] disrespect for the law and the administration of justice." . . . Accordingly, "[a]s with any remedial device, the application of the rule has been restricted to those areas where its remedial objectives are thought most efficaciously served." . . .

Close attention to those remedial objectives has characterized our recent decisions concerning the scope of the Fourth Amendment exclusionary rule. The Court has, to be sure, not seriously questioned, "in the absence of a more efficacious sanction, the continued application of the rule to suppress evidence from the [prosecution's] case where a Fourth Amendment violation has been substantial and deliberate. . . ." Nevertheless, the balancing approach that has evolved in various contexts — including criminal trials — "forcefully suggest[s] that the exclusionary rule be more generally modified to permit the introduction of evidence obtained in the reasonable good-faith belief that a search or seizure was in accord with the Fourth Amendment." . . .

. . . .

When considering the use of evidence obtained in violation of the Fourth Amendment in the prosecution's case-in-chief, moreover, we have declined to adopt a per se or but for rule that would render inadmissible any evidence that came to light through a chain of causation that began with an illegal arrest. . . . We also have held that a witness' testimony may be admitted even when his identity was discovered in an unconstitutional search. . . .

. . . .

As yet, we have not recognized any form of good-faith exception to the Fourth Amendment exclusionary rule. But the balancing approach that has evolved during the years of experience with the rule provides strong support for the modification currently urged upon us. As we discuss below, our evaluation of the costs and benefits of suppressing reliable physical evidence seized by officers reasonably relying on a warrant issued by a detached and neutral magistrate leads to the conclusion that such evidence should be admissible in the prosecution's case-in-chief.

Because a search warrant "provides the detached scrutiny of a neutral magistrate, which is a more reliable safeguard against improper searches than the hurried judgment of a law enforcement officer 'engaged in the often competitive enterprise of ferreting out crime,'" . . . we have expressed a strong preference for warrants and declared that "in a doubtful or marginal case a search under a warrant may be sustainable where without one it would fail." . . . Reasonable minds frequently may differ on the question whether a particular affidavit establishes probable cause, and we have thus concluded that the preference for warrants is most appropriately effectuated by according "great deference" to a magistrate's determination. . . .

Deference to the magistrate, however, is not boundless. It is clear, first, that the deference accorded to a magistrate's finding of probable cause does not preclude inquiry into the knowing or reckless falsity of the affidavit on which that determination was based. . . .

Second, the courts must also insist that the magistrate purport to "perform his 'neutral and detached' function and not serve merely as a rubber stamp for the police." . . . A magistrate failing to "manifest that neutrality and detachment demanded of a judicial officer when presented with a warrant application" and who acts instead as "an adjunct law enforcement officer" cannot provide valid authorization for an otherwise unconstitutional search. . . .

Third, reviewing courts will not defer to a warrant based on an affidavit that does not "provide the magistrate with a substantial basis for determining the existence of probable cause." . . . "Sufficient information must be presented to the magistrate to allow that official to determine probable cause; his action cannot be a mere ratification of the bare conclusions of others." . . . Even if the warrant application was supported by more than a "bare bones" affidavit, a reviewing court may properly conclude that, notwithstanding the deference that magistrates deserve, the warrant was invalid because the magistrate's probable-cause determination reflected an improper analysis of the totality of the circumstances . . . or because the form of the warrant was improper in some respect.

Only in the first of these three situations, however, has the Court set forth a rationale for suppressing evidence obtained pursuant to a search warrant; in the other areas, it has simply excluded such evidence without considering whether Fourth Amendment interests will be advanced. To the extent that proponents of exclusion rely on its behavioral effects on judges and magistrates in these areas, their reliance is misplaced. . . .

. . . Judges and magistrates are not adjuncts to the law enforcement team; as neutral judicial officers, they have no stake in the outcome of particular criminal prosecutions. The threat of exclusion thus cannot be expected significantly to deter them. Imposition of the exclusionary sanction is not necessary meaningfully to inform judicial officers of their errors, and we cannot conclude that admitting evidence obtained pursuant to a warrant while at the same time declaring that the warrant was somehow defective will in any way reduce judicial officers' professional incentives to comply with the Fourth Amendment, encourage them to repeat their mistakes, or lead to the granting of all colorable warrant requests.

If exclusion of evidence obtained pursuant to a subsequently invalidated warrant is to have any deterrent effect, therefore, it must alter the behavior of individual law enforcement officers or the policies of their departments. One could argue that applying the exclusionary rule in cases where the police failed to demonstrate probable cause in the warrant application deters future inadequate presentations or "magistrate shopping" and thus promotes the ends of the Fourth Amendment. Suppressing evidence obtained pursuant to a technically defective warrant supported by probable cause also might encourage officers to scrutinize more closely the form of the warrant and to point out suspected judicial errors. We find such arguments speculative and conclude that suppression of evidence obtained pursuant to a warrant should be ordered only on a case-by-case basis and only in those unusual cases in which exclusion will further the purposes of the exclusionary rule.

We have frequently questioned whether the exclusionary rule can have any deterrent effect when the offending officers acted in the objectively reasonable belief that their conduct did not violate the Fourth Amendment. "No empirical researcher, proponent or opponent of the rule, has yet been able to establish with any assurance whether the rule has a deterrent effect...."

....

This is particularly true, we believe, when an officer acting with objective good faith has obtained a search warrant from a judge or magistrate and acted within its scope. In most such cases, there is no police illegality and thus nothing to deter. It is the magistrate's responsibility to determine whether the officer's allegations establish probable cause and, if so, to issue a warrant comporting in form with the requirements of the Fourth Amendment....

We conclude that the marginal or nonexistent benefits produced by suppressing evidence obtained in objectively reasonable reliance on a subsequently invalidated search warrant cannot justify the substantial costs of exclusion. We do not suggest, however, that exclusion is always inappropriate in cases where an officer has obtained a warrant and abided by its terms.... Nevertheless, the officer's reliance on the magistrate's probable-cause determination and on the technical sufficiency of the warrant he issues must be objectively reasonable.... [A]nd it is clear that in some circumstances the officer will have no reasonable grounds for believing that the warrant was properly issued.

Suppression therefore remains an appropriate remedy if the magistrate or judge in issuing a warrant was misled by information in an affidavit that the affiant knew was false or would have known was false except for his reckless disregard of the truth.... The exception we recognize today will also not apply in cases where the issuing magistrate wholly abandoned his judicial role in the manner condemned in *Lo-Ji Sales, Inc.* v. *New York*... (1979); in such circumstances, no reasonably well-trained officer should rely on the warrant. Nor would an officer manifest objective good faith in relying on a warrant based on an affidavit "so lacking in indicia or probable cause as to render official belief in its existence entirely un-

reasonable."... Finally, depending on the circumstances of the particular case, a warrant may be so facially deficient — *i.e.*, in failing to particularize the place to be searched or the things to be seized — that the executing officers cannot reasonably presume it to be valid....

When the principles we have enunciated today are applied to the facts of this case, it is apparent that the judgment of the Court of Appeals cannot stand....

Accordingly, the judgment of the Court of Appeals is *Reversed*.

[JUSTICE BLACKMUN wrote a concurring opinion.]

JUSTICE BRENNAN, with whom JUSTICE MARSHALL joins, dissenting.

Ten years ago in *United States* v. *Calandra*... (1974), I expressed the fear that the Court's decision "may signal that a majority of my colleagues have positioned themselves to reopen the door [to evidence secured by official lawlessness] still further and abandon altogether the exclusionary rule in search-and-seizure cases."... Since then, in case after case, I have witnessed the Court's gradual but determined strangulation of the rule. It now appears that the Court's victory over the Fourth Amendment is complete. That today's decision represents the *piece de resistance* of the Court's past efforts cannot be doubted, for today the Court sanctions the use in the prosecution's case-in-chief of illegally obtained evidence against the individual whose rights have been violated — a result that had previously been thought to be foreclosed.

The Court seeks to justify this result on the ground that the "costs" of adhering to the exclusionary rule in cases like those before us exceed the "benefits." But the language of deterrence and of cost/benefit analysis, if used indiscriminately, can have a narcotic effect. It creates an illusion of technical precision and ineluctability. It suggests that not only constitutional principle but also empirical data supports the majority's result. When the Court's analysis is examined carefully, however, it is clear that we have not been treated to an honest assessment of the merits of the exclusionary rule, but have instead been drawn into a curious world where the "costs" of excluding illegally obtained evidence loom to exaggerated heights and where the "benefits" of such exclusion are made to disappear with a mere wave of the hand.

The majority ignores the fundamental constitutional importance of what is at stake here. While the machinery of law enforcement and indeed the nature of crime itself have changed dramatically since the Fourth Amendment became part of the Nation's fundamental law in 1791, what the Framers understood then remains true today — that the task of combatting crime and convicting the guilty will in every era seem of such critical and pressing concern that we may be lured by the temptations of expediency into forsaking our commitment to protecting individual liberty and privacy. It was for that very reason that the Framers of the Bill of Rights insisted that law enforcement efforts be permanently and unambiguously restricted in order to preserve personal freedoms. In the constitutional scheme they ordained, the sometimes unpopular task of ensuring that the government's enforcement efforts remain within the strict boundaries fixed by the Fourth Amendment was entrusted to the courts. . . . If those independent tribunals lose their resolve, however, as the Court has done today, and give way to the seductive call of expediency, the vital guarantees of the Fourth Amendment are reduced to nothing more than a "form of words." . . .

A proper understanding of the broad purposes sought to be served by the Fourth Amendment demonstrates that the principles embodied in the exclusionary rule rest upon a far firmer constitutional foundation than the shifting sands of the Court's deterence rationale. But even if I were to accept the Court's chosen method of analyzing the question posed by these cases, I would still conclude that the Court's decision cannot be justified.

. . . .

At bottom, the Court's decision turns on the proposition that the exclusionary rule is merely a " 'judicially created remedy designed to safeguard Fourth Amendment rights generally through its deterrent effect, rather than a personal constitutional right.' " . . . This view of the scope of the Amendment relegates the judiciary to the periphery. Because the only constitutionally cognizable injury has already been "fully accomplished" by the police by the time a case comes before the courts, the Constitution is not itself violated if the judge decides to admit the tainted evidence. Indeed, the most the judge *can* do is wring his hands and hope that perhaps by excluding such evidence he can deter future transgressions by the police.

Such a reading appears plausible, because, as critics of the exclusionary rule never tire of repeating, the Fourth Amendment makes no express provision for the exclusion of evidence secured in violation of its commands. A short answer to this claim, of course, is that many of the Constitution's most vital imperatives are stated in general terms and the task

of giving meaning to these precepts is therefore left to subsequent judicial decision-making in the context of concrete cases. . . .

A more direct answer may be supplied by recognizing that the Amendment, like other provisions of the Bill of Rights, restrains the power of the government as a whole; it does not specify only a particular agency and exempt all others. The judiciary is responsible, no less than the executive, for ensuring that constitutional rights are respected.

When that fact is kept in mind, the role of the courts and their possible involvement in the concerns of the Fourth Amendment comes into sharper focus. Because seizures are executed principally to secure evidence, and because such evidence generally has utility in our legal system only in the context of a trial supervised by a judge, it is apparent that the admission of illegally obtained evidence implicates the same constitutional concerns as the initial seizure of that evidence. Indeed, by admitting unlawfully seized evidence, the judiciary becomes a part of what is in fact a single governmental action prohibited by the terms of the Amendment. Once that connection between the evidence-gathering role of the police and the evidence-admitting function of the courts is acknowledged, the plausibility of the Court's interpretation becomes more suspect. . . .

The Court evades this principle by drawing an artificial line between the constitutional rights and responsibilities that are engaged by actions of the police and those that are engaged when a defendant appears before the courts. According to the Court, the substantive protections of the Fourth Amendment are wholly exhausted at the moment when police unlawfully invade an individual's privacy and thus no substantive force remains to those protections at the time of trial when the government seeks to use evidence obtained by the police.

I submit that such a crabbed reading of the Fourth Amendment casts aside the teaching of those Justices who first formulated the exclusionary rule, and rests ultimately on an impoverished understanding of judicial responsibility in our constitutional scheme. For my part, "[t]he right of the people to be secure in their persons, houses, papers and effects, against unreasonable searches and seizures" comprises a personal right to exclude all evidence secured by means of unreasonable searches and seizures. The right to be free from the initial invasion of privacy and the right of exclusion are coordinate components of the central embracing right to be free from unreasonable searches and seizures.

Such a conception of the rights secured by the Fourth Amendment was unquestionably the original basis of what has come to be called the exclusionary rule when it was formulated in *Weeks* v. *United States* . . . (1914). . . .

. . . .

. . . A new phase in the history of the rule, however, opened with the Court's decision in *Wolf* v. *Colorado* (1949). Although that decision held that the security of one's person and privacy protected by the Fourth Amendment was "implicit in the 'concept of ordered liberty' and as such enforceable against the States through the Due Process Clause" of the Fourteenth Amendment . . . the Court went on, in what can only be regarded as a *tour de force* of constitutional obfuscation, to say that the "ways of enforcing such a basic right raise questions of a different order." Notwithstanding the force of the *Weeks* doctrine that the Fourth Amendment required exclusion, a state court was free to admit illegally seized evidence, according to the Court in *Wolf,* so long as the state had devised some other "effective" means of vindicating a defendant's Fourth Amendment rights.

Twelve years later, in *Mapp* v. *Ohio* (1961), however, the Court restored the original understanding of the *Weeks* case by overruling the holding of *Wolf* and repudiating its rationale. . . .

Despite this clear pronouncement, however, the Court since *Calandra* has gradually pressed the deterrence rationale for the rule back to center stage. . . . The various arguments advanced by the Court in this campaign have only strengthened my conviction that the deterrence theory is both misguided and unworkable. . . .

. . . .

By remaining within its redoubt of empiricism and by basing the rule solely on the deterrence rationale, the Court has robbed the rule of legitimacy. A doctrine that is explained as if it were an empirical proposition but for which there is only limited empirical support is both inherently unstable and an easy mark for critics. The extent of this Court's fidelity to Fourth Amendment requirements, however, should not turn on such statistical uncertainties. . . . Rather than seeking to give effect to the liberties secured by the Fourth Amendment through guesswork about deterrence, the Court should restore to its proper place the principle framed 70 years ago in *Weeks* that an individual whose privacy has been invaded in violation of the Fourth Amendment has a right grounded in that Amendment to prevent the government from subsequently making use of any evidence so obtained.

. . . .

Even if I were to accept the Court's general approach to the exclusionary rule, I could not agree with today's result. There is no question that in the hands of the present Court the deterrence rationale has proved to be a powerful tool for confining the scope of the rule. . . .

. . . .

Significantly, the Court points to none, and, indeed as the Court acknowledges . . . recent studies have demonstrated that the "costs" of the exclusionary rule — calculated in terms of dropped prosecutions and lost convictions — are quite low. Contrary to the claims of the rule's critics that exclusion leads to "the release of countless guilty criminals," . . . these studies have demonstrated that federal and state prosecutors very rarely drop cases because of potential search and seizure problems. . . . Of course, these data describe only the costs attributable to the exclusion of evidence in all cases; the costs due to the exclusion of evidence in the narrower category of cases where police have made objectively reasonable mistakes must necessarily be even smaller. The Court, however, ignores this distinction and mistakenly weighs the aggregated costs of exclusion in *all* cases, irrespective of the circumstances that led to exclusion, . . . against the potential benefits associated with only those cases in which evidence is excluded because police reasonably but mistakenly believe that their conduct does not violate the Fourth Amendment. . . . When such faulty scales are used, it is little wonder that the balance tips in favor of restricting the application of the rule.

What then supports the Court's insistence that this evidence be admitted? Apparently, the Court's only answer is that even though the costs of exclusion are not very substantial, the potential deterrent effect in these circumstances is so marginal that exclusion cannot be justified. The key to the Court's conclusion in this respect is its belief that the prospective deterrent effect of the exclusionary rule operates only in those situations in which police officers, when deciding whether to go forward with some particular search, have reason to know that their planned conduct will violate the requirements of the Fourth Amendment. . . . If these officers in fact understand (or reasonably should understand because the law is well-settled) that their proposed conduct will offend the Fourth Amendment and that, consequently, any evidence they seize will be suppressed in court, they will refrain from conducting the planned search. In those circumstances, the incentive system created by the exclusionary rule will have the hoped-for deterrent effect. But in situations where police officers reasonably (but mistakenly) believe that their planned conduct satisfies Fourth Amendment requirements — presumably either (a) because they are acting on the basis of an apparently valid warrant, or (b) because their conduct is only later determined to be invalid as a result of a subsequent change in the law or the resolution of an unsettled question of law—then such officers will have no reason to refrain from conducting the search and the exclusionary rule will have no effect.

. . . .

The flaw in the Court's argument, however, is that its logic captures only one comparatively minor element of the generally acknowledged deterrent purposes of the exclusionary rule. To be sure, the rule operates to some extent to deter future misconduct by individual officers who have had evidence suppressed in their own cases. But what the Court overlooks is that the deterrence rationale for the rule is not designed to be, nor should it be thought of as, a form of "punishment" of individual police officers for their failures to obey the restraints imposed by the Fourth Amendment. . . . Instead, the chief deterrent function of the rule is its tendency to promote institutional compliance with Fourth Amendment requirements on the part of law enforcement agencies generally. Thus, as the Court has previously recognized, "over the long term, [the] demonstration [provided by the exclusionary rule] that our society attaches serious consequences to violation of constitutional rights is thought to encourage those who formulate law enforcement policies, and the officers who implement them, to incorporate Fourth Amendment ideals into their value system." It is only through such an institution-wide mechanism that information concerning Fourth Amendment standards can be effectively communicated to rank and file officers.

. . . .

After today's decision, however, that institutional incentive will be lost. Indeed, the Court's "reasonable mistake" exception to the exclusionary rule will tend to put a premium on police ignorance of the law. . . .

Although the Court brushes these concerns aside, a host of grave consequences can be expected to result from its decision to carve this new exception out of the exclusionary rule. A chief consequence of today's decision will be to convey a clear and unambiguous message to magistrates that their decisions to issue warrants are now insulated from subsequent judicial review. . . .

Moreover, the good faith exception will encourage police to provide only the bare minimum of information in future warrant applications. The police will now know that if they can secure a warrant, so long as the circumstances of its issuance are not "entirely unreasonable," all police conduct pursuant to that warrant will be protected from further judicial review. . . .

. . . .

When the public, as it quite properly has done in the past as well as in the present, demands that those in government increase their efforts to combat crime, it is all too easy for those government officials to seek expedient solutions. In contrast to such costly and difficult measures as building more prisons, improving law enforcement methods, or hiring more prosecutors and judges to relieve the overburdened court systems in the country's metropolitan areas, the relaxation of Fourth Amendment standards seems a tempting, costless means of meeting the public's demand for better law enforcement. In the long run, however, we as a society pay a heavy price for such expediency, because as Justice Jackson observed, the rights guaranteed in the Fourth Amendment "are not mere second-class rights but belong in the catalog of indispensable freedoms." . . . Once lost, such rights are difficult to recover. There is hope, however, that in time this or some later Court will restore these precious freedoms to their rightful place as a primary protection for our citizens against overreaching officialdom.

I dissent.

[JUSTICE STEVENS wrote a dissenting opinion.]

Chimel v. California

395 U.S. 752 (1969)
Vote: 7–2

Police armed with an arrest warrant but not a search warrant went to the Chimel home. They entered the home with the consent of Mrs. Chimel. When Mr. Chimel arrived, the police presented him with the warrant and informed him that he was under arrest in connection with a burglary of a coin shop. At that time one of the officers also asked for permission to "look around" the house. Chimel objected, but was informed that a search was permissible anyway "on the basis of a lawful arrest." Accompanied by Mrs. Chimel, the officers then proceeded to undertake a forty-five to sixty minute search of the entire house, in the process discovering coins and other items that were later introduced into evidence at his trial. Chimel was convicted and sought to have his conviction overturned on grounds that this evidence was seized in violation of the Fourth Amendment. The appellate courts upheld Chimel's conviction, whereupon he petitioned the Supreme Court to issue a writ of certiorari.

MR. Justice Stewart delivered the opinion of the Court.

Only last Term in *Terry* v. *Ohio* . . . (1968), we emphasized that "the police must, whenever practicable, obtain advance judicial approval of searches and seizures through the warrant procedure," . . . and that "[t]he scope of [a] search must be 'strictly tied to and justified by' the circumstances which rendered its initiation permissible.'" . . . The search undertaken by the officer in that "stop and frisk" case was sustained under that test, because it was no more than a "protective . . . search for weapons." But in a companion case, *Sibron* v. *New York* . . . (1968), we applied the same standard to another set of facts and reached a contrary result, holding that a policeman's action in thrusting his hand into a suspect's pocket had been neither motivated by nor limited to the objective of protection. Rather, the search had been made in order to find narcotics, which were in fact found.

A similar analysis underlies the "search incident to arrest" principle, and marks its proper extent. When an arrest is made, it is reasonable for the arresting officer to search the person arrested in order to remove any weapons that the latter might seek to use in order to resist arrest or effect his escape. Otherwise, the officer's safety might well be endangered, and the arrest itself frustrated. In addition, it is entirely reasonable for the arresting officer to search for and seize any evidence on the arrestee's person in order to prevent its concealment or destruction. And the area into which an arrestee might reach in order to grab a weapon or evidentiary items must, of course, be governed by a like rule. A gun on a table or in a drawer in front of one who is arrested can be as dangerous to the arresting officer as one concealed in the clothing of the person arrested. There is ample justification, therefore, for a search of the arrestee's person and the area "within his immediate control" — construing that phrase to mean the area from within which he might gain possession of a weapon or destructible evidence.

There is no comparable justification, however, for routinely searching any room other than that in which an arrest occurs — or, for that matter, for searching through all the desk drawers or other closed or concealed areas in that room itself. Such searches, in the absence of well-recognized exceptions, may be made only under the authority of a search warrant. The "adherence to judicial processes" mandated by the Fourth Amendment requires no less.

. . . .

It is argued in the present case that it is "reasonable" to search a man's house when he is arrested in it. But that argument is founded on little more than a subjective view regarding the acceptability of certain sorts of police conduct, and not on considerations relevant to Fourth Amendment interests. Under such an unconfined analysis, Fourth Amendment protection in this area would approach the evaporation point. It is not easy to explain why, for instance, it is less subjectively "reasonable" to search a man's house when he is arrested on his front lawn — or just down the street — than it is when he happens to be in the house at the time of arrest. . . .

. . . No consideration relevant to the Fourth Amendment suggests any point of rational limitation, once the search is allowed to go beyond the area from which the person arrested might obtain weapons or evidentiary items. The only reasoned distinction is one between a search of the person arrested and the area within his reach on the one hand, and more extensive searches on the other.

. . . .

Application of sound Fourth Amendment principles to the facts of this case produces a clear result. The search here went far beyond the petitioner's person and the area from within which he might have obtained either a weapon or something that could have been used as evidence against him. There was no constitutional justification, in the absence of a search warrant, for extending the search beyond that area. The scope of the search was, therefore, "unreasonable" under the Fourth and Fourteenth Amendments, and the petitioner's conviction cannot stand.

Reversed.

[MR. JUSTICE HARLAN wrote a concurring opinion.]

MR. JUSTICE WHITE, with whom MR. JUSTICE BLACK joins, dissenting.

In light of the uniformity of judgment of the Congress, past judicial decisions, and common practice rejecting the proposition that arrest warrants are essential wherever it is practicable to get them, the conclusion is inevitable that such arrests and accompanying searches are reasonable, at least until experience teaches the contrary. It must very often be the case that by the time probable cause to arrest a man is accumulated, the man is aware of police interest in him or for other good reasons is on the verge of flight. Moreover, it will likely be very difficult to determine the probability of his flight. Given this situation, it may be best in all cases simply to allow the arrest if there is probable cause, especially since that issue can be determined very shortly after the arrest.

Nor are the stated assumptions at all fanciful. It was precisely these facts which moved the Congress to grant to the FBI the power to arrest without a warrant without any showing of probability of flight. Both the Senate and House committees quoted the letter of the Acting Deputy Attorney General, Peter Campbell Brown, who in asking for the new legislation asserted: "Although it is recognized that in any felony case the person to be arrested may attempt to flee, it is also recognized that in any such case in which the defendant is arrested without a warrant in an emergency situation, such defendant may be able to present a rather convincing argument that he did not intend to flee.". . . Some weight should be accorded this factual judgment by law enforcement officials, adopted by the Congress.

If circumstances so often require the warrantless arrest that the law generally permits it, the typical situation will find the arresting officers lawfully on the premises without arrest or search warrant. Like the majority, I would permit the police to search the person of a suspect and the area under his immediate control either to assure the safety of the officers or to prevent the destruction of evidence. And like the majority, I see nothing in the arrest alone furnishing probable cause for a search of any broader scope. However, where as here the existence of probable cause is independently established and would justify a warrant for a broader search for evidence, I would follow past cases and permit such a search to be carried out without a warrant, since the fact of arrest supplies an exigent circumstance justifying police action before the evidence can be removed, and also alerts the suspect to the fact of the search so that he can immediately seek judicial determination of probable cause in an adversary proceeding, and appropriate redress.

This view, consistent with past cases, would not authorize the general search against which the Fourth Amendment was meant to guard, nor would it broaden or render uncertain in any way whatsoever the scope of searches permitted under the Fourth Amendment. The issue in this case is not the breadth of the search, since there was clearly probable cause for the search which was carried out. No broader search than if the officers had a warrant would be permitted. The only issue is whether a search warrant was required as a precondition to that search. It is agreed that such a warrant would be required absent exigent circumstances. I would hold that the fact of arrest supplies such an exigent circumstance, since the police had lawfully gained entry to the premises to effect the arrest and since delaying the search to secure a warrant would have involved the risk of not recovering the fruits of the crime.

The majority today proscribes searches for which there is probable cause and which may prove fruitless unless carried out immediately. This rule will have no added effect whatsoever in protecting the rights of the criminal accused at trial against introduction of evidence seized without probable cause. Such evidence could not be introduced under the old rule. Nor does the majority today give any added protection to the right of privacy of those whose houses there is probable cause to search. A warrant would still be sworn out for those houses, and the privacy of their owners invaded. The only possible justification for the majority's rule is that in some instances arresting officers may search when they have no probable cause to do so and that such unlawful searches might be prevented if the officers first sought a warrant from a magistrate. Against the possible protection of privacy in that class of cases, in which the privacy of the house has already been invaded by entry to make the arrest — an entry for which the majority does not assert that any warrant is necessary — must be weighed the risk of destruction of evidence for which there is probable cause to search, as a result of delays in obtaining a search warrant. Without more basis for radical change than the Court's opinion reveals, I would not upset the balance of these interests which has been struck by the former decisions of this Court.

In considering searches incident to arrest, it must be remembered that there will be immediate opportunity to challenge the probable cause for the search in an adversary proceeding. The suspect has been apprised of the search by his very presence at the scene, and having been arrested, he will soon be brought into contact with people who can explain his rights. . . .

An arrested man, by definition conscious of the police interest in him, and provided almost immediately with a lawyer and a judge, is in an excellent position to dispute the reasonableness of his arrest and contemporaneous search in a full adversary proceeding. I would uphold the constitutionality of this search contemporaneous with an arrest since there were probable cause both for the search and for the arrest, exigent circumstances involving the removal or destruction of evidence, and satisfactory opportunity to dispute the issues of probable cause shortly thereafter. In this case, the search was reasonable.

Coolidge v. New Hampshire

403 U.S. 433 (1971)
Vote: 5–4

On January 13, 1964, Pamela Mason, a fourteen-year-old girl from Manchester, New Hampshire, left home during a heavy snowstorm, apparently in response to a man's telephone call for a baby-sitter. Eight days later, her body was found by the side of a highway several miles away. She had been murdered. In response to the event, the police began a massive investigation. On January 28, acting on a tip from a neighbor, the police went to Coolidge's home to question him. As a result of the questioning, they grew increasingly suspicious of Coolidge. After further investigation and questioning of his wife, the police returned with a warrant authorizing a search of his house and automobile.

The warrant was issued by the Attorney General of New Hampshire, who was acting under a law (later repealed) that allowed him, as a justice of the peace, to issue such warrants. At this same time, the Attorney General was also directing the investigation into the murder. The searches and seizure of the automobile under this warrant produced incriminating evidence that was used to convict Coolidge. Upon appeal, the New Hampshire Supreme Court upheld the conviction, whereupon Coolidge petitioned the Supreme Court for a writ of certiorari, which it granted.

MR. JUSTICE STEWART delivered the opinion of the Court.

The petitioner's first claim is that the warrant authorizing the seizure and subsequent search of his 1951 Pontiac automobile was invalid because not issued by a "neutral and detached magistrate."...

The classic statement of the policy underlying the warrant requirement of the Fourth Amendment is that of Mr. Justice Jackson, writing for the Court in *Johnson* v. *United States* ... [1948].

The point of the Fourth Amendment, which often is not grasped by zealous officers, is not that it denies law enforcement the support of the usual inferences which reasonable men draw from evidence. Its protection consists in requiring that those inferences be drawn by a neutral and detached magistrate instead of being judged by the officer engaged in the often competitive enterprise of ferreting out crime. Any assumption that evidence sufficient to support a magistrate's disinterested determination to issue a search warrant will justify the officers in making a search without a warrant would reduce the Amendment to a nullity and leave the people's homes secure only in the discretion of police officers.... When the right of privacy must reasonably yield to the right of search is, as a rule, to be decided by a judicial officer, not by a policeman or government enforcement agent.

In this case, the determination of probable cause was made by the chief "government enforcement agent" of the State—the Attorney General—who was actively in charge of the investigation and later was to be chief prosecutor at the trial. To be sure, the determination was formalized here by a writing bearing the title "Search Warrant," whereas in *Johnson* there was no piece of paper involved, but the State has not attempted to uphold the warrant on any such artificial basis. Rather, the State argues that the Attorney General, who was unquestionably authorized as a justice of the peace to issue warrants under then-existing state law, did in fact act as a "neutral and detached magistrate." Further, the State claims that *any* magistrate, confronted with the showing of probable cause made by the Manchester chief of police, would have issued the warrant in question. To the first proposition it is enough to answer that there could hardly be a more appropriate setting than this for a *per se* rule of disqualification rather than a case-by-case evaluation of all the circumstances. Without disrespect to the state law enforcement agent here involved, the whole point of the basic rule so well expressed by Mr. Justice Jackson is that prosecutors and policemen simply cannot be asked to maintain the requisite neutrality with regard to their own investigations—the "competitive enterprise" that must rightly engage their single-minded attention.... As for the proposition that the existence of probable cause renders noncompliance with the warrant procedure an irrelevance, it is enough to cite *Agnello* v. *United States* ... decided in 1925:

Belief, however well founded, that an article sought is concealed in a dwelling house furnishes no justification for a search of that place without a warrant. And such searches are held unlawful notwithstanding facts unquestionably showing probable cause.

. . . .

We find no escape from the conclusion that the seizure and search of the Pontiac automobile cannot constitutionally rest upon the warrant issued by the state official who was the chief investigator and prosecutor in this case. Since he was not the neutral and detached magistrate required by the Constitution, the search stands on no firmer ground than if there had been no warrant at all. If the seizure and search are to be justified, they must, therefore, be justified on some other theory.

The State proposes three distinct theories to bring the facts of this case within one or another of the exceptions to the warrant requirement. . . .

The State's first theory is that the seizure on February 19 and subsequent search of Coolidge's Pontiac were "incident" to a valid arrest. We assume that the arrest of Coolidge inside his house was valid, so that the first condition of a warrantless "search incident" is met. . . . And since the events in issue took place in 1964, we assess the State's argument in terms of the law as it existed before *Chimel v. California*... which substantially restricted the "search incident" exception to the warrant requirement, but did so only prospectively. . . . But even under pre-*Chimel* law, the State's position is untenable.

. . . [T]his Court has repeatedly held that, "[a] search may be incident to an arrest "only if it is substantially contemporaneous with the arrest and is confined to the *immediate* vicinity of the arrest. . . ." . . . There is nothing in search-incident doctrine (as opposed to the special rules for automobiles and evidence in "plain view,". . .) that suggests a different result where the arrest is made inside the house and the search outside and at some distance away.

. . . .

The second theory put forward by the State to justify a warrantless seizure and seach of the Pontiac car is that. . . the police officer may make a warrantless search of an automobile whenever they have probable cause to do so, and. . . whenever the police may make a legal contemporaneous search. . . they may also seize the car, take it to the police station, and search it there. . . .

. . . .

The underlying rationale of [such a theory] is that there is

a necessary difference between a search of a store, dwelling house or other structure in respect of which a proper official warrant readily may be obtained, and a search of a ship, motor boat, wagon or automobile, for contraband goods, where *it is not practicable to secure a warrant* because the vehicle can be quickly moved out of the locality or jurisdiction in which the warrant must be sought."...

In this case, the police had known for some time of the probable role of the Pontiac car in the crime. Coolidge was aware that he was a suspect in the Mason murder, but he had been extremely cooperative throughout the investigation, and there was no indication that he meant to flee. He had already had ample opportunity to destroy any evidence he thought incriminating. There is no suggestion that, on the night in question, the car was being used for any illegal purpose, and it was regularly parked in the driveway of his house. The opportunity for search was thus hardly "fleeting." The objects that the police are assumed to have had probable cause to search for in the car were neither stolen nor contraband nor dangerous.

. . . .

The word "automobile" is not a talisman in whose presence the Fourth Amendment fades away and disappears. . . . In short, by no possible stretch of the legal imagination can this be made into a case where "it is not practicable to secure a warrant," and the "automobile exception," despite its label, is simply irrelevant.

The State's third theory in support of the warrantless seizure and search of the Pontiac car is that the car itself was an "instrumentality of the crime," and as such might be seized by the police on Coolidge's property because it was in plain view. . . .

The rationale for the "plain view" exception is evident if we keep in mind the two distinct constitutional protections served by the warrant requirement. First, the magistrate's scrutiny is intended to eliminate altogether searches not based on probable cause. The premise here is that *any* intrusion in the way of search or seizure is an evil, so that no intrusion at all is justified without a careful prior determination of necessity. . . . The second, distinct objective is that those searches deemed necessary should be as limited as possible. Here, the specific evil is the "general warrant" abhorred by the colonists, and the problem is not that of intrusion *per se,* but of general, exploratory rummaging in a person's belongings. . . . The warrant accomplishes this second objective by requiring a "particular description" of the things to be seized.

The "plain view" doctrine is not in conflict with the first objective because plain view does not occur until a search is in progress. In each case, this initial intrusion is justified by a warrant or by an exception such as "hot pursuit" or search incident to a lawful arrest, or by an extraneous valid reason for the officer's presence. And, given the initial intrusion, the seizure of an object in plain view is consistent with the second objective, since it does not convert the search into a general or exploratory one. As against the minor peril to Fourth Amendment protections, there is a major gain in effective law enforcement. Where, once an otherwise lawful search is in progress, the police inadvertently come upon a piece of evidence, it would often be a needless inconvenience, and sometimes dangerous — to the evidence or to the police themselves — to require them to ignore it until they have obtained a warrant particularly describing it.

The limits on the doctrine are implicit in the statement of its rationale. The first of these is that plain view *alone* is never enough to justify the warrantless seizure of evidence. This is simply a corollary of the familiar principle discussed above, that no amount of probable cause can justify a warrantless search or seizure absent "exigent circumstances." Incontrovertible testimony of the senses that an incriminating object is on premises belonging to a criminal suspect may establish the fullest possible measure of probable cause. But even where the object is contraband, this Court has repeatedly stated and enforced the basic rule that the police may not enter and make a warrantless seizure. . . .

The second limitation is that the discovery of evidence in plain view must be inadvertent. The rationale of the exception to the warrant requirement, as just stated, is that a plain-view seizure will not turn an initially valid (and therefore limited) search into a "general" one, while the inconvenience of procuring a warrant to cover an inadvertent discovery is great. But where the discovery is anticipated, where the police know in advance the location of the evidence and intend to seize it, the situation is altogether different. The requirement of a warrant to seize imposes no inconvenience whatever, or at least none which is constitutionally cognizable in a legal system that regards warrantless searches as *"per se* unreasonable" in the absence of "exigent circumstances."

If the initial intrusion is bottomed upon a warrant that fails to mention a particular object, though the police know its location and intend to seize it, then there is a violation of the express constitutional requirement of "Warrants . . . particularly describing . . . [the] things to be seized." The initial intrusion may, of course, be legitimated not by a warrant but by one of the exceptions to the warrant requirement, such as hot pursuit or search incident to lawful arrest. But to extend the scope of such an intrusion to the seizure of objects — not contraband nor stolen nor dangerous in themselves — which the police know in advance they will find in plain view and intend to seize, would fly in the face of the basic rule that no amount of probable cause can justify a warrantless seizure.

In the light of what has been said, it is apparent that the "plain view" exception cannot justify the police seizure of the Pontiac car in this case. The police had ample opportunity to obtain a valid warrant; they knew the automobile's exact description and location well in advance; they intended to seize it when they came upon Coolidge's property. And this is not a case involving contraband or stolen goods or objects dangerous in themselves.

The seizure was therefore unconstitutional, and so was the subsequent search at the station house. Since evidence obtained in the course of the search was admitted at Coolidge's trial, the judgment must be reversed and the case remanded to the New Hampshire Supreme Court. . . .

MR. JUSTICE HARLAN, concurring.

From the several opinions that have been filed in this case it is apparent that the law of search and seizure is due for an overhauling. State and federal law enforcement officers and prosecutorial authorities must find quite intolerable the present state of uncertainty, which extends even to such an everyday question as the circumstances under which police may enter a man's property to arrest him and seize a vehicle believed to have been used during the commission of a crime.

I would begin this process of re-evaluation by overruling *Mapp v. Ohio . . .* (1961), and *Ker v. California . . .* (1963). The former of these cases made the federal "exclusionary rule" applicable to the States. The latter forced the State to follow all the ins and outs of this Court's Fourth Amendment decisions, handed down in federal cases.

In combination *Mapp* and *Ker* have been primarily responsible for bringing about serious distortions and incongruities in this field of constitutional law. Basically these have had two aspects, as I believe an examination of our more recent opinions and certiorari docket will show. First, the States have been put in a federal mold with respect to this aspect of criminal law enforcement, thus depriving the country of the opportunity to observe the effects of different procedures in similar settings. . . . Second, in order to leave some room for the States to cope with their own diverse problems, there has been generated a tendency to relax federal requirements under the Fourth Amendment, which now govern state procedures as well. . . . Until we face up to the basic constitutional mistakes of *Mapp* and *Ker,* no solid progress in setting things straight in search and seizure law will, in my opinion, occur.

But for *Mapp* and *Ker,* I would have little difficulty in voting to sustain this conviction, for I do not think that anything the State did in this case could be said to offend those values which are "at the core of the Fourth Amendment." . . .

Because of *Mapp* and *Ker,* however, this case must be judged in terms of federal standards, and on that basis I concur . . . in the judgment of the Court.

MR. CHIEF JUSTICE BURGER, dissenting in part and concurring in part.

This case illustrates graphically the monstrous price we pay for the exclusionary rule in which we seem to have imprisoned ourselves. . . .

On the merits of the case I find not the slightest basis in the record to reverse this conviction. Here again the Court reaches out, strains, and distorts rules that were showing some signs of stabilizing, and directs a new trial which will be held more than seven years after the criminal acts charged.

MR. JUSTICE BLACK, concurring and dissenting.

The Fourth Amendment prohibits unreasonable searches and seizures. The Amendment says nothing about consequences. It certainly nowhere provides for the exclusion of evidence as the remedy for violation. . . .

. . . .

The majority holds that evidence it views as improperly seized in violation of its ever-changing concept of the Fourth Amendment is inadmissible. The majority treats the exclusionary rule as a judge-made rule of evidence designed and utilized to enforce the majority's own notions of proper police conduct. The Court today announces its new rules of police procedure in the name of the Fourth Amendment, then holds that evidence seized in violation of the new "guidelines" is automatically inadmissible at trial. The majority does not purport to rely on the Fifth Amendment to exclude the evidence in this case. Indeed, it could not. The majority prefers instead to rely on "changing times" and the Court's role as it sees it, as the administrator in charge of regulating the contacts of officials with citizens. The majority states that in the absence of a better means of regulation, it applies a court-created rule of evidence.

I readily concede that there is much recent precedent for the majority's present announcement of yet another new set of police operating procedures. By invoking this rulemaking power found not in the words but somewhere in the "spirit" of the Fourth Amendment, the Court has expanded that Amendment beyond recognition. And each new step is justified as merely a logical extension of the step before. . . .

. . . .

Our Government is founded upon a written Constitution. The draftsmen expressed themselves in careful and measured terms corresponding with the immense importance of the powers delegated to them. The Framers of the Constitution, and the people who adopted it, must be understood to have used words in their natural meaning, and to have intended what they said. The Constitution itself contains the standards by which the seizure of evidence challenged in the present case and the admissibility of that evidence at trial is to be measured in the absence of congressional legislation. It is my conclusion that both the seizure of the rifle offered by petitioner's wife and the seizure of the automobile at the time of petitioner's arrest were consistent with the Fourth Amendment and that the evidence so obtained under the circumstances shown in the record in this case could not be excluded under the Fifth Amendment.

MR. JUSTICE BLACKMUN joined MR. JUSTICE BLACK in [parts of his opinion].

MR. JUSTICE WHITE, with whom THE CHIEF JUSTICE joins, [wrote a concurring and dissenting opinion].

Terry v. Ohio
392 U.S. 1 (1968)
Vote: 8–1

The facts of the case are contained in the Court's opinion.

MR. CHIEF JUSTICE WARREN delivered the opinion of the Court.

Petitioner Terry was convicted of carrying a concealed weapon and sentenced to the statutorily prescribed term of one to three years in the penitentiary. Following the denial of a pretrial motion to suppress, the prosecution introduced in evidence two revolvers and a number of bullets seized from Terry and a co-defendant, Richard Chilton, by Cleveland Police Detective Martin McFadden. At the hearing on the motion to suppress this evidence, Officer McFadden testified that while he was patrolling in plain clothes in downtown Cleveland at approximately 2:30 in the afternoon of October 31, 1963, his attention was attracted by two men, Chilton and Terry, standing on the corner of Huron Road and Euclid Avenue. He had never seen the two men before, and he was unable to say precisely what first drew his eye to them. However, he testified that he had been a policeman for 39 years and a detective for 35 and that he had been assigned to patrol this vicinity of downtown Cleveland for shoplifters and pickpockets for 30 years. He explained that he had developed routine habits of observation over the years and that he would "stand and watch people or walk and watch people at many intervals of the day." He added: "Now, in this case when I looked over they didn't look right to me at the time."

His interest aroused, Officer McFadden took up a post of observation in the entrance to a store 300 to 400 feet away from the two men. "I get more purpose to watch them when I seen their movements," he testified. He saw one of the men leave the other one and walk southwest on Huron Road, past some stores. The man paused for a moment and looked in a store window, then walked on a short distance, turned around and walked back toward the corner, pausing once again to look in the same store window. He rejoined his companion at the corner, and the two conferred briefly. Then the second man went through the same series of motions, strolling down Huron Road, looking in the same window, walking on a short distance, turning back, peering in the store window again, and returning to confer with the first man at the corner. The two men repeated this ritual alternately between five and six times apiece — in all, roughly a dozen trips. At one point, while the two were standing together on the corner, a third man approached them and engaged them briefly in conversation. This man then left the two others and walked west on Euclid Avenue. Chilton and Terry resumed their measured pacing, peering, and conferring. After this had gone on for 10 to 12 minutes, the two men walked off together, heading west on Euclid Avenue, following the path taken earlier by the third man.

By this time Officer McFadden had become thoroughly suspicious. He testified that after observing their elaborately casual and oft-repeated reconnaissance of the store window on Huron Road, he suspected the two men of "casing a job, a stick-up," and that he considered it his duty as a police officer to investigate further. He added that he feared "they may have a gun." Thus, Officer McFadden followed Chilton and Terry and saw them stop in front of Zucker's store to talk to the same man who had conferred with them earlier on the street corner. Deciding that the situation was ripe for direct action, Officer McFadden approached the three men, identified himself as a police officer and asked for their names. At this point his knowledge was confined to what he had observed. He was not acquainted with any of the three men by name or by sight, and he had received no information concerning them from any other source. When the men "mumbled something" in response to his inquiries, Officer McFadden grabbed petitioner Terry, spun him around so that they were facing the other two, with Terry between McFadden and the others, and patted down the outside of his clothing. In the left breast pocket of Terry's overcoat Officer McFadden felt a pistol. He reached inside the overcoat pocket, but was unable to remove the gun. At this point, keeping Terry between himself and the others, the officer ordered all three men to enter Zucker's store. As they went in, he removed Terry's overcoat completely, removed a .38-caliber revolver from the pocket and ordered all three men to face the wall with their hands raised. Officer McFadden proceeded to pat down the outer clothing of Chilton and the third man, Katz. He discovered another revolver in the outer pocket of Chilton's overcoat, but no weapons were found on Katz. The officer testified that he only patted the men down to see whether they had weapons, and that he did not put his hands beneath the outer garments of either Terry or Chilton until he felt their guns. So far as appears from the record, he never placed his hands beneath Katz' outer garments. Officer McFadden seized Chilton's gun, asked the proprietor of the store to call a police wagon, and took all three men to the station, where Chilton and Terry were formally charged with carrying concealed weapons.

On the motion to suppress the guns the prosecution took the position that they had been seized following a search incident to a lawful arrest. The trial court rejected this theory, stating that it "would be stretching the facts beyond reasonable comprehension" to find that Officer McFadden had had probable cause to arrest the men before he patted them down for weapons. However, the court denied the defendants' motion on the ground that Officer McFadden, on the basis of his experience, "had reasonable cause to believe . . . that the defendants were conducting themselves suspiciously, and some interrogation should be made of their action." Purely for his own protection, the court held, the officer had the right to pat down the outer clothing of these men, who he had reasonable cause to believe might be armed. The court distinguished between an investigatory "stop" and an arrest, and between a "frisk" of the outer clothing for weapons and a full-blown search for evidence of crime. The frisk, it held, was essential to the proper performance of the officer's investigatory duties, for without it "the answer to the police officer may be a bullet, and a loaded pistol discovered during the frisk is admissible."

After the court denied their motion to suppress, Chilton and Terry waived jury trial and pleaded not guilty. The court adjudged them guilty, and the Court of Appeals for the Eighth Judicial District, Cuyahoga County, affirmed. . . . The Supreme Court of Ohio dismissed their appeal. . . . We granted certiorari. . . . We affirm the conviction.

Our first task is to establish at what point in this encounter the Fourth Amendment becomes relevant. That is, we must decide whether and when Officer McFadden "seized" Terry and whether and when he conducted a "search." There is some suggestion in the use of such terms as "stop" and "frisk" that such police conduct is outside the purview of the Fourth Amendment because neither action rises to the level of a "search" or "seizure" within the meaning of the Constitution. We emphatically reject this notion. It is quite plain that the Fourth Amendment governs "seizures" of the person which do not eventuate in a trip to the station house and prosecution for crime — "arrests" in traditional terminology. It must be recognized that whenever a police officer accosts an individual and restrains his freedom to walk away, he has "seized" that person. And it is nothing less than sheer torture of the English language to suggest that a careful exploration of the outer surfaces of a person's clothing all over his or her body in an attempt to find weapons is not a "search." Moreover, it is simply fantastic to urge that such a procedure performed in public by a policeman while the citizen stands helpless, perhaps facing a wall with his hands raised, is a "petty indignity." It is a serious intrusion upon the sanctity of the person, which may inflict great indignity and arouse strong resentment, and it is not to be undertaken lightly.

The danger in the logic which proceeds upon distinctions between a "stop" and an "arrest," or "seizure" of the person, and between a "frisk" and a "search" is two-fold. It seeks to isolate from constitutional scrutiny the initial stages of the contact between the policeman and the citizen. And by suggesting a rigid all-or-nothing model of justification and regulation under the Amendment, it obscures the utility of limitations upon the scope, as well as the initiation, of police action as a means of constitutional regulation. This Court has held in the past that a search which is reasonable at its inception may violate the Fourth Amendment by virtue of its intolerable intensity and scope. . . . The scope of the search must be "strictly tied to and justified by" the circumstances which rendered its initiation permissible. *Warden* v. *Hayden,* 387 U.S. 294, 310 (1967) (Mr. Justice Fortas, concurring). . . .

The distinctions of classical "stop-and-frisk" theory thus serve to divert attention from the central inquiry under the Fourth Amendment — the reasonableness in all the circumstances of the particular governmental invasion of a citizen's personal security. "Search" and "seizure" are not talismans. We therefore reject the notions that the Fourth Amendment does not come into play at all as a limitation upon police conduct if the officers stop short of something called a "technical arrest" or a "full-blown search."

In this case there can be no question, then, that Officer McFadden "seized" petitioner and subjected him to a "search" when he took hold of him and patted down the outer surfaces of his clothing. We must decide whether at that point it was reasonable for Officer McFadden to have interfered with petitioner's personal security as he did. And in determining whether the seizure and search were "unreasonable" our inquiry is a dual one — whether the officer's action was justified at its inception, and whether it was reasonably related in scope to the circumstances which justified the interference in the first place.

If this case involved police conduct subject to the Warrant Clause of the Fourth Amendment, we would have to ascertain whether "probable cause" existed to justify the search and seizure which took place. However, that is not the case. We do not retreat from our holdings that the police must, whenever practicable, obtain advance judicial approval of searches and seizures through the warrant procedure, . . . or that in most instances failure to comply with the warrant requirement can only be excused by exigent circumstances. . . . But we deal here with an entire rubric of police conduct—necessarily swift action predicated upon the on-the-spot observations of the officer on the beat—which historically has not been, and as a practical matter could not be, subjected to the warrant procedure. Instead, the conduct involved in this case must be tested by the Fourth Amendment's general proscription against unreasonable searches and seizures.

Nonetheless, the notions which underlie both the warrant procedure and the requirement of probable cause remain fully relevant in this context. In order to assess the reasonableness of Officer McFadden's conduct as a general proposition, it is necessary "first to focus upon the governmental interest which allegedly justifies official intrusion upon the constitutionally protected interests of the private citizen," for there is "no ready test for determining reasonableness other than by balancing the need to search [or seize] against the invasion which the search [or seizure] entails."*Camara* v. *Municipal Court* . . . (1967). And in justifying the particular intrusion the police officer must be able to point to specific and articulable facts which, taken together with rational inferences from those facts, reasonably warrant that intrusion. The scheme of the Fourth Amendment becomes meaningful only when it is assured that at some point the conduct of those charged with enforcing the laws can be subjected to the more detached, neutral scrutiny of a judge who must evaluate the reasonableness of a particular search or seizure in light of the particular circumstances. And in making that assessment it is imperative that the facts be judged against an objective standard: would the facts available to the officer at the moment of the seizure or the search "warrant a man of reasonable caution in the belief" that the action taken was appropriate? . . . Anything less would invite intrusions upon constitutionally guaranteed rights based on nothing more substantial than inarticulate hunches, a result this Court has consistently refused to sanction. . . . And simple "'good faith on the part of the arresting officer is not enough.'" . . . If subjective good faith alone were the test, the protections of the Fourth Amendment would evaporate, and the people would be 'secure in their persons, houses, papers, and effects,' only in the discretion of the police." . . .

Applying these principles to this case, we consider first the nature and extent of the governmental interests involved. One general interest is of course that of effective crime prevention and detection; it is this interest which underlies the recognition that a police officer may in appropriate circumstances and in an appropriate manner approach a person for purposes of investigating possibly criminal behavior even though there is no probable cause to make an arrest. It was this legitimate investigative function Officer McFadden was discharging when he decided to approach petitioner and his companions. He had observed Terry, Chilton, and Katz go through a series of acts, each of them perhaps innocent in itself, but which taken together warranted further investigation. . . .

. . . It would have been poor police work indeed for an officer of 30 years' experience in the detection of thievery from stores in this same neighborhood to have failed to investigate this behavior further.

The crux of this case, however, is not the propriety of Officer McFadden's taking steps to investigate petitioner's suspicious behavior, but rather, whether there was justification for McFadden's invasion of Terry's personal security by searching him for weapons in the course of that investigation. . . . [W]e cannot blind ourselves to the need for law enforcement officers to protect themselves and other prospective victims of violence in situations where they may lack probable cause for an arrest. When an officer is justified in believing that the individual whose suspicious behavior he is investigating at close range is armed and presently dangerous to the officer or to others, it would appear to be clearly unreasonable to deny the officer the power to take necessary measures to determine whether the person is in fact carrying a weapon and to neutralize the threat of physical harm.

We must still consider, however, the nature and quality of the intrusion on individual rights which must be accepted if police officers are to be conceded the right to search for weapons in situations where probable cause to arrest for crime is lacking. Even a limited search of the outer clothing for weapons constitutes a severe, though brief, intrusion upon cherished personal security, and it must surely be an annoying, frightening, and perhaps humiliating experience. . . .

. . . .

Our evaluation of the proper balance that has to be struck in this type of case leads us to conclude that there must be a narrowly drawn authority to permit a reasonable search for weapons for the protection of the police officer, where he has reason to believe that he is dealing with an armed and dangerous individual, regardless of whether he has probable cause to arrest the individual for a crime. The officer need not be absolutely certain that the individual is armed; the issue is whether a reasonably prudent man in the circumstances would be warranted in the belief that his safety or that of others was in danger. . . .

We conclude that the revolver seized from Terry was properly admitted in evidence against him. At the time he seized petitioner and searched him for weapons, Officer McFadden had reasonable grounds to believe that petitioner was armed and dangerous, and it was necessary for the protection of himself and others to take swift measures to discover the true facts and neutralize the threat of harm if it materialized. The policeman carefully restricted his search to what was appropriate to the discovery of the particular items which he sought. Each case of this sort will, of course, have to be decided on its own facts. We merely hold today that where a police officer observes unusual conduct which leads him reasonably to conclude in light of his experience that criminal activity may be afoot and that the persons with whom he is dealing may be armed and presently dangerous, where in the course of investigating this behavior he identifies himself as a policeman and makes reasonable inquiries, and where nothing in the initial stages of the encounter serves to dispel his reasonable fear for his own or others' safety, he is entitled for the protection of himself and others in the area to conduct a carefully limited search of the outer clothing of such persons in an attempt to discover weapons which might be used to assault him. Such a search is a reasonable search under the Fourth Amendment, and any weapons seized may properly be introduced in evidence against the person from whom they were taken.

Affirmed.

[MR. JUSTICE BLACK concurred in the judgment.]

[JUSTICES HARLAN and WHITE wrote separate concurring opinions.]

MR. JUSTICE DOUGLAS, dissenting.

I agree that petitioner was "seized" within the meaning of the Fourth Amendment. I also agree that frisking petitioner and his companions for guns was a "search." But it is a mystery how that "search" and that "seizure" can be constitutional by Fourth Amendment standards, unless there was "probable cause" to believe that (1) a crime had been committed or (2) a crime was in the process of being committed or (3) a crime was about to be committed.

The opinion of the Court disclaims the existence of "probable cause." If loitering were in issue and that was the offense charged, there would be "probable cause" shown. But the crime here is carrying concealed weapons; and there is no basis for con-

cluding that the officer had "probable cause" for believing that that crime was being committed. Had a warrant been sought, a magistrate would, therefore, have been unauthorized to issue one, for he can act only if there is a showing of "probable cause." We hold today that the police have greater authority to make a "seizure" and conduct a "search" than a judge has to authorize such action. We have said precisely the opposite over and over again.

Delaware v. Prouse

440 U.S. 648 (1979)
Vote: 8–1

A Delaware highway patrol officer stopped Prouse's car. As he approached the car the officer smelled marijuana, which he then observed in plain view and seized. Prouse was subsequently indicted for illegal possession of a controlled substance. At his trial, Prouse's attorneys filed a motion to suppress the marijuana. The officer testified that prior to stopping the automobile he had observed no violations or any suspicious behavior by the driver. Nor had he seen any equipment violations. He further testified that he had made the stop only to check the driver's license and registration, and that the stop was "routine." The officer was not acting pursuant to any official standards, guidelines, or procedures pertaining to document spot checks. Official rules were silent on such spot checks.

The trial court granted the motion to suppress, finding that the stop and detention were wholly capricious and therefore violative of the Fourth Amendment. Upon appeal, the Delaware Supreme Court affirmed, and the state petitioned the United States Supreme Court for a writ of certiorari, which was granted.

MR. JUSTICE WHITE delivered the opinion of the Court.

. . . We agree that the States have a vital interest in ensuring that only those qualified to do so are permitted to operate motor vehicles, that these vehicles are fit for safe operation, and hence that licensing, registration, and vehicle inspection requirements are being observed. . . .

The question remains, however, whether in the service of these important ends the discretionary spot check is a sufficiently productive mechanism to justify the intrusion upon Fourth Amendment interests which such stops entail. On the record before us, that question must be answered in the negative. Given the alternative mechanisms available, both those in use and those that might be adopted, we are unconvinced that the incremental contribution to highway safety of the random spot check justifies the practice under the Fourth Amendment.

. . . It seems common sense that the percentage of all drivers on the road who are driving without a license is very small and that the number of licensed drivers who will be stopped in order to find one unlicensed operated will be large indeed. . . . In terms of actually discovering unlicensed drivers or deterring them from driving, the spot check does not appear sufficiently productive to qualify as a reasonable law enforcement practice under the Fourth Amendment.

Much the same can be said about the safety aspects of automobiles as distinguished from drivers. . . .

. . . When there is not probable cause to believe that a driver is violating any one of the multitude of applicable traffic and equipment regulations — or other articulable basis amounting to reasonable suspicion that the driver is unlicensed or his vehicle unregistered — we cannot conceive of any legitimate basis upon which a patrolman could decide that stopping a particular driver for a spot check would be more productive than stopping any other driver. This kind of standardless and unconstrained discretion is the evil the Court has discerned when in previous cases it has insisted that the discretion of the official in the field be circumscribed, at least to some extent. . . .

The "grave danger" of abuse of discretion . . . does not disappear simply because the automobile is subject to state regulation resulting in numerous instances of police-citizen contact. . . . Only last Term we pointed out that "if the government intrudes . . . the privacy interest suffers whether the government's motivation is to investigate violations of criminal laws or breaches of other statutory or regulatory standards." . . .

An individual operating or traveling in an automobile does not lose all reasonable expectation of privacy simply because the automobile and its use are subject to government regulation. Automobile travel is a basic, pervasive, and often necessary mode of transportation to and from one's home, workplace, and leisure activities. Many people spend more hours each day traveling in cars than walking on the streets. Undoubtedly, many find a greater sense of security and privacy in traveling in an automobile than they do in exposing themselves by pedestrian or other modes of travel. Were the individual subject to unfettered governmental intrusion every time he entered an automobile, the security guaranteed by the Fourth Amendment would be seriously circumscribed. . . .

Accordingly, we hold that except in those situations in which there is at least articulable and reasonable suspicion that a motorist is unlicensed or that an automobile is not registered, or that either the vehicle or an occupant is otherwise subject to seizure for violation of law, stopping an automobile and detaining the driver in order to check his driver's license and the registration of the automobile are unreasonable under the Fourth Amendment. This holding does not preclude the State of Delaware or other States from developing methods for spot checks that involve less intrusion or that do not involve the unconstrained exercise of discretion. Questioning of all oncoming traffic at roadblock-type stops is one possible alternative. We hold only that persons in automobiles on public roadways may not for that reason alone have their travel and privacy interfered with at the unbridled discretion of police officers. The judgment below is affirmed.

So ordered.

[MR. JUSTICE BLACKMUN wrote a concurring opinion, which MR. JUSTICE POWELL joined.]

MR. JUSTICE REHNQUIST, dissenting.

. . . No one questions that the State may require the licensing of those who drive on its highways and the registration of vehicles which are driven on those highways. If it may insist on these requirements, it obviously may take steps necessary to enforce compliance. The reasonableness of the enforcement measure chosen by the State is tested by weighing its intrusion on the motorists' Fourth Amendment interests against its promotion of the State's legitimate interests. . . .

In executing this balancing process, the Court concludes that given the alternative mechanisms available, discretionary spot checks are not a "sufficiently productive mechanism" to safeguard the State's admittedly "vital interest in ensuring that only those qualified to do so are permitted to operate motor vehicles, that these vehicles are fit for safe operation, and hence that licensing, registration, and vehicle inspection requirements are being observed." . . . Foremost among the alternative methods of enforcing traffic and vehicle safety regulations, according to the Court, is acting upon observed violations, for "drivers without licenses are presumably the less safe drivers whose propensities may well exhibit themselves."... Noting that "finding an unlicensed driver among those who commit traffic violations is a much more likely event than finding an unlicensed driver by choosing randomly from the entire universe of drivers," *ibid.,* the Court concludes that the contribution to highway safety made by random stops would be marginal at best. The State's primary interest, however, is in traffic safety, not in apprehending unlicensed motorists for the sake of apprehending unlicensed motorists. The whole point of enforcing motor vehicle safety regulations is to remove from the road the unlicensed driver before he demonstrates why he is unlicensed. The Court would apparently prefer that the State check licenses and vehicle registrations as the wreckage is being towed away.

Nor is the Court impressed with the deterrence rationale, finding it inconceivable that an unlicensed driver who is not deterred by the prospect of being involved in a traffic violation or other incident requiring him to produce a license would be deterred by the possibility of being subjected to a spot check. The Court arrives at its conclusion without the benefit of a shred of empirical data in this record suggesting that a system of random spot checks would fail to deter violators. In the absence of such evidence, the State's determination that random stops would serve a deterrence function should stand.

On the other side of the balance, the Court advances only the most diaphanous of citizen interests. Indeed, the Court does not say that these interests can never be infringed by the State, just that the State must infringe them en masse rather than citizen by citizen. To comply with the Fourth Amendment, the State need only subject *all* citizens to the same "anxiety" and "inconvenien[ce]" to which it now subjects only a few.

... Although a system of discretionary stops could conceivably be abused, the record before us contains no showing that such abuse is probable or even likely. Nor is there evidence in the record that a system of random license checks would fail adequately to further the State's interest in deterring and apprehending violators. Nevertheless, the Court concludes "[o]n the record before us" that the random spot check is not "a sufficiently productive mechanism to justify the intrusion upon Fourth Amendment interests which such stops entail."... I think that the Court's approach reverses the presumption of constitutionality accorded acts of the States. The burden is not upon the State to demonstrate that its procedures are consistent with the Fourth Amendment, but upon respondent to demonstrate that they are not....

... Absent an equal protection violation, the fact that random stops may entail "a possibly unsettling show of authority,"... and "may create substantial anxiety," seems an insufficient basis to distinguish for Fourth Amendment purposes between a roadblock stopping all cars and the random stop at issue here. Accordingly, I would reverse the judgment of the Supreme Court of Delaware.

Michigan v. Summers

452 U.S. 692 (1981)
Vote: 6–3

In TERRY V. OHIO (1968), the Court first separated the Fourth Amendment's reasonableness requirement from its probable cause provision, thereby creating an exception to the rule requiring probable cause to conduct searches and seizures. The Court in TERRY went to great pains to carve out an extremely limited exception, which was based in part upon a combination of a limited search (a pat-down as opposed to a full-scale search), short duration, and an important governmental interest (protecting the safety of police officers in a threatening situation). But once this exception was created, a strong dynamic to enlarge upon it was set in motion. In short order the Court was confronted with a series of other situations that presented strong arguments for treatment as exceptions of the general rule that official search and seizure in criminal cases must be supported by probable cause. In some of these cases the Court has declined to extend the exception, for example, *Dunaway* v. *New York,* 442 U.S. 200 (1978); DELAWARE V. PROUSE, 440 U.S. 648 (1979); *Brown* v. *Texas,* 448 U.S. 47 (1979); and *Ybarra* v. *Illinois,* 444 U.S. 85 (1979). But in others it has found a reasonable basis for applying the TERRY exception and in so doing has enlarged upon it. See *Adams* v. *Williams,* 407 U.S. 143 (1972), *United States* v. *Brigoni-Ponce,* 422 U.S.

873 (1975), and *United States* v. *Martinez-Fuerte,* 428 U.S. 543 (1976).

Thus, despite the assertion of Justice Stevens in the case below, we may be witnessing a process by which the general rule is being eaten by the exceptions. This of course is the concern of the dissenters, who see in this case still one more bite from the general rule. They are particularly disturbed by the expansiveness of Justice Stevens' reasoning, which they view as an invitation to broaden the exceptions still more. More generally, the majority opinion also suggests a subtle shift in approach, a move from a rights-oriented analysis in Fourth Amendment jurisprudence to a balancing of interests approach, a shift that is facilitated by the detachment of the reasonableness requirement from the probable cause requirement. If a search or seizure must only be "reasonable," any number of valid state interests can be put forward to be balanced against the individual's interests in being secure from search and seizure. If TERRY-like exceptions continue to be expanded, will not the Fourth Amendment be turned on its head and be transformed from an absolute prohibition against search and seizure unless there is probable cause to a new and broad positive grant of authority to law enforcement officials?

Reread Justice Douglas' dissent in TERRY. He warns against creating even a limited exception, fearing that once the first step is taken others will surely follow. Do you agree with him? If not, where and how would you draw the line? Note that even the dissenters in *Summers* acknowledge a category of exceptions considerably broader than the one first provided for in TERRY. Still, they try to draw a line; the nature of the exception here is qualitatively different from those in TERRY and cases that immediately followed. Here, they argue, the exception goes beyond the recognized concerns incidental to the core of law enforcement and deals with the core itself. They express fear that in this case the Court is doing away with probable cause simply in order to enhance the ability of police to conduct investigations that may lead to probable cause to arrest, clearly a goal that

appears to fly in the face of the Fourth Amendment. More generally, contrast Justice Stevens' language in the case below with observations by Justice Robert Jackson in *Johnson* v. *United States,* 333 U.S. 10 (1948):

> The point of the Fourth Amendment, which often is not grasped by zealous officers, is not that it denies law enforcement the support of the usual inferences which reasonable men draw from evidence. Its protection consists in requiring that those inferences be drawn by a neutral and detached magistrate instead of being judged by the officer engaged in the often competitive enterprise of ferreting out crime. Any assumption that evidence sufficient to support a magistrate's disinterested determination to issue a search warrant will justify the officers in making a search without a warrant would reduce the Amendment to a nullity and leave the people's homes secure only in the discretion of police officers. Crime, even in the privacy of one's own quarters, is, of course, of grave concern to society, and the law allows such crime to be reached on proper showing. The right of officers to thrust themselves into a home is also a grave concern, not only to the individual but to a society which chooses to dwell in reasonable security and freedom from surveillance. When the right of privacy must reasonably yield to the right of search is, as a rule, to be decided by a judicial officer, not by a policeman or government enforcement agent.

This case arose when police officers about to execute a warrant to search a house for narcotics encountered Summers leaving the house. They requested his assistance and detained him for the duration of the search, although they did not have probable cause to arrest him at the time. After finding narcotics in the house and ascertaining that the house belonged to Summers, the police arrested him, searched him, and found narcotics in his pocket. At his trial for possession of heroin on his person, Summers moved to suppress the evidence as the product of an illegal search in violation of the Fourth Amendment. The trial judge granted the motion and quashed the information, a decision that was upheld by the Michigan Supreme Court. From the outset, it was conceded that at the time of Summers' detention, the police did not have probable cause to arrest him. Thus the issue before the Court was the scope of the government's authority when executing a search warrant to search premises and whether Summers' seizure can be justified under a TERRY-like exception to the probable cause requirement. The Court quickly disposes of the first issue and turns to focus on the second.

JUSTICE STEVENS delivered the opinion of the Court.

The dispositive question in this case is whether the initial detention of respondent violated his constitutional right to be secure against an unreasonable seizure of his person. The State attempts to justify the eventual search of respondent's person by arguing that the authority to search premises granted by the warrant implicitly included the authority to search persons on those premises, just as that authority included an authorization to search furniture and containers in which the particular things described might be concealed. But as the Michigan Court of Appeals correctly noted, even if otherwise acceptable, this argument could not justify the initial detention of respondent outside the premises described in the warrant.... Our appraisal of the validity of the search of respondent's person therefore depends upon a determination whether the officers had the authority to require him to re-enter the house and to remain there while they conducted their search.

In assessing the validity of respondent's initial detention, we note first that it constituted a "seizure" within the meaning of the Fourth Amendment. The State does not contend otherwise, and the record demonstrates that respondent was not free to leave the premises while the officers were searching his home. It is also clear that respondent was not formally arrested until after the search was completed. The dispute therefore involves only the constitutionality of a pre-arrest "seizure" which we assume was unsupported by probable cause.

In *Dunaway* v. *New York* [1978] the Court reaffirmed the general rule that an official seizure of the person must be supported by probable cause, even if no formal arrest is made. In that case police officers located a murder suspect at a neighbor's house, took him into custody, and transported him to the police station, where interrogation ultimately produced a confession. Because the suspect was not arrested until after he had confessed, and because he presumably would have been set free if probable cause had not been established during his questioning, the State argued that the pre-arrest detention should not be equated with an arrest and should be upheld as

"reasonable" in view of the serious character of the crime and the fact that the police had an articulable basis for suspecting that Dunaway was involved.... The Court firmly rejected the State's argument, noting that "the detention of petitioner was in important respects indistinguishable from a traditional arrest."... We stated:

> Indeed, any 'exception' that could cover a seizure as intrusive as that in this case would threaten to swallow the general rule that Fourth Amendment seizures are 'reasonable' only if based on probable cause.
>
> "The central importance of the probable-cause requirement to the protection of a citizen's privacy afforded by the Fourth Amendment's guarantees cannot be compromised in this fashion. 'The requirement of probable cause has roots that are deep in our history.'... Hostility to seizures based on mere suspicion was a prime motivation for the adoption of the Fourth Amendment, and decisions immediately after its adoption affirmed that 'common rumor or report, suspicion, or even "strong reason to suspect" was not adequate to support a warrant for arrest.'... The familiar threshold standard of probable cause for Fourth Amendment seizures reflects the benefit of extensive experience accommodating the factors relevant to the 'reasonableness' requirement of the Fourth Amendment, and provides the relative simplicity and clarity necessary to the implementation of a workable rule....

Although we refused in *Dunaway* to find an exception that would swallow the general rule, our opinion recognized that some seizures significantly less intrusive than an arrest have withstood scrutiny under the reasonableness standard embodied in the Fourth Amendment. In these cases the intrusion on the citizen's privacy "was so much less severe" than that involved in a traditional arrest that "the opposing interests in crime prevention and detection and in the police officer's safety" could support the seizure as reasonable....

In the first such case, *Terry* v. *Ohio* [1968], the Court recognized the narrow authority of police officers who suspect criminal activity to make limited intrusions on an individual's personal security based on less than probable cause. The Court approved a "frisk" for weapons as a justifiable response to an officer's reasonable belief that he was dealing with a possibly armed and dangerous suspect. In the second such case, *Adams* v. *Williams*... [1972], the

Court relied on *Terry* to hold that an officer could forcibly stop a suspect to investigate an informant's tip that the suspect was armed and carrying narcotics. And in *United States* v. *Brignoni-Ponce...* [1975], the Court held that the special enforcement problems confronted by roving Border Patrol agents, though not sufficient to justify random stops of vehicles near the Mexican border to question their occupants about their citizenship, . . . were adequate to support vehicle stops based on the agents' awareness of specific articulable facts indicating that the vehicle contained illegal aliens. The Court reasoned that the difficulty in patrolling the long Mexican border and the interest in controlling the influx of illegal aliens justified the limited intrusion, usually lasting no more than a minute, involved in the stop. . . .

These cases recognize that some seizures admittedly covered by the Fourth Amendment constitute such limited intrusions on the personal security of those detained and are justified by such substantial law enforcement interests that they may be made on less than probable cause, so long as police have an articulable basis for suspecting criminal activity. In these cases, as in *Dunaway,* the Court was applying the ultimate standard of reasonableness embodied in the Fourth Amendment. They are consistent with the general rule that every arrest, and every seizure having the essential attributes of a formal arrest, is unreasonable unless it is supported by probable cause. But they demonstrate that the exception for limited intrusions that may be justified by special law enforcement interests is not confined to the momentary, on-the-street detention accompanied by a frisk for weapons involved in *Terry* and *Adams.* Therefore, in order to decide whether this case is controlled by the general rule, it is necessary to examine both the character of the official intrusion and its justification.

Of prime importance in assessing the intrusion is the fact that the police had obtained a warrant to search respondent's house for contraband. A neutral and detached magistrate had found probable cause to believe that the law was being violated in that house and had authorized a substantial invasion of the privacy of the persons who resided there. The detention of one of the residents while the premises were searched, although admittedly a significant restraint on his liberty, was surely less intrusive than the search itself. Indeed, we may safely assume that most citizens — unless they intend flight to avoid arrest — would elect to remain in order to observe the search of their possessions. Furthermore, the type of detention imposed here is not likely to be exploited by the officer or unduly prolonged in order to gain more information, because the information the officers seek normally will be obtained through the search and not through the detention. Moreover, because the detention in this case was in respondent's own residence, it could add only minimally to the public stigma associated with the search itself and would involve neither the inconvenience nor the indignity associated with a compelled visit to the police station. In sharp contrast to the custodial interrogation in *Dunaway,* the detention of this respondent was "substantially less intrusive" than an arrest. . . .

In assessing the justification for the detention of an occupant of premises being searched for contraband pursuant to a valid warrant, both the law enforcement interest and the nature of the "articulable facts" supporting the detention are relevant. Most obvious is the legitimate law enforcement interest in preventing flight in the event that incriminating evidence is found. Less obvious, but sometimes of greater importance, is the interest in minimizing the risk of harm to the officers. Although no special danger to the police is suggested by the evidence in this record, the execution of a warrant to search for narcotics is the kind of transaction that may give rise to sudden violence or frantic efforts to conceal or destroy evidence. The risk of harm to both the police and the occupants is minimized if the officers routinely exercise unquestioned command of the situation. . . . Finally, the orderly completion of the search may be facilitated if the occupants of the premises are present. Their self-interest may induce them to open locked doors or locked containers to avoid the use of force that is not only damaging to property but may also delay the completion of the task at hand.

It is also appropriate to consider the nature of the articulable and individualized suspicion on which the police base the detention of the occupant of a home subject to a search warrant. We have already noted that the detention represents only an incremental intrusion on personal liberty when the search of a home has been authorized by a valid warrant. The existence of a search warrant, however, also provides an objective justification for the detention. A judicial officer has determined that police have probable cause to believe that someone in the home is committing a crime. Thus a neutral magistrate rather than an officer in the field has made the critical determination that the police should be given a special authorization to thrust themselves into the privacy of a home. The connection of an occupant to that home gives the police officer an easily identifiable and certain basis for determining that suspicion of criminal activity justifies a detention of that occupant.

In *Payton* v. *New York*... we held that police officers may not enter a private residence to make a routine felony arrest without first obtaining a warrant....

That holding is relevant today. If the evidence that a citizen's residence is harboring contraband is sufficient to persuade a judicial officer that an invasion of the citizen's privacy is justified, it is constitutionally reasonable to require that citizen to remain while officers of the law execute a valid warrant to search his home. Thus, for Fourth Amendment purposes, we hold that a warrant to search for contraband founded on probable cause implicitly carries with it the limited authority to detain the occupants of the premises while a proper search is conducted.

Because it was lawful to require respondent to reenter and to remain in the house until evidence establishing probable cause to arrest him was found, his arrest and the search incident thereto were constitutionally permissible. The judgment of the Supreme Court of Michigan must therefore be reversed.

It is so ordered.

JUSTICE STEWART, with whom JUSTICE BRENNAN and JUSTICE MARSHALL join, dissenting.

The Court is correct in stating that "some seizures significantly less intrusive than an arrest have withstood scrutiny under the reasonableness standard embodied in the Fourth Amendment." But to escalate this statement into some kind of a general rule is to ignore the protections that the Fourth Amendment guarantees to us all. There are only two types of seizures that need not be based on probable cause. The first, represented by the *Terry* line of cases, is a limited stop to question a person and to perfom a pat-down for weapons when the police have reason to believe that he is armed and dangerous.... The second is a brief stop of vehicles near our international borders to question occupants of the vehicles about their citizenship....

From these two special exceptions to the general prohibition on seizures not based on probable cause, the Court leaps to the very broad idea that courts may approve a wide variety of seizures not based on probable cause, so long as the courts find, after balancing the law enforcement purposes of the police conduct against the severity of their intrusion, that the seizure appears "reasonable." But those two lines of cases do not represent some sort of exemplary balancing test for Fourth Amendment cases. Rather, they represent two isolated exceptions to

the general rule that the Fourth Amendment itself has already performed the constitutional balance between police objectives and personal privacy. The seizure permitted by the Court today, the detention of a person at his home while the police execute a search warrant for contraband inside it, is categorically different from those two special exceptions to the warrant and probable-cause requirement, and poses a significantly greater threat to the protections guaranteed by the Constitution.

The common denominator of the *Terry* cases and the border checkpoint cases is the presence of some governmental interest independent of the ordinary interest in investigating crime and apprehending suspects, an interest important enough to overcome the presumptive constitutional restraints on police conduct. At issue in *Terry* was "more than the governmental interest in investigating crime; in addition, there is the more immediate interest of the police officer in taking steps to assure himself that the person with whom he is dealing is not armed with a weapon that could unexpectedly and fatally be used against him."...

Similarly, in *Adams* v. *Williams*... the officer had received an informant's tip, not amounting to probable cause, that Williams was carrying narcotics and a gun. The Court held that the officer acted legally in reaching into the car and intruding on Williams' person to see if Williams indeed was in possession of a lethal weapon. In so holding, the Court made clear that what justified this intrusion on Williams' person was not the possibility of finding contraband narcotics, but rather the officer's need to protect himself from harm by seizing the suspected gun....

In *United States* v. *Brignoni-Ponce, supra,* the Court approved a limited stop of vehicles by patrols of immigration officers near the Mexican border, but in doing so it stressed the unique governmental interest in preventing the illegal entry of aliens. The Court held that brief stops and inquiries based on less than probable cause to search or arrest were necessary because the entry of undocumented aliens creates "significant economic and social problems, competing with citizens and legal resident aliens for jobs, and generating extra demand for social services."... And in *United States* v. *Martinez-Fuerte*... upholding similarly brief stops and inquiries at permanent check-points, the Court relied on the unique difficulty of patrolling a 2,000-mile long and virtually uninhabited border area, a difficulty that would prove insuperable if the Government could stop a vehicle only on the basis of probable cause to believe that that particular vehicle contained illegal entrants.

It seems clear, therefore, that before a court can uphold a detention on less than probable cause on the ground that it is "reasonable" in the light of the competing interests, the government must demonstrate an important purpose beyond the normal goals of criminal investigation, or must demonstrate an extraordinary obstacle to such investigation.

What the Court approves today is justified by no such special governmental interest or law enforcement need. There were only two governmental purposes supporting the detention of the respondent. One was "the legitimate law enforcement interest in preventing flight in the event that incriminating evidence is found." The other was that "the orderly completion of the search may be facilitated if the occupants of the premises are present." Unlike the law enforcement objectives that justified the police conduct in *Terry* and the border stop cases, these objectives represented nothing more than the ordinary police interest in discovering evidence of crime and apprehending wrongdoers. And the Fourth and Fourteenth Amendments impose significant restraints upon these traditional police activities, even though the police and the courts may find those restraints unreasonably inconvenient.

If the police, acting without probable cause, can seize a person to make him available for arrest in case probable cause is later developed to arrest him, the requirement of probable cause for arrest has been turned upside down. And if the police may seize a person without probable cause in order to "facilitate" the execution of a warrant that did not authorize his arrest, the fundamental principle that the scope of a search and seizure can be justified only by the scope of the underlying warrant has suffered serious damage. There is no authority in this Court for the principle that the police can engage in searches and seizures without probable cause simply because to do so enhances their ability to conduct investigations which may eventually lead to probable cause....

Beyond the issue of the governmental interest justifying the detention, I question the Court's view that the detention here is of the limited, unintrusive sort that permits the Court to engage in a "reasonableness" balancing test.... *Terry* v. *Ohio* "defined a special category of Fourth Amendment 'seizures' so *substantially less intrusive* than arrests that the general rule requiring probable cause to make Fourth Amendment 'seizures' reasonable could be replaced by a balancing test." As we then noted in *Dunaway*, the patdown searches in *Terry, Adams,* and *Mimms* were declared legal because they were extremely limited in time and in the degree of personal intrusion.... The Court also noted that in the border cases, the stops normally consumed less than a minute and involved no more than brief interroga-

tion.... Thus, in the rare cases in which the Court has permitted an independent balancing of interests, the police intrusion has been extremely narrow. Moreoever, the Court has required that the stop and inquiry or search be "reasonably related in scope to the justification for their initiation,"... and, under that requirement, the unusual governmental or law enforcement interests justifying the patdown stops and border stops have provided a limiting principle ensuring the narrowness of the police action. The detention approved by the Court today, however, is of a very different order.

The explicit holding of the Court is that "a warrant to search for contraband founded on probable cause implicitly carries with it the limited authority to detain the occupants of the premises while a proper search is conducted."... Though on superficial reading, this language may suggest a minor intrusion of brief duration, a detention "while a proper search is being conducted" can mean a detention of several hours. The police thereby make the person a prisoner in his own home for a potentially very long period of time. Moreover, because of the questionable nature of the governmental interest asserted by the State and acknowledged by the Court in this case, the requirement that the scope of the intrusion be reasonably related to its justification does not provide a limiting principle for circumscribing the detention. If the purpose of the detention is to help the police make the search, the detention can be as long as the police find it necessary to protract the search.

In *Dunaway,* the Court reaffirmed that the "'long-prevailing standards' of probable cause embodied 'the best compromise that has been found for accommodating [the] often opposing interests' in 'safeguard[ing] citizens from rash and unreasonable interferences with privacy' and in 'seek[ing] to give fair leeway for enforcing the law in the community's protection.'"... Because the present case presents no occasion for departing from this principle, I respectfully dissent.

Katz v. U.S.

389 U.S. 347 (1967)
Vote: 8–1

A literal reading of the Fourth Amendment's prohibition against unreasonable searches and seizures suggests that it prohibits only the physical trespass and invasion of one's person or home and the seizure of one's belongings. However, early in its consideration of the matter, the Court construed the language of this provision broadly, "in light of its spirit." In 1878, the Court extended the Fourth Amendment's protection to sealed letters while in possession of the U.S. postal service (*Ex parte Jackson,* 1878).

In *Olmstead* v. *U.S.,* 277 U.S. 438 (1928), the Court was urged to extend the protections of the Fourth Amendment to the telephone, by then an important tool of communication, but by a closely divided vote it refused to take this step, insisting instead that the Fourth Amendment was meant only to limit physical trespass and the seizure of tangible objects—books, papers, and the like. The majority went on to suggest that protection of the privacy of telecommunications should originate with the Congress, not the Court.

In their celebrated dissents, Justices Holmes and Brandeis took issue with the Court's narrow interpretation of the Fourth Amendment and urged that the telephone be brought under the protection of the Fourth Amendment. Brandeis argued that "clauses guaranteeing the individual protection against specific abuses of power must have [the] capacity of adapting to a changing world." In the wake of *Olmstead,* Congress passed a law which in effect prohibited the use in federal courts of evidence obtained from wiretaps. Over the years, the Court interpreted this statute broadly and at the same time began bringing surreptitious electronic listening devices under the discipline of the Fourth Amendment. In 1967, the Court essentially abandoned its position in *Olmstead* and held that wiretapping must meet Fourth Amendment standards. In *Berger* v. *New York,* 388 U.S. 41 (1967), a sharply divided Court ruled on a New York statute requiring judicial authorization for electronic eavesdropping if a police officer above the rank of sergeant, a district attorney, or the state attorney general said that there was a "reasonable basis to believe" that evidence of a crime would be revealed. The Court held that the statute was insufficiently limited to pass Fourth Amendment standards; also that the two-month time limit permitted for eavesdropping was exces-

sive. While some interpreted this decision to mean that electronic eavesdropping per se was unconstitutional, this view was quickly put to rest in *Katz,* decided six months later.

MR. JUSTICE STEWART delivered the opinion of the Court.

The petitioner was convicted in the District Court for the Southern District of California under an eight-count indictment charging him with transmitting wagering information by telephone from Los Angeles to Miami and Boston, in violation of a federal statute. At trial the Government was permitted, over the petitioner's objection, to introduce evidence of the petitioner's end of telephone conversations, overheard by FBI agents who had attached an electronic listening and recording device to the outside of the public telephone booth from which he had placed his calls. In affirming his conviction, the Court of Appeals rejected the contention that the recordings had been obtained in violation of the Fourth Amendment, because "[t]here was no physical entrance into the area occupied by [the petitioner]." We granted certiorari in order to consider the constitutional questions thus presented.

The petitioner has phrased those questions as follows:

A. Whether a public telephone booth is a constitutionally protected area so that evidence obtained by attaching an electronic listening recording device to the top of such a booth is obtained in violation of the right to privacy of the user of the booth.

B. Whether physical penetration of a constitutionally protected area is necessary before a search and seizure can be said to be violative of the Fourth Amendment to the United States Constitution.

We decline to adopt this formulation of the issues. In the first place, the correct solution of Fourth Amendment problems is not necessarily promoted by incantation of the phrase "constitutionally protected area." Secondly, the Fourth Amendment cannot be translated into a general constitutional "right to privacy." That Amendment protects individual privacy against certain kinds of governmental intrusion, but its protections go further, and often have nothing to do with privacy at all. Other provisions of the Constitution protect personal privacy from other forms of governmental invasion. But the protection of a person's *general* right to privacy—his right to be let alone by other people — is, like the protection of his property and of his very life, left largely to the law of the individual States.

Because of the misleading way the issues have been formulated, the parties have attached great significance to the characterization of the telephone booth from which the petitioner placed his calls. The petitioner has strenuously argued that the booth was a "constitutionally protected area." The Government has maintained with equal vigor that it was not. But this effort to decide whether or not a given "area," viewed in the abstract, is "constitutionally protected" deflects attention from the problem presented by this case. For the Fourth Amendment protects people, not places. What a person knowingly exposes to the public, even in his own home or office, is not a subject of Fourth Amendment protection. . . . But what he seeks to preserve as private, even in an area accessible to the public, may be constitutionally protected. . . .

The Government stresses the fact that the telephone booth from which the petitioner made his calls was constructed partly of glass, so that he was as visible after he entered it as he would have been if he had remained outside. But what he sought to exclude when he entered the booth was not the intruding eye — it was the uninvited ear. He did not shed his right to do so simply because he made his calls from a place where he might be seen. No less than an individual in a business office, in a friend's apartment, or in a taxicab, a person in a telephone booth may rely upon the protection of the Fourth Amendment. One who occupies it, shuts the door behind him, and pays the toll that permits him to place a call is surely entitled to assume that the words he utters into the mouthpiece will not be broadcast to the world. To read the Constitution more narrowly is to ignore the vital role that the public telephone has come to play in private communication.

The Government contends, however, that the activities of its agents in this case should not be tested by Fourth Amendment requirements, for the surveillance technique they employed involved no physical penetration of the telephone booth from which the petitioner placed his calls. It is true that the absence of such penetration was at one time thought to foreclose further Fourth Amendment inquiry . . . for that Amendment was thought to limit only searches and seizures of tangible property. But "[t]he premise that property interests control the right of the Government to search and seize has been discredited." . . . Thus, although a closely divided Court supposed in *Olmstead* that surveillance without any trespass and without the seizure of any material ob-

ject fell outside the ambit of the Constitution, we have since departed from the narrow view on which that decision rested. Indeed, we have expressly held that the Fourth Amendment governs not only the seizure of tangible items, but extends as well to the recording of oral statements, overheard without any "technical trespass under . . . local property law." Once this much is acknowledged, and once it is recognized that the Fourth Amendment protects people — and not simply "areas" — against unreasonable searches and seizures, it becomes clear that the reach of that Amendment cannot turn upon the presence or absence of a physical intrusion into any given enclosure.

We conclude that the underpinnings of *Olmstead* and *Goldman* have been so eroded by our subsequent decisions that the "trespass" doctrine there enunciated can no longer be regarded as controlling. The Government's activities in electronically listening to and recording the petitioner's words violated the privacy upon which he justifiably relied while using the telephone booth and thus constituted a "search and seizure" within the meaning of the Fourth Amendment. The fact that the electronic device employed to achieve that end did not happen to penetrate the wall of the booth can have no constitutional significance.

The question remaining for decision, then, is whether the search and seizure conducted in this case complied with constitutional standards. In that regard, the Government's position is that its agents acted in an entirely defensible manner. They did not begin their electronic surveillance until investigation of the petitioner's activities had established a strong probability that he was using the telephone in question to transmit gambling information to persons in other States, in violation of federal law. Moreover, the surveillance was limited, both in scope and in duration, to the specific purpose of establishing the contents of the petitioner's unlawful telephonic communications. The agents confined their surveillance to the brief periods during which he used the telephone booth, and they took great care to overhear only the conversations of the petitioner himself.

Accepting this account of the Government's actions as accurate, it is clear that this surveillance was so narrowly circumscribed that a duly authorized magistrate, properly notified of the need for such investigation, specifically informed of the basis on which it was to proceed, and clearly apprised of the precise intrusion it would entail, could constitutionally have authorized, with appropriate safeguards, the very limited search and seizure that the Government asserts in fact took place. . . .

The Government urges that, because its agents relied upon the decisions in *Olmstead* and *Goldman,* and because they did no more here than they might properly have done with prior judicial sanction, we should retroactively validate their conduct. That we cannot do. It is apparent that the agents in this case acted with restraint. Yet the inescapable fact is that this restraint was imposed by the agents themselves, not a judicial officer. . . . In the absence of such safeguards, this Court has never sustained a search upon the sole ground that officers reasonably expected to find evidence of a particular crime and voluntarily confined their activities to the least intrusive means consistent with that end. . . . "Over and again this Court has emphasized that the mandate of the [Fourth] Amendment requires adherence to judicial processes,". . . and that searches conducted outside the judicial process, without prior approval by judge or magistrate, are *per se* unreasonable under the Fourth Amendment subject only to a few specifically established and well-delineated exceptions.

The Government does not question these basic principles. Rather, it urges the creation of a new exception to cover this case. It argues that surveillance of a telephone booth should be exempted from the usual requirement of advance authorization by a magistrate upon a showing of probable cause. We cannot agree. . . .

Judgment reversed.

MR. JUSTICE MARSHALL took no part in the consideration or decision of this case.

[MR. JUSTICE DOUGLAS, with whom MR. JUSTICE BRENNAN joined, concurred in the judgment of the Court.]

[MR. JUSTICE HARLAN concurred in the judgment of the Court.]

[MR. JUSTICE WHITE concurred in the judgment of the Court.]

MR. JUSTICE BLACK, dissenting.

If I could agree with the Court that eavesdropping carried on by electronic means (equivalent to wiretapping) constitutes a "search" or "seizure," I would be happy to join the Court's opinion. . . .

Since I see no way in which the words of the Fourth Amendment can be construed to apply to eavesdropping, that closes the matter for me. In interpreting the Bill of Rights, I willingly go as far as a liberal construction of the language takes me, but I simply cannot in good conscience give a meaning to words which they have never before been thought to have and which they certainly do not have in common ordinary usage. I will not distort the words of the Amendment in order to "keep the Constitution up to date" or "to bring it into harmony with the times." It was never meant that this Court have such power, which in effect would make us a continuously functioning constitutional convention.

With this decision the Court has completed, I hope, its rewriting of the Fourth Amendment, which started only recently when the Court began referring incessantly to the Fourth Amendment not so much as a law against *unreasonable* searches and seizures as one to protect an individual's privacy. By clever word juggling the Court finds it plausible to argue that language aimed specifically at searches and seizures of things that can be searched and seized may, to protect privacy, be applied to eavesdropped evidence of conversations that can neither be searched nor seized. Few things happen to an individual that do not affect his privacy in one way or another. Thus, by arbitrarily substituting the Court's language, designed to protect privacy, for the Constitution's language, designed to protect against unreasonable searches and seizures, the Court has made the Fourth Amendment its vehicle for holding all laws violative of the Constitution which offend the Court's broadest concept of privacy. . . .

The Fourth Amendment protects privacy only to the extent that it prohibits unreasonable searches and seizures of "persons, houses, papers, and effects." No general right is created by the Amendment so as to give this Court the unlimited power to hold unconstitutional everything which affects privacy. Certainly the Framers, well acquainted as they were with the excesses of governmental power, did not intend to grant this Court such omnipotent lawmaking authority as that. The history of governments proves that it is dangerous to freedom to repose such powers in courts.

For these reasons I respectfully dissent.

Dalia v. U.S.

441 U.S. 238 (1979)
Vote: 5–4

Title III of the Crime Control Act of 1968 permits courts to authorize electronic surveillance through telephone taps and bugging devices by government officials in specified situations and upon a showing of probable cause.

In March 1973, federal law enforcement officials applied to the United States District Court of New Jersey seeking authorization to tap the office telephones of Larry Dalia, whom they had reason to believe was engaged in the theft of goods being shipped in interstate commerce. The Court authorized a wiretap for twenty days or until the purpose of the interception was achieved, whichever came first, and limited the wiretap to the types of communications relevant to the investigation at hand. At the end of twenty days, officials asked for and were granted an extension on the telephone wiretap and for the first time requested the Court's permission to bug Dalia's office in order to intercept oral communications. Finding reason to believe that his office was being used to plan interstate thefts, the Court granted permission to bug the office. Although the Court's order did not explicitly authorize surreptitious entry into Dalia's office, FBI agents broke into the office in the middle of the night to install the bug and later to remove it.

At trial, Dalia unsuccessfully moved to have the evidence obtained through the bug suppressed, though he was subsequently convicted of the theft charges. His conviction was affirmed by the United States Court of Appeals, and the case reached the Supreme Court by writ of certiorari.

MR. JUSTICE POWELL delivered the opinion of the Court.

Petitioner first contends that the Fourth Amendment prohibits covert entry of private premises in all cases, irrespective of the reasonableness of the entry or the approval of a court. He contends that Title III is unconstitutional insofar as it enables courts to authorize covert entries for the installation of electronic bugging devices.

In several cases this Court has implied that in some circumstances covert entry to install electronic bugging devices would be constitutionally acceptable if done pursuant to a search warrant. Thus, for example, in *Irvine* v. *California* . . . (1954), the plurality stated that in conducting electronic surveillance, state police officers had "flagrantly, deliberately, and persistently violated the fundamental principle declared by the Fourth Amendment as a restriction on the Federal Government." . . . It emphasized that the bugging equipment was installed through a covert entry of the defendant's home "*without a search warrant* or other process." . . . (emphasis added). Similarly, in *Silverman* v. *United States* . . . (1961), it was noted that "[t]his Court has never held that a federal officer may *without warrant* and without consent physically entrench into a man's office or home, there secretly observe or listen, and relate at the man's subsequent criminal trial what was seen or heard." (Emphasis added.) Implicit in decisions such as *Silverman* and *Irvine* has been the Court's view that covert entries are constitutional in some circumstances, at least if they are made pursuant to warrant.

Moreover, we find no basis for a constitutional rule proscribing all covert entries. It is well established that law officers constitutionally may break and enter to execute a search warrant where such entry is the only means by which the warrant effectively may be executed. . . . Petitioner nonetheless argues that covert entries are unconstitutional for their lack of notice. This argument is frivolous, as was indicated in *Katz* v. *United States* . . . (1967), where the Court stated that "officers need not announce their purpose before conducting an otherwise [duly] authorized search if such an announcement would provoke the escape of the suspect or the destruction of critical evidence." In *United States* v. *Donovan*, 429 U.S. 413, 429 n. 19 (1977), we held that Title III provided a constitutionally adequate substitute for advance notice by requiring that once the surveillance operation is completed the authorizing judge must cause notice to be served on those subjected to surveillance. See 18 U.S.C. §2518(8)(d). There is no reason why the same notice is not equally sufficient with respect to electronic surveillances requiring covert entry. We make explicit, therefore, what has long been implicit in our decisions dealing with this subject: The Fourth Amendment does not prohibit *per se* a covert entry performed for the purpose of installing otherwise legal electronic bugging equipment.

Petitioner's second contention is that Congress has not given the courts statutory authority to approve covert entries for the purpose of installing electronic surveillance equipment, even if constitutionally it could have done so. Petitioner emphasizes that although Title III sets forth with meticulous care the circumstances in which electronic surveillance is permitted, there is no comparable indication in the statute that covert entry ever may be ordered. . . .

Title III does not refer explicitly to covert entry. The language, structure, and history of the statute, however, demonstrate that Congress meant to authorize courts — in certain specified circumstances — to approve electronic surveillance without limitation on the means necessary to its accomplishment, so long as they are reasonable under the circumstances. Title III provides a comprehensive scheme for the regulation of electronic surveillance, prohibiting all secret interception of communications except as authorized by certain state and federal judges in response to applications from specified federal and state law enforcement officials. . . . Although Congress was fully aware of the distinction between bugging and wiretapping . . . Title III by its terms deals with each form of surveillance in essentially the same manner. . . . Orders authorizing interceptions of either wire or oral communications may be entered only after the court has made specific determinations concerning the likelihood that the interception will disclose evidence of criminal conduct. . . . Moreover, with respect to both wiretapping and bugging, an authorizing court must specify the exact scope of the surveillance undertaken, enumerating the parties whose communications are to be overheard (if they are known), the place to be monitored, and the agency that will do the monitoring. . . .

The plain effect of the detailed restrictions of §2518 is to guarantee that wiretapping or bugging occurs only when there is a genuine need for it and only to the extent that it is needed. Once this need has been demonstrated in accord with the requirements of §2518, the courts have broad authority to "approv[e] interception of wire or oral communications," 18 U.S.C. §§2516(1), (2), subject of course to constitutional limitations. Nowhere in Title III is there any indication that the authority of courts under §2518 is to be limited to approving those methods of interception that do not require covert entry for installation of the intercepting equipment.

The legislative history of Title III underscores Congress' understanding that courts would authorize electronic surveillance in situations where covert entry of private premises was necessary. Indeed, a close examination of that history reveals that Congress did not explicitly address the question of covert entries in the Act only because it did not perceive surveillance requiring such entries to differ in any important way from that performed without entry. Testimony before subcommittees considering Title III and related bills indicated that covert entries were a necessary part of most electronic bugging operations. . . .

. . . .

Finally, Congress' purpose in enacting the statute would be largely thwarted if we were to accept peti-

tioner's invitation to read into Title III a limitation on the courts' authority under §2518. Congress permitted limited electronic surveillance under Title III because it concluded that both wiretapping and bugging were necessary to enable law enforcement authorities to combat successfully certain forms of crime. Absent covert entry, however, almost all electronic bugging would be impossible. . . .

In sum, we conclude that Congress clearly understood that it was conferring power upon the courts to authorize covert entries ancillary to their responsibility to review and approve surveillance applications under the statute. To read the statute otherwise would be to deny the "respect for the policy of Congress [that] must save us from inputing to it a self-defeating, if not disingenuous purpose." . . .

Petitioner's final contention is that, if covert entries are to be authorized under Title III, the authorizing court must explicitly set forth its approval of such entries before the fact. . . .

The Fourth Amendment requires that search warrants be issued only "upon probable cause, supported by Oath or affirmation, and particularly describing the place to be searched, and the persons or things to be seized." Finding these words to be "precise and clear," *Stanford* v. *Texas* . . . (1965), this Court has interpreted them to require only three things. First, warrants must be issued by neutral, disinterested magistrates. . . . Second, those seeking the warrant must demonstrate to the magistrate their probable cause to believe that "the evidence sought will aid in a particular apprehension or conviction" for a particular offense. . . . Finally, "warrants must particularly describe the 'things to be seized,'" as well as the place to be searched. . . .

It would extend the Warrant Clause to the extreme to require that, whenever it is reasonably likely that Fourth Amendment rights may be affected in more than one way, the court must set forth precisely the procedures to be followed by the executing officers. Such an interpretation is unnecessary, as we have held — and the Government concedes — that the manner in which a warrant is executed is subject to later judicial review as to its reasonableness. See *Zurcher* v. *Stanford Daily* (1978). . . . More important, we would promote empty formalism were we to require magistrates to make explicit what unquestionably is implicit in bugging authorizations: that a covert entry, with its attendant interference with Fourth Amendment interests, may be necessary for the installation of the surveillance equipment. . . . We conclude, therefore, that the Fourth Amendment does not require that a Title III electronic surveillance order include a specific authorization to enter covertly the premises described in the order.

The judgment of the Court of Appeals is

Affirmed.

MR. JUSTICE BRENNAN, with whom MR. JUSTICE STEWART joins [in part]... concurring in part and dissenting in part.... [Omitted.]

MR. JUSTICE STEVENS, with whom MR. JUSTICE BRENNAN and MR. JUSTICE MARSHALL join, dissenting.

The perpetrators of these break-ins were agents of the Federal Bureau of Investigation. Their office, however, carries with it no general warrant to trespass on private property. Without legislative or judicial sanction, the conduct of these agents was unquestionably "unreasonable" and therefore prohibited by the Fourth Amendment. Moreover, that conduct violated the Criminal Code of the State of New Jersey unless it was duly authorized.

The only consideration that arguably might legitimate these "otherwise tortious and possibly criminal" invasions of petitioner's private property, is the fact that a federal judge had entered an order authorizing the agents to use electronic equipment to intercept oral communications at petitioner's office. The order, however, did not describe the kind of equipment to be used and made no reference to an entry, covert or otherwise, into private property. Nor does any statute expressly permit such activity or even authorize a federal judge to enter orders granting federal agents a license to commit criminal trespass. The initial question this case raises, therefore, is whether this kind of power should be read into a statute that does not expressly grant it.

In my opinion, there are three reasons, each sufficient by itself, for refusing to do so. First, until Congress has stated otherwise, our duty to protect the rights of the individual should hold sway over the interest in more effective law enforcement. Second, the structural detail of this statute precludes a reading that converts silence into thunder. Third, the legislative history affirmatively demonstrates that Congress never contemplated the situation now before the Court.

"Congress, like this Court, has an obligation to obey the mandate of the Fourth Amendment."... But Congress is better equipped than the Judiciary to make the empirical judgment that a previously unauthorized investigative technique represents a "reasonable" accommodation between the privacy interests protected by the Fourth Amendment and effective law enforcement. Throughout our history, therefore, it has been Congress that has taken the lead in granting new authority to invade the citizen's privacy. It is appropriate to accord special deference to Congress whenever it has expressly balanced the need for a new investigatory technique against the undesirable consequences of any intrusion or constitutionally protected interests in privacy....

But no comparable deference should be given federal intrusions on privacy that are not expressly authorized by Congress. In my view, a proper respect for Congress' important role in this area, as well as our tradition of interpreting statutes to avoid constitutional issues, compels this conclusion.

Today the Court has gone even further [than in three prior cases] in finding an implicit grant of Executive power in Title III. That Title "does not refer explicitly to covert entry" of any kind, much less to entries that are tortious or criminal.... Nevertheless, the Court holds that Congress, without having said so explicitly, has authorized the agents of a national police force in carrying out a surveillance order to break into private premises in violation of state law. Moreover, the Court finds in the silent statute an open-ended authorization to effect such illegal entries without an explicit judicial determination that there is probable cause to believe they are necessary or even appropriate. In my judgment, it is most unrealistic to assume that Congress granted such broad and controversial authority to the Executive without making its intention to do so unmistakably plain. This is the paradigm case in which "the exact words of the statute provide the surest guide to determining Congress' intent." I would not enlarge the coverage of the statute beyond its plain meaning.

....

Because it is not supported by either the text of the statute or the scraps of relevant legislative history, I fear that the Court's holding may reflect an unarticulated presumption that national police officers have the power to carry out a surveillance order by whatever means may be necessary unless explicitly prohibited by the statute or by the Constitution.

But surely the presumption should run the other way. Congressional silence should not be construed to authorize the Executive to violate state criminal laws or to encroach upon constitutionally protected privacy interests. Before confronting the serious constitutional issues raised by the Court's reading of Title III, we should insist upon an unambiguous statement by Congress that this sort of police conduct may be authorized by a court and that a specific showing of necessity, or at least probable cause, must precede such an authorization. Without a legislative mandate that is both explicit and specific, I would presume that this flagrant invasion of the citizen's privacy is prohibited. . . .

I respectfully dissent.

U.S. v. Place

462 U.S. 696 (1983)
Vote: 9–0

Once TERRY created an exception to the probable cause requirement, a powerful force was set in motion to expand upon it. As we saw in MICHIGAN V. SUMMERS (1981) and will see in NEW JERSEY V. T.L.O. (1985), a number of cases have done just this. TERRY also sharpened the focus on the issue of what constitutes a search or a seizure within the meaning of the Fourth Amendment, an issue also raised in the electronic surveillance cases of *Olmstead* and KATZ. In KATZ, the Court brought at least certain forms of surveillance (conversations from a public telephone in the immediate case) within the protection of the Fourth Amendment. In so doing KATZ put forward a framework with which to understand the privacy rights inherent in the Fourth Amendment, emphasizing a person's "legitimate expectations of privacy."

In the case below the Court deals with the issue of invasion of privacy in connection with the exposure of a traveler's luggage to a trained narcotics detection dog. Although this issue was not addressed directly by the trial or appellate courts or briefed before the Supreme Court, the Court's opinion goes out of its way to emphasize that such dog sniffs are sui generis and do not constitute searches for Fourth Amendment purposes. The concurring opinions take the majority to task on this, claiming that it need not have addressed the issue, and arguing that dog sniffing of luggage even in public places is a more complicated problem than the majority realizes.

Just one year later, in *United States* v. *Jacobsen*, 466 U.S. 109 (1984), the Court was confronted with another such detection device, this time a chemical test that reveals only whether or not a particular substance is cocaine. Drawing on *Place*, the Court in *Jacobsen* held that use of the test upon packages that had been seized without a warrant by law enforcement officials did not constitute a search within the Fourth Amendment because there is no "legitimate expectation of privacy" in possessing cocaine.

The facts in the case below are as follows: Place's behavior aroused suspicion of law enforcement officials while he was waiting in line to purchase a ticket at the Miami airport. They asked him for identification and for permission to search his luggage. He provided identification and consented to the search, but since his flight was about to depart, the police decided not to search. Still suspicious but lacking probable cause to arrest, the officials telephoned Drug Enforcement Agency (DEA) officials in New York, who were on hand when Place arrived at La Guardia airport. At this time, Place refused to consent to a search of his luggage. The agents then took his luggage across the city to Kennedy Airport, where it was subjected to a "sniff test" by a trained narcotics detection dog. At this point, ninety minutes had elapsed since the seizure of the luggage. After the sniff test indicated drugs, the police obtained a search warrant, and upon opening one of the suitcases discovered a large quantity of cocaine. Place was subsequently charged with various drug offenses. The district court denied a motion to suppress the evidence, but the court of appeals reversed, holding that the ninety-minute seizure of luggage without probable cause exceeded the limited type of investigative stop and pat-down permitted in TERRY and its progeny. Although the Court, in the opinion below, eventually decides this case on a TERRY basis, it goes out of its way to give its approval to dog sniffs of luggage in public places, and it is for this reason that we consider it here following KATZ.

At first blush, KATZ appears to be a liberal and expansive decision. But in light of this case, is it fair to say, as one scholar has, that KATZ is a "two-edged sword capable of cutting both ways"? Can you think of other types of "searches" of closed containers that allow officials to detect contraband without additionally revealing what else may be within?

JUSTICE O'CONNOR delivered the opinion of the Court.

In this case, the Government asks us to recognize the reasonableness under the Fourth Amendment of warrantless seizures of personal luggage from the custody of the owner on the basis of less than probable cause, for the purpose of pursuing a limited course of investigation, short of opening the luggage, that would quickly confirm or dispel the authorities' suspicion. Specifically, we are asked to apply the principles of *Terry* v. *Ohio* to permit such seizures on the basis of reasonable, articulable suspicion, premised on objective facts, that the luggage contains contraband or evidence of a crime. In our view, such application is appropriate.

In *Terry* the Court first recognized "the narrow authority of police officers who suspect criminal activity to make limited intrusions on an individual's personal security based on less than probable cause.". . . In approving the limited search for weapons, or "frisk," of an individual the police reasonably believed to be armed and dangerous, the Court implicitly acknowledged the authority of the police to make a *forcible stop* of a person when the officer has reasonable, articulable suspicion that the person has been, is, or is about to be engaged in criminal activity. . . .

The exception to the probable-cause requirement for limited seizures of the person recognized in *Terry* and its progeny rests on a balancing of the competing interests to determine the reasonableness of the type of seizure involved within the meaning of "the Fourth Amendment's general proscription against unreasonable searches and seizures.". . . We must balance the nature and quality of the intrusion on the individual's Fourth Amendment interests against the importance of the governmental interests alleged to justify the intrusion. When the nature and extent of the detention are minimally intrusive of the individual's Fourth Amendment interests, the opposing law enforcement interests can support a seizure based on less than probable cause.

We examine first the governmental interest offered as a justification for a brief seizure of luggage from the suspect's custody for the purpose of pursuing a limited course of investigation. The Government contends that, where the authorities possess specific and articulable facts warranting a reasonable belief that a traveler's luggage contains narcotics, the governmental interest in seizing the luggage briefly to pursue further investigation is substantial. We agree. . . .

Respondent suggests that, absent some special law enforcement interest such as officer safety, a generalized interest in law enforcement cannot justify an intrusion on an individual's Fourth Amendment interests in the absence of probable cause. Our prior cases, however, do not support this proposition. In *Terry*, we described the governmental interests supporting the initial seizure of the person as "effective crime prevention and detection; it is this interest which underlies the recognition that a police officer may in appropriate circumstances and in an appropriate manner approach a person for purposes of investigating possible criminal behavior even though there is no probable cause to make an arrest.". . . Similarly, in *Michigan* v. *Summers* we identified three law enforcement interests that justified limited detention of the occupants of the premises during execution of a valid search warrant: "preventing flight in the event that incriminating evidence is found," "minimizing the risk of harm" both to the officers and the occupants, and "orderly completion of the search.". . . The test is whether those interests are sufficiently "substantial,". . . not whether they are independent of the interest in investigating crimes effectively and apprehending suspects. The context of a particular law enforcement practice, of course, may affect the determination whether a brief intrusion on Fourth Amendment interests on less than probable cause is essential to effective criminal investigation. Because of the inherently transient nature of drug courier activity at airports, allowing police to make brief investigative stops of persons at airports on reasonable suspicion of drug-trafficking substantially enhances the likelihood that police will be able to prevent the flow of narcotics into distribution channels.

Against this strong governmental interest, we must weight the nature and extent of the intrusion upon the individual's Fourth Amendment rights when the police briefly detain luggage for limited investigative purposes. On this point, respondent Place urges that the rationale for a *Terry* stop of the person is wholly inapplicable to investigative detentions of personality. Specifically, the *Terry* exception to the probable-cause requirement is premised on the notion that a *Terry*-type stop of the person is substantially less intrusive of a person's liberty interests than a formal arrest. In the property context, however, Place urges, there are no degrees of intrusion. Once the owner's property is seized, the dispossession is absolute.

We disagree. The intrusion on possessory interests occasioned by a seizure of one's personal effects can vary both in its nature and extent. The seizure may be made after the owner has relinquished control of the property to a third party or, as here, from the immediate custody and control of the owner. Moreover, the police may confine their investigation to an on-the-spot inquiry — for example, immediate exposure of the luggage to a trained narcotics detection dog — or transport the property to another location. Given the fact that seizures of property can vary in intrusiveness, some brief detentions of personal effects may be so minimally intrusive of Fourth Amendment interests that strong countervailing governmental interests will justify a seizure based only on specific articulable facts that the property contains contraband or evidence of a crime.

In sum, we conclude that when an officer's observations lead him reasonably to believe that a traveler is carrying luggage that contains narcotics, the principles of *Terry* and its progeny would permit the officer to detain the luggage briefly to investigate the circumstances that aroused his suspicion, provided that the investigative detention is properly limited in scope.

The purpose for which respondent's luggage was seized, of course, was to arrange its exposure to a narcotics detection dog. Obviously, if this investigative procedure is itself a search requiring probable cause, the initial seizure of respondent's luggage for the purpose of subjecting it to the sniff test — no matter how brief — could not be justified on less than probable cause. . . .

The Fourth Amendment "protects people from unreasonable government intrusions into their legitimate expectations of privacy." . . . We have affirmed that a person possesses a privacy interest in the contents of personal luggage that is protected by the Fourth Amendment. . . . A "canine sniff" by a well-trained narcotics detection dog, however, does not require opening the luggage. It does not expose non-contraband items that otherwise would remain hidden from public view, as does, for example, an officer's rummaging through the contents of the luggage. Thus, the manner in which information is obtained through this investigative technique is much less intrusive than a typical search. Moreover, the sniff discloses only the presence or absence of narcotics, a contraband item. Thus, despite the fact that the sniff tells the authorities something about the contents of the luggage, the information obtained is limited. This limited disclosure also ensures that the owner of the property is not subjected to the embarrassment and inconvenience entailed in less discriminate and more intrusive investigative methods.

In these respects, the canine sniff is *sui generis*. We are aware of no other investigative procedure that is so limited both in the manner in which the information is obtained and in the content of the information revealed by the procedure. Therefore, we conclude that the particular course of investigation that the agents intended to pursue here — exposure of respondent's luggage, which was located in a public place, to a trained canine — did not constitute a "search" within the meaning of the Fourth Amendment.

There is no doubt that the agents made a "seizure" of Place's luggage for purposes of the Fourth Amendment when, following his refusal to consent to a search, the agent told Place that he was going to take the luggage to a federal judge to secure issuance of a warrant. . . . We therefore examine whether the agents' conduct in this case was such as to place the seizure within the general rule requiring probable cause for a seizure or within *Terry's* exception to that rule.

At the outset, we must reject the Government's suggestion that the point at which probable cause for seizure of luggage from the person's presence becomes necessary is more distant than in the case of a *Terry* stop of the person himself. The premise of the Government's argument is that seizures of property are generally less intrusive than seizures of the person. While true in some circumstances, that premise is faulty on the facts we address in this case. The precise type of detention we confront here is seizure of personal luggage from the immediate possession of the suspect for the purpose of arranging exposure to a narcotics detection dog. Particularly in the case of detention of luggage within the traveler's immediate possession, the police conduct intrudes on both the suspect's possessory interest in his luggage as well as his liberty interest in proceeding with his itinerary. . . . Therefore, when the police seize luggage from the suspect's custody, we think the limitations applicable to investigative detentions of the person should define the permissible scope of an investigative detention of the person's luggage on less than probable cause. Under this standard, it is clear that the police conduct here exceeded the permissible limits of a *Terry*-type investigative stop.

The length of the detention of respondent's luggage alone precludes the conclusion that the seizure was reasonable in the absence of probable cause. Although we have recognized the reasonableness of seizures longer than the momentary ones involved in *Terry, Adams,* and *Brignoni-Ponce*, see *Michigan* v.

Summers, the brevity of the invasion of the individual's Fourth Amendment interests is an important factor in determining whether the seizure is so minimally intrusive as to be justifiable on reasonable suspicion. Moreover, in assessing the effect of the length of the detention, we take into account whether the police diligently pursue their investigation. We note that here the New York agents knew the time of Place's scheduled arrival at LaGuardia, had ample time to arrange for their additional investigation at that location, and thereby could have minimized the intrusion on respondent's Fourth Amendment interests. Thus, although we decline to adopt any outside time limitation for a permissible *Terry* stop, we have never approved a seizure of the person for the prolonged 90-minute period involved here and cannot do so on the facts presented by this case. . . .

Although the 90-minute detention of respondent's luggage is sufficient to render the seizure unreasonable, the violation was exacerbated by the failure of the agents to accurately inform respondent of the place to which they were transporting his luggage, of the length of time he might be dispossessed, and of what arrangements would be made for return of the luggage if the investigation dispelled the suspicion. In short, we hold that the detention of respondent's luggage in this case went beyond the narrow authority possessed by police to detain briefly luggage reasonably suspected to contain narcotics.

We conclude that, under all of the circumstances of this case, the seizure of respondent's luggage was unreasonable under the Fourth Amendment. Consequently, the evidence obtained from the subsequent search of his luggage was inadmissible, and Place's conviction must be reversed. The judgment of the Court of Appeals, accordingly, is affirmed.

It is so ordered.

JUSTICE BRENNAN, with whom JUSTICE MARSHALL joins, concurring in the result.

. . . .

I have had occasion twice in recent months to discuss the limited scope of the exception to the Fourth Amendment's probable cause requirement created by *Terry* and its progeny. . . . Unfortunately, the unwarranted expansion of that exception which the Court endorses today forces me to elaborate on my previously expressed views.

. . . .

It is clear that *Terry,* and the cases that followed it, permit only brief investigative stops and extremely limited searches based on reasonable suspicion. They do not provide the police with a commission to employ whatever investigative techniques they deem appropriate. . . . "[T]he scope of a *Terry*-type 'investigative' stop and any attendant search must be extremely limited or the *Terry* exception would 'swallow the general rule that Fourth Amendment seizures [and searches] are "reasonable" only if based on probable cause.'" . . .

. . . .

. . . *Terry* and the cases that followed it authorize a brief "investigative" stop of an individual based on reasonable suspicion and a limited search for weapons if the officer reasonably suspects that the individual is armed and presently dangerous. The purpose of this brief stop is "to determine [the individual's] identity or to maintain the status quo momentarily while obtaining more information. . . ." Anything more than a brief stop "must be based on consent or probable cause." . . . It is true that *Terry* stops may involve seizures of personal effects incidental to the seizure of the person involved. Obviously, an officer cannot seize a person without also seizing the personal effects that the individual has in his possession at the time. But there is a difference between incidental seizures of personal effects and seizures of property independent of the seizure of the person.

The Fourth Amendment protects "effects" as well as people from unreasonable searches and seizures. . . . "[T]he [Fourth] Amendment protects two different interests of the citizen — the interest in retaining possession of property and the interest in maintaining personal privacy." . . . "A seizure threatens the former, a search the latter." Even if an item is not searched, therefore, its seizure implicates a protected Fourth Amendment interest. For this reason, seizures of property must be based on probable cause. . . . Neither *Terry* nor its progeny changed this rule.

In this case, the officers' seizure of respondent and their later independent seizure of his luggage implicated separate Fourth Amendment interests. First, respondent had a protected interest in maintaining his personal security and privacy. *Terry* allows this interest to be overcome, and authorizes a limited intrusion, if the officers have reason to suspect that criminal activity is afoot. Second, respondent had a protected interest in retaining possession of his personal effects. While *Terry* may authorize seizures of personal effects incident to a lawful seizure of the person, nothing in the *Terry* line of cases authorizes the police to seize personal property, such as luggage, independent of the seizure of the person. Such seizures significantly expand the scope of a *Terry* stop and may not be effected on less than probable cause. Obviously, they also significantly expand the scope of the intrusion.

The officers did not develop probable cause to arrest respondent during their encounter with him. . . . Therefore, they had to let him go. But despite the absence of probable cause to arrest respondent, the officers seized his luggage and deprived him of possession. Respondent, therefore, was subjected not only to an invasion of his personal security and privacy, but also to an independent dispossession of his personal effects based simply on reasonable suspicion. It is difficult to understand how this intrusion is not more severe than a brief stop for questioning or even a limited, on-the-stop patdown search for weapons.

In my view, as soon as the officers seized respondent's luggage, independent of their seizure of him, they exceeded the scope of a permissible *Terry* stop and violated respondent's Fourth Amendment rights. In addition, the officers' seizure of respondent's luggage violated the established rule that seizures of personal effects must be based on probable cause. Their actions, therefore, should not be upheld.

The Court acknowledges that seizures of personal property must be based on probable cause. . . . Despite this recognition, the Court employs a balancing test drawn from *Terry* to conclude that personal effects may be seized based on reasonable suspicion. . . . [But] the *Terry* balancing test should not be wrenched from its factual and conceptual moorings.

There are important reasons why balancing inquiries should not be conducted except in the most limited circumstances. *Terry* and the cases that followed it established "isolated exceptions to the general rule that the Fourth Amendment itself has already performed the constitutional balance between police objectives and personal privacy." . . . "[T]he protections intended by the Framers could all too easily disappear in the consideration and balancing of the multifarious circumstances presented by different cases, especially when that balancing may be done in the first instance by police officers engaged in the 'often competitive enterprise of ferreting out crime.'" . . . The truth of this proposition is apparent when one considers that the Court today has employed a balancing test "to swallow the general rule that [seizures of property] are 'reasonable' only if based on probable cause." . . .

The Court also suggests today, in a discussion unnecessary to the judgment, that exposure of respondent's luggage to a narcotics detection dog "did not constitute a 'search' within the meaning of the Fourth Amendment." . . .

[But] the issue is more complex than the Court's discussion would lead one to believe. . . . [T]he use of electronic detection techniques that enhance human perception implicates "especially sensitive concerns." . . . Obviously, a narcotics detection dog is not an electronic detection device. Unlike the electronic "beeper" in *Knotts* [in which the Court upheld the use of a tracking beeper in a suspect's package], however, a dog does more than merely allow the police to do more efficiently what they could do using only their own senses. A dog adds a new and previously unobtainable dimension to human perception. The use of dogs, therefore, represents a greater intrusion into an individual's privacy. Such use implicates concerns that are at least as sensitive as those implicated by the use of certain electronic detection devices. . . .

I have expressed the view that dog sniffs of people constitute searches. See *Doe* v. *Renfrow* . . . (1981). In *Doe,* I suggested that sniffs of inanimate objects might present a different case. . . . In any event, I would leave the determination of whether dog sniffs of luggage amount to searches, and the subsidiary question of what standards should govern such intrusions, to a future case providing an appropriate, and more informed, basis for deciding these questions.

Justice Douglas was the only dissenter in *Terry.* He stated that "[t]here have been powerful hydraulic pressures throughout our history that bear heavily on the Court to water down constitutional guarantees and give the police the upper hand." . . . Today, the Court uses *Terry* as a justification for submitting to these pressures. Their strength is apparent, for even when the Court finds that an individual's Fourth Amendment rights have been violated it cannot resist the temptation to weaken the protections the Amendment affords.

JUSTICE BLACKMUN, with whom JUSTICE MARSHALL joins, concurring in the judgment.

Because I agree with the Court that there is a significant law enforcement interest in interdicting illegal drug traffic in the Nation's airports . . . a limited intrusion caused by a temporary seizure of luggage for investigative purposes could fall within the *Terry* exception. The critical threshold issue is the intrusiveness of the seizure. In this case, the seizure went well beyond a minimal intrusion and therefore cannot fall within the *Terry* exception.

The Court's resolution of the status of dog sniffs under the Fourth Amendment is troubling for a different reason. The District Court expressly observed that Place "does not contest the validity of sniff searches *per se.*" . . . While Place may have pos-

of the inquiry. But even if I believed that a "balancing test" appropriately replaces the judgment of the Framers of the Fourth Amendment, I would nonetheless object to the cursory short-sighted "test" that the Court employs to justify its predictable weakening of Fourth Amendment protections. In particular, the test employed by the Court vastly overstates the social costs that a probable-cause standard entails and, though it plausibly articulates the serious privacy interests at stake, inexplicably fails to accord them adequate weight in striking the balance.

The Court begins to articulate its "balancing test" by observing that "the government's need for effective methods to deal with breaches of public order" is to be weighed on one side of the balance. . . . Of course, this is not correct. It is not the government's need for effective enforcement methods that should weigh in the balance, for ordinary Fourth Amendment standards — including probable cause — may well permit methods for maintaining the public order that are perfectly effective. If that were the case, the governmental interest in having effective standards would carry no weight at all as a justification for *departing* from the probable-cause standard. Rather, it is the costs of applying probable cause as opposed to applying some lesser standard that should be weighed on the government's side.

In order to tote up the costs of applying the probable-cause standard, it is thus necessary first to take into account the nature and content of that standard, and the likelihood that it would hamper achievement of the goal — vital not just to "teachers and administrators," . . . of maintaining an effective educational setting in the public schools. . . .

. . . .

A legitimate balancing test whose function was something more substantial than reaching a predetermined conclusion acceptable to this Court's impressions of what authority teachers need would therefore reach rather a different result than that reached by the Court today. On one side of the balance would be the costs of applying traditional Fourth Amendment standards — the "practical" and "flexible" probable-cause standard where a full-scale intrusion is sought, a lesser standard in situations where the intrusion is much less severe and the need for greater authority compelling. Whatever costs were toted up on this side would have to be discounted by the costs of applying an unprecedented and ill-defined "reasonableness under all the circumstances" test that will leave teachers and administrators uncertain as to their authority and will encourage excessive fact-based litigation.

On the other side of the balance would be the serious privacy interests of the student, interests that the Court admirably articulates in its opinion . . . but which the Court's new ambiguous standard places in serious jeopardy. I have no doubt that a fair assessment of the two sides of the balance would necessarily reach the same conclusion that, as I have argued above, the Fourth Amendment's language compels — that school searches like that conducted in this case are valid only if supported by probable cause.

. . . .

In the past several Terms, the Court has produced a succession of Fourth Amendment opinions in which "balancing tests" have been applied to resolve various questions concerning the proper scope of official searches. The Court has begun to apply a "balancing test" to determine whether a particular category of searches intrudes upon expectations of privacy that merit Fourth Amendment protection. . . . It applies a "balancing test" to determine whether a warrant is necessary to conduct a search. . . . In today's opinion, it employs a "balancing test" to determine what standard should govern the constitutionality of a given category of searches. . . . Should a search turn out to be unreasonable after application of all of these "balancing tests" the Court then applies an additional "balancing test" to decide whether the evidence resulting from the search must be excluded. . . .

All of these "balancing tests" amount to brief nods by the Court in the direction of a neutral utilitarian calculus while the Court in fact engages in an unanalyzed exercise of judicial will. Perhaps this doctrinally destructive nihilism is merely a convenient umbrella under which a majority that cannot agree on a genuine rationale can conceal its differences. . . . And it may be that the real force underlying today's decision is the belief that the Court purports to reject — the belief that the unique role served by the schools justifies an exception to the Fourth Amendment on their behalf. If so, the methodology of today's decision may turn out to have as little influence in future cases as will its result, and the Court's departure from traditional Fourth Amendment doctrine will be confined to the schools.

On my view, the presence of the word "unreasonable" in the text of the Fourth Amendment does not grant a shifting majority of this Court the authority to answer *all* Fourth Amendment questions by consulting its momentary vision of the social good. Full-scale searches unaccompanied by probable cause violate the Fourth Amendment. I do not pretend that our traditional Fourth Amendment doctrine automatically answers all of the different legal questions that occasionally arise. I do contend, however, that this Court has an obligation to provide some coherent framework to resolve such questions on the basis of more than a conclusory recitation of the results of a "balancing test." The Fourth Amendment itself supplies that framework and, because the Court today fails to heed its message, I must respectfully dissent.

[JUSTICE STEVENS, with whom JUSTICE MARSHALL joins, and with whom JUSTICE BRENNAN joined in part, wrote an opinion concurring in part and dissenting in part.]

Wyman v. James

400 U.S. 309 (1971)
Vote: 6–3

Among the most publicized of welfare abusers are AFDC mothers who falsely claim that their children have no father living with them and claim more dependents than they in fact have. Welfare officials have long tried to root out such abuses. At one time many agencies conducted unannounced "midnight raids" on the homes of welfare recipients to verify the absence of a father and to confirm the number of eligible children. While such practices were generally regarded as abusive and have been stopped, officials continue to seek other, more acceptable methods for detecting cheaters. One alternative was provided for in New York State and New York City statutes and regulations. New York law required caseworkers to make periodic home visits to ensure that welfare funds were being spent properly. They also required that these visits be made during the day and that advance notice be given. Benefits could be terminated if welfare recipients did not open their homes for periodic visits.

In this case, a class action suit that affected thousands of similarly situated women, an AFDC mother, Ms. James, refused to allow a caseworker to enter her home as required by state and city regulations, although she did offer to meet with him at another mutually convenient site

and to provide information relevant to his inquiry. Ms. James' refusal to allow the home visit eventually resulted in an agency ruling to terminate her AFDC benefits. Ms. James then sued the Commissioner of the New York Department of Social Services, seeking an order to enjoin termination of her benefits. A federal district court ruled in her favor, and Wyman, then Commissioner of the New York Department of Social Services, appealed to the United States Supreme Court.

MR. JUSTICE BLACKMUN delivered the opinion of the Court.

When a case involves a home and some type of official intrusion into that home, as this case appears to do, an immediate and natural reaction is one of concern about Fourth Amendment rights and the protection which that Amendment is intended to afford. Its emphasis indeed is upon one of the most precious aspects of personal security in the home: "The right of the people to be secure in their persons, houses, papers, and effects. . . ." This Court has characterized that right as "basic to a free society.". . . And over the years the Court consistently has been most protective of the privacy of the dwelling. . . .

This natural and quite proper protective attitude, however, is not a factor in this case, for the seemingly obvious and simple reason that we are not concerned here with any search by the New York social service agency in the Fourth Amendment meaning of that term. It is true that the governing statute and regulations appear to make mandatory the initial home visit and the subsequent periodic "contacts" (which may include home visits) for the inception and continuance of aid. It is also true that the caseworker's posture in the home visit is perhaps, in a sense, both rehabilitative and investigative. But this latter aspect, we think, is given too broad a character and far more emphasis than it deserves if it is equated with a search in the traditional criminal law context. We note, too, that the visitation in itself is not forced or compelled, and that the beneficiary's denial of permission is not a criminal act. If consent to the visitation is withheld, no visitation takes place. The aid then never begins or merely ceases, as the case may be. There is no entry of the home and there is no search.

If, however, we were to assume that a caseworker's home visit, before or subsequent to the beneficiary's initial qualification for benefits, somehow (perhaps because the average beneficiary might feel she is in no position to refuse consent to the visit), and despite its interview nature, does possess some of the characteristics of a search in the traditional sense, we nevertheless conclude that the visit does not fall within the Fourth Amendment's proscription. This is because it does not descend to the level of unreasonableness. . . .

There are a number of factors that compel us to conclude that the home visit proposed for Mrs. James is not unreasonable:

1. The public's interest in this particular segment of the area of assistance to the unfortunate is protection and aid for the dependent child whose family requires such aid for that child. The focus is on the *child* and, further, it is on the child who is *dependent*. There is no more worthy object of the public's concern. The dependent child's needs are paramount, and only with hesitancy would we relegate those needs, in the scale of comparative values, to a position secondary to what the mother claims as her rights.

2. The agency, with tax funds provided from federal as well as from state sources, is fulfilling a public trust. The State, working through its qualified welfare agency, has appropriate and paramount interest and concern in seeing and assuring that the intended and proper objects of that tax-produced assistance are the ones who benefit from the aid it dispenses. Surely it is not unreasonable, in the Fourth Amendment sense or in any other sense of that term, that the State have at its command a gentle means, of limited extent and of practical and considerate application, of achieving that assurance.

3. One who dispenses purely private charity naturally has an interest in and expects to know how his charitable funds are utilized and put to work. The public, when it is the provider, rightly expects the same. It might well expect more, because of the trust aspect of public funds, and the recipient, as well as the caseworker, has not only an interest but an obligation.

4. The emphasis of the New York statutes and regulations is upon the home, upon "close contact" with the beneficiary, upon restoring the aid recipient "to a condition of self-support," and upon the relief of his distress. . . .

5. The home visit, it is true, is not required by federal statute or regulation. But it has been noted that the visit is "the heart of welfare administration"; that it affords "a personal, rehabilitative orientation, unlike that of most federal programs"; and that the "more pronounced service orientation" effected by Congress with the 1956 amendments to the Social Security Act "gave redoubled importance to the practice of home visiting." . . .

6. The means employed by the New York agency are significant. Mrs. James received written notice several days in advance of the intended home visit. The date was specified. . . . Privacy is emphasized. The applicant-recipient is made the primary source of information as to eligibility. Outside informational sources, other than public records, are to be consulted only with the beneficiary's consent. Forcible entry or entry under false pretenses or visitation outside working hours or snooping in the home are forbidden. . . .

7. Mrs. James, in fact, on this record presents no specific complaint of any unreasonable intrusion of her home and nothing that supports an inference that the desired home visit had as its purpose the obtaining of information as to criminal activity. She complains of no proposed visitation at an awkward or retirement hour. She suggests no forcible entry. She refers to no snooping. She describes no impolite or reprehensible conduct of any kind. She alleges only, in general and nonspecific terms, that on previous visits and, on information and belief, on visitation at the home of other aid recipients, "questions concerning personal relationships, beliefs and behavior are raised and pressed which are unnecessary for a determination of continuing eligibility." Paradoxically, this same complaint could be made of a conference held elsewhere than in the home, and yet this is what is sought by Mrs. James. The same complaint could be made of the census taker's questions. . . . What Mrs. James appears to want from the agency that provides her and her infant son with the necessities for life is the right to receive those necessities upon her own informational terms, to utilize the Fourth Amendment as a wedge for imposing those terms, and to avoid questions of any kind.

8. We are not persuaded, as Mrs. James would have us be, that all information pertinent to the issue of eligibility can be obtained by the agency through an interview at a place other than the home, or, as the District Court majority suggested, by examining a lease or a birth certificate, or by periodic medical examinations, or by interviews with school personnel. . . .

9. The visit is not one by police or uniformed authority. It is made by a caseworker of some training whose primary objective is, or should be, the welfare, not the prosecution, of the aid recipient for whom the worker has profound responsibility. As

has already been stressed, the program concerns dependent children and the needy families of those children. It does not deal with crime or with the actual or suspected perpetrators of crime. The caseworker is not a sleuth but rather, we trust, is a friend to one in need.

10. The home visit is not a criminal investigation, does not equate with a criminal investigation, and despite the announced fears of Mrs. James and those who would join her, is not in aid of any criminal proceeding. If the visitation serves to discourage misrepresentation or fraud, such a byproduct of that visit does not impress upon the visit itself a dominant criminal investigative aspect. And if the visit should, by chance, lead to the discovery of fraud and a criminal prosecution should follow, then, even assuming that the evidence discovered upon the home visitation is admissible, an issue upon which we express no opinion, that is a routine and expected fact of life and a consequence no greater than that which necessarily ensues upon any other discovery by a citizen of criminal conduct.

11. The warrant procedure, which the plaintiff appears to claim to be so precious to her, even if civil in nature, is not without its seriously objectionable features in the welfare context. If a warrant could be obtained (the plaintiff affords us little help as to how it would be obtained), it presumably could be applied for *ex parte*, its execution would require no notice, it would justify entry by force, and its hours for execution would not be so limited as those prescribed for home visitation. The warrant necessarily would imply conduct either criminal or out of compliance with an asserted governing standard. Of course, the force behind the warrant argument, welcome to the one asserting it, is the fact that it would have to rest upon probable cause, and probable cause in the welfare context, as Mrs. James concedes, requires more than the mere need of the caseworker to see the child in the home and to have assurance that the child is there and is receiving the benefit of the aid that has been authorized for it. In this setting the warrant argument is out of place.

It seems to us that the situation is akin to that where an Internal Revenue Service agent, in making a routine civil audit of a taxpayer's income tax return, asks that the taxpayer produce for the agent's review some proof of a deduction the taxpayer has asserted to his benefit in the computation of his tax. If the taxpayer refuses, there is, absent fraud, only a disallowance of the claimed deduction and a consequent additional tax. The taxpayer is fully within his "rights" in refusing to produce the proof, but in maintaining and asserting those rights a tax detri-

ment results and it is a detriment of the taxpayer's own making. So here Mrs. James has the "right" to refuse the home visit, but a consequence in the form of cessation of aid, similar to the taxpayer's resultant additional tax, flows from that refusal. The choice is entirely hers, and nothing of constitutional magnitude is involved.

Camara v. *Municipal Court*... (1967), and its companion case, *See* v. *City of Seattle*... (1967), both by a divided Court, are not inconsistent with our result here. Those cases concerned, respectively, a refusal of entry to city housing inspectors checking for a violation of a building's occupancy permit, and a refusal of entry to a fire department representative interested in compliance with a city's fire code. In each case a majority of this Court held that the Fourth Amendment barred prosecution for refusal to permit the desired warrantless inspection. *Frank* v. *Maryland*... (1959), a case that reached an opposing result and that concerned a request by a health officer for entry in order to check the source of a rat infestation, was *pro tanto* overruled. Both *Frank* and *Camara* involved dwelling quarters. *See* had to do with a commercial warehouse.

But the facts of the three cases are significantly different from those before us. . . . The community welfare aspects, of course, were highly important, but each case arose in a criminal context where a genuine search was denied and prosecution followed.

In contrast, Mrs. James is not being prosecuted for her refusal to permit the home visit and is not about to be so prosecuted. Her wishes in that respect are fully honored. We have not been told, and have not found, that her refusal is made a criminal act by any applicable New York or federal statute. The only consequence of her refusal is that the payment of benefits ceases. Important and serious as this is, the situation is no different than if she had exercised a similar negative choice initially and refrained from applying for AFDC benefits. If a statute made her refusal a criminal offense, and if this case were one concerning her prosecution under that statute, *Camara* and *See* would have conceivable pertinency.

Our holding today does not mean, of course, that a termination of benefits upon refusal of a home visit is to be upheld against constitutional challenge under all conceivable circumstances. The early morning mass raid upon homes of welfare recipients is not unknown. . . . But that is not this case. Facts of that kind present another case for another day.

We therefore conclude that the home visitation as structured by the New York statutes and regulations is a reasonable administrative tool; that it serves a valid and proper administrative purpose for the dispensation of the AFDC program; that it is not an unwarranted invasion of personal privacy; and that it violates no right guaranteed by the Fourth Amendment.

Reversed and remanded with directions to enter a judgment of dismissal.

MR. JUSTICE WHITE concurred in the judgment . . . of the Court. . . .

MR. JUSTICE DOUGLAS, dissenting.

We are living in a society where one of the most important forms of property is government largesse which some call the "new property." The payrolls of government are but one aspect of that "new property." Defense contracts, highway contracts, and the other multifarious forms of contracts are another part. So are subsidies to air, rail, and other carriers. So are disbursements by government for scientific research. So are TV and radio licenses to use the air space which of course is part of the public domain. Our concern here is not with those subsidies but with grants that directly or indirectly implicate the *home life* of the recipients.

In 1969 roughly 127 billion dollars were spent by the federal, state, and local governments on "social welfare." To farmers alone almost four billion dollars were paid, in part for not growing certain crops. Almost 129,000 farmers received $5,000 or more, their total benefits exceeding $1,450,000,000. Those payments were in some instances very large, a few running a million or more a year. But the majority were payments under $5,000 each.

Yet almost every beneficiary whether rich or poor, rural or urban, has a "house" — one of the places protected by the Fourth Amendment against "unreasonable searches and seizures." The question in this case is whether receipt of largesse from the government makes the *home* of the beneficiary subject to access by an inspector of the agency of oversight, even though the beneficiary objects to the intrusion and even though the Fourth Amendment's procedure for access to one's *house* or *home* is not followed. The penalty here is not, of course, invasion of the privacy of Barbara James, only her loss of federal or state largesse. That, however, is merely rephrasing the problem. Whatever the semantics, the central question is whether the government by force of its largesse has the power to "buy up" rights guaranteed by the Constitution. But for the assertion of her constitutional right, Barbara James in this case would have received the welfare benefit.

. . . If the regime under which Barbara James lives were enterprise capitalism as, for example, if she ran a small factory geared into the Pentagon's procurement program, she certainly would have a right to deny inspectors access to her *home* unless they came with a warrant.

If the welfare recipient was not Barbara James but a prominent, affluent cotton or wheat farmer receiving benefit payments for not growing crops, would not the approach be different? Welfare in aid of dependent children, like social security and unemployment benefits, has an aura of suspicion. There doubtless are frauds in every sector of public welfare whether the recipient be a Barbara James or someone who is prominent or influential. But constitutional rights — here the privacy of the *home* — are obviously not dependent on the poverty or on the affluence of the beneficiary. It is the precincts of the *home* that the Fourth Amendment protects; and their privacy is as important to the lowly as to the mighty.

It may be that in some tenements one baby will do service to several women and call each one "mom." It may be that other frauds, less obvious, will be perpetrated. But if inspectors want to enter the precincts of the home against the wishes of the lady of the house, they must get a warrant. The need for exigent action as in cases of "hot pursuit" is not present, for the lady will not disappear; nor will the baby.

I would place the same restrictions on inspectors entering the *homes* of welfare beneficiaries as are on inspectors entering the *homes* of those on the payroll of government, or the *homes* of those who contract with the government, or the *homes* of those who work for those having government contracts. The values of the *home* protected by the Fourth Amendment are not peculiar to capitalism as we have known it; they are equally relevant to the new form of socialism which we are entering. Moreover, as the numbers of functionaries and inspectors multiply, the need for protection of the individual becomes indeed more essential if the values of a free society are to remain.

MR. JUSTICE MARSHALL, whom MR. JUSTICE BRENNAN joins, dissenting.

Simply stated, the issue in this case is whether a state welfare agency can require all recipients of AFDC benefits to submit to warrantless "visitations" of their homes. In answering that question, the majority dodges between constitutional issues to reach a result clearly inconsistent with the decisions of this Court. We are told that there is no search involved in this case; that even if there were a search, it would not be unreasonable; and that even if this were an unreasonable search, a welfare recipient waives her right to object by accepting benefits. I emphatically disagree with all three conclusions....

The Court's assertion that this case concerns no search "in the Fourth Amendment meaning of that term" is neither "obvious" nor "simple." I should have thought that the Fourth Amendment governs all intrusions by agents of the public upon personal security.... In an era of rapidly burgeoning governmental activities and their concomitant inspectors, caseworkers, and researchers, a restriction of the Fourth Amendment to "the traditional criminal law context" tramples the ancient concept that a man's home is his castle....

Even if the Fourth Amendment does not apply to each and every governmental entry into the home, the welfare visit is not some sort of purely benevolent inspection. No one questions the motives of the dedicated welfare caseworker. Of course, caseworkers seek to be friends but the point is that they are also required to be sleuths. The majority concedes that the "visitation" is partially investigative, but claims that this investigative aspect has been given too much emphasis. Emphasis has indeed been given. Time and again, in briefs and at oral argument, appellants emphasized the need to enter AFDC homes to guard against welfare fraud and child abuse, both of which are felonies....

Conceding for the sake of argument that someone might view the "visitation" as a search, the majority nonetheless concludes that such a search is not unreasonable. However, its mode of reaching that conclusion departs from the entire history of Fourth Amendment case law. Of course, the Fourth Amendment test is reasonableness, but in determining whether a search is reasonable, this Court is not free merely to balance, in a totally ad hoc fashion, any number of subjective factors. An unbroken line of cases holds that, subject to a few narrowly drawn exceptions, any search without a warrant is constitutionally unreasonable.... In this case, no suggestion that evidence will disappear, that a criminal will escape, or that an officer will be injured, justifies the failure to obtain a warrant. Instead, the majority asserts what amounts to three state interests that allegedly render this search reasonable. None of these interests is sufficient to carve out a new exception to the warrant requirement.

First, it is argued that the home visit is justified to protect dependent children from "abuse" and "exploitation." These are heinous crimes, but they are not confined to indigent households. Would the ma-

jority sanction, in the absence of probable cause, compulsory visits to all American homes for the purpose of discovering child abuse? Or is this Court prepared to hold as a matter of constitutional law that a mother, merely because she is poor, is substantially more likely to injure or exploit her children? Such a categorical approach to an entire class of citizens would be dangerously at odds with the tenets of our democracy.

Second, the Court contends that caseworkers must enter the homes of AFDC beneficiaries to determine eligibility. Interestingly, federal regulations do not require the home visit. In fact, the regulations specify the recipient himself as the primary source of eligibility information thereby rendering an inspection of the home only one of several alternative secondary sources. The majority's implication that a biannual home visit somehow assures the verification of actual residence or actual physical presence in the home strains credulity in the context of urban poverty. Despite the caseworker's responsibility for dependent children, he is not even required to see the children as a part of the home visit....

We are told that the plight of Mrs. James is no different from that of a taxpayer who is required to document his right to a tax deduction, but this analogy is seriously flawed. The record shows that Mrs. James has offered to be interviewed anywhere other than her home, to answer any questions, and to provide any documentation that the welfare agency desires. The agency curtly refused all these offers and insisted on its "right" to pry into appellee's home. Tax exemptions are also governmental "bounty." A true analogy would be an Internal Revenue Service requirement that in order to claim a dependency exemption, a taxpayer *must* allow a specially trained IRS agent to invade the home for the purpose of questioning the occupants and looking for evidence that the exemption is being properly utilized for the benefit of the dependent. If such a system were even proposed, the cries of constitutional outrage would be unanimous.

Appellants offer a third state interest that the Court seems to accept as partial justification for this search. We are told that the visit is designed to rehabilitate, to provide aid. This is strange doctrine indeed. A paternalistic notion that a complaining citizen's constitutional rights can be violated so long as the State is somehow helping him is alien to our Nation's philosophy. More than 40 years ago, Mr. Justice Brandeis warned:

> Experience should teach us to be most on our guard to protect liberty when the

Government's purposes are beneficient. *Olmstead* v. *United States* . . . (1928) (dissenting opinion).

Although the Court does not agree with my conclusion that the home visit is an unreasonable search, its opinion suggests that even if the visit were unreasonable, appellee has somehow waived her right to object. Surely the majority cannot believe that valid Fourth Amendment consent can be given under the threat of the loss of one's sole means of support. Nor has Mrs. James waived her rights. Had the Court squarely faced the question of whether the State can condition welfare payments on the waiver of clear constitutional rights, the answer would be plain. The decisions of this Court do not support the notion that a State can use welfare benefits as a wedge to coerce "waiver" of Fourth Amendment rights. . . .

The Right to Counsel

The prevailing English doctrine regarding right to counsel at the time of the American revolution prohibited counsel in felony cases but permitted them in misdemeanors. This position, which was not abandoned until 1836 in England, held that counsel was not necessary in felony cases because the court itself would take care to see that defendants' rights were protected. In contrast, counsel was deemed more important in lesser cases, which presumably might be tried by lay judges. The right to counsel provision was inserted into the Sixth Amendment in direct response to this English limitation, a provision that also has been adopted by all the states, either as constitutional guarantees or through statute.

However, throughout most of our history, this constitutional right to counsel has meant only that those accused of crimes had the right, if they so chose and could afford it, to have assistance of counsel at trial. As early as 1790, Congress provided for the appointment of counsel at public expense for those unable to afford one in cases involving capital crimes, and several of the states made similar provisions. It was not until the end of the nineteenth century, though, that the Supreme Court was asked to consider whether the Sixth Amendment required appointment of counsel where the accused could not afford one. And it was not until 1928, in response to the infamous trial of the "Scottsboro boys," that the Court began to consider the claim of a right to *appointed*

counsel in *state* courts. Thus like so many other provisions of the Bill of Rights, the formative cases charting the meaning of right to counsel are commingled with the issues of extending the protections of the Bill of Rights to the states by means of the Due Process Clause of the Fourteenth Amendment.

The decisive Supreme Court ruling in this formative period was *Powell* v. *Alabama,* 287 U.S. 45 (1932), which overturned the conviction of four indigent black teenage boys in Alabama who had been tried, convicted, and sentenced to death for raping a white woman, under conditions that the Court found to be a travesty of justice. While the Court held that the entire proceedings violated due process, it emphasized the lack of counsel in a capital case. This ruling, in effect, created a right to appointed counsel for indigents in exceptional circumstances, although the ruling rested upon the Court's interpretation of the Due Process Clause in the Fourteenth Amendment rather than the Sixth Amendment's right to counsel provision.

After *Powell,* the task facing the Court was to determine precisely what factors constituted exceptional circumstances. The difficulty of this task is illustrated in the 1942 decision *Betts* v. *Brady,* 316 U.S. 455 (1942), which is discussed at some length in the landmark right to counsel case, GIDEON V. WAINWRIGHT, 372 U.S. 335 (1963). During this same period, the Court began interpreting the Sixth Amendment's right to counsel provision as it applied to federal courts. The Court's broad interpretations of this provision created what the dissenters in *Brady* saw as an unconscionable double standard — greater constitutional protections afforded defendants in federal courts than were granted to defendants in state courts.

This tension was finally resolved in 1963, when, in GIDEON V. WAINWRIGHT, the Court extended the right to appointed counsel in state courts in all *felony* cases for those unable to afford one, in effect incorporating the Sixth Amendment into the Fourteenth and creating one standard for federal and state courts alike. Twelve years later, in *Argersinger* v. *Hamlin,* 407 U.S. 25 (1972), the Court extended the right to counsel provision to cover all misdemeanor cases that might result in incarceration. Utmost in the minds of Chief Justice Burger, and Justices Powell and Rehnquist, who concurred in the *Argersinger* judgment but not with the Court's reasoning, was the cost of extending an automatic right to counsel to defendants in vast numbers of lesser cases. They also expressed the fear that the majority's logic would eventually extend the right to counsel to all petty offenses, even those involving small fines. This fear was later quelled when the Court drew the line and refused to extend the right to counsel to a defendant in a case involving a charge of theft where the defendant was convicted and fined $50.00 (SCOTT V. ILLINOIS, 440 U.S. 367, 1979). It should be noted that in this case, Scott was charged with an offense that carried the maximum penalty of a $500 fine, one year in jail, or both. One might reasonably ask how one would know that this case was "petty" in advance of the outcome.

But even as some issues are resolved, others emerge. The logic of the importance of counsel has led some judges in cases involving serious charges to appoint counsel over defendants' strenuous objections and insistence that they wanted to represent themselves. Thus the inevitable question: Is there a right *not* to have counsel? The Court answered this question in the affirmative in FARETTA V. CALIFORNIA, 422 U.S. 840 (1975), but not without vigorous dissent.

Other issues remain: At what stages in the lengthy criminal process is counsel available —

early at the pretrial process? Late at appeal? Is access to appointed counsel at these stages to be as readily available as it is those with private counsel? In the pretrial process, involving a suspect in police custody, the Sixth Amendment right to counsel merges with the Fifth Amendment right against self-incrimination. This is one of the central issues in MIRANDA V. ARIZONA, 384 U.S. 436 (1966), where the Court ruled that the arresting officer must affirmatively warn the suspect of his rights to remain silent and to counsel. Regarding other issues, the Court has not differentiated in any significant way between those with publicly appointed as opposed to privately retained counsel, but in a series of cases beginning with *Escobedo* v. *Illinois,* 378 U.S. 478 (1964), the Court has held that counsel must be made available once a suspect is taken into custody. In MIRANDA V. ARIZONA, 348 U.S. 436 (1966), the Court went still further and required the police at arrest to advise suspects of their right to silence and right of counsel to be present at interrogation. One year later, in *United States* v. *Wade,* 388 U.S. 218 (1967), the Court overturned the conviction of a man who was exhibited to witnesses before trial at a postindictment lineup conducted for identification purposes without notice to and in the absence of his appointed counsel. Still, based on extralegal practicalities, you might ask yourself whether access in these early stages is or can be equalized. Well-to-do suspects may have a personal attorney whom they can call at arrest. Public defenders are not routinely made available until the first appearance in court, often after one to three days in custody.

In the 1970s the Court drew the line for right to counsel at the early stages of the victim identification process. In *Kirby* v. *Illinois,* 406 U.S. 682 (1972), the Court upheld an identification derived from a "show up" where the suspect was confronted by the victim in the police station without his lawyer present or having been informed of his right to have counsel present. A year later, in *United States* v. *Ash,* 413 U.S. 300 (1973), the Court held that presence of counsel at photo lineups (where police present the victim or witness with a number of photographs, including one of the suspect) was not required by the Sixth Amendment.

At the other end of the process — appeal — the Court has set limits on the amount of resources that constitutionally must be made available for poor people. In *Ross* v. *Moffitt*, 417 U.S. 600 (1974), the Court reaffirmed a 1963 ruling, *Douglas* v. *California*, 372 U.S. 353, that required an indigent's right to appointed counsel for first appeal, but went on to hold that there was no constitutional right to appointed counsel in a second appeal from an intermediate to a higher appellate court.

With the universal right to counsel in serious criminal cases and the dramatic expansion of public defender organizations, it is not surprising that another type of right to counsel issue would emerge: the right to *effective assistance* of counsel. Criminal courts, and particularly the lower courts, are organized to process large volumes of cases quickly and routinely, belying the myth of quiet deliberation and careful preparation that is supposed to attend criminal proceedings. Increasingly, the issue of effective assistance of counsel is being raised by bar associations, law school professors, and courts, and we can expect this to be one of the primary right to counsel issues of the future.

An indication of these developments is seen in two cases handed down at the end of the 1983 term. In *United States* v. *Cronic*, 466 U.S. 648 (1984), the Court held that external conditions of representation such as inexperience and amount of time allowed for preparation were insufficient to establish constitutionally defective assistance of counsel. Defendants contesting the effectiveness of their counsel's assistance, the Court held, must demonstrate specific defects in their attorney's actual performance. In a companion case, *Strickland* v. *Washington*, 466 U.S. 668 (1984), the Court elaborated on this standard:

> The defendant must show that there is a reasonable probability that, but for counsel's unprofessional errors, the result of the proceeding would have been different. A reasonable probability is a probability sufficient to undermine confidence in the outcome.

Despite this relatively stringent standard, we can expect more cases in this area of right to counsel law.

Cases

Gideon v. Wainwright

> 372 U.S. 335 (1963)
> Vote: 9–0

The facts of the case are contained in the Court's opinion.

MR. JUSTICE BLACK delivered the opinion of the Court.

Petitioner was charged in a Florida state court with having broken and entered a poolroom with intent to commit a misdemeanor. This offense is a felony under Florida law. Appearing in court without funds and without a lawyer, petitioner asked the court to appoint counsel for him, whereupon the following colloquy took place:

The Court: Mr. Gideon, I am sorry, but I cannot appoint Counsel to represent you in this case. Under the laws of the State of Florida, the only time the Court can appoint Counsel to represent a Defendant is when that person is charged with a capital offense. I am sorry, but I will have to deny your request to appoint Counsel to defend you in this case.

The Defendant: The United State Supreme Court says I am entitled to be represented by Counsel.

Put to trial before a jury, Gideon conducted his defense about as well as could be expected from a layman. He made an opening statement to the jury, cross-examined the State's witnesses, presented witnesses in his own defense, declined to testify himself, and made a short argument "emphasizing his innocence to the charge contained in the Information filed in this case." The jury returned a verdict of guilty, and petitioner was sentenced to serve five years in the state prison. . . . Since 1942, when *Betts v. Brady* was decided by a divided Court, the problem of a defendant's federal constitutional right to counsel in a state court has been a continuing source of controversy and litigation in both state and federal courts. To give this problem another review here, we granted certiorari. . . . Since Gideon was proceeding *in forma pauperis*, we appointed counsel to represent him and requested both sides to discuss in their briefs and oral arguments the following: "Should this Court's holding in *Betts* v. *Brady*, . . . [1942], be reconsidered?"

I

The facts upon which Betts claimed that he had been unconstitutionally denied the right to have counsel appointed to assist him are strikingly like the facts upon which Gideon here bases his federal constitutional claim. . . . Treating due process as "a concept less rigid and more fluid than those envisaged in other specific and particular provisions of the Bill of Rights," the Court held that refusal to appoint counsel under the particular facts and circumstances in the *Betts* case was not so "offensive to the common and fundamental ideas of fairness" as to amount to a denial of due process. Since the facts and circumstances of the two cases are so nearly indistinguishable, we think the *Betts* v. *Brady* holding if left standing would require us to reject Gideon's claim that the Constitution guarantees him the assistance of counsel. Upon full reconsideration we conclude that *Betts* v. *Brady* should be overruled.

II

The Sixth Amendment provides, "In all criminal prosecutions, the accused shall enjoy the right . . . to have the Assistance of Counsel for his defence." We have construed this to mean that in federal courts counsel must be provided for defendants unable to employ counsel unless the right is competently and intelligently waived. Betts argued that this right is extended to indigent defendants in state courts by the Fourteenth Amendment. In response the Court stated that, while the Sixth Amendment laid down "no rule for the conduct of the States, the question recurs whether the constraint laid by the Amendment upon the national courts expresses a rule so fundamental and essential to a fair trial, and so, to due process of law, that it is made obligatory upon the States by the Fourteenth Amendment." . . . On

the basis of this historical data the Court concluded that "appointment of counsel is not a fundamental right, essential to a fair trial." . . . It was for this reason the *Betts* Court refused to accept the contention that the Sixth Amendment's guarantee of counsel for indigent federal defendants was extended to or, in the words of that Court, "made obligatory upon the States by the Fourteenth Amendment." . . .

We think the Court in *Betts* had ample precedent for acknowledging that those guarantees of the Bill of Rights which are fundamental safeguards of liberty immune from federal abridgment are equally protected against state invasion by the Due Process Clause of the Fourteenth Amendment. This same principle was recognized, explained, and applied in *Powell* v. *Alabama* . . . (1932), a case upholding the right of counsel, where the Court held that despite sweeping language to the contrary in *Hurtado* v. *California* . . . (1884), the Fourteenth Amendment "embraced" those "fundamental principles of liberty and justice which lie at the base of all our civil and political institutions," even though they had been "specifically dealt with in another part of the federal Constitution." . . .

We accept *Betts* v. *Brady*'s assumption, based as it was on our prior cases, that a provision of the Bill of Rights which is "fundamental and essential to a fair trial" is made obligatory upon the States by the Fourteenth Amendment. We think the Court in *Betts* was wrong, however, in concluding that the Sixth Amendment's guarantee of counsel is not one of these fundamental rights. Ten years before *Betts* v. *Brady*, this Court, after full consideration of all the historical data examined in *Betts*, had unequivocally declared that "the right to the aid of counsel is of this fundamental character." . . . While the Court at the close of its *Powell* opinion did by its language, as this Court frequently does, limit its holding to the particular facts and circumstances of that case, its conclusions about the fundamental nature of the right to counsel are unmistakable. Several years later, in 1936, the Court reemphasized what it had said about the fundamental nature of the right to counsel in this language:

> We concluded that certain fundamental rights, safeguarded by the first eight amendments against federal action, were also safeguarded against state action by the due process of law clause of the Fourteenth Amendment, and among them the fundamental right of the accused to the aid of counsel in a criminal prosecution. *Grosjean* v. *American Press Co.* . . . (1936).

And again in 1938 this Court said:

> [The assistance of counsel] is one of the safeguards of the Sixth Amendment deemed necessary to insure fundamental human rights of life and liberty. . . . The Sixth Amendment stands as a constant admonition that if the constitutional safeguards it provides be lost, justice will not 'still be done.' *Johnson* v. *Zerbst* . . . (1938).

In light of these and many other prior decisions of this Court, it is not surprising that the *Betts* Court, when faced with the contention that "one charged with crime, who is unable to obtain counsel, must be furnished counsel by the State," conceded that "[e]xpressions in the opinions of this court lend color to the argument. . . ." . . . The fact is that in deciding as it did — that "appointment of counsel is not a fundamental right, essential to a fair trial" — the Court in *Betts* v. *Brady* made an abrupt break with its own well-considered precedents. In returning to these old precedents, sounder we believe than the new, we but restore constitutional principles established to achieve a fair system of justice. Not only these precedents but also reason and reflection require us to recognize that in our adversary system of criminal justice, any person haled into court, who is too poor to hire a lawyer, cannot be assured a fair trial unless counsel is provided for him. This seems to us to be an obvious truth. Governments, both state and federal, quite properly spend vast sums of money to establish machinery to try defendants accused of crime. Lawyers to prosecute are everywhere deemed essential to protect the public's interest in an orderly society. Similarly, there are few defendants charged with crime, few indeed, who fail to hire the best lawyers they can get to prepare and present their defenses. That government hires lawyers to prosecute and defendants who have the money hire lawyers to defend are the strongest indications of the widespread belief that lawyers in criminal courts are necessities, not luxuries. The right of one charged with crime to counsel may not be deemed fundamental and essential to fair trials in some countries, but it is in ours. From the very beginning, our state and national constitutions and laws have laid great emphasis on procedural and substantive safeguards designed to assure fair trials before impartial tribunals in which every defendant stands equal before the law. This noble idea cannot be realized if the poor man charged with crime has to face his accusers without a lawyer to assist him. A defendant's need for a lawyer is nowhere better stated than in the moving words of Mr. Justice Sutherland in *Powell* v. *Alabama:*

> The right to be heard would be, in many cases, of little avail if it did not comprehend the right to be heard by counsel. Even the intelligent and educated layman has small and sometimes no skill in the science of law. If charged with crime, he is incapable, generally, of determining for himself whether the indictment is good or bad. He is unfamiliar with the rules of evidence. Left without the aid of counsel he may be put on trial without a proper charge, and convicted upon incompetent evidence, or evidence irrelevant to the issue or otherwise inadmissible. He lacks both the skill and knowledge adequately to prepare his defense, even though he have a perfect one. He requires the guiding hand of counsel at every step in the proceedings against him. Without it, though he be not guilty, he faces the danger of conviction because he does not know how to establish his innocence. . . .

The Court in *Betts* v. *Brady* departed from the sound wisdom upon which the Court's holding in *Powell* v. *Alabama* rested. Florida, supported by two other States, has asked that *Betts* v. *Brady* be left intact. Twenty-two States, as friends of the Court, argue that *Betts* was "an anachronism when handed down" and that it should now be overruled. We agree.

The judgment is reversed and the cause is remanded to the Supreme Court of Florida for further action not inconsistent with this opinion.

Reversed.

[Mr. Justice Douglas joined in the opinion of the Court, and also wrote a brief concurring opinion.]

My Brother Harlan is of the view that a guarantee of the Bill of Rights that is made applicable to the States by reason of the Fourteenth Amendment is a lesser version of that same guarantee as applied to the Federal Government. Mr. Justice Jackson shared that view. But that view has not prevailed and rights protected against state invasion by the Due Process Clause of the Fourteenth Amendment are not watered-down versions of what the Bill of Rights guarantees.

[Mr. Justice Clark concurred in the result.]

Mr. Justice Harlan, concurring.

I agree that *Betts* v. *Brady* should be overruled, but consider it entitled to a more respectful burial than has been accorded, at least on the part of those of us who were not on the Court when that case was decided.

I cannot subscribe to the view that *Betts* v. *Brady* represented "an abrupt break with its own well-considered precedents."... In 1932, in *Powell* v. *Alabama,* 287 U.S. 45, a capital case, this Court declared that under the particular facts there presented—"the ignorance and illiteracy of the defendants, their youth, the circumstances of public hostility... and above all that they stood in deadly peril of their lives"...—the state court had a duty to assign counsel for the trial as a necessary requisite of due process of law. It is evident that these limiting facts were not added to the opinion as an afterthought; they were repeatedly emphasized... and were clearly regarded as important to the result.

Thus when this Court, a decade later, decided *Betts* v. *Brady,* it did no more than to admit of the possible existence of special circumstances in noncapital as well as capital trials, while at the same time insisting that such circumstances be shown in order to establish a denial of due process. The right to appointed counsel had been recognized as being considerably broader in federal prosecutions... but to have imposed these requirements on the States would indeed have been "an abrupt break" with the almost immediate past. The declaration that the right to appointed counsel in state prosecutions, as established in *Powell* v. *Alabama,* was not limited to capital cases was in truth not a departure from, but an extension of, existing precedent.

. . . .

In noncapital cases, the "special circumstances" rule has continued to exist in form while its substance has been substantially and steadily eroded. . . . The Court has come to recognize, in other words, that the mere existence of a serious criminal charge constituted in itself special circumstances requiring the services of counsel at trial. In truth the *Betts* v. *Brady* rule is no longer a reality.

. . . .

The special circumstances rule has been formally abandoned in capital cases, and the time has now come when it should be similarly abandoned in noncapital cases, at least as to offenses which, as the one involved here, carry the possibility of a substantial prison sentence. (Whether the rule should extend to *all* criminal cases need not now be decided.) This indeed does no more than to make explicit something that has long since been foreshadowed in our decisions.

In agreeing with the Court that the right to counsel in a case such as this should now be expressly recognized as a fundamental right embraced in the Fourteenth Amendment,... I do not understand the Court to depart from the principles laid down in *Palko* v. *Connecticut*... or to embrace the concept that the Fourteenth Amendment "incorporates" the Sixth Amendment as such.

Scott v. Illinois

> 440 U.S. 367 (1979)
> Vote: 5–4

In *Argersinger* v. *Hamlin,* 407 U.S. 25 (1972), the Supreme Court extended its ruling in Gideon v. Wainwright to misdemeanor cases. Since the vast majority of criminal cases involve misdemeanors, *Argersinger* was a dramatic expansion of the right to counsel provision that has had profound implications for the nation's courts. However, *Argersinger* was not clear on precisely where the line separating eligible from ineligible defendants was drawn. This issue is the subject of *Scott.*

Petitioner Scott was charged with shoplifting merchandise valued at less than $150.00, a misdemeanor punishable under Illinois law by a fine of up to $500 or one year in jail, or both. He was not represented by counsel at his bench trial, where he was convicted and fined $50. Scott appealed his conviction, claiming that his constitutional rights had been violated because Illinois had not provided him with counsel at public expense. The Illinois Supreme Court rejected his contention, and the United States Supreme Court agreed to accept his petition for a writ of certiorari.

Mr. Justice Rehnquist delivered the opinion of the Court.

Betts v. *Brady,* . . . (1942), held that not every indigent defendant accused in a state criminal prosecution was entitled to appointment of counsel. A determination had to be made in each individual case whether failure to appoint counsel was a denial of fundamental fairness. *Betts* was in turn overruled in *Gideon* v. *Wainwright*... (1963).

Several Terms later the Court held in *Duncan* v. *Louisiana,* 391 U.S. 145 (1968), that the right to jury trial in federal court guaranteed by the Sixth

Amendment was applicable to the States by virtue of the Fourteenth Amendment. The Court held, however, that "[i]t is doubtless true that there is a category of petty crimes or offenses which is not subject to the Sixth Amendment jury trial provision and should not be subject to the Fourteenth Amendment jury trial requirement here applied to the States. Crimes carrying possible penalties up to six months do not require a jury trial if they otherwise qualify as petty offenses. . . ." In *Baldwin* v. *New York*, . . . (1970), the controlling opinion of Mr. Justice White concluded that "no offense can be deemed 'petty' for purposes of the right to trial by jury where imprisonment for more than six months is authorized."

In *Argersinger* the State of Florida urged that a similar dichotomy be employed in the right-to-counsel area: any offense punishable by less than six months in jail should not require appointment of counsel for an indigent defendant. The *Argersinger* Court rejected this analogy, however, observing that "the right to trial by jury has a different genealogy and is brigaded with a system of trial to a judge alone."

The number of separate opinions in *Gideon, Duncan, Baldwin,* and *Argersinger* suggests that constitutional line drawing becomes more difficult as the reach of the Constitution is extended further, and as efforts are made to transpose lines from one area of Sixth Amendment jurisprudence to another. The process of incorporation creates special difficulties, for the state and federal contexts are often different and application of the same principle may have ramifications distinct in degree and kind. The range of human conduct regulated by state criminal laws is much broader than that of the federal criminal laws, particularly on the "petty" offense part of the spectrum. As a matter of constitutional adjudication, we are, therefore, less willing to extrapolate an already extended line when, although the general nature of the principle sought to be applied is clear, its precise limits and their ramifications become less so. We have now in our decided cases departed from the literal meaning of the Sixth Amendment. And we cannot fall back on the common law as it existed prior to the enactment of that Amendment, since it perversely gave less in the way of right to counsel to accused felons than to those accused of misdemeanors. . . .

In *Argersinger* the Court rejected arguments that social cost or a lack of available lawyers militated against its holding, in some part because it thought these arguments were factually incorrect. . . . But they were rejected in much larger part because of the Court's conclusion that incarceration was so severe a sanction that it should not be imposed as a result of a criminal trial unless an indigent defendant had been offered appointed counsel to assist in his defense, regardless of the cost to the States implicit in such a rule. The Court in its opinion repeatedly referred to trials "where an accused is deprived of his liberty," . . . and to "a case that actually leads to imprisonment even for a brief period." . . . The Chief Justice in his opinion concurring in the result also observed that "any deprivation of liberty is a serious matter." . . .

Although the intentions of the *Argersinger* Court are not unmistakably clear from its opinion, we conclude today that *Argersinger* did indeed delimit the constitutional right to appointed counsel in state criminal proceedings. Even were the matter *res nova,* we believe that the central premise of *Argersinger* — that actual imprisonment is a penalty different in kind from fines or the mere threat of imprisonment — is eminently sound and warrants adoption of actual imprisonment as the line defining the constitutional right to appointment of counsel. *Argersinger* has proved reasonably workable, whereas any extension would create confusion and impose unpredictable, but necessarily substantial, costs on 50 quite diverse States. We therefore hold that the Sixth and Fourteenth Amendments to the United States Constitution require only that no indigent criminal defendant be sentenced to a term of imprisonment unless the State has afforded him the right to assistance of appointed counsel in his defense. The judgment of the Supreme Court of Illinois is accordingly

Affirmed.

MR. JUSTICE BRENNAN, with whom MR. JUSTICE MARSHALL and MR. JUSTICE STEVENS join, dissenting.

The Court, in an opinion that at best ignores the basic principles of prior decisions, affirms Scott's conviction without counsel because he was sentenced only to pay a fine. In my view, the plain wording of the Sixth Amendment and the Court's precedents compel the conclusion that Scott's uncounseled conviction violated the Sixth and Fourteenth Amendments and should be reversed.

The Court's opinion intimates that the Court's precedents ordaining the right to appointed counsel for indigent accuseds in state criminal proceedings fail to provide a principled basis for deciding this case. That is demonstrably not so. The principles developed in the relevant precedents are clear and sound. The Court simply chooses to ignore them.

Gideon v. *Wainwright* held that, because representation by counsel in a criminal proceeding is "fundamental and essential to a fair trial," . . . the Sixth

Amendment right to counsel was applicable to the States through the Fourteenth Amendment.

Earlier precedents had recognized that the assistance of appointed counsel was critical, not only to equalize the sides in an adversary criminal process, but also to give substance to other constitutional and procedural protections afforded criminal defendants. *Gideon* established the right to appointed counsel for indigent accuseds as a categorical requirement, making the Court's former case-by-case due-process analysis . . . unnecessary in cases covered by its holding. *Gideon* involved a felony prosecution, but that fact was not crucial to the decision; its reasoning extended, in the words of the Sixth Amendment, to *"all* criminal prosecutions."

Argersinger v. *Hamlin* took a cautious approach toward implementing the logical consequences of *Gideon's* rationale. The petitioner in *Argersinger* had been sentenced to jail for 90 days after conviction — at a trial without counsel — of carrying a concealed weapon, a Florida offense carrying an authorized penalty of imprisonment up to six months and a fine up to $1,000. The State, relying on *Duncan* v. *Louisiana* . . . (1968), and *Baldwin* v. *New York* . . . (1970), urged that the Sixth Amendment right to counsel, like the right to jury trial, should not apply to accuseds charged with "petty" offenses punishable by less than six months imprisonment. But *Argersinger* refused to extend the "petty" offense limitation to the right to counsel. The Court pointed out that the limitation was contrary to the express words of the Sixth Amendment, which guarantee its enumerated rights "[i]n all criminal prosecutions"; that the right to jury trial was the only Sixth Amendment right applicable to the States that had been held inapplicable to "petty offenses"; that this limitation had been based on historical considerations peculiar to the right to jury trial; and that the right to counsel was more fundamentally related to the fairness of criminal prosecutions than the right to jury trial and was in fact essential to the meaningful exercise of other Sixth Amendment protections.

Although its analysis, like that in *Gideon* and other earlier cases, suggested that the Sixth Amendment right to counsel should apply to all state criminal prosecutions, *Argersinger* held only that an indigent defendant is entitled to appointed counsel, even in petty offenses punishable by six months of incarceration or less, if he is likely to be sentenced to incarceration for any time if convicted. The question of the right to counsel in cases in which incarceration was authorized but would not be imposed was expressly reserved.

In my view petitioner could prevail in this case without extending the right to counsel beyond what was assumed to exist in *Argersinger.* Neither party in that case questioned the existence of the right to counsel in trials involving "non-petty" offenses punishable by more than six months in jail. The question the Court addressed was whether the right applied to some "petty" offenses to which the right to jury trial did not extend. The Court's reasoning in applying the right to counsel in the case before it — that the right to counsel is more fundamental to a fair proceeding than the right to jury trial and that the historical limitations on the jury trial right are irrelevant to the right to counsel — certainly cannot support a standard for the right to counsel that is more restrictive than the standard for granting a right to jury trial. . . . *Argersinger* thus established a "two dimensional" test for the right to counsel: the right attaches to any "non-petty" offense punishable by more than six months in jail and in addition to any offense where actual incarceration is likely regardless of the maximum authorized penalty. . . .

The offense of "theft" with which Scott was charged is certainly not a "petty" one. It is punishable by a sentence of up to one year in jail. Unlike many traffic or other "regulatory" offenses, it carries the moral stigma associated with common-law crimes traditionally recognized as indicative of moral depravity. The State indicated at oral argument that the services of a professional prosecutor were considered essential to the prosecution of this offense. . . . Likewise, nonindigent defendants charged with this offense would be well advised to hire the "best lawyers they can get." Scott's right to the assistance of appointed counsel is thus plainly mandated by the logic of the Court's prior cases, including *Argersinger* itself.

But rather than decide consonant with the assumption in regard to non-petty offenses that was both implicit and explicit in *Argersinger,* the Court today retreats to the indefensible position that the *Arsersinger* "actual imprisonment" standard is the *only* test for determining the boundary of the Sixth Amendment right to appointed counsel in state misdemeanor cases, thus necessarily deciding that in many cases (such as this one) a defendant will have no right to appointed counsel even when he has a constitutional right to a jury trial. This is simply an intolerable result. Not only is the "actual imprisonment" standard unprecedented as the exclusive test, but the problems inherent in its application demonstrate the superiority of an "authorized imprisonment" standard that would require the appointment of counsel for indigents accused of any offense for which imprisonment for any time is authorized.

First, the authorized imprisonment standard more faithfully implements the principles of the Sixth Amendment identified in *Gideon*. The procedural rules established by state statutes are geared to the nature of the potential penalty for an offense, not to the actual penalty imposed in particular cases. The authorized penalty is also a better predictor of the stigma and other collateral consequences that attach to conviction of an offense. With the exception of *Argersinger,* authorized penalties have been used consistently by this Court as the true measures of the seriousness of offenses. . . . Imprisonment is a sanction particularly associated with criminal offenses; trials of offenses punishable by imprisonment accordingly possess the characteristics found by *Gideon* to require the appointment of counsel. By contrast, the actual imprisonment standard, as the Court's opinion in this case demonstrates, denies the right to counsel in criminal prosecutions to accuses who suffer the severe consequences of prosecution other than imprisonment.

Second, the "authorized imprisonment" test presents no problems of administration. It avoids the necessity for time-consuming consideration of the likely sentence in each individual case before trial and the attendant problems of inaccurate predictions, unequal treatment, and apparent and actual bias.

Finally, the "authorized imprisonment" test ensures that courts will not abrogate legislative judgments concerning the appropriate range of penalties to be considered for each offense. Under the actual imprisonment standard, "[t]he judge will . . . be forced to decide in advance of trial — and without hearing the evidence — whether he will forgo entirely his judicial discretion to impose some sentence of imprisonment and abandon his responsibility to consider the full range of punishments established by the legislature. His alternatives, assuming the availability of counsel, will be to appoint counsel and retain the discretion vested in him by law, or to abandon this discretion in advance and proceed without counsel." . . . The authorized imprisonment standard, on the other hand, respects the allocation of functions between legislatures and courts in the administration of the criminal justice system.

The apparent reason for the Court's adoption of the "actual imprisonment" standard for all misdemeanors is concern for the economic burden that an "authorized imprisonment" standard might place on the States. But, with all respect, that concern is both irrelevant and speculative.

This Court's role in enforcing constitutional guarantees for criminal defendants cannot be made dependent on the budgetary decisions of state governments. . . .

In any event, the extent of the alleged burden on the States is, as the Court admits . . . speculative. Although more persons are charged with misdemeanors punishable by incarceration than are charged with felonies, a smaller percentage of persons charged with misdemeanors qualify as indigent, and misdemeanor cases as a rule require far less attorney time.

Furthermore, public defender systems have proved economically feasible, and the establishment of such systems to replace appointment of private attorneys can keep costs at acceptable levels even when the number of cases requiring appointment of counsel increases dramatically. The public defender system alternative also answers the argument that an authorized imprisonment standard would clog the courts with inexperienced appointed counsel.

Perhaps the strongest refutation of respondent's alarmist prophecies that an authorized imprisonment standard would wreak havoc on the States is that the standard has not produced that result in the substantial number of States that already provide counsel in all cases where imprisonment is authorized — States that include a large majority of the country's population and a great diversity of urban and rural environments. Moreover, of those States that do not yet provide counsel in all cases where *any* imprisonment is authorized, many provide counsel when periods of imprisonment longer than 30 days, 3 months, or 6 months are authorized. In fact, Scott would be entitled to appointed counsel under the current laws of at least 33 States.

It may well be that adoption by this Court of an authorized imprisonment standard would lead state and local governments to re-examine their criminal statutes. A state legislature or local government might determine that it no longer desired to authorize incarceration for certain minor offenses in light of the expense of meeting the requirements of the Constitution. In my view this re-examination is long overdue. In any event, the Court's actual imprisonment standard must inevitably lead the courts to make this re-examination, which plainly should more properly be a legislative responsibility.

The Court's opinion turns the reasoning of *Argersinger* on its head. It restricts the right to counsel, perhaps the most fundamental Sixth Amendment right, more narrowly than the admittedly less fundamental right to jury trial. The abstract pretext that "constitutional line drawing becomes more difficult as the reach of the Constitution is extended further, and as efforts are made to transpose lines from one area of Sixth Amendment jurisprudence to another," cannot camouflage the anomalous result the Court reaches. . . .

[JUSTICE POWELL wrote a concurring opinion. JUSTICE BLACKMUN wrote a dissenting opinion.]

Faretta v. California

422 U.S. 806 (1975)
Vote: 6–3

Anthony Faretta was charged with grand theft, a felony, at arraignment in Los Angeles County Superior Court. The judge assigned a public defender to represent him. Before the trial date, however, Faretta requested permission to represent himself. After questioning Faretta, the trial court judge decided to allow Faretta to represent himself; the judge then reversed himself before the actual trial and insisted that Faretta be represented by a public defender. He further refused Faretta's request to be allowed to serve as co-counsel in his own defense. Faretta was convicted at trial, and the California Court of Appeals affirmed both his conviction and the decision of the trial court judge to deny self-representation. The Supreme Court granted certiorari.

MR. JUSTICE STEWART delivered the opinion of the Court.

. . . The question before us now is whether a defendant in a state criminal trial has a constitutional right to proceed *without* counsel when he voluntarily and intelligently elects to do so. Stated another way, the question is whether a State may constitutionally hale a person into its criminal courts and there force a lawyer upon him, even when he insists that he wants to conduct his own defense. It is not an easy question, but we have concluded that a State may not constitutionally do so.

. . . The Sixth Amendment does not provide merely that a defense shall be made for the accused; it grants to the accused personally the right to make his defense. It is the accused, not counsel, who must be "informed of the nature and cause of the accusation," who must be "confronted with the witnesses against him," and who must be accorded "compulsory process for obtaining witnesses in his favor." Although not stated in the Amendment in so many words, the right to self-representation—to make one's own defense personally—is thus necessarily implied by the structure of the Amendment. The right to defend is given directly to the accused; for it is he who suffers the consequences if the defense fails.

The counsel provision supplements this design. It speaks of the "assistance" of counsel, and an assistant, however expert, is still an assistant. The language and spirit of the Sixth Amendment contemplate that counsel, like the other defense tools guaranteed by the Amendment, shall be an aid to a willing defendant—not an organ of the State interposed between an unwilling defendant and his right to defend himself personally. To thrust counsel upon the accused, against his considered wish, thus violates the logic of the Amendment. In such a case, counsel is not an assistant, but a master; and the right to make a defense is stripped of the personal character upon which the Amendment insists. . . .

[The roots of the Sixth Amendment in English history are traced.]

. . . .

In sum, there is no evidence that the colonists and the Framers ever doubted the right of self-representation, or imagined that this right might be considered inferior to the right of assistance of counsel. To the contrary, the colonists and the Framers, as well as their English ancestors, always conceived of the right to counsel as an "assistance" for the accused, to be used at his option, in defending himself. The Framers selected in the Sixth Amendment a form of words that necessarily implies the right of self-representation. That conclusion is supported by centuries of consistent history.

There can be no blinking the fact that the right of an accused to conduct his own defense seems to cut against the grain of this Court's decisions holding that the Constitution requires that no accused can be convicted and imprisoned unless he has been accorded the right to the assistance of counsel. . . .

But it is one thing to hold that every defendant, rich or poor, has the right to the assitance of counsel, and quite another to say that a State may compel a defendant to accept a lawyer he does not want. The value of state-appointed counsel was not unappreciated by the Founders, yet the notion of compulsory counsel was utterly foreign to them. And whatever else may be said of those who wrote the Bill of Rights, surely there can be no doubt that they understood the inestimable worth of free choice.

It is undeniable that in most criminal prosecutions

defendants could better defend with counsel's guidance than by their own unskilled efforts. But where the defendant will not voluntarily accept representation by counsel, the potential advantage of a lawyer's training and experience can be realized, if at all, only imperfectly. To force a lawyer on a defendant can only lead him to believe that the law contrives against him. Moreover, it is not inconceivable that in some rare instances, the defendant might in fact present his case more effectively by conducting his own defense. Personal liberties are not rooted in the law of averages. The right to defend is personal. The defendant, and not his lawyer or the State, will bear the personal consequences of a conviction. It is the defendant, therefore, who must be free personally to decide whether in his particular case counsel is to his advantage. And although he may conduct his own defense ultimately to his own detriment, his choice must be honored out of "that respect for the individual which is the lifeblood of the law."...

. . . .

In forcing Faretta, under these circumstances, to accept against his will a state-appointed public defender, the California courts deprived him of his constitutional right to conduct his own defense. Accordingly, the judgment before us is vacated, and the case is remanded for further proceedings not inconsistent with this opinion.

MR. CHIEF JUSTICE BURGER, with whom MR. JUSTICE BLACKMUN and MR. JUSTICE REHNQUIST join, dissenting.

This case... is another example of the judicial tendency to constitutionalize what is thought "good." That effort fails on its own terms here, because there is nothing desirable or useful in permitting every accused person, even the most uneducated and inexperienced, to insist upon conducting his own defense to criminal charges. Moreover, there is no constitutional basis for the Court's holding, and it can only add to the problems of an already malfunctioning criminal justice system. I therefore dissent.

As the Court seems to recognize, . . . the conclusion that the rights guaranteed by the Sixth Amendment are "personal" to an accused reflects nothing more than the obvious fact that it is he who is on trial and therefore has need of a defense. But neither that nearly trivial proposition nor the language of the Amendment, which speaks in uniformly mandatory terms, leads to the further conclusion that the right to counsel is merely supplementary and may be dispensed with at the whim of the accused. Rather, this Court's decisions have consistently included the right

to counsel as an integral part of the bundle making up the larger "right to a defense as we know it."...

. . . .

. . . [B]oth the "spirit and logic" of the Sixth Amendment are that every person accused of crime shall receive the fullest possible defense; in the vast majority of cases this command can be honored only by means of the expressly guaranteed right to counsel, and the trial judge is in the best position to determine whether the accused is capable of conducting his defense. True freedom of choice and society's interest in seeing that justice is achieved can be vindicated only if the trial court retains discretion to reject any attempted waiver of counsel and insist that the accused be tried according to the Constitution. This discretion is as critical an element of basic fairness as a trial judge's discretion to decline to accept a plea of guilty. . . .

The Court's attempt to support its result by collecting data from prior decisions is no more persuasive than its analysis of the Sixth Amendment. Considered in context, the cases upon which the Court relies to "beat its path" either lead it nowhere or point it in precisely the opposite direction. [The opinion then reviews these cases.]

. . . .

In short, what the Court represents as a well-traveled road is in reality a constitutional trail which it is blazing for the first time today, one that has not even been hinted at in our previous decisions. Far from an interpretation of the Sixth Amendment, it is a perversion of the provision to which we gave full meaning in *Gideon* v. *Wainwright* and *Argersinger* v. *Hamlin*.

. . . I hesitate to participate in the Court's attempt to use history to take it where legal analysis cannot. Piecing together shreds of English legal history and early state constititional and statutory provisions, without a full elaboration of the context in which they occurred or any evidence that they were relied upon by the drafters of our Federal Constitution, creates more questions than it answers and hardly provides the firm foundation upon which the creation of new constitutional rights should rest. We are well reminded that this Court once employed an exhaustive analysis of English and colonial practices regarding the right to counsel to justify the conclusion that it was fundamental to a fair trial and, less than 10 years later, used essentially the same material to conclude that it was not. Compare *Powell* v. *Alabama* . . . with *Betts* v. *Brady*. . . .

As if to illustrate this point, the single historical fact cited by the Court which would appear truly relevant to ascertaining the meaning of the Sixth Amendment proves too much. As the Court points out, *ante,* at 2539, §35 of the Judiciary Act of 1789 provided a statutory right to self-representation in federal criminal trials. The text of the Sixth Amendment, which expressly provides only for a right to counsel, was proposed the day after the Judiciary Act was signed. It can hardly be suggested that the Members of the Congress of 1789, then few in number, were unfamiliar with the Amendment's carefully structured language, which had been under discussion since the 1787 Constitutional Convention. . . .

. . . .

Society has the right to expect that, when courts find new rights implied in the Constitution, their potential effect upon the resources of our criminal justice system will be considered. However, such considerations are conspicuously absent from the Court's opinion in this case.

It hardly needs repeating that courts at all levels are already handicapped by the unsupplied demand for competent advocates, with the result that it often takes far longer to complete a given case than experienced counsel would require. If we were to assume that there will be widespread exercise of the newly discovered constitutional right to self-representation, it would almost certainly follow that there will be added congestion in the courts and that the quality of justice will suffer. Moreover, the Court blandly assumes that once an accused has elected to defend himself he will be bound by his choice and not be heard to complain of it later. . . . This assumption ignores the role of appellate review, for the reported cases are replete with instances of a convicted defendant being relieved of a deliberate decision even when made *with the advice of counsel.* . . . It is totally unrealistic, therefore, to suggest that an accused will always be held to the consequences of a decision to conduct his own defense. Unless, as may be the case, most persons accused of crime have more wit than to insist upon the dubious benefit that the Court confers today, we can expect that many expensive and good-faith prosecutions will be nullified on appeal for reasons that trial courts are now deprived of the power to prevent.

[MR. JUSTICE BLACKMUN, with whom the CHIEF JUSTICE and MR. JUSTICE REHNQUIST joined, also wrote a dissenting opinion.]

Confessions and Self-Incrimination

The Fifth Amendment provides in part that "[n]o person . . . shall be compelled in any criminal case to be a witness against himself." This "right to silence" was included in the Bill of Rights as a limit on the newly established national government, and at the time of its adoption, the constitutions of all the states contained similar provisions.

The source of this right is the ancient maxim, *nemo tenetur seipsum prodere,* which means "no man is bound to accuse himself." In limited form the right to silence has long been recognized in the common law, although dramatic events in the sixteenth century broadened its coverage and elevated it to a fundamental right. When it first emerged as a general right, this protection against self-incrimination meant only that a person on trial for a criminal charge could not be compelled to answer questions to his detriment unless he had first been properly appraised of the charges against him. This was the position that John Lilburne insisted upon when in 1637 he was brought before an ecclesiastical proceeding in England. An ardent Puritan, Lilburne was suspected of smuggling religious tracts into England from Holland. At the proceedings he was questioned widely about a host of activities and associates. He refused to cooperate with his interrogators, insisting that the questions had nothing to do with the charges against him and that the court was simply trying to "ensnare" him on other issues because it lacked sufficient evidence to convict him of the charges for which he had been arrested. Both at this and later similar proceedings Lilburne stood firm, and his silence earned him lengthy periods of imprisonment for contempt of court. His stubborn refusal aroused public opinion and the support of political notables, and when the Parliament was reconvened after a long absence, some of its members took up his cause and in a flurry of activity ordered Lilburne freed, provided restitution for him, abolished the Star Chamber and the High Commission, and eliminated the power to compel testimony by the remaining ecclesiastical courts. With this latter action, the first parliamentary recognition of the modern right to silence came into existence.

It is important to understand Lilburne's position and the nature of the new protection his actions helped secure. Lilburne's resistance was not based upon a flat refusal to cooperate with his captors. Rather, he refused to take an oath requiring truthful answers to *all* questions put to him. All Lilburne insisted upon was that he first be informed of the subject matter of the questioning and that he did not have to answer questions extending beyond it. In Lilburne's case the right to silence meant only that no person should be put on trial and compelled to answer incriminating questions without first having been properly accused. But once set in motion this limited right gained momentum and breadth and eventually evolved into a general right to silence by the criminally accused at trial. At the time of the adoption of the Constitution, this understanding was entrenched in the common law.

Self-Incrimination, Police Interrogation, and Federalism

Although the right to silence at trial has long been recognized under the common law, the related issue of controlling interrogations made prior to trial has a much shorter and equally controversial history. The first efforts to subject pretrial interrogation to the scrutiny of the law dealt with the issue of coerced confessions, and by the time of the adoption of the Constitution, English courts had formulated the rule that "a confession forced from the mind by the flattery of hope, or by the torture of fear," was to be rejected on the grounds that it was unreliable. In the United States the rule regarding coerced confessions followed English practice and appeared first as a common law rule of evidence rather than a constitutional principle. As a result, despite an early ruling by the Supreme Court in *United States* v. *Bram,* 297 U.S. 278 (1897), the issue of the admissibility at trial of involuntary or coerced confessions obtained during pretrial interrogation did not emerge as a constitutional issue until the 1930s, when the Court first began reviewing a variety of questionable and racially motivated practices employed by state law enforcement officials. One such case was *Brown* v. *Mississippi,* 297 U.S. 278 (1936). In that case, Brown and two other black men had confessed to the murder of a white man after more than two days of continuous torture by a group of white vigilantes. The Mississippi high court upheld the conviction on the grounds that their attorney had not challenged the introduction of the confessions at trial. This ruling was appealed to the United States Supreme Court, which held that the conviction was "void for want of the essential elements of due process."

Thus the Court began the slow process of developing a constitutional protection against the introduction of involuntary confessions in state courts. The Court's approach during the 1930s and 1940s led to a case-by-case assessment of the circumstances surrounding each interrogation. If a majority found that the circumstances under which the incriminating statements obtained were repugnant to a sense of "fundamental fairness," it would rule the confession involuntary and inadmissable under the Fourteenth Amendment's Due Process Clause.

Although the Court's Fourteenth Amendment rulings on state actions were presumably applicable to federal officials through the Due Process Clause of the Fifth Amendment, the Court never made such a position explicit during this period. Instead, the Court's decisions regarding involuntary confessions in federal proceedings rested primarily on interpretations of the federal rules of criminal procedure, which in turn had been promulgated under the Court's supervisory power over the administration of criminal justice in federal proceedings, rules that presumably could be abrogated by Congress. These federal cases differed from the state cases in that they did not involve claims of involuntariness due to third-degree police tactics. In these cases the Court was confronted with techniques that were acceptable under the evolving due process standards, which emphasized torture and threat, but were nevertheless troublesome because they had been obtained after hours or even days of sustained questioning in isolation and close confinement.

The first major case in which the court confronted this issue was *McNabb* v. *United States,* 318 U.S. 332 (1943). In this case three suspects were interrogated singly and together for almost forty-eight hours before being presented in court. Confessions obtained during this period were subsequently introduced at trial. In overturning the conviction the Supreme Court indicated that even though the confessions may have met the voluntariness standards under due process, the delay in presenting the arrestees to a federal judicial officer nevertheless violated their right to a prompt presentment required by the federal rules of criminal procedure. In a series of cases following *McNabb,* the Court sought to clarify the purpose of the prompt presentment rule, reasoning that "delay must not be of a nature to give opportunity for the extraction of a confession" (*Mallory* v. *United States,* 354 U.S. 449, 1957). But even as it sought to provide a rationale for this rule for federal courts, the language used by the Court became intertwined with Fifth Amendment considerations and elevated the issue to constitutional status.

One consequence of these developments was a dual set of standards, one for state courts based upon the Due Process Clause of the Fourteenth Amendment, and one for federal courts based upon un undifferentiated reliance upon the federal rules of criminal procedure, federal common law, and vague references to the Fifth Amendment's prohibition against self-incrimination. As this double standard became sharper, there was pressure to bring the two sets of standards closer together. The controversy has never been fully settled and still evokes considerable debate,

but over the years the gap has lessened as a result of Supreme Court rulings in federal cases that have shifted their rationale to a constitutional basis. Also, rulings in both federal and state cases have linked and broadened the meanings of the Fifth Amendment protection against self-incrimination and the Sixth Amendment's right to counsel, and incorporated both provisions into the Fourteenth Amendment. See *Malloy* v. *Hogan,* 378 U.S. 1 (1964) and GIDEON V. WAINWRIGHT, 372 U.S. 335 (1963). Another key case in these developments was *Massiah* v. *United States,* 377 U.S. 201 (1964), in which the Supreme Court ruled that Massiah's Sixth Amendment right to counsel had been violated when evidence deliberately elicited from him by a federal undercover informant after his indictment and in the absence of counsel was introduced into court. This ruling significantly expanded the breadth of the Court's concern with the prohibition against compelled testimony and directly linked this provision with the Sixth Amendment's right to counsel, even in pretrial contact with law enforcement officers. And because it was decided after GIDEON V. WAINWRIGHT, *Massiah* carried the implication that the states were also bound by the ruling. These rulings generated considerable controversy. Both *Mallory* and *Massiah* were decided by 5 to 4 decisions, with the minority justices penning sharp dissents. But by themselves these rulings were not momentous, since federal officials have a relatively limited role in law enforcement. And at the time, at least in the eyes of some, the Court's rulings could be overturned, if needed, by Congress because they rested upon a subconstitutional foundation. Others saw the Court's action in these cases as part of a broader constitutional revolution with far-reaching implications for the states. Events proved this view to be correct.

The controversy generated by the Court's rulings for the federal system in *Massiah* paled in comparison to the fire-storm that greeted the Court's rulings in *Malloy* v. *Hogan,* 378 U.S. 1 (1964), *Escobedo* v. *Illinois,* 378 U.S. 478 (1964), and MIRANDA V. ARIZONA, 384 U.S. 436 (1966).

Malloy explicitly incorporated the Fifth Amendment into the Fourteenth via the Due Process Clause. *Escobedo* not only applied to the states the Court's prior rulings on suspect's pretrial rights to silence and counsel, it went well beyond them and held that a suspect who had made incriminating statements to police shortly after being taken into custody had been denied his Sixth Amendment right to counsel because the police had not allowed him to consult with his attorney. The Court thus pushed forward the point at which it sought to provide active protection for the right to silence, and by stressing the absence of counsel, it deemphasized the need for the accused to demonstrate compulsion in the questioning. Less than three years later, in another closely divided ruling, a five-man majority amplified and extended this concern. While *Massiah* and *Escobedo* had attempted to effect a practical right to silence by pushing back in time the point at which counsel was to be made available to a suspect, the accused still had the burden demonstrating that his incriminating statements made in early contact had not been voluntary. MIRANDA shifted the burden to the police. This complicated and controversial ruling required the police not only to make counsel available prior to questioning, but required them to affirmatively warn all arrestees of their right to silence and their right to an attorney before any questioning commenced. Arguing that coercion not only entailed brutal third-degree techniques, but could also include subtle forms of deception, the Court in effect placed the burden upon the police to demonstrate that incriminating information obtained through custodial interrogations was the product of a knowing and voluntary waiver of the right to silence and counsel. Absent demonstration, the Court held, such evidence was inadmissable.

In MIRANDA, the Court stressed that the conditions of custodial interrogation rendered the voluntariness of any subsequent confession highly suspect. But as you read the cases in this section, consider in what manner, if any, the warnings mandated by MIRANDA alter the conditions of custodial interrogation. Is there any more reason to believe that a suspect's decision to waive his or her rights and submit to interrogation is "voluntary" than there is to believe that pre-MIRANDA confessions were voluntary? Do the police continue to use trickery after MIRANDA? Can they? If not, what is the aim of MIRANDA? And what constitutes "custody"?

Reaction to MIRANDA was swift and fierce. Police groups regarded it as a vote of no confidence. Coming, as it did, on the heels of a host of other decisions protecting the rights of the criminally accussed (e.g., the exclusionary rule and expansion of the right to counsel), and during a period that some saw as Supreme Court–sanctioned civil rights disturbances, many public officials vigorously condemned the court for handcuffing the police and unleashing the forces of lawlessness. Although more moderate in tone, the minority opinions in MIRANDA and cases that followed from it echoed some of these same sentiments.

Since MIRANDA, and especially in the last years of the Burger court, a long series of cases have sought to define what distinguishes a "conversation" with police from a police "interrogation" and what constitutes a knowing and voluntary waiver of an arrestee's MIRANDA rights. While these decisions have significantly restricted the scope of MIRANDA, until 1984 they had not directly challenged the underlying rationale of the ruling.

But in the 1983 term a majority was mustered to mount a more fundamental attack on MIRANDA. In NEW YORK V. QUARLES, 467 U.S. 649 (1984), the court punched a direct hole in MIRANDA when it created a "public safety" exception to the requirement that suspects in police custody be warned of their rights before being questioned. This case arose when police, responding to a call of a woman who had just been raped at gunpoint, trailed a suspect into a grocery store. Upon apprehending a man who matched the woman's description, the first question the police asked was "Where is your gun?" He revealed its location and both his response and the gun were admitted into evidence at trial. The Court reasoned that the police officers had acted reasonably in asking the gun question before issuing the MIRANDA warning, since had they issued the warning first, the suspect might not have revealed the location of the gun. Under the circumstances, the Court continued, it was desirable to locate the gun immediately, since otherwise it might have been found by someone who inadvertently could have hurt himself or someone else. Even Justice O'Connor, normally critical of rulings constricting the police, dissented in part, criticizing the Court for creating a vague exception that would confuse police and invite protracted litigation. Other dissenters focused on the fact situation — it was late at night, the store was empty, there were a number of police officers who could easily have searched for the gun — to question the assumption that the facts were compelling enough to warrant an exception to a long-standing and clear rule.

This same term the Court created another exception to a constitutionally based exclusionary rule, this one stemming from the Sixth Amendment's right to counsel provision (*Nix* v. *Williams,* 467 U.S. 431, 1984). In this, the celebrated "Christian burial case," Williams had been taken into custody. In the process of being transported to a police station in a nearby town, Williams was questioned by police, who, disregarding his MIRANDA rights (and explicit instructions given them by his attorney over the telephone prior to departure), pressed Williams to lead them to the body of the little girl he was suspected of killing, so her parents could take comfort in the fact that she had had a Christian burial during the Christmas season. Williams cooperated and led the police to the body. In one important Supreme Court decision, *Brewer* v. *Williams,* 430 U.S. 387 (1977), the Court overturned his conviction on grounds that Williams' statement to the police, which was admitted into evidence, had been obtained in violation of his MIRANDA rights.

The *Brewer* Court was bitterly divided, and a concurring opinion in effect invited retrial of the case, in which the statement would be excluded but the evidence obtained from it would be included. This occurred and Williams was again con-

victed of first-degree murder. The issue of the evidence derived from the suppressed statement came before the Supreme Court in *Nix* v. *Williams,* and six justices voted to carve out an "inevitable discovery" exception to the Sixth Amendment's exclusionary rule. In so doing the Court reasoned that searchers (there were over two hundred combing the vicinity) ultimately or inevitably would have discovered the victim's body even had Williams, whose statement it acknowledged had been taken in violation of his Sixth Amendment rights, not been questioned by the police.

Both QUARLES and *Nix* v. *Williams* represent important cutbacks by the Court on the constitutional rulings of the Warren Court. But one may ask whether they will ameliorate long-standing complaints of the Warren Court rulings. Recall that one of the major criticisms of the Warren Court was that its rulings imposed confusing and unworkable rules on the police. However, whatever its vices, MIRANDA had the virtue of clarity. Now, whatever their virtues, the "public safety" and "inevitable discovery" exceptions carved out by the Burger Court and embraced even more fully by the Rehnquist Court have the vice of ambiguity and uncertainty. In QUARLES, the concurring opinion of Justice O'Connor — certainly one of the more law-and-order–oriented justices on the current Court — speaks eloquently on this point. Also, contrast the varying assessments of danger given by Justices Rehnquist and Marshall in QUARLES. If they so disagree, even with the benefit of hindsight and leisure, can we reasonably expect police in the midst of an arrest encounter to make an informed choice? Given this problem, in what direction do you think courts are likely to err — for the police or for the arrestee?

Although the Burger Court did not overrule MIRANDA or any of the other Warren Court rulings protecting the rights of the criminally accused, it did chip away at some of them. Under Chief Justice Rehnquist, this tendency has accelerated. A growing number of justices have mounted a near head-on attack of MAPP, and have been aggressive in limiting the scope of MIRANDA. Although it appears that the police have come to accommodate MIRANDA, still there is pressure to restrict it, and a growing majority of justices have been responsive. In 1987 the Rehnquist Court upheld admission of a confession by a suspect who continued to talk to the police after having been given a MIRANDA warning, but who later was found to be psychotic after having told a court-appointed psychiatrist that he was following the "voice of God" (*Colorado* v. *Connelly,* 479 U.S. 157, 1987). And in another 1987 decision, the Court, by a vote of 5 to 4, upheld the introduction at trial of a tape-recorded conversation between an arrestee and his wife made while he was in custody and after he had been warned of his MIRANDA rights. Although he had indicated he did not want to talk to police until he had consulted with a lawyer, the police placed an operating tape recorder on a table in plain sight when his wife came to visit him. Incriminating statements that he made, and which were recorded, were later introduced into evidence at trial. The Supreme Court held that since there was no evidence that the wife had been used as a ploy to get the suspect to talk, the conversation was not interrogation within the meaning of MIRANDA and thus could be introduced at trial (*Arizona* v. *Mauro,* 481 U.S. 520, 1987). Two years later, in a 5 to 4 split, the Court upheld the conviction of an arrestee who had received a "modified" version of the MIRANDA warning, in which the arresting officer advised a suspect that council would be appointed "if and when you go to court." (*Duckworth* v. *Eagan* 57 LW 4942, 1989).

Despite this chipping away, MIRANDA remains durable. This is suggested by an important case in the 1987–88 term, *Arizona* v. *Roberson,* 451 U.S. 477, which reinforced MIRANDA. *Edwards,* which strengthened an earlier ruling on the same issue, held that the invocation of the right to counsel by an in-custody defendant bars further police-initiated, counselless interrogation not only for the crime under investigation at the time the request is made, but for additional, unrelated offenses of which the defendant is also suspected.

Related Issues

Since it was first called upon to interpret the Fifth Amendment's provision that "[n]o person shall be compelled in any criminal case to be a witness against himself," the Supreme Court has given broad meaning to the term "criminal case," interpreting the prohibition to be a ban on compulsory testimony in *any* governmental investigation, whether by police, grand jury, criminal or civil courts, internal revenue agents, legislative bodies, and so on, in which answers might be used subsequently as incriminating evidence in a proceeding where criminal-like sanctions could be applied.

However, this right to silence is not without limits. It serves only to protect the witness herself or himself, not others who might be damaged by the compelled testimony. Furthermore, the witness must explicitly claim this right or be deemed to have waived it. And it is the court, not the witness, who makes the final judgment in this claim. Nor does the provision protect witnesses if there is no possibility of subsequent criminal prosecution, even though the testimony may reveal criminal activity or personally embarrassing information. Thus the Court has permitted compelled testimony if information revealed in this testimony is barred from use in criminal proceedings or barred from use as a link in a chain of information that is used to prove criminal activity.

This principle of immunity is simple enough in theory and widely accepted, but it evokes considerable controversy in efforts to operationalize it. The central issue is whether witnesses should be granted *use* immunity or *transactional* immunity. *Use* immunity means that information obtained directly or indirectly through compelled testimony cannot be used as evidence in any subsequent criminal proceeding. But criminal prosecution for the actions related to the testimony is still permitted, provided that the prosecution can show that its case in no way relied upon this testimony. In contrast, *transactional* immunity grants the witness *total* immunity from criminal prosecution for any activity revealed or related to the testimony given under a grant of immunity, regardless of whether the prosecution relied upon any of this information. It is a grant of absolute immunity. The problems of each type are obvious. In the former, it is difficult to prove that information revealed in testimony was not used by law enforcement officials; in the latter, there is a very real fear that a clever witness will take an "immunity bath" by revealing all his criminal activities in order to prevent future criminal liability for them.

While Congress had provided for transactional immunity in some circumstances earlier in this century, more recently it has followed a narrower course. In 1970, it adopted a comprehensive immunity statute that provided for what has come to be known as use-derivative use immunity. The Supreme Court later upheld a challenge to this statute in KASTIGAR V. UNITED STATES, 406 U.S. 441 (1972). The Court's view and the various theories of immunity, including the position that immunity itself undermines the protection against self-incrimination, are explored in the various opinions in this case.

Over the years, the Court has extended the Fifth Amendment privilege against self-incrimination well beyond its original criminal contours, to cover juvenile proceedings (IN RE GAULT 387 U.S. 1, 1967); to protect loss of citizenship in administrative proceedings (*Kennedy* v. *Mendoza-Martinez,* 372 U.S. 144, 1963); and to protect against automatic loss of employment for those who invoke the protection of the Fifth Amendment by refusing to

sign a "waiver of immunity" and to testify before investigative bodies (GARDNER V. BRODERICK, 392 U.S. 273, 1968). In each of these areas, the Court, reasoning by analogy, found that the penal intent of the official actions so closely resembled criminal sanctions that the Fifth Amendment's protections should cover them.

Still, the Court has been reluctant to chart out a broader contour for the Amendment. Despite the urge to use the Amendment's protection against self-incrimination to protect witnesses during dragnet legislative investigations of the McCarthy era, the Court has never embraced the idea that the Amendment should protect against infamy and disgrace. Nor, despite occasionally involving the Fifth Amendment in discussions of a general right to privacy, e.g., GRISWOLD V. CONNECTICUT, 381 U.S. 479 (1965), has the Court embraced any broader rationale. Absent the possibility of criminal-like sanctions, the Court is prepared to permit compelled disclosure or to search for other means for protecting privacy in the face of governmental intrusiveness of a dubious nature. For Court scrutiny of testimony compelled by legislative committees, see Chapter 2, especially McGRAIN V. DAUGHERTY, 273 U.S. 135 (1927), WATKINS V. UNITED STATES, 345 U.S. 178 (1957), and BARENBLATT V. UNITED STATES, 360 U.S. 109 (1959). See also GRAVEL V. UNITED STATES, 408 U.S. 606 (1972), and UNITED STATES V. NIXON, 418 U.S. 683 (1974).

Cases

Miranda v. Arizona

384 U.S. 436 (1966)
Vote 5–4

Miranda is the culmination of a series of cases that expanded the rights of the criminally accused and significantly altered long-standing interrogation practices of law enforcement officers.

In essence, *Miranda* sought to narrow the gap between those rights available to the criminally accused in the courtroom and those available to them at earlier stages of the criminal process while in police custody. It placed affirmative obligations on law enforcement officials to warn suspects of their rights and to honor these rights when invoked.

Miranda's immediate antecedent was *Escobedo* v. *Illinois,* 378 U.S. 478 (1964), in which the Court held that the rights to counsel and silence applied to the pretrial stage when it "shifts from investigatory to accusatory." In this case the police neither warned Escobedo of his right to silence nor honored his request to consult with his attorney (who was waiting to see his client in an adjoining room at the police station). The Supreme Court subsequently held that Escobedo's conviction, based in part upon incriminating evidence obtained during this interrogation, was invalid.

In *Miranda* the Court reiterated its commitment to these pretrial rights and attempted to effect a procedure to secure them. Its major tool was the requirement that the police warn suspects of their rights to silence and counsel. The Court sought to give meaning to this requirement by obligating the police to demonstrate that any incriminating evidence they obtain from questioning suspects is the result of a knowing and voluntary waiver of rights by the suspects. In the absence of such a waiver this information cannot be introduced as evidence at trial.

Miranda represents the high-water mark of the Warren Court's expansion of the rights of the criminally accused. Since then, the membership of the Court has changed significantly and so too have its decisions in this area. Subsequent cases illustrate the ways the Court has distinguished *Miranda* to give it a narrower interpretation.

In the case from which this decision takes its name, Ernesto Miranda was arrested at home and taken into custody at a Phoenix police station. The record indicates that he was not advised of his right to appointed counsel, and there were conflicting statements from police officers as to whether he was warned that anything he said could be used against him. After two hours of interrogation, during which there is no indication that threats of physical violence were made, the officers emerged with a written confession signed by Miranda. At the top of the statement was a typed paragraph stating that the confession was made voluntarily, without threats or promises of immunity and "with full knowledge of my legal rights, understanding any statement I make may be used against me." Against

objections of his counsel, this written statement was admitted into evidence at trial. Miranda was found guilty and sentenced to twenty to thirty years' imprisonment for each count of kidnapping and rape. The Supreme Court of Arizona upheld his conviction, whereupon Miranda petitioned to the Supreme Court for a writ of certiorari.

MR. CHIEF JUSTICE WARREN delivered the opinion of the Court.

The cases before us raise questions which go to the roots of our concepts of American criminal jurisprudence: the restraints society must observe consistent with the Federal Constitution in prosecuting individuals for crime. More specifically, we deal with the admissibility of statements obtained from an individual who is subjected to custodial police interrogation and the necessity for procedures which assure that the individual is accorded his privilege under the Fifth Amendment to the Constitution not to be compelled to incriminate himself.

. . . .

We start here, as we did in *Escobedo,* with the premise that our holding is not an innovation in our jurisprudence, but is an application of principles long recognized and applied in other settings. We have undertaken a thorough re-examination of the *Escobedo* decision and the principles it announced, and we reaffirm it. That case was but an explication of basic rights that are enshrined in our Constitution — that "No person . . . shall be compelled in any criminal case to be a witness against himself," and that "the accused shall . . . have the Assistance of Counsel" — rights which were put in jeopardy in that case through official overbearing. These precious rights were fixed in our Constitution only after centuries of persecution and struggle. And in the words of Chief Justice Marshall, they were secured "for ages to come, and . . . designed to approach immortality as nearly as human institutions can approach it." . . .

Our holding will be spelled out with some specificity in the pages which follow but briefly stated it is this: the prosecution may not use statements, whether exculpatory or inculpatory, stemming from custodial interrogation of the defendant unless it demonstrates the use of procedural safeguards effective to secure the privilege against self-incrimination. By custodial interrogation, we mean questioning initiated by law enforcement officers after a person has been taken into custody or otherwise deprived of his freedom of action in any significant way. As for the procedural safeguards to be employed, unless other fully effective means are devised to inform accused persons of their right of silence and to assure a continuous opportunity to exercise it, the following measures are required. Prior to any questioning, the person must be warned that he has a right to remain silent, that any statement he does make may be used as evidence against him, and that he has a right to the presence of an attorney, either retained or appointed. The defendant may waive effectuation of these rights, provided the waiver is made voluntarily, knowingly and intelligently. If, however, he indicates in any manner and at any stage of the process that he wishes to consult with an attorney before speaking there can be no questioning. Likewise, if the individual is alone and indicates in any manner that he does not wish to be interrogated, the police may not question him. The mere fact that he may have answered some questions or volunteered some statements on his own does not deprive him of the right to refrain from answering any further inquiries until he has consulted with an attorney and thereafter consents to be questioned.

I

The constitutional issue we decide in each of these cases is the admissibility of statements obtained from a defendant questioned while in custody or otherwise deprived of his freedom of action in any significant way. In each, the defendant was questioned by police officers, detectives, or a prosecuting attorney in a room in which he was cut off from the outside world. In none of these cases was the defendant given a full and effective warning of his rights at the outset of the interrogation process. In all the cases, the questioning elicited oral admissions, and in three of them, signed statements as well which were admitted at their trials. They thus all share salient features — incommunicado interrogation of individuals in a police-dominated atmosphere, resulting in self-incriminating statements without full warnings of constitutional rights.

An understanding of the nature and setting of this in-custody interrogation is essential to our decisions today. The difficulty in depicting what transpires at such interrogations stems from the fact that in this country they have largely taken place incommunicado. From extensive factual studies undertaken in the early 1930s, including the famous Wickersham Report to Congress by a Presidential Commission, it is clear that police violence and the "third degree" flourished at that time. In a series of cases decided by this Court long after these studies, the police resorted to physical brutality — beating, hanging,

whipping — and to sustained and protracted questioning incommunicado in order to extort confessions. The Commission on Civil Rights in 1961 found much evidence to indicate that "some policemen still resort to physical force to obtain confessions," 1961 Comm'n on Civil Rights Rep., Justice, pt. 5, 17. The use of physical brutality and violence is not, unfortunately, relegated to the past or to any part of the country. Only recently in Kings county, New York, the police brutally beat, kicked and placed lighted cigarette butts on the back of a potential witness under interrogation for the purpose of securing a statement incriminating a third party. . . .

The examples given above are undoubtedly the exception now, but they are sufficiently widespread to be the object of concern. Unless a proper limitation upon custodial interrogation is achieved — such as these decisions will advance — there can be no assurance that practices of this nature will be eradicated in the foreseeable future. . . .

. . . [W]e stress that the modern practice of in-custody interrogation is psychologically rather than physically oriented. As we have stated before ". . . this Court has recognized that coercion can be mental as well as physical, and that the blood of the accused is not the only hallmark of an unconstitutional inquisition." . . . Interrogation still takes place in privacy. Privacy results in secrecy and this in turn results in a gap in our knowledge as to what in fact goes on in the interrogation rooms. A valuable source of information about present police practices, however, may be found in various police manuals and texts which document procedures employed with success in the past, and which recommend various other effective tactics. These texts are used by law enforcement agencies themselves as guides. It should be noted that these texts professedly present the most enlightened and effective means presently used to obtain statements through custodial interrogation. . . . [The Court then reviews relevant portions of standard texts on criminal investigation and interrogation.]

. . . .

From these representative samples of interrogation techniques, the setting prescribed by the manuals and observed in practice becomes clear. In essence, it is this: To be alone with the subject is essential to prevent distraction and to deprive him of any outside support. The aura of confidence in his guilt undermines his will to resist. He merely confirms the preconceived story the police seek to have him describe. Patience and persistence, at times relentless questioning are employed. To obtain a confession, the interrogator must "patiently maneuver himself or his quarry into a position from which the desired objective may be attained." When normal procedures fail to produce the needed result, the police may resort to deceptive stratagems such as giving false legal advice. It is important to keep the subject off balance, for example, by trading on his insecurity about himself or his surroundings. The police then persuade, trick, or cajole him out of exercising his constitutional rights. Even without employing brutality, the "third degree" or the specific stratagems described above, the very fact of custodial interrogation exacts a heavy toll on individual liberty and trades on the weakness of individuals. . . .

II

We sometimes forget how long it has taken to establish the privilege against self-incrimination, the sources from which it came and the fervor with which it was defended. Its roots go back into ancient times. Perhaps the critical historical event shedding light on its origins and evolution was the trial of one John Lilburn, a vocal anti-Stuart Leveller, who was made to take the Star Chamber Oath in 1637. The oath would have bound him to answer all questions posed to him on any subject. . . .

On account of the Lilburn Trial, Parliament abolished the inquisitorial Court of Star Chamber and went further in giving him generous reparation. The lofty principles to which Lilburn had appealed during his trial gained popular acceptance in England. These sentiments worked their way over to the Colonies and were implanted after great struggle into the Bill of Rights. . . .

Thus we may view the historical development of the privilege as one which groped for the proper scope of governmental power over the citizen. As a "noble principle often transcends its origins," the privilege has come rightfully to be recognized in part as an individual's substantive right, a "right to a private enclave where he may lead a private life. That right is the hallmark of our democracy.". . . We have recently noted that the privilege against self-incrimination — the essential mainstay of our adversary system — is founded on a complex of values. . . . All these policies point to one overriding thought: the constitutional foundation underlying the privilege is the respect a government — state or federal — must accord to the dignity and integrity of its citizens. To maintain a "fair state-individual balance," to require the government "to shoulder the entire load," 8 Wigmore, Evidence 317 (McNaughton rev. 1961), to respect the inviolability of the human personality, our accusatory system of criminal justice demands that the government seeking to punish an individual pro-

duce the evidence against him by its own independent labors, rather than by the cruel, simple expedient of compelling it from his own mouth. . . . In sum, the privilege is fulfilled only when the person is guaranteed the right "to remain silent unless he chooses to speak in the unfettered exercise of his own will.". . .

III

Today, then, there can be no doubt that the Fifth Amendment privilege is available outside of criminal court proceedings and serves to protect persons in all settings in which their freedom of action is curtailed in any significant way from being compelled to incriminate themselves. We have concluded that without proper safeguards the process of in-custody interrogation of persons suspected or accused of crime contains inherently compelling pressures which work to undermine the individual's will to resist and to compel him to speak where he would not otherwise do so freely. In order to combat these pressures and to permit a full opportunity to exercise the privilege against self-incrimination, the accused must be adequately and effectively apprised of his rights and the exercise of those rights must be fully honored.

It is impossible for us to forsee the potential alternatives for protecting the privilege which might be devised by Congress or the States in the exercise of their creative rule-making capacities. Therefore we cannot say that the Constitution necessarily requires adherence to any particular solution for the inherent compulsions of the interrogation process as it is presently conducted. Our decision in no way creates a constitutional straitjacket which will handicap sound efforts at reform, nor is it intended to have this effect. We encourage Congress and the States to continue their laudable search for increasingly effective ways of protecting the rights of the individual while promoting efficient enforcement of our criminal laws. However, unless we are shown other procedures which are at least as effective in apprising accused persons of their right of silence and in assuring a continuous opportunity to exercise it, the following safeguards must be observed.

At the outset, if a person in custody is to be subjected to interrogation, he must first be informed in clear and unequivocal terms that he has the right to remain silent. For those unaware of the privilege, the warning is needed simply to make them aware of it — the threshold requirement for an intelligent decision as to its exercise. More important, such a warning is an absolute prerequisite in overcoming the inherent pressures of the interrogation atmosphere. It is not just the subnormal or woefully ignorant who succumb to an interrogator's imprecations, whether implied or expressly stated, that the interrogation will continue until a confession is obtained or that silence in the face of accusation is itself damning and will bode ill when presented to a jury. Further, the warning will show the individual that his interrogators are prepared to recognize his privilege should he choose to exercise it.

. . . .

The warning of the right to remain silent must be accompanied by the explanation that anything said can and will be used against the individual in court. This warning is needed in order to make him aware not only of the privilege, but also of the consequences of forgoing it. . . .

. . . .

An individual need not make a pre-interrogation request for a lawyer. While such request affirmatively secures his right to have one, his failure to ask for a lawyer does not constitute a waiver. No effective waiver of the right to counsel during interrogation can be recognized unless specifically made after the warnings we here delineate have been given. . . .

Accordingly we hold that an individual held for interrogation must be clearly informed that he has the right to consult with a lawyer and to have the lawyer with him during interrogation under the system for protecting the privilege we delineate today. As with the warnings of the right to remain silent and that anything stated can be used in evidence against him, this warning is an absolute prerequisite to interrogation. No amount of circumstantial evidence that the person may have been aware of this right will suffice to stand in its stead. Only through such a warning is there ascertainable assurance that the accused was aware of this right.

. . . [I]t is necessary to warn him not only that he has the right to consult with an attorney, but also that if he is indigent a lawyer will be appointed to represent him. Without this additional warning, the admonition of the right to consult with counsel would often be understood as meaning only that he can consult with a lawyer if he has one or has the funds to obtain one. . . .

. . . .

If the interrogation continues without the presence of an attorney and a statement is taken, a heavy burden rests on the government to demonstrate that the defendant knowingly and intelligently waived his privilege against self-incrimination and his right to retained or appointed counsel. . . .

. . . .

Our decision is not intended to hamper the traditional function of police officers in investigating crime. . . . When an individual is in custody on probable cause, the police may, of course, seek out evidence in the field to be used at trial against him. Such investigation may include inquiry of persons not under restraint. General on-the-scene questioning as to facts surrounding a crime or other general questioning of citizens in the fact-finding process is not affected by our holding. It is an act of responsible citizenship for individuals to give whatever information they may have to aid in law enforcement. In such situations the compelling atmosphere inherent in the process of in-custody interrogation is not necessarily present.

In dealing with statements obtained through interrogation, we do not purport to find all confessions inadmissible. Confessions remain a proper element in law enforcement. Any statement given freely and voluntarily without any compelling influences is, of course, admissible in evidence. The fundamental import of the privilege while an individual is in custody is not whether he is allowed to talk to the police without the benefit of warnings and counsel, but whether he can be interrogated. There is no requirement that police stop a person who enters a police station and states that he wishes to confess to a crime, or a person who calls the police to offer a confession or any other statement he desires to make. Volunteered statements of any kind are not barred by the Fifth Amendment and their admissibility is not affected by our holding today.

To summarize, we hold that when an individual is taken into custody or otherwise deprived of his freedom by the authorities in any significant way and is subjected to questioning, the privilege against self-incrimination is jeopardized. Procedural safeguards must be employed to protect the privilege, and unless other fully effective means are adopted to notify the person of his right of silence and to assure that the exercise of the right will be scrupulously honored, the following measures are required. He must be warned prior to any questioning that he has the right to remain silent, that anything he says can be used against him in a court of law, that he has the right to the presence of an attorney, and that if he cannot afford an attorney one will be appointed for him prior to any questioning if he so desires. Opportunity to exercise these rights must be afforded to him throughout the interrogation. After such warnings have been given, and such opportunity afforded him, the individual may knowingly and intelligently waive these rights and agree to answer questions or make a statement. But unless and until such warnings and waiver are demonstrated by the prosecution at trial, no evidence obtained as a result of interrogation can be used against him.

IV

If the individual desires to exercise his privilege, he has the right to do so. This is not for the authorities to decide. An attorney may advise his client not to talk to police until he has had an opportunity to investigate the case, or he may wish to be present with his client during any police questioning. In doing so an attorney is merely exercising the good professional judgment he has been taught. This is not cause for considering the attorney a menace to law enforcement. He is merely carrying out what he is sworn to do under his oath — to protect to the extent of his ability the rights of his client. In fulfilling this responsibility the attorney plays a vital role in the administration of criminal justice under our Constitution.

In announcing these principles, we are not unmindful of the burdens which law enforcement officials must bear, often under trying circumstances. We also fully recognize the obligations of all citizens to aid in enforcing the criminal laws. This Court, while protecting individual rights, has always given ample latitude to law enforcement agencies in the legitimate exercise of their duties. The limits we have placed on the interrogation process should not constitute an undue interference with a proper system of law enforcement. . . .

It is also urged that an unfettered right to detention for interrogation should be allowed because it will often redound to the benefit of the person questioned. When police inquiry determines that there is no reason to believe that the person has committed any crime, it is said, he will be released without need for further formal procedures. The person who has committed no offense, however, will be better able to clear himself after warnings with counsel present than without. It can be assumed that in such circumstances a lawyer would advise his client to talk freely to police in order to clear himself.

Custodial interrogation, by contrast, does not necessarily afford the innocent an opportunity to clear themselves. A serious consequence of the present practice of the interrogation alleged to be beneficial for the innocent is that many arrests "for investigation" subject large numbers of innocent persons to detention and interrogation. In one of the cases before us, No. 584, *California* v. *Stewart,* police held four persons, who were in the defendant's house at the time of the arrest, in jail for five days until defendant confessed. At that time they were finally released. Police stated that there was "no evidence to connect them with any crime." Available statistics on the extent of this practice where it is condoned indicated that these four are far from alone in being sub-jected to arrest, prolonged detention, and interrogation without the requisite probable cause.

Over the years the Federal Bureau of Investigation has compiled an exemplary record of effective law enforcement while advising any suspect or arrested person, at the outset of an interview, that he is not required to make a statement, that any statement may be used against him in court, that the individual may obtain the services of an attorney of his own choice and, more recently, that he has a right to free counsel if he is unable to pay. A letter received from the Solicitor General in response to a question from the Bench makes it clear that the present pattern of warnings and respect for the rights of the individual followed as a practice by the FBI is consistent with the procedure which we delineate today.

It is also urged upon us that we withhold decision on this issue until state legislative bodies and advisory groups have had an opportunity to deal with these problems by rule making. We have already pointed out that the Constitution does not require any specific code of procedures for protecting the privilege against self-incrimination during custodial interrogation. Congress and the States are free to develop their own safeguards for the privilege, so long as they are fully as effective as those described above in informing accused persons of their right of silence and in affording a continuous opportunity to exercise it. In any event, however, the issues presented are of constitutional dimensions and must be determined by the courts. The admissibility of a statement in the face of a claim that it was obtained in violation of the defendant's constitutional rights is an issue the resolution of which has long since been undertaken by this Court. Judicial solutions to problems of constitutional dimension have evolved decade by decade. As courts have been presented with the need to enforce constitutional rights, they have found means of doing so. . . . Where rights secured by the Constitution are involved, there can be no rule making or legislation which would abrogate them.

MR. JUSTICE CLARK, dissenting in part and concurring in part.

Custodial interrogation has long been recognized as "undoubtedly an essential tool in effective law enforcement." Recognition of this fact should put us on guard against the promulgation of doctrinaire rules. Especially is this true where the Court finds that "the Constitution has prescribed" its holdings and where the light of our past cases is to the contrary. Indeed, even in *Escobedo* the Court never hinted that an affirmative "waiver" was a prerequisite to questioning; that the burden of proof as to waiver was on the prosecution; that the presence of counsel — absent a waiver — during interrogation was required; that a waiver can be withdrawn at the will of the accused; that counsel must be furnished during an accusatory stage to those unable to pay; nor that admissions and exculpatory statements are "confessions." To require all those things at one gulp should cause the Court to choke. . . .

The rule prior to today . . . depended upon "a totality of circumstances evidencing an involuntary . . . admission of guilt."

I would continue to follow that rule. Under the "totality of circumstances" rule, . . . I would consider in each case whether the police officer prior to custodial interrogation added the warning that the suspect might have counsel present at the interrogation and, further, that a court would appoint one at his request if he was too poor to employ counsel. In the absence of warnings, the burden would be on the State to prove that counsel was knowingly and intelligently waived or that in the totality of the circumstances, including the failure to give the necessary warnings, the confession was clearly voluntary.

Rather than employing the arbitrary Fifth Amendment rule which the Court lays down I would follow the more pliable dictates of the Due Process Clauses of the Fifth and Fourteenth Amendments which we are accustomed to administering and which we know from our cases are effective instruments in protecting persons in police custody. In this way we would not be acting in the dark nor in one full sweep changing the traditional rules of custodial interrogation which this Court has for so long recognized as a justifiable and proper tool in balancing individual rights against the rights of society. It will be soon enough to go further when we are able to appraise with somewhat better accuracy the effect of such a holding.

I would affirm the convictions in *Miranda* v. *Arizona,* No. 759; *Vignera* v. *New York,* No. 760; and *Westover* v. *United States,* No. 761. In each of those cases I find from the circumstances no warrant for reversal. In *California* v. *Stewart,* No. 584, I would dismiss the writ of certiorari for want of a final judgment, 28 U.S.C. §1257(3) (1964 ed.); but if the merits are to be reached I would affirm on the ground that the State failed to fulfill its burden, in the absence of a showing that appropriate warnings were given, of proving a waiver or a totality of circumstances showing voluntariness. Should there be a retrial, I would leave the State free to attempt to prove these elements.

MR. JUSTICE HARLAN, whom MR. JUSTICE STEWART and MR. JUSTICE WHITE join, dissenting.

I believe the decision of the Court represents poor constitutional law and entails harmful consequences for the country at large. How serious these consequences may prove to be only time can tell. But the basic flaws in the Court's justification seem to me readily apparent now once all sides of the problem are considered.

. . . .

While the fine points of this scheme are far less clear than the Court admits, the tenor is quite apparent. The new rules are not designed to guard against police brutality or other unmistakably banned forms of coercion. Those who use third-degree tactics and deny them in court are equally able and destined to lie as skillfully about warnings and waivers. Rather, the thrust of the new rules is to negate all pressures, to reinforce the nervous or ignorant suspect, and ultimately to discourage any confession at all. The aim in short is toward "voluntariness" in a utopian sense, or to view it from a different angle, voluntariness with a vengeance.

To incorporate this notion into the Constitution requires a strained reading of history and precedent and a disregard of the very pragmatic concerns that alone may on occasion justify such strains. I believe that reasoned examination will show that the Due Process Clauses provide an adequate tool for coping with confessions and that, even if the Fifth Amendment privilege against self-incrimination be invoked, its precedents taken as a whole do not sustain the present rules. Viewed as a choice based on pure policy, these new rules prove to be a highly debatable, if not one-sided, appraisal of the competing interests, imposed over widespread objection, at the very time when judicial restraint is most called for by the circumstances.

. . . .

What the Court largely ignores is that its rules impair, if they will not eventually serve wholly to frustrate, an instrument of law enforcement that has long and quite reasonably been thought worth the price paid for it. There can be little doubt that the Court's new code would markedly decrease the number of confessions. To warn the suspect that he may remain silent and remind him that his confession may be used in court are minor obstructions. To require also an express waiver by the suspect and an end to questioning whenever he demurs must heavily handicap questioning. And to suggest or provide counsel for the suspect simply invites the end of the interrogation. . . .

How much harm this decision will inflict on law enforcement cannot fairly be predicted with accuracy. Evidence on the role of confessions is notoriously incomplete. . . . We do know that some crimes cannot be solved without confessions, that ample expert testimony attests to their importance in crime control, and that the Court is taking a real risk with society's welfare in imposing its new regime on the country. The social costs of crime are too great to call the new rules anything but a hazardous experimentation.

While passing over the costs and risks of its experiment, the Court portrays the evils of normal police questioning in terms which I think are exaggerated. Albeit stringently confined by the due process standards interrogation is no doubt often inconvenient and unpleasant for the suspect. However, it is no less so for a man to be arrested and jailed, to have his house searched, or to stand trial in court, yet all this may properly happen to the most innocent given probable cause, a warrant, or an indictment. Society has always paid a stiff price for law and order, and peaceful interrogation is not one of the dark moments of the law.

This brief statement of the competing considerations seems to me ample proof that the Court's preference is highly debatable at best and therefore not to be read into the Constitution. . . .

New York v. Quarles

467 U.S. 649 (1984)
Vote: 5–1–3

Two police officers were on patrol in New York City late one night when a woman approached their car and told them she had just been raped by a man whose clothing she described in detail. She also told the officers that the man had entered a nearby supermarket and that he was carrying a gun. One of the officers entered the store, spotted the suspect, and, after a brief pursuit, in which the officer held his drawn gun, cornered and captured the suspect.

Assisted by three other police officers who had just arrived, the first officer frisked the suspect and discovered an empty shoulder holster. After handcuffing him, the officer asked him where his gun was. The suspect nodded in the direction of some empty cartons and responded, "The gun is over there." The officer then retrieved a loaded .38 caliber revolver from one of the cartons, formally placed Quarles under arrest, and then read him his MIRANDA rights. Quarles then indicated he

would be willing to answer questions without an attorney present and did so.

In subsequent prosecution for possession of a weapon (the state did not pursue the charge of rape for reasons unknown to the Supreme Court), the judge excluded both Quarles' statement — "The gun is over there" — and the gun itself on grounds that they were both tainted by the officer's MIRANDA violation. This ruling was affirmed by the New York State Court of Appeals and arrived at the United States Supreme Court by writ of certiorari.

The day before the Supreme Court handed down this decision, it ruled on *Nix* v. *Williams*, 467 U.S. 431 (1984), in which it carved out an "inevitable discovery" exception that allows evidence obtained in violation of Sixth Amendment rights to be introduced if that evidence would "inevitably" or "ultimately" have been discovered anyway.

One of the continuing criticisms of law enforcement officials is that the rulings of the Warren Court are ambiguous and confusing to police, who have to apply them in tense situations. By creating these two exceptions, does the Court move towards greater or less clarity of MIRANDA? Compare the assessments of relative danger in the QUARLES case by Justices Rehnquist and Marshall. If they cannot agree in this situation, how can we expect police officers to?

JUSTICE REHNQUIST delivered the opinion of the Court.

The Fifth Amendment guarantees that "[n]o person . . . shall be compelled in any criminal case to be a witness against himself." . . . In *Miranda* this Court for the first time extended the Fifth Amendment privilege against compulsory self-incrimination to individuals subjected to custodial interrogation by the police. . . . The Fifth Amendment itself does not prohibit all incriminating admissions; "[a]bsent some officially *coerced* self-accusation, the Fifth Amendment privilege is not violated by even the most damning admissions." . . . The *Miranda* Court, however, presumed that interrogation in certain custodial circumstances is inherently coercive and held that statements made under those circumstances are inadmissible unless the suspect is specifically informed of his *Miranda* rights and freely decides to forgo those rights. The prophylactic *Miranda* warnings therefore are "not themselves rights protected by the Constitution but [are] instead measures to insure that the right against compulsory self-incrimination [is] protected." *Michigan* v. *Tucker* . . . (1974). Requiring *Miranda* warnings before custodial interrogation provides "practical reinforcement" for the Fifth Amendment right. *Michigan* v. *Tucker.*

In this case we have before us no claim that respondent's statements were actually compelled by police conduct which overcame his will to resist. . . . Thus the only issue before us is whether Officer Kraft was justified in failing to make available to respondent the procedural safeguards associated with the privilege against compulsory self-incrimination since *Miranda.*

The New York Court of Appeals was undoubtedly correct in deciding that the facts of this case come within the ambit of the *Miranda* decision as we have subsequently interpreted it. We agree that respondent was in police custody because we have noted that "the ultimate inquiry is simply whether there is a 'formal arrest or restraint on freedom of movement' of the degree associated with a formal arrest." . . . Here Quarles was surrounded by at least four police officers and was handcuffed when the questioning at issue took place. As the New York Court of Appeals observed, there was nothing to suggest that any of the officers were any longer concerned for their own physical safety. . . . The New York Court of Appeals' majority declined to express an opinion as to whether there might be an exception to the *Miranda* rule if the police had been acting to protect the public, because the lower courts in New York had made no factual determination that the police had acted with that motive.

We hold that on these facts there is a "public safety" exception to the requirement that *Miranda* warnings be given before a suspect's answers may be admitted into evidence, and that the availability of that exception does not depend upon the motivation of the individual officers involved. In a kaleidoscopic situation such as the one confronting these officers, where spontaneity rather than adherence to a police manual is necessarily the order of the day, the application of the exception which we recognize today should not be made to depend on *post hoc* findings at a suppression hearing concerning the subjective motivation of the arresting officer. Undoubtedly most police officers, if placed in Officer Kraft's position, would act out of a host of different, instinctive, and largely unverifiable motives — their own safety, the safety of others, and perhaps as well the desire to obtain incriminating evidence from the suspect.

Whatever the motivation of individual officers in such a situation, we do not believe that the doctrinal underpinnings of *Miranda* require that it be applied in all its rigor to a situation in which police officers ask questions reasonably prompted by a concern for the public safety. The *Miranda* decision was based in large part on this Court's view that the warnings which it required police to give to suspects in custody would reduce the likelihood that the suspects would fall victim to constitutionally impermissible practices of police interrogation in the presumptively coercive environment of the station house. . . . The dissenters warned that the requirement of *Miranda* warnings would have the effect of decreasing the number of suspects who respond to police questioning. . . . The *Miranda* majority, however, apparently felt that whatever the cost to society in terms of fewer convictions of guilty suspects, that cost would simply have to be borne in the interest of enlarged protection for the Fifth Amendment privilege.

The police in this case, in the very act of apprehending a suspect, were confronted with the immediate necessity of ascertaining the whereabouts of a gun which they had every reason to believe the suspect had just removed from his empty holster and discarded in the supermarket. So long as the gun was concealed somewhere in the supermarket, with its actual whereabouts unknown, it obviously posed more than one danger to the public safety: an accomplice might make use of it, a customer or employee might later come upon it.

In such a situation, if the police are required to recite the familiar *Miranda* warnings before asking the whereabouts of the gun, suspects in Quarles' position might well be deterred from responding. Procedural safeguards which deter a suspect from responding were deemed acceptable in *Miranda* in order to protect the Fifth Amendment privilege; when the primary social cost of those added protections is the possibility of fewer convictions, the *Miranda* majority was willing to bear that cost. Here, had *Miranda* warnings deterred Quarles from responding to Officer Kraft's question about the whereabouts of the gun, the cost would have been something more than merely the failure to obtain evidence useful in convicting Quarles. Officer Kraft needed an answer to his question not simply to make his case against Quarles but to insure that further danger to the public did not result from the concealment of the gun in a public area.

We conclude that the need for answers to questions in a situation posing a threat to the public safety outweighs the need for the prophylactic rule protecting the Fifth Amendment's privilege against self-incrimination. We decline to place officers such as Officer Kraft in the untenable position of having to consider, often in a matter of seconds, whether it best serves society for them to ask the necessary questions without the *Miranda* warnings and render whatever probative evidence they uncover inadmissible, or for them to give the warnings in order to preserve the admissibility of evidence they might uncover but possibly damage or destroy their ability to obtain that evidence and neutralize the volatile situation confronting them.

In recognizing a narrow exception to the *Miranda* rule in this case, we acknowledge that to some degree we lessen the desirable clarity of that rule. At least in part in order to preserve its clarity, we have over the years refused to sanction attempts to expand our *Miranda* holding. See, *e.g., Minnesota* v. *Murphy*... (1984) (refusal to extend *Miranda* requirements to interviews with probation officers); *Fare* v. *Michael C.* ... (1979) (refusal to equate request to see a probation officer with request to see a lawyer for *Miranda* purposes); *Beckwith* v. *United States*... (1976) (refusal to extend *Miranda* requirements to questioning in non-custodial circumstances). As we have in other contexts, we recognize here the importance of a workable rule "to guide police officers, who have only limited time and expertise to reflect on and balance the social and individual interests involved in the specific circumstances they confront." *Dunaway* v. *New York*... (1979). But as we have pointed out, we believe that the exception which we recognize today lessens the necessity of that on-the-scene balancing process. The exception will not be difficult for police officers to apply because in each case it will be circumscribed by the exigency which justifies it. We think police officers can and will distinguish almost instinctively between questions necessary to secure their own safety or the safety of the public and questions designed solely to elicit testimonial evidence from a suspect.

The facts of this case clearly demonstrate that distinction and an officer's ability to recognize it. Officer Kraft asked only the question necessary to locate the missing gun before advising respondent of his rights. It was only after securing the loaded revolver and giving the warnings that he continued with investigatory questions about the ownership and place of purchase of the gun. The exception which we recognize today, far from complicating the thought processes and the on-the-scene judgments of police officers, will simply free them to follow their legitimate instincts when confronting situations presenting a danger to the public safety.

We hold that the Court of Appeals in this case erred in excluding the statement, "the gun is over there," and the gun because of the officer's failure to read respondent his *Miranda* rights before attempting to locate the weapon. Accordingly we hold that it also erred in excluding the subsequent statements as illegal fruits of a *Miranda* violation. We therefore reverse and remand for further proceedings not inconsistent with this opinion.

It is so ordered.

JUSTICE O'CONNOR, concurring in part in the judgment and dissenting in part.

In *Miranda* v. *Arizona*... the Court held unconstitutional, because inherently compelled, the admission of statements derived from in-custody questioning not preceded by an explanation of the privilege against self-incrimination and the consequences of foregoing it. Today, the Court concludes that overriding considerations of public safety justify the admission of evidence — oral statements and a gun — secured without the benefit of such warnings. In so holding, the Court acknowledges that it is departing from prior precedent, and that it is "lessen[ing] the desirable clarity of [the *Miranda* rule]." Were the Court writing from a clean slate, I could agree with its holding. But *Miranda* is now the law and, in my view, the Court has not provided sufficient justification for departing from it or for blurring its now clear strictures. Accordingly, I would require suppression of the initial statement taken from respondent in this case. On the other hand, nothing in *Miranda* or the privilege itself requires exclusion of nontestimonial evidence derived from informal custodial interrogation, and I therefore agree with the Court that admission of the gun in evidence is proper.

. . . .

The distinction between testimonial and nontestimonial evidence was explored in some detail in *Schmerber* v. *California* [1966], a decision this Court handed down within a week of deciding *Miranda*. The defendant in *Schmerber* had argued that the privilege against self-incrimination barred the state from compelling him to submit to a blood test, the results of which would be used to prove his guilt at trial. The State, on the other hand, had urged that the privilege prohibited it only from compelling the accused to make a formal testimonial statement against himself in an official legal proceeding. This Court rejected both positions. It favored an approach that protected the "accused only from being compelled to testify against himself, or otherwise provide the State with evidence of a testimonial or communicative nature." The blood tests were admissible because they were neither testimonial nor communicative in nature.

The Court has applied this bifurcated approach in its subsequent cases as well. For example, in *United States* v. *Wade,* where admission of a line-up identification was approved, the Court emphasized that no question was presented as to the admissibility of anything said or done at the lineup.... Likewise, in *Michigan* v. *Tucker,* where evidence derived from a technical *Miranda* violation was admitted, the Court noted that no statement taken without *Miranda* warnings was being admitted into evidence.... Thus, based on the distinction first articulated in *Schmerber,* "a strong analytical argument can be made for an intermediate rule whereby[,] although [the police] cannot require the suspect to speak by punishment or force, the nontestimonial [evidence derived from] speech that is [itself] excludable for failure to comply with the *Miranda* code could still be used."...

...[W]hatever case can be made for suppression evaporates when the statements themselves are not admitted, given the rationale of the *Schmerber* line of cases. Certainly interrogation which provides leads to other evidence does not offend the values underlying the Fifth Amendment privilege any more than the compulsory taking of blood samples, fingerprints, or voice exemplars, all of which may be compelled in an "attempt to discover evidence that might be used to prosecute [a defendant] for a criminal offense."... Use of a suspect's answers "merely to find other evidence establishing his connection with the crime [simply] differs only by a shade from the permitted use for that purpose of his body or his blood."... The values underlying the privilege may justify exclusion of an unwarned person's out-of-court statements.... But when the only evidence to be admitted is derivative evidence such as a gun — derived not from actual compulsion but from a statement taken in the absence of *Miranda* warnings — those values simply cannot require suppression, at least no more so than they would for other such nontestimonial evidence.

On the other hand, if a suspect is subject to abusive police practices and actually or overtly compelled to speak, it is reasonable to infer both an unwillingness to speak and a perceptible assertion of the privilege.... Thus, when the *Miranda* violation consists of a deliberate and flagrant abuse of the accused's constitutional rights, amounting to a denial of due process, application of a broader exclusionary rule is warranted. Of course, "a defendant raising [such] a coerced-confession claim... must first prevail in a voluntariness hearing before his confession and evidence derived from it [will] become inadmissible."... By contrast, where the accused proves only that the police failed to administer the *Miranda* warnings, exclusion of the statement itself is all that will and should be required. Limitation of the *Miranda* prohibition to testimonial use of the statements themselves adequately serves the purposes of the privilege against self-incrimination.

JUSTICE MARSHALL, with whom JUSTICE BRENNAN and JUSTICE STEVENS join, dissenting.

Earlier this Term, the four members of the majority joined an opinion stating: "[Q]uestions of historical fact... must be determined, in the first instance, by state courts and deferred to, in the absence of 'convincing evidence' to the contrary, by the federal courts."... In this case, there was convincing, indeed almost overwhelming, evidence to support the New York court's conclusion that Quarles' hidden weapon did not pose a risk either to the arresting officers or to the public. The majority ignores this evidence and sets aside the factual findings of the New York Court of Appeals. More cynical observers might well conclude that a state court's findings of fact "deserve[] a 'high measure of deference,'"... only when deference works against the interests of a criminal defendant.

The majority's treatment of the legal issues presented in this case is no less troubling than its abuse of the facts. Before today's opinion, the Court had twice concluded that, under *Miranda* v. *Arizona,* police officers conducting custodial interrogations must advise suspects of their rights before any questions concerning the whereabouts of incriminating weapons can be asked. *Rhode Island* v. *Innis*... (1980) (dicta); *Orozco* v. *Texas*... (1969) (holding). Now the majority departs from these cases and rules that police may withhold *Miranda* warnings whenever custodial interrogations concern matters of public safety.

Before today's opinion, the procedures established in *Miranda* v. *Arizona* had "the virtue of informing police and prosecutors with specificity as to what they may do in conducting custodial interrogation, and of informing courts under what circumstances statements obtained during such interrogations are not admissible."... In a chimerical quest for public safety, the majority has abandoned the rule that brought eighteen years of doctrinal tranquility to the field of custodial interrogations. As the majority candidly concedes, a public-safety exception destroys forever the clarity of *Miranda* for both law enforcement officers and members of the judiciary. The Court's candor cannot mask what a serious loss the administration of justice has incurred.

This case is illustrative of the chaos the "public-safety" exception will unleash. . . .

If after plenary review two appellate courts so fundamentally differ over the threat to public safety presented by the simple and uncontested facts of this case, one must seriously question how law enforcement officers will respond to the majority's new rule in the confusion and haste of the real world. . . . Not only will police officers have to decide whether the objective facts of an arrest justify an unconsented custodial interrogation; they will also have to remember to interrupt the interrogation and read the suspect his *Miranda* warnings once the focus of the inquiry shifts from protecting the public's safety to ascertaining the suspect's guilt. Disagreements of the scope of the "public-safety" exception and mistakes in its application are inevitable.

. . .

Though unfortunate, the difficulty of administering the "public-safety" exception is not the most profound flaw in the majority's decision. . . .

The majority's error stems from a serious misunderstanding of *Miranda* v. *Arizona* and of the Fifth Amendment upon which that decision was based. The majority implies that *Miranda* consisted of no more than a judicial balancing act in which the benefits of "enlarged protection for the Fifth Amendment privilege" were weighed against "the cost to society in terms of fewer convictions of guilty suspects." Supposedly because the scales tipped in favor of the privilege against self-incrimination, the *Miranda* Court erected a prophylactic barrier around statements made during custodial interrogations. The majority now proposes to return to the scales of social utility to calculate whether *Miranda's* prophylactic rule remains cost-effective when threats to the public's safety are added to the balance. The results of the majority's "test" are announced with pseudo-scientific precision. . . .

. . . .

Miranda v. *Arizona* was the culmination of a century-long inquiry into how this Court should deal with confessions made during custodial interrogations. Long before *Miranda,* the Court had recognized that the Federal Government was prohibited from introducing at criminal trials compelled confessions, including confessions compelled in the course of custodial interrogations. In 1924, Justice Brandeis was reciting settled law when he wrote: "[A] confession obtained by compulsion must be excluded whatever may have been the character of the compulsion, and whether the compulsion was applied in a judicial proceeding or otherwise." . . .

Prosecutors in state courts were subject to similar constitutional restrictions. Even before *Malloy* v. *Hogan,* . . . (1964), formally applied the Self-Incrimination Clause of the Fifth Amendment to the States, the Due Process Clause constrained the States from extorting confessions from criminal defendants. *Chambers* v. *Florida* . . . (1940); *Brown* v. *Mississippi* . . . (1936). Indeed, by the time of *Malloy,* the constraints of the Due Process Clause were almost as stringent as the requirements of the Fifth Amendment itself. . . .

When *Miranda* reached this Court, it was undisputed that both the States and the Federal Government were constitutionally prohibited from prosecuting defendants with confessions coerced during custodial interrogations. As a theoretical matter, the law was clear. In practice, however, the courts found it exceedingly difficult to determine whether a given confession had been coerced. Difficulties of proof and subleties of interrogation technique made it impossible in most cases for the judiciary to decide with confidence whether the defendant had voluntarily confessed his guilt or whether his testimony had been unconstitutionally compelled. Courts around the country were spending countless hours reviewing the facts of individual custodial interrogations.

Miranda dealt with these practical problems. After a detailed examination of police practices and a review of its previous decisions in the area, the Court in *Miranda* determined that custodial interrogations are inherently coercive. The Court therefore created a constitutional presumption that statements made during custodial interrogations are compelled in violation of the Fifth Amendment and are thus inadmissible in criminal prosecutions. As a result of the Court's decision in *Miranda,* a statement made during a custodial interrogation may be introduced as proof of a defendant's guilt only if the prosecution demonstrates that the defendant knowingly and intelligently waived his constitutional rights before making the statement. The now-familiar *Miranda* warnings offer law-enforcement authorities a clear, easily administered device for ensuring that criminal suspects understand their constitutional rights well enough to waive them and to engage in consensual custodial interrogation.

In fashioning its "public-safety" exception to *Miranda,* the majority makes no attempt to deal with the constitutional presumption established by that case. The majority does not argue that police questioning about issues of public safety is any less coercive than custodial interrogations into other matters. The majority's only contention is that police officers could more easily protect the public if *Miranda* did not apply to custodial interrogations concerning the public's safety. But *Miranda* was not a decision about public safety; it was a decision about coerced confessions. Without establishing that interrogations concerning the public's safety are less likely to be coercive than other interrogations, the majority cannot endorse the "public-safety" exception and remain faithful to the logic of *Miranda* v. *Arizona*.

The majority's avoidance of the issue of coercion may not have been inadvertent. It would strain credulity to contend that Officer Kraft's questioning of respondent Quarles was not coercive. In the middle of the night and in the back of an empty supermarket, Quarles was surrounded by four armed police officers. His hands were handcuffed behind his back. . . .

That the application of the "public-safety" exception in this case entailed coercion is no happenstance. The majority's *ratio decidendi* is that interrogating suspects about matters of public safety *will* be coercive. In its cost-benefit analysis, the Court's strongest argument in favor of a public-safety exception to *Miranda* is that the police would be better able to protect the public's safety if they were not always required to give suspects their *Miranda* warnings. The crux of this argument is that, by deliberately withholding *Miranda* warnings, the police can get information out of suspects who would refuse to respond to police questioning were they advised of their constitutional rights. The "public-safety" exceptions is efficacious precisely because it permits police officers to coerce criminal defendants into making involuntary statements.

. . . .

The irony of the majority's decision is that the public's safety can be perfectly well protected without abridging the Fifth Amendment. If a bomb is about to explode or the public is otherwise imminently imperiled, the police are free to interrogate suspects without advising them of their constitutional rights. . . .

To a limited degree, the majority is correct that there is a cost associated with the Fifth Amendment's ban on introducing coerced self-incriminating statements at trial. Without a "public-safety" exception, there would be occasions when a defendant incriminated himself by revealing a threat to the public, and the State was unable to prosecute because the defendant retracted his statement after consulting with counsel and the police cannot find independent proof of guilt. Such occasions would not, however, be common. The prosecution does not always lose the use of incriminating information revealed in these situations. After consulting with counsel, a suspect may well volunteer to repeat his statement in hopes of gaining a favorable plea bargain or more lenient sentence. The majority thus overstates its case when it suggests that a police officer must necessarily choose between public safety and admissibility.

But however frequently or infrequently such cases arise, their regularity is irrelevant. The Fifth Amendment prohibits compelled self-incrimination. As the Court has explained on numerous occasions, this prohibition is the mainstay of our adversarial system of criminal justice. Not only does it protect us against the inherent unreliability of compelled testimony, but it also ensures that criminal investigations will be conducted with integrity and that the judiciary will avoid the taint of official lawlessness. . . . The policies underlying the Fifth Amendment's privilege against self-incrimination are not diminished simply because testimony is compelled to protect the public's safety. The majority should not be permitted to elude the Amendment's absolute prohibition simply by calculating special costs that arise when the public's safety is at issue. Indeed, were constitutional adjudication always conducted in such an *ad hoc* manner, the Bill of Rights would be a most unreliable protector of individual liberties.

Having determined that the Fifth Amendment renders inadmissible Quarles' response to Officer Kraft's questioning, I have no doubt that our precedents require that the gun discovered as a direct result of Quarles' statement must be presumed inadmissible as well. . . .

. . . .

Accordingly, I would affirm the order of the Court of Appeals to the extent that it found Quarles' testimony inadmissible under the Fifth Amendment, would vacate the order to the extent that it suppressed Quarles' gun, and would remand the matter for reconsideration in light of *Nix* v. *Williams* [1984]. [This case permits introduction into evidence of tainted "fruits" that inevitably would have been discovered in the absence of the questioning.]

Gardner v. Broderick

392 U.S. 273 (1968)
Vote: 9–0

Gardner, a New York City Police officer, was called before a grand jury investigating alleged bribery and corruption of police officers. He was advised that the grand jury would be questioning him about his activities. Gardner was further advised of his rights and asked to sign a "waiver of immunity," being told that in accordance with state and city law, he would lose his job if he did not sign the waiver. Gardner refused and subsequently lost his job. He sued for reinstatement and back pay.

Gardner's dismissal was upheld by the New York courts, whereupon he appealed to the Supreme Court of the United States.

MR. JUSTICE FORTAS delivered the opinion of the Court.

The question presented in the present case is whether a policeman who refuses to waive the protections which the privilege gives him may be dismissed from office because of that refusal.

About a year and a half after New York City discharged petitioner for his refusal to waive this immunity, we decided *Garrity* v. *New Jersey* . . . (1967). In that case, we held that when a policeman had been compelled to testify by the threat that otherwise he would be removed from office, the testimony that he gave could not be used against him in a subsequent prosecution. Garrity had not signed a waiver of immunity and no immunity statute was applicable in the circumstances. . . .

The New York Court of Appeals considered that *Garrity* did not control the present case. It is true that *Garrity* related to the attempted use of compelled testimony. It did not involve the precise question which is presented here: namely, whether a State may discharge an officer for refusing to waive a right which the Constitution guarantees to him. The New York Court of Appeals also distinguished our post-*Garrity* decision in *Spevack* v. *Klein,* supra. In *Spevack,* we ruled that a lawyer could not be disbarred solely because he refused to testify at a disciplinary proceeding on the ground that his testimony would tend to incriminate him. The Court of Appeals concluded that *Spevack* does not control the present case because different considerations apply in the case of a public official such as a policeman. A lawyer, it stated, although licensed by the state is not an employee. This distinction is now urged upon us. It is argued that although a lawyer could not constitutionally be confronted with Hobson's choice between self-incrimination and forfeiting his means of livelihood, the same principle should not protect a policeman. Unlike the lawyer, he is directly, immediately, and entirely responsible to the city or State

which is his employer. He owes his entire loyalty to it. He has no other "client" or principal. He is a trustee of the public interest, bearing the burden of great and total responsibility to his public employer. Unlike the lawyer who is directly responsible to his client, the policeman is either responsible to the State or to no one.

We agree that these factors differentiate the situations. If appellant, a policeman, had refused to answer questions specifically, directly, and narrowly relating to the performance of his official duties, without being required to waive his immunity with respect to the use of his answers or the fruits thereof in a criminal prosecution of himself, *Garrity* v. *New Jersey,* supra, the privilege against self-incrimination would not have been a bar to his dismissal.

The facts of this case, however, do not present this issue. Here, petitioner was summoned to testify before a grand jury in an investigation of alleged criminal conduct. He was discharged from office, not for failure to answer relevant questions about his official duties, but for refusal to waive a constitutional right. He was dismissed for failure to relinquish the protections of the privilege against self-incrimination. The Constitution of New York State and the City Charter both expressly provided that his failure to do so, as well as his failure to testify, would result in dismissal from his job. He was dismissed solely for his refusal to waive the immunity to which he is entitled if he is required to testify despite his constitutional privilege. . . .

. . . New York City discharged him for refusal to execute a document purporting to waive his constitutional rights and to permit prosecution of himself on the basis of his compelled testimony. Petitioner could not have assumed — and certainly he was not required to assume — that he was being asked to do an idle act of no legal effect. In any event, the mandate of the great privilege against self-incrimination does not tolerate the attempt, regardless of its ultimate effectiveness, to coerce a waiver on the immunity it confers on penalty of the loss of employment. It is clear that petitioner's testimony was demanded before the grand jury in part so that it might be used to prosecute him, and not solely for the purpose of securing an accounting of his performance of his public trust. If the latter had been the only purpose, there would have been no reason to seek to compel petitioner to waive his immunity.

Proper regard for the history and meaning of the privilege against self-incrimination, applicable to the States under our decision in *Malloy* v. *Hogan* . . . (1964), and for the decisions of this Court, dictate the conclusion that the provision of the New York

ernment, acting without colorable right, coerces a defendant into incriminating himself.

We conclude that the immunity provided by 18 U.S.C. §6002 leaves the witness and the prosecutorial authorities in substantially the same position as if the witness had claimed the Fifth Amendment privilege. The immunity therefore is coextensive with the privilege and suffices to supplant it. The judgment of the Court of Appeals for the Ninth Circuit accordingly is

Affirmed.

MR. JUSTICE MARSHALL, dissenting.

. . . .

The Court recognizes that an immunity statute must be tested by that standard, that the relevant inquiry is whether it "leaves the witness and the prosecutorial authorities in substantially the same position as if the witness had claimed the Fifth Amendment privilege." . . . I assume, moreover, that in theory that test would be met by a complete ban on the use of the compelled testimony, including all derivative use, however remote and indirect. But I cannot agree that a ban on use will in practice be total, if it remains open for the government to convict the witness on the basis of evidence derived from a legitimate independent source. The Court asserts that the witness is adequately protected by a rule imposing on the government a heavy burden of proof if it would establish the independent character of evidence to be used against the witness. But in light of the inevitable uncertainties of the fact-finding process, . . . a greater margin of protection is required in order to provide a reliable guarantee that the witness is in exactly the same position as if he had not testified. That margin can be provided only by immunity from prosecution for the offenses to which the testimony relates, i.e., transactional immunity.

I do not see how it can suffice merely to put the burden of proof on the government. First, contrary to the Court's assertion, the Court's rule does leave the witness "dependent for the preservation of his rights upon the integrity and good faith of the prosecuting authorities." . . . For the information relevant to the question of taint is uniquely within the knowledge of the prosecuting authorities. They alone are in a position to trace the chains of information and investigation that lead to the evidence to be used in a criminal prosecution. A witness who suspects that his compelled testimony was used to develop a lead will be hard pressed indeed to ferret out the evidence necessary to prove it. And of course it is no answer to say he need not prove it, for though the Court puts the burden of proof on the government, the government will have no difficulty in meeting its burden by mere assertion if the witness produces no contrary evidence. The good faith of the prosecuting authorities is thus the sole safeguard of the witness' rights. Second, even their good faith is not a sufficient safeguard. For the paths of information through the investigative bureaucracy may well be long and winding, and even a prosecutor acting in the best of faith cannot be certain that somewhere in the depths of his investigative apparatus, often including hundreds of employees, there was not some prohibited use of the compelled testimony. . . . The Court today sets out a loose net to trap tainted evidence and prevent its use against the witness, but it accepts an intolerably great risk that tainted evidence will in fact slip through that net.

In my view the Court turns reason on its head when it compares a statutory grant of immunity to the "immunity" that is inadvertently conferred by an unconstitutional interrogation. The exclusionary rule of evidence that applies in that situation has nothing whatever to do with this case. Evidence obtained through a coercive interrogation, like evidence obtained through an illegal search, is excluded at trial because the Constitution prohibits such methods of gathering evidence. The exclusionary rules provide a partial and inadequate remedy to some victims of illegal police conduct, and a similarly partial and inadequate deterrent to police officers. An immunity statute, on the other hand, is much more ambitious than any exclusionary rule. It does not merely attempt to provide a remedy for past police misconduct, which never should have occurred. An immunity statute operates in advance of the event, and it authorizes — even encourages — interrogation that would otherwise be prohibited by the Fifth Amendment. . . .

. . . .

. . . [A]n immunity statute must be tested by a standard far more demanding than that appropriate for an exclusionary rule fashioned to deal with past constitutional violations. Measured by that standard, the statute approved today by the Court fails miserably. I respectfully dissent. . . .

[JUSTICE DOUGLAS also wrote a dissenting opinion.]

Other Criminal Justice Issues: Punishment and Fairness

The early landmark cases expanding the right to fair trial and the protection against coerced confessions contain three common features: they involved criminal defendants who were black, poor, and charged with capital offenses. As constitutional victories imposing higher standards on the administration of criminal justice were effective in curbing the worst abuses related to the first two of these three factors, increased attention was directed at the third, and in the 1960s, the NAACP Legal Defense Fund, Inc., mounted a direct assault on the death penalty. While death penalty issues had reached the high court several times before, this time the death penalty per se was under challenge as violative of the Eighth Amendment's prohibition against cruel and unusual punishment as applied to the states via the Fourteenth Amendment.

In early skirmishes, the Court ruled that persons opposed to the death penalty could not automatically be excluded from juries in capital cases (*Witherspoon* v. *Illinois,* 391 U.S. 510, 1968), and ruled unconstitutional a statute providing for a maximum of death after trial but only life imprisonment for those who plead guilty (*United States* v. *Jackson,* 390 U.S. 570, 1968). In another important case, one which some hoped would put an end to the death sentence, *Furman* v. *Georgia,* 408 U.S. 238 (1972), a hopelessly fragmented Court (there were nine separate opinions) held that as *then administered* the death penalty constituted cruel and unusual punishment and also violated due process. While the five justices in the majority agreed in result, they disagreed on their specific reasons. Three argued that the imposition of the dealth penalty under any circumstances was constitutionally impermissible. Two more argued that as administered current laws permitted too much room for arbitrariness and caprice in the administration of this most awesome of penalties.

Four dissenters, all appointees of Richard Nixon, voted to uphold the current laws.

Furman had the effect of voiding the death penalty in all of the states that provided for capital punishment (39 and the District of Columbia), and as a consequence removed the threat of death for 648 men and women who were then on death row. It also served as an invitation to state legislatures to rewrite the laws in a way that would overcome the objections of the two majority justices who did not oppose the death penalty per se.

Most of those states that had the death penalty prior to *Furman* quickly adopted new laws to meet *Furman* standards. Some of the new statutes mandated the penalty of death upon conviction for a very limited number of offenses, while others separated determination of guilt from the sentencing phase of the trial, and went on to specify detailed guidelines to be followed by judges and juries when deciding whether to prescribe the death penalty.

These statutes in turn were soon before the Supreme Court. In two companion cases both types of provisions were challenged. In *Woodson* v. *North Carolina,* 428 U.S. 280 (1976), a bare majority held that a statute providing for a *mandatory* death sentence violated the Eighth Amendment. Here, too, each justice had separate reasons, but the sentiment of those who did not oppose capital punishment per se was that such a statute did not permit judges and juries sufficient opportunity to consider aggravating and mitigating factors in individual cases and therefore was too rigid. But in GREGG V. GEORGIA, 428 U.S. 153 (1976), the second of these companion cases, a bare majority voted to uphold Georgia's revised death sentence law. The separate opinions of the majority reasoned that Georgia had struck an acceptable balance between structuring the sentencing decision and permitting flexibility to consider aggravating and mitigating factors in individual cases. In a plurality opinion, Justice Stewart reviewed the process the judge and jury must go through before imposing a death sentence and found it acceptable.

But nothing in GREGG directly limits the prosecutor's discretion to charge a capital or noncapital offense or to introduce or withhold aggravating or enhancing information. His or her discretion is not affected by the decision and remains substantial. What do you think the Court would do if confronted with statistical data that revealed that a higher proportion of blacks than of whites is charged with aggravating (and hence capital) factors? What would you do if you found that one of two equally culpable defendants had pled guilty and received a life sentence, while the other had been sentenced to death after being found guilty at trial? Would it make a difference if the former had agreed to testify for the prosecution? Given what you know about plea bargaining (see BORDENKIRCHER V. HAYES, 1977), how "structured" in practice do you think the sentencing process is or can be?

The Court has addressed some of these and related issues, and no doubt will continue to do so for some time. For instance, in *Coker* v. *Georgia*, 433 U.S. 584 (1977), the Court invoked the principle of proportionality in holding that a death sentence was excessive for rape. In *Enmund* v. *Florida*, 458 U.S. 782 (1982), the Court held the death penalty to be excessive for conviction through involvement in felony murder where the defendant did not take a life or use, or attempt to use, lethal force.

More recently the Court has dealt with the issue of lengthy delays of appeals following imposition of death sentences, the issue of excluding opponents of death penalty from jury service, and the issue of proportionality in the administration of the death penalty. In several cases in the early 1980s, Justice Rehnquist writing for the Court took some of his colleagues and lower court judges to task for allowing "endlessly drawn-out legal proceedings" in death penalty appeals and for granting "numerous procedural protections unheard of for other crimes" (*Coleman* v. *Balkom*,

451 U.S. 949, 1981). In *Gray* v. *Mississippi*, 481 U.S. 648 (1987), a fragmented Court reaffirmed its 1963 ruling in *Witherspoon* v. *Illinois* (1968), which held that persons could not be excluded automatically from juries in capital cases on the basis of their opposition to the death penalty.

The Court has addressed the issue of proportionality of sentencing in death penalty cases. After appearing to firmly root the principle of proportionality and extend it to non–death-penalty cases, the Court began to retreat. In *Pully* v. *Harris*, 465 U.S. 37 (1984), it held that states are not constitutionally required to review each death sentence to determine if it is proportional with sentences imposed in other, similar cases. This view was broadened and reaffirmed in decisions handed down in 1987. In *Tison* v. *Arizona*, 481 U.S. 137 (1987), the Court upheld a law that provided for the death penalty for those convicted in a felony murder, even though some of them were directly involved only in the felony and not the murder. However, in *Sumner* v. *Shuman*, 107 S.Ct. 2716 (1987), the Court held that a statute mandating the death penalty for a prison inmate who is convicted of murder while serving a life sentence without possibility of parole is unconstitutional because it does not allow the sentencing authority an opportunity to consider as possible mitigating factors the defendant's character and prior record and the circumstances of the particular offense. In a biting dissent, Justice White emphasized the conditions built into the law, and argued that "the Constitution does not bar a state legislature from determining, in this limited class of cases, that as a matter of law, no amount of mitigating evidence could ever be sufficient to outweigh the aggravating factors."

Perhaps the most important death penalty case since GREGG is MCCLESKEY V. KEMP, 481 U.S. 279 (1987), in which the Court rejected a proportionality argument suggested by a study that showed statistically significant racial disparities in the imposition of the death penalty. This case rested on painstaking research by Iowa law professor David Baldus, who found, even when controlling for legally relevant factors, that black defendants with white victims were much more likely to be convicted of capital offenses and sentenced to death than were other defendants. Although the Court split 5 to 4 on this issue, the firmness with which the majority disposed of the evidence of disparity suggests that it will be some time before the issue will be raised again.

During the 1987–88 and 1988–89 terms, with one notable exception, the Court's death penalty cases focused on the mechanics of the process of balancing aggravating and mitigating circumstances that are crucial to shaping the discretion of sentencing juries. The one exception was *Thompson* v. *Oklahoma*, 108 S.Ct. 2687 (1988), which held that a state cannot execute someone who was 15 years old when he or she committed the capital offense. A plurality of four agreed that a "national consensus" drew the line at the death penalty for defendants under 16 years of age, although the fifth and deciding vote was by Justice O'Connor, who indicated that a state could execute children younger than 16, but only if the "legislature had spoken clearly" on the matter by setting a minimum age for the death penalty.

Ironically, the issue of proportionality has fared better in non–death-penalty cases. In *Weems* v. *United States*, 217 U.S. 349 (1910), the Supreme Court held that a sentence handed down by a court in the Philippines (then an official dependency of the United States) constituted cruel and unusual punishment. In that case, the defendant had been convicted of falsifying a public document and sentenced to fifteen years of *cadena temporal*, a form of imprisonment that included hard labor in chains and permanent civil disabilities. In its opinion in *Weems*, the Court stressed the petty nature of the offense and the offensive nature of the penalty, and went on to say that "punishment for crime should be graduated and proportioned to offense." Fifty years later, in *Robinson* v. *California*, 370 U.S. 660 (1960), the Court held that a statute providing for a ninety-day sentence for the crime of being "addicted to the use of narcotics" violated the Eighth Amendment. In overturning the California law, the Court emphasized that the statute criminalized a "condition" or "state of being" rather than an "action," and as such the use of the criminal sanction for what should be regarded as an "illness" to be treated as a civil, not criminal, matter was inappropriate.

More recently, the Court has been asked to review the *length* of prison terms for their proportionality. But many fear the consequences of such a step, for it would in effect constitutionalize the appellate review of sentencing, and in so doing place a heavy burden on an already overworked federal judiciary. This seemed to be the message in the majority's decision in *Rummel* v. *Estelle*, 445 U.S. 263 (1980), in which a majority of five held that a life sentence imposed after a third nonviolent conviction did *not* constitute cruel and unusual punishment. However, just two years later, in SOLEM V. HELM (1983), the Court, again in a 5 to 4 decision — due to an apparent shift in Justice Blackmun's thinking — held that a life sentence under a habitual-offender statute for someone convicted of six prior nonviolent offenses constituted disproportionate and hence cruel and unusual punishment. While the majority attempted to distinguish SOLEM from *Rummel*, in his dissent, Chief Justice Burger took the majority to task for its abrupt abandonment of a precedent that had only just been established. Unless there is still another reversal by the Court, SOLEM has the potential for involving the federal courts in overseeing a change as significant and far reaching as any that it has ever faced in the criminal process. However, recent decisions suggest that the Court is retreating from its interest in proportionality of sentencing (*Pulley* v. *Harris*, 465 U.S. 37 (1984), and McCLESKEY V. KEMP (1987). They pull back not only from SOLEM v. Helm but from some of the dicta in GREGG V. GEORGIA as well. However, there are now two lines of precedent, one emphasizing the need for proportionality and the other discounting it.

One of the things that makes sentencing reform so problematic and hence sentence review so difficult is the widespread practice of plea bargaining. This no doubt is one of the reasons appellate courts are so reluctant to embrace a sentencing review function. While the trial continues to be celebrated in myth and theory, in fact the vast majority of all convictions in American courts are secured through guilty pleas. Many of these guilty pleas involve prosecutorial discretion to define the seriousness of the offense or, as in the case of SOLEM, to invoke habitual offender provisions in the law. To the extent that this occurs, formal definitions of offense at conviction may not accurately reflect seriousness of actual behavior. This, of course, wreaks havoc with any sentencing scheme that attaches precise sentences to specific offenses. Indeed, the more carefully calibrated such sentencing schemes are, the greater the likelihood that plea bargaining will distort the process.

Typically, plea bargaining involves the agreement of the accused to plead guilty in exchange for leniency of treatment by the prosecutor. The prosecutor may agree to reduce the seriousness of the charge, drop secondary charges, ignore habitual offender options, or the like in exchange for a plea of guilty. The benefits to both parties are obvious: the defendant obtains certainty and more lenient treatment than is likely if convicted after trial, while the prosecutor gains the certainty of conviction and is spared the expense of trial.

Plea bargaining raises serious questions about equity in sentencing, problems that take on increased significance if, as SOLEM V. HELM suggests, the principle of proportionality is a constitutional mandate. Plea bargaining also raises other due process issues. What happens, for instance, if the prosecutors renege on their bargain at the sentencing stage? For years, officials in the criminal justice system ignored such questions; indeed, they often pretended that plea bargaining did not even exist. However, in recent years officials increasingly have become open and frank about the practice, and the Supreme Court has put its seal of approval on the process, although not without reservations and vigorous dissent in *Brady* v. *United States,* 397 U.S. 742 (1970). Since then it has handed down a number of decisions designed to structure the process and promote its integrity. The Court has held that a defendant has the right to withdraw the plea of guilty if a prosecutor fails to keep a promise at a later stage of the process (*Santobello* v. *New York,* 401 U.S. 257, 1971), although it has also ruled that a trial court can accept the plea of guilty even though the defendant maintains innocence and pleads guilty only in order to avoid a harsher sentence if convicted at trial (*North Carolina* v. *Alford,* 400 U.S. 25, 1970). BORDENKIRCHER V. HAYES (1977) raises a number of other questions that even more clearly link plea bargaining with sentencing and in so doing reveals the vast powers of the prosecutor to affect sentencing. BORDENKIRCHER was decided before SOLEM. How do you think the present court would deal with BORDENKIRCHER in light of SOLEM?

The Court has been vigorous in supporting other aspects of law enforcement as well. Most notably in two important cases in the 1980s, it upheld the policy of "preventive detention," which provides for pretrial detention without opportunity for bail for those arrestees who may be a danger to the community. In 1984 Justice Rehnquist, for the Court, upheld a New York statute that authorized pretrial detention of accused juveniles after a finding that there was a serious risk they might, before adjudication, "commit an act which if committed by an adult would be a crime" (*Schall* v. *Martin,* 467 U.S. 253, 1984). Justice Rehnquist argued that the statute was not punitive because minors are always under some form of custody, and that it "serves the legitimate state objective of protecting both the juvenile and society from the hazards of pretrial crime." In a predictably vigorous dissent, Justice Marshall assailed the Court's logic, arguing that such detention was inherently punitive and that most juveniles, including those in the case under question, are typically released after adjudication without receiving a custodial sentence.

In 1987 the Court finally addressed the issue of pretrial preventive detention for adults, an issue it had ducked in 1969 when, in response from President Nixon and Attorney General John Mitchell, the Congress had adopted preventive detention for the District of Columbia. By the 1980s, this same type of law had gained considerable popularity, having been embraced by a number of states and, in the Bail Reform Act of 1984, by the Congress, for the entire federal system. This Act allows federal courts to detain, prior to trial, arrestees charged with certain serious felonies, if the prosecutor demonstrates by "clear and convincing" evidence that no release conditions "will reasonably assure . . . the safety of any other person and the community." In response to a due process challenge, Justice Rehnquist, for the Court, characterized preventive detention as regulatory rather than punitive, and then proceeded to apply a balancing test, by which the interests of the community clearly outweighed the interests of the individual defendants (*United States* v. *Salerno,* 481 U.S. 739, 1987). Responding to the Eighth Amendment challenge that it violates the prohibition against excessive bail, he argued that this provision "says nothing about whether bail shall be available at all," and rejected the argument that historically the sole purpose of bail has been to assure the accused's appearance at trial.

These two decisions, together with the other Burger Court and Rehnquist Court rulings dealing with the rights of the criminally accused and the sentenced, add up to a ringing vote of confidence in current law enforcement practices. These decisions loosen earlier bonds established by the Court to limit the power and more carefully scrutinize the activities of law enforcement officials. It remains to be seen how much further the Court will go in dismantling the safeguards that it erected in the 1960s and 1970s around the criminally accused and the sentenced. Ironically, many of these cutbacks are coming just as a new generation of criminal justice professionals have come to accept the enhanced rights that were thrust upon their agencies twenty years earlier.

Cases

Gregg v. Georgia

428 U.S. 153 (1979)
Vote: 7–2

Troy Gregg was charged with and convicted of armed robbery and murder. In accordance with Georgia law, adopted in the wake of *Furman* v. *Georgia,* 408 U.S. 238 (1972), the trial was bifurcated into a guilt-determination stage and a sentencing stage. At the guilt stage, the jury found Gregg guilty of two counts of armed robbery and two counts of murder. At the penalty stage, neither the prosecutor nor the defense attorney offered any additional evidence. Both spoke at length about the propriety of capital punishment and reviewed the weight of the evidence of guilt.

The trial judge instructed the jury that it could recommend either a death sentence or life imprisonment on each count. He further charged the jury that it was free to consider the facts and circumstances in mitigation or aggravation presented by either of the attorneys. He then instructed the jury that it "would not be authorized to consider [imposing] the sentence of death" unless it first found beyond a reasonable doubt in at least one of the following three aggravating circumstances: the murder was committed while the offender was engaged in the commission of other capital felonies; the murder was for the purpose of receiving money and the automobile of the victims; and the murder was outrageously and wantonly vile, horrible, and inhuman, in that it involved the depravity of the mind of the defendant. Finding the first and second of these circumstances, the jury returned a verdict of death, as required by the post-*Furman* law. As also required by law, the Supreme Court of Georgia reviewed the record of this case and compared the sentence with other sentences in similar cases. It then affirmed the conviction and sentence.

The United States Supreme Court granted Gregg's petition for a writ of certiorari, which challenged the imposition of the death sentence as "cruel and unusual" punishment in violation of the Eighth and Fourteenth Amendments.

MR. JUSTICE STEWART, MR. JUSTICE POWELL, and MR. JUSTICE STEVENS announced the judgment of the Court and filed an opinion delivered by MR. JUSTICE STEWART.

The history of the prohibition of "cruel and unusual" punishment already has been reviewed by this Court at length. The phrase first appeared in the English Bill of rights in 1689, which was drafted by Parliament at the accession of William and Mary. . . . The English version appears to have been directed against punishments unauthorized by statute and beyond the jurisdiction of the sentencing court, as well as those disproportionate to the offense involved. . . . The American draftsmen, who adopted the English phrasing in drafting the Eighth Amendment, were primarily concerned, however, with proscribing "tortures" and other "barbarous" methods of punishment. . . .

In the earliest cases raising Eighth Amendment claims, the Court focused on particular methods of execution to determine whether they were too cruel to pass constitutional muster. The constitutionality of the sentence of death itself was not at issue, and the criterion used to evaluate the mode of execution was its similarity to "torture" and other "barbarous" methods. . . .

But the Court has not confined the prohibition embodied in the Eighth Amendment to "barbarous" methods that were generally outlawed in the 18th century. Instead, the Amendment has been interpreted in a flexible and dynamic manner. The Court early recognized that "a principle to be vital must be capable of wider application than the mischief which gave it birth." . . .

. . . [T]he Eighth Amendment has not been regarded as a static concept. As Chief Justice Warren said, in an oft-quoted phrase, "[t]he Amendment must draw its meaning from the evolving standards of democracy that mark the progress of a maturing society." . . . Thus, an assessment of contemporary values concerning the infliction of a challenged sanc-

tion is relevant to the application of the Eighth Amendment." . . .

But our cases also make clear that public perceptions of standards of decency with respect to criminal sanctions are not conclusive. A penalty also must accord with "the dignity of man," which is the "basic concept underlying the Eighth Amendment." . . . This means, at least, that the punishment not be "excessive." When a form of punishment in the abstract (in this case, whether capital punishment may ever be imposed as a sanction for murder) rather than in the particular (the propriety of death as a penalty to be applied to a specific defendant for a specific crime) is under consideration, the inquiry into "excessiveness" has two aspects. First, the punishment must not involve the unnecessary and wanton infliction of pain. . . . Second, the punishment must not be grossly out of proportion to the severity of the crime.

Of course, the requirements of the Eighth Amendment must be applied with an awareness of the limited role to be played by the courts. This does not mean that judges have no role to play, for the Eighth Amendment is a restraint upon the exercise of legislative power.

But, while we have an obligation to insure that constitutional bounds are not overreached, we may not act as judges as we might as legislators.

Therefore, in assessing a punishment selected by a democratically elected legislature against the constitutional measure, we presume its validity. We may not require the legislature to select the least severe penalty possible so long as the penalty selected is not cruelly inhumane or disporportionate to the crime involved. And a heavy burden rests on those who would attack the judgment of the representatives of the people.

. . . .

The imposition of the death penalty for the crime of murder has a long history of acceptance both in the United States and England. The common-law rule imposed a mandatory death sentence on all convicted murderers. . . . And the penalty continued to be used into the 20th century by most American States, although the breadth of the common-law rule was diminished, initially by narrowing the class of murders to be punished by death and subsequently by widespread adoption of laws expressly granting juries the discretion to recommend mercy. . . .

It is apparent from the text of the Constitution itself that the existence of capital punishment was accepted by the Framers. At the time the Eighth Amendment was ratified, capital punishment was a common sanction in every State. Indeed, the First

Congress of the United States enacted legislation providing death as the penalty for specified crimes. . . . The Fifth Amendment, adopted at the same time as the Eighth, contemplated the continued existence of the capital sanction by imposing certain limits on the prosecution of capital cases:

> No person shall be held to answer for a capital, or otherwise infamous crime, unless on a presentment or indictment of a Grand Jury; . . . nor shall any person be subject for the same offense to be twice put in jeopardy of life or limb; . . . nor be deprived of life, liberty, or property, without due process of law. . . .

And the Fourteenth Amendment, adopted over three-quarters of a century later, similarly contemplates the existence of the capital sanction in providing that no State shall deprive any person of "life, liberty, or property" without due process of law.

For nearly two centuries, this Court repeatedly, and often expressly, has recognized that capital punishment is not invalid *per se.* . . .

Four years ago, the petitioners in *Furman* and its companion cases predicated their argument primarily upon the asserted proposition that standards of decency had evolved to the point where capital punishment no longer could be tolerated. The petitioners in those cases said, in effect, that the evolutionary process had come to an end, and that standards of decency required that the Eighth Amendment be construed finally as prohibiting capital punishment for any crime regardless of its depravity and impact on society. This view was accepted by two Justices. Three other Justices were unwilling to go so far; focusing on the procedures by which convicted defendants were selected for the death penalty rather than on the actual punishment inflicted, they joined in the conclusion that the statutes before the Court were constitutionally invalid.

The petitioners in the capital cases before the Court today renew the "standards of decency" argument, but developments during the four years since *Furman* have undercut substantially the assumptions upon which their argument rested. Despite the continuing debate, dating back to the 19th century, over the morality and utility of capital punishment, it is now evident that a large proportion of American society continues to regard it as an appropriate and necessary criminal sanction.

The most marked indication of society's endorsement of the death penalty for murder is the legislative response to *Furman*. The legislatures of at least 35 States have enacted new statutes that provide for the death penalty for at least some crimes that result in the death of another person. And the Congress of the United States, in 1974, enacted a statute providing the death penalty for aircraft piracy that results in death. . . .

. . . .

As we have seen, however, the Eighth Amendment demands more than that a challenged punishment be acceptable to contemporary society. The Court also must ask whether it comports with the basic concept of human dignity at the core of the Amendment. . . . Although we cannot "invalidate a category of penalties because we deem less severe penalties adequate to serve the ends of penology, . . . the sanction imposed cannot be so totally without penological justification that it results in the gratuitous infliction of suffering. . . .

The death penalty is said to serve two principle social purposes: retribution and deterrence of capital crimes by prospective offenders.

In part, capital punishment is an expression of society's moral outrage at particularly offensive conduct. This function may be unappealing to many, but it is essential in an ordered society that asks its citizens to rely on legal processes rather than self-help to vindicate their wrongs. "Retribution is no longer the dominant objective of the criminal law," . . . but neither is it a forbidden objective nor one inconsistent with our respect for the dignity of men. . . .

Statistical attempts to evaluate the worth of the death penalty as a deterrent to crimes by potential offenders have occasioned a great deal of debate. The results simply have been inconclusive. . . .

The value of capital punishment as a deterrent of crime is a complex factual issue the resolution of which properly rests with the legislatures, which can evaluate the results of statistical studies in terms of their own local conditions and with a flexibility of approach that is not available to the courts. . . .

In sum, we cannot say that the judgment of the Georgia legislature that capital punishment may be necessary in some cases is clearly wrong. Considerations of federalism, as well as respect for the ability of a legislature to evaluate, in terms of its particular state, the moral consensus concerning the death penalty and its social utility as a sanction, require us to conclude, in the absence of more convincing evidence, that the inflation of death as a punishment for murder is not without justification and thus is not unconstitutionally severe.

Finally, we must consider whether the punishment of death is disproportionate in relation to the crime for which it is imposed. There is no question that death as a punishment is unique in its severity and irrevocability. . . . When a defendant's life is at stake, the Court has been particularly sensitive to insure that every safeguard is observed. . . . But we are concerned here only with the imposition of capital punishment for the crime of murder, and when a life has been taken deliberately by the offender, we cannot say that the punishment is invariably disproportionate to the crime. It is an extreme sanction, suitable to the most extreme of crimes.

We hold that the death penalty is not a form of punishment that may never be imposed, regardless of the circumstances of the offense, regardless of the character of the offender, and regardless of the procedure followed in reaching the decision to impose it.

We now consider whether Georgia may impose the death penalty on the petitioner in this case.

While *Furman* did not hold that the infliction of the death penalty *per se* violates the Constitution's ban on cruel and unusual punishment, it did recognize that the penalty of death is different in kind from any other punishment imposed under our system of criminal justice. Because of the uniqueness of the death penalty, *Furman* held that it could not be imposed under sentencing procedures that created a substantial risk that it would be inflicted in an arbitrary and capricious manner. MR. JUSTICE WHITE concluded that "the death penalty is exacted with great infrequency even for the most atrocious crimes and . . . there is no meaningful basis for distinguishing the few cases in which it is imposed from the many cases in which it is not." . . . Indeed, the death sentences examined by the Court in *Furman* were "cruel and unusual in the same way that being struck by lightning is cruel and unusual. For, of all the people convicted of [capital crimes], many just as reprehensible as these, the petitioners [in *Furman* were] among a capriciously selected random handful upon which the sentence of death has in fact been imposed. . . . [T]he Eighth and Fourteenth Amendments cannot tolerate the infliction of a sentence of death under legal systems that permit this unique penalty to be so wantonly and so freakishly imposed." . . .

Furman mandates that where discretion is afforded a sentencing body on a matter so grave as the determination of whether a human life should be taken or spared, that discretion must be suitably directed and limited so as to minimize the risk of wholly arbitrary and capricious action.

. . . .

. . . [T]he concerns expressed in *Furman* that the penalty of death not be imposed in an arbitrary or capricious manner can be met by a carefully drafted statute that ensures that the sentencing authority is given adequate information and guidance. As a general proposition these concerns are best met by a system that provides for a bifurcated proceeding at which the sentencing authority is apprised of the information relevant to the imposition of sentence and provided with standards to guide its use of the information.

We do not intend to suggest that only the above-described procedures would be permissible under *Furman* or that any sentencing system constructed along these general lines would inevitably satisfy the concerns of *Furman,* for each distinct system must be examined on an individual basis. Rather, we have embarked upon this general exposition to make clear that it is possible to construct capital-sentencing systems capable of meeting *Furman's* constitutional concerns.

We now turn to consideration of the constitutionality of Georgia's capital-sentencing procedures. In the wake of *Furman,* Georgia amended its capital punishment statute, but chose not to narrow the scope of its murder provisions. . . . Thus, now as before *Furman,* in Georgia "[a] person commits murder when he unlawfully and with malice aforethought, either express or implied, causes the death of another human being." . . . All persons convicted of murder "shall be punished by death or by imprisonment for life." . . .

Georgia did act, however, to narrow the class of murderers subject to capital punishment by specifying 10 statutory aggravating circumstances, one of which must be found by the jury to exist beyond a reasonable doubt before a death sentence can ever be imposed. In addition, the jury is authorized to consider any other appropriate aggravating or mitigating circumstances. . . . The jury is not required to find any mitigating circumstance in order to make a recommendation of mercy that is binding on the trial court, . . . but it must find a *statutory* aggravating circumstance before recommending a sentence of death.

These procedures require the jury to consider the circumstances of the crime and the criminal before it recommends sentence. No longer can a Georgia jury do as Furman's jury did: reach a finding of the defendant's guilt and then, without guidance or direction, decide whether he should live or die. Instead, the jury's attention is directed to the specific circumstances of the crime: Was it committed in the course of another capital felony? Was it committed for money? Was it committed upon a peace officer or judicial officer? Was it committed in a particularly heinous way or in a manner that endangered the lives of many persons? In addition, the jury's attention is focused on the characteristics of the person who committed the crime: Does he have a record of prior convictions for capital offenses? Are there any special facts about this defendant that mitigate against imposing capital punishment (*e.g.,* his youth, the extent of his cooperation with the police, his emotional state at the time of the crime)? As a result, while some jury discretion still exists, "the discretion to be exercised is controlled by clear and objective standards so as to produce non-discriminatory application."...

As an important additional safeguard against arbitrariness and caprice, the Georgia statutory scheme provides for automatic appeal of all death sentences to the State's supreme court. That court is required by statute to review each sentence of death and determine whether it was imposed under the influence of passion or prejudice, whether the evidence supports the jury's finding of a statutory aggravating circumstance, and whether the sentence is disproportionate compared to those sentences imposed in similar cases....

In short, Georgia's new sentencing procedures require as a prerequisite to the imposition of the death penalty, specific jury findings as to the circumstances of the crime or the character of the defendant. Moreover to guard further against a situation comparable to that presented in *Furman,* the Supreme Court of Georgia compares each death sentence with the sentences imposed on similarly situated defendants to ensure that the sentence of death in a particular case is not disproportionate. On their face these procedures seem to satisfy the concerns of *Furman.* No longer should there be "no meaningful basis for distinguishing the few cases in which [the death penalty] is imposed from the many cases in which it is not."...

The petitioner contends, however, that the changes in the Georgia sentencing procedures are only cosmetic, that the arbitrariness and capriciousness condemned by *Furman* continue to exist in Georgia — both in traditional practices that still remain and in the new sentencing procedures adopted in response to *Furman.*

First, the petitioner focuses on the opportunities for discretionary action that are inherent in the processing of any murder case under Georgia law. He notes that the state prosecutor has unfettered authority to select those persons whom he wishes to prosecute for a capital offense and to plea bargain with them. Further, at the trial the jury may choose to convict a defendant of a lesser included offense rather than find him guilty of a crime punishable by death, even if the evidence would support a capital verdict. And finally, a defendant who is convicted and sentenced to die may have his sentence com-

muted by the Governor of the State and the Georgia Board of Pardons and Paroles.

The existence of these discretionary stages is not determinative of the issues before us. At each of these stages an actor in the criminal justice system makes a decision which may remove a defendant from consideration as a candidate for the death penalty. *Furman,* in contrast, dealt with the decision to impose the death sentence on a specific individual who had been convicted of a capital offense. Nothing in any of our cases suggests that the decision to afford an individual defendant mercy violates the Constitution. *Furman* held only that, in order to minimize the risk that the death penalty would be imposed on a capriciously selected group of offenders, the decision to impose it had to be guided by standards so that the sentencing authority would focus on the particularized circumstances of the crime and the defendant.

....

The basic concern of *Furman* centered on those defendants who were being condemned to death capriciously and arbitrarily. Under the procedures before the Court in that case, sentencing authorities were not directed to give attention to the nature or circumstances of the crime committed or to the character or record of the defendant. Left unguided, juries imposed the death sentence in a way that could only be called freakish. The new Georgia sentencing procedures, by contrast, focus the jury's attention on the particularized nature of the crime and the particularized characteristics of the individual defendant. While the jury is permitted to consider any aggravating or mitigating circumstances, it must find and identify at least one statutory aggravating factor before it may impose a penalty of death. In this way the jury's discretion is channeled. No longer can a jury wantonly and freakishly impose the death sentence; it is always circumscribed by the legislative guidelines. In addition, the review function of the Supreme Court of Georgia affords additional assurance that the concerns that prompted our decision in *Furman* are not present to any significant degree in the Georgia procedure applied here.

For the reasons expressed in this opinion, we hold that the statutory system under which Gregg was sentenced to death does not violate the Constitution. Accordingly, the judgment of the Georgia Supreme Court is

Affirmed.

[CHIEF JUSTICE BURGER and JUSTICES WHITE, REHNQUIST, and BLACKMUN concurred and joined in a separate concurring opinion.]

MR. JUSTICE BRENNAN, dissenting.

This Court inescapably has the duty, as the ultimate arbiter of the meaning of our Constitution, to say whether, when individuals condemned to death stand before our Bar, "moral concepts" require us to hold that the law has progressed to the point where we should declare that the punishment of death, like punishments on the rack, the screw and the wheel, is no longer morally tolerable in our civilized society. My opinion in *Furman* v. *Georgia* concluded that our civilization and the law had progressed to this point and that therefore the punishment of death, for whatever crime and under all circumstances, is "cruel and unusual" in violation of the Eighth and Fourteenth Amendments of the Constitution. I shall not again canvass the reasons that led to that conclusion. I emphasize only that foremost among the "moral concepts" recognized in our cases and inherent in the Clause is the primary moral principle that the State, even as it punishes, must treat its citizens in a manner consistent with their intrinsic worth as human beings — a punishment must not be so severe as to be degrading to human dignity. A judicial determination whether the punishment of death comports with human dignity is therefore not only permitted but compelled by the Clause. . . .

. . . .

The fatal constitutional infirmity in the punishment of death is that it treats "members of the human race as nonhumans, as objects to be toyed with and discarded. [It is] thus inconsistent with the fundamental premise of the Clause that even the vilest criminal remains a human being possessed of common human dignity." *Id.*, at 273. As such it is a penalty that "subjects the individual to a fate forbidden by the principle of civilized treatment guaranteed by the [Clause]." I therefore would hold, on that ground alone, that death is today a cruel and unusual punishment prohibited by the Clause. "Justice of this kind is obviously no less shocking than the crime itself, and the new 'official' murderer, far from offering redress for the offense committed against society, adds instead a second defilement to the first."

MR. JUSTICE MARSHALL, dissenting.

In *Furman* I concluded that the death penalty is constitutionally invalid for two reasons. First, the death penalty is excessive. . . . And second, the American people, fully informed as to the purposes of the death penalty and its liabilities, would in my view reject it as morally unacceptable. . . .

Since the decision in *Furman,* the legislatures of 35 States have enacted new statutes authorizing the imposition of the death sentence for certain crimes, and Congress has enacted a law providing the death penalty for air piracy resulting in death. . . . I would be less than candid if I did not acknowledge that these developments have a significant bearing on a realistic assessment of the moral acceptability of the death penalty to the American people. But if the constitutionality of the death penalty turns, as I have urged, on the opinion of an *informed* citizenry, then even the enactment of new death statutes cannot be viewed as conclusive. In *Furman,* I observed that the American people are largely unaware of the information critical to a judgment of the morality of the death penalty, and concluded that if they were better informed they would consider it shocking, unjust, and unacceptable. . . . A recent study, conducted after the enactment of the post-*Furman* statutes, has confirmed that the American people knew little about the death penalty, and that the opinions of an informed public would differ significantly from those of a public unaware of the consequences and effects of the death penalty.

Even assuming, however, that the post-*Furman* enactment of statutes authorizing the death penalty renders the prediction of the views of an informed citizenry an uncertain basis for a constitutional decision, the enactment of those statutes has no bearing whatsoever on the conclusion that the death penalty is unconstitutional because it is excessive. An excessive penalty is invalid under the Cruel and Unusual Punishments Clause "even though popular sentiment may favor" it. . . . The inquiry here, then, is simply whether the death penalty is necessary to accomplish the legitimate legislative purposes in punishment, or whether a less severe penalty — life imprisonment — would do as well. . . .

The two purposes that sustain the death penalty as nonexcessive in the Court's view are general deterrence and retribution. . . . The available evidence, I concluded in *Furman,* was convincing that "capital punishment is not necessary as a deterrent to crime in our society." . . .

. . . The evidence I reviewed in *Furman* remains convincing, in my view, that "capital punishment is not necessary as a deterrent to crime in our society." . . . The justification for the death penalty must be found elsewhere.

The other principal purpose said to be served by the death penalty is retribution. . . . It is this notion that I find to be the most disturbing aspect of today's unfortunate decision.

. . . .

In a related vein, it may be suggested that the expression of moral outrage through the imposition of the death penalty serves to reinforce basic moral values — that it marks some crimes as particularly offensive and therefore to be avoided. The argument is akin to a deterrence argument, but differs in that it contemplates the individual's shrinking from antisocial conduct not because he fears punishment, but because he has been told in the strongest possible way that the conduct is wrong. This contention, like the previous one, provides no support for the death penalty. It is inconceivable that any individual concerned about conforming his conduct to what society says is "right" would fail to realize that murder is "wrong" if the penalty were simply life imprisonment.

The foregoing contentions — that society's expression of moral outrage through the imposition of the death penalty pre-empts the citizenry from taking the law into its own hands and reinforces moral values — are not retributive in the purest sense. They are essentially utilitarian in that they portray the death penalty as valuable because of its beneficial results. These justifications for the death penalty are inadequate because the penalty is, quite clearly I think, not necessary to the accomplishment of those results.

There remains for consideration, however, what might be termed the purely retributive justification for the death penalty — that the death penalty is appropriate, not because of its beneficial effect on society, but because the taking of the murderer's life is itself morally good. . . .

. . . The mere fact that the community demands the murderer's life in return for the evil he has done can not sustain the death penalty, for as the plurality reminds us, "the Eighth Amendment demands more than that a challenged punishment be acceptable to contemporary society." . . . To be sustained under the Eighth Amendment, the death penalty must "[comport] with the basic concept of human dignity at the core of the Amendment," . . . the objective in imposing it must be "[consistent] with our respect for the dignity of other men." . . . Under these standards, the taking of life "because the wrong-doer deserves it" surely must fall, for such a punishment has as its very basis the total denial of the wrong-doer's dignity and worth.

The death penalty, unnecessary to promote the goal of deterrence or to further any legitimate notion of retribution, is an excessive penalty forbidden by the Eighth and Fourteenth Amendments. I respectfully dissent from the Court's judgment upholding the sentences of death imposed upon the petitioners in these cases.

McCleskey v. Kemp

481 U.S. 279 (1987)
Vote: 5–4

After GREGG, opponents of capital punishment began examining the ways capital cases were actually handled in the criminal justice system — from the initial decision to charge to the final decision to sentence. The most careful and complete such study was undertaken by Iowa law professor David Baldus and his colleagues, who found statistically significant disparities by race in the ways capital cases were handled by Georgia officials and juries. Their most striking finding was that, even when controlling for legally relevant factors, black defendants with white victims were much more likely to be convicted of capital offenses and sentenced to death than were other defendants. The study by Baldus and his colleagues was used to challenge McCleskey's sentence of death. He had been convicted of killing a white police officer.

JUSTICE POWELL delivered the opinion of the Court.

. . . .

. . . In support of his claim, McCleskey proffered a statistical study performed by Professors David C. Baldus, George Woodworth, and Charles Pulanski (the Baldus study) that purports to show a disparity in the imposition of the death sentence in Georgia based on the race of the murder victim and, to a lesser extent, the race of the defendant. The Baldus study is actually two sophisticated statistical studies that examine over 2,000 murder cases that occurred in Georgia during the 1970s. The raw numbers collected by Professor Baldus indicate that defendants charged with killing white persons received the death penalty in 11% of the cases, but defendants charged with killing blacks received the death penalty in only 1% of the cases. The raw numbers also indicate a reverse racial disparity according to the race of the defendant: 4% of the black defendants received the death penalty, as opposed to 7% of the white defendants.

Baldus also divided the cases according to the combination of the race of the defendant and the race of the victim. He found that the death penalty was assessed in 22% of the cases involving black defendants and white victims; 8% of the cases involving white defendants and white victims; 1% of the cases involving black defendants and black victims; and 3% of the cases involving white defendants and black victims. Similarly, Baldus found that prosecutors sought the death penalty in 70% of the cases involving black defendants and white victims; 32% of the cases involving white defendants and white victims; 15% of the cases involving black defendants and black victims; and 19% of the cases involving white defendants and black victims.

Baldus subjected his data to an extensive analysis, taking account of 230 variables that could have explained the disparities on nonracial grounds. One of his models concludes that, even after taking account of 39 nonracial variables, defendants charged with killing white victims were 4.3 times as likely to receive a death sentence as defendants charged with killing blacks. According to this model, black defendants were 1.1 times as likely to receive a death sentence as other defendants. Thus, the Baldus study indicates that black defendants, such as McCleskey, who kill white victims have the greatest likelihood of receiving the death penalty.

....

... [T]o prevail under the Equal Protection Clause, McCleskey must prove that the decision-makers in *his* case acted with discriminatory purpose. He offers no evidence specific to his own case that would support an inference that racial considerations played a part in his sentence. Instead, he relies solely on the Baldus study....

The Court has accepted statistics as proof of intent to discriminate in certain limited contexts. First, this Court has accepted statistical disparities as proof of an equal protection violation in the selection of the jury venire in a particular district. Although statistical proof normally must present a "stark" pattern to be accepted as the sole proof of discriminatory intent under the Constitution, ... "[b]ecause of the nature of the jury-selection task, ... we have permitted a finding of constitutional violation even when the statistical pattern does not approach [such] extremes." ... Second, this Court has accepted statistics in the form of multiple regression analysis to prove statutory violations under Title VII....

But the nature of the capital sentencing decision, and the relationship of the statistics to that decision, are fundamentally different from the corresponding elements in the venire-selection or Title VII cases. Most importantly, each particular decision to impose the death penalty is made by a petit jury selected from a properly constituted venire. Each jury is unique in its composition, and the Constitution requires that

its decision rest on consideration of innumerable factors that vary according to the characteristics of the individual defendant and the facts of the particular capital offense. . . .

Thus, the application of an inference drawn from the general statistics to a specific decision in a trial and sentencing simply is not comparable to the application of an inference drawn from general statistics to a specific venire-selection or Title VII case. . . .

. . . .

McCleskey also argues that the Baldus study demonstrates that the Georgia capital sentencing system violates the Eighth Amendment . . . [and that it] is arbitrary and capricious in *application,* and therefore his sentence is excessive, because racial considerations may influence capital sentencing decisions in Georgia. We now address this claim.

. . . .

At most, the Baldus study indicates a discrepancy that appears to correlate with race. Apparent disparities in sentencing are an inevitable part of our criminal justice system. The discrepancy indicated by the Baldus study is "a far cry from the major systemic defects identified in *Furman.*". As this Court has recognized, any mode for determining guilt or punishment "has its weaknesses and the potential for misuse." . . . Despite these imperfections, our consistent rule has been that constitutional guarantees are met when "the mode [for determining guilt or punishment] itself has been surrounded with safeguards to make it as fair as possible." . . . Where the discretion that is fundamental to our criminal process is involved, we decline to assume that what is unexplained is invidious. In light of the safeguards designed to minimize racial bias in the process, the fundamental value of jury trial in our criminal justice system, and the benefits that discretion provides to criminal defendants, we hold that the Baldus study does not demonstrate a constitutionally significant risk of racial bias affecting the Georgia capital-sentencing process.

. . . .

. . . McCleskey's arguments are best presented to the legislative bodies. It is not the responsibility— or indeed even the right—of this Court to determine the appropriate punishment for particular crimes. It is the legislatures, the elected representatives of the people, that are "constituted to respond to the will and consequently the moral values of the people." . . .

Accordingly, we affirm the judgment of the Court of Appeals for the Eleventh Circuit.

It is so ordered.

JUSTICE BRENNAN, with whom JUSTICE MARSHALL

joins, and with whom JUSTICE BLACKMUN and JUSTICE STEVENS join [in part], dissenting.

. . . .

The Court today holds that Warren McCleskey's sentence was constitutionally imposed. It finds no fault in a system in which lawyers must tell their clients that race casts a large shadow on the capital sentencing process. . . .

. . . .

The statistical evidence in this case thus relentlessly documents the risk that McCleskey's sentence was influenced by racial considerations. . . . In light of the gravity of the interest at stake, petitioner's statistics on their face are a powerful demonstration of the type of risk that our Eighth Amendment jurisprudence has consistently condemned.

Evaluation of McCleskey's evidence cannot rest solely on the numbers themselves. We must also ask whether the conclusion suggested by those numbers is consonant with our understanding of history and human experience. Georgia's legacy of a race-conscious criminal justice system, as well as this Court's own recognition of the persistent danger that racial attitudes may affect criminal proceedings, indicate that McCleskey's claim is not a fanciful product of mere statistical artifice.

. . . .

The Court . . . maintains that accepting McCleskey's claim would impose a threat to all sentencing because of the prospect that a correlation might be demonstrated between sentencing outcomes and other personal characteristics. Again, such a view is indifferent to the considerations that enter into a determination of whether punishment is "cruel and unusual." Race is a consideration whose influence is expressly constitutionally proscribed. . . .

. . . .

. . . [I]t has been scarcely a generation since this Court's first decision striking down racial segregation, and barely two decades since the legislative prohibition of racial discrimination in major domains of national life. These have been honorable steps, but we cannot pretend that in three decades we have completely escaped the grip of a historical legacy spanning centuries. Warren McCleskey's evidence confronts us with the subtle and persistent influence of the past. His message is a disturbing one to a society that has formally repudiated racism, and a frustrating one to a Nation accustomed to regarding its destiny as the product of its own will. Nonetheless, we ignore him at our peril, for we remain imprisoned by the past as long as we deny its influence in the present.

The Court's decision today will not change what attorneys in Georgia tell other Warren McCleskeys about their chances of execution. Nothing will soften the harsh message they must convey, nor alter the prospect that race undoubtedly will continue to be a topic of discussion. McCleskey's evidence will not have obtained judicial acceptance, but that will not affect what is said on death row. However many criticisms of today's decision may be rendered, these painful conversations will serve as the most eloquent dissents of all.

[JUSTICE BLACKMUN, with whom JUSTICE MARSHALL and JUSTICE STEVENS joined and with whom JUSTICE BRENNAN joined in part, also wrote a dissenting opinion.]

Solem v. Helm

463 U.S. 277 (1983)
Vote: 5–4

In 1964, 1966, and 1969, Jerry Helm was convicted of third-degree burglary. In 1972, he was convicted of obtaining money under false pretenses. In 1973, he was convicted of grand larceny. And in 1975, he was convicted of a third-offense, driving while intoxicated. None of these offenses involved crime against a person and all involved alcohol. Again, in 1979, Helm was arrested and pled guilty to the charge of uttering a "no account" check of $100. Ordinarily, the maximum penalty for such an offense is five years' imprisonment and a $5000 fine. However, as a result of his criminal record, Helm was subject to South Dakota's criminal recidivist statute, which provided that when an offender has been convicted of at least three prior offenses, the maximum penalty for the current offense could be enhanced to life imprisonment without possibility of parole. Even here, however, the Governor retained discretionary authority to pardon and commute sentence.

After serving two years, Helm petitioned the Governor to commute his sentence to a fixed term of years (thereby making him eligible for parole). After this request was denied, Helm sought habeas corpus relief in federal district court. Citing a 1980 Supreme Court decision, *Rummel* v. *Estelle,* 445

U.S. 263, which upheld life sentence with possibility of parole for a habitual offender, the district court denied relief. However, the United States Court of Appeals distinguished *Rummel* from *Helm,* in part because it found that Helm's sentence was "grossly disproportionate to the nature of the offense." It then ordered the District Court to issue the writ and release Helm unless the state resentenced. The case reached the Supreme Court upon a petition of certiorari by prison warden, Herman Solem, acting in behalf of the state.

JUSTICE POWELL delivered the opinion of the Court.

The principle that a punishment should be proportionate to the crime is deeply rooted and frequently repeated in common-law jurisprudence. In 1215 three chapters of Magna Carta were devoted to the rule that "amercements" may not be excessive. And the principle was repeated and extended in the First Statute of Westminister... (1275). These were not hollow guarantees, for the royal courts relied on them to invalidate disproportionate punishments.... When prison sentences became the normal criminal sanctions, the common law recognized that these, too, must be proportional. See, *e.g., Hodge*s v. *Humkin* ... (1615)(Croke, J.)("imprisonment ought always to be according to the quality of the offence").

The English Bill of Rights repeated the principle of proportionality in language that was later adopted in the Eighth Amendment: "excessive Baile ought not to be required nor excessive Fines imposed nor cruell and unusuall Punishments inflicted." 1 W. & M., sess. 2, ch. 2 (1689). Although the precise scope of this provision is uncertain, it at least incorporated "the longstanding principle of English law that the punishment... should not be, by reason of its excessive length or severity, greatly disproportionate to the offense charged."...

When the Framers of the Eighth Amendment adopted the language of the English Bill of Rights, they also adopted the English principle of proportionality. Indeed, one of the consistent themes of the era was that Americans had all the rights of English subjects.... Thus our Bill of Rights was designed in part to ensure that these rights were preserved. Although the Framers may have intended the Eighth Amendment to go beyond the scope of its English counterpart, their use of the language of the English Bill of Rights is convincing proof that they intended to provide at least the same protection — including the right to be free from excessive punishments.

The constitutional principle of proportionality has been recognized explicitly in this Court for almost a century. In the leading case of *Weems* v. *United States*... (1910), the defendant had been convicted of falsifying a public document and sentenced to 15 years of "cadena temporal," a form of imprisonment that included hard labor in chains and permanent civil disabilities. The Court noted "that it is a precept of justice that punishment for crime should be graduated and proportioned to offense,"... and held that the sentence violated the Eighth Amendment. The Court endorsed the principle of proportionality as a constitutional standard, ... and determined that the sentence before it was "cruel in its excess of imprisonment,"... as well as in its shackles and restrictions.

The Court next applied the principle to invalidate a criminal sentence in *Robinson* v. *California*... (1962). A 90-day sentence was found to be excessive for the crime of being "addicted to the use of narcotics." The Court explained that "imprisonment for ninety days is not, in the abstract, a punishment which is either cruel or unusual."... Thus there was no question of an inherently barbaric punishment. "But the question cannot be considered in the abstract. Even one day in prison would be a cruel and unusual punishment for the 'crime' of having a common cold." *Ibid.*

Most recently, the Court has applied the principle of proportionality to hold capital punishment excessive in certain circumstances. *Enmund* v. *Florida*... (1982)(death penalty excessive for felony murder when defendant did not take life, attempt to take life, or intend that a life be taken or that lethal force be used); *Coker* v. *Georgia*... (1977)(plurality opinion) ("sentence of death is grossly disproportionate and excessive punishment for the crime of rape");... (POWELL, J., concurring in the judgment in part and dissenting in part)("ordinarily death is disproportionate punishment for the crime of raping an adult woman"). And the Court has continued to recognize that the Eighth Amendment proscribes grossly disproportionate punishments, even when it has not been necessary to rely on the proscription....

... When we have applied the proportionality principle in capital cases, we have drawn no distinction with cases of imprisonment.... It is true that the "penalty of death differs from all other forms of criminal punishment, not in degree but in kind."... As a result, "our decisions [in] capital cases are of limited assistance in deciding the constitutionality of the punishment" in a noncapital case.... We agree, therefore, that, "[o]utside the context of capital punishment, *successful* challenges to the proportionality of particular sentences [will be] exceedingly rare,"... This does not mean, however, that proportionality analysis is entirely inapplicable in noncapital cases.

In sum, we hold as a matter of principle that a criminal sentence must be proportionate to the crime for which the defendant has been convicted. Reviewing courts, of course, should grant substantial deference to the broad authority that legislatures necessarily possess in determining the types and limits of punishments for crimes, as well as to the discretion that trial courts possess in sentencing convicted criminals. But no penalty is *per se* constitutional. As the Court noted in *Robinson* v. *California,*... a single day in prison may be unconstitutional in some circumstances.

When sentences are reviewed under the Eighth Amendment, courts should be guided by objective factors that our cases have recognized. First, we look to the gravity of the offense and the harshness of the penalty....

Second, it may be helpful to compare the sentences imposed on other criminals in the same jurisdiction. If more serious crimes are subject to the same penalty, or to less serious penalties, that is some indication that the punishment at issue may be excessive....

Third, courts may find it useful to compare the sentences imposed for commission of the same crime in other jurisdictions....

Application of these factors assumes that courts are competent to judge the gravity of an offense, at least on a relative scale. In a broad sense this assumption is justified, and courts traditionally have made these judgments—just as legislatures must make them in the first instance. Comparisons can be made in light of the harm caused or threatened to the victim of society, and the culpability of the offender. Thus in *Enmund* the Court determined that the petitioner's conduct was not as serious as his accomplices' conduct. Indeed, there are widely shared views as to the relative seriousness of crimes.... For example, as the criminal laws make clear, nonviolent crimes are less serious than crimes marked by violence or the threat of violence....

There are other accepted principles that courts may apply in measuring the harm caused or threatened to the victim or society. The absolute magnitude of the crime may be relevant. Stealing a million dollars is viewed as more serious than stealing a hundred dollars—a point recognized in statutes distinguishing petty theft from grand theft.... Few would dispute that a lesser included offense should not be punished more severely than the greater offense....It also is generally recognized that attempts are less serious than completed crimes.... Similarly, an accessory after the fact should not be subject to a higher penalty than the principal....

Turning to the culpability of the offender, there are again clear distinctions that courts may recognize and apply. In *Enmund* the Court looked at the petitioner's lack of intent to kill in determining that he was less culpable than his accomplices.... Most would agree that negligent conduct is less serious than intentional conduct. South Dakota, for example, ranks criminal acts in ascending order of seriousness as follows: negligent acts, reckless acts, knowing acts, intentional acts, and malicious acts....

This list is by no means exhaustive. It simply illustrates that there are generally accepted criteria for comparing the severity of different crimes on a broad scale, despite the difficulties courts face in attempting to draw distinctions between similar crimes.

Application of the factors that we identify also assumes that courts are able to compare different sentences. This assumption, too, is justified. The easiest comparison, of course, is between capital punishment and noncapital punishments, for the death penalty is different from other punishments in kind rather than degree. For sentences of imprisonment, the problem is not so much one of ordering, but one of line-drawing. It is clear that a 25-year sentence generally is more severe than a 15-year sentence, but in most cases it would be difficult to decide that the former violates the Eighth Amendment while the latter does not. Decisions of this kind, although troubling, are not unique to this area. The courts are constantly called upon to draw similar lines in a variety of contexts.

. . . .

It remains to apply the analytical framework established by our prior decisions to the case before us. We first consider the relevant criteria, viewing Helm's sentence as life imprisonment without possibility of parole. We then consider the State's argument that the possibility of commutation is sufficient to save an otherwise unconstitutional sentence.

Helm's crime was "one of the most passive felonies a person could commit."... It involved neither violence nor threat of violence to any person. The $100 face value of Helm's "no account" check was not trivial, but neither was it a large amount. One hundred dollars was less than half the amount South Dakota required for a felonious theft. It is easy to see why such a crime is viewed by society as among the less serious offenses....

Helm, of course, was not charged with uttering a "no account" check, but also with being an habitual offender. And a State is justified in punishing a recidivist more severely than it punishes a first offender. Helm's status, however, cannot be considered in the abstract. His prior offenses, although classified as felonies, were all relatively minor.* All were nonviolent and none was a crime against a person. Indeed, there was no minimum amount in either the burglary or the false pretenses statutes, . . . and the minimum amount covered by the grand larceny statute was fairly small. . . .

Helm's present sentence is life imprisonment without possibility of parole. Barring executive clemency, . . . Helm will spend the rest of his life in the state penitentiary. This sentence is far more severe than the life sentence we considered in *Rummel* v. *Estelle.* Rummel was likely to have been eligible for parole within 12 years of his initial confinement, a fact on which the Court relied heavily. . . . Helm's sentence is the most severe punishment that the State could have imposed on any criminal for any crime. . . . Only capital punishment, a penalty not authorized in South Dakota when Helm was sentenced, exceeds it.

We next consider the sentences that could be imposed on other criminals in the same jurisdiction. When Helm was sentenced, a South Dakota court was required to impose a life sentence for murder. . . . No other crime was punishable so severely on the first offense. . . .

Helm's habitual offender status complicates our analysis, but relevant comparisons are still possible. Under [the habitual offender statute], the penalty for a second or third felony is increased by one class. Thus a life sentence was mandatory when a second or third conviction was for treason, first degree manslaughter, first degree arson, or kidnapping, and a life sentence would have been authorized when a second or third conviction was for such crimes as attempted murder, placing an explosive device on an aircraft, or first degree rape. Finally, the statute under which Helm was sentenced, authorized life imprisonment after three prior convictions, regardless of the crimes.

In sum, there were a handful of crimes that were necessarily punished by life imprisonment. . . . There

*Helm, who was 36 years old when he was sentenced, is not a professional criminal. The record indicates an addiction to alcohol, and a consequent difficulty in holding a job. His record involves no instance of violence of any kind. Incarcerating him for life without possibility of parole is unlikely to advance the goals of our criminal justice system in any substantial way. Neither Helm nor the State will have an incentive to pursue clearly needed treatment for his alcohol problem, or any other program of rehabilitation.

was a larger group for which life imprisonment was authorized in the discretion of the sentencing judge. . . . Finally, there was a large group of very serious offenses for which life imprisonment was not authorized, including a third offense of heroin dealing or aggravated assault.

Criminals committing any of these offenses ordinarily would be thought more deserving of punishment than one uttering a "no account" check — even when the bad-check writer had already committed six minor felonies. Moreover, there is no indication in the record that any habitual offender other than Helm has ever been given the maximum sentence on the basis of comparable crimes. . . .

Finally, we compare the sentences imposed for commission of the same crime in other jurisdictions. . . . It appears that Helm was treated more severely than he would have been in any other State.

The State argues that the present case is essentially the same as *Rummel* v. *Estelle,* for the possibility of parole in that case is matched by the possibility of executive clemency here. The State reasons that the Governor could commute Helm's sentence to a term of years. We conclude, however, that the South Dakota commutation system is fundamentally different from the parole system that was before us in *Rummel.*

. . . [I]t is possible to predict, at least to some extent, when parole might be granted. Commutation, on the other hand, is an *ad hoc* exercise of executive clemency. A Governor may commute a sentence at any time for any reason without reference to any standards. . . .

The Constitution requires us to examine Helm's sentence to determine if it is proportionate to his crime. Applying objective criteria, we find that Helm has received the penultimate sentence for relatively minor criminal conduct. He has been treated more harshly than other criminals in the State who have committed more serious crimes. He has been treated more harshly than he would have been in any other jurisdiction, with the possible exception of a single State. We conclude that his sentence is significantly disproportionate to his crime, and is therefore prohibited by the Eighth Amendment. The judgment of the Court of Appeals is accordingly

Affirmed.

CHIEF JUSTICE BURGER, with whom JUSTICE WHITE, JUSTICE REHNQUIST, and JUSTICE O'CONNOR join, dissenting.

The controlling law governing this case is crystal clear, but today the Court blithely discards any concept of *stare decisis,* trespasses gravely on the authority of the States, and distorts the concept of proportionality of punishment by tearing it from its moorings in capital cases. Only two Terms ago we held in *Rummel* v. *Estelle,* 445 U.S. 263 (1980), that life sentence imposed after only a *third* nonviolent felony conviction did not constitute cruel and unusual punishment under the Eighth Amendment. Today, the Court ignores its recent precedent and holds that a life sentence imposed after a *seventh* felony conviction constitutes cruel and unusual punishment under the Eighth Amendment. Moreover, I reject the fiction that all Helm's crimes were innocuous or nonviolent. Among his felonies were three burglaries and a third conviction for drunk driving. By comparison Rummel was a relatively "model citizen." Although today's holding cannot rationally be reconciled with *Rummel,* the Court does not purport to overrule *Rummel.* I therefore dissent.

I

It is true, as we acknowledge in *Rummel,* that the "Court has on occasion stated that the Eighth Amendment prohibits imposition of a sentence that is grossly disproportionate to the severity of a crime." . . . But even a cursory review of our cases shows that this type of proportionality review has been carried out only in a very limited category of cases, and never before in a case involving solely a sentence of imprisonment. In *Rummel,* we said that the proportionality concept of the capital punishment cases was inapposite because of the "unique nature of the death penalty. . . ." "Because a sentence of death differs in kind from any sentence of imprisonment, no matter how long, our decisions applying the prohibition of cruel and unusual punishments to capital cases are of limited assistance in deciding the constitutionality of the punishment meted out to Rummel."

The *Rummel* Court also rejected the claim that *Weems* v. *United States,* . . . (1910), required it to determine whether Rummel's punishment was "disproportionate" to his crime. In *Weems,* the Court had struck down as cruel and unusual punishment a sentence of *cadena temporal* imposed by a Phillipine Court. This bizarre penalty, which was unknown to Anglo-Saxon law, entailed a minimum of 12 years' imprisonment chained day and night at the wrists and ankles, hard and painful labor while so chained, and a number of "accessories" including lifetime civil disabilities. . . .

. . . However, the *Rummel* Court emphasized that drawing lines between different sentences of imprisonment would thrust the Court inevitably "into the basic line-drawing process that is pre-eminently the province of the legislature" and produce judgments that were no more than the visceral reactions of individual Justices.

The *Rummel* Court categorically rejected the very analysis adopted by the Court today. Rummel had argued that various objective criteria existed by which the Court could determine whether his life sentence was proportional to his crimes. In rejecting Rummel's contentions, the Court explained why each was insufficient to allow it to determine in an *objective* manner whether a given sentence of imprisonment is proportionate to the crime for which it is imposed.

First, it rejected the distinctions Rummel tried to draw between violent and nonviolent offenses, noting that "the absence of violence does not always affect the strength of society's interest in deterring a particular crime or in punishing a particular individual." . . . Similarly, distinctions based on the amount of money stolen are purely "subjective" matters of line drawing. . . .

Second, the Court squarely rejected Rummel's attempt to compare his sentence with the sentence he would have received in other States — an argument that the Court today accepts. The *Rummel* Court explained that such comparisons are flawed for several reasons. . . . For one, the criminal laws of the various states vary widely. Another . . . is that some states have comprehensive provisions for parole and others do not. . . . Perhaps most important, such comparisons trample on fundamental concepts of federalism. Different states surely may view particular crimes as more or less severe than other states. . . .

Finally, we flatly rejected Rummel's suggestion that we measure his sentence against the sentences imposed by Texas for other crimes:

. . . .

If there were any doubts as to the meaning of *Rummel,* they were laid to rest last Term in *Hutto* v. *Davis* . . . (1982). . . . There a United States District Court held that a 40-year sentence for the possession of nine ounces of marijuana violated the Eighth Amendment. . . .

. . . While the doctrine of *stare decisis* does not absolutely bind the Court to its prior opinions, a decent regard for the orderly development of the law and the administration of justice requires that directly controlling cases be either followed or candidly overruled.

II

Although historians and scholars have disagreed about the Framers' original intentions, the more common view seems to be that the Framers viewed the Cruel and Unusual Punishments Clause as prohibiting the kind of torture meted out during the reign of the Stuarts. Moreover, it is clear that until 1892, over 100 years after the ratification of the Bill of Rights, not a single Justice of this Court even asserted the doctrine adopted for the first time by the Court today. The prevailing view up to now has been that the Eighth Amendment reaches only the *mode* of punishment and not the length of a sentence of imprisonment. In light of this history, it is disingenuous for the Court blandly to assert that "[t]he constitutional principle of proportionality has been recognized explicitly in this Court for almost a century." . . . That statement seriously distorts history and our cases.

By asserting the power to review sentences of imprisonment for excessiveness the Court launches into uncharted and unchartable waters. Today it holds that a sentence of life imprisonment, without the possibility of parole, is excessive punishment for a seventh allegedly "nonviolent" felony. How about the eighth "nonviolent" felony? The ninth? The twelfth? Suppose one offense was a simple assault? Or selling liquor to a minor? Or statutory rape? Or price-fixing? The permutations are endless and the Court's opinion is bankrupt of realistic guiding principles. Instead, it casually lists several allegedly "objective" factors and arbitrarily asserts that they show respondent's sentence to be "significantly disproportionate" to his crimes. . . .

There is a real risk that this holding will flood the appellate courts with cases in which equally arbitrary lines must be drawn. . . . To require appellate review of all sentences of imprisonment—as the Court's opinion necessarily does—will "administer the *coup de grace* to the courts of appeal as we know them." . . . This is judicial usurpation with a vengence; Congress has pondered for decades the concept of appellate review of sentences and has hesitated to act.

III

Even if I agreed that the Eighth Amendment prohibits imprisonment "disproportionate to the crime committed," . . . I reject the notion that respondent's sentence is disproportionate to his crimes for, if we are to have a system of laws, not men, *Rummel* is controlling.

. . . .

The Court's opinion necessarily reduces to the proposition that a sentence of life imprisonment with the possibility of commutation, but without possibility of parole, is so much more severe than a life sentence with the possibility of parole that one is excessive while the other is not. This distinction does not withstand scrutiny; a well-behaved "lifer" in respondent's position is most unlikely to serve for life.

IV

It is indeed a curious business for this court to so far intrude into the administration of criminal justice to say that a state legislature is barred by the Constitution from identifying its habitual criminals and removing them from the streets. Surely seven felony convictions warrant the conclusion that respondent is incorrigible. It is even more curious that the Court should brush aside controlling precedents that are barely in the bound volumes of United States Reports. . . .

Bordenkircher v. Hayes

434 U.S. 357 (1977)
Vote: 5–4

In 1973, Paul Lewis Hayes was indicted by a Kentucky grand jury for forgery of a check for $88.30, then a felony offense punishable by a term of two to ten years (a penalty that was subsequently repealed in 1975). After arraignment, Hayes' attorney met with the prosecutor to discuss a possible plea agreement. During these conferences the prosecutor offered to recommend a sentence of five years if Hayes would plead guilty and "save the court the inconvenience and necessity of a trial." He also indicated that if Hayes would not plead guilty he would return to the grand jury and seek an indictment under the state's Habitual Criminal Act (also repealed in 1975), which would subject Hayes to a mandatory life sentence since he had two prior felony convictions. The first conviction was in 1971, when Hayes was seventeen, for "detaining a female," for which he served five years in a reformatory; the second in 1970, for robbery, for which he received a five-year suspended sentence and probation.

Hayes refused to plead guilty. In turn, the prosecutor secured the additional indictment under the habitual criminal statute, and Hayes was subsequently convicted and sentenced to life imprisonment.

The Kentucky court of appeals rejected Hayes' contention that the enhancement charge for habitual felony, initiated solely because he had refused to plead guilty, constituted a violation of his constitutional right to due process. The United States District Court denied his writ for a petition of habeas corpus, holding that it found no constitutional defects in the indictment and sentencing process. The United States Court of Appeals reversed, reasoning that the prosecutor's conduct during the pretrial process violated principles that "protected defendants from the vindictive exercise of a prosecutor's discretion," and ordered that Hayes be discharged from prison once he had completed the lawful term for forgery. The State of Kentucky, acting through its penitentiary superintendent, Bordenkircher, successfully petitioned the United States Supreme Court for a writ of certiorari.

MR. JUSTICE STEWART delivered the opinion of the Court.

We have recently had occasion to observe: "Whatever might be the situation in an ideal world, the fact is that the guilty plea and the often concomitant plea bargain are important components of this country's criminal justice system. Properly administered they can benefit all concerned." . . . The open acknowledgment of this previously clandestine practice has led this court to recognize the importance of counsel during plea negotiations, . . . the need for a public record indicating that a plea was knowingly and voluntarily made, . . . and the requirement that a prosecutor's plea-bargaining promise must be kept, *Santobello* v. *New York* . . . [1971]. . . .

. . . .

To punish a person because he has done what the law plainly allows him to do is a due process violation of the most basic sort, . . . and for an agent of the State to pursue a course of action whose objective is to penalize a person's reliance on his legal rights is "patently unconstitutional." . . . But in the "give-and-take" of plea bargaining, there is no such element of punishment or retaliation so long as the accused is free to accept or reject the prosecution's offer.

Plea bargaining flows from "the mutuality of advantage" to defendants and prosecutors, each with his own reasons for wanting to avoid trial. . . . Defendants advised by competent counsel and protected by other procedural safeguards are presumptively capable of intelligent choice in response to prosecutorial persuasion, and unlikely to be driven to false self-condemnation. . . . Indeed, acceptance of the basic legitimacy of plea bargaining necessarily implies rejection of any notion that a guilty plea is involuntary in a constitutional sense simply because it is the end result of the bargaining process. By hypothesis, the plea may have been induced by promises of a recommendation of a lenient sentence or a reduction of charges, and thus by fear of the possibility of a greater penalty upon conviction after a trial. . . .

While confronting a defendant with the risk of more severe punishment clearly may have a "discouraging effect on the defendant's assertion of his trial rights, the imposition of these difficult choices [is] an inevitable" — and permissible — "attribute of any legitimate system which tolerates and encourages the negotiation of pleas." . . . It follows that, by tolerating and encouraging the negotiation of pleas, this Court has necessarily accepted as constitutionally legitimate the simple reality that the prosecutor's interest at the bargaining table is to persuade the defendant to forgo his right to plead not guilty.

It is not disputed here that Hayes was properly chargeable under the recidivist statute, since he had in fact been convicted of two previous felonies. In our system, so long as the prosecutor has probable cause to believe that the accused committed an offense defined by statute, the decision whether or not to prosecute, and what charge to file or bring before a grand jury, generally rests entirely in his discretion. Within the limits set by the legislature's constitutionally valid definition of chargeable offenses, "the conscious exercise of some selectivity in enforcement is not in itself a federal constitutional violation" so long as "the selection was [not] deliberately based upon an unjustifiable standard such as race, religion, or other arbitrary classification." . . . To hold that the prosecutor's desire to induce a guilty plea is an "unjustifiable standard," which, like race or religion, may play no part in his charging decision, would contradict the very premises that underlie the concept of plea bargaining itself. Moreover, a rigid constitutional rule that would prohibit a prosecutor from acting forthrightly in his dealings with the defense could only invite unhealthy subterfuge that would drive the practice of plea bargaining back into the shadows from which it has so recently emerged. . . .

There is no doubt that the breadth of discretion that our country's legal system vests in prosecuting attorneys carries with it the potential for both individual and institutional abuse. And broad though that discretion may be, there are undoubtedly constitutional limits upon its exercise. We hold only that the course of conduct engaged in by the prosecutor in this case, which no more than openly presented the defendant with the unpleasant alternatives of forgoing trial or facing charges on which he was plainly subject to prosecution, did not violate the Due Process Clause of the Fourteenth Amendment.

Accordingly, the judgment of the Court of Appeals is

Reversed.

[MR. JUSTICE BLACKMUN, with whom MR. JUSTICE BRENNAN and MR. JUSTICE MARSHALL joined, wrote a dissenting opinion.]

MR. JUSTICE POWELL, dissenting.

Although I agree with much of the Court's opinion, I am not satisfied that the result in this case is just or that the conduct of the plea bargaining met the requirements of due process.

Respondent was charged with the uttering of a single forged check in the amount of $88.30. Under Kentucky law, this offense was punishable by a prison term of from 2 to 10 years, apparently without regard to the amount of the forgery. During the course of plea bargaining, the prosecutor offered respondent a sentence of five years in consideration of a guilty plea. I observe, at this point, that five years in prison for the offense charged hardly could be characterized as a generous offer. Apparently respondent viewed the offer in this light and declined to accept it; he protested that he was innocent and insisted on going to trial. Respondent adhered to this position even when the prosecutor advised that he would seek a new indictment under the State's Habitual Criminal Act which would subject respondent, if convicted, to a mandatory life sentence because of two prior felony convictions.

The prosecutor's initial assessment of respondent's case led him to forgo an indictment under the habitual criminal statute. The circumstances of respondent's prior convictions are relevant to this assessment and to my view of the case. Respondent was 17 years old when he committed his first offense. He was charged with rape but pleaded guilty to the lesser included offense of "detaining a female." One of the other participants in the incident was sentenced to life imprisonment. Respondent was sent not to prison but to a reformatory where he served five years. Respondent's second offense was robbery. This time he was found guilty by a jury and was sentenced to five years in prison, but he was placed on probation and served no time. Although respondent's prior convictions brought him within the terms of the Habitual Criminal Act, the offenses themselves did not result in imprisonment; yet the addition of a conviction on a charge involving $88.30 subjected respondent to a mandatory sentence of imprisonment for life. Persons convicted of rape and murder often are not punished so severely.

No explanation appears in the record for the prosecutor's decision to escalate the charge against respondent other than respondent's refusal to plead guilty. The prosecutor has conceded that his purpose was to discourage respondent's assertion of constitutional rights, and the majority accepts this characterization of events....

It seems to me that the question to be asked under the circumstances is whether the prosecutor reasonably might have charged respondent under the Habitual Criminal Act in the first place. The deference that courts properly accord the exercise of a prosecutor's discretion perhaps would foreclose judicial criticism if the prosecutor originally had sought an indictment under that Act, as unreasonable as it would have seemed. But here the prosecutor evidently made a reasonable, responsible judgment not to subject an individual to a mandatory life sentence when his only new offense had societal implications as limited as those accompanying the uttering of a single $88 forged check and when the circumstances of his prior convictions confirmed the inappropriateness of his applying the habitual criminal statute.* I think it may be inferred that the prosecutor himself deemed it unreasonable and not in the public interest to put this defendant in jeopardy of a sentence of life imprisonment.

There may be situations in which a prosecutor would be fully justified in seeking a fresh indictment for a more serious offense. The most plausible justification might be that it would have been reasonable and in the public interest initially to have charged the defendant with the greater offense. In most cases a court could not know why the harsher indictment was sought, and an inquiry into the prosecutor's motive would neither be indicated nor likely to be fruitful. In those cases, I would agree with the majority that the situation would not differ materially from one in which the higher charge was brought at the outset....

But this is not such a case. Here, any inquiry into the prosecutor's purpose is made unnecessary by his candid acknowledgment that he threatened to procure and in fact procured the habitual criminal indictment because of respondent's insistence on exercising his constitutional rights....

The plea-bargaining process, as recognized by this Court, is essential to the functioning of the criminal-justice system. It normally affords genuine benefits to defendants as well as to society. And if the system

*Indeed, the Kentucky Legislature subsequently determined that the habitual criminal statute under which respondent was convicted swept too broadly and did not identify adequately the kind of prior convictions that should trigger its application. At least one of respondent's two prior convictions would not satisfy the criteria of the revised statute; and the impact of the statute, when applied, has been reduced significantly in situations, like this one, where the third offense is relatively minor.

is to work effectively, prosecutors must be accorded the widest discretion, within constitutional limits, in conducting bargaining. This is especially true when a defendant is represented by counsel and presumably is fully advised of his rights. Only in the most exceptional case should a court conclude that the scales of the bargaining are so unevenly balanced as to arouse suspicion. In this case, the prosecutor's actions de-

nied respondent due process because their admitted purpose was to discourage and then to penalize with unique severity his exercise of constitutional rights. Implementation of a strategy calculated solely to deter the exercise of constitutional rights is not a constitutionally permissible exercise of discretion. I would affirm the opinion of the Court of Appeals on the facts of this case.

Fair Procedure in the Administrative Process: The New Substantive Due Process?

The Fifth and Fourteenth Amendments provide, in part, that "life, liberty or property" cannot be taken without "due process of law." As we have seen, during the late nineteenth century these provisions first were used to protect property and only later extended to protect the criminally accused. They are protean phrases whose meaning continues to grow and adapt to new conditions. Thus, periodically, the Court must confront three sets of issues: What is "due process?" "How much process is due?" And what is meant by "life," "liberty," and "property?" Combined, these issues raise the general question, what constitutes a fair hearing? We will examine recent answers to this question as it applies to a wide array of decisions involving juvenile courts, school discipline, welfare benefits, and social security payments. The list could be extended for the question involves the central issues of modern administrative law.

In a very real sense the most important developments in the "due process revolution" begun in the 1960s involve the way the Constitution has been interpreted to require governmental and quasi-governmental institutions to structure their relationships with individuals, businesses, and each other. In this enterprise of subjecting a variety of governmental functions to the strictures of due process, the Court has been both activist and sweeping, and in so doing has generated considerable controversy both among its members (decisions are often sharply divided) and outside, where its opinions have been praised for their sensitivity to the complexities of the bureaucratic state

and condemned for usurping the functions of other governmental units.

Some critics have labeled these developments the "new substantive due process," a comparison to the Court's rulings on economic regulation during the early part of this century, in which a majority of justices sought to read their own economic philosophies into the due process clauses (see Chapter 5). The upshot of that earlier controversy was an eventual retreat and judicial deference to the legislative and administrative process. Regarding the new substantive due process, too, some justices, often in sharp dissent, counsel similar deference. And there have been changes in direction as the Warren Court justices have been replaced by appointees of Presidents Nixon, Ford, and Reagan. Compare, for instance, Justice Fortas' sweeping language in IN RE GAULT, 387 U.S. 1, decided in 1967 at perhaps the height of the Warren Court's activism, with the style of the majority opinion in MATHEWS V. ELDRIDGE, 424 U.S. 319 (1976), decided nine years and five new justices later. Still, as you read MATHEWS in light of the other cases preceding it, ask whether it signals a real "retreat" or simply a consolidation and specification of the "outer boundaries" of the new substantive due process.

One of the Court's boldest decisions in the noncriminal area of due process is IN RE GAULT (1967), in which it undertook a wide-ranging assessment of juvenile court practices and ordered major changes in the structure and organization of juvenile proceedings. At the time, this decision was criticized by some, including Justice Stewart in dissent, because it appeared that the Court had reached out and "picked" an obscure case in order to find a vehicle for working its own revolutionary will upon the juvenile court systems of the fifty states. Others criticized the decision for weakening the framework on which the nonadversarial structure of juvenile proceedings had rested since the turn of this century. Still, many if not most of those closely connected with juvenile courts welcomed the decision and pointed out that the requirements imposed by GAULT were already standard policy in the most well-regarded state juvenile court systems.

Some anticipated that GAULT was the opening move in a drive to impose the complete set of standards of criminal courts upon juvenile courts, but this has not come to pass. In a series of decisions since GAULT, a divided Court, with many of the GAULT majority in dissent, has ruled that while the standard of proof in a juvenile hearing must be the traditional criminal court standard of "beyond a reasonable doubt" (rather than the "preponderance of the evidence," which has been the standard in some juvenile proceedings) (*In re Winship,* 397 U.S. 358, 1970), the Court has *not* imposed a right to a jury trial on juvenile proceedings (*McKeiver* v. *Pennsylvania,* 403 U.S. 528, 1971), nor has it actively invited further constitutional scrutiny of juvenile proceedings.

Historically, the law has distinguished between "rights" and "privileges." Rights have generally been treated as possessions of individuals, and are to be carefully protected if government seeks to take them away, while privileges are benefits provided by government, which can exercise its own discretion in granting and withholding them. Consequently, those whose rights are threatened (e.g., property holders in the face of eminent domain) have been accorded considerable legal and constitutional protections. Those who receive privileges such as public education, welfare, or employment have been accorded lesser protections.

However, the institutionalization of the modern welfare state, with its myriad social services, has caused a rethinking of this rights/privileges dis-tinction. To distinguish these social services from traditional constitutional rights, but to elevate them in legal importance above mere privileges, a new term — "entitlements" — has been coined to describe certain forms of legislatively created, benefit-producing activities. Increasingly, entitlements have been accorded constitutional protections akin to the protections once reserved for rights, and in recent years both the range of activities characterized as entitlements and the amount of court-imposed due process required to administer them has been expanded.

An influential article by Charles Reich in the *Yale Law Journal* (1964), "The New Property," has shaped modern thinking about these issues. Reich argued that for most people, wealth provided by government has become more important than traditional forms of private wealth; thus it should be accorded the constitutional protections available to traditional forms of private wealth. For instance Reich observed, wealth obtained through Social Security, unemployment compensation, veterans' benefits, and various welfare schemes constitutes a major source of income for millions of people. Jobs, both through direct employment by government and indirectly by private companies depending wholly or primarily on government contracts, provide a livelihood for millions more. Government-required certification and licenses are conditions for doing business for still others. Numerous others depend upon government-controlled prices, subsidies, and protection. And as both public and private employers establish educational requirements as prerequisites for employment, a high school diploma, a B.A., and a certificate of training take on property-like qualities they once did not possess.

Reich's view is that this government-produced and -controlled "wealth" should be regarded as the equivalent of traditional forms of property, and as such should be constitutionally protected. Just as the courts insist upon high standards of fair procedure when government is involved in depriving people of their traditional forms of "liberty" or "property," they should do the same when reviewing procedures for dispensing, terminating, and administering these new forms of property. Reich's vision has gained acceptance in the courts. Indeed, the most widespread and deeply felt consequence of the "due process revolution" has been the constitutionalization of decision making in a bewildering array of governmental agencies.

By constitutionalizing this process, the Supreme Court has imposed revolutionary changes on the entire structure of government and many private government contractors. The Court has required oversight by the federal courts in ways that pale in comparison to appellate court involvement in the administration of criminal justice, an area which historically has been supervised by the courts anyway. Now, routinely, courts may be asked to review the most minute decisions of government agencies, while these bodies, in turn, have been forced to create detailed provisions for dispensing and withholding claims to the "new property." The Federal Communications Commission must hold lengthy hearings accessible to the public when deciding whether to grant or revoke radio and television broadcast rights. Courts are involved in supervising the administration of schools, prisons, hospitals. Courts require universities to establish detailed procedures for dropping students who fail and for dealing with those charged with plagiarism. Government employees are constitutionally entitled to a detailed hearing procedure before being dismissed for whatever reasons. Professional licensing procedures, even if administered by private organizations, are subject to review in the courts for fairness.

In essence, by the mid 1970s, the administration of virtually the entire complex array of benefits and services provided by the modern welfare and administrative state had been constitutionalized and thereby subjected to judicial review in the federal courts. And as traditional forms of standing and jurisdiction have eroded, numerous individuals and groups are now able to bring suits into federal courts challenging the decisions of a plethora of governmental bodies. Furthermore, as the standards for fair hearing have evolved, the likelihood

of victory — or at least stalemate and delay — of such parties increases, and this further swells their ranks. As a consequence, questions about judicial capacity and competence must be taken seriously.

Although our emphasis here is on procedure, we should not forget that examinations of the process by which decisions are made is a concern with substance. We saw this in the examination of the "economic due process" cases involving the "freedom of contract" and in the death penalty cases, in which some justices focused on the sentencing process while others argued against the "cruel and unusual" substance of the policy. Keep this close relationship between substance and procedure in mind when you read the cases in this section. To what extent do you think the justices seize upon procedure as a vehicle for overriding the expert decisions of others and impose their own policy preferences? One clue is how broad and wide-ranging the Court's rulings are. To the extent that the Court does act as a substantive policy maker, what limits are there on its expertise? its capacity? Do federal judges have the time and knowledge to make informed judgments on all issues that come before them? If not, how do they select? But if the courts do not protect the interests of those often-vulnerable people making claims to the "new property," who will? To what extent should the courts defer to experts in legislatively created agencies? These, of course, are the questions asked about the Court's "substantive due process rulings" in the economic regulation cases. The answer there was to withdraw and defer. Should the Court do the same here?

Numerous cases involving claims of protection of the new forms of property could be presented. They deal with such issues as income and benefits, employment, occupational licensing, government-controlled franchises, government contracts, subsidies, the use of public lands and resources, and the distribution of government services. The Supreme Court has rendered important decisions in all these areas. We have selected but four cases to illustrate the range of issues, the variety of approaches, and the evolving views of the justices as turnover occurs on the Court.

Obviously, governmental functions vary widely, and the challenge to the Court has been to fashion requirements for fair hearings that are appropriate to particular circumstances. Not surprisingly, the Court has met this challenge by adopting a balancing approach that considers factors distinctive to each setting. Compare the requirements imposed on the four quite different institutions in the cases below. IN RE GAULT deals with criminal-like conduct of juveniles. GOSS V. LOPEZ (1975) involves disciplinary proceedings in public schools. GOLD-BERG V. KELLY (1970) reviews a decision to terminate welfare payments, and MATHEWS V. ELDRIDGE (1976) involves a claim against the Social Security Administration. In each case the Court held that minimal constitutional requirements for a fair hearing differed markedly. GAULT requires the highest standards and GOSS the lowest, with GOLDBERG and MATHEWS in between. Is there a logic to this sequence? Note that in GOLDBERG, the Court upholds the claims of the individual, while in MATHEWS it does not, attempting to distinguish MATHEWS from GOLDBERG. Are you convinced?

Note also that MATHEWS was decided in 1976, after the departure of two members of the GOLD-BERG majority and the addition of three new appointees (Powell, Rehnquist, and Stevens, although the last did not sit in this case). Finally, it is instructive to point out that GOSS V. LOPEZ was decided 5 to 4, with the most recent appointees joining in dissent. While this would seem to suggest the likelihood of an abrupt shift with the addition of more Republican-appointed Justices, the pattern since MATHEWS has been mixed. Justice Stevens is by no means a consistent nay-sayer, and beginning in the early 1980s, Justice Blackmun showed an increased willingness to support claims of individuals in the "new property" cases. Furthermore, a careful reading of MATHEWS does not so much reveal a majority set on dismantling the fair-hearing requirements of GOLDBERG as it shows a Court with a desire to establish outer boundaries. A great many "new property" claimants continue to gain victories in the federal courts.

Perhaps the only firm opponents to these developments are Chief Justice Rehnquist and Justice Scalia, who consistently take a position of deference to the other branches and to the states. But this view is not shared by anyone else on the Court. The others — to varying degrees — are willing to embrace active judicial oversight of the administrative process. It is for this reason that so many conservative court watchers, such as Donald Horowitz, author of *The Courts and Social Policy* (1977), have argued that judicial activism is now firmly institutionalized, embraced by conservative and liberal judges alike. Their differences, he seems to be saying, pale in comparison to similarities in their willingness to tolerate constitutional review of so many administrative functions.

Cases

In re Gault

387 U.S. 1 (1967)
Vote: 7–2

Gerald Gault, age fifteen, was taken into custody as a result of a complaint that he had made lewd telephone calls. After hearings before a juvenile court judge, he was judged delinquent and ordered committed to the Arizona State Industrial School for up to six years.

The circumstances of Gault's detention and hearing are as follows: Upon the complaint of a neighbor, Mrs. Cook, police took Gerald and a friend into custody. Gerald's parents were not notified at the time and later learned of his detention from another neighbor. During police custody, Gerald was not advised of his rights to remain silent and to representation by counsel. The family did not receive a copy of the petition filed by the police for a court hearing. The complainant, Mrs. Cook, did not appear at any of the hearings. The police report was vague on the number and nature of the calls to Mrs. Cook, and the little evidence available was unclear as to whether Gerald or his friend made the offensive remarks. At some of the proceedings the juvenile court judge appeared to be confused as to what precisely Gerald was charged with. Still, the court declared Gerald to be delinquent and committed him into custody for a maximum of six years.

If Gerald were an adult and had been charged with the same crime, the sentence for his offense would have been a maximum imprisonment of two months and a fine of from $5 to $50.

Arizona law did not permit an appeal in juvenile cases, so the Gaults filed a petition in state court for a writ of habeas corpus. In it they challenged a variety of procedures of the state Juvenile Code. (See the list at the outset of the Court's opinion.) The superior court dismissed the writ and the Arizona Supreme Court affirmed the dismissal. The Gaults then appealed to the United States Supreme Court.

MR. JUSTICE FORTAS delivered the opinion of the Court.

. . . [A]ppellants . . . urge that we hold the Juvenile Code of Arizona invalid on its face or as applied in this case because, contrary to the Due Process Clause of the Fourteenth Amendment, the juvenile is taken from the custody of his parents and committed to a state institution pursuant to proceedings in which the Juvenile Court has virtually unlimited discretion, and in which the following basic rights are denied:

1. Notice of the charges;
2. Right to counsel;
3. Right to confrontation and cross-examination;
4. Privilege against self-incrimination;
5. Right to a transcript of the proceedings; and
6. Right to appellate review.

    . . . .

. . . As to these proceedings, there appears to be little current dissent from the proposition that the Due Process Clause has a role to play. The problem is to ascertain the precise impact of the due process requirement upon such proceedings.

From the inception of the juvenile court system, wide differences have been tolerated — indeed insisted upon — between the procedural rights accorded to adults and those of juveniles. In practically all jurisdictions, there are rights granted to adults which are withheld from juveniles. In addition to the specific problems involved in the present case, for example, it has been held that the juvenile is not entitled to bail, to indictment by grand jury, to a public trial or to trial by jury. It is frequent practice that rules governing the arrest and interrogation of adults by the police are not observed in the case of juveniles.

The history and theory underlying this development are well-known, but a recapitulation is necessary for purposes of this opinion. The Juvenile Court movement began in this country at the end of the last century. From the juvenile court statute adopted in Illinois in 1899, the system has spread to every State in the Union, the District of Columbia, and Puerto Rico. The constitutionality of Juvenile Court laws has been sustained in over 40 jurisdictions against a variety of attacks.

The early reformers were appalled by adult procedures and penalties, and by the fact that children could be given long prison sentences and mixed in jails with hardened criminals. They were profoundly convinced that society's duty to the child could not be confined by the concept of justice alone. They believed that society's role was not to ascertain whether the child was "guilty" or "innocent," but "What is he, how has he become what he is, and what had best be done in his interest and in the interest of the state to save him from a downward career." The child — essentially good, as they saw it — was to be made "to feel that he is the object of [the state's] care and solicitude," not that he was under arrest or on trial. The rules of criminal procedure were therefore altogether inapplicable. The apparent rigidities, technicalities, and harshness which they observed in both substantive and procedural criminal law were therefore to be discarded. The idea of crime and punishment was to be abandoned. The child was to be "treated" and "rehabilitated" and the procedures, from apprehension through institutionalization, were to be "clinical" rather than punitive.

These results were to be achieved, without coming to conceptual and constitutional grief, by insisting that the proceedings were not adversary, but that the state was proceeding as *parens patriae*. The Latin phrase proved to be a great help to those who sought to rationalize the exclusion of juveniles from the constitutional scheme; but its meaning is murky and its historic credentials are of dubious relevance. [The phrase was taken from chancery practice, where, however, it was used to describe the power of the state to act *in loco parentis* for the purpose of protecting the property interests and the person of the child.] But there is no trace of the doctrine in the history of criminal jurisprudence. At common law, children under seven were considered incapable of possessing criminal intent. Beyond that age, they were subjected to arrest, trial, and in theory to punishment like adult offenders. In these old days, the state was not deemed to have authority to accord them fewer procedural rights than adults.

The right of the state, as *parens patriae,* to deny to the child procedural rights available to his elders was elaborated by the assertion that a child, unlike an adult, has a right "not to liberty but to custody." He can be made to attorn to his parents, to go to school, etc. If his parents default in effectively performing their custodial functions — that is, if the child is "delinquent" — the state may intervene. In doing so, it does not deprive the child of any rights, because he has none. It merely provides the "custody" to which the child is entitled. On this basis, proceedings involving juveniles were described as "civil" not "criminal" and therefore not subject to the requirements which restrict the state when it seeks to deprive a person of his liberty.

Accordingly, the highest motives and most enlightened impulses led to a peculiar system for juveniles, unknown to our law in any comparable context. The constitutional and theoretical basis for this particular system is — to say the least — debatable. And in practice, as we remarked in the *Kent* case, *supra,* the results have not been entirely satisfactory. Juvenile Court history has again demonstrated that unbridled discretion, however benevolently motivated, is frequently a poor substitute for principle and procedure. In 1937, Dean Pound wrote: "The powers of the Star Chamber were a trifle in comparison with those of our juvenile courts. . . ." The absence of substantive standards has not necessarily meant that children receive careful, compassionate, individualized treatment. The absence of procedural rules based upon constitutional principle has not always produced fair, efficient, and effective procedures. Departures from established principles of due process have frequently resulted not in enlightened procedure, but in arbitrariness. The Chairman of the Pennsylvania Council of Juvenile Court Judges has recently observed: "Unfortunately, loose procedures, high-handed methods and crowded court calendars, either singly or in combination, all too often, have resulted in depriving some juveniles of fundamental rights that have resulted in a denial of due process."

. . . .

It is claimed that juveniles obtain benefits from the special procedures applicable to them which more than offset the disadvantages of denial of the substance of normal due process. As we shall discuss, the observance of due process standards, intelligently and not ruthlessly administered, will not compel the States to abandon or displace any of the substantive benefits of the juvenile process. But it is important, we think, that the claimed benefits of the juvenile process should be candidly appraised. Neither sentiment nor folklore should cause us to shut our eyes, for example, to such startling findings as that reported in an exceptionally reliable study of repeaters or recidivism conducted by the Stanford Research Institute for the President's Commission on Crime in the District of Columbia. This Commission's Report states:

> In fiscal 1966 approximately 66 percent of the 16- and 17-year-old juveniles referred to the court by the Youth Aid Division had been before the court previously. In 1965, 56 percent of those in the Receiving Home were repeaters. The SRI study revealed that 61 percent of the sample Juvenile Court referrals in 1965 had been previously referred at least once and that 42 percent had been referred at least twice before.

Certainly, these figures and the high crime rates among juveniles to which we have referred could not lead us to conclude that the absence of constitutional protections reduces crime, or that the juvenile system, functioning free of constitutional inhibitions as it has largely done, is effective to reduce crime or rehabilitate offenders. We do not mean by this to denigrate the juvenile court process or to suggest that there are not aspects of the juvenile system relating to offenders which are valuable. But the features of the juvenile system which its proponents have asserted are of unique benefit will not be impaired by constitutional domestication. For example, the commendable principles relating to the processing and treatment of juveniles separately from adults are in no way involved or affected by the procedural issues under discussion. Further, we are told that one of the important benefits of the special juvenile court procedures is that they avoid classifying the juvenile as a "criminal." The juvenile offender is now classed as a "delinquent." There is, of course, no reason why this should not continue. It is disconcerting, however, that this term has come to involve only slightly less stigma than the term "criminal" applied to adults. It is also emphasized that in practically all jurisdictions, statutes provide that an adjudication of the child as a delinquent shall not operate as a civil disability or disqualify him for civil service appointment. There is no reason why the application of due process requirements should interfere with such provisions.

. . . .

Further, it is urged that the juvenile benefits from informal proceedings in the court. The early conception of the Juvenile Court proceeding was one in which a fatherly judge touched the heart and conscience of the erring youth by talking over his problems, by paternal advice and admonition, and in which, in extreme situations, benevolent and wise institutions of the State provided guidance and help "to save him from a downward career." Then, as now, goodwill and compassion were admirably prevalent. But recent studies have, with surprising unanimity, entered sharp dissent as to the validity of this gentle conception. They suggest that the appearance as well as the actuality of fairness, impartiality and orderliness — in short, the essentials of due process — may be a more impressive and more therapeutic attitude so far as the juvenile is concerned. . . .

Ultimately, however, we confront the reality of that portion of the Juvenile Court process with which we deal in this case. A boy is charged with misconduct. The boy is committed to an institution where he may be restrained of liberty for years. It is of no constitutional consequence — and of limited practical meaning — that the institution to which he is committed is called an Industrial School. The fact of the matter is that, however euphemistic the title, a "receiving home" or an "industrial school" for juveniles is an institution of confinement in which the child is incarcerated for a greater or lesser time. His world becomes "a building with whitewashed walls, regimented routine and institutional hours. . . ." Instead of mother and father and sisters and brothers and friends and classmates, his world is peopled by guards, custodians, state employees, and "delinquents" confined with him for anything from waywardness to rape and homicide.

In view of this, it would be extraordinary if our Constitution did not require the procedural regularity and the exercise of care implied in the phrase "due process." Under our Constitution, the condition of being a boy does not justify a kangaroo court. The traditional ideas of Juvenile Court procedure, indeed, contemplated that time would be available and care would be used to establish precisely what the juvenile did and why he did it — was it a prank of adolescence or a brutal act threatening serious consequences to himself or society unless corrected? Under traditional notions, one would assume that in a case like that of Gerald Gault, where the juvenile appears to have a home, a working mother and father, and an older brother, the Juvenile Judge would have made a careful inquiry and judgment as to the possibility that the boy could be disciplined and dealt with at home, despite his previous transgressions. Indeed, so far as appears in the record before us, except for some conversation with Gerald about his school work and his "wanting to go to... Grand Canyon with his father," the points to which the judge directed his attention were little different from those that would be involved in determining any charge of violation of a penal statute. The essential difference between Gerald's case and a normal criminal case is that safeguards available to adults were discarded in Gerald's case. The summary procedure as well as the long commitment was possible because Gerald was 15 years of age instead of over 18.

If Gerald had been over 18, he would not have been subject to Juvenile Court proceedings. For the particular offense immediately involved, the maximum punishment would have been a fine of $5 to $50, or imprisonment in jail for not more than two months. Instead, he was committed to custody for a maximum of six years. If he had been over 18 and had committed an offense to which such a sentence might apply, he would have been entitled to substantial rights under the Constitution of the United States as well as under Arizona's laws and constitution. The United States Constitution would guarantee him rights and protections with respect to arrest, search and seizure, and pretrial interrogation. It would assure him of specific notice of the charges and adequate time to decide his course of action and to prepare his defense. He would be entitled to clear advice that he could be represented by counsel, and, at least if a felony were involved, the State would be required to provide counsel if his parents were unable to afford it. If the court acted on the basis of his confession, careful procedures would be required to assure its voluntariness. If the case went to trial, confrontation and opportunity for cross-examination would be guaranteed. So wide a gulf between the State's treatment of the adult and of the child requires a bridge sturdier than mere verbiage, and reasons more persuasive than cliché can provide. As Wheeler and Cottrell have put it, "The rhetoric of the juvenile court movement had developed without any necessarily close correspondence to the realities of court and institutional routines." [The Court then held that in juvenile proceedings due process requires: (1) adequate and timely notice; (2) a right to counsel; and that (3) "absent a valid confession, a determination of delinquency and an order to a state institution cannot be sustained in the absence of sworn testimony subjected to the opportunity for cross-examination." The Court did not rule on the failure to provide a transcript and on the right to appellate review.]

[JUSTICES BLACK and WHITE wrote separate concurring opinions. JUSTICE HARLAN concurred in part and dissented in part.]

MR. JUSTICE STEWART, dissenting.

The Court today uses an obscure Arizona case as a vehicle to impose upon thousands of juvenile courts throughout the Nation restrictions that the constitution made applicable to adversary criminal trials. I believe the Court's decision is wholly unsound as a matter of constitutional law, and sadly unwise as a matter of judicial policy.

Juvenile proceedings are not criminal trials. They are not civil trials. They are simply not adversary proceedings. Whether treating with a delinquent child, a neglected child, a defective child, or a dependent child, a juvenile proceeding's whole purpose and mission is the very opposite of the mission and purpose of a prosecution in a criminal court. The object of the one is correction of a condition. The object of the other is conviction and punishment for a criminal act.

. . . .

The inflexible restrictions that the Constitution so wisely made applicable to adversary criminal trials have no inevitable place in the proceedings of those public social agencies known as juvenile or family courts. And to impose the Court's long catalog of requirements upon juvenile proceedings in every area of the country is to invite a long step backwards into the nineteenth century. In that era there were no juvenile proceedings, and a child was tried in a conventional criminal court with all the trappings of a conventional criminal trial. . . .

A State in all its dealings must, of course, accord every person due process of law. And due process may require that some of the same restrictions which the Constitution has placed upon criminal trials must be imposed on juvenile proceedings. For example, I suppose that all would agree that a brutally coerced confession could not constitutionally be considered in a juvenile court hearing. But it surely does not follow that the testimonial privilege against self-incrimination is applicable in all juvenile proceedings. Similarly, due process clearly requires timely notice of the purpose and scope of any proceedings affecting the relationship of parent and child. . . . But it certainly does

not follow that notice of a juvenile hearing must be framed with all the technical niceties of a criminal indictment. . . .

In any event, there is no reason to deal with issues such as these in the present case. The Supreme Court of Arizona found that the parents of Gerald Gault "knew of their right to counsel, to subpoena and cross examine witnesses, of the right to confront the witnesses against Gerald and the possible consequences of a finding of delinquency." . . . It further found that "Mrs. Gault knew the exact nature of the charge against Gerald from the day he was taken to the detention home." . . . And . . . no issue of compulsory self-incrimination is presented by this case.

I would dismiss the appeal.

Goss v. Lopez

419 U.S. 565 (1975)
Vote: 5–4

Dwight Lopez and a group of other students at Central High School and McGuggey Junior High School in Columbus, Ohio, were suspended for up to ten days in connection with disturbances at the schools. Several students, including Lopez, challenged these suspensions in federal district court.

At the time, Ohio law empowered school principals to suspend pupils for misconduct for up to ten days or to expel them. The law required notification to parents of such actions within twenty-four hours and required that the reasons for the suspensions be stated. It further provided that students who were expelled, or their parents, could appeal in person to the Board of Education.

The students argued that these procedures did not meet constitutional standards of due process because they did not accord them a hearing, either prior to suspension or within a reasonable time thereafter. Lopez and his fellow students asked the Court to enjoin school administrators to remove all references to such suspensions from their records and to declare the Ohio law governing suspensions unconstitutional.

A three-judge district court held for the students. The defendant school administrators appealed to the United States Supreme Court.

MR. JUSTICE WHITE delivered the opinion of the Court.

At the outset, appellants contend that because there is no constitutional right to an education at public expense, the Due Process Clause does not protect against expulsions from the public school system. This position misconceives the nature of the issue and is refuted by prior decisions. The Fourteenth Amendment forbids the State to deprive any person of life, liberty or property without due process of law. Protected interests in property are normally "not created by the Constitution. Rather, they are created and their dimensions are defined" by an independent source such as state statutes or rules entitling the citizen to certain benefits. . . .

Accordingly, a state employee who under state law, or rules promulgated by state officials, has a legitimate claim of entitlement to continued employment absent sufficient cause for discharge may demand the procedural protections of due process. . . . So may welfare recipients who have statutory rights to welfare as long as they maintain the specified qualifications. *Goldberg* v. *Kelly* . . . (1970). *Morrissey* v. *Brewer,* . . . (1972), applied the limitations of the Due Process Clause to governmental decisions to revoke parole, although a parolee has no constitutional right to that status. In like vein was *Wolff* v. *McDonald* . . . (1974), where the procedural protections of the Due Process Clause were triggered by official cancellation of a prisoner's good-time credits accumulated under state law, although those benefits were not mandated by the Constitution.

. . . .

Although Ohio may not be constitutionally obligated to establish and maintain a public school system, it has nevertheless done so and has required its children to attend. Those young people do not "shed their constitutional rights" at the schoolhouse door. . . . "The Fourteenth Amendment, as now applied to the States, protects the citizen against the State itself and all of its creatures . . . Boards of Education not excepted." . . . The authority possessed by the State to prescribe and enforce standards of conduct in its schools, although concededly very broad, must be exercised consistently with constititional safeguards. Among other things, the State is constrained to recognize a student's legitimate entitlement to a public education as a property interest which is protected by the Due Process Clause and which may not be taken away for misconduct without adherence to the minimum procedures required by that clause.

The Due Process Clause also forbids arbitrary deprivations of liberty. "Where a person's good name, reputation, honor, or integrity is at stake because of what the government is doing to him," the minimal requirements of the clause must be satisfied. . . . School authorities here suspended appellees from school for periods of up to 10 days based on charges of misconduct. If sustained and recorded, those charges could seriously damage the student's standing with their fellow pupils and their teachers as well as interfere with later opportunities for higher education and employment. It is apparent that the claimed right of the State to determine unilaterally and without process whether that misconduct has occurred immediately collides with the requirements of the Constitution.

Appellants proceed to argue that even if there is a right to a public education protected by the Due Process Clause generally, the clause comes into play only when the State subjects a student to a "severe detriment or grievous loss." The loss of 10 days, it is said, is neither severe nor grievous and the Due Process Clause is therefore of no relevance. Appellee's argument is again refuted by our prior decisions; for in determining "whether due process requirements apply in the first place, we must look not to the 'weight' but the the *nature* of the interest at stake." . . . Appellees were excluded from school only temporarily, it is true, but the length and consequent severity of a deprivation, while another factor to weigh in determining the appropriate form of hearing, "is not decisive of the basic right" to a hearing of some kind. . . . The Court's view has been that as long as a property deprivation is not *de minimis,* its gravity is irrelevant to the question whether account must be taken of the Due Process Clause. . . . A 10-day suspension from school is not *de minimis* in our view and may not be imposed in complete disregard of the Due Process Clause.

. . . .

"Once it is determined that due process applies, the question remains what process is due." . . . We turn to that question, fully realizing as our cases regularly do that the interpretation and application of the Due Process Clause are intensely practical matters and that "the very nature of due process negates any concept of inflexible porcedures universally applicable to every imaginable situation." . . .

There are certain bench marks to guide us, however. . . . [M]any controversies have raged about the cryptic and abstract words of the Due Process Clause but there can be no doubt that at a minimum they require that deprivation of life, liberty or property by adjudication be preceded by notice and opportunity for hearing appropriate to the nature of the case." . . . "[T]he fundamental requisite of due process of law is the opportunity to be heard," . . . a right that "has little reality or worth unless one is informed that the matter is pending and can choose for himself whether to . . .

contest."... At the very minimum, therefore, students facing suspension and the consequent interference with a protected property interest must be given *some* kind of notice and afforded *some* kind of hearing. "Parties whose rights are to be affected are entitled to be heard; and in order that they may enjoy that right they must first be notified."...

It also appears from our cases that the timing and content of the notice and the nature of the hearing will depend on appropriate accommodation of the competing interests involved....

We do not believe that school authorities must be totally free from notice and hearing requirements if their schools are to operate with acceptable efficiency. Students facing temporary suspension have interests qualifying for protection of the Due Process Clause, and due process requires, in connection with a suspension of 10 days or less, that the student be given oral or written notice of the charges against him and, if he denies them, an explanation of the evidence the authorities have and an opportunity to present his side of the story. The clause requires at least these rudimentary precautions against unfair or mistaken findings of misconduct and arbitrary exclusion from school.

There need be no delay between the time "notice" is given and the time of the hearing. In the great majority of cases the disciplinarian may informally discuss the alleged misconduct with the student minutes after it has occurred. We hold only that, in being given an opportunity to explain his version of the facts at this discussion, the student first be told what he is accused of doing and what the basis of the accusation is. Lower courts which have addressed the question of the *nature* of the procedures required in short suspension cases have reached the same conclusion.... Since the hearing may occur almost immediately following the misconduct, it follows that as a general rule notice and hearing should precede removal of the student from school. We agree with the District Court, however, that there are recurring situations in which prior notice and hearing cannot be insisted upon. Students whose presence poses a continuing danger to persons or property or an ongoing threat of disrupting the academic process may be immediately removed from school. In such cases, the necessary notice and rudimentary hearing should follow as soon as practicable, as the District Court indicated.

In holding as we do, we do not believe that we have imposed procedures on school disciplinarians which are inappropriate in a classroom setting. Instead we have imposed requirements which are, if anything, less than a fair-minded school principal would impose upon himself in order to avoid unfair suspensions....

We stop short of construing the Due Process Clause to require, countrywide, that hearings in connection with short suspensions must afford the student the opportunity to secure counsel, to confront and cross-examine witnesses supporting the charge or to call his own witnesses to verify his version of the incident. Brief disciplinary suspensions are almost countless. To impose in each such case even truncated trial type procedures might well overwhelm administrative facilities in many places and, by diverting resources, cost more than it would save in educational effectiveness. Moreover, further formalizing the suspension process and escalating its formality and adversary nature may not only make it too costly as a regular disciplinary tool but also destroy its effectiveness as part of the teaching process....

We should also make it clear that we have addressed ourselves solely to the short suspension, not exceeding 10 days. Longer suspensions or expulsions for the remainder of the school term, or permanently, may require more formal procedures. Nor do we put aside the possibility that in unusual situations, although involving only a short suspension, something more than the rudimentary procedures will be required. HOLDING:

The District Court found each of the suspensions involved here to have occurred without a hearing, either before or after the suspension, and that each suspension was therefore invalid and the statute unconstitutional insofar as it permits such suspensions without notice or hearing. Accordingly, the judgment is

Affirmed.

MR. JUSTICE POWELL, with whom THE CHIEF JUSTICE, MR. JUSTICE BLACKMUN, and MR. JUSTICE REHNQUIST join, dissenting.

The Court today invalidates an Ohio statute that permits student suspensions from school without a hearing "for not more than ten days." The decision unnecessarily opens avenues for judicial intervention in the operation of our public schools that may affect adversely the quality of education. The Court holds for the first time that the federal courts, rather than educational officials and state legislatures, have the authority to determine the rules applicable to routine classroom discipline of children and teenagers in the public schools. It justifies this unprecedented intrusion into the process of elementary and secondary education by identifying a new constitutional right: the right of a student not to be suspended for as much as a single day without notice and a due process hearing either before or promptly following the suspension.

The Court's decision rests on the premise that, under Ohio law, education is a property interest protected by the Fourteenth Amendment's Due Process Clause and therefore that any suspension requires notice and a hearing. In my view, a student's interest in education is not infringed by a suspension within the limited period prescribed by Ohio law. Moreover, to the extent that there may be some arguable infringement, it is too speculative, transitory and insubstantial to justify imposition of a *constitutional* rule.

. . . .

No one can foresee the ultimate frontiers of the new "thicket" the Court now enters. Today's ruling appears to sweep within the protected interest in education a multitude of discretionary decisions in the educational process. Teachers and other school authorities are required to make many decisions that may have serious consequences for the pupil. They must decide, for example, how to grade the student's work, whether a student passes or fails a course, whether he is to be promoted, whether he is required to take certain subjects, whether he may be excluded from interscholastic athletics or other extracurricular activities, whether he may be removed from one school and sent to another, whether he may be bused long distances when available schools are nearby, and whether he should be placed in a "general," "vocational," or "college-preparatory" track.

In these and many similar situations claims of impairment of one's educational entitlement identical in principle to those before the Court today can be asserted with equal or greater justification. Likewise, in many of these situations, the pupil can advance the same types of speculative and subjective injury given critical weight in this case. The District Court, relying upon generalized opinion evidence, concluded that a suspended student may suffer psychological injury in one or more of the ways set forth in the margin below. The Court appears to adopt this rationale. . . .

It hardly need be said that if a student, as a result of a day's suspension, suffers "a blow" to his "self-esteem," "feels powerless," views "teachers with resentment," or feels "stigmatized by his teachers," identical psychological harms will flow from many other routine and necessary school decisions. The student who is given a failing grade, who is not promoted, who is excluded from certain extracurricular activities, who is assigned to a school reserved for children of less than average ability, or who is placed in the "vocational" rather than the "college-preparatory" track, is unlikely to suffer any less psychological injury than if he were suspended for a day for a relatively minor infraction.

. . . .

Not so long ago, state deprivations of the most significant forms of state largesse were not thought to require due process protection on the ground that the deprivation resulted only in the loss of a state provided "benefit." . . . In recent years the Court, wisely in my view, has rejected the "wooden distinction between 'rights' and 'privileges'" . . . and looked instead to the significance of the state created or enforced right and to the substantiality of the alleged deprivation. Today's opinion appears to abandon this reasonable approach by holding in effect that government infringement of any interest to which a person is entitled, no matter what the interest or how inconsequential the infringement, requires *constitutional* protection. As it is difficult to think of any less consequential infringement than suspension of a junior high school student for a single day, it is equally difficult to perceive any principled limit to the new reach of procedural due process.

Goldberg v. Kelly

397 U.S. 254 (1970)
Vote: 6–3

John Kelly and others were recipients of financial aid under the federally assisted program Aid to Families with Dependent Children (AFDC) or under New York State's general Home Relief program. They brought a class action suit, alleging that New York State and New York City officials, acting in accordance with state and local regulations, terminated their aid without prior notice and hearing, and thus deprived them of property without due process of law. While the suits were pending in the courts, the State and City adopted procedures for notice and hearing, and the suits were amended to challenge the adequacy of the new procedures, which the claimants still maintained were constitutionally inadequate.

The relevant requirements of these new provisions governing discontinuation and termination of aid under the city-administered program and considered by the Court here are as follows: A caseworker who doubts a recipient's eligibility must first discuss the issue with the recipient, and if the caseworker concludes that the recipient is no longer eligible, he or she recommends termination to a supervisor. If the latter concurs, he or she sends the recipient a letter stating reasons for the proposed termination and giving notice that the recipient has seven days to request a higher official to review the record and consider any written statement the recipient may wish to submit. If the reviewing official affirms the determination of ineligibility, aid is stopped immediately and the recipient is informed in writing of the reasons. This letter also informs the recipient that the recipient may request a post-termination hearing before an independent hearing officer, at which time the recipient may appear personally, offer oral evidence, confront and cross-examine adverse witnesses, and have a record made of the hearing.

Appellees Kelly et al. challenged these procedures, arguing that they provided no opportunity for personal appearance before the reviewing official, for oral presentation of evidence, or for confrontation and cross-examination of adverse witnesses *prior* to termination of benefits.

A three-judge district court ruled that only an evidentiary hearing *before* termination of benefits would satisfy constitutional standards, overturned the termination orders, and ordered changes in the regulations. City officials appealed to the United States Supreme Court.

Mr. Justice Brennan delivered the opinion of the Court.

The constitutional issue to be decided... is the narrow one whether the Due Process Clause requires that the recipient be afforded an evidentiary hearing *before* the termination of benefits....

Appellant does not contend that procedural due process is not applicable to the termination of welfare benefits. Such benefits are a matter of statutory entitlement for persons qualified to receive them. Their termination involves state action that adjudicates important rights. The constitutional challenge cannot be answered by an argument that public assistance benefits are "a 'privilege' and not a 'right.'"... Relevant constitutional restraints apply as much to the withdrawal of public assistance benefits as to disqualification for unemployment compensation... or to denial of a tax exemption... or to discharge from public employment.... The extent to which procedural due process must be afforded the recipient is influenced by the extent to which he may be "condemned to suffer grievous loss,"... and depends upon whether the recipient's interest in avoiding that loss outweighs the governmental interest in summary adjudication. Accordingly... "consideration of what procedures due process may require under any given set of circumstances must begin with a determination of the precise nature of the government function involved as well as of the private interest that has been affected by governmental action."...

It is true, of course, that some governmental benefits may be administratively terminated without affording the recipient a pre-termination evidentiary hearing. But we agree with the District Court that when welfare is discontinued, only a pre-termination evidentiary hearing provides the recipient with procedural due process.... For qualified recipients, welfare provides the means to obtain essential food, clothing, housing, and medical care.... Thus the crucial factor in this context — a factor not present in the case of the blacklisted government contractor, the discharged government employee, the taxpayer denied a tax exemption, or virtually anyone else whose governmental largesse is ended — is that termination of aid pending resolution of a controversy over eligibility may deprive an *eligible* recipient of the very means by which to live while he waits. Since he lacks independent resources, his situation becomes immediately desperate. His need to concentrate upon finding the means for daily subsistence, in turn, adversely affects his ability to seek redress from the welfare bureaucracy.

Moreover, important governmental interests are promoted by affording recipients a pre-termination evidentiary hearing. From its founding the Nation's basic commitment has been to foster the dignity and well-being of all persons within its borders. We have come to recognize that forces not within the control of the poor contribute to their poverty. This perception, against the background of our traditions, has significantly influenced the development of the contemporary public assistance system. Welfare, by meeting the basic demands of subsistence, can help bring within the reach of the poor the same opportunities that are available to others to participate meaningfully in the life of the community. At the same time, welfare guards against the societal malaise that may flow from a widespread sense of unjustified frustration and insecurity. Public assistance, then, is not mere charity, but a means to "promote the general Welfare, and secure the Blessings of Liberty to ourselves and our Posterity." The same governmental interests which counsel the provision of welfare, counsel as well its uninterrupted provision to those eligible to receive it; pre-termination evidentiary hearings are indispensable to that end.

Appellant does not challenge the force of these considerations but argues that they are outweighed by countervailing governmental interests in conserving fiscal and administrative resources. These interests, the argument goes, justify the delay of any evidentiary hearing until after discontinuance of the grants. Summary adjudication protects the public fisc by stopping payments promptly upon discovery of reason to believe that a recipient is no longer eligible. Since most terminations are accepted without challenge, summary adjudication also conserves both the fisc and administrative time and energy by reducing the number of evidentiary hearings actually held.

We agree with the District Court, however, that these governmental interests are not overriding in the welfare context. The requirement of a prior hearing doubtless involves some greater expense, and the benefits paid to ineligible recipients pending decision at the hearing probably cannot be recouped, since these recipients are likely to be judgment-proof. But the State is not without weapons to minimize these increased costs. Much of the drain on fiscal and administrative resources can be reduced by developing procedures for prompt pre-termination hearings and by skillful use of personnel and facilities. Indeed, the very provision for a post-termination evidentiary hearing in New York's Home Relief program is itself cogent evidence that the State recognizes the primacy of the public interest in correct eligibility determinations and therefore in the provision of procedural safeguards. Thus, the interest of the eligible recipient in uninterrupted receipt of public assistance, coupled with the State's interest that his payments not be erroneously terminated, clearly outweighs the State's competing concern to prevent any increase in its fiscal and administrative burdens. . . .

. . . [T]he pre-termination hearing need not take the form of a judicial or quasi-judicial trial. We bear in mind that the statutory "fair hearing" will provide the recipient with a full administrative review. Accordingly, the pre-termination hearing has one function only: to produce an initial determination of the validity of the welfare department's grounds for discontinuance of payments in order to protect a recipient against an erroneous termination of his benefits. . . . Thus, a complete record and a comprehensive opinion, which would serve primarily to facilitate judicial review and to guide future decisions, need not be provided at the pre-termination stage. We recognize, too, that both welfare authorities and

recipients have an interest in relatively speedy resolution of questions of eligibility, that they are used to dealing with one another informally, and that some welfare departments have very burdensome caseloads. These considerations justify the limitation of the pre-termination hearing to minimum procedural safeguards, adapted to the particular characteristics of welfare recipients, and to the limited nature of the controversies to be resolved. We wish to add that we, no less than the dissenters, recognize the importance of not imposing upon the States or the Federal Government in this developing field of law any procedural requirements beyond those demanded by rudimentary due process.

"The fundamental requisite of due process of law is the opportunity to be heard." . . . The hearing must be "at a meaningful time and in a meaningful manner." . . . In the present context these principles require that a recipient have timely and adequate notice detailing the reasons for a proposed termination, and an effective opportunity to defend by confronting any adverse witnesses and by presenting his own arguments and evidence orally. These rights are important in cases such as those before us, where recipients have challenged proposed terminations as resting on incorrect or misleading factual premises or on misapplication of rules or policies to the facts of particular cases.

The city's procedures presently do not permit recipients to appear personally with or without counsel before the official who finally determines continued eligibility. Thus a recipient is not permitted to present evidence to that official orally, or to confront or cross-examine adverse witnesses. These omissions are fatal to the constitutional adequacy of the procedures.

The opportunity to be heard must be tailored to the capacities and circumstances of those who are to be heard. It is not enough that a welfare recipient may present his position to the decision maker in writing or second-hand through his caseworker. Written submissions are an unrealistic option for most recipients, who lack the educational attainment necessary to write effectively and who cannot obtain professional assistance. Moreover, written submissions do not afford the flexibility of oral presentations; they do not permit the recipient to mold his argument to the issues the decision maker appears to regard as important. Particularly where credibility and veracity are at issue, as they must be in many termination proceedings, written submissions are a wholly unsatisfactory basis for decision. The second-hand presentation to the decision maker by the caseworker has its own deficiencies; since the caseworker usually gathers the facts upon which the charge of ineligibility rests, the presentation of the recipient's side of the controversy cannot safely be left to him. Therefore a recipient must be allowed to state his position orally. . . .

In almost every setting where important decisions turn on questions of fact, due process requires an opportunity to confront and cross-examine adverse witnesses. . . . Welfare recipients must therefore be given an opportunity to confront and cross-examine the witnesses relied on by the department.

"The right to be heard would be, in many cases, of little avail if it did not comprehend the right to be heard by counsel." . . . We do not say that counsel must be provided at the pre-termination hearing, but only that the recipient must be allowed to retain an attorney if he so desires. Counsel can help delineate the issues, present the factual contentions in an orderly manner, conduct cross-examination, and generally safeguard the interests of the recipient. We do not anticipate that this assistance will unduly prolong or otherwise encumber the hearing. . . .

Finally, the decision maker's conclusion as to a recipient's eligibility must rest solely on the legal rules and evidence adduced at the hearing. . . . To demonstrate compliance with this elementary requirement, the decision maker should state the reasons for his determination and indicate the evidence he relied on, . . . though his statement need not amount to a full opinion or even formal findings of fact and conclusions of law. And, of course, an impartial decision maker is essential. . . . [P]rior involvement in some aspects of a case will not necessarily bar a welfare official from acting as a decision maker. He should not, however, have participated in making the determination under review.

Affirmed.

MR. JUSTICE BLACK, dissenting.

The more than a million names on the relief rolls in New York, and the more than nine million names on the rolls of all the 50 States were not put there at random. The names are there because state welfare officials believed that those people were eligible for assistance. Probably in the officials' haste to make out the lists many names were put there erroneously in order to alleviate immediate suffering, and undoubtedly some people are drawing relief who are not entitled under the law to do so. Doubtless some draw relief checks from time to time who know they are not eligible, either because they are not actually in need or for some other reason. Many of those who thus draw undeserved gratuities are without sufficient property to enable the Government to col-

lect back from them any money they wrongfully receive. But the Court today holds that it would violate the Due Process Clause of the Fourteenth Amendment to stop paying those people weekly or monthly allowances unless the Government first affords them a full "evidentiary hearing" even though welfare officials are persuaded that the recipients are not rightfully entitled to receive a penny under the law. In other words, although some recipients might be on the lists for payment wholly because of deliberate fraud on their parts, the Court holds that the Government is helpless and must continue, until after an evidentiary hearing, to pay money that it does not owe, never has owed, and never could owe. I do not believe there is any provision in our Constitution that should thus paralyze the Government's efforts to protect itself against making payments to people who are not entitled to them.

Particularly do I not think that the Fourteenth Amendment should be given such an unnecessarily broad construction. That Amendment came into being primarily to protect Negroes from discrimination, and while some of its language can and does protect others, all know that the chief purpose behind it was to protect ex-slaves. . . . The Court, however, relies upon the Fourteenth Amendment and in effect says that failure of the Government to pay a promised charitable installment to an individual deprives that individual of *his own property,* in violation of the Due Process Clause of the Fourteenth Amendment. It somewhat strains credulity to say that a government's promise of charity to an individual is property belonging to that individual when the Government denies that the individual is honestly entitled to receive such a payment. . . .

The procedure required today as a matter of constitutional law finds no precedent in our legal system. Reduced to its simplest terms, the problem in this case is similar to that frequently encountered when two parties have an ongoing legal relationship which requires one party to make periodic payments to the other. Often the situation arises where the party "owing" the money stops paying it and justifies his conduct by arguing that the recipient is not legally entitled to payment. The recipient can, of course, disagree and go to court to compel payment. But I know of no situation in our legal system in which the person alleged to owe money to another is required by law to continue making payments to a judgment-proof claimant without the benefit of any security or bond to insure that these payments can be recovered if he wins his legal argument. Yet today's decision in no way obligates the welfare recipient to pay back any benefits wrongfully received

able difficulty in drawing a clear line between civil or legal rights, which were protected, and purely social or private preferences, which were not. For instance, did the Fourteenth Amendment grant Congress the authority to prohibit privately owned railways, hotels, restaurants, and theaters from excluding people on the basis of race? from segregating patrons by race? Could states segregate pupils in public schools by race? Could courts enforce contracts that contain racially discriminatory provisions? Does Congress have the authority to prohibit public accommodations from excluding or segregating patrons by race? These are but a few of the questions that were to come before the Supreme Court in the wake of the Fourteenth Amendment.

Although not many challenges to racial discrimination came before the Court prior to the 1930s (most of the early equal protection cases involved challenges to economic regulations), the few race-related cases that were handed down during the first decades after adoption of the Fourteenth Amendment seized upon this civil/social distinction, and in so doing permitted all but the most blatant forms of state-sanctioned racial discrimination. Indeed, the system of apartheid that grew up in the American South in the early twentieth century was fostered in no small part by the Supreme Court's interpretation of the equal protection provision. This approach is illustrated by three cases decided by 1896, one of which upheld the claims of a black plaintiff and the other two of which rejected them. Together they outlined a philosophy that shaped the Court's approach to race relations for over half a century.

In *Strauder* v. *West Virginia*, 100 U.S. 303 (1880), the Court overturned the state conviction of a black man found guilty of murder, because state law had excluded blacks from petit juries. The Court observed that "the very fact that colored people are singled out and expressly denied by statute all right to participate in the administration of the law, as jurors, because of their color, though they are citizens, and may be in other respects fully qualified, is practically a brand upon them, affixed by the law, an assertion of their infe-

riority, and stimulant to that race prejudice which is an impediment of securing to individuals of that race that equal justice which the law aims to secure to all others."

Three years later, in the CIVIL RIGHTS CASES, 109 U.S. 3 (1883), the Court held unconstitutional the Civil Rights Act of 1875, which prohibited racial discrimination by proprietors of hotels, theaters, and railways, arguing that such practices were *private* matters not within the purview of the Fourteenth Amendment and Congress' power to enforce it. The power of Congress to enforce the provisions of the Fourteenth Amendment, the Court held, was limited to "counteracting such laws as the states may adopt or enforce, and which by the amendment they are prohibited from making." The Fourteenth amendment, it continued, "does not authorize Congress to create a code of municipal law for the regulation of private rights; but to provide modes of redress against the operation of state laws, and the action of state officers, executive or judicial, when these are subversive to the fundamental rights specified in the amendment."

This decision drew a lone dissent from Justice John Marshall Harlan, who argued that Congress "under its express power to enforce [the Fourteenth Amendment]... may enact laws of a direct and primary character, operating upon states, their officers and agents, and also upon, at least, such individuals and corporations as exercise public functions and wield power and authority under the state." "Public conveyances, inns and places of public amusement," he continued, "all operated under a web of government licenses" that in effect made them agents of the public and as such constituted state action within the purview of the Fourteenth Amendment and congressional authority. But this view was not to gain acceptance until well into the twentieth century, and even now Congress remains cautious about its authority under the Fourteenth Amendment.

In PLESSY V. FURGUSON, 163 U.S. 537 (1896), the Court sought to harmonize the tensions inherent in the civil/social equality distinction. To this end, it put its seal of approval on a state law requiring users of public services to be segregated by race, a practice which at the time was widespread in public schools in the North and probably deemed acceptable by many supporters of the Fourteenth Amendment. In upholding a Louisiana statute requiring that railway companies provide separate accommodations for black and white passengers, PLESSY transformed this practice into the constitutional doctrine of "separate but equal." (Ironically, the case originally arose because Plessy, arguing that he was white, had refused to sit in the black coach.) Building on *Strauder,* Justice Brown, for the majority, elaborated on the distinction between social and civil rights, arguing that "[t]he object of the [Fourteenth] amendment was undoubtedly to enforce the absolute equality of the two races before the law . . . [but] in the nature of things it could not have been intended to abolish distinctions based upon color, or to enforce social, as distinquished from political, equality, or a commingling of the two races upon terms unsatisfactory to either." He continued:

> We consider the underlying fallacy of the plaintiff's argument to consist in the assumption that the enforced separation of the two races stamps the colored race with a badge of inferiority. If this be so, it is not by reason of anything found in the act, but solely because the colored race chooses to put that construction upon it. [The] argument also assumes that social prejudices may be overcome by legislation, and that equal rights cannot be secured to the negro except by an enforced commingling of the two races. We cannot accept this proposition. If the two races are to meet upon terms of social equality, it must be the result [of] voluntary consent of individuals. . . . Legislation is powerless to eradicate racial instincts, or to abolish distinctions based upon physical differences, and the attempt to do so can only result in accentuation of the difficulties of the present situation.

PLESSY occasioned another powerful and prophetic dissent by Justice Harlan. Arguing that the clear intent of the state law was to discriminate against blacks, he asserted, "There is no caste here. The Constitution is colorblind, and neither knows nor tolerates classes among citizens." He continued, "In my opinion, the judgment this day rendered will, in time, prove to be quite as perni-

cious as the decision made by this tribunal in the *Dred Scott case.*"

PLESSY, significant enough in an era when the dominant mode of intercity transportation was the train, supplied the constitutional and moral basis for the web of Jim Crow laws that effectively created a system of apartheid in the American South for the first two-thirds of the twentieth century, dividing people by race in public transportation, accommodations, theaters, recreation facilities, employment, restaurants, schools, and the like. This constitutional wall separating the races was not seriously breached until the 1960s.

During the first decade of the twentieth century, the "separate but equal" doctrine embraced in PLESSY served as window dressing for state policies whose clear intent was to discriminate against and deny public services to blacks. Indeed, the courts even honored this limited notion of equality in the breach when they accepted segregated facilities that were clearly not equal by anyone's stretch of imagination. And in *Cumming* v. *Richmond County Board of Education,* 175 U.S. 528 (1899), the Supreme Court permitted a state to altogether deny a high school education to blacks even though such education was available to whites.

Despite such interpretations, the Court did from time to time strike down state practices whose obvious intent was racial discrimination. In *Yick Wo* v. *Hopkins,* 118 U.S. 356 (1886), the Court overturned a San Francisco ordinance that made it unlawful to operate a laundry in a wooden building without special consent of the board of supervisors. Although the ordinance was ostensibly a public safety measure, the city did not dispute the allegation that it really was designed to put Chinese launderers out of business (310 of the 320 Chinese laundries in the city were in wooden buildings), or the fact that Caucasians were routinely granted exemptions to the requirement while Chinese were not. Again, in *Guinn* v. *United States,* 283 U.S. 347 (1915), the Court declared unconstitutional the "grandfather clauses" of several Southern states, which provided that men whose grandfathers had been eligible to vote were excused from having to meet stringent literacy tests, a device that in effect permitted easy registration for whites and made registration virtually impossible for blacks. And after some indecision, the Court also overturned the so-called "white primary," a practice based on the argument that a political party was a private organization that could, if it wished, exclude blacks from membership and voting (*Smith* v. *Allwright,* 321 U.S. 649, 1944).

But decisions such as these were few and far between during the first half of the twentieth century. More typically, the Court's earlier rulings in the CIVIL RIGHTS CASES (1883) and PLESSY (1896) provided the justification for state-sanctioned discrimination and national inaction. Cases from the South upheld discriminatory practices against blacks, and cases from the West upheld discrimination against Asians and Chicanos.

Even as the Court gave a narrow meaning to the Equal Protection Clause as it pertained to racial issues, it was called upon to interpret the clause in regard to economic regulation. Indeed, the very first equal protection claim to be decided by the Supreme Court involved an economic — not a racial — issue. In the SLAUGHTER HOUSE CASES, 16 Wall. 36 (1873), the Court gave short shrift to an argument that plaintiff butchers had been denied equal protection by a New Orleans ordinance regulating the meat processing industry, and went on to express doubt "whether any action of a state not directed by way of discrimination against the negroes as a class, or on account of their race, will ever be held to come within the purview of this provision." And nearly forty years later, in *Lindsley* v. *Natural Carbonic Gas Co.,* 220 U.S. 61 (1911), the Court elaborated an even more restraintist view, saying that: (1) while all classifications discriminate in some way, states have wide latitude to classify so long as the classification is not purely arbitrary; (2) as long as there is some reasonable basis for the regulation, classifications do not have to have "mathematical nicety" (e.g., they can be over- or under-inclusive), even if they work hardships on some; (3) if it is possible to conceive of a state of facts under which the challenged classification scheme could be upheld, that state of facts must be presumed to be present at the time of the adoption of the law; and (4) the burden of demonstrating that the classification scheme under challenge is arbitrary and unreasonable is on the challenger. This test gives great deference to legislatures, and it is difficult to imagine many regulations falling from its weight.

Yet during this same period, another line of cases yielded a quite different approach. In the 1880s, the Court, with several new Justices, seized upon the equal protection provision of the Fourteenth Amendment to overturn state laws regulating economic activity. "As a general proposition," the majority observed in *Gulf, C. & S. F. Ry* v. *Ellis,* 165 U.S. 150 (1897), "[it] is undeniably true [that] it is not within the scope of the Fourteenth Amendment to withhold from States the power of classification." But, it continued, such classification must be "based upon some reasonable ground — some difference which bears a just and proper relation to the attempted classification — and is not a mere arbitrary selection." But having said this, the Court then went on to invalidate a regulation requiring railroad defendants (but not others) to pay attorneys' fees of successful plaintiffs. In *Connolly* v. *Union Sewer Pipe Co.,* 184 U.S. 540 (1902), the Court invalidated a state antitrust law because it applied to business but not to farm operations. And in *Truax* v. *Corrigan,* 257 U.S. 312 (1921), it used the Equal Protection Clause to invalidate a restriction on antilabor injunctions because they were limited in scope to protect only some and not all property. The argument used by the Court to invalidate state laws in these and other cases was its insistence upon the need for careful scrutiny of the "reasonableness" of the substance of the regulations. By expanding the traditional test's concern for reasonableness in relation to the aim of the regulation (presumed to be acceptable), to the reasonableness of the aim itself, the Court embraced what has been termed "substantive equal protection," and in so doing embarked on a career of second-guessing state legislatures and overturning regulations affecting business and the economy. Between 1897 and the mid-1930s the Court struck down over twenty major state and local economic regulations on equal protection grounds. This trend came to a halt with Roosevelt's reelection and the constitutional crisis precipitated by his court-packing plan of 1937. Just as this crisis ended the Court's embrace of an economic "substantive due process," so too it put an end to an economic "substantive equal protection."

The Roosevelt Court's response was to "return" to a procedural notion of due process and equal protection, a shift that initially gave great deference to the states. In a series of cases in the 1940s and 1950s, the Court upheld state laws that granted family members of river pilots license preferences (*Kotch* v. *Board of River Port Pilots Commissioners,* 330 U.S. 552, 1947); wives and daughters of male bar owners preferences in employment in such establishments (Goesaert et al. v. Cleary, 335 U.S. 464, 1948); and restricted the sale of prescription eyeglasses to licensed opticians (*Williamson* v. *Lee Optical Co.,* 348 U.S. 483, 1955).

But even as the Court was consolidating its position of restraint and deference to legislatures on economic issues, it accelerated its scrutiny of government actions that limited individual rights and liberties or focused on weak groups. The manifesto for this apparent double standard—deference to legislatures on economic issues and active scrutiny of civil rights and liberties issues—was Justice Stone's famous footnote four in the Carolene Products case, 304 U.S. 144 (1938), in which he outlined a new and special role for the courts.

Footnote four argues that the federal courts have a special obligation to scrutinize carefully the constitutionality of legislation when it affects rights specifically protected in the Bill of Rights (e.g., freedom of speech), restricts participation in the political process (e.g., denies someone the right to vote), or is directed at an "insular minority" (e.g., a racial or religious minority, which is not able to protect itself in the political process because of small numbers or historical circumstances). In Chapter 5, we traced the rise of this

theory of special stewardship as it affected the process of nationalizing provisions in the Bill of Rights, and in this and the following chapter we will examine its impact on the Equal Protection Clause, first as it affected blacks and then as it was extended to other groups.

The watershed case in the development of the special stewardship approach as it applied to the equal protection guarantee was Brown v. Board of Education, 347 U.S. 484 (1954), in which the Court, under the leadership of newly appointed Chief Justice Earl Warren, handed down a unanimous ruling declaring segregation in public schools to be unconstitutional. Effectively killing Plessy v. Ferguson, the Court held that separate educational facilities in public schools were inherently unequal and therefore violative of the equal protection guarantee of the Fourteenth Amendment. The Court's ruling in this case voided long-standing dual school systems and school attendance laws in over a dozen states and in the District of Columbia (via the Fifth Amendment's Due Process Clause), and directly affected the daily lives of several million schoolchildren. By extension, it soon led to rulings to desegregate other types of public facilities.

The Court's message in Brown was clear, and resistance was fierce. School boards ignored the ruling. Southern governors openly defied it. Lower courts made disingenuous distinctions. Lawsuits dragged on for years. Black parents seeking to enroll their children in previously all-white schools did so at risk of life and limb, and often saw their children graduate before courts would rule on their claims. And when finally pressed to the wall, school boards dismantled the formal structure of dual systems but recreated segregation through redrawing school attendance boundaries, separating students within the same school, and the like.

Out of their experience trying to implement Brown and give meaning to Justice Stone's theory of special stewardship, several of the Justices embraced the emerging strict scrutiny test to supplement the traditional, or *ordinary,* scrutiny test which, they felt, was too deferential to government and placed too much burden on plaintiffs. Strict scrutiny, which the Court had earlier claimed to use in the Japanese relocation case (KOREMATSU V. UNITED STATES (1944)), is distinguished from ordinary scrutiny in several ways: The Court adopts a skeptical rather than deferential stance when assessing classifications involving "suspect categories" such as race or limiting "fundamental rights." Strict scrutiny shifts the burden of proof from those who challenge a classification to those who use it. Whether directly or indirectly, classifications, under strict scrutiny, must meet higher standards than those judged by ordinary scrutiny — defenders must demonstrate a "compelling state interest" and prove that there are no other alternatives.

Not surprisingly, most classifications challenged under the traditional test are upheld, while most classifications and many systems whose effect is to distinguish by "suspect" classification fall under the weight of strict scrutiny. In a very real sense, the outcome of a case is likely to be determined by the test selected, and it is because of this that so much controversy exists over the two tiers of tests.

While justices since KOREMATSU have always wanted to scrutinize racial classifications carefully, there has never been a time when all nine justices have accepted this double tier of tests as a *general* framework. Justice Harlan vigorously resisted the move to extend strict scrutiny from the outset. Writing in dissent in SHAPIRO V. THOMPSON, 394 U.S. 618 (1969), he observed that this "equal protection doctrine of relatively recent vintage . . . reflects to an unusual degree the current notion that this Court possesses a peculiar wisdom all its own whose capacity to lead this Nation out of its present troubles is contained only by the limits of judicial ingenuity in contriving new constitutional principles to meet each problem as it arises." Other justices have followed in this vein. Scholars have ridiculed the Courts' two-tier approach as "Lochnering," a reference to the now-repudiated decision in LOCHNER V. NEW YORK, 198 U.S. 45 (1905), in which the Court overturned state-mandated maximum-hours regulations for bakers.

A related controversy has to do with the meanings of "fundamental rights" and "suspect cate-

gories," an important issue since they trigger a shift in presumptions and burdens of proof. Some justices want inclusive and flexible definitions, while others want to limit them to specific provisions in the Constitution. During the 1960s, the former view prevailed, as the Court ruled that privacy and freedom to travel were "fundamental rights" and alienage and parentage were "suspect categories." Still more rights and categories not singled out in the Constitution, such as health, education, wealth, and gender, were put forward as candidates for special treatment by the Court but have never been clearly elevated to these special categories.

Since the 1960s developments in this area have been mixed, as justices have continued to disagree among themselves, and as changes on the Court have reduced the number of proponents of a two-tier approach. The result is that although not abandoned, this approach is facing a growing challenge. One consequence has been the development of still a third test, "ordinary scrutiny with a bite," or so-called "middle-level scrutiny." This latest test surfaced in several cases challenging gender-based classifications. Unable to obtain enough support to elevate gender to a suspect category, liberal justices were able to convince enough other colleagues that a more-than-ordinary scrutiny should be employed in sex discrimination cases. Thus, for instance, in CRAIG V. BOREN (1976), this middle-level test was first articulated and invoked to invalidate an Oklahoma statute that established twenty-one and eighteen as the beer-purchasing age for men and women, respectively. Since then this test has gone on to lead a precarious life in several other sex discrimination cases, to be discussed later.

Controversy over the adoption, scope, and coverage of this two- or three-tier set of tests has not been an abstract debate. Rather, it has emerged as the Court has been forced to deal with a great variety of concrete problems. Perhaps more than anything, the tests first emerged in response to resistance to Court rulings on seemingly neutral policies that in fact perpetuated discriminatory practices. The Court felt compelled to make it easier for plaintiffs to challenge race relations cases; thus the history of these tests, and the shift in presumptions and proofs, must be understood in the context of the quest for racial equality. For this reason, we first examine the history of the Court's handling of racial discrimination cases. In Chapter 11 we examine other efforts to extend this expansive approach to gender, wealth, alienage, and age.

The history of the Court's approach to combat racial discrimination can be divided into three periods: (1) early development (1938–1954); (2) BROWN and its immediate aftermath (1955–1969); (3) affirmative integration (1970–present). During the first two periods, the Court was united in its resolve to attack segregation of public facilities, but during the third and continuing period, this consensus has broken down, as justices have differed among themselves on the limits of constitutional protections.

Pre-Brown Developments — The Erosion of Separate but Equal

For years after PLESSY V. FERGUSON (1896), the Court avoided a direct application of the separate but equal principle to education, but in doing so, it demonstrated that even this weak principle of equality was fraudulent. Not only did PLESSY reinforce segregation, the Court's continued inaction condoned state-sactioned shabby treatment of blacks, Chicanos, Asians, Jews, and other ethnic minorities. It was not until 1938 that the Court even began to take seriously the "equal" portion of the "separate but equal" equation. In *Missouri ex rel. Gaines* v. *Canada,* 305 U.S. 676 (1938), the Court overturned a Missouri policy that excluded blacks from the state law school and provided them with tuition to law schools in neighboring states. Missouri and other states immediately responded by establishing black-only law schools. The question then became: How vigorous would the Court be in comparing equality of the separate facilities? This question was partially answered twelve years later, in *McLaurin* v.

Oklahoma State Regents, 339 U.S. 637 (1950). Unable to deny admission to blacks and to offer to pay their tuition elsewhere, and unwilling to duplicate specialized graduate school facilities, the Oklahoma legislature voted to admit blacks to its previously all-white university graduate programs but insisted they remain segregated. Classrooms, libraries, and cafeterias were to have special areas for blacks and whites. In a unanimous ruling, the Court struck down this provision, arguing that such restrictions impaired and inhibited the educational opportunities of black students. That same term the Court handed down an even more far-reaching decision, *Sweatt* v. *Painter,* 339 U.S. 629 (1950). Sweatt refused to attend a recently created black-only law school, which had only twenty-three students, and sought a court order to gain admission to the University of Texas law school in Austin. In his opinion for the Court, Chief Justice Vinson contrasted the two schools and found the black law school to be vastly inferior on every count — including faculty, student body, size, library, and alumni. He then went on to compare other intangible factors and concluded that a separate minority law school, however nice the facilities, could not be an effective "proving ground for legal learning and practice." In effect, the Chief Justice was saying that separate law school facilities were inherently unequal.

These rulings were heartening to opponents of apartheid, but in practice meant very little, since so few blacks qualified for postgraduate training. The real goal was to attack segregation in the elementary and secondary schools, and it was this issue to which opponents of segregation turned. Their goal was no longer equality of separate facilities, but the death of the separate but equal doctrine itself. To this end, the NAACP Legal Defense Fund created test cases by stipulating that facilities and resources in dual school systems were equal even when they were not. One such case involved the dual school system in Topeka, Kansas, where in fact some of the physical facilities for black pupils were newer and better than those for whites.

One of five cases joined together for oral argument, BROWN V. BOARD OF EDUCATION (1954), was first argued before the Court in December 1952. In June 1953, the Court requested additional oral argument for that October, and directed the litigants to address themselves to the intent of Congress and the state legislatures that drafted and adopted the Fourteenth Amendment. The Court also asked to hear the litigants' views on whether the Amendment was intended to abolish the then-common practice of racial segregation in public schools. In the interim, President Eisenhower appointed Earl Warren to succeed Carl Vinson as Chief Justice. Finally, in June 1954, the Court handed down its momentous ruling. In a brief opinion for a unanimous Court, Chief Justice Warren noted that the intent of those who drafted and adopted the Fourteenth Amendment was "inconclusive," and went on to rule that segregation in public schools was a violation of the equal protection guarantee of the Fourteenth Amendment. While not explicitly overruling PLESSY V. FERGUSON, the Court held that "separate facilities are inherently unequal." Thus began the next chapter in the constitutional struggle for racial equality, the battle to dismantle dual school systems. This move came to involve the federal courts in a process of social change of unprecedented magnitude.

Dismantling Dual School Systems

While some of the border states quietly complied with BROWN, the immediate response of public officials in the Deep South was to do little other than condemn the Court in vitriolic language and reaffirm their commitment to segregation. Crude opposition took the form of blatantly racist appeals, while the more sophisticated couched their opposition in terms of "states rights." In the immediate aftermath of BROWN, both Congress and President Eisenhower stood aloof, thereby creating a vacuum of national support for school desegregation and reinforcing the resolve of opponents. The Court unwittingly contributed to this opposition in its follow-up ruling, BROWN V. BOARD OF EDUCATION (BROWN II), 349 U.S. 294 (1955), which, while re-

affirming its order to dismantle segregated school systems, added the qualifier "with all deliberate speed." This phrase was probably inserted as a necessary compromise in order to obtain a unanimous opinion, but opponents of desegregation interpreted it to mean an imperceptibly slow crawl.

After BROWN the Court did not hand down a major school desegregation case for over ten years. There were certainly numerous opportunities for it to have affirmed an important Fifth Circuit Court of Appeals decision. And when it did act to extend the logic of BROWN to public golf courses, swimming pools, and the like, it did so in brief per curiam opinions. Critics have attacked the Court for its silence during this long and stormy period, but others have defended its actions, pointing out that BROWN had spoken with eloquent simplicity and that the appellate courts — most particularly the Fifth Circuit — were actively giving meaning to BROWN.

The various circuit courts of appeal increasingly became involved in a process of reviewing and systematically knocking down a host of obstacles erected by recalcitrant school officials and legal fictions dreamed up by a handful of sympathetic district court judges. Many trial courts were also active in this regard. No doubt the judges were emboldened in their actions by the eventual ground swell of national support for the increasingly visible and vocal civil rights movement and the crudeness of so many of its opponents. The violence and threats against small children seeking to attend integrated schools after court orders, the threats and vilification against federal district court judges who ordered desegregation, and the moral mission of the civil rights movement seared the conscience of the nation.

A series of dramatic incidents in the late 1950s transformed this movement into a national crusade. Among them was the Montgomery bus boycott (protesting policies that required blacks to ride in the rear of buses), which catapulted Martin Luther King, Jr., into national prominence. Another was resistance in Arkansas to a court order to admit black students to Central High School in

Little Rock, an order which was openly flaunted by Arkansas Governor Orville Faubus and the state legislature. In the face of the threat of violence, President Eisenhower reluctantly ordered the national guard into the city to enforce the court order. National television coverage revealed the depth and viciousness of antagonism that greeted the handful of youngsters on their way to school as they were surrounded by national guardsmen and further galvanized national support for school desegregation.

Throughout the late 1950s and 1960s, the lower courts continued to knock down obstacles erected to thwart the ruling in Brown. In doing so, they pierced the veils of formalism and sought to determine the actual effects of local policies. When it reentered the fray, the Supreme Court reinforced its ruling in Brown, and in the mid-1960s made more visible its resolve to combat racial segregation in the public schools. The Court held that "voluntary student transfer plans" were unacceptable, because, even though their purposes appeared to be "neutral," their clear intent and effect was to maintain segregation (*Goss* v. *Board of Education,* 373 U.S. 683, 1963). And when a Maryland county closed all of its public schools rather than submit to a court order to desegregate, the Court ordered the schools reopened, thereby creating what some have argued is a constitutional right to education (*Griffin* v. *County School Board of Prince Edward County,* 377 U.S. 218, 1964).

In *Green* v. *County School Board of New Kent County,* 391 U.S. 430 (1968), the Court invalidated "freedom of choice" attendance plans, which, while racially neutral on their face, reinforced long-standing attendance patterns. *Green* was another turning point. Until then, the Court had focused on the *intent* of school officials and had rejected desegregation plans because on their face there was clear intent to discriminate. But in *Green,* the Court faced a more subtle effort to maintain segregation, and met the challenge by expanding its focus to include not only intent but "effect" as well. This change made it easier for plaintiffs to bring suits and more difficult for school boards to devise

plausible but ineffective plans. "The burden on the school board today," wrote Justice Brennan in *Green,* "is to come forward with a plan that promises realistically to work and promises realistically to work now." The Court's growing impatience was underscored a year later, when in another terse, sharply worded per curiam opinion, the Court announced that the era of "all deliberate speed" was over (*Alexander* v. *Holmes County Board of Education,* 396 U.S. 19, 1969).

Green and *Alexander* were the last major school desegregation cases by the Warren Court and among the last major school desegregation decisions by a unanimous Court. Even as these decisions signified a stepped-up vigilance by the Court, the winds of change were shifting. Warren retired in 1969, and President Nixon—never a friend of the civil rights movement and a long-standing critic of the Court—replaced him with a "strict constructionist," Warren Burger, a judge with a conservative record on the Court of Appeals for the District of Columbia. During the next three years, President Nixon made three more appointments.

The civil rights movement of the early 1960s, which had galvanized widespread support for school desegregation, had by the end of the decade become fragmented. And, at least in the eyes of many, it had been replaced by the "black power movement," whose objectives and tactics were not as compatible with the constitutional focus of the earlier movement. And school desegregation was moving north. Thus the "effects" emphasis announced by the Court in *Green* was to be implemented by a changing Court, in a shifting climate, and over a broadened locale.

Affirmative School Integration

Despite these many changes, the Court did not retreat from its commitment to school desegregation. Indeed, opinions written by Chief Justice Burger shortly after he assumed office were considerably more far-reaching than anything penned by Earl Warren. It was only after this further expansion of power of the federal courts that consensus on the Court finally collapsed.

This collapse was due to differences over the nature and scope of remedies that lower courts could use and more particularly to the appropriate tests to identify racial discrimination. And it is important to note that this conflict arose when desegregation efforts moved North. Because the South had a history of state-imposed dual school systems, litigants had only to show discriminatory effects (e.g., one-race schools) to raise a strong case that they were due to the lingering effects of intentional racial discrimination. But the North had no such history of state-mandated dual school systems. As a consequence, some of the justices insisted upon a stronger showing of discriminatory intent before approving the types of lower court remedies originally designed to dismantle the lingering effects of dual school systems in the South. This regional factor helps explain why the Court could speak with unanimity and such firmness in SWANN ET AL. V. CHARLOTTE-MECKLENBURG BOARD OF EDUCATION, 403 U.S. 912 (a Southern case) in 1971 but lack such firmness and unanimity soon after in KEYES ET AL. V. SCHOOL DISTRICT NO. 1, 413 U.S. 189 (1973) (a case arising in Denver, Colorado) and in MILLIKEN V. BRADLEY, 418 U.S. 717 (1974) (Detroit, Michigan). It also helps explain why Justice Powell, who is from Virginia, could in effect accuse his colleagues of a double standard that included more stringent tests for the South. The intent/effect distinction was reinforced by a regional expansion, and the divisions on the Court must be understood in terms of both these factors.

One of the earliest issues that divided the Court in the 1970s was the extent of the authority of federal courts to redraw school district boundaries. In *United States* v. *Scotland New City School Board,* 407 U.S. 484 (1972), it voided a decision by a predominantly white city to withdraw from a county school system, a move that would have left the county schools 89 percent black. Here, the Court had no trouble identifying race, rather than the desire for "local autonomy," as a major factor in the city's decision. But the next year, the Court

was evenly split in a review of a district court order requiring several predominantly white school districts adjacent to Richmond, Virginia, to merge with that city's school district to achieve a racial balance in all the districts. The 4 to 4 vote (Justice Powell did not participate because he had been involved in earlier desegregation controversies when he had served on the Richmond school board in the 1960s) meant that the appellate court's ruling overturning the ordered merger stood, although the decision supposedly has no precedential value. While the Richmond case was inconclusive, it did reveal sharp strains among the justices, indicating that a growing number thought that district courts were exceeding constitutional powers in their orders to desegregate.

Still, in 1971, the Court handed down a unanimous ruling approving of a wide variety of remedies available to district court judges in SWANN. And in KEYES, a divided Court boldly extended school desegregation to the North, where segregation in the public schools had never been statutorily sanctioned. In SWANN, Chief Justice Burger, for the Court, upheld a district court ruling that, after finding systematic state-sanctioned racial segregation, had ordered remedial actions such as the use of explicit racial balances or quotas for each school in the district; the total elimination of one-race schools; the alteration of attendance zones; and extensive busing of pupils. Chief Justice Burger's opinion in this case went a long way to demonstrate that he was not "the President's justice," as many critics alleged.

Affirmative desegregation orders in the South had always been justified on grounds that they were needed to completely dismantle the lingering effects of long-standing dual school systems. However, there had been no such de jure segregation in the North. Officials there claimed that whatever segregation existed was de facto, due to private housing patterns and not public policy. But proponents of school integration alleged that much segregation in the North was due to racially motivated gerrymandering of school attendance boundaries, tracking systems, and publicly sanctioned housing and zoning policies. The net result, they argued, was that many Northern cities had subtle but nevertheless effective state-sanctioned policies of racial segregation. Furthermore, they pointed out, the language in *Green* and SWANN emphasized the effects — disproportionate racial balances in school attendance — not simply the intent of public officials.

KEYES was the first major school desegregation case in the North to reach the Supreme Court. It arose in Denver, a rapidly growing city with a long history of relatively amicable race relations and no history of publicly announced segregation. Yet as the Court reviewed the extent of segregation in that city's public schools, plus the nature of its attendance boundaries in one section of the city, it concluded that there was officially sanctioned segregation and upheld a district court order to remedy it. This decision significantly expanded the meaning of de jure segregation and emboldened supporters of school desegregation. Dissenters on the Court criticized the majority for overreaching, complaining that the Court had sanctioned a systemwide remedy for a problem that was limited to one small section of the district.

Since KEYES, the Court has wavered in its interpretation of de jure segregation and the scope of remedial action to correct it. One indication of this is seen in a Detroit case, MILLIKEN V. BRADLEY (1974), in which a majority of five, over bitter dissents, invalidated a district court's order to merge the predominantly black Detroit school district with the predominantly white districts surrounding it. The majority argued that because there had been no showing of segregation outside the suburban districts, they were improperly drawn into the remedy. Justice Marshall, in dissent, argued that the lower court record amply demonstrated the complicity of some of the outlying districts and that, furthermore, all the districts were creatures of the state, which through its action and inaction had permitted the pattern of segregation to develop. Why, he asked, should the Court be willing to redraw boundaries of electoral districts to remedy equal protection complaints of voters — as was done in the reapportionment cases — but re-strict itself to remedies solely within the "offending" unit in racially based cases?

In fact, MILLIKEN did not rule out entirely intergovernmental remedies, and two years later a divided Court upheld a metropolitanwide plan to overcome racially motivated practices in the location of low-income public housing projects in Chicago and its suburbs (*Hills* v. *Gautreaux,* 425 U.S. 284, 1976). There, the Court held that an area-wide plan was appropriate because there had been a finding of discrimination by officials in both Chicago and its suburbs.

KEYES appeared to signal the willingness of at least some of President Nixon's appointees to embrace an "effects" test rather than the more restrictive "intent" test. The effects/intent distinction is important because it determines who shoulders the burden of proving discrimination and the nature of that proof. The former standard places the burden of proof on users of classifications that yield disproportionate effects, while the latter shifts the responsibility of proving discrimination to plaintiffs who are alleging discrimination, requiring them to prove intent.

The acceptance of an "effects" test by some of the Nixon appointees was greeted with relief by proponents of desegregation. But with continued turnover on the Court, this development dissolved even before it jelled. The Court's retreat is seen in PASADENA CITY BOARD OF EDUCATION V. SPANGLER, 427 U.S. 424 (1976), in which the four Nixon appointees (Burger, Rehnquist, Powell, and Blackmun) joined with Justices White and Stewart to form a majority that overturned an elaborate systemwide desegregation order by a district court that required annual adjustments of attendance boundaries to reflect shifting racial populations. Once a district with a history of racial discrimination has reached a point of "racial neutrality" in attendance, Justice Rehnquist argued for the Court, courts cannot continue to force it to adopt remedies to overcome resegregation due to voluntary housing preferences. All segregation, he argued, is not prohibited by the Equal Protection Clause, only that which is sanctioned by state action. In dissent, Justice Marshall took issue with the majority's interpretation of the facts, arguing that the Court was ignoring the fact that Pasadena had never exhibited good faith in implementing the original desegregation order and thus required continued supervision. Still, what most sharply distinguishes the two positions is Rehnquist's emphasis on intent versus Marshall's emphasis on effects, and the inferences each draws from his initial focus.

The Court's "retreat" from an effects emphasis is further evidenced in two nonschool-related cases, one handed down the same term as PASADENA, the other the following year. In the first case, the Court sustained a District of Columbia personnel test for applicants to the police force against a challenge that it was racially discriminatory because a disproportionate number of blacks failed it and because it bore no relationship to job performance (WASHINGTON ET AL. V. DAVIS ET AL., 426 U.S. 229, 1976). Writing for a majority of seven, Justice White found that there was a reasonable employment-related basis for the test, but he did reaffirm the Court's willingness to look beneath the surface of even reasonable policies to search for evidence of racial discrimination. Still, the opinion's emphasis on "purpose and intent" seems to represent a step back from the emphasis on "effects" in *Green* and KEYES, and in an earlier and successful challenge to another personnel test, *Griggs* v. *Duke Power Co.,* 401 U.S. 424 (1971). Intent was emphasized over effects again the following year, in an equal housing case where the Court stated that "racially discriminatory intent or purpose is required to show a violation of the equal protection clause . . . [and that] disproportionate impact is [only] a starting point." This view was underscored in three more cases handed down in the mid-1970s: *School District of Omaha* v. *U.S.,* 431 U.S. 667 (1977); *Dayton Board of Education* v. *Brinkman,* 433 U.S. 406 (1977); and *Austin Independent School District* v. *U.S.,* 429 U.S. 990 (1976).

But just as the Court began to emphasize the de jure, *intent* standard, it appeared to return once again to stress the *effects,* or disproportionate impact, test. In COLUMBUS BOARD OF EDUCATION V. PENICK, 433 U.S. 449 (1979), the Court upheld a far-reaching court order to desegregate and in so doing nearly obliterated any distinction between de jure and de facto segregation. As you read this case, ask what it would have taken for Columbus to have convinced the Court that it had not discriminated, that segregation in the city's schools was purely natural and not the consequence of official policy. What would it take for the city to satisfy the Court and be free of the continuing supervision?

Other recent cases have also demonstrated the ambivalence of the Court over the choice of tests and the range of remedies. In *Armour* v. *Nix,* 446 U.S. 930 (1980), it affirmed a lower court ruling barring an interdistrict desegregation plan for Atlanta area schools. But in *Delaware State Board* v. *Evans,* 446 U.S. 923 (1980), it upheld a lower court order requiring extensive busing between the city of Wilmington and eleven surrounding county districts.

Despite this apparent ambivalence and the marked differences among the current justices on some issues, all nine justices remain firmly committed to use by federal courts of a variety of remedies to overcome segregation in public schools. This view was reinforced in a 1983 decision rebuffing a request to cut back the range of permissible remedies available to district courts, in *Metropolitan County Board of Education of Nashville* v. *Kelly,* 459 U.S. 1183. Here, the Department of Justice had intervened to ask the Court to ban such remedies as busing, interdistrict mergers, and race-conscious rezoning, but a unanimous Court reaffirmed its commitment to SWANN and to the use of such remedies.

Still, tensions on the Court remain and are focused in part on the intent and effects standards, a distinction which parallels and reinforces differences between the traditional or ordinary scrutiny test on one hand and the strict scrutiny test on the other. This controversy involves many other issues besides race and public schools, and we will return to it in Chapter 11 when considering cases dealing with gender, alienage, age, and other classifications.

The Doctrine of State Action

Earlier we made a distinction between public and private action, noting that the Civil War Amendments were designed to put an end only to public or state action that discriminated. This prohibition against discriminatory state action was also echoed in the Civil Rights Acts of 1866 and 1875. In principle, this distinction is clear and unexceptional. Few would dispute the claim that the right of privacy permits individuals the right to discriminate in their personal affairs. But in a complex society in which government is intertwined in many organized private activities, and where many private institutions serve public functions, the boundary is difficult to draw. Nevertheless, it is possible to discern differences in scope of coverage. Initially, the Court gave a circumscribed meaning to state action, but in recent years it has significantly expanded the concept.

In 1883, the Court held that the Fourteenth Amendment forbade only those discriminatory actions "sanctioned in some way by the state" or "done under state authority." Thus the Court held racial discrimination by proprietors of theaters, restaurants, hotels, and railway companies, which had been banned by the Civil Rights Act of 1875, was private policy, and hence beyond the scope of Congress' power to prohibit (CIVIL RIGHTS CASES, 109 U.S. 3, 1883). Coupled with the separate but equal doctrine of PLESSY V. FERGUSON, this view of state action provided a firm constitutional basis for the web of Jim Crow laws that ensnared the South in the early part of this century.

Following the growth of Jim Crow laws, segregation in housing was first accomplished through zoning ordinances requiring segregated housing. Widely adopted in municipalities across the country, such ordinances were eventually challenged in the courts. When the issue reached the Court in 1917, it ruled that such zoning constituted an unconstitutional interference with property (*Buchanan* v. *Warley,* 245 U.S. 60, 1917). But this did not put an end to legally sanctioned segregation in housing. Proponents of segregation turned to still another device, the restrictive covenant, a legally

binding provision in a deed or lease which specifies the conditions of sale, use, and lease — often in perpetuity — of property. Throughout the early twentieth century such provisions were routinely appended to property deeds to exclude purchase or lease of property by blacks, Jews, Catholics, and members of other ethnic and religious groups. When these covenants were first challenged in the courts, they were upheld. Although clearly discriminatory, the Supreme Court initially ruled racially restrictive covenants were not unconstitutional when they were made by private individuals and not the state (*Corrigan* v. *Buckley,* 271 U.S. 323, 1926).

This view held until 1948, when in SHELLEY V. KRAEMER, 334 U.S. 1 (1948), the Supreme Court agreed to reconsider its position on restrictive covenants. In his opinion for a unanimous Court (three justices not participating), Chief Justice Vinson distinguished between making and enforcing restrictive covenants. Private parties, he said, have a right to enter into racially restrictive agreements if they so choose. But, he continued, such agreements cannot be enforced by courts because doing so would involve the state in the discriminatory action. "State action," the Chief Justice wrote, "refers to exertions of state power in all forms."

Throughout the late 1940s, 1950s, and 1960s, the Supreme Court continued to give an expansive interpretation to the doctrine of "state action" and the closely associated concept "under color of state law." In 1945, it held that injurious and abusive actions of a white sheriff had been "under color of state law" and therefore constituted public, not private, action, which was redressable in federal courts (*Screws* v. *U.S.,* 325 U.S. 91, 1945). Subsequent Court rulings in the 1950s through the 1970s took this position further and, in combination with Section 1983 of Title 42 of the United States Code, provided a rationale for prosecution and civil suits in federal courts for violations of civil rights of private individuals by local officials — through their action or inaction — acting under "color of law." Thus, in *Monroe* v. *Pape,* 365 U.S. 176 (1961), the Court held that police brutality constituted state action within the meaning of Section 1983. In

Scheuer v. *Rhodes,* 416 U.S. 323 (1974), an action commenced in the wake of the National Guard shooting of four Kent State students, the Court held that state officers are not protected through sovereign immunity if they acted under state law in a manner violative of the Constitution. In *Rizzo* v. *Goode,* 423 U.S. 362 (1976), the Court upheld a lower ruling that "official indifference" to the unlawful discriminatory practices of the Philadelphia police department constituted unconstitutional state action.

Thus, we see, the concepts of state action and "under color of law" are elastic and have been stretched. But are there no limits? Must the state sanction the substance of all private contracts the courts are called upon to enforce? In a complex society, almost any action, however "private," can be connected to the state. When is the connection so tenuous that there is *no* state action?

This is precisely the issue raised but left open in SHELLEY V. KRAEMER, and clarified in a pair of subsequent cases. The first case arose when a restaurant that leased space from a parking facility owned and operated by an agency of the City of Wilmington, Delaware, refused service to a black. Rejecting the restaurant's claim that it was a private organization and thus could discriminate, the Court held that the discrimination constituted unconstitutional state action because the restaurant was located on public property leased to the restaurant by the parking authority (*Burton* v. *Wilmington Parking Authority,* 365 U.S. 775, 1961). The state's failure to take the steps necessary to assure there would be no discrimination by its business partner, the Court reasoned, constituted state involvement in the restaurant's policy and hence "state action" in violation of the Fourteenth Amendment.

While the Civil Rights Act of 1964 (outlawing racial discrimination in public facilities involved in interstate commerce) and various state antidiscrimination laws have reduced the need to rely on "state action" doctrine to combat discrimination in public facilities, the doctrine is still important and the question still remains: How far does state action extend into the private sphere? An answer

was forthcoming in MOOSE LODGE NO. 107 V. IRVIS, 407 U.S. 163 (1972). In this case, the Court was confronted with a policy of the Moose Lodge, a national fraternal society, which restricted membership and guests in its local lodges to Caucasian males. The case arose when K. Leroy Irvis, the Minority leader of the Pennsylvania House of Representatives, was refused service at a Moose Lodge in Harrisburg. In court, Irvis did not quarrel directly with the policy that restricted Moose Lodge membership and guests to Caucasian males. It was, he conceded, a private club, which received no governmental subsidies, was not open to the general public, and was not on public property. But the Lodge did have a state-granted liquor license, and this, he maintained, was enough to implicate the state in the Lodge's discriminatory action. In federal district court, seeking injunctive relief under 42 U.S.C. 1983, Irvis asked the court to revoke Moose Lodge's liquor license so long as it continued to discriminate. The district court found that Irvis had been denied service as a guest, and ordered the liquor license to be revoked until the Lodge changed its policy. This ruling was appealed and overturned by a sharply divided Supreme Court. Writing for a majority of six, Justice Rehnquist, not then Chief Justice, distinguished this case from the "symbiotic relationship between lessor and lessee that was present in *Burton.*" The Fourteenth Amendment, he continued, does not prohibit discrimination by an otherwise private entity simply because it receives state benefits or is subject to standard state regulations. Extending the state action doctrine to include such state-furnished services as electricity, water, and police and fire protection, Rehnquist reasoned, would "utterly emasculate the distinction between private as distinguished from State conduct." In contrast, the dissenters sharply distinguished between routine government regulations and state grants of a limited number of liquor licenses. They had no problem voting to uphold the ruling of the district court.

If you are persuaded by the dissenters' arguments in MOOSE LODGE V. IRVIS, you must still confront the issue posed by Justice Rehnquist.

Unless you are prepared to "utterly emasculate" any distinction between public and private, you must draw a line between purely private and state action. Where would you draw it? What if, as has been the case in some controversies, racial discrimination is by private schools whose *students* receive federal aid? What if it is justified on religious grounds? Could a state, in its zeal to eradicate discrimination, condition receipt of federally guaranteed student loans upon a promise by the recipient not to join private clubs that discriminate? If you are not satisfied by Justice Rehnquist's efforts, where would you draw the line?

Power of the Federal Government to Combat Racial Discrimination

The post–Civil War Reconstruction Era witnessed a flurry of civil rights activity initiated by Radical Republicans in the Congress — the adoption of the Thirteenth, Fourteenth, and Fifteenth Amendments, and the enactment of a number of civil rights acts giving effect to the guarantees of these amendments. For a brief period, these actions had an impact. Federal troops were stationed in the South, and national officials had responsibility for overseeing the transition from slavery to freedom. Blacks voted in large numbers and were elected to public office throughout the South. But this burst of enthusiasm was divisive and short-lived. White Southerners bitterly resented occupation by federal troops, and the Republican party, badly split between the Radicals in Congress and moderates, increasingly turned its attention to other issues.

No doubt preoccupation with economic development and westward expansion was the major reason for the demise of national interest in the protection of the civil liberties of the newly freed slaves. But two more proximate causes can also be identified. The disputed outcome of the presidential election of 1876 threw the decision into a Congress sharply divided between pro-Southern Democrats in the House and Radical Republicans who controlled the Senate. After working out a compromise in which the Democrats gained a number of

concessions, including withdrawal of federal troops from the South, Republican Rutherford B. Hayes was declared the winner over the Democratic candidate, Samuel J. Tilden. Thus ended Reconstruction and congressional interest in civil rights.

What was lost in the Congress was not carried on by the Supreme Court. From the outset, its justices had not been enthusiastic about the new amendments or the civil rights acts that followed. We have already seen how the Court transformed the Due Process Clause into an instrument to protect property, while at the same time giving it a narrow reading as it applied to the civil rights of blacks. In the same vein, the Court gave short shrift to the civil rights legislation enacted by the Congress in the aftermath of the Civil War. Nowhere is this more clearly illustrated than in the CIVIL RIGHTS CASES, 109 U.S. 3 (1883), in which the Court declared unconstitutional major portions of the Civil Rights Act of 1875.

Eighty years later, the civil rights movement of the 1950s and 1960s rekindled interest in protection of civil rights. Spurred on by the Court's ruling in BROWN V. BOARD OF EDUCATION, and by mounting pressure from a broad spectrum of civil rights activists, the Congress was once more prodded into action. Between 1957 and 1968, a period which has come to be known as the Second Reconstruction, the Congress enacted a series of increasingly potent civil rights acts. Each of them, in turn, was duly challenged in the courts. This time the Supreme Court responded expansively, giving broad meaning both to the Fourteenth Amendment and to Congress' powers to combat racial discrimination under the Civil War Amendments. In HEART OF ATLANTA MOTEL V. UNITED STATES, 379 U.S. 241 (1964), the Court upheld provisions in the Civil Rights Act of 1964, which prohibited discrimination in public accommodations if their operations affected interstate commerce. And in SOUTH CAROLINA V. KATZENBACH, 383 U.S. 301 (1966), a nearly unanimous Court gave an expansive interpretation of Congress' authority under Section 2 of the Fifteenth Amendment, which authorizes it to take "appropriate" measures in the states to protect against racial discrimination in voting. This Act provided for extensive federal presence and activity in states with low minority participation in elections and granted federal officials authority to monitor and prescribe requirements for the entire electoral process, from specifying voter qualifications to counting ballots. The impact of this intervention has been enormous, as blacks who previously had been intimidated flocked to the polls. Throughout the South, blacks now constitute a significant force in electoral politics and hold a substantial number of important elected offices.

Minorities have long been discriminated against in access to housing, and one of the highest priorities of civil rights groups has been adoption of fair housing laws that prohibit discrimination in the sale and rental of houses and apartments. Overriding objections that it was ushering in the demise of property rights, Congress enacted the Civil Rights Act of 1968, the first national fair housing law to be passed in more than a century. Exempting only small rental units (which came to be known as Mrs. Murphy's boardinghouses) and houses sold by owners without the service of a broker, this law, it was estimated at the time, covered more than three-quarters of all housing units in the United States.

But even as this act was being signed into law, the Court was asked to interpret a still broader antidiscrimination law enacted by Congress in 1866, which had lain all but dormant for over a century. This act prohibited *all* racial discrimination, private or public, in the sale and rental of property, exempting neither Mrs. Murphy boardinghouses nor owner-sold units. Thus the Court was faced with the dilemma of having to interpret a sweeping old law in the face of a much more limited new law. Turning aside the argument that the Court should deal with the earlier law in light of the recent sentiments of the contemporary Congress, in a sweeping decision the Court upheld the 1866 law (JONES V. MAYER CO., 392 U.S. 409, 1968).

Following the Congress of 1866, the Court selected as its starting point the Thirteenth Amendment, which grants Congress authority to enforce the prohibition against slavery and involuntary servitude by "appropriate legislation." Agreeing with the 1866 Congress that denial of access to housing because of race constituted an unconstitutional "badge of slavery," the Court went on to uphold the law, taking what is perhaps its boldest step in interpreting the power of the Congress to tackle the problems of racial discrimination.

But perhaps the most effective way Congress has sought to combat racial discrimination has been to condition receipt of federal funds upon guarantees not to discriminate. Indeed, it was not until threats were made to withhold federal funds that local schools throughout the South began to respond seriously to the myriad court orders to desegregate. In a society in which the federal government occupies such a prominent role, this power of the purse is enormous. It has been expanded still further as Congress has applied it to third parties as well. Thus students otherwise eligible to receive governmentally guaranteed educational loans may not use them to pay costs at private schools that discriminate. Recipients of federal grants must promise not only not to discriminate, but not to do business with others who do. And with this power to prohibit comes the power to investigate and supervise. Thus in recent years much of the most effective civil rights enforcement has rested on a statutory and administrative rather than constitutional basis.

After twenty years of relatively strong federal administration, support for civil rights enforcement eroded in the early 1980s under the Reagan administration. While not directly challenging the constitutionality of the major civil rights acts of the 1960s and 1970s, the Reagan administration took aim at the administrative mechanisms constructed by various federal agencies to combat racial discrimination. The President directed the Department of Education to relax its monitoring of discrimination in the nation's primary and secondary schools, and in a number of cases ordered the Department of Justice to intervene on the side of local school boards resisting court orders to desegregate. His administration urged an end to many affirmative action programs to combat employment discrimination. And during his term of office, the number of employment discrimination suits approved by the Equal Employment Opportunity Commission (EEOC) dropped sharply. More generally, the efforts of the EEOC and the Department of Housing and Urban Development (HUD) to negotiate voluntary settlements in discrimination cases were significantly curtailed. While President Reagan was criticized for presiding over a "dangerous deterioration in Federal enforcement of civil rights laws," his supporters contended that his administration was simply restoring a proper balance to the enforcement of civil rights laws, an evenhanded approach that would not penalize innocent nonminority members, infringe upon rights of property, privacy, and religious freedom, or erode still further principles of federalism. The Bush administration has pursued the same general course, although less zealously.

This divisive national debate is reflected in rulings of the Supreme Court. The consensus and unanimity that characterized the Court's race relations decisions in the 1950s and 1960s gave way to sharply divided rulings throughout the 1970s and 1980s. While the Court continues to affirm the authority of the Congress to enact civil rights legislation and the lower courts to take a wide variety of actions to remedy specific findings of discrimination, the justices disagree on interpretations of the breadth of coverage of specific legislative provisions, the nature and amount of evidence necessary to prove discrimination, and the authority of public bodies to embrace affirmative action programs in the absence of a prior finding of discrimination.

The result is a retreat from the bold rulings on both the Constitution and the civil rights acts that had characterized the Court's rulings in the 1960s and 1970s. Increasingly the Court is reluctant to approve remedial actions in the absence of a finding of intentional discrimination, and to give expansive readings to the civil rights acts. This change is illustrated by the Court's shift in approach to section 1 of the Civil Rights Act of 1866, whose broad prohibition against discrimination in housing was upheld in JONES V. MAYER (1968). In 1976, the Court upheld another provision of the Act, which prohibits discrimination in contracts, and ruled that the provision also applies to private parties, *Runyon* v. *McCrary,* 485 U.S. 617. However by

1989, a reconstituted Court seriously considered overruling *Runyon.* In *Patterson* v. *McLean Credit Union,* 57 LW 4705 (1989), in a 5 to 4 vote, the Court ruled that although the Act did apply to the formation of private contracts, it did *not* protect against discrimination arising under conditions of employment under these contracts. This decision, it appears, signals the direction the Court will be taking in the 1990s.

Affirmative Action

The preceding discussion has focused on what the Constitution prohibits and what courts and legislatures can do to combat unconstitutional practices. We now turn to examine a different question: How far can government go in adopting preferential treatment of minorities, in the absence of a specific finding of discrimination, to pursue the goal of integration? Does affirmative action run afoul of the mandate of equal treatment? Is compensatory discrimination justifiable under the Constitution? Can, for instance, government adopt "benign quotas" to foster a stable, integrated public housing development? Can schools? Can government, in the absence of a finding of discrimination, give preferential treatment to racial minorities to combat the lingering and historic *general* effects of racial discrimination? Or, taking Justice Harlan's observation in PLESSY V. FERGUSON (1896) literally, is the Constitution color "blind"? Are all race-conscious policies unconstitutional?

We have already seen that the Court has given partial answers to some of these questions. Public officials can adopt race-conscious policies, and the courts may require such adoptions, if they are designed to remedy specific instances of discrimination. Thus, for instance, preferential hiring and promotion of minorities can be justified if it is a remedy to counter past discrimination.

But until 1978, the Court had never squarely faced the issue of preferential treatment per se. That is, all its prior rulings had addressed *remedial* actions, taken after a finding of intentional discrimination. In 1974, the Court ducked the opportunity to rule on a law school's affirmative action program fashioned to address a general social problem rather than as a remedy to a specific finding of discrimination (*DeFunis* v. *Odegaard,* 416 U.S. 312). But the issue resurfaced in 1978, in a challenge to the preferential admissions policy established by the medical school at the University of California at Davis. Founded in 1968, the medical school had had no history of racial discrimination in admissions. Yet in 1971 it had adopted a separate admissions system for "disadvantaged" applicants from several minority groups (blacks, Chicanos, Asians, and American Indians). The special system involved an elaborate two-tiered process. First, minority students were separated, if they so chose, into a special pool of applicants whose backgrounds were assessed to determine if they were "disadvantaged" due to financial or educational deprivation. Minority students who met this requirement were then ranked and granted admission in sequence until they comprised 16 percent of the entering class. While all students admitted met the school's minimum entrance requirements, there was no question that, overall, the students in the special program had records and academic qualifications markedly inferior to those of many unsuccessful white applicants. Allan Bakke was one such unsuccessful applicant. In his suit, Bakke alleged, and the school agreed, that but for the special race-conscious program he would have been admitted.

In overturning the Davis preferential system, the Court was badly fragmented (REGENTS OF THE UNIVERSITY OF CALIFORNIA V. BAKKE, 438 U.S. 265, 1978). Six justices wrote separate opinions and no single opinion commanded majority support. Four justices thought that the Davis quota system violated Title VI of the Civil Rights Act of 1964, which provided in part that "No person in the United States shall, on the ground of race, color, or national origin, be excluded from participation in, be denied the benefits of, or be subject to discrimination under any program or activity receiving Federal financial assistance." Adhering to the principle that the Court should decide on the narrowest grounds possible, these justices argued that in the absence of a Court determination of prior racial discrimination, Title VI required color-blind treatment of applicants in federally supported programs (such as the Davis medical school pro-

gram). But four other justices supported the Davis plan, arguing that the quota violated neither Title VI nor the Equal Protection Clause of the Fourteenth Amendment. They accepted the university's contention that preferential treatment is permissible to remedy "past societal discrimination." Title VI, they argued, was designed to help blacks overcome the cumulative effects of a long history of discrimination, and they were disturbed that it could be used to undermine the very goals it was designed to pursue.

Justice Powell sat in the balance. He agreed with the four justices who argued that race-conscious admissions policies were acceptable under Title VI and the Constitution, but he also agreed that they should be administered with the utmost caution and care. The Davis quota system, he felt, was too rigid because it disregarded "individual rights." In contrast, he cited with approval the admissions policy of Harvard Law College. Harvard, he pointed out, acknowledged that one of its goals was a "diverse" student body. Thus, in addition to academic qualifications, Harvard "took into consideration" a variety of factors, including region, family, background, personal experience, and race. This difference between the Davis and Harvard policies was crucial to Powell because, conceivably, for any individual applicant, one "weakness" could be offset by another "strength." After reading the case, ask yourself if this difference is substantial. What difference does it make if race is a necessary condition for a limited number of admissions decisions or simply one important factor which is considered? Might not Davis simply be more honest than Harvard?

It is important to underscore the narrowness of BAKKE. It does not prohibit preferential treatment or race-conscious admissions policies per se. Nor does it hold that all benign quotas are prohibited by the Constitution. Despite this, there were many who predicted that BAKKE would put an end to affirmative action programs. This has not occurred.

Indeed, since BAKKE the Supreme Court has handed down a number of decisions upholding affirmative action plans. Some justices, most notably Chief Justice Rehnquist and Justices White, Scalia, and Kennedy are unequivocally opposed to affirmative action unless it is a narrowly tailored remedy following a judicial finding of intentional discrimination. In contrast, Justices Marshall, Brennan, and Blackmun are enthusiastic supporters of affirmative action. The remaining justices walk a complex course, accepting certain plans and rejecting others. The result is a confused jurisprudence filled with twists and turns, but one that for the most part has yielded majorities that have upheld a variety of affirmative action plans.

In UNITED STEELWORKERS OF AMERICA, AFL-CIO v. WEBER, 488 U.S. 193 (1979), the Court, by a vote of 5 to 2 (two justices not participating), upheld an affirmative action plan arrived at after negotiations between the steelworkers' union and the Kaiser Aluminum Co. The plan, which called for a fixed percentage of blacks to be selected for the company's skilled-craft training programs, had been adopted after the union produced figures revealing that blacks, historically, had been significantly underrepresented in the company's higher-paid skilled craft jobs proportionate to their numbers in the local work force. Despite the plan's Davis-like formula, a majority of justices approved it. For some the distinction between the private action of Kaiser Aluminum and the state action of the University of California was crucial. However, given the government's involvement in overseeing labor-management negotiations, is this distinction compelling?

The next year, in FULLILOVE V. KLUTZNICK (1980), the Court, by a vote of 6 to 3, upheld a provision in the federal Public Works Employment Act of 1977, which required that at least 10 percent of the funds granted to state and local governments to be spent for projects be "set aside" for minority-owned businesses. In their several opinions, the justices who constituted a majority (there was no single majority opinion) tried to distinguish this situation from that in BAKKE. Some characterized it as a remedy following from a congressional "finding" of prior discrimination in the building trades industry. Others pointed out that it was "temporary" and remedial in nature, and not a permanent policy. However, the several dissenters challenged these arguments, contrasting

Congress' sloppy fact-finding process unfavorably with the meticulous process required by courts before they can impose race-conscious remedies. Furthermore, some dissenters noted that the "temporary" remedial policy was still in force years after its adoption.

In *Firefighters' Local* v. *Stotts*, 467 U.S. 561 (1985), the Court appeared to be charting a new and more restrictive course when it reversed a lower court order prohibiting a fire department from implementing a layoff policy of last hired, first fired. In that case the district court had enjoined the department from following this long-standing policy in order to protect minority employees with less seniority than nonminorities who had been hired under a consent decree supervised by the court. Justice White, for the Court, held that such a plan had to be limited to protecting only those individual members of minority groups who could demonstrate that they had been "actual victims" of discrimination. Only after such a finding, he reasoned, could the Court order "make-whole relief." Absent such a finding, he continued, Title VII of the Civil Rights Act of 1964 protects bona fide seniority rules.

Stotts was reaffirmed and expanded a year later in a case involving layoffs of teachers. In *Wygant* v. *Jackson,* 476 U.S. 267 (1986), five justices struck down a contractually arranged layoff plan that modified the traditional seniority system in order to protect minority employees by limiting minority layoffs to a level that could not exceed the overall percentage of minorities employed. In holding that this plan violated the Civil Rights Act, the Court emphasized that the system had not been adopted to benefit specific victims of discrimination and was justified as a general effort to "remedy societal discrimination" and to provide "role models" for minority students. In rejecting these arguments, the Court pointed out that the school board's plan worked against "innocent people," and went on to insist that remedies involving layoffs must be in response to findings of prior discrimination and must be drawn narrowly and constructed so they will not result in "serious disruptions" of the lives of particular innocent individuals.

Affirmative action and the issue of minority set-asides took still another turn in 1989, when by a vote of 6 to 3 the Court ruled that a city's set-aside plan for minority-owned businesses was unconstitutional (CITY OF RICHMOND V. J. A. CROSON CO., 107 S.Ct. 706, 1989). Writing for a highly fragmented Court, Justice O'Connor distinguished Richmond's plan from the Congressional plan it upheld in FULLILOVE in 1980. Even though the Court in FULLILOVE conceded that Congress had not made a specific finding of discrimination, Justice O'Connor argued that the plan passed constitutional muster because it rested on the sweeping powers of Congress to regulate interstate commerce and Congress' "unique remedial powers" under the Fourteenth Amendment. In striking down Richmond's similar plan, the Court asserted that neither states nor their subdivisions possess such equivalent authority, and thus they cannot engage in similar types of affirmative action. Although the RICHMOND Court attempts to distinguish the two cases in terms of differences between the powers of Congress and those of the states, it is also important to note that a presidential administration and several new justices intervened in the eight years between the two decisions. A clean majority now either insists on using the strict scrutiny standard when reviewing all types of race-based classifications — benign or discriminatory — or opposes all race-based classifications unless they are remedial, that is, are part of a corrective measure ordered by a court after a finding of purposeful discrimination.

Stotts, Wygant, and RICHMOND were major victories for opponents of affirmative action. However, Justices Marshall, Brennan, and Blackmun, dissenters in Stotts, Wygant, and RICHMOND, have been joined by other justices to form slim majorities in other far-reaching decisions that uphold affirmative action hiring and promotion plans.

In LOCAL 28 OF THE SHEETMETAL WORKERS' INTERNATIONAL ASSOC. V. EEOC, 478 U.S. 421 (1986), the Court upheld a lower court order that had established a 29 percent nonwhite membership goal in a union with a "long and persistent pattern of discrimination." And in a companion case,

Local No. 93, International Assoc. of Firefighters v. Cleveland, 478 U.S. 501 (1986), the Court ruled that section 706(g) of Title VII of the Civil Rights Act of 1964 does not prohibit employers or unions from entering into a *voluntary* hiring agreement as part of a consent decree that provides for preferential consideration of members of minority groups who are not actual victims of discrimination.

The following year, in the most important affirmative action case since BAKKE, the Court, in an expansive opinion, upheld a county's *voluntary* affirmative action plan to promote more women in an agency that traditionally had maintained segregated job classifications (JOHNSON V. TRANSPORTATION AGENCY, SANTA CLARA COUNTY, 480 U.S. 616, 1987). These decisions, actively opposed by the Reagan administration, constituted important victories for advocates of affirmative action.

We have then two divergent sets of decisions: one supportive of affirmative action and minority set-asides; and the other opposed to the use of racial (or gender) quotas and set-asides unless part of a narrowly-tailored, judicially-crafted remedy. Although there has been an effort by some justices to reconcile these two lines of decisions, most justices are firmly ensconced in one camp or the other. Furthermore a growing number of justices is openly hostile to the use of race or gender-related considerations of any sort. Indeed one reason that the Court has not been more aggressive in ruling against affirmative action programs has been the reluctance of some of the justices to reject or overrule precedent. However, as a group, the recent appointees to the Court are opposed to affirmative action, and as new justices come to replace the dwindling number of supporters, a majority is likely to emerge that will want to limit race-conscious policies to remedial actions after a judicial determination of discrimination. At the same time this majority is likely to insist upon a narrow interpretation of discrimination; one that emphasizes intent over effects and one that increases the burden of proof on the plaintiffs.

Cases

Plessy v. Ferguson

163 U.S. 537 (1896)
Vote: 7–1

While abolition of slavery was un-equivocally secured by the Civil War, many of the hopes that blacks held for Reconstruction were dashed by the reaction that followed the presidential election of 1876. Despite the great Civil War Amendments, the goal of resurgent white racists was to reassert white domination throughout the South. This control was effected through economic domination and reinforced by Jim Crow laws that limited black participation in public affairs and restricted black access to public facilities.

One such law, which gave rise to this case, was an 1890 Louisiana statute that required separate railway carriages for whites and blacks, and made passengers refusing to comply with the law subject to fine or imprisonment. This case was precipitated when Homer Adolph Plessy insisted on sitting in the white section of the train and was forcibly ejected and charged with violating the statute. At the time and in initial litigation, Plessy, who was seven-eighths Caucasian and one-eighth African, argued that because the mixture of colored blood was not discernible in him, he was entitled to sit in the white coach. Consequently, he argued that the Louisiana act violated the Thirteenth Amendment's prohibition against involuntary servitude because it reinforced a "badge of slavery"; further, it violated Fourteenth Amendment provisions for privileges and immunities and equal protection because it was unduly restrictive. The Court gave short shrift to the first two arguments (which are omitted in the opinion below) and then turned to deal with the equal protection claim.

Plessy is one of the most infamous cases in American constitutional history. Not only does the Court engage in some of the most dissembling language ever to come from its bench and ignore the clear aim of the state law, its expansive opinion supplied the constitutional doctrine of "separate but equal," which provided the moral and legal bases for the web of Jim Crow laws that ensnared the South in a system of apartheid for nearly two-thirds of a century.

Contrast the Court's opinion with the dissent of Justice Harlan, the author of perhaps the most prophetic dissent ever to be penned by a justice.

MR. JUSTICE BROWN delivered the opinion of the Court.

The object of the Fourteenth Amendment was undoubtedly to enforce the absolute equality of the two races before the law, but in the nature of things it could not have been intended to abolish distinctions based upon color, or to enforce social, as distinguished from political equality, or a commingling of the two races upon terms unsatisfactory to either. Laws permitting, and even requiring, their separation in places where they are liable to be brought into contact do not necessarily imply the inferiority of either race to the other, and have been generally, if not universally, recognized as within the competency of the state legislatures in the exercise of their police power. The most common instance of this is connected with the establishment of separate schools for white and colored children, which has been held to be a valid exercise of the legislative power even by courts of States where the political rights of the colored race have been longest and most earnestly enforced.

One of the earliest of these cases is that of *Roberts* v. *City of Boston,* 5 Cush. 198, in which the Supreme Judicial Court of Massachusetts held that the general school committee of Boston had power to make provision for the instruction of colored children in separate schools established exclusively for them, and to prohibit their attendance upon the other schools. . . . It was held that the powers of the committee extended to the establishment of separate schools for children of different ages, sexes and colors, and that they might also establish special schools for poor and neglected children, who have become too old to attend the primary school, and yet have not acquired the rudiments of learning, to enable them to enter the ordinary schools. Similar laws have been enacted by Congress under its general power of legislation over the District of Columbia, as well as by the legislatures of many of the States, and have been generally, if not uniformly, sustained by the courts.

Laws forbidding the intermarriage of the two races may be said in a technical sense to interfere with the freedom of contract, and yet have been universally recognized as within the police power of the State.

The distinction between laws interfering with the political equality of the negro and those requiring the separation of the two races in schools, theatres and railway carriages has been frequently drawn by this court. Thus in *Strauder* v. *West Virginia,* 100 U.S. 303, it was held that a law of West Virginia limiting to white male persons, 21 years of age and citizens of the State, the right to sit upon juries, was a discrimination which implied a legal inferiority in civil society, which lessened the security of the right of the colored race, and was a step toward reducing them to a condition of servility. . . .

. . . .

So far, then, as a conflict with the Fourteenth Amendment is concerned, the case reduces itself to the question whether the statute of Louisiana is a reasonable regulation, and with respect to this there must necessarily be a large discretion on the part of the legislature. In determining the question of reasonableness it is at liberty to act with reference to the established usages, customs, and traditions of the people, and with a view to the promotion of their comfort, and the preservation of the public peace and good order. Gauged by this standard, we cannot say that a law which authorizes or even requires the separation of the two races in public conveyances is unreasonable, or more obnoxious to the Fourteenth Amendment than the acts of Congress requiring separate schools for colored children in the District of Columbia, the constitutionality of which does not seem to have been questioned, or the corresponding acts of state legislatures.

We consider the underlying fallacy of the plaintiff's argument to consist in the assumption that the enforced separation of the two races stamps the colored race with a badge of inferiority. If this be so, it is not by reason of anything found in the act, but solely because the colored race chooses to put that construction upon it. The argument necessarily assumes that if, as has been more than once the case, and is not unlikely to be so again, the colored race should become the dominant power in the state legislature, and should enact a law in precisely similar terms, it would thereby relegate the white race to an inferior position. We imagine that the white race, at least, would not acquiesce in this assumption. The argument also assumes that social prejudices may be overcome by legislation, and that equal rights cannot be secured to the negro except by an enforced commingling of the two races. We cannot accept this proposition. If the two races are to meet upon terms of social equality, it must be the result of natural affinities, a mutual appreciation of each other's merits and a voluntary consent of individuals. As was said by the Court of Appeals of New York in *People* v. *Gallagher,* 93 N.Y. 438, 448, "this end can neither be accomplished nor promoted by laws which conflict with the general sentiment of the community upon whom they are designed to operate. When the government, therefore, has secured to each of its citizens equal rights before the law and equal opportunities for improvement and progress, it has accomplished the end for which it was organized and performed all of the functions respecting social advantages with which it is endowed." Legislation is powerless to eradicate racial instincts or to abolish distinctions based upon physical differences, and the attempt to do so can only result in accentuating the difficulties of the present situation. If the civil and political rights of both races be equal, one cannot be inferior to the other civilly or politically. If one race be inferior to the other socially, the Constitution of the United States cannot put them upon the same plane.

. . . .

The judgment of the court below is, therefore,

Affirmed.

MR. JUSTICE HARLAN, dissenting.

In respect of civil rights, common to all citizens, the Constitution of the United States does not, I think, permit any public authority to know the race of those entitled to be protected in the enjoyment of such rights. Every true man has pride of race, and under appropriate circumstances, when the rights of others, his equals before the law, are not to be affected, it is his privilege to express such pride and to take such action based upon it as to him seems proper. But I deny that any legislative body or judicial tribunal may have regard to the race of citizens when the civil rights of those citizens are involved. Indeed, such legislation, as that here in question, is inconsistent not only with that equality of rights which pertains to citizenship, National and State, but with the personal liberty enjoyed by every one within the United States.

The Thirteenth Amendment does not permit the withholding or the deprivation of any right necessarily inhering in freedom. It not only struck down the institution of slavery as previously existing in the United States, but it prevents the imposition of any burdens or disabilities that constitute badges of slavery or servitude. It decreed universal civil freedom in this country. This court has so adjudged. But that amendment having been found inadequate to the protection of the rights of those who had been in slavery, it was followed by the Fourteenth Amendment, which added greatly to the dignity and glory of American citizenship, and to the security of personal liberty, by declaring that "all persons born or naturalized in the United States, and subject to the jurisdiction thereof, are citizens of the United States and of the State wherein they reside," and that "no State shall make or enforce any law which shall abridge the privileges or immunities of citizens of the United States; nor shall any State deprive any person of life, liberty or property without due process of law, nor deny to any person within its jurisdiction the equal protection of the laws." These two amendments, if enforced according to their true intent and meaning, will protect all the civil rights that pertain to freedom and citizenship. Finally, and to the end that no citizen should be denied, on account of his race, the privilege of participating in the political control of his country, it was declared by the Fifteenth Amendment that "the right of citizens of the United States to vote shall not be denied or abridged by the United States or by any State on account of race, color or previous condition of servitude."

These notable additions to the fundamental law were welcomed by the friends of liberty throughout the world. They removed the race line from our governmental systems. They had, as this court has said, a common purpose, namely, to secure "to a race recently emancipated, a race that through many generations have been held in slavery, all the civil rights that the superior race enjoy." They declared, in legal effect, this court has further said, "that the law in the States shall be the same for the black as for the white; that all persons, whether colored or white, shall stand equal before the laws of the States, and, in regard to the colored race, for whose protection the amendment was primarily designed, that no discrimination shall be made against them by law because of their color." We also said: "The words of the amendment, it is true, are prohibitory, but they contain a necessary implication of a positive immunity or right, most valuable to the colored race — the right to exemption from unfriendly legislation against them distinctively as colored — exemption from legal discriminations, implying inferiority in civil society, lessening the security of their enjoyment of the rights which others enjoy, and discriminations which

are steps towards reducing them to the condition of a subject race." It was, consequenty, adjudged that a state law that excluded citizens of the colored race from juries, because of their race and however well qualified in other respects to discharge the duties of jurymen, was repugnant to the Fourteenth Amendment. *Strauder* v. *West Virginia* (1880)....

It was said in argument that the statute of Louisiana does not discriminate against either race, but prescribes a rule applicable alike to white and colored citizens. But this argument does not meet the difficulty. Every one knows that the statute in question had its origin in the purpose, not so much to exclude white persons from railroad cars occupied by blacks, as to exclude colored people from coaches occupied by or assigned to white persons. Railroad corporations of Louisiana did not make discrimination among whites in the matter of accommodation for travellers. The thing to accomplish was, under the guise of giving equal accommodation for whites and blacks, to compel the latter to keep to themselves while travelling in railroad passenger coaches. No one would be so wanting in candor as to assert the contrary. The fundamental objection, therefore, to the statute is that it interferes with the personal freedom of citizens. "Personal liberty," it has been well said, "consists in the power of locomotion, of changing situation, or removing one's person to whatsoever places one's own inclination may direct, without imprisonment or restraint, unless by due course of law." If a white man and a black man choose to occupy the same public conveyance on a public highway, it is their right to do so, and no government, proceeding alone on grounds of race, can prevent it without infringing the personal liberty of each.

....

The white race deems itself to be the dominant race in this country. And so it is, in prestige, in achievements, in education, in wealth and in power. So, I doubt not, it will continue to be for all time, if it remains true to its great heritage and holds fast to the principles of constitutional liberty. But in view of the Constitution, in the eye of the law, there is in this country no superior, dominant, ruling class of citizens. There is no caste here. Our Constitution is colorblind, and neither knows nor tolerates classes among citizens. In respect of civil rights, all citizens are equal before the law. The humblest is the peer of the most powerful. The law regards man as man, and takes no account of his surroundings or of his color when his civil rights as guaranteed by the supreme law of the land are involved. It is, therefore, to be regretted that this high tribunal, the final expositor of the fundamental law of the land, has reached the conclusion that it is competent for a

State to regulate the enjoyment by citizens of their civil rights solely upon the basis of race.

In my opinion, the judgment this day rendered will, in time, prove to be quite as pernicious as the decision made by this tribunal in the *Dred Scott case.* It was adjudged in that case that the descendants of Africans who were imported into this country and sold as slaves were not included nor intended to be included under the word "citizens" in the Constitution, and could not claim any of the rights and privileges which that instrument provided for and secured to citizens of the United States; that at the time of the adoption of the Constitution they were "considered as a subordinate and inferior class of beings, who had been subjugated by the dominant race, and, whether emancipated or not, yet remained subject to their authority, and had no rights or privileges but such as those who held the power and the government might choose to grant them." 19 How. 393, 404. The recent amendments of the Constitution, it was supposed, had eradicated these principles from our institutions. But it seems that we have yet, in some of the States, a dominant race — a superior class of citizens, which assumes to regulate the enjoyment of civil rights, common to all citizens, upon the basis of race. The present decision, it may well be apprehended, will not only stimulate aggressions, more or less brutal and irritating, upon the admitted rights of colored citizens, but will encourage the belief that it is possible, by means of state enactments, to defeat the beneficent purposes which the people of the United States had in view when they adopted the recent amendments of the Constitution, by one of which the blacks of this country were made citizens of the United States and of the States in which they respectively reside, and whose privileges and immunities, as citizens, the States are forbidden to abridge. Sixty millions of whites are in no danger from the presence here of eight millions of blacks. The destinies of the two races in this country are indissolubly linked together, and the interests of both require that the common government of all shall not permit the seeds of race hate to be planted under the sanction of law. What can more certainly arouse race hate, what more certainly create and perpetuate a feeling of distrust between these races, than state enactments, which in fact proceed on the ground that colored citizens are so inferior and degraded that they cannot be allowed to sit in public coaches occupied by white citizens? That, as all will admit, is the real meaning of such legislation as was enacted in Louisiana.

. . . .

. . . It is scarcely just to say that a colored citizen should not object to occupying a public coach as-

signed to his own race. He does not object, nor, perhaps, would he object to separate coaches for his race, if his rights under the law were recognized. But he objects, and ought never to cease objecting to the proposition, that citizens of the white and black races can be adjudged criminals because they sit, or claim the right to sit, in the same public coach on a public highway.

The arbitrary separation of citizens, on the basis of race, while they are on a public highway, is a badge of servitude wholly inconsistent with the civil freedom and the equality before the law established by the Constitution. It cannot be justified upon any legal grounds.

. . . I am constrained to withhold my assent from the opinion and judgment of the majority.

Mr. Justice Brewer did not hear the argument or participate in the decision of this case.

Brown v. Board of Education (Brown I)

> 347 U.S. 484 (1954)
> Vote: 9–0

Brown v. Board of Education (Brown II)

> 349 U.S. 294 (1955)
> Vote: 9–0

Perhaps the most pernicious application of Plessy's separate but equal doctrine was the creation of racially segregated schools throughout the South. But even this doctrine was honored in the breach as public officials and the Court tolerated widely disparate educational facilities and opportunities for blacks and whites. This separate and unequal treatment was not seriously challenged by the Court for nearly forty years after Plessy, and when it was challenged the Court moved slowly and cautiously.

Between 1938 and 1950, the Court ruled on several challenges to racially segregated educational programs. All were at the postgraduate level and, at most, involved only a tiny handful of students. In each of these cases the Court held that separate programs or arrangements for blacks were unacceptable because they did not offer the same level of opportunity as was available to whites. In the last of these cases, *Sweatt* v. *Painter,* 339 U.S. 629 (1950), the Court held the law school that Texas had opened for blacks was vastly inferior to the white-only University of Texas Law School, and ordered that the latter admit black students. In its opinion, the Court compared the two schools on a number of factors that "are incapable of objective measurement... such as reputation of the faculty, experience of the administration, position and influence of the alumni, standing in the community, traditions and prestige." The handwriting was on the wall. After this, it was only a matter of time before the separate but equal doctrine would fall completely.

This opportunity arose in the case below. Actually one of several cases joined together for argument before the Court, *Brown* was an especially interesting test case because it arose not in the Deep South but in Kansas, the home of many ardent abolitionists during the years before the Civil War. *Brown* was also an ideal test case for another reason. Unlike earlier cases that reached the Court, there was a reasonable basis to the claim that the *tangible* facilities provided black pupils in Topeka were equal or even superior to those provided whites. Thus the case forced the Court to deal with the "separate" portion of the PLESSY doctrine.

But *Brown* presented still more imposing problems for the Court. All the earlier inroads into the separate but equal doctrine had dealt with postgraduate university programs involving only a tiny handful of adult students. *Brown* addressed the issue of racial segregation in primary and secondary schools of fifteen states, which by law had mandated "dual school systems." Its ruling altered long-standing policies and administrative arrangements of thousands of school districts in over a dozen states and the daily lives of millions of youngsters. It was for a court ruling truly revolutionary. For this reason, after the historic 1954 ruling, the Court ordered additional argument with respect to the equitable remedies to be used to oversee the massive task of dismantling dual school systems throughout the South. The result was a second opinion, *Brown* v. *Board of Education,* 349 U.S. 294 (1955), known as Brown II to distinguish it from the 1954 ruling, Brown I. Relevant portions of Brown II follow the 1954 case. Note the Court's use of the phrase "all deliberate speed." Do you think this helped or hurt the Court in subsequent years?

BROWN I
MR. CHIEF JUSTICE WARREN delivered the opinion of the Court.

These cases come to us from the States of Kansas, South Carolina, Virginia, and Delaware. They are premised on different facts and different local conditions, but a common legal question justifies their consideration together in this consolidated opinion.

In each of the cases, minors of the Negro race, through their legal representatives, seek the aid of the courts in obtaining admission to the public schools of their community on a nonsegregated basis. In each instance, they had been denied admission to schools attended by white children under laws requiring or permitting segregation according to race. This segregation was alleged to deprive the plaintiffs of the equal protection of the laws under the Fourteenth Amendment. In each of the cases other than the Delaware case, a three-judge federal district court denied relief to the plaintiffs on the so-called "separate but equal" doctrine announced by this Court in *Plessy* v. *Ferguson,* 163 U.S. 537. Under that doctrine, equality of treatment is accorded when the races are provided substantially equal facilities, even though these facilities be separate. In the Delaware case, the Supreme Court of Delaware adhered to that doctrine, but ordered that the plaintiffs be admitted to the white schools because of their superiority to the Negro schools.

The plaintiffs contend that segregated public schools are not "equal" and cannot be made "equal," and that hence they are deprived of the equal protection of the laws. Because of the obvious importance of the question presented, the Court took jurisdiction. Argument was heard in the 1952 Term, and reargument was heard this Term on certain questions propounded by the Court.

Reargument was largely devoted to the circumstances surrounding the adoption of the Fourteenth Amendment in 1868. It covered exhaustively consideration of the Amendment in Congress, ratification by the states, then-existing practices in racial segregation, and the views of proponents and opponents of the Amendment. This discussion and our own investigation convince us that, although these sources cast some light, it is not enough to resolve the problem with which we are faced. At best, they are inconclusive. The most avid proponents of the post-War Amendments undoubtedly intended them to remove all legal distinctions among "all persons born or naturalized in the United States." Their opponents, just as certainly, were antagonistic to both the letter and the spirit of the Amendments and wished them to have the most limited effect. What others in Congress and the state legislatures had in mind cannot be determined with any degree of certainty.

An additional reason for the inconclusive nature of the Amendment's history, with respect to segregated schools, is the status of public education at that time. In the South, the movement toward free common schools, supported by general taxation, had not yet taken hold. Education of white children was largely in the hands of private groups. Education of Negroes was almost nonexistent, and practically all of the race were illiterate. In fact, any education of Negroes was forbidden by law in some states. Today, in contrast, many Negroes have achieved outstanding success in the arts and sciences as well as in the business and professional world. It is true that public school education at the time of the Amendment had advanced further in the North, but the effect of the Amendment on Northern States was generally ignored in the congressional debates. Even in the North, the conditions of public education did not approximate those existing today. The curriculum was usually rudimentary; ungraded schools were common in rural areas; the school term was but three months a year in many states; and compulsory school attendance was virtually unknown. As a consequence, it is not surprising that there should be so little in the history of the Fourteenth Amendment relating to its intended effect on public education.

In the first cases in this Court construing the Fourteenth Amendment, decided shortly after its adoption, the Court interpreted it as proscribing all state-imposed discriminations against the Negro race. The doctrine of "separate but equal" did not make its appearance in this Court until 1896 in the case of *Plessy* v. *Ferguson, supra,* involving not education but transportation. American courts have since labored with the doctrine for over half a century. In this Court, there have been six cases involving the "separate but equal" doctrine in the field of public education. In *Cumming* v. *County Board of Education...* and *Gong Lum* v. *Rice...* the validity of the doctrine itself was not challenged. In more recent cases, all on the graduate school level, inequality was found in that specific benefits enjoyed by white students were denied to Negro students of the same educational qualifications. *Missouri ex rel. Gaines* v. *Canada,... Sipuel* v. *Oklahoma,... Sweatt* v. *Painter,... McLaurin* v. *Oklahoma State Regents....* In none of these cases was it necessary to re-examine the doctrine to grant relief to the Negro plaintiff. And in *Sweatt* v. *Painter, supra,* the Court expressly reserved decision on the question whether *Plessy* v. *Ferguson* should be held inapplicable to public education.

In the instant cases, that question is directly presented. Here, unlike *Sweatt* v. *Painter,* there are findings below that the Negro and white schools involved have been equalized, or are being equalized, with respect to buildings, curricula, qualifications and salaries of teachers, and other "tangible" factors. Our decision, therefore, cannot turn on merely a comparison of these tangible factors in the Negro and white schools involved in each of the cases. We must look instead to the effect of segregation itself on public education.

In approaching this problem, we cannot turn the clock back to 1868 when the Amendment was adopted, or even to 1896 when *Plessy* v. *Ferguson* was written. We must consider public education in the light of its full development and its present place in American life throughout the Nation. Only in this way can it be determined if segregation in public schools deprives these plaintiffs of the equal protection of the laws.

Today, education is perhaps the most important function of state and local governments. Compulsory school attendance laws and the great expenditures for education both demonstrate our recognition of the importance of education to our democratic society. It is required in the performance of our most basic public responsibilities, even service in the armed forces. It is the very foundation of good citizenship. Today it is a principal instrument in awakening the child to cultural values, in preparing him for later professional training, and in helping him to adjust normally to his environment. In these days, it is doubtful that any child may reasonably be expected to succeed in life if he is denied the opportunity of an education. Such an opportunity, where the state has undertaken to provide it, is a right which must be made available to all on equal terms.

We come then to the question presented: Does segregation of children in public schools solely on the basis of race, even though the physical facilities and other "tangible" factors may be equal, deprive the children of the minority group of equal educational opportunities? We believe that it does.

In *Sweatt* v. *Painter, supra,* in finding that a segregated law school for Negroes could not provide them equal educational opportunities, this Court relied in large part on "those qualities which are incapable of objective measurement but which make for greatness in a law school." In *McLaurin* v. *Oklahoma State Regents, supra,* the Court, in requiring that a Negro admitted to a white graduate school be treated like all other students, again resorted to intangible considerations: ". . . his ability to study, to engage in discussions and exchange views with other students, and, in general, to learn his profession." Such considerations apply with added force to children in grade and high schools. To separate them from others of similar age and qualifications solely because of their race generates a feeling of inferiority as to their status in the community that may affect their hearts and minds in a way unlikely ever to be undone. The effect of this separation on the educational opportunities was well stated by a finding in the Kansas case by a court which nevertheless felt compelled to rule against the Negro plaintiffs:

> Segregation of white and colored children in public schools has a detrimental effect upon the colored children. The impact is greater when it has the sanction of the law; for the policy of separating the races is usually interpreted as denoting the inferiority of the negro group. A sense of inferiority affects the motivation of the child to learn. Segregation with the sanction of law, therefore, has a tendency to [retard] the educational and mental development of negro children and to deprive them of some of the benefits they would receive in a racial[ly] integrated school system.

Whatever may have been the extent of psychological knowledge at the time of *Plessy* v. *Ferguson,* this finding is amply supported by modern authority.* Any language in *Plessy* v. *Ferguson* contrary to this finding is rejected.

We conclude that in the field of public education the doctrine of "separate but equal" has no place. Separate educational facilities are inherently unequal.

*K. B. Clark, Effect of Prejudice and Discrimination on Personality Development (Midcentury White House Conference on Children and Youth, 1950); Witmer and Kotinsky, Personality in the Making (1952); c. VI; Deutscher and Chein, The Psychological Effects of Enforced Segregation: A Survey of Social Science Opinion, 26 J. Psychol. 259 (1948); Chein, What are the Psychological Effects of Segregation Under Conditions of Equal Facilities?, 3 Int. J. Opinion and Attitude Res. 229 (1949); Brameld, Educational Costs, in Discrimination and National Welfare (MacIver, ed., 1949), 44–48; Frazier, The Negro in the United States (1949), 674–681. And see generally Myrdal, An American Dilemma (1944).

Therefore, we hold that the plaintiffs and others similarly situated for whom the actions have been brought are, by reason of the segregation complained of, deprived of the equal protection of the laws guaranteed by the Fourteenth Amendment. This disposition makes unnecessary any discussion whether such segregation also violates the Due Process Clause of the Fourteenth Amendment.

Because these are class actions, because of the wide applicability of this decision, and because of the great variety of local conditions, the formulation of decrees in these cases presents problems of considerable complexity. On reargument, the consideration of appropriate relief was necessarily subordinated to the primary question—the constitutionality of segregation in public education. We have now announced that such segregation is a denial of the equal protection of the laws. In order that we may have the full assistance of the parties in formulating decrees, the cases will be restored to the docket, and the parties are requested to present further argument. . . .

BROWN II (1955)

MR. CHIEF JUSTICE WARREN delivered the opinion of the Court.

These presentations [at reargument] were informative and helpful to the Court in its consideration of the complexities arising from the transition to a system of public education freed of racial discrimination. The presentations also demonstrated that substantial steps to eliminate racial discrimination in public schools have already been taken, not only in some of the communities in which these cases arose, but in some of the states appearing as *amici curiae,* and in other states as well. . . .

Full implementation of these constitutional principles may require solution of varied local school problems. School authorities have the primary responsibility for elucidating, assessing, and solving these problems; courts will have to consider whether the action of school authorities constitutes good faith implementation of the governing constitutional principles. Because of their proximity to local conditions and the possible need for further hearings, the courts which originally heard these cases can best perform this judicial appraisal. Accordingly, we believe it appropriate to remand the cases to those courts.

In fashioning and effectuating the decrees, the courts will be guided by equitable principles. Traditionally, equity has been characterized by a practical flexibility in shaping its remedies and by a facility for adjusting and reconciling public and private needs. These cases call for the exercise of these traditional attributes of equity power. At stake is the personal interest of the plaintiffs in admission to public schools as soon as practicable on a nondiscriminatory basis. To effectuate this interest may call for elimination of a variety of obstacles in making the transition to school systems operated in accordance with the constitutional principles set forth in our May 17, 1954, decision. Courts of equity may properly take into account the public interest in the elimination of such obstacles in a systematic and effective manner. But it should go without saying that the vitality of these constitutional principles cannot be allowed to yield simply because of disagreement with them.

While giving weight to these public and private considerations, the courts will require that the defendants make a prompt and reasonable start toward full compliance with our May 17, 1954, ruling. Once such a start has been made, the courts may find that additional time is necessary to carry out the ruling in an effective manner. The burden rests upon the defendants to establish that such time is necessary in the public interest and is consistent with good faith compliance at the earliest practicable date. To that end, the courts may consider problems related to administration, arising from the physical condition of the school plant, the school transportation system, personnel, revision of school districts and attendance areas into compact units to achieve a system of determining admission to the public schools on a nonracial basis, and revision of local laws and regulations which may be necessary in solving the foregoing problems. They will also consider the adequacy of any plans the defendants may propose to meet these problems and to effectuate a transition to a racially nondiscriminatory school system. During this period of transition, the courts will retain jurisdiction of these cases.

The . . . cases are remanded to the District Courts to take such proceedings and enter such orders and decrees consistent with this opinion as are necessary and proper to admit to public schools on a racially nondiscriminatory basis with all deliberate speed the parties to these cases. . . .

It is so ordered.

Swann et al. v. Charlotte-Mecklenburg Board of Education

403 U.S. 912 (1971)
Vote: 9–0

For years after BROWN, schools in the South remained segregated. When prodded by increasingly active district courts, local officials formally dismantled their dual school systems. But by maintaining neighborhood schools, gerrymandering attendance zones, resisting busing, and granting "freedom of choice" transfer plans, public schools remained largely segregated. The patience of the justices on the Supreme Court began to wear thin. In a number of decisions they pierced the formalisms erected to thwart implementation of BROWN and insisted that concrete steps be taken to dismantle segregated school systems. Finally, in *Green v. County School Board of New Kent County,* 391 U.S. 430 (1968), the Court called a halt to the era of "all deliberate speed" and announced it was time to develop "a plan that promises to work, and . . . to work now."

But even as the Court was embracing stronger language and encouraging district courts to take even more aggressive roles in designing remedial desegregation orders, a new president, Richard Nixon, who had campaigned on an antibusing platform, was directing the Department of Justice and the Department of Health, Education, and Welfare to move more cautiously and to urge restraint in the use of desegregation remedies. This new turn of events was not lost on Southern officials, who, buoyed by presidential support, increased their resolve to resist desegregation orders and especially those requiring busing.

The case below arose in these crosscurrents. For years the school district of Charlotte-Mecklenburg, North Carolina, like many others throughout the South, had done little to desegregate its schools. Finally, in 1968, after lengthy litigation it adopted a plan that made some efforts towards desegregation but still left around 60 percent of its black pupils in a handful of all-black schools. Additional litigation was initiated in 1969, in light of the Court's strong language in *Green v. New Kent County,* and after extensive negotiations, study, and resistance, the district court imposed a plan on a reluctant school board that called for the use of racial balances, or quotas, for each school, elimination of one-race schools, remedial altering of school attendance zones, and extensive busing.

Given the Nixon administration's opposition to some of these remedies and a North Carolina antibusing statute, opponents of the plan appealed.

The Court of Appeals for the Fifth Circuit accepted most parts of the wide-ranging plan, but rejected those portions which required pairing and busing to desegregate elementary schools, arguing that they were unreasonable burdens for such young children and the school district. The case eventually arrived at the Supreme Court by writ of certiorari, and the Court agreed to review the validity of the state's antibusing law and the acceptability of the range of remedies ordered by the district court.

Note that the Court's opinion was written by Chief Justice Burger, who just a few months before had been President Nixon's first appointment to the Supreme Court.

MR. CHIEF JUSTICE BURGER delivered the opinion of the Court.

We granted certiorari in this case to review important issues as to the duties of school authorities and the scope of powers of federal courts under this Court's mandates to eliminate racially separate public schools established and maintained by state action.

This case and those argued with it arose in States having a long history of maintaining two sets of schools in a single school system deliberately operated to carry out a governmental policy to separate pupils in schools solely on the basis of race. That was what *Brown* v. *Board of Education* was all about. These cases present us with the problem of defining in more precise terms than heretofore the scope of the duty of school authorities and district courts in implementing *Brown I* and the mandate to eliminate dual systems and establish unitary systems at once. . . .

. . . .

The construction of new schools and the closing of old ones are two of the most important functions of local school authorities and also two of the most complex. They must decide questions of location and capacity in light of population growth, finances, land values, site availability, through an almost endless list of factors to be considered. The result of this will be a decision which, when combined with one technique or another of student assignment, will determine the racial composition of the student body in each school in the system. Over the long run, the consequences of the choices will be far reaching. People gravitate toward school facilities, just as schools are located in response to the needs of people.

The location of schools may thus influence the patterns of residential development of a metropolitan area and have important impact on composition of inner-city neighborhoods.

In the past, choices in this respect have been used as a potent weapon for creating or maintaining a state-segregated school system. In addition to the classic pattern of building schools specifically intended for Negro and white students, school authorities have sometimes, since *Brown,* closed schools which appeared likely to become racially mixed through changes in neighborhood residential patterns. This was sometimes accompanied by building new schools in the areas of white suburban expansion farthest from Negro population centers in order to maintain the separation of the races with a minimum departure from the formal principles of "neighborhood zoning." Such a policy does more than simply influence the short-run composition of the student body of a new school. It may well promote segregated residential patterns which, when combined with "neighborhood zoning," further lock the school system into the mold of separation of the races. Upon a proper showing a district court may consider this in fashioning a remedy.

In ascertaining the existence of legally imposed school segregation, the existence of a pattern of school construction and abandonment is thus a factor of great weight. In devising remedies where legally imposed segregation has been established, it is the responsibility of local authorities and district courts to see to it that future school construction and abandonment are not used and do not serve to perpetuate or re-establish the dual system. When necessary, district courts should retain jurisdiction to assure that these responsibilities are carried out. . . .

The central issue in this case is that of student assignment, and there are essentially four problem areas:

(1) to what extent racial balance or racial quotas may be used as an implement in a remedial order to correct a previously segregated system;

(2) whether every all-Negro and all-white school must be eliminated as an indispensable part of a remedial process of desegregation;

(3) what the limits are, if any, on the rearrangement of school districts and attendance zones, as a remedial measure; and

(4) what the limits are, if any, on the use of transportation facilities to correct state-enforced racial school segregation.

(1) *Racial Balances or Racial Quotas.*

. . . .

In this case it is urged that the District Court has imposed a racial balance requirement of 71%–29%

on individual schools. The fact that no such objective was actually achieved — and would appear to be impossible — tends to blunt that claim, yet in the opinion and order of the District Court of December 1, 1969, we find that court directing

> that efforts should be made to reach a 71–29 ratio in the various schools so that there will be no basis for contending that one school is racially different from the others, . . . [t]hat no school [should] be operated with an all-black or predominantly black student body, [and] [t]hat pupils of all grades [should] be assigned in such a way that as nearly as practicable the various schools at various grade levels have about the same proportion of black and white students.

The District Judge went on to acknowledge that variation "from that norm may be unavoidable." This contains intimations that the "norm" is a fixed mathematical racial balance reflecting the pupil constituency of the system. If we were to read the holding of the District Court to require, as a matter of substantive constitutional right, any particular degree of racial balance or mixing, that approach would be disapproved and we would be obliged to reverse. The constitutional command to desegregate schools does not mean that every school in every community must always reflect the racial composition of the school system as a whole.

As the voluminous record in this case shows, the predicate for the District Court's use of the 71%–29% ratio was twofold: first, its express finding, approved by the Court of Appeals and not challenged here, that a dual school system had been maintained by the school authorities at least until 1969; second, its finding, also approved by the Court of Appeals, that the school board had totally defaulted in its acknowledged duty to come forward with an acceptable plan of its own, notwithstanding the patient efforts of the District Judge who, on at least three occasions, urged the board to submit plans. As the statement of facts shows, these findings are abundantly supported by the record. It was because of this total failure of the school board that the District Court was obliged to turn to other qualified sources, and Dr. Finger was designated to assist the District Court to do what the board should have done.

We see therefore that the use made of mathematical ratios was no more than a starting point in the process of shaping a remedy, rather than an inflexible requirement. From that starting point the District Court proceeded to frame a decree that was within its discretionary powers, as an equitable remedy for the particular circumstances. As we said in *Green,* a school authority's remedial plan or a district court's remedial decree is to be judged by its effectiveness. Awareness of the racial composition of the whole school system is likely to be a useful starting point in shaping a remedy to correct past constitutional violations. In sum, the very limited use made of mathematical ratios was within the equitable remedial discretion of the District Court.

(2) *One-race Schools.*

The record in this case reveals the familiar phenomenon that in metropolitan areas minority groups are often found concentrated in one part of the city. In some circumstances certain schools may remain all or largely of one race until new schools can be provided or neighborhood patterns change. Schools all or predominately of one race in a district of mixed population will require close scrutiny to determine that school assignments are not part of state-enforced segregation.

In light of the above, it should be clear that the existence of some small number of one-race, or virtually one-race, schools within a district is not in and of itself the mark of a system that still practices segregation by law. The district judge or school authorities should make every effort to achieve the greatest possible degree of actual desegregation and will thus necessarily be concerned with the elimination of one-race schools. No *per se* rule can adequately embrace all the difficulties of reconciling the competing interests involved; but in a system with a history of segregation the need for remedial criteria of sufficient specificity to assure a school authority's compliance with its constitutional duty warrants a presumption against schools that are substantially disproportionate in their racial composition. Where the school authority's proposed plan for conversion from a dual to a unitary system comtemplates the continued existence of some schools that are all or predominately of one race, they have the burden of showing that such school assignments are genuinely nondiscriminatory. The court should scrutinize such schools, and the burden upon the school authorities will be to satisfy the court that their racial composition is not the result of present or past discriminatory action on their part.

An optional majority-to-minority transfer provision has long been recognized as a useful part of every desegregation plan. Provision for optional transfer of those in the majority racial group of a particular school to other schools where they will be in the minority is an indispensable remedy for those students willing to transfer to other schools in order to lessen the impact on them of the state-imposed stigma of segregation. In order to be effective, such a transfer arrangement must grant the transferring student free transportation and space must be made available in the school to which he desires to move.

(3) *Remedial Altering of Attendance Zones.*

The maps submitted in these cases graphically demonstrate that one of the principal tools employed by school planners and by courts to break up the dual school system has been a frank — and sometimes drastic — gerrymandering of school districts and attendance zones. An additional step was pairing, "clustering," or "grouping" of schools with attendance assignments made deliberately to accomplish the transfer of Negro students out of formerly segregated Negro schools and transfer of white students to formerly all-Negro schools. More often than not, these zones are neither compact nor contiguous: indeed they may be on opposite ends of the city. As an interim corrective measure, this cannot be said to be beyond the broad remedial powers of a court.

Absent a constitutional violation there would be no basis for judicially ordering assignment of students on a racial basis. All things being equal, with no history of discrimination, it might well be desirable to assign pupils to schools nearest their homes. But all things are not equal in a system that has been deliberately constructed and maintained to enforce racial segregation. The remedy for such segregation may be administratively awkward, inconvenient, and even bizarre in some situations and may impose burdens on some; but all awkwardness and inconvenience cannot be avoided in the interim period when remedial adjustments are being made to eliminate the dual school systems.

No fixed or even substantially fixed guidelines can be established as to how far a court can go, but it must be recognized that there are limits. The objective is to dismantle the dual school system. "Racially neutral" assignment plans proposed by school authorities to a district court may be inadequate; such plans may fail to counteract the continuing effects of past school segregation resulting from discriminatory location of school sites or distortion of school size in order to achieve or maintain an artificial racial separation. When school authorities present a district court with a "loaded game board," affirmative action in the form of remedial altering of attendance zones is proper to achieve truly nondiscriminatory assignments. In short, an assignment plan is not acceptable simply because it appears to be neutral.

. . . .

We hold that the pairing and grouping of noncontiguous school zones is a permissible tool and such action is to be considered in light of the objectives sought. . . .

(4) *Transportation of Students.*

The scope of permissible transportation of students as an implement of a remedial decree has never been defined by this Court and by the very nature of the problem it cannot be defined with precision. No rigid guidelines as to student transportation can be given for application to the infinite variety of problems presented in thousands of situations. Bus transportation has been an integral part of the public education system for years, and was perhaps the single most important factor in the transition from the one-room schoolhouse to the consolidated school. Eighteen million of the Nation's public school children, approximately 39%, were transported to their schools by bus in 1969–1970 in all parts of the country.

The importance of bus transportation as a normal and accepted tool of educational policy is readily discernible in this and the companion case. The Charlotte school authorities did not purport to assign students on the basis of geographically drawn zones until 1965 and then they allowed almost unlimited transfer privileges. The District Court's conclusion that assignment of children to the school nearest their home serving their grade would not produce an effective dismantling of the dual system is supported by the record.

Thus the remedial techniques used in the District Court's order were within that court's power to provide equitable relief; implementation of the decree is well within the capacity of the school authority.

. . . .

The Court of Appeals, searching for a term to define the equitable remedial power of the district courts, used the term "reasonableness." In *Green, supra,* this Court used the term "feasible" and by implication, "workable," "effective," and "realistic" in the mandate to develop "a plan that promises realistically to work, and . . . to work *now.*" On the facts of this case, we are unable to conclude that the order of the District Court is not reasonable, feasible and workable. However, in seeking to define the scope of remedial power or the limits on remedial power of courts in an area as sensitive as we deal with here, words are poor instruments to convey the sense of basic fairness inherent in equity. Substance, not semantics, must govern, and we have sought to suggest the nature of limitations without frustrating the appropriate scope of equity.

At some point, these school authorities and others like them should have achieved full compliance with this Court's decision in *Brown I.* The systems would then be "unitary" in the sense required by our decisions in *Green* and *Alexander.*

It does not follow that the communities served by such systems will remain demographically stable, for in a growing, mobile society, few will do so. Neither school authorities nor district courts are constitutionally required to make year-by-year adjustments of the racial composition of student bodies once the affirmative duty to desegregate has been accomplished and racial discrimination through official action is eliminated from the system. This does not mean that federal courts are without power to deal with future problems; but in the absence of a showing that either the school authorities or some other agency of the State has deliberately attempted to fix or alter demographic patterns to affect the racial composition of the schools, further intervention by a district court should not be necessary.

For the reasons herein set forth, the judgment of the Court of Appeals is affirmed as to those parts in which it affirmed the judgment of the District Court. The order of the District Court... is also

Affirmed.

Keyes et al. v. School District No. 1, Denver, Colorado

413 U.S. 189 (1973)
Vote: 6–2

Keyes et al. brought suit in federal district court against the Denver school district, alleging that it had engaged in intentional segregation of schools in the Park Hills section of the district. They subsequently expanded their suit to challenge segregation in other sections of the city, particularly the predominantly black core-city schools. Denver defended against these latter allegations by arguing that segregation there was due to housing patterns, not racially motivated policies.

The district court found that the school district had engaged in deliberate segregation in the Park Hills section and ordered relief, but it denied further relief for other sections of the city. It held that segregative intent in these other sections had not been proven and that proof of such intent would be required for each section of the city before broader relief would be granted. The court of appeals affirmed the district court's rulings on these issues, holding that the single instance of intentional segregation was insufficient to prove an overall policy of segregation and thus warrant districtwide relief.

Keyes et al. then petitioned the Supreme Court for a writ of certiorari. The issue before the Court was whether a finding of deliberate segregation in one significant portion of a district is sufficient to shift the burden to school officials to prove that segregation in other parts of the district is not likewise motivated by segregative intent.

MR. JUSTICE BRENNAN delivered the opinion of the Court.

This school desegregation case concerns the Denver, Colorado, school system. That system has never been operated under a constitutional or statutory provision that mandated or permitted racial segregation in public education. Rather, the gravamen of this action, brought in June 1969 in the District Court for the District of Colorado by parents of Denver schoolchildren, is that respondent School Board alone, by use of various techniques such as the manipulation of student attendance zones, schoolsite selection and a neighborhood school policy, created or maintained racially or ethnically (or both racially and ethnically) segregated schools throughout the school district, entitling petitioners to a decree directing desegregation of the entire school district.

. . . .

. . . [W]here plaintiffs prove that the school authorities have carried out a systematic program of segregation affecting a substantial portion of the students, schools, teachers, and facilities within the school system, it is only common sense to conclude that there exists a predicate for a finding of the existence of a dual school system. Several considerations support this conclusion. First, it is obvious that a practice of concentrating Negroes in certain schools by structuring attendance zones or designating "feeder" schools on the basis of race has the reciprocal effect of keeping other nearby schools predominantly white. Similarly, the practice of building a school... to a certain size and in a certain location, "with conscious knowledge that it would be a segregated school," has a substantial reciprocal effect on the racial composition of other nearby schools. So also, the use of mobile classrooms, the drafting of student transfer policies, the transportation of students, and the assignment of faculty and staff, on racially identifiable bases, have the clear effect of earmarking schools according to their racial composition, and this, in turn, together with the elements of student assignment and school construction, may have a profound reciprocal effect on the racial composition of residential neighborhoods within a metropolitan area, thereby causing further racial concentration within the schools. . . .

. . . .

. . . [W]e hold that a finding of intentionally segregative school board actions in a meaningful portion of a school system, as in this case, creates a presumption that other segregated schooling within the system is not adventitious. It establishes, in other words, a prima facie case of unlawful segregative design on the part of school authorities, and shifts to those authorities the burden of proving that other segregated schools within the system are not also the result of intentionally segretative actions. This is true even if it is determined that different areas of the school district should be viewed independently of each other because, even in that situation, there is high probability that where school authorities have effectuated an intentionally segregative policy in a meaningful portion of the school system, similar impermissible considerations have motivated their actions in other areas of the system. We emphasize that the differentiating factor between *de jure* segregation and so-called *de facto* segregation to which we referred in *Swann* is *purpose* or *intent* to segregate. Where school authorities have been found to have practiced purposeful segregation in part of a school system, they may be expected to oppose system-wide desegregation, as did the respondents in this case, on the ground that their purposefully segregative actions were isolated and individual events, thus leaving plaintiffs with the burden of proving otherwise. But at that point where an intentionally segregative policy is practiced in a meaningful or significant segment of a school system, as in this case, the school authorities cannot be heard to argue that plaintiffs have proved only "isolated and individual" unlawfully segregative actions. In that circumstance, it is both fair and reasonable to require that the school authorities bear the burden of showing that their actions as to other segregated schools within the system were not also motivated by segregative intent.

. . . .

In discharging that burden, it is not enough, of course, that the school authorities rely upon some allegedly logical, racially neutral explanation for their actions. Their burden is to adduce proof sufficient to support a finding that segregative intent was not among the factors that motivated their actions. The courts below attributed much significance to the fact that many of the Board's actions in the core city area antedated our decision in *Brown*. We reject any suggestion that remoteness in time has any relevance to the issue of intent. If the actions of school authorities were to any degree motivated by segregative intent and the segregation resulting from those actions continues to exist, the fact of remoteness in time certainly does not make those actions any less "intentional."

This is not to say, however, that the prima facie case may not be met by evidence supporting a finding that a lesser degree of segregated schooling in the core city area would not have resulted even if the Board had not acted as it did. In *Swann*, we suggested that at some point in time the relationship between past segregative acts and present segregation may become so attenuated as to be incapable of supporting a finding of *de jure* segregation warranting judicial intervention. We made it clear, however, that a connection between past segregative acts and present segregation may be present even when not apparent and that close examination is required before concluding that the connection does not exist. Intentional school segregation in the past may have been a factor in creating a natural environment for the growth of further segregation. Thus, if respondent School Board cannot disprove segregative intent, it can rebut the prima facie case only by showing that its past segregative acts did not create or contribute to the current segregated condition of the core city schools.

The respondent School Board invoked at trial its "neighborhood school policy" as explaining racial and ethnic concentrations within the core city schools, arguing that since the core city area population had long been Negro and Hispanic, the concentrations were necessarily the result of residential patterns and not of purposefully segregative policies. We have no occasion to consider in this case whether a "neighborhood school policy" of itself will justify racial or ethnic concentrations in the absence of a finding that school authorities have committed acts constituting *de jure* segregation. It is enough that we hold that the mere assertion of such a policy is not dispositive where, as in this case, the school authorities have been found to have practiced *de jure* segregation in a meaningful portion of the school system by techniques that indicate that the *neighborhood school* concept has not been maintained free of manipulation. . . .

MR. JUSTICE WHITE took no part in the decision of this case.

MR. JUSTICE DOUGLAS [concurring, said in part]:

I think it is time to state that there is no constitutional difference between *de jure* and *de facto* segregation, for each is the product of state actions or policies. If a "neighborhood" or "geographical" unit has been created along racial lines by reason of the play of restrictive covenants that restrict certain areas to "the elite," leaving the "undesirables" to move elsewhere, there is state action in the constitutional sense because the force of law is placed behind those covenants.

There is state action in the constitutional sense when public funds are dispersed by urban development agencies to build racial ghettoes.

Where the school district is racially mixed and the races are segregated in separate schools, where black teachers are assigned almost exclusively to black schools, where the school board closed existing schools located in fringe areas and built new schools in black areas and in distant white areas, where the school board continued the "neighborhood" school policy at the elementary level, these actions constitute state action. They are of a kind quite distinct from the classical *de jure* type of school segregation. Yet calling them *de facto* is a misnomer, as they are only more subtle types of state action that create or maintain a wholly or partially segregated school system. . . .

When a State forces, aids, or abets, or helps create a racial "neighborhood," it is a travesty of justice to treat that neighborhood as sacrosanct in the sense that its creation is free from the taint of state action.

The Constitution and Bill of Rights have described the design of a pluralistic society. The individual has the right to seek such companions as he desires. But a State is barred from creating by one device or another ghettoes that determine the school one is compelled to attend.

MR. JUSTICE POWELL, concurring in part and dissenting in part.

The Court's decision today, while adhering to the *de jure/de facto* distinction, will require the application of the *Green/Swann* doctrine of "affirmative duty" to the Denver School Board despite the absence of any history of state-mandated school segregation. The only evidence of a constitutional violation was found in various decisions of the School Board. I concur in the Court's position that the public school authorities are the responsible agency of the State, and that if the affirmative-duty doctrine is sound constitutional law for Charlotte, it is equally so for Denver. I would not, however, perpetuate the *de jure/de facto* distinction nor would I leave to petitioners the initial tortuous effort of identifying "segregative acts" and deducing "segregative intent." I would hold, quite simply, that where segregated public schools exist within a school district to a substantial degree, there is a prima facie case that the duly constituted public authorities (I will usually refer to them collectively as the "school board") are sufficiently responsible to warrant imposing upon them a nationally applicable burden to demonstrate they nevertheless are operating a genuinely integrated school system.

The principal reason for abandonment of the *de jure/de facto* distinction is that, in view of the evolution of the holding in *Brown I* into the affirmative-duty doctrine, the distinction no longer can be justified on a principled basis. In decreeing remedial requirements for the Charlotte/Mecklenburg school district, *Swann* dealt with a metropolitan, urbanized area in which the basic causes of segregation were generally similar to those in all sections of the country, and also largely irrelevant to the existence of historic, state-imposed segregation at the time of the *Brown* decision. Further, the extension of the affirmative-duty concept to include compulsory student transportation went well beyond the mere remedying of that portion of school segregation for which former state segregation laws were ever responsible. Moreover, as the Court's opinion today abundantly demonstrates, the facts deemed necessary to establish *de jure* discrimination present problems of subjective intent which the courts cannot fairly resolve.

MR. JUSTICE REHNQUIST, dissenting.

. . . [T]he fact that invidious racial discrimination is prohibited by the Constitution in the North as well as the South must not be allowed to obscure the equally important fact that the consequences of manipulative drawing of attendance zones in a school district the size of Denver does not necessarily result in denial of equal protection to all minority students within that district. There are significant differences between the proof which would support a claim such as that alleged by plaintiffs in this case, and the total segregation required by statute which existed in *Brown*.

The Court's opinion obscures that factual differences between the situation shown by the record to have existed in Denver and the situations dealt with in earlier school desegregation opinions of the Court. . . .

. . . .

. . . [I]n a school district the size of Denver's, it is quite conceivable that the School Board might have engaged in the racial gerrymandering of the attendance boundary between two particular schools in order to keep one largely Negro and Hispanic, and the other largely Anglo, as the District Court found to have been the fact in this case. Such action would have deprived affected minority students who were the victims of such gerrymandering of their constitutional right to equal protection of the laws. But if the school board had been evenhanded in its drawing of the attendance lines for other schools in the district, minority students required to attend other schools within the district would have suffered no such deprivation. It certainly would not reflect normal English usage to describe the entire district as "segregated" on such a state of facts, and it would be a quite unprecedented application of principles of equitable relief to determine that if the gerrymandering of one attendance zone were proved, particular racial mixtures could be required by a federal district court for every school in the district.

It is quite possible, of course, that a school district purporting to adopt racially neutral boundary zones might, with respect to every such zone, invidiously discriminate against minorities, so as to produce substantially the same result as was produced by the statutorily decreed segregation involved in *Brown.* If that were the case, the consequences would necessarily have to be the same as were the consequences in *Brown.* But, in the absence of a statute requiring segregation, there must necessarily be the sort of factual inquiry which was unnecessary in those jurisdictions where racial mixing in the schools was forbidden by law.

Milliken v. Bradley

418 U.S. 717 (1974)
Vote: 5–4

As early as 1967, Judge Skelly Wright of the District of Columbia raised the possibility of a metropolitanwide remedy to overcome segregation in predominantly black communities (*Hobson v. Hansen,* 269 F. Supp. 401, 1967). In a comprehensive desegregation order for the District of Columbia, he noted the schools in that city were so heavily black that they could not be meaningfully integrated without involving some exchange with the predominantly white suburbs ringing the city. But Wright was deterred from such a remedy, no doubt because it would have challenged

fundamental aspects of federalism (metropolitan Washington consists of the District and communities in two states).

The metropolitanwide issue was again raised in the case below. Detroit, like Washington, is a city with a predominantly black school-age population, ringed by suburbs whose schools are predominantly white. But unlike Washington, an interdistrict remedy for Detroit would not clash with the principles of federalism. Indeed, since all units of local government are but creatures of the state, it might be argued that when violations of the Constitution are involved, there is no strong interest in respecting the integrity of local boundaries.

This case arose when, in response to a finding of de jure segregation in Detroit's schools, a district court ordered a metropolitanwide remedy that involved busing of students between Detroit and its neighboring school districts. When the issue reached the Supreme Court, a bare majority rejected the plan, arguing that the district court had exceeded its authority because there was no finding of any intent to segregate by officials in the suburban districts drawn into the court's plan. Detroit's remedy, it argued, must be restricted to the central city itself. Chief Justice Burger's opinion for a bare majority occasioned three sharp dissents, which challenge the majority's assertion that there was no finding of intent in the surrounding districts and go on to insist that it is the state and not the local districts that are responsible for educational policies. Why should this make a difference? Compare the majority's defense of local school districts here with the Court's treatment of local units of government in the reapportionment decisions. Are the two sets of decisions consistent? Can you distinguish between the two sets of issues?

Mr. Chief Justice Burger delivered the opinion of the Court.

We granted certiorari in these consolidated cases to determine whether a federal court may impose a multidistrict, areawide remedy to a single district *de jure* segregation problem absent any finding that the other included school districts have failed to operate unitary school systems within their districts, absent any claim or finding that the boundary lines of any affected school district were established with the purpose of fostering racial segregation in public schools, absent any finding that the included districts committed acts which effected segregation within the other districts, and absent a meaningful opportunity for the included neighboring school districts to present evidence or be heard on the propriety of a multidistrict remedy or on the question of constitutional violations by those neighboring districts.

. . . .

. . . In *Brown* v. *Board of Education,* 349 U.S. 294 (1955) (*Brown II*), the Court's first encounter with the problem of remedies in school desegregation cases, the Court noted that:

> In fashioning and effectuating the decrees the courts will be guided by equitable principles. Traditionally, equity has been characterized by a practical flexibility in shaping its remedies and by a facility for adjusting and reconciling public and private needs.

In further refining the remedial processes, *Swann* held, the task is to correct, by a balancing of the individual and collective interests, "the condition that offends the Constitution." A federal remedial power may be exercised "only on the basis of a constitutional violation" and, "[a]s with any equity case, the nature of the violation determines the scope of the remedy."

Proceeding from these basic principles, we first note that in the District Court the complaints sought a remedy aimed at the *condition* alleged to offend the Constitution — the segregation within the Detroit City school district. The court acted on this theory of the case and in its initial ruling on the "Desegregation Area" stated:

> The task before this court, therefore, is now, and . . . has always been, how to desegregate the Detroit public schools.

Thereafter, however, the District Court abruptly rejected the proposed Detroit-only plans on the ground that "while it would provide a racial mix more in keeping with the Black-White proportions of the student population, [it] would accentuate the racial identifiability of the [Detroit] district as a Black school system, and would not accomplish desegregation." . . . Accordingly, the District Court proceeded to redefine the relevant area to include areas of predominantly white pupil population in order to ensure that "upon implementation, no school, grade or classroom [would be] substantially disproportionate to the overall racial composition" of the entire metropolitan area.

While specifically acknowledging that the District Court's findings of a condition of segregation were limited to Detroit, the Court of Appeals approved the use of a metropolitan remedy. . . .

Viewing the record as a whole, it seems clear that the District Court and the Court of Appeals shifted the primary focus from a Detroit remedy to the metropolitan area only because of their conclusion that total desegregation of Detroit would not produce the racial balance which they perceived as desirable. Both courts proceeded on an assumption that the Detroit schools could not be truly desegregated — in their view of what constituted desegregation — unless the racial composition of the student body of each school substantially reflected the racial composition of the population of the metropolitan area as a whole. The metropolitan area was then defined as Detroit plus 53 of the outlying school districts. . . .

Here the District Court's approach to what constituted "actual desegregation" raises the fundamental question, not presented in *Swann,* as to the circumstances in which a federal court may order desegregation relief that embraces more than a single school district. The court's analytical starting point was its conclusion that school district lines are no more than arbitrary lines on a map "drawn for political convenience." Boundary lines may be bridged where there has been a constitutional violation calling for interdistrict relief, but, the notion that school district lines may be casually ignored or treated as a mere administrative convenience is contrary to the history of public education in our country. No single tradition in public education is more deeply rooted than local control over the operation of schools; local autonomy has long been thought essential both to the maintenance of community concern and support for public schools and to the quality of the educational process. Thus, in *San Antonio School District* v. *Rodriguez* [1973], we observed that local control over the educational process affords citizens an opportunity to participate in decision-making, permits the structuring of school programs to fit local needs, and encourages "experimentation, innovation and a healthy competition for educational excellence." . . .

. . . .

The controlling principle consistently expounded in our holdings is that the scope of the remedy is determined by the nature and extent of the constitutional violation. Before the boundaries of separate and autonomous school districts may be set aside by consolidating the separate units for remedial purposes or by imposing a cross-district remedy, it must first be shown that there has been a constitutional violation within one district that produces a significant segregative effect in another district. Specifically it must be shown that racially discriminatory acts of the state or local school districts, or of a single school district have been a substantial cause of inter-district segregation. Thus an inter-district remedy might be in order where the racially discriminatory acts of one or more school districts caused racial segregation in an adjacent district, or where district lines have been deliberately drawn on the basis of race. In such circumstances an inter-district remedy would be appropriate to eliminate the inter-district segregation directly caused by the constitutional violation. Conversely, without an inter-district violation and inter-district effect, there is no constitutional wrong calling for an inter-district remedy.

The record before us, voluminous as it is, contains evidence of *de jure* segregated conditions only in the Detroit schools; indeed, that was the theory on which the litigation was initially based and on which the District Court took evidence. With no showing of significant violation by the 53 outlying school districts and no evidence of any inter-district violation or effect, the court went beyond the original theory of the case as framed by the pleadings and mandated a metropolitan area remedy. To approve the remedy ordered by the court would impose on the outlying districts, not shown to have committed any constitutional violation, a wholly impermissible remedy based on a standard not hinted at in *Brown I* and *II* or any holding of this Court.

. . . .

The constitutional right of the Negro respondents residing in Detroit is to attend a unitary school system in that district. Unless petitioners drew the district lines in a discriminatory fashion, or arranged for White students residing in the Detroit district to attend schools in Oakland and Macomb Counties, they were under no constitutional duty to make provisions for Negro students to do so. The view of the dissenters, that the existence of a dual system *in Detroit* can be made the basis for a decree requiring cross-district transportation of pupils cannot be supported on the grounds that it represents merely the devising of a suitably flexible remedy for the violation of rights already established by our prior decisions. It can be supported only by drastic expansion of the constitutional right itself, an expansion without any support in either constitutional principle or precedent.

. . . .

We conclude that the relief ordered by the District Court and affirmed by the Court of Appeals was based upon an erroneous standard and was unsupported by record evidence that acts of the outlying districts affected the discrimination found to exist in the schools of Detroit. Accordingly, the judgment of the Court of Appeals is vacated and the case is remanded for further proceedings consistent with this opinion leading to prompt formulation of a decree directed to eliminating the segregation found to exist in Detroit city schools, a remedy which has been delayed since 1970.

Reversed and remanded.

[MR. JUSTICE STEWART wrote a concurring opinion.]

MR. JUSTICE DOUGLAS, dissenting.

The Court of Appeals has acted responsibly in these cases and we should affirm its judgment. This was the fourth time the case was before it over a span of less than three years. The Court of Appeals affirmed the District Court on the issue of segregation and on the "Detroit-only" plans of desegregation. The Court of Appeals also approved in principle the use of a metropolitan area plan, vacating and remanding only to allow the other affected school districts to be brought in as parties and in other minor respects.

. . . .

When we rule against the metropolitan area remedy we take a step that will likely put the problems of the Blacks and our society back to the period that antedated the "separate but equal" regime of *Plessy* v. *Ferguson*. The reason is simple.

The inner core of Detroit is now rather solidly black; and the blacks, we know, in many instances are likely to be poorer, just as were the Chicanos in *San Antonio Independent School District* v. *Rodriguez*. By that decision the poorer school districts must pay their own way. It is therefore a foregone conclusion that we have now given the States a formula whereby the poor must pay their own way.

Today's decision given *Rodriguez* means that there is no violation of the Equal Protection Clause though the schools are segregated by race and though the Black schools are not only "separate" but "inferior."

So far as equal protection is concerned we are now in a dramatic retreat from the 8-to-1 decision in 1896 that Blacks could be segregated in public facilities provided they received equal treatment.

MR. JUSTICE WHITE, with whom MR. JUSTICE DOUGLAS, MR. JUSTICE BRENNAN, and MR. JUSTICE MARSHALL join, dissenting.

Regretfully, and for several reasons, I can join neither the Court's judgment nor its opinion. The core of my disagreement is that deliberate acts of segregation and their consequences will go unremedied, not because a remedy would be infeasible or unreasonable in terms of the usual criteria governing school desegregation cases, but because an effective remedy would cause what the Court considers to be undue administrative inconvenience to the State. The result is that the State of Michigan, the entity at which the Fourteenth Amendment is directed, has successfully insulated itself from its duty to provide effective desegregation remedies by vesting sufficient power over its public schools in its local school districts. If this is the case in Michigan, it will be the case in most States.

I am surprised that the Court, sitting at this distance from the State of Michigan, claims better insight than the Court of Appeals and the District Court as to whether an interdistrict remedy for equal protection violations practiced by the State of Michigan would involve undue difficulties for the State in the management of its public schools. In the area of what constitutes an acceptable desegregation plan, "we must of necessity rely to a large extent, as this Court has for more than 16 years, on the informed judgment of the district courts in the first instance and on courts of appeals." Obviously, whatever difficulties there might be, they are surmountable; for the Court itself concedes that had there been sufficient evidence of an interdistrict violation, the District Court could have fashioned a single remedy for the districts implicated rather than a different remedy for each district in which the violation had occurred or had an impact.

I am even more mystified how the Court can ignore the legal reality that the constitutional violations, even if occurring locally, were committed by governmental entities for which the State is responsible and that it is the State that must respond to the command of the Fourteenth Amendment. An interdistrict remedy for the infringements that occurred in this case is well within the confines and powers of the State, which is the governmental entity ultimately responsible for desegregating its schools. . . .

Until today, the permissible contours of the equitable authority of the district courts to remedy the unlawful establishment of a dual school system have been extensive, adaptable, and fully responsive to the ultimate goal of achieving "the greatest possible degree of actual desegregation." There are indeed limitations on the equity powers of the federal judiciary, but until now the Court has not accepted the proposition that effective enforcement of the Fourteenth Amendment could be limited by political or administrative boundary lines demarcated by the very State responsible for the constitutional violation and for the disestablishment of the dual system. Un-

til now the Court has instead looked to practical considerations in effectuating a desegregation decree, such as excessive distance, transportation time and hazards to the safety of the school children involved in a proposed plan. That these broad principles have developed in the context of dual school systems compelled or authorized by state statute at the time of *Brown* v. *Board of Education,* does not lessen their current applicability to dual systems found to exist in other contexts, like that in Detroit, where intentional school segregation does not stem from the compulsion of state law, but from deliberate individual actions of local and state school authorities directed at a particular school system. . . .

The result reached by the Court certainly cannot be supported by the theory that the configuration of local governmental units is immune from alteration when necessary to redress constitutional violations. In addition to the well-established principles already noted, the Court has elsewhere required the public bodies of a State to restructure the State's political subdivisions to remedy infringements of the constitutional rights of certain members of its populace, notably in the reapportionment cases. . . .

MR. JUSTICE MARSHALL, with whom MR. JUSTICE DOUGLAS, MR. JUSTICE BRENNAN, and MR. JUSTICE WHITE join, dissenting.

In *Brown* v. *Board of Education* (1954), this Court held that segregation of children in public schools on the basis of race deprives minority group children of equal educational opportunities and therefore denies them the equal protection of the laws under the Fourteenth Amendment. This Court recognized then that remedying decades of segregation of public education would not be an easy task. Subsequent events, unfortunately, have seen that prediction bear bitter fruit. But however imbedded old ways, however ingrained old prejudices, this Court has not been diverted from its appointed task of making "a living truth" of our constitutional ideal of equal justice under law. *Cooper* v. *Aaron* (1958).

After 20 years of small, often difficult steps toward that great end, the Court today takes a giant step backwards. Notwithstanding a record showing widespread and pervasive racial segregation in the educational system provided by the State of Michigan for children in Detroit, this Court holds that the District Court was powerless to require the State to remedy its constitutional violation in any meaningful fashion. Ironically purporting to base its result on the principle that the scope of the remedy in a desegregation case should be determined by the nature and the extent of the constitutional violation, the Court's answer is to provide no remedy at all for the violation proved in this case, thereby guaranteeing that Negro children in Detroit will receive the same separate and inherently unequal education in the future as they have been unconstitutionally afforded in the past.

I cannot subscribe to this emasculation of our constitutional guarantee of equal protection of the laws and must respectfully dissent. Our precedents, in my view, firmly establish that where, as here, state-imposed segregation has been demonstrated, it becomes the duty of the State to eliminate root and branch all vestiges of racial discrimination and to achieve the greatest possible degree of actual desegregation. I agree with both the District Court and the Court of Appeals that, under the facts of this case, this duty cannot be fulfilled unless the State of Michigan involves outlying metropolitan area school districts in its desegregation remedy. Furthermore, I perceive no basis either in law or in the practicalities of the situation justifying the State's interposition of school district boundaries as absolute barriers to the implementation of an effective desegregation remedy. Under established and frequently used Michigan procedures, school district lines are both flexible and permeable for a wide variety of purposes, and there is no reason why they must now stand in the way of meaningful desegregation relief.

The rights at issue in this case are too fundamental to be abridged on grounds as superficial as those relied on by the majority today. We deal here with the right of all of our children, whatever their race, to an equal start in life and to an equal opportunity to reach their full potential as citizens. Those children who have been denied that right in the past deserve better than to see fences thrown up to deny them that right in the future. Our Nation, I fear, will be ill-served by the Court's refusal to remedy separate and unequal education, for unless our children begin to learn together, there is little hope that our people will ever learn to live together.

... [T]he district Court's decision to expand its desegregation decree beyond the geographical limits of the city of Detroit rested in large part on its conclusions (A) that the State of Michigan was ultimately responsible for curing the condition of segregation within the Detroit city schools, and (B) that a Detroit-only remedy would not accomplish this task. In my view, both of these conclusions are well supported by the facts of this case and by this Court's precedents.

... Adequate desegregation of the Detroit system was also hampered by discriminatory restrictions placed by the State on the use of transportation within Detroit. While state aid for transportation was provided by statute for suburban districts, many of which were highly urbanized, aid for intra-city transportation was excepted. One of the effects of this restriction was to encourage the construction of small walk-in neighborhood schools in Detroit, thereby lending aid to the intentional policy of creating a school system which reflected, to the greatest extent feasible, extensive residential segregation. Indeed, that one of the purposes of the transportation restriction was to impede desegregation was evidenced when the Michigan Legislature amended the State Transportation Aid Act to cover intra-city transportation but expressly prohibited the allocation of funds for cross busing of students within a school district to achieve racial balance.

Washington et al. v. Davis et al.

426 U.S. 229 (1976)
Vote: 7–2

This case deals with employment personnel tests; yet there is an obvious and important connection with the education cases in this section. Like SWANN, KEYES, and MILLIKEN, cases already discussed, and PASADENA V. SPANGLER and COLUMBUS V. PENICK, which follow, this case wrestles with the intent/effects controversy, with the conditions under which the balance of proof shifts, and with the duration and scope of remedial actions. After reading this and the following two cases, PASADENA and COLUMBUS, ask yourself if there is a consistent thread in the Court's rulings from SWANN through COLUMBUS. If so, what is it?

This case arose when two men, both black, whose applications to become police officers in the District of Columbia had been rejected, brought suit against the District and city officials, claiming that the Police Department's recruiting procedures were racially discriminatory and violated the Fifth Amendment's Due Process Clause. Specifically, they argued that the standard personnel test, Test 21, generally administered to prospective government employees to determine levels of verbal skills, bore no relationship to job performance and excluded a disproportionately high number of black applicants.

The district court, noting the absence of any claim of intentional discrimination, went on to find that: (1) while substantial, the number of black police officers in the District was not proportionate to the city's population; (2) a higher percentage of blacks failed the test than whites; and (3) the test had not been validated to establish its reliability for measuring subsequent job performance. These findings, the district court ruled, were sufficient to shift the burden of proof of the reasonableness of the test to city officials. Having done this, the district court went on to consider the city's arguments in favor of the test: 44 percent of the new police officers recruited with Test 21 were black, a figure equal to the number of 20- to 29-year-old blacks in the recruiting area. Experts testified that the test was in fact a useful indicator of training school performance, one that neither intentionally nor unintentionally discriminated against otherwise qualified blacks. In light of this, the Court granted a summary judgment in favor of the city.

The court of appeals reversed and directed summary judgment in favor of the unsuccessful job applicants. In doing so, it applied the standards enunciated by the Supreme Court in *Griggs* v. *Duke Power Co.,* 401 U.S. 242 (1971), which had rejected another personnel test because it conflicted with Title VII of the Civil Rights Act of 1964. In *Griggs* the Court construed Title VII to prohibit the use of personnel tests that operate to exclude members of minority groups, unless the employer demonstrates that such tests are "substantially related to job performance." Although this case did not raise Title VII issues, the court of appeals was guided by prior Title VII rulings and held that the lack of discriminatory intent in the enactment and administration of Test 21 was irrelevant; the critical fact was that four times as many blacks as whites failed the test. Such disproportionate effects, it ruled, was sufficient to establish a constitutional violation. Washington, D.C. officials petitioned the Supreme Court for a writ of certiorari.

MR. JUSTICE WHITE delivered the opinion of the Court.

Because the Court of Appeals erroneously applied the legal standards applicable to Title VII cases in resolving the constitutional issue before it, we reverse its judgment in respondents' favor....

As the Court of Appeals understood Title VII, employees or applicants proceeding under it need not concern themselves with the employer's possibly discriminatory purpose but instead may focus solely on the racially differential impact of the challenged hiring or promotion practices. This is not the constitutional rule. We have never held that the constitutional standard for adjudicating claims of invidious racial discrimination is identical to the standards applicable under Title VII, and we decline to do so today.

The central purpose of the Equal Protection Clause of the Fourteenth Amendment is the prevention of official conduct discriminating on the basis of race. It is also true that the Due Process Clause of the Fifth Amendment contains an equal protection component prohibiting the United States from invidiously discriminating between individuals or groups. *Bolling* v. *Sharpe* ... (1954). But our cases have not embraced the proposition that a law or other official act, without regard to whether it reflects a racially discriminatory purpose, is unconstitutional *solely* because it has a racially disproportionate impact.

Almost 100 years ago, *Strauder* v. *West Virginia,* ... (1880), established that the exclusion of Negroes from grand and petit juries in criminal proceedings violated the Equal Protection Clause, but the fact that a particular jury or a series of juries does not statistically reflect the racial composition of the community does not in itself make out an invidious discrimination forbidden by the Clause. "A purpose to discriminate must be present which may be proven by systematic exclusion of eligible jurymen of the proscribed race or by unequal application of the law to such an extent as to show intentional discrimination." ... A defendant in a criminal case is entitled "to require that the State not deliberately and systematically deny to members of his race the right to participate as jurors in the administration of justice." ...

The rule is the same in other contexts. *Wright* v. *Rockefeller,* (1964), upheld a New York congressional apportionment statute against claims that district lines had been racially gerrymandered. The challenged districts were made up predominantly of whites or of minority races, and their boundaries were irregularly drawn. The challengers did not prevail because they failed to prove that the New York Legislature "was either motivated by racial considerations or in fact drew the districts on racial lines"; the plaintiffs had not shown that the statute "was the product of a state contrivance to segregate on the basis of race or place of origin."... The dissenters were in agreement that the issue was whether the "boundaries... were purposefully drawn on racial lines."...

The school desegregation cases have also adhered to the basic equal protection principle that the invidious quality of a law claimed to be racially discriminatory must ultimately be traced to a racially discriminatory purpose. That there are both predominantly black and predominantly white schools in a community is not alone violative of the Equal Protection Clause. The essential element of *de jure* segregation is "a current condition of segregation resulting from intentional state action." *Keyes* v. *School Dist. No. 1*... (1973). "The differentiating factor between *de jure* segregation and so-called *de facto* segregation... is *purpose* or *intent* to segregate."... The Court has also recently rejected allegations of racial discrimination based solely on the statistically disproportionate racial impact of various provisions of the Social Security Act because "[t]he acceptance of appellants' constitutional theory would render suspect each difference in treatment among the grant classes, however lacking in racial motivation and however otherwise rational the treatment might be." *Jefferson* v. *Hackney* (1972)....

This is not to say that the necessary discriminatory racial purpose must be express or appear on the face of the statute, or that a law's disproportionate impact is irrelevant in cases involving Constitution-based claims of racial discrimination. A statute, otherwise neutral on its face, must not be applied so as invidiously to discriminate on the basis of race. *Yick Wo* v. *Hopkins*... (1886). It is also clear from the cases dealing with racial discrimination in the selection of juries that the systematic exclusion of Negroes is itself such an "unequal application of the law... as to show intentional discrimination."... A prima facie case of discriminatory purpose may be proved as well by the absence of Negroes on a particular jury combined with the failure of the jury commissioners to be informed of eligible Negro jurors in a community... or with racially nonneutral selection procedures.... Within a prima facie case made out, "the burden of proof shifts to the State to rebut the presumption of unconstitutional action by showing that permissible racially neutral selection criteria and procedures have produced the monochromatic result."...

Necessarily, an invidious discriminatory purpose may often be inferred from the totality of the relevant facts, including the fact, if it is true, that the law bears more heavily on one race than another. It is also not infrequently true that the discriminatory impact — in the jury cases for example, the total or seriously disproportionate exclusion of Negroes from jury venires — may for all practical purposes demonstrate unconstitutionality because in various circumstances the discrimination is very difficult to explain on nonracial grounds. Nevertheless, we have not held that a law, neutral on its face and serving ends otherwise within the power of government to pursue, is invalid under the Equal Protection Clause simply because it may affect a greater proportion of one race than of another. Disproportionate impact is not irrelevant, but it is not the sole touchstone of an invidious racial discrimination forbidden by the Constitution. Standing alone, it does not trigger the rule... that racial classifications are to be subjected to the strictest scrutiny and are justifiable only by the weightiest of considerations.

There are some indications to the contrary in our cases. In *Palmer* v. *Thompson*... (1971), the city of Jackson, Miss., followed a court decree to this effect, desegregated all of its public facilities save five swimming pools which had been operated by the city and which, following the decree, were closed by ordinance pursuant to a determination by the city council that closure was necessary to preserve peace and order and that integrated pools could not be economically operated. Accepting the finding that the pools were closed to avoid violence and economic loss, this Court rejected the argument that the abandonment of this service was inconsistent with the outstanding desegregation decree and that the otherwise seemingly permissible ends served by the ordinance could be impeached by demonstrating that racially invidious motivations had prompted the city council's action. The holding was that the city was not overtly or covertly operating segregated pools and was extending identical treatment to both whites and Negroes. The opinion warned against grounding decision on legislative purpose or motivation, thereby lending support for the proposition that the operative effect of the law rather than its purpose is the paramount factor. But the holding of the case was that the legitimate purpose of the ordinance — to preserve peace and avoid deficits — were not open to impeachment by evidence that the councilmen were actually motivated by racial considerations. Whatever dicta the opinion may contain, the decision did not involve, much less invalidate, a statute or ordinance having neutral purposes but disproportionate racial consequences.

....

Both before and after *Palmer* v. *Thompson*, however, various Courts of Appeals have held in several contexts, including public employment, that the substantially disproportionate racial impact of a statute or official practice standing alone and without regard to discriminatory purpose, suffices to prove racial discrimination violating the Equal Protection Clause absent some justification going substantially beyond what would be necessary to validate most other legislative classifications. The cases impressively demonstrate that there is another side to the issue; but, with all due respect, to the extent that those cases rested on or expressed the view that proof of discriminatory racial purpose is unnecessary in making out an equal protection violation, we are in disagreement.

As an initial matter, we have difficulty understanding how a law establishing a racially neutral qualification for employment is nevertheless racially discriminatory and denies "any person... equal protection of the laws" simply because a greater proportion of Negroes fail to qualify than members of other racial or ethnic groups. Had respondents, along with all others who had failed Test 21, whether white or black, brought an action claiming that the test denied each of them equal protection of the laws as compared with those who had passed with high enough scores to qualify them as police recruits, it is most unlikely that their challenge would have been sustained. Test 21, which is administered generally to prospective Government employees, concededly seeks to ascertain whether those who take it have acquired a particular level of verbal skill; and it is untenable that the Constitution prevents the Government from seeking modestly to upgrade the communicative abilities of its employees rather than to be satisfied with some lower level of competence, particularly where the job requires special ability to communicate orally and in writing. Respondents, as Negroes, could no more successfully claim that the test denied them equal protection than could white applicants who also failed. The conclusion would not be different in the face of proof that more Negroes than whites had been disqualified by Test 21. That other Negroes also failed to score well would, alone, not demonstrate that respondents individually were being denied equal protection of the laws by the application of an otherwise valid qualifying test being administered to prospective police recruits.

Nor on the facts of the case before us would the disproportionate impact of Test 21 warrant the conclusion that it is a purposeful device to discriminate against Negroes and hence an infringement of the constitutional rights of respondents as well as other black applicants. As we have said, the test is neutral on its face and rationally may be said to serve a purpose the Government is constitutionally empowered to pursue. Even agreeing with the District Court that the differential racial effect of Test 21 called for further inquiry, we think the District Court correctly held that the affirmative efforts of the Metropolitan Police Department to recruit black officers, the changing racial composition of the recruit classes and of the force in general, and the relationship of the test to the training program negated any inference that the Department discriminated on the basis of race or that "a police officer qualifies on the color of his skin rather than ability." 348 F. Supp., at 18.

Under Title VII, Congress provided that when hiring and promotion practices disqualifying substantially disproportionate numbers of blacks are challenged, discriminatory purpose need not be proved, and that it is an insufficient response to demonstrate some rational basis for the challenged practices. It is necessary, in addition, that they be "validated" in terms of job performance in any one of several ways, perhaps by ascertaining the minimum skill, ability, or potential necessary for the position at issue and determining whether the qualifying tests are appropriate for the selection of qualified applicants for the job in question. However this process proceeds, it involves a more probing judicial review of, and less deference to, the seemingly reasonable acts of administrators and executives than is appropriate under the Constitution where special racial impact, without discriminatory purpose, is claimed. We are not disposed to adopt this more rigorous standard for the purposes of applying the Fifth and the Fourteenth Amendments in cases such as this.

A rule that a statute designed to serve neutral ends is nevertheless invalid, absent compelling justification, if in practice it benefits or burdens one race more than another would be far reaching and would raise serious questions about, and perhaps invalidate, a whole range of tax, welfare, public service, regulatory, and licensing statutes that may be more burdensome to the poor and to the average black than to the more affluent white.

Given that rule, such consequences would perhaps be likely to follow. However, in our view, extension of the rule beyond those areas where it is already applicable by reason of statute, such as in the field of public employment, should await legislative prescription.

. . . .

The judgment of the Court of Appeals accordingly is
Reversed.

[MR. JUSTICE STEWART concurred.]

[MR. JUSTICE STEVENS wrote a concurring opinion.]

[MR. JUSTICE BRENNAN, joined by MR. JUSTICE MARSHALL, wrote a dissenting opinion.]

Pasadena City Board of Education v. Spangler

427 U.S. 424 (1976)
Vote: 6–2

In 1968, students and parents in Pasadena, California, brought suit against officials seeking relief from allegedly unconstitutional segregation in the public schools. In 1970, the district court found in their favor and ordered the school board to submit desegregation plans that, among other things, would assure that there would be no school "with a majority of minority students." This plan, known as the "Pasadena Plan," was subsequently submitted to and approved by the court. In 1974, school officials asked the district court to eliminate the "no majority" provision of the order, arguing that they had complied with the order during school year 1970–71, and that subsequent resegregation that appeared to be inconsistent with the order was due to private patterns of relocation, factors for which neither the school board nor the Plan were responsible.

The district court denied this request, finding that the school district had complied with the "no majority" provision only during the Plan's first year, and that it had not complied fully with other portions of the Plan regarding desegregation of administration and faculties. This judgment was affirmed by a divided court of appeals, whereupon the school board successfully petitioned the Supreme Court for a writ of certiorari.

MR. JUSTICE REHNQUIST delivered the opinion of the Court.

We do not have before us any issue as to the validity of the District Court's original judgment, since petitioners' predecessors did not appeal from it. . . . All that is now before us are the questions of whether the District Court was correct in denying relief when petitioners in 1974 sought to modify the "no majority" requirements as then interpreted by the District Court.

. . . .

When the District Court's order in this case, as interpreted and applied by that court, is measured against what this Court said in its intervening decision in *Swann* v. *Board of Education* . . . (1971), regarding the scope of the judicially created relief which might be available to remedy violations of the Fourteenth Amendment, we think the inconsistency between the two is clear. The District Court's interpretation of the order appears to contemplate the "substantive constitutional right [to a] particular degree of racial balance or mixing" which the Court in *Swann* expressly disapproved. It became apparent, at least by the time of the 1974 hearing, that the District Court viewed this portion of its order not merely as a "starting point in the process of shaping a remedy," which *Swann* indicated would be appropriate, but instead as an "inflexible requirement," to be applied anew each year to the school population within the attendance zone of each school.

The District Court apparently believed it had authority to impose this requirement even though subsequent changes in the racial mix in the Pasadena schools might be caused by factors for which the defendants could not be considered responsible. Whatever may have been the basis for such a belief in 1970, in *Swann* the Court cautioned that "it must be recognized that there are limits" beyond which a court may not go in seeking to dismantle a dual school system. These limits are in part tied to the necessity of establishing that school authorities have in some manner caused unconstitutional segregation, for "[a]bsent a constitutional violation there would be no basis for judicially ordering assignment of students on a racial basis." While the District Court found such a violation in 1970, and while this unappealed finding afforded a basis for its initial requirement that the defendants prepare a plan to remedy such racial segregation, its adoption of the Pasadena Plan in 1970 established a racially neutral system of student assignment in the PUSD. Having done that, we think that in enforcing its order so as to require annual readjustment of attendance zones so that there would not be a majority of any minority in any Pasadena public school, the District Court exceeded its authority.

. . . .

There was also no showing in this case that those post-1971 changes in the racial mix of some Pasadena schools which were focused upon by the lower courts were in any manner caused by segregative actions chargeable to the defendants. The District

Court rejected petitioners' assertion that the movement was caused by so-called "white flight" traceable to the decree itself. It stated that the "trends evidenced in Pasadena closely approximate the state-wide trends in California schools, both segregated and desegregated." The fact that black student enrollment at 5 out of 32 of the regular Pasadena schools came to exceed 50% during the 4-year period from 1970 to 1974 apparently resulted from people randomly moving into, out of, and around the PUSD area. This quite normal pattern of human migration resulted in some changes in the demographics of Pasadena's residential patterns, with resultant shifts in the racial makeup of some of the schools. But as these shifts were not attributed to any segregative actions on the part of the petitioners, we think this case comes squarely within the sort of situation foreseen in *Swann:*

> It does not follow that the communities served by [unitary] systems will remain demographically stable, for in a growing, mobile society, few will do so. Neither school authorities nor district courts are constitutionally required to make year-by-year adjustments of the racial composition of student bodies once the affirmative duty to desegregate has been accomplished and racial discrimination through official action is eliminated from the system.

It may well be that petitioners have not yet totally achieved the unitary system contemplated by this quotation from *Swann.* There has been, for example, dispute as to the petitioners' compliance with those portions of the plan specifying procedures for hiring and promoting teachers and administrators. But that does not undercut the force of the principle underlying the quoted language from *Swann.* In this case the District Court approved a plan designed to obtain racial neutrality in the attendance of students at Pasadena's public schools. No one disputes that the initial implementation of this plan accomplished *that* objective. That being the case, the District Court was not entitled to require the PUSD to rearrange its attendance zones each year so as to ensure that the racial mix desired by the court was maintained in perpetuity. For having once implemented a racially neutral attendance pattern in order to remedy the perceived constitutional violations on the part of the defendants, the District Court had fully performed its function of providing the appropriate remedy for previous racially discriminatory attendance patterns.

MR. JUSTICE STEVENS took no part in the consideration or decision of this case.

MR. JUSTICE MARSHALL, with whom MR. JUSTICE BRENNAN joins, dissenting.

I cannot agree with the Court that the District Court's refusal to modify the "no majority of any minority" provision of its order was erroneous. Because at the time of the refusal "racial discrimination through official action" . . . had apparently not yet been eliminated from the Pasadena school system, it is my view that the District Court did not abuse its discretion in refusing to dissolve a major part of its order.

. . . .

The Court's conclusion that modification of the District Court's order is mandated is apparently largely founded on the fact that during the Pasadena Plan's first year, its implementation did result in no school's having a majority of minority students. According to the Court, it follows from our decision in *Swann, supra,* that as soon as the school attendance zone scheme had been successful, even for a very short period, in fulfilling its objectives, the District Court should have relaxed its supervision over that aspect of the desegregation plan. It is irrelevant to the Court that the system may not have achieved "'unitary' status in all other respects such as the hiring and promoting of teachers and administrators."

In my view, the Court, in so ruling, has unwarrantedly extended our statement in *Swann* that "[n]either school authorities nor district courts are constitutionally required to make year-by-year adjustments of the racial composition of student bodies *once the affirmative duty to desegregate has been accomplished and racial discrimination through official action is eliminated from the system.*" That statement recognizes on the one hand that a fully desegregated school system may not be compelled to adjust its attendance zones to conform to changing demographic patterns. But on the other hand, it also appears to recognize that *until* such a unitary system is established, a district court may act with broad discretion — discretion which includes the adjustment of attendance zones — so that the goal of a wholly unitary system might be sooner achieved.

In insisting that the District Court largely abandon its scrutiny of attendance patterns, the Court might well be insuring that a unitary school system in which segregation has been eliminated "root and branch," *Green* v. *County School Board . . .* (1968), will never be achieved in Pasadena. For at the point that the Pasadena system is in compliance with the aspects of the plan specifying procedures for hiring and promoting teachers and administrators, it may be that the attendance patterns within the system will be such as to once again manifest substantial aspects of a segregated system. It seems to me singularly unwise for the Court to risk such a result.

We have held that "[o]nce a right and a violation have been shown, the scope of a district court's equitable powers to remedy past wrongs is broad, for breadth and flexibility are inherent in equitable remedies." *Swann* v. *Board of Education*. As the Court recognizes, there is no issue before us as to the validity of the District Court's original judgment that unconstitutional segregation existed in the Pasadena school system. Thus there is no question as to there being both a "right and a violation." Moreover, at least as of the time that the District Court acted on the request for modification, the violation had not yet been entirely remedied. Particularly, given the breadth of discretion normally accorded a district court in fashioning equitable remedies, I see no reason to require the District Court in a case such as this to modify its order prior to the time that it is clear that the entire violation has been remedied and a unitary system has been achieved. We should not compel the District Court to modify its order unless conditions have changed so much that "dangers, once substantial, have become attenuated to a shadow." I, for one, cannot say that the District Court was in error in determining that such attenuation had not yet taken place and that modification of the order would "surely be to sign the death warrant of the Pasadena Plan and its objectives." Accordingly, I dissent.

Columbus Board of Education v. Penick

443 U.S. 449 (1979)
Vote: 7–2

In 1976, 32 percent of the school population in Columbus, Ohio, was black, and 70 percent of the students in the citywide district attended schools that were either 80 percent or more black or white. This was challenged as unconstitutional by minority students and parents. After lengthy hearings, the federal district court ruled that the public schools in Columbus were "openly and intentionally segregated on the basis of race" as of 1954, when BROWN V. BOARD OF EDUCATION was decided, and that since then the school board had failed to take enough measures to eliminate that segregation. The district court further found that the school board had responded to a growing school-age population in Columbus since the 1950s by adjusting its policies and locating new schools in such a way as to foster continued segregation. It found that the board had "approved optional attendance zones, discontiguous attendance areas and boundary changes which have maintained and enhanced racial imbalance," and concluded that segregation in the Columbus schools resulted directly from "intentional segregative *acts and omissions*" in violation of the Equal Protection Clause (emphasis added).

One issue in this case is how active a school board must be in combating racial segregation if it is to avoid being in violation of the Constitution. On this point the district court found that the board had not been active enough. Of the 103 schools built by the board between 1950 and 1975, eighty-seven opened with "racially identifiable" student bodies and seventy-one remained that way as of the mid-1970s. "This result," the district court continued, "was reasonably forseeable under the circumstances in light of the sites selected, and the [fact that] the Board was repeatedly warned that it was, without apparent justification, choosing sites that would maintain or foster segregation." The district court drew "the inference of segregative intent from the Columbus defendants' failures, after notice, to consider predictable racial consequences of their acts and omissions when alternatives were available which would have eliminated or lessened racial imbalance."

The school board maintained that the 1954 date seized upon by the district court was arbitrary, that its site selection policies were based upon racially neutral criteria, and that the segregation found in the city's schools was due to housing patterns beyond the responsibility of the school board.

After losing in the district court, Columbus challenged, in the court of appeals, the district court's standard for finding "segregative intent," arguing that inferences drawn from attendance figures, and not from demonstration of purposeful or intentional actions, obliterated the distinction between de jure and de facto segregation. For all practical purposes, this meant that any segregation, regardless of cause, would be sufficient evidence from which to infer unconstitutional intent. This, the board argued, was inconsistent with the prior rulings of the Supreme Court. What once required proof, it maintained, was now true by definition; the district court's standard put them in an impossible position.

Notwithstanding this complaint, the Supreme Court upheld the rulings of the lower courts. After reading this case, ask what it would take for the Columbus school board to successfully demonstrate that it was no longer segregating its students by race.

MR. JUSTICE WHITE delivered the opinion of the Court.

... [W]e cannot fault the conclusion of the District Court and the Court of Appeals that at the time of trial there was systemwide segregation in the Columbus schools that was the result of recent and remote intentionally segregative actions of the Columbus Board. While appearing not to challenge most of the subsidiary findings of historical fact, ... petitioners dispute many of the factual inferences drawn from these facts by the two courts below. On this record, however, there is no apparent reason to disturb the factual findings and conclusions entered by the District Court and strongly affirmed by the Court of Appeals after its own examination of the record.

Nor do we discern that the judgments entered below rested on any misapprehension of the controlling law. It is urged that the courts below failed to heed the requirements of *Keyes, Washington* v. *Davis* ... (1976), and *Arlington Heights* v. *Metropolitan Housing Dev. Corp.* ... (1977), that a plaintiff seeking to make out an equal protection violation on the basis of racial discrimination must show purpose. Both courts, it is argued, considered the requirement satisfied if it were shown that disparate impact would be the natural and foreseeable consequence of the practices and policies of the Board, which, it is said, is nothing more than equating impact with intent, contrary to the controlling precedent.

The District Court, however, was amply cognizant of the controlling cases. It understood that to prevail the plaintiffs were required to "'prove not only that segregated schooling exists but also that it was brought about or maintained by intentional state action,'" that is, that the school officials had "intended to segregate."... The District Court also recognized that under those cases disparate impact and foreseeable consequences, without more, do not establish a constitutional violation. Nevertheless, the District Court correctly noted that actions having foreseeable and anticipated disparate impact are relevant evidence to prove the ultimate fact, forbidden purpose. Those cases do not forbid "the foreseeable effects standard from being utilized as one of the several kinds of proofs from which an inference of segregative intent may be properly drawn." Adherence to a particular policy or practice, "with full knowledge of the predictable effects of such adherence upon racial imbalance in a school system is one factor among many others which may be considered by a court in determining whether an inference of segregative intent should be drawn." The District Court thus stayed well within the requirements of *Washington* v. *Davis* and *Arlington Heights*. ...

It is also urged that the District Court and the Court of Appeals failed to observe the requirements of our recent decision in *Dayton I,* which reiterated the accepted rule that the remedy imposed by a court of equity should be commensurate with the violation ascertained, and held that the remedy for the violations that had then been established in that case should be aimed at rectifying the "incremental segregative effect" of the discriminatory acts identified. In *Dalton I,* only a few apparently isolated discriminatory practices had been found; yet a systemwide remedy had been imposed without proof of a systemwide impact. Here, however, the District Court repeatedly emphasized that it had found purposefully segregative practices with current, systemwide impact. ...

....

Nor do we perceive any misuse of *Keyes,* where we held that purposeful discrimination in a substantial part of a school system furnishes a sufficient basis for an inferential finding of a systemwide discriminatory intent unless otherwise rebutted, and that given the purpose to operate a dual school system one could infer a connection between such a purpose and racial separation in other parts of the school system. There was no undue reliance here on the inferences permitted by *Keyes,* or upon those recognized by *Swann.* Furthermore, the Board was given ample opportunity to counter the evidence of segregative purpose and current, systemwide impact, and the findings of the courts below were against it in both respects.

Because the District Court and the Court of Appeals committed no prejudicial errors of fact or law, the judgment appealed from must be

Affirmed.

MR. JUSTICE STEWART, with whom THE CHIEF JUSTICE joins, concurring.

. . . .

. . . As I understood the Court's opinions in these cases, if such an officially authorized segregated school system can be found to have existed in 1954, then any current racial separation in the schools will be presumed to have been caused by acts in violation of the Constitution. Even if, as the Court says, this presumption is rebuttable, the burden is on the school board to rebut it. And, when the factual issues are as elusive as these, who bears the burden of proof can easily determine who prevails in the litigation.

I agree that a school district in violation of the Constitution in 1954 was under a duty to remedy that violation. So was a school district violating the Constitution in 1964, and so is one violating the Constitution today. But this duty does not justify a complete shift of the normal burden of proof.

MR. JUSTICE POWELL, dissenting.

. . . The Court indulges the courts below in their stringing together of a chain of "presumptions," not one of which is close enough to reality to be reasonable. This chain leads inexorably to the remarkable conclusion that the absence of integration found to exist in a high percentage of the 241 schools in Columbus and Dayton was caused entirely by intentional violations of the Fourteenth Amendment by the school boards of these two cities. Although this conclusion is tainted on its face, is not supported by evidence in either case, and as a general matter seems incredible, the courts below accepted it as the necessary premise for requiring as a matter of *constitutional law* a systemwide remedy prescribing racial balance in each and every school.

There are unintegrated schools in every major urban area in the country that contains a substantial minority population. This condition results primarily from familiar segregated housing patterns, which—in turn—are caused by social, economic, and demographic forces for which no school board is responsible. These causes of the greater part of the school segregation problem are not newly discovered. Nearly a decade ago, Professor Bickel wrote:

> In most of the larger urban areas, demographic conditions are such that no policy that a court can order, and a school board, a city or even a

state has the capability to put into effect, will in fact result in the foreseeable future in racially balanced public schools. Only a reordering of the environment involving economic and social policy on the broadest conceivable front might have an appreciable impact. A. Bickel, the Supreme Court and the Idea of Progress 132, and n. 47 (1970).

Federal courts, including this Court today, continue to ignore these indisputable facts. Relying upon fictions and presumptions in school cases that are irreconcilable with principles of equal protection law applied in all other cases, see, *e.g., Personnel Administrator of Massachusetts* v. *Feeney* . . . (1979); *Arlington Heights* v. *Metropolitan Housing Dev. Corp.* . . . (1977); *Washington* v. *Davis* . . . (1976), federal courts prescribe systemwide remedies without relation to the causes of the segregation found to exist, and implement their decrees by requiring extensive transportation of children of all school ages.

The type of state-enforced segregation that *Brown I* properly condemned no longer exists in this country. This is not to say that school boards — particularly in the great cities of the North, Midwest, and West — are taking all reasonable measures to provide integrated educational opportunities. As I indicated in my separate opinion in *Keyes* v. *School Dist. No. 1, Denver, Colo.* (1973), *de facto* segregation has existed on a large scale in many of these cities, and often it is indistinguishable in effect from the type of *de jure* segregation outlawed by *Brown.* Where there is proof of intentional segregative action or inaction, the federal courts must act, but their remedies should not exceed the scope of the constitutional violation. . . . Systemwide remedies such as were ordered by the courts below, and today are approved by this Court, lack any principled basis when the absence of integration in all schools cannot reasonably be attributed to discriminatory conduct.

Holding the school boards of these two cities responsible for *all* of the segregation in the Dayton and Columbus systems and prescribing fixed racial ratios in every school as the constitutionally required remedy necessarily implies a belief that the same school boards — under court supervision — will be capable of bringing about and maintaining the desired racial balance in each of these schools. The experience in city after city demonstrates that this is an illusion. The process of resegregation, stimulated by resentment against judicial coercion and concern as to the effect of court supervision of education, will follow today's decisions as surely as it has in other cities subjected to similar sweeping decrees.

The orders affirmed today typify intrusions on local and professional authorities that affect adversely the quality of education. They require an extensive reorganization of both school systems, including the reassignment of almost half of the 96,000 students in the Columbus system and the busing of some 15,000 students in Dayton. They also require reassignments of teachers and other staff personnel, reorganization of grade structures, and the closing of certain schools. The orders substantially dismantle and displace neighborhood schools in the face of compelling economic and educational reasons for preserving them. This wholesale substitution of judicial legislation for the judgments of elected officials and professional educators derogates the entire process of public education. Moreover, it constitutes a serious interference with the private decisions of parents as to how their children will be educated. These harmful consequences are the inevitable byproducts of a judicial approach that ignores other relevant factors in favor of an exclusive focus on racial balance in every school.

These harmful consequences, moreover, in all likelihood will provoke responses that will defeat the integrative purpose of the courts' orders. Parents, unlike school officials, are not bound by these decrees and may frustrate them through the simple expedient of withdrawing their children from a public school system in which they have lost confidence. In spite of the substantial costs often involved in relocation of the family or in resort to private education, experience demonstrates that many parents view these alternatives as preferable to submitting their children to court-run school systems. In the words of a leading authority:

> An implication that should have been seen all along but can no longer be ignored is that a child's enrollment in a given public school is not determined by a governmental decision alone. It is a joint result of a governmental decision (the making of school assignments) and parental decisions, whether to remain in the same residential location, whether to send their child to a private school, or which school district to move into when moving into a metropolitan area. The fact that the child's enrollment is a result of two decisions operating jointly means that government policies must, to be effective, anticipate parental decisions and obtain the parents' active cooperation in implementing school policies. Coleman, New Incentives for Desegregation, 7 Human Rights, No. 3, pp. 10, 13 (1978).

At least where inner-city populations comprise a large proportion of racial minorities and surrounding suburbs remain white, conditions that exist in most large American cities, the demonstrated effect of compulsory integration is a substantial exodus of whites from the system. It would be unfair and misleading to attribute this phenomenon to a racist response to integration *per se*. It is at least as likely that the exodus is in substantial part a natural reaction of the displacement of professional and local control that occurs when courts go into the business of restructuring and operating school systems.

Nor will this resegregation be the only negative effect of court-coerced integration on minority children. Public schools depend on community support for their effectiveness. When substantial elements of the community are driven to abandon these schools, their quality tends to decline, sometimes markedly. Members of minority groups, who have relied especially on education as a means of advancing themselves, also are likely to react to this decline in quality by removing their children from public schools. As a result, public school enrollment increasingly will become limited to children from families that either lack the resources to choose alternatives or are indifferent to the quality of education. The net effect is an overall deterioration in public education, the one national resource that traditionally has made this country a land of opportunity for diverse ethnic and racial groups.

If public education is not to suffer further, we must "return to a more balanced evaluation of the recognized interests of our society in achieving desegregation with other educational and societal interests a community may legitimately assert." The ultimate goal is to have quality school systems in which racial discrimination is neither practiced nor tolerated. It has been thought that ethnic and racial diversity in the classroom is a desirable component of sound education in our country of diverse populations, a view to which I subscribe. The question that courts in their single-minded pursuit of racial balance seem to ignore is how best to move toward this goal.

For a decade or more after *Brown I*, the courts properly focused on dismantling segregated school systems as a means of eliminating state-imposed discrimination and furthering wholesome diversity in the schools. Experience in recent years, however, has cast serious doubt upon the efficacy of far-reaching judicial remedies directed not against specific constitutional violations, but rather imposed on an entire school system on the fictional assumption that the existence of identifiable black or white schools is caused entirely by intentional segregative conduct, and is evidence of system-wide discrimination. In my view, some federal courts — now led by this Court — are pursuing a path away from rather than toward the desired goal. While these courts conscientiously view their judgments as mandated by the Constitution (a view that would have astonished constitutional scholars throughout most of our history), the fact is that restructuring and overseeing the operation of major public school systems — as ordered in these cases — fairly can be viewed as social engineering that hardly is appropriate for the federal judiciary.

The time has come for a thoughtful re-examination of the proper limits of the role of courts in confronting the intractable problems of public education in our complex society. Proved discrimination by state or local authorities should never be tolerated, and it is a first responsibility of the judiciary to put an end to it where it has been proved. But many courts have continued also to impose wide-ranging decrees, and to retain ongoing supervision over school systems. Local and state legislative and administrative authorities have been supplanted or relegated to initiative-stifling roles as minions of the courts. Indeed, there is reason to believe that some legislative bodies have welcomed judicial activism with respect to a subject so inherently difficult and so politically sensitive that the prospect of others confronting it seems inviting. Federal courts no longer should encourage this deference by the appropriate authorities — no matter how willing they may be to defer. Courts are the branch least competent to provide long-range solutions acceptable to the public and most conducive to achieving both diversity in the classroom and quality education.

. . . .

After all, and in spite of what many view as excessive government regulation, we are a free society — perhaps the most free of any in the world. Our people instinctively resent coercion, and perhaps most of all when it affects their children and the opportunities that only education affords them. It is now reasonably clear that the goal of diversity that we call integration, if it is to be lasting and conducive to quality education, must have the support of parents who so frequently have the option to choose where their children will attend school. Courts, of course, should confront discrimination wherever it is found to exist. But they should recognize limitations on judicial action inherent in our system and also the limits of effective judicial power. The primary and continuing responsibility for public education, including the bringing about and maintaining of desired diversity, must be left with school officials and public authorities.

MR. JUSTICE REHNQUIST, with whom MR. JUSTICE POWELL joins, dissenting.

The Court suggests a radical new approach to desegregation cases in systems without a history of statutorily mandated separation of the races: if a district court concludes — employing what in honesty must be characterized as an irrebuttable presumption — that there was a "dual" school system at the time of *Brown I* (1954), it must find post-1954 constitutional violations in a school board's failure to take every affirmative step to integrate the system. Put differently, *racial imbalance* at the time the complaint is filed is sufficient to support a systemwide, racial balance, school busing remedy if the district court can find *some* evidence of discriminatory purpose prior to 1954, without any inquiry into the causal relationship between those pre-1954 violations and current segregation in the school system.

Civil Rights Cases

109 U.S. 3 (1883)
Vote: 8–1

The post–Civil War period witnessed the adoption of the Thirteenth, Fourteenth, and Fifteenth Amendments, each of which provided sweeping protection for the newly freed slaves and granted Congress authority over the states to enforce their provisions. Acting on this authority, between 1866 and 1875, Congress enacted eleven major civil rights acts, which extended federal protection against deprivations of rights to accommodations, the use of courts, voting, the purchase of property, and enjoyment of other civil rights.

One such statute was the Civil Rights Act of 1875, which provided in part "That all persons within the jurisdiction of the United States shall be entitled to the full and equal enjoyment of the accommodations, advantages, facilities and privileges of inns, public conveyances . . . and other places of public amusement; subject only to the conditions and limitations established by law, and applicable alike to citizens of every race and color, regardless of any previous condition of servitude." The Act further provided "That any person who shall violate the foregoing section by denying to any citizen, except for reasons by law . . . shall for every such offense forfeit and pay the sum of $500 to the person aggrieved thereby, . . . and shall also for every such offense, be deemed guilty of misdemeanor."

Several cases arising in connection with these provisions were consolidated for argument before the United States Supreme Court. Two cases stemmed from indictments for denying blacks accommodations in an inn; two arose when blacks were denied seats in a theater; and two more arose when black women were denied seats reserved for whites in a railroad car. The aggrieved parties argued that the Act was based upon two premises: First, the Fourteenth Amendment authorized Congress to prohibit discrimination by the state and by private providers of public service traditionally subject to public regulation. Second, congressional authority to enforce the Fourteenth Amendment extended beyond official state laws that discriminated to also cover situations where the states, through inaction, denied persons their constitutional rights. In contrast, the appellees contended that the discriminatory behavior under challenge was private action not within the scope of the Fourteenth Amendment, and that the provisions of the Civil Rights Act under which the cases had been brought were unconstitutional.

Mr. Justice Bradley delivered the opinion of the court.

. . . [I]t is the purpose of the law to declare that, in the enjoyment of the accommodations and privileges of inns, public conveyances, theaters and other places of public amusement, no distinction shall be made between citizens of different race or color, or between those who have and those who have not been slaves. Its effect is, to declare that, in all inns, public conveyances and places of amusement, colored citizens, whether formerly slaves or not, and citizens of other races, shall have the same accommodations and privileges in all inns, public conveyances, and places of amusement as are enjoyed by white citizens. . . .

Has Congress constitutional power to make such a law? Of course, no one will contend that the power

to pass it was contained in the Constitution before the adoption of the last three Amendments. . . .

. . . It is state action of a particular character that is prohibited. Individual invasion of individual rights is not the subject matter of the Amendment. It has a deeper and broader scope. It nullifies and makes void all state legislation, and state action of every kind, which impairs the privileges and immunities of citizens of the United States, or which injures them in life, liberty or property without due process of law, or which denies to any of them the equal protection of the laws. It not only does this, but . . . invests Congress with power to enforce it by appropriate legislation. To enforce what? To enforce the prohibition. To adopt appropriate legislation for correcting the effects of such prohibited state laws and state Acts, and thus to render them effectually null, void and innocuous. This is the legislative power conferred upon Congress, and this is the whole of it. It does not invest Congress with power to legislate upon subjects which are within the domain of state legislation; but to provide modes of relief against state legislation or state action, of the kind referred to. It does not authorize Congress to create a code of municipal law for the regulation of private rights; but to provide modes of redress against the operation of state laws, and the action of state officers executive or judicial, when these are subversive of the fundamental rights specified in the Amendment. Positive rights and privileges are undoubtedly secured by the 14th Amendment; but they are secured by way of prohibition against state laws and state proceedings affecting those rights and privileges, and by power given to Congress to legislate for the purpose of carrying such prohibition into effect; and such legislation must, necessarily, be predicated upon such supposed state laws or state proceedings, and be directed to the correction of their operation and effect. . . .

And so in the present case, until some state law has been passed or some state action through its officers or agents has been taken, adverse to the rights of citizens sought to be protected by the 14th Amendment, no legislation of the United States under said Amendment, nor any proceeding under such legislation, can be called into activity; for the prohibitions of the Amendment are against state laws and acts done under state authority. Of course, legislation may and should be provided in advance to meet the exigency when it arises; but it should be adapted to the mischief and wrong which the Amendment was intended to provide against; and that is, state laws, or state action of some kind, adverse to the rights of the citizen secured by the

Amendment. Such legislation cannot properly cover the whole domain of rights appertaining to life, liberty and property, defining them and providing for their vindication. That would be to establish a code of municipal law regulative of all private rights between man and man in society. It would be to make Congress take the place of the State Legislatures and to supersede them. It is absurd to affirm that, because the rights of life, liberty and property, which include all civil rights that men have, are, by the Amendment, sought to be protected against invasion on the part of the State without due process of law, Congress may, therefore, provide due process of law for their vindication in every case; and that, because the denial by a State to any persons, of the equal protection of the laws, is prohibited by the Amendment, therefore Congress may establish laws for their equal protection. In fine, the legislation which Congress is authorized to adopt in this behalf is not general legislation upon the rights of the citizen, but corrective legislation, that is, such as may be necessary and proper for counteracting such laws as the States may adopt or enforce, and which, by the Amendment, they are prohibited from making or enforcing, or such acts and proceedings as the States may commit or take, and which, by the Amendment, they are prohibited from committing or taking. It is not necessary for us to state, if we could, what legislation would be proper for Congress to adopt. It is sufficient for us to examine whether the law in question is of that character.

An inspection of the law shows that it makes no reference whatever to any supposed or apprehended violation of the 14th Amendment on the part of the States. It is not predicated on any such view. It proceeds *ex directo* to declare that certain acts committed by individuals shall be deemed offenses, and shall be prosecuted and punished by proceedings in the courts of the United States. It does not profess to be corrective of any constitutional wrong committed by the States; it does not make its operation to depend upon any such wrong committed. It applies equally to cases arising in States which have the justest laws respecting the personal rights of citizens, and whose authorities are ever ready to enforce such laws, as to those which arise in States that may have violated the prohibition of the Amendment. In other words, it steps into the domain of local jurisprudence, and lays down rules for the conduct of individuals in society towards each other, and imposes sanctions for the enforcement of those rules, without referring in any manner to any supposed action of the State or its authorities.

If this legislation is appropriate for enforcing the prohibitions of the Amendment, it is difficult to see where it is to stop. Why may not Congress with equal show of authority enact a code of laws for the enforcement and vindication of all rights of life, liberty and property? If it is supposable that the States may deprive persons of life, liberty and property without due process of law, and the Amendment itself does suppose this, why should not Congress proceed at once to prescribe due process of law for the protection of every one of these fundamental rights, in every possible case, as well as to prescribe equal privileges in inns, public conveyances and theaters? The truth is, that the implication of a power to legislate in this manner is based upon the assumption that if the States are forbidden to legislate or act in a particular way on a particular subject, and power is conferred upon Congress to enforce the prohibition, this gives Congress power to legislate generally upon that subject, and not merely power to provide modes of redress against such state legislation or action. The assumption is certainly unsound. It is repugnant to the 10th Amendment of the Constitution which declares that powers not delegated to the United States by the Constitution, nor prohibited by it to the States, are reserved to the States respectively or to the people.

. . . .

In this connection it is proper to state that civil rights, such as are guarantied by the Constitution against state aggression, cannot be impaired by the wrongful acts of individuals, unsupported by state authority in the shape of laws, customs or judicial or executive proceedings. The wrongful act of an individual, unsupported by any such authority, is simply a private wrong, or a crime of that individual; an invasion of the rights of the injured party, it is true, whether they affect his person, his property or his reputation; but if not sanctioned in some way by the State, or not done under state authority, his rights remain in full force, and may presumably be vindicated by resort to the laws of the State for redress. An individual cannot deprive a man of his right to vote, to hold property, to buy and to sell, to sue in the courts or to be a witness or a juror; he may, by force or fraud, interfere with the enjoyment of the right in a particular case; he may commit an assault against the person or commit murder, or use ruffian violence at the polls, or slander the good name of a fellow citizen; but, unless protected in these wrongful acts by some shield of state law or state authority, he cannot destroy or injure the right; he will only render himself amenable to satisfaction or punishment; and amenable therefor to the laws of the State where the wrongful acts are committed. Hence, in all those cases where the Constitution seeks to protect the rights of the citizen against discriminative and unjust laws of the State by prohibiting such laws, it is not individual offenses, but abrogation and denial of rights, which it denounces, and for which it clothes the Congress with power to provide a remedy. This abrogation and denial of rights, for which the States alone were or could be responsible, was the great seminal and fundamental wrong which was intended to be remedied. And the remedy to be provided must necessarily be predicated upon that wrong. It must assume that in the cases provided for, the evil or wrong actually committed rests upon some state law or state authority for its excuse and perpetration.

Of course, these remarks do not apply to those cases in which Congress is clothed with direct and plenary powers of legislation over the whole subject, accompanied with an express or implied denial of such power to the States, as in the regulation of commerce with foreign Nations, among the several States. . . .

If the principles of interpretation which we have laid down are correct, as we deem them to be, and they are in accord with the principles laid down in the cases before referred to, as well as in the recent case of *U.S.* v. *Harris,* decided at the last Term of this court, it is clear that the law in question cannot be sustained by any grant of legislative power made to Congress by the 14th Amendment. That Amendment prohibits the States from denying to any person the equal protection of the laws, and declares that Congress shall have power to enforce, by appropriate legislation, the provisions of the Amendment. The law in question, without any reference to adverse state legislation on the subject, declares that all persons shall be entitled to equal accommodations and privileges of inns, public conveyances and places of public amusement, and imposes a penalty upon any individual who shall deny to any citizen such equal accommodations and privileges. This is not corrective legislation; it is primary and direct; it takes immediate and absolute possession of the subject of the right of admission to inns, public conveyances and places of amusement. It supersedes and displaces state legislation on the same subject, or only allows it permissive force. It ignores such legislation, and assumes that the matter is one that belongs to the domain of national regulation. Whether it would not have been a more effective protection of the rights of citizens to have clothed Congress with

plenary power over the whole subject, is not now the question. What we have to decide is, whether such plenary power has been conferred upon Congress by the 14th Amendment; and, in our judgment, it has not.

. . . [W]hether Congress, in the exercise of its power to regulate commerce amongst the several States, might or might not pass a law regulating rights in public conveyances passing from one State to another, is also a question which is not now before us, as the sections in question are not conceived in any such view.

But the power of Congress to adopt direct and primary, as distinguished from corrective, legislation on the subject in hand, is sought, in the second place, from the 13th Amendment, which abolishes slavery. . . .

This Amendment, as well as the 14th, is undoubtedly self-executing without any ancillary legislation, so far as its terms are applicable to any existing state of circumstances. By its own unaided force and effect, it abolished slavery and established universal freedom. Still, legislation may be necessary and proper to meet all the various cases and circumstances to be affected by it, and to prescribe proper modes of redress for its violation in letter or spirit. And such legislation may be primary and direct in its character; for the Amendment is not a mere prohibition of state laws establishing or upholding slavery, but an absolute declaration that slavery or involuntary servitude shall not exist in any part of the United States.

. . . .

But is there any similarity between such servitudes and a denial by the owner of an inn, a public conveyance, or a theater, of its accommodations and privileges to an individual, even though the denial be founded on the race or color of that individual? Where does any slavery or servitude, or badge of either, arise from such an act of denial? Whether it might not be a denial of a right which, if sanctioned by the state law, would be obnoxious to the prohibitions of the 14th Amendment, is another question. But what has it to do with the question of slavery?

. . . .

. . . It would be running the slavery argument into the ground, to make it apply to every act of discrimination which a person may see fit to make as to the guests he will entertain, or as to the people he will take into his coach or cab or car, or admit to his concert or theater or deal with in other matters of intercourse or business. Innkeepers and public carriers, by the laws of all the States, so far as we are aware,

are bound, to the extent of their facilities, to furnish proper accommodation to all unobjectionable persons who in good faith apply for them. If the laws themselves make any unjust discrimination, amenable to the prohibitions of the 14th Amendment, Congress has full power to afford a remedy, under that Amendment and in accordance with it.

When a man has emerged from slavery, and by the aid of beneficent legislation has shaken off the inseparable concomitants of that state, there must be some state in the progress of his elevation when he takes the rank of a mere citizen, and ceases to be the special favorite of the laws, and when his rights, as a citizen or a man, are to be protected in the ordinary modes by which other men's rights are protected. There were thousands of free colored people in this country before the abolition of slavery, enjoying all the essential rights of life, liberty and property the same as white citizens; yet no one, at that time, thought that it was any invasion of their personal *status* as freemen because they were not admitted to all the privileges enjoyed by white citizens, or because they were subjected to discriminations in the enjoyment of accommodations in inns, public conveyances and places of amusement. Mere discriminations on account of race or color were not regarded as badges of slavery. . . .

MR. JUSTICE HARLAN, dissenting.

The opinion in these cases proceeds, it seems to me, upon grounds entirely too narrow and artificial. I cannot resist the conclusion that the substance and spirit of the recent Amendments of the Constitution have been sacrificed by a subtle and ingenious verbal criticism. . . .

The court adjudges, I think erroneously, that Congress is without power, under either the 13th or 14th Amendment, to establish such regulations. . . .

. . . .

The 13th Amendment, it is conceded, did something more than to prohibit slavery as an *institution,* resting upon distinctions of race, and upheld by positive law. My brethren admit that it established and decreed universal *civil freedom* throughout the United States. But did the freedom thus established involve nothing more than exemption from actual slavery? Was nothing more intended than to forbid any man from owning another as property? Was it the purpose of the Nation simply to destroy the institution, and then remit the race, theretofore held in bondage, to the several States for such protection, in their civil rights, necessarily growing out of

freedom, as those States, in their discretion, might choose to provide? . . .

. . . .

. . . [T]he power of Congress under the 13th Amendment is not necessarily restricted to legislation against slavery as an institution upheld by positive law, but may be exerted to the extent, at least, of protecting the liberated race against discrimination, in respect of legal rights belonging to freemen, where such discrimination is based upon race.

. . . [A] keeper of an inn is in the exercise of a *quasi* public employment. The law gives him special privileges and he is charged with certain duties and responsibilities to the public. The public nature of his employment forbids him from discriminating against any person asking admission as a guest on account of the race or color of that person.

. . . As to places of public amusement. It may be argued that the managers of such places have no duties to perform with which the public are, in any legal sense, concerned, or with which the public have any right to interfere; and that the exclusion of a black man from a place of public amusement, on account of his race; or the denial to him, on that ground, of equal accommodations at such places, violates no legal right for the vindication of which he may invoke the aid of the courts. My answer is, that places of public amusement, within the meaning of the Act of 1875, are such as are established and maintained under direct license of the law. The authority to establish and maintain them comes from the public. The colored race is a part of that public. The local government granting the license represents them as well as all other races within its jurisdiction. . . .

. . . .

The doctrines of *Munn* v. *Illinois* [1877] have never been modified by this court, and I am justified, upon the authority of that case, in saying that places of public amusement, conducted under the authority of the law, are clothed with a public interest, because used in a manner to make them of public consequence and to affect the community at large. The law may, therefore, regulate, to some extent, the mode in which they shall be conducted and, consequently, the public have rights in respect of such places, which may be vindicated by the law. It is, consequently, not a matter purely of private concern.

Congress has not, in these matters, entered the domain of state control and supervision. It does not, as I have said, assume to prescribe the general conditions and limitations under which inns, public conveyances and places of public amusement, shall be conducted or managed. It simply declares, in effect, that since the Nation has established universal freedom in this country, for all time, there shall be no discrimination, based merely upon race or color, in respect of the accommodations and advantages of public conveyances, inns and places of public amusement.

I am of the opinion that such discrimination practiced by corporations and individuals in the exercise of their public or *quasi* public functions is a badge of servitude, the imposition of which Congress may prevent under its power, by appropriate legislation, to enforce the 13th Amendment; and consequently, without reference to its enlarged power under the 14th Amendment, the Act of March 1, 1875, is not, in my judgement, repugnant to the Constitution.

It remains now to consider these cases with reference to the power Congress has possessed since the adoption of the 14th Amendment. Much that has been said as to the power of Congress under the 13th Amendment is applicable to this branch of the discussion, and will not be repeated.

. . . .

The assumption that [the Fourteenth] Amendment consists wholly of prohibition upon state laws and state proceedings in hostility to its provisions, is unauthorized by its language. The first clause of the 1st section — "All persons born or naturalized in the United States, and subject to the jurisdiction thereof, are citizens of the United States, and of the State wherein they reside" — is of a distinctly affirmative character. In its application to the colored race, previously liberated, it created and granted, as well citizenship of the United States, as citizenship of the State in which they respectively resided. It introduced all of that race, whose ancestors had been imported and sold as slaves, at once, into the political community knwon as the "People of the United States." They became, instantly, citizens of the United States, *and* of their respective States. . . .

The citizenship thus acquired, by that race, in virtue of an affirmative grant from the Nation, may be protected, not alone by the judicial branch of the government, but by congressional legislation of a primary direct character; thus, because the power of Congress is not restricted to the enforcement of prohibitions upon state laws or state action. It is, in terms distinct and positive, to enforce "the *provisions* of *this article*" of Amendment; not simply those of a prohibitive character, but the provisions — *all* of the provisions — affirmative and prohibitive, of the Amendment. It is, therefore, a grave misconception to suppose that the 5th section of the Amendment has reference exclusively to express prohibitions upon state laws or state action. If any right was created by that Amendment, the grant of power, through appropriate legislation, to enforce its provisions, authorizes Congress, by means of legislation, operating throughout the entire Union, to guard, secure and protect that right.

. . . .

This court has always given a broad and liberal construction to the Constitution, so as to enable Congress, by legislation, to enforce rights secured by that instrument. The legislation which Congress may enact, in execution of its power to enforce the provisions of this Amendment, is such as may be appropriate to protect the right granted. The word "appropriate" was undoubtedly used with reference to its meaning, as established by repeated decisions of this court. Under given circumstances, that which the court characterizes as corrective legislation might be deemed by Congress appropriate and entirely sufficient. Under other circumstances primary direct legislation may be required. But it is for Congress, not the judiciary, to say that legislation is appropriate; that is, best adapted to the end to be attained. The judiciary may not, with safety to our institutions, enter the domain of legislative discretion, and dictate the means which Congress shall employ in the exercise of its granted powers. That would be sheer usurpation of the functions of a coordinate department, which, if often repeated, and permanently acquiesced in, would work a radical change in our system of government. . . .

My brethren say, that when a man has emerged from slavery and by the aid of beneficent legislation has shaken off the inseparable concomitants of that state, there must be some stage in the progress of his elevation when he takes the rank of a mere citizen, and ceases to be the special favorite of the laws, and when his rights as a citizen, or a man, are to be protected in the ordinary modes by which other men's rights are protected. It is, I submit, scarcely just to say that the colored race has been the special favorite of the laws. The Statute of 1875, now adjudged to be unconstitutional, is for the benefit of citizens of every race and color. What the Nation, through Congress, has sought to accomplish in reference to that race, is — what had already been done in every State of the Union for the white race — to secure and protect rights belonging to them as freemen and citizens; nothing more. It was not deemed enough "to help the feeble up, but to support him after." The one underlying purpose of congressional legislation has been to enable the black race to take the rank of mere citizens. The difficulty has been to compel a recognition of the legal right of the black race to take the rank of citizens, and to secure the enjoyment of privileges belonging, under the law, to them as a component part of the people for whose welfare and happiness government is ordained. At every step, in this direction, the Nation has been confronted with class tyranny, which a contemporary English historian says is, of all tyrannies, the most intolerable. "For it is ubiquitous in its operation, and weighs, perhaps, most heavily on those whose obscurity or distance would withdraw them from the notice of a single despot." Today, it is the colored race which is denied, by corporations and individuals wielding public authority, rights fundamental in their freedom and citizenship. At some future time, it may be that some other race will fall under the ban of race discrimination. If the constitutional Amendments be enforced, according to the intent with which, as I conceive, they were adopted, there cannot be in this Republic, any class of human beings in practical subjection to another class, with power in the latter to dole out to the former just such privileges as they may choose to grant. The supreme law of the land has decreed that no authority shall be exercised in this country upon the basis of discrimination, in respect of civil rights, against freemen and citizens because of their race, color or previous condition of servitude. To that decree — for the due enforcement of which, by appropriate legislation, Congress has been invested with express power — every one must bow, whatever may have been, or whatever now are, his individual views as to the wisdom or policy, either of the recent changes in the fundamental law, or of the legislation which has been enacted to give them effect.

For the reasons stated I feel constrained to withhold my assent to the opinion of the court.

Shelley v. Kraemer

> 334 U.S. 1 (1948)
> Vote: 6–0

On February 16, 1911, a group of landowners in a residential section of St. Louis signed an agreement that provided in part that "no part of said property or any portion thereof shall be, for said term of fifty-five years, occupied by any person not of the Caucasian race, it being intended hereby to restrict the use of said property for said period of time against the occupancy as owners or tenants of any portion of said property for resident or other purpose by people of the Negro or Mongolian Race." On August 11, 1945, pursuant to a contract of sale, the Shelleys, who were black, received a warranty deed to a parcel of land that had been covered by this restrictive covenant. This transaction was effected by a third party, who was white, and at the time of purchase the Shelleys had no knowledge of the restrictive agreement. On October 9, 1945, Kraemer et al., owners of other property subject to the restrictive agreement, brought suit in state court asking that the Shelleys be restrained from taking possession of the property, that they be divested of title to the property, and that title revert to the prior owner or some other person as the court should direct.

The trial court denied the requested relief on technical ground (not all the parties to the agreement had in fact signed it), but upon appeal the Supreme Court of Missouri reversed the trial court and directed that the relief requested by Kraemer et al. be granted.

At the time the Missouri high court rendered its decision, the Shelleys were occupying the house they thought they had purchased.

MR. CHIEF JUSTICE VINSON delivered the opinion of the Court.

These cases present for our consideration questions relating to the validity of the court enforcement of private agreements, generally described as restrictive covenants, which have as their purpose the exclusion of persons of designated race or color from the ownership or occupancy of real property. Basic constitutional issues of obvious importance have been raised.

. . . .

It cannot be doubted that among the civil rights intended to be protected from discriminatory state action by the Fourteenth Amendment are the rights to acquire, enjoy, own and dispose of property. Equality in the enjoyment of property rights was regarded by the framers of that Amendment as an essential precondition to the realization of other basic civil rights and liberties which the Amendment was intended to guarantee. Thus §1987 of the Revised Statutes, derived from §1 of the Civil Rights Act of 1866 which was enacted by Congress while the Fourteenth Amendment was also under consideration, provides:

> All citizens of the United States shall have the same right, in every State and Territory, as is enjoyed by white citizens thereof to inherit, purchase, lease, sell, hold, and convey real and personal property.

This Court has given specific recognition to the same principle. *Buchanan* v. *Warley* . . . (1917).

It is likewise clear that restrictions on the right of occupancy of the sort sought to be created by the private agreements in these cases could not be squared with the requirements of the Fourteenth Amendment if imposed by state statute or local ordinance. We do not understand respondents to urge the contrary. In the case of *Buchanan* v. *Warley,* a unanimous Court declared unconstitutional the provisions of a city ordinance which denied to colored persons the right to occupy houses in blocks in which the greater number of houses were occupied by white persons, and imposed similar restrictions on white persons with respect to blocks in which the greater number of houses where occupied by colored persons. During the course of the opinion in that case, this Court stated: "The Fourteenth Amendment and these statutes enacted in furtherance of its purpose operate to qualify and entitle a colored man to acquire property without state legislation discriminating against him solely because of color."

. . . .

But the present cases, unlike [*Buchanan*], do not involve action by state legislatures or city councils. Here the particular patterns of discrimination and the areas in which the restrictions are to operate, are determined, in the first instance, by the terms of agreements among private individuals. Participation of the State consists in the enforcement of the restrictions so defined. The crucial issue with which we are here confronted is whether this distinction removes these cases from the operation of the prohibitory provisions of the Fourteenth Amendment.

Since the decision of this Court in the *Civil Rights Cases* . . . (1883), the principle has become firmly embedded in our constitutional law that the action inhibited by the first section of the Fourteenth Amendment is only such action as may fairly be said to be that of the States. That Amendment erects no shield against merely private conduct, however discriminatory or wrongful.

We conclude, therefore, that the restrictive agreements standing alone cannot be regarded as violative of any rights guaranteed to petitioners by the Fourteenth Amendment. So long as the purposes of those agreements are effectuated by voluntary adherence to their terms, it would appear clear that there has been no action by the State and the provisions of the Amendment have not been violated.

But here these was more. These are cases in which the purposes of the agreements were secured only by judicial enforcement by state courts of the restrictive terms of the agreements. The respondents urge that judicial enforcement of private agreements does not amount to state action; or, in any event, the participation of the State is so attenuated in character as not to amount to state action within the meaning of the Fourteenth Amendment. Finally, it is suggested, even if the States in these cases may be deemed to have acted in the constitutional sense, their action did not deprive petitioners of rights guaranteed by the Fourteenth Amendment. We move to a consideration of these matters.

That the action of state courts and judicial officers in their official capacities is to be regarded as action of the State within the meaning of the Fourteenth Amendment, is a proposition which has long been established by decisions of this Court. . . .

. . . .

One of the earliest applications of the prohibitions contained in the Fourteenth Amendment to action of state judicial officials occurred in cases in which Negroes had been excluded from jury service in criminal prosecutions by reason of their race or color. These cases demonstrate, also, the early recognition by this Court that state action in violation of the Amendment's provisions is equally repugnant to the constitutional commands whether directed by state statute or taken by a judicial official in the absence of statute. Thus, in *Strauder* v. *West Virginia* (1880), this Court declared invalid a state statute restricting jury service to white persons as amounting to a denial of the equal protection of the laws to the colored defendant in that case. In the same volume of the reports, the Court in *Ex parte Virginia, supra,* held that a similar discrimination imposed by the action of a state judge denied rights protected by the Amendment, despite the fact that the language of the state statute relating to jury service contained no such restrictions.

The action of the state courts in imposing penalties or depriving parties of other substantive rights without providing adequate notice and opportunity to defend, has, of course, long been regarded as a denial of the due process of law guaranteed by the Fourteenth Amendment....

In numerous cases, this Court has reversed criminal convictions in state courts for failure of those courts to provide the essential ingredients of a fair hearing. Thus it has been held that convictions obtained in state courts under the domination of a mob are void. Convictions obtained by coerced confessions, by the use of perjured testimony known by the prosecution to be such, or without the effective assistance of counsel, have also been held to be exertions of state authority in conflict with the fundamental rights protected by the Fourteenth Amendment.

But the examples of state judicial action which have been held by this Court to violate the Amendment's commands are not restricted to situations in which the judicial proceedings were found in some manner to be procedurally unfair. It has been recognized that the action of state courts in enforcing a substantive common-law rule formulated by those courts, may result in the denial of rights guaranteed by the Fourteenth Amendment, even though the judicial proceedings in such cases may have been in complete accord with the most rigorous conceptions of procedural due process.

The short of the matter is that from the time of the adoption of the Fourteenth Amendment until the present, it has been the consistent ruling of this Court that the action of the States to which the Amendment has reference includes action of state courts and state judicial officials. Although, in construing the terms of the Fourteenth Amendment, differences have from time to time been expressed as to whether particular types of state action may be said to offend the Amendment's prohibitory provisions, it has never been suggested that state court action is immunized from the operation of those provisions simply because the act is that of the judicial branch of the state government.

. . . .

We have no doubt that there has been state action in these cases in the full and complete sense of the phrase. The undisputed facts disclose that petitioners were *willing* purchasers of properties upon which they desired to establish homes. The owners of the properties were willing sellers; and the contracts of sale were accordingly consummated. It is clear that but for the active intervention of the state courts, supported by the full panoply of state power, petitioners would have been free to occupy the properties in question without restraint.

These are not cases, as has beeen suggested, in which the States have merely abstained from action,

leaving private individuals free to impose such discriminations as they see fit. Rather, these are cases in which the States have made available to such individuals the full coercive power of government to deny to petitioners, on the grounds of race or color, the enjoyment of property rights in premises which petitioners are willing and financially able to acquire and which the grantors are willing to sell. The difference between judicial enforcement and nonenforcement of the restrictive covenants is the difference to petitioners between being denied rights of property available to other members of the community and being accorded full enjoyment of those rights on an equal footing.

. . . We have noted that previous decisions of this Court have established the proposition that judicial action is not immunized from the operation of the Fourteenth Amendment simply because it is taken pursuant to the state's common-law policy. Nor is the Amendment ineffective simply because the particular pattern of discrimination, which the State has enforced, was defined initially by the terms of a private agreement. State action, as that phrase is understood for the purposes of the Fourteenth Amendment, refers to exertions of state power in all forms. And when the effect of that action is to deny rights subject to the protection of the Fourteenth Amendment, it is the obligation of this Court to enforce the constitutional commands.

We hold that in granting judicial enforcement of the restrictive agreements in these cases, the States have denied petitioners the equal protection of the laws and that, therefore, the action of the state courts cannot stand. We have noted that freedom from discrimination by the States in the enjoyment of property rights was among the basic objectives sought to be effectuated by the framers of the Fourteenth Amendment. That such discrimination has occurred in these cases is clear. Because of the race or color of these petitioners they have been denied rights of ownership or occupancy enjoyed as a matter of course by other citizens of different race or color....

Respondents urge, however, that since the state courts stand ready to enforce restrictive covenants excluding white persons from the ownership or occupancy of property covered by such agreements, enforcement of covenants excluding colored persons may not be deemed a denial of equal protection of the laws to the colored persons who are thereby affected. This contention does not bear scrutiny. The parties have directed our attention to no case in which a court, state or federal, has been called upon to enforce a covenant excluding members of the white majority from ownership or occupancy of real property on grounds of race or color. But there are more fundamental considerations. The rights created by the first section of the Fourteenth Amendment are, by its terms, guaranteed to the individual. The rights established are personal rights. It is, therefore, no answer to these petitioners to say that the courts may also be induced to deny white persons rights of ownership and occupancy on grounds of race or color. Equal protection of the laws is not achieved through indiscriminate imposition of inequalitites.

Nor do we find merit in the suggestion that property owners who are parties to these agreements are denied equal protection of the laws if denied access to the courts to enforce the terms of restrictive covenants and to assert property rights which the state courts have held to be created by such agreements. The Constitution confers upon no individual the right to demand action by the State which results in the denial of equal protection of the laws to other individuals. . . .

. . . .

For the reasons stated, the judgment of the Supreme Court of Missouri . . . must be

Reversed.

MR. JUSTICE REED, MR. JUSTICE JACKSON, and MR. JUSTICE RUTLEDGE took no part in the consideration or decision of these cases.

Moose Lodge No. 107 v. Irvis

407 U.S. 163 (1972)
Vote: 6–3

K. Leroy Irvis, a black man and majority leader of the Pennsylvania House of Representatives, was refused service by the Moose Lodge in Harrisburg, Pennsylvania, a local branch of a national fraternal organization that operates as a private club. Each local lodge is bound by the national constitution and by-laws, which restrict membership to "white male Caucasians" and which permit members to bring only Caucasians as guests on their premises.

After being refused service, Irvis brought suit against the Pennsylvania Liquor Authority and the Moose Lodge, seeking injunctive relief that would require the Liquor Authority to revoke the Moose Lodge's liquor license so long as it maintained its discriminatory membership and guest policies. The district court ruled against Irvis, since he had neither applied for nor been denied membership in the Moose Lodge, nor did he have standing to sue as a taxpayer. But the district court did rule that Irvis had standing to challenge the Moose Lodge's guest policy, and went on to hold that although the Lodge members' right to privacy allowed them to exclude blacks if they so chose, they could not hold a state-granted liquor license at the same time. In its opinion, the district court relied upon the "state action" doctrine of SHELLEY V. KRAEMER (1948) and *Burton* v. *Wilmington Parking Authority,* 365 U.S. 775 (1961). In *Burton,* the Supreme Court held that a privately operated restaurant that leased its premises from a governmental agency could not refuse service to blacks, because the state was implicated, through the lease, in the restaurant's policies.

In the opinion below, Justice Rehnquist, for the majority on the Supreme Court, distinguishes the *Moose Lodge* controversy from both previous cases. Is he convincing? If not, where would you draw the distinction between public and private? Or should one be drawn?

MR. JUSTICE REHNQUIST delivered the opinion of the Court.

Moose Lodge is a private club in the ordinary meaning of that term. It is a local chapter of a national fraternal organization having well-defined requirements for membership. It conducts all of its activities in a building that is owned by it. It is not publicly funded. Only members and guests are permitted in any lodge of the order; one may become a guest only by invitation of a member or upon invitation of the house committee.

Appellee, while conceding the right of private clubs to choose members upon a discriminatory basis, asserts that the licensing of Moose Lodge to serve liquor by the Pennsylvania Liquor Control Board amounts to such State involvement with the club's activities as to make its discriminatory practices forbidden by the Equal Protection Clause of the Fourteenth Amendment. The relief sought and obtained by appellee in the District Court was an injunction forbidding the licensing by the liquor authority of Moose Lodge until it ceased its discriminatory practices. We conclude that Moose Lodge's refusal to serve food and beverages to a guest by reason of the fact that he was a Negro does not, under the circumstances here presented, violate the Fourteenth Amendment.

In 1883, this Court in *The Civil Rights Cases* . . . set forth the essential dichotomy between discriminatory action by the State, which is prohibited by the Equal Protection Clause, and private conduct, "however discriminatory or wrongful," against which that clause "erects no shield," *Shelley* v. *Kramer,* (1948). That dichotomy has been subsequently reaffirmed in *Shelley* v. *Kramer, Burton* v. *Wilmington Parking Authority,* (1951).

While the principle is easily stated, the question of whether particular discriminatory conduct is private, on the one hand, or amounts to "State action," on the other hand, frequently admits of no easy answer. "Only by sifting facts and weighing circumstances can the nonobvious involvement of the State in private conduct be attributed its true significance."

Our cases make clear that the impetus for the forbidden discrimination need not originate with the State if it is state action that enforces privately originated discrimination. *Shelley* v. *Kraemer.* The Court held in *Burton* v. *Wilmington Parking Authority,* that a private restaurant owner who refused service because of a customer's race violated the Fourteenth Amendment, where the restaurant was located in a building owned by a state-created parking authority and leased from the authority. The Court, after a comprehensive review of the relationship between the lessee and the parking authority concluded that the latter had "so far insinuated itself into a position of interdependence with Eagle [the restaurant owner] that it must be recognized as a joint participant in the challenged activity, which, on that account, cannot be considered to have been so 'purely private' as to fall without the scope of the Fourteenth Amendment."

The Court has never held, of course, that discrimination by an otherwise private entity would be violative of the Equal Protection Clause if the private entity receives any sort of benefit or service at all from the State, or if it is subject to state regulation in any degree whatever. Since state-furnished services include such necessities of life as electricity, water, and police and fire protection, such a holding would utterly emasculate the distinction between private as distinguished from State conduct set forth in *The Civil Rights Cases,* and adhered to in subsequent decisions. Our holdings indicate that where the impetus for the discrimination is private, the State must have "significantly involved itself with invidious discriminations," in order for the discriminatory action to fall within the ambit of the constitutional prohibition.

Our prior decisions dealing with discriminatory refusal of service in public eating places are significantly different factually from the case now before us. *Peterson* v. *City of Greenville,* . . . (1963), dealt with trespass prosecution of persons who "sat in" at a restaurant to protest its refusal of service to Negroes. There the Court held that although the ostensible initiative for the trespass prosecution came from the proprietor, the existence of a local ordinance requiring segregation of races in such places was tantamount to the State having "commanded a particular result." With one exception, . . . there is no suggestion in this record that the Pennsylvania statutes and regulations governing the sale of liquor are intended either overtly or covertly to encourage discrimination.

In *Burton,* the Court's full discussion of the facts in its opinion indicates the significant differences between that case and this.

Here there is nothing approaching the symbiotic relationship between lessor and lessee that was present in *Burton,* where the private lessee obtained the benefit of locating in a building owned by the State-created parking authority, and the parking authority was enabled to carry out its primary public purpose of furnishing parking space by advantageously leasing portions of the building constructed for that purpose to commercial lessees such as the owner of the Eagle Restaurant. Unlike *Burton,* the Moose Lodge building is located on land owned by it, not by any public authority. Far from apparently holding itself out as a place of public accommodation, Moose Lodge quite ostentatiously proclaims the fact that it is not open to the public at large. Nor is it located and operated in such surroundings that although private in name, it discharges a function or performs a service that would otherwise in all likelihood be performed by the State. In short, while Eagle was a public restaurant in a public building, Moose Lodge is a private social club in a private building.

With the exception hereafter noted, the Pennsylvania Liquor Control Board plays absolutely no part in establishing or enforcing the membership or guest policies of the club which it licenses to serve liquor. There is no suggestion in this record that the Pennsylvania Act, either as written or as applied, discriminates against minority groups either in their right to apply for club licenses themselves or in their right to purchase and be served liquor in places of public accommodation. The only effect that the state licensing of Moose Lodge to serve liquor can be said to have on the right of any other Pennsylvanian to buy or be served liquor on premises other than those of Moose Lodge is that for some purposes club licenses are counted in the maximum number of licenses which may be issued in a given municipality. Basically each municipality has a quota of one retail license for each 1,500 inhabitants. Licenses issued to hotels, municipal golf courses and airport restaurants are not counted in this quota, nor are club licenses until the maximum number of retail licenses is reached. Beyond that point, neither additional retail licenses nor additional club licenses may be issued so long as the number of issued and outstanding retail licenses remains above the statutory maximum.

The District Court was at pains to point out in its opinion what it considered to be the "pervasive" nature of the regulation of private clubs by the Pennsylvania Liquor Control Board. As that court noted, an applicant for a club license must make such physical alterations in its premises as the board may require, must file a list of the names and addresses of its members and employees, and must keep extensive financial records. The board is granted the right to inspect the licensed premises at any time when patrons, guests or members are present.

However detailed this type of regulation may be in some particulars, it cannot be said to in any way foster or encourage racial discrimination. Nor can it be said to make the State in any realistic sense a partner or even a joint venturer in the club's enterprise. The limited effect of the prohibition against obtaining additional club licenses when the maximum number of retail licenses allotted to a municipality has been issued, when considered together with the availability of liquor from hotel, restaurant, and retail licensees falls far short of conferring upon club licensees a monopoly in the dispensing of liquor in any given municipality or in the State as a whole. We therefore hold that, with the exception hereafter noted, the operation of the regulatory scheme enforced by the Pennsylvania Liquor Control Board does not sufficiently implicate the State in the discriminatory guest policies of Moose Lodge so as to make the latter "State action" within the ambit of the Equal Protection Clause of the Fourteenth Amendment.

The District Court found that the regulations of the Liquor Control Board adopted pursuant to statute affirmatively require that "every club licensee shall adhere to all the provisions of its constitution and by-laws." Appellant argues that the purpose of this provision "is purely and simply and plainly the prevention of subterfuge," pointing out that the *bona fides* of a private club, as opposed to a place of public accommodation masquerading as a private club, is a matter with which the State Liquor Control Board may legitimately concern itself. Appellee concedes this to be the case, and expresses disappointment with the District Court at this point. There can be no doubt that the label "private club" can and has been used to evade both regulations of State and local liquor authorities, and statutes requiring places of public accommodation to serve all persons without regard to race, color, religion, or national origin. . . .

The effect of this particular regulation on Moose Lodge under the provisions of the constitution placed in the record in the court below would be to place State sanctions behind its discriminatory membership rules, but not behind its guest practices, which were not embodied in the constitution of the lodge. Had there been no change in the relevant circumstances since the making of the record in the District Court, our holding in Part I of this opinion that appellee has standing to challenge only the guest practices of Moose Lodge would have a bearing on our disposition of this issue. Appellee stated upon oral argument, though, and Moose Lodge conceded in its Brief that the bylaws of the Supreme Lodge have been altered since the lower court decision to make applicable to guests the same sort of racial restrictions as are presently applicable to members.

Even though the Liquor Control Board regulation in question is neutral in its terms, the result of its application in a case where the constitution and by-laws of a club required racial discrimination would be to invoke the sanctions of the State to enforce a concededly discriminatory private rule. State action, for purposes of the Equal Protection Clause, may emanate from rulings of administrative and regulatory agencies as well as from legislative or judicial action. *Shelley* v. *Kraemer, supra,* makes it clear that the application of state sanctions to enforce such a rule would violate the Fourteenth Amendment. Although the record before us is not as clear as one would like, appellant has not persuaded us that the District Court should have denied any and all relief.

Appellee was entitled to a decree enjoining the enforcement of §113.09 of the regulations promulgated by the Pennsylvania Liquor Control Board insofar as that regulation requires compliance by Moose Lodge with provisions of its constitution and by-laws containing racially discriminatory provisions. He was entitled to no more. The judgment of the District Court is reversed, and the cause remanded with instructions to enter a decree in conformity with this opinion.

Reversed and remanded.

MR. JUSTICE DOUGLAS, with whom MR. JUSTICE MARSHALL joins, dissenting.

My view of the First Amendment and the related guarantees of the Bill of Rights is that they create a zone of privacy which precludes government from interfering with private clubs or groups. The associational rights which our system honors permits all white, all black, all brown, and all yellow clubs to be formed. They also permit all Catholic, all Jewish, or all agnostic clubs to be established. Government may not tell a man or woman who his or her associates must be. The individual can be as selective as he desires. So the fact that the Moose Lodge allows only Caucasians to join or come as guests is constitutionally irrelevant, as is the decision of the Black Muslims to admit to their services only members of their race.

The problem is different, however, where the public domain is concerned. . . . [W]here restaurants or other facilities serving the public are concerned and licenses are obtained from the State for operating the business, the "public" may not be defined by the proprietor to include only people of his choice; nor may a State or municipal service be granted only to some.

Those cases are not precisely apposite, however, for a private club, by definition, is not in the public domain. And the fact that a private club gets some kind of permit from the State or municipality does not make it *ipso facto* a public enterprise or undertaking, any more than the grant to a householder of a permit to operate an incinerator puts the householder in the public domain. We must therefore examine whether there are special circumstances involved in the Pennsylvania scheme which differentiate the liquor license possessed by Moose Lodge from the incinerator permit.

Pennsylvania has a state store system of alcohol distribution. Resale is permitted by hotels, restaurants, and private clubs which all must obtain licenses from the Liquor Control Board. The scheme of regulation is complete and pervasive; and the state courts have sustained many restrictions on the licensees. . . . Once a license is issued the licensee must comply with many detailed requirements or risk suspension or revocation of the license. Among these requirements is Regulation No. 113.09 which says "Every club licensee shall adhere to all the provisions of its Constitution and By-laws." This regulation means, as applied to Moose Lodge, that it must adhere to the racially discriminatory provision of the Constitution of its Supreme Lodge that "The membership of the lodge shall be composed of male persons of the Caucasian or White race above the age of twenty-one years, and not married to someone other than the Caucasian or White race, who are of good moral character, physically and mentally normal, who shall profess a belief in a Supreme Being."

It is argued that this regulation only aims at the prevention of subterfuge and at enforcing Pennsylvania's differentiation between places of public accommodation and bona fide private clubs. It is also argued that the regulation only gives effect to the constitutionally protected rights of privacy and of association. But I cannot so read the regulation. While those other purposes are embraced in it, so is the restrictive membership clause. And we have held that "a State is responsible for the discriminatory act of a private party when the State, by its law, has compelled the act." It is irrelevant whether the law is statutory, or an administrative regulation. And it is irrelevant whether the discriminatory act was instigated by the regulation, or was independent of it. The result, as I see it, is the same as though Pennsylvania had put into its liquor licenses a provision that the license may not be used to dispense liquor to Blacks, Browns, Yellows — or atheists or agnostics. Regulation No. 113.09 is thus an invidious form of state action.

Were this regulation the only infirmity in Pennsylvania's licensing scheme, I would perhaps agree with the majority that the appropriate relief would be a decree enjoining its enforcement. But there is another flaw in the scheme not so easily cured. Liquor licenses in Pennsylvania, unlike driver's licenses, or marriage licenses, are not freely available to those who meet racially neutral qualifications. There is a complex quota system, which the majority accurately describes. What the majority neglects to say is that the Harrisburg quota, where Moose Lodge No. 107 is located, has been full for many years. No more club licenses may be issued in that city.

This state-enforced scarcity of licenses restricts the ability of blacks to obtain liquor, for liquor is commercially available *only* at private clubs for a significant portion of each week. Access by blacks to places that serve liquor is further limited by the fact that the state quota is filled. A group desiring to form a nondiscriminatory club which would serve blacks must purchase a license held by an existing club, which can exact a monopoly price for the transfer. The availability of such a license is speculative at best, however, for, as Moose Lodge itself concedes, without a liqour license a fraternal organization would be hard-pressed to survive.

Thus, the State of Pennsylvania is putting the weight of its liquor license, concededly a valued and important adjunct to a private club, behind racial discrimination.

MR. JUSTICE BRENNAN, with whom MR. JUSTICE MARSHALL joins, dissenting.

When Moose Lodge obtained its liquor license, the State of Pennsylvania became an active participant in the operation of the Lodge bar. Liquor licensing laws are only incidentally revenue measures; they are primarily pervasive regulatory schemes under which the State dictates and continually supervises virtually every detail of the operation of the licensee's business. Very few, if any, other licensed businesses experience such complete state involvement. Yet the Court holds that that involvement does not constitute "state action" making the Lodge's refusal to serve a guest liquor solely because of his race a violation of the Fourteenth Amendment. The vital flaw in the Court's reasoning is its complete disregard of the fundamental value underlying the "state action" concept. . . .

. . . .

This is thus a case requiring application of the principle that until today has governed our determinations of the existence of "state action": "Our prior decisions leave no doubt that the mere existence of efforts by the State, through legislation or otherwise, to authorize, encourage, or otherwise support racial discrimination in a particular facet of life constitutes illegal state involvement in those pertinent private acts of discrimination that subsequently occur."

I therefore dissent and would affirm the final decree entered by the District Court.

Heart of Atlanta Model v. U.S.

379 U.S. 241 (1964)
See pp. 216–218.

South Carolina v. Katzenbach

383 U.S. 301 (1966)
See pp. 252–256.

Jones v. Mayer Co.

392 U.S. 409 (1968)
Vote: 7–2

In April 1968, Congress enacted the Fair Housing Act of 1968, the nation's first fair housing law to be passed in more than a century. The complicated act, designed to be implemented in stages, prohibited discrimination in the sale and rental of federally assisted housing, covered virtually all multiple-unit dwellings and single-family residences not owned by private individuals. The act, eventually, was to be extended to forbid real estate agents and home mortgage institutions from discriminating in the sale, rental, and financing of privately owned single-family homes and investment properties. Although broad in coverage — by some estimates, it covered over three quarters of all housing units in the United States — its provisions with respect to rentals and sales exempted what came to be known as "Mrs. Murphy's boardinghouses," owner-occupied apartments of four units or less, and owner-occupied single-family dwellings.

As Congress was debating the provisions of the 1968 act, Joseph Lee Jones, a black resident of St. Louis County, Missouri, was in the courts seeking redress because he had been unable to purchase a house in Paddock Woods, Missouri, due to his race. He based his challenge upon an 1866 Act of Congress (reenacted in 1870 after passage of the Fourteenth Amendment and incorporated as 42 U.S.C. section 1982), which provided in part that "All citizens of the United States shall have the same right, in every State and Territory, as is enjoyed by white citizens thereof to inherit, purchase, lease, sell, hold, and convey real and personal property." The federal district court denied his request for injunctive relief in the form of an order to the Mayer Co. to sell him property. The court of appeals affirmed this ruling, upholding the constitutionality of Section 1982, but giving it a narrow interpretation. It concluded that Section 1982 applied only to state action and not to private refusals to sell. The Supreme Court granted Jones' petition for a writ of certiorari.

Before the Court, the Mayer Company claimed that Section 1982 was unconstitutional. Jones countered that the prohibition against racial discrimination in Section 1982 was valid under Congress' authority to enforce the Thirteenth Amendment's prohibition against slavery and involuntary servitude. He also argued that Mayer's court-enforced discrimination amounted to state action, which was prohibited by the Equal Protection Clause of the Fourteenth Amendment. In its opinion, the Supreme Court upheld Section 1982 on Thirteenth Amendment grounds, and thus found it unnecessary to rule on the state action–Fourteenth Amendment argument.

The context of time and events is important. While the Fair Housing Act of 1968 contained a great many remedies and provided for federal intervention to combat racial discrimination in the housing market, the language of the act adopted nearly one hundred years earlier was far more sweeping. It covered *all* housing units, even Mrs. Murphy's boardinghouse. Thus the Supreme Court was called upon to interpret a sweeping provision in an old law just after Congress had consciously rejected such sweeping language when adopting the new law.

Furthermore, when earlier the Supreme Court had interpreted similarly sweeping language in other Reconstruction-era statutes, it had held some of them to be unconstitutional and given narrow meaning to others. See, for example, the CIVIL RIGHTS CASES (1883). Should any of this have made a difference? Did it?

MR. JUSTICE STEWART delivered the opinion of the Court.

This Court last had occasion to consider the scope of 42 U.S.C. §1982 in 1948, in *Hurd* v. *Hodge*. That case arose when property owners in the District of Columbia sought to enforce racially restrictive covenants against the Negro purchasers of several homes on their block. A federal district court enforced the restrictive agreements by declaring void the deeds of the Negro purchasers. It enjoined further attempts to sell or lease them the properties in question and directed them to "remove themselves and all of their personal belongings" from the premises within 60 days. The Court of Appeals for the District of Columbia affirmed, and this Court granted certiorari to decide whether §1982 . . . barred enforcement of the racially restrictive agreements in that case.

That result, this Court concluded, was prohibited by §1982. To suggest otherwise, the Court said, "is to reject the plain meaning of language."

Hurd v. *Hodge* squarely held, therefore, that a Negro citizen who is denied the opportunity to purchase the home he wants "[s]olely because of [his] race and color," has suffered the kind of injury that §1982 was designed to prevent. The basic source of the injury in *Hurd* was, of course, the action of private individuals — white citizens who had agreed to exclude Negroes from a residential area. But an arm of the Government — in that case, a federal court — had assisted in the enforcement of that agreement.

Thus *Hurd* v. *Hodge, supra,* did not present the question whether *purely* private discrimination, unaided by any action on the part of government, would violate §1982 if its effects were to deny a citizen the right to rent or buy property solely because of his race or color.

. . . .

We begin with the language of the statute itself. In plain and unambiguous terms, §1982 grants to all citizens, without regard to race or color, "the same right" to purchase and lease property "as is enjoyed by white citizens."

On its face, . . . §1982 appears to prohibit *all* discrimination against Negroes in the sale or rental of property — discrimination by private owners as well as discrimination by public authorities. Indeed, even the respondents seem to concede that, if §1982 "means what it says" — to use the words of the respondents' brief — then it must encompass every racially motivated refusal to sell or rent and cannot be confined to officially sanctioned segregation in housing. Stressing what they consider to be the revolutionary implications of so literal a reading of §1982, the respondents argue that Congress cannot possibly have intended any such result. Our examination of the relevant history, however, persuades us that Congress meant exactly what it said.

. . . .

In attempting to demonstrate the contrary, the respondents rely heavily upon the fact that the Congress which approved the 1866 statute wished to eradicate the recently enacted Black Codes — laws which had saddled Negroes with "onerous disabilities and burdens, and curtailed their rights . . . to such an extent that their freedom was of little value. . . ." *Slaughter-House Cases.* The respondents suggest that the only evil Congress sought to eliminate was that of racially discriminatory laws in the former Confederate States. But the Civil Rights Act was drafted to apply throughout the country, and its language was far broader than would have been necessary to strike down discriminatory statutes.

That broad language, we are asked to believe, was a mere slip of the legislative pen. We disagree. For the same Congress that wanted to do away with the Black Codes *also* had before it an imposing body of evidence pointing to the mistreatment of Negroes by private individuals and unofficial groups, mistreatment unrelated to any hostile state legislation. "Accounts in newspapers North and South, Freedmen's Bureau and other official documents, private reports and correspondence were all adduced" to show that "private outrage and atrocity" was "daily inflicted on freedmen. . . ." The congressional debates are replete with references to private injustices against Negroes — references to white employers who refused to pay their Negro workers, white planters who agreed among themselves not to hire freed slaves without the permission of their former masters, white citizens who assaulted Negroes or who combined to drive them out of their communities.

Indeed, one of the most comprehensive studies then before Congress stressed the prevalence of private hostility toward Negroes and the need to protect them from the resulting persecution and discrimination. The report noted the existence of laws virtually prohibiting Negroes from owning or renting property in certain towns, but described such laws as "mere isolated cases," representing "the local outcroppings of a spirit . . . found to prevail elsewhere" — a spirit expressed, for example, by lawless acts of brutality directed against Negroes who traveled to areas where they were not wanted. The report concluded that, even if anti-Negro legislation were "repealed in all the States lately in rebellion," equal treatment for the Negro would not yet be secured.

In this setting, it would have been strange indeed if Congress had viewed its task as encompassing merely the nullification of racist laws in the former rebel States. That the Congress which assembled in the Nation's capital in December 1865 in fact had a broader vision of the task before it became clear early in the session, when three proposals to invalidate discriminatory state statutes were rejected as "too narrowly conceived." From the outset it seemed clear, at least to Senator Trumbull of Illinois, Chairman of the Judiciary Committee, that stronger legislation might prove necessary. . . .

. . . .

In light of the concerns that led Congress to adopt it and the contents of the debates that preceded its passage, it is clear that the Act was designed to do just what its terms suggest: to prohibit all racial discrimination, whether or not under color of law, with respect to the rights enumerated therein — including the right to purchase or lease property.

Nor was the scope of the 1866 Act altered when it was re-enacted in 1870, some two years after the ratification of the Fourteenth Amendment. It is quite true that some members of Congress supported the Fourteenth Amendment "in order to eliminate doubt as to the constitutional validity of the Civil Rights Act as applied to the States." But it certainly does not follow that the adoption of the Fourteenth Amendment or the subsequent readoption of the Civil Rights Act were meant somehow to *limit* its application to state action. The legislative history furnishes not the slightest factual basis for any such speculation, and

the conditions prevailing in 1870 make it highly implausible. For by that time most, if not all, of the former Confederate States, then under the control of "reconstructed" legislatures, had formally repudiated racial discrimination, and the focus of congressional concern had clearly shifted from hostile statutes to the activities of groups like the Ku Klux Klan, operating wholly outside the law.

Against this background, it would obviously make no sense to assume, without any historical support whatever, that Congress made a silent decision in 1870 to exempt private discrimination from the operation of the Civil Rights Act of 1866. "The cardinal rule is that repeals by implication are not favored." All Congress said in 1870 was that the 1866 law "is hereby re-enacted." That is all Congress meant.

As we said in a somewhat different setting two Terms ago, "We think that history leaves no doubt that, if we are to give [the law] the scope that its origins dictate, we must accord it a sweep as broad as its language." "We are not at liberty to seek ingenious analytical instruments," to carve from §1982 an exception for private conduct — even though its application to such conduct in the present context is without established precedent. And, as the Attorney General of the United States said at the oral argument of this case, "The fact that the statute lay partially dormant for many years cannot be held to diminish its force today."

The remaining question is whether Congress has power under the Constitution to do what §1982 purports to do: to prohibit all racial discrimination, private and public, in the sale and rental of property. Our starting point is the Thirteenth Amendment, for it was pursuant to that constitutional provision that Congress originally enacted what is now §1982. . . .

As its text reveals, the Thirteenth Amendment "is not a mere prohibition of State laws establishing or upholding slavery, but an absolute declaration that slavery or involuntary servitude shall not exist in any part of the United States." *Civil Rights Cases* [1883]. It has never been doubted, therefore, "that the power vested in Congress to enforce the article by appropriate legislation," includes the power to enact laws "direct and primary, operating upon the acts of individuals, whether sanctioned by State legislation or not."

Thus, the fact that §1982 operates upon the unofficial acts of private individuals, whether or not sanctioned by state law, presents no constitutional problem. If Congress has the power under the Thirteenth Amendment to eradicate conditions that prevent Negroes from buying and renting property because of their race or color, then no federal statute calculated to achieve that objective can be thought to exceed the constitutional power of Congress simply because it reaches beyond state action to regulate the conduct of private individuals. The constitutional question in this case, therefore, comes to this: Does the authority of Congress to enforce the Thirteenth Amendment "by appropriate legislation" include the power to eliminate all racial barriers to the acquisition of real and personal property? We think the answer to that question is plainly yes.

"By its own unaided force and effect," the Thirteenth Amendment "abolished slavery, and established universal freedom." Whether or not the Amendment *itself* did any more than that—a question not involved in this case—it is at least clear that the Enabling Clause of that Amendment empowered Congress to do much more. For that clause clothed "Congress with power to pass *all laws necessary and proper for abolishing all badges and incidents of slavery in the United States.*"

. . . Surely Congress has the power under the Thirteenth Amendment rationally to determine what are the badges and the incidents of slavery, and the authority to translate that determination into effective legislation. Nor can we say that the determination Congress has made is an irrational one. For this Court recognized long ago that, whatever else they may have encompassed, the badges and incidents of slavery—its "burdens and disabilities"—included restraints upon "those fundamental rights which are the essence of civil freedom, namely, the same right . . . to inherit, purchase, lease, sell and convey property, as is enjoyed by white citizens." *Civil Rights Cases* [1883]. Just as the Black Codes, enacted after the Civil War to restrict the free exercise of those rights, were substitutes for the slave system, so the exclusion of Negroes from white communities became a substitute for the Black Codes. And when racial discrimination herds men into ghettos and makes their ability to buy property turn on the color of their skin, then it too is a relic of slavery.

Negro citizens North and South, who saw in the Thirteenth Amendment a promise of freedom—freedom to "go and come at pleasure" and to "buy and sell when they please"—would be left with "a mere paper guarantee" if Congress were powerless to assure that a dollar in the hands of a Negro will purchase the same thing as a dollar in the hands of a white man. At the very least, the freedom that Congress is empowered to secure under the Thirteenth Amendment includes the freedom to buy whatever a white man can buy, the right to live wherever a white man can live. If Congress cannot say that being a free man means at least this much, then the

Thirteenth Amendment made a promise the Nation cannot keep.

. . . .

. . . The judgment is

Reversed.

[MR. JUSTICE DOUGLAS wrote a concurring opinion.]

[MR. JUSTICE HARLAN, with whom MR. JUSTICE WHITE concurred, wrote a dissenting opinion.]

Regents of the University of California v. Bakke

438 U.S. 265 (1978)
Vote: 5–4

Racial discrimination cases in education considered up to this point have focused on standards for identifying unconstitutional segregation and have explored the range of court-ordered remedies permitted by the Supreme Court to overcome it. *Bakke* takes these issues one significant step forward. It deals with reverse discrimination, the use of racial quotas, in the absence of a finding of prior discrimination, for the benign purpose of increasing rather than excluding minorities. While racially conscious zoning, goals, and quotas had been approved by the Supreme Court before, in SWANN V. CHARLOTTE-MECKLENBURG BOARD OF EDUCATION, such racially conscious policies had all been adopted as *remedies* after judicial findings of prior segregation. This case is different. Here the medical school of the University of California at Davis had no history of racial discrimination. Indeed, it was only a few years old at the time this case arose and from its founding had actively sought minority applicants. Thus, what makes this case distinctive is that the Davis medical school *voluntarily* adopted a policy of preferential treatment for disadvantaged minorities as part of an effort to overcome a general and historic problem.

To this end it devised a special admissions program for "disadvantaged minorities," which worked in coordination with its regular admission system.

Sixteen out of the one hundred entering places were reserved for disadvantaged blacks, Chicanos, Asians, and American Indians who met acceptable standards for admission. Minority applicants had the choice of being considered under this special program or the regular admissions program. Non-minorities, even if from a disadvantaged background, could be considered only under the regular system. No definition of "disadvantage" was ever formally adopted by the school, but those in the special pool of applicants were screened by a committee to determine if they had experienced economic or educational deprivation. If candidates passed this hurdle, those who were acceptable for admission were ranked according to their qualifications, except that the special program did not cut off at a 2.5 grade point average, as did the regular program. The top candidates in the special pool were then admitted in order until there were sixteen acceptances. Applicants in the regular pool were selected by a similar process until eighty-four places were filled. Applicants in the special program were never directly compared to those in the regular program, although all those admitted under both systems were qualified to study medicine.

Overall, those admitted under the special program had lower grade point averages, MCAT (Medical College Aptitude Test) scores, and "benchmark" scores (a composite index based upon a number of factors, including assessments after interviews by Davis faculty) than the average for the regular admittees and many unsuccessful applicants considered in the regular process.

One such unsuccessful regular applicant was Allan Bakke, a 37-year-old engineer of Norwegian ancestry who had twice been rejected for admission to the Davis medical school. On most of the standard criteria considered by the school, his scores were higher than the average for regular admittees. His overall grade point average was 3.51, in contrast to an average of 3.29 for the regular admittees, and his scores on the verbal, quantitative, science, and general information portions of the MCAT were similarly higher. The contrast

was even greater with the averages of the special admittees, whose overall grade point average was 2.62 and whose average MCAT scores were considerably lower than Bakke's.

After being denied admission for a third time, Bakke filed suit in the Superior Court of California, alleging that the special admissions program operated to exclude him on the basis of his race in violation of the California Constitution, the Fourteenth Amendment of the United States Constitution, and Section 601 of Title VI of the Civil Rights Act of 1964. But for the special admissions program, he maintained, he would have been accepted at the Davis medical school. The trial court found that Davis' special program operated as an unconstitutional racial quota. On appeal, the California Supreme Court agreed with the University's goal of wanting to integrate the medical profession and to increase the number of physicians willing to serve members of minority groups, but concluded that the special admissions program was "not the least intrusive means of achieving these goals." Without passing on state constitutional or federal statutory questions, the California high court held that the Equal Protection Clause of the Fourteenth Amendment required that "no applicant may be rejected because of his race, in favor of another who is less qualified, as measured by standards applied without regard to race." The University then petitioned the Supreme Court for a writ of certiorari.

In its decision, a majority of five on the Supreme Court held for Bakke, who was subsequently admitted to and graduated from the Davis medical school. In deciding the case, the Court was badly splintered. There were six different opinions, none of which commanded a majority. Four justices — Stevens, Burger, Stewart, and Rehnquist — held that the Davis quota system was a violation of Title VI of the Civil Rights Act of 1964, which provides in part that "No person in the United States shall, on the grounds of race, color, or national origin, be excluded from participation in, be denied the benefits of, or be subjected to discrimination under any program or activity receiving Federal financial assistance." Four other justices — Brennan, Marshall, White, and Blackmun — were of the opinion that the Davis quota system violated neither the Constitution nor the Civil Rights Act of 1964, and voted to uphold the Davis plan. Justice Powell took a middle position, saying that universities could consider race in the admissions process as part of a legitimate effort to diversify their student bodies, but that Davis had gone too far because it did not permit "individual comparisons." Thus by a vote of 5 to 4, the Court held that race could be taken into consideration in admissions, but by a vote of 5 to 4, it held that Davis' affirmative action program was invalid. The three other opinions, all from justices who concurred with Brennan, elaborated on important additional issues they believed were raised in the case.

At the time, this case generated considerable public interest. Over sixty amicus curiae briefs were filed. Many thought that all affirmative action programs were at stake and that admissions procedures of universities across the country were on trial. But as you read the case, ask what, precisely, the court did prohibit. Despite the outcome, do you think Justice Powell was closer to Justice Stevens or to Justice Brennan? Also consider Justice Marshall's opinion in light of the following figures: between 1970 and 1974, the Davis special program admitted fifty-three Asians, thirty-nine Chicanos, twenty-seven blacks, and apparently no American Indians. Did the program accomplish the goals he attributed to it? Would this make a difference to him? There is, of course, no way of knowing how many "disadvantaged" whites might have been admitted under the program had it been broadened to include them. But one might ask, would a quota system open to "disadvantaged" persons in general pass muster? Why should it? What precisely is the purpose of any affirmative action program in the absence of a special finding of prior discrimination? Finally, contrast this case with the next five cases, UNITED STEELWORKERS OF AMERICA V. WEBER (1979), FULLILOVE V. KLUTZNICK (1980), CITY OF RICHMOND V. J. A. CROSON CO. (1989), LOCAL 28 OF THE SHEETMETAL

WORKERS' INTERNATIONAL ASSOC. V. EEOC (1986), and JOHNSON V. TRANSPORTATION AGENCY (1987). Can you draw an acceptable distinction among the Court's rulings in these six cases?

MR. JUSTICE POWELL announced the judgment of the court.

. . . .

II

In this Court the parties neither briefed nor argued the applicability of Title VI of the Civil Rights Act of 1964. Rather, as had the California court, they focused exclusively upon the validity of the special admissions program under the Equal Protection Clause. Because it was possible, however, that a decision on Title VI might obviate resort to constitutional interpretation, see *Ashwander* v. *TVA,* (1936), we requested supplementary briefing on the statutory issue.

. . . .

B

The language of §601, like that of the Equal Protection Clause, is majestic in its sweep:

> No person in the United States shall, on the ground of race, color, or national origin, be excluded from participation in, be denied the benefits of, or be subjected to discrimination under any program or activity receiving Federal financial assistance.

The concept of "discrimination," like the phrase "equal protection of the laws," is susceptible to varying interpretations. . . . We must, therefore, seek whatever aid is available in determining the precise meaning of the statute before us. Examination of the voluminous legislative history of Title VI reveals a congressional intent to halt federal funding of entities that violate a prohibition of racial discrimination similar to that of the Constitution. . . .

The problem confronting Congress was discrimination against Negro citizens at the hands of recipients of federal moneys. . . . Over and over again, proponents of the bill detailed the plight of Negroes seeking equal treatment in such programs. There simply was no reason for Congress to consider the validity of hypothetical preferences that might be accorded minority citizens; the legislators were dealing with the real and pressing problem of how to guarantee those citizens equal treatment.

Further evidence of the incorporation of a constitutional standard into Title VI appears in the repeated refusals of the legislation's supporters precisely to define the term "discrimination." Opponents sharply criticize this failure, but proponents of the bill merely replied that the meaning of "discrimination" would be made clear by reference to the Constitution or other existing law. For example, Senator Humphrey noted the relevance of the Constitution:

> As I have said, the bill has a simple purpose. That purpose is to give fellow citizens — Negroes — the same rights and opportunities that white people take for granted. This is no more than what was preached by the prophets, and by Christ Himself. It is no more than what our Constitution guarantees.

In view of the clear legislative intent, Title VI must be held to proscribe only those racial classifications that would violate the Equal Protection Clause or the Fifth Amendment.

III

A

Petitioner does not deny that decisions based on race or ethnic origin by faculties and administrations of state universities are renewable under the Fourteenth Amendment. For his part, respondent does not argue that all racial or ethnic classifications are *per se* invalid. See *e.g., Hirabayashi* v. *United States* (1943); *Korematsu* v. *United States* (1944); *Lee* v. *Washington* (1968); *United Jewish Organizations* v. *Carey* (1977). The parties do disagree as to the level of judicial scrutiny to be applied to the special admissions program. Petitioner argues that the court below erred in applying strict scrutiny, as this inexact term has been applied in our cases. That level of review, petitioner asserts, should be reserved for classifications that disadvantage "discrete and insular minorities." See *United States* v. *Carolene Products Co.* . . . n. 4 (1938). Respondent, on the other hand, contends that the California court correctly rejected the notion that the degree of judicial scrutiny accorded a particular racial or ethnic classification hinges upon membership in a discrete and insular minority and duly recognized that the "rights established [by the Fourteenth Amendment] are personal rights." *Shelley* v. *Kraemer* (1948).

En route to this crucial battle over the scope of judicial review, the parties fight a sharp preliminary action over the proper characterization of the special admissions program. Petitioner prefers to view it as establishing a "goal" of minority representation in the medical school. Respondent, echoing the courts below, labels it a racial quota.

This semantic distinction is beside the point: the special admissions program is undeniably a classification based on race and ethnic background. To the extent that there existed a pool of at least minimally qualified minority applicants to fill the 16 special admissions seats, white applicants could compete only for 84 seats in the entering class, rather than the 100 open to minority applicants. Whether this limitation is described as a quota or a goal, it is a line drawn on the basis of race and ethnic status.

The guarantees of the Fourteenth Amendment extend to persons. Its language is explicit: "No state shall . . . deny to any person within its jurisdiction the equal protection of the laws." It is settled beyond question that the "rights created by the first section of the Fourteenth Amendment are, by its terms, guaranteed to the individual. The guarantee of equal protection cannot mean one thing when applied to one individual and something else when applied to a person of another color. If both are not accorded the same protection, then it is not equal.

Nevertheless, petitioner argues that the court below erred in applying strict scrutiny to the special admissions programs because white males, such as respondent, are not a "discrete and insular minority" requiring extraordinary protection from the majoritarian political process. *Carolene Products Co.* This rationale, however, has never been invoked in our decisions as a prerequisite to subjecting racial or ethnic distinctions to close scrutiny. Nor has this Court held that discreteness and insularity constitute necessary preconditions to a holding that a particular classification is invidious. See, *e.g., Skinner* v. *Oklahoma* (1942); *Carrington* v. *Rash* (1965). These characteristics may be relevant in deciding whether or not to add new types of classifications to the list of "suspect" categories or whether a particular classification survives close examination. Racial and ethnic classifications, however, are subject to stringent examination without regard to these additional characteristics. We declared as much in the first cases explicitly to recognize racial distinctions as suspect:

> Distinctions between citizens solely because of their ancestry are by their very nature odious to a free people whose institutions are founded upon the doctrine of equality. *Hirabayashi.* . . . [A]ll legal restrictions which curtail the rights of a single racial group are immediately suspect. That is not to say that all such restrictions are unconstitutional. It is

to say that courts must subject them to the most rigid scrutiny. *Korematsu.*

The Court has never questioned the validity of those pronouncements. Racial and ethnic distinctions of any sort are inherently suspect and thus call for the most exacting judicial examination.

B

This perception of racial and ethnic distinctions is rooted in our Nation's constitutional and demographic history. The Court's initial view of the Fourteenth Amendment was that its "one pervading purpose" was "the freedom of the slave race, the security and firm establishment of that freedom, and the protection of the newly-made freeman and citizen from the oppressions of those who had formerly exercised dominion over him." *Slaughter-House Cases* (1873). The Equal Protection Clause, however, was "[v]irtually strangled in its infancy by post-civil-war judicial reactionism." It was relegated to decades of relative desuetude while the Due Process Clause of the Fourteenth Amendment, after a short germinal period, flourished as a cornerstone in the Court's defense of property and liberty of contract. See, *e.g., Mugler* v. *Kansas* (1887); *Allgeyer* v. *Louisiana* (1897); *Lochner* v. *New York* (1905). In that cause, the Fourteenth Amendment's "one pervasive purpose" was displaced. See, *e.g., Plessy* v. *Ferguson* (1896). It was only as the era of substantive due process came to a close, see, *e.g., Nebbia* v. *New York* (1934); *West Coast Hotel* v. *Parrish* (1937), that the Equal Protection Clause began to attain a genuine measure of vitality.

By that time it was no longer possible to peg the guarantees of the Fourteenth Amendment to the struggle for equality of one racial minority. During the dormancy of the Equal Protection Clause, the United States had become a nation of minorities. Each had to struggle — and to some extent struggles still — to overcome the prejudices not of a monolithic majority, but of a "majority" composed of various minority groups of whom it was said — perhaps unfairly in many cases — that a shared characteristic was a willingness to disadvantage other groups. As the Nation filled with the stock of many lands, the reach of the Clause was gradually extended to all ethnic groups seeking protection from official discrimination. . . . The guarantees of equal protection, said the Court in *Yick Wo,* "are universal in their application, to all persons within the territorial jurisdiction, without regard to any differences of race, of color, or of nationality; and the equal protection of the laws is a pledge of the protection of equal laws."

Although many of the Framers of the Fourteenth Amendment conceived of its primary function as bridging the vast distance between members of the Negro race and the white "majority," *Slaughter-House Cases,* the Amendment itself was framed in universal terms, without reference to color, ethnic origin, or condition of prior servitude. As this Court recently remarked in interpreting the 1866 Civil Rights Act to extend to claims of racial discrimination against white persons, "the 39th Congress was intent upon establishing in federal law a broader principle than would have been necessary to meet the particular and immediate plight of the newly freed Negro slaves." And that legislation was specifically broadened in 1870 to ensure that "all persons," not merely "citizens," would enjoy equal rights under the law. . . .

Over the past 30 years, this Court has embarked upon the crucial mission of interpreting the Equal Protection Clause with the view of assuring to all persons the "protection of equal laws," in a Nation confronting a legacy of slavery and racial discrimination. Because the landmark decisions in this area arose in response to the continued exclusion of Negroes from the mainstream of American society, they could be characterized as involving discrimination by the "majority" white race against the Negro minority. But they need not be read as depending upon that characterization for their results. It suffices to say that "[o]ver the years, this Court consistently repudiated [d]istinctions between citizens solely because of their ancestry as being 'odious to a free people whose institutions are founded upon the doctrine of equality.'"

Petitioner urges us to adopt for the first time a more restrictive view of the Equal Protection Clause and hold that discrimination against members of the white "majority" cannot be suspect if its purpose can be characterized as "benign." The clock of our liberties, however, cannot be turned back to 1868. It is far too late to argue that the guarantee of equal protection to *all* persons permits the recognition of special wards entitled to a degree of protection greater than that accorded others. "The Fourteenth Amendment is not directed solely against discrimination due to a 'two-class theory' — that is, based upon differences between 'white' and Negro."

Once the artificial line of a "two-class theory" of the Fourteenth Amendment is put aside, the difficulties entailed in varying the level of judicial review according to a perceived "preferred" status of a particular racial or ethnic minority are intractable. The concepts of "majority" and "minority" necessarily reflect temporary arrangements and political judgments. As observed above, the white "majority" itself is composed of various minority groups, most of which can lay claim to a history of prior discrimination at the hands of the state and private individuals. Not all of these groups can receive preferential treatment and corresponding judicial tolerance of distinctions drawn in terms of race and nationality, for then the only "majority" left would be a new minority of White Anglo-Saxon Protestants. There is no principled basis for deciding which groups would merit "heightened judicial solicitude" and which would not. Courts would be asked to evaluate the extent of the prejudice and consequent harm suffered by various minority groups. Those whose societal injury is thought to exceed some arbitrary level of tolerability then would be entitled to preferential classifications at the expense of individuals belonging to other groups. Those classifications would be free from exacting judicial scrutiny. As these preferences began to have their desired effect, and the consequences of past discrimination were undone, new judicial rankings would be necessary. The kind of variable sociological and political analysis necessary to produce such rankings simply does not lie within the judicial competence — even if they otherwise were politically feasible and socially desirable.

Moreover, there are serious problems of justice connected with the idea of preference itself. First, it may not always be clear that a so-called preference is in fact benign. Courts may be asked to validate burdens imposed upon individual members of particular groups in order to advance the group's general interest. See *United Jewish Organizations* v. *Carey*. Nothing in the Constitution supports the notion that individuals may be asked to suffer otherwise impermissible burdens in order to enhance the societal standing of their ethnic groups. Second, preferential programs may only reinforce common stereotypes holding that certain groups are unable to achieve success without special protection based on a factor having no relationship to individual worth. Third, there is a measure of inequity in forcing innocent persons in respondent's position to bear the burdens of redressing grievances not of their making.

By hitching the meaning of the Equal Protection Clause to these transitory considerations, we would be holding, as a constitutional principle, that judicial scrutiny of classifications touching on racial and ethnic background may vary with the ebb and flow of political forces. Disparate constitutional tolerance of such classifications well may serve to exacerbate racial and ethnic antagonisms rather than alleviate them. Also, the mutability of a constitutional principle, based upon shifting political and social judgments, undermines the chances for consistent application of the Constitution from one generation to the next, a critical feature of its coherent interpretation. In expounding the Constitution, the Court's role is to discern "principles sufficiently absolute to give them roots throughout the community and continuity over significant periods of time, and to lift them above the level of the pragmatic political judgments of a particular time and place."

If it is the individual who is entitled to judicial protection against classifications based upon his racial or ethnic background because such distinctions impinge upon personal rights, rather than the individual only because of his membership in a particular group, then constitutional standards may be applied consistently. Political judgments regarding the necessity for the particular classification may be weighed in the constitutional balance, *Korematsu* v. *United States* (1944), but the standard of justification will remain constant. This is as it should be, since those political judgments are the product of rough compromise struck by contending groups within the democratic process. When they touch upon an individual's race or ethnic background, he is entitled to a judicial determination that the burden he is asked to bear on that basis is precisely tailored to serve a compelling governmental interest. The Constitution guarantees that right to every person regardless of his background.

Petitioner contends that on several occasions this Court has approved preferential classifications without applying the most exacting scrutiny. Most of the cases upon which petitioner relies are drawn from three areas: school desegregation, employment discrimination, and sex discrimination. Each of the cases cited presented a situation materially different from the facts of this case.

The school desegregation cases are inapposite. Each involved remedies for clearly determined constitutional violations. . . . Here, there was no judicial determination of constitutional violation as a predicate for the formulation of a remedial classification.

The employment discrimination cases also do not advance petitioner's cause. . . . But we have never approved preferential classifications in the absence of proven constitutional or statutory violations.

Nor is petitioner's view as to the applicable standard supported by the fact that gender-based classifications are not subjected to this level of scrutiny. Gender-based distinctions are less likely to create the analytical and practical problems present in preferential programs premised on racial or ethnic criteria. With respect to gender there are only two possible classifications. The incidence of the burdens imposed by preferential classifications is clear. There are no rival groups who can claim that they, too, are entitled to preferential treatment. Classwide questions as to the group suffering previous injury and groups which fairly can be burdened are relatively manageable for reviewing courts. The resolution of these same questions in the context of racial and ethnic preferences presents far more complex and intractable problems than gender-based classifications. More importantly, the perception of racial classifications as inherently odious stems from a lengthy and tragic history that gender-based classifications do not share. In sum, the Court has never viewed such classification as inherently suspect or as comparable to racial or ethnic classifications for the purpose of equal-protection analysis.

. . . .

In this case . . . there has been no determination by the legislature or a responsible administrative agency that the University engaged in a discriminatory practice requiring remedial efforts. Moreover, the operation of petitioner's special admissions program is quite different from the remedial measures approved in [other] cases. It prefers the designated minority groups at the expense of other individuals who are totally foreclosed from competition for the 16 special admissions seats in every medical school class. Because of that foreclosure, some individuals are excluded from enjoyment of a state-provided benefit — admission to the medical school — they otherwise would receive. When a classification denies an individual opportunities or benefits enjoyed by others solely because of his race or ethnic background, it must be regarded as suspect.

IV

We have held that in "order to justify the use of a suspect classification, a State must show that its purpose or interest is both constitutionally permissible and substantial, and that its use of the classification is 'necessary . . . to the accomplishment' of its purpose or the safeguarding of its interest." The special admissions program purports to serve the purposes of: (i) "reducing the historic deficit of traditionally disfavored minorities in medical schools and the medical profession," Brief for Petitioner 32; (ii) countering the effects of societal discrimination; (iii) increasing the number of physicians who will practice in communities currently underserved; and (iv) obtaining the educational benefits that flow from an ethnically diverse student body. It is necessary to decide which, if any, of these purposes is substantial enough to support the use of a suspect classification.

If petitioner's purpose is to assure within its student body some specified percentage of a particular group merely because of its race or ethnic origin,

such a preferential purpose must be rejected not as insubstantial but as facially invalid. Preferring members of any one group for no reason other than race or ethnic origin is discrimination for its own sake. This the Constitution forbids. . . .

B

The State certainly has a legitimate and substantial interest in ameliorating, or eliminating where feasible, the disabling effects of identified discrimination. The line of school desegregation cases, commencing with *Brown,* attests to the importance of this state goal and the commitment of the judiciary to affirm all lawful means toward its attainment. In the school cases, the States were required by court order to redress the wrongs worked by specific instances of racial dis-·crimination. That goal was far more focused than the remedying of the effects of "societal discrimination," an amorphous concept of injury that may be ageless in its reach into the past.

We have never approved a classification that aids persons perceived as members of relatively victimized groups at the expense of other innocent individuals in the absence of judicial, legislative, or administrative findings of constitutional or statutory violations. After such findings have been made, the governmental interest in preferring members of the injured groups at the expense of others is substantial, since the legal rights of the victims must be vindicated. In such a case, the extent of the injury and the consequent remedy will have been judicially, legislatively, or administratively defined. Also, the remedial action usually remains subject to continuing oversight to assure that it will work the least harm possible to other innocent persons competing for the benefit. Without such findings of constitutional or statutory violations, it cannot be said that the government has any greater interest in helping one individual than in refraining from harming another. Thus, the government has no compelling justification for inflicting such harm.

Petitioner does not purport to have made, and is in no position to make, such findings. Its broad mission is education, not the formulation of any legislative policy or the adjudication of particular claims of illegality. For reasons similar to those stated in Part III of this opinion, isolated segments of our vast governmental structures are not competent to make those decisions, at least in the absence of legislative mandates and legislatively determined criteria. Before relying upon these sorts of findings in establishing a racial classification, a governmental body must have the authority and capability to establish, in the record, that the classification is responsive to identified discrimination. Lacking this capability, petitioner has not carried its burden of justification on this issue.

Hence, the purpose of helping certain groups whom the faculty of the Davis Medical School perceived as victims of "societal discrimination" does not justify a classification that imposes disadvantages upon persons like respondent, who bear no responsibility for whatever harm the beneficiaries of the special admissions program are thought to have suffered. To hold otherwise would be to convert a remedy heretofore reserved for violations of legal rights into a privilege that all institutions throughout the Nation could grant at their pleasure to whatever groups are perceived as victims of societal discrimination. This is a step we have never approved.

C

Petitioner identifies, as another purpose of its program, improving the delivery of health care services to communities currently underserved. It may be assumed that in some situations a State's interest in facilitating the health care of its citizens is sufficiently compelling to support the use of a suspect classification. But there is virtually no evidence in the record indicating that petitioner's special admissions program is either needed or geared to promote that goal.

D

The fourth goal asserted by petitioner is the attainment of a diverse student body. This clearly is a constitutionally permissible goal for an institution of higher education. Academic freedom, though not a specifically enumerated constitutional right, long has been viewed as a special concern of the First Amendment. The freedom of a university to make its own judgments as to education includes the selection of its student body.

. . . .

Thus, in arguing that its universities must be accorded the right to select those students who will contribute the most to the "robust exchange of ideas," petitioner invokes a countervailing constitutional interest, that of the First Amendment. In this light, petitioner must be viewed as seeking to achieve a goal that is of paramount importance in the fulfillment of its mission.

It may be argued that there is greater force to these views at the undergraduate level than in a medical school where the training is centered primarily on professional competency. But even at the graduate level, our tradition and experience lend support to the view that the contribution of diversity is substantial. . . . Physicians serve a heterogenous population. An otherwise qualified medical student with a particular background — whether it be ethnic, geographic, culturally advantaged or disadvantaged — may bring to a professional school of medicine experiences, outlooks and ideas that enrich the training of its student body and better equip its graduates to render with understanding their vital service to humanity.

Ethnic diversity, however, is only one element in a range of factors a university properly may consider in attaining the goal of a heterogeneous student body. Although a university must have wide discretion in making the sensitive judgments as to who should be admitted, constitutional limitations protecting individual rights may not be disregarded. Respondent urges — and the courts below have held — that petitioner's dual admissions program is a racial classification that impermissibly infringes his rights under the Fourteenth Amendment. As the interest of diversity is compelling in the context of a university's admissions program, the question remains whether the program's racial classification is necessary to promote this interest.

V

A

It may be assumed that the reservation of a specified number of seats in each class for individuals from the preferred ethnic groups would contribute to the attainment of considerable ethnic diversity in the student body. But petitioner's argument that this is the only effective means of serving the interest of diversity is seriously flawed. In a most fundamental sense the argument misconceives the nature of the state interest that would justify consideration of race or ethnic background. It is not an interest in simple ethnic diversity, in which a specified percentage of the student body is in effect guaranteed to be members of selected ethnic groups, with the remaining percentage an undifferentiated aggregation of students. The diversity that furthers a compelling state interest encompasses a far broader array of qualifications and characteristics of which racial or ethnic origin is but a single though important element. Petitioner's special admissions program, focused *solely* on ethnic diversity, would hinder rather than further attainment of genuine diversity.

Nor would the state interest in genuine diversity be served by expanding petitioner's two-track system into a multitrack program with a prescribed number of seats set aside for each identifiable category of applicants. Indeed, it is inconceivable that a university would thus pursue the logic of petitioner's two-track program to the illogical end of insulating each category of applicants with certain desired qualifications from competition with all other applicants.

The experience of other university admissions programs, which take race into account in achieving the educational diversity valued by the First Amendment, demonstrates that the assignment of a fixed number of places to a minority group is not a necessary means toward that end. An illuminating example is found in the Harvard College program:

> In recent years Harvard College has expanded the concept of diversity to include students from disadvantaged economic, racial and ethnic groups. Harvard College now recruits not only Californians or Louisianans but also blacks and Chicanos and other minority students.

> In practice, this new definition of diversity has meant that race has been a factor in some admission decisions. When the Committee on Admissions reviews the large middle group of applicants who are 'admissible' and deemed capable of doing good work in their courses, the race of an applicant may tip the balance in his favor just as geographic origin or a life spent on a farm may tip the balance in other candidates' cases. A farm boy from Idaho can bring something to Harvard College that a Bostonian cannot offer. Similarly, a black student can usually bring something that a white person cannot offer.

> In Harvard college admissions the Committee has not set target-quotas for the number of blacks, or of musicians, football players, physicists or Californians to be admitted in a given year. . . . But that awareness [of the necessity of including more than a token number of black students] does not mean that the Committee sets the minimum number of blacks or of people from west of the Mississippi who are to be admitted. It means only that in choosing among thousands of applicants who are not only 'admissible' academically but have other strong qualities, the Committee, with a number of criteria in mind, pays some attention to distribution among many types and categories of students.

In such an admissions program, race or ethnic background may be deemed a "plus" in a particular applicant's file, yet it does not insulate the individual from comparison with all other candidates for the available seats. The file of a particular black applicant may be examined for his potential contribution to diversity without the factor of race being decisive when compared, for example, with that of an applicant identified as an Italian-American if the latter is thought to exhibit qualities more likely to promote beneficial educational pluralism. Such qualities could include exceptional personal talents, unique work or service experience, leadership potential, maturity, demonstrated compassion, a history of overcoming disadvantage, ability to communicate with the poor, or other qualifications deemed important. In short, an admissions program operated in this way is flexible enough to consider all pertinent elements of diversity in light of the particular qualifications of each applicant, and to place them on the same footing for consideration, although not necessarily according them the same weight. Indeed, the weight attributed to a particular quality may vary from year to year depending upon the "mix" both of the student body and the applicants for the incoming class.

This kind of program treats each applicant as an individual in the admissions process. The applicant who loses out on the last available seat to another candidate receiving a "plus" on the basis of ethnic background will not have been foreclosed from all consideration for that seat simply because he was not the right color or had the wrong surname. It would mean only that his combined qualifications, which may have included similar nonobjective factors, did not outweigh those of the other applicant. His qualifications would have been weighed fairly and competitively, and he would have no basis to complain of unequal treatment under the Fourteenth Amendment.

It has been suggested that an admissions program which considers race only as one factor is simply a subtle and more sophisticated — but no less effective — means of according racial preference than the Davis program. A facial intent to discriminate, however, is evident in petitioner's preference program and not denied in this case. No such facial infirmity exists in an admissions program where race or ethnic background is simply one element — to be weighed fairly against other elements — in the selection process. "A boundary line," as Mr. Justice Frankfurter remarked in another connection, "is none the worse for being narrow." And a Court would not assume that a university, professing to employ a facially nondiscriminatory admissions policy, would operate it as a cover for the functional equivalent of a quota system. In short, good faith would be presumed in the absence of a showing to the contrary in the manner permitted by our cases.

B

In summary, it is evident that the Davis special admissions program involves the use of an explicit racial classification never before countenanced by this Court. It tells applicants who are not Negro, Asian, or "'Chicano" that they are totally excluded from a specific percentage of the seats in an entering class. No matter how strong their qualifications, quantitative and extracurricular, including their own potential for contribution to educational diversity, they are never afforded the chance to compete with applicants from the preferred groups for the special admission seats. At the same time, the preferred applicants have the opportunity to compete for every seat in the class.

The fatal flaw in petitioner's preferential program is its disregard of individual rights as guaranteed by the Fourteenth Amendment. Such rights are not absolute. But when a State's distribution of benefits or imposition of burdens hinges on the color of a person's skin or ancestry, that individual is entitled to a demonstration that the challenged classification is necessary to promote a substantial state interest. Petitioner has failed to carry this burden. For this reason, that portion of the California court's judgment holding petitioner's special admissions program invalid under the Fourteenth Amendment must be affirmed.

C

In enjoining petitioner from ever considering the race of any applicant, however, the courts below failed to recognize that the State has a substantial interest that legitimately may be served by a properly devised admissions program involving the competitive consideration of race and ethnic origin. For this reason, so much of the California court's judgment as enjoins petitioner from any consideration of the race of any applicant must be

Reversed.

Opinion of MR. JUSTICE BRENNAN, MR. JUSTICE WHITE, MR. JUSTICE MARSHALL, and MR. JUSTICE BLACKMUN, concurring in the judgment in part and dissenting.

The Court today, in reversing in part the judgment of the Supreme Court of California, affirms the constitutional power of Federal and State Government to act affirmatively to achieve equal opportunity for all. The difficulty of the issue presented — whether Government may use race-conscious programs to redress the continuing effects of past discrimination — and the mature consideration which each of our Brethren has brought to it have resulted in many opinions, no single one speaking for the Court. But this should not and must not mask the central meaning of today's opinions: Government may take race into account when it acts not to demean or insult any racial group, but to remedy disadvantages cast on minorities by past racial prejudice, at least when appropriate findings have been made by judicial, legislative, or administrative bodies with competence to act in this area.

II

In our view, Title VI prohibits only those uses of racial criteria that would violate the Fourteenth Amendment if employed by a State or its agencies; it does not bar the preferential treatment of racial minorities as a means of remedying past societal discrimination to the extent that such action is consistent with the Fourteenth Amendment. The legislative history of Title VI, administrative regulations interpreting the statute, subsequent congressional and executive action, and the prior decisions of this Court compel this conclusion. None of these sources lends support to the proposition that Congress intended to bar all race-conscious efforts to extend the benefits of federally financed programs to minorities who have been historically excluded from the full benefits of American life.

[Part of Section II, omitted here, reviewed the legislative history of Title VI of the Civil Rights Act of 1964 and concluded that it was not intended to bar all race-conscious programs. The opinion then turned to address the equal protection issue.]

III
A

The assertion of human equality is closely associated with the proposition that differences in color or creed, birth or status, are neither significant nor relevant to the way in which persons should be treated. Nonetheless, the position that such factors must be "[c]onstitutionally an irrelevance," *Edwards* v. *California* (1941) (Jackson, J., concurring), summed up by the shorthand phrase "[o]ur Constitution is colorblind," *Plessy* v. *Ferguson* (1896) (Harlan, J., dissenting), has never been adopted by this Court as the proper meaning of the Equal Protection Clause. Indeed, we have expressly rejected this proposition on a number of occasions.

Our cases have always implied that an "overriding statutory purpose," *McLaughlin* v. *Florida* (1964), could be found that would justify racial classifications. See *e.g., ibid.; Loving* v. *Virginia* (1967); *Korematsu*

v. *United States* (1944); *Hirabayashi* v. *United States* (1943). More recently, in *McDaniel* v. *Barresi* (1971), this Court unanimously reversed the Georgia Supreme Court which had held that a desegregation plan voluntarily adopted by a local school board, which assigned students on the basis of race, was *per se* invalid because it was not colorblind. And in *North Carolina State Board of Ed.* v. *Swann* (1971), we held, again unanimously, that a statute mandating colorblind school assignment plans could not stand "against the background of segregation," since such a limit on remedies would "render illusory the promise of *Brown* [*I*]."

We conclude, therefore, that racial classifications are not *per se* invalid under the Fourteenth Amendment. Accordingly, we turn to the problem of articulating what our role should be in reviewing state action that expressly classifies by race.

B

Respondent argues that racial classifications are always suspect and, consequently, that this Court should weigh the importance of the objectives served by Davis' special admissions program to see if they are compelling. In addition, he asserts that this Court must inquire whether, in its judgment, there are alternatives to racial classifications which would suit Davis' purposes. Petitioner, on the other hand, states that our proper role is simply to accept petitioner's determination that the racial classifications used by its program are reasonably related to what it tells us are its benign purposes. We reject petitioner's view, but, because our prior cases are in many respects inapposite to that before us now, we find it necessary to define with precision the meaning of that inexact term, "strict scrutiny."

Unquestionably we have held that a government practice or statute which restricts "fundamental rights" or which contains "suspect classifications" is to be subjected to "strict scrutiny" and can be justified only if it furthers a compelling government purpose and, even then, only if no less restrictive alternative is available. But no fundamental right is involved here. . . . Nor do whites as a class have any of the "traditional indicia of suspectness: the class is not saddled with such disabilities, or subjected to such a history of purposeful unequal treatment, or regulated to such a position of political powerlessness as to command extraordinary protection from the majoritarian political process." . . .

Moreover, if the University's representations are credited, this is not a case where racial classifications are "irrelevant and therefore prohibited." . . . Nor

has anyone suggested that the University's purposes contravene the cardinal principle that racial classifications that stigmatize — because they are drawn on the presumption that one race is inferior to another or because they put the weight of government behind racial hatred and separatism — are invalid without more. . . .

On the other hand, the fact that this case does not fit neatly into our prior analytic framework for race cases does not mean that it should be analyzed by applying the very loose rational-basis standard of review that is the very least that is always applied in equal protection cases. " '[T]he mere recitation of a benign, compensatory purpose is not an automatic shield which protects against any inquiry into the actual purposes underlying a statutory scheme.' " . . . Instead, a number of considerations — developed in gender discrimination cases but which carry even more force when applied to racial classifications — lead us to conclude that racial classifications designed to further remedial purposes " 'must serve important governmental objectives and must be substantially related to achievement of those objectives.' " . . .

First, race, like "gender-based classifications, too often [has] been inexcusably utilized to stereotype and stigmatize politically powerless segments of society." . . . While a carefully tailored statute designed to remedy past discrimination could avoid these vices, . . . we nonetheless have recognized that the line between honest and thoughtful appraisal of the effect of past discrimination and paternalistic stereotyping is not so clear and that a statute based on the latter is patently capable of stigmatizing all women with a badge of inferiority. . . . State programs designed ostensibly to ameliorate the effects of past racial discrimination obviously create the same hazard of stigma, since they may promote racial separatism and reinforce the views of those who believe that members of racial minorities are inherently incapable of succeeding on their own. . . .

Second, race, like gender and illegitimacy, is an immutable characteristic which its possessors are powerless to escape or set aside. While a classification is not *per se* invalid because it divides classes on the basis of an immutable characteristic, it is nevertheless true that such divisions are contrary to our deep belief that "legal burdens should bear some relationship to individual responsibility or wrongdoing," and that advancement sanctioned, sponsored, or approved by the State should ideally be based on individual merit or achievement, or at least on factors within the control of an individual.

Because this principle is so deeply rooted it might be supposed that it would be considered in the legislative process and weighed against the benefits of programs preferring individuals because of their race. But this is not necessarily so: The "natural consequence of our governing processes [may well be] that the most 'discrete and insular' of whites ... will be called upon to bear the immediate, direct costs of benign discrimination." Moreover, it is clear from our cases that there are limits beyond which majorities may not go when they classify on the basis of immutable characteristics. Thus, even if the concern for individualism is weighed by the political process, that weighing cannot waive the personal rights of individuals under the Fourteenth Amendment.

In sum, because of the significant risk that racial classifications established for ostensibly benign purposes can be misused, causing effects not unlike those created by invidious classifications, it is inappropriate to inquire only whether there is any conceivable basis that might sustain such a classification. Instead, to justify such a classification an important and articulated purpose for its use must be shown. In addition, any statute must be stricken that stigmatizes any group or that singles out those least well represented in the political process to bear the brunt of a benign program. Thus our review under the Fourteenth Amendment should be strict—not "'strict' in theory and fatal in fact," because it is stigma that causes fatality—but strict and searching nonetheless.

IV

Davis' articulated purpose of remedying the effects of past societal discrimination is, under our cases, sufficiently important to justify the use of race-conscious admissions programs where there is a sound basis for concluding that minority underrepresentation is substantial and chronic, and that the handicap of past discrimination is impeding access of minorities to the medical school.

A

At least since *Green v. County School Board* (1968), it has been clear that a public body which has itself been adjudged to have engaged in racial discrimination cannot bring itself into compliance with the Equal Protection Clause simply by ending its unlawful acts and adopting a neutral stance. Three years later, *Swann v. Charlotte-Mecklenburg Board of Ed.,* (1971), and its companion cases reiterated that racially neutral remedies for past discrimination were inadequate where consequences of past discriminatory acts influence or control present decisions. And the Court further held both that courts could enter de-

segregation orders which assigned students and faculty by reference to race, and that local school boards could *voluntarily* adopt desegregation plans which made express reference to race if this was necessary to remedy the effects of past discrimination. Moreover, we stated that school boards, even in the absence of a judicial finding of past discrimination, could voluntarily adopt plans which assigned students with the end of creating racial pluralism by establishing fixed ratios of black and white students in each school. In each instance, the creation of unitary school systems, in which the effects of past discrimination had been "eliminated root and branch," was recognized as a compelling social goal justifying the overt use of race.

Finally, the conclusion that state educational institutions may constitutionally adopt admissions programs designed to avoid exclusion of historically disadvantaged minorities, even when such programs explicitly take race into account, finds direct support in our cases construing congressional legislation designed to overcome the present effects of past discrimination. Congress can and has outlawed actions which have a disproportionately adverse and unjustified impact upon members of racial minorities and has required or authorized race-conscious action to put individuals disadvantaged by such impact in the position they otherwise might have enjoyed. Such relief does not require as a predicate proof that recipients of preferential advancement have been individually discriminated against; it is enough that each recipient is within a general class of persons likely to have been the victims of discrimination. Nor is it an objection to such relief that preference for minorities will upset the settled expectations of nonminorities. In addition, we have held that Congress, to remove barriers to equal opportunity, can and has required employers to use test criteria that fairly reflect the qualifications of minority applicants vis-à-vis nonminority applicants, even if this means interpreting the qualifications of an applicant in light of his race.

These cases cannot be distinguished simply by the presence of judicial findings of discrimination, for race-conscious remedies have been approved where such findings have not been made. *McDaniel v. Barresi* [1971]. Indeed, the requirement of a judicial determination of a constitutional or statutory violation as a predicate for race-conscious remedial actions would be self-defeating. Such a requirement would severely undermine efforts to achieve voluntary compliance with the requirements of law. And, our society and jurisprudence have always stressed the value of voluntary efforts to further the objectives of the law. Judicial intervention is a last resort to achieve cessation of illegal conduct or the remedying of its effects rather than a prerequisite to action.

Nor can our cases be distinguished on the ground that the entity using explicit racial classifications had itself violated §1 of the Fourteenth Amendment or an antidiscrimination regulation, for again race-conscious remedies have been approved where this is not the case. Moreover, the presence or absence of past discrimination by universities or employers is largely irrelevant to resolving respondent's constitutional claims. . . . If it was reasonable to conclude — as we hold that it was — that the failure of minorities to qualify for admission at Davis under regular procedures was due principally to the effects of past discrimination, then there is a reasonable likelihood that, but for pervasive racial discrimination, respondent would have failed to qualify for admission even in the absence of Davis' special admissions program.

Thus, our cases under Title VII of the Civil Rights Act have held that, in order to achieve minority participation in previously segregated areas of public life, Congress may require or authorize preferential treatment for those likely disadvantaged by societal racial discrimination. Such legislation has been sustained even without a requirement of findings of intentional racial discrimination by those required or authorized to accord preferential treatment, or a case-by-case determination that those to be benefited suffered from racial discrimination. These decisions compel the conclusion that States also may adopt race-conscious programs designed to overcome substantial, chronic minority underrepresentation where there is reason to believe that the evil addressed is a product of past racial discrimination.

. . . .

. . . Nothing whatever in the legislative history of either the Fourteenth Amendment or the Civil Rights Acts even remotely suggests that the States are foreclosed from furthering the fundamental purpose of equal opportunity to which the Amendment and those Acts are addressed. Indeed, voluntary initiatives by the States to achieve the national goal of equal opportunity have been recognized to be essential to its attainment. "To use the Fourteenth Amendment as a sword against such state power would stultify that Amendment." We therefore conclude that Davis' goal of admitting minority students disadvantaged by the effects of past discrimination is sufficiently important to justify use of race-conscious admissions criteria.

B

Properly construed, therefore, our prior cases unequivocally show that a state government may adopt race-conscious programs if the purpose of such programs is to remove the disparate racial impact its actions might otherwise have and if there is reason to believe that the disparate impact is itself the product of past discrimination, whether its own or that of society at large. There is no question that Davis' program is valid under this test.

Certainly, on the basis of the undisputed factual submissions before this Court, Davis had a sound basis for believing that the problem of underrepresentation of minorities was substantial and chronic and that the problem was attributable to handicaps imposed on minority applicants by past and present racial discrimination. Until at least 1973, the practice of medicine in this country was, in fact, if not in law, largely the prerogative of whites. In 1950, for example, while Negroes comprised 10% of the total population, Negro physicians constituted only 2.2% of the total number of physicians. The overwhelming majority of these, moreover, were educated in two predominantly Negro medical schools, Howard and Meharry. By 1970, the gap between the proportion of Negroes in medicine and their proportion in the population had widened: The number of Negroes employed in medicine remained frozen at 2.2% while the Negro population had increased to 11.1%. The number of Negro admittees to predominantly white medical schools, moreover, had declined in absolute numbers during the years 1955 to 1964.

Moreover, Davis had very good reason to believe that the national pattern of underrepresentation of minorities in medicine would be perpetuated if it retained a single admissions standard. For example, the entering classes in 1968 and 1969, the years in which such a standard was used, included only one Chicano and two Negroes out of 100 admittees. Nor is there any relief from this pattern of underrepresentation in the statistics for the regular admissions program in later years.

Davis clearly could conclude that the serious and persistent underrepresentation of minorities in medicine depicted by these statistics is the result of handicaps under which minority applicants labor as a consequence of a background of deliberate, purposeful discrimination against minorities in education and in society generally, as well as in the medical profession. From the inception of our national life, Negroes have been subjected to unique legal disabilities impairing access to equal educational opportunity. Under slavery, penal sanctions were imposed upon anyone attempting to educate Negroes. After enactment of the Fourteenth Amendment the States continued to deny Negroes equal educational opportunity, enforcing a strict policy of segregation that itself stamped Negroes as inferior, *Brown*, which relegated minorities to inferior educational institutions, and which denied them intercourse in the mainstream of professional life necessary to advancement. See *Sweatt v. Painter* (1950). Segregation was not limited to public facilities, moreover, but was enforced by criminal penalties against private action as well. Thus, as late as 1908, this Court enforced a state criminal conviction against a private college for teaching Negroes together with whites. *Berea College* v. *Kentucky.*

Green v. *County School Board,* (1968), gave explicit recognition to the fact that the habit of discrimination and the cultural tradition of race prejudice cultivated by centuries of legal slavery and segregation were not immediately dissipated when *Brown I* announced the constitutional principle that equal educational opportunity and participation in all aspects of American life could not be denied on the basis of race. Rather, massive official and private resistance prevented, and to a lesser extent still prevents, attainment of equal opportunity in education at all levels and in the professions. The generation of minority students applying to Davis Medical School since it opened in 1968—most of whom were born before or about the time *Brown I* was decided—clearly have been victims of this discrimination. Judicial decrees recognizing discrimination in public education in California testify to the fact of widespread discrimination suffered by California-born minority applicants; many minority group members living in California, moreover, were born and reared in school districts in southern States segregated by law. Since separation of school children by race "generates a feeling of inferiority as to their status in the community that may affect their hearts and minds in a way unlikely ever to be undone," *Brown I,* the conclusion is inescapable that applicants to medical school must be few indeed who endured the effects of *de jure* segregation, the resistance to *Brown I,* or the equally debilitating pervasive private discrimination fostered by our long history of official discrimination, and yet come to the starting line with an education equal to whites.

C

The second prong of our test—whether the Davis program stigmatizes any discrete group or individual and whether race is reasonably used in light of the program's objectives—is clearly satisfied by the Davis program.

It is not even claimed that Davis' program in any way operates to stigmatize or single out any discrete and insular, or even any identifiable, nonminority group. Nor will harm comparable to that imposed upon racial minorities by exclusion or separation on grounds of race be the likely result of the program. It does not, for example, establish an exclusive preserve for minority students apart from and exclusive of whites. Rather, its purpose is to overcome the effects of segregation by bringing the races together. True, whites are excluded from participation in the special admissions program, but this fact only operates to reduce the number of whites to be admitted in the regular admissions program in order to permit admission of a reasonable percentage—less than their proportion of the California population—of otherwise underrepresented qualified minority applicants.

Nor was Bakke in any sense stamped as inferior by the Medical School's rejection of him. Indeed, it is conceded by all that he satisfied those criteria regarded by the School as generally relevant to academic performance better than most of the minority members who were admitted. Moreover, there is absolutely no basis for concluding that Bakke's rejection as a result of Davis' use of racial preference will affect him throughout his life in the same way as the segregation of the Negro school children in *Brown I* would have affected them. Unlike discrimination against racial minorities, the use of racial preferences for remedial purposes does not inflict a pervasive injury upon individual whites in the sense that wherever they go or whatever they do there is a significant likelihood that they will be treated as second-class citizens because of their color. This distinction does not mean that the exclusion of a white resulting from the preferential use of race is not sufficiently serious to require justification; but it does mean that the injury by such a policy is not distinguishable from disadvantages caused by a wide range of government actions, none of which has ever been thought impermissible for that reason alone.

In addition, there is simply no evidence that the Davis program discriminates intentionally or unintentionally against any minority group which it purports to benefit. The program does not establish a quota in the invidious sense of a ceiling on the number of minority applicants to be admitted. Nor can the program reasonably be regarded as stigmatizing the program's beneficiaries or their race as inferior. The Davis program does not simply advance less qualified applicants; rather, it compensates applicants, whom it is uncontested are fully qualified to study medicine, for educational disadvantage which it was reasonable to conclude was a product of state-fostered discrimination. Once admitted, these students must satisfy the same degree requirements as regularly admitted students; they are taught by the same faculty in the same classes; and their performance is evaluated by the same standards by which regularly admitted students are judged. Under these circumstances, their performance and degrees must be regarded equally with the regularly admitted students with whom they compete for standing. Since minority graduates cannot justifiably be regarded as less well qualified than nonminority graduates by virtue of the special admissions program, there is no reasonable basis to conclude that minority graduates at schools using such programs would be stigmatized as inferior by the existence of such programs.

D

We disagree with the lower court's conclusion that the Davis program's use of race was unreasonable in light of its objectives. First, as petitioner argues, there are no practical means by which it could achieve its ends in the foreseeable future without the use of race-conscious measures. With respect to any factor (such as poverty or family educational background) that may be used as a substitute for race as an indicator of past discrimination, whites greatly outnumber racial minorities simply because whites make up a far larger percentage of the total population and therefore far outnumber minorities in absolute terms at every socioeconomic level. For example, of a class of recent medical school applicants from families with less than $10,000 income, at least 71% were white. Of all 1970 families headed by a person *not* a high school graduate which included children under 18, 80% were white and 20% were racial minorities. Moreover, while race is positively correlated with differences in GPA and MCAT scores, economic disadvantage is not. Thus, it appears that economically disadvantaged whites do not score less well than economically advantaged whites, while economically advantaged blacks score less well than do disadvantaged whites. These statistics graphically illustrate that the University's purpose to integrate its classes by compensating for past discrimination could not be achieved by a general preference for the economically disadvantaged or the children of parents of limited education unless such groups were to make up the entire class.

Second, the Davis admissions program does not simply equate minority status with disadvantage. Rather, Davis considers on an individual basis each applicant's personal history to determine whether he or she has likely been disadvantaged by racial discrimination. The record makes clear that only minority applicants likely to have been isolated from the mainstream of American life are considered in the special program; other minority applicants are eligible only through the regular admissions program. True, the procedure by which disadvantage is de-

tected is informal, but we have never insisted that educators conduct their affairs through adjudicatory proceedings, and such insistence here is misplaced. A case-by-case inquiry into the extent to which each individual applicant has been affected, either directly or indirectly, by racial discrimination, would seem to be, as a practical matter, virtually impossible, despite the fact that there are excellent reasons for concluding that such effects generally exist. When individual measurement is impossible or extremely impractical, there is nothing to prevent a State from using categorical means to achieve its end, at least where the category is closely related to the goal. And it is clear from our cases that specific proof that a person has been victimized by discrimination is not a necessary predicate to offering him relief where the probability of victimization is great.

E

Finally, Davis' special admissions program cannot be said to violate the Constitution simply because it has set aside a predetermined number of places for qualified minority applicants rather than using minority status as a positive factor to be considered in evaluating the applications of disadvantaged minority applicants. For purposes of constitutional adjudication, there is no difference between the two approaches. In any admissions program which accords special consideration to disadvantaged racial minorities, a determination of the degree of preference to be given is unavoidable, and any given preference that results in the exclusion of a white candidate is no more or less constitutionally acceptable than a program such as that at Davis. . . .

The "Harvard" program, as those employing it readily concede, openly and successfully employs a racial criterion for the purpose of ensuring that some of the scarce places in institutions of higher education are allocated to disadvantaged minority students. That the Harvard approach does not also make public the extent of the preference and the precise workings of the system while the Davis program employs a specific, openly stated number, does not condemn the latter plan for purposes of Fourteenth Amendment adjudication. It may be that the Harvard plan is more acceptable to the public than is the Davis "quota." If it is, any State, including California, is free to adopt it in preference to a less acceptable alternative, just as it is generally free, as far as the Constitution is concerned, to abjure granting any racial preferences in its admissions program. But there is no basis for preferring a particular preference program simply because in achieving the same goals that the Davis Medical School is pursuing, it proceeds in a manner that is not immediately apparent to the public.

IV

Accordingly, we would reverse the judgment of the Supreme Court of California holding the Medical School's special admissions program unconstitutional and directing respondent's admission, as well as that portion of the judgment enjoining the Medical School from according any consideration to race in the admissions program.

[MR. JUSTICE WHITE wrote a separate opinion, which argued that Title VI did not authorize a private cause of action by an aggrieved party. His views on the merits of Title VI and the equal protection issue are included in the opinion of JUSTICES BRENNAN, WHITE, MARSHALL, and BLACKMUN. But he also joined in parts of JUSTICE POWELL'S opinion.]

MR. JUSTICE MARSHALL.

I agree with the judgment of the Court only insofar as it permits a university to consider the race of an applicant in making admissions decisions. I do not agree that petitioner's admissions program violates the Constitution. For it must be remembered that, during most of the past 200 years, the Constitution as interpreted by this Court did not prohibit the most ingenious and pervasive forms of discrimination against the Negro. Now, when a State acts to remedy the effects of that legacy of discrimination, I cannot believe that this same Constitution stands as a barrier.

I

[This section traces the history of the treatment of blacks in the United States from its founding until the present.]

II

The position of the Negro today in America is the tragic but inevitable consequence of centuries of unequal treatment. Measured by any benchmark of comfort or achievement, meaningful equality remains a distant dream for the Negro.

A Negro child today has a life expectancy which is shorter by more than five years than that of a white child. The Negro child's mother is over three times more likely to die of complications in childbirth, and the infant mortality rate for Negroes is nearly twice that for whites. The median income of the Negro family is only 60% that of the median of a white family,

and the percentage of Negroes who live in families with incomes below the poverty line is nearly four times greater than that of whites.

When the Negro child reaches working age, he finds that America offers him significantly less than it offers his white counterpart. For Negro adults, the unemployment rate is twice that of whites, and the unemployment rate for Negro teenagers is nearly three times that of white teenagers. A Negro male who completes four years of college can expect a median annual income of merely $110 more than a white male who has only a high school diploma. Although Negroes represent 11.5% of the population, they are only 1.2% of the lawyers and judges, 2% of the physicians, 2.3% of the dentists, 1.1% of the engineers and 2.6% of the college and university professors.

The relationship between those figures and the history of unequal treatment afforded to the Negro cannot be denied. At every point from birth to death the impact of the past is reflected in the still disfavored position of the Negro.

In light of the sorry history of discrimination and its devastating impact on the lives of Negroes, bringing the Negro into the mainstream of American life should be a state interest of the highest order. To fail to do so is to ensure that America will forever remain a divided society.

III

I do not believe that the Fourteenth Amendment requires us to accept that fate. Neither its history nor our past cases lend any support to the conclusion that a University may not remedy the cumulative effects of society's discrimination by giving consideration to race in an effort to increase the number and percentage of Negro doctors.

IV

While I applaud the judgment of the Court that a university may consider race in its admissions process, it is more than a little ironic that, after several hundred years of class-based discrimination against Negroes, the Court is unwilling to hold that a class-based remedy for that discrimination is permissible. In declining to so hold, today's judgment ignores the fact that for several hundred years Negroes have been discriminated against, not as individuals, but rather solely because of the color of their skins. It is unnecessary in 20th century America to have individual Negroes demonstrate that they have been victims of racial discrimination; the racism of our society has been so pervasive that none, regardless of wealth or position, has managed to escape its impact. The experience of Negroes in America has been different in kind, not just in degree, from that of other ethnic groups. It is not merely the history of slavery alone but also that a whole people were marked as inferior by the law. And that mark has endured. The dream of America as the great melting pot has not been realized for the Negro; because of his skin color he never even made it into the pot.

These differences in the experience of the Negro make it difficult for me to accept that Negroes cannot be afforded greater protection under the Fourteenth Amendment where it is necessary to remedy the effects of past discrimination. In the *Civil Rights Cases,* the Court wrote that the Negro emerging from slavery must cease "to be the special favorite of the laws." We cannot in light of the history of the last century yield to that view. Had the Court in that Case and others been willing to "do for human liberty and the fundamental rights of American citizenship, what it did . . . for the protecton of slavery and the rights of the masters of fugitive slaves," we would not need now to permit the recognition of any "special wards."

Most importantly, had the Court been willing in 1896, in *Plessy* v. *Ferguson,* to hold that the Equal Protection Clause forbids differences in treatment based on race, we would not be faced with this dilemma in 1978. We must remember, however, that the principle that the "Constitution is color-blind" appeared only in the opinion of the lone dissenter. The majority of the Court rejected the principle of color blindness, and for the next 60 years, from *Plessy* to *Brown* v. *Board of Education,* ours was a Nation where, *by law,* an individual could be given "special" treatment based on the color of his skin.

It is because of a legacy of unequal treatment that we now must permit the institutions of this society to give consideration to race in making decisions about who will hold the positions of influence, affluence and prestige in America. For far too long, the doors to those positions have been shut to Negroes. If we are ever to become a fully integrated society, one in which the color of a person's skin will not determine the opportunities available to him or her, we must be willing to take steps to open those doors. I do not believe that anyone can truly look into America's past and still find that a remedy for the effects of that past is impermissible.

. . . .

I fear that we have come full circle. After the Civil War our government started several "affirmative action" programs. This Court in the *Civil Rights Cases* and *Plessy* v. *Ferguson* destroyed the movement to-ward complete equality. For almost a century no action was taken, and this nonaction was with the tacit approval of the courts. Then we had *Brown* v. *Board of Education* and the Civil Rights Acts of Congress, followed by numerous affirmative action programs. *Now,* we have this Court again stepping in, this time to stop affirmative action programs of the type used by the University of California.

MR. JUSTICE BLACKMUN.

I participate fully, of course, in the opinion . . . that bears the names of my Brothers BRENNAN, WHITE, MARSHALL, and myself. I add only some general observations that hold particular significance for me, and then a few comments on equal protection.

I

At least until the early 1970's, apparently only a very small number, less than 2%, of the physicians, attorneys, and medical and law students in the United States were members of what we now refer to as minority groups. In addition, approximately three-fourths of our Negro physicians were trained at only two medical schools. If ways are not found to remedy that situation, the country can never achieve its professed goal of a society that is not race conscious.

I yield to no one in my earnest hope that the time will come when an "affirmative action" program is unnecessary and is, in truth, only a relic of the past. I would hope that we could reach this stage within a decade at the most. But the story of *Brown* v. *Board of Education* (1954), decided almost a quarter of a century ago, suggests that that hope is a slim one. At some time, however, beyond any period of what some would claim is only transitional inequality, the United States must and will reach a stage of maturity where action along this line is no longer necessary. Then persons will be regarded as persons, and discrimination of the type we address today will be an ugly feature of history that is instructive but that is behind us.

The number of qualified, indeed highly qualified, applicants for admission to existing medical schools in the United States far exceeds the number of places available. Wholly apart from racial and ethnic considerations, therefore, the selection process inevitably results in the denial of admission to many *qualified* persons, indeed, to far more than the number of those who are granted admission. Obviously, it is a denial to the deserving. This inescapable fact is brought into sharp focus here because Allan Bakke is not himself charged with discrimination and yet is the one who is disadvantaged, and because the Medical

School of the University of California at Davis itself is not charged with historical discrimination.

....

It is somewhat ironic to have us so deeply disturbed over a program where race is an element of consciousness, and yet to be aware of the fact, as we are, that institutions of higher learning, albeit more on the undergraduate than the graduate level, have given conceded preferences up to a point to those possessed of athletic skills, to the children of alumni, to the affluent who may bestow their largess on the institutions, and to those having connections with celebrities, the famous, and the powerful.

Programs of admission to institutions of higher learning are basically a responsibility for academicians and for administrators and the specialists they employ. The judiciary, in contrast, is ill-equipped and poorly trained for this. The administration and management of educational institutions are beyond the competence of judges and are within the special competence of educators, provided always that the educators perform within legal and constitutional bounds. For me, therefore, interference by the judiciary must be the rare exception and not the rule.

I am not convinced, as MR. JUSTICE POWELL seems to be, that the difference between the Davis program and the one employed by Harvard is very profound or constitutionally significant. The line between the two is a thin and indistinct one. In each, subjective application is at work. Because of my conviction that admission programs are primarily for the educators, I am willing to accept the representation that the Harvard program is one where good faith in its administration is practiced as well as professed. I agree that such a program, where race or ethnic background is only one of many factors, is a program better formulated than Davis' two-track system. The cynical, of course, may say that under a program such as Harvard's one may accomplish covertly what Davis concedes it does openly. I need not go that far, for despite its two-track aspect, the Davis program, for me, is within constitutional bounds, though perhaps barely so. It is surely free of stigma, and I am not willing to infer a constitutional violation.

It is worth noting, perhaps, that governmental preference has not been a stranger to our legal life. We see it in veterans' preferences. We see it in the aid-to-the-handicapped programs. We see it in the progressive income tax. We see it in the Indian programs. We may excuse some of these on the ground that they have specific constitutional protection or, as with Indians, that those benefited are wards of the Government. Nevertheless, these preferences exist and may not be ignored. And in the admissions field, as I have indicated, educational institutions have always used geography, athletic ability, anticipated financial largess, alumni pressure, and other factors of that kind.

....

I suspect that it would be impossible to arrange an affirmative action program in a racially neutral way and have it successful. To ask that this be so is to demand the impossible. In order to get beyond racism, we must first take account of race. There is no other way. And in order to treat some persons equally, we must treat them differently. We cannot — we dare not — let the Equal Protection Clause perpetrate racial supremacy.

MR. JUSTICE STEVENS, with whom THE CHIEF JUSTICE, MR. JUSTICE STEWART, and MR. JUSTICE REHNQUIST join, concurring in the judgment in part and dissenting in part.

It is always important at the outset to focus precisely on the controversy before the Court. It is particularly important to do so in this case because correct identification of the issues will determine whether it is necessary or appropriate to express any opinion about the legal status of any admissions program other than petitioner's.

II

... In this case, we are presented with a constitutional question of undoubted and unusual importance. Since, however, a dispositive statutory claim was raised at the very inception of this case, and squarely decided in the portion of the trial court judgment affirmed by the California Supreme Court, it is our plain duty to confront it. Only if petitioner should prevail on the statutory issue would it be necessary to decide whether the University's admissions program violated the Equal Protection Clause of the Fourteenth Amendment.

III

Section 601 of the Civil Rights Act of 1964 provides:

> No person in the United States shall, on the ground of race, color, or national origin, be excluded from participation in, be denied the benefits of, or be subjected to discrimination under any program or activity receiving Federal financial assistance.

The University, through its special admissions policy, excluded Bakke from participation in its program of medical education because of his race. The University also acknowledges that it was, and still is, receiving federal financial assistance. The plain language of the statute therefore requires affirmance of the judgment below. A different result cannot be justified unless that language misstates the actual intent of the Congress that enacted the statute or the statute is not enforceable in a private action. Neither conclusion is warranted.

. . . .

. . . [T]he proponents of Title VI assumed that the Constitution itself required a colorblind standard on the part of government, but that does not mean that the legislation only codifies an existing constitutional prohibition. The statutory prohibition against discrimination in federally funded projects contained in §601 is more than a simple paraphrasing of what the Fifth or Fourteenth Amendment would require. The Act's proponents plainly considered Title VI consistent with their view of the Constitution and they sought to provide an effective weapon to implement that view. As a distillation of what the supporters of the Act believed the Constitution demanded of State and Federal Governments, §601 has independent force, with language and emphasis in addition to that found in the Constitution.

As with other provisions of the Civil Rights Act, Congress' expression of its policy to end racial discrimination may independently proscribe conduct that the Constitution does not. However, we need not decide the congruence — or lack of congruence — of the controlling statute and the Constitution since the meaning of the Title VI ban on exclusion is crystal clear: Race cannot be the basis of excluding anyone from participation in a federally funded program.

In short, nothing in the legislative history justifies the conclusion that the broad language of §601 should not be given its natural meaning. We are dealing with a distinct statutory prohibition, enacted at a particular time with particular concerns in mind; neither its language nor any prior interpretation suggests that its place in the Civil Rights Act, won after long debate, is simply that of a constitutional appendage. In unmistakable terms the Act prohibits the exclusion of individuals from federally funded programs because of their race. As succinctly phrased during the Senate debate, under Title VI it is not "permissible to say 'yes' to one person, but to say 'no' to another person, only because of the color of his skin."

. . . .

The University's special admissions program violated Title VI of the Civil Rights Act of 1964 by excluding Bakke from the medical school because of his race. It is therefore our duty to affirm the judgment ordering Bakke admitted to the University.

Accordingly, I concur in the Court's judgment insofar as it affirms the judgment of the Supreme Court of California. To the extent that it purports to do anything else, I respectfully dissent.

United Steelworkers of America, AFL-CIO v. Weber

443 U.S. 193 (1979)
Vote: 5–2

In 1974, the United Steelworkers of America and Kaiser Aluminum and Chemical Corporation entered into a collective bargaining agreement over conditions and terms of employment at several Kaiser plants. The agreement included an affirmative action plan designed to eliminate the conspicuous racial imbalance in Kaiser's then almost exclusively white craftwork force by reserving for black employees 50 percent of all openings in its craft training programs until the percentage of black craftworkers in each of its plants was equal to the percentage of blacks in the local work force.

This litigation arose from the affirmative action plan in one Kaiser plant where prior to 1974 only 1.83 percent of the craftwork force was black, even though the local work force was approximately 39 percent black. Pursuant to the national agreement, when this Kaiser plant established a special program to train its unskilled workers for the better-paying craft positions, it modified the standard seniority system of selection so that 50 percent of the trainees would be black. During the program's first year of operation, seven black and six white trainees were selected. The most-senior black trainee had less seniority than several workers whose bids for admission to the program were rejected.

One white applicant was Brian Weber, who, despite his seniority over the blacks accepted into the program, found his application rejected. He instituted a class action suit in federal district court, alleging that because the affirmative action program had resulted in junior black employees receiving traning in preference to senior white employees, he and others similarly situated had been discriminated against in violation of the provisions of Sections 703(a) and (d) of Title VII of the Civil Rights Act of 1974 (that made it unlawful to "discriminate . . . because of race" in hiring and in the selection of apprentices for training programs). The district court held that the affirmative action plan did violate Title VII. This ruling was affirmed by the court of appeals, whereupon the Steelworkers petitioned the Supreme Court for a writ of certiorari.

Can you reconcile the Court's ruling here with its ruling in BAKKE?

MR. JUSTICE BRENNAN delivered the opinion of the Court.

We emphasize at the outset the narrowness of our inquiry. Since the Kaiser-USWA plan does not involve state action, this case does not present an alleged violation of the Equal Protection Clause of the Fourteenth Amendment. Further, since the Kaiser-USWA plan was adopted voluntarily, we are not concerned with what Title VII requires or with what a court might order to remedy a past proved violation of the Act. The only question before us is the narrow statutory issue of whether Title VII *forbids* private employers and unions from voluntarily agreeing upon bona fide affirmative action plans that accord racial preferences in the manner and for the purpose provided in the Kaiser-USWA plan. . . .

Respondent argues that Congress intended in Title VII to prohibit all race-conscious affirmative action plans. Respondent's argument rests upon a literal interpretation of §§703(a) and (d) of the Act. Those sections make it unlawful to "discriminate . . . because of . . . race" in hiring and in the selection of apprentices for training programs. . . .

Respondent's argument is not without force. But it overlooks the significance of the fact that the Kaiser-USWA plan is an affirmative action plan voluntarily adopted by private parties to eliminate traditional patterns of racial segregation. In this context respondent's reliance upon a literal construction of §§703(a) and (d) . . . is misplaced. It is a "familiar rule, that a thing may be within the letter of the statute and yet not within the statute, because not within its spirit, nor within the intention of its makers." . . . The prohibition against racial discrimination in §§703(a) and (d) of Title VII must therefore be read against the background of the legislative history of Title VII and the historical context from which the Act arose. . . . Examination of these sources makes clear that an interpretation of the sections that forbade all race-

conscious affirmative action would "bring about an end completely at variance with the purpose of the statute" and must be rejected. . . .

Congress' primary concern in enacting the prohibition against racial discrimination in Title VII of the Civil Rights Act of 1964 was with "the plight of the Negro in our economy." . . . unless blacks were able to secure jobs "which have a future." . . .

Accordingly, it was clear to Congress that "[t]he crux of the problem [was] to open employment opportunities for Negroes in occupations which have been traditionally closed to them," . . . and it was to this problem that Title VII's prohibition against racial discrimination in employment was primarily addressed.

It plainly appears from the House Report accompanying the Civil Rights Act that Congress did not intend wholly to prohibit private and voluntary affirmative action efforts as one method of solving this problem. The Report provides:

> No bill can or should lay claim to eliminating all of the causes and consequences of racial and other types of discrimination against minorities. There is reason to believe, however, that national leadership provided by the enactment of Federal legislation dealing with the most troublesome problems *will create an atmosphere conducive to voluntary or local resolution of other forms of discrimination.* (Emphasis supplied).

Given this legislative history, we cannot agree with respondent that Congress intended to prohibit the private sector from taking effective steps to accomplish the goal that Congress designed Title VII to achieve. The very statutory words intended as a spur or catalyst to cause "employers and unions to self-examine and to self-evaluate their employment practices and to endeavor to eliminate, so far as possible, the last vestiges of an unfortunate and ignominious page in this country's history," cannot be interpreted as an absolute prohibition against all private, voluntary, race-conscious affirmative action efforts to hasten the elimination of such vestiges. It would be ironic indeed if a law triggered by a Nation's concern over centuries of racial injustice and intended to improve the lot of those who had "been excluded from the American dream for so long," constituted the first legislative prohibition of all voluntary, private, race-conscious efforts to abolish traditional patterns of racial segregation and hierarchy.

Our conclusion is further reinforced by examination of the language and legislative history of §703(j) of Title VII. Opponents of Title VII raised two related arguments against the bill. First, they argued that the Act would be interpreted to *require* employers with racially imbalanced work forces to grant preferential treatment to racial minorities in order to integrate. Second, they argued that employers with racially imbalanced work forces would grant preferential treatment to racial minorities, even if not required to do so by the Act. Had Congress meant to prohibit all race-conscious affirmative action, as respondent urges, it easily could have answered both objections by providing that Title VII would not require or *permit* racially preferential integration efforts. But Congress did not choose such a course. Rather Congress added §703(j) which addresses only the first objection. The section provides that nothing contained in Title VII "shall be interpreted to *require* any employer...to grant preferential treatment... to any group because of the race...of such... group on account of" a *de facto* racial imbalance in the employer's work force. The section does *not* state that "nothing in Title VII shall be interpreted to *permit*" voluntary affirmative efforts to correct racial imbalances. The natural inference is that Congress chose not to forbid all voluntary race-conscious affirmative action.

The reasons for this choice are evident from the legislative record. Title VII could not have been enacted into law without substantial support from legislators in both Houses who traditionally resisted federal regulation in private business. Those legislators demanded as a price for their support that "management prerogatives, and union freedoms... be left undisturbed to the greatest extent possible." Section 703(j) was proposed by Senator Dirksen to allay any fears that the Act might be interpreted in such a way as to upset this compromise. The section was designed to prevent §703 of Title VII from being interpreted in such a way as to lead to undue "Federal Government interference with private businesses because of some Federal employee's ideas about racial balance or racial imbalance." Clearly, a prohibition against all voluntary, race-conscious, affirmative action efforts would disserve these ends. Such a prohibition would augment the powers of the Federal Government and diminish traditional management prerogatives while at the same time impeding attainment of the ultimate statutory goals. In view of this legislative history and in view of Congress' desire to avoid undue federal regulation of private businesses, use of the word "require" rather than the phrase "require or permit" in §703(j) fortified the conclusion that Congress did not intend to limit traditional business freedom to such a degree as to prohibit all voluntary, race-conscious affirmative action.

We therefore hold that Title VII's prohibition in §§703(a) and (d) against racial discrimination does not condemn all private, voluntary, race-conscious affirmative action plans.

We need not today define in detail the line of demarcation between permissible and impermissible action plans. It suffices to hold that the challenged Kaiser-USWA affirmative action plan falls on the permissible side of the line. The purposes of the plan mirror those of the statute. Both were designed to break down old patterns of racial segregation and hierarchy. Both were structured to "open employment opportunities for Negroes in occupations which have been traditionally closed to them."

At the same time, the plan does not unnecessarily trammel the interests of the white employees. The plan does not require the discharge of white workers and their replacement with new black hirees. Nor does the plan create an absolute bar to the advancement of white employees; half of those trained in the program will be white. Moreover, the plan is a temporary measure; it is not intended to maintain racial balance, but simply to eliminate a manifest racial imbalance. Preferential selection of craft trainees at the Gramercy plant will end as soon as the percentage of black skilled craftworkers in the Gramercy plant approximates the percentage of blacks in the local labor force.

We conclude, therefore, that the adoption of the Kaiser-USWA plan for the Gramercy plant falls within the area of discretion left by Title VII to the private sector voluntarily to adopt affirmative action plans designed to eliminate conspicuous racial imbalance in traditionally segregated job categories. Accordingly, the judgment of the Court of Appeals for the Fifth Circuit is

Reversed.

MR. JUSTICE POWELL and MR. JUSTICE STEVENS took no part in the consideration or decision of these cases.

[MR. JUSTICE BLACKMUN wrote a concurring opinion.]

MR. CHIEF JUSTICE BURGER, dissenting.

The Court reaches a result I would be inclined to vote for were I a Member of Congress considering a proposed amendment of Title VII. I cannot join the Court's judgment, however, because it is contrary to the explicit language of the statute and arrived at by means wholly incompatible with long-established principles of separation of powers. Under the guise of statutory "construction," the Court effectively rewrites Title VII to achieve what it regards as a desirable result. It "amends" the statute to do precisely what both its sponsors and its opponents agreed the statute was *not* intended to do.

When Congress enacted Title VII after long study and searching debate, it produced a statute of extraordinary clarity, which speaks directly to the issue we consider in this case. In §703(d) Congress provided:

> It shall be an unlawful employment practice for any employer, labor organization, or joint labor-management committee controlling apprenticeship or other training or retraining, including on-the-job training programs, to discriminate against any individual because of his race, color, religion, sex, or national origin in admission to, or employment in, any program established to provide apprenticeship or other training.

Often we have difficulty interpreting statutes either because of imprecise drafting or because legislative compromises have produced genuine ambiguities. But here there is no lack of clarity, no ambiguity. The quota embodied in the collective-bargaining agreement between Kaiser and the Steelworkers unquestionably discriminates on the basis of race against individual employees seeking admission to on-the-job training programs. And, under the plain language of §703(d), that is "an *unlawful* employment practice."

. . . .

Arguably, Congress may not have gone far enough in correcting the effects of past discrimination when it enacted Title VII. The gross discrimination against minorities to which the Court adverts — particularly against Negroes in the building trades and craft unions — is one of the dark chapters in the otherwise great history of the American labor movement. And, I do not question the importance of encouraging voluntary compliance with the purposes and policies of Title VII. But that statute was conceived and enacted to make discrimination against *any* individual illegal, and I fail to see how "voluntary compliance" with the no-discrimination principle that is the heart and soul of Title VII as currently written will be achieved by permitting employers to discriminate against some individuals to give preferential treatment to others.

Until today, I had thought the Court was of the unanimous view that "[d]iscriminatory preference for any group, minority or majority, is precisely and only what Congress has proscribed" in Title VII. *Griggs* v. *Duke Power Co.,* 401 U.S. 424, 431 (1971). Had Congress intended otherwise, it very easily could have drafted language allowing what the Court permits today. Far from doing so, Congress expressly

prohibited in §§703(a) and (d) the very discrimination against Brian Weber which the Court today approves. If "affirmative action" programs such as the one presented in this case are to be permitted, it is for Congress, not this Court, to so direct.

MR. JUSTICE REHNQUIST, with whom THE CHIEF JUSTICE joins, dissenting.

In a very real sense, the Court's opinion is ahead of its time: it could more appropriately have been handed down five years from now, in 1984, a year coinciding with the title of a book from which the Court's opinion borrows, perhaps subconsciously, at least one idea. Orwell describes in his book a governmental official of Oceania, one of the three great world powers, denouncing the current enemy, Eurasia, to an assembled crowd:

> It was almost impossible to listen to him without being first convinced and then maddened. . . . The speech had been proceeding for perhaps twenty minutes when a messenger hurried onto the platform and a scrap of paper was slipped into the speaker's hand. He unrolled and read it without pausing in his speech. Nothing altered in his voice or manner, or in the content of what he was saying, but suddenly the names were different. Without words said, a wave of understanding rippled through the crowd. Oceania was at war with Eastasia . . . The banners and posters with which the square was decorated were all wrong! . . .
>
> [T]he speaker had switched from one line to the other actually in mid-sentence, not only without a pause, but without even breaking the syntax. G. Orwell, Nineteen Eighty-Four 181–182 (1949).

Today's decision represents an equally dramatic and equally unremarked switch in this Court's interpretation of Title VII.

The operative sections of Title VII prohibit racial discrimination in employment *simpliciter.* Taken in its normal meaning, and as understood by all Members of Congress who spoke to the issue during the legislative debates, see *infra,* at 231–251, this language prohibits a covered employer from considering race when making an employment decision, whether the race be black or white. . . .

We have never wavered in our understanding that Title VII "prohibits *all* racial discrimination in employment, without exception for any group of particular employees." In *Griggs* v. *Duke Power Co.* (1971), our first occasion to interpret Title VII, a unanimous

Court observed that "[d]iscriminatory preference, for any group, minority or majority, is precisely and only what Congress has proscribed." And in our most recent discussion of the issue, we uttered words seemingly dispositive of this case: "It is clear beyond cavil that the obligation imposed by Title VII is to provide an equal opportunity for *each* applicant regardless of race, without regard to whether members of the applicant's race are already proportionately represented in the work force." *Furnco Construction Corp.* v. *Waters* (1978).

Today, however, the Court behaves much like the Orwellian speaker earlier described, as if it had been handed a note indicating that Title VII would lead to a result unacceptable to the Court if interpreted here as it was in our prior decisions. Accordingly, without even a break in syntax, the Court rejects "a literal construction of §703(a)" in favor of newly discovered "legislative history," which leads it to a conclusion directly contrary to that compelled by the "uncontradicted legislative history" unearthed in our other prior decisions. Now we are told that the legislative history of Title VII shows that employers are free to discriminate on the basis of race: an employer may, in the Court's words, "trammel the interests of the white employees" in favor of black employees in order to eliminate "racial imbalance." Our earlier interpretations of Title VII, like the banners and posters decorating the square in Oceania, were all wrong.

. . . .

Thus, by a *tour de force* reminiscent not of jurists such as Hale, Holmes, and Hughes, but of escape artists such as Houdini, the Court eludes clear statutory language, "uncontradicted" legislative history, and uniform precedent in concluding that employers are, after all, permitted to consider race in making employment decisions. It may be that one or more of the principal sponsors of Title VII would have preferred to see a provision allowing preferential treatment of minorities written into the bill. Such a provision, however, would have to have been expressly or impliedly excepted from Title VII's explicit prohibition on all racial discrimination in employment. There is no such exception in the Act. And a reading of the legislative debates concerning Title VII, in which proponents and opponents alike uniformly denounced discrimination in favor of, as well as discrimination against, Negroes, demonstrates clearly that any legislator harboring an unspoken desire for such a provision could not possibly have succeeded in enacting it into law.

Quite simply, Kaiser's racially discriminatory admission quota is flatly prohibited by the plain language of Title VII. This normally dispositive fact, however,

gives the Court only momentary pause. An "interpretation" of the statute upholding Weber's claim would, according to the Court, "'bring about an end completely at variance with the purpose of the statute.'" To support this conclusion, the Court calls upon the "spirit" of the Act, which it divines from passages in Title VII's legislative history indicating that enactment of the statute was prompted by Congress' desire "'to open employment opportunities for Negroes in occupations which [had] been traditionally closed to them.'" . . . But the legislative history invoked by the Court to avoid the plain language of §§703(a) and (d) simply misses the point. To be sure, the reality of employment discrimination against Negroes provided the primary impetus for passage of Title VII. But this fact by no means supports the proposition that Congress intended to leave employers free to discriminate against white persons. In most cases, "[l]egislative history . . . is more vague than the statute we are called upon to interpret." . . . Here, however, the legislative history of Title VII is as clear as the language of §§703(a) and (d), and it irrefutably demonstrates that Congress meant precisely what it said in §§703(a) and (d) — that *no* racial discrimination in employment is permissible under Title VII, not even preferential treatment of minorities to correct racial imbalance.

. . . .

Our task in this case, like any other case involving the construction of a statute, is to give effect to the intent of Congress. To divine that intent, we traditionally look first to the words of the statute and, if they are unclear, then to the statute's legislative history. Finding the desired result hopelessly foreclosed by these conventional sources, the Court turns to a third source — the "spirit" of the Act. But close examination of what the Court proffers as the spirit of the Act reveals it as the spirit animating the present majority, not the 88th Congress. For if the spirit of the Act eludes the cold words of the statute itself, it rings out with unmistakable clarity in the words of the elected representatives who made the Act law. It is *equality*.

There is perhaps no device more destructive to the notion of equality than the *numerus clausus* — the quota. Whether described as "benign discrimination" or "affirmative action," the racial quota is nonetheless a creator of castes, a two-edged sword that must demean one in order to prefer another. In passing Title VII, Congress outlawed *all* racial discrimination, recognizing that no discrimination based on race is benign, that no action disadvantaging a person because of his color is affirmative. With today's holding, the Court introduces into Title VII a tolerance for the very evil that the law was intended to eradicate, without offering even a clue as to what the limits on that tolerance may be. We are told simply that Kaiser's racially discriminatory admission quota "falls on the permissible side of the line." By going not merely *beyond,* but directly *against* Title VII's language and legislative history, the Court has sown the wind. Later courts will face the impossible task of reaping the whirlwind.

Fullilove v. Klutznick

448 U.S. 448 (1980)
Vote: 6–3

The Court's school desegregation decisions upholding the use of race-conscious policies by lower courts all involve plans that had been authorized by trial courts under their powers of equitable remedy following a finding of segregation in the school district to which the plan applies. In BAKKE, a crucial factor for some justices was that there had been no judicial finding of past discrimination by the medical school and that the policy was not "remedial" in the strict sense of the term. But BAKKE does not give much guidance in determining what type of fact-finding process is required to prove prior discrimination. Nor does it tell us which public agents can engage in such fact-finding or construct remedies involving the use of racial quotas. Although some justices questioned the capacity of the medical school faculty to undertake such an enterprise, they were silent on the authority of other public bodies. Thus, after BAKKE many important questions remained unanswered. To pass constitutional muster, must all "benign" racial quotas be preceded by a *judicial* finding of prior discrimination? Are such quotas permitted *only* as part of an equitable remedy constructed by a court? Or do other governmental bodies, say, legislatures and executive agencies, possess constitutionally acceptable capabilities and authority? If so, which ones? The following case begins to answer this question.

The case arose as a challenge to the "minority business enterprise" (MBE) provision of the Public Works Employment Act of 1977, which requires in part that, absent an administrative waiver, at least 10 percent of federal funds granted for local public works projects must be used by the state or local grantee to procure services or supplies from businesses owned by minority-group members, defined as United States citizens "who are Negroes, Spanish-speaking, Orientals, Indians, Eskimos, and Aleuts." Under detailed implementing regulations grantee state and local governments and their private prime contractors are required to seek out all available MBEs, provide technical assistance as needed, waive bonding requirements where feasible, and give MBEs other types of assistance to aid them in the intricacies of the bidding and contracting process. Regulations promulgated pursuant to the Act also provide that MBEs can receive contracts, even though they are not the lowest bidders, if their bids reflect "merely attempts to cover costs inflated by the present effects of prior disadvantage." Guidelines further provide for administrative waiver of the 10 percent MBE requirement on a case-by-case basis if it is administratively infeasible to meet them. The legislative history and structure of the Public Works Employment Act of 1977 indicates that it was perceived by many in Congress to be a temporary measure, to provide temporary jobs, and to stimulate the economy rather than become a permanent mechanism for funneling federal funds to state and local governments for public works. The legislative history also suggests that the MBE provision was regarded by at least some of its supporters to be a "remedial" measure to overcome a specific and limited finding by Congress of prior discrimination in the building trades. These factors were emphasized by Chief Justice Burger in his opinion for the plurality. Still, years later, the 10 percent MBE provision remains federal policy.

MR. CHIEF JUSTICE BURGER announced the judgment of the Court, and delivered an opinion, in which MR. JUSTICE WHITE and MR. JUSTICE POWELL joined.

[Deleted from the opinion is a long opening section recounting the legislative history of Public Works and Employment Act of 1977 and of the limited and remedial objectives of its Minority Business Employment (MBE) provision, and a section that holds that the MBE provision does not fall outside the scope of Congress' spending and interstate commerce powers and is within its enforcement power of Section 5 of the Fourteenth Amendment.]

. . . .

As a threshold matter, we reject the contention that in the remedial context the Congress must act in a wholly "color-blind" fashion. In *Swann* v. *Charlotte-Mecklenburg Board of Education.* . . . (1971), we rejected this argument in considering a court-formulated school desegregation remedy on the basis that examination of the racial composition of student bodies was an unavoidable starting point and that racially based attendance assignments were permissible so long as no absolute racial balance of each school was required. . . .

In [this and other] school desegregation cases we dealt with the authority of a federal court to formulate a remedy for unconstitutional racial discrimination. However, the authority of a court to incorporate racial criteria into a remedial decree also extends to statutory violations. Where federal antidiscrimination laws have been violated, an equitable remedy may in the appropriate case include a racial or ethnic factor. . . .

When we have discussed the remedial powers of a federal court, we have been alert to the limitation that "[t]he power of the federal courts to restructure the operation of local and state governmental entities 'is not plenary. . . .' [A] federal court is required to tailor 'the scope of the remedy' to fit the nature and extent of the . . . violation."

Here we deal . . . not with the limited remedial powers of a federal court, . . . but with the broad remedial powers of Congress. It is fundamental that in no organ of government, state or federal, does there repose a more comprehensive remedial power than in the Congress, expressly charged by the Constitution with competence and authority to enforce equal protection guarantees. Congress not only may induce voluntary action to assure compliance with existing federal statutory or constitutional antidiscrimination provisions, but also, where Congress has authority to declare certain conduct unlawful, it may, as here, authorize and induce state action to avoid such conduct.

. . . .

It is not a constitutional defect in this program that it may disappoint the expectations of nonminority firms. When effectuating a limited and properly tailored remedy to cure the effects of prior discrimination, such "a sharing of the burden" by innocent parties is not impermissible. The actual "burden"

shouldered by nonminority firms is relatively light in this connection when we consider the scope of this public works program as compared with overall construction contracting opportunities. Moreover, although we may assume that the complaining parties are innocent of any discriminatory conduct, it was within congressional power to act on the assumption that in the past some nonminority businesses may have reaped competitive benefit over the years from the virtual exclusion of minority firms from these contracting opportunities.

Another challenge to the validity of the MBE program is the assertion that it is underinclusive — that it limits its benefit to specified minority groups rather than extending its remedial objectives to all businesses whose access to government contracting is impaired by the effects of disadvantage or discrimination. Such an extension would, of course, be appropriate for Congress to provide; it is not a function for the courts.

. . . .

The Congress has not sought to give select minority groups a preferred standing in the construction industry, but has embarked on a remedial program to place them on a more equitable footing with respect to public contracting opportunities. There has been no showing in this case that Congress has inadvertently effected an invidious discrimination by excluding from coverage an identifiable minority group that has been the victim of a degree of disadvantage and discrimination equal to or greater than that suffered by the groups encompassed by the MBE program. . . .

It is also contended that the MBE program is overinclusive — that it bestows a benefit on businesses identified by racial or ethnic criteria which cannot be justified on the basis of competitive criteria or as a remedy for the present effects of identified prior discrimination. . . .

It is significant that the administrative scheme provides for waiver and exemption. Two fundamental congressional assumptions underlie the MBE program: (1) that the present effects of past discrimination have impaired the competitive position of businesses owned and controlled by members of minority groups; and (2) that affirmative efforts to eliminate barriers to minority-firm access, and to evaluate bids with adjustment for the present effects of past discrimination, would assure that at least 10% of the federal funds granted under the Public Works Employment Act of 1977 would be accounted for by contracts with available, qualified, bona fide minority business enterprises. Each of these assumptions may be rebutted in the administrative process.

. . . .

Affirmed.

[MR. JUSTICE POWELL wrote a separate concurring opinion.]

MR. JUSTICE MARSHALL, with whom MR. JUSTICE BRENNAN and MR. JUSTICE BLACKMUN join, concurring in the judgment.

... [B]ecause a racial classification ostensibly designed for remedial purposes is susceptible to misuse, it may be justified only by showing "an important and articulated purpose for its use." "In addition any statute must be stricken that stigmatizes any group or that singles out those least well represented in the political process to bear the brunt of a benign program." ... In our view, then, the proper inquiry is whether racial classifications designed to further remedial purposes serve important governmental objectives and are substantially related to achievement of those objectives.

Judged under this standard, the 10% minority set-aside provision at issue in this case is plainly constitutional. Indeed, the question is not even a close one. ...

Because the means chosen by Congress to implement the set-aside provision are substantially related to the achievement of its remedial purpose, the provision also meets the second prong of our *Bakke* test. Congress reasonably determined that race-conscious means were necessary to break down the barriers confronting participation by minority enterprises in federally funded public works projects. That the set-aside creates a quota in favor of qualified and available minority business enterprises does not necessarily indicate that it stigmatizes. ... Since under the set-aside provision a contract may be awarded to a minority enterprise only if it is qualified to do the work, the provision stigmatizes as inferior neither a minority firm that benefits from it nor a nonminority firm that is burdened by it. Nor does the set-aside "establish a quota in the invidious sense of a ceiling," on the number of minority firms that can be awarded public works contracts. In addition, the set-aside affects only a miniscule amount of the funds annually expended in the United States for construction work.

In sum, it is clear to me that the racial classifications employed in the set-aside provision are substantially related to the achievement of the important and congressionally articulated goal of remedying the present effects of past racial discrimination. The provision, therefore, passes muster under the equal protection standard I adopted in *Bakke*.

....

MR. JUSTICE STEWART, with whom MR. JUSTICE REHNQUIST joins, dissenting.

... Today, the Court upholds a statute that accords a preference to citizens who are "Negroes, Spanish-speaking, Orientals, Indians, Eskimos, and Aleuts," for much the same reasons. I think today's decision is wrong for the same reason that *Plessy v. Ferguson* was wrong, and I respectfully dissent.

....

The Court's attempt to characterize the law as a proper remedial measure to counteract the effects of past or present racial discrimination is remarkably unconvincing. The Legislative Branch of government is not a court of equity. It has neither the dispassionate objectivity nor the flexibility that are needed to mold a race-conscious remedy around the single objective of eliminating the effects of past or present discrimination.

But even assuming that Congress has the power, under §5 of the Fourteenth Amendment or some other constitutional provision, to remedy previous illegal racial discrimination, there is no evidence that Congress has in the past engaged in racial discrimination in its disbursement of federal contracting funds. The MBE provision thus pushes the limits of any such justification far beyond the equal protection standard of the Constitution. Certainly, nothing in the Constitution gives Congress any greater authority to impose detriments on the basis of race than is afforded the Judicial Branch. And a judicial decree that imposes burdens on the basis of race can be upheld only where its sole purpose is to eradicate the actual effects of illegal race discrimination.

....

There are those who think that we need a new Constitution, and their views may someday prevail. But under the Constitution we have, one practice in which government may never engage is the practice of racism—not even "temporarily" and not even as an "experiment."

For these reasons, I would reverse the judgment of the Court of Appeals.

[MR. JUSTICE STEVENS wrote a separate dissenting opinion.]

City of Richmond v. J.A. Croson Co.

109 S. Ct. 706 (1989)
Vote: 6–3

Richmond, Virginia, adopted a Minority Business Utilization Plan requiring prime contractors awarded city construction contracts to subcontract at least 30 percent of the dollar amount of each contract to one or more "Minority Business Enterprises," which the Plan defined as a business from anywhere in the country at least 51 percent of which is owned and controlled by black, Spanish-speaking, Oriental, Indian, Eskimo, or Aleut citizens. Although the city declared that the plan was remedial, it introduced no direct evidence that the city had previously discriminated on the basis of race in letting contracts or that its prime contractors had discriminated against minority subcontractors.

However, the City Council did consider a statistical study that revealed that although the city's population was 50 percent black, only 0.67 percent of its prime construction contracts had been awarded to minority businesses in recent years, and that there were virtually no minority members in various local contractors' associations. The Council also received and considered various national studies that the Congress had considered in passing the minority set-aside program that was upheld in FULLILOVE.

For all practical purposes, the city's minority set-aside program was identical to the federal act, the one major difference being that the city specified a 30 percent rather than a 10 percent set-aside. But even here it was following the same formula that Congress had used, except that Richmond is 50 percent black whereas the country as a whole is just over 10 percent black.

There are, however, two important factors that distinguish this case from FULLILOVE. Five years after FULLILOVE, and after the appointment of several new justices, the Court handed down *Wygant v. Jackson Board of Education* (476 U.S. 267, 1986). Second, FULLILOVE involved an Act of Congress, whereas this case involved an action by a city council. As you will see, both of these sets of factors are important. In *Wygant* a majority of justices, some of whom oppose *all* nonremedial racial classifications and some of whom insist that the strict scrutiny standard is required when reviewing all racial classifications — benign as well as discriminatory — vacated a plan for race-based layoffs that had been agreed to by a teachers' union and a local school district in order to preserve positions

for minority teachers. The plurality stated that despite the plan's benign intent, it failed both prongs of the strict scrutiny standard because (1) it was not justified by a compelling governmental interest, since the record revealed no prior discrimination by the Board involved; and (2) the agreement was not narrowly tailored to accomplish a remedial purpose. In the case below a majority adheres to *Wygant,* and some of the justices make much of the fact that the Richmond City Council is not the United States Congress.

[JUSTICE O'CONNOR announced the judgment of the Court and delivered the opinion of the Court, in parts of which THE CHIEF JUSTICE, JUSTICE WHITE, and JUSTICE KENNEDY join.]

. . . .

Appellant and its supporting *amici* rely heavily on *Fullilove* for the proposition that a city council, like Congress, need not make specific findings of discrimination to engage in race-conscious relief. Thus, appellant argues "[i]t would be a perversion of federalism to hold that the federal government has a compelling interest in remedying the effects of racial discrimination in its own public works program, but a city government does not." . . .

What appellant ignores is that Congress, unlike any State or political subdivision, has a specific constitutional mandate to enforce the dictates of the Fourteenth Amendment. The power to "enforce" may at times also include the power to define situations which *Congress* determines threaten principles of equality and to adopt prophylactic rules to deal with those situations. . . . The Civil War Amendments themselves worked a dramatic change in the balance between congressional and state power over matters of race. Speaking of the Thirteenth and Fourteenth Amendments in *Ex parte Virginia,* . . . (1880), the Court stated: "They were intended to be, what they really are, limitations of the powers of the States and enlargements of the power of Congress."

That Congress may identify and redress the effects of society-wide discrimination does not mean that, *a fortiori,* the States and their political subdivisions are free to decide that such remedies are appropriate. Section 1 of the Fourteenth Amendment is an explicit *constraint* on state power, and the States must undertake any remedial efforts in accordance with that provision. To hold otherwise would be to cede control over the content of the Equal Protection Clause to the 50 state legislatures and their myriad political subdivisions. The mere recitation of a benign or compensatory purpose for the use of a racial classification would essentially entitle the States to exercise the full power of Congress under §5 of the Fourteenth Amendment and insulate any racial classification from judicial scrutiny under §1. We believe that such a result would be contrary to the intentions of the Framers of the Fourteenth Amendment, who desired to place clear limits on the States' use of race as a criterion for legislative action, and to have the federal courts enforce those limitations. . . .

. . . Thus, our treatment of an exercise of congressional power in *Fullilove* cannot be dispositive here. In the *Slaughter-House Cases* . . . the Court noted that the Civil War Amendments granted "additional powers to the Federal government," and laid "additional restraints upon those of the States." . . .

It would seem equally clear, however, that a state or local subdivision (if delegated the authority from the State) has the authority to eradicate the effects of private discrimination within its own legislative jurisdiction. This authority must, of course, be exercised within the constraints of §1 of the Fourteenth Amendment. . . .

Thus, if the city could show that it had essentially become a "passive participant" in a system of racial exclusion practiced by elements of the local construction industry, we think it clear that the city could take affirmative steps to dismantle such a system. It is beyond dispute that any public entity, state or federal, has a compelling interest in assuring that public dollars, drawn from the tax contributions of all citizens, do not serve to finance the evil of private prejudice. . . .

. . . .

Classifications based on race carry a danger of stigmatic harm. Unless they are strictly reserved for remedial settings, they may in fact promote notions of racial inferiority and lead to a politics of racial hostility. . . . We thus reaffirm the view . . . that the standard of review under the Equal Protection Clause is not dependent on the race of those burdened or benefited by a particular classification. . . .

Our continued adherence to the standard of review . . . does not, as JUSTICE MARSHALL's dissent suggests, . . . indicate that we view "racial discrimination as largely a phenomenon of the past" or that "government bodies need no longer preoccupy themselves with rectifying racial injustice." As we indicate below, . . . States and their local subdivisions have many legislative weapons at their disposal both to punish and prevent present discrimination and to remove arbitrary barriers to minority advancement. Rather, our interpretation . . . stems from our agree-

ment with the view expressed by Justice Powell in *Bakke*, that "[t]he guarantee of equal protection cannot mean one thing when applied to one individual and something else when applied to a person of another color." . . .

Under the standard proposed by JUSTICE MARSHALL's dissent, "[r]ace-conscious classifications designed to further remedial goals" . . . are forthwith subject to a relaxed standard of review. How the dissent arrives at the legal conclusion that a racial classification is "designed to further remedial goals," without first engaging in an examination of the factual basis for its enactment and the nexus between its scope and that factual basis we are not told. However, once the "remedial" conclusion is reached, the dissent's standard is singularly deferential, and bears little resemblance to the close examination of legislative purpose we have engaged in when reviewing classifications based either on race or gender. . . . The dissent's watered-down version of equal protection review effectively assures that race will always be relevant in American life, and that the "ultimate goal" of "eliminat[ing] entirely from governmental decisionmaking such irrelevant factors as a human being's race" . . . will never be achieved.

Even were we to accept a reading of the guarantee of equal protection under which the level of scrutiny varies according to the ability of different groups to defend their interests in the representative process, heightened scrutiny would still be appropriate in the circumstances of this case. One of the central arguments for applying a less exacting standard to "benign" racial classifications is that such measures essentially involve a choice made by dominant racial groups to disadvantage themselves. If one aspect of the judiciary's role under the Equal Protection Clause is to protect "discrete and insular minorities" from majoritarian prejudice or indifference, see *United States* v. *Carolene Products Co.* . . . (1938), some maintain that these concerns are not implicated when the "white majority" places burdens upon itself. . . .

In this case, blacks comprise approximately 50% of the population of the city of Richmond. Five of the nine seats on the City Council are held by blacks. The concern that a political majority will more easily act to the disadvantage of a minority based on unwarranted assumptions or incomplete facts would seem to militate for, not against, the application of heightened judicial scrutiny in this case. . . .

. . . .

. . . Appellant argues that it is attempting to remedy various forms of past discrimination that are alleged to be responsible for the small number of minority businesses in the local contracting industry. Among these the city cites the exclusion of blacks from skilled construction trade unions and training programs. This past discrimination has prevented them "from following the traditional path from laborer to entrepreneur." . . . The city also lists a host of nonracial factors which would seem to face a member of any racial group attempting to establish a new business enterprise, such as deficiencies in working capital, inability to meet bonding requirements, unfamiliarity with bidding procedures, and disability caused by an inadequate track record. . . .

While there is no doubt that the sorry history of both private and public discrimination in this country has contributed to a lack of opportunities for black entrepreneurs, this observation, standing alone, cannot justify a rigid racial quota in the awarding of public contracts in Richmond, Virginia. Like the claim that discrimination in primary and secondary schooling justifies a rigid racial preference in medical school admissions, an amorphous claim that there has been past discrimination in a particular industry cannot justify the use of an unyielding racial quota.

It is sheer speculation how many minority firms there would be in Richmond absent past societal discrimination, just as it was sheer speculation how many minority medical students would have been admitted to the medical school at Davis absent past discrimination in educational opportunities. Defining these sorts of injuries as "identified discrimination" would give local governments license to create a patchwork of racial preferences based on statistical generalizations about any particular field of endeavor.

These defects are readily apparent in this case. The 30% quota cannot in any realistic sense be tied to any injury suffered by anyone. . . .

None of [the] "findings" [presented to the Court], singly or together, provide the city of Richmond with a "strong basis in evidence for its conclusion that remedial action was necessary." . . . There is nothing approaching a prima facie case of a constitutional or statutory violation by *anyone* in the Richmond construction industry. . . .

The District Court accorded great weight to the fact that the city council designated the Plan as "remedial." But the mere recitation of a "benign" or legitimate purpose for a racial classification, is entitled to little or no weight. . . .

The District Court also relied on the highly conclusionary statement of a proponent of the Plan that there was racial discrimination in the construction industry "in this area, and the State, and around the nation." It also noted that the city manager had re-lated his view that racial discrimination still plagued the construction industry in his home city of Pittsburg. These statements are of little probative value in establishing identified discrimination in the Richmond construction industry. The factfinding process of legislative bodies is generally entitled to a presumption of regularity and deferential review by the judiciary. . . . But when a legislative body chooses to employ a suspect classification, it cannot rest upon a generalized assertion as to the classification's relevance to its goals. . . .

Reliance on the disparity between the number of prime contracts awarded to minority firms and the minority population of the city of Richmond is similarly misplaced. There is no doubt that "[w]here gross statistical disparities can be shown, they alone in a proper case may constitute prima facie proof of a pattern or practice of discrimination" under Title VII. . . . But it is equally clear that "[w]hen special qualifications are required to fill particular jobs, comparisons to the general population (rather than to the smaller group of individuals who possess the necessary qualifications) may have little probative value." . . .

In the employment context, we have recognized that for certain entry level positions or positions requiring minimal training, statistical comparisons of the racial composition of an employer's workforce to the racial composition of the relevant population may be probative of a pattern of discrimination. . . . But where special qualifications are necessary, the relevant statistical pool for purposes of demonstrating discriminatory exclusion must be the number of minorities qualified to undertake the particular task. . . .

In this case, the city does not even know how many MBEs in the relevant market are qualified to undertake prime or subcontracting work in public construction projects. . . . Nor does the city know what percentage of total city construction dollars minority firms now receive as subcontractors on prime contracts let by the city.

. . . .

As noted by the court below, it is almost impossible to assess whether the Richmond Plan is narrowly tailored to remedy prior discrimination since it is not linked to identified discrimination in any way. We limit ourselves to two observations in this regard.

First, there does not appear to have been any consideration of the use of race-neutral means to increase minority business participation in city contracting. . . .

Second, the 30% quota cannot be said to be narrowly tailored to any goal, except perhaps outright racial balancing. It rests upon the "completely unrealistic" assumption that minorities will choose a particular trade in lockstep proportion to their representation in the local population. . . .

Since the city must already consider bids and waivers on a case-by-case basis, it is difficult to see the need for a rigid numerical quota. . . .

Given the existence of an individualized procedure, the city's only interest in maintaining a quota system rather than investigating the need for remedial action in particular cases would seem to be simple administrative convenience. But the interest in avoiding the bureaucratic effort necessary to tailor remedial relief to those who truly have suffered the effects of prior discrimination cannot justify a rigid line drawn on the basis of a suspect classification. . . . Under Richmond's scheme, a successful black, Hispanic, or Oriental entrepreneur from anywhere in the country enjoys an absolute preference over other citizens based solely on their race. We think it obvious that such a program is not narrowly tailored to remedy the effects of prior discrimination.

. . . .

Nothing we say today precludes a state or local entity from taking action to rectify the effects of identified discrimination within its jurisdiction. If the city of Richmond had evidence before it that nonminority contractors were systematically excluding minority businesses from subcontracting opportunities it could take action to end the discriminatory exclusion. Where there is a significant statistical disparity between the number of qualified minority contractors willing and able to perform a particular service and the number of such contractors actually engaged by the locality or the locality's prime contractors, an inference of discriminatory exclusion could arise. . . . Under such circumstances, the city could act to dismantle the closed business system by taking appropriate measures against those who discriminate on the basis of race or other illegitimate criteria. . . . In the extreme case, some form of narrowly tailored racial preference might be necessary to break down patterns of deliberate exclusion.

Nor is local government powerless to deal with individual instances of racially motivated refusals to employ minority contractors. Where such discrimination occurs, a city would be justified in penalizing the discriminator and providing appropriate relief to the victim of such discrimination. . . . Moreover, evidence of a pattern of individual discriminatory acts can, if supported by appropriate statistical proof, lend support to a local government's determination that broader remedial relief is justified.

Even in the absence of evidence of discrimination, the city has at its disposal a whole array of race-neutral devices to increase the accessibility of city contracting opportunities to small entrepreneurs of all races. Simplification of bidding procedures, relaxation of bonding requirements, and training and financial aid for disadvantaged entrepreneurs of all races would open the public contracting market to all those who have suffered the effects of past societal discrimination or neglect. Many of the formal barriers to new entrants may be the product of bureaucratic inertia more than actual necessity, and may have a disproportionate effect on the opportunities open to new minority firms. Their elimination or modification would have little detrimental effect on the city's interests and would serve to increase the opportunities available to minority business without classifying individuals on the basis of race. The city may also act to prohibit discrimination in the provision of credit or bonding by local suppliers and banks. Business as usual should not mean business pursuant to the unthinking exclusion of certain members of our society from its rewards.

. . . .

. . . Because the city of Richmond has failed to identify the need for remedial action in the awarding of its public construction contracts, its treatment of its citizens on a racial basis violates the dictates of the Equal Protection Clause. Accordingly, the judgment of the Court of Appeals for the Fourth Circuit is *Affirmed.*

[JUSTICE STEVENS concurred in part with the opinion above and in the judgment.]

[JUSTICE KENNEDY concurred in part in the opinion above and in the judgment.]

JUSTICE SCALIA, concurring in the judgment.

I agree with much of the Court's opinion, and, in particular, with its conclusion that strict scrutiny must be applied to all governmental classification by race, whether or not its asserted purpose is "remedial" or "benign." . . . I do not agree, however, with the Court's dicta suggesting that, despite the Fourteenth Amendment, state and local governments may in some circumstances discriminate on the basis of race in order (in a broad sense) "to ameliorate the effects of past discrimination." . . . The benign purpose of compensating for social disadvantages, whether they have been acquired by reason of prior discrimination or otherwise, can no more be pursued by the illegitimate means of racial discrimination than can other assertedly benign purposes we have repeatedly rejected.

. . . .

In my view there is only one circumstance in which the States may act *by race* to "undo the effects of past discrimination": where that is necessary to eliminate their own maintenance of a system of unlawful racial classification. If, for example, a state agency has a discriminatory pay scale compensating black employees in all positions at 20% less than their nonblack counterparts, it may assuredly promulgate an order raising the salaries of "all black employees" by 20%.... This distinction explains our school desegregation cases, in which we have made plain that States and localities sometimes have an obligation to adopt race-conscious remedies....

....

A State can, of course, act "to undo the effects of past discrimination" in many permissible ways that do not involve classification by race. In the particular field of state contracting, for example, it may adopt a preference for small businesses, or even for new businesses—which would make it easier for those previously excluded by discrimination to enter the field. Such programs may well have racially disproportionate impact, but they are not based on race. And, of course, a State may "undo the effects of past discrimination" in the sense of giving the identified victim of state discrimination that which it wrongfully denied him—for example, giving to a previously rejected black applicant the job that, by reason of discrimination, had been awarded to a white applicant, even if this means terminating the latter's employment. In such a context, the white job-holder is not being selected for disadvantageous treatment because of his race, but because he was wrongfully awarded a job to which another is entitled. That is worlds apart from the system here, in which those to be disadvantaged are identified solely by race.

....

It is plainly true that in our society blacks have suffered discrimination immeasurably greater than any directed at other racial groups. But those who believe that racial preferences can help to "even the score" display, and reinforce, a manner of thinking by race that was the source of the injustice and that will, if it endures within our society, be the source of more injustice still. The relevant proposition is not that it was blacks, or Jews, or Irish who were discriminated against, but that it was individual men and women, "created equal," who were discriminated against. And the relevant resolve is that that should never happen again. Racial preferences appear to "even the score" (in some small degree) only if one embraces the proposition that our society is appropriately viewed as divided into races, making it right

that an injustice rendered in the past to a black man should be compensated for by discriminating against a white. Nothing is worth that embrace. Since blacks have been disproportionately disadvantaged by racial discrimination, any race-neutral remedial program aimed at the disadvantaged *as such* will have a disproportionately beneficial impact on blacks. Only such a program, and not one that operates on the basis of race, is in accord with the letter and the spirit of our constitution.

Since I believe that the appellee here had a constitutional right to have its bid succeed or fail under a decisionmaking process uninfected with racial bias, I concur in the judgment of the Court.

JUSTICE MARSHALL, with whom JUSTICE BRENNAN and JUSTICE BLACKMUN join, dissenting.

... The essence of the majority's position is that Richmond has failed to catalogue adequate findings to prove that past discrimination has impeded minorities from joining or participating fully in Richmond's construction contracting industry. I find deep irony in second-guessing Richmond's judgment on this point. As much as any municipality in the United States, Richmond knows what racial discrimination is; a century of decisions by this and other federal courts has richly documented the city's disgraceful history of public and private racial discrimination. In any event, the Richmond City Council *has* supported its determination that minorities have been wrongly excluded from local construction contracting. Its proof includes statistics showing that minority-owned businesses have received virtually no city contracting dollars and rarely if ever belonged to area trade associations; testimony by municipal officials that discrimination has been widespread in the local construction industry; and the same exhaustive and widely publicized federal studies relied on in *Fullilove,* studies which showed that pervasive discrimination in the Nation's tight-knit construction industry had operated to exclude minorities from public contracting. These are precisely the types of statistical and testimonial evidence which, until today, this Court had credited in cases approving of race-conscious measures designed to remedy past discrimination.

More fundamentally, today's decision marks a deliberate and giant step backward in this Court's affirmative action jurisprudence. Cynical of one municipality's attempt to redress the effects of past racial discrimination in a particular industry, the majority launches a grapeshot attack on race-conscious remedies in general. The majority's unnecessary pronouncements will inevitably discourage or prevent governmental entities, particularly States and localities, from acting to rectify the scourge of past discrimination. This is the harsh reality of the majority's decision, but it is not the Constitution's command.

. . . .

. . . The members of the Richmond City Council were well aware of . . . exhaustive congressional findings, a point the majority, tellingly, elides. The transcript of the session at which the Council enacted the local set-aside initiative contains numerous references to the 6-year-old congressional set-aside program, to the evidence of nationwide discrimination barriers described above, and to the *Fullilove* decision itself. . . .

The City Council's members also heard testimony that, although minority groups made up half of the city's population, only .67% of the $24.6 million which Richmond had dispensed in construction contracts during the five years ending in March 1983 had gone to minority-owned prime contractors. . . . They heard testimony that the major Richmond area construction trade associations had virtually no minorities among their hundreds of members. Finally, they heard testimony from city officials as to the exclusionary history of the local construction industry. As the District Court noted, not a single person who testified before the City Council denied that discrimination in Richmond's construction industry had been widespread. . . . So long as one views Richmond's local evidence of discrimination against the backdrop of systematic nationwide racial discrimination which Congress had so painstakingly identified in this very industry, this case is readily resolved.

"Agreement upon a means for applying the Equal Protection Clause to an affirmative-action program has eluded this Court every time the issue has come before us." . . . My view has long been that race-conscious classifications designed to further remedial goals "must serve important governmental objectives and must be substantially related to achievement of those objectives" in order to withstand constitutional scrutiny. . . . Analyzed in terms of this two-prong standard, Richmond's set-aside, like the federal program on which it was modeled, is "plainly constitutional." . . .

A
1

Turning first to the governmental interest inquiry, Richmond has two powerful interests in setting aside a portion of public contracting funds for minority-owned enterprises. The first is the city's interest in eradicating the effects of past racial discrimination. It is far too late in the day to doubt that remedying

such discrimination is a compelling, let alone an important, interest. . . .

Richmond has a second compelling interest in setting aside, where possible, a portion of its contracting dollars. That interest is the prospective one of preventing the city's own spending decisions from reinforcing and perpetuating the exclusionary effects of past discrimination. . . .

The majority pays only lip service to this additional governmental interest. . . . But our decisions have often emphasized the danger of the government tacitly adopting, encouraging, or furthering racial discrimination even by its own routine operations. In *Shelley* v. *Kraemer* . . . (1948), this Court recognized this interest as a constitutional command, holding unanimously that the Equal Protection Clause forbids courts to enforce racially restrictive covenants even where such covenants satisfied all requirements of state law and where the State harbored no discriminatory intent. . . .

The majority is wrong to trivialize the continuing impact of government acceptance or use of private institutions or structures once wrought by discrimination. When government channels all its contracting funds to a white-dominated community of established contractors whose racial homogeneity is the product of private discrimination, it does more than place its imprimatur on the practices which forged and which continue to define that community. It also provides a measurable boost to those economic entities that have thrived within it, while denying important economic benefits to those entities which, but for prior discrimination, might well be better qualified to receive valuable government contracts. In my view, the interest in ensuring that the government does not reflect and reinforce prior private discrimination in dispensing public contracts is every bit as strong as the interest in eliminating private discrimination — an interest which this Court has repeatedly deemed compelling. . . . The more government bestows its rewards on those persons or businesses that were positioned to thrive during a period of private racial discrimination, the tighter the dead-hand grip of prior discrimination becomes on the present and future. Cities like Richmond may not be constitutionally required to adopt set-aside plans. . . . But there can be no doubt that when Richmond acted affirmatively to stem the perpetuation of patterns of discrimination through its own decisionmaking, it served an interest of the highest order.

2

The remaining question with respect to the "governmental interest" prong of equal protection analysis is whether Richmond has proffered satisfactory proof of past racial discrimination to support its twin interests in remediation and in governmental nonperpetuation. Although the Members of this Court have differed on the appropriate standard of review for race-conscious remedial measures, . . . we have always regarded this factual inquiry as a practical one. Thus, the Court has eschewed rigid tests which require the provision of particular species of evidence, statistical or otherwise. At the same time we have required that government adduce evidence that, taken as a whole, is sufficient to support its claimed interest and to dispel the natural concern that it acted out of mere "paternalistic stereotyping, not on a careful consideration of modern social conditions." . . .

    . . . .

The varied body of evidence on which Richmond relied provides a "strong," "firm," and "unquestionably legitimate" basis upon which the City Council could determine that the effects of past racial discrimination warranted a remedial and prophylactic governmental response. As I have noted, . . . Richmond acted against a backdrop of congressional and Executive Branch studies which demonstrated with such force the nationwide pervasiveness of prior discrimination that Congress presumed that "'present economic inequities'" in construction contracting resulted from "'past discriminatory systems.'" . . . [T]o suggest that the facts on which Richmond has relied do not provide a sound basis for its finding of past racial discrimination simply blinks credibility.

    . . . .

No one, of course, advocates "blind judicial deference" to the findings of the City Council or the testimony of city leaders. The majority's suggestion that wholesale deference is what Richmond seeks is a classic straw-man argument. But the majority's trivialization of the testimony of Richmond's leaders is dismaying in a far more serious respect. By disregarding the testimony of local leaders and the judgment of local government, the majority does violence to the very principles of comity within our federal system which this court has long championed. Local officials, by virtue of their proximity to, and their expertise with, local affairs, are exceptionally well-qualified to make determinations of public good "within their respective spheres of authority." . . . The majority, however, leaves any traces of comity behind in its headlong rush to strike down Richmond's race-conscious measure.

    . . . .

B

In my judgment, Richmond's set-aside plan also comports with the second prong of the equal protec-

tion inquiry, for it is substantially related to the interests it seeks to serve in remedying past discrimination and in ensuring that municipal contract procurement does not perpetuate that discrimination. The most striking aspect of the city's ordinance is the similarity it bears to the "appropriately limited" federal set-aside provision upheld in *Fullilove*. . . . Like the federal provision, Richmond's is limited to five years in duration, and was not renewed when it came up for reconsideration in 1988. Like the federal provision, Richmond's contains a waiver provision freeing from its subcontracting requirements those nonminority firms that demonstrate that they cannot comply with its provisions. . . . Like the federal provision, Richmond's has a minimal impact on innocent third parties. While the measure affects 30% of *public* contracting dollars, that translates to only 3% of overall Richmond area contracting. . . .

Finally, like the federal provision, Richmond's does not interfere with any vested right of a contractor to a particular contract; instead it operates entirely prospectively. Richmond's initiative affects only future economic arrangements and imposes only a diffuse burden on nonminority competitors — here, businesses owned or controlled by nonminorities which seek subcontracting work on public construction projects. . . .

These factors, far from "justify[ing] a preference of any size or duration," . . . are precisely the factors to which this Court looked in *Fullilove*. . . .

III

I would ordinarily end my analysis at this point and conclude that Richmond's ordinance satisfies both the governmental interest and substantial relationship prongs of our Equal Protection Clause analysis. However, I am compelled to add more, for the majority has gone beyond the facts of this case to announce a set of principles which unnecessarily restrict the power of governmental entities to take race-conscious measures to redress the effects of prior discrimination.

Today, for the first time, a majority of this Court has adopted strict scrutiny as its standard of Equal Protection Clause review of race-conscious remedial measures. . . . This is an unwelcome development. A profound difference separates governmental actions that themselves are racist, and governmental actions that seek to remedy the effects of prior racism or to prevent neutral governmental activity from perpetuating the effects of such racism. . . .

Racial classifications "drawn on the presumption that one race is inferior to another or because they put the weight of government behind racial hatred and separatism" warrant the strictest judicial scrutiny because of the very irrelevance of these rationales. . . . By contrast, racial classifications drawn for the purpose of remedying the effects of discrimination that itself was race-based have a highly pertinent basis: the tragic and indelible fact that discrimination against blacks and other racial minorities in this Nation has pervaded our Nation's history and continues to scar our society. . . .

In concluding that remedial classifications warrant no different standard of review under the Constitution than the most brute and repugnant forms of state-sponsored racism, a majority of this Court signals that it regards racial discrimination as largely a phenomenon of the past, and that government bodies need no longer preoccupy themselves with rectifying racial injustice. I, however, do not believe this Nation is anywhere close to eradicating racial discrimination or its vestiges. In constitutionalizing its wishful thinking, the majority today does a grave disservice not only to those victims of past and present racial discrimination in this Nation whom government has sought to assist, but also to this Court's long tradition of approaching issues of race with the utmost sensitivity.

. . . .

The majority today sounds a full-scale retreat from the Court's longstanding solicitude to race-conscious remedial efforts "directed toward deliverance of the century-old promise of equality of economic opportunity." . . . The new and restrictive tests it applies scuttle one city's effort to surmount its discriminatory past, and imperil those of dozens more localities. I, however, profoundly disagree with the cramped vision of the Equal Protection Clause which the majority offers today and with its application of that vision to Richmond, Virginia's, laudable set-aside plan. The battle against pernicious racial discrimination or its effects is nowhere near won. I must dissent.

JUSTICE BLACKMUN, with whom JUSTICE BRENNAN joins, dissenting.

I join JUSTICE MARSHALL's perceptive and incisive opinion revealing great sensitivity toward those who have suffered the pains of economic discrimination in the construction trades for so long.

I never thought that I would live to see the day when the city of Richmond, Virginia, the cradle of the Old Confederacy, sought on its own, within a narrow confine, to lessen the stark impact of persistent discrimination. But Richmond, to its great credit, acted. Yet this Court, the supposed bastion of equality, strikes down Richmond's efforts as though discrimination had never existed or was not demonstrated in this particular litigation. JUSTICE MARSHALL convincingly discloses the fallacy and the shallowness of that

approach. History is irrefutable, even though one might sympathize with those who — though possibly innocent in themselves — benefit from the wrongs of past decades.

So the Court today regresses. I am confident, however, that, given time, it one day again will do its best to fulfill the great promises of the Constitution's Preamble and of the guarantees embodied in the Bill of Rights — a fulfillment that would make this Nation very special.

Local 28 of the Sheetmetal Workers' International Assoc. v. EEOC

478 U.S. 421 (1986)
Vote: 5–1–3

In 1975, a federal district court held that Local 28 of the sheetmetal workers' union had discriminated against nonwhites in recruitment, selection, training, and admission to the union, in violation of Title VII of the Civil Rights Act of 1964, and in a remedial order gave the union six years to reach a 29 percent nonwhite membership goal. This figure represented the proportion of nonwhites in the relevant labor pool in the area. The court also emphasized that its order was a temporary remedy designed to overcome a "long and persistent pattern of discrimination."

Local 28, with support from the Reagan administration, argued that the court's order violated Section 706(g), the enforcement provisions of Title VII, which, they argued, provide race-conscious relief only for those who have been victims of discrimination. In this case, Local 28 admitted a prior history of discrimination but argued that the relief was overly broad in that it benefitted those who were not identifiable victims of its prior practices of discrimination.

The court of appeals affirmed the district court's order, and when the issue reached the Supreme Court, Local 28 was supported by the Solicitor General.

JUSTICE BRENNAN announced the judgment of the Court and delivered the opinion of the court [in part] and an opinion [in part] in which JUSTICE MARSHALL, JUSTICE BLACKMUN, and JUSTICE STEVENS join.

. . . .

IV

Petitioners, joined by the Solicitor General, argue that the membership goal, the Fund order, and other orders which require petitioners to grant membership preferences to nonwhites are expressly prohibited by §706(g), 42 U.S.C. §2000e–5(g), which defines the remedies available under Title VII. Petitioners and the Solicitor General maintain that §706(g) authorizes a district court to award preferential relief only to the actual victims of unlawful discrimination. They maintain that the membership goal and the Fund violate this provision, since they require petitioners to admit to membership, and otherwise to extend benefits to black and Hispanic individuals who are not the identified victims of unlawful discrimination. We reject this argument, and hold that §706(g) does not prohibit a court from ordering, in appropriate circumstances, affirmative race-conscious relief as a remedy for past discrimination. Specifically, we hold that such relief may be appropriate where an employer or a labor union has engaged in persistent or egregious discrimination, or where necessary to dissipate the lingering effects of pervasive discrimination.

A

Section 706(g) states:

> If the court finds that the respondent has intentionally engaged in or is intentionally engaging in an unlawful employment practice, . . . the court may enjoin the respondent from engaging in such unlawful employment practice, and order such affirmative action as may be appropriate, which may include, but is not limited to, reinstatement or hiring or employees, with or without back pay, . . . or any other equitable relief as the court deems appropriate. . . . No order of the court shall require the admission or reinstatement of an individual as a member of a union, or the hiring, reinstatement, or promotion of an individual as an employee, or the payment to him of any back pay, if such individual was refused admission, suspended, or expelled, or was refused employment or advancement or was suspended or discharged for any reason other than discrimination on account of race, color, religion, sex, or national origin in violation of . . . this title. . . .

The language of §706(g) plainly expresses Congress's intent to vest district courts with broad discretion to award "appropriate" equitable relief to remedy unlawful discrimination. . . . Nevertheless, petitioners and the Solicitor General argue that the last sentence of §706(g) prohibits a court from ordering an employer or labor union to take affirmative steps to eliminate discrimination which might incidentally benefit individuals who are not the actual victims of discrimination. This reading twists the plain language of the statute.

The last sentence of §706(g) prohibits a court from ordering a union to admit an individual who was "refused admission . . . for any reason other than discrimination." It does not, as petitioners and the Solicitor General suggest, say that a court may order relief only for the actual victims of past discrimination. The sentence on its face addresses only the situation where a plaintiff demonstrates that a union (or an employer) has engaged in unlawful discrimination, but the union can show that a particular individual would have been refused admission even in the absence of discrimination, for example because that individual was unqualified. In these circumstances, §706(g) confirms that a court could not order the union to admit the unqualified individual. . . . In this case, neither the membership goal nor the Fund order required petitioners to admit to membership individuals who had been refused admission for reasons unrelated to discrimination. Thus, we do not read §706(g) to prohibit a court from ordering the kind of affirmative relief the District Court awarded in this case.

. . .

The availability of race-conscious affirmative relief under §706(g) as a remedy for a violation of Title VII also furthers the broad purposes underlying the statute. Congress enacted Title VII based on its determination that racial minorities were subject to pervasive and systematic discrimination in employment. "[I]t was clear to Congress that '[t]he crux of the problem [was] to open employment opportunities for Negroes in occupations which have been traditionally closed to them,' . . . and it was to this problem that Title VII's prohibition against racial discrimination in employment was primarily addressed." *Steelworkers* v. *Weber* . . . (1979). . . . Title VII was designed "to achieve equality of employment opportunities and remove barriers that have operated in the past to favor an identifiable group of white employees over other employees." . . . In order to foster equal employment opportunities, Congress gave the lower courts broad power under §706(g) to fashion "the most complete relief possible" to remedy past discrimination. . . .

In most cases, the court need only order the employer or union to cease engaging in discriminatory practices, and award make-whole relief to the individuals victimized by those practices. In some instances, however, it may be necessary to require the employer or union to take affirmative steps to end discrimination effectively to enforce Title VII. Where an employer or union has engaged in particularly longstanding or egregious discrimination, an injunction simply reiterating Title VII's prohibition against discrimination will often prove useless and will only result in endless enforcement litigation. In such cases, requiring recalcitrant employers or unions to hire and to admit qualified minorities roughly in proportion to the number of qualified minorities in the work force may be the only effective way to ensure the full enjoyment of the rights protected by Title VII. . . .

Further, even where the employer or union formally ceases to engage in discrimination, informal mechanisms may obstruct equal employment opportunities. An employer's reputation for discrimination may discourage minorities from seeking available employment. . . . In these circumstances, affirmative race-conscious relief may be the only means available "to assure equality of employment opportunities and to eliminate those discriminatory practices and devices which have fostered racially stratified job environments to the disadvantage of minority citizens.". . . Affirmative action "promptly operates to change the outward and visible signs of yesterday's racial distinctions and thus, to provide an impetus to the process of dismantling the barriers, psychological or otherwise, erected by past practices.". . .

Finally, a district court may find it necessary to order interim hiring or promotional goals pending the development of nondiscriminatory hiring or promotion procedures. In these cases, the use of numerical goals provides a compromise between two unacceptable alternatives: an outright ban on hiring or promotions, or continued use of a discriminatory selection procedure.

We have previously suggested that courts may utilize certain kinds of racial preferences to remedy past discrimination under Title VII. . . . *Fullilove* v. *Klutznick,* . . . (1980). . . .

. . .

Despite the fact that the plain language of §706(g) and the purposes of Title VII suggest the opposite, petitioners and the Solicitor General maintain that the legislative history indicates that Congress intended that affirmative relief under §706(g) benefit only the identified victims of past discrimination. To support this contention, petitioners and the Solicitor General rely principally on statements made throughout the House and Senate debates to the effect that Title VII would not require employers or labor unions to adopt quotas or preferences that would benefit racial minorities.

Our examination of the legislative history of Title VII convinces us that, when examined in context, the statements relied upon by petitioners and the Solicitor General do not indicate that Congress intended to limit relief under §706(g) to that which benefits only the actual victims of unlawful discrimination. Rather, these statements were intended largely to reassure opponents of the bill that it would not require employers or labor unions to use racial quotas or to grant preferential treatment to racial minorities in order to avoid being charged with unlawful discrimination. . . . The bill's supporters insisted that this would not be the intent and effect of the legislation, and eventually agreed to state this expressly in §703(j), 42 U.S.C. §2000e–2(j). Contrary to the arguments made by the petitioners and the Solicitor General, these statements do not suggest that a court may not order preferential relief under §706(g) when appropriate to remedy past discrimination. Rather, it is clear that the bill's supporters only wished to emphasize that an employer would not violate the statute merely by having a racially imbalanced work force, and, consequently, that a court could not order an employer to adopt racial preferences merely to correct such an imbalance.

. . . .

[M]any opponents of Title VII argued that an employer could be found guilty of discrimination under the statute simply because of a racial imbalance in his work force, and would be compelled to implement racial "quotas" to avoid being charged with liability. . . . At the same time, supporters of the bill insisted that employers would not violate Title VII simply because of racial imbalance, and emphasized that neither the Commission nor the courts could compel employers to adopt quotas solely to facilitate racial balancing. . . . The debate concerning what Title VII did and did not require culminated in the adoption of §703(j), which stated expressly that the statute did not require an employer or labor union to adopt quotas or preferences simply because of a racial imbalance. However, while Congress strongly opposed the use of quotas or preferences merely to maintain racial balance, it gave no intimation as to whether such measures would be acceptable as *remedies* for Title VII violations.

Congress' failure to consider this issue is not surprising, since there was relatively little civil rights litigation prior to the adoption of the 1964 Civil

Rights Act. More importantly, the cases that had been litigated had not resulted in the sort of affirmative-action remedies that, as later became apparent, would sometimes be necessary to eliminate effectively the effects of past discrimination. Thus, the use of racial preferences as a *remedy* for past discrimination simply was not an issue at the time Title VII was being considered. Our task then, is to determine whether Congress intended to preclude a district court from ordering affirmative action in appropriate circumstances as a remedy for past discrimination. . . . Our examination of the legislative policy behind Title VII leads us to conclude that Congress did not intend to prohibit a court from exercising its remedial authority in that way. Congress deliberately gave the district courts broad authority under Title VII to fashion the most complete relief possible to eliminate "the last vestiges of an unfortunate and ignominious page in this country's history." . . . As we noted above, affirmative race-conscious relief may in some instances be necessary to accomplish this task. In the absence of any indication that Congress intended to limit a district court's remedial authority in a way which would frustrate the court's ability to enforce Title VII's mandate, we decline to fashion such a limitation ourselves.

· · ·

Our reading of the scope of the district court's remedial powers under §706(g) is confirmed by the contemporaneous interpretations of the EEOC and the Justice Department. Following the enactment of the Civil Rights Act of 1964, both the Justice Department and the EEOC, the two federal agencies charged with enforcing Title VII, steadfastly maintained that race-conscious remedies for unlawful discrimination are available under the statute. Both agencies have, in appropriate cases, sought court orders and consent decrees containing such provisions. . . .

· · ·

. . . [O]ur interpretation of §706(g) is confirmed by the legislative history of the Equal Employment Opportunity Act of 1972, 86 Stat. 103, which amended Title VII in several respects. One such change modified the language of §706(g) to empower a court to order "such affirmative action as may be appropriate, which may include, *but is not limited to* reinstatement or hiring of employees . . . *or any other equitable relief as the court deems appropriate.*" . . . This language was intended "to give the courts wide discretion exercising their equitable powers to fashion the most complete relief possible." . . . While the

section-by-section analysis undertaken in the Conference Committee Report stressed the need for "make-whole" relief for the "victims of unlawful discrimination,". . . nowhere did Congress suggest that a court lacked the power to award preferential remedies that might benefit nonvictims. Indeed, the Senate's rejection of two other amendments supports a contrary conclusion.

. . . .

· · ·

Finally, petitioners and the Solicitor General find support for their reading of §706(g) in several of our decisions applying that provision. Petitioners refer to several cases for the proposition that court-ordered remedies under §706(g) are limited to make-whole relief benefiting actual victims of past discrimination. . . . *Albemarle Paper Co.* v. *Moody* . . . (1975). This reliance is misguided. The cases cited hold only that a court may order relief designed to make individual victims of racial discrimination whole. . . . None of these decisions suggested that individual "make-whole" relief was the *only* kind of remedy available under the statute. On the contrary, several cases emphasized that the district court's remedial powers should be exercised both to eradicate the effects of unlawful discrimination as well as to make the victims of past discrimination whole. . . . Neither do these cases suggest that §706(g) prohibits a court from ordering relief which might benefit nonvictims; indeed several cases acknowledged that the district court has broad authority to "devise prospective relief designed to assure that employers found to be in violation of [Title VII] eliminate their discriminatory practices and the effects therefrom." . . .

Petitioners claim to find their strongest support in *Firefighters* v. *Stotts,* 467 U.S. 561 . . . (1984). In *Stotts,* the city of Memphis, Tennessee had entered into a consent decree requiring affirmative steps to increase the proportion of minority employees in its Fire Department. Budgetary cuts subsequently forced the city to lay off employees; under the city's last-hired, first-fired seniority system, many of the black employees who had been hired pursuant to the consent decree would have been laid off first. These employees sought relief, and the District Court, concluding that the proposed layoffs would have a racially discriminatory effect, enjoined the city from applying its seniority policy "insofar as it will decrease the percentage of black[s] that are presently employed." . . . We held that the District Court exceeded its authority.

First, we rejected the claim that the District Court was merely enforcing the terms of the consent decree since the parties had expressed no intention to depart from the existing seniority system in the event of layoffs. Second, we concluded that the District Court's order conflicted with §703(h) of Title VII, which "permits the routine application of a seniority system absent proof of an intention to discriminate."... Since the District Court had found the proposed layoffs were not motivated by a discriminatory purpose, we held that the court erred in enjoining the city from applying its seniority system in making the layoffs.

We also rejected the Court of Appeals' suggestion that the District court's order was justified by the fact that, had plaintiffs prevailed at trial, the court could have entered an order overriding the city's seniority system.... [We] observed that a court may abridge a bona fide seniority system in fashioning a Title VII remedy only to make victims of intentional discrimination whole, that is, a court may award competitive seniority to individuals who show that they had been discriminated against. However, because none of the firefighters protected by the court's order was a proven victim of illegal discrimination, we reasoned that at trial the District Court would have been without authority to override the city's seniority system, and therefore the court could not enter such an order merely to effectuate the purposes of the consent decree.

While not strictly necessary to the result, we went on to comment "... that a court can award competitive seniority only when the beneficiary of the award has actually been a victim of illegal discrimination is consistent with the policy behind §706(g)" which, we noted, "is to provide 'make-whole' relief only to those who have been actual victims of illegal discrimination."... Relying on this language, petitioners, joined by the Solicitor General, argue that both the membership goal and the Fund order contravene the policy behind §706(g) since they extend preferential relief to individuals who were not the actual victims of illegal discrimination. We think that argument both reads *Stotts* too broadly and ignores the important differences between *Stotts* and this case.

. . . .

. . .

Although we conclude that §706(g) does not foreclose a district court from instituting some sorts of racial preferences where necessary to remedy past discrimination, we do not mean to suggest that such relief is always proper. While the fashioning of "appropriate" remedies for a particular Title VII violation invokes the "equitable discretion of the district courts,"... we emphasize that a court's judgment should be guided by sound legal principles. In particular, the court should exercise its discretion with an eye towards Congress' concern that race-conscious affirmative measures not be invoked simply to create a racially balanced work force. In the majority of Title VII cases, the court will not have to impose affirmative action as a remedy for past discrimination, but need only order the employer or union to cease engaging in discriminatory practices and award make-whole relief to the individuals victimized by those practices. However, in some cases, affirmative action may be necessary in order effectively to enforce Title VII. As we noted before, a court may have to resort to race-conscious affirmative action when confronted with an employer or labor union that has engaged in persistent or egregious discrimination. Or, such relief may be necessary to dissipate the lingering effects of pervasive discrimination. Whether there might be other circumstances that justify the use of court-ordered affirmative action is a matter that we need not decide here. We note only that a court should consider whether affirmative action is necessary to remedy past discrimination in a particular case before imposing such measures, and that the court should also take care to tailor its orders to fit the nature of the violation it seeks to correct. In this case, several factors lead us to conclude that the relief ordered by the District Court was proper.

First, both the District Court and the Court of Appeals agreed that the membership goal and Fund order were necessary to remedy petitioners' pervasive and egregious discrimination....

. . . .

Second, the District Court's flexible application of the membership goal gives strong indication that it is not being used simply to achieve and maintain racial balance, but rather as a benchmark against which the court could gauge petitioners' efforts to remedy past discrimination....

Third, both the membership goal and the Fund order are temporary measures....

Finally, we think it significant that neither the membership goal nor the Fund order "unnecessarily trammel the interests of white employees."... Petitioners concede that the District Court's orders did not require any member of the union to be laid off, and did not discriminate against *existing* union members....

. . . .

... While white applicants for union membership may be denied certain benefits available to their non-white counterparts, the court's orders do not stand as an absolute bar to the admission of such individuals; again, a majority of those entering the union after entry of the court's orders have been white. We therefore conclude that the District Court's orders do not violate the equal protection safeguards of the Constitution.

. . . .

JUSTICE POWELL, concurring in part and concurring in the judgment. [omitted]

JUSTICE O'CONNOR, concurring in part and dissenting in part.

. . . I would reverse the judgment of the Court of Appeals on statutory grounds insofar as the membership "goal" and the Fund order are concerned, and I would not reach petitioners' constitutional claims. I agree . . . that the membership "goal" in this case operates as a rigid racial quota that cannot feasibly be met through good-faith efforts by Local 28. In my view, §703(j), 42 U.S.C. §2000e–(j), and §706(g), 42 U.S.C. §2000e–5(g), read together, preclude courts from ordering racial quotas such as this. I therefore dissent from the Court's judgment insofar as it affirms the use of these mandatory quotas.

. . . .

I do not question that petitioners' past violations of Title VII were egregious, or that in some respects they exhibited inexcusable recalcitrance in the face of the District Court's earlier remedial orders. But the timetable with which petitioners were ordered to comply was quite unrealistic and clearly could not be met by good-faith efforts on petitioners' part. In sum, the membership goal operates as a rigid membership quota, which will in turn spawn a sharp curtailment in the opportunities of nonminorities to be admitted to the apprenticeship program. . . .

Whether the unequivocal rejection of racial quotas by the Congress that enacted Title VII is said to be expressed in §706(g), in §703(j), or in both, a "remedy" such as this membership quota cannot stand. . . . Accordingly, I would reverse the judgment of the Court of Appeals on statutory grounds . . . without reaching petitioners' constitutional claims.

JUSTICE WHITE, dissenting.

As the Court observes, the general policy under Title VII is to limit relief for racial discrimination in employment practices to actual victims of the discrimination. But I agree that §706(g) does not bar relief for nonvictims in all circumstances. Hence, I generally agree with [p]arts . . . of the Court's opinion. It may also be that this is one of those unusual cases where nonvictims of discrimination were entitled to a measure of the relief ordered by the District Court and affirmed by the Court of Appeals.

But Judge Winter, in dissent below, was correct in concluding that critical parts of the remedy ordered in this case were excessive under §706(g), absent findings that those benefiting from the relief had been victims of discriminatory practices by the union. As Judge Winter explained and contrary to the Court's views, the cumulative effect of the revised affirmative action plan and the contempt judgments against the union established not just a minority membership goal but also a strict racial quota that the union was required to attain. We have not heretofore approved this kind of racially discriminatory hiring practice, and I would not do so now. Beyond this, I am convinced, as Judge Winter was, that holding the union in contempt for failing to attain the membership quota during a time of economic doldrums in the construction industry and a declining demand for the union skills involved in this case was for all practical purposes equivalent to a judicial insistence that the union comply even if it required the displacement of nonminority workers by members of the plaintiff class. The remedy is inequitable in my view, and for this reason I dissent from the judgment affirming the Court of Appeals.

JUSTICE REHNQUIST, with whom the CHIEF JUSTICE joins, dissenting. [omitted]

Johnson v. Transportation Agency, Santa Clara County

480 U.S. 616 (1987)
Vote: 6–3

In 1978, the Santa Clara County Transit District Board of Supervisors adopted an affirmative action plan for the County's Transportation Agency. The plan provided that in making promotions to positions with a traditionally segregated job classification in which women had been significantly underrepresented, the agency was authorized to consider as one factor the sex of a qualified applicant. The board based this policy on a finding that women as well as ethnic minorities were represented, in the agency as a whole and in several job categories, in numbers far lower than their proportion in the county labor force.

In the job classification relevant to this case, none of the 238 skilled craftworkers was a woman.

The plan noted that this underrepresentation in part reflected the fact that women had traditionally not been employed in certain positions and had not been motivated to pursue them "because of the limited opportunities that have existed in the past for them to work in such classifications." The plan also extended similar considerations to ethnic minorities.

The agency stated that the plan was intended to achieve "a statistically measurable yearly improvement in hiring, training and promotion of minorities and women throughout the Agency in all major job classifications where they are underrepresented" and specified its ideal as attaining a work force whose composition reflected the proportion of minorities and women in the area labor force. However, the plan acknowledged that a number of other factors also affected employment, and it did not set aside any specific number of positions for women or minorities. Rather, it authorized the consideration of ethnicity and sex as a factor when evaluating "qualified candidates" for positions in which members of such groups were poorly represented.

One such position in which women were underrepresented was that of road dispatcher, which was one of the agency's 238 skilled craft positions. In 1979, when a position became vacant, nine applicants were deemed qualified. After interviews during which all the applicants received evaluation scores, seven were certified as eligible for appointment by the agency. Mr. Johnson was tied for second place in this ranking; Ms. Joyce ranked fourth. After a second set of interviews, communication with the county's Affirmative Action Office, and consideration of the fact that the agency employed no women in any skilled craft position and had never appointed a woman as a road dispatcher, the director of the agency selected Ms. Joyce over Mr. Johnson for the position.

Johnson filed a complaint alleging that he had been denied promotion on the basis of his sex, in violation of Title VII of the Civil Rights Act of 1964. The district court found that Johnson was more qualified than Joyce and that her sex was the "determining factor in her selection." The court of appeals reversed and found for the county. With support from the Reagan administration, Johnson pursued his case to the Supreme Court.

JUSTICE BRENNAN delivered the opinion of the Court:
. . . .
In reviewing the employment decision at issue in this case, we must first examine whether that decision was made pursuant to a plan prompted by concerns similar to those of the employer in *Weber*. Next, we must determine whether the effect of the plan on males and non-minorities is comparable to the effect of the plan in that case.

As an initial matter, the Agency adopted as a benchmark for measuring progress in eliminating underrepresentation the long-term goal of a work force that mirrored in its major job classifications the percentage of women in the area labor market. Even as it did so, however, the Agency acknowledged that such a figure could not by itself necessarily justify taking into account the sex of applicants for positions in all job categories. For positions requiring specialized training and experience, the Plan observed that the number of minorities and women "who possess the qualifications required for entry into such job classifications is limited." . . . The Plan therefore directed that annual short-term goals be formulated that would provide a more realistic indication of the degree to which sex should be taken into account in filling particular positions. . . . The Plan stressed that such goals "should not be construed as 'quotas' that must be met," but as reasonable aspirations in correcting the imbalance in the Agency's work force. . . .
. . . .
. . . [H]ad the Plan simply calculated imbalances in all categories according to the proportion of women in the area labor pool, and then directed that hiring be governed solely by those figures, its validity fairly could be called into question. This is because analysis of a more specialized labor pool normally is necessary in determining underrepresentation in some positions. If a plan failed to take distinctions in qualifications into account in providing guidance for actual employment decisions, it would dictate mere blind hiring by the numbers, for it would hold supervisors to "achievement of a particular percentage of minority employment or membership . . . regardless of circumstances such as economic conditions or the number of qualified minority applicants. . . ."

The Agency's Plan emphatically did not authorize such blind hiring. It expressly directed that numerous factors be taken into account in making hiring decisions, including specifically the qualifications of female applicants for particular jobs. . . .

. . . Given the obvious imbalance in the Skilled Craft category, and given the Agency's commitment to eliminating such imbalances, it was plainly not unreasonable for the Agency to determine that it was appropriate to consider as one factor the sex of Ms. Joyce in making its decision. The promotion of Joyce thus satisfies the first requirement enunciated in *Weber,* since it was undertaken to further an affirmative action plan designed to eliminate Agency work force imbalances in traditionally segregated job categories.

We next consider whether the Agency Plan unnecessarily trammeled the rights of male employees or created an absolute bar to their advancement. In contrast to the plan in *Weber,* which provided that 50% of the positions in the craft training program were exclusively for blacks, and to the consent decree upheld last term in *Firefighters* v. *Cleveland* . . . (1986), which required the promotion of specific numbers of minorities, the Plan sets aside no positions for women. The Plan expressly states that "[t]he 'goals' established for each Division should not be construed as 'quotas' that must be met." Rather, the Plan merely authorizes that consideration be given to affirmative action concerns when evaluating qualified applicants. . . . The Plan thus resembles the "Harvard Plan" approvingly noted by JUSTICE POWELL in *University of California Regents* v. *Bakke* . . . (1978), which considers race along with other criteria in determining admission to the college. . . . Similarly, the Agency Plan requires women to compete with all other qualified applicants. *No* persons are automatically excluded from consideration: *all* are able to have their qualifications weighed against those of other applicants.

In addition, petitioner had no absolute entitlement to the road dispatcher position. Seven of the applicants were classified as qualified and eligible, and the Agency Director was authorized to promote any of the seven. Thus, denial of the promotion unsettled no legitimate firmly rooted expectation on the part of the petitioner. Furthermore, while the petitioner in this case was denied a promotion, he retained his employment with the Agency, at the same salary and with the same seniority, and remained eligible for other promotions.

Finally, the Agency's Plan was intended to *attain* a balanced work force, not to maintain one. . . .

The Agency acknowledged the difficulties that it would confront in remedying the imbalance in its work force, and it anticipated only gradual increases in the representation of minorities and women. It is thus unsurprising that the Plan contains no explicit end data, for the Agency's flexible, case-by-case approach was not expected to yield to success in a brief period of time. Express assurance that a program is only temporary may be necessary if the program actually sets aside positions according to specific numbers. This is necessary both to minimize the effect of the program on other employees, and to ensure that the plan's goals "[are] not being used simply to achieve and maintain . . . balance, but rather as a benchmark against which" the employer may measure its progress in eliminating the underrepresentation of minorities and women. In this case, however, substantial evidence shows that the Agency has sought to take a moderate, gradual approach to eliminating the imbalance in its work force, one which establishes realistic guidance for employment decisions, and which visits minimal intrusion on the legitimate expectations of other employees. Given this fact, as well as the Agency's express commitment to "attain" a balanced work force, there is ample assurance that the Agency does not seek to use its Plan to maintain a permanent racial and sexual balance.

. . . .

We therefore hold that the Agency appropriately took into account as one factor the sex of Diane Joyce in determining that she should be promoted to the road dispatcher position. The decision to do so was made pursuant to an affirmative action plan that represents a moderate, flexible, case-by-case approach to effecting a gradual improvement in the representation of minorities and women in the Agency's work force. Such a plan is fully consistent with Title VII, for it embodies the contribution that voluntary employer action can make in eliminating the vestiges of discrimination in the workplace. Accordingly, the judgment of the Court of Appeals is

Affirmed.

[JUSTICE STEVENS wrote a separate concurring opinion.]

[JUSTICE O'CONNOR concurred in the judgment.]

[JUSTICE WHITE wrote a separate dissenting opinion.]

JUSTICE SCALIA, with whom THE CHIEF JUSTICE joins, and with whom JUSTICE WHITE joins in [part], dissenting.

With a clarity which, had it not proven so unavailing, one might well recommend as a model of statutory draftmanship, Title VII of the Civil Rights Act of 1964 declares:

It shall be an unlawful employment practice for an employer

(1) to fail or refuse to hire or to discharge any individual, or otherwise to discriminate against any individual with respect to his compensation, terms, conditions, or privileges of employment, because of such individual's race, color, religion, sex, or national origin; or

(2) to limit, segregate, or classify his employees or applicants for employment in any way which would deprive or tend to deprive any individual of employment opportunities or otherwise adversely affect his status as an employee, because of such individual's race, color, religion, sex, or national origin. . . .

The Court today completes the process of converting this from a guarantee that race or sex will *not* be the basis for employment determinations, to a guarantee that it often *will*. . . .

Several salient features of Santa Clara's affirmative action plan should be noted. Most importantly, the plan's purpose was assuredly not to remedy prior sex discrimination by the Agency. It could not have been, because there was no prior sex discrimination to remedy. The majority, in cataloguing the Agency's alleged misdeeds, . . . neglects to mention the District Court's finding that the agency "has not discriminated in the past, and does not discriminate in the present against women in regard to employment opportunities in general and promotions in particular." . . .

Not only was the plan not directed at the results of past sex discrimination by the Agency, but its objective was not to achieve the state of affairs that this Court has dubiously assumed would result from an absence of discrimination — an overall work force "more or less representative of the racial and ethnic composition of the population in the community." . . . Rather, the oft-stated goal was to mirror the racial and sexual composition of the entire county labor force, not merely in the Agency work force as a whole, but in each and every individual job category at the Agency. In a discrimination-free world, it would obviously be a statistical oddity for every job category to match the racial and sexual composition of even that portion of the county work force *qualified* for that job; it would be utterly miraculous for each of them to match, as the plan expected, the composition of the *entire* work force. . . .

The most significant proposition of law established by today's decision is that racial or sexual discrimination is permitted under Title VII when it is intended to overcome the effect, not of the employer's own

discrimination, but of societal attitudes that have limited the entry of certain races, or of a particular sex, into certain jobs. . . . While Mr. Johnson does not advance a constitutional claim here, it is most unlikely that Title VII was intended to place a lesser restraint on discrimination by public actors than is established by the Constitution. . . .

. . . .

. . . [T]oday's decision goes well beyond merely allowing racial or sexual discrimination in order to eliminate the effects of prior societal *discrimination*. The majority opinion often uses the phrase "traditionally segregated job category" to describe the evil against which the plan is legitimately (according to the majority) directed. As originally used in *Steelworkers* v. *Weber* . . . (1979), that phrase described skilled jobs from which employers and unions had systematically and intentionally excluded black workers — traditionally segregated jobs, that is, in the sense of conscious, exclusionary discrimination. . . . But that is assuredly not the sense in which the phrase is used here. . . . It is a "traditionally segregated job category" *not* in the *Weber* sense, but in the sense that, because of long-standing social attitudes, it has not been regarded *by women themselves* as desirable work. . . . There are, of course, those who believe that the social attitudes which cause women themselves to avoid certain jobs and to favor others are as nefarious as conscious, exclusionary discrimination. Whether or not that is so (and there is assuredly no consensus on the point equivalent to our national consensus against intentional discrimination), the two phenomena are certainly distinct. And it is the alteration of social attitudes, rather than the elimination of discrimination, which today's decision approves as justification for state-enforced discrimination. This is an enormous expansion, undertaken without the slightest justification or analysis.

I have omitted from the foregoing discussion the most obvious respect in which today's decision o'erleaps, without analysis, a barrier that was thought still to be overcome. . . . In *Weber*, . . . and in later decisions, this Court has repeatedly emphasized that *Weber* involved only a private employer. This distinction between public and private employers has several possible justifications. *Weber* rested in part on the assertion that the Congress did not wish to intrude too deeply into private employment decisions. . . . Another reason for limiting *Weber* to private employers is that state agencies, unlike private actors, are subject to the Fourteenth Amendment. . . .

In truth, however, [the Act] draws no distinction between private and public employers, and the only good reason for creating such a distinction would be to limit the damage of *Weber*. It would be better, in my view, to acknowledge that case as fully applicable precedent, and to use the Fourteenth Amendment ramifications — which *Weber* did not address and which are implicated for the first time here — as the occasion for reconsidering and overruling [*Weber*]. . . .

In addition to complying with the commands of the statute, abandoning *Weber* would have the desirable side-effect of eliminating the requirement of willing suspension of disbelief that is currently a credential for reading our opinions in the affirmative action field — from *Weber* itself, which demanded belief that the corporate employer adopted the affirmative action program "voluntarily," rather than under practical compulsion from government contracting agencies. . . .

. . . .

It is unlikely that today's result will be displeasing to politically elected officials, to whom it provides the means of quickly accomodating the demands of organized groups to achieve concrete, numerical improvements in the economic status of particular constituencies. Nor will it displease the world of corporate and governmental employers (many of whom have filed briefs as amici in the present case, all on the side of Santa Clara), for whom the cost of hiring less qualified workers is often substantially less — and infinitely more predictable — than the cost of litigating Title VII cases and of seeking to convince federal agencies by nonnumerical means that no discrimination exists. In fact, the only losers in the process are the Johnsons of the country, for whom Title VII has been not merely repealed but actually inverted. The irony is that these individuals — predominantly unknown, unaffluent, unorganized — suffer this injustice at the hands of a Court fond of thinking itself the champion of the politically impotent. I dissent.

CHAPTER 11

Social Change and the Fourteenth Amendment: The "New Equal Protection" and the Right of Privacy and Autonomy

The "New Equal Protection"

With BROWN V. BOARD OF EDUCATION (1954), the Supreme Court unleashed a powerful force in American constitutional law. Once perceived, the logic of BROWN was quickly extended to other areas. Throughout the 1960s, an era of political activism generally, a long line of interests queued up to plead their causes before the justices of the Supreme Court, and in Chief Justice Earl Warren and his brethren, they found responsive champions. The 1960s witnessed what can only be called a constitutional revolution, whose goal was equality and whose most effective weapon was the Fourteenth Amendment. During this revolution the Court invoked the Equal Protection Clause to work fundamental changes in the structure of the American system of representative government and to extend the mantle of constitutional protection to groups of all sorts: ethnic minorities, women, the poor, aliens, the illegitimate, the uneducated, the elderly, and other identifiable groups. And the Court seized upon the Equal Protection Clause in conjunction with various other constitutional provisions to fashion previously undreamt of rights of privacy, travel, and education.

Although the Warren Court was firmly united in its determination to eradicate the lingering effects of racial segregation, the justices were not so united when they were asked to extend the expanded equality principle of BROWN to these other groups. As the equal protection revolution spread, divisions on the Court intensified. Early in the 1960s, rumblings were occasionally voiced in the dissents of Justices Harlan and Stewart, who warned against judicial usurpation of the legislative function, invoked the values of federalism, and warned against an overextended judiciary. Justice Black, too, castigated his fellow liberals for reading their own values into the Equal Protection Clause. These voices of restraint were amplified and extended after the 1968 presidential election, and in rapid succession four "strict constructionist" justices were appointed by President Nixon: Chief

Justice Warren Burger and Associate Justices Rehnquist, Blackmun, and Powell. Justices Powell and Blackmun, however, proved to be less predictable than many had thought. And so has Justice Stevens, President Ford's sole appointee. Still, even with President Reagan's appointment of Justices O'Connor, Scalia, and Kennedy, no clear and consistently conservative majority has emerged. Some of the recent appointees are strong believers in stare decisis, and so are reluctant to overrule decisions with which they disagree. One consequence: Despite the many changes on the Court, the "new equal protection" remains alive, if not well. Still, given the conservative views of a growing number of justices, what may not be achieved quickly through abrupt overrulings may come about more slowly through new distinctions and reinterpretations. In the long run, evolution may produce the same results as counterrevolution.

The cases in this chapter trace these developments. We can readily assess the nature of the changes in the Court's direction following the transition from Warren to Burger and on to Rehnquist to determine how the widely anticipated counterrevolution has fared. Overall, the Warren Court's decisions have held up remarkably well. In some areas they have been extended, in other areas boundaries have been drawn, and in a few areas they have been trimmed back. Still, unlike recent rulings on criminal procedure, none of the major equal protection developments made by the Warren Court have been significantly cut back or abandoned. Indeed, some of the Court's most dramatic acts of judicial legislation occurred under Chief Justice Burger.

But since the hey-day of the Warren Court in the mid-1960s, consistent, clear liberal activism has been replaced with an inconsistent, ideosyncratic activism, liberal in some areas and conservative in others. This state of affairs reflects the power of precedent, the importance of the remaining Warren Court liberals, and the failure of appointing presidents to accurately gauge all the views of their appointees. It also reflects the pragmatic approach taken by Chief Justice Burger and one or two other

justices. Whatever the full explanation, the anticipated counterrevolution of the Burger Court did not materialize, and it remains to be seen whether it will under Chief Justice Rehnquist and the growing number of newly appointed conservative justices.

The Burger Court was characterized by drift and divisiveness. Some of the most vitriolic opinions ever penned by justices on the Supreme Court were written during his tenure and involved differences arising from the "new equal protection" and the emerging constitutional right to privacy, as justices who agreed in result nevertheless disagreed among themselves as to reasons and disagreed still more bitterly with those who supported opposite results. As the conservative majority has grown, the sharp divisions that characterized equal protection decisions under Chief Justice Burger have moderated. With his promotion to Chief Justice, William Rehnquist has curbed his earlier tendency for strident language and solo opinions, and appears to be trying to foster a consensus among the Court's emerging majority. Certainly, the complicated divisions and sharp language that characterized the Court's equal protection decisions in the 1970s have been moderated in recent years. Still, the new conservative majority is not a monolithic bloc. Some justices are more reluctant than others to overrule precedent, and some follow their own paths, causing them to diverge from one another from time to time, in both reasoning and outcome.

One of the major controversies that continues to divide the justices involves standards for judging equal protection claims that involve "suspect groups" or allegations of infringement of "fundamental rights." We introduced this controversy in the previous chapter, so we need comment on it only briefly here. The traditional test of the so-called "old equal protection" was to ascertain "reasonableness," an approach that granted considerable deference to legislatures. Under it, a classification scheme was presumed reasonable if after ordinary scrutiny it was found to be reasonably related to the aim of the legislature (which in turn was presumed to be valid). In contrast, the "new equal protection" insists upon greater judicial vigilance if classifications employ or impinge disproportionately upon "suspect categories" of people, or if they appear to encroach upon "fundamental" rights even though they pursue valid legislative aims. In such instances, the Court is to give strict scrutiny to the classifications and require their makers to show that there is a "compelling" need to employ them. Disagreements among the justices as to the value of this two-tier approach have sharply divided the Court, as have disagreements as to the precise meaning, extent, and applicability of each of these approaches. These divisions became painfully apparent during the 1970s, when the number of dissenting, concurring, partially concurring and dissenting opinions proliferated. They continue into the 1990s, but with some signs of abatement. In certain respects, the controversy has been compounded with the emergence of a third test, the so-called middle level of scrutiny that has been embraced by some of the justices and used most explicitly in sex discrimination cases.

With this general introduction, we turn to thread our way through the maze of issues and arguments in the cases that illustrate the "old," the "new," and the newest approaches to equal protection. While the quality of reasoning, the lack of clear and consistent positions, and the bewildering number of different tests and opinions may be frustrating, there is no doubt that the *impact* of these decisions has been far reaching.

Reapportionment

In 1945 a group of voters in Illinois filed a suit in federal district court alleging that they were being denied their constitutional rights because they were underrepresented in Congress. Eventually they asked the Supreme Court to insist that congressional districts be territorily compact and of equal population. By a vote of 4 to 3, the justices declined to rule on this request (*Colegrove v. Green*, 328 U.S. 549, 1946). Justice Frankfurter,

writing for the Court, held that apportionment was a "political question" beyond the competence of courts. He wrote, "Courts ought not to enter into the political thicket. The remedy for unfairness in districting is to secure state legislatures that will apportion properly, or to invoke the ample powers of Congress." Despite the slim majority (three justices dissented, there was one vacancy on the Court, and Justice Jackson was on leave as special prosecutor at Nuremburg), Justice Frankfurter's firm opinion appeared to put an end to the quest of urban interests to use the courts to break the backs of rural-dominated legislatures.

Colegrove had never seriously been challenged before the federal courts when, in 1960, the Court agreed to hear another type of representation issue. This case arose after the Alabama legislature had gerrymandered the long-standing boundaries of the city of Tuskegee, changing it from a simple square to a twenty-eight-sided figure, to remove all but a handful of blacks from the city's population. Rejecting the state's argument that the issue was a nonjusticiable "political question," Justice Frankfurter, writing for the majority, held that the actions of the state clearly constituted unconstitutional racial discrimination (*Gomillion* v. *Lightfoot*, 364 U.S. 339, 1960). But he went to some length to distinguish this case from *Colegrove*, arguing that it presented a "readily isolated" instance of racial discrimination which "lifted the issue out of the 'political question' area and into the conventional sphere of constitutional litigation." Despite this effort, *Gomillion* can be seen as an important bridging case. If the court can correct abuses of electoral representation arising from racial discrimination, why should it not correct other types of abuses as well—malapportionment, for instance?

Two years later, it did precisely this. In BAKER V. CARR, 369 U.S. 186 (1962), the Court overruled *Colegrove* and, despite the vigorous dissents of Justices Frankfurter and Harlan, plunged headlong into the "political thicket." In BAKER, the Court held that it possessed jurisdiction of the subject matter and that federal courts had power to offer relief. It then returned the case to the district court for trial. As in *Gomillion,* the facts in BAKER V. CARR were extreme and hence especially compelling for a Court committed to equality. Despite state constitutional amendments requiring decennial reapportionment and guaranteeing other forms of representational fairness, a badly malapportioned Tennessee legislature had not reapportioned itself in over sixty years. One district was over fifteen times larger than the next, and the entire state was gerrymandered into a crazy-quilt designed to perpetuate rural domination despite a large urban population.

Some interpreted BAKER as paving the way for a "reasonableness" standard in apportionment, a standard which would have allowed states considerable leeway in structuring systems of representation. But in short order it became clear that the justices had something more in mind in assessing the standards for apportionment not only in congressional districts but for state and local electoral districts, of all sorts. In the early 1960s, the Court overturned Georgia's county-unit system of selecting its governor (this was a winner-take-all, electoral-college-like scheme that in the past had permitted candidates who lost general elections to ascend to the governorship) (*Gray* v. *Sanders,* 372 U.S. 368, 1963); held that congressional districts must be substantially equal in population (*Wesberry* v. *Sanders,* 376 U.S. 1, 1964); and extended the equal population principle to both houses of state legislatures (REYNOLDS V. SIMS, 377 U.S. 533, 1964).

REYNOLDS presents the Court's boldest statement on the issue. It is radically egalitarian and individualistic and came to be summarized as "one man, one vote" (later amended to "one person, one vote"). Categorically rejecting the federal analogy for states (which would allow at least one chamber of a bicameral legislature to be based upon traditional geographical units—most frequently counties—just as each state, regardless of population, is represented in Congress by two Senators), the Court in REYNOLDS insisted on strict population equality in both houses. In a subsequent decision the Court underscored this insis-

tence when it overturned a "federal" system for a state legislature even after it had been endorsed by an overwhelming majority of voters in a statewide referendum (*Lucas* v. *44th General Assembly,* 377 U.S. 712, 1964).

How strict would the Court be in insisting on population equality? The answer was soon forthcoming: "very." In 1969 the Court overturned an apportionment scheme for congressional districts in Missouri that had a maximum deviation between the largest and smallest districts of less than .6 percent (*Kirkpatrick* v. *Preisler,* 494 U.S. 526, 1969), differences which the state had justified with a desire to respect long-standing and traditional boundaries of units of state and local government and natural geographical divisions.

But even as the Court was insisting on increasing mathematical exactitude in applying the equal population principle, the original architects of reapportionment were being replaced by justices who resisted such precision. The Court's rulings in the 1970s and 1980s reflect this shift; they have been characterized by relaxation of the equal population principle for *state* legislative districts, but not wholesale abandonment of it. While the Court is clearly moving in the direction of a "reasonableness" standard that would permit states considerable flexibility and respect traditional boundaries in establishing state legislative districts, it has not yet moved forcefully to articulate a set of basic standards, and its decisions appear ad hoc and inconsistent.

The first clear indication of this new development was MAHAN V. HOWELL, 410 U.S. 315 (1973). Here, Justice Rehnquist, writing for a majority of five, held that states have some leeway to deviate from the "equal-population principle" in apportioning districts in either or both houses of their legislatures *if* that variation is based upon "legitimate considerations incident to the effectuation of a rational state policy." "Respect for boundaries or political subdivisions," he continued, was one such reasonable basis. A decade later the Court carried this modification one step further when, in a 5 to 4 vote, it upheld a Wyoming state legislature's apportionment scheme which followed county lines even though it allowed a maximum population deviation of 89 percent (*Brown* v. *Thomson,* 103 S.Ct. 2960, 1983). But the same day *Brown* was decided, the court, also by a 5 to 4 vote (Justice O'Connor was the pivotal vote), overturned a New Jersey congressional apportionment plan even though it permitted only a maximum population deviation of 0.6984 percent, a figure smaller than the Census Bureau's margin of error for reporting population figures (*Karcher* v. *Daggett,* 103 S.Ct. 2653, 1983)! These sharp divisions suggest that this area will be in flux for some time to come. Yet these decisions also reveal a trend towards incremental modification and not an abandonment of the Warren Court's "one person, one vote" principle.

The Court's involvement in legislative apportionment has precipitated a host of related issues which it has approached in a flexible way. While it has extended the equal population principle to legislativelike units of local government of all sorts (city councils, county boards, and the like), it has stopped short of saying that all "special district governments" comprised of elected representatives must be selected on a one person, one vote basis. Thus, for instance, it upheld a scheme for selecting regional governing bodies by allowing each constituent school district one vote even though the districts were not of equal population (*Sailors* v. *Board of Education,* 387 U.S. 105, 1967). *Brown* v. *Thompson* will encourage still greater variations. However in 1989 it ruled unconstitutional New York City's complicated scheme for selecting the powerful Board of Estimate, which, among other things, provided for one member from each of the city's boroughs regardless of their population, and provided for a weighted voting system that gave some members more power than others, *Bd. of Estimate* v. *Morris,* 109 S.Ct. 1433.

The Court's willingness to disregard traditional boundaries of congressional districts for the principle of "strict equality" has paved the way for considerable political and at times ethnic gerrymandering in apportionment. The Court's insistence on districts of equal population (a moving target in a state with growing or shifting population) has encouraged dominant parties in legislatures to disregard traditional units and voting blocs of like-minded citizens to fashion new districts that reinforce their dominance. Federal courts have generally tolerated a fair amount of gerrymandering, although they have insisted upon a secondary principle of compactness and have been vigilant in protecting against racial discrimination or diluting the concentrated electoral power of racial minorities in reapportionment. But to the extent that the Court tries to preserve the power of traditional voting blocs in reapportioned districts, it acknowledges a competing theory of representation — a pluralist notion of representation of interests through groups — that is at fundamental odds with the radically individual-based theory of representation inherent in the "one person, one vote" doctrine. This, of course, was one of the tensions debated in the *Federalist Papers* and one of the reasons for the creation of a bicameral Congress, with one house based upon geographical representation and the other based upon population. For cases raising such issues, see *United Jewish Organizations* v. *Carey,* 430 U.S. 144 (1977); *Gaffney* v. *Cummings,* 412 U.S. 735 (1973); and *Wright* v. *Rockefeller,* 376 U.S. 52 (1964).

When BAKER V. CARR was handed down, it was followed by a great many prophecies that the Court's entry into the political thicket would precipitate a constitutional crisis between the Court and the Congress or the Court and the states. Others were jubilant, expecting that reapportionment would liberate state legislatures from the tyranny of domination by rural minorities. In fact, neither of these prophecies came true. While BAKER and its progeny did plunge the federal courts headlong into the continuing task of overseeing reapportionment and judicial mapmaking, its actions have not precipitated even a continuing national issue. The Court's entry into the political thicket is a two-edged sword. In some areas Republicans benefit, while in others Democrats do. Furthermore, a great many state legislators secretly welcome the periodic prodding by the federal courts. Court involvement in reapportionment is now a well-institutionalized, routine feature of political life.

Despite this, the optimistic predictions of a rebirth of the cities did not materialize after reapportionment, in part because the problems of the cities stem from far more than underrepresentation in Congress and in state legislatures. Also, it is the suburbs that have experienced the real gains from reapportionment, and they often have more in common with rural areas and small towns than with central cities. Thus we see a revolution that wasn't.

Suspect Classifications

Wealth. In 1949, Joseph Tussman and Jacobus ten Broek wrote an article arguing that classifications based upon wealth or property, like those of race, were to be viewed with disfavor in light of the Equal Protection Clause of the Fourteenth Amendment ["The Equal Protection of the Laws," 37 *California Law Review* (1949) 341]. Just a few years later the Warren Court came to embrace such a view, and since the 1950s the Court has scrutinized a wide variety of policies and classifications that differentially affect people of varying financial means. For a short while in the 1960s it appeared that the Court was going to elevate wealth to a "suspect category," which meant that states would have to show a "compelling interest" before policies discriminating by income would be upheld. But second thoughts and changes on the Court intervened and wealth was not declared a suspect class.

The Court's concern with the differential effects of wealth began long before Earl Warren's appointment as Chief Justice. Although not tied to the Equal Protection Clause, many of the fair-trial/right-to-counsel cases considered in Chapter 5 can be considered as wealth-related rulings. And in *Edwards* v. *California*, 314 U.S. 160 (1941), the Court invalidated California's "anti-Okie" statute enacted during the Great Depression to stem the

tide of emigrants from the Dust Bowl, which had made it a misdemeanor to knowingly bring into the state a nonresident indigent. In striking down this law the Court relied not upon the Equal Protection Clause but on the Commerce Clause, arguing that the restriction retarded the free movement of people in interstate commerce.

A bridging case between these early cases and the Court's modern equal protection approach to wealth is *Griffin* v. *Illinois,* 351 U.S. 12 (1956). By 1956 the Court had gone a long way toward expanding the rights of poor criminal defendants at trial by making counsel available to them at public expense. In *Griffin,* the Court extended this reasoning and required states to pay for trial transcripts of poor people in criminal appeals. *Griffin* was significant because some justices rested their positions not on grounds of fair trial or due process but on equal protection grounds, and because of Justice Black's expansive opinion. "In criminal trials," he wrote for the majority, "a State can no more discriminate on account of poverty than on account of religions, race, or color." This comparison of poverty with race was significant and ten years later was strengthened still more when the Court struck down state poll taxes as violations of the Equal Protection Clause (*Harper* v. *Virginia Board of Elections,* 383 U.S. 663, 1966). While the Court was aware that poll taxes of a few dollars had been imposed by Southern states as one of a number of seemingly neutral devices to prevent blacks (who were also overwhelmingly poor) from voting, it is significant that in *Harper* the Court chose to rest its opposition to poll taxes on income discrimination, not racial discrimination, grounds, as it emphasized the "fundamental" right to vote. This line of decisions opened the door for a direct equal protection attack on other wealth-related policies and classifications, which at the time many thought would serve to make distributive justice a constitutional mandate.

But such an expansive course did not develop. Although the Court has gone a long way toward protecting the rights of poor people, it has not embraced a distributive justice concept of the Equal

Protection Clause. At first it was cautious and indirect, and in recent years has firmly rejected wealth as a suspect category. Still it has not rejected all considerations of wealth.

The Court's concern with policies that impinge differentially on wealth has taken two different forms. First, and perhaps most important, it has insisted upon greater care in the administration of public programs that dispense such government largess (i.e., wealth) as welfare, health care, and social services. In effect the Court has transformed such benefits from privileges to be dispensed at the discretion of individual public officials to "entitlements" (rights) that must be administered evenhandedly according to standards of due process. See, for example, GOLDBERG V. KELLY, 397 U.S. 254 (1970). And more generally, the Court has extended the requirements of due process to cover a variety of other types of "new property," such as educational certification, access to government contracts, and access to the regulation process, in an effort to see that they are dispensed and withheld in an orderly and fair fashion.

Second, and more relevant to this chapter, the Court has been willing to scrutinize at least *some* wealth-based classifications and policies to determine if they discriminate in light of the Equal Protection Clause. In taking this approach, the Court has overturned a number of policies on grounds that they discriminate against the poor. Many of the policies it has overturned remove obstacles that block poor people's access to the legal process. Thus, for instance, the Court has declared unconstitutional a state law requiring a filing fee before a court would grant a divorce (*Boddie* v. *Connecticut*, 401 U.S. 371, 1971) and a Wisconsin statute requiring a father with child support responsibilities to first demonstrate compliance with his obligations before remarrying (*Zablicki* v. *Redhail*, 434 U.S. 374, 1978).

But in other cases alleging discrimination against the poor, the Court has rebuffed constitutional challenges. It has upheld as constitutional a filing fee applicable to indigents as a condition for petitioning for bankruptcy; state statutes providing for

only limited protection before eviction of tenants for nonpayment of rent (*Lindsey* v. *Normet*, 405 U.S. 56, 1972); disconnecting utilities for nonpayment (*Memphis Light, Gas and Water Division* v. *Craft*, 436 U.S. 1, 1978); and repossession of furniture for nonpayment (*Flagg Brothers, Inc.* v. *Brooks*, 436 U.S. 149, 1978). Similarly, the Court has been reluctant to rely upon the Equal Protection Clause to find discrimination through local zoning laws and other measures that restrict the amount and types of low income housing that can be built in local communities (WARTH V. SELDIN, 422 U.S. 490, 1975).

The Court's most important statement on wealth and discrimination is found in a case that directly affects the lives of millions of people. One issue in SAN ANTONIO INDEPENDENT SCHOOL DISTRICT V. RODRIGUEZ, 411 U.S. 1 (1973), was whether access to equal educational opportunities, like access to the ballot box and access to courts, was a "fundamental right" limitations on which should be subject to "strict scrutiny." The specific issue dealt with how public education was to be financed. At the time, public schools in forty-nine of the fifty states were financed primarily through local property taxes, a system which allowed wide variations in the per pupil expenditures of different school districts within a state. Plaintiffs in RODRIGUEZ argued that poor districts were discriminated against because, although they might have higher property tax rates than wealthier districts, they could still raise less money for their schools. They argued that the Equal Protection Clause prohibited a system of financing public schools through local property taxes and proposed that the Constitution require a statewide system of financing that provided equal per pupil expenditures to all students, regardless of variations in aggregate wealth of local districts. By a narrowly divided vote, the Court rejected this contention, thereby dashing hopes of using the Equal Protection Clause as a significant vehicle of distributive justice. It should be noted, however, that even though the Court has held that the Constitution does not require statewide financing of public schools, a number of states have moved toward it, either through legislative initiative or, as in the case of New Jersey, through state supreme court rulings based upon provisions in state constitutions.

While the controversy over abortion is thought of primarily as a battle between the supporters of "right to life" and supporters of the "right to privacy and autonomy," once ROE V. WADE, 410 U.S. 113 (1973), established the constitutional right to abortion, the controversy introduced important equal protection issues. After ROE V. WADE, opponents of abortion diversified their tacks. One successful effort was to limit access to abortions by prohibiting use of public funds to pay for elective abortions, a policy adopted by a number of states in the wake of ROE V. WADE and upheld by a sharply divided Court in MAHER V. ROE, 432 U.S. 464 (1977). Appellants in MAHER argued that such a policy discriminated against poor people because those who could afford abortions were free to obtain them, and because the state did pay for normal childbirth and other medical procedures for poor people. Justice Powell, writing for a slim majority, rejected the argument and reasoned that the lower court has "misconceived the nature and scope of the fundamental right [to abortion] recognized in *Roe*," and that "financial need alone [does not identify] a suspect class for purposes of Equal Protection analysis." This approach was reaffirmed three years later in *Harris* v. *McRae*, 448 U.S. 297 (1980), which upheld the so-called Hyde Amendment prohibiting the use of federal funds for abortions financed through state-administered medical benefit programs. In effect the Court's position is that while women are free to obtain abortions if they choose (and can afford them), there is no state obligation to provide abortions for poor women *even* when it pays for other and more expensive types of pregnancy-related medical services.

The Court's current approach to wealth and the Equal Protection Clause might best be summed up by a dissent penned by Justice Harlan, in 1963, just as it appeared the Court was going to embrace a strict standard in scrutinizing wealth-related policies. In dissent in *Douglas* v. *California,* 372 U.S. 353 (1963), Justice Harlan warned:

> Every financial exaction which the State imposes on a uniform basis is more easily satisfied by the well-to-do than by the indigent. . . . The Equal Protection Clause does not impose on the States "an affirmative duty to lift the handicaps flowing from differences in economic circumstances." To so construe it would be to read into the Constitution a philosophy of leveling that would be foreign to many of our basic concepts of the proper relations between government and society. The State may have a moral obligation to eliminate the evils of poverty, but it is not required by the Equal Protection Clause to give to some whatever others can afford.

If you grant this, then why should the Constitution require that poor people accused of crimes be provided with free defense counsel, while poor women are deprived of public assistance to obtain abortions? More generally, why should the Court strike down wealth-related obstacles to access to courts and marriage but not school resources and abortions? Can you draw a firm distinction between where the Constitution should and should not attempt to ameriliorate the discriminatory effects of poverty. If you don't draw the line here, where would you draw it?

Gender. Parallels in developments in the constitutional rights of women and blacks are striking. Both groups were initially disenfranchised in ways that required constitutional amendments to correct (the Thirteenth, Fourteenth, and Fifteenth Amendments for blacks, the Nineteenth for women). (The proposed Equal Rights Amendment (ERA) passed Congress in 1972, but fell two short of the required thirty-eight ratifying state legislatures.) Both groups met with hostile receptions when they first pressed their claims for civil rights. And both groups were able to secure basic constitutional protections only after intense and prolonged political struggle and initial defeat before the Court. Two major differences between these groups' constitutional struggles are that developments of women's rights have lagged several decades behind parallel developments for blacks, and that women have not been as successful in convincing the Court to subject gender-based classifications to rigorous scrutiny as racial minorities have been with respect to racial classifications. Still, in recent decades the Supreme Court has taken significant steps to extend the mantle of constitutional protections to both groups, and many of the gains made by blacks through constitutional law subsequently have been obtained by women through a combination of constitutional rulings and expansive legislation.

While it was the Warren Court that took the first dramatic steps to embrace the modern conception of racial equality under the Constitution, the equivalent steps for women's rights were taken by the Burger Court (*Reed* v. *Reed,* 404 U.S. 71, 1971). Indeed, in the only significant women's rights case handed down during the tenure of Chief Justice Earl Warren, the Court unanimously upheld a state law which excluded women from jury duty unless they specifically volunteered to serve (*Hoyt* v. *Florida,* 368 U.S. 57, 1961), a type of discrimination that was struck down when it was directed at blacks nearly eighty years earlier (*Strauder* v. *West Virginia,* 100 U.S. 303, 1980). The Court's decision in *Hoyt* continued a tradition begun ninety years earlier, when in *Bradwell* v. *Illinois,* 16 Wall. 130 (1873), the first equal protection case ever to be argued before it, the Court sustained the refusal of the Illinois Supreme Court to admit Myra Bradwell to the state bar solely because she was a woman and the common law did not permit women to be admitted to the bar.

The Court's initial approach to women's Fourteenth Amendment claims during this long period is represented in this volume by GOESAERT ET AL. V. CLEARY, 335 U.S. 464 (1948). Here, with Justice Frankfurter writing for a majority of six, the Court upheld a Michigan statute which prohibited a woman from tending bar in a licensed establishment unless she was "the wife or daughter of the male owner." In his opinion, Justice Frankfurter, using what would later come to be known as the "ordinary scrutiny" test, found it easy to dismiss Ms. Goesaert's arguments, claiming that the

Michigan legislature may have had good reasons for adopting the law, and thus the Court should defer to its judgment. Between *Bradwell* and *Reed* even those few decisions that might be viewed as furthering women's interests must be judged in retrospect as patronizing. Between the 1880s and the mid-1930s, the Court overturned many important pieces of social welfare legislation on grounds that they violated the Due Process and Equal Protection Clauses of the Fourteenth Amendment. Among the occasional exceptions to this general policy were a few statutes designed to benefit selected groups or to prohibit a handful of "immoral" practices which a majority of justices thought might require special legislative attention. Thus state laws upholding prohibition of liquor, gambling, and the like were upheld on grounds of morality, and a few state laws regulating maximum hours for women and children were upheld on grounds that unlike adult males these groups were vulnerable and in need of special protection.

One such exception was MULLER V. OREGON, 208 U.S. 412 (1908), in which the Court, convinced by the famous "Brandeis brief" submitted in behalf of the state, upheld Oregon's statute which regulated working hours for women. And in one of the first major decisions after President Roosevelt unveiled his Court-packing plan, the Court upheld similar legislation protecting women and children in the District of Columbia (WEST COAST HOTEL CO. V. PARISH, 300 U.S. 379, 1937). Here, too, some of the justices emphasized the special conditions of women and children to justify their support of the statute. Regarded as liberal at the time (since more general legislation in the same vein was being struck down by the Court), the Court's reasoning in these cases is now widely regarded as deficient.

The Court's equivalent to BROWN V. BOARD OF EDUCATION for women was *Reed* v. *Reed,* 404 U.S. 71, handed down in 1971 in an opinion written by Chief Justice Burger. In that case, a unanimous Court struck down an Idaho statute which gave preference to males over females to serve as administrators of estates, presumably to reduce intrafamily rivalry and facilitate administrative convenience. The Court held that the Idaho law constituted an "arbitrary legislative choice" unreasonable on its face.

Reed precipitated a host of cases, and during the balance of the decade, the Burger Court handed down a string of important decisions broadening women's rights under the Fourteenth Amendment and under civil rights legislation of the 1960s and 1970s. Probably the most significant of these decisions was FRONTIERO V. RICHARDSON, 411 U.S. 677 (1973), in which the Court voided a statute which allowed a male in the armed services an automatic right to claim his spouse as a dependent for purposes of obtaining increased benefits but did not allow the same for a female. This decision paved the way for the general principle that unless the Court is presented with a strong reason, the Fourteenth Amendment prohibits differential treatment of men and women. As obvious as this may now seem, it must be remembered that until 1971, the Supreme Court had *never* struck down a law because it discriminated against women. And even today, the justices differ sharply among themselves as to how "strong" the state's reason must be before they use the Fourteenth Amendment to strike down gender-based classifications. Similarly, the Court has not been as quick to rely upon an expansive conception of *state action* to nullify sex disrimination by private parties as it has with respect to racial discrimination. On the other hand, it has put more "bite" in the reasonableness test when applied to women's rights issues than when applied to issues of economic regulation.

Unlike the cases that followed from BROWN V. BOARD OF EDUCATION (1954), the women's rights cases following *Reed* did not enjoy a solid and broad base of support among the justices. Early on, Justice Rehnquist articulated a position which allows no special scrutiny of sex-based classifications and gives great deference to legislatures; only occasionally has he joined with colleagues to declare state-created gender-based classifications unconstitutional. At the other extreme were Justices Douglas, White, Brennan, and Marshall, who

in FRONTIERO and later cases urged that *all* gender-based classifications are inherently suspect and should be voided unless, after strict scrutiny, the state can show that it has a compelling interest in maintaining them and has no other available alternatives.

Other justices, most notably Justices Stevens, Blackmun, and O'Connor, appear to have developed a middle position, embracing a third test somewhere between ordinary and strict scrutiny (which Professor Gunther of the Stanford Law School has termed "ordinary scrutiny with a bite") to assess women's rights claims. Falling between Rehnquist, on one side, and Marshall and Brennan, on the other, these justices are often pivotal in the outcomes of sex discrimination cases. Given these differences in basic approach, it is hardly surprising that divisions on the Court in sex discrimination cases have been sharper than the equivalent decisions in race discrimination cases.

Outcomes, too, have been mixed. While the Court has swept aside a great many laws discriminating against women, a solid majority has refused to hold that gender-related classifications per se are constitutionally suspect. Indeed, the Court has found a great many such classifications to be acceptable, and a number of the more important decisions broadening the rights of women have rested upon statutory, not constitutional, law, most particularly Title VII of the Civil Rights Act of 1964.

While the Burger Court overturned many laws and policies discriminating against women, it also upheld a number of gender-related policies, including a number of policies that single out women for "benign" treatment. While it is impossible to discern a clear line of development in these cases because the majorities have been slim and divided and because of changes on the Court, still it is possible to outline some major features of these three lines of cases.

In the first line, most of the gender-based policies the Court has found to be defective rest upon a traditional or stereotyped notion of a woman's role in society. Thus, for instance, in *Reed* the court rejected the implied logic of the preference given to males, which was that as breadwinners and heads of households men should be preferred to women. Similarly, in *Stanton* v. *Stanton,* 421 U.S. 7 (1975), the court (Justice Rehnquist dissenting) held unconstitutional a Utah law that provided for lower age of majority for girls than for boys in connection with parental obligation to pay child support. The following year the Court overturned an Oklahoma statute which provided for a lower drinking age for women than for men (CRAIG V. BOREN, 429 U.S. 190, 1976). Similarly, the Court has struck down other state and federal laws premised upon a belief that men are breadwinners and women are dependents. See, for example, *Orr* v. *Orr,* 440 U.S. 268 (1979), in which the court struck down an Alabama law providing that men but not women were liable for postdivorce alimony; *Califano* v. *Westcott,* 443 U.S. 76 (1979), which overturned a section of the Social Security Act providing benefits to needy dependent children in the event of a father's unemployment but not a mother's; and *Wengler* v. *Druggists Mutual Insurance Co.,* 446 U.S. 142 (1980), which struck down Missouri's workers' compensation law requiring husbands to provide proof of dependence on their spouses' earnings but did not require wives to prove such dependence. In these cases the Court seems to be saying that even if such assumptions contain a grain of truth, they are unacceptable because a legislature could easily construct a more reasonable and accurate classification system. But not all traditional (stereotyped?) sex roles are constitutionally suspect in the eyes of the Justices. In *Rostker* v. *Goldberg,* 453 U.S. 57 (1971), Justice Rehnquist, writing for a majority of six, upheld the constitutionality of the Military Selective Service Act's provisions for male-only draft registration. Citing the need to defer to the Congress, the fact that Congress had considered the sex discrimination issue at length in its deliberations on this policy, and Congress' historical authority to raise and regulate armies and navies, the Court concluded "that the Congress had acted well within its constitutional authority when it authorized the regis-

tration of men and not women under the Military Selective Service Act."

In the second line of decisions, the Court has upheld a number of gender-based classifications. Not surprisingly, many of them involve policies related to childbirth and pregnancy, necessarily gender-specific. For instance, the Court upheld a California disability insurance scheme which excluded from coverage normal pregnancy (GEDULDIG V. AIELLO, 417 U.S. 484, 1974), and a private employer's disability plan which excluded pregnancies from coverage (*General Electric Co.* v. *Gilbert,* 429 U.S. 125, 1976). In these cases the Court rejected the claim that women were singled out and discriminated against by health plans which did not provide pregnancy benefits even though they provided for male-only medical coverage. Some of these rulings were subsequently overruled by Congress in amendments to civil rights legislation.

In a third line of decisions, the Court has upheld several statutes and policies using sex-based classifications for "benign" purposes. Thus, by a 5 to 4 vote, the Court upheld a federal law on mandatory Navy discharges which guaranteed women thirteen years of service but which required automatic discharge for men if they twice failed to be promoted, something that could occur in a period of less than thirteen years (*Schlesinger* v. *Ballard,* 419 U.S. 498, 1975). Here, the Court accepted the Navy's argument that the longer time for women was a reasonable compensatory policy because women were excluded from combat opportunities and hence were less likely to be promoted as rapidly as men. Similarly, a sharply divided Court upheld a Florida law which granted widows but not widowers a property tax exemption after the loss of spouse (*Kahn* v. *Shevlin,* 416 U.S. 351, 1974). Here, the Court accepted the state's argument and evidence that a woman is more likely to be hard-pressed financially after the death of her husband than a husband would be after the death of his wife. For this same reason, the Court, four years later, upheld a federal statute allowing wives to exclude three more of their low-earning years than husbands in computing average wage for purposes of fixing social security retirement benefits (*Califano* v. *Webster,* 430 U.S. 313, 1977).

Many of the most important sex discrimination cases handed down by the Supreme Court have rested on statutory, not constitutional, grounds. While such decisions have generally (although not uniformly) upheld women's rights claims, they have caused some concern among advocates of women's rights because they rest upon a somewhat shaky foundation, one that could be removed by a future Congress. It was precisely for this reason that the women's rights movement was so vigorous in its pursuit of the Equal Rights Amendment (ERA) during the 1970s and early 1980s, and was so disappointed when in 1982 it fell just two states short of ratification. (The ERA was approved by thirty-six states, with combined populations of well over 75 percent of the American population.)

One area in which the Court's rulings on statutory-based rights for women have been important is employment. While the Court has ruled that certain forms of employment discrimination violate the Fourteenth Amendment, generally it has relied upon Title VII of the Civil Rights Act of 1964, its amendments, and other equal rights legislation to fashion its approach to sex discrimination in the marketplace. In 1984, for instance, a unanimous court interpreted Title VII of the Civil Rights Act of 1964 to prohibit sex discrimination in decisions to grant partnerships by law firms, a ruling which by extension applies to accounting and consulting firms and hundreds of other private, partnership concerns (*Hishon* v. *King and Spaulding,* 104 S.Ct. 2229, 1984). However a 1989 ruling gave an extremely narrow ruling to 42 USC 1981, which prohibits racial discrimination in the enforcement of contracts, *Patterson* v. *McLean Credit Union,* 109 S.Ct. 2363.

There has been considerable litigation involving employee-administered pension plans and life insurance policies, which traditionally have relied heavily upon gender-based actuarial tables in determining contributions to and benefits from pension plans and the amount of insurance premiums. Because, on average, women live longer than men,

such gender-based classifications have long been common. But in a series of cases beginning in the 1970s, the Court has considered challenges to such schemes in light of both the Fourteenth Amendment and the 1964 Civil Rights Act, which forbids employers to "discriminate against any individual with respect to his compensation . . . because of such individual's sex, . . . deprive or tend to deprive any individual of employment opportunities . . . because of such individual's . . . sex, and . . . [discriminate] with respect to . . . compensation, terms, conditions, or privileges of employment."

Here, too, results have been mixed, but generally supportive of women's claims. In 1976 the Court, by a vote of 6 to 3, ruled that the exclusion of pregnancy benefits from a general employees' medical insurance plan did not constitute a violation of Title VII (*General Electric Co.* v. *Gilbert,* 429 U.S. 125, 1976). But one year later the Court ruled that Title VII prohibited an employer from taking away seniority benefits from women who went on pregnancy leaves (*Nashville Gas* v. *Satty,* 434 U.S. 136, 1977). In both cases, the Court relied heavily on the Fourteenth Amendment–based decision in GEDULDIG V. AIELLO. In 1978 the Court handed down another Title VII case, this time overturning a rule requiring female employees of the Los Angeles Department of Water and Power to make larger monthly contributions to a pension fund than male employees, a policy which the city had defended because women live longer than men (*Los Angeles Department of Water and Power* v. *Manhart, et al.,* 435 U.S. 702, 1978). In 1983 the Court relied on Title VII to strike down policies of granting women lower monthly pension payments than men, again rejecting the rationale that women, on average, live longer (*Arizona* v. *Norris,* 103 S.Ct. 3492. In this case, the Court squarely rejected the claim that such a scheme was fair, because, in fact, on average, men and women received equal total benefits. (Although women received smaller monthly payments than men, they live longer, so the total they received turned out to be the same.) Title VII, the Court asserted, forbids gender as a basis for determining compensation and benefits, even though it might be shown to be actuarially reasonable or valid. The upshot of these cases, as Justice Rehnquist noted in his separate opinion in *Manhart,* was to prohibit use of "gender-based actuarial tables [that] have been in use since at least 1843 [and whose] statistical validity has been repeatedly verified."

While it may appear foolish to abandon nearly 150 years of "verified" experience, consider the following: on average, whites live longer than blacks. Would you defend a policy of higher pension benefits for blacks than whites, or of lower life insurance premiums for whites than blacks? Such race classifications may also have a "valid" actuarial basis, but have long been prohibited by legislation and court rulings. If race can be banned for such uses, why not gender? Would you allow for higher life insurance premiums for fat people than for thin people? Smokers over nonsmokers? Catholics over Protestants? Old people over younger people? Returning to Oklahoma's drinking age differences considered in CRAIG V. BOREN, are you prepared to uphold the law because you are persuaded that, on average, young men drink more heavily and are involved in driving accidents more frequently? If so, would you be willing to uphold relaxed drinking restrictions on Italian Catholics and Jews or favor fat people over thin people because studies reveal that, on average, they have fewer alcohol-related problems than the population at large? What issues are involved in relying on such classifications? Why should some be banned and others accepted?

After reflecting on these issues, consider whether you would support the ill-fated proposal for an Equal Rights Amendment:

> Equality of rights under the law shall not be denied or abridged by the United States or by a state on account of sex. The Congress shall have the power to enforce, by appropriate legislation, the provisions of this article.

Would such an amendment ban all gender-based classifications, or only render such classifications constitutionally suspect? Why do you think advocates of the ERA have not been content to rely upon the Fourteenth Amendment and legislation?

Three other issues in women's rights cases have arisen which have close parallels to race discrimination issues decided earlier by the Court. In PERSONNEL ADMINISTRATOR OF MASSACHUSETTS V. FEENEY, 422 U.S. 256 (1979), the Court was asked to declare Massachusetts' absolute preference for veterans in its civil service hiring to be unconstitutional because, although gender neutral on its face, it had the effect of making it next to impossible for women to obtain well-paying jobs in the civil service. Rejecting the analogy to *Griggs* v. *Duke Power Co.,* 401 U.S. 424 (1971), in which the Court overturned a race-neutral employment test because blacks failed it at a disproportionately high rate, the Court applied heightened ordinary scrutiny and upheld the Massachusetts law as a bona fide policy benefitting veterans.

In what is properly a case involving the First Amendment right of association and privacy, the Supreme Court upheld a decision by the Minnesota Department of Human Rights ordering the state chapters of the Jaycees, a civic organization whose national by-laws restricted membership to men, to admit women (*Roberts* v. *United States Jaycees,* 104 S.Ct. 3244, 1984). In response to the challenge that the Minnesota statute, as interpreted by the Department of Human Rights, infringed upon the Jaycees' "right of *intimate* association," the Court found that "the local chapters of the Jaycees are neither small nor selective," and that much of the "activity central to the... association involves the participation of strangers." Thus Justice Brennan, writing for the Court, concluded that the Jaycees chapters "lack the distinctive characteristics that might afford constitutional protection to the decision of its members to exclude women." In response to another Jaycees' argument, that the Minnesota statute infringed upon its "freedom of *expressive* association," Justice Brennan likened the Jaycees to a quasi-commercial organization with less than full free expression rights. He then went on to question whether admitting women would have any noticeable impact on members' freedom of expression, but concluded: "In any event, even if enforcement of the Act causes some incidental abridgement of the Jaycees' protected speech, that effect is no greater than is necessary to accomplish the State's legitimate purposes." While Justice Rehnquist and O'Connor concurred only in the result and Chief Justice Burger and Justice Blackmun did not participate, it is still significant that there were no dissenting votes in this case.

The issue of discrimination against males — a variation on the BAKKE and WEBER themes — emerged in MISSISSIPPI UNIVERSITY FOR WOMEN V. HOGAN, 102 S.Ct. 3331 (1982), where for the first time the Court considered the constitutionality of state-supported single-sex colleges. In an opinion written by Justice O'Connor, the Court ordered the nation's last state-funded women's university to admit males to its college of nursing, a decision which was lamented by Justice Powell in a dissent emphasizing the value of diversity and freedom of choice.

Other Classifications. Once race was firmly ensconced as a constitutionally suspect classification, pressure mounted to include other groups in this category. As we have seen, gender attained the status of a semisuspect category; in this section we consider efforts of still other groups. One of the earliest and most successful efforts — indeed, it preceded the Warren Court's concern with racial discrimination — is seen in KOREMATSU V. UNITED STATES, 323 U.S. 214 (1944), the decision that upheld the internment of people of Japanese ancestry (citizens and noncitizens alike) in detention camps during World War II, but in dicta observed that "all legal restrictions which curtail the civil rights of a single racial group are immediately suspect," a view that was later refined and transformed into the constitutional doctrine of "suspect category" triggering strict scrutiny. Not only was the dicta in KOREMATSU repeated in BROWN V. BOARD OF EDUCATION (1954) and the racial discrimination cases that followed,

the strict scrutiny test was employed by the Court to scrutinize a host of laws restricting the rights of aliens generally.

Even after the transformation from Warren to Burger, the Court continued to strike down laws restricting rights and opportunities of aliens, and it appeared that *alienage* classifications of all sorts would automatically receive strict scrutiny. For instance, in *Graham* v. *Richardson,* 403 U.S. 365 (1971), the Court reiterated the view that a classification based on alienage is "inherently suspect and subject to close judicial scrutiny," and went on to hold unconstitutional a state law which denied welfare benefits to otherwise eligible lawfully admitted resident aliens. Several later cases affirmed this position, as the Court struck down laws prohibiting aliens from practicing law (*In re Griffiths,* 413 U.S. 717, 1973), and working as engineers (*Examining Board* v. *Flores de Otero,* 426 U.S. 572, 1976).

More recently, however, the Court appears to have shifted and has upheld a number of state laws restricting aliens. Thus in *Perkins* v. *Smith,* 426 U.S. 913 (1976), it affirmed a ruling excluding aliens from juries; in *Foley* v. *Connelie,* 435 U.S. 291 (1978), it upheld New York State's exclusion of aliens from the state police force; and in AMBACH V. NORWICK, 441 U.S. 68 (1979), it upheld a state law limiting public school teaching positions to United States citizens. Still, in 1982, the Court ruled that minor children of illegal alien immigrants did have the constitutional right to a free public education (*Plyler* v. *Doe,* 102 S.Ct. 2382, 1982). Thus, the Court now has two lines of precedents, one striking down and the other upholding laws limiting the rights of aliens, and a majority can seize upon either line it wishes. After reading AMBACH, see if you can clearly distinguish rationales for those laws the Court has struck down and those it has upheld. Why doesn't the Court in AMBACH cite KOREMATSU as a precedent?

Our society provides an array of protections and benefits to children of deceased parents, and it is also a society in which a substantial number of births occur out of wedlock. Thus it is not surprising that the Court has been urged to declare *illegitimacy* a suspect category. While the Court has not acceded to this request, it has come close, using "ordinary scrutiny with a bite" to strike down a number of laws denying illegitimate children rights possessed by legitimate children. For instance, the Court has struck down a state law denying illegitimate children the right to sue for damages for the wrongful death of their mother (*Levy* v. *Louisiana,* 391 U.S. 68, 1968).

But here too the Court has developed two lines of precedents, one eliminating restrictions on the illegitimate and the other upholding them. Thus in *Weber* v. *Aetna Casualty & Surety Co.,* 406 U.S. 164 (1972), the Court, over a vigorous dissent by Justice Rehnquist, held that a workers' compensation statute denying equal recovery rights to unacknowledged illegitimate children while granting them to other children served "no legitimate state interest, compelling or otherwise." But four years later the Court upheld a requirement that placed an extra burden of proof of dependency upon a divorced father's illegitimate children who claim social security benefits (*Mathews* v. *Lucas,* 427 U.S. 495, 1976). And so it goes: two lines of conflicting precedents and a tangle of separate opinions based upon ordinary, strict, and middle-level scrutiny.

Strict scrutiny and suspect classifications were initially justified to guarantee basic constitutional protections to "insular minorities" and "powerless" groups, who were not in positions to help themselves in the face of unsympathetic majorities. Perhaps it was inevitable that the federal courts were asked to extend these concepts to protect *institutionalized persons, the handicapped,* and *the retarded,* all groups which for quite different reasons are clearly not in good positions to help themselves in the political arena. A landmark case in this development was *Wyatt* v. *Stickney,* 325 F.Supp. 781 (1971), in which Judge Frank M. Johnson, Jr., of the Federal District Court for Northern Alabama, handed down a far-reaching decision challenging the constitutionality of the conditions and treatment in Alabama's mental hospitals. His decision, which amounts to a Bill of

Rights for institutionalized people of all sorts (in hospitals, reformatories, jails, and prisons), found the food, facilities, lack of treatment, size and competence of staff, level of funding, and the like to be so pitiful as to be a denial of basic human and constitutional standards. Since then, numerous other federal courts have rendered similar rulings, declaring conditions in a variety of state-run institutions to be constitutionally wanting. In so doing, they have catapulted the federal courts into an oversight role nearly as detailed and as complex as the one thrust upon them in the school desegregation cases. The first substantial Supreme Court ruling in this vein was O'CONNOR V. DONALDSON, 422 U.S. 563 (1975), which held that a person who is not dangerous cannot be held against his will in an institution without receiving treatment. But in this decision the Court fell short of declaring a fundamental right to treatment, as some liberals had wanted.

Typically, the Supreme Court has declined to hear appeals in most institutional-conditions cases, thereby allowing district courts considerable discretion in exercising their equitable powers to tackle abuses in such institutions. But in recent years the Court has grown less sympathetic to the institutionalized, especially confined criminals and those awaiting trial. Thus, for instance, in *Bell* v. *Wolfish,* 411 U.S. 520 (1979), the Court upheld a jailer's broad discretion to limit the privacy of pre-trial detainees, and in *Rhodes* v. *Chapman,* 452 U.S. 337 (1981), it rejected complaints that long-term prison inmates were being doubled up in cells built for one, observing that "the Constitution does not mandate comfortable prisons." Still, many lower court decisions and a handful of Supreme Court decisions have had the effect of mandating considerable improvements in conditions, procedures, and privacy of confined persons of all sorts. Thus here, too, there are two somewhat contradictory lines of precedents from which to draw. For instance, in *Youngberg* v. *Romeo,* 457 U.S. 315 (1982), the Court ruled that retarded persons committed to state mental institutions had a constitutional right to safe conditions, to be free from unnecessary restraints, and to receive a minimum of training in safe-care skills. Only two years earlier, in *Pennhurst State School and Hospital* v. *Halderman,* 451 U.S. 1 (1981), the Court had denied that federal legislation created any rights for the developmentally disabled.

Classifications by *age* have also met with mixed review by the Court, and the most important gains against age discrimination have been made in the Congress. This legislation has clearly made a difference. In MASSACHUSETTS BOARD OF RETIREMENT V. MURGIA, 427 U.S. 307 (1976), the Court refused to declare age a suspect classification and knock down a law mandating retirement at age fifty for state police officers. But subsequent congressional legislation expanded the protection against age discrimination, going well beyond what the Court held was required by the Constitution, and as a consequence a fifty-nine-year-old test pilot was restored to his job with back pay (*McDonnell Douglas* v. *Houghton,* 434 U.S. 966, 1977). An important amendment, in 1974, to the Age Discrimination in Employment Act of 1967 expanded the definition of employers to include state and local governments, a move that was unsuccessfully challenged under the Tenth Amendment by the State of Wyoming when a game warden did not want to retire at age fifty-five (*EEOC* v. *Wyoming,* 960 U.S. 226, 1983).

More generally, equal protection developments through the 1980s reveal a Court that, while refusing to roll back the gains established in the 1960s and early 1970s, is clearly no longer keen on expanding the sweeping language of its race relations decisions to other disadvantaged groups. But when Congress has taken up such concerns, in most instances the Court has been willing to back it up by giving broad interpretation to the host of equal opportunity laws adopted in the 1960s and 1970s. Only recently have a substantial number of justices begun to seriously question such legislation on federalism grounds or, as in the case of the rights of the handicapped, begun to impose restrictive interpretation on expansive laws. As these issues continue to be raised before a Court in transition, we can expect even greater changes in the 1990s.

Fundamental Rights

The Court has long held that the Constitution protects rights not specifically identified in the Constitution. Even the modern architect of judicial restraint, Justice Frankfurter, held that the Fourteenth Amendment protected rights not specifically listed or implied in the first eight amendments. But precisely what such rights are, how they are to be discovered, and how to develop constitutional protection for them remains problematic. We have already encountered this controversial two-tier approach in the recent cases involving First Amendment freedoms, rights that all justices have long recognized as "fundamental," and in cases involving race. But the issue becomes much more problematic when we turn to rights not specifically identified in the Constitution. The first nonenumerated right to gain a special protected status in this scheme was the right to vote. But this elevation of voting to a fundamental right is hardly problematic given the Fifteenth Amendment, which guarantees citizens the right to vote irrespective of race, the Court's history of combating racial discrimination in connection with voting in the South, its involvement in reapportionment, and the Voting Rights Act of 1965.

The argument that there are nonenumerated "fundamental rights" that, if encroached, trigger especially searching judicial scrutiny can be traced to the CAROLENE PRODUCTS footnote number four and to the Court's decision in *Skinner* v. *Oklahoma,* 316 U.S. 535 (1942), which overturned a statute providing for sterilization of those convicted two or more times of felonies involving moral terpitude. In his expansive opinion for the Court, Justice Douglas noted that an individual so punished "is forever deprived of a basic liberty," and went on to argue that such legislation must be subject to searching judicial scrutiny. "Marriage and procreation," he continued, are "fundamental rights" to be jealously guarded by the Court. As we will see, more recently the Court has returned to consider such matters further, first in its decision striking down antimiscegenation statutes, *Loving v. Virginia,* 388 U.S. 1 (1967), and more recently in its birth control and abortion decisions.

Over the years, a number of candidates for nonenumerated fundamental rights have been put forward. We have already considered one such claim in SAN ANTONIO INDEPENDENT SCHOOL DISTRICT V. RODRIGUEZ, 441 U.S. 1 (1973), in which the Court refused to declare wealth a suspect category or to designate equal educational resources a fundamental right. Among other candidates that have been put forward as fundamental rights are travel, welfare, treatment, and medical care.

Only the right to *travel* has been enshrined as fundamental, although in light of *Regan* v. *Wald,* 104 S.Ct. 3026 (1984), upholding an executive ban on travel to Cuba, this is a very shaky "fundamental" right. The issue of travel initially came before the Court in a series of cases in the 1950s and early 1960s in which the Court considered various restrictions on international travel (by refusing or confiscating passports) for those who refused to take an oath that they were not members of the Communist party (*Kent* v. *Dulles,* 357 U.S. 116, 1958); were members of Communist organizations (*Aptheker* v. *Secretary of State,* 378 U.S. 500, 1964); or travelled to places disapproved of by the State Department (*Zemel* v. *Rusk,* 381 U.S. 1, 1965). In these and other cases, international travel was treated as an aspect of the First Amendment rights of assembly and expression, and domestic travel was protected as an aspect of interstate commerce, although dicta in these cases suggested that travel was an independent right by itself.

But even this incremental elevation did not automatically guarantee that travel would become a fundamental right whose encroachment would trigger strict judicial scrutiny. This step was achieved in SHAPIRO V. THOMPSON, 349 U.S. 618 (1969), a case which combined the claim of a fundamental

constitutional right to travel with the claim of a fundamental right to welfare. This decision, which declared the right to travel a fundamental right to be protected by strict scrutiny, was handed down shortly before Chief Justice Warren left the bench, and represents the high-water mark in his Court's embrace of the fundamental rights approach. It also presents the controversy over the two-tier approach to constitutional protection of rights in its sharpest focus, as Justice Rehnquist, in dissent, excoriates his colleagues for their activist ways.

Since SHAPIRO, the travel–welfare-rights combination has resurfaced before the Court several times in a variety of challenges to state residency requirements for welfare and medical care. See, for example, *Memorial Hospital* v. *Maricopa County,* 415 U.S. 250 (1974), in which the Court struck down a one-year residency requirement before an indigent could receive nonemergency medical treatment at public expense.

Welfare as a fundamental right was the issue in DANDRIDGE V. WILLIAMS, 397 U.S. 471 (1970), a decision in which the Court, under the leadership of newly appointed Chief Justice Burger, called an abrupt halt to the long march many thought SHAPIRO had begun. The case involved a challenge to the absolute limit of $250 per month on the amount of a grant under a state-administered Social Security program, regardless of the size of the family or its actual need. Writing for a majority of six, Justice Stewart acknowledged that the issue involved pressing economic needs, but went on to hold that welfare was not a fundamental right and to rule that ordinary scrutiny was sufficient to judge the constitutionality of such legislation. The Court has continued to adhere to this view in welfare rights cases and in so doing has upheld a number of restrictive policies criticized as discriminatory because they are insufficiently sensitive to actual needs. These include *Richardson* v. *Belcher,* 404 U.S. 78 (1971), upholding automatic reduction in Social Security payments to adjust for workers' compensation awards, and *Jefferson* v. *Hackney,* 406 U.S. 535 (1972), upholding a Texas policy limiting welfare payments to 75 percent of the standard need of welfare recipients.

Despite these decisions, the Court has not withdrawn altogether from the scrutiny of welfare rights. As we saw in Chapter 5, the Court has come to regard a variety of government-created "entitlements" as new forms of property to be protected by the Due Process Clauses of the Fifth and Fourteenth Amendments. Taking this approach, the Court throughout the 1970s and 1980s continued to review and strike down a number of welfare requirements and practices on due process grounds. Indeed, this emphasis on property rights is nicely illustrated in Stewart's opinion in DANDRIDGE, where he compares welfare laws with New Deal legislation regulating business. Arguing that just as the Court eventually came to defer to legislatures in matters of business regulation, so it should defer to legislatures on social welfare issues. In both types of cases, Stewart argued, ordinary scrutiny of legislation remains the proper test.

Still, the Court has never explicitly rejected the strict scrutiny approach of SHAPIRO. Thus here, too, the Court has two lines of precedents from which to draw, depending upon the propensities of a majority of justices. More generally, in SHAPIRO and DANDRIDGE, we see the Court in conflict with itself, a conflict that years later has still not been fully resolved, as other candidates are put forward for designation as fundamental rights. Dicta in some of the early school desegregation cases suggested that education was such a right (*Griffin* v. *County School Board,* 377 U.S. 218, 1964), although as you will see in RODRIGUEZ, when pressed the Court rejected the argument. Similarly, in a series of cases that challenged zoning laws that excluded low-income housing from a community, the Court refused to declare decent housing a fundamental right (WARTH V. SELDIN, 422 U.S. 490, 1975). But the Court came quite close to declaring treatment of mental illness a fundamental right for at least those nondangerous people the state sought to institutionalize (O'CONNOR V. DONALDSON, 422 U.S. 563, 1975). Since then, however, it has tended to approach institutional condition-and-treatment issues on due process rather than equal protection or fundamental rights grounds. This approach is suggested by CLEBURNE V. CLEBURNE (1987), in which the Court rejected the argument that the mentally handicapped are a "suspect category" to be protected by strict scrutiny, but then went on to apply the traditional rational relation test in a creative way to overturn a city's regulation that restricted opportunities for this vulnerable population.

Conclusion

The failure of the Burger Court to extend suspect classifications and fundamental rights did not mean a counterrevolution. Although some rights were trimmed, none of the major equal protection decisions has yet been forcefully repudiated. And while recent Court decisions called a halt to developments in some areas, and rolled back the boundaries in others, the Burger Court engaged in some remarkable acts of judicial legislation of its own. It remains to be seen if the Rehnquist Court mounts a revolution.

To date, however, the continuity through the Warren, Burger, and Rehnquist Courts has often been obscured by the pyrotechnics sparked by debate over the two-tier approach. But even as the Nixon, Ford, and Reagan appointees have questioned or repudiated this approach, some of them have come to accept "ordinary scrutiny with a bite" and, in so doing, have made precarious alliances with the liberals on the Court.

Justice O'Connor's behavior on the Court suggests another reason why, despite the changes on the Court, there has been continuity. Although willing to adopt a conservative stance when confronting new issues, she is deferential to precedent. In several decisions, most notably those dealing with abortion and affirmative action, she has criticized Chief Justice Rehnquist and Justices White, Scalia, and Kennedy for their willingness to disregard precedent and act as if they were writing on a clean slate. Thus we see that stare decisis serves to curb the impulses of some of the justices and fosters continuity.

Another possible direction of the Court is indicated in CITY OF CLEBURNE V. CLEBURNE LIVING CENTER, 473 U.S. 432 (1985). In that case the Court had been urged to designate the mentally retarded as a suspect class and use heightened scrutiny to review and strike down a city's zoning ordinance and special use permit requirement, which had been invoked to prevent the establishment of a group home for the mentally retarded. In his opinion, which was joined by five other justices, Justice White ruled that the mentally retarded do not constitute a suspect or quasi-suspect class, and held that the zoning ordinance in question should be assessed by the traditional "rational relation" test. This test asks the less stringent question, "Is the regulation related to a legitimate governmental purpose?" In the past fifty years the Court's answer to this question has almost always been yes.

However in CLEBURNE the Court surprised a great many people by holding that there was no reasonable relation between the city's zoning goals and its ordinance and its requirement for a special use permit. This case is important for two reasons. First, as Justice Marshall suggested in his concurring opinion, the Court in fact had engaged in a searching inquiry into the motives and aims of the city's regulations, something that is neither required nor normally done under the rational relation test. Marshall persuasively argued that the Court was subscribing to a form of heightened scrutiny even though it refused to use that term. Second, this decision may pump life into the rational relation test, after years of decrepitude in the wake of the New Deal. In this case the petitioners, the mentally retarded, constituted a particularly sympathetic group. But as we noted in Chapter 5, in the future the Court may be willing to employ a more robust rational relation test to protect a variety of other interests against "unreasonable" governmental regulation. Whatever CLEBURNE signals for the future Court's role in reviewing "economic regulations," it is clear that even the recent, conservative appointees to the Court have not wholly rejected a special role for the Court in protecting the politically powerless and socially vulnerable. While they do not like the complex protective apparatus constructed by the Warren Court, they are willing to pursue similar aims through flexible use of the traditional approach.

Cases

Baker v. Carr

369 U.S. 186 (1962)
See pp. 69–77.

Reynolds v. Sims

377 U.S. 533 (1964)
Vote: 8–1

Three years after its decision in BAKER V. CARR, the Court handed down a series of decisions on the merits of various schemes of apportionment in six different states. None of the schemes passed constitutional muster. We reprint here the principal decision in this set of cases, in which the Court announces its "one person, one vote" standard and insists that it must apply to *both* houses of a bicameral state legislature. In so doing, the Court rejects the "federal analogy" embraced by a number of states, including Alabama, which would allow for at least one house to be based upon representation of a geographical area (usually county), just as each state is allowed two senators regardless of population.

In subsequent cases, the Court was confronted with the issue of how precisely this new equal population standard should be applied.

The present case arose when voters from "underrepresented" state legislative districts filed suit alleging that their diluted vote denied them equal protection of the law.

MR. CHIEF JUSTICE WARREN delivered the opinion of the Court.

A predominant consideration in determining whether a State's legislative apportionment scheme constitutes an invidious discrimination violative of rights asserted under the Equal Protection Clause is that the rights allegedly impaired are individual and personal in nature. . . . While the result of a court decision in a state legislative apportionment controversy may be to require the restructuring of the geographical distribution of seats in a state legislature, the judicial focus must be concentrated upon ascertaining whether there has been any discrimination against certain of the State's citizens which constitutes an impermissible impairment of their constitutionally protected right to vote. Like *Skinner* v. *Oklahoma* such a case "touches a sensitive and important area of human rights," and "involves one of the basic civil rights of man," presenting questions of alleged "individuous discriminations . . . against groups or types of individuals in violation of the constitutional guaranty of just and equal laws." Undoubtedly, the right of suffrage is a fundamental matter in a free and democratic society. Especially since the right to exercise the franchise in a free and unimpaired manner is preservative of other basic civil and political rights, any alleged infringement of the right of citizens to vote must be carefully and meticulously scrutinized. Almost a century ago, in *Yick Wo* v. *Hopkins,* the Court referred to "the political franchise of voting" as "a fundamental political right, because preservative of all rights."

Legislators represent people, not trees or acres. Legislators are elected by voters, not farms or cities or economic interests. As long as ours is a representative form of government, and our legislatures are those instruments of government elected directly by and directly representative of the people, the right to elect legislators in a free and unimpaired fashion is a bedrock of our political system. It could hardly be gainsaid that a constitutional claim had been asserted by an allegation that certain otherwise qualified voters had been entirely prohibited from voting for members of their state legislature. And, if a State should provide that the votes of citizens in one part of the State should be given two times, or five times, or 10 times the weight of votes of citizens in another part of the State, it could hardly be contended that the right to vote of those residing in the disfavored areas had not been effectively diluted. It would appear extraordinary to suggest that a State could be constitutionally permitted to enact a law providing that certain of the State's voters could vote two, five, or 10 times for their legislative representatives, while voters living elsewhere could vote only once. And it is inconceivable that a state law to the effect that, in counting votes for legislators, the votes of citizens in one part of the State would be multiplied by two, five, or 10, while the votes of persons in another area would be counted only at face value, could be constitutionally sustainable. Of course, the effect of state legislative districting schemes which give the same number of representatives to unequal numbers of constituents is identical. Overweighting and overevaluation of the votes of those living here has the certain effect of dilution and undervaluation of the votes of those living there. The resulting discrimination against those individual voters living in disfavored areas is easily demonstrable mathematically. Their right to vote is simply not the same right to vote as that of those living in a favored part of the State. Two, five, or 10 of them must vote before the effect of their voting is equivalent to that of their favored neighbor. Weighting the votes of citizens differently, by any method or means, merely because of where they happen to reside, hardly seems justifiable. One must be ever aware that the Constitution forbids "sophisticated as well as simple-minded modes of discrimination." . . .

State legislatures are, historically, the fountainhead of representative government in this country. A number of them have their roots in colonial times, and substantially antedate the creation of our Nation and our Federal Government. In fact, the first formal stirrings of American political independence are to be found, in large part, in the views and actions of several of the colonial legislative bodies. With the birth of our National Government, and the adoption and ratification of the Federal Constitution, state legislatures retained a most important place in our Nation's governmental structure. But representative government is in essence self-government through the medium of elected representatives of the people, and each and every citizen has an inalienable right to full and effective participation in the political processes of his State's legislative bodies. Most citizens can achieve this participation only as qualified voters through the election of legislators to represent them.

Full and effective participation by all citizens in state government requires, therefore, that each citizen have an equally effective voice in the election of members of his state legislature. Modern and viable state government needs, and the Constitution demands, no less.

Logically, in a society ostensibly grounded on representative government, it would seem reasonable that a majority of the people of a State could elect a majority of that State's legislators. To conclude differently, and to sanction minority control of state legislative bodies, would appear to deny majority rights in a way that far surpasses any possible denial of minority rights that might otherwise be thought to result. Since legislatures are responsible for enacting laws by which all citizens are to be governed, they should be bodies which are collectively responsive to the popular will. And the concept of equal protection has been traditionally viewed as requiring the uniform treatment of persons standing in the same relation to the governmental action questioned or challenged. With respect to the allocation of legislative representation, all voters, as citizens of a State, stand in the same relation regardless of where they live. Any suggested criteria for the differentiation of citizens are insufficient to justify any discrimination, as to the weight of their votes, unless relevant to the permissible purposes of legislative apportionment. Since the achieving of fair and effective representation for all citizens is concededly the basic aim of legislative apportionment, we conclude that the Equal Protection Clause guarantees the opportunity for equal participation by all voters in the election of state legislators. Diluting the weight of votes because of place of residence impairs basic constitutional rights under the Fourteenth Amendment just as much as invidious discriminations based upon factors such as race or economic status. Our constitutional system amply provides for the protection of minorities by means other than giving them majority control of state legislatures. And the democratic ideals of equality and majority rule, which have served this Nation so well in the past, are hardly of any less significance for the present and the future.

We are told that the matter of apportioning representation in a state legislature is a complex and many-faceted one. We are advised that States can rationally consider factors other than population in apportioning legislative representation. We are admonished not to restrict the power of the States to impose differing views as to political philosophy on their citizens. We are cautioned about the dangers of entering into political thickets and mathematical quagmires. Our answer is this: a denial of constitutionally protected rights demands judicial protection; our oath and our office require no less of us. As stated in *Gomillion* v. *Lightfoot:*

> When a State exercises power wholly within the domain of state interest, it is insulated from federal judicial review. But such insulation is not carried over when state power is used as an instrument for circumventing a federally protected right.

To the extent that a citizen's right to vote is debased, he is that much less a citizen. The fact that an individual lives here or there is not a legitimate reason for overweighting or diluting the efficacy of his vote. The complexions of societies and civilizations change, often with amazing rapidity. A nation once primarily rural in character becomes predominantly urban. Representation schemes once fair and equitable become archaic and outdated. But the basic principle of representative government remains, and must remain, unchanged — the weight of a citizen's vote cannot be made to depend on where he lives. Population is, of necessity, the starting point for consideration and the controlling criterion for judgment in legislative apportionment controversies. A citizen, a qualified voter, is no more nor less so because he lives in the city or on the farm. This is the clear and strong command of our Constitution's Equal Protection Clause. This is an essential part of the concept of a government of laws and not men. This is at the heart of Lincoln's vision of "government of the people, by the people, [and] for the people." The Equal Protection Clause demands no less than substantially equal state legislative representation for all citizens, of all places as well as of all races.

We hold that, as a basic constitutional standard, the Equal Protection Clause requires that the seats in both houses of a bicameral state legislature must be apportioned on a population basis. Simply stated, an individual's right to vote for state legislators is unconstitutionally impaired when its weight is in a substantial fashion diluted when compared with votes of citizens living in other parts of the State. Since, under neither the existing apportionment provisions nor either of the proposed plans was either of the houses of the Alabama Legislature apportioned on a population basis, the District Court correctly held that all three of these schemes were constitutionally invalid. Furthermore, the existing apportionment, and also to a lesser extent the apportionment under the Crawford-Webb Act, presented little more than crazy quilts, completely lacking in rationality, and could be found invalid on that basis alone. Although the District Court presumably found the apportionment of the Alabama House of Representatives under the 67-Senator Amendment to be acceptable, we conclude that the deviations from a strict population basis are too egregious to permit us to find that that body, under this proposed plan, was apportioned sufficiently on a population basis so as to permit the arrangement to be constitutionally sustained. Although about 43% of the State's total population would be required to comprise districts which could elect a majority in that body, only 39 of the 106 House seats were actually to be distributed on a population basis, as each of Alabama's 67 counties was given at least one representative, and population-variance ratios of close to 5-to-1 would have existed. While mathematical nicety is not a constitutional requisite, one could hardly conclude that the Alabama House, under the proposed constitutional amendment, had been apportioned sufficiently on a population basis to be sustainable under the requirements of the Equal Protection Clause. And none of the other apportionments of seats in either of the bodies of the Alabama Legislature, under the three plans considered by the District Court, came nearly as close to approaching the required constitutional standard as did that of the House of Representatives under the 67-Senator Amendment.

Legislative apportionment in Alabama is signally illustrative and symptomatic of the seriousness of this problem in a number of the States. At the time this litigation was commenced, there had been no reapportionment of seats in the Alabama Legislature for over 60 years. Legislative inaction, coupled with the unavailability of any political or judicial remedy, had resulted, with the passage of years, in the perpetuated scheme becoming little more than an irrational anachronism. Consistent failure by the Alabama Legislature to comply with state constitutional requirements as to the frequency of reapportionment and the bases of legislative representation resulted in a minority strangle hold on the State Legislature. Inequality of representation in one house added to the inequality in the other. With the crazy-quilt existing apportionment virtually conceded to be invalid, the Alabama Legislature offered two proposed plans for consideration by the District Court, neither of which was to be effective until 1966 and neither of which provided for the apportionment of even one of the two houses on a population basis. We find that the court below did not err in holding that neither of these proposed reapportionment schemes, considered as a whole, "meets the necessary constitutional requirements." And we conclude that the District Court acted properly in considering these two proposed plans, although neither was to become effective until

the 1966 election and the proposed constitutional amendment was scheduled to be submitted to the State's voters in November 1962. Consideration by the court below of the two proposed plans was clearly necessary in determining whether the Alabama Legislature had acted effectively to correct the admittedly existing malapportionment, and in ascertaining what sort of judicial relief, if any, should be afforded.

Since neither of the houses of the Alabama Legislature, under any of the three plans considered by the District Court, was apportioned on a population basis, we would be justified in proceeding no further. However, one of the proposed plans, that contained in the so-called 67-Senator Amendment, at least superficially resembles the scheme of legislative representation followed in the Federal Congress. Under this plan, each of Alabama's 67 counties is allotted one senator, and no counties are given more than one Senate seat. Arguably, this is analogous to the allocation of two Senate seats, in the Federal Congress, to each of the 50 States, regardless of population. Seats in the Alabama House, under the proposed constitutional amendment, are distributed by giving each of the 67 counties at least one, with the remaining 39 seats being allotted among the more populous counties on a population basis. This scheme, at least at first glance, appears to resemble that prescribed for the Federal House of Representatives, where the 435 seats are distributed among the States on a population basis, although each State, regardless of its population, is given at least one Congressman. Thus, although there are substantial differences in underlying rationale and result, the 67-Senator Amendment, as proposed by the Alabama Legislature, at least arguably presents for consideration a scheme analogous to that used for apportioning seats in Congress.

Much has been written since our decision in *Baker v. Carr* about the applicability of the so-called federal analogy to state legislative apportionment arrangements. After considering the matter, the court below concluded that no conceivable analogy could be drawn between the federal scheme and the apportionment of seats in the Alabama Legislature under the proposed constitutional amendment. We agree with the District Court, and find the federal analogy inapposite and irrelevant to state legislative districting schemes. Attempted reliance on the federal analogy appears often to be little more than an after-the-fact rationalization offered in defense of maladjusted state apportionment arrangements. The original constitutions of 36 of our States provided that representation in both houses of the state legislature would be based completely, or predominantly, on population. And the Founding Fathers clearly had no intention of establishing a pattern or model for the apportionment of seats in state legislatures when the system of representation in the Federal Congress was adopted. Demonstrative of this is the fact that the Northwest Ordinance, adopted in the same year, 1787, as the Federal Constitution, provided for the apportionment of seats in territorial legislatures solely on the basis of population.

The system of representation in the two Houses of the Federal Congress is one ingrained in our Constitution, as part of the law of the land. It is one conceived out of compromise and concession indispensable to the establishment of our federal republic. Arising from unique historical circumstances, it is based on the consideration that in establishing our type of federalism a group of formerly independent States bound themselves together under one national government. Admittedly, the original 13 States surrendered some of their sovereignty in agreeing to join together "to form a more perfect Union." But at the heart of our constitutional system remains the concept of separate and distinct governmental entitites which have delegated some, but not all, of their formerly held powers to the single national government. The fact that almost three-fourths of our present States were never in fact independently sovereign does not detract from our view that the so-called federal analogy is inapplicable as a sustaining precedent for state legislative apportionments. The developing history and growth of our republic cannot cloud the fact that, at the time of the inception of the system of representation in the Federal Congress, a compromise between the larger and smaller States on this matter averted a deadlock in the Constitutional Convention which had threatened to abort the birth of our Nation. In rejecting an asserted analogy to the federal electoral college in *Gray* v. *Sanders,* we stated:

> We think the analogies to the electoral college, to districting and redistricting, and to other phases of the problems of representation in state or federal legislatures or conventions are inapposite. The inclusion of the electoral college in the Constitution, as the result of specific historical concerns, validated the collegiate principle despite its inherent numerical inequality, but implied nothing about the use of the analogous system by a State in a state-wide election. No such specific accommodation of the latter was ever undertaken, and therefore no validation of its numerical inequality ensued.

Political subdivisions of States — counties, cities, or whatever — never were and never have been considered as sovereign entities. Rather, they have been regarded as subordinate governmental instrumentalities created by the State to assist in the carrying out of state governmental functions. . . . [T]hese governmental units are "created as convenient agencies for exercising such of the governmental powers of the State as may be entrusted to them," and the "number, nature and duration of the powers conferred upon [them] . . . and the territory over which they shall be exercised rests in the absolute discretion of the State." The relationship of the States to the Federal Government could hardly be less analogous.

Thus, we conclude that the plan contained in the 67-Senator Amendment for appportioning seats in the Alabama Legislature cannot be sustained by recourse to the so-called federal analogy. Nor can any other inequitable state legislative apportionment scheme be justified on such an asserted basis. This does not necessarily mean that such a plan is irrational or involves something other than a "republican form of government." We conclude simply that such a plan is impermissible for the States under the Equal Protection Clause, since perforce resulting, in virtually every case, in submergence of the equal-population principle in at least one house of a state legislature.

Since we find the so-called federal analogy inapposite to a consideration of the constitutional validity of state legislative apportionment schemes, we necessarily hold that the Equal Protection Clause requires both houses of a state legislature to be apportioned on a population basis. The right of a citizen to equal representation and to have his vote weighed equally with those of all other citizens in the election of members of one house of a bicameral state legislature would amount to little if States could effectively submerge the equal-population principle in the apportionment of seats in the other house. If such a scheme were permissible, an individual citizen's ability to exercise an effective voice in the only instrument of state government directly representative of the people might be almost as effectively thwarted as if neither house were apportioned on a population basis. Deadlock between the two bodies might result in compromise and concession on some issues. But in all too many cases the more probable result would be frustration of the majority will through minority veto in the house not apportioned on a population basis, stemming directly from the failure to accord adequate overall legislative representation to all of the State's citizens on a nondiscriminatory basis. In summary, we can perceive no constitutional difference, with respect to the geographical distribution of state legislative representation, between the two houses of a bicameral state legislature.

We do not believe that the concept of bicameralism is rendered anachronistic and meaningless when the predominant basis of representation in the two state legislative bodies is required to be the same — population. A prime reason for bicameralism, modernly considered, is to insure mature and deliberate consideration of, and to prevent precipitate action on, proposed legislative measures. Simply because the controlling criterion for apportioning representation is required to be the same in both houses does not mean that there will be no differences in the composition and complexion of the two bodies. Different constituencies can be represented in the two houses. One body could be composed of single-member districts while the other could have at least some multimember districts. The length of terms of the legislators in the separate bodies could differ. The numerical size of the two bodies could be made to differ, even significantly, and the geographical size of the districts from which legislators are elected could also be made to differ. And apportionment in one house could be arranged so as to balance off minor inequities in the representation of certain areas in the other house. In summary, these and other factors could be, and are presently in many States, utilized to engender differing complexions and collective attitudes in the two bodies of a state legislature, although both are apportioned substantially on a population basis.

By holding that as a federal constitutional requisite both houses of a state legislature must be apportioned on a population basis, we mean that the Equal Protection Clause requires that a State make an honest and good faith effort to construct districts, in both houses of its legislature, as nearly of equal population as is practicable. We realize that it is a practical impossibility to arrange legislative districts so that each one has an identical number of residents, or citizens, or voters. Mathematical exactness or precision is hardly a workable constitutional requirement.

In *Wesberry* v. *Sanders,* the Court stated that congressional representation must be based on population as nearly as is practicable. In implementing the basic constitutional principle of representative government as enunciated by the Court in *Wesberry* — equality of population among districts — some distinctions may well be made between congressional and state legislative representation. Since, almost invariably, there is a significantly larger number of seats in state legislative bodies to be distributed within a State than congressional seats, it may be feasible to use political subdivision lines to a greater extent in establishing state legislative districts than in congressional districting while still affording adequate representation to all parts of the State. To do so would be constitutionally valid, so long as the resulting apportionment was one based substantially on population and the equal-population principle was not diluted in any significant way. Somewhat more flexibility may therefore be constitutionally permissible with respect to state legislative apportionment than in congressional districting. Lower courts can and assuredly will work out more concrete and specific standards for evaluating state legislative apportionment schemes in the context of actual litigation. For the present, we deem it expedient not to attempt to spell out any precise constitutional tests. What is marginally permissible in one State may be unsatisfactory in another, depending on the particular circumstances of the case. Developing a body of doctrine on a case-by-case basis appears to us to provide the most satisfactory means of arriving at detailed constitutional requirements in the area of state legislative apportionment. Thus, we proceed to state here only a few rather general considerations which appear to us to be relevant.

A State may legitimately desire to maintain the integrity of various political subdivisions, insofar as possible, and provide for compact districts of contiguous territory in designing a legislative apportionment scheme. Valid considerations may underlie such aims. Indiscriminate districting, without any regard for political subdivision or natural or historical boundary lines, may be little more than an open invitation to partisan gerrymandering. Single-member districts may be the rule in one State, while another State might desire to achieve some flexibility by creating multimember or floterial districts. Whatever the means of accomplishment, the overriding objective must be substantial equality of population among the various districts, so that the vote of any citizen is approximately equal in weight to that of any other citizen in the State.

History indicates, however, that many States have deviated, to a greater or lesser degree, from the equal-population principle in the apportionment of seats in at least one house of their legislatures. So long as the divergences from a strict population standard are based on legitimate considerations incident to the effectuation of a rational state policy, some deviations from the equal-population principle are constitutionally permissible with respect to the apportionment of seats in either or both of the two houses of a bicameral state legislature. But neither history alone, nor economic or other sorts of group interests, are permissible factors in attempting to justify disparities from population-based representations. Citizens, not history or economic interests, cast votes. Considerations of area alone provide an insufficient justification for deviations from the equal-population principle. Again, people, not land or trees or pastures, vote. Modern developments and improvements in transportation and communications make rather hollow, in the mid-1960's, most claims that deviations from population-based representation can validly be based solely on geographical considerations. Arguments for allowing such deviations in order to insure effective representation for sparsely settled areas and to prevent legislative districts from becoming so large that the availability of access of citizens to their representatives is impaired are today, for the most part, unconvincing.

A consideration that appears to be of more substance in justifying some deviations from population-based representation in state legislatures is that of insuring some voice to political subdivisions, as political subdivisions. Several factors make more than insubstantial claims that a State can rationally consider according political subdivisions some independent representation in at least one body of the state legislature, as long as the basic standard of equality of population among districts is maintained. Local governmental entities are frequently charged with various responsibilities incident to the operation of state government. In many States much of the legislature's activity involves the enactment of so-called local legislation, directed only to the concerns of particular political subdivisions. And a State may legitimately desire to construct districts along political subdivision lines to deter the possibilities of gerrymandering. However, permitting deviations from population-based representation does not mean that each local governmental unit or political subdivision can be given separate representation, regardless of population. Carried too far, a scheme of giving at least one seat in one house to each political subdivision (for example, to each county) could easily result, in many States, in a total subversion of the equal-population principle in that legislative body. This would be especially true in a State where the number of counties is large and many of them are sparsely populated, and the number of seats in the legislative body being apportioned does not significantly exceed the number of counties. Such a result, we conclude, would be constitutionally impermissible. And careful judicial scrutiny must of course be given, in evaluating state apportionment schemes, to the character as well as the degree of deviations from a strict population basis. But if, even as a result of a clearly rational state policy of according some legislative representation to political subdivisions, population is submerged as the controlling consideration in the apportionment of seats in the particular legislative body, then the right of all of the State's citizens to cast an effective and adequately weighted vote would be unconstitutionally impaired.

One of the arguments frequently offered as a basis for upholding a State's legislative apportionment arrangement, despite substantial disparities from a population basis in either or both houses, is grounded on congressional approval, incident to admitting States into the Union, of state apportionment plans containing deviations from the equal-population principle. Proponents of this argument contend that congressional approval of such schemes, despite their disparities from population-based representation, indicates that such arrangements are plainly sufficient as establishing a "republican form of government." As we stated in *Baker* v. *Carr,* some questions raised under the Guaranty Clause are nonjusticiable, where "political" in nature and where there is a clear absence of judicially manageable standards. Nevertheless, it is not inconsistent with this view to hold that, despite congressional approval of state legislative apportionment plans at the time of admission into the Union, even though deviating from the equal-population principle here enunciated, the Equal Protection Clause can and does require more. And an apportionment scheme in which both houses are based on population can hardly be considered as failing to satisfy the Guaranty Clause requirement. Congress presumably does not assume, in admitting States into the Union, to pass on all constitutional questions relating to the character of state governmental organization. In any event, congressional approval, however well-considered, could hardly validate an unconstitutional state legislative apportionment. Congress simply lacks the constitutional power to insulate States from attack with respect to alleged deprivations of individual constitutional rights.

That the Equal Protection Clause requires that both houses of a state legislature be apportioned on a population basis does not mean that States cannot adopt some reasonable plan for periodic revision of their apportionment schemes. Decennial reapportionment appears to be a rational approach to readjustment of legislative representation in order to take into account population shifts and growth. Reallocation of legislative seats every 10 years coincides with the prescribed practice in 41 of the States, often honored more in the breach than the observance, however. Illustratively, the Alabama Constitution requires decennial reapportionment, yet the last reapportionment of the Alabama Legislature, when this suit was brought, was in 1901. Limitations on the frequency of reapportionment are justified by the need for stability and continuity in the organization of the legislative system, although undoubtedly reapportioning no more frequently than every 10 years leads to some imbalance in the population of districts toward the end of the decennial period and also to the development of resistance to change on the part of some incumbent legislators. In substance, we do not regard the Equal Protection Clause as requiring daily, monthly, annual or biennial reapportionment, so long as a State has a reasonably conceived plan for periodic readjustment of legislative representation. While we do not intend to indicate that decennial reapportionment is a constitutional requisite, compliance with such an approach would clearly meet their minimal requirements for maintaining a reasonably current scheme of legislative representation. And we do not mean to intimate that more frequent reapportionment would not be constitutionally permissible or practicably desirable. But if reapportionment were accomplished with less frequency, it would assuredly be constitutionally suspect.

. . . .

. . . [We] affirm the judgment below and remand the cases for further proceedings consistent with the views stated in this opinion.

It is so ordered.

MR. JUSTICE CLARK, concurring in the affirmance.

The Court goes much beyond the necessities of this case in laying down a new "equal population" principle for state legislative apportionment. This principle seems to be an offshoot of *Gray* v. *Sanders* (1963), *i.e.,* "one person, one vote," modified by the "nearly as is practicable" admonition of *Wesberry* v. *Sanders,* 376 U.S. 1, 8 (1964). Whether "nearly as is practicable" means "one person, one vote" qualified by "approximately equal" or "some deviations" or by the impossibility of "mathematical nicety" is not clear from the majority's use of these vague and meaningless phrases. But whatever the standard, the Court applies it to each house of the State Legislature.

It seems to me that all the Court need say in this case is that each plan considered by the trial court is "a crazy quilt," clearly revealing invidious discrimination in each house of the Legislature and therefore violative of the Equal Protection Clause.

I, therefore, do not reach the question of the so-called "federal analogy." But in my view, if one house of the State Legislature meets the population standard, representation in the other house might include some departure from it so as to take into account, on a rational basis, other factors in order to afford some representation to the various elements of the State.

MR. JUSTICE STEWART, concurring in part.

All of the parties have agreed with the District Court's findings that legislative inaction for some 60 years in the face of growth and shifts in population has converted Alabama's legislative apportionment plan enacted in 1901 into one completely lacking in rationality. Accordingly, . . . I would affirm the judgment of the District Court holding that this apportionment violated the Equal Protection Clause.

I also agree with the Court that it was proper for the District Court, in framing a remedy, to adhere as closely as practicable to the apportionments approved by the representatives of the people of Alabama, and to afford the State of Alabama full opportunity, consistent with the requirements of the Federal Constitution, to devise its own system of legislative apportionment.

MR. JUSTICE HARLAN, dissenting.

In these cases the Court holds that seats in the legislatures of six States are apportioned in ways that violate the Federal Constitution. Under the Court's ruling it is bound to follow that the legislatures in all but a few of the other 44 States will meet the same fate. These decisions . . . have the effect of placing basic aspects of state political systems under the pervasive overlordship of the federal judiciary. Once again, I must register my protest. . . .

. . . What is done today deepens my conviction that judicial entry into this realm is profoundly ill-advised and constitutionally impermissible. . . . I believe that the vitality of our political system, on which in the last analysis all else depends, is weakened by reliance on the judiciary for political reform; in time a complacent body politic may result.

These decisions also cut deeply into the fabric of our federalism. What must follow from them may eventually appear to be the product of State Legislatures. Nevertheless, no thinking person can fail to recognize that the aftermath of these cases, however desirable it may be thought in itself, will have been achieved at the cost of a radical alteration in the relationship between the States and the Federal Government, more particularly the Federal Judiciary. Only one who has an overbearing impatience with the federal system and its political processes will believe that that cost was not too high or was inevitable.

Finally, these decisions give support to a current mistaken view of the Constitution and the constitutional function of this Court. This view, in a nutshell, is that every major social ill in this country can find its cure in some constitutional "principle," and that this Court should "take the lead" in promoting reform when other branches of government fail to act. The Constitution is not a panacea for every blot upon the public welfare, nor should this Court, ordained as a judicial body, be thought of as a general haven for reform movements. The Constitution is an instrument of government, fundamental to which is the premise that in a diffusion of governmental authority lies the greatest promise that this Nation will realize liberty for all its citizens. This Court, limited in function in accordance with that premise, does not serve its high purpose when it exceeds its authority, even to satisfy justified impatience with the slow workings of the political process. For when, in the name of constitutional interpretation, the Court *adds* something to the Constitution that was deliberately excluded from it, the Court in reality substitutes its view of what should be so for the amending process.

I dissent in each of these cases, believing that in none of them have the plaintiffs stated a cause of action. To the extent that *Baker* v. *Carr*, expressly or by implication, went beyond a discussion of jurisdictional doctrines independent of the substantive issues involved here, it should be limited to what it in fact was: an experiment in venturesome constitutionalism. . . .

Mahan v. Howell

410 U.S. 315 (1973)
Vote: 5–3

In a series of cases after BAKER V. CARR, 369 U.S. 186 (1962), and REYNOLDS V. SIMS, 377 U.S. 533 (1964), the Court continued to elaborate on its one person, one vote doctrine. In doing so, it appeared to be developing a position of ever-increasing precision for constructing legislative districts. Along the way, it emphatically rejected the federal analogy that would allow at least one house of a state legislature to be based upon geographical representation (*Lucas* v. *44th*

General Assembly, 377 U.S. 713, 1964), a decision which at the time was widely interpreted to mean that lines based upon traditional units of government would have to be abandoned if they could not accommodate the equal population principle. An important statement of this development was *Kirkpatrick* v. *Preisler,* 494 U.S. 526 (1969), in which the Court overturned a congressional redistricting plan which had allowed a maximum deviation in population of only 6.8 percent.

In the case below, the district court invalidated Virginia's state legislative reapportionment plan, which in part had recognized county lines at the expense of strict population equality. (The plan resulted in a maximum deviation between the largest and smallest districts of 16 percent.) In devising its own reapportionment plan, the district court was guided by *Kirkpatrick.* The district court's ruling and plan was appealed by the state.

The opinion below represents a marvelous example of "distinguishing." Rather than view the Court's reapportionment decisions as a single line of increasingly precise rulings, the majority here reaches into the air, divides the Court's prior rulings into those dealing with congressional districts and those dealing with state and local legislative districts, and then reaches back to the early landmark case of REYNOLDS V. SIMS to extract language that supports something less rigorous that pure population equality for *state* legislative districts. There the Court spoke of "*substantial*" equality and votes of citizens of "*approximately*" equal weight" (emphasis added).

In his opinion for the majority, then-Justice Rehnquist states (creates?) a (new?) principle: the Court will be more tolerant of deviation from the equal population principle in state legislative districts than in congressional legislative districts. Contrast this with the dissenters' position, which recognizes no such distinction between state legislative and congressional districts. Which side do you agree with? Why? If you accept the majority's position, how much leeway from population equality does the Constitution tolerate? Recall that the Court's decisions have held that the Fourteenth

Amendment bans the "federal analogy" for representation in state legislatures. What *principle* of representation can you discover in Justice Rehnquist's opinion? While the principle held by the dissenters may be easier to identify and articulate, we can still ask how equal "equal" must be. Note, for instance, that the census is taken only every ten years, and that we live in a mobile society. Also, even in the census, there is a generally recognized margin of error. Similarly, in some districts a substantial population is highly fluid; for example, around universities, military bases, and winter vacation areas. In other areas, a higher-than-average portion of the population is under the voting age. Are such factors relevant?

Since he has consistently opposed the Court's approach to reapportionment, the distinction articulated by Justice Rehnquist may merely be a strategic ploy in a general assault on the equal population principle. In 1973, he joined in a decision to overturn a congressional reapportionment plan on the basis of the *Kirkpatrick* precedent, but in a concurring opinion he indicated he did so reluctantly, and that had he been on the Court at the time *Kirkpatrick* was decided, he would have dissented. In *Mahan*, Rehnquist finally may have found the majority he desired to begin his long-planned assault on the principle. And since then he has been consistent in his efforts. In 1984, he abandoned the reserve expressed in 1973, and dissented in a congressional redistricting case which the majority thought was covered by *Kirkpatrick* (*Karcher* v. *Dagget*, 103 S.Ct. 2653, 1983). In a companion case, Rehnquist wrote the majority opinion upholding a state legislative districting plan upon the strength of *Mahan,* which recognized county lines and permitted a maximum variation between the largest and smallest districts of 89 percent (*Brown* v. *Thompson*, 103 S.Ct. 2690, 1983).

Both these 1983 decisions were decided by votes of 5 to 4, with Justice Sandra Day O'Connor casting the pivotal vote with the liberal remnant of the *Mahan* minority to overturn the congressional districting plan, but then abandoning them to join with Justice Rehnquist and a conservative bloc to uphold Wyoming's state districting plan. Thus we see that despite the two principles — one for state legislatures, one for congressional districts — Justice Rehnquist is consistent in his opposition to the population principle across the board. In contrast, other justices are equally consistent in their embrace of a single principle. Perhaps only Justice O'Connor really believes in the two-principle approach to reapportionment.

MR. JUSTICE REHNQUIST delivered the opinion of the Court.

The statute apportioning the House provided for a combination of 52 single-member, multimember, and floater delegate districts from which 100 delegates would be elected. As found by the lower court, the ideal district in Virginia consisted of 46,485 persons per delegate, and the maximum percentage variation from that ideal under the Act was 16.4%, . . . the 12th district being overrepresented by 6.8% and the 16th district being underrepresented by 9.6%. The population ratio between these two districts was 1.18 to 1. The average percentage variance under the plan was ±3.89%, and the minimum population percentage necessary to elect a majority of the House was 49.29%. Of the 52 districts, 35 were within 4% of perfection and nine exceeded a 6% variance from the ideal. With one exception, the delegate districts followed political jurisdictional lines of the counties and cities. That exception, Fairfax County, was allotted 10 delegates but was divided into two five-member districts.

Relying on *Kirkpatrick* v. *Preisler* (1969); *Wells* v. *Rockefeller* (1969), and *Reynolds* v. *Sims* (1964), the District Court concluded that the 16.4% variation was sufficient to condemn the House statute under the "one person, one vote" doctrine. While it noted that the variances were traceable to the desire of the General Assembly to maintain the integrity of traditional county and city boundaries, and that it was impossible to draft district lines to overcome unconstitutional disparities and still maintain such integrity, it held that the State proved no governmental necessity for strictly adhering to political subdivision lines. Accordingly, it undertook its own redistricting and devised a plan having a percentage variation of slightly over 10% from the ideal district, a percentage it believed came "within passable constitutional limits as 'a good-faith effort to achieve absolute equality.' *Kirkpatrick* v. *Preisler*. . . ."

Appellants contend that the District Court's reliance on *Kirkpatrick* v. *Preisler, supra,* and *Wells* v.

Rockefeller, supra, in striking down the General Assembly's reapportionment plan was erroneous, and that proper application of the standards enunciated in *Reynolds* v. *Sims, supra,* would have resulted in a finding that the statute was constitutional.

In *Kirkpatrick* v. *Preisler* and *Wells* v. *Rockefeller,* this Court invalidated state reapportionment statutes for federal congressional districts having maximum percentage deviations of 5.97% and 13.1% respectively. The express purpose of these cases was to elucidate the standard first announced in the holding of *Wesberry* v. *Sanders* (1964), that "the command of Art. I, §2, that Representatives be chosen 'by the People of the several States' means that as nearly as is practicable one man's vote in a congressional election is to be worth as much as another's." And it was concluded that that command "permits only the limited population variances which are unavoidable despite a good faith effort to achieve absolute equality, or for which justification is shown." The principal question thus presented for review is whether or not the Equal Protection Clause of the Fourteenth Amendment likewise permits only "the limited population variances which are unavoidable despite a good faith effort to achieve absolute equality" in the context of state legislative reapportionment.

This Court first recognized that the Equal Protection Clause requires both houses of a bicameral state legislature to be apportioned substantially on a population basis in *Reynolds* v. *Sims, supra.* In so doing, it suggested that in the implementation of the basic constitutional principle — equality of population among the districts — more flexibility was constitutionally permissible with respect to state legislative reapportionment than in congressional redistricting. Consideration was given to the fact that, almost invariably, there is a significantly larger number of seats in state legislative bodies to be distributed within a state than congressional seats, and that therefore it may be feasible for a State to use political subdivision lines to a greater extent in establishing state legislative districts than congressional districts while still affording adequate statewide representation. Another possible justification for deviation from population-based representation in state legislatures was stated to be:

> [T]hat of insuring some voice to political subdivisions, as political subdivisions. Several factors make more than insubstantial claims that a State can rationally consider according political subdivisions some independent representation in at least one body of the state legislature, as long as the basic standard of

equality of population among districts is maintained. Local governmental entities are frequently charged with various responsibilities incident to the operation of state government. In many States much of the legislature's activity involves the enactment of so-called local legislation, directed only to the concerns of particular political subdivisions. And a State may legitimately desire to construct districts along political subdivision lines to deter the possibilities of gerrymandering. . . .

The Court reiterated that the overriding objective in reapportionment must be "substantial equality of population among the various districts, so that the vote of any citizen is approximately equal in weight to that of any other citizen in the state."

By contrast, the Court in *Wesberry* v. *Sanders,* recognized no excuse for the failure to meet the objective of equal representation for equal numbers of people in congressional districting other than the practical impossibility of drawing equal districts with mathematical precision. Thus, whereas population alone has been the sole criterion of constitutionality in congressional redistricting under Art. I, §2, broader latitude has been afforded the States under the Equal Protection Clause in state legislative redistricting because of the considerations enumerated in *Reynolds* v. *Sims, supra.* The dichotomy between the two lines of cases has consistently been maintained. In *Kirkpatrick* v. *Preisler,* for example, one asserted justification for population variances was that they were necessarily a result of the State's attempt to avoid fragmenting political subdivisions by drawing congressional district lines along existing political subdivision boundaries. This argument was rejected in the congressional context. But in *Abate* v. *Mundt* (1971), an apportionment for a county legislature having a maximum deviation from equality of 11.9% was upheld in the face of an equal protection challenge, in part because New York had a long history of maintaining the integrity of existing local government units within the county.

Application of the "absolute equality" test of *Kirkpatrick* and *Wells* to state legislative redistricting may impair the normal functioning of state and local governments. Such an effect is readily apparent from an analysis of the District Court's plan in this case. Under Art. VII, §§2 and 3 of Virginia's Constitution, the General Assembly is given extensive power to enact special legislation regarding the organization of, and the exercise of governmental powers by, counties, cities, towns, and other political subdivisions. The statute redistricting the House of Delegates consistently sought to avoid the fragmentation of such subdivisions, assertedly to afford them a voice in Richmond to seek such local legislation.

....

We conclude, therefore, that the constitutionality of Virginia's legislative redistricting plan was not to be judged by the more stringent standards that *Kirkpatrick* and *Wells* make applicable to congressional reapportionment, but instead by the equal protection test enunciated in *Reynolds* v. *Sims, supra*. We reaffirm its holding that "the Equal Protection Clause requires that a State make an honest and good faith effort to construct districts, in both houses of its legislature, as nearly of equal population as is practicable."... We likewise reaffirm its conclusion that "[s]o long as the divergences from a strict population standard are based on legitimate considerations incident to the effectuation of a rational state policy, some deviations from the equal-population principle are constitutionally permissible with respect to the apportionment of seats in either or both of the two houses of a bicameral state legislature."

The asserted justification for the divergences in this case — the State's policy of maintaining the integrity of political subdivision lines — is not a new one to this Court.

....

We are not prepared to say that the decision of the people of Virginia to grant the General Assembly the power to enact local legislation dealing with the political subdivisions is irrational. And if that be so, the decision of the General Assembly to provide representation to subdivisions *qua* subdivisions in order to implement that constitutional power is likewise valid when measured against the Equal Protection Clause of the Fourteenth Amendment. The inquiry then becomes whether it can reasonably be said that the state policy urged by Virginia to justify the divergences in the legislative reapportionment plan of the House is, indeed, furthered by the plan adopted by the legislature, and whether, if so justified, the divergences are also within tolerable limits. For a State's policy urged in justification of disparity in district population, however rational, cannot constitutionally be permitted to emasculate the goal of substantial equality.

There was uncontradicted evidence offered in the District Court to the effect that the legislature's plan, subject to minor qualifications, "produces the minimum deviation above and below the norm, keeping intact political boundaries...." That court itself recognized that equality was impossible if political boundaries were to be kept intact in the process of districting. But it went on to hold that since the State "proved no governmental necessity for strictly

adhering to political subdivision lines," the legislative plan was constitutionally invalid. As we noted above, however, the proper equal protection test is not framed in terms of "governmental necessity," but instead in terms of a claim that a State may "rationally consider."

....

Appellees argue that the traditional adherence to such lines is no longer a justification since the Virginia constitutional provision regarding reapportionment, ... neither specifically provides for apportionment along political subdivision lines nor draws a distinction between the standards for congressional and legislative districting. The standard in each case is described in the "as nearly as is practicable" language used in *Wesberry* v. *Sanders, supra*, and *Reynolds* v. *Sims, supra*. But, as we have previously indicated, the latitude afforded to States in legislative redistricting is somewhat broader than that afforded to them in congressional redistricting. Virginia was free as a matter of federal constitutional law to construe the mandate of its Constitution more liberally in the case of legislative redistricting than in the case of congressional redistricting, and the plan adopted by the legislature indicates that it has done so.

We also reject the argument that, because the State is not adhering to its tradition of respecting the boundaries of political subdivisions in congressional and State Senate redistricting, it may not do so in the case of redistricting for the House of Delegates. Nothing in the fact that Virginia has followed the constitutional mandate of this Court in the case of congressional redistricting, or that it has chosen in some instances to ignore political subdivision lines in the case of the State Senate, detracts from the validity of its consistently applied policy to have at least one house of its bicameral legislature responsive to voters of political subdivisions as such.

We hold that the legislature's plan for apportionment of the House of Delegates may reasonably be said to advance the rational state policy of respecting the boundaries of political subdivisions. The remaining inquiry is whether the population of disparities among the districts that have resulted from the pursuit of this plan exceed constitutional limits. We conclude that they do not.

....

Neither courts nor legislatures are furnished any specialized calipers that enable them to extract from the general language of the Equal Protection Clause of the Fourteenth Amendment the mathematical formula that establishes what range of percentage deviations is permissible, and what is not. The 16-odd percent maximum deviation that the District Court found to exist in the legislative plan for the reapportionment of the House is substantially less than the percentage deviations that have been found invalid in the previous decisions of this Court. While this percentage may well approach tolerable limits, we do not believe it exceeds them. Virginia has not sacrificed substantial equality to justifiable deviations.

The policy of maintaining the integrity of political subdivision lines in the process of reapportioning a state legislature, the policy consistently advanced by Virginia as a justification for disparities in population among districts that elect members to the House of Delegates, is a rational one. It can reasonably be said, upon examination of the legislative plan, that it does in fact advance that policy. The population disparities that are permitted thereunder result in a maximum percentage deviation that we hold to be within tolerable constitutional limits. We, therefore, hold the General Assembly's plan for the reapportionment of the House of Delegates constitutional and reverse the District Court's conclusion to the contrary.

. . . .

Affirmed in part, reversed in part.

MR. JUSTICE POWELL took no part in the consideration or decision of these cases.

MR. JUSTICE BRENNAN, with whom MR. JUSTICE DOUGLAS and MR. JUSTICE MARSHALL join, concurring in part and dissenting in part.

The holdings of our prior decisions can be restated in two unequivocal propositions. First, the paramount goal of reapportionment must be the drawing of district lines so as to achieve precise equality in the population of each district. "[T]he Equal Protection Clause requires that a State make an honest and good faith effort to construct districts, in both houses of its legislature, as nearly of equal population as is practicable." *Reynolds* v. *Sims;* see also *Kirkpatrick* v. *Preisler.* The Constitution does not permit a State to relegate considerations of equality to secondary status and reserve as the primary goal of apportionment the service of some other state interest.

Second, it is open to the State, in the event that it should fail to achieve the goal of population equality, to attempt to justify its failure by demonstrating that precise equality could not be achieved without jeopardizing some critical governmental interest. The Equal Protection Clause does not exalt the principle of equal representation to the point of nullifying every competing interest of the State. But we have held firmly to the view that variations in weight accorded each vote can be approved only where the State meets its burden of presenting cogent reasons

in explanation of the variations, and even then only where the variations are small. See, *e.g., Abate* v. *Mundt* (1971); *Kirkpatrick* v. *Preisler, Swann* v. *Adams.*

The validity of these propositions and their applicability to the case before us are not at all diminished by the fact that *Kirkpatrick* v. *Preisler* and *Wells* v. *Rockefeller* (1969) — two of the many cases in which the propositions were refined and applied — concerned the division of States into federal congressional districts rather than legislative reapportionment. Prior to today's decision, we have never held that different constitutional *standards* are applicable to the two situations. True, there are significant differences between congressional districting and legislative apportionment, and we have repeatedly recognized those differences. In *Reynolds* v. *Sims,* for example, we termed "more than insubstantial" the argument that "a State can rationally consider according political subdivisions some independent representation in at least one body of the state legislature, as long as the basic standard of equality of population among districts is maintained." But the recognition of these differences is hardly tantamount to the establishment of two distinct controlling standards. What our decisions have made clear is that certain state interests that are pertinent to legislative reapportionment can have no possible relevance to congressional districting. Thus, the need to preserve the integrity of political subdivisions as political subdivisions may, in some instances, justify small variations in the population of districts from which state legislators are elected. But that interest can hardly be asserted in justification of malapportioned congressional districts. *Kirkpatrick* v. *Preisler, supra.* While the State may have a broader range of interests to which it can point in attempting to justify a failure to achieve precise equality in the context of legislative apportionment, it by no means follows that the State is subject to a lighter burden of proof or that the controlling constitutional standard is in any sense distinguishable.

Our concern in *Kirkpatrick* v. *Preisler* was with the constitutional requirement that "as nearly as is practicable one man's vote in a congressional election is to be worth as much as another's." We rejected the State's argument that "there is a fixed numerical or percentage population variance small enough to be considered *de minimis* and to satisfy without question the 'as nearly as practicable' standard. . . . Since 'equal representation for equal numbers of people [is] the fundamental goal for the House of Representatives,' the 'as nearly as practicable' standard requires that the State make a good-faith effort to achieve precise mathematical equality. . . ."

Moreover, we held... that "[i]t was the burden of the State 'to present... acceptable reasons for the variations among the populations of the various... districts....'"

The principles that undergirded our decision in *Kirkpatrick* v. *Preisler* are the very principles that supported our decision in *Swann* v. *Adams,* a case involving the apportionment of a state legislature. The opinion in *Kirkpatrick* does not suggest that a different standard might be applicable to congressional districting. On the contrary, the "as nearly as practicable" standard with which we were concerned is identical to the standard that *Reynolds* v. *Sims* specifically made applicable to controversies over state legislative apportionment. And the holding in *Kirkpatrick* that the State must bear the burden of justifying deviations from population equality not only rested squarely and exclusively on our holding in *Swann* v. *Adams,* but even defined the test by quotation from *Swann.*

In *Swann* v. *Adams* we held that variations in the population of legislative districts must be justified by the State by presentation of "acceptable reasons for the variations." And a comparison of the opinion for the Court in *Swann* with the views expressed by two Justices in dissent decisively refutes any suggestion that unequal representation will be upheld so long as some rational basis for the discrimination can be found. A showing of necessity, not rationality, is what our decision in *Swann* requires.

... [E]ven assuming that the Commonwealth's plan can be considered free of any "taint of arbitrariness or discrimination," appellants have failed to meet their burden of justifying the inequalities. They insist that the legislature has followed a consistent practice of drawing district lines in conformity with county boundaries. But a showing that a State has followed such a practice is still a long step from the necessary showing that the State *must* follow that practice. Neither in the Virginia Constitution nor in any Act of the Assembly has Virginia explicitly indicated any interest in preserving the integrity of county lines or in providing representation of political subdivisions as political subdivisions. On the contrary, the Constitution establishes a single standard for both legislative apportionment and congressional districting, and that standard requires only that lines be drawn so as to insure, "as nearly as is practicable," representation in proportion to population. And the origins of the constitutional provision make clear that equality in district population, not the representation of political subdivisions, is the Commonwealth's pre-eminent goal.

Moreover, in asserting its interest in preserving the integrity of county boundaries, the Commonwealth offers nothing more than vague references to "local legislation," without describing such legislation with precision, without indicating whether such legislation amounts to a significant proportion of the legislature's business, and without demonstrating that the District Court's plan would materially affect the treatment of such legislation.

. . . .

... [T]he best that can be said of appellant's efforts to secure county representation is that the plan can be effective only with respect to some unspecified but in all likelihood small number of issues that affect a single county and that are overwhelmingly important to the voters of that county; and even then it provides effective representation only where the affected county represents a large enough percentage of the voters in the district to have a significant impact on the election of the delegate. But even if county representation were, in fact, a strong and legitimate goal of the Commonwealth, and even if the 1971 plan did represent a rational effort to serve that goal, it is still not clear that the legislature's plan should be upheld. The plan prepared by the District Court would achieve a much higher degree of equality in district population, and it would accomplish that salutary goal with minimal disruption of the legislature's effort to avoid fragmenting counties. Of the 134 political subdivisions in the Commonwealth, only 12 would be divided by the District Court's plan. More significant, the number of persons resident in voting districts that would be cut out of one county or city and shifted to another is 64,738, out of the total state population of 4,648,494. Thus, even making each of the logical and empirical assumptions implicit in the view that violating county lines would effectively disenfranchise certain persons on certain local issues, the number of persons affected would still be less than 1½% of the total state population.

On this record — without any showing of the specific need for county representation or a showing of how such representation can be meaningfully provided to small counties whose votes would be submerged in a multicounty district — I see no basis whatsoever for upholding the Assembly's 1971 plan and the resulting substantial variations in district population. Accordingly, I would affirm the judgment of the District Court holding the plan invalid under the Equal Protection Clause of the Fourteenth Amendment.

Korematsu v. U.S.

323 U.S. 214 (1944)
See pp. 156–160.

San Antonio Independent School District v. Rodriguez

411 U.S. 1 (1973)
Vote: 5–4

In Texas, as in most other states, public schools are financed through a combination of revenue from local property taxes and direct grants from the state. Typically, state aid is designed to help equalize variations in per-pupil expenditures caused by differences in the local tax base. This was one of the objectives in the state aid formula in Texas at the time of this suit. Still, it was revealed that the amount of taxable property varied so greatly from district to district that, despite the state aid, there were gross disparities in local per-pupil expenditures. Indeed, in some instances, even though districts poor in terms of total aggregate taxable wealth were taxed at a rate twice as high as wealthier districts, they could only raise half as much money per pupil as the wealthy districts. Because of the continued inequalities of resources available to local schools, parents in a poor school district filed suit in federal district court claiming that the state's school financing scheme was unconstitutional. They won their case in the district court, whereupon the state appealed.

MR. JUSTICE POWELL delivered the opinion of the Court.

Texas virtually concedes that its historically rooted dual system of financing education could not withstand the strict judicial scrutiny that this Court has found appropriate in reviewing legislative judgments that interfere with fundamental constitutional rights or that involve suspect classifications. If, as previous decisions have indicated, strict scrutiny means that the State's system is not entitled to the usual presumption of validity, that the State rather than the complainants must carry a "heavy burden of justification," that the State must demonstrate that its educational system has been structured with "precision" and is "tailored" narrowly to serve legitimate objectives and that it has selected the "least drastic means" for effectuating its objectives, the Texas financing system and its counterpart in virtually every other State will not pass muster. The State candidly admits that "[n]o one familiar with the

Texas system would contend that it has yet achieved perfection." Apart from its concession that educational finance in Texas has "defects" and "imperfections," the State defends the system's rationality with vigor and disputes the District Court's finding that it lacks a "reasonable basis."

This, then, establishes the framework for our analysis. We must decide, first, whether the Texas system of financing public education operates to the disadvantage of some suspect class or impinges upon a fundamental right explicitly or implicitly protected by the Constitution, thereby requiring strict judicial scrutiny. If so, the judgment of the District Court should be affirmed. If not, the Texas scheme must still be examined to determined whether it rationally furthers some legitimate, articulated state purpose and therefore does not constitute an invidious discrimination. . . .

The District Court's opinion does not reflect the novelty and complexity of the constitutional questions posed by appellees' challenge to Texas' system of school finance. In concluding that strict judicial scrutiny was required, that court relied on decisions dealing with the rights of indigents to equal treatment in the criminal trial and appellate processes, and on cases disapproving wealth restrictions on the right to vote. Those cases, the District Court concluded, established wealth as a suspect classification. Finding that the local property tax system discriminated on the basis of wealth, it regarded those precedents as controlling. It then reasoned, based on decisions of this Court affirming the undeniable importance of education, that there is a fundamental right to education and that, absent some compelling state justification, the Texas system could not stand.

We are unable to agree that this case, which in significant aspects is *sui generis,* may be so neatly fitted into the conventional mosaic of constitutional analysis under the Equal Protection Clause. Indeed, for the several reasons that follow, we find neither the suspect classification nor the fundamental interest analysis persuasive.

The wealth discrimination discovered by the District Court in this case . . . is quite unlike any of the forms of wealth discrimination heretofore reviewed by this Court. . . .

. . . .

. . . The individuals or groups of individuals who constituted the class discriminated against in our prior cases shared two distinguishing characteristics: because of their impecunity they were completely unable to pay for some desired benefit, and as a consequence, they sustained an absolute deprivation of a meaningful opportunity to enjoy that benefit. In *Griffin* v. *Illinois* (1956), and its progeny, the Court invalidated state laws that prevented an indigent criminal defendant from acquiring a transcript, or an adequate substitute for a transcript, for use at several stages of the trial and appeal process. The payment requirements in each case were found to occasion *de facto* discrimination against those who, because of their indigency, were totally unable to pay for transcripts. And, the Court in each case emphasized that no constitutional violation would have been shown if the State had provided some "adequate substitute" for a full stenographic transcript. . . .

Likewise, in *Douglas* v. *California* (1963), a decision establishing an indigent defendant's right to court-appointed counsel on direct appeal, the Court dealt only with defendants who could not pay for counsel from their own resources and who had no other way of gaining representation. *Douglas* provides no relief for those on whom the burdens of paying for a criminal defense are, relatively speaking, great but not insurmountable. Nor does it deal with relative differences in the quality of counsel acquired by the less wealthy.

. . . .

. . . Even a cursory examination, however, demonstrates that neither of the two distinguishing characteristics of wealth classifications can be found here. First, in support of their charge that the system discriminates against the "poor," appellees have made no effort to demonstrate that it operates to the peculiar disadvantage of any class fairly definable as indigent, or as composed of persons whose incomes are beneath any designated poverty level. Indeed, there is reason to believe that the poorest families are not necessarily clustered in the poorest property districts. . . .

Second, neither appellees nor the District Court addressed the fact that, unlike each of the foregoing cases, lack of personal resources has not occasioned an absolute deprivation of the desired benefit. The argument here is not that the children in districts having relatively low assessable property values are receiving no public education; rather, it is that they are receiving a poorer quality education than that available to children in districts having more assessable wealth. Apart from the unsettled and disputed question whether the quality of education may be determined by the amount of money expended for it, a sufficient answer to appellees' argument is that at least where wealth is involved the Equal Protection Clause does not require absolute equality or precisely equal advantages. . . .

For these two reasons—the absence of any evidence that the financing system discriminates against any definable category of "poor" people or that it results in the absolute deprivation of education—the

disadvantaged class is not susceptible to identification in traditional terms.

. . . .

We thus conclude that the Texas system does not operate to the peculiar disadvantage of any suspect class. But in recognition of the fact that this Court has never heretofore held that wealth discrimination alone provides an adequate basis for invoking strict scrutiny, appellees have not relied solely on this contention. They also assert that the State's system impermissibly interferes with the exercise of a "fundamental" right and that accordingly the prior decisions of this Court require the application of the strict standard of judicial review. . . . *Shapiro* v. *Thompson* (1969). It is this question—whether education is a fundamental right, in the sense that it is among the rights and liberties protected by the Constitution—which has so consumed the attention of courts and commentators in recent years.

In *Brown* v. *Board of Education* (1954), a unanimous Court recognized that "education is perhaps the most important function of state and local governments." . . . This theme, expressing an abiding respect for the vital role of education in a free society, may be found in numerous opinions of Justices of this Court writing both before and after *Brown* was decided.

Nothing this Court holds today in any way detracts from our historic dedication to public education. But the importance of a service performed by the State does not determine whether it must be regarded as fundamental for purposes of examination under the Equal Protection Clause. . . .

Lindsey v. *Normet* (1972), decided only last Term, firmly reiterates that social importance is not the critical determinant for subjecting state legislation to strict scrutiny. The complainants in that case, involving a challenge to the procedural limitations imposed on tenants in suits brought by landlords under Oregon's Forcible Entry and Wrongful Detainer Law, urged the Court to examine the operation of the statute under "a more stringent standard than mere rationality." . . . The tenants argued that the statutory limitations implicated "fundamental interests which are particularly important to the poor," such as the "need for decent shelter" and the "right to retain peaceful possession of one's home." MR. JUSTICE WHITE's analysis, in his opinion for the Court, is instructive:

> We do not denigrate the importance of decent, safe, and sanitary housing. But the Constitution does not provide judicial remedies for every social and economic ill. We are unable to perceive in that document any

constitutional guarantee of access to dwellings of a particular quality or any recognition of the right of a tenant to occupy the real property of his landlord beyond the term of his lease, without the payment of rent. . . . *Absent constitutional mandate,* the assurance of adequate housing and the definition of landlord-tenant relationships are legislative, not judicial, functions.

Similarly, in *Dandridge* v. *Williams* . . . (1970), the Court's explicit recognition of the fact that the "administration of public welfare assistance . . . involves the most basic economic needs of impoverished human beings." . . . provided no basis for departing from the settled mode of constitutional analysis of legislative classifications involving questions of economic and social policy. As in the case of housing, the central importance of welfare benefits to the poor was not an adequate foundation for requiring the State to justify its law by showing some compelling state interest.

The lesson of these cases in addressing the question now before the Court is plain. It is not the province of this Court to create substantive constitutional rights in the name of guaranteeing equal protection of the laws. Thus the key to discovering whether education is "fundamental" is not to be found in comparisons of the relative societal significance of education as opposed to subsistence or housing. Nor is it to be found by weighing whether education is as important as the right to travel. Rather, the answer lies in assessing whether there is a right to education explicitly or implicitly guaranteed by the Constitution.

Education, of course, is not among the rights afforded explicit protection under our Federal Constitution. Nor do we find any basis for saying it is implicitly so protected. As we have said, the undisputed importance of education will not alone cause this Court to depart from the usual standard for reviewing a State's social and economic legislation. It is appellees' contention, however, that education is distinguishable from other services and benefits provided by the State because it bears a peculiarly close relationship to other rights and liberties accorded protection under the Constitution. Specifically, they insist that education is itself a fundamental personal right because it is essential to the effective exercise of First Amendment freedoms and to intelligent utilization of the right to vote. In asserting a nexus between speech and education, appellees urge that the right to speak is meaningless unless the speaker is capable of articulating his thoughts intelligently and persuasively. The "marketplace of ideas" is an empty forum for those lacking basic communicative tools. Likewise, they argue that the corollary right to receive information becomes little more than a hollow privilege when the recipient has not been taught to read, assimilate, and utilize available knowledge.

A similar line of reasoning is pursued with respect to the right to vote. . . .

We need not dispute any of these propositions. The Court has long afforded zealous protection against unjustifiable governmental interference with the individual's rights to speak and to vote. Yet we have never presumed to possess either the ability or the authority to guarantee to the citizenry the most *effective* speech or the most *informed* electoral choice. . . .

Even if it were conceded that some identifiable quantum of education is a constitutionally protected prerequisite to the meaningful exercise of either right, we have no indication that the present levels of educational expenditure in Texas provide an education that falls short. Whatever merit appellees' argument might have if a State's financing system occasioned an absolute denial of educational opportunities to any of its children, that argument provides no basis for finding an interference with fundamental rights where only relative differences in spending levels are involved and where — as is true in the present case — no charge fairly could be made that the system fails to provide each child with an opportunity to acquire the basic minimal skills necessary for the enjoyment of the rights of speech and of full participation in the political process.

Furthermore, the logical limitations on appellees' nexus theory are difficult to perceive. How, for instance, is education to be distinguished from the significant personal interests in the basics of decent food and shelter? Empirical examination might well buttress an assumption that the ill-fed, ill-clothed, and ill-housed are among the most ineffective participants in the political process and that they derive the least enjoyment from the benefits of the First Amendment. If so appellees' thesis would cast serious doubt on the authority of *Dandridge* v. *Williams,* . . . and *Lindsey* v. *Normet.* . . .

We have carefully considered each of the arguments supportive of the District Court's finding that education is a fundamental right or liberty and have found those arguments unpersuasive. In one further respect we find this a particularly inappropriate case in which to subject state action to strict judicial scrutiny. The present case, in another basic sense, is significantly different from any of the cases in which the Court has applied strict scrutiny to state or federal legislation touching upon constitutionally protected rights. Each of our prior cases involved legislation which "deprived," "infringed," or "interferred" with the free exercise of some such fundamental personal right or liberty. . . . A critical distinction between those cases and the one now before us lies in what Texas is endeavoring to do with respect to education. . . .

. . . Every step leading to the establishment of the system Texas utilizes today — including the decisions permitting localities to tax and expend locally, and creating and continuously expanding state aid — was implemented in an effort to *extend* public education and to improve its quality. Of course, every reform that benefits some more than others may be criticized for what it fails to accomplish. But we think it plain that, in substance, the thrust of the Texas system is affirmative and reformatory and, therefore, should be scrutinized under judicial principles sensitive to the nature of the State's efforts and to the rights reserved to the States under the Constitution.

. . . .

We need not rest our decision, however, solely on the inappropriateness of the strict scrutiny test. A century of Supreme Court adjudication under the Equal Protection Clause affirmatively supports the application of the traditional standard of review, which requires only that the State's system be shown to bear some rational relationship to legitimate state purposes. This case represents far more than a challenge to the manner in which Texas provides for the education of its children. We have here nothing less than a direct attack on the way in which Texas has chosen to raise and disburse state and local tax revenues. We are asked to condemn the State's judgment in conferring on political subdivisions the power to tax local property to supply revenues for local interests. In so doing, appellees would have the Court intrude in an area in which it has traditionally deferred to state legislatures. This Court has often admonished against such interferences with the State's fiscal policies under the Equal Protection Clause. . . .

Thus we stand on familiar ground when we continue to acknowledge that the Justices of this Court lack both the expertise and the familiarity with local problems so necessary to the making of wise decisions with respect to the raising and disposition of public revenues. Yet we are urged to direct the States either to alter drastically the present system or to throw out the property tax altogether in favor of some other form of taxation. No scheme of taxation, whether the tax is imposed on property, income, or purchases of goods and services, has yet been devised which is free of all discriminatory impact. In such a complex arena in which no perfect alternatives exist, the Court does well not to impose too rigorous a standard of scrutiny lest all local fiscal schemes become subjects of criticism under the Equal Protection Clause.

In addition to matters of fiscal policy, this case also involves the most persistent and difficult questions of educational policy, another area in which this Court's lack of specialized knowledge and experience counsels against premature interference with the informed judgments made at the state and local levels. Education, perhaps even more than welfare assistance, presents a myriad of "intractable economic, social, and even philosophical problems." The very complexity of the problems of financing and managing a statewide public school system suggest that "there will be more than one constitutionally permissible method of solving them," and that, within the limits of rationality, "the legislature's efforts to tackle the problems" should be entitled to respect. . . .

It must be remembered also that every claim arising under the Equal Protection Clause has implications for the relationship between national and state power under our federal system. Questions of federalism are always inherent in the process of determining whether a State's laws are to be accorded the traditional presumption of constitutionality, or are to be subjected instead to rigorous judicial scrutiny. . . .

The foregoing considerations buttress our conclusion that Texas' system of public school finance is an inappropriate candidate for strict judicial scrutiny. These same considerations are relevant to the determination whether that system, with its conceded imperfections, nevertheless bears some rational relationship to a legitimate state purpose. It is to this question that we next turn our attention.

. . . .

. . . Because of differences in expenditure levels occasioned by disparities in property tax income, appellees claim that children in less affluent districts have been made the subject of invidious discrimination. The District Court found that the State had failed even "to establish a reasonable basis" for a system that results in different levels of per pupil expenditure. We disagree.

. . . .

Appellees do not question the propriety of Texas' dedication to local control of education. To the contrary, they attack the school finance system precisely because, in their view, it does not provide the same level of local control and fiscal flexibility in all districts. Appellees suggest that local control could be preserved and promoted under other financing systems that resulted in more equality in educational expenditures. While it is no doubt true that reliance on local property taxation for school revenues provides less freedom of choice with respect to expenditures for some districts than for others, the existence of "some inequality" in the manner in which the State's rationale is achieved is not alone a sufficient basis for striking down the entire system. *McGowan* v. *Maryland* (1961). It may not be condemned simply because it imperfectly effectuates the State's goals. *Dandridge* v. *Williams*. Nor must the financing system fail because, as appellees suggest, other methods of satisfying the State's interest, which occasion "less drastic" disparities in expenditures, might be conceived. Only where state action impinges on the exercise of fundamental constitutional rights or liberties must it be found to have chosen the least restrictive alternative. Cf. *Dunn* v. *Blumstein* (1972); *Shelton* v. *Tucker* (1960). It is also well to remember that even those districts that have reduced ability to make free decisions with respect to how much they spend on education still retain under the present system a large measure of authority as to how available funds will be allocated....

Appellees further urge that the Texas system is unconstitutionally arbitrary because it allows the availability of local taxable resources to turn on "happenstance." They see no justification for a system that allows, as they contend, the quality of education to fluctuate on the basis of the fortuitous positioning of the boundary lines of political subdivisions and the location of valuable commercial and industrial property. But any scheme of local taxation—indeed the very existence of identifiable local governmental units—requires the establishment of jurisdictional boundaries that are inevitably arbitrary....

Moreover, if local taxation for local expenditure is an unconstitutional method of providing for education then it may be an equally impermissible means of providing other necessary services customarily financed largely from local property taxes, including local police and fire protection, public health and hospitals, and public utility facilities of various kinds. We perceive no justification for such a severe denegration of local property taxation and control as would follow from appellees' contentions. It has simply never been within the constitutional prerogative of this Court to nullify statewide measures for financing public services merely because the burdens or benefits thereof fall unevenly depending upon the relative wealth of the political subdivisions in which citizens live.

In sum, to the extent that the Texas system of school finance results in unequal expenditures between children who happen to reside in different districts, we cannot say that such disparities are the product of a system that is so irrational as to be invidiously discriminatory. Texas has acknowledged its shortcomings and has persistently endeavored—not without some success—to ameliorate the differences in levels of expenditures without sacrificing the benefits of local participation. The Texas plan is not the result of hurried, ill-conceived legislation. It certainly is not the product of purposeful discrimination against any group or class. On the contrary, it is rooted in decades of experience in Texas and elsewhere, and in major part is the product of responsible studies by qualified people. In giving substance to the presumption of validity to which the Texas system is entitled, *Lindsey* v. *National Carbonic Gas Co.* (1911), it is important to remember that at every stage of its development it has constituted a "rough accommodation" of interests in an effort to arrive at practical and workable solutions. One also must remember that the system here challenged is not peculiar to Texas or to any other State. In its essential characteristics the Texas plan for financing public education reflects what many educators for a half century have thought was an enlightened approach to a problem for which there is no perfect solution. We are unwilling to assume for ourselves a level of wisdom superior to that of legislators, scholars, and educational authorities in 49 States, especially where the alternatives proposed are only recently conceived and nowhere yet tested. The constitutional standard under the Equal Protection Clause is whether the challenged state action rationally furthers a legitimate state purpose or interest. We hold that the Texas plan abundantly satisfies this standard.

[MR. JUSTICE STEWART wrote a concurring opinion. MR. JUSTICE BRENNAN wrote a brief dissenting opinion. MR. JUSTICE WHITE, with whom MR. JUSTICE DOUGLAS and MR. JUSTICE BRENNAN joined, wrote a dissenting opinion.]

MR. JUSTICE MARSHALL, with whom MR. JUSTICE DOUGLAS concurs, dissenting.

The Court today decides, in effect, that a State may constitutionally vary the quality of education which it offers its children in accordance with the amount of taxable wealth located in the school districts within which they reside. The majority's decision represents an abrupt departure from the mainstream of recent state and federal court decisions concerning the unconstitutionality of state educational financing schemes dependent upon taxable local wealth. More unfortunately, though, the majority's holding can only be seen as a retreat from our historic commitment to equality of educational opportunity....

In my judgment, the right of every American to an equal start in life, so far as the provision of a state service as important as education is concerned, is far too vital to permit state discrimination on grounds as tenuous as those presented by this record. . . .

The Court acknowledges that "substantial interdistrict disparities in school expenditures" exist in Texas, and that these disparities are "largely attributable to differences in the amounts of money collected through local property taxation." But instead of closely examining the seriousness of these disparities and the invidiousness of the Texas financing scheme, the Court undertakes an elaborate exploration of the efforts Texas has purportedly made to close the gaps between its districts in terms of levels of district wealth and resulting educational funding. Yet, however praiseworthy Texas' equalizing efforts, the issue in this case is not whether Texas is doing its best to ameliorate the worst features of a discriminatory scheme, but rather whether the scheme itself is in fact unconstitutionally discriminatory in the face of the Fourteenth Amendment's guarantee of equal protection of the laws. When the Texas financing scheme is taken as a whole, I do not think it can be doubted that it produces a discriminatory impact on substantial numbers of the school-age children of the State of Texas.

. . . .

The appellants do not deny the disparities in educational funding caused by variations in taxable district property wealth. They do contend, however, that whatever the differences in per pupil spending among Texas districts, there are no discriminatory consequences for the children of the disadvantaged districts. They recognize that what is at stake in this case is the quality of the public education provided Texas children in the districts in which they live. But appellants reject the suggestion that the quality of education in any particular district is determined by money — beyond some minimal level of funding which they believe to be assured every Texas district. . . . In their view, there is simply no denial of equal educational opportunity to any Texas school children as a result of the widely varying per pupil spending power provided districts under the current financing scheme.

In my view, though, even an unadorned restatement of this contention is sufficient to reveal its absurdity. . . . It is an inescapable fact that if one district has more funds available per pupil than another district, the former will have greater choice in educational planning than will the latter. In this regard, I believe the question of discrimination in educational quality must be deemed to be an objective one that looks to what the State provides its children, not to what the children are able to do with what they receive. . . .

At the very least, in view of the substantial interdistrict disparities in funding and in resulting educational inputs shown by appellees to exist under the Texas financing scheme, the burden of proving that these disparities do not in fact affect the quality of children's education must fall upon appellants. Yet appellants made no effort in the District Court to demonstrate that educational quality is not affected by variations in funding and in resulting inputs. And, in this Court, they have argued no more than that the relationship is ambiguous. This is hardly sufficient to overcome appellees' prima facie showing of state-created discrimination between the school children of Texas with respect to objective educational opportunity.

. . . .

This Court has repeatedly held that state discrimination which either adversely affects a "fundamental interest" or is based on a distinction of a suspect character . . . must be carefully scrutinized to ensure that the scheme is necessary to promote a substantial, legitimate state interest. The majority today concludes, however, that the Texas scheme is not subject to such a strict standard of review under the Equal Protection Clause. Instead, in its view, the Texas scheme must be tested by nothing more than that lenient standard of rationality which we have traditionally applied to discriminatory state action in the context of economic and commercial matters. By so doing the Court avoids the telling task of searching for a substantial state interest which the Texas financing scheme, with its variations in taxable district property wealth, is necessary to further. I cannot accept such an emasculation of the Equal Protection Clause in the context of this case.

. . . .

The Court seeks solace for its action today in the possibility of legislative reform. The Court's suggestions of legislative redress and experimentation will doubtless be of great comfort to the school children of Texas' disadvantaged districts, but considering the vested interests of wealthy school districts in the preservation of the status quo, they are worth little more. The possibility of legislative action is, in all events, no answer to this Court's duty under the Constitution to eliminate unjustified state discrimination. In this case we have been presented with an instance of such discrimination, in a particularly invidious form, against an individual interest of large constitutional and practical importance. To support the demonstrated discrimination in the provision of educational opportunity the State has offered a justi-fication which, on analysis, takes on at best an ephemeral character. Thus, I believe that the wide disparities in taxable district property wealth inher-ent in the local property tax element of the Texas fi-nancing scheme render that scheme violative of the Equal Protection Clause.

I would therefore affirm the judgment of the Dis-trict Court.

Warth v. Seldin

> 422 U.S. 490 (1975)
> See pp. 59–63.

Muller v. Oregon

> 208 U.S. 412 (1908)
> See pp. 366–367.

West Coast Hotel Co. v. Parrish

> 300 U.S. 379 (1937)
> See pp. 367–370

Goesaert et al. v. Cleary

> 335 U.S. 464 (1948)
> Vote: 6–3

The facts of this case are contained in the opinion.

MR. JUSTICE FRANKFURTER delivered the opinion of the Court.

As part of the Michigan system for controlling the sale of liquor, bartenders are required to be licensed in all cities having a population of 50,000 or more, but no female may be licensed unless she be "the wife or daughter of the male owner" of a licensed li-quor establishment. The case is here on direct ap-peal from an order of the District Court... denying an injunction to restrain the enforcement of the Michigan law. The claim, denied below... and re-newed here, is that Michigan cannot forbid females generally from being barmaids and at the same time make an exception in favor of the wives and daugh-ters of the owners of liquor establishments. Beguil-ing as the subject is, it need not detain us long. To ask whether or not the Equal Protection of the Laws Clause of the Fourteenth Amendment barred Michi-gan from making the classification the State has made between wives and daughters of owners of li-quor places and wives and daughters of non-owners, is one of those rare instances where to state the question is in effect to answer it.

We are, to be sure, dealing with a historic calling. We meet the alewife, sprightly and ribald, in Shake-speare, but centuries before him she played a role in the social life of England. The Fourteenth Amend-ment did not tear history up by the roots, and the regulation of the liquor traffic is one of the oldest and most untrammeled of legislative powers. Michigan could, beyond question, forbid all women from work-ing behind a bar. This is so despite the vast changes in the social and legal position of women. The fact that women may not have achieved the virtues that men have long claimed as their prerogatives and now indulge in vices that men have long practiced, does not preclude the States from drawing a sharp line between the sexes, certainly in such matters as the regulation of the liquor traffic. See the Twenty-First Amendment and *Carter* v. *Virginia,* 321 U.S. 131. The Constitution does not require legislatures to re-flect sociological insight, or shifting social standards, any more than it requires them to keep abreast of the latest scientific standards.

While Michigan may deny to all women opportuni-ties for bartending, Michigan cannot play favorites among women without rhyme or reason. The Con-stitution in enjoining the equal protection of the laws upon States precludes irrational discrimination as be-tween persons or groups of persons in the incidence of a law. But the Constitution does not require situ-ations "which are different in fact or opinion to be treated in law as though they were the same." Since bartending by women may, in the allowable legisla-tive judgment, give rise to moral and social problems against which it may devise preventive measures, the legislature need not go to the full length of prohibi-tion if it believes that as to a defined group of females other factors are operating which either eliminate or reduce the moral and social problems otherwise call-ing for prohibition. Michigan evidently believes that the oversight assured through ownership of a bar by a barmaid's husband or father minimizes hazards that may confront a barmaid without such protecting oversight. This Court is certainly not in a position to gainsay such belief by the Michigan legislature. If it is entertainable, as we think it is, Michigan has not violated its duty to afford equal protection of its laws. We cannot cross-examine either actually or argumentatively the mind of Michigan legislators nor question their motives. Since the line they have drawn is not without a basis in reason, we cannot give ear to the suggestion that the real impulse behind this legislation was an unchivalrous desire of male bartenders to try to monopolize the calling.

It would be an idle parade of familiar learning to review the multitudinous cases in which the constitutional assurance of the equal protection of the laws has been applied. The generalities on this subject are not in dispute; their application turns peculiarly on the particular circumstances of a case. Thus, it would be a sterile inquiry to consider whether this case is nearer to the nepotic pilotage law of Louisiana, sustained in *Kotch* v. *Pilot Commissioners* [1948], than it is to the Oklahoma sterilization law, which fell in *Skinner* v. *Oklahoma* [1942]. Suffice it to say that "A statute is not invalid under the Constitution because it might have gone farther than it did, or because it may not succeed in bringing about the result that it tends to produce."

Nor is it unconstitutional for Michigan to withdraw from women the occupation of bartending because it allows women to serve as waitresses where liquor is dispensed. The District Court has sufficiently indicated the reasons that may have influenced the legislature in allowing women to be waitresses in a liquor establishment over which a man's ownership provides control. Nothing need be added to what was said below as to the other grounds on which the Michigan law was assailed.

Judgment affirmed.

MR. JUSTICE RUTLEDGE, with whom MR. JUSTICE DOUGLAS and MR. JUSTICE MURPHY join, dissenting.

While the equal protection clause does not require a legislature to achieve "abstract symmetry" or to classify with "mathematical nicety," that clause does require lawmakers to refrain from invidious distinctions of the sort drawn by the statute challenged in this case.

The statute arbitrarily discriminates between male and female owners of liquor establishments. A male owner, although he himself is always absent from his bar, may employ his wife and daughter as barmaids. A female owner may neither work as a barmaid herself nor employ her daughter in that position, even if a man is always present in the establishment to keep order. This inevitable result of the classification be-

lies the assumption that the statute was motivated by a legislative solicitude for the moral and physical well-being of women who, but for the law, would be employed as barmaids. Since there could be no other conceivable justification for such discrimination against women owners of liquor establishments, the statute should be held invalid as a denial of equal protection.

Frontiero v. Richardson

411 U.S. 677 (1973)
Vote: 8–1

Federal law permitted a serviceman to claim his wife as a "dependent" without regard to whether she was in fact dependent upon him for any part of her support. However it also provided that a servicewoman could not claim her husband as a "dependent" unless he was in fact dependent upon her for over one-half of his support.

Under other laws, a member of the uniformed services with dependents was entitled to an increased "basic allowance for quarters" and a member's dependents were provided comprehensive medical and dental care. Sharron Frontiero, a lieutenant in the Air Force, sought increased quarters allowances and housing and medical benefits for her husband, on the ground that he was her "dependent." Although such benefits as she had applied for would automatically have been granted with respect to the wife of a male member of the uniformed services, her application was denied because she failed to demonstrate that her husband was dependent upon her for more than one-half of his support.

The Frontieros sought a permanent injunction against the continued enforcement of these statutes and an order directing equal treatment of males and females when providing dependents' benefits. The district court upheld these provisions, whereupon the Frontieros appealed.

MR. JUSTICE BRENNAN announced the judgment of the Court in an opinion in which MR. JUSTICE DOUGLAS, MR. JUSTICE WHITE, and MR. JUSTICE MARSHALL join.

At the outset, appellants contend that classifications based upon sex, like classifications based upon race, alienage, and national origin, are inherently suspect and must therefore be subjected to close judicial scrutiny. We agree and, indeed, find at least implicit support for such an approach in our unanimous decision only last Term in *Reed* v. *Reed* (1971).

In *Reed,* the Court considered the constitutionality of an Idaho statute providing that, when two individuals are otherwise equally entitled to appointment as administrator of an estate, the male applicant must be preferred to the female. Appellant, the mother of the deceased, and appellee, the father, filed competing petitions for appointment as administrator of their son's estate. Since the parties, as parents of the deceased, were members of the same entitlement class, the statutory preference was invoked and the father's petition was therefore granted. Appellant claimed that this statute, by giving a mandatory preference to males over females without regard to their individual qualifications, violated the Equal Protection Clause of the Fourteenth Amendment.

The Court noted that the Idaho statute "provides that different treatment be accorded to the applicants on the basis of their sex; it thus establishes a classification subject to scrutiny under the Equal Protection Clause." Under "traditional" equal protection analysis, a legislative classification must be sustained unless it is "patently arbitrary" and bears no rational relationship to a legitimate governmental interest.

In an effort to meet this standard, appellee contended that the statutory scheme was a reasonable measure designed to reduce the workload on probate courts by eliminating one class of contests. Moreover, appellee argued that the mandatory preference for male applicants was in itself reasonable since "men [are] as a rule more conversant with business affairs than . . . women." Indeed, appellee maintained that "it is a matter of common knowledge, that women still are not engaged in politics, the professions, business or industry to the extent that men are." And the Idaho Supreme Court, in upholding the constitutionality of this statute, suggested that the Idaho Legislature might reasonably have "concluded that in general men are better qualified to act as an administrator than are women."

Despite these contentions, however, the Court held the statutory preference for male applicants unconstitutional. In reaching this result, the Court implicitly rejected appellee's apparently rational explanation of the statutory scheme, and concluded that, by ignoring the individual qualifications of particular applicants, the challenged statute provided "dissimi-

lar treatment for men and women who are . . . similarly situated." The Court therefore held that, even though the State's interest in achieving administrative efficiency "is not without some legitimacy," "[t]o give a mandatory preference to members of either sex over members of the other, merely to accomplish the elimination of hearings on the merits, is to make the very kind of arbitrary legislative choice forbidden by the [Consttution]. . . ." This departure from "traditional" rational basis analysis with respect to sex-based classifications is clearly justified.

There can be no doubt that our Nation has had a long and unfortunate history of sex discrimination. Traditionally, such discrimination was rationalized by an attitude of "romantic paternalism" which, in practical effect, put women not on a pedestal, but in a cage. Indeed, this paternalistic attitude became so firmly rooted in our national consciousness that, exactly 100 years ago, a distinguished member of this Court was able to proclaim:

> Man is, or should be, woman's protector and defender. The natural and proper timidity and delicacy which belongs to the female sex evidently unfits it for many of the occupations of civil life. The constitution of the family organization, which is founded in the divine ordinance, as well as in the nature of things, indicates the domestic sphere as that which properly belongs to the domain and functions of womanhood. The harmony, not to say identity, of interests and views which belong, or should belong, to the family institution is repugnant to the ideas of a woman adopting a distinct and independent career from that of her husband. . . .
>
> . . . The paramount destiny and mission of woman are to fulfil the noble and benign offices of wife and mother. This is the law of the Creator. *Bradwell* v. *Illinois* (1873).

As a result of notions such as these, our statute books gradually became laden with gross, stereotypical distinctions between the sexes and, indeed, throughout much of the 19th century the position of women in our society was, in many respects, comparable to that of blacks under the pre-Civil War slave codes. Neither slaves nor women could hold office, serve on juries, or bring suit in their own names, and married women traditionally were denied the legal capacity to hold or convey property or to serve as legal guardians of their own children. . . . And although blacks were guaranteed the right to vote in 1870, women were denied even that right — which is itself "preservative of other basic civil and political rights" — until adoption of the Nineteenth Amendment half a century later.

It is true, of course, that the position of women in America has improved markedly in recent decades. Nevertheless, it can hardly be doubted that, in part because of the high visibility of the sex characteristic, women still face pervasive, although at times more subtle, discrimination in our educational institutions, on the job market and, perhaps most conspicuously, in the political arena. . . .

Moreover, since sex, like race and national origin, is an immutable characteristic determined solely by the accident of birth, the imposition of special disabilities upon the members of a particular sex because of their sex would seem to violate "the basic concept of our system that legal burdens should bear some relationship to individual responsibility. . . ." And what differentiates sex from such nonsuspect statutes as intelligence or physical disability, and aligns it with the recognized suspect criteria, is that the sex characteristic frequently bears no relation to ability to perform or contribute to society. As a result, statutory distinctions between the sexes often have the effect of invidiously relegating the entire class of females to inferior legal status without regard to the actual capabilities of its individual members.

We might also note that, over the past decade, Congress has itself manifested an increasing sensitivity to sex-based classifications. In Title VII of the Civil Rights Act of 1964, for example, Congress expressly declared that no employer, labor union, or other organization subject to the provisions of the Act shall discriminate against any individual on the basis of "race, color, religion, *sex,* or national origin." Similarly, the Equal Pay Act of 1963 provides that no employer covered by the Act "shall discriminate . . . between employees on the basis of *sex.*" And §1 of the Equal Rights Amendment, passed by Congress on March 22, 1972, and submitted to the legislatures of the States for ratification, declares that "[e]quality of rights under the law shall not be denied or abridged by the United States or by any State on account of sex." Thus, Congress has itself concluded that classifications based upon sex are inherently invidious, and this conclusion of a coequal branch of Government is not without significance to the question presently under consideration.

With these considerations in mind, we can only conclude that classifications based upon sex, like classifications based upon race, alienage, or national origin, are inherently suspect, and must therefore be subjected to strict judicial scrutiny. Applying the analysis mandated by that stricter standard of review, it is clear that the statutory scheme now before us is constitutionally invalid.

The sole basis of the classification established in the challenged statutes is the sex of the individuals involved. . . . [A] female member of the uniformed services seeking to obtain housing and medical benefits for her spouse must prove his dependency in fact, whereas no such burden is imposed upon male members. In addition, the statutes operate so as to deny benefits to a female member, such as appellant Sharron Frontiero, who provides less than one-half of her spouse's support, while at the same time granting such benefits to a male member who likewise provides less than one-half of his spouse's support. Thus, to this extent at least, it may fairly be said that these statutes command "dissimilar treatment for men and women who are . . . similarly situated."

Moreover, the Government concedes that the differential treatment accorded men and women under these statutes serves no purpose other than mere "administrative convenience." In essence, the Government maintains that, as an empirical matter, wives in our society frequently are dependent upon their husbands, while husbands rarely are dependent upon their wives. Thus, the Government argues that Congress might reasonably have concluded that it would be both cheaper and easier simply conclusively to presume that wives of male members are financially dependent upon their husbands, while burdening female members with the task of establishing dependency in fact.

The Government offers no concrete evidence, however, tending to support its view that such differential treatment in fact saves the Government any money. In order to satisfy the demands of strict judicial scrutiny, the Government must demonstrate, for example, that it is actually cheaper to grant increased benefits with respect to *all* male members, than it is to determine which male members are in fact entitled to such benefits and to grant increased benefits only to those members whose wives actually meet the dependency requirement. Here, however, there is substantial evidence that, if put to the test, many of the wives of male members would fail to qualify for benefits. And in light of the fact that the dependency determination with respect to the husbands of female members is presently made solely on the basis of affidavits, rather than through the more costly hearing process, the Government's explanation of the statutory scheme is, to say the least, questionable.

In any case, our prior decisions make clear that, although efficacious administration of governmental programs is not without some importance, "the Constitution recognizes higher values than speed and efficiency." And when we enter the realm of "strict judicial scrutiny," there can be no doubt that "administrative convenience" is not a shibboleth, the mere recitation of which dictates constitutionality. See *Shapiro* v. *Thompson* (1969); *Carrington* v. *Rash* (1965). On the contrary, any statutory scheme which draws a sharp line between the sexes, *solely* for the purpose of achieving administrative convenience, necessarily commands "dissimilar treatment for men and women who are . . . similarly situated," and therefore involves the "very kind of arbitrary legislative choice forbidden by the [Constitution]. . . ." *Reed* v. *Reed* [1971]. We therefore conclude that, by according differential treatment to male and female members of the uniformed services for the sole purpose of achieving administrative convenience, the challenged statutes violate the Due Process Clause of the Fifth Amendment insofar as they require a female member to prove the dependency of her husband.

Reversed.

MR. JUSTICE STEWART concurs in the judgment, agreeing that the statutes before us work an invidious discrimination in violation of the Constitution. *Reed* v. *Reed*. . . .

MR. JUSTICE POWELL, with whom THE CHIEF JUSTICE and MR. JUSTICE BLACKMUN join, concurring in the judgment.

I agree that the challenged statutes constitute an unconstitutional discrimination against service women in violation of the Due Process Clause of the Fifth Amendment, but I cannot join the opinion of MR. JUSTICE BRENNAN, which would hold that all classifications based upon sex, "like classifications based upon race, alienage, and national origin," are "inherently suspect and must therefore be subjected to close judicial scrutiny."

It is unnecessary for the Court in this case to characterize sex as a suspect classification, with all of the far-reaching implications of such a holding. *Reed* v. *Reed* (1971), which abundantly supports our decision today, did not add sex to the narrowly limited group of classifications which are inherently suspect. In my view, we can and should decide this case on the authority of *Reed* and reserve for the future any expansion of its rationale.

There is another, and I find compelling, reason for deferring a general categorizing of sex classifications as invoking the strictest test of judicial scrutiny. The Equal Rights Amendment, which if adopted will resolve the substance of this precise question, has been approved by the Congress and submitted for ratification by the States. If this Amendment is duly adopted, it will represent the will of the people accomplished in the manner prescribed by the Constitution. By acting prematurely and unnecessarily, as I view it, the Court has assumed a decisional responsibility at the very time when state legislatures, functioning within the traditional democratic process, are debating the proposed Amendment. It seems to me that this reaching out to pre-empt by judicial action a major political decision which is currently in process of resolution does not reflect appropriate respect for duly prescribed legislative processes.

There are times when this Court, under our system, cannot avoid a constitutional decision on issues which normally should be resolved by the elected representatives of the people. But democratic institutions are weakened, and confidence in the restraint of the Court is impaired, when we appear unnecessarily to decide sensitive issues of broad social and political importance at the very time they are under consideration within the prescribed constitutional processes.

[MR. JUSTICE REHNQUIST dissented.]

Geduldig v. Aiello

417 U.S. 484 (1974)
Vote: 6–3

California had a disability insurance scheme for private employees temporarily disabled from working by an injury or illness not covered by workers' compensation. Under it employees contributed up to one percent of their salary to a disability fund. The program excluded several types of disabilities, including disabilities arising from normal pregnancies and childbirth. Carolyn Aiello and three other women, all of whom were otherwise eligible for benefits, filed a suit in federal district court challenging California's exclusion of normal pregnancy from coverage, alleging that it was invidious discrimination that denied them equal protection of the laws. A three-judge district court supported their contention, whereupon Geduldig, Director of Human Resources Development for the state, appealed.

MR. JUSTICE STEWART delivered the opinion of the Court.

It is clear that California intended to establish this benefit system as an insurance program that was to function essentially in accordance with insurance concepts. Since the program was instituted in 1946, it has been totally self-supporting, never drawing on general state revenues to finance disability or hospital benefits. The Disability Fund is wholly supported by the one percent of wages annually contributed by participating employees. At oral argument, counsel for the appellant informed us that in recent years between 90% and 103% of the revenue to the Disability Fund has been paid out in disability and hospital benefits. This history strongly suggests that the one-percent contribution rate, in addition to being easily computable, bears a close and substantial relationship to the level of benefits payable and to the disability risks insured under the program.

Over the years California has demonstrated a strong commitment not to increase the contribution rate above the one-percent level. The State has sought to provide the broadest possible disability protection that would be affordable by all employees, including those with very low incomes. Because any larger percentage or any flat dollar-amount rate of contribution would impose an increasingly regressive levy bearing most heavily upon those with the lowest incomes, the State has resisted any attempt to change the required contribution from the one-percent level. The program is thus structured, in terms of the level of benefits and the risks insured, to maintain the solvency of the Disability Fund at a one-percent annual level of contribution.

In ordering the State to pay benefits for disability accompanying normal pregnancy and delivery, the District Court acknowledged the State's contention "that coverage of these disabilities is so extraordinarily expensive that it would be impossible to maintain a program supported by employee contributions if these disabilities are included." 359 F. Supp., at 798. There is considerable disagreement between the parties with respect to how great the increased costs would actually be but they would clearly be substantial. For purposes of analysis the District Court accepted the State's estimate, which was in excess of $100 million annually, and stated; "[I]t is clear that including these disabilities would not destroy the program. The increased costs could be accommodated quite easily by making reasonable changes in the contribution rate, the maximum benefits allowable, and the other variables affecting the solvency of the program."

Each of these "variables"—the benefit level deemed appropriate to compensate employee disability, the risks selected to be insured under the program, and the contribution rate chosen to maintain the solvency of the program and at the same time to permit low-income employees to participate with minimal personal sacrifice—represents a policy determination by the State. The essential issue in this case is whether the Equal Protection Clause requires such policies to be sacrificed or compromised in order to finance the payment of benefits to those whose disability is attributable to normal pregnancy and delivery.

We cannot agree that the exclusion of this disability from coverage amounts to invidious discrimination under the Equal Protection Clause. California does not discriminate with respect to the persons or groups which are eligible for disability insurance protection under the program. The classification challenged in this case relates to the asserted underinclusiveness of the set of risks that the State has selected to insure. Although California has created a program to insure most risks of employment disability, it has not chosen to insure all such risks, and this decision is reflected in the level of annual contributions exacted from participating employees. This Court has held that, consistently with the Equal Protection Clause, a State "may take one step at a time, addressing itself to the phase of the problem which seems most acute to the legislative mind. . . . The legislature may select one phase of one field and apply a remedy there, neglecting the others. . . ." Particularly with respect to social welfare programs, so long as the line drawn by the State is rationally supportable, the courts will not interpose their judgment as to the appropriate stopping point. "[T]he Equal Protection Clause does not require that a State must choose between attacking every aspect of a problem or not attacking the problem at all."

The District Court suggested that moderate alterations in what it regarded as "variables" of the disability insurance program could be made to accommodate the substantial expense required to include normal pregnancy within the program's protection. The same can be said, however, with respect to the other expensive class of disabilities that are excluded from coverage—short-term disabilities. If the Equal Protection Clause were thought to compel disability payments for normal pregnancy, it is hard to perceive why it would not also compel payments for short-term disabilities suffered by participating employees.

It is evident that a totally comprehensive program would be substantially more costly than the present program and would inevitably require state subsidy, a higher rate of employee contribution, a lower scale of benefits for those suffering insured disabilities, or some combination of these measures. There is nothing in the Constitution, however, that requires the State to subordinate or compromise its legitimate interests solely to create a more comprehensive social insurance program than it already has.

The State has a legitimate interest in maintaining the self-supporting nature of its insurance program. Similarly, it has an interest in distributing the available resources in such a way as to keep benefit payments at an adequate level for disabilities that are covered, rather than to cover all disabilities inadequately. Finally, California has a legitimate concern in maintaining the contribution rate at a level that will not unduly burden participating employees, particularly low-income employees who may be most in need of the disability insurance.

These policies provide an objective and wholly non-invidious basis for the State's decision not to create a more comprehensive insurance program than it has. There is no evidence in the record that the selection of the risks insured by the program worked to discriminate against any definable group or class in terms of the aggregate risk protection derived by that group or class from the program. There is no risk from which men are protected and women are not. Likewise, there is no risk from which women are protected and men are not.

The appellee simply contends that, although she has received insurance protection equivalent to that provided all other participating employees, she has suffered discrimination because she encountered a risk that was outside the program's protection. For the reasons we have stated, we hold that this contention is not a valid one under the Equal Protection Clause of the Fourteenth Amendment.

The stay heretofore issued by the Court is vacated, and the judgment of the District Court is

Reversed.

Mr. Justice Brennan, with whom Mr. Justice Douglas and Mr. Justice Marshall join, dissenting.

. . . Because I believe that *Reed* v. *Reed* (1971), and *Frontiero* v. *Richardson* (1973), mandate a stricter standard of scrutiny which the State's classification fails to satisfy, I respectfully dissent.

California's disability insurance program was enacted to supplement the State's unemployment insurance and workmen's compensation programs by providing benefits to wage earners to cushion the economic effects of income loss and medical expenses resulting from sickness or injury. . . .

To achieve the Act's broad humanitarian goals, the legislature fashioned a pooled-risk disability fund covering all employees at the same rate of contribution, regardless of individual risk. . . . [C]ompensation is paid for virtually all disabling conditions without regard to cost, voluntariness, uniqueness, predictability, or "normalcy" of the disability.* Thus, for example, workers are compensated for costly disabilities such as heart attacks, voluntary disabilities such as cosmetic surgery or sterilization, disabilities unique to sex or race such as prostatectomies or sickle-cell anemia, pre-existing conditions inevitably resulting in disability such as degenerative arthritis or cataracts, and "normal" disabilities such as removal of irritating wisdom teeth or other orthodontia.

Despite the Code's broad goals and scope of coverage, compensation is denied for disabilities suffered in connection with a "normal" pregnancy — disabilities suffered only by women. Disabilities caused by pregnancy, however, like other physically disabling conditions covered by the Code, require medical care, often include hospitalization, anesthesia and surgical procedures, and may involve genuine risk to life. Moreover, the economic effects caused by pregnancy-related disabilities are functionally indistinguishable from the effects caused by any other disability: wages are lost due to a physical inability to work, and medical expenses are incurred for the delivery of the child and for postpartum care. In my view, by singling out for less favorable treatment a gender-linked disability peculiar to women, the State has created a double standard for disability compensation: a limitation is imposed upon the disabilities for which women workers may recover, while men receive full compensaton for all disabilities suffered, including those that affect only or primarily their sex, such as prostatectomies, circumcision, hemophilia, and gout. In effect, one set of rules is applied to females and another to males. Such dissimilar treatment of men and women, on the basis of physical characteristics inextricably linked to one sex, inevitably constitutes sex discrimination.

. . . .

*While the Code technically excludes from coverage individuals under court commitment for dipsomania, drug addiction, or sexual psychopathy, . . . the Court was informed by the Deputy Attorney General of California at oral argument that court commitment for such disabilities is "a fairly archaic practice" and that "it would be unrealistic to say that they constitute valid exclusions." . . .

In the past, when a legislative classification has turned on gender, the Court has justifiably applied a standard of judicial scrutiny more strict than that generally accorded economic or social welfare programs. Compare *Reed* v. *Reed* . . . (1971), and *Frontiero* v. *Richardson* . . . (1973), with *Dandridge* v. *Williams* . . . (1970), and *Jefferson* v. *Hackney* . . . (1972). Yet, by its decision today, the Court appears willing to abandon that higher standard of review without satisfactorily explaining what differentiates the gender-based classification employed in this case from those found unconstitutional in *Reed* and *Frontiero*. The Court's decision threatens to return men and women to a time when "traditional" equal protection analysis sustained legislative classifications that treated differently members of a particular sex solely because of their sex. See, *e.g., Muller* v. *Oregon* (1908); *Goesaert* v. *Cleary* (1948); *Hoyt* v. *Florida* (1961).

I cannot join the Court's apparent retreat. I continue to adhere to my view that "classifications based upon sex, like classifications based upon race, alienage, or national origin, are inherently suspect, and must therefore be subjected to strict judicial scrutiny." *Frontiero* v. *Richardson, supra,* at 688. When, as in this case, the State employs a legislative classification that distinguishes between beneficiaries solely by reference to gender-linked disability risks, "[t]he Court is not . . . free to sustain the statute on the ground that it rationally promotes legitimate governmental interests; rather, such suspect classifications can be sustained only when the State bears the burden of demonstrating that the challenged legislation serves overriding or compelling interests that cannot be achieved either by a more carefully tailored legislative classification or by the use of feasible, less drastic means.

The State has clearly failed to meet that burden in the present case. The essence of the State's justification for excluding disabilities caused by a normal pregnancy from its disability compensation scheme is that covering such disabilities would be too costly. To be sure, as presently funded, inclusion of normal pregnancies "would be substantially more costly than the present program." The present level of benefits for insured disabilities could not be maintained without increasing the employee contribution rate, raising or lifting the yearly contribution ceiling, or securing state subsidies. But whatever role such monetary considerations may play in traditional equal protection analysis, the State's interest in preserving the fiscal integrity of its disability insurance program simply cannot render the State's use of a suspect classification constitutional. For while "a State has a valid interest in preserving the fiscal integrity of its

programs[,] . . . a State may not accomplish such a purpose by invidious distinctions between classes of its citizens. . . . The saving of welfare costs cannot justify an otherwise invidious classification." *Shapiro* v. *Thompson* (1969). Thus, when a statutory classification is subject to strict judicial scrutiny, the State "must do more than show that denying [benefits to the excluded class] saves money." *Memorial Hospital* v. *Maricopa County* (1974). See also *Graham* v. *Richardson* (1971).

Moreover, California's legitimate interest in fiscal integrity could easily have been achieved through a variety of less drastic, sexually neutral means. . . .

I would therefore affirm the judgment of the District Court.

Craig v. Boren

429 U.S. 190 (1976)
Vote: 7–2

Oklahoma law forbade the sale of 3.2 percent beer to males under the age of 21 and to females under the age of 18. This law was challenged in federal district court by Craig, a male between the ages of 18 and 21 years of age, and Whitener, a licensed vendor of 3.2 percent beer. They sought declaratory and injunctive relief against enforcement of this gender-based differential on the ground that it constituted invidious discrimination against males 18–20 years of age. A three-judge district court sustained the constitutionality of the law and dismissed the action, whereupon Craig and Whitener appealed.

MR. JUSTICE BRENNAN delivered the opinion of the Court.

. . . [In upholding Oklahoma's law] the district Court recognized that *Reed* v. *Reed* was controlling. In applying the teachings of that case, the court found the requisite important governmental objective in the traffic-safety goal proffered by the Oklahoma Attorney General. It then concluded that the statistics introduced by the appellees established that the gender-based distinction was substantially related to achievement of that goal.

We accept for purposes of discussion the District Court's identification of the objective underlying §§241 and 245 as the enhancement of traffic safety. Clearly, the protection of public health and safety represents an important function of state and local governments. However, appellees' statistics in our view cannot support the conclusion that the gender-based distinction closely serves to achieve that objective and therefore the distinction cannot under *Reed* withstand equal protection challenge.

The appellees introduced a variety of statistical surveys. First, an analysis of arrest statistics for 1973 demonstrated that 18–20-year-old male arrests for "driving under the influence" and "drunkenness" substantially exceeded female arrests for that same age period. Similarly, youths aged 17–21 were found to be overrepresented among those killed or injured in traffic accidents, with males again numerically exceeding females in this regard. Third, a random roadside survey in Oklahoma City revealed that young males were more inclined to drive and drink beer than were their female counterparts. Fourth, Federal Bureau of Investigation nationwide statistics exhibited a notable increase in arrests for "driving under the influence." Finally, statistical evidence gathered in other jurisdictions, particularly Minnesota and Michigan, was offered to corroborate Oklahoma's experience by indicating the pervasivenes of youthful participation in motor vehicle accidents following the imbibing of alcohol. Conceding that "the case is not free from doubt," the District Court nonetheless concluded that this statistical showing substantiated "a rational basis for the legislative judgment underlying the challenged classification."

Even were this statistical evidence accepted as accurate, it nevertheless offers only a weak answer to the equal protection question presented here. The most focused and relevant of the statistical surveys, arrests of 18–20-year-olds for alcohol-related driving offenses, exemplifies the ultimate unpersuasiveness of this evidentiary record. Viewed in terms of the correlation between sex and the actual activity that Oklahoma seeks to regulate — driving while under the influence of alcohol — the statistics broadly establish that .18% of females and 2% of males in that age group were arrested for that offense. While such a disparity is not trivial in a statistical sense, it hardly can form the basis for employment of a gender line in a classifying device. Certainly if maleness is to serve as a proxy for drinking and driving, a correlation of 2% must be considered an unduly tenuous "fit." Indeed, prior cases have consistently rejected the use of sex as a decision-making factor even though the statutes in question certainly rested on far more predictive empirical relationships than this.

Moreover, the statistics exhibit a variety of other short-comings that seriously impugn their value to equal protection analysis. Setting aside the obvious methodological problems, the surveys do not adequately justify the salient features of Oklahoma's gender-based traffic-safety law. None purports to measure the use and dangerousness of 3.2% beer as opposed to alcohol generally, a detail that is of particular importance since, in light of its low alcohol level, Oklahoma apparently considers the 3.2% beverage to be "nonintoxicating." Moreover, many of the studies, while graphically documenting the unfortunate increase in driving while under the influence of alcohol, make no effort to relate their findings to age-sex differentials as involved here. Indeed, the only survey that explicitly centered its attention upon young drivers and their use of beer — albeit apparently not of the diluted 3.2% variety — reached results that hardly can be viewed as impressive in justifying either a gender or age classification.

There is no reason to belabor this line of analysis. It is unrealistic to expect either members of the judiciary or state officials to be well versed in the rigors of experimental or statistical technique. But this merely illustrates that proving broad sociological propositions by statistics is a dubious business, and one that inevitably is in tension with the normative philosophy that underlies the Equal Protection Clause. Suffice it to say that the showing offered by the appellees does not satisfy us that sex represents a legitimate, accurate proxy for the regulation of drinking and driving. In fact, when it is further recognized that Oklahoma's statute prohibits only the selling of 3.2% beer to young males and not their drinking the beverage once acquired (even after purchase by their 18–20-year-old female companions), the relationship between gender and traffic safety becomes far too tenuous to satisfy *Reed's* requirement that the gender-based difference be substantially related to achievement of the statutory objective.

We hold, therefore, that under *Reed,* Oklahoma's 3.2% beer statute invidiously discriminates against males 18–20 years of age.

Appellees argue, however, that §§241 and 245 enforce state policies concerning the sale and distribution of alcohol and by force of the Twenty-first Amendment should therefore be held to withstand the equal protection challenge. The District Court's response to this contention is unclear. The court assumed that the Twenty-first Amendment "strengthened" the State's police powers with respect to alcohol regulation, but then said that "the standards of review that [the Equal Protection Clause] mandates are not relaxed." Our view is, and we hold, that the Twenty-first Amendment does not save the invidious gender-based discrimination from invalidation as a denial of equal protection of the laws in violation of the Fourteenth Amendment.

....

It is true that *California* v. *LaRue* (1972), relied upon the Twenty-first Amendment to "strengthen" the State's authority to regulate live entertainment at establishments licensed to dispense liquor, at least when the performances "partake more of gross sexuality than of communication." Nevertheless, the Court has never recognized sufficient "strength" in the Amendment to defeat an otherwise established claim of invidious discrimination in violation of the Equal Protection Clause. Rather, *Moose Lodge No. 107* v. *Irvis* (1972) establishes that state liquor regulatory schemes cannot work invidious discriminations that violate the Equal Protection Clause.

Following this approach, both federal and state courts uniformly have declared the unconstitutionality of gender lines that restrain the activities of customers of state-regulated liquor establishments irrespective of the operation of the Twenty-first Amendment. Even when state officials have posited sociological or empirical justifications for these gender-based differentiations, the courts have struck down discriminations aimed at an entire class under the guise of alcohol regulation. In fact, social science studies that have uncovered quantifiable differences in drinking tendencies dividing along both racial and ethnic lines strongly suggest the need for application of the Equal Protection Clause in preventing discriminatory treatment that almost certainly would be perceived as invidious.* In sum, the principles embodied in the Equal Protection Clause are not to be

*Thus, if statistics were to govern the permissibility of state alcohol regulation without regard to the Equal Protection Clause as a limiting principle, it might follow that States could freely favor Jews and Italian Catholics at the expense of all other Americans, since available studies regularly demonstrate that the former two groups exhibit the lowest rates of problem drinking. Similarly, if a State were allowed simply to depend upon demographic characteristics of adolescents in identifying problem drinkers, statistics might support the conclusion that only black teenagers should be permitted to drink, followed by Asian-Americans and Spanish-Americans. "Whites and American Indians have the lowest proportions of abstainers and the highest proportions of moderate/heavy and heavy drinkers."

In the past, some States have acted upon their notions of the drinking propensities of entire groups in fashioning their alcohol policies. The most typical recipient of this treatment has been the American Indian; indeed, several States established criminal sanctions for the sale of alcohol to an Indian or "half or quarter breed Indian." While Indian-oriented provisions were the most common, state alcohol beverage prohibitions also have been directed at other groups, notably German, Italian and Catholic immigrants. The repeal of most of these laws signals society's perception of the unfairness and questionable constitutionality of singling out groups to bear the brunt of alcohol regulation.

rendered inapplicable by statistically measured but loose-fitting generalities concerning the drinking tendencies of aggregate groups. We thus hold that the operation of the Twenty-first Amendment does not alter the application of equal protection standards that otherwise govern this case.

We conclude that the gender-based differential contained in Okla. Stat., Tit. 37, §245 (1976 Supp.) constitutes a denial of the equal protection of the laws to males aged 18–20 and reverse the judgment of the District Court.

It is so ordered.

[MR. JUSTICE POWELL wrote a concurring opinion.]

MR. JUSTICE STEVENS, concurring.

There is only one Equal Protection Clause. It requires every State to govern impartially. It does not direct the courts to apply one standard of review in some cases and a different standard in other cases. Whatever criticism may be leveled at a judicial opinion implying that there are at least three such standards applies with the same force to a double standard.

I am inclined to believe that what has become known as the two-tiered analysis of equal protection claims does not describe a completely logical method of deciding cases, but rather is a method the Court has employed to explain decisions that actually apply a single standard in a reasonably consistent fashion. I also suspect that a careful explanation of the reasons motivating particular decisions may contribute more to an identification of that standard than an attempt to articulate it in all-encompassing terms. It may therefore be appropriate for me to state the principal reasons which persuaded me to join the Court's opinion.

In this case, the classification is not as obnoxious as some the Court has condemned, nor as inoffensive as some the Court has accepted. It is objectionable because it is based on an accident of birth, because it is a mere remnant of the now almost universally rejected tradition of discriminating against males in this age bracket, and because, to the extent it reflects any physical difference between males and females, it is actually perverse.* The question then is whether the traffic safety justification put forward by the State is sufficient to make an otherwise offensive classification acceptable.

The classification is not totally irrational. For the evidence does indicate that there are more males than females in this age bracket who drive and also more who drink. Nevertheless, there are several rea-

*Because males are generally heavier than females, they have a greater capacity to consume alcohol without impairing their driving ability than do females.

sons why I regard the justification as unacceptable. It is difficult to believe that the statute was actually intended to cope with the problem of traffic safety, since it has only a minimal effect on access to a not very intoxicating beverage and does not prohibit its consumption. Moreover, the empirical data submitted by the State accentuates the unfairness of treating all 18–20-year-old males as inferior to their female counterparts. The legislation imposes a restraint on 100% of the males in the class allegedly because about 2% of them have probably violated one or more laws relating to the consumption of alcoholic beverages. It is unlikely that this law will have a significant deterrent effect either on that 2% or on the law-abiding 98%. But even assuming some such slight benefit, it does not seem to me that an insult to all of the young men of the State can be justified by visiting the sins of the 2% on the 98%.

[MR. JUSTICE BLACKMUN concurred in part.]

MR. JUSTICE STEWART, concurring in the judgment.

The disparity created by these Oklahoma statutes amounts to total irrationality. For the statistics upon which the State now relies, whatever their other shortcomings, wholly fail to prove or even suggest that 3.2% beer is somehow more deleterious when it comes into the hands of a male aged 18–20 than of a female of like age. The disparate statutory treatment of the sexes here, without even a colorably valid justification of explanation, thus amounts to invidious discrimination.

MR. CHIEF JUSTICE BURGER, dissenting.

At the outset I cannot agree that appellant Whitener has standing arising from her status as a saloon-keeper to assert the constitutional rights of her customers. In this Court "a litigant may only assert his own constitutional rights or immunities.". . . There are a few, but strictly limited exceptions to that rule; despite the most creative efforts, this case fits within none of them.

. . . .

In sum, permitting a vendor to assert the constitutional rights of vendees whenever those rights are arguably infringed introduces a new concept of constitutional standing to which I cannot subscribe.

On the merits, we have only recently recognized that our duty is not "to create substantive constitutional rights in the name of guaranteeing equal protection of the laws." *San Antonio School Dist.* v. *Rodriguez* . . . (1973). Thus, even interests of such importance in our society as public education and housing do not qualify as "fundamental rights" for

equal protection purposes because they have no textually independent constitutional status. Though today's decision does not go so far as to make gender-based classifications "suspect," it makes gender a disfavored classification. Without an independent constitutional basis supporting the right asserted or disfavoring the classification adopted, I can justify no substantive constitutional protection other than the normal protection afforded by the Equal Protection Clause.

The means employed by the Oklahoma Legislature to achieve the objectives sought may not be agreeable to some judges, but since eight Members of the Court think the means not irrational, I see no basis for striking down the statute as violative of the Constituion simply because we find it unwise, unneeded, or possibly even a bit foolish.

With MR. JUSTICE REHNQUIST, I would affirm the judgment of the District Court.

MR. JUSTICE REHNQUIST, dissenting.

The Court's disposition of this case is objectionable on two grounds. First is its conclusion that *men* challenging a gender-based statute which treats them less favorably than women may invoke a more stringent standard of judicial review than pertains to most other types of classifications. Second is the Court's enunciation of this standard, without citation to any source, as being that "classifications by gender must serve *important* governmental objectives and must be *substantially* related to achievement of those objectives." The only redeeming feature of the Court's opinion, to my mind, is that it apparently signals a retreat by those who joined the plurality of opinion in *Frontiero* v. *Richardson* (1973), from their view that sex is a "suspect" classification for purposes of equal protection analysis. I think the Oklahoma statute challenged here need pass only the "rational basis" equal protection analysis expounded in cases such as *McGowan* v. *Maryland* (1961), and *Williamson* v. *Lee Optical Co.* (1955), and I believe that it is constitutional under that analysis.

In *Frontiero* v. *Richardson, supra,* the opinion for the plurality sets forth the reasons of four Justices for concluding that sex should be regarded as a suspect classification for purposes of equal protection analysis. The reasons center on our Nation's "long and unfortunate history of sex discrimination" which has been reflected in a whole range of restrictions on the legal rights of women, not the least of which have concerned the ownership of property and participation in the electoral process. Noting that the pervasive and persistent nature of the discrimination experienced by women is in part the result of their ready identifiability, the plurality rested its invocation of strict scrutiny largely upon the fact that "statutory distinctions between the sexes often have the effect of invidiously relegating the entire class of females to inferior legal status without regard to the actual capabilities of its individual members."

Subsequent to *Frontiero,* the Court has declined to hold that sex is a suspect class, and no such holding is imported by the Court's resolution of this case. However, the Court's application here of an elevated or "intermediate" level scrutiny, like that invoked in cases dealing with discrimination against females, raises the question of why the statute here should be treated any differently from countless legislative classifications unrelated to sex which have been upheld under a minimum rationality standard.

Most obviously unavaliable to support of any kind of special scrutiny in this case, is a history or pattern of past discrimination, such as was relied on by the plurality in *Frontiero* to support its invocation of strict scrutiny. There is no suggestion in the Court's opinion that males in this age group are in any way peculiarly disadvantaged, subject to systematic discriminatory treatment, or otherwise in need of special solicitude from the courts.

The Court does not discuss the nature of the right involved, and there is no reason to believe that it sees the purchase of 3.2% beer as implicating any important interest, let alone one that is "fundamental" in the constitutional sense of invoking strict scrutiny. Indeed, the Court's accurate observation that the statute affects the selling but not the drinking of 3.2% beer, *ante,* at 204, further emphasizes the limited effect that it has on even those persons in the age group involved. There is, in sum, nothing about the statutory classification involved here to suggest that it affects an interest, or works against a group, which can claim under the Equal Protection Clause that it is entitled to special judicial protection.

It is true that a number of our opinions contain broadly phrased dicta implying that the same test should be applied to all classifications based on sex, whether affecting females or males. . . . However, before today, no decision of this Court has applied an elevated level of scrutiny to invalidate a statutory discrimination harmful to males, except where the statute impaired an important personal interest protected by the Constitution. There being no such interest here, and there being no plausible argument that this is a discrimination against females, the Court's reliance on our previous sex-discrimination cases is ill-founded. It treats gender classification as a talisman which — without regard to the rights involved or the persons affected — calls into effect a heavier burden of judicial review.

The Court's conclusion that a law which treats males less favorably than females "must serve important governmental objectives and must be substantially related to achievement of those objectives" apparently comes out of thin air. The Equal Protection Clause contains no such language, and none of our previous cases adopt that standard. I would think we have had enough difficulty with the two standards of review which our cases have recognized — the norm of "rational basis," and the "compelling state interest" required where a "suspect classification" is involved — so as to counsel weightily against the insertion of still another "standard" between those two. How is this Court to divine what objectives are important? How is it to determine whether a particular law is "substantially" related to the achievement of such objective, rather than related in some other way to its achievement? Both of the phrases used are so diaphanous and elastic as to invite subjective judicial preferences or prejudices relating to particular types of legislation, masquerading as judgments whether such legislation is directed at "important" objectives or, whether the relationship to those objectives is "substantial" enough.

I would have thought that if this Court were to leave anything to decision by the popularly elected branches of the Govenment, where no constitutional claim other than that of equal protection is invoked, it would be the decision as to what governmental objectives to be achieved by law are "important," and which are not. As for the second part of the Court's new test, the Judicial Branch is probably in no worse position than the Legislative or Executive Branches to determine if there is *any* rational relationship between a classification and the purpose which it might be thought to serve. But the introduction of the adverb "substantially" requires courts to make subjective judgments as to operational effects, for which neither expertise nor their access to data fits them. And even if we manage to avoid both confusion and the mirroring of our own preferences in the development of this new doctrine, the thousands of judges in other courts who must interpret the Equal Protection Clause may not be so fortunate.

The applicable rational-basis test is one which

> permits the States a wide scope of discretion in enacting laws which affect some groups of citizens differently than others. The constitutional safeguard is offended only if the classification rests on grounds wholly irrelevant to the achievement of the State's objective. State legislatures are presumed to have acted within their constitutional power despite the fact that, in practice, their laws result in

some inequality. A statutory discrimination will not be set aside if any state of facts reasonably may be conceived to justify it. *McGowan* v. *Maryland.*

Our decisions indicate that application of the Equal Protection Clause in a context not justifying an elevated level of scrutiny does not demand "mathematical nicety" or the elimination of all inequality. Those cases recognize that the practical problems of government may require rough accommodations of interests, and hold that such accommodations should be respected unless no reasonable basis can be found to support them. Whether the same ends might have been better or more precisely served by a different approach is no part of the judicial inquiry under the traditional minimum rationality approach. . . .

Personnel Administrator of Massachusetts v. Feeney

442 U.S. 256 (1979)
Vote: 7–2

Helen B. Feeney, who is not a veteran, brought an action alleging that Chapter 31.23 of Massachusetts General Laws providing for absolute lifetime preference for veterans in the civil service inevitably operated to exclude women from consideration for the best Massachusetts civil service jobs and thus denied her equal protection of the laws. Under Chapter 31.23, all veterans who qualify for state civil service positions must be considered for appointment ahead of any qualifying nonveterans. This law, gender-neutral on its face, also allows veterans to exercise this preference at any time and as many times as they wish. In Helen Feeney's case it meant that despite higher scores on the merit selection tests, she was invariably passed over for positions in favor of men who had lower scores but were veterans. After numerous such experiences during a decade of active effort, Ms. Feeney commenced litigation, claiming that the Massachusetts law was unconstitutional.

When this litigation began, over 98 percent of the veterans of Massachusetts were male, and only 1.8 percent were female. Fully one-quarter of the population of the state were veterans. During the decade between 1963 and 1973, when Ms. Feeney was actively but unsuccessfully seeking advancement in the state civil service, over 47,000 new permanent appointments were made. Of those hired, 43 percent were women and 57 percent men, but a large percentage of the female appointees filled lower-paying positions for which males traditionally do not apply. On each of fifty "sample eligible lists" that were part of the trial court record, one or more women who would have been certified as eligible for appointment on the basis of test results were passed over in favor of male veterans with lower test scores.

This case was tried twice before a federal district court. In both instances, the Court concluded that the Massachusetts "absolute preference" policy was unconstitutional.

MR. JUSTICE STEWART delivered the opinion of the Court.

. . . The sole question for decision on this appeal is whether Massachusetts, in granting an absolute lifetime preference to veterans, has discriminated against women in violation of the Equal Protection Clause of the Fourteenth Amendment.

The equal protection guarantee of the Fourteenth Amendment does not take from the States all power of classification. *Massachusetts Bd. of Retirement* v. *Murgia.* Most laws classify, and many affect certain groups unevenly, even though the law itself treats them no differently from all other members of the class described by the law. When the basic classification is rationally based, uneven effects upon particular groups within a class are ordinarily of no constitutional concern. The calculus of effects, the manner in which a particular law reverberates in a society, is a legislative and not a judicial responsibility. *Dandridge* v. *Williams* (1970); *San Antonio School Dist.* v. *Rodriguez* (1973). In assessing an equal protection challenge, a court is called upon only to measure the basic validity of the legislative classification. When some other independent right is not at stake, see, *e.g., Shapiro* v. *Thompson,* and when there is no "reason to infer antipathy," it is presumed that "even improvident decisions will eventually be rectified by the democratic process. . . ."

Certain classifications, however, in themselves supply a reason to infer antipathy. Race is the paradigm. A racial classification, regardless of purported motivation, is presumptively invalid and can be upheld only upon an extraordinary justification. *Brown* v. *Board of Education* (1954). This rule applies as well to a classification that is ostensibly neutral but is an obvious pretext for racial discrimination. But, as was made clear in *Washington* v. *Davis* (1974), and *Arlington Heights* v. *Metropolitan Housing Dev. Corp.* (1975), even if a neutral law has a disproportionately adverse effect upon a racial minority, it is unconstitutional under the Equal Protection Clause only if that impact can be traced to a discriminatory purpose.

Classifications based upon gender, not unlike those based upon race, have traditionally been the touchstone of pervasive and often subtle discrimination. This Court's recent cases teach that such classifications must bear a close and substantial relationship to important governmental objectives, *Craig* v. *Boren* (1976); and are in many settings unconstitutional. Although public employment is not a constitutional right, *Massachusetts Bd. of Retirement* v. *Murgia*, (1976), and the States have wide discretion in framing employee qualifications, these precedents dictate that any state law overtly or covertly designed to prefer males over females in public employment would require an exceedingly persuasive justification to withstand a constitutional challenge under the Equal Protection Clause of the Fourteenth Amendment.

The cases of *Washington* v. *Davis,* and *Arlington Heights* v. *Metropolitan Housing Dev. Corp.,* recognize that when a neutral law has a disparate impact upon a group that has historically been the victim of discrimination, an unconstitutional purpose may still be at work. But those cases signaled no departure from the settled rule that the Fourteenth Amendment guarantees equal laws, not equal rights. *Davis* upheld a job-related employment test that white people passed in proportionately greater numbers than Negroes, for there had been no showing that racial discrimination entered into the establishment or formulation of the test. *Arlington Heights* upheld a zoning board decision that tended to perpetuate racially segregated housing patterns, since, apart from its effect, the board's decision was shown to be nothing more than an application of a constitutionally neutral zoning policy. Those principles apply with equal force to a case involving alleged gender discrimination.

When a statute gender-neutral on its face is challenged on the ground that its effects upon women are disproportionately adverse, a twofold inquiry is thus appropriate. The first question is whether the statutory classification is indeed neutral in the sense that it is not gender based. If the classification itself, covert or overt, is not based upon gender, the second question is whether the adverse effect reflects invidious gender-based discrimination. In this second inquiry, impact provides an "important starting point," but purposeful discrimination is "the condition that offends the Constitution."

It is against this background of precedent that we consider the merits of the case before us.

The question whether ch. 31, §23, establishes a classification that is overtly or covertly based upon gender must first be considered. . . .

If the impact of this statute could not be plausibly explained on a neutral ground, impact itself would signal that the real classification made by the law was in fact not neutral. But there can be but one answer to the question whether this veteran preference excludes significant numbers of women from preferred state jobs because they are women or because they are nonveterans. Apart from the facts that the definition of "veterans" in the statute has always been neutral as to gender and that Massachusetts has consistently defined veteran status in a way that has been inclusive of women who have served in the military, this is not a law that can plausibly be explained only as a gender-based classification. Indeed, it is not a law that can rationally be explained on that ground. Veteran status is not uniquely male. Although few women benefit from the preference, the nonveteran class is not substantially all female. To the contrary, significant numbers of nonveterans are men, and all nonveterans — male as well as female — are placed at a disadvantage. Too many men are affected by ch. 31, §23, to permit the inference that the statute is but a pretext for preferring men over women.

Moreover, as the District Court implicitly found, the purposes of the statute provide the surest explanation for its impact. Just as there are cases in which impact alone can unmask an invidious classification, cf. *Yick Wo* v. *Hopkins,* (1883), there are others in which — notwithstanding impact — the legitimate noninvidious purposes of a law cannot be missed. This is one. The distinction made in ch. 31, §23, is, as it seems to be, quite simply between veterans and nonveterans, not between men and women.

The dispositive question, then, is whether the appellee has shown that a gender-based discriminatory purpose has, at least in some measure, shaped the Massachusetts veterans' preference legislation. As did the District Court, she points to two basic factors which in her view distinguish ch. 31, §23, from the neutral rules at issue in the *Washington* v. *Davis* and *Arlington Heights* cases. The first is the nature of the preference, which is said to be demonstrably gender-biased in the sense that it favors a status reserved under federal military policy primarily to men. The second concerns the impact of the absolute life-time preference upon the employment opportunities of women, an impact claimed to be too inevitable to have been unintended. The appellee contends that these factors, coupled with the fact that the preference itself has little if any relevance to actual job performance, more than suffice to prove the discriminatory intent required to establish a constitutional violation.

The contention that this veterans' preference is "inherently nonneutral" or "gender-biased" presumes that the State, by favoring veterans, intentionally incorporated into its public employment policies the panoply of sex-based and assertedly discriminatory federal laws that have prevented all but a handful of women from becoming veterans. There are two serious difficulties with this argument. First, it is wholly at odds with the District Court's central finding that Massachusetts has not offered a preference to veterans for the purpose of discriminating against women. Second, it cannot be reconciled with the assumption made by both the appellee and the District Court that a more limited hiring preference for veterans could be sustained. Taken together, these difficulties are fatal.

To the extent that the status of veteran is one that few women have been enabled to achieve, every hiring preference for veterans, however modest or extreme, is inherently gender-biased. If Massachusetts by offering such a preference can be said intentionally to have incorporated into its state employment policies the historical gender-based federal military personnel practices, the degree of the preference would or should make no constitutional difference. Invidious discrimination does not become less so because the discrimination accomplished is of a lesser magnitude. Discriminatory intent is simply not amenable to calibration. It either is a factor that has influenced the legislative choice or it is not. The District Court's conclusion that the absolute veterans' preference was not originally enacted or subsequently reaffirmed for the purpose of giving an advantage to males as such necessarily compels the conclusion that the State intended nothing more than to prefer "veterans." Given this finding, simple logic suggests that an intent to exclude women from significant public jobs was not at work in this law. To reason that it was, by describing the preference as "inherently nonneutral" or "gender-biased," is merely to restate the fact of impact, not to answer the question of intent.

To be sure, this case is unusual in that it involves a law that by design is not neutral. The law overtly prefers veterans as such. As opposed to the written test at issue in *Davis,* it does not purport to define a job-related characteristic. To the contrary, it confers upon a specifically described group — perceived to be particularly deserving — a competitive headstart. But the District Court found, and the appellee has not disputed, that this legislative choice was legitimate. The basic distinction between veterans and nonveterans, having been found not gender-based, and the goals of the preference having been found worthy, ch. 31 must be analyzed as is any other neutral law that casts a greater burden upon women as a group than upon men as a group. The enlistment policies of the Armed Services may well have discriminated on the basis of sex. But this history of discrimination against women in the military is not on trial in this case.

The appellee's ultimate argument rests upon the presumption, common to the criminal and civil law, that a person intends the natural and foreseeable consequences of his voluntary actions. Her position was well stated in the concurring opinion in the District Court.

> Conceding . . . that the goal here was to benefit the veteran, there is no reason to absolve the legislature from awareness that the means chosen to achieve this goal would freeze women out of all those state jobs actively sought by men. To be sure, the legislature did not wish to harm women. But the cutting-off of women's opportunities was an inevitable concomitant of the chosen scheme — as inevitable as the proposition that if tails is up, heads must be down. Where a law's consequences are *that* inevitable, can they meaningfully be described as unintended?

This rhetorical question implies that a negative answer is obvious, but it is not. The decision to grant a preference to veterans was of course "intentional." So, necessarily, did an adverse impact upon nonveterans follow from that decision. And it cannot seriously be argued that the Legislature of Massachusetts could have been unaware that most veterans are men. It would thus be disingenuous to say that the adverse consequences of this legislation for women were unintended, in the sense that they were not volitional or in the sense that they were not foreseeable.

"Discriminatory purpose," however, implies more than intent as volition or intent as awareness of consequences. It implies that the decisionmaker, in this case a state legislature, selected or reaffirmed a particular course of action at least in part "because of," not merely "in spite of," its adverse effects upon an identifiable group. Yet nothing in the record demonstrates that this preference for veterans was originally devised or subsequently re-enacted because it would accomplish the collateral goal of keeping women in a stereotypic and predefined place in the Massachusetts Civil Service.

To the contrary, the statutory history shows that the benefit of the preference was consistently offered to "any person" who was a veteran. That benefit has been extended to women under a very broad statutory definition of the term veteran. The preference formula itself, which is the focal point of this challenge, was first adopted — so it appears from this record — out of a perceived need to help a small group of older Civil War veterans. It has been reaffirmed and extended only to cover new veterans. When the totality of legislative actions establishing and extending the Massachusetts veterans' preference are considered, the law remains what it purports to be: a preference for veterans of either sex over nonveterans of either sex, not for men over women.

Veterans' hiring preferences represent an awkward — and, many argue, unfair — exception to the widely shared view that merit and merit alone should prevail in the employment policies of government. After a war, such laws have been enacted virtually without opposition. During peacetime, they inevitably have come to be viewed in many quarters as undemocratic and unwise. Absolute and permanent preferences, as the troubled history of this law demonstrates, have always been subject to the objection that they give the veteran more than a square deal. But the Fourteenth Amendment "cannot be made a refuge from ill-advised . . . laws." The substantial edge granted to veterans by ch. 31, §23, may reflect unwise policy. The appellee, however, has simply failed to demonstrate that the law in any way reflects a purpose to discriminate on the basis of sex.

The judgment is reversed, and the case is remanded for further proceedings consistent with this opinion.

It is so ordered.

[MR. JUSTICE STEVENS, with whom MR. JUSTICE WHITE joined, wrote a brief concurring opinion.]

MR. JUSTICE MARSHALL, with whom MR. JUSTICE BRENNAN joins, dissenting.

Although acknowledging that in some circumstances, discriminatory intent may be inferred from the inevitable or foreseeable impact of a statute, the Court concludes that no such intent has been established here. I cannot agree. In my judgment, Massachusetts' choice of an absolute veterans' preference system evinces purposeful gender-based discrimination. And because the statutory scheme bears no substantial relationship to a legitimate governmental objective, it cannot withstand scrutiny under the Equal Protection Clause.

The District Court found that the "prime objective" of the Massachusetts veterans' preference statute was to benefit individuals with prior military service. Under the Court's analysis, this factual determination "necessarily compels the conclusion that the State intended nothing more than to prefer 'veterans.' Given this finding, simple logic suggests that an intent to exclude women from significant public jobs was not at work in this law." I find the Court's logic neither simple nor compelling.

That a legislature seeks to advantage one group does not, as a matter of logic or common sense, exclude the possibility that it also intends to disadvantage another. Individuals in general and lawmakers in particular frequently act for a variety of reasons. As this Court recognized in *Arlington Heights* v. *Metropolitan Housing Dev. Corp.* (1977), "[r]arely can it be said that a legislature or administrative body operating under a broad mandate made a decision motivated solely by a single concern." Absent an omniscience not commonly attributed to the judiciary, it will often be impossible to ascertain the sole or even dominant purpose of a given statute. Thus, the critical constitutional inquiry is not whether an illicit consideration was the primary or but-for cause of a decision, but rather whether it had an appreciable role in shaping a given legislative enactment. Where there is "proof that a discriminatory purpose has been *a* motivating factor in the decision, . . . judicial deference is no longer justified."

Moreover, since reliable evidence of subjective intentions is seldom obtainable, resort to inference based on objective factors is generally unavoidable. To discern the purposes underlying facially neutral policies, this Court has therefore considered the degree, inevitability, and foreseeability of any disproportionate impact as well as the alternatives reasonably available.

In the instant case, the impact of the Massachusetts statute on women is undisputed. Any veteran with a passing grade on the civil service exam must be placed ahead of a nonveteran, regardless of their respective scores. The District Court found that, as a practical matter, this preference supplants test results as a determinant of upper-level civil service appointments. Because less than 2% of the women in Massachusetts are veterans, the absolute-preference formula has rendered desirable state civil service employment an almost exclusively male prerogative.

As the District Court recognized, this consequence follows foreseeably, indeed inexorably, from the long history of policies severely limiting women's participation in the military. Although neutral in form, the statute is anything but neutral in application. It inescapably reserves a major sector of public employment to "an already established class which, as a matter of historical fact, is 98% male." Where the foreseeable impact of a facially neutral policy is so disproportionate, the burden should rest on the State to establish that sex-based considerations played no part in the choice of the particular legislative scheme.

Clearly, that burden was not sustained here. The legislative history of the statute reflects the Commonwealth's patent appreciation of the impact the preference system would have on women, and an equally evident desire to mitigate that impact only with respect on certain traditionally female occupations. Until 1971, the statute and implementing civil service regulations exempted from operation of the preference any job requisitions "especially calling for women." In practice, this exemption, coupled with the absolute preference for veterans, has created a gender-based civil service hierarchy, with women occupying low-grade clerical and secretarial jobs and men holding more responsible and remunerative positions.

Thus, for over 70 years, the Commonwealth has maintained, as an integral part of its veterans' preference system, an exemption relegating female civil service applicants to occupations traditionally filled by women. Such a statutory scheme both reflects and perpetuates precisely the kind of archaic assumptions about women's roles which we have previously held invalid. Particularly when viewed against the range of less discriminatory alternatives available to assist veterans,* Massachusetts' choice of a formula that so severely restricts public employment opportunities for women cannot reasonably be thought gender-neutral. The Court's conclusion to the contrary — that "nothing in the record" evinces a "collateral goal of keeping women in a stereotypic and predefined place in the Massachusetts Civil Service," — displays a singularly myopic view of the facts established below.

To survive challenge under the Equal Protection Clause, statutes reflecting gender-based discrimina-

*Only four States afford a preference comparable in scope to that of Massachusetts.... Other States and the Federal Government grant point or tie-breaking preferences that do not foreclose opportunities for women....

tion must be substantially related to the achievement of important governmental objectives. Appellants here advance three interests in support of the absolute-preference system: (1) assisting veterans in their readjustment to civilian life; (2) encouraging military enlistment; and (3) rewarding those who have served their country. Although each of those goals is unquestionably legitimate, the "mere recitation of a benign, compensatory purpose" cannot of itself insulate legislative classifications from constitutional scrutiny. And in this case, the Commonwealth has failed to establish a sufficient relationship between its objectives and the means chosen to effectuate them.

With respect to the first interest, facilitating veterans' transition to civilian status, the statute is plainly overinclusive. By conferring a permanent preference, the legislation allows veterans to invoke their advantage repeatedly, without regard to their date of discharge. As the record demonstrates, a substantial majority of those currently enjoying the benefits of the system are not recently discharged veterans in need of readjustment assistance.

Nor is the Commonwealth's second asserted interest, encouraging military service, a plausible justification for this legislative scheme. In its original and subsequent re-enactments, the statute extended benefits retroactively to veterans who had served during a prior specified period. If the Commonwealth's "actual purpose" is to induce enlistment, this legislative design is hardly well suited to that end. For I am unwilling to assume what appellants made no effort to prove, that the possibility of obtaining an *ex post facto* civil service preference significantly influenced the enlistment decisions of Massachusetts residents. Moreover, even if such influence could be presumed, the statute is still grossly overinclusive in that it bestows benefits on men drafted as well as those who volunteered.

Finally, the Commonwealth's third interest, rewarding veterans, does not "adequately justify the salient features" of this preference system. Where a particular statutory scheme visits substantial hardship on a class long subject to discrimination, the legislation cannot be sustained unless "'carefully tuned to alternative considerations.'" Here, there are a wide variety of less discriminatory means by which Massachusetts could effect its compensatory purposes. For example, a point preference system, such as that maintained by many States and the Federal Government, or an absolute preference for a limited duration, would reward veterans without excluding all qualified women from upper-level civil service positions. Apart from public employment, the Commonwealth, can, and does, afford assistance to veterans in various ways, including tax abatements, educational subsidies, and special programs for needy veterans. Unlike these and similar benefits, the costs of which are distributed across the taxpaying public generally, the Massachusetts statute exacts a substantial price from a discrete group of individuals who have long been subject to employment discrimination, and who, "because of circumstances totally beyond their control, have [had] little if any chance of becoming members of the preferred class."

In its present unqualified form, the veterans' preference statute precludes all but a small fraction of Massachusetts women from obtaining any civil service position also of interest to men. Given the range of alternatives available, this degree of preference is not constitutionally permissible.

I would affirm the judgment of the court below.

Mississippi University for Women v. Hogan

458 U.S. 718 (1982)
Vote: 5–4

From its founding in 1884, Mississippi University for Women (MUW), a state-supported university, limited its enrollment to women. In 1974, MUW established a four-year baccalaureate program in nursing, one of three such programs in the state. In 1979, Joe Hogan, an experienced registered nurse living and working in the city in which MUW is located, applied for admission to the baccalaureate program in nursing. Although he was otherwise qualified, he was denied admission solely because of his sex. However, school officials informed him that he could audit courses, even a full complement of courses, although he could not enroll in them for credit.

Hogan filed an action in district court claiming the single-sex admissions policy violated the Equal Protection Clause of the Fourteenth Amendment.

JUSTICE O'CONNOR delivered the opinion of the Court.

We begin our analysis aided by several firmly-established principles. Because the challenged policy expressly discriminates among applicants on the basis of gender, it is subject to scrutiny under the Equal Protection Clause of the Fourteenth Amendment. *Reed* v. *Reed*... (1971). That this statute discriminates against males rather than against females does not exempt it from scrutiny or reduce the standard of review. Our decisions also establish that the party seeking to uphold a statute that classifies individuals on the basis of their gender must carry the burden of showing an "exceedingly persuasive justification" for the classification. The burden is met only by showing at least that the classification serves "important governmental objectives and that the discriminatory means employed" are "substantially related to the achievement of those objectives."

Although the test for determining the validity of a gender-based classification is straightforward, it must be applied free of fixed notions concerning the roles and abilities of males and females. Care must be taken in ascertaining whether the statutory objective itself reflects archaic and stereotypic notions. Thus, if the statutory objective is to exclude or "protect" members of one gender because they are presumed to suffer from an inherent handicap or to be innately inferior, the objective itself is illegitimate.

If the State's objective is legitimate and important, we next determine whether the requisite direct, substantial relationship between objective and means is present. The purpose of requiring that close relationship is to assure that the validity of a classification is determined through reasoned analysis rather than through the mechanical application of traditional, often inaccurate, assumptions about the proper roles of men and women. The need for the requirement is amply revealed by reference to the broad range of statutes already invalidated by this Court, statutes that relied upon the simplistic, outdated assumption that gender could be used as a "proxy for other, more germane bases of classification," *Craig* v. *Boren* (1976), to establish a link between objective and classification.

Applying this framework, we now analyze the arguments advanced by the State to justify its refusal to allow males to enroll for credit in MUW's School of Nursing.

The State's primary justification for maintaining the single-sex admissions policy of MUW's School of Nursing is that it compensates for discrimination against women and, therefore, constitutes educational affirmative action. Pet. Brief 8. As applied to the School of Nursing, we find the State's argument unpersuasive.

In limited circumstances, a gender-based classification favoring one sex can be justified if it intentionally and directly assists members of the sex that is disproportionately burdened. See *Schlesinger* v.

Ballard (1975). However, we consistently have emphasized that "the mere recitation of a benign, compensatory purpose is not an automatic shield which protects against any inquiry into the actual purposes underlying a statutory scheme." The same searching analysis must be made, regardless of whether the State's objective is to eliminate family controversy, *Reed* v. *Reed*, to achieve administrative efficiency, *Frontiero* v. *Richardson*, or to balance the burdens borne by males and females.

It is readily apparent that a State can evoke a compensatory purpose to justify an otherwise discriminatory classification only if members of the gender benefited by the classification actually suffer a disadvantage related to the classification. We considered such a situation in *Califano* v. *Webster* (1977), which involved a challenge to a statutory classification that allowed women to eliminate more low-earning years than men for purposes of computing Social Security retirement benefits. Although the effect of the classification was to allow women higher monthly benefits than were available to men with the same earning history, we upheld the statutory scheme, noting that it took into account that women "as such have been unfairly hindered from earning as much as men" and "work[ed] directly to remedy" the resulting economic disparity.

A similar pattern of discrimination against women influenced our decision in *Schlesinger* v. *Ballard* (1975). There, we considered a federal statute that granted female Naval officers a 13-year tenure of commissioned service before mandatory discharge, but accorded male officers only a nine-year tenure. We recognized that, because women were barred from combat duty, they had had fewer opportunities for promotion than had their male counterparts. By allowing women an additional four years to reach a particular rank before subjecting them to mandatory discharge, the statute directly compensated for other statutory barriers to advancement.

In sharp contrast, Mississippi has made no showing that women lacked opportunities to obtain training in the field of nursing or to attain positions of leadership in that field when the MUW School of Nursing opened its door or that women currently are deprived of such opportunities. In fact, in 1970, the year before the School of Nursing's first class enrolled, women earned 94 percent of the nursing baccalaureate degrees conferred in Mississippi and 98.6 percent of the degrees earned nationwide.... As one would expect, the labor force reflects the same predominance of women in nursing. When MUW's School of Nursing began operation, nearly 98 percent of all employed registered nurses were female.

Rather than compensate for discriminatory barriers faced by women, MUW's policy of excluding males from admission to the School of Nursing tends to perpetuate the stereotyped view of nursing as an exclusively woman's job. By assuring that Mississippi allots more openings in its state-supported nursing schools to women than it does to men, MUW's admissions policy lends credibility to the old view that women, not men, should become nurses, and makes the assumption that nursing is a field for women a self-fulfilling prophecy. Thus, we conclude that, although the State recited a "benign, compensatory purpose," it failed to establish that the alleged objective is the actual purpose underlying the discriminatory classification.

The policy is invalid also because it fails the second part of the equal protection test, for the State has made no showing that the gender-based classification is substantially and directly related to its proposed compensatory objective. To the contrary, MUW's policy of permitting men to attend classes as auditors fatally undermines its claim that women, at least those in the School of Nursing, are adversely affected by the presence of men.

. . . .

Thus, considering both the asserted interest and the relationship between the interest and the methods used by the State, we conclude that the State has fallen far short of establishing the "exceedingly persuasive justification" needed to sustain the gender-based classification. Accordingly, we hold that MUW's policy of denying males the right to enroll for credit in its School of Nursing violates the Equal Protection Clause of the Fourteenth Amendment.

CHIEF JUSTICE BURGER, dissenting.

I agree generally with JUSTICE POWELL's dissenting opinion. I write separately, however, to emphasize that the Court's holding today is limited to the context of a professional nursing school.... Since the Court's opinion relies heavily on its finding that women have traditionally dominated the nursing profession, ... it suggests that a State might well be justified in maintaining, for example, the option of an all-women's business school or liberal arts program.

[JUSTICE BLACKMUN dissented.]

JUSTICE POWELL, with whom JUSTICE REHNQUIST joins, dissenting.

The Court's opinion bows deeply to conformity. Left without honor — indeed, held unconstitutional — is an element of diversity that has characterized much of American education and enriched much of American life. The Court in effect holds today that no State now may provide even a single institution of higher learning open only to women students. It gives no need to the efforts of the State of Mississippi to provide abundant opportunities for young men and young women to attend coeducational institutions, and none to the preferences of the more than 40,000 young women who over the years have evidenced their approval of an all-women's college by choosing Mississippi University for Women (MUW) over seven coeducational universities within the State. The Court decides today that the Equal Protection Clause makes it unlawful for the State to provide women with a traditionally popular and respected choice of educational environment. It does so in a case instituted by one man, who represents no class, and whose primary concern is personal convenience.

It is undisputed that women enjoy complete equality of opportunity in Mississippi's public system of higher education. Of the State's eight universities and 16 junior colleges, all except MUW are coeducational. At least two other Mississippi universities would have provided respondent with the nursing curriculum that he wishes to pursue. No other male has joined in his complaint. The only groups with any personal acquantance with MUW to file *amicus* briefs are female students and alumnae of MUW. And they have emphatically rejected respondent's arguments, urging that the State of Mississippi be allowed to continue offering the choice from which they have benefited.

Nor is respondent significantly disadvantaged by MUW's all-female tradition. His constitutional complaint is based upon a single asserted harm: that he must *travel* to attend the state-supported nursing schools that concededly are available to him. The Court characterizes this injury as one of "inconvenience." This description is fair and accurate, though somewhat embarrassed by the fact that there is, of course, no constitutional right to attend a state-supported university in one's home town. Thus the Court, to redress respondent's injury of inconvenience, must rest its invalidation of MUW's single-sex program on a mode of "sexual stereotype" reasoning that has no application whatever to the respondent or to the "wrong" of which he complains. At best this is anomalous. And ultimately the anomaly reveals legal error — that of applying a heightened equal protection standard, developed in cases of genuine sexual stereotyping, to a narrowly utilized state classification that provides an *additional* choice for women. Moreover, I believe that Mississippi's educational system should be upheld in this case even if this inappropriate method of analysis is applied.

Coeducation, historically, is a novel educational theory. From grade school through high school, college, and graduate and professional training, much of the nation's population during much of our history has been educated in sexually segregated classrooms. At the college level, for instance, until recently some of the most prestigious colleges and universities — including most of the Ivy League — had long histories of single-sex education. . . .

The sexual segregation of students has been a reflection of, rather than an imposition upon, the preference of those subject to the policy. It cannot be disputed, for example, that the highly qualified women attending the leading women's colleges could have earned admission to virtually any college of their choice. Women attending such colleges have chosen to be there, usually expressing a preference for the special benefits of single-sex institutions. Similar decisions were made by the colleges that elected to remain open to women only.

The arguable benefits of single-sex colleges also continue to be recognized by students of higher education. The Carnegie Commission on Higher Education has reported that it "favor[s] the continuation of colleges for women. They provide an element of diversity . . . and [an environment in which women] generally . . . speak up more in their classes, . . . hold more positions of leadership on campus, . . . and have more role models and mentors among women teachers and administrators." A 10-year empirical study by the Cooperative Institutional Research Program of the American Counsel of Education and the University of California, Los Angeles also has affirmed the distinctive benefits of single-sex colleges and universities.

Despite the continuing expressions that single-sex institutions may offer singular advantages to their students, there is no doubt that coeducational institutions are far more numerous. But their numerical predominance does not establish — in any sense properly cognizable by a court — that individual preferences for single-sex education are misguided or illegitimate, or that a State may not provide its citizens with a choice.

The issue in this case is whether a State transgresses the Constitution when — within the context of a public system that offers a diverse range of campuses, curricula, and educational alternatives — it seeks to accommodate the legitimate personal preferences of those desiring the advantages of an all-women's college. In my view, the Court errs seriously by assuming — without argument or discussion—that the equal protection standard generally applicable to sex discrimination is appropriate here. That standard was designed to free women from "archaic and overbroad generalizations. . . ." In no previous case have we applied it to invalidate state efforts to *expand* women's choices. Nor are there prior sex discrimination decisions by this Court in which a male plaintiff, as in this case, had the choice of an equal benefit.

. . . .

By applying heightened equal protection analysis to this case, the Court frustrates the liberating spirit of the Equal Protection Clause. It forbids the States from providing women with an opportunity to choose the type of university they prefer. And yet it is these women whom the Court regards as the *victims* of an illegal, stereotyped perception of the role of women in our society. The Court reasons this way in a case in which no woman has complained, and the only complainant is a man who advances no claims on behalf of anyone else. His claim, it should be recalled, is not that he is being denied a substantive educational opportunity, or even the right to attend an all-male or a coeducational college. It is *only* that the colleges open to him are located at inconvenient distances.

The Court views this case as presenting a serious equal protection claim of sex discrimination. I do not, and I would sustain Mississippi's right to continue MUW on a rational basis analysis. But I need not apply this "lowest tier" of scrutiny. I can accept for present purposes the standard applied by the Court: that there is a gender-based distinction that must serve an important governmental objective by means that are substantially related to its achievement. The record in this case reflects that MUW has a historic position in the State's educational system dating back to 1884. More than 2,000 women presently evidence their preference for MUW by having enrolled there. The choice is one that discriminates invidiously against no one. And the State's purpose in preserving that choice is legitimate and substantial. Generations of our finest minds, both among educators and students, have believed that single-sex, college-level institutions afford distinctive benefits. There are many persons, of course, who have different views. But simply because there are these differences is no reason—certainly none of constitutional dimension—to conclude that no substantial state interest is served when such a choice is made available.

. . . .

In sum, the practice of voluntarily chosen single-sex education is an honored tradition in our country, even if it now rarely exists in state colleges and universities. Mississippi's accommodation of such student choices is legitimate because it is completely consensual and is important because it permits students to decide for themselves the type of college education they think will benefit them most. Finally, Mississippi's policy is substantially related to its long-respected objective.

A distinctive feature of America's tradition has been respect for diversity. This has been characteristic of the peoples from numerous lands who have built our country. It is the essence of our democratic system. At stake in this case as I see it is the preservation of a small aspect of this diversity. But that aspect is by no means insignificant, given our heritage of available choice between single-sex and coeducational institutions of higher learning. The Court answers that there is discrimination—not just that which may be tolerable, as for example between those candidates for admission able to contribute most to an educational institution and those able to contribute less—but discrimination of constitutional dimension. But, having found "discrimination," the Court finds it difficult to identify the victims. It hardly can claim that women are discriminated against. A constitutional case is held to exist solely because one man found it inconvenient to travel to any of the other institutions made available to him by the State of Mississippi. In essence he insists that he has a right to attend a college in his home community. This simply is not a sex discrimination case. The Equal Protection Clause was never intended to be applied to this kind of case.

Johnson v. Transportation Agency, Santa Clara County

107 S.Ct. 1442 (1987)
See pp. 792–796.

Korematsu v. U.S.

323 U.S. 214 (1944)
See pp. 156–160.

Ambach v. Norwich

441 U.S. 68 (1979)
Vote: 5–4

New York Education Law 3001(3) forbids permanent certification as a public school teacher of any person who is not a United States citizen, unless that person has manifested an intention to apply for citizenship. Ms. Norwich, a subject of Great Britain, was married to a United States citizen and had resided in this country for ten years at the time she made application for a teaching certificate for nursery school through sixth grade. This application was denied by Ambach, Commissioner of Education of the State of New York, who cited Section 3001(3). Norwich filed suit in federal court, seeking to enjoin enforcement of the law. Applying "close judicial scrutiny," the district court held that the statute was overbroad because it excluded all resident aliens from all teaching jobs regardless of the subject to be taught, the alien's nationality, the alien's relationship to this country, and the alien's willingness to substitute some other sign of loyalty to this nation's political values. New York appealed.

As you read the majority and minority opinions, see if you can clearly distinguish between those restrictions the Court has upheld and those it has overturned in cases handed down since World War II. Then look at the dates of these decisions. Is there an underlying principle at work, or are the changes best explained by shifts in the temper of the times and changes on the Court? Does the Court appear to be returning to a deference to legislatures that it so willingly adopted in an earlier era? Are there any differences in the way the Court goes about upholding New York's restrictions on aliens in this case and the Court's willingness to uphold the executive order that applied to citizens as well as aliens in KOREMATSU? Why isn't KOREMATSU cited in the opinion?

MR. JUSTICE POWELL delivered the opinion of the Court.

The decisions of this Court regarding the permissibility of statutory classifications involving aliens have not formed an unwavering line over the years. State regulation of the employment of aliens long has been subject to constitutional constraints. In *Yick Wo* v. *Hopkins* (1886), the Court struck down an ordinance which was applied to prevent aliens from running laundries, and in *Truax* v. *Raich* (1915), a law requiring at least 80% of the employees of certain businesses to be citizens was held to be an unconstitutional infringement of an alien's "right to work for a living in the common occupations of the community...." At the same time, however, the Court also has recognized a greater degree of latitude for the States when aliens were sought to be excluded from public employment. At the time *Truax* was decided, the governing doctrine permitted States to exclude aliens from various activities when the restriction pertained to "the regulation or distribution of the public domain, or of the common property or resources of the people of the State...." Hence, as part of a larger authority to forbid aliens from owning land, *Frick* v. *Webb* (1923); *Webb* v. *O'Brien* (1923); *Porterfield* v. *Webb* (1923); *Terrace* v. *Thompson* (1923); *Blythe* v. *Hinckley* (1901); *Hauenstein* v. *Lynham* (1880); harvesting wildlife, *Patsone* v. *Pennsylvania* (1914); *McCready* v. *Virginia* (1877); or maintaining an inherently dangerous enterprise, *Ohio ex rel. Clarke* v. *Deckebach* (1927), States permissibly could exclude aliens from working on public construction projects, *Crane* v. *New York* (1915), and, it appears, from engaging in any form of public employment at all....

Over time, the Court's decisions gradually have restricted the activities from which States are free to exclude aliens. The first sign that the Court would question the constitutionality of discrimination against aliens even in areas affected with a "public interest" appeared in *Oyama* v. *California* (1948). The Court there held that statutory presumptions designed to discourage evasion of California's ban on alien landholding discriminated against the citizen children of aliens. The same Term, the Court held that the "ownership" a State exercises over fish found in its territorial waters "is inadequate to justify California in excluding any or all aliens who are lawful residents of the State from making a living by fishing in the ocean off its shores while permitting all others to do so." *Takahashi* v. *Fish & Game Comm'n* (1948). This process of withdrawal from the former doctrine culminated in *Graham* v. *Richardson* (1971), which for the first time treated classifications based on alienage as "inherently suspect and subject to close judicial scrutiny." Applying *Graham*, this Court has held invalid statutes that prevented aliens from entering a State's classified civil service, *Sugarman* v. *Dougall* (1973), practicing law, *In re Griffiths* (1973), working as an engineer, *Examining Board* v. *Flores de Otero* (1976), and receiving state educational benefits, *Nyquist* v. *Mauclet* (1977).

Although our more recent decisions have departed substantially from the public-interest doctrine of *Truax's* day, they have not abandoned the general principle that some state functions are so bound up with the operation of the State as a governmental entity as to permit the exclusion from those functions of all persons who have not become part of the process of self-government. In *Sugarman,* we recognized that a State could, "in an appropriately defined class of positions, require citizenship as a qualification for office." . . . The exclusion of aliens from such governmental positions would not invite as demanding scrutiny from this Court.

Applying the rational-basis standard, we held last Term that New York could exclude aliens from the ranks of its police force. *Foley* v. *Connelie* (1978). Because the police function fulfilled "a most fundamental obligation of government to its constituency" and by necessity cloaked policemen with substantial discretionary powers, we viewed the police force as being one of those appropriately defined classes of positions for which a citizenship requirement could be imposed. Accordingly, the State was required to justify its classification only "by a showing of some rational relationship between the interest sought to be protected and the limiting classification."

The rule for governmental functions, which is an exception to the general standard applicable to classifications based on alienage, rests on important principles inherent in the Constitution. The distinction between citizens and aliens, though ordinarily irrelevant to private activity, is fundamental to the definition and government of a State. The Constitution itself refers to the distinction no less than 11 times indicating that the status of citizenship was meant to have significance in the structure of our government. The assumption of that status, whether by birth or naturalization, denotes an association with the polity which, in a democratic republic, exercises the powers of governance. The form of this association is important: an oath of allegiance or similar ceremony cannot substitute for the unequivocal legal bond citizenship represents. It is because of this special significance of citizenship that governmental entities, when exercising the functions of government, have wider latitude in limiting the participation of noncitizens.

In determining whether, for purposes of equal protection analysis, teaching in public schools constitutes a governmental function, we look to the role of public education and to the degree of responsibility and discretion teachers possess in fulfilling that role. Each of these considerations supports the conclusion that public school teachers may be regarded as performing a task "that go[es] to the heart of representative government."

Public education, like the police function, "fulfills a most fundamental obligation of government to its constituency." The importance of public schools in the preparation of individuals for participation as citizens, and in the preservation of the values on which our society rests, long has been recognized by our decisions.

. . . [A] State properly may regard all teachers as having an obligation to promote civic virtues and understanding in their classes, regardless of the subject taught. Certainly a State also may take account of a teacher's function as an example for students, which exists independently of particular classroom subjects. In light of the foregoing considerations, we think it clear that public school teachers come well within the "governmental function" principle recognized in *Sugarman* and *Foley.* Accordingly, the Constitution requires only that a citizenship requirement applicable to teaching in the public schools bear a rational relationship to a legitimate state interest.

As the legitimacy of the State's interest in furthering the educational goals outlined above is undoubted, it remains only to consider whether §3001(3) bears a rational relationship to this interest. The restriction is carefully framed to serve its purpose, as it bars from teaching only those aliens who have demonstrated their unwillingness to obtain United States citizenship. Appellees, and aliens similarly situated, in effect have chosen to classify themselves. They prefer to retain citizenship in a foreign country with the obligations it entails of primary duty and loyalty. They have rejected the open invitation extended to qualify for eligibility to teach by applying for citizenship in this country. The people of New York, acting through their elected representatives, have made a judgment that citizenship should be a qualification for teaching the young of the State in the public schools, and §3001(3) furthers that judgment.

Reversed.

MR. JUSTICE BLACKMUN, with whom MR. JUSTICE BRENNAN, MR. JUSTICE MARSHALL, and MR. JUSTICE STEVENS join, dissenting.

Once again the Court is asked to rule upon the constitutionality of one of New York's many statutes that impose a requirement of citizenship upon a person before that person may earn his living in a specified occupation. These New York statutes, for the most part, have their origin in the frantic and overreactive days of the First World War when attitudes of parochialism and fear of the foreigner were the order of the day.

As the Court acknowledges, its decisions regarding the permissibility of statutory classifications concerning aliens "have not formed an unwavering line over the years." Thus, just last Term, in *Foley* v. *Connelie* (1978), the Court upheld against equal protection challenge the New York statute limiting appointment of members of the state police force to citizens of the United States. The touchstone, the Court indicated, was that "citizenship may be a relevant qualification for fulfilling 'important nonelective executive, legislative, and judicial positions' held by 'officers who participate directly in the formulation, execution, or review of broad public policy.'" For such positions, a State need show only some rational relationship between the interest sought to be protected and the limiting classification. Police, it then was felt, were clothed with authority to exercise an almost infinite variety of discretionary powers that could seriously affect members of the public. They thus fell within the category of important officers who participate directly in the execution of "broad public policy." The Court was persuaded that citizenship bore a rational relationship to the special demands of police positions, and that a State therefore could constitutionally confine that public responsibility to citizens of the United States.

On the other hand, the Court frequently has invalidated a state provision that denies a resident alien the right to engage in specified occupational activity: *Yick Wo* v. *Hopkins* (1886) (ordinance applied so as to prevent Chinese subjects from engaging in the laundry business); *Truax* v. *Raich* (1915) (statute requiring an employer's work force to be composed of not less than 80% "qualified electors or native-born citizens"); *Takahashi* v. *Fish & Game* (1948) (limitation of commercial fishing licenses to persons not "ineligible to citizenship"); *Sugerman* v. *Dougall* (New York statute relating to permanent positions in the "competitive class" of the state civil service); *In re Griffiths* (1973) (the practice of law); *Nelson* v. *Miranda* (1973), summarily aff'g. (Ariz. 1972) (social service worker and teacher); *Examining Board* v. *Flores de Otero* (1976) (the practice of civil engineering). See also *Nyquist* v. *Mauclet* (New York statute barring certain resident aliens from state financial assistance for higher education).

Indeed, the Court has held more than once that state classifications based on alienage are "inherently suspect and subject to close judicial scrutiny." And "[a]lienage classifications by a State that do not withstand this stringent examination cannot stand."

There is thus a line, most recently recognized in *Foley* v. *Connelie,* between those employments that a State in its wisdom constitutionally may restrict to United States citizens, on the one hand, and those employments, on the other, that the State may not deny to resident aliens. For me, the present case falls on the *Sugarman-Griffiths-Flores de Otero-Mauclet* side of that line, rather than on the narrowly isolated *Foley* side.

. . . .

But the Court, to the disadvantage of appellees, crosses the line from *Griffiths* to *Foley* by saying, that the "distinction between citizens and aliens, though ordinarily irrelevant to private activity, is fundamental to the definition and government of a State." It then concludes that public school teaching "constitutes a governmental function," *ibid.,* and that public school teachers may be regarded as performing a task that goes "to the heart of representative government." The Court speaks of the importance of public schools in the preparation of individuals for participation as citizens, and in the preservation of the values on which our society rests. After then observing that teachers play a critical part in all this, the Court holds that New York's citizenship requirement is constitutional because it bears a rational relationship to the State's interest in furthering these educational goals.

I perceive a number of difficulties along the easy road the Court takes to this conclusion:

First, the New York statutory structure itself refutes the argument. Section 3001(3) provides for exceptions with respect to alien teachers "employed pursuant to regulations adopted by the commissioner of education permitting such employment," provides another exception for persons ineligible for United States citizenship because of oversubscribed quotas. Also, New York is unconcerned with any citizenship qualification for teachers in the private schools of the State, even though the record indicates that about 18% of the pupils at the elementary and secondary levels attend private schools. . . . And the stark fact that the State permits some aliens to sit on certain local school boards, reveals how shallow and indistinct is New York's line of demarcation between citizenship and noncitizenship. The Court's attempted rationalization of this fact hardly extinguishes the influence school board members, including these otherwise "disqualified" resident aliens, possess in school administration, in the selection of faculty, and in the approval of textbooks and instructional materials.

Second, the New York statute is all-inclusive in its disqualifying provisions: "No person shall be employed or authorized to teach in the public schools of the state who is . . . [n]ot a citizen." It sweeps indiscriminately. It is "neither narrowly confined nor precise in its application," nor limited to the accomplishment of substantial state interests.

Third, the New York classification is irrational. Is it better to employ a poor citizen teacher than an excellent resident alien teacher? Is it preferable to have a citizen who has never seen Spain or a Latin American country teach Spanish to eighth graders and to deny that opportunity to a resident alien who may have lived for 20 years in the culture of Spain or

Latin America? The State will know how to select its teachers responsibly, wholly apart from citizenship, and can do so selectively and intelligently.

Fourth, it is logically impossible to differentiate between this case concerning teachers and *In re Griffiths* concerning attorneys. If a resident alien *may not* constitutionally be barred from taking a state bar examination and thereby becoming qualified to practice law in the courts of a State, how is one to comprehend why a resident alien *may* constitutionally be barred from teaching in the elementary and secondary levels of a State's public schools? One may speak proudly of the role model of the teacher, of his ability to mold young minds, of his inculcating force as to national ideals, and of his profound influence in the impartation of our society's values. Are the attributes of an attorney any the less? He represents us in our critical courtroom controversies even when citizenship and loyalty may be questioned. He stands as an officer of every court in which he practices. He is responsible for strict adherence to the announced and implied standards of professional conduct and to the requirements of evolving ethical codes and for honesty and integrity in his professional and personal life. Despite the almost continuous criticism leveled at the legal profession, he, too, is an influence in legislation, in the community, and in the role-model figure that the professional person enjoys. . . .

If an attorney has a constitutional right to take a bar examination and practice law, despite his being a resident alien, it is impossible for me to see why a resident alien, otherwise completely competent and qualified, as these appellees concededly are, is constitutionally disqualified from teaching in the public schools of the great State of New York. The District Court expressed it well and forcefully when it observed that New York's exclusion "seems repugnant to the very heritage the State is seeking to inculcate."

I respectfully dissent.

Massachusetts Board of Retirement v. Murgia

427 U.S. 307 (1976)
Vote: 7–1

A Massachusetts statute mandated retirement at the age of fifty for all uniformed state police officers. Four months before his mandatory retirement, Officer Murgia passed the state's comprehensive physical exam and was pronounced in excellent physical shape and capable of performing the duties of a uniformed officer. Still, he was forced to retire at age fifty. He sued, claiming the law violated his equal protection rights. He won at the district court, which said it did not have to decide whether to use ordinary or strict scrutiny since the Massachusetts law would fall on the lesser of the two tests. Massachusetts appealed.

Apart from its outcome, this case is interesting for Justice Marshall's dissent, which rejects the two-tier (ordinary scrutiny and strict scrutiny) approach to Fourteenth Amendment claims, and argues that the Court has sub silentio abandoned it in civil rights cases for a more flexible and variable approach whose minimum rational-test position has considerably more bite than the rational-relation position traditionally used to assess economic regulations. By now you are in a position to make a judgment. Is he correct? If so, does he adequately articulate what the Court's new "real" approach is?

PER CURIAM

We need state only briefly our reasons for agreeing that strict scrutiny is not the proper test for determining whether the mandatory retirement provision denies appellee equal protection. *San Antonio School District* v. *Rodriguez* (1973) reaffirmed that equal protection analysis requires strict scrutiny of a legislative classification only when the classification impermissibly interferes with the exercise of a fundamental right or operates to the peculiar disadvantage of a suspect class. Mandatory retirement at age 50 under the Massachusetts statute involves neither situation.

This Court's decisions give no support to the proposition that a right of governmental employment *per se* is fundamental. Accordingly, we have expressly stated that a standard less than strict scrutiny "has consistently been applied to state legislation restricting the availability of employment opportunities."

Nor does the class of uniformed state police officers over 50 constitute a suspect class for purposes of equal protection analysis. [We] observe that a suspect class is one "saddled with such disabilities, or subjected to such a history of purposeful unequal treatment, or relegated to such a position of political powerlessness as to command extraordinary protection from the majoritarian political process." While the treatment of the aged in this Nation has not been wholly free of discrimination, such persons, unlike, say, those who have been discriminated against on the basis of race or national origin, have not experienced a "history of purposeful unequal treatment" or been subjected to unique disabilities on the basis of stereotyped characteristics not truly indicative of their abilities. The class subject to the compulsory retirement feature of the Massachusetts statute consists of uniformed state police officers over the age of 50. It cannot be said to discriminate only against the elderly. Rather, it draws the line at a certain age in middle life. But even old age does not define a "discrete and insular" group in need of "extraordinary protection from the majoritarian political process." Instead, it marks a stage that each of us will reach if we live out our normal span. Even if the statute could be said to impose a penalty upon a class defined as the aged, it would not impose a distinction sufficiently akin to those classifications that we have found suspect to call for strict judicial scrutiny.

Under the circumstances, it is unnecessary to subject the State's resolution of competing interests in this case to the degree of critical examination that our cases under the Equal Protection Clause recently have characterized as "strict judicial scrutiny."

We turn then to examine this state classification under the rational-basis standard. This inquiry employs a relatively relaxed standard reflecting the Court's awareness that the drawing of lines that create distinctions is peculiarly a legislative task and an unavoidable one. Perfection in making the necessary classifications is neither possible nor necessary. Such action by a legislature is presumed to be valid.

In this case, the Massachusetts statute clearly meets the requirements of the Equal Protection Clause, for the State's classification rationally furthers the purpose identified by the State: Through mandatory retirement at age 50, the legislature seeks to protect the public by assuring physical preparedness of its uniformed police. Since physical ability generally declines with age, mandatory retirement at 50 serves to remove from police service those whose fitness for uniformed work presumptively has diminished with age. This clearly is rationally related to the State's objective. There is no indication that §26(3)(a) has the effect of excluding from service so few officers who are in fact unqualified as to render age 50 a criterion wholly unrelated to the objective of the statute.

That the State chooses not to determine fitness more precisely through individualized testing after age 50 is not to say that the objective of assuring physical fitness is not rationally furthered by a maximum-age limitation. It is only to say that with regard to the interest of all concerned, the State perhaps has not chosen the best means to accomplish this purpose. But where rationality is the test, a State "does not violate the Equal Protection Clause merely because the classifications made by its laws are imperfect."

We do not make light of the substantial economic and psychological effects premature and compulsory retirement can have on an individual; nor do we denigrate the ability of elderly citizens to continue to contribute to society. The problems of retirement have been well documented and are beyond serious dispute. But "[w]e do not decide today that the [Massachusetts statute] is wise, that it best fulfills the relevant social and economic objectives that [Massachusetts] might ideally espouse, or that a more just and humane system could not be devised." We decide only that the system enacted by the Massachusetts Legislature does not deny appellee equal protection of the laws.

The judgment is reversed.

MR. JUSTICE STEVENS took no part in the consideration or decision of this case.

MR. JUSTICE MARSHALL, dissenting.

Today the Court holds that it is permissible for the Commonwealth of Massachusetts to declare that members of its state police force who have been proved medically fit for service are nonetheless legislatively unfit to be policemen and must be terminated—involuntarily "retired"—because they have reached the age of 50. Although we have called the right to work "of the very essence of the personal freedom and opportunity that it was the purpose of the [Fourteenth] Amendment to secure," the Court finds that the right to work is not a fundamental right. And, while agreeing that "the treatment of the aged in this Nation has not been wholly free of discrimination," the Court holds that the elderly are not a suspect class. Accordingly, the Court undertakes the scrutiny mandated by the bottom tier of its two-tier equal protection framework, finds the challenged legislation not to be "wholly unrelated" to its objective, and holds, therefore, that it survives equal protection attack. I respectfully dissent.

Although there are signs that its grasp on the law is weakening, the rigid two-tier model still holds sway as the Court's articulated description of the equal protection test. Again, I must object to its perpetuation. The model's two fixed modes of analysis, strict scrutiny and mere rationality, simply do not describe the inquiry the Court has undertaken — or should undertake — in equal protection cases. Rather, the inquiry has been much more sophisticated and the Court should admit as much. It has focused upon the character of the classification in question, the relative importance to individuals in the class discriminated against of the governmental benefits that they do not receive, and the state interests asserted in support of the classification.

Although the Court outwardly adheres to the two-tier model, it has apparently lost interest in recognizing further "fundamental" rights and "suspect" classes. In my view, this result is the natural consequence of the limitations of the Court's traditional equal protection analysis. If a statute invades a "fundamental" right or discriminates against a "suspect" class, it is subject to strict scrutiny. If a statute is subject to strict scrutiny, the statute always, or nearly always, is struck down. Quite obviously, the only critical decision is whether strict scrutiny should be invoked at all. It should be no surprise, then, that the Court is hesitant to expand the number of categories of rights and classes subject to strict scrutiny, when each expansion involves the invalidation of virtually every classification bearing upon a newly covered category.

But however understandable the Court's hesitancy to invoke strict scrutiny, all remaining legislation should not drop into the bottom tier, and be measured by the mere rationality test. For that test, too, when applied as articulated, leaves little doubt about the outcome: the challenged legislation is always upheld. See *New Orleans v. Dukes* (overruling *Morey v. Doud* (1957), the only modern case in which this Court has struck down an economic classification as irrational). It cannot be gainsaid that there remain rights, not now classified as "fundamental," that remain vital to the flourishing of a free society, and classes, not now classified as "suspect," that are unfairly burdened by invidious discrimination unrelated to the individual worth of their members. Whatever we call these rights and classes, we simply cannot forgo all judicial protection against discriminatory legislation bearing upon them, but for the rare instances when the legislative choice can be termed "wholly irrelevant" to the legislative goal.

While the Court's traditional articulation of the rational-basis test does suggest just such an abdication, happily the Court's deeds have not matched its words. Time and again, met with cases touching upon the prized rights and burdened classes of our society, the Court has acted only after a reasonably probing look at the legislative goals and means, and at the significance of the personal rights and interests invaded. These cases make clear that the Court has rejected, albeit *sub silentio,* its most deferential statements of the rationality standard in assessing the validity under the Equal Protection Clause of much noneconomic legislation.

But there are problems with deciding cases based on factors not encompassed by the applicable standards. First, the approach is rudderless, affording no notice to interested parties of the standards governing particular cases and giving no firm guidance to judges who, as a consequence, must assess the constitutionality of legislation before them on an *ad hoc* basis. Second, and not unrelatedly, the approach is unpredictable and requires holding this Court to standards it has never publicly adopted. Thus, the approach presents the danger that, as I suggest has happened here, relevant factors will be misapplied or ignored. All interests not "fundamental" and all classes not "suspect" are not the same; and it is time for the Court to drop the pretense that, for purposes of the Equal Protection Clause, they are.

The danger of the Court's verbal adherence to the rigid two-tier test, despite its effective repudiation of that test in the cases, is demonstrated by its efforts here. There is simply no reason why a statute that tells able-bodied police officers, ready and willing to work, that they no longer have the right to earn a living in their chosen profession merely because they are 50 years old should be judged by the same minimal standards of rationality that we use to test economic legislation that discriminates against business interests. Yet, the Court today not only invokes the minimal level of scrutiny, it wrongly adheres to it. Analysis of the three factors I have identified above — the importance of the governmental benefits denied, the character of the class, and the asserted state interests — demonstrates the Court's error.

Whether "fundamental" or not, "'the right of the individual . . . to engage in any of the common occupations of life'" has been repeatedly recognized by this Court as falling within the concept of liberty guaranteed by the Fourteenth Amendment. . . . Even if the right to earn a living does not include the right to work for the government, it is settled that because of the importance of the interest involved, we have always carefully looked at the reasons asserted for depriving a government employee of his job.

While depriving any government employee of his job is a significant deprivation, it is particularly burdensome when the person deprived is an older citizen. Once terminated, the elderly cannot readily find alternative employment. The lack of work is not only economically damaging, but emotionally and physically draining. Deprived of his status in the community and of the opportunity for meaningful activity, fearful of becoming dependent on others for his support, and lonely in his new-found isolation, the involuntarily retired person is susceptible to physical and emotional ailments as a direct consequence of his enforced idleness. Ample clinical evidence supports the conclusion that mandatory retirement poses a direct threat to the health and life expectancy of the retired person, and these consequences of termination for age are not disputed by appellants. Thus, an older person deprived of his job by the government loses not only his right to earn a living, but, too often, his health as well, in sad contradiction of Browning's promise: "The best is yet to be,/The last of life, for which the first was made."

Nor only are the elderly denied important benefits when they are terminated on the basis of age, but the classification of older workers is itself one that merits judicial attention. Whether older workers constitute a "suspect" class or not, it cannot be disputed that they constitute a class subject to repeated and arbitrary discrimination in employment. . . .

. . . .

. . . I agree that the purpose of the mandatory retirement law is legitimate, and indeed compelling. The Commonwealth has every reason to assure that its state police officers are of sufficient physical strength and health to perform their jobs. In my view, however, the means chosen, the forced retirement of officers at age 50, is so overinclusive that it must fall.

All potential officers must pass a rigorous physical examination. Until age 40, this same examination must be passed every two years — when the officer re-enlists — and, after age 40, every year, Appellants have conceded that "[w]hen a member passes his re-enlistment or annual physical, he is found to be qualified to perform all of the duties of the Uniformed Branch of the Massachusetts State Police." If a member fails the examination, he is immediately terminated or refused re-enlistment. Thus, the only members of the state police still on the force at age 50 are those who have been determined — repeatedly — by the Commonwealth to be physically fit for the job. Yet, all of these physically fit officers are automatically terminated at age 50. Appellants do not seriously assert that their testing is no longer effective at age 50, nor do they claim that continued testing would serve no purpose because officers over 50 are no longer physically able to perform their jobs. Thus the Commonwealth is in the position of already individually testing its police officers for physical fitness, conceding that such testing is adequate to determine the physical ability of an officer to continue on the job, and conceding that that ability may continue after age 50. In these circumstances, I see no reason at all for automatically terminating those officers who reach the age of 50; indeed, that action seems the height of irrationality.

Accordingly, I conclude that the Commonwealth's mandatory retirement law cannot stand when measured against the significant deprivation the Commonwealth's action works upon the terminated employees. I would affirm the judgment of the District Court.

Shapiro v. Thompson

> 394 U.S. 618 (1969)
> See pp. 316–320.

Dandridge v. Williams

> 397 U.S. 471 (1970)
> Vote: 6–3

Like every state in the Union, Maryland participates in the Federal Aid to Families with Dependent Children (AFDC) program, established by 42 U.S.C. Section 601, and initiated under the Social Security Act of 1935. Under this jointly financed program, a state computes the so-called "standard of need" of each eligible family unit and receives a percentage of this from the federal government, to which it adds a variable state contribution. In administering these welfare programs, some states provide that every family shall receive grants sufficient to meet fully this standard of need. Others provide that each family shall receive a percentage of this determined need. And still others provide grants to families in full accord with the standard of need but impose an upper limit on the total amount any one family may receive. Along with several other states, Maryland followed this last course of action. Under its "maximum grant regulation," it placed a ceiling of about $250 per month on an AFDC grant, regardless of the size of the family or its actual need.

Williams and family, recipients of AFDC aid, challenged this ceiling, alleging that it was prohibited by the Social Security Act and the Equal Protection Clause of the Fourteenth Amendment. The district court held the Maryland regulation "invalid on its face for overreaching" and thus violative of the Equal Protection Clause. Maryland appealed. The Supreme Court held that the Maryland regulation is not prohibited by the Social Security Act establishing the AFDC program (this part of the Court's and dissenters' opinions are omitted), and then went on to consider the constitutional objections to the regulation.

MR. JUSTICE STEWART delivered the opinion of the Court.

... Maryland says that its maximum grant regulation is wholly free of any invidiously discriminatory purpose or effect, and that the regulation is rationally supportable on at least four entirely valid grounds. The regulation can be clearly justified, Maryland argues, in terms of legitimate state interests in encouraging gainful employment, in maintaining an equitable balance in economic status as between welfare families and those supported by a wage-earner, in providing incentives for family planning, and in allocating available public funds in such a way as fully to meet the needs of the largest possible number of families. The District Court, while apparently recognizing the validity of at least some of these state concerns, nonetheless held that the regulation "is invalid on its face for overreaching," that it violates the Equal Protection Clause "[b]ecause it cuts too broad a swath on an indiscriminate basis as applied to the entire group of AFDC eligibles to which it purports to apply. ... "

If this were a case involving government action claimed to violate the First Amendment guarantee of free speech, a finding of "overreaching" would be significant and might be crucial. For when otherwise valid governmental regulation sweeps so broadly as to impinge upon activity protected by the First Amendment, its very overbreadth may make it unconstitutional. But the concept of "overreaching" has no place in this case. For here we deal with state regulation in the social and economic field, not affecting freedoms guaranteed by the Bill of Rights, and claimed to violate the Fourteenth Amendment only because the regulation results in some disparity in grants of welfare payments to the largest AFDC families. For this Court to approve the invalidation of

state economic or social regulation as "overreaching" would be far too reminiscent of an era when the Court thought the Fourteenth Amendment gave it power to strike down state laws "because they may be unwise, improvident, or out of harmony with a particular school of thought." *Williamson* v. *Lee Optical* [1955]. That era long ago passed into history.

In the area of economics and social welfare, a State does not violate the Equal Protection Clause merely because the classifications made by its laws are imperfect. If the classification has some "reasonable basis," it does not offend the Constitution simply because the classification "is not made with mathematical nicety or because in practice it results in some inequality." "The problems of government are practical ones and may justify, if they do not require, rough accommodations — illogical, it may be, and unscientific." ... "A statutory discrimination will not be set aside if any state of facts reasonably may be conceived to justify it."

To be sure, the cases cited, and many others enunciating this fundamental standard under the Equal Protection Clause, have in the main involved state regulation of business or industry. The administration of public welfare assistance, by contrast, involves the most basic economic needs of impoverished human beings. We recognize the dramatically real factual difference between the cited cases and this one, but we can find no basis for applying a different constitutional standard. It is a standard that has consistently been applied to state legislation restricting the availability of employment opportunities. *Goesaert* v. *Cleary* [1948], *Kotch* v. *Board of River Port Pilot Comm'rs* [1947]. And it is a standard that is true to the principle that the Fourteenth Amendment gives the federal courts no power to impose upon the States their views of what constitutes wise economic or social policy.

Under this long-established meaning of the Equal Protection Clause, it is clear that the Maryland maximum grant regulation is constitutionally valid. We need not explore all the reasons that the State advances in justification of the regulation. It is enough that a solid foundation for the regulation can be found in the State's legitimate interest in encouraging employment and in avoiding discrimination between welfare families and the families of the working poor. By combining a limit on the recipient's grant with permission to retain money earned, without reduction in the amount of the grant, Maryland provides an incentive to seek gainful employment. And by keying the maximum family AFDC grants to the minimum wage a steadily employed head of a household receives, the State maintains some semblance of an equitable balance between families on welfare and those supported by an employed breadwinner.

It is true that in some AFDC families there may be no person who is employable. It is also true that with respect to AFDC families whose determined standard of need is below the regulatory maximum, and who therefore receive grants equal to the determined standard, the employment incentive is absent. But the Equal Protection Clause does not require that a State must choose between attacking every aspect of a problem or not attacking the problem at all. It is enough that the State's action be rationally based and free from invidious discrimination. The regulation before us meets that test.

We do not decide today that the Maryland regulation is wise, that it best fulfills the relevant social and economic objectives that Maryland might ideally espouse, or that a more just and humane system could not be devised. Conflicting claims of morality and intelligence are raised by opponents and proponents of almost every measure, certainly including the one before us. But the intractable economic, social, and even philosophical problems presented by public welfare assistance programs are not the business of this Court. The Constitution may impose certain procedural safeguards upon systems of welfare administration, *Goldberg* v. *Kelly* [1970]. But the Constitution does not empower this Court to second-guess state officials charged with the difficult responsibility of allocating limited public welfare funds among the myriad of potential recipients. Cf. *Steward Mach. Co.* v. *Davis* [1937].

The judgment is reversed.

[MR. JUSTICE DOUGLAS, dissenting, said in part:]
. . . I do not find it necessary to reach the constitutional argument in this case, for in my view the Maryland regulation is inconsistent with the terms and purposes of the Social Security Act.

MR. JUSTICE MARSHALL, whom MR. JUSTICE BRENNAN joins, dissenting.
. . . The Court holds today that regardless of the arbitrariness of a classification it must be sustained if any state goal can be imagined that is arguably furthered by its effects. This is so even though the classification's underinclusiveness or overinclusiveness clearly demonstrates that its actual basis is something other than that asserted by the State, and even though the relationship between the classification and the state interests which it purports to serve is so tenuous that it could not seriously be maintained that the classification tends to accomplish the ascribed goals.

The Court recognizes, as it must, that this case involves "the most basic economic needs of impoverished human beings," and that there is therefore a "dramatically real factual difference" between the instant case and those decisions upon which the Court relies. The acknowledgment that these dramatic differences exist is a candid recognition that the Court's decision today is wholly without precedent. I cannot subscribe to the Court's sweeping refusal to accord the Equal Protection Clause any role in this entire area of the law. . . .

. . . I believe that in overruling the decision of this and every other district court that has passed on the validity of the maximum grant device, the Court both reaches the wrong result and lays down an insupportable test for determining whether a State has denied its citizens the equal protection of the laws.

. . . .

In the instant case, the only distinction between those children with respect to whom assistance is granted and those children who are denied such assistance is the size of the family into which the child permits himself to be born. The class of individuals with respect to whom payments are actually made (the first four or five eligible dependent children in a family), is grossly underinclusive in terms of the class that the AFDC program was designed to assist, namely, *all* needy dependent children. Such underinclusiveness manifests "a prima facie violation of the equal protection requirement of reasonable classification," compelling the State to come forward with a persuasive justification for the classification.

The Court never undertakes to inquire for such a justification; rather it avoids the task by focusing upon the abstract dichotomy between two different approaches to equal protection problems that have been utilized by this Court.

Under the so-called "traditional test," a classification is said to be permissible under the Equal Protection Clause unless it is "without any reasonable basis." . . . On the other hand, if the classification affects a "fundamental right," then the state interest in perpetuating the classification must be "compelling" in order to be sustained. See, *e.g., Shapiro* v. *Thompson* [1968].

This case simply defies easy characterization in terms of one or the other of these "tests." The cases relied on by the Court, in which a "mere rationality" test was actually used, *e.g., Williamson* v. *Lee Optical Co.* (1955), are most accurately described as involving the application of equal protection reasoning to the regulation of business interests. The extremes to which the Court has gone in dreaming up rational bases for state regulation in that area may in many instances be ascribed to a healthy revulsion from the Court's earlier excesses in using the Constitution to protect interests that have more than enough power to protect themselves in the legislative halls. This case, involving the literally vital interests of a powerless minority— poor families without breadwinners— is far removed from the area of business regulation, as the Court concedes. Why then is the standard used in those cases imposed here? We are told no more than that this case falls in "the area of economics and social welfare," with the implication that from there the answer is obvious.

In my view, equal protection analysis of this case is not appreciably advanced by the *a priori* definition of a "right," fundamental or otherwise. Rather, concentration must be placed upon the character of the classification in question, the relative importance to individuals in the class discriminated against of the governmental benefits that they do not receive, and the asserted state interests in support of the classification. As we said only recently, "In determining whether or not a state law violates the Equal Protection Clause, we must consider the facts and circumstances behind the law, the interests which the State claims to be protecting, and the interests of those who are disadvantaged by the classification."

It is the individual interests here at stake that, as the Court concedes, most clearly distinguish this case from the "business regulation" equal protection cases. AFDC support to needy dependent children provides the stuff that sustains those children's lives: food, clothing, shelter. And this Court has already recognized several times that when a benefit, even a "gratuitous" benefit, is necessary to sustain life, stricter constitutional standards, both procedural and substantive, are applied to the deprivation of that benefit.

Nor is the distinction upon which the deprivation is here based— the distinction between large and small families— one that readily commends itself as a basis for determining which children are to have support approximating subsistence and which are not. Indeed, governmental discrimination between children on the basis of a factor over which they have no control— the number of their brothers and sisters— bears some resemblance to the classification between legitimate and illegitimate children which we condemned as a violation of the Equal Protection Clause in *Levy* v. *Louisiana* (1968).

The asserted state interests in the maintenance of the maximum grant regulation, on the other hand,

are hardly clear. In the early stages of this litigation, the State attempted to rationalize the maximum grant regulation on the theory that it was merely a device to conserve state funds, in the language of the motion to dismiss, "a legitimate way of allocating the State's limited resources available for AFDC assistance." Indeed, the initial opinion of the District Court concluded that the sole reason for the regulation, as revealed by the record, was "to fit the total needs of the State's dependent children, as measured by the State's standards of their subsistence requirements, into an inadequate State appropriation." The District Court quite properly rejected this asserted justification, for "[t]he saving of welfare costs cannot justify an otherwise invidious classification." *Shapiro* v. *Thompson* [1968]. See *Goldberg* v. *Kelly* [1970].

. . . Maryland has urged that the maximum grant regulation serves to maintain a rough equality between wage-earning families and AFDC families, thereby increasing the political support for— or perhaps reducing the opposition to— the AFDC program. It is questionable whether the Court really relies on this ground, especially when in many States the prescribed family maximum bears no such relation to the minimum wage. But the Court does not indicate that a different result might obtain in other cases. Indeed, whether elimination of the maximum would produce welfare incomes out of line with other incomes in Maryland is itself open to question on this record. . . . And it is too late to argue that political expediency will sustain discrimination not otherwise supportable. Cf. *Cooper* v. *Aaron* (1958).

Vital to the employment-incentive basis found by the Court to sustain the regulation is, of course, the supposition that an appreciable number of AFDC recipients are in fact employable. For it is perfectly obvious that limitations upon assistance cannot reasonably operate as a work incentive with regard to those who cannot work or who cannot be expected to work. In this connection, Maryland candidly notes that "only a very small percentage of the total universe of welfare recipients are employable." The State, however, urges us to ignore the "total universe" and to concentrate attention instead upon the heads of AFDC families. Yet the very purpose of the AFDC program since its inception has been to provide assistance for dependent *children*. The State's position is thus that the State may deprive certain needy children of assistance to which they would otherwise be entitled in order to provide an arguable work incentive for their parents. But the State may not wield its economic whip in this fashion when the effect is to cause a deprivation to needy dependent children in order to correct an arguable fault of their parents.

Even if the invitation of the State to focus upon the heads of AFDC families is accepted, the minimum rationality of the maximum grant regulation is hard to discern. The District Court found that of Maryland's more than 32,000 AFDC families, only about 116 could be classified as having employable members, and, of these, the number to which the maximum grant regulation was applicable is not disclosed by the record. . . . In short, not only has the State failed to establish that there is a substantial or even a significant proportion of AFDC heads of households as to whom the maximum grant regulation arguably serves as a viable and logical work incentive, but it is also indisputable that the regulation at best is drastically *over-inclusive* since it applies with equal vigor to a very substantial number of persons who like appellees are completely disabled from working.

Finally, it should be noted that, to the extent there is a legitimate state interest in encouraging heads of AFDC households to find employment, application of the maximum grant regulation is also grossly *under-inclusive* because it singles out and affects only large families. No reason is suggested why this particular group should be carved out for the purpose of having unusually harsh "work incentives" imposed upon them. Not only has the State selected for special treatment a small group from among similarly situated families, but it has done so on a basis—family size—that bears no relation to the evil that the State claims the regulation was designed to correct. There is simply no indication whatever that heads of large families, as opposed to heads of small families, are particularly prone to refuse to seek or to maintain employment.

The State has presented other arguments to support the regulation. However, they are not dealt with specifically by the Court, and the reason is not difficult to discern. The Court has picked the strongest available; the others suffer from similar and greater defects. Moreover, it is relevant to note that both Congress and the State have adopted other measures that deal specifically with exactly those interests the State contends are advanced by the maximum grant regulation. Thus, for example, employable AFDC recipients are required to seek employment through the congressionally established Work Incentive Program, which provides an elaborate system of counseling, training, and incentive payments for heads of AFDC families. The existence

of these alternatives does not, of course, conclusively establish the invalidity of the maximum grant regulation. It is certainly relevant, however, in appraising the overall interest of the State in the maintenance of the regulation.

In the final analysis, Maryland has set up an AFDC program structured to calculate and pay the minimum standard of need to dependent children. Having set up that program, however, the State denies some of those needy children the minimum subsistence standard of living, and it does so on the wholly arbitrary basis that they happen to be members of large families. One need not speculate too far on the actual reason for the regulation, for in the early stages of this litigation the State virtually conceded that it set out to limit the total cost of the program along the path of least resistance. Now, however, we are told that other rationales can be manufactured to support the regulation and to sustain it against a fundamental constitutional challenge.

However, these asserted state interests, which are not insignificant in themselves, are advanced either not at all or by complete accident by the maximum grant regulation. Clearly they could be served by measures far less destructive of the individual interests at stake. Moreover, the device assertedly chosen to further them is at one and the same time both grossly underinclusive—because it does not apply at all to a much larger class in an equal position—and grossly overinclusive—because it applies so strongly against a substantial class as to which it can rationally serve no end. Were this a case of pure business regulation, these defects would place it beyond what has heretofore seemed a borderline case, see, *e.g.*, *Railway Express Agency* v. *New York* (1949), and I do not believe that the regulation can be sustained even under the Court's "reasonableness" test.

In any event, it cannot suffice merely to invoke the spectre of the past and to recite from *Lindsley* v. *Natural Carbonic Gas Co.* and *Williamson* v. *Lee Optical Co.* to decide the case. Appellees are not a gas company or an optical dispenser; they are needy dependent children and families who are discriminated against by the State. The basis of that discrimination—the classification of individuals into large and small families—is too arbitrary and too unconnected to the asserted rationale, the impact on those discriminated against—the denial of even a subsistence existence—too great, and the supposed interests served too contrived and attenuated to meet the requirements of the Constitution. In my view Maryland's maximum grant regulation is invalid under the Equal Protection Clause of the Fourteenth Amendment.

I would affirm the judgment of the District Court.

O'Connor v. Donaldson

422 U.S. 563 (1975)
Vote: 9–0

Kenneth Donaldson was civilly committed to confinement as a mental patient in a Florida state hospital and was kept in custody there against his will for nearly fifteen years. Throughout his confinement, Donaldson repeatedly, but unsuccessfully, demanded his release, claiming that he was neither dangerous nor mentally ill, and that, at any rate, the hospital was not providing treatment for his supposed illness. Finally, Donaldson brought a "1983 suit," under 42 U.S.C. Section 1983, in federal district court, alleging that O'Connor, the hospital's superintendent, and others had deprived him of his constitutional right to liberty. At his trial there was uncontradicted testimony that Donaldson had posed no danger to others during his confinement or at any other time in his life. Evidence also revealed that his confinement was a simple regime of enforced custodial care and not a program designed to alleviate or cure his supposed illness. After trial, a jury returned a verdict awarding Donaldson damages for his unlawful confinement and the court ordered his release. This outcome was sustained upon appeal, whereupon O'Connor petitioned the Supreme Court for a writ of certiorari.

Although the Court is reluctant to address the issue, does this decision establish a constitutional right to treatment for those confined to mental hospitals? Does it signal an aspect of an emerging constitutional right to privacy and autonomy? Why is this decision unanimous in upholding Donaldson's claims, when shortly before the Court denied that welfare was a fundamental right?

MR. JUSTICE STEWART delivered the opinion of the Court.

The Court of Appeals affirmed the judgment of the District Court in a broad opinion dealing with "the far-reaching question whether the Fourteenth Amendment guarantees a right to treatment to persons involuntarily civilly committed to state mental hospitals." 493 F. 2d, at 509. The appellate court held that when, as in Donaldson's case, the rationale for confinement is that the patient is in need of treatment, the Constitution requires that minimally adequate treatment in fact be provided. The court further expressed the view that, regardless of the grounds for involuntary civil commitment, a person confined against his will at a state mental institution has "a constitutional right to receive such individual treatment as will give him a reasonable opportunity to be cured or to improve his mental condition." Conversely, the court's opinion implied that it is constitutionally permissible for a State to confine a mentally ill person against his will in order to treat his illness, regardless of whether his illness renders him dangerous to himself or others.

We have concluded that the difficult issues of constitutional law dealt with by the Court of Appeals are not presented by this case in its present posture. Specifically, there is no reason now to decide whether mentally ill persons dangerous to themselves or to others have a right to treatment upon compulsory confinement by the State, or whether the State may compulsorily confine a nondangerous, mentally ill individual for the purpose of treatment. As we view it, this case raises a single, relatively simple, but nonetheless important question concerning every man's constitutional right to liberty.

The jury found that Donaldson was neither dangerous to himself nor dangerous to others, and also found that, if mentally ill, Donaldson had not received treatment. That verdict, based on abundant evidence, makes the issue before the Court a narrow one. We need not decide whether, when, or by what procedures a mentally ill person may be confined by the State on any of the grounds which, under contemporary statutes, are generally advanced to justify involuntary confinement of such a person — to prevent injury to the public, to ensure his own survival or safety, or to alleviate or cure his illness. For the jury found that none of the above grounds for continued confinement was present in Donaldson's case.

Given the jury's findings, what was left as justification for keeping Donaldson in continued confinement? The fact that state law may have authorized confinement of the harmless mentally ill does not itself establish a constitutionally adequate purpose for the confinement. Nor is it enough that Donaldson's original confinement was founded upon a constitutionally adequate basis, if in fact it was, because even if his involuntary confinement was initially permissible, it could not constitutionally continue after that basis no longer existed.

A finding of "mental illness" alone cannot justify a State's locking a person up against his will and keeping him indefinitely in simple custodial confinement. Assuming that that term can be given a reasonably precise content and that the "mentally ill" can be identified with reasonable accuracy, there is still no constitutional basis for confining such persons involuntarily if they are dangerous to no one and can live safely in freedom.

May the State confine the mentally ill merely to ensure them a living standard superior to that they enjoy in the private community? That the State has a proper interest in providing care and assistance to the unfortunate goes without saying. But the mere presence of mental illness does not disqualify a person from preferring his home to the comforts of an institution. Moreover, while the State may arguably confine a person to save him from harm, incarceration is rarely if ever a necessary condition for raising the living standards of those capable of surviving safely in freedom, on their own or with the help of family or friends.

May the State fence in the harmless mentally ill solely to save its citizens from exposure to those whose ways are different? One might as well ask if the State, to avoid public unease, could incarcerate all who are physically unattractive or socially eccentric. Mere public intolerance or animosity cannot constitutionally justify the deprivation of a person's physical liberty.

In short, a State cannot constitutionally confine without more a nondangerous individual who is capable of surviving safely in freedom by himself or with the help of willing and responsible family members or friends. Since the jury found, upon ample evidence, that O'Connor, as an agent of the State, knowingly did so confine Donaldson, it properly concluded that O'Connor violated Donaldson's constitutional right to freedom.

MR. CHIEF JUSTICE BURGER, concurring.

. . . .

There can be no doubt that involuntary commitment to a mental hospital, like involuntary confinement of an individual for any reason, is a deprivation of liberty which the State cannot accomplish without due process of law. Commitment must be justified on the basis of a legitimate state interest, and the reasons for committing a particular individual must be established in an appropriate proceeding. Equally important, confinement must cease when those reasons no longer exist.

The Court of Appeals purported to be applying these principles in developing the first of its theories supporting a constitutional right to treatment. It first identified what it perceived to be the traditional bases for civil commitment — physical dangerousness to oneself or others, or a need for treatment — and stated:

> [W]here, as in Donaldson's case, the rationale for confinement is the *'parens patriae'* rationale that the patient is in need of treatment, the due process clause requires that minimally adequate treatment be in fact provided. . . . To deprive any citizen of his or her liberty upon the altruistic theory that the confinement is for humane therapeutic reasons and then fail to provide adequate treatment violates the very fundamentals of due process.

The Court of Appeals did not explain its conclusion that the rationale for respondent's commitment was that he needed treatment. The Florida statutes in effect during the period of his confinement did not require that a person who had been adjudicated incompetent and ordered committed either be provided with psychiatric treatment or released, and there was no such condition in respondent's order of commitment. More important, the instructions which the Court of Appeals read as establishing an absolute constitutional right to treatment did not require the jury to make any findings regarding the specific reasons for respondent's confinement or to focus upon any rights he may have had under state law. Thus, the premise of the Court of Appeals' first theory must have been that, at least with respect to persons who are not physically dangerous, a State has no power to confine the mentally ill except for the purpose of providing them with treatment.

That proposition is surely not descriptive of the power traditionally exercised by the States in this area. Historically, and for a considerable period of time, subsidized custodial care in private foster homes or boarding houses was the most benign form of care provided incompetent or mentally ill persons for whom the States assumed responsibility. Until well into the 19th century the vast majority of such persons were simply restrained in poorhouses, almshouses, or jails. See A. Deutsch, The Mentally Ill in America, 38-54, 114-131 (2d ed. 1949). The few States that established institutions for the mentally ill during this early period were concerned primarily with providing a more humane place of confinement and only secondarily with "curing" the persons sent there.

As the trend toward state care of the mentally ill expanded, eventually leading to the present statutory schemes for protecting such persons, the dual functions of institutionalization continued to be recognized. While one of the goals of this movement was to provide medical treatment to those who could benefit from it, it was acknowledged that this could not be done in all cases and that there was a large range of mental illness for which no known "cure" existed. In time, providing places for the custodial confinement of the so-called "dependent insane" again emerged as the major goal of the State's programs in this area and continued to be so well into this century. See D. Rothman, The Discovery of the Asylum (1971).

In short, the idea that States may not confine the mentally ill except for the purpose of providing them with treatment is of very recent origin, and there is no historical basis for imposing such a limitation on state power. Analysis of the sources of the civil commitment power likewise lends no support to that notion. There can be little doubt that in the exercise of its police power a State may confine individuals solely to protect society from the dangers of significant antisocial acts or communicable disease. Additionally, the States are vested with the historic *parens patriae* power, including the duty to protect "persons under legal disabilities to act for themselves." The classic example of this role is when a State undertakes to act as "the general guardian of all infants, idiots, and lunatics."

Of course, an inevitable consequence of exercising the *parens patriae* power is that the ward's personal freedom will be substantially restrained, whether a guardian is appointed to control his property, he is placed in the custody of a private third party, or committed to an institution. Thus, however the power is implemented, due process requires that it not be invoked indiscriminately. At a minimum, a particular scheme for protection of the mentally ill must rest upon a legislative determination that it is compatible with the best interests of the affected class and that its members are unable to act for themselves. Moreover, the use of alternative forms of protection may be motivated by different considerations, and the justifications for one may not be invoked to rationalize another.

However, the existence of some due process limitations on the *parens patriae* power does not justify the further conclusion that it may be exercised to confine a mentally ill person only if the purpose of the confinement is treatment. Despite many recent advances in medical knowledge, it remains a stubborn fact that there are many forms of mental illness which are not understood, some which are untreatable in the sense that no effective therapy has yet been discovered for them, and that rates of "cure" are generally low. There can be little responsible debate regarding "the uncertainty of diagnosis in this field and the tentativeness of professional judgment." Similarly, as previously observed, it is universally recognized as fundamental to effective therapy that the patient acknowledge his illness and cooperate with those attempting to give treatment; yet the failure of a large proportion of mentally ill persons to do so is a common phenomenon. It may be that some persons in either of these categories, and there may be others, are unable to function in society and will suffer real harm to themselves unless provided with care in a sheltered environment. At the very least, I am not able to say that a state legislature is powerless to make that kind of judgment.

Alternatively, it has been argued that a Fourteenth Amendment right to treatment for involuntarily confined mental patients derives from the fact that many of the safeguards of the criminal process are not present in civil commitment. The Court of Appeals described this theory as follows:

> [A] due process right to treatment is based on the principle that when the three central limitations on the government's power to detain — that detention be in retribution for a specific offense; that it be limited to a fixed term; and that it be permitted after a proceeding where the fundamental procedural safeguards are observed — are absent, there must be a *quid pro quo* extended by the government to justify confinement. And the *quid pro quo* most commonly recognized is the provision of rehabilitative treatment.

To the extent that this theory may be read to permit a State to confine an individual simply because it is willing to provide treatment, regardless of the subject's ability to function in society, it raises the gravest of constitutional problems, and I have no doubt the Court of Appeals would agree on this score. As a justification for a constitutional right to such treatment, the *quid pro quo* theory suffers from equally serious defects.

It is too well established to require extended discussion that due process is not an inflexible concept. Rather, its requirements are determined in particular instances by identifying and accommodating the interests of the individual and society. Where claims that the State is acting in the best interests of an individual are said to justify reduced procedural and substantive safeguards, this Court's decisions require that they be "candidly appraised." However, in so doing judges are not free to read their private notions of public policy or public health into the Constitution.

The *quid pro quo* theory is a sharp departure from, and cannot coexist with, these due process principles. As an initial matter, the theory presupposes that essentially the same interests are involved in every situation where a State seeks to confine an individual; that assumption, however, is incorrect. It is elementary that the justification for the criminal process and the unique deprivation of liberty which it can impose requires that it be invoked only for commission of a specific offense prohibited by legislative enactment. But it would be incongruous to apply the same limitation when quarantine is imposed by the State to protect the public from a highly communicable disease.

A more troublesome feature of the *quid pro quo* theory is that it elevates a concern for essentially procedural safeguards into a new substantive constitutional right. Rather than inquiring whether strict standards of proof or periodic redetermination of a patient's condition are required in civil confinement, the theory accepts the absence of such safeguards but insists that the State provide benefits which, in the view of a court, are adequate "compensation" for confinement. In light of the wide divergence of medical opinion regarding the diagnosis of and proper therapy for mental abnormalities, that prospect is especially troubling in this area and cannot be squared with the principle that "courts may not substitute for the judgments of legislators their own understanding of the public welfare, but must instead concern themselves with the validity of the methods which the legislature has selected." Of course, questions regarding the adequacy of procedure and the power of a State to continue particular confinements are ultimately for the courts, aided by expert opinion to the extent that is found helpful. But I am not persuaded that we should abandon the traditional limitations on the scope of judicial review.

In sum, I cannot accept the reasoning of the Court of Appeals and can discern no other basis for equating an involuntarily committed mental patient's unquestioned constitutional right not to be confined without due process of law with a constitutional right to *treatment*. Given the present state of medical knowledge regarding abnormal human behavior and its treatment, few things would be more fraught with peril than to irrevocably condition a State's power to protect the mentally ill upon the providing of "such treatment as will give [them] a realistic opportunity to be cured." Nor can I accept the theory that a State may lawfully confine an individual thought to need treatment and justify that deprivation of liberty solely by providing some treatment. Our concepts of due process would not tolerate such a "tradeoff." Because the Court of Appeals' analysis could be read as authorizing those results, it should not be followed.

City of Cleburne v. Cleburne Living Center

473 U.S. 432 (1985)
See pp. 370–373.

The Rights of Privacy and Autonomy

As fundamental as it is to individual liberty, a right to privacy is nowhere to be found in the Constitution. Yet over the years the Court has articulated such a right, at first piece-meal and as a derivative by-product of other, explicit protections. But in GRISWOLD V. CONNECTICUT, 381 U.S. 479 (1965), the Court asserted the right of privacy as an independent constitutional right. Since then, it has enlarged upon and reaffirmed this new right. In this section we trace the antecedents and origins of this development, and then turn to consider recent cases and circumstances that shape the contours and limits of this newest constitutional right. This development constitutes one of the boldest acts of judicial legislation in the Court's history, a development significant enough in itself but one that is all the more remarkable because many of the major steps were taken not by the activist Warren Court, but under the leadership of Warren Burger and with considerable support from the Nixon appointees, and some of the Reagan appointees.

While certain aspects of privacy have long been protected under the common law, one of the earliest calls for an independent constitutionally-based right to privacy was an article by Samuel Warren and Louis Brandeis, "The Right to Privacy," 4 *Harvard Law Review* 193 (1890), in which they argued that privacy should not be understood simply as an aspect of the right of property, as it traditionally had been, but as an aspect of personal liberty. "The right to be left alone," they argued, was first and foremost a personal, not a property, right. Nearly forty years later, after his appointment to and long service on the Supreme Court, Justice Brandeis reiterated this view in his dissent in *Olmstead* v. *United States,* 277 U.S. 438 (1928). In that case the majority held that the Fourth Amendment's prohibition against warrantless searches and seizures did not prohibit warrantless wiretaps of telephones, because conversations were not "things" — like books, papers, and personal effects — which were protected by the Fourth Amendment. In what is perhaps his most eloquent and most quoted dissent, Justice Brandeis took issue with this reasoning and argued that the Fourth and Fifth Amendments were designed to protect *persons* and should be flexible enough to adapt to new technologies. He wrote:

> The protection guaranteed by the [Fourth and Fifth] Amendments is much broader in scope. The makers of our constitution undertook to secure conditions favorable to the pursuit of happiness. They recognized the significance of man's spiritual nature, of his feelings and of his intellect. They knew that only a part of the pain, pleasure, and satisfaction of life are to be found in material things. They sought to protect Americans in their beliefs, their thoughts, their emotions, and their sensations. They conferred as against the government the right to be let alone — the most comprehensive of rights and the right most valued by civilized men.

As we have seen, the Court eventually came to accept Brandeis' view of the Fourth Amendment when it overruled *Olmstead* in KATZ V. UNITED STATES, 389 U.S. 437 (1967). But as significant as this development was, KATZ and related cases did not create a *general* right to privacy. They restricted themselves to invasions of privacy in which subsequent criminal prosecution is at issue.

The Court has found privacy rights in other constitutional provisions as well, most notably the First Amendment's protections of free speech and religious freedom. In protecting the freedom of expression inherent in the First Amendment, the Court, in effect, has created a zone of autonomy or privacy within which individuals are free from governmental intrusion. People have, the Court has held, an absolute right to free thought and conscience, as well as considerable freedom to express themselves either actively or passively. Thus, in interpreting the First Amendment broadly, the Court has gone a long way towards recognizing those values of privacy and autonomy — the right to left alone — that Warren and Brandeis so eloquently wrote about one hundred years ago.

But the First Amendment cuts two ways. Since mid-century, the Court has significantly expanded the right of the press and has used the First Amendment to curtail libel law. In so doing it has facilitated media access to private areas of life once jealously guarded by libel laws. See, for example, NEW YORK TIMES CO. V. SULLIVAN, 376 U.S. 254 (1964).

Still other First Amendment issues have affected privacy. For a time at least, it appeared that the Court was going to deal with the issue of regulation of obscenity and pornography through a privacy-based approach. This was suggested in STANLEY V. GEORGIA, 394 U.S. 557 (1969), in which the Court overturned a conviction for possession of obscene materials because that possession was purely for private use, not public use or commercial distribution. But the Court has not extended this privacy principle to other situations and appears to have abandoned the general approach. Since STANLEY, it has upheld a conviction for showing obscene movies even when the theater in which they were shown did not thrust its wares upon an unsuspecting public and restricted access to adults (PARIS ADULT THEATRE I V. SLATON, 413 U.S. 49, 1973). And more recently, the Court rejected a privacy argument when it upheld a conviction for violating sodomy laws which involved privately taken photographs of sexual acts of consenting adults in their own home (BOWERS V. HARDWICK, 478 U.S. 186, 1986).

Like so many other constitutional developments, the Court's recent decisions on the right to privacy can be traced to earlier civil rights decisions. In NAACP V. ALABAMA, 357 U.S. 449 (1958), the Court held unconstitutional an Alabama law compelling disclosure of NAACP membership lists on grounds that such disclosure would abridge the rights of members to engage in lawful associations. There was, the Court found, "an uncontroverted showing that on past occasions revelation of memberships had exposed these members to economic reprisal, loss of employment, threat of physical coercion, and other manifestations of public hostility." As a consequence, the Court concluded, NAACP members had a right of privacy which included a protection against disclosure of membership. In its decision the Court emphasized the particular circumstances of this case, but it did go on to defend its ruling on more general grounds, emphasizing the right to be able to join together collectively and associate freely without fear of recrimination. The sweeping language of this case resurfaced seven years later in GRISWOLD V. CONNECTICUT, 381 U.S. 479 (1965), a case in which the Court took a great leap forward and created a general constitutional right of privacy.

Drawing on dicta from prior cases, Justice Douglas, for the Court in GRISWOLD, referred to "penumbras, formed by emanations" from the First, Fourth, and Fifth as well as the Third and Ninth Amendments. By concluding that the whole is more than the sum of its parts, the Court created an independent constitutional right of privacy. GRISWOLD was not without its detractors. Predictably enough, Justice Black dissented, criticizing the majority for its failure to tie its decision to a "specific constitutional provision." While the reasoning in GRISWOLD may have been controversial, the situation that gave rise to the case was much less so. GRISWOLD arose as a test case to challenge a long-dormant Connecticut law which made it a crime to use or dispense for use contraceptives. In the Court's striking down of this law, Jus-

tice Douglas spoke of a right of "marital privacy," one "older than the Bill of Rights" itself.

Reaction to GRISWOLD was immediate and intense. While there was no widespread lamentation for the death of the Connecticut statute, there was considerable concern that a powerful new force in the hands of the activist Warren Court had been unleashed. Some welcomed such prospects and envisioned larger developments, but many were critical of the Court's brazen act of judicial legislation, seeing in it a great potential for mischief.

The larger developments envisioned by some liberals have not materialized, but in subsequent decisions the Court has reiterated an independent constitutional right to privacy, and staked out a limited yet intensely controversial scope for this new right. The most important interpretations of this new right have focused on sexual activities, women's reproductive freedom, and abortion. These issues have catapulted the Court into the center of a storm of controversy more intense and politically divisive than any generated by the Warren Court.

Bodily Autonomy and Abortion

Expansive in its reasoning, GRISWOLD was in fact a narrow decision. It overturned a statute, long in disuse, prohibiting the *use* of contraceptives by married couples. At first little happened and GRISWOLD stood alone, a great potential but possibly an isolated decision which served the limited purpose of striking down an archaic and unenforced law. But in 1972 the Court took another step toward defining this new right to privacy when it declared unconstitutional a Massachusetts law prohibiting distribution of contraceptives to unmarried persons (*Eisenstadt* v. *Baird*, 405 U.S. 438, 1972). GRISWOLD had given life to an important new constitutional right to privacy, not only for married couples, but for people generally. But subsequent events suggest that this move may only succeed in defining a limited range of rights of sexual association and not the expansive new *general* right to privacy that some initially predicted. Still, whatever its contours, GRISWOLD is a bold bit of judicial policymaking.

The next giant step in expanding this right of sexual privacy and perhaps establishing still another right to bodily autonomy was ROE V. WADE, 410 U.S. 113 (1973), and a companion case, DOE v. BOLTON, 410 U.S. 179 (1973), to many the most significant decisions ever handed down by the Supreme Court. In these cases the Court held the right to privacy allowed an adult woman in consultation with her physician the freedom to decide whether or not to have an abortion. In his opinion for the majority (White and Rehnquist dissented), Justice Blackmun, formerly of Rochester, Minnesota (home of the famous Mayo Clinic), divided pregnancy into three stages and held that during the first trimester the decision to abort was a private matter to be determined entirely by the woman and her doctor. During the second trimester, Blackmun continued, the state could impose reasonable procedures for abortions, such as requiring that they be performed in a clinic. And during the third trimester, the state could completely regulate abortions, provided that the abortion did not jeopardize a woman's health.

Even as ROE was greeted with enthusiasm by women's rights groups and liberals, it met with fierce opposition from the Catholic Church and from well-organized anti-abortion, or pro-life, groups. These opposition groups have sought to have it overturned on subsequent appeals and through constitutional amendment, but have had considerable success in stemming its impact by erecting barriers to access to abortions by barring government funds to pay for them. Given the intensity of feelings on both sides of this issue and the importance a decision to abort or not has in the lives of so many millions of people, it is not surprising that after ROE the Court was inundated with appeals on this and closely related issues. During the late 1970s and 1980s the Court heard more appeals on abortion and contraceptives than any other kind of case, and abortion became a major political issue.

The giant step of ROE was followed with numerous important tiny steps that reinforced and consolidated the Court's commitment to the constitutional right of privacy and women's reproductive autonomy. In these cases the Court generally gave short shrift to absolute veto rights for husbands of women who wanted abortions and parents of unmarried minors who wanted abortions (*Planned Parenthood* v. *Danforth,* 428 U.S. 52, 1976). See also *Bellotti* v. *Baird,* 443 U.S. 622 (1979), in which a unanimous Court struck down a Massachusetts law requiring an unmarried minor to receive the consent of both parents for an abortion, or if parental consent was not obtained, authorization from a state judge if the judge could conclude that an abortion was in the woman's "best interest." (Even Justice Rehnquist joined in this decision, but with a condition: "only until this Court is willing to reconsider *Danforth.*") For a while, the Court, with but few minor exceptions, continued to broaden the scope of ROE by striking down a wide variety of impediments to access to abortions and birth control, often in response to requests by "pro-life" groups. For instance, in *Carey* v. *Population Services International,* 431 U.S. 678 (1977), the Court invalidated a New York law prohibiting "the distribution of non-medical contraceptives to adults except through licensed pharmacies, and prohibiting anyone other than a physician from distributing them to those under sixteen."

Despite this, opposition to the ROE decision remained and intensified. Legislatures imposed limitations on public assistance to pay for abortions, with the result being that middle-class women have easy access to abortions while poor women do not. The action raises questions of equal protection as well as privacy. But in MAHER V. ROE, 432 U.S. 464 (1977), the Court sustained a Connecticut law allowing medicaid funds to be used to reimburse women for the costs of childbirth but prohibiting their use to pay for all but "medically necessary" abortions. Such restrictions were reaffirmed three years later in *Harris* v. *McRae,* 448 U.S. 297 (1980), which upheld the so-called Hyde Amendment, a provision now regularly appended to many pieces of legislation, which prohibits use of federal monies to pay for nontherapeutic abortions. These decisions, coupled with changes on the Court, led opponents to redouble their efforts to get the Court to reverse its stance on ROE.

Initially the Court stood firm in striking down obstacles to access to abortions in the open market. Thus in *Bigelow* v. *Virginia,* 421 U.S. 809 (1975), it struck down a statute restricting advertisements for abortion clinics, a decision that may have resuscitated the life of a First Amendment protection for commercial speech as well. But in *H. L.* v. *Matheson,* 450 U.S. 398 (1981), the Court upheld a Utah statute requiring parental notification prior to an abortion's being performed on an unmarried minor. Here, Chief Justice Burger, writing for the majority, distinguished between Utah's law and the laws struck down in *Danforth* and *Bellotti* on the grounds that Utah provided only for parental notification, while the others had allowed parental and spousal veto.

However the Court's commitment to the right of reproductive autonomy was again dramatically reaffirmed in both 1983 and 1986. In 1983, in a sweeping decision, it struck down a local ordinance that required a twenty-four hour notice before abortions could take place, that all abortions in the second and third trimesters be performed in hospitals (rather than less expensive clinics), and that doctors must be vigorous in informing women of antiabortion views and the consequences of abortion, *Akron* v. *Akron Center for Reproductive Health,* 462 U.S. 416 (1983). This decision was strongly supported by a solid majority, although this time Justice O'Connor, the Court's first woman and its first appointee since anti-abortion foes began concentrating on the Supreme Court appointment process, joined with Justices White and Rehnquist in dissent.

Three years later, in *Thornburgh* v. *American College of Obstetricians and Gynecologists,* 476 U.S. 747 (1986), the issue of state laws limiting access to abortions again came before the Court. In this case, the state sought to defend its laws as being within the restrictions of ROE and *Akron,* but the Reagan administration entered the suit and in arguments before the Court urged that ROE be overruled. In a vigorous opinion by Justice Black-

mun, the author of ROE, a majority of five reaffirmed ROE V. WADE and invalidated Pennsylvania's provisions. Justice White, in dissent, joined by Justice Rehnquist, launched a full-scale attack on ROE, and received some additional support from Chief Justice Burger and Justice O'Connor.

Abortion emerged as a major campaign issue in the 1988 Presidential election, placing the victor, George Bush, on record as a staunch opponent of abortion. Furthermore, the abortion issue became a litmus test in the confirmation hearings for William Sullivan as Secretary of the Department of Health and Human Services. No doubt, it will continue to be an issue in the nomination and confirmation proceedings of future Supreme Court justices as well.

After the 1988 election, sensing that the tide was turning in their favor, opponents of abortion stepped up their efforts to get states to enact restrictive abortion legislation and press the Supreme Court to overrule ROE V. WADE. Thus, during the October 1988 term, the Solicitor General again asked the Court to overrule ROE V. WADE, and in July 1989 the Court stopped only a short step from doing so. The case was WEBSTER V. REPRODUCTIVE HEALTH SERVICES, 57 LW 5023 (1989), which involved a Missouri statute that restricted abortions in three ways: It defined human life as beginning at conception; mandated costly and time-consuming tests, prior to performing a late abortion, to determine whether the fetus is viable; and restricted information about abortions that can be provided by employees in public hospitals and private hospitals receiving public funds. The Missouri law, upheld by the trial court, was overturned under ROE by the Eighth Circuit Court of Appeals. On appeal, Missouri asked the Supreme Court not only to reverse the Eighth Circuit and uphold the statute, but to overrule ROE as well. Two days after the November 1988 election the Solicitor-General filed an amicus brief, identical to the one submitted in *Thornburgh,* asking the Court to use WEBSTER as the opportunity to reconsider and overrule ROE.

Between *Thornburgh,* decided in 1986, and WEBSTER, decided in 1989, President Reagan had named two additional justices to the Supreme Court, Antonin Scalia and Anthony Kennedy. In both appointments, the would-be justices' views on abortion had been significant factors in their nominations and confirmation hearings, and in WEBSTER, both performed according to predictions. They joined with Justices White, Rehnquist, and O'Connor in upholding the Missouri statute that severely restricted access to abortions. Despite the Solicitor-General's argument to overrule ROE, the plurality opinion argued that the Missouri statute could be upheld without having to do so. This was possible because Justice Rehnquist for the plurality offered a tortured interpretation of ROE. It not only drew a predictable dissent from Justice Blackmun, but as well a separate opinion from Justice Scalia who argued that WEBSTER had overruled ROE *sub silento*. He accused the plurality of irresponsibility for not biting the bullet and directly overruling ROE. The three liberal octogenarians, Blackmun, Marshall, and Brennan dissented, arguing that the Missouri statute should be struck down. And Justice Stevens wrote a separate dissent, focusing his objection to the Missouri statute's definition of life, which, he argued, ran afoul of the First Amendment's Establishment Clause.

There is no question that Justice Scalia is correct. But by writing an opinion that upheld WEBSTER without explicitly overruling ROE, the Court has invited a prolonged period of litigation. As Justice Scalia put it, "It thus appears that the mansion of constitutionalized abortion-law, constructed overnight in ROE v. WADE, must be disassembled door-jamb by door-jamb, and never entirely brought down, no matter how wrong it may be." We can expect that throughout the 1990s, the Court will be asked to continue this task of piece-meal dismantelling.

Other Issues

While GRISWOLD, ROE, and their progeny focus on the general right of privacy and autonomy in matters of sexual intimacy, in fact the Court has been active in protecting only conventional heterosexual relationships, mostly within the context of the family, and has turned aside efforts to extend the mantle of constitutional protection to nontraditional sexual relationships and living arrangements. In *Village of Belle Terre* v. *Boraas,* 416 U.S. 1 (1974), it upheld a city zoning ordinance that restricted housing to conventional families over the privacy claims of students and unmarried couples who were living together in single-family dwellings in violation of the ordinance. And the following year, only a bare majority could be mustered to overturn a single-family zoning ordinance that, in the case at hand, had the effect of prohibiting a grandmother, her son, and two of her grandchildren from inhabiting the same house (MOORE V. CITY OF EAST CLEVELAND, 1977).

After ducking for a number of years the issue of laws criminalizing homosexual conduct, the Court finally faced it squarely in BOWERS V. HARDWICK, 478 U.S. 186 (1986). There, by a vote of 5 to 4, the Court upheld a Georgia statute making it a crime punishable by twenty years' imprisonment to engage in sodomy. In this case, Hardwick challenged the statute, claiming that it placed him, a practicing homosexual, in continuing danger of arrest and prosecution. Although the statute made no distinction between heterosexual and homosexual sodomy, in his decision for the Court, Justice White framed the issue as one of a "fundamental right [of] homosexuals to engage in sodomy," and went on to reject such an idea. Echoing the language of Justice Frankfurter, he argued that homosexual conduct was not "deeply rooted in this nation's history and traditions," and that to succeed, the particular liberty at issue had to be "implicit in the concept of ordered liberty."

These cases suggest that even though the Court has been bold and active in creating rights to protect sexual activity and reproductive freedoms, its preference has tilted strongly to the conventional and the orthodox. Apart from the intense political opposition its decisions have generated, the Court's selective application of this right to privacy may create a problem of consistency in rationale. The strongest justification for judicial activism in protecting individuals from intrusive governments is that there are some insular minorities who, because of their small numbers, political weakness, and peculiarities of beliefs, are not likely to secure support in legislative assemblies. Yet the Court's decisions in this area have tended disproportionately to benefit the politically powerful and to slight those who are not. Those involved in traditional marital or sexual relationships, those who are more well-off, and those living in conventional nuclear families fare fairly well under the Court's rulings in the privacy area. But those who might be more closely linked to "insular minorities," those involved in nontraditional sexual relationships, the poor, and those preferring "alternative" living arrangements have fared much less well. Thus, ironically, those who as a group may be less in need of the helping hand of judicial activism have in fact received it, while those most in need have not. The Court's 1989 ruling in WEBSTER indicates that even the more conventional relationships may not continue to enjoy constitutional protection if the Court decides to rethink GRISWOLD as it has ROE.

This brief review has only scratched the surface of the issues that will continue to be rethought by the Court during the 1990s. Additionally there are a host of related issues the Court will face. Increasingly, courts are being asked to decide important questions of life and death, as cases involving the use of extended life support systems for severely retarded and malformed newborns, the elderly, and the critically injured are litigated. In conjunction with medical authorities, philosophers, and legislatures, the courts are addressing a rapidly growing list of questions. What interests and whose interests are involved in administering or withholding critical life-support devices to the malformed newborn? the terminally ill? the pained elderly? How is death to be defined? Whose privacy and autonomy rights are involved in such decisions? To date the Supreme Court has chosen not to address these issues, preferring instead to allow lower courts considerable discretion to handle such issues on a case-by-case basis, and no

doubt wanting to encourage legislatures, in conjunction with the medical profession, to develop policy in this area. Indeed, new technologies challenge the Court's assumption in ROE V. WADE, that a fetus is viable only in the third trimester. No doubt the Court is reluctant to adopt other positions that technological advancement may soon refute. Still, in a society that reveres the law as much as ours and in which almost all major issues of public policy are eventually translated into constitutional questions, we can expect that in time the Court will enter this thicket as well.

Conclusion

The developments we have just examined have catapulted the Court into one of political theory's classic debates: the quest for individual autonomy versus the impulse for community. Liberal political theory traditionally has emphasized individual rights and individual autonomy and celebrated processes that facilitate their pursuit. Yet liberal theory is subject to criticism. In celebrating process and individualism, it has neglected substance and community. Communitarian critics of liberalism assert that the wholly autonomous individual does not exist, and that as an ideal it is alienating. They argue that human beings are social creatures whose full measure can only find expression in a social context. For them, community is an essential component of human existence, and is to be fostered and cherished.

If in this discussion "family" is considered as community, few would object to these criticisms. However, if *government* is substituted for *community,* there will be considerable debate. Liberals tend not to think of government as the expression of community. Yet if the interconnection between individuals and society suggested by the communitarian critique of liberalism is accepted, then government may have to serve a crucial moral and educative function in expressing, fostering, and perpetuating community values.

The issues of contraception, abortion, and sexual preference raised in the Court's decisions on privacy involve sensitive questions that are closely related to the understanding not only of oneself but also of community. The Court's privacy cases, then, are excursions into moral and social philoso- phy and the nature of society. This explains in part the passion exhibited in discussions of these cases. To expect less intensity would be to fail to appreciate just how profound the issues are.

Cases

Katz v. U.S.

389 U.S. 347 (1967)
See pp. 595–598.

NAACP v. Alabama

357 U.S. 449 (1958)
See pp. 496–499.

Griswold v. Connecticut

privacy

381 U.S. 479 (1965)
Vote: 7–2

Griswold, Executive Director of the Planned Parenthood League of Connecticut, and a colleague were arrested for giving to married persons information, instruction, and medical advice about preventing conception. They were charged with violating an accessory provision of a Connecticut law that "any person who uses any drug, medicinal article or instrument for the purpose of preventing conception shall be fined not less than fifty dollars or imprisoned not less than sixty days nor more than one year or both." They were subsequently convicted as accessories to this offense and fined $100 each. The Supreme Court of Connecticut affirmed their convictions, whereupon they appealed to the United States Supreme Court, claiming that the Connecticut law violated the Fourteenth Amendment.

In overturning this conviction, the Court held the statute violated the constitutional right to privacy. But in trying to show that its decision simply protects "traditional" rights long left alone, does the Court (unwittingly?) exclude nontraditional forms of sexual intimacy?

MR. JUSTICE DOUGLAS delivered the opinion of the Court.

... [W]e are met with a wide range of questions that implicate the Due Process Clause of the Fourteenth Amendment. Overtones of some arguments suggest that *Lochner* v. *New York* ... [1905], should be our guide. But we decline that invitation.... We do not sit as a super-legislature to determine the wisdom, need, and propriety of laws that touch economic problems, business affairs, or social conditions. This law, however, operates directly on an intimate relation of husband and wife and their physician's role in one aspect of that relation.

The association of people is not mentioned in the Constitution nor in the Bill of Rights. The right to educate a child in a school of the parents' choice — whether public or private or parochial — is also not mentioned. Nor is the right to study any particular subject or any foreign language. Yet the First Amendment has been construed to include certain of those rights.

By *Pierce* v. *Society of Sisters* the right to educate one's children as one chooses is made applicable to the States by the force of the First and Fourteenth Amendments. By *Meyer* v. *Nebraska* the same dignity is given the right to study the German language in a private school. In other words, the State may not, consistently with the spirit of the First Amendment, contract the spectrum of available knowledge. The right of freedom of speech and press includes not only the right to utter or to print, but the right to distribute, the right to receive, the right to read, the freedom of inquiry, freedom of thought, and freedom to teach—indeed the freedom of the entire university community. Without those peripheral rights the specific rights would be less secure. And so we reaffirm the principle of the *Pierce* and the *Meyer* cases.

In *NAACP* v. *Alabama* [1958], we protected the "freedom to associate and privacy in one's associations," noting that freedom of association was a peripheral First Amendment right. Disclosure of membership lists of a constitutionally valid association, we held, was invalid "as entailing the likelihood of a substantial restraint upon the exercise by petitioner's members of their right to freedom of association." In other words, the First Amendment has a penumbra where privacy is protected from governmental intrusion. In like context, we have protected forms of "association" that are not political in the customary sense but pertain to the social, legal, and economic benefit of the members. In *Schware* v. *Board of Bar Examiners* we held it not permissible to bar a lawyer from practice, because he had once been a member of the Communist Party. The man's "association with that Party" was not shown to be "anything more than a political faith in a political party" and was not action of a kind proving bad moral character.

Those cases involved more than the "right of assembly"—a right that extends to all irrespective of their race or ideology. The right of "association," like the right of belief (*Board of Education* v. *Barnette*) is more than the right to attend a meeting; it includes the right to express one's attitudes or philosophies by membership in a group or by affiliation with it or by other lawful means. Association in that context is a form of expression of opinion; and while it is not expressly included in the First Amendment its existence is necessary in making the express guarantees fully meaningful.

The foregoing cases suggest that specific guarantees in the Bill of Rights have penumbras, formed by emanations from those guarantees that help give them life and substance. Various guarantees create zones of privacy. The right of association contained in the penumbra of the First Amendment is one, as we have seen. The Third Amendment in its prohibition against the quartering of soldiers "in any house" in time of peace without the consent of the owner is another facet of that privacy. The Fourth Amendment explicitly affirms the "right of the people to be secure in their persons, houses, papers, and effects, against unreasonable searches and seizures." The Fifth Amendment in its Self-Incrimination Clause enables the citizen to create a zone of privacy which government may not force him to surrender to his detriment. The Ninth Amendment provides: "The enumeration in the Constitution, of certain rights, shall not be construed to deny or disparage others retained by the people."

The Fourth and Fifth Amendments were described in *Boyd* v. *United States* as protection against all governmental invasions "of the sanctity of a man's home and the privacies of life." We recently referred in *Mapp* v. *Ohio* [1962] to the Fourth Amendment as creating a "right to privacy, no less important than any other right carefully and particularly reserved to the people."

We have had many controversies over these penumbral rights of "privacy and repose." These cases bear witness that the right of privacy which presses for recognition here is a legitimate one.

The present case, then, concerns a relationship lying within the zone of privacy created by several fundamental constitutional guarantees. And it concerns a law which, in forbidding the *use* of contraceptives rather than regulating their manufacture or sale, seeks to achieve its goals by means having a maximum destructive impact upon that relationship. Such a law cannot stand in light of the familiar principle, so often applied by this Court, that a "governmental purpose to control or prevent activities constitutionally subject to state regulation may not be achieved by means which sweep unnecessarily broadly and thereby invade the area of protected freedoms." *NAACP* v. *Alabama*. Would we allow the police to search the sacred precincts of marital bedrooms for telltale signs of the use of contraceptives? The very idea is repulsive to the notions of privacy surrounding the marriage relationship.

We deal with a right of privacy older than the Bill of Rights—older than our political parties, older than our school system. Marriage is a coming together for better or for worse, hopefully enduring, and intimate to the degree of being sacred. It is an association that promotes a way of life, not causes; a harmony in living, not political faiths; a bilateral loyalty, not commercial or social projects. Yet it is an association for as noble a purpose as any involved in our prior decisions.

Reversed.

MR. JUSTICE GOLDBERG, whom THE CHIEF JUSTICE and MR. JUSTICE BRENNAN join, concurring.

I agree with the Court that Connecticut's birth-control law unconstitutionally intrudes upon the right of marital privacy, and I join in its opinion and judgment. Although I have not accepted the view that "due process" as used in the Fourteenth Amendment incorporates all of the first eight Amendments. I do agree that the concept of liberty protects those personal rights that are fundamental, and is not confined to the specific terms of the Bill of Rights. My conclusion that the concept of liberty is not so restricted and that it embraces the right of marital privacy though that right is not mentioned explicitly in the Constitution is supported both by numerous decisions of this Court, referred to in the Court's opinion, and by the language and history of the Ninth Amendment. In reaching the conclusion that the right of marital privacy is protected, as being within the protected penumbra of specific guarantees of the Bill of Rights, the Court refers to the Ninth Amendment, I add these words to emphasize the relevance of that Amendment to the Court's holding.

. . . .

A dissenting opinion suggests that my interpretation of the Ninth Amendment somehow "broaden[s] the powers of this Court." With all due respect. I believe that it misses the import of what I am saying. I do not take the position that the entire Bill of Rights is incorporated in the Fourteenth Amendment, and I do not mean to imply that the Ninth Amendment is applied against the States by the Fourteenth. Nor do I mean to state that the Ninth Amendment constitutes an independent source of rights protected from infringement by either the States or the Federal Government. Rather, the Ninth Amendment shows a belief of the Constitution's authors that fundamental rights exist that are not expressly enumerated in the first eight amendments and an intent that the list of rights included there not be deemed exhaustive. As any student of this Court's opinions knows, this Court has held, often unanimously, that the Fifth and Fourteenth Amendments protect certain fundamental personal liberties from abridgment by the Federal Government or the States. . . . The Ninth Amendment simply shows the intent of the Constitution's authors that other fundamental personal rights should not be denied such protection or disparaged in any other way simply because they are not specifically listed in the first eight constitutional amendments. I do not see how this broadens the authority of the Court; rather it serves to support what this Court has been doing in protecting fundamental rights.

. . . In sum, the Ninth Amendment simply lends strong support to the view that the "liberty" protected by the Fifth and Fourteenth Amendments from infringement by the Federal Government or the States is not restricted to rights specifically mentioned in the first eight amendments.

. . . .

Although the Connecticut birth-control law obviously encroaches upon a fundamental personal liberty, the State does not show that the law serves any "subordinating [state] interest which is compelling" or that it is "necessary . . . to the accomplishment of a permissible state policy." The State, at most, argues that there is some rational relation between this statute and what is admittedly a legitimate subject of state concern — the discouraging of extra-marital relations. It says that preventing the use of birth-control devices by married persons helps prevent the indulgence by some in such extramarital relations. The rationality of this justification is dubious, particularly in light of the admitted widespread availability to all persons in the State of Connecticut, unmarried as well as married, of birth-control devices for the prevention of disease, as distinguished from the prevention of conception. But, in any event, it is clear that the state interest in safeguarding marital fidelity can be served by a more discriminately tailored statute, which does not, like the present one, sweep unnecessarily broadly, reaching far beyond the evil sought to be dealt with and intruding upon the privacy of all married couples.

. . . .

In sum, I believe that the right of privacy in the marital relation is fundamental and basic — a personal right "retained by the people" within the meaning of the Ninth Amendment. Connecticut cannot constitutionally abridge this fundamental right, which is protected by the Fourteenth Amendment from infringement by the States. I agree with the Court that petitioners' convictions must therefore be reversed.

MR. JUSTICE HARLAN, concurring in the judgment.

I fully agree with the judgment of reversal, but find myself unable to join the Court's opinion. The reason is that it seems to me to evince an approach to this case very much like that taken by my Brothers Black and Stewart in dissent, namely: the Due Process Clause of the Fourteenth Amendment does not touch this Connecticut statute unless the enactment is found to violate some right assured by the letter or penumbra of the Bill of Rights.

. . . .

In my view, the proper constitutional inquiry in this case is whether this Connecticut statute infringes the Due Process Clause of the Fourteenth Amendment because the enactment violates basic values "implicit in the concept of ordered liberty," *Palko* v. *Connecticut.* For reasons stated at length in my dissenting opinion in *Poe* v. *Ullman, supra,* I believe that it does. While the relevant inquiry may be aided by resort to one or more of the provisions of the Bill of Rights, it is not dependent on them or any of their radiations. The Due Process Clause of the

Fourteenth Amendment stands, in my opinion, on its own bottom.

. . . .

Judicial self-restraint will not, I suggest, be brought about in the "due process" area by the historically unfounded incorporation formula long advanced by my Brother Black, and now in part espoused by my Brother Stewart. It will be achieved in this area, as in other constitutional areas, only by continual insistence upon respect for the teachings of history, solid recognition of the basic values that underlie our society, and wise appreciation of the great roles that the doctrines of federalism and separation of powers have played in establishing and preserving American freedoms. Adherence to these principles will not, of course, obviate all constitutional differences of opinion among judges, nor should it. Their continued recognition will, however, go farther toward keeping most judges from roaming at large in the constitutional field than will the interpolation into the Constitution of an artificial and largely illusory restriction on the content of the Due Process Clause.

[MR. JUSTICE WHITE wrote a concurring opinion.]

[MR. JUSTICE BLACK, with whom MR. JUSTICE STEWART joins, dissenting.]

The Court talks about a constitutional "right of privacy" as though there is some constitutional provision or provisions forbidding any law ever to be passed which might abridge the "privacy" of individuals. But there is not. There are, of course, guarantees in certain specific constitutional provisions which are designed in part to protect privacy at certain times and places with respect to certain activities. Such, for example, is the Fourth Amendment's guarantee against "unreasonable searches and seizures." But I think it belittles that Amendment to talk about it as though it protects nothing but "privacy." . . .

One of the most effective ways of diluting or expanding a constitutionally guaranteed right is to substitute for the crucial word or words of a constitutional guarantee another word or words, more or less flexible and more or less restricted in meaning. This fact is well illustrated by the use of the term "right of privacy" as a comprehensive substitute for the Fourth Amendment's guarantee against "unreasonable searches and seizures." "Privacy" is a broad, abstract and ambiguous concept which can easily be shrunken in meaning but which can also, on the other hand, easily be interpreted as a constitutional ban against many things other than searches and seizures. I have expressed the view many times that First Amendment freedoms, for example, have suf-

fered from a failure of the courts to stick to the simple language of the First Amendment in construing it, instead of invoking multitudes of words substituted for those the Framers used. For these reasons I get nowhere in this case by talk about a constitutional "right of privacy" as an emanation from one or more constitutional provisions. I like my privacy as well as the next one, but I am nevertheless compelled to admit that government has a right to invade it unless prohibited by some specific constitutional provision. For these reasons I cannot agree with the Court's judgment and the reasons it gives for holding this Connecticut law unconstitutional.

. . . .

I realize that many good and able men have eloquently spoken and written, sometimes in rhapsodical strains, about the duty of this Court to keep the Constitution in tune with the times. The idea is that the Constitution must be changed from time to time and that this Court is charged with a duty to make those changes. For myself, I must with all deference reject that philosophy. The Constitution makers knew the need for change and provided for it. Amendments suggested by the people's elected representatives can be submitted to the people or their selected agents for ratification. That method of change was good for our Fathers, and being somewhat old-fashioned I must add it is good enough for me. And so, I cannot rely on the Due Process Clause or the Ninth Amendment or any mysterious and uncertain natural law concept as a reason for striking down this state law. The Due Process Clause with an "arbitrary and capricious" or "shocking to the conscience" formula was liberally used by this Court to strike down economic legislation in the early decades of this century, threatening, many people thought, the tranquility and stability of the Nation. See, *e.g., Lochner* v. *New York* [1905]. That formula, based on subjective considerations of "natural justice," is no less dangerous when used to enforce this Court's views about personal rights than those about economic rights. I had thought that we had laid that formula, as a means for striking down state legislation, to rest once and for all in cases like *West Coast Hotel Co.* v. *Parrish.*

MR. JUSTICE STEWART, whom MR. JUSTICE BLACK joins, dissenting.

In the course of its opinion the Court refers to no less than six Amendments to the Constitution: the First, the Third, the Fourth, the Fifth, the Ninth, and the Fourteenth. But the Court does not say which of these Amendments, if any, it thinks is infringed by this Connecticut law.

We *are* told that the Due Process Clause of the Fourteenth Amendment is not, as such, the "guide" in this case. With that much I agree. There is no claim that this law, duly enacted by the Connecticut Legislature, is unconstitutionally vague. There is no claim that the appellants were denied any of the elements of procedural due process at their trial, so as to make their convictions constitutionally invalid. And, as the Court says, the day has long passed since the Due Process Clause was regarded as a proper instrument for determining "the wisdom, need, and propriety" of state laws.

As to the First, Third, Fourth, and Fifth Amendments. I can find nothing in any of them to invalidate this Connecticut law, even assuming that all those Amendments are fully applicable against the States. It has not even been argued that this is a law "respecting an establishment of religion, or prohibiting the free exercise thereof." And surely, unless the solemn process of constitutional adjudication is to descend to the level of a play on words, there is not involved here any abridgment of "the freedom of speech, or of the press; or the right of the people peaceably to assemble, and to petition the Government for a redress of grievances." No soldier has been quartered in any house. There has been no search, and no seizure. Nobody has been compelled to be a witness against himself.

The Court also quotes the Ninth Amendment, and my Brother GOLDBERG'S concurring opinion relies heavily upon it. But to say that the Ninth Amendment has anything to do with this case is to turn somersaults with history. The Ninth Amendment, like its companion the Tenth, which this Court held "states but a truism that all is retained which has not been surrendered" was framed by James Madison and adopted by the States simply to make clear that the adoption of the Bill of Rights did not alter the plan that the *Federal* Government was to be a government of express and limited powers, and that all rights and powers not delegated to it were retained by the people and the individual States. Until today no member of this Court has ever suggested that the Ninth Amendment meant anything else, and the idea that a federal court could ever use the Ninth Amendment to annul a law passed by the elected representatives of the people of the State of Connecticut would have caused James Madison no little wonder.

What provision of the Constitution, then, does make this state law invalid? The Court says it is the right of privacy "created by several fundamental constitutional guarantees." With all deference, I can find no such general right of privacy in the Bill of Rights, in any other part of the Constitution, or in any case ever before decided by this Court.

Stanley v. Georgia

> 394 U.S. 557 (1969)
> See pp. 530–532.

Roe v. Wade

> 410 U.S. 113 (1973)
> See pp. 38–44.

Maher v. Roe

> 432 U.S. 464 (1977)
> Vote: 7–2

A Connecticut regulation limited state medicaid benefits for first-trimester abortions only to those certified by a doctor as medically necessary. It enforced this provision through a system of prior authorization from its Department of Social Services and a refusal to reimburse hospitals costs for noncertified abortions. Connecticut medicaid regulations also authorized full payment for qualifying individuals for costs associated with normal childbirth.

Susan Roe (a pseudonym), an unwed mother of three and eligible for medicaid, was unable to obtain an abortion because of her physician's refusal to certify that the procedure was medically necessary. In a suit brought in federal district court against Edward Maher, Commissioner of Social Services for the State of Connecticut, she attacked the validity of the regulation, alleging that it violated her constitutional rights under the Due Process and Equal Protection Clauses of the Fourteenth Amendment.

Although it found no independent constitutional right to a state-financed abortion, the district court held that the Equal Protection Clause forbids the exclusion of nontherapeutic abortions from state welfare programs that generally subsidize the medical expenses incident to pregnancy and childbirth. "Abortion and childbirth, when stripped of the sensitive moral arguments surrounding the abortion controversy," the district court said, "are simply two alternative medical methods of dealing with pregnancy." It then rejected the state's claim of a fiscal interest in such regulations, stating that the claim was "wholly chimerical because abortion is the least expensive medical response to a pregnancy." It then went on to find that the regulation intruded upon a "fundamental interest" and enjoined the state from requiring the certificate of medical necessity for medicaid-funded abortions. The district court also barred other restrictive provisions designed to prevent medicaid-funded abortions. The state appealed.

In the decision below, the Court overturns the district court ruling. This decision gave new strength to foes of abortion, who have been successful in getting many state legislatures and the United States Congress to bar the use of public monies to pay for abortions. In Congress such provisions are called "Hyde Amendments," after their original author, Representative Hyde, and are regularly attached to pieces of legislation. One such version, much more restrictive than the Connecticut regulation considered below, was adopted in 1976 and reads as follows:

> None of the funds provided by this joint resolution shall be used to perform abortions except where the life of the mother would be endangered if the fetus were carried to term; or except for such medical procedures necessary for the victims of rape or incest when such rape or incest has been reported promptly to a law enforcement agency or public health services.

Since then, various versions of this "Hyde Amendment" have been adopted by Congress. The above provision was challenged in federal courts and upheld by the Supreme Court in *Harris* v. *McRae,* 448 U.S. 297 (1980). In *Harris,* the Court did acknowledge that such a restriction impinged upon a constitutional right recognized in ROE V. WADE, but went on to hold that the reason-

ing in MAHER applied to the Hyde Amendments as well. While government cannot place obstacles to a woman's freedom of choice, the *Harris* majority reasoned, "it need not remove those not of its own creation. . . . Whether freedom of choice that is constitutionally protected warrants federal subsidization is a question for Congress to answer, not a matter of constitutional entitlement."

JUSTICE POWELL delivered the opinion of the Court:

The Constitution imposes no obligation on the States to pay the pregnancy-related medical expenses of indigent women, or indeed to pay any of the medical expenses of indigents. But when a State decides to alleviate some of the hardships of poverty by providing medical care, the manner in which it dispenses benefits is subject to constitutional limitations. Appellees' claim is that Connecticut must accord equal treatment to both abortion and childbirth, and may not evidence a policy preference by funding only the medical expenses incident to childbirth. This challenge to the classifications established by the Connecticut regulation presents a question arising under the Equal Protection Clause of the Fourteenth Amendment. The basic framework of analysis of such a claim is well-settled:

> We must decide, first, whether [state legislation] operates to the disadvantage of some suspect class or impinges upon a fundamental right explicitly or implicitly protected by the Constitution, thereby requiring strict judicial scrutiny. . . . If not, the [legislative] scheme must still be examined to determine whether it rationally furthers some legitimate, articulated state purpose and therefore does not constitute an invidious discrimination . . . *San Antonio School District* v. *Rodriguez* (1973).

. . . Applying this analysis here, we think the District Court erred in holding that the Connecticut regulation violated the Equal Protection Clause of the Fourteenth Amendment.

This case involves no discrimination against a suspect class. An indigent woman desiring an abortion does not come within the limited category of disadvantaged classes so recognized by our cases. Nor does the fact that the impact of the regulation falls upon those who cannot pay lead to a different conclusion. In a sense, every denial of welfare to an indigent creates a wealth classification as compared to nonindigents who are able to pay for the desired goods or services. But this Court has never held that financial need alone identifies a suspect class for purposes of equal protection analysis. See *Rodriguez, supra... Dandridge* v. *Williams* (1970). Accordingly, the central question in this case is whether the regulation "impinges upon a fundamental right explicitly or implicitly protected by the Constitution." The District Court read our decisions in *Roe* v. *Wade, supra,* and the subsequent cases applying it, as establishing a fundamental right to abortion and therefore concluded that nothing less than a compelling state interest would justify Connecticut's different treatment of abortion and childbirth. We think the District Court misconceived the nature and scope of the fundamental right recognized in *Roe.*

At issue in *Roe* was the constitutionality of a Texas law making it a crime to procure or attempt to procure an abortion, except on medical advice for the purpose of saving the life of the mother. Drawing on a group of disparate cases restricting governmental intrusion, physical coercion, and criminal prohibition of certain activities, we concluded that the Fourteenth Amendment's concept of personal liberty affords constitutional protection against state interference with certain aspects of an individual's personal "privacy," including a woman's decision to terminate her pregnancy.

The Texas statute imposed severe criminal sanctions on the physicians and other medical personnel who performed abortions, thus drastically limiting the availability and safety of the desired service. We held that only a compelling state interest would justify such a sweeping restriction on a constitutionally protected interest, and we found no such state interest during the first trimester. Even when judged against this demanding standard, however, the State's dual interests in the health of the pregnant woman and the potential life of the fetus were deemed sufficient to justify substantial regulation of abortions in the second and third trimesters. "These interests are separate and distinct. Each grows in substantiality as the woman approaches term and, at a point during pregnancy, each becomes 'compelling.'" In the second trimester, the State's interest in the health of the pregnant woman justifies state regulation reasonably related to that concern. At viability, usually in the third trimester, the State's interest in the potential life of the fetus justifies prohibition with criminal penalties, except where the life or health of the mother is threatened.

The Texas law in *Roe* was a stark example of impermissible interference with the pregnant woman's decision to terminate her pregnancy. In subsequent cases, we have invalidated other types of restric-

tions, different in form but similar in effect, on the woman's freedom of choice.

. . . .

The Connecticut regulation before us is different in kind from the laws invalidated in our previous abortion decisions. The Connecticut regulation places no obstacles — absolute or otherwise — in the pregnant woman's path to an abortion. An indigent woman who desires an abortion suffers no disadvantage as a consequence of Connecticut's decision to fund childbirth; she continues as before to be dependent on private sources for the service she desires. The State may have made childbirth a more attractive alternative, thereby influencing the woman's decision, but it has imposed no restriction on access to abortions that was not already there. The indigency that may make it difficult — and in some cases, perhaps, impossible — for some women to have abortions is neither created nor in any way affected by the Connecticut regulation. We conclude that the Connecticut regulation does not impinge upon the fundamental right recognized in *Roe.*

Our conclusion signals no retreat from *Roe* or the cases applying it. There is a basic difference between direct state interference with a protected activity and state encouragement of an alternative activity consonant with legislative policy. Constitutional concerns are greatest when the State attempts to impose its will by force of law; the State's power to encourage actions deemed to be in the public interest is necessarily far broader.

This distinction is implicit in two cases cited in *Roe* in support of the pregnant woman's right under the Fourteenth Amendment. *Meyer* v. *Nebraska* (1923), involved a Nebraska law making it criminal to teach foreign languages to children who had not passed the eighth grade. Nebraska's imposition of a criminal sanction on the providers of desired services makes *Meyer* closely analogous to *Roe.* In sustaining the constitutional challenge brought by a teacher convicted under the law, the Court held that the teacher's "right thus to teach and the right of parents to engage him so as to instruct their children" were "within the liberty of the Amendment." In *Pierce* v. *Society of Sisters* (1925), the Court relied on *Meyer* to invalidate an Oregon criminal law requiring the parent or guardian of a child to send him to a public school, thus precluding the choice of a private school. Reasoning that the Fourteenth Amendment's concept of liberty "excludes any general power of the State to standardize its children by forcing them to accept instruction from public teachers only," the Court held that the law "unreasonably interfere[d] with the liberty of parents and guardians to direct the upbringing and education of children under their control."

Both cases invalidated substantial restrictions on constitutionally protected liberty interests: in *Meyer,* the parent's right to have his child taught a particular foreign language; in *Pierce,* the parent's right to choose private rather than public school education. But neither case denied to a State the policy choice of encouraging the preferred course of action. Indeed, in *Meyer* the Court was careful to state that the power of the State "to prescribe a curriculum" that included English and excluded German in its free public schools "is not questioned." Similarly, *Pierce* casts no shadow over a State's power to favor public education by funding it—a policy choice pursued in some States for more than a century....

The question remains whether Connecticut's regulation can be sustained under the less demanding test of rationality that applies in the absence of a suspect classification or the impingement of a fundamental right. This test requires that the distinction drawn between childbirth and nontherapeutic abortion by the regulation be "rationally related" to a "constitutionally permissible" purpose. *Lindsey* v. *Normet* (1972). We hold that the Connecticut funding scheme satisfies this standard.

Roe itself explicitly acknowledged the State's strong interest in protecting the potential life of the fetus. That interest exists throughout the pregnancy, "grow[ing] in substantiality as the woman approaches term."...

The decision whether to expend state funds for nontherapeutic abortion is fraught with judgments of policy and value over which opinions are sharply divided. Our conclusion that the Connecticut regulation is constitutional is not based on a weighing of its wisdom or social desirability, for this Court does not strike down state laws "because they may be unwise, improvident, or out of harmony with a particular school of thought." Indeed, when an issue involves policy choices as sensitive as those implicated by public funding of nontherapeutic abortions, the appropriate forum for their resolution in a democracy is the legislature. We should not forget that "legislatures are ultimate guardians of the liberties and welfare of the people in quite as great a degree as the courts."

In conclusion, we emphasize that our decision today does not proscribe government funding of nontherapeutic abortions. It is open to Congress to require provision of medicaid benefits for such abortions as a condition of state participation in the medicaid program. Also, Connecticut is free—through normal democratic processes—to decide that such benefits should be provided. We hold only that the Constitution does not require a judicially imposed resolution of these difficult issues.

[MR. CHIEF JUSTICE BURGER wrote a concurring opinion.]

MR. JUSTICE BRENNAN, with whom MR. JUSTICE MARSHALL and MR. JUSTICE BLACKMUN join, dissenting.

. . . .

The Court's premise is that only an equal protection claim is presented here. Claims of interference with enjoyment of fundamental rights have, however, occupied a rather protean position in our constitutional jurisprudence. Whether or not the Court's analysis may reasonably proceed under the Equal Protection Clause, the Court plainly errs in ignoring, as it does, the unanswerable argument of appellee, and holding of the District Court, that the regulation unconstitutionally impinges upon her claim of privacy derived from the Due Process Clause.

Roe v. *Wade* and cases following it hold that an area of privacy invulnerable to the State's intrusion surrounds the decision of a pregnant woman whether or not to carry her pregnancy to term. The Connecticut scheme clearly infringes upon that area of privacy by bringing financial pressures on indigent women that force them to bear children they would not otherwise have...

. . . .

...*Doe* v. *Bolton,* the companion to *Roe,* in addition to striking down the Georgia criminal prohibition against elective abortions, struck down the procedural requirements of certification of hospitals, of approval by a hospital committee, and of concurrence in the abortion decision by two doctors other than the woman's own doctor. None of these requirements operated as an absolute bar to elective abortions in the manner of the criminal prohibitions present in the other aspect of the case or in *Roe,* but this was not sufficient to save them from unconstitutionality. In *Planned Parenthood* we struck down a requirement for spousal consent to an elective abortion which the Court characterizes today simply as an "absolute obstacle" to a woman obtaining an abortion. But the obstacle was "absolute" only in the limited sense that a woman who was unable to persuade her spouse to agree to an elective abortion was prevented from obtaining one. Any woman whose husband agreed, or could be persuaded to agree, was free to obtain an abortion, and the State never imposed directly any prohibition of its own. This requirement was qualitatively different from the criminal statutes that the Court today says are comparable, but we nevertheless found it unconstitutional.

Webster v. Reproductive Health Services

> 109 S.Ct. 3040 (1989)
> Vote: 5–4

With their success in MAHER (1977) abortion opponents intensified their efforts to secure state legislation restricting access to abortions under the ROE framework, even as they continued their campaign to get it overruled. The former turned on finding ways to appeal to those justices who felt bound by precedent but might be persuaded to narrow it. The latter turned on their success in influencing the appointment of new justices who would be willing to reconsider and reject ROE altogether. These concerns were joined in *Thornburgh* v. *American College of Obstetricians and Gynecologists,* 476 U.S. 747 (1986), in which the Court ruled on Pennsylvania's Abortion Control Act of 1982. The most controversial features of this act involved a mandated procedure for securing informed consent, and a detailed specification of the nature of information physicians were required to provide patients. When these procedures were challenged in court as being unconstitutionally invasive of women's rights, lawyers for the State argued that they did not conflict with the precedents established by ROE, MAHER and or any other prior abortion cases. However when the case reached the Supreme Court, the Solicitor-General at the behest of the Reagan administration filed an *amicus curiae* brief asking the Court to overrule ROE. In a passionate opinion announcing the judgment of the Court, Justice Blackmun, the author of ROE, reaffirmed that decision and ruled that the key provisions in the Pennsylvania statute were unconstitutional. The four dissenters varied in their reasoning. Justice O'Connor emerged

as a swing vote in future abortion cases, when she announced that she would have upheld the Pennsylvania law because it did not conflict with ROE. Chief Justice Burger, as well as Justice White and then-Justice Rehnquist indicated that it was time to rethink and reject ROE altogether.

This opportunity to rethink ROE reemerged three years later in a case challenging a 1986 Missouri statute which placed even more restrictions on women and doctors than had the recently rejected Pennsylvania law. The case, WEBSTER v. REPRODUCTIVE HEALTH SERVICES, is reprinted below. The challenged provisions of the Missouri law are stated at the outset of the plurality opinion by Justice Rehnquist. An especially controversial feature of the law is the statement of "findings" set forth in its preamble, which announces that "the life of each human being begins at conception," and that "unborn children have protectable interests in life, health, and well-being." Taken at face value this is a claim that the state has authority to protect the fetus from the moment of conception, a view clearly at odds with the tripartite framework set forth in ROE.

Between 1986 when *Thornburgh* overturned Pennsylvania's restrictive abortion law and WEBSTER, the Court experienced some significant changes in membership. Justice Scalia replaced Chief Justice Burger and Justice Rehnquist was elevated to Chief Justice. And Justice Kennedy replaced Justice Powell. The result was a net increase in one hardline opponent of a constitutional right to abortion (Kennedy for Powell), and the elevation of an outspoken opponent of ROE to Chief Justice. No doubt it was this change that led the Solicitor-General to resubmit the same *amicus* brief he had used in *Thornburgh,* and again request that the Court overrule ROE.

The results in the case below reflect this shift. In a five to four vote, the Court upheld the sorts of restrictive provisions that earlier it would have rejected. However even with the changes a majority could not be mustered to overrule ROE. As she had been in earlier cases, Justice O'Connor was the swing vote with respect to upholding the ROE framework. She wrote separately arguing that the provisions at hand did not implicate the broader ROE framework. But she was alone in this regard. All other justices understood WEBSTER as a significant attack on ROE. Writing for the plurality, Justice Rehnquist acknowledges in Part II-D, the most important part of his opinion, that the decision will "modify and narrow ROE and succeeding cases." He is attacked for this from both sides. Justice Scalia argues that he is being disingenuous since Part II-D in effect repudiates the tripartite framework, the heart of ROE, and asserts that the Court should have had the courage of its convictions and directly overruled ROE in a forthright manner. Similarly, dissenters Blackmun, Marshall, Brennan, and Stevens all regard the opinion as rejecting the core of ROE.

Although the Chief Justice may have been trying to be a statesperson in his opinion, as Justice Scalia suggests (others think he was being Machiavellian in the absence of a majority to overrule ROE), it is clear that WEBSTER does not provide the definitive solution to the Court's abortion problem. Indeed it is likely to increase the Court's involvement in this area. Opponents of abortion will be encouraged to press for even more restrictive legislation, while proponents will hope to regroup and get the Court to redraw lines so that not all constitutional protection for women who want abortions will be lost. Much will depend on future appointments to the Court and to the leadership role that Justice O'Connor may be given in this area.

CHIEF JUSTICE REHNQUIST announced the judgment of the Court and delivered the opinion of the Court with respect to Parts I, II-A, II-B, and II-C, and an opinion with respect to Parts II-D and III, in which JUSTICE WHITE and JUSTICE KENNEDY join.

. . . .

I

In June 1986, the Governor of Missouri signed into law [a statute] which amended existing state law concerning unborn children and abortions. The Act consisted of 20 provisions, 5 of which are now before the Court. The first provision, or preamble, contains "findings" by the state legislature that "[t]he life of each human being begins at conception," and that "unborn children have protectable interests in life, health, and well-being." Mo. Rev. Stat. §§1.205.1(1), (2) (1986). The Act further requires that all Missouri laws be interpreted to provide unborn children with the same rights enjoyed by other persons, subject to the Federal Constitution and this Court's precedents. §1.205.2. Among its other provisions, the Act requires that, prior to performing an abortion on any woman whom a physician has reason to believe is 20 or more weeks pregnant, the physician ascertain whether the fetus is viable by performing "such medical examinations and tests as are necessary to make a finding of the gestational age, weight, and lung maturity of the unborn child." §188.029. The Act also prohibits the use of public employees and facilities to perform or assist abortions not necessary to save the mother's life, and it prohibits the use of public funds, employees, or facilities for the purpose of "encouraging or counseling" a woman to have an abortion not necessary to save her life. §§188.205, 188.210, 188.215.

In July 1986, five health professionals employed by the State and two nonprofit corporations brought this class action in the United States District Court for the Western District of Missouri to challenge the constitutionality of the Missouri statute. Plaintiffs, appellees in this Court, sought declaratory and injunctive relief on the ground that certain statutory provisions violated the First, Fourth, Ninth, and Fourteenth Amendments to the Federal Constitution. They asserted violations of various rights, including the "privacy rights of pregnant women seeking abortions"; the "woman's right to an abortion"; the right[t] to privacy in the physician-patient relationship"; the physician's "righ[t] to practice medicine"; the pregnant woman's "right to life due to inherent risks involved in childbirth"; and the woman's right to "receive . . . adequate medical advice and treatment" concerning abortion.

. . . .

. . . Following a 3-day trial in December 1986, the District Court declared seven provisions of the Act unconstitutional and enjoined their enforcement. These provisions included the preamble, Mo. Rev. Stat. §1.205 (1986); the "informed consent" provision, which required physicians to inform the pregnant woman of certain facts before performing an abortion, §188.039; the requirement that post-16-week abortions be performed only in hospitals, §188.025; the mandated tests to determine viability, §188.029; and the prohibition on the use of public funds, employees, and facilities to perform or assist nontherapeutic abortions, and the restrictions on the use of public funds, employees, and facilities to encourage or counsel women to have such abortions, §§188.205, 188.210, 188.215.... The Court of Appeals for the Eighth Circuit affirmed, with one exception not relevant to this appeal....

II

Decision of this case requires us to address four sections of the Missouri Act: (a) the preamble; (b) the prohibition on the use of public facilities or employees to perform abortions; (c) the prohibition on public funding of abortion counseling; and (d) the requirement that physicians conduct viability tests prior to performing abortions. We address these *seriatim.*

A

The Act's preamble, as noted, sets forth "findings" by the Missouri legislature that "[t]he life of each human being begins at conception," and that "[u]nborn children have protectable interests in life, health, and well-being." Mo. Rev. Stat. §§1.205.1(1), (2) (1986). The Act then mandates that state laws be interpreted to provide unborn children with "all the rights, privileges, and immunities available to other persons, citizens, and residents of this state," subject to the Constitution and this Court's precedents. §1.205.2. In invalidating the preamble, the Court of Appeals relied on this Court's dictum that "'a State may not adopt one theory of when life begins to justify its regulation of abortions.'"... It rejected Missouri's claim that the preamble was "abortion-neutral," and "merely determine[d] when life begins in a non-abortion context, a traditional state prerogative." The court thought that "[t]he only plausible inference" from the fact that "every remaining section of the bill save one regulates the performance of abortions" was that "the state intended its abortion regulations to be understood against the backdrop of its theory of life."

The State contends that the preamble itself is precatory and imposes no substantive restrictions on abortions, and that appellees therefore do not have standing to challenge it.... Appellees, on the other hand, insist that the preamble is an operative part of the Act intended to guide the interpretation of other provisions of the Act.... It will be time enough for federal courts to address the meaning of the preamble should it be applied to restrict the activities of appellees in some concrete way. Until then, this Court "is not empowered to decide... abstract propositions, or to declare, for the government of future cases, principles or rules of law which cannot

affect the result as to the thing in issue in the case before it." We therefore need not pass on the constitutionality of the Act's preamble.

B

Section 188.210 provides that "[i]t shall be unlawful for any public employee within the scope of his employment to perform or assist an abortion, not necessary to save the life of the mother," while §188.215 makes it "unlawful for any public facility to be used for the purpose of performing or assisting an abortion not necessary to save the life of the mother." The Court of Appeals held that these provisions contravened this Court's abortion decisions. We take the contrary view.

. . . .

The Court of Appeals... reasoned that the ban on the use of public facilities "could prevent a woman's chosen doctor from performing an abortion because of his unprivileged status at other hospitals or because a private hospital adopted a similar anti-abortion stance." It also thought that "[s]uch a rule could increase the cost of obtaining an abortion and delay the timing of it as well."

We think that this analysis is much like that which we rejected in *Maher*.... [T]he State's decision here to use public facilities and staff to encourage childbirth over abortion "places no governmental obstacle in the path of a woman who chooses to terminate her pregnancy." Just as Congress' refusal to fund abortions in *McRae* left "an indigent woman with at least the same range of choice in deciding whether to obtain a medically necessary abortion as she would have had if Congress had chosen to subsidize no health care costs at all," Missouri's refusal to allow public employees to perform abortions in public hospitals leaves a pregnant woman with the same choices as if the State had chosen not to operate any public hospitals at all. The challenged provisions only restrict a woman's ability to obtain an abortion to the extent that she chooses to use a physician affiliated with a public hospital. This circumstance is more easily remedied, and thus considerably less burdensome, than indigency, which "may make it difficult — and in some cases, perhaps, impossible — for some women to have abortions" without public funding. Having held that the State's refusal to fund abortions does not violate *Roe v. Wade,* it strains logic to reach a contrary result for the use of public facilities and employees. If the State may "make a value judgment favoring childbirth over abortion and... implement that judgment by the allocation of public funds,"

surely it may do so through the allocation of other public resources, such as hospitals and medical staff.
. . . .

C [omitted]

D

Section 188.029 of the Missouri Act provides:

Before a physician performs an abortion on a woman he has reason to believe is carrying an unborn child of twenty or more weeks gestational age, the physician shall first determine if the unborn child is viable by using and exercising that degree of care, skill, and proficiency commonly exercised by the ordinarily skillful, careful, and prudent physician engaged in similar practice under the same or similar conditions. In making this determination of viability, the physician shall perform or cause to be performed such medical examinations and tests as are necessary to make a finding of the gestational age, weight, and lung maturity of the unborn child and shall enter such findings and determination of viability in the medical record of the mother.

As with the preamble, the parties disagree over the meaning of this statutory provision. The State emphasizes the language of the first sentence, which speaks in terms of the physician's determination of viability being made by the standards of ordinary skill in the medical profession. Appellees stress the language of the second sentence, which prescribes such "tests as are necessary" to make a finding of gestational age, fetal weight, and lung maturity.

The Court of Appeals read §188.029 as requiring that after 20 weeks "doctors *must* perform tests to find gestational age, fetal weight and lung maturity." The court indicated that the tests needed to determine fetal weight at 20 weeks are "unreliable and inaccurate" and would add $125 to $250 to the cost of an abortion. It also stated that "amniocentesis, the only method available to determine lung maturity, is contrary to accepted medical practice until 28–30 weeks of gestation, expensive, and imposes significant health risks for both the pregnant woman and the fetus."
. . . .

We think the viability-testing provision makes sense only if the second sentence is read to require only those tests that are useful to making subsidiary findings as to viability. If we construe this provision to require a physician to perform those tests needed to make the three specified findings *in all circumstances,* including when the physician's reasonable professional judgment indicates that the tests would be irrelevant to determining viability or even dangerous to the mother and the fetus, the second sentence of §188.029 would conflict with the first sentence's *requirement* that a physician apply his reasonable professional skill and judgment. It would also be incongruous to read this provision, especially the word "necessary," to require the performance of tests irrelevant to the expressed statutory purpose of determining viability. It thus seems clear to us that the Court of Appeals' construction of §188.029 violates well-accepted canons of statutory interpretation used in the Missouri courts. . . .

The viability-testing provision of the Missouri Act is concerned with promoting the State's interest in potential human life rather than in maternal health. Section 188.029 creates what is essentially a presumption of viability at 20 weeks, which the physician must rebut with tests indicating that the fetus is not viable prior to performing an abortion. It also directs the physician's determination as to viability by specifying consideration, if feasible, of gestational age, fetal weight, and lung capacity. The District Court found that "the medical evidence is uncontradicted that a 20-week fetus is *not* viable," and that "23½ to 24 weeks gestation is the earliest point in pregnancy where a reasonable possibility of viability exists." But is also found that there may be a 4-week error is estimating gestational age, which supports testing at 20 weeks.

In *Roe* v. *Wade,* the Court recognized that the State has "important and legitimate" interests in protecting maternal health and in the potentiality of human life. During the second trimester, the State "may, if it chooses, regulate the abortion procedure in ways that are reasonably related to maternal health." After viability, when the State's interest in potential human life was held to become compelling, the State "may, if it chooses, regulate, and even proscribe, abortion except where it is necessary, in appropriate medical judgment for the preservation of the life or health of the mother."
. . . .

We think that the doubt cast upon the Missouri statute by [prior] cases is not so much a flaw in the statute as it is a reflection of the fact that the rigid trimester analysis of the course of a pregnancy enunciated in *Roe* has resulted in subsequent cases . . . making constitutional law in this area a virtual Procrustean bed. Statutes specifying elements of informed consent to be provided abortion patients, for example, were invalidated if they were thought to "structur[e] . . . the dialogue between the woman and her physician." . . .

Stare decisis is a cornerstone of our legal system, but it has less power in constitutional cases, where, save for constitutional amendments, this Court is the only body able to make needed changes. We have not refrained from reconsideration of a prior construction of the Constitution that has proved "unsound in principle and unworkable in practice." *Garcia* v. *San Antonio Metropolitan Transit Authority* (1985); *Erie R. Co.* v. *Tompkins* (1938). We think the *Roe* trimester framework falls into that category.

In the first place, the rigid *Roe* framework is hardly consistent with the notion of a Constitution cast in general terms, as ours is, and usually speaking in general principles, as ours does. The key elements of the *Roe* framework — trimesters and viability — are not found in the text of the Constitution or in any place else one would expect to find a constitutional principle. Since the bounds of the inquiry are essentially indeterminate, the result has been a web of legal rules that have become increasingly intricate, resembling a code of regulations rather than a body of constitutional doctrine. As JUSTICE WHITE has put it, the trimester framework has left this Court to serve as the country's *"ex officio* medical board with powers to approve or disapprove medical and operative practices and standards throughout the United States."

In the second place, we do not see why the State's interest in protecting potential human life should come into existence only at the point of viability, and that there should therefore be a rigid line allowing state regulation after viability but prohibiting it before viability. The dissenters in *Thornburgh,* writing in context of the *Roe* trimester analysis, would have recognized this fact by positing against the "fundamental right" recognized in *Roe* the State's "compelling interest" in protecting potential human life throughout pregnancy. . . .

The tests that §188.029 requires the physician to perform are designed to determine viability. The State here has chosen viability as the point at which its interest in potential human life must be safeguarded. It is true that the tests in question increase the expense of abortion, and regulate the discretion of the physician in determining the viability of the fetus. Since the tests will undoubtedly show in many cases that the fetus is not viable, the tests will have been performed for what were in fact second-trimester abortions. But we are satisfied that the re-

quirement of these tests permissibly furthers the State's interest in protecting potential human life, and we therefore believe §188.029 to be constitutional.

. . . .

III

Both appellants and the United States as *Amicus Curiae* have urged that we overrule our decision in *Roe* v. *Wade.* The facts of the present case, however, differ from those at issue in *Roe.* Here, Missouri has determined that viability is the point at which its interest in potential human life must be safeguarded. In *Roe,* on the other hand, the Texas statute criminalized the performance of *all* abortions, except when the mother's life was at stake. This case therefore affords us no occasion to revisit the holding of *Roe,* which was that the Texas statute unconstitutionally infringed the right to an abortion derived from the Due Process Clause, and we leave it undisturbed. To the extent indicated in our opinion, we would modify and narrow *Roe* and succeeding cases.

Because none of the challenged provisions of the Missouri Act properly before us conflict with the Constitution, the judgment of the Court of Appeals is *Reversed.*

JUSTICE O'CONNOR, concurring in part and concurring in the judgment.

I concur in Parts I, II-A, II-B, and II-C of the Court's opinion. [However I differ with respect to Part II-D.]

. . . .

Unlike the plurality [in II-D], I do not understand these viability testing requirements to conflict with any of the Court's past decisions concerning state regulation of abortion. Therefore, there is no necessity to accept the State's invitation to reexamine the constitutional validity of *Roe* v. *Wade. . . .*

. . . .

Finally, and rather half-heartedly, the plurality suggests that the marginal increase in the cost of an abortion created by Missouri's viability testing provision may make §188.029, even as interpreted, suspect under this Court's decision in *Akron* striking down a second-trimester hospitalization requirement. I dissented from the court's opinion in *Akron* because it was my view that, even apart from *Roe's* trimester framework which I continue to consider problematic, the *Akron* majority had distorted and misapplied its own standard for evaluating state regulation of abortion which the Court had applied with fair consistency in the past: that, previability, "a regulation imposed on a lawful abortion is not unconstitutional unless it unduly burdens the right to seek an abortion."

It is clear to me that requiring the performance of examinations and tests useful to determining whether a fetus is viable, when viability is possible, and when it would not be medically imprudent to do so, does not impose an undue burden on a woman's abortion decision. On this ground alone I would reject the suggestion that §188.029 as interpreted is unconstitutional. More to the point, however, just as I see no conflict between §188.029 . . . or any decision of this Court concerning a State's ability to give effect to its interest in potential life, I see no conflict between §188.029 and the Court's opinion in *Akron.* The second-trimester hospitalization requirement struck down in *Akron* imposed, in the majority's view, "a heavy, and unnecessary, burden" more than doubling the cost of "women's access to a relatively inexpensive, otherwise accessible, and safe abortion procedure." By contrast, the cost of examinations and tests that could usefully and prudently be performed when a woman is 20–24 weeks pregnant to determine whether the fetus is viable would only marginally, if at all, increase the cost of an abortion. . . .

. . . Accordingly, because the Court of Appeals misinterpreted Mo. Rev. Stat. §188.029, and because, properly interpreted, §188.029 is not inconsistent with any of this Court's prior precedents, I would reverse the decision of the Court of Appeals.

JUSTICE SCALIA, concurring in part and concurring in the judgment.

I join Parts I, II-A, II-B, and II-C of the opinion of THE CHIEF JUSTICE. As to Part II-D, I share JUSTICE BLACKMUN's view that it effectively would overrule *Roe* v. *Wade.* I think that should be done, but would do it more explicitly. . . .

The outcome of today's case will doubtless be heralded as a triumph of judicial statesmanship. It is not that, unless it is statesmanlike needlessly to prolong this Court's self-awarded sovereignty over a field where it has little proper business since the answers to most of the cruel questions posed are political and not juridical — a sovereignty which therefore quite properly, but to the great damage of the Court, makes it the object of the sort of organized public pressure that political institutions in a democracy ought to receive.

. . . .

The Court has often spoken more broadly than needed in precisely the fashion at issue here, announcing a new rule of constitutional law when it could have reached the identical result by applying the rule thereby displaced. . . .

The real question, then, is whether there are valid reasons to go beyond the most stingy possible holding today. It seems to me there are not only valid but compelling ones. Ordinarily, speaking no more broadly than is absolutely required avoids throwing settled law into confusion; doing so today preserves a chaos that is evident to anyone who can read and count. Alone sufficient to justify a broad holding is the fact that our retaining control, through *Roe,* of what I believe to be, and many of our citizens recognize to be, a political issue, continuously distorts the public perception of the role of this Court. We can now look forward to at least another Term with carts full of mail from the public, and streets full of demonstrators, urging us — their unelected and life-tenured judges who have been awarded those extraordinary, undemocratic characteristics precisely in order that we might follow the law despite the popular will — to follow the popular will. Indeed, I expect we can look forward to even more of that than before, given our indecisive decision today. . . .

. . . Given the Court's newly contracted abstemiousness, what will it take, one must wonder, to permit us to reach [the] fundamental question? The result of our vote today is that we will not reconsider that prior opinion, even if most of the Justices think it is wrong, unless we have before us a statute that in fact contradicts it — and even then (under our newly discovered "no-broader-than-necessary" requirement) only minor problematical aspects of *Roe* will be reconsidered, unless one expects State legislatures to adopt provisions whose compliance with *Roe* cannot even be argued with a straight face. It thus appears that the mansion of constitutionalized abortion-law, constructed overnight in *Roe* v. *Wade,* must be disassembled door-jamb by door-jamb, and never entirely brought down, no matter how wrong it may be.

Of the four courses we might have chosen today — to reaffirm *Roe,* to overrule it explicitly, to overrule it *sub silentio,* or to avoid the question — the last is the least responsible. On the question of the constitutionality of §188.029, I concur in the judgment of the Court and strongly dissent from the manner in which it has been reached.

JUSTICE BLACKMUN, with whom JUSTICE BRENNAN and JUSTICE MARSHALL join, concurring in part and dissenting in part.

Today, *Roe* v. *Wade* (1973), and the fundamental constitutional right of women to decide whether to terminate a pregnancy, survive but are not secure. Although the Court extricates itself from this case without making a single, even incremental, change in the law of abortion, the plurality and JUSTICE SCALIA would overrule *Roe* (the first silently, the other explicitly) and would return to the States virtually unfettered authority to control the quintessentially intimate, personal, and life-directing decision whether to carry a fetus to term. Although today, no less than yesterday, the Constitution and the decisions of this Court prohibit a State from enacting laws that inhibit women from the meaningful exercise of that right, a plurality of this court implicitly invites every state legislature to enact more and more restrictive abortion regulations in order to provoke more and more test cases, in the hope that sometime down the line the Court will return the law of procreative freedom to the severe limitations that generally prevailed in this country before January 22, 1973. Never in my memory has a plurality announced a judgment of this Court that so foments disregard for the law and for our standing decisions.

Nor in my memory has a plurality gone about its business in such a deceptive fashion. At every level of its review, from its effort to read the real meaning out of the Missouri statute, to its intended evisceration of precedents and its deafening silence about the constitutional protections that it would jettison, the plurality obscures the portent of its analysis. With feigned restraint, the plurality announces that its analysis leaves *Roe* "undisturbed," albeit "modif[ied] and narrow[ed]." But this disclaimer is totally meaningless. The plurality opinion is filled with winks, and nods, and knowing glances to those who would do away with *Roe* explicitly, but turns a stone face to anyone in search of what the plurality conceives as the scope of a woman's right under the Due Process Clause to terminate a pregnancy free from the coercive and brooding influence of the State. The simple truth is that *Roe* would not survive the plurality's analysis, and that the plurality provides no substitute for *Roe's* protective umbrella.

I fear for the future. I fear for the liberty and equality of the millions of women who have lived and come of age in the 16 years since *Roe* was decided. I fear for the integrity of, and public esteem for, this Court.

I dissent.

I

...[T]ucked away at the end of its opinion, the plurality suggests a radical reversal of the law of abortion; and there, primarily, I direct my attention.

In the plurality's view, the viability-testing provision imposes a burden on second-trimester abortions as a way of furthering the State's interest in protecting the potential life of the fetus. Since under the *Roe* framework, the State may not fully regulate abortion in the interest of potential life (as opposed to maternal health) until the third trimester, the plurality finds it necessary, in order to save the Missouri testing provision, to throw out *Roe's* trimester framework. In flat contradiction to *Roe,* the plurality concludes that the State's interest in potential life is compelling before viability, and upholds the testing provision because it "permissibly furthers" that state interest.

A

At the outset, I note that in its haste to limit abortion rights, the plurality compounds the errors of its analysis by needlessly reaching out to address constitutional questions that are not actually presented. The conflict between §188.029 and *Roe's* trimester framework, which purportedly drives the plurality to reconsider our past decisions, is a contrived conflict: the product of an aggressive misreading of the viability-testing requirement and a needlessly wooden application of the *Roe* framework.

The plurality's reading of §188.029 (also joined by JUSTICE O'CONNOR) is irreconcilable with the plain language of the statute and is in derogation of this Court's settled view that "'district courts and courts of appeals are better schooled in and more able to interpret the laws of their respective States.'" Abruptly setting aside the construction of §188.029 adopted by both the District Court and Court of Appeals as "plain error," the plurality reads the viability-testing provision as requiring only that before a physician may perform an abortion on a woman whom he believes to be carrying a fetus of 20 or more weeks gestational age, the doctor must determine whether the fetus is viable and, as part of that exercise, must, to the extent feasible and consistent with sound medical practice, conduct tests necessary to make findings of gestational age, weight, and lung maturity. But the plurality's reading of the provision, according to which the statute requires the physician to perform tests only in order to determine *viability,* ignores the statutory language explicitly directing that "the physician *shall* perform or cause to be performed such medical examinations and tests as are *necessary to make a finding of the gestational age, weight, and lung maturity* of the unborn child and *shall* enter such findings" in the mother's medical record. §188.029 (emphasis added). The statute's plain language requires the physician to undertake whatever tests are necessary to determine gestational age, weight, and lung maturity, regardless of whether the tests are necessary to a finding of viability, and regardless of whether the tests subject the pregnant woman or the fetus to additional health risks or add substantially to the cost of an abortion.

Had the plurality read the statute as written, it would have had no cause to reconsider the *Roe* framework. As properly construed, the viability-testing provision does not pass constitutional muster under even a rational-basis standard, the least restrictive level of review applied by this Court. By mandating tests to determine fetal weight and lung maturity for every fetus thought to be more than 20 weeks gestational age, the statute requires physicians to undertake procedures, such as amniocentesis, that, in the situation presented, have no medical justification, impose significant additional health risks on both the pregnant woman and the fetus, and bear no rational relation to the State's interest in protecting fetal life. As written, §188.029 is an arbitrary imposition of discomfort, risk, and expense, furthering no discernible interest except to make the procurement of an abortion as arduous and difficult as possible. Thus, were it not for the plurality's tortured effort to avoid the plain import of §188.029, it could have struck down the testing provision as patently irrational irrespective of the *Roe* framework.

The plurality eschews this straightforward resolution, in the hope of precipitating a constitutional crisis. Far from avoiding constitutional difficulty, the plurality attempts to engineer a dramatic retrenchment in our jurisprudence by exaggerating the conflict between its untenable construction of §188.029 and the *Roe* trimester framework.

No one contests that under the *Roe* framework the State, in order to promote its interest in potential human life, may regulate and even proscribe non-therapeutic abortions once the fetus becomes viable. *Roe*, 410 U.S., at 164–165. If, as the plurality appears to hold, the testing provision simply requires a physician to use appropriate and medically sound tests to determine whether the fetus is actually viable when the estimated gestational age is greater than 20 weeks (and therefore within what the District Court found to be the margin of error for viability, then I see little or no conflict with *Roe*. Nothing in *Roe*, or any of its progeny, holds that a State may not effectuate its compelling interest in the potential life of a viable fetus by seeking to ensure that no viable fetus is mistakenly aborted because of the inherent lack of precision in estimates of gestational age. A requirement that a physician make a finding of viability, one way or the other, for every fetus that falls within the range of possible viability does

no more than preserve the State's recognized authority. Although, as the plurality correctly points out, such a testing requirement would have the effect of imposing additional costs on second-trimester abortions where the tests indicated that the fetus was not viable, these costs would be merely incidental to, and a necessary accommodation of, the State's unquestioned right to prohibit non-therapeutic abortions after the point of viability. In short, the testing provision, as construed by the plurality is consistent with the *Roe* framework and could be upheld effortlessly under current doctrine.

How ironic it is, then, and disingenuous, that the plurality scolds the Court of Appeals for adopting a construction of the statute that fails to avoid constitutional difficulties. By distorting the statute, the plurality manages to avoid invalidating the testing provision on what should have been noncontroversial constitutional grounds; having done so, however, the plurality rushes headlong into a much deeper constitutional thicket, brushing past an obvious basis for upholding §188.029 in search of a pretext for scuttling the trimester framework. Evidently, from the plurality's perspective, the real problem with the Court of Appeals' construction of §188.029 is not that it raised a constitutional difficulty, but that it raised the wrong constitutional difficulty — one not implicating *Roe*. The plurality had remedied that, traditional canons of construction and judicial forbearance notwithstanding.

B

Having set up conflict between §188.029 and the *Roe* trimester framework, the plurality summarily discards *Roe*'s analytic core as "'unsound in principle and unworkable in practice.'" This is so, the plurality claims, because the key elements of the framework do not appear in the text of the Constitution, because the framework more closely resembles a regulatory code than a body of constitutional doctrine, and because under the framework the State's interest in potential human life is considered compelling only after viability, when, in fact, that interest is equally compelling throughout pregnancy. The plurality does not bother to explain these alleged flaws in *Roe*. Bald assertion masquerades as reasoning. The object, quite clearly, is not to persuade, but to prevail.

1

The plurality opinion is far more remarkable for the arguments that it does not advance than for those that it does. The plurality does not even mention, much less join, the true jurisprudential debate underlying this case: whether the Constitution includes an "unenumerated" general right to privacy as recognized in many of our decisions, most notably *Griswold* v. *Connecticut,* 381 U.S. 479 (1965), and *Roe,* and, more specifically, whether and to what extent such a right to privacy extends to matters of childbearing and family life, including abortion. See, *e.g., Eisenstadt* v. *Baird* (1972) (contraception); *Loving* v. *Virginia* (1967) (marriage); *Skinner* v. *Oklahoma ex re.* Williamson (1942) (procreation); *Pierce* v. *Society of Sisters* (1925) (childrearing). These are questions of unsurpassed significance in this Court's interpretation of the Constitution, and mark the battleground upon which this case was fought, by the parties, by the Solicitor General as *amicus* on behalf of petitioners, and by an unprecedented number of *amici.* On these grounds, abandoned by the plurality, the Court should decide this case.

But rather than arguing that the text of the Constitution makes no mention of the right to privacy, the plurality complains that the critical elements of the *Roe* framework—trimesters and viability—do not appear in the Constitution and are, therefore, somehow inconsistent with a Constitution cast in general terms. *Ante,* at 20. Were this a true concern, we would have to abandon most of our constitutional jurisprudence. As the plurality well knows, or should know, the "critical elements" of countless constitutional doctrines nowhere appear in the Constitution's text. The Constitution makes no mention, for example, of the First Amendment's "actual malice" standard for proving certain libels, of the standard for determining when speech is obscene. Similarly, the Constitution makes no mention of the rational-basis test, or the specific verbal formulations of intermediate and strict scrutiny by which this Court evaluates claims under the Equal Protection Clause. The reason is simple. Like the *Roe* framework, these tests or standards are not, and do not purport to be, rights protected by the Constitution. Rather, they are judge-made methods for evaluating and measuring the strength and scope of constitutional rights or for balancing the constitutional rights of individuals against the competing interests of government.

With respect to the *Roe* framework, the general constitutional principle, indeed the fundamental constitutional right, for which it was developed is the right to privacy, a species of "liberty" protected by the Due Process Clause, which under our past decisions safeguards the right of women to exercise some control over their own role in procreation. As

we recently reaffirmed in *Thornburgh* v. *American College of Obstetricians and Gynecologists* (1986), few decisions are "more basic to individual dignity and autonomy" or more appropriate to that "certain private sphere of individual liberty" that the Constitution reserves from the intrusive reach of government than the right to make the uniquely personal, intimate, and self-defining decision whether to end a pregnancy. It is this general principle, the " 'moral fact that a person belongs to himself and not others nor to society as a whole,' " that is found in the Constitution. The trimester framework simply defines and limits that right to privacy in the abortion context to accommodate, not destroy, a State's legitimate interest in protecting the health of pregnant women and in preserving potential human life. Fashioning such accommodations between individual rights and the legitimate interests of government, establishing benchmarks and standards with which to evaluate the competing claims of individuals and government, lies at the very heart of constitutional adjudication. To the extent that the trimester framework is useful in this enterprise, it is not only consistent with constitutional interpretation, but necessary to the wise and just exercise of this Court's paramount authority to define the scope of constitutional rights.

2

The plurality next alleges that the result of the trimester framework has "been a web of legal rules that have become increasingly intricate, resembling a code of regulations rather than a body of constitutional doctrine." Again, if this were a true and genuine concern, we would have to abandon vast areas of our constitutional jurisprudence. The plurality complains that under the trimester framework the Court has distinguished between a city ordinance requiring that second-trimester abortions be performed in clinics and a state law requiring that these abortions be performed in hospitals, or between laws requiring that certain information be furnished to a woman by a physician or his assistant and those requiring that such information be furnished by the physician exclusively. Are these distinctions any finer, or more "regulatory," than the distinctions we have often drawn in our First Amendment jurisprudence, where, for example, we have held that a "release time" program permitting public-school students to leave school grounds during school hours to receive religious instruction does not violate the Establishment Clause, even though a release-time program permitting religious instruction on school grounds does violate the Clause? Compare *Zorach* v. *Clauson* (1952), with *McCollum* v. *Board of Education* (1948). Our Fourth Amendment jurisprudence recognizes factual distinctions no less intricate. . . .

That numerous constitutional doctrines result in narrow differentiations between similar circumstances does not mean that this Court has abandoned adjudication in favor of regulation. Rather, these careful distinctions reflect the process of constitutional adjudication itself, which is often highly fact-specific, requiring such determinations as whether state laws are "unduly burdensome" or "reasonable" or bear a "rational" or "necessary" relation to asserted state interests. . . .

. . . If, in delicate and complicated areas of constitutional law, our legal judgments "have become increasingly intricate," *ante,* at 20, it is not, as the plurality contends, because we have overstepped our judicial role. Quite the opposite: the rules are intricate because we have remained conscientious in our duty to do justice carefully, especially when fundamental rights rise or fall with our decisions.

3

Finally, the plurality asserts that the trimester framework cannot stand because the State's interest in potential life is compelling throughout pregnancy, not merely after viability. The opinion contains not one word of rationale for its view of the State's interest. This "it-is-so-because-we-say-so" jurisprudence constitutes nothing other than an attempted exercise of brute force; reason, much less persuasion, has no place.

. . . .

For my own part, I remain convinced, as six other Members of this Court 16 years ago were convinced, that the *Roe* framework, and the viability standard in particular, fairly, sensibly, and effectively functions to safeguard the constitutional liberties of pregnant women while recognizing and accommodating the State's interest in potential human life. The viability line reflects the biological facts and truths of fetal development; it marks that threshold moment prior to which a fetus cannot survive separate from the woman and cannot reasonably and objectively be regarded as a subject of rights or interests distinct from, or paramount to, those of the pregnant woman. At the same time, the viability standard takes account of the undeniable fact that as the fetus evolves into its postnatal form, and as it loses its dependence on the uterine environment, the State's interest in the fetus' potential human life, and in fostering a regard for human life in general, becomes compel-

ling. As a practical matter, because viability follows "quickening" — the point at which a woman feels movement in her womb — and because viability occurs no earlier than 23 weeks gestational age, it establishes an easily applicable standard for regulating abortion while providing a pregnant woman ample time to exercise her fundamental right with her responsible physician to terminate her pregnancy. . . . In *Roe,* we discharged that responsibility as logic and science compelled. The plurality today advances not one reasonable argument as to why our judgment in that case was wrong and should be abandoned.

C

Having contrived an opportunity to reconsider the *Roe* framework, and then having discarded that framework, the plurality finds the testing provision unobjectionable because it "permissibly furthers the State's interest in protecting potential human life." This newly minted standard is circular and totally meaningless. Whether a challenged abortion regulation "permissibly furthers" a legitimate state interest is the *question* that courts must answer in abortion cases, not the standard for courts to apply. In keeping with the rest of its opinion, the plurality makes no attempt to explain or to justify its new standard, either in the abstract or as applied in this case. Nor could it. The "permissibly furthers" standard has no independent meaning, and consists of nothing other than what a majority of this Court may believe at any given moment in any given case. The plurality's novel test appears to be nothing more than a dressed-up version of rational-basis review, this Court's most lenient level of scrutiny. One thing is clear, however: were the plurality's "permissibly furthers" standard adopted by the Court, for all practical purposes, *Roe* would be overruled.

The "permissibly furthers" standard completely disregards the irreducible minimum of *Roe:* the Court's recognition that a woman has a limited fundamental constitutional right to decide whether to terminate a pregnancy. That right receives no meaningful recognition in the plurality's written opinion. Since, in the plurality's view, the State's interest in potential life is compelling as of the moment of conception, and is therefore served only if abortion is abolished, every hindrance to a woman's ability to obtain an abortion must be "permissible." Indeed, the more severe the hindrance, the more effectively (and permissibly) the State's interest would be furthered. A tax on abortions or a criminal prohibition would both satisfy the plurality's standard. So, for that matter, would a requirement that a pregnant woman memorize and recite today's plurality opinion before seeking an abortion.

The plurality pretends that *Roe* survives, explaining that the facts of this case differ from those in *Roe:* here, Missouri has chosen to assert its interest in potential life only at the point of viability, whereas, in *Roe,* Texas had asserted that interest from the point of conception, criminalizing all abortions, except where the life of the mother was at stake. This, of course, is a distinction without a difference. The plurality repudiates every principle for which *Roe* stands; in good conscience, it cannot possibly believe that *Roe* lies "undisturbed" merely because this case does not call upon the Court to reconsider the Texas statute, or one like it. If the Constitution permits a State to enact any statute that reasonably furthers its interest in potential life, and if that interest arises as of conception, why would the Texas statute fail to pass muster? One suspects that the plurality agrees. It is impossible to read the plurality opinion... without recognizing its implicit invitation to every State to enact more and more restrictive abortion laws, and to assert their interest in potential life as of the moment of conception. All these laws will satisfy the plurality's non-scrutiny, until sometime, a new regime of old dissenters and new appointees will declare what the plurality intends: that *Roe* is no longer good law.

D

Thus, "not with a bang, but a whimper," the plurality discards a landmark case of the last generation, and casts into darkness the hopes and visions of every woman in this country who had come to believe that the Constitution guaranteed her the right to exercise some control over her unique ability to bear children. The plurality does so either oblivious or insensitive to the fact that millions of women, and their families, have ordered their lives around the right to reproductive choice, and that this right has become vital to the full participation of women in the economic and political walks of American life. The plurality would clear the way once again for government to force upon women the physical labor and specific and direct medical and psychological harms that may accompany carrying a fetus to term. The plurality would clear the way again for the State to conscript a woman's body and to force upon her a "distressful life and future."

The result, as we know from experience, would be that every year hundreds of thousands of women, in desperation, would defy the law, and place their health and safety in the unclean and unsympathetic hands of back-alley abortionists, or they would attempt to perform abortions upon themselves, with disastrous results. Every year, many women, especially poor and minority women, would die or suffer debilitating physical trauma, all in the name of enforced morality or religious dictates or lack of compassion, as it may be.

Of the aspirations and settled understandings of American women, of the inevitable and brutal consequences of what it is doing, the tough-approach plurality utters not a word. This silence is callous. It is also profoundly destructive of this Court as an institution. To overturn a constitutional decision is a rare and grave undertaking. To overturn a constitutional decision that secured a fundamental personal liberty to millions of persons would be unprecedented in our 200 years of constitutional history. Although the doctrine of *stare decisis* applies with somewhat diminished force in constitutional cases generally, even in ordinary constitutional cases "any departure from *stare decisis* demands special justification." This requirement of justification applies with unique force where, as here, the Court's abrogation of precedent would destroy people's firm belief, based on past decisions of this Court, that they possess an unabridgeable right to undertake certain conduct.

... Instead, the plurality pretends that it leaves *Roe* standing, and refuses even to discuss the real issue underlying this case: whether the Constitution includes an unenumerated right to privacy that encompasses a woman's right to decide whether to terminate a pregnancy. To the extent that the plurality does criticize the *Roe* framework, these criticisms are pure *ipse dixit.*

This comes at a cost. The doctrine of *stare decisis* "permits society to presume that bedrock principles are founded in the law rather than in the proclivities of individuals, and thereby contributes to the integrity of our constitutional system of government, both in appearance and in fact." Today's decision involves the most politically divisive domestic legal issue of our time. By refusing to explain or to justify its proposed revolutionary revision in the law of abortion, and by refusing to abide not only by our precedents, but also by our canons for reconsidering those precedents, the plurality invites charges of cowardice and illegitimacy to our door. I cannot say that these would be undeserved.

II

For today, at least, the law of abortion stands undisturbed. For today, the women of this Nation still retain the liberty to control their destinies. But the signs are evident and very ominous, and a chill wind blows.

I dissent.

JUSTICE STEVENS, concurring in part and dissenting in part.

... I agree with JUSTICE BLACKMUN, that the record identifies a sufficient number of unconstitutional applications to support the Court of Appeals' judgment invalidating those provisions....

I

It seems to me that in Part II-D of its opinion, the plurality strains to place a construction on §188.029 that enables it to conclude, "[W]e would modify and narrow *Roe* and succeeding cases." That statement is ill-advised because there is no need to modify even slightly the holdings of prior cases in order to uphold §188.029. For the most plausible nonliteral construction, as both JUSTICE BLACKMUN and JUSTICE O'CONNOR have demonstrated, is constitutional and entirely consistent with our precedents.

I am unable to accept JUSTICE O'CONNOR'S construction of the second sentence in §188.029, however, because I believe it is foreclosed by two controlling principles of statutory interpretation. First, it is our settled practice to accept "the interpretation of state law in which the District Court and the Court of Appeals have concurred even if an examination of the state-law issue without such guidance might have justified a different conclusion." Second, "[t]he fact that a particular application of the clear terms of a statute might be unconstitutional does not provide us with a justification for ignoring the plain meaning of the statute." In this case, I agree with the Court of Appeals that the meaning of the second sentence of §188.029 is too plain to be ignored. The sentence twice uses the mandatory term "shall," and contains no qualifying language. If it is implicitly limited to tests that are useful in determining viability, it adds nothing to the requirement imposed by the preceding sentence.

My interpretation of the plain language is supported by the structure of the statute as a whole, particularly the preamble, which "finds" that life "begins at conception" and further commands that state laws shall be construed to provide the maximum protection to "the unborn child at every stage of development." I agree with the District Court that "[o]bviously, the purpose of this law is to protect the potential life of the fetus, rather than to safeguard maternal health." A literal reading of the statute tends to accomplish that goal. Thus it is not "incongruous" to assume that the Missouri Legislature was trying to protect the potential human life of nonviable fetuses by making the abortion decision more costly. On the contrary, I am satisfied that the Court of Appeals, as well as the District Court, correctly concluded that the Missouri Legislature meant exactly what it said in the second sentence of §188.029. I am also satisfied... that the testing provision is manifestly unconstitutional under *Williamson* v. *Lee Optical Co.* "irrespective of the *Roe* [v. *Wade*] framework."

II

The Missouri statute defines "conception" as "the fertilization of the ovum of a female by a sperm of a male," even though standard medical texts equate "conception" with implantation in the uterus, occurring about six days after fertilization. Missouri's declaration therefore implies regulation not only of previability abortions, but also of common forms of contraception such as the IUD and the morning-after pill. Because the preamble, read in context, threatens serious encroachments upon the liberty of the pregnant woman and the health professional, I am persuaded that these plaintiffs, appellees before us, have standing to challenge its constitutionality.

To the extent that the Missouri statute interferes with contraceptive choices, I have no doubt that it is unconstitutional under the Court's holdings in *Griswold* v. *Connecticut* (1965), *Eisenstadt* v. *Baird* (1972), and *Carey* v. *Population Services International* (1977)....

. . . .

One might argue that the *Griswold* holding applies to devices "preventing conception" — that is, fertilization — but not to those preventing implantation, and therefore, that *Griswold* does not protect a woman's choice to use an IUD or take a morning-after pill. There is unquestionably a theological basis for such an argument, just as there was unquestionably a theological basis for the Connecticut statute that the Court invalidated in *Griswold*. Our jurisprudence, however, has consistently required a secular basis for valid legislation. Because I am not aware of any secular basis for differentiating between contraceptive procedures that are effective immediately before and those that are effective immediately after fertilization, I believe it inescapably follows that the preamble to the Missouri statute is invalid under *Griswold* and its progeny.

Indeed, I am persuaded that the absence of any secular purpose for the legislative declarations that life begins at conception and that conception occurs at fertilization makes the relevant portion of the preamble invalid under the Establishment Clause of the First Amendment to the Federal Constitution. This conclusion does not, and could not, rest on the fact that the statement happens to coincide with the tenets of certain religions, or on the fact that the legislators who voted to enact it may have been motivated by religious considerations. Rather, it rests on the fact that the preamble, an unequivocal endorsement of a religious tenet of some but by no means all Christian faiths, serves no identifiable secular purpose. That fact alone compels a conclusion that the statute violates the Establishment Clause.

My concern can best be explained by reference to the position on this issue that was endorsed by St. Thomas Aquinas and widely accepted by the leaders of the Roman Catholic Church for many years. . . .

> "For St. Thomas, as for mediaeval Christendom generally, there is a lapse of time—approximately 40 to 80 days—after conception and before the soul's infusion. . . .
> "For St. Thomas, 'seed and what is not seed is determined by sensation and movement.' What is destroyed in abortion of the unformed fetus is seed, not man. . . .

If the views of St. Thomas were held as widely today as they were in the Middle Ages, and if a state legislature were to enact a statute prefaced with a "finding" that female life begins 80 days after conception and male life begins 40 days after conception, I have no doubt that this Court would promptly conclude that such an endorsement of a particular religious tenet is violative of the Establishment Clause.

In my opinion the difference between that hypothetical statute and Missouri's preamble reflects nothing more than a difference in theological doctrine. The preamble to the Missouri statute endorses the theological position that there is the same secular interest in preserving the life of a fetus during the first 40 or 80 days of pregnancy as there is after viability—indeed, after the time when the fetus has become a "person" with legal rights protected by the Constitution. To sustain that position as a matter of law, I believe Missouri has the burden of identifying the secular interests that differentiate the first 40 days of pregnancy from the period immediately before or after fertilization when, as *Griswold* and related cases establish, the Constitution allows the use of contraceptive procedures to prevent potential life from developing into full personhood. Focusing our attention on the first several weeks of pregnancy is especially appropriate because that is the period when the vast majority of abortions are actually performed.

As a secular matter, there is an obvious difference between the state interest in protecting the freshly fertilized egg and the state interest in protecting a 9-month-gestated, fully sentient fetus on the eve of birth. There can be no interest in protecting the newly fertilized egg from physical pain or mental anguish, because the capacity for such suffering does not yet exist; respecting a developed fetus, however, that interest is valid. In fact, if one prescinds the theological concept of ensoulment—or one accepts St. Thomas Aquinas' view that ensoulment does not occur for at least 40 days, a State has no greater secular interest in protecting the potential life of an embryo that is still "seed" than in protecting the potential life of a sperm or an unfertilized ovum.

There have been times in history when military and economic interests would have been served by an increase in population. No one argues today, however, that Missouri can assert a societal interest in increasing its population as its secular reason for fostering potential life. Indeed, our national policy, as reflected in legislation the Court upheld last Term, is to prevent the potential life that is produced by "pregnancy and childbirth among unmarried adolescents." If the secular analysis were based on a strict balancing of fiscal costs and benefits, the economic costs of unlimited childbearing would outweigh those of abortion. There is, of course, an important and unquestionably valid secular interest in "protecting a young pregnant woman from the consequences of an incorrect decision." Although that interest is served by a requirement that the woman receive medical and, in appropriate circumstances, parental, advice, it does not justify the state legislature's official endorsement of the theological tenet embodied in §§1.205.1(1), (2).

The State's suggestion that the "finding" in the preamble to its abortion statute is, in effect, an amendment to its tort, property, and criminal laws is not persuasive. The Court of Appeals concluded that the preamble "is simply an impermissible state adoption of a theory of when life begins to justify its abortion regulations." Supporting that construction is the state constitutional prohibition against legislative enactments pertaining to more than one subject matter. Moreover, none of the tort, property, or criminal law cases cited by the State was either based on or buttressed by a theological answer to the question of when life begins. Rather, the Missouri courts, as well as a number of other state courts, had already concluded that a "fetus is a 'person,' 'minor,' or 'minor child' within the meaning of their particular wrongful death statutes."

Bolstering my conclusion that the preamble violates the First Amendment is the fact that the intensely divisive character of much of the national debate over the abortion issue reflects the deeply held religious convictions of many participants in the debate. The Missouri Legislature may not inject its endorsement of a particular religious tradition into this debate, for "[t]he Establishment Clause does not allow public bodies to foment such disagreement."

In my opinion the preamble to the Missouri statute is unconstitutional for two reasons. To the extent that it has substantive impact on the freedom to use contraceptive procedures, it is inconsistent with the central holding in *Griswold*. To the extent that it merely makes "legislative findings without operative effect," as the State argues, it violates the Establishment Clause of the First Amendment. Contrary to the theological "finding" of the Missouri Legislature, a woman's constitutionally protected liberty encompasses the right to act on her own belief that — to paraphrase St. Thomas Aquinas — until a seed has acquired the powers of sensation and movement, the life of a human being has not yet begun.

Moore v. City of East Cleveland

431 U.S. 494 (1977)
Vote: 5–4

In *Village of Belle Terre* v. *Boraas,* 416 U.S. 1 (1974), the Supreme Court upheld a village ordinance which restricted land use to one-family dwellings and defined "family" to mean one or more persons related by blood, adoption, or marriage, or not more than two unrelated persons. The case arose when owners of a house in the village, who had leased it to six unrelated students at the State University of New York at Stony Brook were cited for violating the ordinance. In his decision for a majority of seven, Justice Douglas treated the ordinance as a reasonable environmental protection law whose purpose was to foster "family values . . . and the blessings of quiet seclusion and clean air [that] make the area a sanctuary for people."

The case below is a variation on this theme. An East Cleveland housing ordinance limited occupancy of a dwelling unit to members of a single "family" and went on to define "family." The case arose when Inez Moore was charged with violation of the ordinance. Ms. Moore lived with her son, his son, and one of the children of another of her two sons. The boys had lived together with

Ms. Moore, and at least one of their fathers, since the death of one of their mothers. While East Cleveland's complicated definition of "family" allowed for various types of related individuals living together, the Moore household did not qualify under it. When Ms. Moore received notice of violation and an order to comply, she refused to remove one of her grandsons from the house and was subsequently charged with and convicted of a criminal offense. She appealed and lost in the Ohio courts, which cited *Belle Terre* as precedent, whereupon she appealed to the United States Supreme Court.

JUSTICE POWELL delivered the opinion of the Court.

The city argues that our decision in *Village of Belle Terre* v. *Boraas* (1974) requires us to sustain the ordinance attacked here. Belle Terre, like East Cleveland, imposed limits on the types of groups that could occupy a single dwelling unit. [W]e sustained the Belle Terre ordinance on the ground that it bore a rational relationship to permissible state objectives.

But one overriding factor sets this case apart from *Belle Terre*. The ordinance there affected only *unrelated* individuals. It expressly allowed all who were related by "blood, adoption, or marriage" to live together, and in sustaining the ordinance we were careful to note that it promoted "family needs" and "family values." East Cleveland, in contrast, has chosen to regulate the occupancy of its housing by slicing deeply into the family itself. This is no mere incidental result of the ordinance. On its face it selects certain categories of relatives who may live together and declares that others may not. In particular, it makes a crime of a grandmother's choice to live with her grandson in circumstances like those presented here.

When a city undertakes such intrusive regulation of the family the usual judicial deference to the legislature is inappropriate. "This Court has long recognized that freedom of personal choice in matters of marriage and family life is one of the liberties protected by the Due Process Clause of the Fourteenth Amendment." A host of cases, tracing their lineage to *Meyer* v. *Nebraska,* (1923), and *Pierce* v. *Society of Sisters* (1925), have consistently acknowledged a "private realm of family life which the state cannot enter." Of course, the family is not beyond regulation. . . . But when the government intrudes on choices concerning family living arrangements, this Court must examine carefully the importance of the governmental interests advanced and the extent to which they are served by the challenged regulation.

When thus examined, this ordinance cannot survive. The city seeks to justify it as a means of preventing overcrowding, minimizing traffic and parking congestion, and avoiding an undue financial burden on East Cleveland's school system. Although these are legitimate goals, the ordinance before us serves them marginally, at best. For example, the ordinance permits any family consisting only of husband, wife, and unmarried children to live together, even if the family contains a half dozen licensed drivers, each with his or her own car. At the same time it forbids an adult brother and sister to share a household, even if both faithfully use public transportation. The ordinance would permit a grandmother to live with a single dependent son and children, even if his school-age children number a dozen, yet it forces Mrs. Moore to find another dwelling for her grandson John, simply because of the presence of his uncle and cousin in the same household. We need not labor the point. [The ordinance] has but a tenuous relation to alleviation of the conditions mentioned by the city.

The city would distinguish the cases based on *Meyer* and *Pierce*. It points out that none of them "gives grandmothers any fundamental rights with respect to grandsons," and suggests that any constitutional right to live together as a family extends only to the nuclear family — essentially a couple and their dependent children.

To be sure, these cases did not expressly consider the family relationship presented here. They were immediately concerned with freedom of choice with respect to childbearing, or with the rights of parents to the custody and companionship of their own children, or with traditional parental authority in matters of child rearing and education. But unless we close our eyes to the basic reasons why certain rights associated with the family have been accorded shelter under the Fourteenth Amendment's Due Process Clause, we cannot avoid applying the force and rationale of these precedents to the family choice involved in this case.

. . . .

Substantive due process has at times been a treacherous field for this Court. There *are* risks when the judicial branch gives enhanced protection to certain substantive liberties without the guidance of the more specific provisions of the Bill of Rights. As the history of the *Lochner* era demonstrates, there is reason for concern lest the only limits to such judicial intervention become the predilections of those who happen at the time to be Members of this Court. That history counsels caution and restraint. But it does not counsel abandonment, nor does it require what the city urges here: cutting off any protection of family rights at the first convenient, if arbitrary boundary — the boundary of the nuclear family.

Appropriate limits on substantive due process come not from drawing arbitrary lines but rather from careful "respect for the teachings of history [and] solid recognition of the basic values that underlie our society." Our decisions establish that the Constitution protects the sanctity of the family precisely because the institution of the family is deeply rooted in this Nation's history and tradition. It is through the family that we inculcate and pass down many of our most cherished values, moral and cultural.

Ours is by no means a tradition limited to respect for the bonds uniting the members of the nuclear family. The tradition of uncles, aunts, cousins, and especially grandparents sharing a household along with parents and children has roots equally venerable and equally deserving of constitutional recognition. Over the years millions of our citizens have grown up in just such an environment, and most, surely, have profited from it. Even if conditions of modern society have brought about a decline in extended family households, they have not erased the accumulated wisdom of civilization, gained over the centuries and honored throughout our history, that supports a larger conception of the family. Out of choice, necessity, or a sense of family responsibility, it has been common for close relatives to draw together and participate in the duties and the satisfactions of a common home. Decisions concerning child rearing, which *Yoder, Meyer, Pierce* and other cases have recognized as entitled to constitutional protection, long have been shared with grandparents or other relatives who occupy the same household — indeed who may take on major responsibility for the rearing of the children. Especially in times of adversity, such as the death of a spouse or economic need, the broader family has tended to come together for mutual sustenance and to maintain or rebuild a secure home life. This is apparently what happened here.

Whether or not such a household is established because of personal tragedy, the choice of relatives in this degree of kinship to live together may not lightly be denied by the State. *Pierce* struck down an Oregon law requiring all children to attend the State's public schools, holding that the Constitution "excludes any general power of the State to standardize its children by forcing them to accept instruction from public teachers only." By the same token the Constitution prevents East Cleveland from standardizing its children—and its adults—by forcing all to live in certain narrowly defined family patterns.

Reversed.

MR. JUSTICE BRENNAN, with whom MR. JUSTICE MARSHALL joins, concurring.

I join the plurality's opinion. I agree that the Constitution is not powerless to prevent East Cleveland from prosecuting as a criminal and jailing a 63-year-old grandmother for refusing to expel from her home her now 10-year-old grandson who has lived with her and been brought up by her since his mother's death when he was less than a year old. . . . I write only to underscore the cultural myopia of the arbitrary boundary drawn by the East Cleveland ordinance in the light of the tradition of the American home that has been a feature of our society since our beginning as a Nation—the "tradition" in the plurality's words, "of uncles, aunts, cousins, and especially grandparents sharing a household along with parents and children. . . ." The line drawn by this ordinance displays a depressing insensitivity toward the economic and emotional needs of a very large part of our society.

In today's America, the "nuclear family" is the pattern so often found in much of white suburbia. The Constitution cannot be interpreted, however, to tolerate the imposition by government upon the rest of us of white suburbia's preference in patterns of family living. The "extended family" that provided generations of early Americans with social services and economic and emotional support in times of hardship, and was the beachhead for successive waves of immigrants who populated our cities, remains not merely still a pervasive living pattern, but under the goad of brutal economic necessity, a prominent pattern—virtually a means of survival—for large numbers of the poor and deprived minorities of our society. For them compelled pooling of scant resources requires compelled sharing of a household.

The *"extended"* form is especially familiar among black families. We may suppose that this reflects the truism that black citizens, like generations of white immigrants before them, have been victims of economic and other disadvantages that would worsen if they were compelled to abandon extended, for nuclear, living patterns. Even in husband and wife households, 13% of black families compared with 3% of white families include relatives under 18 years old, in addition to the couple's own children. In black households whose head is an elderly woman, as in this case, the contrast is even more striking: 48% of such black households, compared with 10% of counterpart white households, include related minor children not offspring of the head of the household.

I do not wish to be understood as implying that East Cleveland's enforcement of its ordinance is motivated by a racially discriminatory purpose: The record of this case would not support that implication. But the prominence of other than nuclear families among ethnic and racial minority groups, including our black citizens, surely demonstrates that the "extended family" pattern remains a vital tenet of our society. It suffices that in prohibiting this pattern of family living as a means of achieving its objectives, appellee city has chosen a device that deeply intrudes into family associational rights that historically have been central, and today remain central, to a large proportion of our population.

MR. JUSTICE STEVENS, concurring in the judgment.

In my judgment the critical question presented by this case is whether East Cleveland's housing ordinance is a permissible restriction on appellant's right to use her own property as she sees fit.

Long before the original States adopted the Constitution, the common law protected an owner's right to decide how best to use his own property. This basic right has always been limited by the law of nuisance which proscribes uses that impair the enjoyment of other property in the vicinity. But the question whether an individual owner's use could be further limited by a municipality's comprehensive zoning plan was not finally decided until this century.

The holding in *Euclid* v. *Ambler Realty Co.* that a city could use its police power, not just to abate a specific use of property which proved offensive, but also to create and implement a comprehensive plan for the use of land in the community, vastly diminished the rights of individual property owners. It did not, however, totally extinguish those rights. On the contrary, that case expressly recognized that the broad zoning power must be exercised within constitutional limits.

In his opinion for the Court, Mr. Justice Sutherland fused the two express constitutional restrictions on any state interference with private property—that property shall not be taken without due process nor for a public purpose without just compensation—into a single standard: "[B]efore [a zoning] ordinance can be declared unconstitutional, [it must be shown to be] clearly arbitrary and unreasonable, *having no substantial relation to the public health, safety, morals, or general welfare."* This principle was applied in *Nectow* v. *Cambridge* on the basis of a specific finding made by the state trial court that "the health, safety, convenience and general welfare of the inhabitants of the part of the city affected" would not be promoted by prohibiting the landowner's contemplated use, this Court held that the zoning ordinance as applied was unconstitutional.

With one minor exception, between the *Nectow* decision in 1928 and the 1974 decision in *Village of Belle Terre* v. *Boraas,* this Court did not review the substance of any zoning ordinances. The case-by-case development of the constitutional limits on the zoning power has not, therefore, taken place in this Court. On the other hand, during the past half century the broad formulations found in *Euclid* and *Nectow* have been applied in countless situations by the state courts. Those cases shed a revelatory light on the character of the single-family zoning ordinance challenged in this case.

Litigation involving single-family zoning ordinances is common. Although there appear to be almost endless differences in the language used in these ordinances, they contain three principal types of restrictions. First, they define the kind of structure that may be erected on vacant land. Second, they require that a single-family home be occupied only by a "single housekeeping unit." Third, they often require that the housekeeping unit be made up of persons related by blood, adoption, or marriage, with certain limited exceptions.

Although the legitimacy of the first two types of restrictions is well settled, attempts to limit occupancy to related persons have not been successful. The state courts have recognized a valid community interest in preserving the stable character of residential neighborhoods which justifies a prohibition against transient occupancy. Nevertheless, in well-reasoned opinions, the courts of Illinois, New York, New Jersey, California, Connecticut, Wisconsin, and other jurisdictions, have permitted unrelated persons to occupy single-family residences notwithstanding an ordinance prohibiting, either expressly or implicitly, such occupancy.

These cases delineate the extent to which the state courts have allowed zoning ordinances to interfere with the right of a property owner to determine the internal composition of his household. The intrusion on that basic property right has not previously gone beyond the point where the ordinance defines a family to include only persons related by blood, marriage, or adoption. Indeed, . . . state courts have not always allowed the intrusion to penetrate that far. The state decisions have upheld zoning ordinances which regulated the identity, as opposed to the number, of persons who may compose a household only to the extent that the ordinances require such households to remain nontransient, single-housekeeping units.

There appears to be no precedent for an ordinance which excludes any of an owner's relatives from the group of persons who may occupy his residence on a permanent basis. Nor does there appear to be any justification for such a restriction on an owner's use of his property. The city has failed totally to explain the need for a rule which would allow a homeowner to have two grandchildren live with her if they are brothers, but not if they are cousins. Since this ordinance has not been shown to have any "substantial relation to the public health, safety, morals, or general welfare" of the city of East Cleveland, and since it cuts so deeply into a fundamental right normally associated with the ownership of residential property — that of an owner to decide who may reside on his or her property — it must fall under the limited standard of review of zoning decisions which this Court preserved in *Euclid* and *Nectow.* Under that standard, East Cleveland's unprecedented ordinance constitutes a taking of property without due process and without just compensation.

For these reasons, I concur in the Court's judgment.

[MR. CHIEF JUSTICE BURGER dissented.]

MR. JUSTICE STEWART, with whom MR. JUSTICE REHNQUIST joins, dissenting.

In my view, the appellant's claim that the ordinance in question invades constitutionally protected rights of association and privacy is in large part answered by the *Belle Terre* decision. The argument was made there that a municipality could not zone its land exclusively for single-family occupancy because to do so would interfere with protected rights of privacy or association. We rejected this contention, and held that the ordinance at issue "involve[d] no 'fundamental' right guaranteed by the Constitution, such as . . . the right of association, *NAACP* v. *Alabama,* . . . or any rights of privacy, cf. *Griswold* v. *Connecticut* . . . ; *Eisenstadt* v. *Baird.*

The *Belle Terre* decision thus disposes of the appellant's contentions to the extent they focus not on her blood relationships with her sons and grandsons but on more general notions about the "privacy of the home." Her suggestion that every person has a constitutional right permanently to share his residence with whomever he pleases, and that such choices are "beyond the province of legitimate governmental intrusion," amounts to the same argument that was made and found unpersuasive in *Belle Terre.*

To be sure, the ordinance involved in *Belle Terre* did not prevent blood relatives from occupying the same dwelling, and the Court's decision in that case does not, therefore, foreclose the appellant's arguments based specifically on the ties of kinship present in this case. Nonetheless, I would hold, for the reasons that follow, that the existence of those ties does not elevate either the appellant's claim of associational freedom or her claim of privacy to a level invoking constitutional protection.

To suggest that the biological fact of common ancestry necessarily gives related persons constitutional rights of association superior to those of unrelated persons is to misunderstand the nature of the associational freedoms that the Constitution has been understood to protect. Freedom of association has been constitutionally recognized because it is often indispensable to effectuation of explicit First Amendment guarantees. But the scope of the associational right, until now, at least, has been limited to the constitutional need that created it; obviously not every "association" is for First Amendment purposes or serves to promote the ideological freedom that the First Amendment was designed to protect.

The "association" in this case is not for any purpose relating to the promotion of speech, assembly, the press, or religion. And wherever the outer boundaries of constitutional protection of freedom of association may eventually turn out to be, they surely do not extend to those who assert to interest other than the gratification, convenience, and economy of sharing the same residence.

The appellant is considerably closer to the constitutional mark in asserting that the East Cleveland ordinance intrudes upon "the private realm of family life which the state cannot enter." Several decisions of the Court have identified specific aspects of what might broadly be termed "private family life" that are constitutionally protected against state interference.

Although the appellant's desire to share a single-dwelling unit also involves "private family life" in a sense, that desire can hardly be equated with any of the interests protected in the cases just cited. The ordinance about which the appellant complains did not impede her choice to have or not to have children, and it did not dictate to her how her own children were to be nurtured and reared. The ordinance clearly does not prevent parents from living together or living with their unemancipated offspring.

But even though the Court's previous cases are not directly in point, the appellant contends that the importance of the "extended family" in American society requires us to hold that her decision to share her residence with her grandsons may not be interfered with by the State. This decision, like the decisions involved in bearing and raising children, is said to be an aspect of "family life" also entitled to substantive protection under the Constitution. Without pausing to inquire how far under this argument an "extended family" might extend, I cannot agree. When the Court has found that the Fourteenth Amendment placed a substantive limitation on a State's power to regulate, it has been in those rare cases in which the personal interests at issue have been deemed " 'implicit in the concept of ordered liberty.' " The interest that the appellant may have in permanently sharing a single kitchen and a suite of contiguous rooms with some of her relatives simply does not rise to that level. To equate this interest with the fundamental decisions to marry and to bear and raise children is to extend the limited substantive contours of the Due Process Clause beyond recognition.

The appellant also challenges the single-family occupancy ordinance on equal protection grounds. Her claim is that the city has drawn an arbitrary and irrational distinction between groups of people who may live together as a "family" and those who may not. While acknowledging the city's right to preclude more than one family from occupying a single-dwelling unit, the appellant argues that the purposes of the single-family occupancy law would be equally served by an ordinance that did not prevent her from sharing her residence with her two sons and their sons.

This argument misconceives the nature of the constitutional inquiry. In a case such as this one, where the challenged ordinance intrudes upon no substantively protected constitutional right, it is not the Court's business to decide whether its application in a particular case seems inequitable, or even absurd. The question is not whether some other ordinance, drafted more broadly, might have served the city's ends as well or almost as well. The task, rather, is to determine if East Cleveland's ordinance violates the Equal Protection Clause of the United States Constitution. And in performing that task, it must be borne in mind that "[w]e deal with economic and social legislation where legislatures have historically drawn lines which we respect against the charge of violation of the Equal Protection Clause if the law be ' "reasonable, not arbitrary" ' and bears 'a rational relationship to a [permissible] state objective.' [E]very line drawn by a legislature leaves some out that might well have been included. That exercise of discretion, however, is a legislative, not a judicial, function." . . .

Viewed in the light of these principles, I do not think East Cleveland's definition of "family" offends the Constitution. The city has undisputed power to ordain single-family residential occupancy. And that power plainly carries with it the power to say what a "family" is. Here the city has defined "family" to include not only father, mother, and dependent children, but several other close relatives as well. The definition is rationally designed to carry out the legitimate governmental purposes identified in the *Belle Terre* opinion: "The police power is not confined to elimination of filth, stench, and unhealthy places. It is ample to lay out zones where family values, youth values, and the blessings of quiet seclusion and clean air make the area a sanctuary for people."

Obviously, East Cleveland might have as easily and perhaps as effectively hit upon a different definition of "family." But a line could hardly be drawn that would not sooner or later become the target of a challenge like the appellant's. If "family" included all of the householder's grandchildren there would doubtless be the hard case of an orphaned niece or nephew. If, as the appellant suggests, a "family" must include all blood relatives, what of longtime friends? The point is that any definition would produce hardships in some cases without materially advancing the legislative purpose. That this ordinance also does so is no reason to hold it unconstitutional, unless we are to use our power to interpret the United States Constitution as a sort of generalized authority to correct seeming inequity wherever it surfaces. It is not for us to rewrite the ordinance, or substitute our judgment for the discretion of the prosecutor who elected to initiate this litigation.

MR. JUSTICE WHITE, dissenting.

Mr. Justice Powell would apparently construe the Due Process Clause to protect from all but quite important state regulatory interests any right or privilege that in his estimate is deeply rooted in the country's traditions. For me, this suggests a far too expansive charter for this Court. . . . What the deeply rooted traditions of the country are is arguable; which of them deserve the protection of the Due Process Clause is even more debatable. The suggested view would broaden enormously the horizons of the Clause; and, if the interest involved here is any measure of what the States would be forbidden to regulate, the courts would be substantively weighing and very likely invalidating a wide range of measures that Congress and state legislatures think appropriate to respond to a changing economic and social order.

Mrs. Moore's interest in having the offspring of more than one dependent son live with her qualified as a liberty protected by the Due Process Clause; but, because of the nature of that particular interest, the demands of the Clause are satisfied once the Court is assured that the challenged proscription is the produce of a duly enacted or promulgated statute, ordinance, or regulation and that it is not wholly lacking in purpose or utility. That under this ordi-

nance any number of unmarried children may reside with their mother and that this number might be as destructive of neighborhood values as one or more additional grandchildren is just another argument that children and grandchildren may not constitutionally be distinguished by a local zoning ordinance.

That argument remains unpersuasive to me. Here the head of the household may house himself or herself and spouse, their parents, and any number of their unmarried children. A fourth generation may be represented by only one set of grandchildren and then only if born to a dependent child. The ordinance challenged by appellant prevents her from living with both sets of grandchildren only in East Cleveland, an area with a radius of three miles and a population of 40,000. The ordinance thus denies appellant the opportunity to live with all her grandchildren in this particular suburb; she is free to do so in other parts of the Cleveland metropolitan area. If there is power to maintain the character of a single-family neighborhood, as there surely is, some limit must be placed on the reach of the "family." Had it been our task to legislate, we might have approached the problem in a different manner than did the drafters of this ordinance; but I have no trouble in concluding that the normal goals of zoning regulation are present here and that the ordinance serves these goals by limiting, in identifiable circumstances, the number of people who can occupy a single household. The ordinance does not violate the Due Process Clause.

Bowers v. Hardwick

478 U.S. 186 (1986)
(Vote: 5–4)

Hardwick was charged under Section 16-6-2 of a statute that makes it a criminal offense punishable by twenty years' imprisonment to engage in certain sexual acts. Police had found him in his home bedroom engaged in an act of sodomy with another male. Although charges were later dismissed, Hardwick challenged the statute's constitutionality, claiming that his intention to continue as a practicing homosexual placed him in continuing danger of arrest and prosecution. Since Bowers, a man has been convicted under the same act and sentenced to several years' imprisonment for having had oral sex with his wife.

JUSTICE WHITE delivered the opinion of the Court.

. . . .

This case does not require a judgment on whether laws against sodomy between consenting adults in general, or between homosexuals in particular, are wise or desirable. It raises no question about the right or propriety of state legislative decisions to repeal their laws that criminalize homosexual sodomy, or of state court decisions invalidating those laws on state constitutional grounds. The issue presented is whether the Federal Constitution confers a fundamental right upon homosexuals to engage in sodomy and hence invalidates the laws of the many States that still make such conduct illegal and have done so for a very long time. The case also calls for some judgment about the limits of the Court's role in carrying out its constitutional mandate.

We first register our disagreement with the Court of Appeals and with respondent that the Court's prior cases have construed the Constitution to confer a right of privacy that extends to homosexual sodomy and for all intents and purposes have decided this case. The reach of this line of cases was sketched in *Carey* v. *Population Services International.* . . . (1977). *Pierce* v. *Society of Sisters* . . . (1925), and *Meyer* v. *Nebraska* . . . (1923), were described as dealing with child rearing and education; *Prince* v. *Massachusetts* . . . (1944), with family relationships; *Skinner* v. *Oklahoma ex rel. Williamson* . . . (1942), with procreation; *Loving* v. *Virginia* . . . (1967), with marriage; *Griswold* v. *Connecticut* . . . and *Eisenstadt* v. *Baird* . . . with contraception; *Roe* v. *Wade* . . . (1973), with abortion. The latter three cases were interpreted as construing the Due Process Clause of the Fourteenth Amendment to confer a fundamental individual right to decide whether or not to beget or bear a child. . . .

Accepting the decisions in these cases and the above description of them, we think it evident that none of the rights announced in those cases bears any resemblance to the claimed constitutional right of homosexuals to engage in acts of sodomy that is asserted in this case. No connection between family, marriage, or procreation on the one hand and homosexual activity on the other has been demonstrated, either by the Court of Appeals or by respondent. Moreover, any claim that these cases nevertheless stand for the proposition that any kind of private sexual conduct between consenting adults is constitutionally insulted from state proscription is unsupportable. Indeed, the Court's opinion in *Carey* twice asserted that the privacy right, which the *Griswold* line of cases found to be one of the protections provided by the Due Process Clause, did not reach so far. . . .

Precedent aside, however, respondent would have us announce, as the Court of Appeals did, a fundamental right to engage in homosexual sodomy. This we are quite unwilling to do. It is true that despite the language of the Due Process Clauses of the Fifth and Fourteenth Amendments, which appears to focus only on the processes by which life, liberty, or property is taken, the cases are legion in which those Clauses have been interpreted to have substantive content, subsuming rights that to a great extend are immune from federal or state regulation or proscription. Among such cases are those recognizing rights that have little or no textual support in the constitutional language. *Meyers, Prince,* and *Pierce* fall in this category, as do the privacy cases from *Griswold* to *Cary.*

Striving to assure itself and the public that announcing rights not readily identifiable in the Constitution's text involves much more than the imposition of the Justices' own choice of values on the States and the Federal Government, the Court has sought to identify the nature of the rights qualifying for heightened judicial protection. In *Palko* v. *Connecticut* . . . (1937), it was said that this category includes those fundamental liberties that are "implicit in the concept of ordered liberty," such that "neither liberty nor justice would exist if [they] were sacrificed." A different description of fundamental liberties appeared in *Moore* v. *East Cleveland* . . . (1977) (opinion of POWELL, J.), where they are characterized as those liberties that are "deeply rooted in this Nation's history and tradition." . . .

It is obvious to us that neither of these formulations would extend a fundamental right to homosexuals to engage in acts of consensual sodomy. Proscriptions against that conduct have ancient roots. . . . Sodomy was a criminal offense at common law and was forbidden by the laws of the original thirteen States when they ratified the Bill of Rights. In 1868, when the Fourteenth Amendment was ratified, all but 5 of the 37 States in the Union had criminal sodomy laws. In fact, until 1961, all 50 States outlawed sodomy, and today, 24 States and the District of Columbia continue to provide criminal penalties for sodomy performed in private and between consenting adults. . . . Against this background, to claim that a right to engage in such conduct is "deeply rooted in this Nation's history and tradition" or "implicit in the concept of ordered liberty" is, at best, facetious.

Nor are we inclined to take a more expansive view of our authority to discover new fundamental rights imbedded in the Due Process Clause. The Court is most vulnerable and comes nearest to illegitimacy when it deals with judge-made constitutional law having little or no cognizable roots in the language or design of the Constitution. That this is so was painfully demonstrated by the face-off between the Executive and the Court in the 1930's, which resulted in the repudiation of much of the substantive gloss that the Court had placed on the Due Process Clauses of the Fifth and Fourteenth Amendments. There should be, therefore, great resistance to expand the substantive reach of those Clauses, particularly if it requires redefining the category of rights deemed to be fundamental. Otherwise, the Judiciary necessarily takes to itself further authority to govern the country without express constitutional authority. The claimed right pressed on us today falls short of overcoming this resistance.

Respondent, however, asserts that the result should be different where the homosexual conduct occurs in the privacy of the home. He relies on *Stanley* v. *Georgia* . . . (1969), where the Court held that the First Amendment prevents conviction for possessing and reading obscene material in the privacy of his home: "If the First Amendment means anything, it means that a State has no business telling a man, sitting alone in his house, what books he may read or what films he may watch." . . .

Stanley did protect conduct that would not have been protected outside the home, and it partially prevented the enforcement of state obscenity laws; but the decision was firmly grounded in the First Amendment. The right pressed upon us here has no similar support in the text of the Constitution, and it does not qualify for recognition under the prevailing principles for construing the Fourteenth Amendment. Its limits are also difficult to discern. Plainly enough, otherwise illegal conduct is not always immunized whenever it occurs in the home. Victimless crimes, such as the possession and use of illegal drugs, do not escape the law where they are committed at home. *Stanley* itself recognized that its holding offered no protection for the possession in the home of drugs, firearms, or stolen goods. . . . And if respondent's submission is limited to the voluntary sexual conduct between two consenting adults, it would be difficult, except by fiat, to limit the claimed right to homosexual conduct while leaving exposed to prosecution adultery, incest, and other sexual crimes even though they are committed in the home. We are unwilling to start down that road.

Even if the conduct at issue here is not a fundamental right, respondent asserts that there must be a rational basis for the law and that there is none in this case other than the presumed belief of a majority of the electorate in Georgia that homosexual sodomy is immoral and unacceptable. This is said to be an inadequate rationale to support the law. The law, however, is constantly based on notions of morality, and if all laws representing essentially moral choices are to be invalidated under the Due Process Clause, the courts will be very busy indeed. Even respondent makes no such claim, but insists that majority sentiments about the morality of homosexuality should be declared inadequate. We do not agree, and are unpersuaded that the sodomy laws of some 25 States should be invalidated on this basis.

Accordingly, the judgment of the Court of Appeals is

Reversed.

[CHIEF JUSTICE BURGER concurred. (Omitted)]

JUSTICE POWELL, concurring.

I join the opinion of the Court. I agree with the Court that there is no fundamental right — i.e., no substantive right under the Due Process Clause — such as that claimed by respondent, and found to exist by the Court of Appeals. This is not to suggest, however, that respondent may not be protected by the Eighth Amendment of the Constitution. The Georgia statute at issue in this case . . . authorizes a court to imprison a person for up to 20 years for a single private, consensual act of sodomy. In my view, a prison sentence for such conduct — certainly a sentence of long duration — would create a serious Eighth Amendment issue. . . .

In this case, however, respondent has not been tried, much less convicted and sentenced. Moreover, respondent has not raised the Eighth Amendment issue below. For these reasons this constitutional argument is not before us.

JUSTICE BLACKMUN, with whom JUSTICE BRENNAN, JUSTICE MARSHALL, and JUSTICE STEVENS join, dissenting.

This case is no more about "a fundamental right to engage in homosexual sodomy," as the Court purports to declare, . . . than *Stanley* v. *Georgia* . . . (1969), was about a fundamental right to watch obscene movies, or *Katz* v. *United States* . . . (1967), was about a fundamental right to place interstate bets from a telephone booth. Rather, this case is about "the most comprehensive of rights and the right most valued by civilized men," namely, "the right to be let alone." . . .

. . . .

In its haste to reverse the Court of Appeals and hold that the Constitution does not "confe[r] a fundamental right upon homosexuals to engage in sodomy," . . . the Court relegates the actual statute being challenged to a footnote and ignores the procedural posture of the case before it. A fair reading of the statute and of the complaint clearly reveals that the majority has distorted the question this case presents.

First, the Court's almost obsessive focus on homosexual activity is particularly hard to justify in light of the broad language Georgia has used. Unlike the Court, the Georgia Legislature has not proceeded on the assumption that homosexuals are so different from other citizens that their lives may be controlled in a way that would not be tolerated if it limited the choices of those other citizens. . . . Rather, Georgia has provided that "[a] person commits the offense of sodomy when he performs or submits to any sexual act involving the sex organs of one person and the mouth or anus of another" . . . The sex or status of the persons who engage in the act is irrelevant as a matter of state law. In fact, to the extent I can discern a legislative purpose for Georgia's 1968 enactment of Section 16-6-2, that purpose seems to have been to broaden the coverage of the law to reach heterosexual as well as homosexual activity. I therefore see no basis for the Court's decision to treat this case as an "as applied" challenge . . . or for Georgia's attempt, both in its brief and at oral argument, to defend . . . [the act] solely on the grounds that it prohibits homosexual activity. . . .

Second, I disagree with the Court's refusal to consider whether 16-6-2 runs afoul of the Eighth or Ninth Amendments or the Equal Protection Clause of the Fourteenth Amendment. . . . Thus, even if respondent did not advance claims based on the Eighth or Ninth Amendments, or on the Equal Protection Clause, his complaint should not be dismissed if any of those provisions could entitle him to relief. I need not reach either the Eighth Amendment or the Equal Protection Clause issues because I believe that Hardwick has stated a cognizable claim that Section 16-6-2 interferes with constitutionally protected interests in privacy and freedom of intimate association. . . .

. . . .

The Court concludes today that none of our prior cases dealing with various decisions that individuals are entitled to make free of governmental interference "bears any resemblance to the claimed constitutional right of homosexuals to engage in acts of sodomy that is asserted in this case." . . . While it is true that these cases may be characterized by their connection to protection of the family, . . . the Court's conclusion that they extend no further than this boundary ignores the warning in *Moore* v. *East Cleveland* . . . (1977) (plurality opinion), against "clos[ing] our eyes to the basic reasons why certain rights associated with the family have been accorded shelter under the Fourteenth Amendment's Due Process Clause." We protect those rights not because they contribute, in some direct and material way, to the general public welfare, but because they form so central a part of an individual's life. "[T]he concept of privacy embodies the 'moral fact that a person belongs to himself and not others nor to society as a whole.'" . . .

Only the most willful blindness could obscure the fact that sexual intimacy is "a sensitive, key relationship of human existence, central to family life, community welfare, and the development of human personality." . . . The fact that individuals define themselves in a significant way through their intimate sexual relationships with others suggests, in a Nation as diverse as ours, that there may be many "right" ways of conducting those relationships, and that much of the richness of a relationship will come from the freedom an individual has to choose the form and nature of these intensely personal bonds. . . .

. . . .

The behavior for which Hardwick faces prosecution occurred in his own home, a place to which the Fourth Amendment attaches special significance. The Court's treatment of this aspect of the case is symptomatic of its overall refusal to consider the broad principles that have informed our treatment of privacy in specific cases. Just as the right to privacy is more than the mere aggregation of a number of entitlements to engage in specific behavior, so too, protecting the physical integrity of the home is more than merely a means of protecting specific activities that often take place there. . . .

The Court's interpretation of the pivotal case of *Stanley* v. *Georgia* . . . (1969), is entirely unconvincing. *Stanley* held that Georgia's undoubted power to punish the public distribution of constitutionally unprotected, obscene material did not permit the State to punish the private possession of such material. According to the majority here, *Stanley* relied entirely on the First Amendment, and thus, it is claimed, sheds no light on cases not involving printed materials. . . . But that is not what *Stanley* said. Rather, the *Stanley* Court anchored its holding in the Fourth Amendment's special protection for the individual in his home. . . .

The central place that *Stanley* gives JUSTICE BRANDEIS' dissent in *Olmstead,* a case raising *no* First Amendment claim, shows that *Stanley* rested as much on the Court's understanding of the Fourth Amendment as it did on the First. Indeed, in *Paris Adult Theatre I* v. *Slaton* . . . (1973), the Court suggested that reliance on the Fourth Amendment not only supported the Court's outcome in *Stanley* but actually was *necessary* to it: "If obscene material unprotected by the First Amendment in itself carried with it a 'penumbra' of constitutionally protected privacy, this Court would not have found it necessary to decide *Stanley* on the narrow basis of the 'privacy of the home,' which was hardly more than a reaffirmation that 'a man's home is his castle.'"...

....

...[P]etitioner argues, and the Court agrees, that the fact that the acts described in Section 16-6-2 "for hundreds of years, if not thousands, have been uniformly condemned as immoral" is a sufficient reason to permit a State to ban them today....

I cannot agree that either the length of time a majority has held its convictions or the passions with which it defends them can withdraw legislation from this Court's scrutiny.... As JUSTICE JACKSON wrote so eloquently, "we apply the limitations of the Constitution with no fear that freedom to be intellectually and spiritually diverse or even contrary will disintegrate the social organization.... [F]reedom to differ is not limited to things that do not matter much. That would be a mere shadow of freedom. The test of its substance is the right to differ as to things that touch the heart of the existing order. "...It is precisely because the issue raised by this case touches the heart of what makes individuals what they are that we should be especially sensitive to the rights of those whose choices upset the majority.

The assertion that "traditional Judeo-Christian values proscribe" the conduct involved...cannot provide an adequate justification for Section 16-6-2. That certain, but by no means all, religious groups condemn the behavior at issue gives the State no license to impose their judgments on the entire citizenry. The legitimacy of secular legislation depends instead on whether the State can advance some justification for its law beyond its conformity to religious doctrine....

Nor can Section 16-6-2 be justified as a "morally neutral" exercise of Georgia's power to "protect the public environment."... Certainly, some private behavior can affect the fabric of society as a whole.... But the mere fact that intimate behavior may be punished when it takes place in public cannot dictate how States can regulate intimate behavior that occurs in intimate places....

....

It took but three years for the Court to see the error in its analysis in *Minersville School District* v. *Gobitis*... (1940), and to recognize that the threat to national cohesion posed by a refusal to salute the flag was vastly outweighed by the threat to those same values posed by compelling such a salute.... I can only hope that here, too, the Court soon will reconsider its analysis and conclude that depriving individuals of the right to choose for themselves how to conduct their intimate relationships poses a far greater threat to the values more deeply rooted in our Nation's history than tolerance of nonconformity could ever do. Because I think the court today betrays those values, I dissent.

[JUSTICE STEVENS, with whom JUSTICE BRENNAN and JUSTICE MARSHALL joined, dissented. (Omitted)]

APPENDIX I

The Constitution of the United States

Preamble

We the People of the United States, in Order to form a more perfect Union, establish Justice, insure domestic Tranquility, provide for the common Defence, promote the general Welfare, and secure the Blessings of Liberty to ourselves and our Posterity, do ordain and establish this Constitution for the United States of America.

Article I

Section 1. All legislative Powers herein granted shall be vested in a Congress of the United States, which shall consist of a Senate and House of Representatives.

Section 2. (1) The House of Representatives shall be composed of Members chosen every second Year by the People of the several States, and the Electors in each State shall have the Qualifications requisite for Electors of the most numerous Branch of the State Legislature.

(2) No Person shall be a Representative who shall not have attained to the Age of twenty-five Years, and been seven Years a Citizen of the United States, and who shall not, when elected, be an Inhabitant of that State in which he shall be chosen.

(3) Representatives and direct Taxes shall be apportioned among the several States which may be included within this Union, according to their respective Numbers, which shall be determined by adding to the whole Number of free Persons, including those bound to Service for a Term of Years, and excluding Indians not taxed, three-fifths of all other Persons. The actual Enumeration shall be made within three Years after the first Meeting of the Congress of the United States, and within every subsequent Term of ten Years, in such Manner as they shall by Law direct. The Number of Representatives shall not exceed one for every thirty Thousand, but each State shall have at Least one Representative; and until such enumeration shall be made, the State of New Hampshire shall be entitled to chuse three, Massachusetts eight, Rhode Island and Providence Plantations one, Connecticut five, New York six, New Jersey four, Pennsylvania eight, Delaware one, Maryland six, Virginia ten, North Carolina five, South Carolina five, and Georgia three.

(4) When vacancies happen in the Representation from any State, the Executive Authority thereof shall issues Writs of Election to fill such Vacancies.

(5) The House of Representatives shall chuse their Speaker and other Officers; and shall have the sole Power of Impeachment.

Section 3. (1) The Senate of the United States shall be composed of two Senators from each State, chosen by the Legislature thereof, for six Years; and each Senator shall have one Vote.

(2) Immediately after they shall be assembled in Consequence of the first Election, they shall be divided as equally as may be into three Classes. The Seats of the Senators of the first Class shall be vacated at the Expiration of the second Year, of the second Class at the Expiration of the fourth Year, and of the third Class at the Expiration of the sixth Year, so that one-third may be chosen every second Year; and if Vacancies happen by Resignation, or otherwise, during the Recess of the Legislature of any State, the Executive thereof may make temporary Appointments until the next Meeting of the Legislature, which shall then fill such Vacancies.

(3) No Person shall be a Senator who shall not have attained to the Age of thirty Years, and been nine Years a Citizen of the United States, and who shall not, when elected, be an Inhabitant of that State for which he shall be chosen.

(4) The Vice President of the United States shall be President of the Senate, but shall have no Vote, unless they be equally divided.

(5) The Senate shall chuse their other Officers, and also a President pro tempore, in the Absence of the Vice President, or when he shall exercise the Office of President of the United States.

(6) The Senate shall have the sole Power to try all Impeachments. When sitting for that Purpose, they shall be on Oath or Affirmation. When the President of the United States is tried, the Chief Justice shall preside: And no Person shall be convicted without the Concurrence of two-thirds of the Members present.

(7) Judgment in Cases of Impeachment shall not extend further than to removal from Office, and disqualification to hold and enjoy any Office of honor, Trust, or Profit under the United States: but the Party convicted shall nevertheless be liable and subject to Indictment, Trial, Judgment, and Punishment, according to Law.

Section 4. (1) The Times, Places and Manner of holding Elections for Senators and Representatives, shall be prescribed in each State by the Legislature thereof; but the Congress may at any time by Law make or alter such Regulations, except as to the Places of chusing Senators.

(2) The Congress shall assemble at least once in every Year, and such Meeting shall be on the first Monday in December, unless they shall by Law appoint a different Day.

Section 5. (1) Each House shall be the Judge of the Elections, Returns, and Qualifications of its own Members, and a Majority of each shall constitute a Quorum to do Business; but a smaller Number may adjourn from day to day, and may be authorized to compel the Attendance of absent Members, in such Manner, and under such Penalties as each House may provide.

(2) Each House may determine the Rules of its Proceedings, punish its Members for disorderly Behavior, and, with the Concurrence of two-thirds, expel a Member.

(3) Each House shall keep a Journal of its Proceedings, and from time to time publish the same, excepting such Parts as may in their Judgment require Secrecy; and the Yeas and Nays of the Members of either House on any question shall, at the Desire of one-fifth of those Present, be entered on the Journal.

(4) Neither House, during the Session of Congress, shall, without the Consent of the other, adjourn for more than three days, nor to any other Place than that in which the two Houses shall be sitting.

Section 6. (1) The Senators and Representatives shall receive a Compensation for their Services, to be ascertained by Law, and paid out of the Treasury of the United States. They shall in all Cases, except Treason, Felony and Breach of the Peace, be privileged from Arrest during their Attendance at the Session of their respective Houses, and in going to and returning from the same; and for any Speech or Debate in either House, they shall not be questioned in any other Place.

(2) No Senator or Representative shall, during the Time for which he was elected, be appointed to any civil Office under the Authority of the United States, which shall have been created, or the Emoluments whereof shall have been increased during such time; and no Person holding any Office under the United States, shall be a Member of either House during his Continuance in Office.

Section 7. (1) All Bills for raising Revenue shall originate in the House of Representatives; but the Senate may propose or concur with Amendments as on other Bills.

(2) Every Bill which shall have passed the House of Representatives and the Senate, shall, before it become a Law, be presented to the President of the United States; If he approve he shall sign it, but if not he shall return it, with his Objections to the House in which it shall have originated, who shall enter the Objections at large on their Journal, and proceed to reconsider it. If after such Reconsideration two-thirds of that House shall agree to pass the Bill, it shall be sent together with the Objections, to the other House, by which it shall likewise be reconsidered, and if approved by two-thirds of that House, it shall become a Law. But in all such Cases the Votes of both Houses shall be determined by Yeas and Nays, and the Names of the Persons voting for and against the Bill shall be entered on the Journal of each House respectively. If any Bill shall not be returned by the President within ten days (Sundays excepted) after it shall have been presented to him, the Same shall be a Law, in like Manner as if he had signed it, unless the Congress by their Adjournment prevent its Return, in which Case it shall not be a Law.

(3) Every Order, Resolution, or Vote, to Which the Concurrence of the Senate and House of Representatives may be necessary (except on a question of Adjournment) shall be presented to the President of the United States; and before the Same shall take Effect, shall be approved by him, or being disapproved by him, shall be repassed by two-thirds of the Senate and House of Representatives, according to the Rules and Limitations prescribed in the Case of a Bill.

Section 8. (1) The Congress shall have Power To lay and collect Taxes, Duties, Imposts and Excises, to pay the Debts and provide for the common Defence and general Welfare of the United States; but all Duties, Imposts and Excises shall be uniform throughout the United States;

(2) To borrow money on the credit of the United States;

(3) To regulate Commerce with foreign Nations, and among the several States, and with the Indian Tribes;

(4) To establish an uniform Rule of Naturalization, and uniform Laws on the subject of Bankruptcies throughout the United States;

(5) To coin Money, regulate the Value thereof, and of foreign Coin, and fix the Standard of Weights and Measures;

(6) To provide for the Punishment of counterfeiting the Securities and current Coin of the United States;

(7) To Establish Post Offices and Post Roads;

(8) To promote the Progress of Science and useful Arts, by securing for limited Times to Authors and Inventors the exclusive Right to their respective Writings and Discoveries;

(9) To constitute Tribunals inferior to the supreme Court;

(10) To define and punish Piracies and Felonies commited on the high Seas, and Offenses against the Law of Nations;

(11) To declare War, grant Letters of Marque and Reprisal, and make Rules concerning Captures on Land and Water;

(12) To raise and support Armies, but no Appropriation of Money to that Use shall be for a longer Term than two Years;

(13) To provide and maintain a Navy;

(14) To make Rules for the Government and Regulation of the land and naval Forces;

(15) To provide for calling forth the Militia to execute the Laws of the Union, suppress Insurrections and repel Invasions;

(16) To provide for organizing, arming, and disciplining the Militia, and for governing such Part of them as may be employed in the Service of the United States, reserving to the States respectively, the Appointment of the Officers, and the Authority of training the Militia according to the discipline prescribed by Congress;

(17) To exercise exclusive Legislation in all Cases whatsoever, over such District (not exceeding ten Miles square) as may, by Cession of particular States, and the Acceptance of Congress, become the Seat of the Government of the United States, and to exercise like Authority over all Places purchased by the Consent of the Legislature of the State in which the Same shall be, for the Erection of Forts, Magazines, Arsenals, dock-Yards, and other needful Buildings; — And

(18) To make all Laws which shall be necessary and proper for carrying into Execution the foregoing Powers, and all other Powers vested by this Constitution in the Government of the United States, or in any Department or Officer thereof.

Section 9. (1) The Migration or Importation of Such Persons as any of the States now existing shall think proper to admit, shall not be prohibited by the Congress prior to the Year one thousand eight hundred and eight, but a Tax or duty may be imposed on such Importation, not exceeding ten dollars for each Person.

(2) The privilege of the Writ of Habeas Corpus shall not be suspended, unless when in Cases of Rebellion or Invasion the public Safety may require it.

(3) No Bill of Attainder or ex post facto Law shall be passed.

(4) No Capitation, or other direct, Tax shall be laid, unless in Proportion to the Census or Enumeration herein before directed to be taken.

(5) No Tax or Duty shall be laid on Articles exported from any State.

(6) No Preference shall be given by any Regulation of Commerce or Revenue to the Ports of one State over those of another: nor shall Vessels bound to, or from, one State be obliged to enter, clear, or pay Duties to another.

(7) No money shall be drawn from the Treasury, but in Consequence of Appropriations made by Law; and a regular Statement and Account of the Receipts and Expenditures of all public Money shall be published from time to time.

(8) No Title of Nobility shall be granted by the United States: And no Person holding any Office of Profit or Trust under them, shall, without the Consent of the Congress, accept of any present, Emolument, Office, or Title, of any kind whatever, from any King, Prince, or foreign State.

Section 10. (1) No State shall enter into any Treaty, Alliance, or Confederation; grant Letters of Marque and Reprisal; coin Money; emit Bills of Credit; make any Thing but gold and silver Coin a Tender in Payment of Debts; pass any Bill of Attainder, ex post facto Law, or Law impairing the Obligation of Contracts, or grant any Title of Nobility.

(2) No State shall, without the consent of the Congress, lay any Imposts or Duties on Imports or Exports, except what may be absolutely necessary for executing its inspection Laws: and the net Produce of all Duties and Imposts, laid by any State on Imports or Exports, shall be for the Use of the Treasury of the United States; and all such Laws shall be subject to the Revision and Controul of the Congress.

(3) No State shall, without the Consent of Congress, lay any Duty of Tonnage, keep Troops, or Ships of War in time of Peace, enter into any Agreement or Compact with another State, or with a foreign Power, or engage in War, unless ac-

tually invaded, or in such imminent Danger as will not admit of delay.

Article II

Section 1. (1) The executive Power shall be vested in a President of the United States of America. He shall hold his Office during the Term of four Years, and, together with the Vice President, chosen for the same Term, be elected, as follows:

(2) Each State shall appoint, in such Manner as the Legislature thereof may direct, a Number of Electors, equal to the whole Number of Senators and Representatives to which the State may be entitled in the Congress; but no Senator or Representative, or Person holding an Office of Trust or Profit under the United States, shall be appointed an Elector.

(3) The Electors shall meet in their respective States, and vote by Ballot for two Persons, of whom one at least shall not be an Inhabitant of the same State with themselves. And they shall make a List of all the Persons voted for, and of the Number of Voters for each; which List they shall sign and certify, and transmit sealed to the Seat of the Government of the United States, directed to the President of the Senate. The President of the Senate shall, in the Presence of the Senate and House of Representatives, open all the Certificates, and the Votes shall then be counted. The Person having the greatest Number of Votes shall be the President, if such Number be a Majority of the whole Number of Electors appointed; and if there be more than one who have such a Majority, and have an equal Number of Votes, then the House of Representatives shall immediately chuse by Ballot one of them for President; and if no Person have a Majority, then from the five highest on the List the said House shall in like Manner chuse the President. But in chusing the President, the Votes shall be taken by States, the Representation from each State having one Vote; A quorum for this Purpose shall consist of a Member or Members from two-thirds of the States, and a Majority of all

the States shall be necessary to a Choice. In every Case, after the Choice of the President, the Person having the greater Number of Votes of the Electors shall be the Vice President. But if there should remain two or more who have equal Votes, the Senate shall chuse from them by Ballot the Vice President.

(4) The Congress may determine the Time of chusing the Electors, and the Day on which they shall give their Votes; which Day shall be the same throughout the United States.

(5) No person except a natural born Citizen, or a Citizen of the United States, at the time of the Adoption of this Constitution, shall be eligible to the Office of President; neither shall any Person be eligible to that Office who shall not have attained to the Age of thirty-five Years, and been fourteen Years a Resident within the United States.

(6) In case of the removal of the President from Office, or of his Death, Resignation or Inability to discharge the Powers and Duties of the said Office, the Same shall devolve on the Vice President, and the Congress may by Law provide for the Case of Removal, Death, Resignation or Inability, both of the President and Vice President, declaring what Officer shall then act as President, and such Officer shall act accordingly, until the Disability be removed, or a President shall be elected.

(7) The President shall, at stated Times, receive for his Services, a Compensation, which shall neither be increased nor diminished during the Period for which he shall have been elected, and he shall not receive within that Period any other Emolument from the United States, or any of them.

(8) Before he enter on the Execution of his Office, he shall take the following Oath of Affirmation: "I do solemnly swear (or affirm) that I will faithfully execute the Office of President of the United States, and will to the best of my Ability, preserve, protect and defend the Constitution of the United States."

Section 2. (1) The President shall be Commander in Chief of the Army and Navy of the United States, and of the militia in the several States, and of the militia of the several States, when called into the actual Service of the United States; he may require the Opinion, in writing, of the principal Officer in each of the Executive Departments, upon any Subject relating to the Duties of their respective Offices, and he shall have Power to grant Reprieves and Pardons for Offenses against the United States, except in Cases of Impeachment.

(2) He shall have Power, by and with the Advice and Consent of the Senate to make Treaties, provided two-thirds of the Senators present concur; and he shall nominate, and by and with the Advice and Consent of the Senate, shall appoint Ambassadors, other public Ministers and Consuls, Judges of the Supreme Court, and all other Officers of the United States, whose Appointments are not herein otherwise provided for, and which shall be established by Law; but the Congress may by Law vest the Appointment of such inferior Officers, as they think proper, in the President alone, in the Courts of Law, or in the Heads of Departments.

(3) The President shall have Power to fill up all Vacancies that may happen during the Recess of the Senate, by granting Commissions which shall expire at the End of their next Session.

Section 3. He shall from time to time give to the Congress Information of the State of the Union, and recommend to their Consideration such Measures as he shall judge necessary and expedient; he may, on extraordinary Occasions, convene both Houses, or either of them, and in Case of Disagreement between them, with Respect to the Time of Adjournment, he may adjourn them to such Time as he shall think proper; he shall receive Ambassadors and other public Ministers; he shall take Care that the Laws be faithfully executed; and shall Commission all the Officers of the United States.

Section 4. The President, Vice President and all civil Officers of the United States, shall be removed from Office on Impeachment for, and Conviction of, Treason, Bribery, or other high Crimes and Misdemeanors.

Article III

Section 1. The judicial Power of the United States, shall be vested in one supreme Court, and in such inferior Courts as the Congress may from time to time ordain and establish. The Judges, both of the supreme and inferior Courts, shall hold their Offices during good Behaviour, and shall, at stated Times, receive for their Services a Compensation, which shall not be diminished during their Continuance in Office.

Section 2. (1) The judicial Power shall extend to all Cases, in Law and Equity, arising under this Constitution, the Laws of the United States, and Treaties made, or which shall be made, under their Authority;—to all Cases affecting Ambassadors, other public Ministers and Consuls;—to all Cases of admiralty and maritime Jurisdiction;—to Controversies to which the United States shall be a Party;—to Controversies between two or more States—between a State and Citizens of another State;—between Citizens of different States;—between Citizens of the same State claiming Lands under the Grants of different States, and between a State, or the Citizens thereof, and foreign States, Citizens or Subjects.

(2) In all Cases affecting Ambassadors, other public Ministers and Consuls, and those in which a State shall be a Party, the supreme Court shall have original Jurisdiction. In all the other Cases before mentioned, the supreme Court shall have appellate Jurisdiction, both as to Law and Fact, with such Exceptions, and under such Regulations as the Congress shall make.

(3) The trial of all Crimes, except in Cases of Impeachment, shall be by Jury; and such Trial shall be held in the State where the said Crimes shall have been committed; but when not committed within any State, the Trial shall be at such Place or Places as the Congress may by Law have directed.

Section 3. (1) Treason against the United States, shall consist only in levying War against them, or, in adhering to their Enemies, giving them Aid and Comfort. No Person shall be convicted of Treason unless on the Testimony of two Witnesses to the same overt Act, or on Confession in open Court.

(2) The Congress shall have Power to declare the Punishment of Treason, but no Attainder of Treason shall work Corruption of Blood, or Forfeiture except during the Life of the Person Attainted.

Article IV

Section 1. Full Faith and Credit shall be given in each State to the public Acts, Records, and judicial Proceedings of every other State. And the Congress may by general Laws prescribe the Manner in which such Acts, Records and Proceedings shall be proved, and the Effect thereof.

Section 2. (1) The Citizens of each State shall be entitled to all Privileges and Immunities of Citizens in the several States.

(2) A Person charged in any State with Treason, Felony, or other Crime, who shall flee from Justice, and be found in another State, shall on demand of the executive Authority of the State from which he fled, be delivered up, to be removed to the State having Jurisdiction of the Crime.

(3) No Person held to Service or Labour in one State, under the Laws thereof, escaping into another, shall, in Consequence of any Law or Regulation therein, be discharged from such Service or Labour, but shall be delivered up on a Claim of the Party to whom such Service or Labour may be due.

Section 3. (1) New States may be admitted by the Congress into this Union; but no new State shall be formed or erected within the Jurisdiction of any other State; nor any State be formed by the Junction of two or more States, or Parts of States, without the Consent of the Legislatures of the States concerned as well as of the Congress.

(2) The Congress shall have Power to dispose of and make all needful Rules and Regulations respecting the Territory or other Property belonging to the United States; and nothing in this Constitution shall be so construed as to Prejudice any Claims of the United States, or of any particular State.

guarantee clause

Section 4. The United States shall guarantee to every State in this Union a Republican Form of Government, and shall protect each of them against Invasion; and on Application of the Legislature, or of the Executive (when the Legislature cannot be convened) against domestic Violence.

Article V*

The Congress, whenever two-thirds of both Houses shall deem it necessary, shall pro-

*One of the methods provided for in Article V for amending the Constitution has never been implemented—namely, a "Convention for proposing Amendments," which Congress "on the Application of two-thirds of the several States shall call." Between 1975 and 1985, thirty-two states asked for such a convention to deal with the issue of controlling federal expenditures (and the national debt), which is only two states shy of the number that would apparently mandate Congressional action. Since then, the passage of the Gramm-Rudman-Hollings Act, as well as fears that a convention once called could not be limited in subject matter, seems to have deterred the other states.

The lack of precedent has raised other issues of possibly considerable import: (1) Since the calls for convention are not identical, does that give Congress discretion either not to act or to limit or frame the subject matter? (2) How much time should be allowed to elapse between the call by the first state and that by the last? Senator Orrin Hatch (R-Utah) has suggested seven years as an appropriate period during which Congress should be *compelled* to respond, and twelve years as one during which it *might* respond. Such limits have been attached to amendments proposed by Congress. But is it constitutional for Congress, on its own, to delimit state initiatives? The opposite argument—that such calls, once made, would cumulate forever—seems even weaker. (3) It appears settled that once a state ratifies an amendment it may not withdraw its ratification. Since a call for a convention is a less formal step, not an accomplished deed, may *it* be withdrawn by a subsequent legislature? (4) While there is precedent for *state* conventions being limited in subject matter, the only *federal* precedents are the Annapolis and Philadelphia conventions, which took up the issue of commerce and instead replaced the entire Articles of Confederation. Also, Article V speaks of a convention's considering *amendments*. Does this suggest that the convention cannot be limited to framing *an amendment*?

Given the growing number of years since the initial call for a convention, it appears that this call, like that for an equal rights amendment, is dormant.

pose Amendments to this Constitution, or, on the Application of the Legislatures of two-thirds of the several States, shall call a Convention for proposing Amendments, which, in either Case, shall be valid to all Intents and Purposes, as part of this Constitution, when ratified by the Legislatures of three-fourths of the several States, or by Conventions in three-fourths thereof, as the one or the other Mode of Ratification may be proposed by the Congress; Provided that no Amendment which may be made prior to the Year One thousand eight hundred and eight shall in any Manner affect the first and fourth Clauses in the Ninth Section of the first Article; and that no State, without its Consent, shall be deprived of its equal Suffrage in the Senate.

Article VI

(1) All Debts contracted and Engagements entered into, before the Adoption of this Constitution shall be as valid against the United States under this Constitution, as under the Confederation.

(2) This Constitution, and the Laws of the United States which shall be made in Pursuance thereof; and all Treaties made, or which shall be made, under the Authority of the United States, shall be the supreme Law of the Land; and the Judges in every State shall be bound thereby, any Thing in the Constitution or Laws of any State to the Contrary notwithstanding.

(3) The Senators and Representatives before mentioned, and the Members of the several State Legislatures, and all executive and judicial Officers, both of the United States and of the several States, shall be bound by Oath or Affirmation, to support this Constitution; but no religious Test shall ever be required as a Qualification to any Office or public Trust under the United States.

Article VII

The Ratification of the Conventions of nine States shall be sufficient for the Establishment of this Constitution between the States so ratifying the Same.

Articles in addition to, and amendment of, the Constitution of the United States of America, proposed by Congress, and ratified by the legislatures of the several states pursuant to the Fifth Article of the original Constitution.

Amendment I (1791)

Congress shall make no law respecting an establishment of religion, or prohibiting the free exercise thereof; or abridging the freedom of speech, or of the press; or the right of the people peaceably to assemble, and to petition the government for a redress of grievances.

Amendment II (1791)

A well-regulated Militia, being necessary to the security of a free State, the right of the people to keep and bear Arms, shall not be infringed.

Amendment III (1791)

No Soldier shall, in time of peace be quartered in any house, without the consent of the Owner, nor in time of war, but in a manner to be prescribed by law.

Amendment IV (1791)

The right of the people to be secure in their persons, houses, papers, and effects, against unreasonable searches and seizures, shall not be violated, and no Warrants shall issue, but upon probable cause, supported by Oath or affirmation, and particularly describing the place to be searched, and the persons or things to be seized.

Amendment V (1791)

No person shall be held to answer for a capital, or otherwise infamous, crime, unless on a presentment or indictment of a Grand Jury, except in cases arising in the land or naval forces, or in the Militia, when in actual service in time of War or public danger; nor shall any person be subject for the same offence to be twice put in jeopardy of life or limb; nor shall be compelled in any criminal case to be a witness against himself, nor be deprived of life, liberty, or property, without due process of law; nor shall private property be taken for public use, without just compensation.

Amendment VI (1791)

In all criminal prosecutions, the accused shall enjoy the right to a speedy and public trial, by an impartial jury of the State and district wherein the crime shall have been committed, which district shall have been previously ascertained by law, and to be informed of the nature and cause of the accusation; to be confronted with the witnesses against him; to have compulsory process for obtaining witnesses in his favor, and to have the Assistance of Counsel for his defence.

Amendment VII (1791)

In Suits at common law, where the value in controversy shall exceed twenty dollars, the right of trial by jury shall be preserved, and no fact tried by jury, shall be otherwise re-examined in any Court of the United States, than according to the rules of the common law.

Amendment VIII (1791)

Excessive bail shall not be required, nor excessive fines imposed, nor cruel and unusual punishments inflicted.

Amendment IX (1791)

The enumeration in the Constitution, of certain rights, shall not be construed to deny or disparage others retained by the people.

Amendment X (1791)

The powers not delegated to the United States by the Constitution, nor prohibited by it to the States, are reserved to the States respectively, or to the people.

Amendment XI (1798)

The Judicial power of the United States shall not be construed to extend to any suit in law or equity, commenced or prosecuted against one of the United States by Citizens of another State, or by Citizens or Subjects of any Foreign State.

Amendment XII (1804)

The Electors shall meet in their respective states and vote by ballot for President and Vice President, one of whom, at least, shall not be an inhabitant of the same state with themselves; they shall name in their ballots the person voted for as President, and in distinct ballots the person voted for as Vice President, and they shall make distinct lists of all persons voted for as President, and of all persons voted for as Vice President, and of the number of votes for each, which lists they shall sign and certify, and transmit sealed to the seat of the government of the United States, directed to the President of the Senate; — The President of the Senate shall, in the presence of the Senate and House of Representatives, open all the certificates and the votes shall then be counted; — The person having the greatest number of votes for President, shall be the President, if such number be a majority of the whole number of Electors appointed; and if no person have such majority, then from the persons having the highest number not exceeding three on the list of those voted for as President, the House of Representatives shall choose immediately, by ballot, the President. But in choosing the Presdient, the votes shall be taken by states, the representation from each state having one vote; a quorum for this purpose shall consist of a member or members from two-thirds of the states, and a majority of all the states shall be necessary to a choice. And if the House of Representatives shall not choose a President whenever the right of choice shall devolve upon them before the fourth day of March next following, then the Vice President shall act as President, as in the case of the death or other constitutional disability of the President. — The person having the greatest number of votes as Vice President, shall be the Vice President, if such number be a majority of the whole number of Electors appointed, and if no person have a majority, then from the two highest numbers on the list, the Senate shall choose the Vice President; a quorum for the purpose shall consist of two-thirds of the whole number of Senators, and a majority of the whole number shall be necessary to a choice. But no person constitutionally ineligible to the office of President shall be eligible to that of Vice President of the United States.

Amendment XIII (1865)

Section 1. Neither slavery nor involuntary servitude, except as a punishment for crime whereof the party shall have been duly convicted, shall exist within the United States, or any place subject to their jurisdiction.

Section 2. Congress shall have power to enforce this article by appropriate legislation.

Amendment XIV (1868)

Section 1. All persons born or naturalized in the United States, and subject to the jurisdiction thereof, are citizens of the United States and of the State wherein they reside. No State shall make or enforce any law which shall abridge the privileges or immunities of citizens of the United States; nor shall any State deprive any person of life, liberty, or property, without due process of law; nor deny to any person within its jurisdiction the equal protection of the laws.

Section 2. Representatives shall be apportioned among the several States according to their respective numbers, counting the whole number of persons in each State, excluding Indians not taxed. But when the right to vote in any election for the choice of electors for President and Vice President of the United States, Representatives in Congress, the Executive and Judicial officers of a State, or the members of the Legislature thereof, is denied to any of the male inhabitants of such State, being twenty-one years of age, and citizens of the United States, or in any way abridged, except for participation in rebellion, or other crime, the basis of representation therein shall be reduced in the proportion which the number of such male citizens shall bear to the whole number of male citizens twenty-one years of age in such State.

Section 3. No person shall be a Senator or Representative in Congress, or elector of President and Vice President, or hold any office, civil or military, under the United States, or under any State, who having previously taken an oath, as a member of Congress, or as an officer of the United States, or as a member of the State legislature, or as an executive or judicial officer of any State, to support the Constitution of the United States, shall have engaged in insurrection or rebellion against the same, or given aid or comfort to the enemies thereof. But Congress may by a vote of two-thirds of each House, remove such disability.

Section 4. The validity of the public debt of the United States, authorized by law, including debts incurred for payment of pensions and bounties for services in suppressing insurrection or rebellion, shall not be questioned. But neither the United States nor any State shall assume or pay any debt or obligation incurred in aid of insurrection or rebellion against the United States, or any claim for the loss or emancipation of any slave; but all such debts, obligations and claims shall be held illegal and void.

Section 5. The Congress shall have power to enforce, by appropriate legislation, the provisions of this article.

Amendment XV (1870)

Section 1. The right of citizens of the United States to vote shall not be denied or abridged by the United States or by any State on account of race, color, or previous condition of servitude.

Section 2. The Congress shall have power to enforce this article by appropriate legislation.

Amendment XVI (1913)

The Congress shall have power to lay and collect taxes on incomes, from whatever source derived, without apportionment among the several States, and without regard to any census or enumeration.

Amendment XVII (1913)

(1) The Senate of the United States shall be composed of two Senators from each State, elected by the people thereof, for six years; and each Senator shall have one vote. The electors in each State shall have the qualifications requisite for electors of the most numerous branch of the State legislatures.

(2) When vacancies happen in the representation of any State in the Senate, the executive authority of such State shall issue writs of election to fill such vacancies: *Provided,* That the legislature of any State may empower the executive thereof to make temporary appointments until the people fill the vacancies by election as the legislature may direct.

(3) This amendment shall not be so construed as to affect the election or term of any Senator chosen before it becomes valid as part of the Constitution.

Amendment XVIII (1919)

Section 1. After one year from the ratification of this article the manufacture, sale, or transportation of intoxicating liquors within, the importation thereof into, or the exportation thereof from the United States and all territory subject to the jurisdiction thereof for beverage purposes is hereby prohibited.

Section 2. The Congress and the several States shall have concurrent power to enforce this article by appropriate legislation.

Section 3. This article shall be inoperative unless it shall have been ratified as an amendment to the Constitution by the legislatures of the several States, as provided in the Constitution, within seven years from the date of the submission hereof to the States by the Congress.

Amendment XIX (1920)

(1) The right of citizens of the United States to vote shall not be denied or abridged by the United States or by any State on account of sex.

(2) Congress shall have power to enforce this article by appropriate legislation.

Amendment XX (1933)

Section 1. The terms of the President and Vice President shall end at noon on the 20th day of January, and the terms of Senators and Representatives at noon on the 3d day of January, of the years in which said terms would have ended if this article had not been ratified; and the terms of their successors shall then begin.

Section 2. The Congress shall assemble at least once in every year, and such meeting shall begin at noon on the 3d day of January, unless they shall by law appoint a different day.

Section 3. If, at the time fixed for the beginning of the term of the President, the President elect shall have died, the Vice President elect shall become President. If the President shall not have been chosen before the time fixed for the beginning of his term, or if the President elect shall have failed to qualify, then the Vice President elect shall act as President until a President shall have qualified; and the Congress may by law provide for the case wherein neither a President elect nor a Vice President elect shall have qualified, declaring who shall then act as President, or the manner in which one who is to act shall be selected, and such person shall act accordingly until a President or Vice President shall have qualified.

Section 4. The Congress may by law provide for the case of the death of any of the persons from whom the House of Representatives may choose a President whenever the right of choice shall have devolved upon them, and for the case of the death of any of the persons from whom the Senate may choose a Vice President whenever the right of choice shall have devolved upon them.

Section 5. Sections 1 and 2 shall take effect on the 15th day of October following the ratification of this article.

Section 6. This article shall be inoperative unless it shall have been ratified as an amendment to the Constitution by the legislatures of three-fourths of the several States within seven years from the date of its submission.

Amendment XXI (1933)

Section 1. The eighteenth article of amendment to the Constitution of the United States is herby repealed.

Section 2. The transportation or importation into any State, Territory, or possession of the United States for delivery or use therein of intoxicating liquors, in violation of the laws thereof, is hereby prohibited.

Section 3. This article shall be inoperative unless it shall have been ratified as an amendment to the Constitution by conventions in the several States, as provided in the Constitution, within seven years from the date of the submission hereof to the States by the Congress.

Amendment XXII (1951)

Section 1. No person shall be elected to the office of the President more than twice, and no person who has held the office of President, or acted as President, for more than two years of a term to which some other person was elected President shall be elected to the office of President more than once. But this Article shall not apply to any person holding the office of President when this Article was proposed by the Congress, and shall not prevent any person who may be holding the office of President, or acting as President, during the term within which this Article becomes operative from holding the office of President or acting as President during the remainder of such term.

Section 2. This article shall be inoperative unless it shall have been ratified as an amendment to the Constitution by the legislatures of three-fourths of the several States within seven years from the date of its submission to the States by the Congress.

Amendment XXIII (1961)

Section 1. The District constituting the seat of Government of the United States shall appoint in such manner as the Congress may direct:

A number of electors of President and Vice President equal to the whole number of Senators and Representatives in Congress to which the District would be entitled if it were a State, but in no event more than the least populous state; they shall be in addition to those appointed by the states, but they shall be considered, for the purposes of the election of President and Vice President, to be electors appointed by a state; and they shall meet in the District and perform such duties as provided by the twelfth article of amendment.

Section 2. The Congress shall have power to enforce this article by appropriate legislation.

Amendment XXIV (1964)

Section 1. The right of citizens of the United States to vote in any primary or other election for President or Vice President, for electors for President or Vice President, or for Senator or Representative in Congress, shall not be denied or abridged by the United States, or any State by reason of failure to pay any poll tax or other tax.

Section 2. The Congress shall have power to enforce this article by appropriate legislation.

Amendment XXV (1967)

Section 1. In case of the removal of the President from office or of his death or resignation, the Vice President shall become President.

Section 2. Whenever there is a vacancy in the office of the Vice President, the President shall nominate a Vice President who shall take office upon confirmation by a majority vote of both Houses of Congress.

Section 3. Whenever the President transmits to the President pro tempore of the Senate and the Speaker of the House of Representatives his written declaration that he is unable to discharge the powers and duties of his office, and until he transmits to them a written declaration to the contrary, such powers and duties shall be discharged by the Vice President as Acting President.

Section 4. Whenever the Vice President and a majority of either the principal officers of the executive departments or of such other body as Congress may by law provide, transmit to the President pro tempore of the Senate and the Speaker of the House of Representatives their written declaration that the President is unable to discharge the powers and duties of his office, the Vice President shall immediately assume the powers and duties of the office as Acting President.

Thereafter, when the President transmits to the President pro tempore of the Senate and the Speaker of the House of Representatives his written declaration that no inability exists, he shall resume the powers and duties of his office unless the Vice President and a majority of either the principal officers of the executive department or of such other body as Congress may by law provide, transmit within four days to the President pro tempore of the Senate and the Speaker of the House of Representatives their written declaration and the President is unable to discharge the powers and duties of his office. Thereupon Congress shall decide the issue, assembling within forty-eight hours for that purpose if not in session. If the Congress, within twenty-one days after receipt of the latter written declaration, or, if Congress is not in session, within twenty-one days after Congress is required to assemble, determines by two-thirds vote of both Houses that the President is unable to discharge the powers and duties of his office, the Vice President shall continue to discharge the same as Acting President; otherwise, the President shall resume the powers and duties of his office.

Amendment XXVI (1971)

Section 1. The right of citizens of the United States, who are eighteen years of age or older, to vote shall not be denied or abridged by the United States or by any State on account of age.

Section 2. The Congress shall have power to enforce this article by appropriate legislation.

Proposed Equal Rights Amendment*

Section 1. Equality of rights under the law shall not be denied or abridged by the United States or by any State on account of sex.

Section 2. The Congress shall have the power to enforce, by appropriate legislation, the provisions of this article.

Section 3. This amendment shall take effect two years after the date of ratification.

*This amendment was proposed by Congress and submitted to the states in March 1972. In July 1978 Congress extended the deadline for ratification to June 1982, but the amendment failed to gain the requisite support of two-thirds of all state legislatures before the new deadline. The amendment has since been resubmitted to Congress, but is currently dormant.

APPENDIX II

Justices of the United States Supreme Court

The following table shows the composition of the Supreme Court since its inception. The main divisions correspond to the terms in office of the chief justices. Each new line in the table reflects a change in one or more justices; there were no changes in years not listed. For example, in 1803, the year of *Marbury* v. *Madison,* Chief Justice Marshall's colleagues were Paterson, Cushing, Washington, Samuel Chase, and Moore, all of whom were serving on the Court when Marshall was appointed head in 1801; they all served together under Marshall until 1804, when Moore was replaced by Johnson.

Some vacancies on the Court (notably during Reconstruction) have gone unfilled for some time. The lengthier vacancies are marked *vacant* in the table. Blank spaces on the right-hand side do *not* indicate vacancies; they indicate all years when the Court was comprised of fewer than ten members. (Including the chief justice, the Court has consisted of as few as five members — 1789 — and as many as ten — 1863–1870.)

In this century the office of chief justice has been filled three times by the elevation of a justice already serving (White in 1910, Stone in 1941, and Rehnquist in 1981). In the last entry before each such elevation, the name is marked with an asterisk.

JAY, 1789–1795

Year					
1789	Rutledge	Cushing	Wilson	Blair	Iredell
1790	Rutledge	Cushing	Wilson	Blair	Iredell
1791	Johnson, T.	Cushing	Wilson	Blair	Iredell
1793	Paterson	Cushing	Wilson	Blair	Iredell

RUTLEDGE, 1795 (unconfirmed recess appointment)

Year					
1795	Paterson	Cushing	Wilson	Blair	Iredell

ELLSWORTH, 1796–1800

Year					
1796	Paterson	Cushing	Wilson	Chase, Samuel	Iredell
1798	Paterson	Cushing	Washington	Chase, Samuel	Iredell
1799	Paterson	Cushing	Washington	Chase, Samuel	Moore

MARSHALL, 1801–1835

Year						
1801	Paterson	Cushing	Washington	Chase, Samuel	Moore	
1804	Paterson	Cushing	Washington	Chase, Samuel	Johnson, W.	
1806	Livingston	Cushing	Washington	Chase, Samuel	Johnson, W.	
1807	Livingston	Cushing	Washington	Chase, Samuel	Johnson, W.	Todd
1811	Livingston	Story	Washington	Duval	Johnson, W.	Todd
1823	Thompson	Story	Washington	Duval	Johnson, W.	Todd
1826	Thompson	Story	Washington	Duval	Johnson, W.	Trimble
1829	Thompson	Story	Washington	Duval	Johnson, W.	McLean
1830	Thompson	Story	Baldwin	Duval	Johnson, W.	McLean
1835	Thompson	Story	Baldwin	Duval	Wayne	McLean

TANEY, 1836–1864

Year									
1836	Thompson	Story	Baldwin	Barbour	Wayne	McLean	Catron	McKinley	
1837	Thompson	Story	Baldwin	Barbour	Wayne	McLean	Catron	McKinley	
1841	Thompson	Story	Baldwin	Daniel	Wayne	McLean	Catron	McKinley	
1845	Nelson	Woodbury	Baldwin	Daniel	Wayne	McLean	Catron	McKinley	
1846	Nelson	Woodbury	Grier	Daniel	Wayne	McLean	Catron	McKinley	
1851	Nelson	Curtis	Grier	Daniel	Wayne	McLean	Catron	McKinley	
1853	Nelson	Curtis	Grier	Daniel	Wayne	McLean	Catron	Campbell	
1858	Nelson	Clifford	Grier	Daniel	Wayne	McLean	Catron	Campbell	
1862	Nelson	Clifford	Grier	Miller	Wayne	Swayne	Catron	Davis	
1863	Nelson	Clifford	Grier	Miller	Wayne	Swayne	Catron	Davis	Field

CHASE, Salmon, 1864–1873

Year									
1864	Field	Davis	Catron	Swayne	Wayne	Miller	Grier	Nelson	Clifford
1865	Field	Davis	Catron	Swayne	*vacant*	Miller	Grier	Nelson	Clifford
1867	Field	Davis	*vacant*	Swayne	*vacant*	Miller	Grier	Nelson	Clifford
1870		Field	Davis	Swayne	Bradley	Miller	Strong	Nelson	Clifford
1872		Field	Davis	Swayne	Bradley	Miller	Strong	Hunt	Clifford

WAITE, 1874–1888

Year									
1874		Field	Davis	Swayne	Bradley	Miller	Strong	Hunt	Clifford
1877		Field	Harlan	Swayne	Bradley	Miller	Strong	Hunt	Clifford
1880		Field	Harlan	Swayne	Bradley	Miller	Woods	Hunt	Clifford
1881		Field	Harlan	Matthews	Bradley	Miller	Woods	Hunt	Gray
1882		Field	Harlan	Matthews	Bradley	Miller	Woods	Blatchford	Gray

FULLER, 1888–1910

Year									
1888		Field	Harlan	Matthews	Bradley	Miller	Lamar, L.	Blatchford	Gray
1889		Field	Harlan	Brewer	Bradley	Miller	Lamar, L.	Blatchford	Gray
1890		Field	Harlan	Brewer	Bradley	Brown	Lamar, L.	Blatchford	Gray
1892		Field	Harlan	Brewer	Shiras	Brown	Lamar, L.	Blatchford	Gray
1893		Field	Harlan	Brewer	Shiras	Brown	Jackson	Blatchford	Gray
1894		Field	Harlan	Brewer	Shiras	Brown	Jackson	White, E.	Gray
1895		Field	Harlan	Brewer	Shiras	Brown	Peckham	White, E.	Gray
1898		McKenna	Harlan	Brewer	Shiras	Brown	Peckham	White, E.	Gray
1902		McKenna	Harlan	Brewer	Shiras	Brown	Peckham	White, E.	Holmes
1903		McKenna	Harlan	Brewer	Day	Brown	Peckham	White, E.	Holmes
1906		McKenna	Harlan	Brewer	Day	Moody	Peckham	White, E.	Holmes
1909		McKenna	Harlan	Brewer	Day	Moody	Lurton	White, E.*	Holmes

WHITE, E., 1910–1921

Year									
1910		McKenna	Harlan	Hughes	Day	Lamar, J.	Lurton	Holmes	VanDevanter
1912		McKenna	Pitney	Hughes	Day	Lamar, J.	Lurton	Holmes	VanDevanter
1914		McKenna	Pitney	Hughes	Day	Lamar, J.	McReynolds	Holmes	VanDevanter
1916		McKenna	Pitney	Clarke	Day	Brandeis	McReynolds	Holmes	VanDevanter

TAFT, 1921–1930

Year									
1921		McKenna	Pitney	Clarke	Day	Brandeis	McReynolds	Holmes	VanDevanter
1922		McKenna	Pitney	Sutherland	Butler	Brandeis	McReynolds	Holmes	VanDevanter
1923		McKenna	Sanford	Sutherland	Butler	Brandeis	McReynolds	Holmes	VanDevanter
1925		Stone	Sanford	Sutherland	Butler	Brandeis	McReynolds	Holmes	VanDevanter

HUGHES, 1930–1941

Year								
1930	VanDevanter	Holmes	McReynolds	Brandeis	Butler	Sutherland	Roberts	Stone
1932	VanDevanter	Cardozo	McReynolds	Brandeis	Butler	Sutherland	Roberts	Stone
1937	Black	Cardozo	McReynolds	Brandeis	Butler	Sutherland	Roberts	Stone
1938	Black	Cardozo	McReynolds	Brandeis	Butler	Reed	Roberts	Stone
1939	Black	Frankfurter	McReynolds	Douglas	Butler	Reed	Roberts	Stone
1940	Black	Frankfurter	McReynolds	Douglas	Murphy	Reed	Roberts	Stone*

STONE, 1941–1946

Year								
1941	Black	Frankfurter	Byrnes	Douglas	Murphy	Reed	Roberts	Jackson, R.
1943	Black	Frankfurter	Rutledge	Douglas	Murphy	Reed	Roberts	Jackson, R.
1945	Black	Frankfurter	Rutledge	Douglas	Murphy	Reed	Burton	Jackson, R.

VINSON, 1946–1953

Year								
1946	Black	Frankfurter	Rutledge	Douglas	Murphy	Reed	Burton	Jackson, R.
1949	Black	Frankfurter	Minton	Douglas	Clark	Reed	Burton	Jackson, R.

WARREN, 1953–1969

Year								
1953	Black	Frankfurter	Minton	Douglas	Clark	Reed	Burton	Jackson, R.
1955	Black	Frankfurter	Minton	Douglas	Clark	Reed	Burton	Harlan
1956	Black	Frankfurter	Brennan	Douglas	Clark	Reed	Burton	Harlan
1957	Black	Frankfurter	Brennan	Douglas	Clark	Whittaker	Burton	Harlan
1958	Black	Frankfurter	Brennan	Douglas	Clark	Whittaker	Stewart	Harlan
1962	Black	Goldberg	Brennan	Douglas	Clark	White, B.	Stewart	Harlan
1965	Black	Fortas	Brennan	Douglas	Clark	White, B.	Stewart	Harlan
1967	Black	Fortas	Brennan	Douglas	Marshall, T.	White, B.	Stewart	Harlan

BURGER, 1969–1986

Year								
1969	Black	Fortas	Brennan	Douglas	Marshall, T.	White, B.	Stewart	Harlan
1970	Black	Blackmun	Brennan	Douglas	Marshall, T.	White, B.	Stewart	Harlan
1972	Powell	Blackmun	Brennan	Douglas	Marshall, T.	White, B.	Stewart	Rehnquist
1975	Powell	Blackmun	Brennan	Stevens	Marshall, T.	White, B.	Stewart	Rehnquist
1981	Powell	Blackmun	Brennan	Stevens	Marshall, T.	White, B.	O'Connor	Rehnquist*

REHNQUIST, 1986–

Year								
1986	Powell	Blackmun	Brennan	Stevens	Marshall, T.	White, B.	O'Connor	Scalia
1988	Kennedy	Blackmun	Brennan	Stevens	Marshall, T.	White, B.	O'Connor	Scalia

For Further Reading

In addition to Supreme Court opinions (see "A Note on Citations," which follows the Preface), there are numerous other sources of information on constitutional law and the Supreme Court. Students are encouraged to consult the following reference materials and books. We have divided the list into two parts. The first consists of several periodicals and a newspaper that regularly report on current issues in constitutional law. The second part recommends readily available books and articles that, for convenience, are grouped by subject matter of each chapter.

Law reviews. Check your library for the *Index to Legal Periodicals*. It will provide a long list of articles by leading constitutional scholars commenting on current issues before the Court.

The Harvard Law Review. Each November issue is devoted to a careful analysis of the cases handed down by the Supreme Court during the previous term. The issue also contains a lengthy essay on the Court's recent work by a leading scholar.

The Supreme Court Review. Published annually for the past twenty-five years by the University of Chicago Press. Each volume contains several articles on recent issues dealt with by the Supreme Court.

The New York Times. This newspaper offers excellent coverage of the Supreme Court, often printing lengthy extracts of important decisions the day after they are handed down, as well as occasional background pieces on current justices. A good source to keep abreast of current developments while the Court is in session.

Chapter 1
Judicial Review and Court Power

Useful general background works on constitutional history and introductions to constitutional law

Choper, Jesse, Yale Kamisar, and William Lockhart. *Constitutional Law: Cases and Comments,* sixth ed. St. Paul, Minn.: West, 1983.

Kammon, Michael. *A Machine That Would Go of Itself.* New York: Knopf, 1986.

Kelley, Alfred, W. A. Harbison, and H. Belz. *The American Constitution,* sixth ed. New York: Norton, 1982.

Nowak, John, et al. *Constitutional Law,* third ed. St. Paul, Minn.: West, 1986.

O'Brien, David. *Storm Center: The Supreme Court in American Politics.* New York: Norton, 1986.

Prichett, C. Herman. *Constitutional Law of the Federal System.* Englewood Cliffs, N.J.: Prentice-Hall, 1984.

Smith, J. M., and Paul Murphy. *Liberty and Justice — A Historical Record of American Constitutional Development,* revised ed. New York: Knopf, 1968.

Tribe, Laurence. *American Constitutional Law,* second ed. New York: Foundation Press, 1988.

Works on specific aspects of judicial power

Baker, Leonard. *Back to Back: The Duel Between FDR and the Supreme Court.* New York: Macmillan, 1967.

Baum, Lawrence. *The Supreme Court,* second ed. Washington, D.C.: Congressional Quarterly, 1985.

Beard, Charles. *The Supreme Court and the Constitution.* New York: Macmillan, 1912.

Becker, Theodore, and Malcolm Feeley. *The Impact of Supreme Court Decisions,* second ed. New York: Oxford University Press, 1973.

Berger, Raoul. *Congress versus the Supreme Court.* Cambridge, Mass.: Harvard University Press, 1960.

Bickel, Alexander. *The Supreme Court and the Idea of Progress.* New York: Harper & Row, 1970.

Cahn, Edmund. *Supreme Court and Supreme Law.* New York: Simon & Schuster, 1954.

Casper, Gerhard, and Richard Posner. *The Workload of the Supreme Court.* Chicago: American Bar Foundation, 1967.

Choper, Jesse. *Judicial Review and the National Political Process.* Chicago: University of Chicago Press, 1980.

Corwin, Edward S. *The "Higher Law" Background of American Constitutional Law.* Ithaca, N.Y.: Cornell University Press, 1955.

Cover, Robert. *Justice Accused: Anti-Slavery and the Judicial Process.* New Haven, Conn.: Yale University Press, 1974.

"Developments in the Law—Class Actions." *Harvard Law Review* 89 (1976): 1318.

Dunham, Allison, and Phillip Kurland. *Mr. Justice.* Chicago: University of Chicago Press, 1964.

Dworkin, Ronald M. *Law's Empire.* Cambridge, Mass.: Belknap Press, 1986.

Ely, John Hart. *Democracy and Distrust.* Cambridge, Mass.: Harvard University Press, 1980.

Funston, Richard. "The Supreme Court and Critical Elections." *American Political Science Review* (1975): 795.

Garraty, John A. *Quarrels That Have Shaped the Constitution.* New York: Harper & Row, 1962.

Gunther, Gerald. "The Subtle Vices of the Passive Virtues." *Columbia Law Review* 64, no. 1 (1964).

Halpern, Stephen, and Charles Lamb, eds. *Supreme Court Activism and Restraint.* Lexington, Mass.: Heath, 1982.

Henkin, Louis, "Is There a 'Political Question' Doctrine?" *Yale Law Journal* 85 (1971): 597.

Jackson, Robert H. *The Supreme Court in the American System of Government.* Cambridge, Mass.: Harvard University Press, 1954.

Krislov, Samuel. *The Supreme Court in the Political Process.* New York: Macmillan, 1965.

Lewis, Anthony. *Gideon's Trumpet.* New York: Random House, 1964.

Murphy, Walter. *Elements of Judicial Strategy.* Chicago: University of Chicago Press, 1964.

Provine, Doris. *Case Selection in the United States Supreme Court.* Chicago: University of Chicago Press, 1980.

Rabkin, Jeremy. *Judicial Compulsions: How Public Law Distorts Public Policy.* New York, Basic Books, 1989.

Woodward, Bob, and Scott Armstrong. *The Brethren.* New York: Simon & Schuster, 1979.

Chapter 2
President and Congress: Separation of Power and the Balance of Authority

Berger, Raoul. *Executive Privilege: A Constitutional Myth.* Cambridge, Mass.: Harvard University Press, 1974.

———. *Impeachment.* Cambridge, Mass.: Harvard University Press, 1973.

Black, Charles, Jr. *Impeachment.* New Haven, Conn.: Yale University Press, 1974.

Feller, A. "The Tenth Amendment Retires." *American Bar Association Journal* 27 (April 1941): 223.

Fisher, Louis. *Constitutional Conflicts Between Congress and the President* (revised ed. of *The Constitution Between Friends*). Princeton, N.J.: Princeton University Press, 1985.

Harris, J. P. *The Advice and Consent of the Senate.* Berkeley, Calif.: University of California Press, 1953.

Jackson, Robert H. *The Struggle for Judicial Supremacy.* New York: Knopf, 1941.

Morgan, D. L. *Congress and the Constitution.* Cambridge, Mass.: Harvard University Press, 1966.

Murphy, Paul. *The Constitution in Crisis Times: 1918–1969.* New York: Harper & Row, 1972.

Murphy, Walter F. *Congress and the Court.* Chicago: University of Chicago, Press, 1962.

Pritchett, C. Herman. *Congress versus the Supreme Court.* Minneapolis, Minn.: University of Minnesota Press, 1961.

Rossiter, Clinton. *The Supreme Court and the Commander-in-Chief.* Ithaca, N.Y.: Cornell University Press, 1951.

Schmidhauser, John, and L. L. Berg. *The Supreme Court and Congress.* New York: Free Press, 1972.

Scigliano, Robert. *The Supreme Court and the Presidency.* New York: Free Press, 1971.

Chapter 3
The Problems of Yesterday: National Authority over Commerce and Taxation

Cortner, Richard. *The Wagner Act Cases.* Knoxville, Tenn.: University of Tennessee Press, 1964.

Corwin, Edward S. *The Commerce Clause versus States' Rights.* Princeton, N.J.: Princeton University Press, 1936.

Frankfurter, Felix. *The Commerce Clause Under Marshall, Taney and Waite.* Chicago: Quadrangle Books, 1964.

Grodzins, Morton. *The American System: A New View of Government in the United States.* Skokie, Ill.: Rand McNally, 1966.

Howard, A. E. Dick. "State Courts and Constitutional Rights in the Day of the Burger Court." *Virginia Law Review* 62 (1976): 873.

Hyman, H. M. *A More Perfect Union: The Impact of the Civil War on the Constitution.* New York: Knopf, 1973.

Irons, Peter H. *The New Deal Lawyer.* Princeton, N.J.: Princeton University Press, 1982.

Levi, Edward H. *An Introduction to Legal Reasoning.* Chicago: University of Chicago Press, 1948.

Navasky, Victor. *Kennedy Justice.* New York: Atheneum, 1971.

Rottschaefer, Henry. *The Constitution and Socio-Economic Change.* Ann Arbor, Mich.: University of Michigan Press, 1948.

Stern, Robert L. "That Commerce Which Concerns More States Than One." *Harvard Law Review* 47 (1934): 1335.

Twiss, Benjamin. *Lawyers and the Constitution.* Princeton, N.J.: Princeton University Press, 1942.

van Alstyne, William. "The Second Death of Federalism." *Michigan Law Review* 83 (1985): 1709.

Chapter 4
The Other Side of Federalism: State Powers over Commerce and Taxation

Anderson, William. *The Nation and the States: Rival or Partners?* Minneapolis, Minn.: University of Minnesota Press, 1955.

Cooper, Phillip J. *Hard Judicial Choices: Federal District Court Judges and State and Local Officials.* New York: Oxford University Press, 1988.

Cox, Archibald. *The Role of the Supreme Court in American Government.* New York: Oxford University Press, 1976.

Goldwin, R. A., ed. *A Nation of States.* Skokie, Ill.: Rand McNally, 1963.

Krislov, Samuel. Federalism in the Constitution and Constitutional Law. In *Teaching About American Federal Democracy.* Stephen Schecter. Philadelphia: CSF Associates, 1984.

MacMahon, A. W., ed. *Federalism: Mature and Emergent.* New York: Doubleday, 1955.

Marshall, Burke. *Federalism and Civil Rights.* New York: Columbia University Press, 1964.

Mason, Alpheus. *The States' Rights Debate: Anti-Federalism and the Constitution.* New York: Oxford University Press, 1972.

Schmidhauser, John R. *The Supreme Court as Final Arbitrator of Federal-State Relations.* Chapel Hill, N.C.: University of North Carolina Press, 1958.

Chapter 5
Property, the Constitution, and the States

Abraham, Henry J. *The Judicial Process*. New York: Oxford University Press, 1987.

Ackerman, Bruce. *Private Property and the Constitution*. New Haven, Conn.: Yale University Press, 1973.

Commons, John R. *The Legal Foundations of Capitalism*. Madison, Wis.: University of Wisconsin Press, 1924.

Corwin, Edwin S. *Court over the Constitution: A Study of Judicial Review as an Instrument of Popular Government*. Princeton, N.J.: Princeton University Press, 1938.

————. *Liberty Against Government: The Rise, Flowering and Decline of a Famous Judicial Concept*. Baton Rouge, La.: Louisiana State University Press, 1948.

Hayek, F. A. *The Constitution of Liberty*. Chicago: University of Chicago Press, 1960.

McCloskey, Robert G. *The American Supreme Court*. Chicago: University of Chicago Press, 1960.

Posner, Richard. *Economic Analysis of Law*. Boston: Little, Brown, 1984.

Seigan, Bernard H. *Economic Liberties and the Constitution*. Chicago: University of Chicago Press, 1980.

Tiger, Michael, and Madeline Levy. *Law and the Rise of Capitalism*. New York: Monthly Review Press, 1977.

Chapter 6
Nationalization of the Bill of Rights: A Policy in Search of a Theory

Bickel, Alexander, *The Least Dangerous Branch*. Indianapolis, Ind.: Bobbs-Merrill, 1964.

Brant, Irving. *The Bill of Rights*. Indianapolis, Ind.: Bobbs-Merrill, 1965.

Cortner, Richard. *The Supreme Court and the Second Bill of Rights: The Fourteenth Amendment and the Nationalization of Civil Liberties*. Madison, Wis.: University of Wisconsin Press, 1981.

Hand, Learned. *The Bill of Rights*. Cambridge, Mass.: Harvard University Press, 1958.

Hirsch, Harry. *The Enigma of Felix Frankfurter*. New York: Basic Books, 1981.

James, J. B. *The Framing of the Fourteenth Amendment*. Urbana, Ill.: University of Illinois Press, 1956.

Schwartz, Bernard. *The Unpublished Opinions of the Warren Court*. New York: Oxford University Press, 1985.

ten Broek, Jacobus. *The Anti-Slavery Origins of the Fourteenth Amendment*. Berkeley, Calif.: University of California Press, 1951.

Tribe, Lawrence. *Constitutional Choices*. Cambridge, Mass.: Harvard University Press, 1985.

Chapter 7
Freedom of Religion

See also the readings for Chapter 6.

Alley, Robert S. *The Supreme Court on Church and State*. New York: Oxford University Press, 1988.

Dolbare, Kenneth, and Philip Hammond. *The School Prayer Decisions: From Court Policy to Local Practices*. Chicago: University of Chicago Press, 1977.

Konvitz, Milton R. *Religion, Liberty and Conscience: A Constitutional Inquiry*. New York: Viking, 1969.

Pfeffer, Leo. "Freedom and/or Separation: The Constitutional Dilemma of the First Amendment." *Minnesota Law Review* 64 (1980): 561.

Sorauf, Frank. *The Wall of Separation: The Constitutional Politics of Church and State*. Princeton, N.J.: Princeton University Press, 1976.

Chapter 8
Freedom of Expression in America's First 150 Years: A Meager History

Adler, Renata. *Reckless Disregard: Westmoreland v. CBS et al., Sharon v. Time*. New York: Knopf, 1986.

Barron, J. A. *Freedom of the Press for Whom*. Bloomington, Ind.: Indiana University Press, 1973.

Berns, Walter. *Freedom, Virtue and the First Amendment*. Baton Rouge, La.: Louisiana State University Press, 1950.

Cahn, Edmund. *The Great Rights*. New York: Macmillan, 1963.

Clor, H. M. *Obscenity and Public Morality*. Chicago: University of Chicago Press, 1969.

Devlin, Lord Patrick. *The Enforcement of Morals*. New York: Oxford University Press, 1968.

Dworkin, Ronald. *Taking Rights Seriously*. Cambridge, Mass.: Harvard University Press, 1977.

Emerson, Thomas I. *The System of Freedom of Expression*. New York: Random House, 1972.

Hart, H. L. A. *Law, Liberty and Morality*. Stanford, Calif.: Stanford University Press, 1963.

Hook, Sidney. *Heresey, Yes — Conspiracy, No*. New York: Day, 1953.

Krislov, Samuel. *The Supreme Court and Political Freedom*. New York: Free Press, 1968.

Levy, Leonard W. *Emergence of a Free Press* (revised ed. of *Legacy of Suppression*). New York: Oxford University Press, 1985.

Meiklejohn, Alexander. *Political Freedom*. New York: Oxford University Press, 1965.

Nizer, Louis. *The Jury Returns*. New York: Doubleday, 1966.

Shapiro, Martin. *Freedom of Speech*. Englewood Cliffs, N.J.: Prentice-Hall, 1966.

———. *The Pentagon Papers and the Courts*. San Francisco: Chandler, 1972.

Wolff, Robert, Moore Barrington, and Herbert Marcuse. *A Critique of Pure Tolerance*. Boston: Beacon Press, 1965.

Chapter 9
Rights in the Criminal Justice System and Fair Procedure in the Administrative Process

Beaney, William. *The Right to Counsel in American Courts*. Ann Arbor, Mich.: University of Michigan Press, 1955.

Berkson, Larry C. *The Concept of Cruel and Unusual Punishment*. Lexington, Mass.: Lexington Books, 1975.

Black, Charles. *Capital Punishment: The Inevitability of Caprice and Mistake*. New York: Norton, 1983.

Davis, Kenneth Culp. *Discretionary Justice*. Urbana, Ill.: University of Illinois Press, 1971.

Feeley, Malcolm. *The Process Is the Punishment: Handling Cases in a Lower Court*. New York: Russell Sage Foundation, 1979.

Fellman, David. *The Defendants' Rights Today*. Madison, Wis.: University of Wisconsin Press, 1976.

Handler, Joel, and Ellen Jane Hollingsworth. *The Deserving Poor: A Study of Welfare Administration*. New York: Academic Press, 1973.

Herrmann, Robert, Eric Single, and John Boston. *Counsel for the Poor: Criminal Defense in Urban America*. Lexington, Mass.: Heath, 1978.

LaFave, Wayne R. *Arrest: The Decision to Take a Suspect into Custody*. Boston: Little, Brown, 1965.

Levy, Leonard W. *Against the Law: The Nixon Court and Criminal Justice*. New York: Harper & Row, 1974.

———. *Origins of the Fifth Amendment*. New York: Oxford University Press, 1968.

Reich, Charles. "The New Property." *Yale Law Journal* 73 (1964): 733.

Ryerson, Ellen. *The Best-Laid Plans: America's Juvenile Court Experiment*. New York: Hill and Wang, 1978.

Skolnick, Jerome. *Justice Without Trial*. New York: Wiley, 1966.

Vera Institute of Justice. *Felony Arrests*. New York: Longman, 1981.

Weinreb, Lloyd L. *Denial of Justice*. New York: Free Press, 1977.

Westin, Allen F., and M. A. Bakers, *Databanks in a Free Society*. Chicago: Quadrangle, 1973.

Wilson, James Q. *Varities of Police Behavior*. Cambridge, Mass.: Harvard University Press, 1968.

———. *Thinking About Crime*, second ed. New York: Basic Books, 1984.

Chapter 10
Social Change and the Fourteenth Amendment: Race

Dollard, John. *Caste and Class in a Southern Town*. New York: Doubleday, 1957.

Glazer, Nathan. *Affirmative Discrimination*. New York: Basic Books, 1976.

Hamilton, Charles. *The Bench and the Ballot: Southern Federal Judges and Black Voters*. New York: Oxford University Press, 1973.

Higgenbothom, Leon, Jr. *In the Matter of Color: Race and the American Legal Process*. New York: Oxford University Press, 1978.

Kirp, David. *Just Schools: The Idea of Racial Equality in American Schools*. Berkeley, Calif.: University of California Press, 1982.

Myrdal, Gunnar. *An American Dilemma: The Negro Problem and Modern Democracy*. New York: Harper & Row, 1962.

Peltason, Jack. *Fifty-Eight Lonely Men*. Urbana, Ill.: University of Illinois Press, 1962.

Silberman, Charles E. *Crisis in Black and White*. New York: Random House, 1965.

van Woodward, C. *The Strange Career of Jim Crow,* third ed. New York: Oxford University Press, 1973.

Vose, Clement E. *Caucasians Only: The Supreme Court, the NAACP, and the Restrictive Covenant Cases*. Berkeley, Calif.: University of California Press, 1955.

Wilkinson, J. Harvie. *From Brown to Bakke: The Supreme Court and School Integration: 1954–1978*. New York: Oxford University Press, 1979.

Chapter 11
Social Change and the Fourteenth Amendment: The "New Equal Protection" and the Right of Privacy and Autonomy

Berger, Raoul. *Government by Judiciary*. Cambridge, Mass.: Harvard University Press, 1978.

Bickel, Alexander M. *Politics and the Warren Court*. New York: Harper & Row, 1965.

Blasi, Vincent, ed. *The Burger Court: The Counter-Revolution That Wasn't*. New Haven, Conn.: Yale University Press, 1983.

Bumiller, Kristen. *The Civil Rights Society*. Baltimore: Johns Hopkins University Press, 1988.

Daniels, R. *Prejudice: The Decision to Relocate the Japanese Americans*. Philadelphia: Lippincott, 1975.

DeCrow, Karen. *Sexist Justice*. New York: Vintage, 1975.

Dionisopoulos, Allan, and Craig Ducat. *The Right to Privacy: Essays and Cases*. St. Paul, Minn.: West, 1976.

Freeman, J. *Women: A Feminist Perspective*. Palo Alto, Calif.: Mayfield Press, 1975.

Goldstein, Leslie. *The Constitutional Rights of Women*. Madison, Wis.: University of Wisconsin Press, 1987.

Hartz, Louis. *The Liberal Tradition in America,* San Diego: Harcourt Brace Jovanovich, 1955.

Horowitz, Donald. *The Courts and Social Policy*. Washington, D.C.: Brookings Institution, 1977.

Kittrie, Nicholas. *The Right to Be Different*. Baltimore: Johns Hopkins University Press, 1981.

Konowitz, Leo. *Sex Roles in Law and Society*. Albuquerque, N.M.: University of New Mexico Press, 1972.

Lieberman, Jethro. *The Litigious Society*. New York: Basic Books, 1982.

McCann, Michael. *Taking Reform Seriously: Perspectives on Public Interest Liberalism*. Ithaca, N.Y.: Cornell University Press, 1986.

Morgan, Richard E. *Disabling America: The "Rights Industry" in America*. New York: Basic Books, 1984.

O'Brian, David. *Privacy, Law and Public Policy*. New York: Praeger, 1979.

O'Rourke, Timothy. *The Impact of Reapportionment*. New Brunswick, N.J.: Transaction Books, 1980.

Rae, Douglas. *Equalities*. Cambridge, Mass.: Harvard University Press, 1981.

Scheingold, Stuart. *The Politics of Rights*. New Haven, Conn.: Yale University Press, 1974.

Index of Cases

(Those cases in boldface are reprinted in this volume.)

Malloy v. Hogan, 378 U.S. 1 (1964), 630, 645, 647

Manual Enterprises v. Day, 370 U.S. 478 (1962), 473

Mapp v. Ohio, 367 U.S. 643 (1961), 570–572; 381, 557–558, 577, 583–584, 633, 878

Marbury v. Madison, 1 Cranch 137 (1803), 29–32; 4, 10, 14, 21, 46, 49, 71, 80, 147

Marchetti v. U.S., 390 U.S. 39 (1968), 233–235; 183

Marshall v. Gordon, 243 U.S. 521 (1917), 106

Marsh v. Chambers, 463 U.S. 783 (1983), 410, 437

Martinez-Fuerte, U.S. v., 428 U.S. 543 (1976), 568, 591, 594

Martin v. Mott, 25 U.S. (12 Wheat.) 19 (1827), 27, 72, 92

Maryland v. Louisiana, 100 S.Ct. 2114 (1981), 311–314; 273

Maryland v. Wirtz, 392 U.S. 183 (1968), 185, 257, 258, 261

Massachusetts Board of Retirement v. Murgia, 427 U.S. 307 (1976), 859–862; 812, 847, 848

Massachusetts v. Mellon, 262 U.S. 447 (1923), 53, 57, 224

Massachusetts v. Sheppard, 468 U.S. 981 (1984), 558, 572

Massiah v. U.S., 377 U.S. 201 (1964), 630, 631

Mathews v. Eldridge, 424 U.S. 319 (1976), 685–689; 671, 674

Mathews v. Lucas, 427 U.S. 495 (1976), 811

Maxwell v. Dow, 176 U.S. 581 (1900), 388–389, 377

Mayer v. Nebraska (1923), 41

Ex parte McCardle, 7 Wallace 506 (1969), 51–52, 20, 25, 50

McCleskey v. Kemp, 481 U.S. 279 (1987), 661–663; 652, 653

McCollum v. Board of Education, 333 U.S. 203 (1948), 894

McCollum v. Illinois, 333 U.S. 203 (1948), 404

McCray v. U.S., 195 U.S. 27 (1904), 514, 515

McCready v. Virginia, 94 U.S. 391 (1877), 856

McCulloch v. Maryland, 4 Wheat. 316 (1819), 95–99; 50, 84, 171, 180–181, 182, 185, 186, 194, 196, 245, 247, 349

McDaniel v. Barresi, 402 U.S. 39 (1971), 764, 765

McDonnell Douglas v. Houghton, 434 U.S. 966 (1977), 812

McGowan v. Maryland, 366 U.S. 420 (1961), 446–450; 413, 437, 438, 440, 441, 442, 833, 845, 847

McGrain v. Daugherty, 273 U.S. 135 (1927), 104–107; 86, 108, 111, 143, 634

McKeiver v. Pennsylvania, 403 U.S. 528 (1971), 672

McLaughlin v. Florida, 379 U.S. 184 (1964), 763

McLaurin v. Oklahoma State Regents, 339 U.S. 637 (1950), 696, 715, 716

McNabb v. U.S., 318 U.S. 332 (1943), 630

Meek v. Pittinger, 421 U.S. 349 (1975), 407, 434

Memoirs v. Massachusetts, 383 U.S. 413 (1966), 533, 534

Memorial Hospital v. Maricopa County, 415 U.S. 250 (1974), 813, 842

Memphis Light, Gas and Water Division v. Craft, 436 U.S. 1 (1978), 803

Metromedia v. San Diego, 453 U.S. 490 (1981), 539–544

Metropolitan County Board of Education of Nashville v. Kelly, 459 U.S. 1183 (1983), 701

Meyer v. Nebraska, 262 U.S. 390 (1923), 516, 518, 879, 883, 884, 898, 899, 904

Miami Herald Publishing Co. v. Tornillo, 418 U.S. 241 (1974), 511, 512

Michelin Tire Co. v. Wages, 423 U.S. 276 (1976), 272

Michigan v. Long, 463 U.S. 1032 (1983), 381, 562

Michigan v. Summers, 452 U.S. 692 (1981), 590–595; 562, 602, 603, 604–605

Michigan v. Tucker, 417 U.S. 433 (1974), 642, 644

Milk Wagon Drivers Union v. Meadowmoor Dairies, 312 U.S. 287 (1941), 462, 467

Miller v. California, 413 U.S. 15 (1973), 532; 533–535, 474

Ex parte Milligan, 4 Wallace 2 (1866), 150–153; 92

Milliken v. Bradley, 418 U.S. 717 (1974), 724–728; 699, 700

Minersville School District v. Gobitis, 310 U.S. 586 (1940), 412, 442, 443–444, 461, 907

Minnesota Moratorium. *See* Home Building and Loan Association v. Blaisdell

Minnesota Rate Cases, 230 U.S. 352 (1913), 259

Minnesota v. Clover Leaf Creamery Co., 449 U.S. 456 (1981), 301–304; 271

Minnesota v. Murphy, 465 U.S. 420 (1984), 643

Minor v. Board of Education of Cincinnati, 419 F. 2d 1387 (1969), 421

Minor v. Happersett, 21 Wall 162, (1874), 242

Miranda v. Arizona, 384 U.S. 436 (1966), 634–641; 13, 618, 630, 631, 633, 641–646

Mishkin v. New York, 383 U.S. 502 (1966), 530, 534

Mississippi University for Women v. Hogan, 458 U.S. 718 (1982), 852–855; 810

Missouri ex rel. Gaines v. Canada, 305 U.S. 676 (1938), 696, 715

Missouri v. Holland, 252 U.S. 416 (1920), 153–155; 20, 91, 93, 160, 161, 162

Missouri v. Illinois, 180 U.S. 208 (1901), 53

Mistretta v. U.S., 57 LW 4102 (1989), 85–86, 139

Mobile v. Kimball, 102 U.S. 691 (1880), 199

Monroe v. Pape, 365 U.S. 176 (1961), 702

Montoya de Hernandez, U.S. v., 473 U.S. 531 (1985), 563

Moore v. City of East Cleveland, 431 U.S. 494 (1977), 898–903; 875, 904, 906

Moose Lodge No. 107 v. Irvis, 407 U.S. 163 (1972), 747–751; 703–704, 844

Morey v. Doud, 354 U.S. 457 (1957), 336, 861

Morrison, Alexia, Independent Counsel v. Theodore B. Olson, et al., 56 LW 4835 (1988), 139–145

Morrison v. Olson, 108 S.Ct. 2597 (1988), 85

Morrissey v. Brewer, 408 U.S. 471 (1972), 679

Mosley, U.S. v., 238 U.S. 383 (1915), 71

Mountain Timber Co. v. Washington, 243 U.S. 219 (1917), 74

Mueller v. Allen, 463 U.S. 388 (1983), 429–434; 407, 437

Mugler v. Kansas, 123 U.S. 623 (1887), 248; 479, 758

Mulford v. Smith, 307 U.S. 39 (1939), 232–233; 183, 213

Muller v. Oregon, 208 U.S. 412 (1908), 366–367; 334, 368, 369, 805, 835, 842

Munn v. Illinois, 94 U.S. 133 (1877), 358–362; 333, 334, 336, 742

Murdock v. Pennsylvania, 319 U.S. 105 (1943), 411, 412, 415, 464

Murray's Lessee v. Hoboken Land & Improvement Company, 18 How. 272 (1855), 384

Murray v. Curlett, 374 U.S. 203 (1963), 405, 420, 422

Murray v. U.S., 108 S.Ct. 2529 (1988), 558

Muskrat v. U.S., 219 U.S. 346 (1911), 56

About the Authors

Malcolm M. Feeley, a distinguished scholar and author, is a professor of law at the University of California at Berkeley. His previous books, which include *The Process Is the Punishment, The Policy Dilemma,* and *Court Reform on Trial,* have earned awards from the American Bar Association and the American Sociological Association. He has served as consultant to such institutions as the New York Victim Witness Agency and the National Science Foundation.

Samuel Krislov, professor of political science at the University of Minnesota, has served as president of the Midwest Political Science Association and the Law and Society Association. Also a previously published author (*The Supreme Court and Political Freedom, The Supreme Court in the Political Process,* and *Representative Bureaucracy and the American Political System*), he has received fellowships from the Guggenheim and Ford foundations as well as the National Institute of Justice.